Cases and Materials on the Carriage of Goods by Sea

Cases and Materials on the Carriage of Goods by Sea, fourth edition, offers tailored coverage of the most commonly taught topics on Carriage of Goods by Sea courses. Combining a collection of legislative materials, commentaries, scholarly articles, standard forms and up-to-date English case law, it covers the major areas of chartering and bills of lading as well as matters such as exclusion and limitation of liability.

Significant innovations for this edition include:

- Materials on the Rotterdam and Hamburg Rules, and expanded discussion of the Hague-Visby Rules and Charterparties
- Discussion of some of the most important decisions by the senior courts
- Pedagogical features such as end of chapter further reading
- Emphasis on how shipping law operates and is applied in the real world
- A clear, student-friendly text design with a strong emphasis on research and problem solving

This up-to-date collection of materials relating to the carriage of goods by sea will be of value to students of law, researchers and legal practitioners.

Anthony Rogers is Course Director of the LLM in Maritime Law at the City Law School, City University London, UK, where he teaches the Carriage of Goods by Sea course in both London and Piraeus.

Jason Chuah is Professor of Commercial and Maritime Law and Head of Academic Law Programmes at the City Law School, City University London, UK.

The late **Martin Dockray** was Professor of Law at City University London and Head of the Law Department there from 1989 to 2004. His first edition of this book was published in 1987.

Cases and Materials on the Carriage of Goods by Sea

FOURTH EDITION

Anthony Rogers, Jason Chuah and Martin Dockray

Routledge
Taylor & Francis Group

LONDON AND NEW YORK

Fourth edition published 2016
by Routledge
2 Park Square, Milton Park, Abingdon, Oxon, OX14 4RN

and by Routledge
711 Third Avenue, New York, NY 10017

Routledge is an imprint of the Taylor & Francis Group, an informa business

First edition published 1987 by Butterworths Law
Third edition published 2004 by Cavendish Publishing

British Library Cataloguing in Publication Data
A catalogue record for this book is available from the British Library

Library of Congress Cataloging-in-Publication Data
Names: Chuah, Jason, author. | Rogers, Anthony, (Law teacher), author. |
    Dockray, Martin, author.
Title: Cases and materials on the carriage of goods by sea / Jason Chuah,
    Anthony Rogers and Martin Dockray.
Description: Fourth edition. | New York, NY : Routledge, 2016. |
    Includes bibliographical references and index.
Identifiers: LCCN 2015039184| ISBN 9781138809895 (hbk) |
    ISBN 9781138809888 (pbk) | ISBN 9781315749754 (ebk)
Subjects: LCSH: Maritime law—Great Britain—Cases. | Bills of
    lading—Great Britain—Cases.
Classification: LCC KD1818 .C48 2016 | DDC 343.4109/62—dc23
LC record available at http://lccn.loc.gov/2015039184

ISBN: 978-1-138-80989-5 (hbk)
ISBN: 978-1-138-80988-8 (pbk)
ISBN: 978-1-315-74975-4 (ebk)

Typeset in Adobe Caslon Pro
by Apex CoVantage, LLC

MIX
Paper from
responsible sources
FSC   FSC® C013056
www.fsc.org

Printed and bound in Great Britain by
TJ International Ltd, Padstow, Cornwall

Contents

Preface

With some trepidation we have taken on the responsibility of writing the new edition of this work. We know it to be highly regarded in shipping circles as is Martin Dockray himself, although in his case his reputation is not limited to scholarship in the law of carriage of goods by sea. It is now ten years since his death but he is still fondly remembered by staff at the City Law School, City University London and his name lives on there in the form of the Martin Dockray Prize for high achieving City Law School undergraduates. We hope to live up to his high standards of scholarship and to continue to provide context and comment on the twists and turns of the law of carriage of goods by sea.

Much has changed in the last ten years and this is reflected in this present edition. There has been much excitement; some enthusiasm and some mistrust about the proposed Rotterdam Rules, which have been promoted as a possible replacement for the Hague-Visby regime, although this appears to have lapsed into a slough since, at the date of writing (May 2015), only three countries having ratified the convention. The extreme heights of the freight market following the prodigious growth of China and India and the dramatic crash of freight rates since the financial crisis following the collapse of Lehman Brothers bank in September 2008 have translated into litigation and arbitration. We have taken this opportunity to include the recent cases of *The Astra* and *Spar Shipping* in the context of the consequence of failure to pay hire under a time charter. Another recent case to cause controversy in the market, this time with regard to the safe port obligation is *The Ocean Victory*.

As previously, we have preferred cases and judgments that consider the reasons for a rule or which analyse previous case law to those which do not. With regard to style; place names and the names and offices of judges are generally reproduced as originally reported and without note of subsequent changes. Matter omitted is generally indicated by ellipses, whatever the length of the omission. In reproducing cases and other materials, the following are not generally specifically noted: (a) omission of original footnotes; (b) original typographical errors, whether corrected or not; (c) the length and nature of omissions; (d) alterations or substitutions in the form of citations.

Anthony Rogers
Jason Chuah
The City Law School,
City University London.

Acknowledgements

Alison Dockray (Martin's wife): I would like to acknowledge Anthony and Jason's hard work in completing the Fourth Edition. It is very pleasing to know that there will be an updated version of my late husband's book, which is sure to be an enormous bonus to students of the subject.

The authors would also like to thank Andrew and Stuart Reid of Charles M. Willie and Co (Shipping) Ltd, Shipowners of Cardiff and Fotoflite.co.uk (photographers) for kindly allowing us to use the cover photograph.

The publishers and the authors wish to acknowledge with thanks the permissions given by the following to reprint material from the copyright sources listed below:

The Incorporated Council of Law Reporting: *Law Reports; Weekly Law Reports*
Informa Professional Lloyd's of London: *Lloyd's Law Reports*
LexisNexis UK: *All England Law Reports, Law Times Reports, Commercial Case* (reproduced by permission of Reed Elsevier (UK) Ltd trading as LexisNexis UK)
Stopford, M, *Maritime Economics 3rd edn,* Routledge Press.
The United Nations: *Charterparties* 1974, a report of the Secretariat of UNCTAD

Table of Cases

Table of Statutes

*(References in **bold** indicate where material has been reproduced)*

Table of Statutory Instruments

Table of European and International Legislation

*(References in **bold** indicate where material has been reproduced)*

Chapter 1

Introduction

1 Introduction

The law of carriage of goods by sea has contributed greatly to our understanding of both contract and tort law and is of continuing relevance to the development of commercial law providing, as it does, a steady flow of litigation on essential issues such as the nature of the terms of a contract and the effect of any breach.

It is a subject that places high intellectual demands upon those who would study it. However, the law of carriage of goods by sea is also important for those who work in the offices of shipping companies and shipping law firms and this direct connection between the intellectual and the pragmatic is part of its fascination.

In order to fully appreciate its significance it is important to note that while a knowledge of carriage of goods by sea is essential to understand shipping law (a term that more accurately reflects the private law nature of what is more commonly called maritime law), shipping law itself is a key element in international trade law. It is difficult to imagine how a study of shipping law (or maritime law if you will!) can be fully complete without seeing it in its context.

The law of carriage of goods by sea is a distinct part of English law. It has special rules that have no direct counterpart in other areas of domestic law. Nevertheless, for the most part, English law relating to the carriage of goods by sea consists only of the application of general common law ideas, together with a small number of important statutes. The basis of the subject is the law of contract but it also draws on the laws of tort, bailment, agency, property and equity.

But if only familiar principles of general law are involved, how can the law of carriage be said to be distinct? One answer can be found in the way in which general legal ideas have been adapted to meet the special features of the sea trade. Shipping is a truly international business: parties to the business may be located anywhere in the world and duties under a carriage contract may be fulfilled in any coastal state. It is sometimes suggested that this international nature brings with it a pressure for international uniformity of the legal rules. This is open to debate since there are also many examples where sovereign states appear to have responded to attempts at international agreement by acting in the national interest. Nonetheless there are examples of law that has widespread, if not complete application e.g. the Hague-Visby Rules, which we examine later in this book. A significant factor in achieving uniformity is the almost universal use of standard form documents as the basis of most carriage contracts and also the selection of English law and jurisdiction clauses in those contracts, for example in GAFTA (Grain and Feed Trade Association) contracts.

Carriage of goods by sea falls to be performed in special and often hazardous conditions in which it is practically impossible for one party to supervise the work of the other from day to day. This factor was clearly instrumental in the development of the sea carrier's implied duties, including the duty to provide a seaworthy ship and the duty not to deviate from route. It also influenced those parts of the law dealing with the shipper's duty to disclose the dangerous nature of goods shipped, the master's powers of jettison and other extraordinary powers conferred on the master in the event of an emergency.

Another notable feature is that shipping is directly dependent on other commercial activities. Contracts for the carriage of goods by sea are not made in commercial isolation. They are typically entered into in order to sell goods or to give effect to a previous sale. This means that contracts for sea carriage are often of direct interest to persons such as buyers or lenders as well as to the original parties to the contract. Third parties may become involved in the carriage of goods in other ways. Even when a cargo remains in the ownership of a single shipper throughout an ocean voyage it is quite possible that the whole or part of the contract (loading or discharging the cargo, for example) may actually be performed by someone other than the party who originally contracted to carry and deliver. This leads to complex questions about who can sue and who can be sued. In the absence of a statute dealing with the particular problem, in English law satisfactory answers to these questions often involve the creative application of ideas drawn from contract (for example, implication of a contract or of a term), tort (for example, recognition or denial of a duty of care), bailment (terms of bailment) or the law of evidence or of damages.

The widespread use of standard forms has already been mentioned. This use amounts in itself to an important feature of the sea trade. It means that much of the law in this area consists of settled interpretations of common clauses and decisions about the terms that can be implied into contracts of carriage in the absence of express agreement. One consequence of the addiction to the use of standard forms is that judicial decisions on the interpretation of standard terms are of wide interest in the shipping industry, which pays marked attention to the law reports. But the wide use of certain forms also means that a judicial decision that disturbs an accepted construction of a document may retrospectively affect many transactions entered into on the basis of that previously accepted meaning. This may influence the willingness of the courts to reverse a settled interpretation. But so too does the knowledge that shipping circles show no reluctance to make amendments to standard forms in order to avoid anything seen as an unsatisfactory precedent.

So much for some of the special features of the trade; can these special features be proved to have influenced the form of what is mostly judge-made law? It would not be easy to show this in some branches of the common law. But the problem is not so great in the case of the law of carriage by sea. For there is a long tradition of looking at this subject as more than a closed set of technical rules. This means that it is not difficult to collect examples of judgments that determine the law only after consideration of the policy that makes the most sense in the special context in which maritime contracts are performed. The well-known decision in *Behn v Burness* (1863) 3 B & S 751, Exchequer Chamber is a clear example. Other examples from the same chapter include *McAndrew v Adams* (1834) 1 Bing NC 31, Common Pleas and *Bentsen v Taylor* [1893] 2 QB 274, CA. These are not isolated instances.

As we have already noted, the study of the law of carriage of goods by sea is a discrete academic subject but, whilst acknowledging its intellectual status, we should not lose sight of its intimate connection with commercial practice. It is important therefore to set our study of law into its context. The following extract from Stopford, M, *Maritime Economics*, 2009, 3rd edn, Oxford: Routledge at page 61 will help do this.

The sea transport system

The economic model for sea transport saw that over the last 50 years the shipping industry has developed a new transport system based on mechanization and systems technology. Within this system the economic pressures arising from the parcel size distribution and demand differentiation create the demand for different types of shipping service. Today's shipping market has evolved into three separate but closely connected segments: bulk shipping, specialized shipping and liner shipping. Although these segments belong to the same industry, each carries out different tasks and has a very different character.

The transport model is summarized below. Starting at the top of this diagram (row A), world trade splits into three streams; bulk parcels, specialized parcels and general cargo parcels; depending on the PSD function for the commodity and service requirements of each cargo parcel. Large homogeneous parcels such as iron ore, coal and grain are carried by the bulk shipping industry; small parcels of general cargo are carried by the liner shipping industry; and specialized cargoes shipped in large volumes are transported by the specialized shipping industry. These three cargo streams create demand for bulk transport, specialized transport and liner transport (row B). The lower half of the diagram shows how the supply of ships is organized. A major distinction is drawn between the fleets of ships owned by the companies moving their own cargo in their own ships (row C) and the ships owned by independent shipowners (row D) and chartered to the cargo owners in Row C. Between rows C and D are the charter markets where rates for transport are negotiated. This is a highly flexible structure. For example, an oil company might decide to buy its own fleet of tankers to cover half of its oil transport needs and meet the other half by chartering tankers from shipowners. The same applies to the specialized and liner markets.

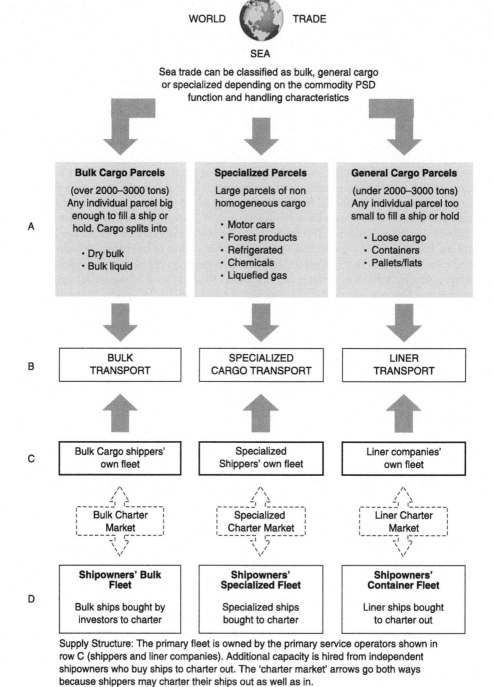

WORLD TRADE

SEA

Sea trade can be classified as bulk, general cargo
or specialized depending on the commodity PSD
function and handling characteristics

Bulk Cargo Parcels

(over 2000–3000 tons)
Any individual parcel big
enough to fill a ship or
hold. Cargo splits into

• Dry bulk
• Bulk liquid

Specialized Parcels

Large parcels of non
homogeneous cargo

• Motor cars
• Forest products
• Refrigerated
• Chemicals
• Liquefied gas

General Cargo Parcels

(under 2000–3000 tons)
Any individual parcel too
small to fill a ship or hold

• Loose cargo
• Containers
• Pallets/flats

A

BULK
TRANSPORT

SPECIALIZED
CARGO TRANSPORT

LINER
TRANSPORT

B

Bulk Cargo shippers'
own fleet

Specialized
Shippers' own fleet

Liner companies'
own fleet

C

Bulk Charter
Market

Specialized
Charter Market

Liner Charter
Market

**Shipowners' Bulk
Fleet**

Bulk ships bought by
investors to charter

**Shipowners'
Specialized Fleet**

Specialized ships
bought to charter

**Shipowners'
Container Fleet**

Liner ships bought
to charter out

D

Supply Structure: The primary fleet is owned by the primary service operators shown in
row C (shippers and liner companies). Additional capacity is hired from independent
shipowners who buy ships to charter out. The 'charter market' arrows go both ways
because shippers may charter their ships out as well as in.

Figure 1.1

The bulk shipping industry carries large parcels of raw materials and bulky semi-manufactures. This is a very distinctive business. Bulk vessels handle few transactions, typically completing about six voyages with a single cargo each year, so the annual revenue depends on half a dozen negotiations per ship each year. In addition, service levels are usually low so little overhead is required to run the ships and organize the cargo. Typically bulk shipping companies have employees in the office for every ship at sea, so a fleet of 50 ships worth $1 billion could be run by a staff of employees, depending on how much of the routine management is subcontracted. In short, bulk shipping businesses focus on minimizing the cost of providing safe transport and managing investment in the expensive ships needed to supply bulk transport.

The liner service transports small parcels of general cargo, which includes manufactured and semi-manufactured goods and many small quantities of bulk commodities malting barley, steel products, non-ferrous metal ores and even waste paper may be transported by liner. For example, a container-ship handles revenue transactions each year, so a fleet of six ships completes transactions per annum. Because there are so many parcels to handle on each voyage, this is a very organization-intensive business. In addition, the transport leg often forms part of an integrated production operation, so speed, reliability and high service levels are important. However, cost is also crucial because the whole business philosophy of international manufacturing depends on cheap transport. With so many transactions, the business relies on published prices, though nowadays prices are generally negotiated with major customers as part of a service agreement. In addition, cargo liners are involved in the through-transport of containers. This is a business where transaction costs are very high and the customers are just as interested in service levels as price.

Specialized shipping services transport difficult cargoes of which the five most important are motor cars, forest products, refrigerated cargo, chemicals and liquefied gas. These trades fall somewhere between bulk and liner; for example, a sophisticated chemical tanker carries parcels a year, often under contracts of affreightment (COAs), but they may take (i.e. individually negotiated) cargoes as well. Service providers in these trades invest in specialized ships and offer higher service levels than bulk shipping companies. Some of the operators become involved in terminals to improve the integration of the cargo-handling operations. They also work with shippers to rationalize and streamline the distribution chain. For example, motor manufacturers and chemical companies place high priority on this and in this sector the pressure for change often comes from its sophisticated clients.

So although the three segments of the shipping industry all carry cargo in ships, they face different tasks in terms of the value and volume of cargo, the number of transactions handled, and the commercial systems employed. Bulk shipping carries the high-volume, price-sensitive cargoes; specialized shipping carries those higher-value cargoes such as cars, refrigerated cargo, forest products and chemicals; the container business transports small parcels; and air freight does the rush jobs. But these segments also overlap, leading to intense competition for the minor bulk cargoes such as forest products, scrap, refrigerated cargo and even grain.

Definition of 'bulk shipping'

Bulk shipping developed as the major sector in the decades following the Second World War. A fleet of specialist crude oil tankers was built to service the rapidly expanding economies of Western Europe and Japan, with smaller vessels for the carriage of oil products and liquid chemicals. In the dry bulk trades, several important industries, notably steel, aluminium and fertilizer manufacture, turned to foreign suppliers for their high-quality raw materials and a fleet of large bulk carriers was built to service the trade, replacing the obsolete 'tweendeckers previously used to transport bulk commodities. As a result, bulk shipping became a rapidly expanding sector of the shipping industry, and bulk tonnage now accounts for about three-quarters of the world merchant fleet.

Most of the bulk cargoes are drawn from the raw material trades such as oil, iron ore, coal and grain, and are often described as bulk commodities on the assumption that, for example, all iron ore is shipped in bulk. In the case of iron ore this is a reasonable assumption, but many smaller commodity trades are shipped partly in bulk and partly as general cargo; for example, a shipload of forest products would be rightly classified as bulk cargo but consignments of logs still travel as general cargo in a few trades. There are three main categories of bulk cargo:

- Liquid bulk requires tanker transportation. The main ones are crude oil, oil products, liquid chemicals such as caustic soda, vegetable oils, and wine. The size of individual consignments varies from a few thousand tons to half a million tons in the case of crude oil.
- The five major bulks – iron ore, grain, coal, phosphates and bauxite – are homogeneous bulk cargoes which can be transported satisfactorily in a conventional dry bulk carrier or multi-purpose (MPP) stowing at 45–55 cubic feet per ton.
- Minor bulks covers the many other commodities that travel in shiploads. The most important are steel products, steel scrap, cement, gypsum, non-ferrous metal ores, sugar, salt, sulphur, forest products, wood chips and chemicals.

Definition of 'liner shipping'

The operation of liner services is a very different business. General cargo consignments are too small to justify setting up a bulk shipping operation. In addition, they are often high-value or delicate, requiring a special shipping service for which the shippers prefer a fixed tariff rather than a fluctuating market rate. There are no hard-and-fast rules about what constitutes general cargo- boxes, bales, machinery, 1,000 tons of steel products, 50 tons of bagged malting barley are typical examples. The main classes of general cargo from a shipping viewpoint are as follows:

- Loose cargo, individual items, boxes, pieces of machinery, etc., each of which must be handled and stowed separately. All general cargo used to be shipped this way, but now almost all has been unitized in one way or another.
- Containerized cargo, standard boxes, usually 8 feet wide, often 8 feet 6 inches high and mostly 20 or 40 feet long, filled with cargo. This is now the principal form of general cargo transport.
- Palletized cargo, for example cartons of apples, are packed onto standard pallets, secured by straps or pallet stretch film for easy stacking and fast handling.
- Pre-slung cargo, small items such as planks of wood lashed together into standard- sized packages.
- Liquid cargo travels in deep tanks, liquid containers or drums.
- Refrigerated cargo, perishable goods that must be shipped, chilled or frozen, in insulated holds or refrigerated containers.
- Heavy and awkward cargo, large and difficult to stow.

Until the mid-1960s most general cargo (called 'break-bulk' cargo) travelled loose and each item had to be packed in the hold of a cargo liner using 'dunnage' (pieces of wood or burlap) to keep it in place. This labour-intensive operation was slow, expensive, difficult to plan and the cargo was exposed to the risk of damage or pilferage. As a result cargo liners spent two-thirds of their time in port and cargo-handling costs escalated to more than one-quarter of the total shipping cost, making it difficult for liner operators to provide the service at an economic cost, and their profit margins were squeezed.

The shipping industry's response was to 'unitize' the transport system, applying the same technology which had been applied successfully on the production lines in manufacturing industry. Work was standardized, allowing investment to increase productivity. Since cargo handling was the main bottleneck, the key was to pack the cargo into internationally accepted standard units which could be handled quickly and cheaply with specially designed equipment. At the outset many systems of unitization were examined, but the two main contenders were pallets and containers. Pallets are flat trays, suitable for handling by fork-lift truck, on which single or multiple units can be packed for easy handling. Containers are standard boxes into which individual items are packed. The first deep-sea container service was introduced in 1966 and in the next 20 years containers came to dominate the transport of general cargo, with shipments of over 50 million units per year.

Definition of 'specialized shipping'

'Specialized' shipping sits somewhere between the liner and the bulk shipping sectors and has characteristics of both. Although it is treated as a separate sector of the business, the dividing line is not particularly well defined. The principal distinguishing feature of these specialized trades is that they use ships designed to carry a specific cargo type and provide a service which is targeted at a particular customer group. Buying specialized ships is risky and is only worthwhile if the cargoes have handling or storage characteristics which make it worth investing in ships designed to improve transport performance of that specific cargo.

. . .

Arranging employment for a ship

When a ship is chartered or a freight rate is agreed, the ship is said to be 'fixed'. Fixtures are arranged in much the same way as any major international hiring or subcontracting operation. Shipowners have vessels for hire, charterers have cargo to transport, and brokers put the deal together. Let us briefly consider the part played by each of these.

The shipowner comes to the market with a ship available, free of cargo. The ship has a particular speed, cargo capacity, dimensions and cargo-handling gear. Existing contractual commitments will determine the date and location at which it will become available. For example, it may be a Handymax bulk carrier currently on a voyage from the US Gulf to deliver grain to Japan, so it will be 'open' (available for hire) in Japan from the anticipated date at which the grain has been discharged, say 12 May. Depending upon his chartering strategy, the shipowner may be looking for a short charter for the vessel or a long charter.

The shipper or charterer may be someone with a volume of cargo to transport from one location to another or a company that needs an extra ship for a period of time. The quantity, timing and physical characteristics of the cargo will determine the type of shipping contract required. For example, the shipper may have a cargo of 50,000 tons of coal to ship from Newcastle, New South Wales, to Rotterdam. Such a cargo might be very attractive to a bulk carrier operator discharging coal in Japan and looking for a cargo to reposition into the North Atlantic, because he has only a short ballast leg from Japan to Australia and then a full cargo back to Europe. So how does the shipper contact the shipowner?

Often the principal (i.e. the owner or charterer) will appoint a shipbroker to act for him. The broker's task is to discover what cargoes or ships are available; what expectations the owners/charterers have about what they will be paid or pay; and what is reasonable given the state of the market. With this information they negotiate the deal for their client, often intense competition with other brokers. Brokers provide other services, including post-fixture processing, dealing with disputes, and providing accounting services in respect of freight, demurrage, etc. Some owners or shippers carry out these tasks themselves. However, this requires a staff and management structure which only very large companies can justify. For this reason most owners and charterers use one or more brokers. Since broking is all about information, brokers tend to gather in shipping centres. London remains the biggest, with other major centres in New York, Tokyo, Hong Kong, Singapore, Piraeus, Oslo and Hamburg.

Four types of contractual arrangement are commonly used, each of which distributes costs and responsibilities in a slightly different way. Under a voyage charter, the shipowner contracts to carry a specific cargo in a specific ship for a negotiated price per ton which covers all the costs. A variant on the same theme is the contract of affreightment, in which the shipowner contracts to carry regular tonnages of cargo for an

1. Voyage Charter *Master instructed by:-* Owner	2. Time charter *Master instructed by:-* Owner for ship and charterer for cargo	3. Bare boat *Master appointed by:-* Charterer
Revenue depends on: Quantity of cargo & rate per unit of cargo	*Revenue depends on*: Hire rate, duration and off-hire time	*Revenue depends on*: Hire rate & duration
Costs paid by owner:	**Costs paid by owner:**	**Costs paid by owner:**
1. Capital costs Capital Brokerage	*1. Capital costs* Capital Brokerage	*1. Capital costs* Capital Brokerage
2. Operating costs Wages Provisions Maintenance Repairs Stores & supplies Lube oil Water Insurance Overheads	*2. Operating costs* Wages Provisions Maintenance Repairs Stores & supplies Lube oil Water Insurance Overheads	Operating costs: note that under bare boat these are paid by the charterer
3. Port costs Port charges Stevadoring charges Cleaning holds Cargo claims *4. Bunkers, etc* Canal transit dues Bunker fuel	Voyage costs: note that under time- charter and bare boat contracts these costs are paid by the charterer	

4. Contract of Affreightment (COA): cost profile same as voyage charter

Figure 1.2

agreed price per ton, again covering all the costs. The time charter is an agreement between owner and charterer to hire the ship, complete with crew, for a fee per day, month or year. In this case the shipowner pays the capital costs and operating expenses, whilst the charterer pays the voyage costs. The owner continues to manage the ship, but the charterer instructs the master where to go and what cargo to load and discharge. Finally the bare boat charter hires out the ship without crew or any operational responsibilities, so in this case the owner just pays the capital costs- it is really a financing arrangement, requiring no ship management expertise on the part of the owner.

The voyage charter

A voyage charter provides transport for a specific cargo from port A to port B for a fixed price per ton. For example, a grain trader may have 25,000 tons of grain to transport from Port Cartier in Canada to Tilbury in the UK. So what does he do? He calls his broker and tells him that he needs transport for the cargo. The broker will fix (i.e. charter) a ship for the voyage at a negotiated freight rate per ton of cargo, say $5.20. The terms will be set out in a charter-party and, if all goes well, the ship arrives on the due date, loads the cargo, transports it to Tilbury, discharges and the transaction is complete.

If the voyage is not completed within the terms of charter-party then there will be a claim. For example, if laytime (i.e. port time) at Tilbury is specified as 7 days and the time counted in port is 10 days, the owner submits a claim for 3 days' demurrage to the charterer. Conversely, if the ship spends only 5 days in port, the charterer will submit a claim for 2 days' despatch to the owner. The rates for demurrage and despatch are stated in dollars per day in the charter-party.

The calculation of demurrage and despatch does not normally present problems, but cases do arise where the charterer disputes the owner's right to demurrage. Demurrage becomes particularly important when there is port congestion. During the 1970s there were delays of up to 6 months in discharging cargo in the Middle East and Lagos, while during the coal boom of 1979 bulk carriers had to wait several months to load coal at Baltimore and Hampton Roads. These are extremes, but during very strong markets such as 2007 when Capesize bulk carriers were earning over $200,000 a day and iron ore ports were congested, even a few days demurrage can be significant. In cases where the demurrage cannot be accurately predicted it is important to the shipowner that he receives a demurrage payment equivalent to his daily hire charge.

The contract of affreightment

The contract of affreightment is a little more complicated. The shipowner agrees to carry a series of cargo parcels for a fixed price per ton. For example, the shipper may have a contract to supply 10 consignments of 50,000 tons of coal from Colombia to Rotterdam at two-monthly intervals. He would like to arrange for the shipment in a single contract at an agreed price per ton and leave the details of each voyage to the shipowner. This allows the shipowner to plan the use of his ships in the most efficient manner. He can switch cargo between vessels to give the best possible operating pattern and consequently a lower charter rate. He may also be able to arrange backhaul cargoes which improve the utilization of the ship. Companies who specialize in COAs sometimes describe their business as industrial shipping; because their aim is to provide a service. Since a long-term contract is involved, COAs involve a greater commitment to servicing the shipper and providing an efficient service.

Most COA business is in the major dry bulk cargoes of iron ore and coal, and the major customers are the steel mills of Europe and the Far East. The problem in negotiating COAs is that the precise volume and timing of cargo shipments are not generally known in advance. Cargo volume may be specified as a range (e.g. minimum x and maximum y tons), while timing may rely on generalizations such as 'The shipments under the contract shall be evenly spread over the contract period'.

The time charter

A time charter gives the charterer operational control of the ships carrying his cargo, while leaving ownership and management of the vessel in the hands of the shipowner. The length of the charter may be the time taken to complete a single voyage (trip charter) or a period of months or years (period charter). When on charter, the shipowner continues to pay the operating costs of the vessel (i.e. the crew, maintenance and repair), but the charterer directs the commercial operations of the vessel and pays all voyage expenses (i.e. bunkers, port charges and canal dues) and cargo-handling costs. With a time charter, the shipowner has a clear basis for preparing the ship's budget, since he knows the ship operating costs from experience and is in receipt of a fixed daily or monthly charter rate (e.g. $5,000 per day). Often the shipowner will use a long time charter from a major corporation, such as a steel mill or an oil company, as security for a loan to purchase the ship needed for the trade.

Although simple in principle, in practice time charters are complex and involve risks for both parties. Details of the contractual agreement are set out in the charter-party. The shipowner must state the vessel's speed, fuel consumption and cargo capacity. The terms of hire will be adjusted if the ship does not perform to these standards. The charter-party will also set out the conditions under which the vessel is regarded as 'off-hire' for example, during emergency repairs, when the charterer does not pay the charter hire. Long time charters also deal with such matters as the adjustment to the hire charge in the event of the vessel being laid up, and will set out certain conditions under which the charterer is entitled to terminate the arrangement- for example, if the owner fails to run the ship efficiently.

There are three reasons why subcontracting may be attractive. First, the shipper may not wish to become a shipowner, but his business requires the use of a ship under his control. Second, the time charter may work out cheaper than buying, especially if the owner has lower costs, due to lower overheads and larger fleet. This seems to have been one of the reasons why oil companies subcontracted so much of their transport in the 1960s. Third, the charterer may be a speculator taking a position in anticipation of a change in the market.

Time chartering to industrial clients is a prime source of revenue for the shipowner. The availability of time charters varies from cargo to cargo and with business circumstances. In the early 1970s about 80% of oil tankers owned by independent shipowners were on time charter to oil companies. The figure below shows that twenty years later the position had reversed and only about 20% were on time charter. In short, there had been a major change of policy by the oil companies, in response to changing circumstances in the tanker market and the oil industry.

The bare boat charter

Finally, if a company wishes to have full operational control of the ship, but does not wish to own it, a bare boat charter is arranged. Under this arrangement the investor, not necessarily a professional shipowner, purchases the vessel and hands it over to the charterer for a specified period, usually 10–20 years. The charterer manages the vessel and pays all operating and voyage costs. The owner, who is often a financial institution such as a life insurance company, is not active in the operation of a vessel and does not require any specific maritime skills. It is just an investment. The advantages are that the shipping company does not tie up its capital and the nominal owner of the ship may obtain a tax benefit.

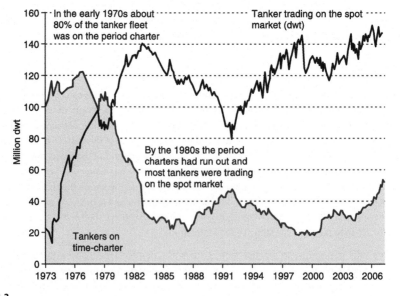

Figure 1.3

2 Chartered shipping

Charterparties will be used where the charterer has a shipload of cargo to move. Where smaller quantities of cargo are concerned then the shipper may (possibly through a freight forwarder) contract with the operators of a liner service. If the bulk (or tramp as it was once popularly called) ship can be compared to a taxi i.e. because it is willing to call wherever it is needed, then the liner is akin to a bus i.e. regularly traveling along a fixed and advertised route.

3 Liner shipping

In liner shipping the terms of the contract are traditionally printed on the bill of lading, which is a receipt for the goods issued by the carrier. At the end of the voyage the carrier will demand that this receipt be produced and surrendered. In this way, the bill of lading operates like a cloakroom ticket. However, this is a ticket that can be transferred by the shipper to someone else. Often it will be a buyer or sub-buyer of the goods from the shipper who will eventually produce the bill of lading and claim delivery from the carrier.

Although a bill of lading may itself be a contract (or evidence of a contract) of affreightment, there is in practice no rigid distinction between operations governed by charterparties and those in which a bill of lading makes an appearance. Where a vessel is under charter it very often happens that bills of lading are issued. If a vessel is voyage chartered to carry the charterer's own goods, the charterer may want a bill of lading in order to be able to prove, if a dispute arises, that goods were delivered to the carrier. And if the charterer wishes to be able to sell the goods before retaking possession from the carrier, he will want the receipt to be in the transferable form of a bill of lading. Moreover, if a vessel is being operated by a charterer who wishes to trade with it and make a profit by carrying goods belonging to other shippers, it is almost inevitable that bills of lading will be issued to those shippers. We examine the features of the bill of lading in Chapter 5.

In the past, contracts were often made both informally and indirectly. The judgment in *Heskell v Continental Express* (1950) 83 Ll L Rep 438 (a case involving liner shipping) contains a description of a process in which no contract was concluded until goods were loaded or accepted for loading. Having learned from an advertisement or otherwise of a date and place of sailing, a shipper would forward his goods to the dock or berth. At the docks, a dock receipt or a mate's receipt would be given in exchange for the goods. The shipper or his agent would then prepare a draft bill of lading in the form used by the particular line and deliver it to the shipowner or his agent. Meanwhile the various consignments of what might be a very mixed cargo would be loaded and stowed on board, the location of a particular parcel depending on its size, shape and other properties, including density and packing as well as on the order in which its port of discharge would be reached in the course of the voyage. A good deal of manual labour was needed to stow break-bulk cargo on a liner. After loading, the draft bill of lading would be checked against the earlier receipt, signed by the master or more often an agent employed by the shipping line and issued to the shipper or his agent in exchange for the freight. In these circumstances, the contract between shipper and carrier depended on the contents of advertisements, and on any public and private statements, trade practice and prior dealings, as well as on the terms printed on the bill of lading.

Containers and computers have changed all this. Probably the most noticeable physical change in UK liner shipping since *Heskell* has been that conventional break-bulk services to many destinations have been replaced by container shipping. A typical general purpose container is manufactured to the International Organization for Standardization's agreed dimensions of 8ft in width by 8ft 6in high by 20ft in length; it is made of steel and capable of carrying up to 24 tons weight. Other lengths (for example, 40ft), heights and materials are also used. Refrigerated and other non-standard containers are available, including open top, half-height, ventilated containers and tank containers for liquids.

The vessel on which such a container is loaded is also likely to be very different from the type of general purpose liner in use when *Heskell* was decided. Today's liner is likely to be specially designed for carrying containers; a fully or partly cellular container ship uses a cell guide system to enable quick mechanical stowage of containers either by shore-based cranes or possibly by the ship's own gear.

From the point of view of a shipper who wants to move either a full container load (FCL) or less than full container load (LCL), it has been said that containers have a number of advantages. Goods shipped move faster and are better protected from damage and theft; a container can be sealed before the start of a journey. It may not then be necessary for the contents to be touched until the seal is broken when the box is opened at its destination.

Containerisation has also resulted in the development of integrated transport services in which carriers are willing to contract to carry from door-to-door or from terminal-to-terminal, and not simply from port-to-port, or 'tackle to tackle' as it is sometimes known. This feature is acknowledged in the changes proposed in the Rotterdam Rules (of which more later). When a shipper reserves space with a carrier for door-to-door transport of his goods, a container can be delivered to the shipper's own premises where it can be packed ('stuffed') and later collected for delivery by road to a container terminal where it will be stored until loaded on board ship. Carriers who offer this multimodal type of transport service are often referred to as Combined Transport or Through Transport Operators. As a matter of terminology, some parts of the UK shipping industry use 'combined transport' to refer to a contract under which the carrier contracts as a principal to carry out the performance of the whole of a transport by two or more modes of transport, while in 'through transport' the carrier contracts as principal in respect of one stage of a journey but only as the agent of the owner of the goods to arrange all other stages. It is, however, important to appreciate that many bills of lading do not recognise this distinction and use the terms 'through'/'combined' transport indiscriminately.

Containers also have advantages from the point of view of the sea carrier. Mechanical handling is quicker and cheaper than traditional methods of loading and stowing. Quicker handling means that container vessels need to spend less time in port and can spend more time at sea so that their productivity is improved. Container ships are faster, more sophisticated and more expensive than their break-bulk counterparts. High costs are involved in building the necessary shore facilities and in providing enough ships of the right size to take advantage of economies of scale and yet at the same time provide the frequent and regular service needed by shippers. This is one reason why some shipowners have chosen not to operate independently in containerised liner trades but instead to amalgamate with others or to join consortia that operate the vessels owned by their members. This development has itself given rise to new and difficult questions of legal liability for loss or damage to goods both as between consortium members and Shippers on the one hand and as between consortium members themselves on the other.

A number of other important changes have also occurred since *Heskell* was decided. In UK outbound liner shipping, the mate's receipt is now a comparative rarity. Export cargo to be carried by a line is forwarded for shipment accompanied by a standard shipping note or a dangerous goods note prepared in several copies by or on behalf of the shipper. A copy of the Shipping Note is signed and returned to the shipper to acknowledge receipt. And it is now common for the bill of lading to be prepared by the carrier by computer from details supplied when the shipper reserved space on a vessel.

An alternative to a bill of lading is also available. A sea waybill is also a receipt for goods issued by a carrier and may contain evidence of the terms of a contract of affreightment in much the same way as a bill of lading. But unlike a bill of lading, a sea waybill does not have to be presented at destination in order to obtain delivery of the goods. Delivery is made to a nominated consignee against proof of identity. A sea waybill may be used in preference to a bill of lading if, for example, it is likely that goods that have been shipped will reach their destination before a bill of lading (as on short sea routes in Europe) and if the shipper does not need a bill of lading in order to obtain payment for or to transfer the title to the goods while they are in the possession of the carrier. The sea waybill unlike the bill of lading is not a negotiable instrument, an essential feature in, for example, commodity trading. See our later remarks on bills of lading Chapter 5.

The chartering process and the charter market

United Nations Conference on Trade and Development (UNCTAD), From *Charter Parties*, report by the Secretariat of UNCTAD, ©1974 United Nations, Reprinted with the permission of the United Nations

(1) The chartering process

A Bargaining position of contracting parties
52 Charterparties are contracts that are negotiated in a free market governed by the prevailing factors of the shipping supply and demand situation. Characteristically, conditions in the freight market are constantly changing, at one stage favouring owners and at another charterers. The state of the market at a particular time is an important factor influencing the bargaining position of the contracting parties.

53 The actual structure of the shipping industry has also an effect on the bargaining position. In chartering, the offer of shipping services in response to an inquiry for shipping space is made by tramp vessel owners who, lacking regular customers, need continuously to find such employment for their vessels as they can under prevailing market conditions. The shipowner's position is not then generally one of domination and the voyage or time charterer is frequently in a position to negotiate the contract on an equal footing, depending on the state of the market at the time.

54 In some trades, it is not unusual for the charterer to occupy the more powerful position in terms of share of the market and financial strength. Charterers, whether appearing in the voyage market or in the time charter market, are often, through their own organisations, in command of large cargo tonnage, as in some of the grain, coal and ore trades. This concentration of bargaining strength on the cargo shipping side appears to have been growing in recent years. To counter this development, shipowners are forming joint ventures in which owners are chartering their vessels to a jointly owned ship-operating company that, in turn, charters the vessels to shippers. A variety of arrangements as regards the management of individual vessels and other matters are possible in the formation and operation of such shipping pools.

B Standard charterparty forms
55 Voyage and time charterparties are, as a rule, concluded on the basis of standard contract forms, and such documentation therefore plays a role of considerable importance in present chartering practice.

56 A brief account follows of the development of standard charterparty forms, of the organisations dealing with their issue and of the different types in common use, following which some general aspects of these documents are discussed.

The development of standard charterparty forms

57 It was in the nineteenth century that shipowners and charterers first concerned themselves with the drafting of standard charterparty forms. Such forms were originally drafted and employed by individual contracting parties, but joint action was later undertaken by groups of shipowners and charterers. An early development began with parties involved in chartering in particular trades co-operating on the joint issue of agreed documents. The establishment in 1862 of the Mediterranean and Black Sea Freight Committee may be cited as an example; this organisation, composed of shipowners, merchants and brokers, issued several standard charterparty forms for the grain trade from the Black Sea and the Mediterranean.

58 In the present century, two organisations have played, and still play, a significant role in the development of internationally utilised standard forms, namely, the Chamber of Shipping of the United Kingdom in London, founded in 1878, and the Baltic and International Maritime Council in Copenhagen (BIMCO), founded in 1905 under the name of the Baltic and White Sea Conference. The work on documentary matters is performed by the Chamber of Shipping through its Documentary Committee and by BIMCO through its Documentary Council. These bodies have issued or approved a great number of standard charterparty forms many of which are so-called 'agreed' documents, as they result from negotiations between charterer and shipper interests, on the one hand, and shipowner interests, on the other; listed as being in current use are four forms for time chartering, including the much used Baltime form, and more than 60 forms for voyage chartering, comprising special forms for most main commodities, as well as general trade forms. In chartering practice, these documents are generally referred to as 'approved' or 'official' forms.

59 Besides the Chamber of Shipping/BIMCO documents – hereafter called approved forms – there are various long-standing standard charterparty forms which are in widespread use in different trades. Mention might be made of the 'C (Ore)7' form, originally devised by the British government to cover ore imports during the First World War, the 'Americanised Welsh Coal Charter 1953', the 'Africanphos 1950' for shipments of phosphate from Morocco, the 'Sugar Charter Party-Steam (London Form)' in general use for cereal shipments from the United States and Canada, and, for time charters, the 'New York Produce Exchange Time Charter'.

60 A further type of standard charterparty form is the so-called 'private' form (sometimes called 'house charterparty'), which is issued and employed by individual firms, usually charterers enjoying more or less of a monopoly in a particular trade and therefore in a position generally to impose their own form on the shipowner. Such private forms, of which there exist a great number, are common in, for example, the ore, fertilizer and oil trades.

General aspects of standard charterparty forms

61 It is the view of some authorities that where standard forms or particular clauses therein are completed by one party to the contract enjoying a dominant position *vis-à-vis* the other, through protection of his own interests the contract may tend to become unduly favourable to him to the detriment of the other party. In shipping this may be illustrated by the practices which prevailed in respect of liner bills of lading prior to the introduction of the Hague Rules. The situation as regards charterparties does not, however, lend itself to any generalisation of this kind.

62 It is true that some existing charterparty forms may be said to be generally biased in favour of one side, or to contain clauses on particular points which may be considered as unduly detrimental to the interests of one of the parties; in this regard, particular attention needs to be drawn to the so-called private forms mentioned above which, in the main, are documents issued by charterers. On the other hand, many standard forms are considered to represent a fair equilibrium between the interests of the parties; and it should be recalled in this context that many forms in common use are agreed documents, implying that they have been negotiated between owner and charterer interests.

63 As regards the drafting of the standard documentation in current use in chartering, this has been criticised as sometimes lacking in logical and systematic order, and, further, as often containing unclear expressions, lacunae, and provisions of little commercial or legal importance. While this is true in the case of several standard forms of an early origin, attention should be drawn to the fact that considerable improvement in documentary practice has been achieved by the work done over the last few decades by the Chamber of Shipping and BIMCO. Those two organisations have issued a number of modern documents, most of them agreed documents, which to a great extent have done away with earlier deficiencies.

64 Despite deficiencies of the kind that may still remain in certain documents, it is generally recognised that standard forms – as far as concerns approved or otherwise well known and commonly used forms – serve significant practical purposes and play an important role in maritime commerce as instruments for facilitating and improving the functioning of the contracting procedure.

65 As to the advantages to be derived from the use of such forms, it should be pointed out, firstly, that often the parties to a charter contract are domiciled in different countries and that the negotiations, which to a great extent are carried out through the intermediary of one or several brokers, are often performed under considerable time pressure. By basing the negotiations on a standard form, the contents of which are well known or readily available to both sides, the parties can concentrate their attention on the particular points on which they require an individual regulation, leaving all other questions to be regulated by the terms of the standard form. The use of a standard form, moreover, means that the parties run no risk of being caught out by an unusual clause or a clause imposing unreasonable or unexpected burdens on them; this, in turn, means cheaper freight rates since the owner does not have to reckon on the freight to cover him for such risks. Generally speaking, it reduces the risk of misunderstandings and ensuing disputes arising in respect of the matters covered by the contract.

66 The employment of standard forms in international chartering has an important effect also from a general legal standpoint, in that they contribute to international uniformity; disparities between regulations prescribed in the various legal systems are partly neutralised, so that similar cases taken to litigation or arbitration will tend, to a certain extent, to bring the same result, irrespective of the jurisdiction under which they are decided. Litigation and submission to arbitration is also thereby reduced. The fact that standard forms are very largely drafted in the English language and are based on English legal thinking supports this tendency toward international uniformity.

67 It should be stressed, however, that the charterparty, whether a voyage or a time charter, is an individual contract, and that the widely varying conditions under which chartering is done set a limit to the possibility of using stereotyped contract terms framed to suit a large number of cases. Thus, time charterparties, especially for long charter periods, must to a considerable extent be tailor-made to meet the particular requirements of the parties. As to voyage charterparties, these are often concluded by the charterer pursuant to the conclusion of a sales contract respecting the cargo to be shipped, and their terms are then made to conform with that contract. Consequently, the standard forms may be amended in various respects, and clauses are often added in order to adapt the contract to the wishes and requirements of the parties. Such amendments, unless made with skill and care, may easily lead to inconsistencies and subsequent difficulties in respect of the construction of the charter; in fact, most charterparty disputes arise from ambiguities created by changes in the standard text or from unclear drafting of additional clauses inserted in the form . . .

(2) The charter market

A The marketplace
110 Finding the right ship or the right cargo among the hundreds of possibilities existing in world shipping at one particular time may seem like searching for the proverbial needle in the haystack. Yet the process of mating cargo with ship can be performed very quickly.

111 The efficiency of the chartering process can be attributed to three dominant characteristics of the charter market:

(a) The large number of shipowners, charterers and shipbrokers the world over;

(b) The availability of rapid modern communications, principally long-distance telex and telephone networks; and

(c) The prevalence of numerous charter market information sources providing late market status reports, as trade newspapers and magazines, shipbrokers' daily information sheets and special studies from a variety of sources.

112 In addition, the world shipping fraternity is an avid reader of the daily news, with special emphasis on weather, economic, trade and crop reports as well as political events. Any current development in those areas may have an important influence on the availability of shipping and on the level of market freight rates. Knowledgeable shipowners and charterers commence a particular chartering transaction with full background information on existing market conditions. Thus, bargaining over freight rates may be limited to a narrow range of rates, with relatively lengthier discussion taking place concerning other specific charter terms.

113 The existence of shipbrokers greatly facilitates the speed and efficiency of the chartering process. The role of the shipbroker is to provide expertise and information at the time these are required by his clients. The expertise takes the form of a knowledge and understanding of ships and trades that enables him to meld the two to the mutual satisfaction of owner and charterer. The shipbroker's information must be highly specific as to the availability of ships and cargoes, together with the freight rates that each may command.

114 A shipbroker is likely to specialise in particular categories of ships and trades. In this process he acquires and maintains an appreciation of the economic factors underlying the trades which he can utilise in interpreting the needs of shipowner and charterer clients alike. The shipbroker's role is that of an intermediary. In this role his communications between principals must reflect the realities of the market place.

115 A standard commission rate for shipbrokers is 2.5 per cent of the gross charter revenue. If the owner and charterer are each represented by a broker normally the commission is equally shared between the two. Many of the larger shipowners and charterers perform their own brokering functions in order to avoid commission, as this can amount to large sums in the case of long-term charters.

116 The charter market is actually composed of many sectoral markets which are generally noncompeting. Vessel class distinctions exist for reasons of vessel type or size. Tankers, as a rule, do not engage in the dry cargo trades although they may from time to time enter the grain trades. Ore carriers, whose holds are small, are not suitable for the carriage of lighter commodities such as grain.

117 Specialised vessels, as LNG (liquid natural gas) tankers or other special product tankers, cannot compete with bulk carriers or other vessels of more generalised characteristics. Conversely, combination carriers in the market will cross over between the tanker and dry-cargo trades to seek the employment offering the greatest return. Large tankers and large dry-cargo carriers are most economically employed in long-haul trades. Small vessels cannot compete effectively in these long trades: they are generally most economical in coastal or short deep-sea shipping services. Despite the many differences in vessel sizes and types, a high degree of interchangeability in the employment of vessels does exist at the margin, so that movements in one sector of the market quickly affect the whole chartering market. Small tankers can carry oil even though they are more costly to operate than large tankers.

118 The charter market is also divided by length of charter: the short-term 'spot' market and the longer-term 'period' market. Short-term chartering may take the form of voyage charters or trip time charters (trip charters). The period market includes longer-term time charters, multiple (consecutive) voyage charters and long-term freighting contracts.

119 In contrast with the open charter market, there exists a very sizeable and growing 'closed' or private charter market wherein the fixture details are not publicly reported. In the negotiation of many charters, particularly the long-term sort, owners and charterers are reluctant to publicise the terms of the charter fixtures. For good reason, owners may have agreed to lower rates than might have been expected and widespread knowledge of such rates might 'spoil' the market. Similarly, charterers may not wish their transport costs to become known for reasons of competitiveness. However, the existence of such charters generally becomes known to the market even though information on specific terms may be lacking. The industry 'grapevine' is often very efficient in providing the missing information. Ironically, the level of charter rates negotiated in these non-reported fixtures is believed to be influenced by the reported level of open-market freight rates.

B Comparison of voyage and time charter costs (earnings)

120 Shipowners and charterers each have a choice between chartering on a voyage or on a time charter basis with the selection of the particular form of charter dependent on a variety of factors. For the shipper (charterer) the frequency, regularity and expected duration of the shipping need are important considerations. The additional workload on the shipper's organisation required by a time charter as compared with a voyage charter will also be considered.

121 For the shipowner, organisational requirements may be a dictating factor since shipowning companies staff, or conversely do not staff, to handle the additional workload associated with voyage charters. However, the shipowner's expectations of future freight market levels as compared with existing levels are frequently an overriding factor in his choice between voyage or time charter. If freight rates are at what the owner considers to be peak levels, he tends to fix his vessels in long-term charters which usually means chartering on a time charter basis, while preferring shorter-term voyage charters when he believes future market rates will rise. For the charterer and shipowner alike, the comparative cost (earnings) of the voyage and the time charter is of great interest. The cost-earnings calculations concerning the two types are not directly comparable since, as has been noted, voyage charters are contracts to transport cargo on a tonnage basis and time charters contract for the lifting capacity of a vessel on a time basis. There exists a need, therefore, for charterers and owners to compare the cost (earnings) relationship of chartering opportunities offered as voyage or time charters. The ability to make such a comparison is basic in the bargaining process associated with the negotiation of a charterparty . . .

C Fixing a voyage charter

125 The process of voyage chartering begins with an expression of a shipping requirement by a prospective charterer to his broker for a voyage charter which may be generally described as '25,000 tons of a commodity between ports A and B, loading date . . . ideas $4.50'. The broker will circulate this information to his shipowner clientele and make the information available to the shipping world generally through daily circulars and telex and telephone circuits to the principal chartering centres of the world, as London, New York, Tokyo and Hong Kong.

126 Responses to the charter offering will be received by the charterer's agent in the form of 'indications' which are relayed to the charterer for reaction and instructions. In a voyage charter, the charterer's main concerns are: the suitability of the vessel size and type, the geographical position of the vessel as affecting its ability to meet required loading dates, the charter rate, loading and discharging rates, laytime, and demurrage and dispatch rates.

127 An owner's consideration of a voyage chartering opportunity will particularly include, in addition to the indicated charter rate, the ports of loading and discharge of the voyage in question, the length of the voyage, and the nature of the cargo to be carried. To the owner the offered charter rate is a dominant but by no means the only consideration. If the discharge port is such as to offer further favourable trading possibilities without an unduly long haul in ballast, the owner will be inclined to accept a lower charter rate. As to voyage length, in general the longer the voyage at a given rate of return, the more attractive the charter to the owner.

128 Owners' responses are usually valid only for a short stated period of time, as 24 hours, so that he may in turn respond to other market offers if the current offer is not accepted. Depending on the 'tone' of the market (ie an indicated plentiful or short supply of tonnage), the charterer will make an early counter-offer or choose to wait if he anticipates that owners may improve their offers.

129 A firm offer for a voyage charter from an owner generally includes the following details:

> Period for which the offer is valid
> Freight rate
> Name of vessel
> Lay days
> Vessel's carrying capacity of the cargo in question
> Loading and discharging ports
> Loading/discharge costs
> Demurrage/dispatch
> Commission
> Charterparty form to be used

130 If, after analysis of the owner's offer, the prospective charterer believes that detailed agreement can be reached, he will make a counter-offer specifying the modifications that are desired. As discussed earlier, the effective cost of the voyage charter to the charterer can be reduced not only by lowering the stated charter rate but also by changes in such terms as those concerned with loading and discharging costs, demurrage and dispatch rates, and commission rates.

131 Voyage charters involving more than a single voyage may require extended interchange to reach agreement on the precise timing of each of the voyages, particularly in the case of longterm voyage charters lasting several years. The negotiations on long-term voyage charters will also require agreement on a variety of alternate charter performance conditions (as, acceptable vessel sizes and cargo loading dates, among others), not usually required in single-voyage charters.

132 A firm offer which is accepted within the period of validity binds the offerer and concludes the negotiations, while acceptance after the expiration of the time limit is considered a counter-offer. Indications or counter-offers bind neither party until formulated and accepted as firm offers. The exchange of offers is usually made in written form by telex or telegram and those made and accepted by telephone are usually confirmed afterwards in writing.

133 Often a firm offer is forwarded or accepted subject to special conditions. A typical example may be that of a merchant who wants to secure shipping space for goods he is about to buy or sell. He may find it practical to have tonnage at hand and negotiate all arrangements for the shipment prior to buying or selling the goods. In such a case his charter offer is made 'subject stem', meaning that he is in no way committed if the purchase or sale of the goods should not materialise. Another example is that of the owner who makes a firm offer 'subject open', meaning that he retains the right to withdraw his offer in case the vessel should be fixed for other business prior to acceptance of the offer in question. Offers with an attached 'subject' proviso should be treated with caution. In general such an offer is no more than an indication. Firm offers given or accepted on this basis do, however, serve a meaningful purpose in keeping the negotiations going and in providing a guide as to why the other party is hesitant.

134 The preparation of the formal voyage charterparty, following agreement on charter terms, is usually an expeditious and straightforward process, particularly for single-voyage charters embodied in a standard form.

135 The administration of the charter during its life requires careful record keeping by both the owner and the charterer to ensure that the payment terms of the various clauses of the charterparty are adhered to. For example, accurate measurement of the cargo loaded must be made in order to compute the charter hire payment. Payments of demurrage or dispatch normally result from each voyage, requiring computations carefully made in accordance with the charterparty terms. Often, agreement on the cost of repairing stevedoring damages does not occur until long after the voyage is completed since the performance of such repairs may not take place until the vessel's next dry-docking period.

D Fixing a time charter

136 The process of searching the market and fixing the charter for vessels to be placed on time charter may vary considerably depending on the contemplated length of the charter. For trip or other short-term charters, the procedures parallel those used for fixing a single-voyage charter. A more selective process is frequently used in the negotiation of time charters of longer duration than, say, one year. Often there is direct negotiation between the charterer and the owner, leaving out shipbrokers to avoid payment of commission.

137 A charterer will have highly specific ideas about the size, type and operating characteristics of the vessel he is seeking to place on time charter for an extended period. In addition, he is likely to have detailed knowledge of the charter status of individual ships of the class he has in mind. Some of those ships may have been employed previously in the charterer's trade and hence he is familiar both with the performance record of the vessel and the reliability of the vessel's owner. Accordingly, the market search may be limited to direct inquiries to one or more owners in order to determine specific vessel availability.

138 The negotiation of a long-term time charter often takes a period of weeks or longer since the wording of each clause will have an important bearing on the overall cost (earnings) under the agreed contract. The negotiation of the rate of hire may well include a series of offers and counter-offers, frequently consisting of varying rates or combinations of rates for different duration periods or extension options. For time charters involving the 'forward' delivery of the vessel (which may be from, say, six months to several years ahead, as in the case of vessels not yet built), the negotiations on rate of hire become more complicated due to uncertainties as to future market freight rate levels. Current rate levels influence the rate of hire under time charters of both near-term and forward delivery. If, during the charter-negotiating period a turning point in market freight rates is experienced, the process of negotiating the charter rate is further complicated by both owner and charterer having to assess the significance of the change.

139 As discussed in paragraphs 97–99, agreement on the clauses pertaining to the performance of the vessel, in terms of average speeds and fuel consumption, is of basic importance. Equal care is required in the negotiation of other charter clauses. For example, agreement should be reached on the treatment of vessel off hire as this relates to the duration of the charter. Under some time charters, the charter period is extended by the off hire time, although many variations of this method are possible.

140 Careful construction of the time charter clauses affects not only its cost (earnings) value to the charterers and owners but also the ease of administering the charter during its operating life. Time charters require extensive and meticulous record-keeping by both owner and charterer, to ensure that sufficient detail is accumulated to serve as the basis for the adjudication of possible claims, many of which may arise, as is often the case, long after the charter has expired. Owners and charterers must provide for the maintenance of these functions within their respective organisations.

Further reading

Brodie, PD, *Illustrated Dictionary of Cargo Handling*, 3rd edn, 2010, London: Informa Law.

Brodie, PD, *Commercial Shipping Handbook*, 3rd edn, 2014, London: Informa law.

Gorton, L, Ihre, R and Sandevarn, A, *Shipbroking and Chartering Practice*, 5th edn, 1999, London: Lloyd's of London.

Griggs, P, 'Obstacles to uniformity of maritime law' (2003) JMLC 191.

Lopez, N, *Best Chartering and Shipping Terms*, 11th edn, 1992, London: Barker & Howard.

Reynolds, F, 'Maritime and other influences on the common law' (2000) LMCLQ 182.

Stopford, M, *Maritime Economics*, 3rd edn, 2009, Oxford: Routledge.

Williams, H, *Chartering Documents*, 4th edn, 1999, London: Lloyd's of London.

Chapter 2

The Vessel and Implied Warranties as to Her Operation

1 Identity of the ship

Charterparties are normally expressed to apply to a particular stated ship, although it may be the case that the parties have agreed that the shipowner has the right to provide a substitute. In the absence of such agreement the charterer cannot be compelled to accept any other vessel. An interesting case on this point is that of *The Super Servant Two* [1990] 1 Lloyd's Rep 1, CA.

Where a specific vessel is chartered but is lost without fault before performance then the contract is frustrated. What about complying with description? If the vessel is described in detail in the charter must she comply strictly with every item of that description? The point was argued in *The Diana Prosperity*.

Reardon Smith Line Ltd v Hansen-Tangen, The Diana Prosperity
[1976] 1 WLR 989

Facts: Hansen-Tangen sub-chartered to Reardon Smith a ship to be built, which was described in the charterparty as 'called yard No 354 at Osaka Zosen' (Osaka Shipbuilding). The Osaka yard had a No 354 on their books, but she was too large for them to build, so construction was sub-contracted to another Japanese yard, Oshima, some 300 miles away. The vessel was number 004 in Oshima's books. Osaka were part-owners of Oshima. Osaka supervised the building and helped in the construction by seconding staff to Oshima.

Held:

Lord Wilberforce: My Lords, these appeals arise out of a charterparty and a subcharterparty both relating to a medium-sized newbuilding tanker to be constructed in Japan. By the time the tanker was ready for delivery the market had collapsed, owing to the oil crisis of 1974, so that the charterers' interest was to escape from their contracts by rejecting the vessel. The ground on which they hoped to do so was that the vessel tendered did not correspond with the contractual description. Both charterparties were on the well known form Shelltime 3. The result of the appeal depends primarily on the view taken of the sub-charterparty between the appellants in the first appeal (Reardon Smith) and the respondents in that appeal (Hansen-Tangen) . . .

. . . the whole case, as regards the first appeal, turns, in my opinion, on the long italicised passage in the subcharter set out above which, for convenience of reference I repeat:

the good Japanese flag (subject to Clause 41) Newbuilding motor tank vessel called Yard No 354 at Osaka Zosen.

I shall refer to this as the 'box' since it appears enclosed in a typed box on the document . . .

The appellants sought, necessarily, to give to the 'box' and the corresponding provision in the intermediate charter contractual effect. They argued that these words formed part of the 'description' of the future goods contracted to be provided, that, by analogy with contracts for the sale of goods, any departure from the description entitled the other party to reject, that there were departures in that the vessel was not built by Osaka and was not Hull No 354. I shall attempt to deal with each of these contentions.

In the first place, I am not prepared to accept that authorities as to 'description' in sale of goods cases are to be extended, or applied, to such a contract as we have here . . . The general law of contract has developed along much more rational lines (eg *Hongkong Fir Shipping Co Ltd v Kawasaki Kisen Kaisha Ltd* [1962] 2 QB 26), in attending to the nature and gravity of a breach or departure rather than in accepting rigid categories which do or do not automatically give a right to rescind, and if the choice were between extending cases under the Sale of Goods Act 1893 into other fields, or allowing more modern doctrine to infect those cases, my preference would be clear. The importance of this line of argument is that Mocatta J and Lord Denning MR used it in the present case so as to reject the appellants' argument on 'description' and I agree with them. But in case it does not appeal to this House, I am also satisfied that the appellants fail to bring the present case within the strictest rules as to 'description'.

In my opinion, the fatal defect in their argument consists in their use of the words 'identity' or 'identification' to bridge two meanings. It is one thing to say of given words that their purpose is to state (identify) an essential part of the description of the goods. It is another to say that they provide one party with a specific indication (identification) of the goods so that he can find them and if he wishes subdispose of them. The appellants wish to say of words which 'identify' the goods in the second sense, that they describe them in the first. I have already given reasons why I can only read the words in the second sense.

The difference is vital. If the words are read in the first sense, then, unless I am right in the legal argument above, each element in them has to be given contractual force. The vessel must, as a matter of contract, and as an essential term, be built by Osaka and must bear their yard number 354; if not, the description is not complied with and the vessel tendered is not that contracted for. If in the second sense, the only question is whether the words provide a means of identifying the vessel. If they fairly do this, they have fulfilled their function. It follows that if the second sense is correct, the words used can be construed much more liberally than they would have to be construed if they were providing essential elements of the description.

The two significant elements (whether in the 'box', or in the intermediate charter) are (i) the yard number 354, (ii) the expression 'built by Osaka Shipbuilding Co Ltd'. (These words do not appear in the 'box' but I will assume, very much in the appellants' favour, that the 'box' has the same meaning as if the word 'built' were used.) The appellants at one time placed great stress on the yard number provision. They contended that by using it the 'owners' assumed an obligation that the vessel should bear a number which would indicate that it would be constructed in the yard, where that number was appropriate, in sequence after vessels bearing earlier yard numbers (350–53). But this argument broke down in face of the fact, certainly known to Sanko which used and introduced the number into the charterparties, that the sequence through 354 was the sequence used at Osaka's yard at Osaka, which yard could not construct the vessel. Thus the use of the yard number for the contracted vessel must have had some other purpose than indicating construction at a particular yard. This turns the argument against the appellants for it shows the words to be 'labelling' words rather than words creating an obligation.

So the question becomes simply whether, as a matter of fact, it can fairly be said that – as a means of identification – the vessel was 'Yard No 354 at Osaka Zosen' or 'built by Osaka Shipping Co Ltd and known as Hull No 354, until named'. To answer this, regard may be had to the actual arrangements for building the vessel and numbering it before named. My Lords, I have no doubt, for the reasons given by the Court of Appeal, that an affirmative answer must be given. I shall not set out the evidence which clearly makes this good. The fact is that the vessel always was Osaka Hull No 354 – though also Oshima No 004 – and equally it can fairly be said to have been 'built' by Osaka as the company which planned, organised and directed the building and contractually engaged with Sculptor to build it, though also it could be said to have been built by Oshima. For the purpose of the identificatory clause, the words used are quite sufficient to cover the facts. No other vessel could be referred to: the reference fits the vessel in question.

There are other facts not to be overlooked. (1) So long as the charterers could identify the nominated vessel they had not the slightest interest in whatever contracting or subcontracting arrangements were made in the course of the building, a fact which no doubt explains the looseness of the language used in the 'box'. (2) In making the arrangements they did for building the vessel, Osaka acted in a perfectly straightforward and open manner. They cannot be said to be substituting one vessel for another; they have not provided any ground on which the charterers can claim that their bargain has not been fulfilled. The contracts all down the chain were closely and appropriately knitted into what Osaka did. (3) If the market had risen instead of falling, it would have been quite impossible for Osaka or Sculptor, or Sanko, to refuse to tender the vessel in accordance with the charters on the ground that it did not correspond with that contracted for. No more on a falling market is there, in my opinion, any ground on which the charterers can reject the vessel. In the end I find this a simple and clear case . . .

Note

On the classification of contractual terms the leading case is *Hongkong Fir Shipping* as is mentioned by Lord Wilberforce above. A useful summary is provided by Lord Scarman in *Bunge Corp v Tradax Export SA* [1981] 1 WLR 711:

> A condition is a term, the failure to perform which entitles the other party to treat the contract as at an end. A warranty is a term, breach of which sounds in damages but does not terminate, or entitle the other party to terminate, the contract. An innominate or intermediate term is one, the effect of non-performance of which the parties expressly or (as is more usual) impliedly agree will depend upon the nature and the consequences of the breach . . . (in which case the court has to decide) whether the breach that has arisen is such as the parties would have said, had they been asked at the time they made their contract: 'it goes without saying that, if that happens, the contract is at an end.'

2 Particular items of description

Modern charterparties usually describe the ship that is the subject of the agreement, making statements, for example, about the vessel's name, class, capacity and location. It is common for a charterparty also to identify the vessel's builder, country of registration, tonnage and present activities. Forms used in some trades go on to deal with the vessel's technical specifications in great detail. Statements of all these types are normally terms of the contract. The cases reproduced in this section deal with the meaning of common descriptive statements in charterparties. They also deal with the way in which particular obligations should be classified. However, some of the cases were decided before *Hongkong Fir Shipping* added innominate/intermediate terms to the standard classification of contractual obligations. Are the older cases still good law, given that a more sophisticated classification is now available? Some of the older decisions were, in any event, made in circumstances that were very different to those prevailing today. If circumstances have changed, it is reasonable to ask if rules should change too. On the other hand, it is also reasonable to ask if further intervention by the courts is really necessary. Charters are negotiated by professionals: if the rule laid down by a well-known case is undesirable, the parties are free to adopt a different solution by making their own wishes clear.

2.1 Flag

In order to trade successfully a ship must be registered in the national registry of a sovereign state. The ship will then fly the flag of that state and the law of that state will then apply to the ship. The choice of flag is often made for fiscal and other financial reasons. However, a statement of the national character of a ship might in some circumstances – during a war, for example – be treated as a term, breach of which would give the charterer the right to decline to take the vessel: *Behn v Burness* (1863) 3 B & S 751. In the absence of an express statement as to nationality, an obligation not to change the flag of a chartered vessel to the detriment of the charterer may be implied.

M Isaacs & Sons Ltd v William McAllum & Co Ltd
[1921] 3 KB 377

Facts: Charterers alleged that a sale of the ship and consequent registration in a different national register was a breach of contract.

Held:

Rowlatt J: The plaintiffs contend that the defendants committed a breach of the charterparty by selling the steamship during the currency of the charterparty. I do not think that the mere fact that the defendants sold the ship during the currency of the charterparty amounted to a breach of the charterparty, especially as the contract of sale contained a clause reserving to the defendants the right to perform personally the obligations of the charterparty.

The plaintiffs, however, say further, that the defendants have committed a breach of the charterparty by selling the steamship during the charterparty to a foreign subject, and so causing a change in her flag. It is not here necessary to inquire whether that action of the defendants would have entitled the plaintiffs to avoid the charterparty. The plaintiffs did not seek to avoid the charterparty. They kept the steamship and continued to avail themselves of her services during the period of the charterparty which has now expired. The charterparty has been performed in the sense that during its currency the steamship has made the various voyages required by the plaintiffs in accordance with the charterparty.

The complaint of the plaintiffs is that there has been a breach of the charterparty, because the services which have been rendered to them by the steamship have been rendered by a ship not of the British flag but of the Greek flag, and that they have thereby suffered damage.

The case has naturally given rise to some discussion as to the terms which are to be implied in a contract of this kind. It is clear that the fact that in this charterparty the steamship was described by an English name, the *City of Hamburg*, did not imply any warranty that it was, or would continue to be, a British ship: see *Clapham v Cologan* (1813) 3 Camp 382, and no claim could be made by the plaintiffs on that ground.

It is said, however, by counsel for the plaintiffs, and it seems to me that they are right in saying so, that where persons enter into a contract for services to be rendered by one of them to the other by means of a specific chattel, there is an implied term in the contract by which the person supplying the chattel undertakes that it shall not be altered so as materially to prejudice the services which are to be rendered by it; and that if it is so altered there is a breach of that term. If a person enters into a contract for the use of a specific thing he does not get what he contracts for if the thing is so altered as to render him services substantially less valuable than, or different from, those contracted for . . .

I therefore think that the question here is whether the defendants by selling the steamship to a Greek subject and so causing her flag to be changed from the British to the Greek flag made such an alteration in her as has materially affected the services which she was to render to the plaintiff under the charterparty. The plaintiffs contend that the defendants by so doing gave them the services of a ship different from and less valuable than that for which they had contracted; and the defendants deny this. Many changes can, no doubt, be made in a chartered ship which do not materially affect her position under the charterparty – such, for example, as altering her colour, or her masts. I have here to consider whether a change in the ship's flag is such a change as materially to affect the ship as the subject matter of the charterparty. I think I must deal with the question generally and without drawing any distinction between different nationalities. I do not think that I can treat the question of a change of flag from the British to the French flag, for example, as distinct for this purpose from a change from the British to the Chinese flag or to the flag of some undeveloped power. That distinction is relevant to the question of damages, but not to the question of breach. I have to face the plain question whether a change in the flag of the chartered ship is a breach of the charterparty as being a material change in the nature of the subject matter. It seems to me that it is. I do not think it could possibly be held that it makes no difference under what flag a ship sails. The law of the flag is of direct importance as affecting the status of the ship. It is also of importance in its collateral effects, as, for instance, in determining the nationality and therefore to some extent the discipline and morals of the crew and in many other respects. It seems to me that in any particular case of this kind there can be no question that the change of flag is a breach of the charterparty, and that the only question is what damages, if any, have resulted from the change of flag. I must therefore hold that it was a breach of this charterparty to change the flag of the steamer during the charterparty.

As to damages, these must depend upon the circumstances of the particular case. I cannot conceive that the transfer of a ship from the flag of a civilised power to that of a wholly uncivilised power would not give rise to damages. Greece, however, is a civilised power and a maritime nation of good standing, and I do not think that the damages in this case can possibly be heavy . . .

2.2 Class

A statement that a vessel is of a particular class has been said to be a condition of a charterparty: *Routh v Macmillan* (1863) 2 H & C 750; *The Apollonius* [1978] 1 Lloyd's Rep 53; *The Seaflower* [2001] 1 Lloyd's Rep 341, CA (note that this case concerned the question of whether or not a tanker had 'Oil Majors' approval; a status valued by tanker operators); and *French v Newgass*, below. But such a statement has been construed as meaning only that at the time of the charter the vessel actually was so classed, not that the classification was correct or that she would continue to be so classed during the charter or that the owners would omit no act necessary to keep her in class.

French v Newgass (1878) 3 CPD 163, CA

Facts: The *William Jackson,* chartered for a voyage from New Orleans to Liverpool, was described in the charter as 'A 1 1/2 Record of American and Foreign Shipping Book. London, 4 Sept, 1786 . . . '. At the time the vessel was so classified. After the ship's arrival in New Orleans, the classification was cancelled by the American and Foreign Shipping Association and the charterer refused to load.

Held:

Brett LJ (Bramwell and Cotton LJJ delivered judgments to the same effect): . . . The question is one solely of construction, and whatever hardship there may be, we have only to construe the written instrument, which in its terms is elliptical. The document states 'A 1 1/2 Record of American and Foreign Shipping Book'. Now, the ordinary meaning of that language is that it refers to the ship, and that she is, at the time of entering into the charterparty, registered as A 1 1/2. The document further speaks of the ship newly classed as above; that relates to what has been done in the book of the American and Foreign Shipping. I am of opinion that the words amount, not only to a warranty, but to a condition, as to the vessel's classification at the time the charterparty was made, and that they must be construed in their grammatical and natural sense; they cannot be added to. No doubt the meaning of words may be extended by custom, if consistent with the written instrument, but here the words are plain, and no addition can be made to them; construing them according to their grammatical meaning, it is a statement as to the actual registration of the vessel. The only argument that can be urged on behalf of the defendant is the argument which was urged in *Hurst v Usborne* (1856) 18 CBNS 144 unsuccessfully, that it is a continuing warranty, and therefore it must be taken to be a statement that the vessel would continue to be of the same class that she was at the time the charterparty was made. Mr Herschell [counsel] proposes to add to the statement; he says that the words are to be construed, not merely that she is newly classed, but that she will continue to be of the same class as she was at the time the charterparty was made; but that construction would refer to the future, whereas the words of the charterparty only refer to the present. If the words suggested were added by implication, the shipowner, no doubt, would have failed to offer a proper ship, but that construction adds to the meaning, and if adopted, the shipowner would have warranted, not only the description of the vessel at the time of the charterparty, but he would have made himself liable for the acts of the authorities at New Orleans, over whom he had no control. It is quite clear that we ought to adhere to the words of the charterparty, and give to them their ordinary meaning. The charterparty contains, as a fact, a statement that the ship is A 1 1/2 Record of American and Foreign Shipping at the time the charterparty was made.

Notes

1   The statement of class was here held to relate to the vessel at the time the charter was made. Other descriptive statements dealt with in this chapter have been interpreted as applying to the vessel at the date of delivery: see *The Apollonius* [1978] 1 Lloyd's Rep 53, below.

2   In *The Seaflower* [2001] 1 Lloyd's Rep 341, the Court of Appeal held that a clause requiring shipowners to obtain the approval of a tanker by a named major oil company within 60 days of the commencement of the charter period was a condition of the contract on breach of which the charterers were entitled to terminate. It was pointed out that while there are similarities between a promise relating to class and to approval by oil majors, the obligations are not identical.

2.3 Cargo capacity

Cargo capacity is normally of great importance to a charterer. If a chartered vessel cannot load all the cargo the charterer wishes to ship, he may be in breach of a contract to sell the goods, miss an intended market or incur extra warehouse or transport expenses on shore as well as the expenses of procuring substitute tonnage. A statement in a charterparty of a vessel's deadweight tonnage (the maximum weight the vessel can lift) or of cubic capacity will usually be treated as a term of the contract. Statements of capacity are often qualified by the word 'about'. Deadweight capacity is sometimes stated generally, although it is often more precisely defined as being measured in certain circumstances (for example, on summer salt water) and as being inclusive or exclusive of bunkers, fresh water or stores. Stowage factors of particular cargoes are detailed in Cufley, CFH, *Ocean Freights*, 1972, London: Staples; reprinted 1983, London: Granada. The two cases in this section establish that it is a question of construction whether a statement in a charterparty of deadweight capacity is to be read as referring to the vessel's abstract lifting capacity (this is the primary meaning) or her capacity to lift a particular type of cargo.

Mackill v Wright Bros & Co Ltd
(1888) 14 App Cas 106

Facts: The *Lauderdale* was chartered to load a general cargo, including a railway locomotive and machinery, at Glasgow for carriage to Karachi. The owners guaranteed that the vessel would carry 2,000 tons deadweight of cargo, including a stated number of pieces of machinery of a given size and type. It was agreed that if the vessel did not carry the guaranteed weight of cargo, there would be a *pro rata* reduction in the lump sum freight.

Held:

Lord Macnaghten: My Lords, the question turns upon the true construction of a charterparty in some respects peculiar. It is a charter for the hire of a vessel for a lump sum from Glasgow to Kurrachee. It has a note in the margin as to the description of part of the proposed cargo, and it contains this guarantee, 'Owners guarantee that the vessel shall carry not less than 2,000 tons dead weight of cargo'. In effect, the charterers say to the owners, 'We want a vessel to carry to Kurrachee a general cargo, including parcels of machinery; we give you the dimensions and number of the largest pieces; will your vessel carry 2,000 tons dead weight?' The owners say 'It will'. That is, I think, something more than a mere guarantee of carrying capacity. It is a guarantee of the vessel's carrying capacity with reference to the contemplated voyage and the description of the cargo proposed to be shipped, so far as that description was made known to the owners . . .

. . . it seems to me that the fair result of the evidence is, that in regard to the machinery which was tendered for shipment and shipped, the cargo was not such a cargo as was contemplated by the charterparty. It contained more large pieces; it was more bulky in comparison to its weight, and it was more awkward for stowage than the terms of the charterparty would naturally have led the owners to expect.

These being the material facts of the case, the clause in the charterparty on which the question turns remains to be considered. The charterparty has this provision: 'Should the vessel not carry the guaranteed dead weight, as above, any expense incurred from this cause to be borne by the owners, and a *pro rata* deduction per ton to be made from the first payment of freight.'

What is the meaning of this provision? What is the event contemplated? Is it the case of the vessel (1) not actually carrying 2,000 tons dead weight from any cause whatever; or (2) not carrying that weight from any cause not attributable to the charterers?

I think it would be unreasonable to read the provision as allowing abatement in the freight in every case of short weight. Such a construction would place the shipowners at the mercy of the charterers. They might fill the whole space at their disposal, and yet the cargo might be much under the contemplated weight, and so the shipowners would lose their full freight without any fault on their part.

I think that the provision was intended to have effect in the event of the vessel not carrying the specified weight, assuming the cargo tendered to be such a cargo as was contemplated by the charterparty, that is, an ordinary general cargo with a fair and reasonable proportion of machinery corresponding as to the largest pieces with the numbers, dimensions, and weights specified in the margin of the charterparty. In other words (to put it most favourably for the charterers), the provision was to come into effect in the event of the vessel not carrying 2,000 tons dead weight from any cause not attributable to the charterers.

I think that the loss of cargo space and the short weight of the cargo carried on the *Lauderdale* were attributable to the charterers. It was their doing . . .

Neither the appellants nor the respondents were, I think, conspicuously reasonable. But the respondents were the more unreasonable of the two, and, what is more to the purpose, I think they took a wrong view of the construction of the charterparty, and of their own position. I therefore agree that the appeal ought to be allowed.

(Lord Halsbury LC and Lord Watson also delivered reasoned judgments.)

W Millar & Co Ltd v Owners of SS Freden [1918] 1 KB 611, CA

Facts: The ship was chartered to carry a full and complete cargo of maize in bags from Durban to the UK. The owners guaranteed the ship's deadweight capacity to be 3,200 tons and freight was to be paid on this quantity. She was full when 3,081 tons had been loaded.

Held:

Swinfen Eady LJ: . . . There is no dispute that the vessel was of a deadweight capacity of 3,200 tons – in other words, that she would take on board a cargo to that extent without sinking the ship below her proper loadline. With regard to the particular cargo of maize she was only able to take on board 3,081 tons 560 lbs, but that was not because her deadweight capacity was not as guaranteed, or had been in any way misrepresented. It was because the cubic capacity of the space on board was insufficient to allow of the stowage of more than 3,081 tons 560 lbs of maize in bags. On the one hand it is said on behalf of the appellants, reading the guarantee of the capacity of the ship in connection with the cargo, that the ship-owners had notice of what the cargo was to be. It was maize in bags, and it is said that the guarantee must be read as if it meant 'We guarantee that the ship on this voyage will be of a capacity to take, and will be able to carry, 3,200 tons of maize in bags'. On the other hand the respondents say 'That is not the language which is used, and that is not what we meant. What we said was, and what we adhere to is, "We guarantee that the ship shall be and is of a deadweight capacity of 3,200 tons, and so it is"'. The guarantee is a measure of the capacity of the ship, the general capacity irrespective of the particular cargo that she was to carry on this voyage.

 . . . Reference was made to *Mackill v Wright* (1888) 14 App Cas 106 [above]. The dispute there was whether the cargo that was actually shipped corresponded to that which was intended, having regard to the representations made at the time the contract was entered into. But it will be observed that the language of the contract there was very different from what we have to consider here. There it was 'the owners guarantee that the vessel shall carry not less than 2,000 tons dead weight of cargo'. Now that must have been a guarantee that the vessel should carry that amount on the voyage in question; and then there was a subsequent clause: 'and should the vessel not carry' – that is, should the vessel not carry on this particular voyage – 'the guaranteed dead weight as above, then any expense incurred from this cause to be borne by the owners and a *pro rata* reduction per ton to be made from the first payment of freight'. So that there was language there pointing to a guarantee with regard to the weight of cargo to be carried on that particular voyage, and not to the general carrying capacity of the ship. Here it is the opposite. The only guarantee is with reference to the general carrying capacity of the ship – a certain deadweight capacity.

 In my opinion the appeal fails and should be dismissed.

(Bankes LJ and Eve J delivered judgments to the same effect.)

Notes

1   A charterparty provided that the ship should 'load a cargo of creosoted sleepers and timbers' and stated that 'charterer has option of shipping 100/200 tons of general cargo' and that 'owners guarantee ship to carry at least about 90,000 cubic feet or 1,500 tons of dead weight of cargo'. The charterers tendered a cargo of the agreed type which did not exceed 90,000 cubic feet. But because the sleepers were of unequal lengths and many were half-round, the ship could load a cargo of only 64,400 cubic feet, 1,120 tons dead weight. The charterers sought damages. Held: the clause was not a guarantee that the ship would carry 90,000 cubic feet of the cargo specified in the charterparty. It was a guarantee of abstract capacity without reference to the particular cargo: *Carnegie v Conner* (1889) 14 QBD 45.

2   Owners guaranteed to place 5,600 tons deadweight cargo capacity and 300,000 cubic feet of bale space at a charterer's disposal. The agreed lump sum freight was to be reduced *pro rata* if the deadweight or bale space were less than the guaranteed figures. The charterers claimed a *pro rata* reduction in respect of 32 tons of necessary dunnage used to stow their cargo. It was held the guarantee was of the vessel's abstract lifting capacity, not capacity to lift that weight of the particular type of cargo shipped or of an average or reasonable cargo: *Re Thomson and Brocklebank* [1918] 1 KB 655.

3 Owners guaranteed dead weight as 7,100 tons and grain capacity as 8,450 tons, with a specific right to deduct from freight *pro rata* for errors. The stated grain capacity was available and was fully utilised by charterers, but deadweight capacity was in fact only 6,728 tons. Held: the charterers were entitled to deduct *pro rata*: *SA Ungheresi Di Armamento Marittimo Oriente v Tyser Line* (1902) 8 Com Cas 25.

4 *'About'*. The *Resolven* was chartered to carry '2,000 tons or thereabouts'. It was held that: '. . . words of elasticity are elastic and their extensiveness runs with the subject matter they refer to. I think that in this instance five per cent may be taken as a fair margin': *The Resolven* (1892) 9 TLR 75, *per* Sir F Jeune P. In *Dreyfus v Parnaso, The Dominator* [1960] 1 Lloyd's Rep 117, Sellers LJ said he would 'regard 331 tons deficiency in a cargo of 10,400 tons, a deficiency of just over three per cent, as fulfilling the obligation to ship about 10,400 tons ... In the absence of any trade evidence on this matter, it is, in my opinion, within a reasonable commercial margin in respect of such cargo'. In *Cargo Ships 'El-Yam' Ltd v Invotra NV* [1958] 1 Lloyd's Rep 39, p 52, Devlin J said that if he had to determine whether a margin of 1.2% was within the phrase 'about 478,000 cubic feet bale capacity' it might have been a point requiring careful consideration, but the point did not in fact arise for decision.

5 A charter of *TFL Prosperity*, a roll-on roll-off vessel designed to carry trailers loaded with containers, provided that the free high of the main deck was 6.10 m. In fact at one critical point, the high was only 6.05 m, so that a trailer double stacked with 40 ft containers could not be loaded on the main deck. The owners were held liable in damages: *Tor Line AB v Alltrans Group* [1984] 1 WLR 50, HL.

3 Time for performance

Charterparties do not all define the time for start of performance in the same way. One option is to agree a specific date on which the vessel is to sail or to be ready to receive cargo. But the uncertainties of maritime trade make prudent shipowners reluctant to fix a specific date unless the vessel is ready to begin at once. An alternative is to state the present position of the vessel and to agree that the ship will sail for the loading port either forthwith or with reasonable despatch. A little more precisely, some standard forms require a statement of present position and an estimate of the date the vessel is expected to be ready to load under the charter.

But if it is commercially unreasonable to expect shipowners to be able to promise performance on a specific date in every case, it is equally unrealistic to expect a charterer to be able to use a vessel whenever it manages to arrive. To avoid arguments about what is realistic or reasonable on the part of a charterer or whether delay by a shipowner has been sufficiently long to enable the charterer to throw up the charter and reject the vessel, it is common for charterparties to specify the earliest date on which the charterer is obliged to commence loading (the lay date) and the latest date on which he is obliged to accept the vessel (the cancellation date). These two dates are sometimes referred to as the lay/can spread. Modern forms in some trades go further and require notification of any changes in the date the vessel is expected ready to load and/or advance notice to be given at specified times before arrival.

3.1 Fixed date obligations

Firm statements in charters that the vessel is in a certain port or sailed on a certain day or is to sail or be ready to receive cargo on or before a certain date are generally important to charterers and so have in the past usually been treated as conditions. The first case in this section has often been criticised as hard on the shipowner; but in context, the decision made good sense.

Behn v Burness (1863) 3 B & S 751, Court of Exchequer Chamber

Facts: The *Martaban*, described as being 'now in the port of Amsterdam', was chartered to proceed with all possible despatch direct to Newport and load a full cargo of coal for Hong Kong. At the time of the charter, the vessel was unavoidably detained by gales at Niewediep, 62 miles and 12 hours sailing time from Amsterdam. She reached Amsterdam four days later and finally sailed for Newport 28 days after the date of the charter.

Held:

Williams J: . . . The question on the present charterparty is confined to the statement of a definite fact – the place of the ship at the date of the contract. Now the place of the ship at the date of the contract, where the ship is in foreign parts and is chartered to come to England, may be the only datum on which the charterer can found his calculations of the time of the ship's arriving at the port of load. A statement is more or less important in proportion as the object of the contract more or less depends upon it. For most charters, considering winds, markets and dependent contracts, the time of a ship's arrival to load is an essential fact, for the interest of the charterer. In the ordinary course of charters in general it would be so: the evidence for the defendant shews it to be actually so in this case. Then, if the statement of the place of the ship is a substantive part of the contract, it seems to us that we ought to hold it to be a condition . . . unless we can find in the contract itself or the surrounding circumstances reason for thinking that the parties did not so intend. If it was a condition and not performed, it follows that the obligation of the charterer dependent thereon, ceased at his option and considerations either of the damage to him or of proximity to performance on the part of the shipowner are irrelevant. So was the decision of *Glaholm v Hays* (2 M & G 257), where the stipulation in a charter of a ship to load at Trieste was that she should sail from England on or before the 4 February, and the nonperformance of this condition released the charterer, notwithstanding the reasons alleged in order to justify the non-performance. So, in *Ollive v Booker* (1 Exch 416), the statement in the charter of a ship which was to load at Marseilles was that she was 'now at sea, having sailed three weeks ago', and it was held to be a condition for the reasons above stated . . . We think these cases well decided, and that they govern the present case . . .

Bentsen v Taylor [1893] 2 QB 274, CA

Facts: By a charterparty dated 29 March, the *Folkvang* was described as 'now sailed or about to sail from a pitch pine port to the UK'. She did not in fact sail from Mobile until 23 April.

Held:

Bowen LJ: . . . The first question we have to consider is, What is the true effect and meaning of the words in the charterparty, 'now sailed or about to sail to the United Kingdom'?

. . . Of course it is often very difficult to decide as a matter of construction whether a representation which contains a promise, and which can only be explained on the ground that it is in itself a substantive part of the contract, amounts to a condition precedent, or is only a warranty. There is no way of deciding that question except by looking at the contract in the light of the surrounding circumstances, and then making up one's mind whether the intention of the parties, as gathered from the instrument itself, will best be carried out by treating the promise as a warranty sounding only in damages, or as a condition precedent by the failure to perform which the other party is relieved of his liability. In order to decide this question of construction, one of the first things you would look to is, to what extent the accuracy of the statement – the truth of what is promised – would be likely to affect the substance and foundation of the adventure which the contract is intended to carry out . . .

It was by the application of that train of reasoning that the court in *Behn v Burness* [above] appears to have come to the conclusion, that if a ship, which at the date of a charterparty is in foreign parts, is chartered to come to England, a statement of the place where she is ought *prima facie* to be construed as a condition precedent . . .

Now, if that is true as regards the place of a ship which is in foreign parts and is chartered to come to England, the same train of reasoning ought to apply to the time at which a ship is stated to have sailed, or to be about to sail, from the place at which she has been loading, unless the language be so vague as to lead anyone to suppose that it was not intended to be a condition precedent. I quite agree that the vagueness or ambiguity of the statement is one of the elements which would influence the court very much in deciding whether the parties intended that the statement should be a promise the fulfilment of which was to be a condition precedent.

That drives us to consider, what is the real meaning of these words. Is there anything in them so vague or so ambiguous that they cannot fairly be treated as a statement of a condition precedent? I agree that a condition precedent ought to be clearly expressed. The statement is, that the ship 'has now sailed or is about to sail'. Having regard to what we have heard of the history of the port of Mobile, I have not the slightest doubt that, if that statement does not mean that the ship has actually sailed, it does mean that she is loaded, or may at all events for business purposes be treated as actually loaded; that she has got past the embarrassments and dangers attendant on loading, and that her sailing is the next thing to be looked for. And, with regard to the suggested ambiguity in the phrase 'about to sail', when it is read in conjunction with the other words, it seems to me clear that it does not mean that the ship is to sail within a 'reasonable' or indefinite time, a statement which might lead to endless difficulties and expense, but that, if she has not already sailed, she is about to sail forthwith. If that is so, then applying the reasoning which lies at the root of *Behn v Burness*, I have no hesitation in saying that I believe the phrase to be a condition precedent. It is a representation the accuracy of which is made a condition precedent, though I do not doubt that the fulfilment of a promise may be equally made a condition precedent . . .

(Lord Esher MR and Kay LJ also delivered reasoned judgments.)

3.2 Reasonable despatch

An obligation to proceed with reasonable despatch is also treated strictly in English law. This obligation will be implied unless the parties have expressly or by implication provided otherwise: *The Kriti Rex* [1996] 2 Lloyd's Rep 171, p 191.

McAndrew v Adams
(1834) 1 Bing NC 31, Common Pleas

Facts: The defendant agreed that the *Swallow* would go in ballast from Portsmouth to St Michael's in the Azores and carry a cargo of oranges direct to London. Instead of proceeding direct to St Michael's, the defendant sailed first to Oporto carrying troops. Shore batteries prevented a landing; the vessel returned the troops to Portsmouth. The charterparty fixed 1 December as the earliest date on which the charterer was obliged to load; 35 running days were allowed for loading with a further 10 days on demurrage. The charterer was entitled to cancel if the vessel did not arrive at St Michael's by 31 January. The *Swallow* sailed for St Michael's on 6 December; she loaded there and returned to London, arriving on 1 February, by which time the market price of oranges had fallen.

Held:

Tindal CJ: . . . And the question here is, whether the defendant sailed within a reasonable time according to the terms of his charterparty. All the authorities concur in stating, that the voyage must be commenced within a reasonable time; and they are all cited and commented upon in *Freeman v Taylor* (1831) 8 Bing 124 and *Mount v Larkins* (1831) 8 Bing 108. If that be the general rule, where there is any delay in a voyage it is incumbent on the party to account for it. In many cases it may be difficult to say what is a reasonable or an unreasonable time for commencing a voyage. It is better, therefore, to refer to the contract itself, and see whether the voyage performed is conformable to that pointed out by the contract.

Now, looking at this contract, I think, with a view to the object of the voyage, its commencement was delayed an unreasonable time. The charterparty was entered into on the 20th of October 1832, and provides, that the *Swallow*:

> being tight, staunch, strong, and in every way fitted for the voyage, shall proceed in ballast to St Michael's.

I do not lay stress on the stipulation for proceeding in ballast, any further than that it seems to refer to a voyage in which the master should not lie by to take in a cargo, which might delay the ship on her voyage. The instrument then goes on:

> shall there receive on board a complete cargo of fruit; and, having been so loaded, shall proceed with the said cargo direct to the port of London.

. . . Now, inasmuch as the parties have stipulated that the lay days shall commence on the 1st of December, it may be inferred that they contemplated the voyage to St Michael's should terminate by that day. If, indeed, by any accident or unforeseen cause, which should excuse the master, the vessel should arrive later, the charterer would have no just cause of action: but the intention at the time was, that the object of the voyage should, if possible, take effect from the 1st of December. That it might have taken effect from that time, is clear; for the voyage usually lasts a fortnight or three weeks, and the vessel sailed for Oporto on the 7th of November.

The instrument then goes on:

> That, in case the vessel should not be arrived at St Michael's, and in readiness to receive her cargo by the 31st of January next, it shall be optional with the agents of the affreighters whether they load or not; and in case they decline loading, the charterparty shall be null and void.

That was to give the charterer the option of repudiating the contract if the vessel should arrive too late for any useful purpose, although if she had been detained by any justifiable cause, he might have no right of action against the owner.

And all the evidence in the cause goes to show that the intention of the parties in entering into this contract was such as I have described: the course of the trade in London, which requires a speedy voyage, and gives advantages to those who are first in the market; and the letter of the 9th of November, in which the plaintiffs say:

> In having taken the *Swallow* to Oporto with passengers, on her way to St Michael's, instead of proceeding direct, we consider you to have deviated from the due performance of the charterparty entered into with us, and we hold you liable for all loss or injury which may arise to the parties interested in consequence of your not proceeding direct.

I think, therefore, that, as the commencement of the voyage was, without any justifiable cause, delayed till the 6th of December, an action lies for the plaintiffs . . .

(The Chief Justice went on to deal with entitlement to damages. Park and Bosanquet JJ delivered judgments to the same effect.)

3.3 Expected ready to load

A statement in a charter of the date that it is expected the vessel will be ready to load (ERTL) will normally be treated as having contractual force, although it will not necessarily be a breach of contract if the ship fails to arrive by an estimated date or time. The leading case on interpretation of clauses of this type is *The Mihalis Angelos*.

Maredelanto Compania Naviera SA v Bergbau-Handel GmbH, The Mihalis Angelos [1971] 1 QB 164, CA

Facts: The *Mihalis Angelos* was chartered for a voyage from Haiphong to Hamburg. The charterparty described the vessel as 'now trading and expected ready to load under this charter about 1 July 1965'. Lay days were not to commence before 1 July 1965; charterers had the option to cancel if the vessel was not ready to load by 20 July 1965.

Held:

Megaw LJ: . . . It is not disputed that when a charter includes the words 'expected ready to load . . . ' a contractual obligation on the part of the shipowner is involved. It is not an obligation that the vessel will be ready to load on the stated date, nor about the stated date, if the date is qualified, as here, by 'about'. The owner is not in breach merely because the vessel arrives much later, or indeed does not arrive at all. The owner is not undertaking that there will be no unexpected delay. But he is undertaking that he honestly and on reasonable grounds believes, at the time of the contract, that the date named is the date when the vessel will be ready to load. Therefore in order to establish a breach of that obligation the charterer has the burden of showing that the owner's contractually expressed expectation was not his honest expectation, or, at the least, that the owner did not have reasonable grounds for it.

In my judgment, such a term in a charterparty ought to be regarded as being a condition of the contract, in the old sense of the word 'condition': that is, that when it has been broken, the other party can, if he wishes, by intimation to the party in breach, elect to be released from performance of his further obligations under the contract; and he can validly do so without having to establish that on the facts of the particular case the breach has produced serious consequences which can be treated as 'going to the root of the contract' or as being 'fundamental' or whatever other metaphor may be thought appropriate for a frustration case. I reach that conclusion for four interrelated reasons.

First, it tends towards certainty in the law. One of the essential elements of law is some measure of uniformity. One of the important elements of the law is predictability. At any rate in commercial law, there are obvious and substantial advantages in having, where possible, a firm and definite rule for a particular class of legal relationship: for example, as here, the legal categorisation of a particular, definable type of contractual clause in common use. It is surely much better, both for shipowners and charterers (and, incidentally, for their advisers), when a contractual obligation of this nature is under consideration, and still more when they are faced with the necessity for an urgent decision as to the effects of a suspected breach of it, to be able to say categorically: 'If a breach is proved, then the charterer can put an end to the contract,' rather than that they should be left to ponder whether or not the courts would be likely, in the particular case, when the evidence has been heard, to decide that in the particular circumstances the breach was or was not such as 'to go to the root of the contract'. Where justice does not require greater flexibility, there is everything to be said for, and nothing against, a degree of rigidity in legal principle.

Second, it would, in my opinion, only be in the rarest case, if ever, that a shipowner could legitimately feel that he had suffered an injustice by reason of the law having given to a charterer the right to put an end to the contract because of the breach by the shipowner of a clause such as this. If a shipowner has chosen to assert contractually, but dishonestly or without reasonable grounds, that he expects his vessel to be ready to load on such-and-such a date, wherein does the grievance lie?

Third, it is, as Mocatta J held, clearly established by authority binding on this court that where a clause 'expected ready to load' is included in a contract for the sale of goods to be carried by sea, that clause is a condition, in the sense that any breach of it enables the buyer to reject the goods without having to show that the dishonest or unreasonable expectation of the seller has in fact been prejudicial to the buyer...

It would, in my judgment, produce an undesirable anomaly in our commercial law if such a clause – 'expected ready to load' – were to be held to have a materially different legal effect where it is contained in a charterparty from that which it has when it is contained in a sale of goods contract...

The fourth reason why I think that the clause should be regarded as being a condition when it is found in a charterparty is that that view was the view of Scrutton LJ so expressed in his capacity as the author of *Scrutton on Charterparties*...

3.4 Combined effect of reasonable despatch and 'expected ready to load undertakings'

An obligation to proceed with reasonable despatch requires the chartered ship to sail for the loading port within a reasonable time, not to sail or to arrive on a particular day: *McAndrew v Adams*, above. An ERTL obligation requires an honest estimate, made on reasonable grounds; it too does not impose a duty to sail or to arrive on a particular day. But when these obligations are combined (and the duty to use reasonable despatch is implied in every case unless expressly excluded) the result, according to the decision in *The North Anglia*, is to produce an absolute duty.

Evera SA Commercial v North Shipping Co Ltd,
The North Anglia [1956] 2 Lloyd's Rep 367

Held:

Devlin J: . . . A charterer manifestly wants, if he can get it, a fixed date for the arrival of the ship at the port of loading. He has to make arrangements to bring down the cargo and to have it ready to load when the ship arrives, and he wants to know, as near as he can, what that date is going to be. On the other hand, it is to the interest of the shipowner, if he can have it, to have the date as flexible as possible. Because of the inevitable delays due to bad weather or other circumstances that there might be in the course of a voyage, he can never be sure that he can arrive at a port on a fixed and certain day. Therefore, in order to accommodate these two views as far as possible, it has been the general practice for a long time past to have a clause under which the shipowner, without pledging himself to a fixed day, gives a date in the charterparty of expected readiness, that is, the date when he expects that he will be ready to load. The protection that is afforded to the charterer under that type of clause is this. As was clearly settled in *Samuel Sanday &*

Co v Keighley, Maxted & Co (1922) 27 Com Cas 296, he is entitled to have that statement of position, as it is called – the statement of expectation as to when the ship arrives or is likely to arrive – made honestly and made on reasonable grounds.

Thus, the result is that, in a perfectly simple case, where at the time when the charterparty was entered into the ship was free to proceed to the port of loading, her obligation is simply to set out in good time so that under normal circumstances she will arrive at the port of loading at or about the day which she has given as being the one when she expects to be ready to load. If something occurs on the voyage to the port of loading which delays the ship without her fault, then the owners under this type of clause are not liable.

The complication arises if the charterparty is made a little ahead so that it is not anticipated by either party that the ship is likely to sail at once for her port of loading. If she is going to have some intervening period, how can she dispose of it?

It was quite clearly settled in *Monroe Brothers Ltd v Ryan* [1935] 2 KB 28 – and I have in mind the point in Greer LJ's judgment (at p 37) where he deals with this particular matter – that the charterers have no right in such circumstances to expect the ship to keep herself free and unoccupied. If the shipowners wish to charter the ship by means of an intervening charterparty, or otherwise to employ her, they are entitled to do so. But if the new engagement into which she enters prevents her from fulfilling her obligations under the next voyage, they take the risk that they will be liable in damages for that. In other words, they take the risk . . . of clashing engagements.

But what then happens, the shipowner having entered into the intervening charter, if the intervening charter interferes with the performance of the second voyage. The simplest case, and one that was settled as long ago as 1907, is the case in which the shipowner, having entered into a charterparty, then deliberately enters into an earlier charterparty which he knows is bound to make him late for the following voyage. In those circumstances there is no need, really, to invoke any principle of difficulty. Manifestly in such circumstances the shipowner who has put it out of his power to perform the engagement which he has entered into is liable in damages. That was so decided in *Thomas Nelson & Sons v Dundee East Coast Shipping Co Ltd* [1907] Sess Cas 927.

The next stage, so to speak, is reached when the shipowner enters into a charter which he honestly anticipates, and with reasonable grounds, will be completed in time to fulfil her earlier obligations, and then, through some circumstances for which he is not responsible, he is delayed on the earlier voyage. That situation was considered by the Court of Appeal in this country in the case of *Monroe Brothers Ltd v Ryan*, above, to which I have already referred. There it was held that the shipowner must nevertheless pay damages.

Then the next stage is reached when the shipowner does not enter into an intervening charter, but is in this position, that when he makes his charter with the charterers who are concerned in the case, he is already under charter to another charterer, and, again, making an honest statement of expectation on reasonable grounds, some delay occurs there for which he is not responsible, with the result that he is late with the second charter. That situation was considered in *Louis Dreyfus & Co v Lauro* (1938) 60 Ll L Rep 94.

The present case introduces yet another new feature. Here when the shipowner made his engagement with the plaintiffs as charterers on August 6, 1953, he had already made an earlier engagement, so that in that respect the situation was comparable to that in *Louis Dreyfus & Co v Lauro* above, but he not merely disclosed the circumstance of the earlier engagement to the charterer, but he set out his estimate with regard to them in full in the charterparty. The substantial question, therefore, which has arisen in this case is whether those words in the charterparty affect the position in such a way as to enable me to distinguish it from *Monroe Brothers Ltd v Ryan* . . .

It is clear that there are two obligations into which the shipowner enters. He enters into the obligation of making an honest and reasonable statement about his position. That he discharged that is not questioned here. But he also entered into an obligation, which is expressed in the printed words of the charter . . . that the ship 'shall with all convenient speed sail and proceed to Fort Churchill'. It is for the breach of that obligation that the ship is being sued in this case, as it was sued in the case of *Monroe Brothers Ltd v Ryan,* above; and the effect of that obligation, it is submitted, combined with the statement of readiness which is made earlier on in the charter, is to impose upon the ship an absolute duty with which . . . the ship has not complied. I think the best way of framing the duty . . . is to take it as it was framed by Branson J in *Louis Dreyfus & Co v Lauro* . . . :

In view of the combination of the expected date and of the implied term that the ship will use all convenient speed to get to her port of loading, the obligation is, as was well put by Mr Mocatta, that she shall start from wherever she may happen to be, at a date when, by proceeding with reasonable dispatch, she will arrive at the port of loading by the expected date.

. . . Under the principle in *Monroe Brothers Ltd v Ryan* the ship is excused if she starts out in good time but something happens on the way to the port of loading. But she is not excused if anything happens before that time which prevents her from starting out upon the expected date . . .

The question therefore arises: Is there anything in the typed words which demands, or enables, me to alter that construction?

. . . if a shipowner wants to make the beginning of one voyage contingent upon the conclusion of the one before, he must say so in clear terms. There is clearly a number of things that would have to be worked out in order that such an arrangement should be made as would be fair to both sides. It may be that the shipowner had it in mind in this case that that was what he wanted. But, if he did have that in mind, he has not put it into such language as would make it plain to any reasonable charterer that the charterer was being invited to accept the risks of delay under an earlier charterparty in which that charterer was not concerned. To pass those risks on to a person who was not a party to that charter requires, in my judgment, if not express language, at least much clearer language than that which has been adopted in the present case . . .

Notes

1   It is a question of construction whether an exclusion clause in a charterparty applies to events occurring before the loading voyage begins. Exclusion clauses do not normally apply before the vessel has begun 'the chartered service'; but chartered service can begin before loading commences: *Barker v McAndrew* (1868) 18 CBNS 759; *Monroe v Ryan* [1935] 2 KB 28; *The Super Servant Two* [1990] 1 Lloyd's Rep 1, CA, p 6.

2   A statement of estimated time of arrival is treated in the same way as a statement of expected readiness to load: *The Myrtos* [1984] 2 Lloyd's Rep 449.

3   The approach adopted in *The North Anglia* was approved by the Court of Appeal in *The Baleares* [1993] 1 Lloyd's Rep 215 where it was held that a reasonable despatch obligation does not remain inoperative until a chartered vessel completes discharge under a preceding fixture and the charterer is not obliged to wait until the vessel leaves the last discharge point before treating the owners as being in breach.

3.5 Cancellation clauses

As we have indicated previously, charterparties contain sophisticated clauses to deal with, what is hoped to be, all possible circumstances. Unfortunately this is not the case; nonetheless a good deal of learning has grown up around these clauses. A common clause is the 'laycan' clause, which derives its name from 'laydays cancelling' and is frequently abbreviated to 'l/c'. This refers to the period of time during which the shipowner must tender a notice of readiness (NOR) to the charterer setting out the fact that the ship has arrived at port and is ready to load. It will contain two dates, for example 'Laydays 26 May Cancelling 3 June'.

You will find this abbreviated as 'laycan 26 May/ 3 June'. The charterer is not obliged to start loading until the first of these dates (if the ship arrives earlier) and may have the option of cancelling the charter if the ship arrives after the second of these dates – in other words the cancelling date.

A shipowner who enters into a charter containing a cancellation clause does not necessarily promise that the ship will arrive by the agreed date. English courts have typically taken the view that a cancelling option depends on non-arrival of the ship, not on a breach of contract by the shipowner.

Marbienes Compania Naviera SA v Ferrostaal AG, The Democritos
[1976] 2 Lloyd's Rep 149, CA

Facts: The *Democritos* was time chartered on the New York Produce Exchange (NYPE) form with a cancelling date of 20 December 1969. The vessel arrived at Durban on 16 December 1969. Her 'tween deck in No 2 hold was found to be collapsed. Repairs would have taken some days so that she might not have been ready by the cancelling date. The master gave a written guarantee that the vessel could load the cargo and loading began.

Held:

Lord Denning MR: . . . It is said by the charterers that the owners were under an absolute obligation to deliver the vessel at Durban by the cancelling date, 20 December 1969 – and this is the point – they were bound to deliver her by that date in a fit condition as required by the charter; and that the owners were in breach of that condition because the vessel was not in a fit state then. The 'tween decks were broken. The charterers admit that they may have waived any right to reject the vessel, but nevertheless they claim that they had a right to sue for damages for the vessel being in an unfit condition. The damages would be for loss incurred by her not being able to carry a full cargo, and also by the time occupied later at Seattle in doing the repairs.

Now there is nothing in this charter which binds the owners positively to deliver by 20 December 1969. The only clue to any time of delivery is to be found in the cancelling clause. There is, of course, an implied term that the owners will use reasonable diligence to deliver the ship in a fit condition by 20 December 1969. But that is not an absolute obligation. So long as they have used reasonable diligence, they are not in breach. In this case it is found that reasonable diligence was used, so there is no breach by them of that implied obligation.

Next the cancelling clause. Its effect is that, although there may have been no breach by the owners nevertheless the charterers are, for their own protection, entitled to cancel if the vessel is not delivered in a proper condition by the cancelling date. That is the sole effect.

On this point the Judge referred to the English cases, particularly *Smith v Dart & Son* (1884) 14 QBD 105 at p 110, when AL Smith J said:

The shipowner does not contract to get there by a certain day, but says: 'If I do not get there you may cancel.'

But we have had the benefit of one or two others. The first is from Scotland, *Nelson & Sons v The Dundee East Coast Shipping Co Ltd* (1907) 44 SLR 661. It was a voyage charter, but Lord M'Laren said this:

If it can be shown that the shipowners had used their best endeavours and that the delay was due to unavoidable accident or perils of the sea, I should have been of opinion that no damages were due. The contract could be cancelled but damages would not be due, for each party would then be within his rights.

... These authorities show that as long as the owner uses reasonable diligence, he is not in breach, but the charterer is entitled to cancel if the vessel is not delivered by the cancelling date ...

The right to exercise an option to cancel depends on non-arrival. But does a ship 'arrive' if she is unseaworthy?

Cheikh Boutros Selim El-Khoury v Ceylon Shipping Lines Ltd, The Madeleine [1967] 2 Lloyd's Rep 224

Facts: The *Madeleine* was fixed on a three-month time charter for world trading. The charterers purported to cancel on the grounds that on the agreed cancellation date the vessel was not in a position in which she could properly be delivered because she did not then possess either a 'deratisation certificate' or a 'deratisation exemption certificate'. Under the law of India, without a certificate she could not sail from Calcutta, the port of delivery, to any port outside India. On the facts, it would have taken two days to obtain the necessary certificate. The charterers purported to cancel at 8.00 am on the cancellation date and again at 8.48 pm on the same day. The shipowners argued that the charterers had no right to cancel in the circumstances or at the times they purported to do so.

Held:

Roskill J: ... Plainly it is for the charterers to establish the right which they have sought to exercise. One begins by asking what right it is which clause 22 confers upon the charterers. That must be a question of the true construction of that clause. I therefore turn back to its language:

Should the Vessel not be delivered by the 2nd day of May 1957 the Charterers to have the option of cancelling.

It is well established that clauses in charterparties cannot be construed in isolation from each other. A charterparty like any other contract must be construed sensibly and in its entirety. Where one has a series of clauses in a standard form which has been in use for a great many years, and which has been interpreted many times by the courts and by arbitrators, the court must look at the provisions as a whole. It is plain, when one looks at clause 22, that it is referring to the nonperformance by the owners of an obligation which they are required elsewhere in the charterparty to perform because the clause starts: 'Should the Vessel not be delivered ... '

Plainly, therefore, that provision has reference to an obligation to deliver and one then turns to see where that obligation is imposed. One turns back to clause 1 in the first instance and one finds there that the vessel is to be delivered and placed at the disposal of the charterers:

... between 9 am and 6 pm, or between 9 am and 2 pm if on Saturday, at CALCUTTA in such available berth where she can safely lie always afloat, she being in every way fitted for ordinary cargo service.

... One has to see what is the obligation which clause 22 postulates that the owners will not perform. The obligation which clause 22 postulates that the owners will not perform is the owners' obligation under clause 1. That obligation is to deliver the vessel not before April 18, between 9 am and 6 pm on a weekday, or between 9 am and 2 pm on a Saturday (and not, I should add, on Sunday or a legal holiday unless the charterers agree then to take her over) in an 'available berth where she can safely lie always afloat, she being in every way fitted for ordinary cargo service'.

... plainly, as a matter of construction, clause 22 is looking back to clause 1 and it is the owners' failure to deliver in accordance with the provisions of clause 1 which gives the charterers the right to cancel under clause 22.

It is important to emphasise that that which the charterers are claiming to exercise is an express contractual right given by clause 22. Their right to cancel does not in any way depend upon any breach of the charterparty by the owners. Entitlement to cancel under clause 22 depends not on any breach by the owners but upon whether the owners have timeously complied with their obligations under clause 1. If they have, there is no right to cancel. If they have not, there is a right to cancel ...

As I have already said, in my judgment, clause 22 cannot be divorced from clause 1. Clause 1 requires the owners to deliver in a condition in which the vessel was in every way fitted for ordinary cargo service ... There was here an express warranty of seaworthiness and unless the ship was timeously delivered in a seaworthy condition, including the necessary certificate from the port health authority, the charterers had the right to cancel. That right, in my judgment, they possessed, and I think that the umpire was wrong in holding that they did not possess it.

That brings me to the second point in the case, namely, whether that right was exercised timeously. I have already dealt with the question of time. In my judgment, the owners cannot say they had the whole of May 10 in which to deliver to avoid cancellation. They had to deliver, in my judgment, not later than 6 pm on May 10 if they were to avoid the risk of the charterparty being cancelled by the charterers ...

[But] both as a matter of construction of the charterparty and as a matter of authority, it is clear law that there is no contractual right to rescind a charterparty under the cancelling clause unless and until the date specified in that clause has been reached. In other words ... there is no anticipatory right to cancel under the clause. I respectfully agree with the passage in the 17th edn of *Scrutton* as correctly stating the law. Of course, the fact that there is no contractual right to cancel in advance does not prevent a charterer seeking to claim the right to rescind in advance of the cancelling date, as the learned editors of *Scrutton* put it 'at common law' ... Where the charterer seeks to say that the contract has been frustrated or that there has been an anticipatory breach which entitles him to rescind, then he has such rights as are given to him at common law.

Note

Roskill J here followed a long-established approach in holding that the charterer was not entitled to exercise a cancelling option before the relevant time had arrived. A unilateral attempt to do so may amount to an anticipatory breach and repudiation of the charter, as it did in the next case.

Fercometal SARL v Mediterranean Shipping Co SA,
The Simona [1989] AC 788

Facts: The *Simona* was chartered to carry a part cargo of steel coils from Durban to Bilbao. The charterers were entitled to cancel the charterparty if the vessel was not ready to load on or before 9 July. On 2 July, the owners requested an extension of the cancellation date. The charterers purported to cancel the contract forthwith and fixed alternative tonnage. The owners did not accept the charterers' repudiation. When the vessel arrived in Durban on 8 July the owners tendered notice of readiness although they were not in fact ready to load. The charterers rejected that notice. On 12 July, when the vessel was still not ready to load, the charterers sent a further notice of cancellation. The owners claimed dead freight. Lords Bridge, Templeman, Oliver and Jauncey agreed with Lord Ackner.

Held:

Lord Ackner: My Lords, this appeal raises one short question: did the respondents (the charterers), in the circumstances . . . lose their right to cancel the charterparty which they had entered into with the appellants (the owners)?

. . . It is important at this stage to emphasise that the charterers' right to cancel given by cl 10 was an independent option, only exercisable if the vessel was not ready to load on or before 9 July 1982. Clause 10 did not impose any contractual obligation on the owners to commence loading by the cancellation date.

. . . It is common ground that the action of the charterers in giving the notice purporting to cancel the contract was premature. It constituted an anticipatory breach and repudiation of the charterparty, because the right of cancellation could not be validly exercised until the arrival of the cancellation date, some seven days hence. It is equally common ground that this repudiation was not accepted by the owners . . .

When one party wrongly refuses to perform obligations, this will not automatically bring the contract to an end. The innocent party has an option. He may either accept the wrongful repudiation as determining the contract and sue for damages or he may ignore or reject the attempt to determine the contract and affirm its continued existence. Cockburn CJ in *Frost v Knight* (1872) LR 7 Ex Ch 111 at 112–13 put the matter thus:

> The law with reference to a contract to be performed at a future time, where the party bound to performance announces prior to the time his intention not to perform it, as established by the cases of *Hochster v De la Tour* (1853) 2 E & B 678 and *The Danube and Black Sea Co v Xenos* (1863) 13 CBNS 825 on the one hand, and *Avery v Bowden* (1855) 5 E & B 714, *Reid v Hoskins* (1856) 6 E & B 953 and *Barwick v Buba* (1857) 2 CBNS 563 on the other, may be thus stated. The promisee, if he pleases, may treat the notice of intention as inoperative, and await the time when the contract is to be executed, and then hold the other party responsible for all the consequences of non-performance: but in that case he keeps the contract alive for the benefit of the other party as well as his own; he remains subject to all the obligations and liabilities under it, and enables the other party not only to complete the contract, if so advised, notwithstanding his previous repudiation of it, but also to take advantage of any supervening circumstance which would justify him in declining to complete it. On the other hand, the promisee may, if he thinks proper, treat the repudiation of the other party as a wrongful putting an end to the contract, and may at once bring his action as on a breach of it and in such action he will be entitled to such damages as would have arisen from the nonperformance of the contract at the appointed time, subject, however, to abatement in respect of any circumstances which may have afforded him the means of mitigating his loss.

. . . The way in which a 'supervening circumstance' may turn out to be to the advantage of the party in default, thus relieving him from liability, is illustrated by *Avery v Bowden*, where the outbreak of the Crimean War between England and Russia made performance of the charterparty no longer legally possible. The defendant, who prior to the outbreak of the war had in breach of contract refused to load, was provided with a good defence to an action for breach of contract, since his repudiation had been ignored. As pointed out by Parker LJ in his judgment ([1987] 2 Lloyd's Rep 236 at 240), the law as stated in *Frost v Knight* and *Johnstone v Milling* has been reasserted in many cases since, and in particular in *Heyman v Darwins Ltd* [1942] AC 356 at 361, where Viscount Simon LC said:

> The first head of claim in the writ appears to be advanced on the view that an agreement is automatically terminated if one party 'repudiates' it. That is not so. As Scrutton LJ said in *Golding v London & Edinburgh Insurance Co Ltd* ((1932) 43 Ll L R 487 at 488): 'I have never been able to understand what effect the repudiation by one party has unless the other accepts it.' If one party so acts or so expresses himself, as to show that he does not mean to accept and

discharge the obligations of a contract any further, the other party has an option as to the attitude he may take up. He may, notwithstanding the so-called repudiation, insist on holding his co-contractor to the bargain and continue to tender due performance on his part. In that event, the co-contractor has the opportunity of withdrawing from his false position, and, even if he does not, may escape ultimate liability because of some supervening event not due to his own fault which excuses or puts an end to further performance.

If an unaccepted repudiation has no legal effect ('a thing writ in water and of no value to anybody': *per* Asquith LJ in *Howard v Pickford Tool Co Ltd* [1951] 1 KB 417 at 421), how can the unaccepted acts of repudiation by the charterers in this case provide the owners with any cause of action? It was accepted in the Court of Appeal by counsel then appearing for the owners that it was an inevitable inference from the findings made by the arbitrators that the *Simona* was not ready to load the charterers' steel at any time prior to the charterers' notice of cancellation on 12 July. Counsel who has appeared before your Lordships for the owners has not been able to depart from this concession. Applying the well established principles set out above, the anticipatory breaches by the charterers not having been accepted by the owners as terminating the contract, the charterparty survived intact with the right of cancellation unaffected. The vessel was not ready to load by close of business on the cancelling date, *viz*, 9 July, and the charterers were therefore entitled to and did give what on the face of it was an effective notice of cancellation . . .

Towards the conclusion of his able address, counsel for the owners sought to raise what was essentially a new point, argued before neither the arbitrators, Leggatt J nor the Court of Appeal. He submitted that the charterers' conduct had induced or caused the owners to abstain from having the ship ready prior to the cancellation date. Of course, it is always open to A, who has refused to accept B's repudiation of the contract, and thereby kept the contract alive, to contend that, in relation to a particular right or obligation under the contract, B is estopped from contending that he, B, is entitled to exercise that right or that he, A, has remained bound by that obligation. If B represents to A that he no longer intends to exercise that right or requires that obligation to be fulfilled by A and A acts on that representation, then clearly B cannot be heard thereafter to say that he is entitled to exercise that right or that A is in breach of contract by not fulfilling that obligation. If, in relation to this option to cancel, the owners had been able to establish that the charterers had represented that they no longer required the vessel to arrive on time because they had already fixed [another vessel] and, in reliance on that representation, the owners had given notice of readiness only after the cancellation date, then the charterers would have been estopped from contending they were entitled to cancel the charterparty. There is, however, no finding of any such representation, let alone that the owners were induced thereby not to make the vessel ready to load by 9 July. On the contrary, the owners on 5 July on two occasions asserted that the vessel would start loading on 8 July and on 8 July purported to tender notice of readiness . . . The non-readiness of the vessel by the cancelling date was in no way induced by the charterers' conduct. It was the result of the owners' decision to load other cargo first.

In short, in affirming the continued existence of the contract, the owners could only avoid the operation of the cancellation clause by tendering the vessel ready to load on time (which they failed to do), or by establishing (which they could not) that their failure was the result of the charterers' conduct in representing that they had given up their option, which representation the owners had acted on by not presenting the vessel on time. I would therefore dismiss the appeal with costs.

Notes

1   The *Niizuru* was time chartered on terms which fixed that the lay/can spread as 20 February/28 April 1992. It was also agreed that the shipowners would 'narrow lay/can to a 15 day spread 25 days prior to the narrowed lay/can'. It was held that compliance with the lay/can narrowing provision was a condition precedent to the delivery of the vessel: *Hyundai Merchant Marine Co Ltd v Karander Maritime Inc, The Niizuru* [1996] 2 Lloyd's Rep 66.

2 In contrast, in *Universal Bulk Carriers Pte Ltd v Andre et Cie SA* [2001] EWCA Civ 588; [2001] 2 Lloyd's Rep 65, the lay/can was 'first half of December' and was to be narrowed by the charterers (not the owners) 32 days in advance. The charterers failed to give notice to narrow and the owners purported to terminate. It was held that the narrowing obligation was not a condition precedent to performance of the contract by the owners and was not a condition of the contract, so that a failure to give notice did not entitle the owners to treat the contract as at an end. The *Niizuru* was distinguished on the grounds that in the present case narrowing the lay/can spread was not important to the owners and any disadvantage to them could be compensated in damages.

4 Speed and fuel consumption

Time charters often contain detailed provisions relating to the speed and fuel consumption of the vessel. These terms are designed to compensate one or other party if the vessel's performance falls below or exceeds stated levels. Clauses may deal in detail with the way in which compliance with agreements about speed and fuel consumption is to be calculated. Promises as to average speed may define the locations and the wind, sea and navigation conditions in which measurements are to be made, perhaps distinguishing between laden and ballast voyages. Forms that exclude, for example, poor weather conditions when calculating a vessel's average performance on a voyage, may thereafter apply the average figure to the vessel's total mileage, making adjustments to take account of actual conditions.

Cosmos Bulk Transport Inc v China National Foreign Trade, The Apollonius [1978] 1 Lloyd's Rep 53

Facts: By a time charter dated 28 August 1974, the *Apollonius* was described as:

> . . . when fully loaded, capable of steaming about 14.5 knots in good weather and smooth water on a consumption of about 38 tons of fuel oil [of a certain specification].

The ship was delivered on 1 November 1974 and ordered to load steel at Fukiyama for delivery at Ensenada, Argentina. She made the voyage from Japan to Argentina at an average speed of 10.61 knots and was redelivered to her owners. Thereafter, following cleaning of her hull in dry dock, her average speed returned to a normal 14.5 knots. An arbitrator found that the cause of the speed reduction was that the hull of the vessel had become encrusted with molluscs during a stay at Whampoa, Canton, between the date of the charter and the date on which the chartered service had commenced. The charterers made a claim for the loss of 5.821 days, made up of 4.821 days due to fouling of the hull and 24 hours due to unnecessary reduction of engine speed. The questions of law for decision by the court were: (a) were charterers entitled to damages for the loss of 4.821 days due to fouling; (b) were charterers entitled to damages for the loss of one day because of failure to prosecute the voyage with utmost diligence?

Held:

Mocatta J: . . . I turn now to the first and most important point of all arising in this case, namely whether the speed warranty in the preamble of the charterparty applies only at the date of the charterparty as is contended by the owners or also or in any case applies at the date of the delivery of the vessel under the charter. The strength of the owners' case on this matter rests on the decision of Atkinson J in *Lorentzen* *v White Shipping Co Ltd* (1942) 74 Ll L Rep 161 which contains an *obiter dictum* favourable to the owners' argument here . . .

The first thing to notice about this statement of Atkinson J is that it was *obiter*, since, as he said, he had to assume that the description in relation to the speed warranty was not true at the date of the charterparty. He was not dealing with a case where there was a breach of a warranty at the date of delivery of a ship under a time charterparty. Secondly, in my judgment little is to be gained from the reference made by Atkinson J to the statement that the classification of a ship as stated in a charterparty is not a condition. In my judgment, the contrary is clearly the case . . .

In addition to this mistake, as I consider it to be, in the reference by Atkinson J to the cases on a vessel's class, another criticism of his reasoning, insofar as his opinion in relation to the speed warranty depended on analogies with the cases on a vessel's class, is that the courts in deciding that a statement as to a vessel's class only applies as at the date that the charterparty is entered into based themselves on very special reasons peculiar to classification . . . I cannot think that analogies drawn with . . . somewhat ancient cases on classification are of much assistance today in the present problem.

. . . Counsel for the owners stressed that the *dictum* of Atkinson J on this point had stood unchallenged since 1942 and that no doubt a number of cases in arbitration had been decided on the basis that the *dictum* was good law and, in all probability, an even greater number of cases had been settled on this basis. I do not feel that this argument is of persuasive weight in the circumstances of this case, since it must be relatively rare for there to be a substantial lapse of time between entering into a time charter of an existing vessel and her delivery thereunder, and, in addition, in most cases . . . it would be immaterial which date was relevant for the decision whether the warranty had or had not been broken.

Counsel for the owners sought to derive support for the owners' case from the principle *noscitur a sociis*, in that in the preamble to this charterparty, in addition to the statement as to the vessel's class, which has been decided to apply only as at that date, there are other statements descriptive of the vessel which are similarly limited in time. It is true that there is a reference inserted especially in the printed form of this preamble providing for the main holds to be clean and available for dry cargo on delivery. This can be argued to be an unique express reference to the date of delivery and on the basis of this an argument founded on the maxim *expressio unius exclusio alterius* might be mounted. I do not, however, think that there is much weight in this submission. It is noticeable that the various items of description contained in the preamble are not all of the same category . . .

The provisions in relation to the ship's capacity in the preamble, which no doubt did apply at the date of the charter, would in my judgment also be applicable at the date of her delivery and it is not impossible that her owners might commit a breach of this term of the charter, if, for example, they were, before delivery, to insert an additional bulkhead or make some other alteration to the structure of the ship which limited the cubic feet grain capacity stated in the preamble. Therefore, I do not think that the associates, if I may so describe them, of the speed warranty in the preamble to this charter are all of one class in respect of the date at which they are applicable. The owners cannot, in my judgment, therefore derive any succour from the well known maxim relied on by counsel . . .

On the other hand, it seems to be clear that the whole purpose of the description of the vessel containing a speed warranty is that when the vessel enters on her service, she will be capable of the speed in question, subject of course to any protection which her owners may obtain if there has been some casualty between the date of the charter and the date of delivery affecting her speed which, under an exceptions clause, protects them from liability in relation to a failure to comply with the warranty. From the charterer's point of view the speed warranty is clearly of very great importance in relation to his calculations as to the rate of hire it will be possible for him to pay, a matter on which his decision would be affected by his calculations as to the time which the ship would take to complete the one trip voyage for which this time charter engaged the *Apollonius*. From the business point of view, I think it is clear that commercial considerations require this description as to the vessel's speed to be applicable as at the date of her delivery whether or not it is applicable at the date of the charter. It may well be that at the date of the charter the vessel will have been completing a previous period of service under a time charter or a very long voyage under a voyage charter including stops in tropical ports, with the result that her bottom has become fouled and her speed thereby affected. In order to guard against such a contingency preventing her from attaining the described speed under the present time charter, the latter not unnaturally contained in cl 50 an option given to the owners of dry-docking her before delivery. From the charterer's point of view, the vital date therefore for the purposes of the description of the vessel, with the one exception in relation to her class to which special considerations and a long line of somewhat ancient decided cases apply, is the date of her delivery . . .

In my judgment there are overwhelming commercial considerations favouring the charterers' argument that the speed warranty, whenever else it may apply, certainly applies at the date of the delivery of a vessel, subject only to the owners being protected from the consequences of any breach of such warranty by any exception clause that may be applicable. I will deal with this last matter shortly. But for these reasons I decline to follow the *dictum* of Atkinson J on this subject and, but for the question as to the protection afforded by cl 13 ['Responsibility and Exemption'], I would answer the first question of law stated for the decision of the court in the affirmative on the basis of breach of the speed warranty . . .

(Mocatta J went on to conclude that the shipowners were protected from the second of the charterers' claims by an exclusion clause and, whether or not they were protected by the same clause against the first claim, on the special facts found by the arbitrator, the vessel was in any event off hire for the relevant period.)

5 The liability of sea carriers

We now turn to examine the basic principles of the liability of a sea carrier for goods that are lost, damaged or destroyed. The law in this area has a long history. Modern English law developed from cases that were decided long before steel hulls and steam engines began to be used in maritime commerce.

We begin by considering the liability at common law of public or common carriers and then looks at the position of the private carrier. Common carriers by sea are unlikely to be found in England today, but the law relating to private carriers is best understood against the older background.

This is important because, in addition to their express contractual obligations, sea carriers are treated in English law as being subject to a number of implied duties. These are:

To provide a seaworthy vessel
To proceed with despatch
To follow a direct or usual route

Although it is as well to note that these common law duties are modified by statute and we discuss this in our comments on the operation of the Hague-Visby Rules.

6 Public carriers

At common law, a distinction was made between the position of public and private carriers. A public or common carrier by sea was someone who held himself out as willing to carry for reward for anyone who wanted to use his services. It does not seem to have been necessary for the goods of several persons to be carried in common, or for the carriage to be between English ports, or even for the ship to follow a fixed itinerary. However, a carrier who carried only for particular persons or who genuinely reserved the right to pick and choose his customers was a private carrier.

A public carrier was subject to a stringent legal regime. If space was available, he was bound to carry with reasonable despatch and at a reasonable cost for anyone who wanted to make use of his services. Goods that were unreasonable in quantity or weight could be refused, and so could goods that were dangerous or not of the type of which he professed to be a carrier. But if goods carried for hire were lost or damaged, a common carrier was absolutely liable, except where the loss or damage was caused by the common law excepted perils, which were losses caused by an act of God, the Queen's (or King's) enemies or by inherent vice of the goods themselves. Damage or loss caused by a general average sacrifice or by the fault of the shipper were also defences at common law.

A common carrier was not, therefore, merely expected to take reasonable care of goods that had been entrusted to him. On the contrary, as the old cases explained, a common carrier was virtually in the position of an insurer of goods against all consequences except the common law excepted perils. Thus he was, for example, liable for loss by theft even if he had not been negligent; and it made no difference whether the goods were stolen from the carrier by strangers or by his own employees. However, the severity of this approach could be mitigated by the common carrier himself, who was free at common law to limit his responsibilities by contract.

The rule imposing this extended liability on common carriers was justified on the ground of public policy. It was said that the carrier was often the only person in a position to know how goods were lost or damaged. So to prevent abuse and to avoid uncertainty, the law held him liable, unless he could prove that the loss or damage was caused 'by the King's enemies, or by such act as could not happen by the intervention of man'.

Coggs v Barnard (1703) 2 Ld Raym 918

Facts: John Coggs brought an action against William Barnard who had undertaken to move casks of brandy belonging to Coggs from a cellar in Holborn in London to one that was closer to the river. One of the casks was staved and 150 gallons were lost. Coggs was successful at trial before a jury, but the case was regarded as raising a difficult point of law, which was then argued before the four judges of the court at Westminster. The judgment of Holt CJ was an important restatement of the liabilities of the various sorts of bailee, one of whom is the carrier.

Held:

Holt CJ: As to the fifth sort of bailment . . . those cases are of two sorts; either a delivery to one that exercises a publick employment, or a delivery to a private person. First if it be a person of the first sort, and he is to have a reward, he is bound to answer for the goods at all events. And this is the case of the common carrier, common hoyman, master of a ship, &c, which case of a master of a ship was first adjudged . . . in the case of *Morse v Slue* (1671) 1 Ventris Rep 190, 238. The law charges this person thus entrusted to carry goods, against all events but acts of God, and of enemies of the King. For though the force be never so great, as if an irresistible multitude of persons should rob him, nevertheless he is chargeable. And this is a politick establishment contrived by the policy of the law for the safety of all persons the necessity of whose affairs oblige them to trust these sorts of persons, that they may be safe in their ways of dealing; for else these carriers might have an opportunity of undoing all persons that had any dealings with them, by combining with thieves, &c, and yet doing it in such a clandestine manner as would not be possible to be discovered.

Notes

1   In English common law no one is obliged to undertake the responsibilities of a common carrier and there are few, if any, sea carriers in this country who choose to do so today. The test for identifying a common carrier is summarised in the next two extracts and shows how this undesirable status is avoided.

2   'Everybody who undertakes to carry for anyone who asks him, is a common carrier. The criterion is, whether he carries for particular persons only, or whether he carries for everyone. If a man holds himself out to do it for everyone who asks him, he is a common carrier; but if he does not do it for everyone, but carries for you and me only, that is a matter of special contract': *Ingate v Christie* (1850) 3 C & K 61, *per* Alderson B.

3   'Did the defendant, while inviting all and sundry to employ him, reserve to himself the right of accepting or rejecting their offers of goods for carriage whether his lorries were full or empty, being guided in his decision by the attractiveness or otherwise of the particular offer and not by his ability or inability to carry having regard to his other engagements? Upon the facts as found by me I answer that question in the affirmative, and in my opinion that answer shows that he is not a common carrier': *Belfast Ropework Co Ltd v Bushell* [1918] 1 KB 210, p 215, *per* Bailhache J.

4   *Act of God.* The common law excepted perils mentioned in the text and in *Coggs v Barnard* include act of God, which has been said to be loss or damage 'due to natural causes directly and exclusively, without human intervention, and that . . . could not have been prevented by any amount of foresight and pains and care reasonably to be expected': *Nugent v Smith* (1876) 1 CPD 423, p 444, *per* James LJ.

5   *King's enemies.* The meaning of this phrase was considered in *Russell v Niemann* (1864) 17 CBNS 163 where cargo was shipped under a bill of lading containing this exception. The shipowner was a subject of the Duke of Mecklenburg and the ship a Mecklenburg ship; the port of loading was in Russia, the port of discharge in England and the shippers either German or Russian. The ship was seized by Danes with whom the Duke was at war. On the question whether the exception referred to the Emperor of Russia, the Queen of England or the Duke, it was held it included enemies of the sovereign of the carrier, whether or not a King.

6   *Inherent vice*: 'anything which by reason of its own inherent qualities was lost without negligence by any one': *Greenshields v Stephens* [1908] AC 431, *per* Earl of Halsbury. In *Gould v South Eastern and Chatham Rly* [1920] 2 KB 186 (a case of inland carriage), Atkin LJ, citing *Story on Bailments*, held that the implied liability of a common carrier did not include responsibility for ordinary wear and tear in transit, ordinary loss or deterioration in quality or quantity such as evaporation or loss or damage through insufficiency of packing.

7 Private carriers

The position of a private carrier by land is less onerous than that of the public carrier. A private carrier by land is not absolutely liable for goods that are lost or damaged while in his possession. At common law, where the rights of the parties are not regulated by an express contract, a private land carrier is only liable, as a bailee who is paid, if he fails to take reasonable care of goods entrusted to him. However, to escape liability, he is obliged to prove that the loss or damage was not caused by his negligence.

The liability at common law of a private carrier by sea, where the rights of the parties are not regulated by an express contract, is less certain. The cases contain inconsistent statements. One view is that all sea carriers are subject to the same rule of strict liability as common carriers. The judgment of Brett LJ in *Liver Alkali* (1874) LR 9 Ex 338 is the best-known statement of this view, although it is not an isolated example: see, for example, *Pandorf v Hamilton* (1885) 16 QBD 635 and *Beaumont-Thomas v Blue Star Line* [1939] 3 All ER 127, p 131.

However, Cockburn CJ's judgment in *Nugent v Smith*, below, rejects Brett LJ's views and treats the private carrier by sea as in the same position as a private carrier by land and therefore as being liable only as a bailee for reward, to exercise reasonable care. Some commentators find support for this view in *dicta* such as that of Willes J in *Grill v General Iron Screw Collier Co* (1866) LR 1 CP 600, p 612 that the 'contract is to carry with reasonable care unless prevented by the excepted perils'.

A third possibility mentioned in several cases is that some classes of sea carriers such as lightermen may have a special status as public-but-not-common-carriers and as such have the same liability as common carriers, while all others are liable only to take reasonable care.

Liver Alkali v Johnson (1874) LR 9 Ex 338, Court of Exchequer Chamber; affirming (1872) LR 7 Ex 267, Court of Exchequer Chamber

Facts: The defendant was a barge owner. He did not ply between fixed termini. With each customer an agreement was made for carriage at a negotiated rate per ton between the places selected by the customer. His customers (including the plaintiffs) did not normally select or agree on a particular barge. A barge was never used to carry the goods of more than one customer at a time. There was no evidence that the defendant had ever refused to let his vessels to anyone who ever applied to him. The defendant argued that he was not a common carrier.

Held:

Blackburn J: It appears by the case stated for this Court on appeal that the defendant was engaged in carrying from Widnes to Liverpool some salt cake of the plaintiffs in a flat on the river Mersey. The goods were injured by reason of the flat getting on a shoal in consequence of a fog. This was a peril of navigation, but could in no sense be called the act of God or of the Queen's enemies.

The jury found that there was no negligence on the part of the defendant.

The question, therefore, raised is, whether the defendant was under the liability of a bailee for hire, viz, to take proper care of the goods, in which case he is not responsible for this loss, or whether he has the more extended liability of a common carrier, viz, to carry the goods safe against all events but acts of God and the enemies of the Queen.

We have purposely confined our expressions to the question, 'whether the defendant has the liability of a common carrier', for we do not think it necessary to inquire whether the defendant is a carrier so as to be liable to an action for not taking goods tendered to him ...

It appears from the evidence stated that the defendant was the owner of several flats, and that he made it his business to send out his flats under the care of his own servants, different persons as required from time to time, to carry cargoes to or from places in the Mersey, but that it always was to carry goods for one person at a time, and that 'he carried for any one who chose to employ him, but that an express agreement was always made as to each voyage or employment of the defendant's flats', which means, as we understand the evidence, that the flats did not go about plying for hire, but were waiting for hire by any one. We think that this describes the ordinary employment of a lighterman, and that, both on authority and principle, a person who exercises this business and employment does, in the absence of something to limit his liability, incur the liability of a common carrier in respect of the goods he carries ...

(Blackburn J then reviewed cases decided between 1671 and 1850 and concluded that the defendant was liable. Mellor, Archibald and Grove JJ concurred.)

Brett J: I cannot come to the conclusion that the defendant in this case was liable whether he was a common carrier or not, because I conclude that he was liable, notwithstanding that I am clearly of opinion that he was not a common carrier ...

It is clear to my mind that a shipowner who publicly professes to own sloops, and to charter them to any one who will agree with him on terms of charter, is not a common carrier, because he does not undertake to carry goods for or to charter his sloop to the first comer. He wants, therefore, the essential characteristic of a common carrier; he is, therefore, not a common carrier, and therefore does not incur at any time any liability on the ground of his being a common carrier. The defendant in the present case, in my opinion, carried on his business like any other owner of sloops or vessels, and was not a common carrier, and was in no way liable as such. But I think that, by a recognised custom of England – a custom adopted and recognised by the Courts in precisely the same manner as the custom of England with regard to common carriers has been adopted and recognised by them – every shipowner who carries goods for hire in his ship, whether by inland navigation, or coastways, or abroad, undertakes to carry them at his own absolute risk, the act of God or of the Queen's enemies alone excepted, unless by agreement between himself and a particular freighter, on a particular voyage, or on particular voyages, he limits his liability by further exceptions ...

I therefore hold that the defendant is liable as a shipowner, upon the custom applicable to him as such, but not liable as a common carrier, upon the custom applicable to that business or employment.

Nugent v Smith (1876) 1 CPD 423, CA; reversing (1876) 1 CPD 19

Facts: The plaintiff shipped two horses on board a steamship plying regularly as a general ship between London and Aberdeen. The horses were shipped without any bill of lading. In the course of the voyage one of the horses died from injuries caused partly by the rolling of the vessel in a severe storm and partly from struggling caused by excessive fright. The plaintiff was awarded damages in the High Court. On appeal, the court held that the defendant was a common carrier, but was not liable for a loss caused by a combination of an act of God and inherent vice. Cockburn CJ went on to consider whether the defendant would have been liable if he had not been a common carrier.

Held:

Cockburn CJ: As the vessel by which the mare was shipped was one of a line of steamers plying habitually between given ports and carrying the goods of all corners as a general ship, and as from this it necessarily follows that the owners were common carriers, it was altogether unnecessary to the decision of the present case to determine the question so elaborately discussed in the judgment of Mr Justice Brett [(1876) 1 CPD 19] as to the liability of the owner of a ship, not being a general ship, but one hired to carry a specific cargo on a particular voyage, to make good loss or damage arising from inevitable accident.

The question being, however, one of considerable importance – though its importance is materially lessened by the general practice of ascertaining and limiting the liability of the shipowner by charterparty or bill of lading – and the question not having before presented itself for judicial decision, I think it right to express my dissent from the reasoning of the Court below, the more so as, for the opinion thus expressed, I not only fail to discover any authority whatever, but find all jurists who treat of this form of bailment carefully distinguishing between the common carrier and the private ship ...

[After considering earlier cases Cockburn CJ continued:] The last case is that of the *Liver Alkali Co v Johnson* [above] ... the Court of Exchequer Chamber held, affirming the judgment of the Court of Exchequer, that the defendant was a common carrier and liable as such. Mr Justice Brett, differing from the majority, held that the defendant was not a common carrier, but, asserting the same doctrine as in the judgment now appealed from, held him liable upon a special custom of the realm attaching to all carriers by sea, of which custom, however, as I have already intimated, I can find no trace whatever. We are, of course, bound by the decision of the Court of Exchequer Chamber in the case referred to as that of a court of appellate jurisdiction, and which, therefore, can only be reviewed by a court of ultimate appeal.

[But] . . . it is obvious that as the decision of the Court of Exchequer Chamber proceeded on the ground that the defendant in that case was a common carrier, the decision is no authority for the position taken in the Court below, that all shipowners are equally liable for loss by inevitable accident. It is plain that the majority of the Court did not adopt the view of Mr Justice Brett. Lastly, while it does not lie within our province to criticise the law we have to administer or to question its policy, I cannot but think that we are not called upon to extend a principle of extreme rigour, peculiar to our own law, and the absence of which in the law of other nations has not been found by experience to lead to the evils for the prevention of which the rule of our law was supposed to be necessary, further than it has hitherto been applied. I cannot, therefore, concur in the opinion expressed in the judgment delivered by Mr Justice Brett, that by the law of England all carriers by sea are subject to the liability which by that law undoubtedly attaches to the common carrier whether by sea or by land . . .

Notes

1   Later cases have interpreted *Liver Alkali* and *Nugent v Smith* in a variety of ways. The decision in *Liver Alkali* was followed in *Hill v Scott* [1895] 2 QB 371, where Lord Russell of Killowen CJ said that there was really no essential difference between the judgments of Blackburn J and Brett J, although he preferred the language of Blackburn J. On appeal, Lord Russell's judgment was affirmed by a Court of Appeal, which included Brett J. But *Liver Alkali* was distinguished in *Consolidated Tea v Oliver's Wharf* [1910] 2 KB 395 where it was said that to attract the liability of a common carrier it was essential that 'the defendants were exercising a public employment'. In *Watkins v Cottell* [1916] 1 KB 10, Avory J said that in *Liver Alkali* the defendant had been held to be a common carrier. To complete the range of possible analyses, in *Belfast Ropework v Bushell*, *Liver Alkali* was spoken of as a case confined to lightermen.

2   There has been little recent consideration of this problem by the courts in England, although the issue has been raised indirectly from time to time: *The Emmanuel C* [1983] 1 Lloyd's Rep 310, construction of exclusion clause; *The Torenia* [1983] 2 Lloyd's Rep 211, burden of proof of cargo claim. Modern cases dealing with performing carriers who are not in contract with the cargo owners – see for example *The Pioneer Container* (Chapter 9) – do not explore the issue but treat the carrier's liability as that of a bailee.

8 Carriage under special contract

Uncertainty about the nature of the liability of a sea carrier at common law might seem to be a serious problem. But for the most part this is a theoretical rather than an important practical difficulty, since most cargoes are carried today, not on bare common law terms, but under contracts (called 'special contracts' or 'special carriage' in the older cases) that deal expressly with the carrier's obligations.

Under an express contract, the carrier's obligations will depend on precise terms of his undertakings and on any terms which must be implied into the contract. Where the contract takes the form of a bill of lading, the carrier's obligation is normally now regarded in English courts as an absolute undertaking to deliver the goods at their destination in the same condition in which they were when shipped, unless prevented by causes mentioned in the contract. The common form statement on a bill of lading that the goods are received 'in apparent good order and condition, for carriage subject to the terms hereof from the port of loading to the port of discharge' is not therefore merely a promise to make reasonable efforts. It is an undertaking to deliver the goods in question in the same order and condition in which they were when shipped, subject only to the exceptions in the contract and to any statutory defences to which the carrier may be entitled. To summarise, a ship must deliver what she received, in the condition she received it, unless relieved by excepted perils or by legislation.

Kay v Wheeler (1867) LR 2 CP 302, Court of Exchequer Chamber

Facts: Coffee was shipped on the defendants' ship *Victoria*, for carriage from Colombo to London under a bill of lading containing the exceptions of 'the act of God, the Queen's enemies, fire, and all and every other dangers and accidents of the sea, rivers, and navigation, of what kind and nature soever'. Part of the cargo was damaged. The defendants argued that they were not common carriers and had used reasonable care, to which the Kelly CB replied: 'In this case the defendants have entered into an express contract to deliver the goods in good condition, except in the four specified cases; and they are therefore liable unless the injury arose from one of the causes so excepted.'

Held:

> **Kelly CB:** The question we have to determine depends on the contract between the parties contained in the bill of lading. That, after stating that certain goods have been shipped in good order and condition, binds the defendants to deliver them in like good order and condition, except in four cases . . . The defendants have delivered the goods in a very different condition from that in which they received them and have therefore broken their contract . . .

Notes: Contractual excepted perils

1   The heart of the common law approach to cargo claims is the rule that a ship must deliver up what she received, in the condition she received it, unless relieved by excepted perils in the contract or by legislation. Until the end of the 18th century bills of lading were very short documents which did not usually add exclusions to the common law excepted perils. But by 1800, the orthodox view in England was that to the traditional form of bills of lading 'additional exceptions are and may be introduced, to take away the responsibility of the master and owners in various cases, for which they would otherwise be responsible'. (*Abbot on Merchant Ships & Seamen*, 1802, London: E & R Brooke, p 176). From about this time a wide variety of exemption clauses began to be introduced into bills of lading and the meaning of standard clauses became a matter of general importance.

2   *Interpretation of exemption clauses.* A cautious approach has been adopted. If a stipulation 'is introduced by way of exception or in favour of one of the parties to the contract . . . we must take care not to give it an extension beyond what is fairly necessary, because those who wish to introduce words in a contract in order to shield themselves ought to do so in clear words': *Burton & Co v English & Co* (1883) 12 QBD 218, p 220, *per* Bowen LJ.

3   *Perils of the sea.* This contractual exemption was one of the earliest to be introduced into bills of lading. The phrase is not interpreted in the same way in all jurisdictions: *The Bunga Seroja* [1999] 1 Lloyd's Rep 512, High Court of Australia. In England a peril or accident is required: something that is fortuitous and unexpected, not something 'due to ordinary wear and tear, nor to the operation of any cause ordinarily incidental to the voyage and therefore to be contemplated': *Hamilton v Pandorf* (1887) App Cas 518, p 530, *per* Lord Herschell. The peril must be a peril *of* the sea, not merely a peril *on* the sea. Perils of the sea are those that are

peculiar to carrying on business on the sea: *Pandorf v Hamilton* (1886) 17 QBD 670, p 675, *per* Lord Esher MR. Wind and waves are perils of the sea; but fire and lightning are not: *Hamilton v Pandorf*, p 527, *per* Lord Bramwell. The accidental incursion of seawater into a vessel at a part of the vessel, and in a manner, where seawater is not expected to enter in the ordinary course of things, is a peril of the sea: *Canada Rice Mills Ltd v Union Marine* [1941] AC 55, PC, *per* Lord Wright. Extraordinary violence of the wind or water is not essential: a collision is a peril of the sea (*The Xantho* (1887) 12 App Cas 503) and can occur in fine weather. Nor is damage by wind or water necessarily required; over-heating of cargo when ventilators are closed to avoid water damage is a peril of the sea. On the other hand, it has also been held that the explosion of machinery and the consumption of the cargo or the ship by rats all lack the necessary connection with the sea: *Thames and Mersey Marine Insurance v Hamilton* (1887) App Cas 484, p 491; *Hamilton v Pandorf*, p 523. But if a rat eats part of a ship and the sea enters through the hole and harms the cargo, then the damage is done by a peril of the sea.

4   *Pirates* have been in the news a great deal in the past ten or so years particularly with regard to activities off the coast of Somalia and in the Gulf of Guinea but they have long been regarded as a peril of the sea: *Pickering v Barkley* (1648) Style 132; *Morse v Slue* (1671) 1 Vent 190. Piracy is defined by the *Oxford English Dictionary* as 'the practice or crime of robbery and depredation on the sea or navigable rivers etc, or by descent from the sea upon the coast, by persons not holding a commission from an established civilised state'. In *The Andreas Lemos* [1982] 2 Lloyd's Rep 483, Staughton J held (in a marine insurance context) that: (1) piracy requires force or the threat of force and is committed when a crew are overpowered by force or terrified into submission; it does not include clandestine theft. 'It is not necessary that the thieves must raise the pirate flag and fire a shot across the victim's bows before they can be called pirates. But piracy is not committed by stealth' (p 491); and (2) piracy can be committed in territorial waters, although only if the ship in question is 'at sea' or if the attack on her can be described as a 'maritime offence' thus excluding attacks where the vessel or the attack cannot be so described because the vessel is, for example, in harbour or moored in a creek or river. Compare *Nesbitt v Lushington* (1792) 4 TR 783 ('Restraint of Princes'), below. See also Hazelwood, SJ, 'The Peril of Pirates' (1983) 2 LMCLQ 283 and s 26(1) of and Sched 5 to the Merchant Shipping and Maritime Security Act 1997.

5   *Strikes.* *Tramp Shipping v Greenwich Marine, The New Horizon* [1972] 2 Lloyd's Rep 314 concerned a vessel chartered for a voyage to St Nazaire with a fixed time for discharge. The charter also provided that time should not count during a strike or lockout of any class of workmen essential to the discharge. The normal course of events at the berth in question was for drivers of cranes and suckers to work round the clock, dividing the 24 hours of the day into three shifts. But when the vessel was ready to discharge, drivers were only working during the day shift in an attempt to improve conditions. The Court of Appeal held that there had been a strike. Lord Denning MR said: '. . . I think a strike is a concerted stoppage of work by men done with a view to improving their wages or conditions, or giving vent to a grievance or making a protest about something or other, or supporting or sympathising with other workmen in such endeavour. It is distinct from a stoppage which is brought about by an external event such as a bomb scare or by apprehension of danger.' Lord Denning MR also said that there could be a strike even though the workmen were not in breach of contract; Stephenson LJ thought there could not be a strike where the employer consents to the stoppage.

6   *Robbers, thieves.* The first word refers to a taking by force that the carrier could not reasonably resist. It does not include theft by pilferage: *De Rothschild v Royal Mail Steam Packet* (1852) 7 Ex 734. 'Thieves' was said in *Taylor v Liverpool and Great Western Steam* (1874) LR 9 QB 546 to be ambiguous and so was construed against the interests of the carrier to mean a

taking by persons from outside the ship and not belonging to it (that is, not crew, passengers or, perhaps, others on board with permission). In this context, theft may also require a violent taking: *Shell v Gibbs* [1982] 1 Lloyd's Rep 369, p 373.

7   *Barratry*. 'Where a captain is engaged in doing that which as an ordinary man of common sense he must know to be a serious breach of his duties to the owners, and is engaged in doing that for his own benefit, then he is acting barratrously': *Mentz, Decker v Maritime Insurance* (1909) 15 Com Cas 17, *per* Hamilton J.

8   *Restraint of princes, rulers, people*. A direct and specific action by sovereign authority does not seem to be needed: an indirect restraint (*Rodoconachi v Elliott* (1874) LR 9 CP 518) or a reasonable fear of seizure has been held sufficient: *Nobel's Explosives v Jenkins* [1896] 2 QB 326. The decision of a court is not an act of princes and rulers: *Finlay v Liverpool and Great Western Steamship* (1870) 23 LT 251; nor is seizure of cargo by a riotous mob a restraint of people, although it may be piracy: *Nesbitt v Lushington* (1792) 4 TR 783.

9 Burden of proof

The general approach taken by English law – that it is for the party who seeks relief to prove the claim – applies to contracts for the carriage of goods by sea as to other civil actions. However, the way in which this general approach is applied to marine cargo claims depends on the special form of the carrier's contract, discussed in the last section.

Govt of Ceylon v Chandris [1965] 2 Lloyd's Rep 204

Facts: The *Agios Vlasios* was chartered to carry rice in bags from Burma to Ceylon. In breach of contract, the charterers detained the vessel on demurrage at Colombo for 120 days. On completion of discharge it was found that some of the bags had been lost or damaged. An umpire found as facts that some of the bags were damaged by condensation and sea water, but that the proportions of damage attributable to each cause could not be stated. The condensation damage was caused by lack of dunnage, by necessary restriction of ventilation and by the long duration of the voyage, but it was impossible to state the proportions of damage so caused. The vessel was not adequately fitted with dunnage for the carriage of rice or with adequate tarpaulins. The charter excepted the owners from liability for loss or damage to goods unless caused by personal act or default or personal want of diligence to make the vessel seaworthy. A special case was stated for the opinion of the court.

Held:

Mocatta J: Mr Staughton (counsel for the charterers) put forward three propositions, which can more conveniently be reframed or re-stated as four in the following terms: first, the general rule is that the burden of proof rests upon the party claiming relief, be he plaintiff in an action or claimant in an arbitration, and this applies both to the liability of the other party and the damages recoverable. Secondly, in a claim for damages for breach of contract of carriage by sea, once it is proved that the goods in question were shipped in good condition (as is the case here) and that a known quantity of those goods is proved to have been delivered damaged, the carrier is liable to pay damages measured by the difference between the sound and damaged values of the goods at the date and place of delivery unless the carrier can establish, and the burden is on him to do so, that the goods were damaged through the operation of an exception in the contract of carriage. Thirdly, and this is a qualification upon the second proposition, if the carrier can only show that some part of the damage to the goods was due to a cause within the exception, he must also show how much of the damage is comprised in that part, otherwise he is liable for the whole.

Fourthly, if part of the damage is shown to be due to a breach of contract by the claimants, then the general rule stated in the first proposition applies, and the claimant must show how much of the damage was caused otherwise than by his breach of contract, failing which he can recover nominal damages only.

The third of the above propositions is based on the well-known *dictum* of Viscount Sumner in *Gosse Millerd v Canadian Government Merchant Marine* [1929] AC 223, at p 241. The *dictum* was *obiter*, but was applied by a Divisional Court in Admiralty in *White & Son (Hull) Ltd v 'Hobsons Bay' (Owners)* (1933) 47 LlL Rep 207, and must have been the basis of innumerable opinions by Counsel and solicitors. Mr Staughton did not seek to challenge its validity in this Court but reserved his right to do so should the case go higher. His answer to it on the facts of this case was, however, this fourth proposition. Viscount Sumner was dealing with a case in which the carrier could only escape from his *prima facie* liability for the whole of the damage by relying upon an exception clause. No question arose of any part of the damage to the cargo having been caused by the plaintiff's fault or breach of contract. Viscount Sumner did not, therefore, have to consider the application of another principle, namely, that a plaintiff cannot recover damages from a defendant for the consequences of his own breach of contract with the defendant. Where such circumstances arise, and they must necessarily be infrequent, if the quantum of damage due to the plaintiff's own breach of contract cannot be ascertained, the latter principle must, in Mr Staughton's submission, apply to the exclusion of Viscount Sumner's *dictum*, otherwise the plaintiff would recover for the whole of the damage to the goods, notwithstanding that part of such damage, albeit unknown in extent, was due to his own breach.

Counsel for the shipowners was not able, as I understood him, to fault the logic or force of Mr Staughton's argument. He did, however, submit (and with this I have the greatest sympathy) that too ready an application either of Viscount Sumner's *dictum* or of counsel for the respondent's fourth proposition was to be deprecated because of their rigidity. Thus, on the one hand, a tribunal should be slow, in a case where the carrier has established that part of the damage is due to an excepted peril, to find that he has failed to adduce sufficient facts from which the quantum of such damage can be inferred. Similarly, on the other hand, when some part of a claimant's goods has undoubtedly been damaged by the carrier's breach of contract and some by the claimant's own breach of contract, the tribunal should be slow to award only nominal damages because of the paucity of primary facts from which the quantum of damages due to the claimant's own breach can be inferred. Juries, arbitrators, judges, and even the Court of Appeal (see, for example, *Silver v Ocean Steamship* [1930] 1 KB 416, *per* Lord Justice Scrutton, at p 429) have not infrequently to make what may in truth be little more than informed guesses at the quantum of damages by drawing inferences from the primary facts proved before them.

In my judgment, Mr Staughton's argument and his fourth proposition are well-founded. In so deciding, I am applying no authority because there is none, but the result follows, in my view, from the principles involved. Moreover, if the final view of the facts here be that some part of the sweat damage to the cargo was due to the claimants' breach of contract in keeping the vessel on demurrage for 120 days and some part was due to the respondent's breach of contract in equipping the ship and caring for the cargo, and if there are no primary facts in evidence from which it is possible to draw an inference as to the quantum of damage attributable to either cause, it is, in my view, more consonant with the practice and tradition of the law that the claimants should fail to recover more than nominal damages than that the respondent should pay for the damage caused by her breach of contract and also that caused by the claimants. The law is not unfamiliar with cases where the plaintiff or the claimant fails owing to inability to discharge the burden of proof falling on him . . .

10 The duty to carry with care

As we have noted before 1800 English bills of lading did not usually contain extensive exclusion clauses. The practice changed in the 19th century. Within 80 years the typical list of exceptions and qualifications in steamship bills of lading was so long that it was said, more or less seriously, that the effect was to exonerate 'shipowners from all liability as carriers, and reduce them substantially to the condition of irresponsible bailees': *Crooks v Allan* (1879) 5 QBD 38, p 40.

The unrestrained use by carriers of exclusion clauses encouraged a close analysis of the nature of carriers' obligations. This process resulted in the identification of a series of duties that are implied at common law and stand alongside the carrier's express promise to carry and deliver: the duty to carry with care, the duty to provide a seaworthy ship, the duty to not depart from the proper route and the implied duty to proceed with reasonable despatch.

11 The carrier's duty of care

Paterson Steamships v Canadian Co-operative Wheat Producers [1934] AC 538, PC

Facts: Wheat was shipped on the appellants' steamship *Sarniadoc* under a bill of lading that incorporated the Canadian Water Carriage of Goods Act 1910. The vessel was stranded and the cargo lost during a gale. The Judicial Committee of the Privy Council held that the Act had to be considered in the light of the shipowner's liability at common law.

Held:

Lord Wright: It will therefore be convenient here, in construing those portions of the Act which are relevant to this appeal, to state in very summary form the simplest principles which determine the obligations attaching to a carrier of goods by sea or water. At common law, he was called an insurer, that is he was absolutely responsible for delivering in like order and condition at the destination the goods bailed to him for carriage. He could avoid liability for loss or damage only by showing that the loss was due to the act of God or the King's enemies. But it became the practice for the carrier to stipulate that for loss due to various specified contingencies or perils he should not be liable: the list of these specific excepted perils grew as time went on. That practice, however, brought into view two separate aspects of the sea carrier's duty which it had not been material to consider when his obligation to deliver was treated as absolute. It was recognized that his overriding obligations might be analysed into a special duty to exercise due care and skill in relation to the carriage of the goods and a special duty to furnish a ship that was fit for the adventure at its inception. These have been described as fundamental undertakings, or implied obligations. If then goods were lost (say) by perils of the seas, there could still remain the inquiry whether or not the loss was also due to negligence or unseaworthiness. If it was, the bare exception did not avail the carrier . . .

Note

Lord Wright's judgment suggests that the carrier's duty of care was developed to prevent unfair reliance by carriers on exclusion clauses. Two other explanations of the origins of the duty of care can be found in the law reports. One is that the duty is simply a consequence of the carrier's position as a bailee. Another explanation is that the duty grew from a standard approach to the interpretation of exclusion clauses ('Negligence . . . came in as an exception on an exception': *The Torenia* [1983] 2 Lloyd's Rep 211). These explanations are not necessarily inconsistent: it seems likely that all three factors played a part in the development of the modern law.

12 Care and perils of the sea

The Xantho **(1887) 12 App Cas 503**

Facts: Goods were shipped on the defendants' vessel at Cronstadt for carriage to Hull under bills of lading that were endorsed to the plaintiffs. The bills of lading contained exceptions for dangers and accidents of the sea. The *Xantho* collided with another vessel in fog and was lost. The plaintiffs brought proceedings for non-delivery. In the House of Lords, the appellant shipowners argued that since collision was a peril of the sea in a policy of insurance, it must also be a peril of the sea in a bill of lading.

Held:

> **Lord Macnaghten** (515): My Lords, in this case the bill of lading on which the question arises is in common form. In the usual terms it states the engagement on the part of the shipowner to deliver the goods entrusted to his care. At the same time it specifies, by way of exception, certain cases in which failure to deliver those goods may be excused. So much for the express terms of the bill of lading. But the shipowner's obligations are not limited and exhausted by what appears on the face of the instrument. Underlying the contract, implied and involved in it . . . there is also an engagement on his part to use due care and skill in navigating the vessel and carrying the goods. Having regard to the duties thus cast upon the shipowner, it seems to follow as a necessary consequence, that even in cases within the very terms of the exception in the bill of lading, the shipowner is not protected if any default or negligence on his part has caused or contributed to the loss.

Note

The Xantho is an important decision but it is far from unique. There are many other clear statements in the cases to the same effect: see, for example, *The Glendarroch* [1894] P 226 and *The Super Servant Two* [1990] 1 Lloyd's Rep 1, CA.

13 Care and fire

Lord Macnaghten's judgment in *The Xantho* suggests that, on analysis, a contract for the carriage of goods by sea can be seen to consist of an absolute promise by the carrier to carry and deliver and a separate implied promise to do so carefully. In the next extract, Scrutton LJ suggests a way in which these two duties can be harmonised.

In Re Polemis and Furness, Withy & Co **[1921] 3 KB 560, CA**

Facts: The steamship *Thrasyvoulos* was lost by fire while being discharged by workmen employed by the charterers. Arbitrators held that the fire was caused by a spark igniting petrol vapour in the hold. The vapour came from leaks from cargo shipped by the charterers. The spark was caused by stevedores employed by the charterers who negligently knocked a plank out of a temporary staging erected in the hold, so that the plank fell into the hold, and in its fall by striking something made the spark which ignited the petrol vapour.

Held:

> **Scrutton LJ:** On these findings the charterers contend that they are not liable [*inter alia*, because] they are protected by an exception of 'fire' which in the charter is 'mutually excepted' . . .
>
> An excepted perils clause, if fully expanded, runs that one of the parties undertakes to do something unless prevented by an excepted peril, in which case he is excused. But where he has an obligation to do some act carefully, if he fails in his obligation, and by his negligence an excepted peril comes into operation and does damage, the excepted peril does not prevent him from acting carefully, and he is liable for damages directly flowing from his breach of his obligation to act carefully, though the breach acts through the medium of an excepted peril. It is a commonplace of mercantile law that if a peril of the sea is brought into operation by the carelessness of the shipowner or his servants, he is liable, though perils of the sea are excepted perils, unless he has also a clause excepting the negligence of his servants. In the same way, though the charterer has an exception of fire in his favour, he will be liable if the fire was directly caused by his servants' negligence, for it was not fire that prevented them from being careful. This disposes of the first defence.

14 Care to avoid consequences

In *Polemis*, above, the negligent conduct occurred before the events to which the excepted peril was said to apply and which caused the damage. The next extract shows how a breach of the carrier's duty of care may occur at a later stage, after initial damage covered by an exemption clause has occurred.

Notara v Henderson (1872) LR 7 QB 225, Court of Exchequer Chamber

Facts: The plaintiffs shipped beans on board the defendants' ship *Trojan*, under a bill of lading, from Alexandria to Glasgow, with leave to call at intermediate ports. The ship called at Liverpool and on leaving the port met with a collision (a peril excepted in the bill of lading) and had to put back for repairs. The beans became wet in consequence of the collision and, on arrival at Glasgow, had deteriorated in value. This deterioration could have been prevented if they had been dried at Liverpool. The plaintiffs sued to recover this loss.

Held:

> **Willes J** (reading the judgment of the Court): The question thus raised is a compound one of law and fact; first, of law, whether there be any duty on the part of the shipowners, through the master, to take active measures to prevent the cargo from being spoilt by damage originally occasioned by sea accidents, without fault on their part, and for the proximate and unavoidable effects of which accident they are exempt from responsibility by the terms of the bill of lading; and secondly, of fact, whether, if there be such a duty, there was, under the circumstances of this case, a breach thereof in not drying the beans . . .
>
> That a duty to take care of the goods generally exists cannot be doubted . . . the duty imposed upon the master, as representing the shipowner, [is] to take reasonable care of the goods entrusted to him, not merely in doing what is necessary to preserve them on board the ship during the ordinary incidents of the voyage, but also in taking reasonable measures to check and arrest their loss, destruction, or deterioration, by reason of accidents, for the necessary effects of which there is, by reason of the exception in the bill of lading, no original liability.
>
> The exception in the bill of lading was relied upon in this court as completely exonerating the shipowner; but it is now thoroughly settled that it only exempts him from the absolute liability of a common

carrier, and not from the consequences of the want of reasonable skill, diligence, and care, which want is popularly described as 'gross negligence'. This is settled, so far as the repairs of the ship are concerned, by the judgment of Lord Wensleydale in *Worms v Storey* (1855) 11 Ex 427, 430; as to her navigation, by a series of authorities collected in *Grill v General Iron Screw Collier Co* (1866) LR 1 C P 600; (1868) 3 CP 476; and as to her management, so far as affects the case of the cargo itself, in *Laurie v Douglas* (1846) 15 M & W 746; where the Court (in a judgment unfortunately not reported at large) upheld a ruling of Pollock, CB, that the shipowner was only bound to take the same care of the goods as a person would of his own goods, viz, 'ordinary and reasonable care'. These authorities and the reasoning upon which they are founded are conclusive to shew that the exemption is from liability for loss which could not have been avoided by reasonable care, skill, and diligence, and that it is inapplicable to the case of a loss arising from the want of such care, and the sacrifice of the cargo by reason thereof, which is the subject-matter of the present complaint. For these reasons we think the shipowners are answerable for the conduct of the master, in point of law, if, in point of fact, he was guilty of a want of reasonable care of the goods in not drying them at Liverpool . . .

(The court held, affirming the judgment of the Court of Queen's Bench, that the facts shewed that the beans might have been taken out and dried and then re-shipped, without unreasonably delaying the voyage; that it was, therefore, the master's duty to have done so, and consequently the defendants were liable.)

15 Exclusion of duty to exercise due care

At common law, just as the parties to a contract could agree to exclude the carrier's liability for particular perils – perils of the sea, for example – so also it was possible to agree expressly that the carrier would not be liable for negligence which caused loss. But English courts adopt a cautious approach to the interpretation of clauses of this type.

The Raphael [1982] 2 Lloyd's Rep 42

Held:

May LJ: . . . if an exemption clause of the kind we are considering excludes liability for negligence expressly, then the Courts will give effect to the exemption. If it does not do so expressly, but its wording is clear and wide enough to do so by implication, then the question becomes whether the contracting parties so intended. If the only head of liability upon which the clause can bite in the circumstances of a given case is negligence, and the parties did or must be deemed to have applied their minds to this eventuality, then clearly it is not difficult for a Court to hold that this was what the parties intended – that this is its proper construction. Indeed, to hold otherwise would be contrary to commonsense. On the other hand if there is a head of liability upon which the clause could bite in addition to negligence then, because it is more unlikely than not a party will be ready to excuse his other contracting party from the consequences of the latter's negligence, the clause will generally be construed as not covering negligence. If the parties did or must be deemed to have applied their minds to the potential alternative head of liability at the time the contract was made then, in the absence of any express reference to negligence, the Courts can sensibly only conclude that the relevant clause was not intended to cover negligence and will refuse so to construe it. In other words, the Court asks itself what in all the relevant circumstances the parties intended the alleged exemption clause to mean.

Note

A vivid example of the approach described by May LJ in *The Raphael* can be found in *Industrie Chimiche v Nea Ninemia* [1983] 1 Lloyd's Rep 310 where Bingham J concluded that 'errors of navigation' in cl 16 of the New York Produce Exchange (NYPE) charter form meant 'non-negligent errors of navigation', reasoning that the clause might have been intended to protect the carrier against claims based on the strict liability of a sea carrier at common law, rather than negligent errors of navigation. This decision was approved by the Court of Appeal in *Seven Seas Transportation Ltd v Pacifico Union Marina Corp, The Satya Kailash and Oceanic Amity* [1984] 1 Lloyd's Rep 588.

16 Burden of proof

The burden of proof in a cargo claim is of course a matter of great importance in legal practice. But the leading cases are also important for the explanation that they provide of the underlying substantive law and are included here for that reason.

The Glendarroch [1894] P 226, CA

Facts: The plaintiffs were shippers and consignees of cement, which was damaged by sea water and became valueless when the *Glendarroch* stranded on St Patrick's Causeway in Cardigan Bay. They brought an action against the defendants for non-delivery. The goods had been shipped under a bill of lading that excepted losses by perils of the sea, but did not relieve the carrier from liability for negligence. The Court of Appeal held that it was for the plaintiffs to prove the contract and for the defendants to prove loss by perils of the sea. If they did so, the burden of proving that the defendants were not entitled to the benefit of the exception on the ground of negligence was on the parties who alleged it, who in this case were the plaintiffs.

Held:

Lord Esher MR: We have to treat this case as if the contract were in the ordinary terms of a bill of lading. The contract being one on the ordinary terms of a bill of lading, the goods are shipped on the terms that the defendant undertakes to deliver them at the end of the voyage unless the loss of the goods during the voyage comes within one of the exceptions in the bill of lading . . .

When you come to the exceptions, among others, there is that one, perils of the sea. There are no words which say 'perils of the sea not caused by the negligence of the captain or crew'. You have got to read those words in by a necessary inference. How can you read them in? They can only be read in, in my opinion, as an exception upon the exceptions. You must read in, 'Except where the loss is by perils of the sea, unless or except that loss is the result of the negligence of the servants of the owner'.

That being so, I think that according to the ordinary course of practice each party would have to prove the part of the matter which lies upon him. The plaintiffs would have to prove the contract and the non-delivery. If they leave that in doubt, of course they fail. The defendants' answer is, 'Yes; but the case was brought within the exception – within its ordinary meaning'. That lies upon them. Then the plaintiffs have a right to say there are exceptional circumstances, viz, that the damage was brought about by the negligence of the defendants' servants, and it seems to me that it is for the plaintiffs to make out that second exception . . .

Joseph Constantine Steamship Line Ltd v Imperial Smelting Corp Ltd, The Kingswood [1941] 2 All ER 165, HL

The decision in *The Glendarroch* was cited with approval in this case.

Held:

Viscount Simon: It is ancient law that, by an implied term of the contract, the shipowner cannot rely on the exception [of perils of the sea] if its operation was brought about either (i) by negligence of his servants, or (ii) by his breach of the implied warranty of seaworthiness. If a ship sails and is never heard of again, the shipowner can claim protection for loss of the cargo under the express exception of perils of the seas. To establish that, must he go on to prove (i) that the perils were not caused by negligence of his servants, and (ii) were not caused by unseaworthiness? I think clearly not. He proves a *prima facie* case of loss by sea perils, and then he is within the exception. If the cargo owner wants to defeat that plea, it is for him by rejoinder to allege and prove either negligence or unseaworthiness. The judgment of the Court of Appeal in *The Glendarroch* is plain authority for this . . .

Note

See further Ezeoke, C, 'Allocating onus of proof in sea cargo claims' (2001) LMCLQ 261.

17 Liability in tort

The sea carrier's contractual rights and duties limit the importance of a duty of care in tort as between the parties to a contract for the carriage of goods by sea. However, tort liability is important where there is actionable fault on the part of someone with whom the owner of the goods is not in contract, typically a sub-carrier or an employee or agent of the contracting carrier, such as a stevedore. The two cases in this section deal with the accrual of the cause of action for negligence, a topic that gives rise to special difficulties in the circumstances in which carriage contracts are performed.

Leigh and Sillivan Ltd v Aliakmon Shipping Co Ltd, The Aliakmon [1986] AC 785

Facts: Leigh and Sillivan were buyers of a cargo of steel coils. The coils were damaged by bad stowage, which caused crushing, condensation and then rust. The damage was done at a time when the risk, but not the legal property in the goods had passed to the buyers. The special terms of the purchase contract agreed between the buyers and the sellers of the steel meant that, in the unusual circumstances of the case, the buyers had no right of action in contract against the owners of *Aliakmon*. The following extract deals with the claim made by the buyers against the shipowners in tort.

Held:

Lord Brandon: . . . My Lords, there is a long line of authority for a principle of law that, in order to enable a person to claim in negligence for loss caused to him by reason of loss of or damage to property, he must have had either the legal ownership of or a possessory title to the property concerned at the time when the loss or damage occurred, and it is not enough for him to have only had contractual rights in relation to such property which have been adversely affected by the loss of or damage to it. The line of authority to which I have referred includes the following cases: *Cattle v Stockton Waterworks Co* (1875) LR 10 QB 453 (contractor doing work on another's land unable to recover from a waterworks company loss suffered by him by reason of that company's want of care in causing or permitting water to leak from a water pipe laid and owned by it on the land concerned); *Simpson & Co v Thomson* (1877) 3 App Cas 279 (insurers of two ships A and B, both owned by C, unable to recover from C loss caused to them by want of care in the navigation of ship A in consequence of which she collided with and damaged ship B); *Société Anonyme de Remorquage à Hélice v Bennetts* [1911] 1 KB 243 (tug owners engaged to tow ship A unable to recover from owners of ship B loss of towage remuneration caused to them by want of care in the navigation of ship B in consequence of which she collided with and sank ship A); *Chargeurs Réunis Compagnie Française de Navigation a Yapeur v English & American Shipping Co* (1921) 9 Ll L R 464 (time charterer of ship A unable to recover from owners of ship B loss caused to them by want of care in the navigation of ship B in consequence of which she collided with and damaged ship A); *The World Harmony* [1967] P 341 (same as preceding case). The principle of law referred to is further supported by the observations of Scrutton LJ in *Elliott Steam Tug Co Ltd v Shipping Controller* [1922] 1 KB 127, 139–140.

None of these cases concerns a claim by cif or c and f buyers of goods to recover from the owners of the ship in which the goods are carried loss suffered by reason of want of care in the carriage of the goods resulting in their being lost or damaged at a time when the risk in the goods, but not yet the legal property in them, has passed to such buyers. The question whether such a claim would lie, however, came up for decision in *Margarine Union GmbH v Cambay Prince Steamship Co Ltd (The Wear Breeze)* [1969] 1 QB 219 . . . Roskill J held [it would] not, founding his decision largely on the principle of law established by the line of authority to which I have referred . . .

[In] *The Mineral Transporter* [1986] AC 1 . . . a collision took place between ships A and B solely by reason of want of care in the navigation of ship B. As a result of the collision ship A was damaged and had to be repaired, and during the period of repair the first plaintiff, who was the time charterer of ship A, suffered loss in the form of wasted payments of hire and loss of profits. The Supreme Court of New South Wales held that the first plaintiff was entitled to recover his loss from the owners of ship B. On appeal to the Privy Council that decision was reversed and it was held that the first plaintiff had no right of suit in respect of his loss. It was urged on the Board that the rule against admitting claims for loss arising solely from a contractual relationship between a plaintiff and the victim of a negligent third party could no longer be supported, and that it was enough that the loss was a direct result of a wrongful act and that it was foreseeable. The judgment of the Board was given by Lord Fraser of Tullybelton who rejected this contention. He made a full examination of the long line of English authority to which I referred earlier, and also of certain Scottish, Australian, Canadian and American decisions. He expressed the conclusion of the Board, at p 25:

> Their Lordships consider that some limit or control mechanism has to be imposed upon the liability of a wrongdoer towards those who have suffered economic damage in consequence of his negligence . . . The common law limitation which has been generally accepted is that stated by Scrutton LJ in *Elliott Steam Tug Co Ltd v Shipping Controller* [1922] 1 KB 127, 139–140 . . . Not only has that rule been generally accepted in many countries including the United Kingdom, Canada, the United States of America and until now Australia, but it has the merit of drawing a definite and readily ascertainable line. It should enable legal practitioners to advise their clients as to their rights with reasonable certainty, and their Lordships are not aware of any widespread dissatisfaction with the rule. These considerations operate to limit the scope of the duty owed by a wrongdoer . . .

Mr Clarke [counsel] said, rightly in my view, that the policy reason for excluding a duty of care in cases like *The Mineral Transporter* and what I earlier called the other non-recovery cases was to avoid the opening of the floodgates so as to expose a person guilty of want of care to unlimited liability to an indefinite number of other persons whose contractual rights have been adversely affected by such want of care. Mr Clarke went on to argue that recognition by the law of a duty of care owed by shipowners to a cif or c and f buyer, to whom the risk but not yet the property in the goods carried in such shipowners' ship has passed, would not of itself open any floodgates of the kind described. It would, he said, only create a strictly limited exception to the general rule, based on the circumstance that the considerations of policy on which that general rule was founded did not apply to that particular case. I do not accept that argument. If an exception to the general rule were to be made in the field of carriage by sea, it would no doubt have to be extended to the field of carriage by land, and I do not think that it is possible to say that no undue increase in the scope of a person's liability for want of care would follow. In any event, where a general rule, which is simple to understand and easy to apply, has been established by a long line of authority over many years, I do not think that the law should allow special pleading in a particular case within the general rule to detract from its application. If such detraction were to be permitted in one particular case, it would lead to attempts to have it permitted in a variety of other particular cases, and the result would be that the certainty, which the application of the general rule presently provides, would be seriously undermined. Yet certainty of the law is of the utmost importance, especially but by no means only, in commercial matters. I therefore think that the general rule, re-affirmed as it has been so recently by the Privy Council in *The Mineral Transporter* [1986] AC 1, ought to apply to a case like the present one . . .

As I said earlier, Mr Clarke submitted that your Lordships should hold that a duty of care did exist in the present case, but that it was subject to the terms of the bill of lading. With regard to this suggestion Sir John Donaldson MR said in the present case [1985] QB 350, 368:

> I have, of course, considered whether any duty of care owed in tort to the buyer could in some way be equated to the contractual duty of care owed to the shipper, but I do not see how this could be done. The commonest form of contract of carriage by sea is one on the terms of the Hague Rules. But this is an intricate blend of responsibilities and liabilities (Article III), rights and immunities (Article IV), limitations in the amount of damages recoverable (Article IV, r 5), time bars (Article III, r 6), evidential provisions (Article III, rr 4 and 6), indemnities (Article III, r 5 and Article IV, r 6) and liberties (Article IV, rr 4 and 6). I am quite unable to see how these can be synthesised into a standard of care.

I find myself suffering from the same inability to understand how the necessary synthesis could be made as the Master of the Rolls.

As I also said earlier, Mr Clarke sought to rely on the concept of a bailment on terms as a legal basis for qualifying the duty of care for which he contended by reference to the terms of the bill of lading. He argued that the buyers, by entering into a c and f contract with the sellers, had impliedly consented to the sellers bailing the goods to the shipowners on the terms of a usual bill of lading which would include a paramount clause incorporating the Hague Rules. I do not consider that this theory is sound. The only bailment of the goods was one by the sellers to the shipowners. That bailment was certainly on the terms of a usual bill of lading incorporating the Hague Rules. But, so long as the sellers remained the bailors, those terms only had effect as between the sellers and the shipowners. If the shipowners as bailees had ever attorned to the buyers, so that they became the bailors in place of the sellers, the terms of the bailment would then have taken effect as between the shipowners and the buyers. Because of what happened, however, the bill of lading never was negotiated by the sellers to the buyers and no attornment by the shipowners ever took place. I would add that, if the argument for the buyers on terms of bailment were correct, there would never have been any need for the Bills of Lading Act 1855 or for the decision of the Court of Appeal in *Brandt v Liverpool, Brazil and River Plate Steam Navigation Co Ltd* [1924] 1 KB 575 to which I referred earlier . . .

My Lords . . . Mr Clarke [also] submitted that any rational system of law ought to provide a remedy for persons who suffered the kind of loss which the buyers suffered in the present case, with the clear implication that, if your Lordships' House were to hold that the remedy for which he contended was not available, it would be lending its authority to an irrational feature of English law. I do not agree with this submission for, as I shall endeavour to show, English law does, in all normal cases, provide a fair and adequate remedy for loss of or damage to goods the subject matter of a cif or c and f contract, and the buyers in this case could easily, if properly advised at the time when they agreed to the variation of the original c and f contract, have secured to themselves the benefit of such a remedy.

As I indicated earlier, under the usual cif or c and f contract the bill of lading issued in respect of the goods is endorsed and delivered by the seller to the buyer against payment by the buyer of the price. When that happens, the property in the goods passes from the sellers to the buyers upon or by reason of such endorsement, and the buyer is entitled, by virtue of section 1 of the Bills of Lading Act 1855, to sue the shipowners for loss of or damage to the goods on the contract contained in the bill of lading. The remedy so available to the buyer is adequate and fair to both parties, and there is no need for any parallel or alternative remedy in tort for negligence. In the present case, as I also indicated earlier, the variation of the original c and f contract agreed between the sellers and the buyers produced a hybrid contract of an extremely unusual character. It was extremely unusual in that what had originally been an ordinary c and f contract became, in effect, a sale ex-warehouse at Immingham, but the risk in the goods during their carriage by sea remained with the buyers as if the sale had still been on a c and f basis. In this situation the persons who had a right to sue the shipowners for loss of or damage to the goods on the contract contained in the bill of lading were the sellers, and the buyers, if properly advised, should have made it a further term of the variation that the sellers should either exercise this right for their account (see *The Albazero* [1977] AC 774) or assign such right to them to exercise for themselves. If either of these two precautions had been taken, the law would have provided the buyers with a fair and adequate remedy for their loss.

These considerations show, in my opinion, not that there is some lacuna in English law relating to these matters, but only that the buyers, when they agreed to the variation of the original contract of sale, did not take the steps to protect themselves which, if properly advised, they should have done. To put the matter quite simply the buyers, by the variation to which they agreed were depriving themselves of the right of suit under section 1 of the Bills of Lading Act 1855 which they would otherwise have had, and commercial good sense required that they should obtain the benefit of an equivalent right in one or other of the two different ways which I have suggested . . .

My Lords, if I had reached a different conclusion on the main question of the existence of a duty of care, and held that such a duty of care, qualified by the terms of the bill of lading, did exist, it would have been necessary to consider the further question whether, on the rather special facts of this case, the shipowners committed any breach of such duty. As it is, however, an answer to that further question is not required.

Notes

1   In the course of his judgment in this case Lord Brandon also rejected suggestions that the buyers could recover as owners of the goods in equity or on the basis of a suggested principle of transferred loss. The Bills of Lading Act 1855 was repealed and replaced by the Carriage of Goods by Sea Act 1992.

2   The decision in *The Aliakmon* stressed the need for a clear and certain general rule defining the ambit of the carrier's duty of care in tort. A rule may be clear, but difficult to apply in practice, as the next case demonstrates and where it is also suggested that an aspect of the general rule is still uncertain.

Homburg Houtiport BV v Agrosin Private Ltd,
The Starsin [2001] EWCA Civ 56; [2001] 1 Lloyd's Rep 437

Facts: Parcels of timber and plywood were carried from three ports in Malaysia to Avonmouth and Antwerp under bills of lading. The cargo was delivered damaged and three claimants, holders of the bills of lading, brought actions in contract and tort. The damage was caused by rain before shipment and then by condensation during the voyage. The stowage was negligent, with inadequate dunnage, inadequate ventilation and improper stowage in one compartment of parcels with different moisture contents. Damage caused by the negligence was progressive throughout the voyage. But at the moment the voyage began, with one exception, the goods were still owned by the shippers and not the claimants. The claimants sought to recover in respect of damage that occurred after they had acquired title.

Held: (*obiter*)

Rix LJ: 77 The traditional view is that a shipowner can only be sued in tort by a cargo-owner whose cargo has suffered damage while on board the vessel by reason of a breach of duty owed to that cargo-owner. Thus damage done to a future owner of the damaged cargo, before the passing of title to that owner, will not give him a cause of action in tort. See *Margarine Union GmbH v Cambay Prince Steamship Co Ltd (The Wear Breeze)* [1969] 1 QB 219 and *Leigh & Sillivan Ltd v Aliakmon Shipping Co Ltd (The Aliakmon)* [1986] AC 785.

78 In the present case, the breach of duty occurred on loading or at latest on completion of loading on Dec 8 in the form of negligent stowage at a time when, other than in the case of Makros Hout, the shippers and not the claimants owned the cargo. The damage caused by that negligence was progressive throughout the voyage and throughout the damaged parcels: it was also inevitable in that it was common ground that there was nothing that could be done to mitigate the effects of the initial breach. The claimants make no claim in respect of the damage which had occurred before they obtained title respectively to their goods, only in respect of the continuing damage which occurred after title had passed. The Judge . . . held that a duty of care was owed at the time of loading to all those, such as the claimants, who would become owners of the cargo during the course of the voyage, that there was a breach of that duty at the outset, and that the cause of action in tort was completed once further damage had occurred after the transfer of title to each claimant in respect of their goods . . .

79 In *The Wear Breeze* and again in *The Aliakmon* the plaintiff cargo-owners never obtained title to the goods until after discharge from the vessels concerned. There never was in those cases any damage caused on board the vessels after title had passed to the purchasers. Nor of course was there any breach by the shipowners of any duty of care at a time when the plaintiffs were owners of cargo on the vessels. Therefore the precise point which has arisen in the present case was never in issue there. The difficulty which has now arisen is to determine whether the rule laid down in those cases was to require both breach of duty and damage to occur at a time when the claimants had title, or whether it is sufficient that damage occurs after the claimants have gained title albeit in respect of a breach of duty which pre-dates the transfer of title. Or to put the matter in another way: is Mr Justice Colman [trial judge] right to say that those cases contemplate that a duty can be owed, and thus broken, to future owners of cargo, or only to those who are owners at the time of breach?

80 One difficulty in answering this problem is that by and large in *The Wear Breeze* Mr Justice Roskill spoke in terms of the time when the negligence occurred, whereas in *The Aliakmon* Lord Brandon of Oakbrook spoke in terms of the time when the damage occurred. If the latter formulation is the correct rule, as Mr Jacobs [counsel for claimants] submits, then it admits of the possibility of Mr Justice Colman's conclusion; whereas if the former formulation is correct, as Mr Berry [counsel for defendants] submits – and *The Wear Breeze* was approved by Lord Brandon – then it is hard to see how Mr Justice Colman's solution can be accepted . . .

94 These are interesting submissions. When all is said and done, it remains true that in *The Wear Breeze*, *The Irene's Success* and *The Aliakmon* the precise issue did not arise because the claimants there never obtained title while the goods were on board the vessel or before all relevant loss had already been suffered. It is also perhaps arguable that, even if it may be said that both Mr Justice Roskill and Lord Brandon considered that no duty of care was owed to the claimants in those cases, they simply did not have in mind the case of a claimant who had actually suffered damage to his goods during the voyage, and after they had become his goods on the voyage. The contrary argument is that there is a firm and well-known rule applying to the carriage of goods, any difficulties in that rule in this context are dealt with in contract by the exceptional statutory effect given to the transfer of a bill of lading, and that it is not necessary or desirable to forego the certainty and simplicity of the old rule to cover exceptional cases where a claimant either has never taken a transfer of the bill of lading or wants to have his own independent remedies against the shipowner in tort as well as against his contract partner under the bill of lading.

95 In my judgment, however, it is not necessary to resolve this point, for in the present case all the damaged goods were treated as having already suffered condensation damage before the transfer of title in them took place (Makros Hout is now revealed as an exception) and in respect of negligence which had already occurred by at latest the start of the voyage. All subsequent condensation damage continuing beyond the transfer of title in the respective parcels was merely the continuation and progression of the damage already suffered. No new negligence, no new mechanism of damage, postdated the transfer of title. It was not submitted that the negligent act of stowage was a continuing breach, merely that the fresh damage which occurred after the claimants had each acquired title created new causes of action in the hands of each new owner of cargo . . .

96 In my judgment, however, the cause of action in respect of the negligent stowage was in the present circumstances completed once and for all when more than insignificant damage was caused by that negligence to the respective parcels of timber. On Mr Justice Colman's findings that would have been not long after the voyage began. That cause of action was possessed by the then owners of that cargo, the shippers or Makros Hout. The principle in question was laid down in *Cartledge v E Jopling & Sons* [1963] AC 758 in the case of personal injury, and in *Pirelli General Cable Works Ltd v Oscar Faber & Partners* [1983] 2 AC 1 in the case of damage to property . . .

105 In my judgment . . . progressive damage originating from one act or omission creates a single cause of action . . . It may be different where entirely different damage is done on different occasions by reason of a different defect, as where, owing to defective hatch covers, one hold is flooded on one day and another hold is flooded on a different day: but that is for another occasion. In my judgment, however, the progressive damage done in this case does not create new causes of action in respect of the later stages of the same progressive damage, even in the hands of a new cargo-owner and even upon the assumption that the new cargo-owner was always within the scope of the shipowner's duty of care. Thus even if the underlying reasoning of Mr Justice Colman on this aspect of the case is correct, further consideration of the nature of the damage and the cause of action in question prevents recovery.

Notes

1   Rix LJ concluded that, with the exception of Makros Hout, the claims in tort must fail. In the case of one other claim it was said pre-transfer condensation damage of something over 5% of the cargo's value was 'more than negligible'.

2   On appeal to the House of Lords, Rix LJ's conclusion (paras 96 and 105, above) was approved. There was no discussion of the unresolved point raised in para 79.

18 Seaworthiness

As explained above, at common law it is an implied term of a contract for the carriage of goods by sea that the carrier will ensure that the ship is seaworthy. This duty is important and complex. It extends far beyond the provision of a ship that is able to remain afloat and move from place to place. The common law duty can, however, be modified or excluded by agreement provided clear words are used. If the intention is not clear, an exclusion or limitation clause in a contract will be interpreted as applying only to the carrier's express undertaking to carry and deliver the cargo. Thus an exception of perils of the sea does not qualify the duty to furnish a seaworthy ship: *Paterson Steamships Ltd v Canadian Co-operative Wheat Producers* [1934] AC 538, PC (see Chapter 3).

The extracts that follow deal first with the general features of the common law doctrine. Later sections deal with particular aspects of the duty, including the fitness of the ship for the particular cargo, the competence of the crew and the extent to which lack of necessary documents can render a ship unfit. The last three sections of the chapter deal with the times at which a ship must be seaworthy, causation and with the remedies available for breach. The Hague and Hague-Visby Rules, when they apply, modify the common law rules.

19 The implied warranty: Origins

The carrier's duty to provide a vessel that was tight, staunch and properly manned and equipped for the voyage was a feature of customary maritime law recognised by many commentators. It was incorporated into modern English law by being treated – as *Lyon v Mells* shows – as an implied promise.

Lyon v Mells (1804) 5 East 428

Facts: The defendant agreed to lighter a quantity of yarn owned by the plaintiffs from the quayside at Hull to a vessel in the dock. The lighter leaked and partly capsized, damaging the yarn. The defendant relied on a public notice that purported to limit the liability of lightermen in the Humber area.

Held:

> **Lord Ellenborough CJ:** ... In every contract for the carriage of goods between a person holding himself forth as the owner of a lighter or vessel ready to carry goods for hire, and the person putting goods on board or employing his vessel or lighter for that purpose, it is a term of the contract on the part of the carrier or lighterman, implied by law, that his vessel is tight and fit for the purpose or employment for which he offers and holds it forth to the public; it is the very foundation and immediate substratum of the contract that it is so: the law presumes a promise to that effect on the part of the carrier without any actual proof; and every reason of sound policy and public convenience requires it should be so.
>
> ... This brings me to consider the terms of the notice ... Every agreement must be construed with reference to the subject matter; and looking at the parties to this agreement (for so I denominate the notice) and the situation in which they stood in point of law to each other, it is clear beyond a doubt that the only object of the owners of the lighters was to limit their responsibility in those cases only where the law would otherwise have made them answer for the neglect of others, and for accidents which it might not be within the scope of ordinary care and caution to provide against. For these reasons, we are of opinion that the plaintiffs are entitled to have their verdict ...

20 The modern doctrine: Summary

Over the last 200 years, the implied duty recognised in *Lyon v Mells* has become increasingly complex. The decision in the next case, *The Eurasian Dream*, contains a valuable restatement of the main features of the modern law, which are considered in the following sections of this chapter.

Papera Traders Co Ltd v Hyundai Merchant Marine Co Ltd, The Eurasian Dream [2002] EWHC 118 (Comm); [2002] 1 Lloyd's Rep 719

Facts: A fire on the car carrier *Eurasian Dream* damaged the vessel's cargo of cars. It was alleged that the loss and damage was caused by unseaworthiness.

Held:

Cresswell J: 125 The classic definition of seaworthiness is contained in the judgment of Lord Justice Scrutton in *FC Bradley & Sons Ltd v Federal Steam Navigation Co* (1926) 24 Ll L Rep 446 at 454, approving a statement from *Carver on Carriage by Sea*:

> The ship must have that degree of fitness which an ordinary careful and prudent owner would require his vessel to have at the commencement of her voyage having regard to all the probable circumstances of it. To that extent the shipowner . . . undertakes absolutely that she is fit, and ignorance is no excuse. If the defect existed, the question to be put is, would a prudent owner have required that it should be made good before sending his ship to sea had he known of it? If he would, the ship was not seaworthy . . .

126 Seaworthiness is not an absolute concept; it is relative to the nature of the ship, to the particular voyage and even to the particular stage of the voyage on which the ship is engaged . . .

127 Seaworthiness must be judged by the standards and practices of the industry at the relevant time, at least so long as those standards and practices are reasonable.

128 The components of the duty (as illustrated by the case law) are as follows:

(1) The vessel must be in a suitable condition and suitably manned and equipped to meet the ordinary perils likely to be encountered while performing the services required of it. This aspect of the duty relates to the following matters.
　(a) The physical condition of the vessel and its equipment.
　(b) The competence / efficiency of the master and crew.
　(c) The adequacy of stores and documentation.
(2) The vessel must be cargoworthy in the sense that it is in a fit state to receive the specified cargo.

Notes

1   The duty to provide a seaworthy ship is here described as both absolute and relative. The standard that the ship must meet is relative. But once that standard has been defined, at common law the shipowner's obligation to meet the standard is absolute: *Steel v State Line Steamship Co* (1877) 3 App Cas 72. It is no excuse that the owner did not know of a defect or that best endeavours were used to make the ship fit: *McFadden v Blue Star Line* [1905] 1 KB 697. The provisions of the Hague-Visby Rules that modify this aspect of common law doctrine are contained in Art III, r 1 and Art IV.

2   The 'ordinary careful and prudent owner' test is not the only verbal formula used to decide if a ship is unseaworthy. An alternative is to ask if the ship, at the relevant moment, was reasonably fit to meet the perils of the voyage.

3   Unseaworthiness can take a number of forms and may relate to the vessel, stores and equipment, the competence and efficiency of the crew and/or to the documentation carried. This classification is best seen as one of convenience rather than a rigid framework into which every defect must fit neatly: defects often overlap the different classes.

4   A ship may be unseaworthy because of trivial as well as serious failings. But not every defect that requires attention will make a ship unseaworthy: *The Fjord Wind* [1999] 1 Lloyd's Rep 307, p 319; *The Pride of Donegal* [2002] EWHC 24 (Comm); [2002] 1 Lloyd's Rep 659. The prudent shipowner might leave some defects to be rectified during the voyage or at a later day.

5   It is not necessary, in order to apply the prudent shipowner test, to identify the precise cause of every mechanical failure: *The Fjord Wind*, p 318. Where a serious failure occurs at sea without outside interference, the natural inference may be that the ship was unseaworthy on sailing. It has also been said that there is 'an inevitable presumption of fact' that a vessel is unseaworthy 'if there is something about it which endangers the safety of the vessel or its cargo or which might cause significant damage to its cargo or which renders it legally or practically impossible for the vessel to go to sea or to load or unload its cargo': *The Arianna* [1987] 2 Lloyd's Rep 376, p 389, *per* Webster J.

6   Examples of defects in the physical condition of a vessel or its equipment rendering it unseaworthy include:

- leaking hull: *Lyon v Mells* (1804) 5 East 428;
- leaking hatch covers: *The Gundulic* [1981] 2 Lloyd's Rep 511;
- leaking sea valve: *McFadden v Blue Star Line* [1905] 1 KB 697;
- porthole not capable of being closed at sea: *Steel v State Line Steamship Co; Dobell v Steamship Rossmore Co Ltd* [1895] 2 QB 408;
- neglecting to put in a nail: *Havelock v Geddes* (1809) 10 East 555;
- crankshaft with flaw in weld: *The Glenfruin* (1885) 10 PD 103;
- defective propeller: *SNIA v Suzuki* (1924) 29 Com Cas 284;
- insufficient spare parts: *The Pride of Donegal* [2002] EWHC 24 [2002] iLloyd's Rep 659;
- unsuitable spare parts: *The Kamsar Voyager* [2002] 2 Lloyd's Rep 57;
- sludge in lubricating oil: *The Kriti Rex* [1996] 2 Lloyd's Rep 171;
- insufficient supply of fuel: *The Vortigern* [1899] P 140;
- contaminated fuel: *The Makedonia* [1962] P 190;
- contaminated cargo tanks and lines: *Vinmar v Theresa* [2001] 2 Lloyd's Rep 1;
- inadequate charts and navigation aids: *The Isla Fernandina* [2000] 2 Lloyd's Rep 15.

21 Cargoworthiness

A ship that can navigate safely may still be unseaworthy in law if it is not fit to carry the agreed cargo. Some commentators prefer to treat cargoworthiness as a distinct obligation, while others regard it as an example of the wider duty to ensure seaworthiness, as it is treated here. This difference is, in practice, one of presentation rather than substance.

Tattersall v National Steamship Co (1884) 12 QBD 297, DC

Facts: The plaintiff shipped cattle on board the defendants' ship *France* for carriage from London to New York under a bill of lading that, among other things, provided that the defendants should not be liable 'for accidents, disease, or mortality, and that under no circumstances shall they be held liable for more than £5 for each of the animals'. The ship had on a previous voyage carried cattle suffering from foot and mouth disease. Some of the cattle shipped under the bill of lading were infected during the voyage. It was found that this was caused by the negligence of the defendants' servants in not cleaning and disinfecting the ship before loading the plaintiff's cattle on board. The plaintiff in consequence suffered damage amounting to more than £5 for each animal.

Held:

> **Day J:** I take it to have been clearly established . . . that where there is a contract to carry goods in a ship there is, in the absence of any stipulation to the contrary, an implied engagement on the part of the person so undertaking to carry that the ship is reasonably fit for the purposes of such carriage. In this case it is clear that the ship was not reasonably fit for the carriage of these cattle. There is, therefore, a breach of their implied engagement by the defendants, and the plaintiff having sustained damage in consequence must be entitled to recover the amount of such damage, unless the defendants are protected by any express stipulation . . .
>
> I have considered the terms of the bill of lading, and, as I construe it, its stipulations which have been relied upon all relate to the carriage of the goods on the voyage, and do not in any way affect the liability for not providing a ship fit for their reception. If the goods had been damaged by any peril in the course of the voyage, which might be incurred in a ship originally fit for the purpose of the carriage of the goods, the case would have been wholly different, but here the goods were not damaged by any such peril, or by any peril which, in my opinion, was contemplated by the parties in framing the bill of lading. They were damaged simply because the defendants' servants neglected their preliminary duty of seeing that the ship was in a proper condition to receive them, and received them into a ship that was not fit to receive them. There is nothing in the bill of lading that I can see to restrict or qualify the liability of the defendants in respect of the breach of this obligation . . .

Note

Other examples of this type of unseaworthiness include:

- defective refrigerating machinery where the cargo was frozen meat: *Maori King v Hughes* [1895] 2 QB 550;
- bullion room not reasonably fit to resist bullion thieves: *Queensland National Bank v P & O* [1898] 1 QB 567;
- ship with no dunnage mats to protect dry cargo: *Hogarth v Walker* [1899] 2 QB 401;
- pumps inadequate for cargo: *Stanton v Richardson* (1872) LR 7 CP 421.

22 Unseaworthiness: Competence of crew

A crew that is inadequate in number, untrained or incompetently led or supervised is just as dangerous as a ship that is sent to sea with inadequate supply of fuel, the wrong charts or a hole in the hull. In all these cases, the vessel will be unseaworthy. The decision in *Clan Line* confirmed the basic principle; the *Eurasian Dream*, below, summarises the position today.

Standard Oil v Clan Line [1924] AC 100

Facts: The vessel's characteristics meant that special precautions had to be taken when ballasting. The owners knew of these peculiarities but the captain did not.

Held:

Lord Atkinson: . . . It is not disputed, I think, that a ship may be rendered unseaworthy by the inefficiency of the master who commands her. Does not that principle apply where the master's inefficiency consists, whatever his general efficiency may be, in his ignorance as to how his ship may, owing to the peculiarities of her structure, behave in circumstances likely to be met with on an ordinary ocean voyage? There cannot be any difference in principle, I think, between disabling want of skill and disabling want of knowledge. Each equally renders the master unfit and unqualified to command, and therefore makes the ship he commands unseaworthy. And the owner who withholds from the master the necessary information should, in all reason, be as responsible for the result of the master's ignorance as if he deprived the latter of the general skill and efficiency he presumably possessed . . .

Papera Traders Co Ltd v Hyundai Merchant Marine Co Ltd,
The Eurasian Dream **[2002] EWHC 118 (Comm); [2002] 1 Lloyd's Rep 719**

Facts: The ship was a purpose-built car carrier. A fire started while the vessel was in port. Cars were being jump-started in the same area in which petrol was being used to prime carburettors. A spark ignited petrol. The fire was not extinguished and cargo and the ship were destroyed. It was alleged that the ship was unseaworthy because there were too few portable radios, working fire extinguishers and sets of breathing apparatus. Other allegations were: that a CO_2 valve was defective and that the master ('a car carrier novice') and crew were ignorant of the peculiar hazards of car carriage and the fire-fighting systems of the ship; that there had been insufficient training in fire fighting; and that the manuals carried on board dealing with fire prevention and control and the precautions to be taken were also inadequate.

Held:

Cresswell J: 129 As to the competence or efficiency of the master and crew:

(1) Incompetence or inefficiency may consist of a 'disabling want of skill' or a 'disabling want of knowledge' . . .

(2) Incompetence or inefficiency is a question of fact, which may be proved from one incident and need not be demonstrated by reference to a series of acts: *The Star Sea* [1997] 1 Lloyd's Rep 360 at 373–374 (*per* Lord Justice Leggatt). However, one mistake or even more than one mistake does not necessarily render a crew-member incompetent: *The Star Sea* at 374 . . .

(3) Incompetence is to be distinguished from negligence and may derive from:
    (a) an inherent lack of ability;
    (b) a lack of adequate training or instruction: eg lack of adequate fire-fighting training;
    (c) a lack of knowledge about a particular vessel and/or its systems: *Standard Oil v Clan Line* [1924] AC 100, 121; *The Farrandoc* [1967] 2 Lloyd's Rep 276; *The Star Sea*;
    (d) a disinclination to perform the job properly . . . ;
    (e) physical or mental disability or incapacity (eg drunkenness, illness) . . .

(4) The test as to whether the incompetence or inefficiency of the master and crew has rendered the vessel unseaworthy is as follows: Would a reasonably prudent owner, knowing the relevant facts, have allowed this vessel to put to sea with this master and crew, with their state of knowledge, training and instruction? (Mr Justice Salmon, *Hongkong Fir Shipping Co Ltd v Kawasaki Kisen Kaisha Ltd* [1962] 2 QB 26 at 34.)

(5) As to causation, unseaworthiness must be 'a cause or, if it is preferred, a real or effective or actual cause [and] in truth, unseaworthiness . . . can never be the sole cause of the loss . . . It must, I think,

> always be only one of several co-operating causes ... I can draw no distinction between cases where the negligent conduct of the master is a cause and cases in which any other cause, such as perils of the seas, or fire, is a co-operating cause ... ' (Lord Wright, *Smith Hogg & Co v Black Sea and Baltic General Insurance Co* [1940] AC 997 at 1005).

Applying these principles, Cresswell J held that the ship was unseaworthy because her equipment and people were inadequate. 'Had the crew ... been properly instructed and trained they ... would have prohibited simultaneous and proximate refuelling/jump-starting and there would not have been a fire.'

23 Lack of necessary documents

The duty to provide a seaworthy ship, as restated in *The Eurasian Dream*, requires the carrier to provide 'adequate documentation'. This aspect of the duty is less well developed than other features. The older common law decisions are reviewed in *The Derby*, which decided that a ship may be seaworthy even where the shipowner does not provide a document that is needed if the ship is to carry on her business without hindrance.

Alfred C Toepfer v Tossa Marine, The Derby [1985] 2 Lloyd's Rep 325, CA

Facts: The vessel was chartered on the New York Produce Exchange (NYPE) form. Line 22 of the charter provided 'vessel on her delivery to be ready to receive cargo ... and in every way fitted for the service'. The vessel was delayed at Leixoes in Portugal when the ITF (an international workers organisation) discovered the vessel did not have and was not qualified to receive an ITF 'blue card', because the crew were not being paid at European rates.

Held:

Kerr LJ: ... The context in which the words 'in every way fitted for the service' occur shows that these words relate primarily to the physical state of the vessel. However, the authorities also show that their scope is wider, in at least two respects. First, in *Hongkong Fir Shipping Co Ltd v Kawasaki Kisen Kaisha Ltd* [1962] 2 QB 26, the words 'she being in every way fitted for ordinary cargo service' in the Baltime form of time charter were treated as forming part of an express warranty that the vessel was seaworthy, and it was held that this warranty required the provision of a sufficient and competent crew to operate the vessel for the purposes of the charter service. I accept that precisely the same reasoning applies to the words 'in every way fitted for the service' in the present case. To that extent, therefore, these words go beyond the purely physical state of the vessel as such. However, I cannot see any basis for any further enlargement of the scope of these words by extracting from them a warranty that the rates of pay and conditions of employment of the crew, with which they expressly declared themselves to be satisfied, must also comply with the requirements, not of any law which is relevant to the vessel, her crew or the vessel's operation under the charter, but also of a self-appointed and extra-legal organization such as the ITF. In my view this is not a meaning which these words can properly bear, let alone in the context in which they appear in the charter.

The second respect in which the scope of these words in line 22 has been held to go beyond the physical state of the vessel is that they have been held to cover the requirement that the vessel must carry certain kinds of documents which bear upon her seaworthiness or fitness to perform the service for which the charter provides. Navigational charts which are necessary for the voyages upon which the vessel may be ordered from time to time are an obvious illustration. For present purposes, however, we are concerned with certificates bearing upon the seaworthiness of the vessel. The nature of such certificates may vary according to the requirements of the law of the vessel's flag or the laws or regulations in force in the countries to which the vessel may be ordered, or which may lawfully be required by the authorities exercising administrative or other functions in the vessel's ports of call pursuant to the laws there in force. Documents falling within this category, which have been considered in the authorities, are certificates concerning the satisfactory state of the vessel which is in some respect related to her physical conditions, and accordingly to her seaworthiness. Their purpose is to provide documentary evidence for the authorities at the vessel's ports of call on matters which would otherwise require some physical inspection of the vessel, and possibly remedial measures – such as fumigation – before the vessel will be accepted as seaworthy in the relevant respect. The nature of description of such certificates, which may accordingly be required to be carried on board to render the vessel seaworthy, must depend on the circumstances and would no doubt raise issues of fact in individual cases. But I do not see any basis for holding that such certificates can properly be held to include documents other than those which may be required by the law of the vessel's flag or by the laws, regulations or lawful administrative practices of governmental or local authorities at the vessel's ports of call. An ITF blue card does not fall within this category, and I can therefore see no reason for including it within the scope of the words in line 22, even in their extended sense as indicated above.

Moreover, I do not consider that the words in line 22 have acquired as a matter of law, any 'expanded meaning', as the arbitrator suggests in para 5 above. The requirement of a deratisation certificate under the laws in force in India in 1957, which was the point at issue in *The Madeleine*, and without which the vessel could not sail to any other country, was in no way different in principle from the 'bill of health' required by the law of Sardinia, which fell to be considered in *Levy v Costerton* (1816) 4 Camp 389. Since a vessel chartered for a voyage from England to Sardinia could not enter and discharge in the port of Cagliari without this document, 'required from all ships even from England', and was consequently delayed by being put under quarantine by the local authorities, it was inevitably held in that case that the vessel had not been ' . . . furnished with everything needful and necessary for such a ship, and for the voyage . . . '.

A decision about half-way in time between 1816 and the present was *Ciampa v British India Steam Navigation Co Ltd* [1915] 2 KB 774. On the appeal before us there was considerable controversy whether the reason for the unseaworthiness of the vessel on arrival in Marseilles in that case was the fact that she had previously called at Mombasa, which was contaminated by a plague, or whether she had a 'foul bill of health' in the sense of some deficiency in her proper documentation. In my view this is irrelevant for present purposes. The vessel was clearly unseaworthy at Marseilles in either event, whether on the ground that the local authorities required her to be fumigated because she had recently called at Mombasa, or because she did not have any document certifying a 'clean bill of health', in the same way as the vessel in *Levy v Costerton*. On whichever basis that decision in 1915 falls to be considered, it is wholly in line with the other two cases decided respectively in 1816 and 1967. The same applies to the 'tonnage certificate' required by Swedish law which was in issue in *Chellew Navigation Co Ltd v AR Appelquist Kolinport AG* (1933) 45 Ll L Rep 190 and (1932) 38 Com Cas 218, which the learned Judge also discussed in his judgment. In that case the umpire held, on the facts, that it was no part of the shipowners' obligation to obtain this certificate, or at any rate not by the time when the charterers had obtained it at their own expense.

I can therefore see no basis for the arbitrator's conclusion in the present case that the words in line 22 of this form of charter-party have somehow acquired an expanded meaning in our law so as to lead to the conclusion that a document in the nature of an ITF blue card can nowadays be held to fall within the requirements imposed upon shipowners by virtue of these words . . .

24 Time at which warranty attaches: The doctrine of stages

At common law, the carrier's duty to provide a seaworthy ship is not a continuing obligation that extends throughout the period covered by the carriage contract. The duty arises only at particular points in time. Two key points are the moment that cargo is loaded and the moment that the ship sails. However, these are not the only relevant times.

The Vortigern [1899] P 140, CA

Facts: The owners of the steamship *Vortigern* sued the defendants to recover the freight due under a charterparty under which shipowners had agreed to carry a cargo of copra to Liverpool from Cebu, Phillipine Islands. The defence was that a portion of the defendants' cargo had been burned as fuel because insufficient coal had been loaded and that the shipowners were in breach of the implied warranty of seaworthiness which attached to the contract of affreightment at the commencement of the voyage.

Held:

> **AL Smith LJ:** . . . The implied warranty which *prima facie* attaches to a charterparty such as the present is that the ship shall be seaworthy for the voyage at the time of sailing, by which is meant that the vessel shall then be in a fit state as to repairs, equipment, and crew, and in all other respects, sufficient to take her in ordinary circumstances to her port of destination, though there is no warranty that the ship shall continue seaworthy during the voyage.
>
> That coals are part of the equipment of a steamship I do not doubt, and if the voyage in this case had been an ordinary voyage, as to which there was no necessity, as regards taking in coal, for dividing it into stages, it cannot be denied that the steamship was unseaworthy when she started from Cebu on her voyage to Liverpool, for the simple reason that she had not then on board an equipment of coal sufficient to take her in ordinary circumstances to her port of destination . . .
>
> In my judgment when a question of seaworthiness arises between either a steamship owner and his underwriter upon a voyage policy, or between a steamship owner and a cargo owner upon a contract of affreightment, and the underwriter or cargo owner establishes that the ship at the commencement of the voyage was not equipped with a sufficiency of coal for the whole of the contracted voyage, it lies upon the shipowner, in order to displace this defence, which is a good one, to prove that he had divided the voyage into stages for coaling purposes by reason of the necessity of the case, and that, at the commencement of each stage, the ship had on board a sufficiency of coal for that stage – in other words, was seaworthy for that stage. If he fails in this he fails in defeating the issue of unseaworthiness which *prima facie* has been established against him. In each case it is a matter for proof as to where the necessity of the case requires that each stage should be, and I think that in the present case the necessity for coaling places at Colombo and Suez has been established.
>
> This question of dividing up voyages into stages, as regards the warranty of seaworthiness, is by no means destitute of authority. There are numerous cases decided upon policies of marine insurance when the voyage is divided into stages, and there is also a case in this Court relating to the warranty of seaworthiness upon a contract of affreightment when the voyage was divided into stages.
>
> As regards the first class of cases it suffices to cite from a judgment of Lord Penzance, when delivering the judgment of the Judicial Committee of the Privy Council, consisting of himself, Sir William Erle, and Giffard LJ in the case of the *Quebec Marine Insurance Co v Commercial Bank of Canada* (1870) LR 3 PC 234 where the numerous prior authorities relating to voyages consisting of different stages are referred to. Lord Penzance says:
>
> > The case of *Dixon v Sadler* (1841) 5 M & W 405 and the other cases which have been cited, leave it beyond doubt that there is seaworthiness for the port, seaworthiness in some cases for the

river, and seaworthiness in some cases, as in a case that has been put forward of a whaling voyage, for some definite, well recognised, and distinctly separate stage of the voyage. This principle has been sanctioned by various decisions; but it has been equally well decided that the vessel in cases where these several distinct stages of navigation involve the necessity of a different equipment or state of seaworthiness, must be properly equipped, and in all respects seaworthy for each of these stages of the voyage respectively at the time when she enters upon each stage, otherwise the warranty of seaworthiness is not complied with. It was argued that the obligation thus cast upon the assured to procure and provide a proper condition and equipment of the vessel to encounter the perils of each stage of the voyage, necessarily involves the idea that between one stage of the voyage and another he should be allowed an opportunity to find and provide that further equipment which the subsequent stage of the voyage requires; and no doubt that is so. But that equipment must, if the warranty of seaworthiness is to be complied with [that is, the warranty at the time of the commencement of the voyage] be furnished before the vessel enters upon that subsequent stage of the voyage which is supposed to require it.

Read into this judgment the word 'shipowner' in the place of 'the assured', and the judgment is in point in the present case.

There is no difference between the implied warranty of seaworthiness which attaches at the commencement of the voyage in the case of an assured shipowner and in the case of a shipowner under a contract of affreightment. In each case the shipowner warrants that his ship is seaworthy at the commencement of the voyage . . .

Note

In *Northumbrian Shipping v Timm* [1939] AC 397, Lord Porter said that the right to determine bunkering stages was probably a matter for the shipowner, 'provided he chooses usual and reasonable stages'. It was also said in this case that refuelling stages should be fixed not later than the start of the voyage, that fuel sufficient for the intended stage and a margin for contingencies should be loaded, but that the allowance for contingencies ought not to be reduced because of the availability en route of alternative bunkering places, even if the charter gives the owner a wide liberty to deviate. This approach to margins seems to coincide with the requirements of marine underwriters: see Kendall, L and Buckley, J, *Business of Shipping*, 7th edn, 2001, Centreville, Maryland: Cornell Maritime, p 183.

AE Reed & Co Ltd v Page, Son and East [1927] 1 KB 743, CA

Facts: The plaintiffs were the consignees of 500 tons of wood pulp which arrived at Erith on the *Borgholm*. They employed the defendants to lighter it to Nine Elms. One of the defendants' barges, *Jellicoe*, had a carrying capacity of 170 tons; 190 tons were put on board. While she was lying alongside the steamer waiting for a tug to tow her to Nine Elms she sank and her cargo was lost. The plaintiffs succeeded in an action for damages. The defendants appealed.

Held:

Scrutton LJ: . . . A ship, when she sails on her voyage, must be seaworthy for that voyage, that is, fit to encounter the ordinary perils which a ship would encounter on such a voyage. But she need not be fit for the voyage before it commences, and when she is loading in port. It is enough if, before she sails, she has completed her equipment and repair. But she must be fit as a ship for the ordinary perils of lying afloat in harbour, waiting to sail. She must, in my view, be fit as a ship, as distinguished from a carrying warehouse, at each stage of her contract adventure, which may, as in *Cohn v Davidson* (1877) 2 QBD 455, commence before loading. And she may as a ship after loading be unfit to navigate because of her stowage, which renders her unsafe as a ship . . .

Looked at from the point of view of a ship to sail the sea, the highest measure of liability will be when she starts on her sea voyage, and this is often spoken of as the stage when the warranty attaches; but what is meant is that it is the time when that highest measure of liability attaches. There are previous stages of seaworthiness as a ship, applicable to proceeding to loading port, loading, and waiting to sail when loading is completed.

On the other hand, the highest measure of liability as a cargo-carrying adventure, that is, of 'cargo-worthiness', is when cargo is commenced to be loaded. It has been decided that if at this stage the ship is fit to receive her contract cargo, it is immaterial that when she sails on her voyage, though fit as a ship to sail, she is unfit by reason of stowage to carry her cargo safely . . .

It was argued that the doctrine of stages was only a question of difference of equipment, and that over-loading was not equipment. But damages unrepaired at the commencement of a new stage, collision during loading, and starting on the voyage with that damage unrepaired, may obviously be unseaworthiness at the commencement of the voyage stage. I see no reason for defining stages only by difference of equipment.

Applying the above statement of the law to the facts of the present case: the barge was sent to the ship's side to carry 170 tons, and she was fit to carry that quantity. The warranty of cargoworthiness was complied with when loading commenced. But then 190 tons were put into her, some 14 per cent more than her proper load. With that cargo in, she had a dangerously low freeboard in calm water. I think at any rate one of her gunwales was awash, and water could continuously enter through cracks, which would be only an occasional source of leakage if she were properly loaded. She had to lie so loaded for some unascertained time in the river till a tug came. The ship was not bound to let the barge lie moored to the ship's side. She might have to navigate under oars to a barge road. She was exposed to all the wash of passing vessels, and the more water she took on board, the more dangerous she would become. It is clear that she was quite unfit to lie in the river for any time exposed to the wash of passing vessels and the natural 'send' of the water. It is still clearer that she was quite unfit to be towed, and that she was in such a condition that she would soon go to the bottom. I am clearly of opinion that the barge was unseaworthy as a barge from the time loading finished, unfit to lie in the river, and still more unfit to be towed . . .

I think in the present case, when the loading was finished and the man in charge, apparently in the ordinary course of his business, left her unattended in the river waiting for a tug, and unfit in fact either to lie in the river or be towed, there was a new stage of the adventure, a new warranty of fitness for that stage, and a breach of that warranty which prevented the exceptions from applying.

25 Unseaworthiness or bad stowage?

It has been said that the duty to provide a seaworthy ship is breached if there is something about the vessel that endangers the safety of the cargo: *The Arianna*, above. Bad stowage is an obvious source of danger. But English courts have been reluctant to treat every case of bad stowage as rendering the ship unseaworthy. There is nothing wrong with this policy. The difficulty is to find a convincing way of reconciling it with established doctrine. The leading case is *Elder Dempster*.

Elder Dempster & Co Ltd v Paterson, Zochonis & Co Ltd [1924] AC 522

Facts: The *Grelwen* loaded casks of palm oil and bags of palm kernels, which were stowed over the casks. On arrival at Hull, it was found that the casks had been crushed by the bags of palm kernels, which were very heavy. The cargo owners claimed damages for breach of the contract of carriage, or alternatively for negligence or breach of duty. If the damage was due to bad stowage, Elder Dempster were protected against liability by the conditions contained in the bills of lading; but if it was due to unseaworthiness, they were liable.

Held:

Viscount Cave: . . . The general principles which should govern the decision are not in doubt. It is well settled that a shipowner or charterer who contracts to carry goods by sea thereby warrants, not only that the ship in which he proposes to carry them shall be seaworthy in the ordinary sense of the word – that is to say, that she shall be tight, staunch and strong, and reasonably fit to encounter whatever perils may be expected on the voyage – but also that both the ship and her furniture and equipment shall be reasonably fit for receiving the contract cargo and carrying it across the sea . . .

It is hardly necessary to add that unseaworthiness and bad stowage are two different things. There are cases, such as *Kopitoff v Wilson* (1876) 1 QBD 377, where, a ship having been injured in consequence of bad stowage, the warranty of seaworthiness of the ship has been held to be broken; but in such cases it is the unseaworthiness caused by bad stowage and not the bad stowage itself which constitutes the breach of warranty. There is no rule that, if two parcels of cargo are so stowed that one can injure the other during the course of the voyage, the ship is unseaworthy: *per* Swinfen Eady LJ in *The Thorsa* [1916] P 257.

Applying these principles to the present case, I have come to the conclusion that the damage complained of was not due to unseaworthiness but to improper stowage. If the fitness or unfitness of the ship is to be ascertained (as was held in *McFadden v Blue Star Line*) at the time of loading, there can be no doubt about the matter. At the moment when the palm oil was loaded the *Grelwen* was unquestionably fit to receive and carry it. She was a well built and well found ship, and lacked no equipment necessary for the carriage of palm oil; and if damage arose, it was due to the fact that after the casks of oil had been stowed in the holds the master placed upon them a weight which no casks could be expected to bear. Whether he could have stowed the cargo in a different way without endangering the safety of the ship is a matter upon which the evidence is conflicting; but if that was impossible, he could have refused to accept some part of the kernels and the oil would then have travelled safely. No doubt that course might have rendered the voyage less profitable to the charterers, but that appears to me for present purposes to be immaterial. The important thing is that at the time of loading the palm oil the ship was fit to receive and carry it without injury; and if she did not do so this was due not to any unfitness in the ship or her equipment, but to another cause.

But it was argued that an owner or charterer loading cargo is to be deemed to warrant the fitness of his ship to receive and carry it, not only at the moment of loading, but also at the time when she sails from the port, and that at the moment when the *Grelwen* left each of her ports of departure she was unfit without 'tween decks to carry the cargo which had then been placed in her holds. My Lords, I think there is some authority for the proposition that the implied warranty of 'seaworthiness for the cargo' extends to fitness for the cargo not only at the time of loading, but also at the time of sailing: see *Cohn v Davidson* (1877) 2 QBD 455, and the observations of Phillimore LJ in *The Thorsa* (above). But it is unnecessary to pursue the point, for the proposition if established will not avail the present respondents. The evidence of the log is conclusive to show that the injury to the casks was caused at or immediately after the time when the cargo was loaded and before the ship sailed, and accordingly that it was not due to any unseaworthiness at the time of sailing. And in any case nothing occurred between the time when the oil was loaded and the time when the ship sailed to make the ship structurally less fit to carry the oil; and it is with reference to the contract cargo – namely, the oil – that the question of fitness must be considered . . .

Notes

1   Should the master of the *Grelwen* have refused to load the palm kernels on top of the casks of oil? Did his willingness to load in this way show incompetence? If so, did his incompetence make the ship unseaworthy in the way suggested above?

2   In *The Thorsa*, chocolate and gorgonzola cheese were stowed in the same hold, which was not ventilated between Genoa and London because of bad weather. The chocolate, which was loaded first, was tainted by the cheese. It was held that the damage was the result of bad stowage and nothing more and that the shipowner was protected by the terms of the bill of lading. This decision treats it as immaterial that when the ship sailed she was unfit by reason of stowage to carry her cargo safely. If this decision is correct – *Elder Dempster* leaves the point open – the result in any case of incompatible consignments turns on the order in which the cargo is loaded and stowed, so that if the cheese had been loaded first in *The Thorsa*, the result would have been reversed. Unattractive though this is, where a contract clearly intends to exclude liability for bad stowage and negligence but not unseaworthiness, some line must be drawn between these matters and this line is drawn, clearly but a little arbitrarily, so that the carrier is not liable for anything occurring after the time of first loading.

26 Causation

To recover for loss or damage to cargo where unseaworthiness is alleged, the claimant must show that the lack of seaworthiness caused the loss or damage complained of: *Kish v Taylor* [1912] AC 604. But unseaworthiness is rarely the sole and exclusive cause of damage or loss of cargo. There are usually other factors that can be said to have caused or contributed to a disaster. What connection should the law demand between a breach of this duty and a loss? Must the unseaworthiness be the sole, dominant, real, substantial or proximate cause or is it enough if it is *a* cause of the loss? The judgments in *Smith, Hogg v Black Sea and Baltic* do not all adopt the same approach.

Smith, Hogg v Black Sea and Baltic General Insurance [1940] AC 997

Facts: The *Lilburn* loaded a cargo of timber for carriage from Soroka to Garston. So much cargo was loaded on deck that on sailing she was dangerously unstable and consequently unseaworthy. When she put into Stornoway to refuel, she fell on her beam ends. Portions of cargo were lost or damaged. The owners claimed a general average contribution. The respondents resisted the claim on the ground that the owners had not exercised due diligence in accordance with the charter to make the vessel seaworthy and that the average act was occasioned by the unseaworthiness. They counterclaimed for loss and damage to cargo. The owners alleged that the accident was the fault of the master (for whose negligence they were not responsible) in taking on bunkers without discharging or reducing the deck cargo.

Held:

Lord Wright: ... Sir Robert Aske [counsel] has strenuously contended on behalf of the appellants, that the master's action, whether or not negligent, was 'novus actus interveniens', which broke the nexus or chain of causation, and reduced the unseaworthiness from 'causa causans' to 'causa sine qua non'. I cannot help deprecating the use of Latin or so-called Latin phrases in this way. They only distract the mind from the true problem which is to apply the principles of English law to the realities of the case ...

Indeed the question what antecedent or subsequent event is a relevant or decisive cause varies with the particular case. If tort, which may in some respects have its own rules, is put aside and the enquiry is limited to contract, the selection of the relevant cause or causes will generally vary with the nature of the contract. I say 'cause or causes' because as Lord Shaw pointed out in *Leyland Shipping Co v Norwich Union Fire Insurance Co* [1918] 1 AC 350, 369 causes may be regarded not so much as a chain, but as a network.

There is always a combination of co-operating causes, out of which the law, employing its empirical or common sense view of causation, will select the one or more which it finds material for its special purpose of deciding the particular case . . .

In carriage of goods by sea, unseaworthiness does not affect the carrier's liability unless it causes the loss, as was held in *The Europa* [1908] P 84 and in *Kish v Taylor* [1912] AC 604 . . .

Apart from express exceptions, the carrier's contract is to deliver the goods safely. But when the practice of having express exceptions limiting that obligation became common, it was laid down that there were fundamental obligations, which were not affected by the specific exceptions, unless that was made clear by express words. Thus an exception of perils of the sea does not qualify the duty to furnish a seaworthy ship or to carry the goods without negligence: see *Paterson Steamships Ltd v Canadian Co-operative Wheat Producers Ltd* (above). From the nature of the contract, the relevant cause of the loss is held to be the unseaworthiness or the negligence as the case may be, not the peril of the sea, where both the breach of the fundamental obligation and the objective peril are co-operating causes. The contractual exception of perils of the seas does not affect the fundamental obligation, unless the contract qualifies the latter in express terms.

To consider these rules, in relation to unseaworthiness, I think the contract may be expressed to be that the shipowner will be liable for any loss in which those other causes covered by exceptions co-operate, if unseaworthiness is a cause, or if it is preferred, a real, or effective or actual cause . . .

In truth, unseaworthiness, which may assume according to the circumstances an almost infinite variety, can never be the sole cause of the loss. At least I have not thought of a case where it can be the sole cause. It must, I think, always be only one of several co-operating causes . . . In this connection I can draw no distinction between cases where the negligent conduct of the master is a cause and cases in which any other cause, such as perils of the seas, or fire, is a co-operating cause. A negligent act is as much a co-operating cause, if it is a cause at all, as an act which is not negligent. The question is the same in either case, it is, would the disaster not have happened if the ship had fulfilled the obligation of seaworthiness, even though the disaster could not have happened if there had not also been the specific peril or action . . .

The sole question, apart from express exception, must then be: 'Was that breach of contract "a" cause of the damage.' It may be preferred to describe it as an effective or real or actual cause though the adjectives in my opinion in fact add nothing. If the question is answered in the affirmative the shipowner is liable though there were other co-operating causes, whether they are such causes as perils of the seas, fire and similar matters, or causes due to human action, such as the acts or omissions of the master, whether negligent or not or a combination of both kinds of cause . . .

In cases of the type now being considered, the negligence, if any, must almost inevitably occur in the course of the voyage, and thus intervene between the commencement of the voyage when the duty to provide a seaworthy ship is broken, and the actual disaster. I doubt whether there could be any event which could supersede or override the effectiveness of the unseaworthiness if it was 'a' cause.

This is clearly so in the facts of this case. The acts of the master in bunkering as he did, and in pumping out the forepeak, whether negligent or not, were indeed more proximate in time to the disaster, and may be said to have contributed to the disaster, but the disaster would not have arisen but for the unseaworthiness, and hence the shipowners are liable . . .

Lord Porter: . . . No doubt those who are either defending themselves or putting forward a counterclaim based upon an allegation of unseaworthiness must prove that the loss was so caused.

But here the loss was, I think, incontestably due to the inability of the ship to take in bunkers by a method which would have been both safe and usual in the case of a seaworthy ship. It was not the coaling that was at fault nor the method adopted: it was the fact that that coaling took place and that method was adopted in a tender ship. If a vessel is to proceed on her voyage, bunkers must be shipped, and though in one sense the change of balance caused by taking in bunkers was responsible for the accident to the *Lilburn*, it was not the dominant cause even if it be necessary to show what the dominant cause was. The master merely acted in the usual way and indeed exercised what he thought was exceptional care in diverting the coal shipped towards the port bunker. In a seaworthy ship his action would have been a safe one. It was the instability of the ship which caused the disaster.

In such circumstances it is unnecessary to decide what would be the result if the loss were attributable partly to the coaling and partly to the unseaworthiness, or to determine whether the fact that the unseaworthiness was a substantial cause even though some other matter relied upon were a substantial cause also, would be enough to make the owners liable for failure to use due care to make the vessel seaworthy.

Note

Lord Wright and Lord Atkin concluded that where unseaworthiness is *a* cause of a loss, the carrier is liable, even though there may be other co-operating causes of the loss that are nearer in time to the disaster. Lord Porter and Lord Romer were more cautious. Confusingly, Lord Maugham agreed with both Lord Porter and Lord Wright. Later decisions, *The Eurasian Dream* for example, have followed the formulation of the law in Lord Wright's judgment. Is there any alternative to Lord Wright's approach where a carrier makes promises that overlap, as in the case of the promise to carry and deliver and the promise to do so in a seaworthy ship? In these circumstances, would it be possible to insist that a cargo claimant could only recover damages by showing that the breach of one of those promises was the exclusive or perhaps the dominant cause of the loss?

27 Burden of proof

In principle, a cargo claimant who alleges that loss or damage has been caused by failure to deliver in accordance with the contract or failure to provide a seaworthy ship may succeed on either ground but bears the burden of proof on both. But a carrier who resists a claim under the first head may find himself providing evidence that establishes liability under the second.

Danske Sukkerfabrikker v Bajamar Compania Naviera, The Torenia
[1983] 2 Lloyd's Rep 211

Facts: The *Torenia* was chartered to load a cargo of sugar at Guayabal, Cuba, for carriage to Denmark. In the course of the voyage she developed an uncontrollable leak when a fracture occurred in her hull; she was abandoned and later sank. The cargo was a total loss. The plaintiffs brought proceedings for non-delivery. At trial, the defendants submitted that, on the basis of *Joseph Constantine Steamship Line Ltd v Imperial Smelting Corp Ltd* [1941] 2 All ER 165, once they had proved the destruction of the goods by a peril of the sea (the fortuitous incursion of sea water), the burden passed to the plaintiffs to prove whatever fault they relied on.

Held:

Hobhouse J: . . . The plaintiffs sought to treat the fact that the vessel's shell plating fractured in weather conditions of a type which ought to have been, and no doubt were, well within the contemplation and expectation of the vessel's owners and crew as liable to be encountered at some stage during the voyage as a wholly neutral occurrence which carried with it no implication of the unfitness of the vessel for that voyage. Whereas in the days of wooden ships or in the days when the design of steel ships and their construction was less well advanced or the forces they were liable to encounter were less well known and understood there may have been many instances where unexplained losses at sea gave rise to no inference of unseaworthiness, it will now be rare for such an inference not to arise in the absence of some overwhelming force of the sea or some occurrence affecting the vessel from outside. In the present case the shipowners, whilst proving the loss of the cargo, have proved also the loss of the vessel in conditions which ought not to have led to the loss of a seaworthy ship. Similarly in proving that the incursion of seawater was fortuitous they have proved that the structure of the vessel was defective . . .

28 Remedies

The primary remedy for any breach of contract is damages. But in some circumstances, breach of an express or implied duty to provide a seaworthy ship may entitle the innocent party to terminate the contract. The *Hongkong Fir*, perhaps the best-known case in this area, has been treated as settling the law in this field for the last 40 years.

Hongkong Fir Shipping v Kawasaki Kisen Kaisha [1962] 2 QB 26, CA

Facts: The plaintiff shipowners time chartered the *Hongkong Fir* to the defendants for 24 months. The vessel was placed at the disposal of the charterers at Liverpool and the same day sailed for Newport News to load coal for carriage to Osaka. Between Liverpool and Osaka she was at sea for about eight and a half weeks, off-hire undergoing repair for about five weeks and had £21,400 spent on her on repairs. While at Osaka, a further 15 weeks and £37,500 were necessary to make her ready for sea. During this period the charterers repudiated the charter and claimed damages for breach of contract. The owners responded that they treated the charterers as having wrongfully repudiated the charter and they too claimed damages. Subsequently the charterers again repudiated the charter and the owners formally accepted the repudiation. In the Court of Appeal, two main issues were argued: (1) Is the seaworthiness obligation a condition the breach of which entitles the charterers to treat the contract as repudiated? (2) Where in breach of contract a party fails to perform it, by what standard does the ensuing delay fall to be measured for the purpose of deciding whether the innocent party is entitled to treat the contract as repudiated?

Held:

Sellers LJ: . . . By clause 1 of the charterparty the shipowners contracted to deliver the vessel at Liverpool 'she being in every way fitted for ordinary cargo service'. She was not fit for ordinary cargo service when delivered because the engine room staff was incompetent and inadequate and this became apparent as the voyage proceeded. It is commonplace language to say that the vessel was unseaworthy by reason of this inefficiency in the engine room.

Ships have been held to be unseaworthy in a variety of ways and those who have been put to loss by reason thereof (in the absence of any protecting clause in favour of a shipowner) have been able to recover damages as for a breach of warranty. It would be unthinkable that all the relatively trivial matters which have been held to be unseaworthiness could be regarded as conditions of the contract or conditions precedent to a charterer's liability and justify in themselves a cancellation or refusal to perform on the part of the charterer . . .

If what is done or not done in breach of the contractual obligation does not make the performance a totally different performance of the contract from that intended by the parties, it is not so fundamental as to undermine the whole contract. Many existing conditions of unseaworthiness can be remedied by attention or repairs, many are intended to be rectified as the voyage proceeds, so that the vessel becomes seaworthy; and, as the judgment points out, the breach of a shipowner's obligation to deliver a seaworthy vessel has not been held by itself to entitle a charterer to escape from the charterparty. The charterer may rightly terminate the engagement if the delay in remedying any breach is so long in fact, or likely to be so long in reasonable anticipation, that the commercial purpose of the contract would be frustrated . . .

Diplock LJ: . . . Every synallagmatic contract contains in it the seeds of the problem: in what event will a party be relieved of his undertaking to do that which he has agreed to do but has not yet done? The contract may itself expressly define some of these events, as in the cancellation clause in a charterparty; but, human prescience being limited, it seldom does so exhaustively and often fails to do so at all. In some classes of contracts such as sale of goods, marine insurance, contracts of affreightment evidenced by bills of lading and those between parties to bills of exchange, Parliament has defined by statute some of the events not provided for expressly in individual contracts of that class; but where an event occurs the occurrence of which neither the parties nor Parliament have expressly stated will discharge one of the parties from further performance of his undertakings, it is for the court to determine whether the event has this effect or not.

The test whether an event has this effect or not has been stated in a number of metaphors all of which I think amount to the same thing: does the occurrence of the event deprive the party who has further undertakings still to perform of substantially the whole benefit which it was the intention of the parties as expressed in the contract that he should obtain as the consideration for performing those undertakings?

. . . What the judge had to do in the present case, as in any other case where one party to a contract relies upon a breach by the other party as giving him a right to elect to rescind the contract, and the contract itself makes no express provision as to this, was to look at the events which had occurred as a result of the breach at the time at which the charterers purported to rescind the charterparty and to decide whether the occurrence of those events deprived the charterers of substantially the whole benefit which it was the intention of the parties as expressed in the charterparty that the charterers should obtain from the further performance of their own contractual undertakings.

One turns therefore to the contract, the Baltime 1939 charter . . . Clause 13, the 'due diligence' clause, which exempts the shipowners from responsibility for delay or loss or damage to goods on board due to unseaworthiness, unless such delay or loss or damage has been caused by want of due diligence of the owners in making the vessel seaworthy and fitted for the voyage, is in itself sufficient to show that the mere occurrence of the events that the vessel was in some respect unseaworthy when tendered or that such unseaworthiness had caused some delay in performance of the charterparty would not deprive the charterer of the whole benefit which it was the intention of the parties he should obtain from the performance of his obligations under the contract – for he undertakes to continue to perform his obligations notwithstanding the occurrence of such events if they fall short of frustration of the contract and even deprives himself of any remedy in damages unless such events are the consequence of want of due diligence on the part of the shipowner.

The question which the judge had to ask himself was, as he rightly decided, whether or not at the date when the charterers purported to rescind the contract, namely, June 6, 1957, or when the shipowners purported to accept such rescission, namely, August 8, 1957, the delay which had already occurred as a result of the incompetence of the engine-room staff, and the delay which was likely to occur in repairing the engines of the vessel and the conduct of the shipowners by that date in taking steps to remedy these two matters, were, when taken together, such as to deprive the charterers of substantially the whole benefit which it was the intention of the parties they should obtain from further use of the vessel under the charterparty . . .

29 Deviation

At common law, it is an implied term of a contract for the carriage of goods by sea that the carrier will not deviate from the proper route without lawful justification. Breach of this duty has serious consequences. The shipowner may not be able to rely on exemption clauses in the contract of carriage if cargo is damaged or lost during or after a deviation and may not be able to enforce other terms of that contract.

30 The origins of the duty not to deviate

The first reported English decision to recognise the sea carrier's implied duty not to deviate from route was *Davis v Garrett* in 1833. It had been held in at least one earlier case that as between the parties to a contract to carry goods by sea, a duty not to deviate could only arise by express agreement. However, a number of writers on maritime and trade law had asserted that there was a general legal duty governing the route to be followed by a carrier. And the duty not to deviate was a well-established feature of the law of marine insurance. The decision in *Davis* put an end to this uncertainty.

Davis v Garrett (1830) 6 Bing 716, Court of Common Pleas

Facts: A cargo of lime was to be carried on the barge *Safety* to London from the river Medway in Kent, act of God, fire and perils of the sea being excepted. At trial, the jury found that as part of a smuggling venture the barge deviated to the East Swale and to Whitstable Bay, which were out of the usual and customary route, where she was caught in a storm. Sea water reached the cargo, the barge caught fire and the master was forced to run her on shore. The lime and the barge were both lost. The plaintiff alleged that the defendant's duty was to carry by the direct usual and customary course. The defendant barge owner argued that he was not liable because (i) the storm and not the deviation was the proximate cause of the loss, which might have occurred even if the *Safety* had taken a direct course; and (ii) that he had not agreed to carry the lime directly to London.

Held:

> **Tindal CJ:** ... As to the first point ... (w)e think that the real answer to the objection is that no wrongdoer can be allowed to apportion or qualify his own wrong; and that as a loss has actually happened while his wrongful act was in operation and force, and which is attributable to his wrongful act, he cannot set up as an answer to the action the bare possibility of a loss, if his wrongful act had never been done. It might admit of a different construction if he could show, not only that the same loss might have happened, but that it must have happened if the act complained of had not been done; but there is no evidence to that extent in the present case ...
>
> [On the second point] ... We cannot but think that the law does imply a duty in the owner of a vessel, whether a general ship or hired for the special purpose of the voyage, to proceed without unnecessary deviation in the usual and customary course.

Notes

1 The judgments in *Davis* do not explain why the court thought that there should be a duty not to deviate. Reports of the case show that counsel for the cargo owner argued that this

obligation was necessary in order to prevent delay, because the risks associated with the usual route were the only things the shipper could take into account when entering into a contract and because a deviation by the carrier would make the shipper's insurance policy on the goods void.

2 There is no suggestion in the report of the judgment that the decision was confined to deviations for an illegal purpose (smuggling) or to dangerous places (*Safety* was not designed for the open sea).

3 The barge owner did not argue that he was protected by the standard form exclusion of liability for 'dangers and accidents of the seas'. It seems likely that both the parties and the court read the exclusion clause as applying only to losses occurring on the proper route.

4 The judgment suggests that after a wrongful deviation a carrier might escape liability for loss or damage to cargo if, but only if, he can show that the loss would also have happened on the proper route. In practice it will be very difficult to show this where the immediate cause of the loss is a storm or other natural force; but it might be possible in the case of losses by fire or inherent vice.

31 Proper route

The parties to a carriage contract can agree on the precise route to be followed if they wish. But what happens if they do not? How is the proper route to be identified?

Reardon Smith Line v Black Sea and Baltic General Insurance [1939] AC 562, HL

Facts: The appellants' vessel *Indian City* was chartered to carry a cargo of ore from Poti in the Black Sea to Sparrow's Point, Baltimore, USA. After loading, she sailed first for Constanza on the west coast of the Black Sea for fuel. The vessel grounded at Constanza and was damaged; part of the cargo had to be jettisoned. The charterers refused to contribute to general average expenses on the grounds that in going to Constanza the ship had deviated from her contractual route, which they said was from Poti to Sparrow's Point by the direct route through Istanbul.

Held:

Lord Porter: . . . It is the duty of a ship, at any rate when sailing upon an ocean voyage from one port to another, to take the usual route between those two ports. If no evidence be given, that route is presumed to be the direct geographical route, but it may be modified in many cases for navigational or other reasons, and evidence may always be given to show what the usual route is, unless a specific route be prescribed by the charter party or bill of lading. In each case therefore when a ship is chartered to sail or when a parcel is shipped upon a liner sailing from one port to another, it is necessary to inquire what the usual route is. In some cases there may be more than one usual route. It would be difficult to say that a ship sailing from New Zealand to this country had deviated from her course whether she sailed by the Suez Canal, the Panama Canal, round the Cape of Good Hope or through the Straits of Magellan. Each might, I think, be a usual route. Similarly the exigencies of bunkering may require the vessel to depart from the direct route or at any rate compel her to touch at ports at which, if she were proceeding under sail, it would be unnecessary for her to call.

It is not the geographical route but the usual route which has to be followed, though in many cases the one may be the same as the other. But the inquiry must always be, what is the usual route, and a route may become a usual route in the case of a particular line though that line is accustomed to follow a course which is not that adopted by the vessels belonging to other lines or to other individuals. It is sufficient if there is a well known practice of that line to call at a particular port.

...No doubt *prima facie* the route direct from Poti to Sparrow's Point through Istanbul would be the ordinary course, but I think that in this case we have evidence sufficient to show that the route has been varied and that the practice of proceeding to Constantza to bunker after loading had become a usual one. It is true that a considerable number of vessels proceeding from Black Sea ports do not call at Constantza for bunkers, and that, if one is to take particulars of Poti and Novorossisk alone, only about one-quarter of the ships proceeding on ocean voyages call at Constantza after loading. It is true also that the journey to Constantza lengthens the voyage by some 200 miles, and that shortly after the accident to the *Indian City* the cost of oil at Constantza increased and the appellants thereafter have taken their bunkers from Algiers instead of Constantza.

All these are matters to be considered, but a short usage, particularly where the obtaining of bunkers is concerned, may still be a sufficient usage to create a usual route...

Note

Moving even a short distance away from route can amount to a deviation. But few cases turn on minor movements at sea away from the ordinary track. In most cases where the doctrine is invoked, the ship has moved off route to call at an unauthorised port in order to take on fuel or to load or discharge other cargo. But calling at the right ports in the wrong order is a deviation and so is carrying a cargo to and then beyond the contracted port of discharge or landing a cargo short of its proper destination: *Cunard Steamship v Buerger* [1927] AC 1.

32 Voluntary departure

Deviation is a voluntary departure from the proper route. A deliberate or conscious breach of contract is not required. However, a ship does not necessarily deviate every time she strays off course.

Rio Tinto v Seed Shipping (1926) 24 Ll L Rep 316

Facts: The charterers shipped a cargo of coal and coke on the defendants' ship *Marjorie Seed* at Glasgow for Huelva. After leaving the Cumbrae the master, not being in perfect health, ordered the helmsman to steer south-south-east, which stranded the ship on rocks off the coast of Ayr. The ordinary course would have been to steer south-south-west. Ship and cargo were totally lost. The plaintiffs sued for the value of the cargo; the defendants pleaded an excepted peril to which the plaintiffs replied that there had been a deviation.

Held:

Roche J: The essence of deviation [is] that the parties contracting have voluntarily substituted another voyage for that which has been insured. A mere departure or failure to follow the contract voyage or route is not necessarily a deviation, or every stranding which occurred in the course of a voyage would be a deviation, because the voyage contracted for, I imagine, is in no case one which essentially involves the necessity of stranding. It is a change of voyage, a radical breach of the contract, that is required to, and essentially does, constitute a deviation . . .

Here I am satisfied, and I find as a fact, that the master never intended to leave the route of the voyage, that is to say, the route of the voyage from Glasgow to Huelva. What he did was to make a mistake as to the compass course which was necessary to take him from the *terminus a quo* to the *terminus ad quem*. To use an analogy which, although analogies are misleading, I think at this stage is in order, he did not adopt another road instead of the road that he had agreed to take, but he got himself into the ditch at the side of the road which he was intending to follow. He was not on another route; he was on the existing route, although he was out of the proper part of the route which he ought to have followed. That is my finding of fact as to what happened; and in my judgment it follows from that that there was not that substitution or change of route which is necessary to constitute a deviation . . .

33 Justifiable deviation: Deviation to save life

At common law, a departure from route can be justified if it is made to save life but not if made only to save property. The common law rule is altered by the Hague and Hague-Visby Rules, when they apply, which allow deviation to save either life or property.

Scaramanga v Stamp (1880) 5 CPD 295, CA

Facts: The *Olympias* was chartered to carry a cargo of wheat from Cronstadt to Gibraltar. Nine days out she sighted the *Arion* whose engine had failed. The weather was fine and the sea smooth, and there would have been no difficulty in taking off the crew. Instead, the master of the *Olympias* agreed to tow the *Arion* into the Texel for £1,000. Having taken the *Arion* in tow, the *Olympias* ran on the Terschelling Sands on the way to the Texel and was lost. The plaintiff claimed the value of his goods, alleging that the goods were not lost by perils of the seas within the exception in the charterparty, but were lost through the wrongful deviation of the defendants' vessel. The defendants pleaded that the deviation was justified, because it was for the purpose of saving the *Arion* and her cargo.

Held:

Cockburn CJ: . . . That there was here a twofold deviation, which, unless the circumstances were such as to justify it, would entitle the plaintiff to recover, cannot be disputed – in the first place, in the departure of the *Olympias* from her proper course in going to the Texel, secondly, in her taking the *Arion* in tow . . . (since) the effect of taking another vessel in tow is necessarily to retard the progress of the towing vessel, and thereby to prolong the risk of the voyage.

[After reviewing the few English authorities on the point, Cockburn CJ said that the effect of American decisions was that] . . . deviation for the purpose of saving life is protected, and involves neither forfeiture of insurance nor liability to the goods' owner in respect of loss which would otherwise be within the exception of 'perils of the seas'. And, as a necessary consequence of the foregoing, deviation for the purpose of communicating with a ship in distress is allowable, inasmuch as the state of the vessel in distress may involve danger to life. On the other hand, deviation for the sole purpose of saving property is not thus privileged, but entails all the usual consequences of deviation . . .

In these propositions I entirely concur . . . The impulsive desire to save human life when in peril is one of the most beneficial instincts of humanity, and is nowhere more salutary in its results than in bringing help to those who, exposed to destruction from the fury of winds and waves, would perish if left without assistance . . . there is neither injustice nor hardship in treating both the merchant and the insurer as making their contracts with the shipowner as subject to this exception to the general rule of not deviating from the appointed course . . .

Deviation for the purpose of saving property stands obviously on a totally different footing. There is here no moral duty to fulfil, which, though its fulfilment may have been attended with danger to life or property, remains unrewarded. There would be much force, no doubt, in the argument that it is to the common interest of merchants and insurers, as well as of shipowners, that ships and cargoes, when in danger of perishing, should be saved, and consequently that, as matter of policy, the same latitude should be allowed in respect of the saving of property as in respect of the saving of life, were it not that the law has provided another, and a very adequate motive for the saving of property, by securing to the salvor a liberal proportion of the property saved – a proportion in which not only the value of the property saved, but also the danger run by the salvor to life or property is taken into account, and in calculating which, if it be once settled that the insurance will not be protected, nor the shipowner freed from liability in respect of loss of cargo, the risk thus run will, no doubt, be included as an element. It would obviously be most unjust if the shipowner could thus take the chance of highly remunerative gain at the risk and possible loss of the merchant or the insurer, neither of whom derive any benefit from the preservation of the property saved . . .

34 Deviation to avoid imminent peril: The extent of permissible deviation

Phelps, James & Co v Hill [1891] 1 QB 605, CA

Facts: Tin and iron plates were shipped on the *Llanduff City* at Swansea for New York. About five days out the vessel and some of her equipment and cargo were damaged in a storm and it was necessary to put back to a port of refuge. She went first to Queenstown where she was ordered by the defendant owners to return to their own yards in Bristol where suitable spare parts were available and where repairs could have been done more cheaply and quickly than elsewhere. It would also have been possible to sell or trans-ship the cargo there. In the Avon, she was run into by another vessel and was sunk. This risk was excepted by the bill of lading. The question was whether there was an unjustifiable deviation in going to Bristol instead of Swansea. The jury at trial found that there had not been an unjustifiable deviation.

Held:

Lopes LJ: The question in this case is whether there was a deviation. If there was a deviation, or, in other words, if the deviation was not justified, the shipowner is liable for a loss by the perils of the sea, and is not protected by the exception of perils in the contract. The voyage must be prosecuted without unnecessary delay or deviation. The shipowner's contract is that he will be diligent in carrying the goods on the agreed voyage, and will do so directly without any unnecessary deviation. But this undertaking is to be understood with reference to the circumstances that arise during the performance of the contract. He is not answerable for delays or deviations which are occasioned or become necessary without default on his part. Where the safety of the adventure under the master's control necessitates that he should go out of his course, he is not only justified in doing so, but it is his duty in the right performance of his contract with the owners of the cargo. The shipowner through his master is bound to act with prudence and skill and care in avoiding dangers and in mitigating the consequences of any disaster which may have happened. The master is bound to take into account the interests of the cargo-owners as well as those of the shipowner. He must act prudently for all concerned . . . Going into a port out of the usual course for necessary repairs, and staying till they are completed, is no deviation, provided it plainly appears that such repairs, under the circumstances and at such port, were reasonably necessary, and the delay not greater than necessary for the completion of such repairs, so as to enable the vessel to proceed on her voyage. The deviation must not be greater than a reasonable necessity demands, having regard to the respective interests of shipowner and cargo-owner. A reasonable necessity implies the existence of such a state of things as, having regard to the interests of all concerned, would properly influence the decision of a reasonably competent and skilful master . . .

35 Justifiable deviation and unseaworthiness

In the last extract, Lopes LJ referred to deviations that become necessary without fault on the part of the carrier. In the next case the carrier was at fault but the deviation was nevertheless held to be justified.

Kish v Taylor [1912] AC 604, HL

Facts: The *Wearside* was chartered to load a full and complete cargo of timber at Mobile or Pensacola. The charterers failed to provide a full cargo so the master attempted to mitigate by obtaining additional cargo from other sources. He was so successful that the *Wearside* was overloaded with deck cargo and became unseaworthy. She sailed, encountered bad weather and had to take refuge in the port of Halifax, where she was repaired and the cargo restowed. On arrival at Liverpool, the shipowners claimed a lien for the charterers' failure to load a full cargo. The cargo owners disputed the existence of the lien, arguing that the deviation to Halifax was not justifiable.

Held:

Lord Atkinson: . . . On the whole . . . I am of opinion that a master, whose ship is, from whatever cause, in a perilous position, does right in making such a deviation from his voyage as is necessary to save his ship and the lives of his crew, and that while the right to recover damages from all breaches of contract, and all wrongful acts committed either by himself or by the owners of his ship, is preserved to those who are thereby wronged or injured, the contract of affreightment is not put an end to by such a deviation, nor are the rights of the owners under it lost . . .

Note

In *Monarch Steamship v Karlshamns Oliefabriker* [1949] AC 196, p 212, Lord Porter referred to *Kish v Taylor* and said that deviation made to remedy unseaworthiness does not amount to unjustifiable deviation but that it might do so if it was established that the owners knew of the vessel's state on sailing. On the general effect of a deviation on a contract of carriage, see the last section of this chapter.

36 Liberty to deviate clauses

At common law the duty not to deviate can be varied or excluded by agreement between the parties to a contract of carriage of goods by sea. In older cases, clauses in bills of lading that purported to confer on a carrier an unrestricted discretion to deviate were interpreted narrowly in English courts. This approach is illustrated here by the decision in *Leduc v Ward*. But as the subsequent extract from *Renton v Palmyra* [1957] AC 149, HL shows, a literal interpretation of a liberty clause may be appropriate in some circumstances.

Leduc v Ward (1888) 20 QBD 475, CA

Facts: The bill of lading stated that the ship was at the port of Fiume and bound for Dunkirk, 'with liberty to call at any ports in any order, and to deviate for the purpose of saving life or property'. Instead of proceeding direct to Dunkirk, the vessel sailed for Glasgow, a total of about 1,200 miles out of the ordinary course of the voyage; ship and cargo were lost near Ailsa Craig, off the mouth of the Clyde. The owners of the goods sued for non-delivery at Dunkirk.

Held:

> **Lord Esher MR:** . . . In the present case liberty is given to call at any ports in any order. It was argued that that clause gives liberty to call at any port in the world. Here, again, it is a question of the construction of a mercantile expression used in a mercantile document, and I think that as such the term can have but one meaning, namely, that the ports, liberty to call at which is intended to be given, must be ports which are substantially ports which will be passed on the named voyage. Of course such a term must entitle the vessel to go somewhat out of the ordinary track by sea of the named voyage, for going into the port of call in itself would involve that. To 'call' at a port is a well-known sea-term; it means to call for the purposes of business, generally to take in or unload cargo, or to receive orders; it must mean that the vessel may stop at the port of call for a time, or else the liberty to call would be idle. I believe the term has always been interpreted to mean that the ship may call at such ports as would naturally and usually be ports of call on the voyage named. If the stipulation were only that she might call at any ports, the invariable construction has been that she would only be entitled to call at such ports in their geographical order; and therefore the words 'in any order' are frequently added, but in any case it appears to me that the ports must be ports substantially on the course of the voyage. It follows that, when the defendants' ship went off the ordinary track of a voyage from Fiume to Dunkirk to a port not on the course of that voyage, such as Glasgow, there was a deviation, and she was then on a voyage different from that contracted for to which the excepted perils clause did not apply; and therefore the shipowners are responsible for the loss of the goods . . .

Notes

1   *Port of call.* Lord Esher described ports of call as 'ports which will be passed on the named voyage'. In *James Morrison & Co v Shaw, Savill and Albion* [1916] 2 KB 783, CA, it was held that there is no hard-and-fast rule that determines whether a port is an intermediate port but that this is a question of interpretation and fact and depends on all circumstances, including the size and class of ship, the nature of the voyage, the usual and customary course, the natural or usual ports of call and the nature and position of the port in question. In that case, it was held that Le Havre was not an intermediate port on a trip from New Zealand to London, even though the deviation added only 54 miles to the voyage.

2   *Main purpose of the contract.* The approach to interpretation adopted in *Leduc v Ward* will not help a cargo owner if a liberty to deviate clause is careful to confer wide express rights on the carrier. But if the liberty conferred is too extensive, the clause may be open to another form of attack. In *Glynn v Margetson* [1891] AC 351, HL, oranges were shipped on the *Zena* for carriage from Malaga to Liverpool. The printed form provided that she had 'liberty to proceed to and stay at any ports in any rotation in the Mediterranean, Levant, Black Sea or Adriatic, or on the coasts of Africa, Spain, Portugal, France, Great Britain and Ireland, for the purpose of delivering coals, cargo or passengers, or for any other purpose whatsoever'. The vessel, on leaving Malaga, did not sail towards Liverpool but in the opposite direction and went first to Burriana about 350 miles from Malaga on the east coast of Spain. The oranges were found damaged on arrival at Liverpool because of the delay. The House of Lords held that the main object and intent of the contract was the carriage of a perishable cargo from Malaga to Liverpool. Since the general words in the printed form would defeat the main purpose of the contract if given full effect, the words were to be given a more limited construction (Lord Herschell) or (Lord Halsbury) if this was not possible, the general words were to be rejected. On the facts, the general words only entitled the owners to call (for the purposes stated) at ports that, in a business sense, could be said to be on the voyage between Malaga and Liverpool.

Renton v Palmyra [1957] AC 149, HL

Facts: Bills of lading issued by the shipowners provided for the carriage of timber in the *Caspiana* from Canada to London or Hull. While the ship was on passage a dock strike broke out in London followed subsequently by a strike at Hull; the shipowners ordered the vessel to proceed to Hamburg where the timber was discharged. The shipowners took no steps to forward it to England but made it available at Hamburg to the holders of the bills of lading on payment of the full freight. In an action against the shipowners for damages for breach of contract, the shipowners contended that they had effected due delivery under the bills of lading and relied on the following printed terms:

> 14 (c) Should it appear that . . . strikes . . . would prevent the vessel from . . . entering the port of discharge or there discharging in the usual manner and leaving again . . . safely and without delay, the master may discharge the cargo at port of loading or any other safe and convenient port . . .
>
> (f) The discharge of cargo under the provisions of this clause shall be deemed due fulfilment of the contract . . .

The House of Lords rejected an argument that since the main object of the contract was the carriage of timber to London or Hull, cl 14 was inconsistent with that object and could be disregarded.

Held:

> **Viscount Kilmuir LC:** . . . It is necessary in considering the authorities on which Mr Mocatta (counsel for the appellants) relies to consider carefully the form of the deviation clauses in each case. They were invariably in so extensive a form that, if they were fully and literally construed, the shipowners had a complete discretion to delay intolerably and so defeat the main object and intent of the contract if they so desired. The distinction between these cases and that before your Lordships' House

has been so well stated by Jenkins LJ [1956] 1 QB 462, 502, that I find it impossible to improve on his words, which I quote:

> ... there is a material difference between a deviation clause purporting to enable the shipowners to delay indefinitely the performance of the contract voyage simply because they choose to do so, and provisions such as those contained in clause 14(c) and (f) in the present case, which are applicable and operative only in the event of the occurrence of certain specified emergencies. The distinction is between a power given to one of the parties which, if construed literally, would in effect enable that party to nullify the contract at will, and a special provision stating what the rights and obligations of the parties are to be in the event of obstacles beyond the control of either arising to prevent or impede the performance of the contract in accordance with its primary terms.

37 Effect of deviation

The law relating to the effect of deviation has changed since *Davis v Garrett*, above, was first decided. At least three different approaches can be identified in later cases.

In the period 1833–90 the orthodox view was that a shipowner was liable for loss or damage to cargo that occurred during a deviation and could not normally rely on exclusion clauses in the contract, which only applied to the planned voyage. Liability for losses that occurred after a deviation when the ship had returned to her intended route was uncertain: *Scaramanga v Stamp*, p 299. A deviation did not give a cargo owner the right to put an end to the contract of carriage, unless perhaps it deprived him of the whole benefit of it: *Freeman v Taylor* (1831) 8 Bing 124; *MacAndrew v Chapple* (1866) 1 CP 643. Failure to carry by an agreed route was not a good reason for refusing to pay freight: *Cole v Shallet* (1682) 3 Lev 41; *Davidson v Gwynne* (1810) 1 Camp 376.

A more radical doctrine was developed in *Balian & Sons v Joly, Victoria & Co* (1890) 6 TLR 345 and *Joseph Thorley Ltd v Orchis Steamship Co* [1907] 1 KB 660, CA. These cases treated the carrier's undertaking not to deviate as a condition precedent to the right to rely on any term of the contract. If the carrier deviated this would put an end to the express contract between the parties from the start of the voyage. The contract was, it was said, 'displaced or avoided'. Under the influence of these decisions, between 1890 and 1936 English courts held that a carrier could not rely on an exclusion clause in a bill of lading in answer to a claim for damage to cargo suffered before, during or after a deviation from route. It was also held in *The Alamosa* (below) that laytime provisions in a charter were no longer enforceable after a deviation on the grounds that the effect of a deviation was 'to wipe out the clauses in the charterparty which were in favour of the shipowner'. But a new view of the effect of deviation emerged in the decision of the House of Lords in the next case.

Hain Steamship Co Ltd v Tate & Lyle Ltd (1936) 41 Com Cas 350, HL

Subsequent US proceedings are reported as *Farr v Hain SS Co Ltd (The Tregenna)* 1941 121 F 2d 940.

Facts: Tate & Lyle were purchasers of sugar that was to be delivered by instalments. The sellers chartered *Tregenna* from Hain Steamship to carry part of the sugar, loading in Cuba and San Domingo. The ship loaded a part cargo in Cuba but, by a mistake for which the shipowners were held responsible, she received no orders for San Domingo and so sailed for her discharge port. She was recalled by the charterers the next day when the mistake was discovered and was directed to complete loading at San Pedro de Macoris in San Domingo, where she arrived a little over a day later than if she had gone direct and after steaming an extra 265 miles. On sailing from San Pedro, she ran aground and was damaged. Part of the cargo was saved and forwarded on another vessel. Claims for freight and for general average were made against Tate & Lyle to whom the bills of lading had been endorsed by the sellers of the sugar. Tate & Lyle argued that the deviation on the way to San Pedro freed them from any liability in respect of the sugar loaded in Cuba. The shipowners replied that any deviation had been waived by the charterers.

Held:

Lord Atkin: . . . My Lords, the effect of a deviation upon a contract of carriage by sea has been stated in a variety of cases but not in uniform language. Everyone is agreed that it is a serious matter. Occasionally language has been used which suggests that the occurrence of a deviation automatically displaces the contract, as by the now accepted doctrine does an event which 'frustrates' a contract. In other cases where the effect of deviation upon the exceptions in the contract had to be considered language is used which Sir Robert Aske (counsel) argued shows that the sole effect is, as it were, to expunge the exceptions clause, as no longer applying to a voyage which from the beginning of the deviation has ceased to be the contract voyage. I venture to think that the true view is that the departure from the voyage contracted to be made is a breach by the shipowner of his contract, a breach of such a serious character that, however slight the deviation, the other party to the contract is entitled to treat it as going to the root of the contract, and to declare himself as no longer bound by any of the contract terms. I wish to confine myself to contracts of carriage by sea, and in the circumstances of such a carriage I am satisfied that by a long series of decisions, adopting in fact commercial usage in this respect, any deviation constitutes a breach of contract of this serious nature. The same view is taken in contracts of marine insurance where there is implied an absolute condition not to deviate. No doubt the extreme gravity attached to a deviation in contracts of carriage is justified by the fact that the insured cargo owner when the ship has deviated has become uninsured. It appears to me inevitable that a breach of contract which results in such momentous consequences well known to all concerned in commerce by sea should entitle the other party to refuse to be bound. It is true that the cargo owner may, though very improbably, be uninsured: it is also true that in these days it is not uncommon for marine insurers to hold the assured covered in case of deviation at a premium to be arranged. But these considerations do not appear to diminish the serious nature of the breach in all the circumstances of sea carriage, and may be balanced by the fact that the ship can and often does take liberties to deviate which prevent the result I have stated. If this view be correct, then the breach by deviation does not automatically cancel the express contract, otherwise the shipowner by his own wrong can get rid of his own contract. Nor does it affect merely the exceptions clauses. This would make those clauses alone subject to a condition of no deviation, a construction for which I can find no justification. It is quite inconsistent with the cases which have treated deviation as precluding enforcement of demurrage provisions. The event falls within the ordinary law of contract. The party who is affected by the breach has the right to say, 'I am not now bound by the contract whether it is expressed in charterparty, bill of lading, or otherwise'. He can, of course, claim his goods from the ship; whether and to what extent he will become liable to pay some remuneration for carriage I do not think arises in this case . . . but I am satisfied that once he elects to treat the contract as at an end he is not bound by the promise to pay the agreed freight any more than by his other promises. But, on the other hand, as he can elect to treat the contract as ended, so he can elect to treat the contract as subsisting; and if he does this with knowledge of his rights he must in accordance with the general law of contract be held bound. No doubt one must be careful to see that the acts of the cargo owner are not misinterpreted when he finds that his goods have been taken off on a voyage to which he did not agree. He could not reasonably be expected to recall the goods when he discovers the ship at a port of call presumably still intending to reach her agreed port of destination. There must be acts which plainly show that the shipper intends to treat the contract as still binding. In the present case where the charterer procured the ship to be recalled to a San Domingo port for the express purpose of continuing to load under the charter, an obligation which of course only existed in pursuance of the express contract, and saw that the ship did receive the cargo stipulated under the subcharter provided by persons who had no right to load except under the subcharter, I am satisfied that there is abundant, indeed conclusive, evidence to justify the report of Branson J that the deviation was waived by the charterers.

The result is that at the time the casualty occurred and the general average sacrifice and expenses were incurred the ship was still under the charter. In respect of the Cuban sugar the charterers appear to have been at the time the owners of the goods, and I think it clear that on principle the contribution falls due from the persons who were owners at the time of the sacrifice, though no doubt it may be passed on to subsequent assignees of the goods by appropriate contractual stipulations. The place of adjustment does not seem to have a bearing on the question against whom the contribution has to be adjusted. It must be remembered that, at any rate so far as the Cuban sugar is concerned, at the time of loss and until transfer of the bills of lading in October Messrs Farr were the only persons in contractual relation with the ship. The bills of lading which they held were in their hands merely receipts for shipment and of course symbols of the goods with which they could transfer the right to possession and the property.

It follows that when the (cargo) arrived at Greenock the Hain Company, who were, through their bills of lading, in possession of the goods, had a claim for contribution against the charterers, and for the reasons given by Greer LJ in his admirable judgment, with which I find myself in entire accord, had a lien on the goods for that contribution.

Now the position of the respondents, Tate & Lyle, has to be considered from two points of view: (1) as indorsees of the bills of lading in circumstances in which the rights and liabilities expressed in the bills of lading would devolve upon them as though the contract contained therein had been made with them (under the Bills of Lading Act); (2) as parties to the Lloyd's bond.

(1)   In respect of the first, in my opinion, the fact of deviation gives the bill-of-lading holder the rights I have already mentioned. On discovery he is entitled to refuse to be bound by the contract. Waiver by the charterer seems on principle to have no bearing upon the rights and liabilities which devolve upon the bill-of-lading holder under the Bills of Lading Act. The consignee has not assigned to him the obligations under the charterparty, nor, in fact, any obligation of the charterer under the bill of lading, for *ex hypothesi* there is none. A new contract appears to spring up between the ship and the consignee of the terms of the bill of lading. One of the terms is the performance of an agreed voyage, a deviation from which is a fundamental breach. It seems to me impossible to see how a waiver of such a breach by the party to the charterparty contract can affect the rights of different parties in respect to the breach by the same event of the bill of lading contract. I think, therefore, that a deviation would admittedly preclude a claim for contribution arising against parties to a subsisting contract of carriage, though no doubt the claim does not arise as a term of the contract, and as the bill of lading holder is entitled to say that he is not bound by the agreed term as to freight the ship could not, in the present circumstances, claim against Tate & Lyle either contribution or freight if they had to rely on the bill of lading alone.

(2)   On the other hand, the terms of the Lloyd's bond appear in the plainest words to give to the ship the right they claim in respect of contribution. The consignees agree to pay to the owners the proper proportion of general average charges 'which may be chargeable upon their respective consignments' or 'to which the shippers or owners of such consignments may be liable to contribute'. General average charges were, as I have said, chargeable by way of lien against the sugar, and the shippers were liable to contribute. The obligation is independent of the bill of lading; there is good consideration in the ship giving up a lien which it claims and giving to the consignees immediate and not delayed delivery. I do not attach any importance in this case to the without-prejudice provisions in the third part of the bond, which affect only the deposit, and would not in any case apply where there was in fact a good claim for contribution against the original shippers. I think, therefore, that the claim of Tate & Lyle which is directed to recovering the deposit made in respect of the Cuban sugar fails, and that the ship's claim for a declaration that there is a valid claim for contribution against the deposit

succeeds. On the ship's claim for the balance of freight in respect of the San Domingo sugar I have come to the conclusion that it must fail. That there is no claim on the express contract, the bill of lading, I have already said. An amendment to claim a *quantum meruit* was, however, allowed, and this has occasioned me some difficulty. I am not prepared at present to adopt the view of Scrutton LJ that in no circumstances can a consignee, whether holder of a bill of lading or not, be liable to pay after a deviation any remuneration for the carriage from which he has benefited. I prefer to leave the matter open, and, in those circumstances, to say that the opinion of the Court of Appeal to the contrary in this case should not be taken as authoritative. In the present case I find that the balance of freight under the charterparty, and therefore under the bill of lading, was to be paid in New York after advice of right delivery and ascertainment of weight. The terms of the cesser clause do not affect this obligation, and consequently the charterer remained and remains still liable for that freight. In these circumstances I am not satisfied that conditions existed under which a promise should be implied whereby the shippers undertook to give to the ship a further and a different right to receive some part of what would be a reasonable remuneration for the carriage. I think, therefore, that the claim for freight fails.

Notes

1   In this case the line of reasoning used in *Balian* and *Orchis Steamship* was abandoned. The House of Lords decided that deviation did not of itself make the contract void *ab initio* and it did not result in the automatic discharge of the agreement. But it was held that deviation was a serious breach of a contract of affreightment and always gave the innocent party the right to bring the contract to an end, in which case he would not be bound by exclusion clauses or by any other promises in the contract, including the promise to pay freight due on delivery. On the other hand, if the innocent party elected to treat the contract as subsisting, the innocent party would continue to be bound by the contract and in particular the shipowner would continue to be entitled to rely on the contractual excepted perils. In the words of Lord Wright MR:

> In the present case the charterers elected to waive the breach, with the result that the charterparty was not abrogated but remained in force. The appellants were thus entitled to . . . rely on the exception of perils of the sea . . .

2   The *Hain* approach is capable of producing very odd results. On this view of the law, if a ship makes a minor and harmless deviation, returns to the contractual route and then delivers the cargo on time and without loss or damage, it seems that the cargo owner can nevertheless bring the contract to an end and avoid liability for contractual payments (such as freight payable on delivery or demurrage at the port of discharge) that become due under the contract after the commencement of the deviation. (Liability on a *quantum meruit* claim is far from certain: cf Goff, R and Jones G, *Unjust Enrichment*, 8th edn, 2011, London: Sweet & Maxwell.) On the other hand, if a vessel deviates, the charterer waives the breach and thereafter the vessel and cargo are lost, *Hain* seems to allow the shipowner to rely on exclusion clauses in the contract in every case, even where the loss actually occurs at places or at times not contemplated by the original contract. In this situation, paradoxically, by affirming the contract, the innocent party changes it.

3   Is *Hain* still good law? The judgments in the case are not in perfect harmony with earlier decisions of the House of Lords in deviation cases and are inconsistent in important

respects with the general law of contract as expounded in more recent decisions. In *Photo Production v Securicor* [1980] AC 827, the House of Lords rejected the idea that by rescinding a contract for a serious breach, the innocent party can bring the whole contract, including any exclusion clauses, to an end. In general the question whether an exclusion clause applies to a particular breach of contract depends on the proper meaning of the clause; there is no general rule of the law of contract that an exclusion clause cannot exclude liability for particularly serious or fundamental breaches. Nevertheless, *Hain* has not been formally overruled. In *Photo Production* Lord Wilberforce said of the deviation cases that (at p 845):

> . . . I suggested in the *Suisse Atlantique* [1967] 1 AC 361 that these cases can be regarded as proceeding upon normal principles applicable to the law of contract generally viz, that it is a matter of the parties' intentions whether and to what extent clauses in shipping contracts can be applied after a deviation, ie a departure from the contractually agreed voyage or adventure. It may be preferable that they should be considered as a body of authority *sui generis* with special rules derived from historical and commercial reasons . . .

4   It is not clear that a special rule is needed to deal with the problems of deviation under a contract to carry goods by sea. It is true that deviation may cause delay and can lead to loss or damage to cargo. And deviation could, in some circumstances, cause a loss of cargo insurance, although it will not necessarily have this effect today when the Standard Cargo Clauses of the Institute of London Underwriters apply. On the other hand, a minor deviation may have no effect at all on a cargo owner: a vessel might depart from route but still arrive on time, at the right place, with the cargo intact, the cargo insurance still in force and no additional premium payable. A rule of law that makes the agreement between the parties unenforceable by the shipowner in these circumstances does not make much sense. For these reasons the view is gaining ground that the law relating to deviation under a contract of affreightment ought to be brought into line with the ordinary law of contract: see *The Antares* [1986] 2 Lloyd's Rep 626, p 633; [1987] 1 Lloyd's Rep 424, CA; *State Trading Corp of India Ltd v M Golodetz Ltd, The Sara D* [1989] 2 Lloyd's Rep 277, CA.

5   *Deviation and demurrage.* In *Hain*, Lord Atkin referred to earlier cases where deviation had been treated as preventing enforcement of demurrage provisions. In *The Alamosa* the vessel was chartered to carry a cargo from the River Plate to Malaga and Seville in that order. After discharging at Malaga within the agreed lay time, she had enough fuel oil to take her to Seville and to discharge there, but not enough to enable her to leave Seville afterwards. The vessel therefore went to Gibraltar having arranged to meet a tanker there. After waiting for two days at Gibraltar for the tanker, which did not arrive, the master took the vessel to Lisbon, which was off the geographical route but was the nearest place at which fuel oil could be obtained. The arbitrator found as a fact that the master acted reasonably in doing so. After taking on fuel, the vessel went to Seville where time taken to discharge exceeded the time fixed by the charter. The owners claimed demurrage in arbitration proceedings. The charterers contended that the ship had deviated from the chartered course and that this deprived the owners of the right to demurrage; the charterers also claimed damages for deviation. On a case stated by the arbitrator, Bailhache J held ((1924) 40 TLR 541) that: 'from the point of deviation all clauses in the contract which were in favour of the shipowners come to an end. The fixed lay days for discharge must go, though the charterers will still remain liable to discharge within a reasonable time.' The owners' claim for demurrage failed.

This judgment was affirmed on appeal to the Court of Appeal. In the House of Lords it was not disputed that the trip to Lisbon was a deviation. However, the owners attempted to justify the deviation by arguing that, if the deviation was reasonably necessary in a business sense, then it was in the course of the voyage which the charter prescribed. This argument was rejected on the grounds that it could only aid the shipowners if it had been proved (which it had not) that all necessary steps had been taken to supply the vessel with fuel at the commencement of the voyage. The judgment of the Court of Appeal was affirmed. Even if proof had been available on the point in question, it is not certain that the shipowners would have been successful. The House of Lords seems to have doubted whether a deviation could be justified if the object was to take on fuel, not to get the ship to the port of discharge, but to take her out of that port after discharge had been completed: *United States Shipping Board v Bunge and Born* (1925) 42 TLR 174.

6   *Deviation and statutory limitation of liability.* The appellants in *Paterson Steamships v Robin Hood Mills* (1937) 58 Ll L Rep 33, p 39, were owners of a cargo of flour/cereals loaded on the *Thordoc* for carriage from Port Arthur (Ontario) to Montreal. Before proceeding on her voyage down Lake Superior, the vessel called at the neighbouring port of Fort William to discharge some boats belonging to the respondents. The *Thordoc* then resumed her chartered voyage in the course of which, because of a faulty compass and the incompetence of the steersman, she stranded at Point Porphyry and was wrecked with great loss and damage to cargo. The appellants obtained judgment for damages in respect of that loss and damage. The respondents then brought the present action to limit their liability under s 503 of the Merchant Shipping Act 1894.

The Privy Council, on appeal from the Exchequer Court of Canada, held that since the loss and damage took place without the actual fault or privity of the respondents in respect of that which caused the loss or damage in question (see Chapter 6), the respondents were entitled to limit their liability. The respondents were not at fault in respect of the improper navigation that caused the stranding merely because there had previously been a deviation. The deviation 'had nothing whatever to do with the loss of, or damage to, cargo now in question. At the time of the stranding any deviation was over and past, and the ship was at a place and on a course proper for her voyage . . .' (*per* Lord Roche).

7   *Deviation and deck cargo.* Cargo stowed on deck is exposed to substantially greater risks than cargo stowed in a hold, so that stowing on deck is a serious breach of a contract to carry in a hold. Unauthorised stowage on deck is sometimes referred to as a quasi deviation. In *Royal Exchange Shipping Co Ltd v Dixon* (1886) 12 App Cas 11, bales of cotton were shipped on the appellants' screw steamer *Egyptian Monarch* for carriage from New Orleans to Liverpool. In breach of contract, some of the cotton was carried on deck. On the voyage the ship went aground and, in order to get her off the master properly, jettisoned the cotton. The endorsees of the bills of lading brought an action against the shipowners to recover the value of the cotton. The House of Lords held that an exception in the bills of lading of 'jettison' was no defence to the claim. It is not clear from the report whether this was conceived as a decision on the construction of the clause, or the application of a rule of law, but in *The Chanda* [1989] 2 Lloyd's Rep 494 it was said that the decision in *Dixon* was based on a principle of construction.

Further reading

Barclay, C, 'Technical aspects of unseaworthiness' (1975) LMCLQ 288.

Baughen, S, 'Does deviation still matter' (1991) LMCLQ 70.

Chorley, R, 'Liberal trends in commercial law' (1940) 3 MLR 287.

Clarke, M, 'Seaworthiness in time charters' (1977) LMCLQ 493.

Coote, B, 'The effect of discharge by breach on exceptions clauses' (1970) 28 Cambridge LJ 221.

Coote, B, 'Deviation and the ordinary law', in Rose, F (ed), *Lex Mercatoria: Essays in Honour of Francis Reynolds*, 2000, London: Lloyd's of London. p 13.

Debattista, C, 'Fundamental breach and deviation' (1989) JBL 22.

Dockray, M, 'Deviation: A doctrine all at sea' (2000) LMCLQ 76.

Goff, R and Jones, G, *Unjust Enrichment*, 8th edn, 2011, London: Sweet & Maxwell.

Grunfeld, C, 'Affreightment – unseaworthiness – causation' (1949) MLR 372.

Lee, J, 'The law of maritime deviation' (1972) 47 Tulane LR 155.

Mills, C, 'The future of deviation' (1983) 4 LMCLQ 587.

Reynolds, F, *The Butterworth Lectures 1990–91*, 1991, London: Butterworths.

Tetley, W and Cleven, B, 'Prosecuting the voyage' (1971) 45 Tulane LR 810.

Chapter 3

Voyage Charterparties, Freight, Laytime and Demurrage

1 Contracts of affreightment

The contract of affreightment traditionally takes one of two forms:

(i) a charterparty, under which the shipowner makes the entire ship available to the charterer;
(ii) a bill of lading, under which the shipowner/carrier undertakes to carry goods of different shippers.

You should also note that it is common practice in the shipping market to use the term 'contract of affreightment' to mean certain agreements made between cargo interests and carriers where shipping space is allocated to the cargo interest on a number of specified ships over a long period. Here there is an overarching agreement to cover the relationship but additionally there may be separate charterparties for particular vessels.

2 The charterparty

The charterparty itself may be one of three types.

We shall take the least relevant for a study of the law of carriage of goods by sea first. This is the demise charterparty and this is also known as the bareboat charter. It is largely outside the scope of this book because it is not a contract of carriage. It is in effect a lease of the vessel. The ship is 'dead' as far as the shipowner is concerned. It is delivered bare of everything, i.e. no bunkers, crew or stores. The charterer is focusing his interest upon the vessel itself and not upon goods to be carried. To the outside world the charterer appears to be the owner of the vessel. It may have the vessel painted in its fleet's colours, it organises the master, crew and equipment of the vessel and it takes responsibility for the vessel's navigation and management.

One test of whether a charter is by demise is found in the judgement of Lord Esher in the leading case of *Baumwoll v Gilchrest* [1892] 1 QB 253 at p 259. He said that it depends upon whether the owner has ' ... parted with the whole possession and control of the ship and to this extent, that he has given to the charterer a power and right independent of him, and without reference to him to do what he pleases with regard to the captain, the crew, and the management and employment of the ship.'

There are a number of consequences of a vessel being demise chartered but in particular:

1. The owner is no longer in possession of the vessel and therefore does not have a *common law lien* if freight remains unpaid (i.e. monies owed to it under the charter).
2. The master is employed by the charterer of the vessel and not by the owner.
3. Bills of lading signed by the master bind the charterer not the owner.
4. If the ship negligently causes a collision it is the charterer not the owner who is liable.
5. Any salvage award earned by the vessel goes to the charterer not the owner.
6. The charterer will be held to be the 'carrier' as far as the Hague/Visby rules are concerned.

Demise charters are used as a means of financing a shipping fleet.

Voyage and demise can be compared to the two extremes of a spectrum. We will examine voyage charters in this chapter and look at time charters in Chapter 4.

With a voyage charter the carrier has the entire management – the captain and crew are its employees. It has control; it pays their wages. It also pays for the bunkers, pilotage, tugs, repairs etc. (except the actual cost of loading the goods).

With a demise charter legal possession is with the charterer and all liabilities fall on the charterer, except for one – depreciation.

The shipowner has only two legal rights:

1.   to obtain payment promptly
2.   to have the ship delivered up to it in the same condition as when it handed her over.

A simple time charter is somewhere in between these extremes. The shipowner provides the crew etc. and the charterer is able to use the vessel within defined limits (both geographical and concerning the cargo) for the period of hire. Remuneration of the carrier in a voyage charter is called 'freight', but in the other two types of charter it is known as 'hire'.

See Lord Denning's judgment in: *The Nanfri, The Benfri and The Lorfri* [1978] 2 Lloyd's Rep 132, CA.

A charterparty is a contract that is negotiated between the parties (i.e. the owner of goods and a carrier of goods) without restriction. The parties may make any agreement they choose, totally by word of mouth, totally in writing or a combination of both, and draw up an individual, bespoke document. However, that is largely an academic point – in commercial reality the charterparty will be in writing and in a standard form.

The standard charters have developed in a number of ways and they will be known by a code name. Those used in a particular trade are one type, for example the coal trade – an example here being the Americanised Welsh Coal Charter (Am Welsh 93). Those used by a dominant firm in a particular market, for example the Shellvoy in the oil industry is another. Then there are those forms drawn up by bodies or associations with an interest in the shipping industry, for example The Baltic and International Maritime Conference (BIMCO) one such being Baltime 1939.

Standard forms are useful in that they assist confidence in international trade. The parties will be aware of the advantages and disadvantages of the common ones and in theory their use should lead to uniformity in practice and legal interpretation.

It is frequently the case that the parties modify or customise a standard form to their needs.

3 Duty to provide a cargo

Many issues arise from the cargo itself. A promise by a charterer to provide a cargo is important, among other things, as the basis of the shipowner's right to earn freight. Words in a charter that excuse a delay in loading will not normally be read as applying to the separate prior duty to tender a cargo.

Grant v Coverdale (1884) 9 App Cas 470

Facts: The plaintiff's vessel *Mennythorpe* was chartered to load a cargo of iron at East Bute Dock, Cardiff. The charterers agreed to load in a fixed time subject to frosts or unavoidable accidents. The charterers had intended that part of the cargo should be taken to the ship from the warehouse by canal. They were unable to load within the fixed time because the canal was frozen. A referee found that while the canal was frozen, the iron could not be taken to the dock by any reasonable means.

Held:

Earl of Selborne LC: . . . it is not denied, and cannot be denied, that unless those words of exception according to their proper construction take this case which has happened out of the demurrage clause, the mere fact of frost or any other thing having impeded the performance of that which the charterer and not the shipowner was bound to perform will not absolve him from the consequences of keeping the ship too long. That was decided under circumstances very similar in many respects, in the case of *Kearon v Pearson* (1861) 7 H & N 386, and decided expressly on the ground, as was pointed out I think by all the learned judges . . . that there was no contract as to the particular place from which the cargo was to come, no contract as to the particular manner in which it was to be supplied, or how it was to be brought to the place of loading, and that therefore it could not be supposed that the parties were contracting about any such thing.

This exception in the contract being limited to 'accidents preventing the loading', the only question is, what is the meaning of 'loading'? and whether this particular frost did, in fact, prevent the loading. There are two things to be done – the operation of loading is the particular operation in which both parties have to concur. Taken literally it is spoken of in the early part of this charterparty as the thing which the shipowner is to do. The ship is to 'proceed to Cardiff East Bute Dock', 'and there load the cargo'. No doubt, for the purpose of loading, the charterer must also do his part; he must have the cargo there to be loaded, and tender it to be put on board the ship in the usual and proper manner. Therefore the business of both parties meets and concurs in that operation of loading. When the charterer has tendered the cargo, and when the operation has proceeded to the point at which the shipowner is to take charge of it, everything after that is the shipowner's business, and everything before the commencement of the operation of loading, those things which are so essential to the operation of loading that they are conditions *sine quibus non* of that operation – everything before that is the charterer's part only. It would appear to me to be unreasonable to suppose, unless the words make it perfectly clear, that the shipowner has contracted that his ship may be detained for an unlimited time on account of impediments, whatever their nature may be, to those things with which he has nothing whatever to do, which precede altogether the whole operation of loading, which are no part whatever of it, but which belong to that which is exclusively the charterer's business. He has to contract for the cargo, he has to buy the cargo, he has to convey the cargo to the place of loading and have it ready there to be put on board; and it is only when he has done those things that the duty and the obligation of the shipowner in respect of the loading arises. These words in the exception are as large as any words can be; they mention 'strikes, frosts, floods, and all other unavoidable accidents preventing the loading'. If therefore you are to carry back the loading to anything necessary to be done by the charterer in order to have the cargo ready to be loaded, no human being can tell where you are to stop. The bankruptcy, for instance, of the person with whom he has contracted for the supply of the iron, or disputes about the fulfilment of the contract, the refusal at a critical point of time to supply the iron, the neglect of the persons who ought to put it on board lighters to come down the canal for any distance or to be brought by sea, or to put it on the railway or bring it in any other way in which it is to be brought; all those things are of course practical impediments to the charterer having the cargo ready to be shipped at the proper place and time; but is it reasonable that the shipowner should be held to be answerable for all those things, and is that within the natural meaning of the word 'loading'? Are those things any part of the operation of loading? Nothing, I suppose, is better established in law with regard to mercantile cases of this kind than the maxim, '*Causa proxima, non remota, spectatur*'; and it appears to me that the fact that this particular wharf was very near the Cardiff East Bute Dock can make no difference in principle if it was not the place of loading. If the cargo had to be brought from this wharf on the Glamorganshire Canal, however near it was, if it had to be brought over a passage which in point of fact was impeded, and over which it was not brought, to the place of loading, to say that the wharf on the Glamorganshire Canal was, upon a fair construction of the words, within the place of loading, appears to me to be no more tenable than if the same thing had been said of a place a mile higher up the canal where, according to the actual contract, the persons were to supply the iron, and where the owner of the iron might have been found.

That really is enough to dispose of the whole argument. The case of *Hudson v Ede* (1868) LR 3 QB 412 was referred to. I understand that case as proceeding upon the same principles, but as containing an admission of this distinction, that where there is, in a proved state of facts, an inevitable necessity that something should be done in order that there should be a loading at the place agreed upon, as for instance that the goods should be brought down part of a river from the only place from which they can be brought, even though that place is a considerable distance off, yet it being practically, according to known mercantile usage, the only place from which they can be brought to be loaded, the parties must be held to have contemplated that the goods should be loaded from that place in the usual manner unless there was an unavoidable impediment. And if the facts had been so about this particular wharf on the Glamorganshire Canal, if that had been the only possible place from which goods could be brought to be loaded at the East Bute Dock, that authority might have applied. But not only was that not the case, but in point of fact cargo not only could be, but actually had been brought up by carts to the East Bute Dock and put on board ship; and I infer from the finding of the referee that the whole might have been done by carting, though I agree that it would have been at an expense which was preposterous and unreasonable if you were to look at the interest of the charterer; but if the charterer has engaged that he will do a certain thing, he must of course pay the damage which arises from his not doing it, whatever the cause of his not doing it may be, whether it be his not being willing to incur an unreasonable expense, or whether it be any other cause.

(Lords Watson, Bramwell and Fitzgerald delivered judgments to the same effect.)

4 A full and complete cargo

A promise to load a full and complete cargo creates a duty to fill the ship, not merely to provide a cargo equal to the capacity of the ship as stated in the charter.

Hunter v Fry (1819) 2 B & A 421, KB

Facts: The plaintiff chartered *Hunter*, which was described in the charterparty as 'of the burden of 261 tons or thereabouts', to the defendants for a circular voyage from London to Madeira, then from Madeira to the West Indies, then back to London with 'a full and complete cargo' of coffee and logwood. The defendants failed to load as great a cargo as the vessel could have carried.

Held:

Abbott CJ: I am of opinion, that the mention of a ship's burden in the description of a ship in the charterparty, in the manner it is here mentioned, is an immaterial circumstance; although it may be made material by the allegation of fraud or other matter. Here, the freighter has not covenanted to load a cargo equivalent to the burden mentioned in the charterparty: he has covenanted to load and put on board a full and complete cargo, and to pay so much per ton for every ton loaded on board. If the covenant had been to pay a gross sum for the voyage, the freighter (upon the arrival of the ship at the foreign port) might have insisted that the captain should take on board as much as the ship would safely contain; and the owner who had covenanted to take a full and complete cargo, would not be justified in saying, that he would take no more than the register tonnage of the ship. It is, indeed, quite impossible that the burden of the ship (as described in the charterparty) should, in every case, be the measure of the precise number of tons which the ship is capable of carrying. That must depend upon the specific gravity of the particular goods; for a ship of given dimensions would be able to carry a larger number of tons, of a given species of goods, that were of a great specific gravity, than she would of another of a less specific gravity, and the freighter would therefore pay freight in proportion to the specific gravity of the goods. Upon the whole, I am of opinion, that the owner was bound to take on board such a number of tons of goods as the ship was capable of containing without injury; and, therefore, that the plaintiff is entitled to have a verdict for £918, which is the difference between the sum actually paid for freight, and that which would have been payable if the shipper had loaded on board a full and complete cargo.

(Bayley, Holroyd and Best JJ delivered judgments to the same effect.)

5 Alternative cargo options

Charters often confer an option on the charterer to select the precise cargo to be loaded. Alternative cargo options can give rise to difficult problems of interpretation where one or more of the prescribed type of cargo is not available or cannot be loaded. In the next case, *Reardon Smith v Ministry of Agriculture*, the charter's preferred cargo was affected by a strike. The case is also the leading authority on computing laytime when the phrase 'weather working days' is used as the measure of the time allowance.

Reardon Smith Line Ltd v Ministry of Agriculture, Fisheries and Food [1963] AC 691

Facts: The *Queen City* was chartered on terms that the vessel:

shall . . . receive on board . . . a full and complete cargo . . . of wheat in bulk . . . and/or barley in bulk, and/or flour in sacks as below which the parties of the second part [*viz*, the charterers] bind themselves shall be shipped . . .

Charterer has the option of loading up to one-third cargo of barley in bulk . . . Charterer has the option of loading up to one-third cargo of flour in sacks . . . [The words were inserted in the printed form in type.]

The vessel was ordered to Vancouver. Notice of readiness to load was given on 18 February 1953. An elevator strike had begun on the night of 16 February and made it impossible for her to load a full and complete cargo of wheat. The charterers did not exercise their option to load part cargoes of barley or flour. The strike having ended on 7 May, the ship began loading on that day and completed a full cargo by 12 May.

Held:

Viscount Radcliffe: . . . Having regard to what has happened and to the form of the exceptions clause, it is at first sight a little difficult, I think, to see how the shipowners can be justified in their claim to be paid demurrage for 75 days as from February 26, on which date, they say, the lay days expired, since it would seem clear that throughout the period of delay the wheat cargo was held up by the strike which is itself an excepted cause.

The owners meet this, in effect, by saying that the charterers have no right to treat their obligation under this charterparty as being simply one to provide a cargo of wheat in bulk, failing an exercise of their option to ship part alternative cargoes of barley or flour. On the contrary, they say, the obligation is essentially an obligation to provide a full and complete cargo of wheat, barley or flour (up to the permitted proportions) as the charterers may select and the mere fact that one of these possible constituents, wheat, is the subject of delay and so within the exceptions clause does not excuse the charterers from their overriding duty to find and ship a full and complete cargo made up of such proportions of these various commodities as the prevailing conditions at Vancouver made it possible to load during the period of the strike.

... But in my view ... the shipowners' interpretation of the basic obligation of the charterparty is misconceived and the charterers' real promise in the opening clause amounts to nothing else than that of providing a full cargo of wheat, unless they should affirmatively decide to vary the make-up of the cargo by substituting barley or flour up to the permitted proportions ...

... It has been apparent throughout the case that the shipowners' argument on this particular issue depends upon the proposition that the parties' rights under the charterparty are governed by principles laid down by the Court of Appeal in 1924 in *Brightman & Co v Bunge y Born Limitada Sociedad* [1924] 2 KB 619 to which I will refer as the *Brightman* case. I think that the decision in the *Brightman* case did lay down certain principles, though not so many or so far-reaching as is sometimes supposed, but in my opinion those principles are not applicable to the relationship established by the charterparty which we are now considering. In order to show why that is so I must make some reference to the essential facts of the *Brightman* case.

Like this, it was a dispute between owners and charterers. The terms of the charterparty had bound the charterers to provide:

> a full and complete cargo of wheat and/or maize and/or rye in bags and/or in bulk, which cargo the said charterers bind themselves to ship.

... The decision of the court was to the effect that some demurrage was payable but not to the whole extent claimed by the owners. In arriving at this decision the principles accepted by the court which are relevant to this appeal are, in my opinion, as follows:

(1) If a shipper has undertaken to ship a full and complete cargo made up of alternative commodities, as in the terms 'wheat and/or maize and/or rye', his obligation is to have ready at the port of shipment a complete cargo within the range of those alternatives. Consequently the fact that he is prevented from loading one of the possible types of cargo by a cause within the exceptions clause, even though that is the type that he has himself selected and provided for, is not an answer to a claim for demurrage. To protect him each of the alternatives or all the alternatives would have to be covered by an excepted cause.

(2) Consistently with this view the shipper's selection of one of the named commodities does not convert the primary obligation to ship a full cargo in one form or the other into a simple obligation to ship a full cargo of the commodity selected. In other words, his selection is not like the exercise of an option to name a port. He may change his mind and alter his choice. He 'retains control of his powers until the final ton is put on the ship', said Atkin LJ [1924] 2 KB 637. This may not be a full statement of the nature or consequences of the right of selection, but I have no doubt that it describes the general situation.

(3) If a shipper finds himself stopped by an excepted cause (eg in that case, the government prohibition) from loading or continuing to load the type of cargo that he has provided for and genuinely intended to ship, he may still rely on delay as covered by the exceptions clause to the extent of a reasonable time 'to consider the position and change [his] cargo' as Scrutton LJ said, or to 'deal with the altered conditions' as Bankes LJ said, or, simply, 'to change over' as Atkin LJ said.

As regards this last principle, I must admit that very careful attention to the three judgments of Bankes, Scrutton and Atkin LJJ has left me uncertain as to its origin or its full implications. I think that on the whole his time for adjustment is better attributed to a term derived from the general position of a shipper under such a charterparty, when confronted with such circumstances, than to a right derived from any possible construction of the exceptions clause itself ...

In my opinion, however, the principle of the *Brightman* case has no application here, because there is here no primary obligation on the charterers to ship a mixed cargo. The primary obligation is to provide a cargo of wheat only, the exceptions clause covers delay in the shipping of wheat, and there is no obligation on the charterers to lose that protection by exercising their option to provide another kind of cargo that is not affected by a cause of delay, even assuming such a cargo to be readily available. Really, that seems to me to contain the whole point of the dispute. There is in this case no duty on the charterers to 'switch' from wheat to barley or flour, because their choice of loading barley or flour is unfettered and is not at any time controlled in their hands by an overriding obligation to put on board by a fixed date a full cargo which must include those commodities, if it cannot consist of wheat alone.

It comes down, then, to a question of construing the opening clause of the charterparty. Under it the vessel is to receive on board 'a full and complete cargo . . . of wheat in bulk . . . and/or barley in bulk and/or flour in sacks'. There are then added the words in typescript 'as below', and this is a qualification which both affects what has gone before and conditions the meaning of what follows, namely, the charterers' undertaking to ship their cargo. The words 'as below' can only refer to the options which are also added in typescript at the foot of the clause, an option to load up to 'one-third cargo of barley in bulk', subject to an increased rate of freight, and an option to load 'up to one-third cargo of flour in bags', also at an increased freight rate. There is no option relating to wheat: wheat is the one commodity not subject to option.

It is said for the shipowners that there is no special significance in the use of the word option in this clause. Charterers who have stipulated for and undertaken to provide mixed or alternative cargoes have an option anyway, since it is they who retain to the end the right of selecting what cargo they are actually to provide; and it is argued that the total effect of the clause is, just as in the *Brightman* case, to leave the charterers under a primary obligation to put on board at the due date a full cargo made up in one or other of the permitted ways.

I do not think that that is the right construction. I cannot agree that, just because even without mentioning an option the charterers would have had a right of choice, the word 'option', when it is expressly mentioned, means no more than this. Wheat, it is to be noted, though linked indifferently with barley and flour as one of the possible cargoes, is, unlike them, not described as the subject of an option. This supports the view that wheat is to be the basic cargo, displaced only if and as the charterers so decide; just as the rate of freight for wheat is to be the basic rate of which other rates are expressed as a variation. Indeed, if the barley and flour options are not intended to be true options in the sense that only the positive exercise of the holder's choice can ever give him any responsibility to load or the shipowners any right to call for those commodities as part of a cargo, I cannot see how the parties could have expressed the option provisions in the way that they did. For, if the language is understood as the shipowners argue that it should be, the phrases introduced by the words 'charterer has the option' convey nothing more than a restriction on the right of selection among the commodities previously mentioned by tying the range of selection down to the permitted proportions; and what is clearly introduced as a right beneficial to the charterers would amount merely to a limitation on their existing power of selection. Moreover, even a short delay in the shipping of the cargo they wanted would turn their right of choice into a burden to ship a cargo they might never require. I cannot think that this was the bargain of the parties . . .

(Lords Cohen, Keith, Evershed and Devlin agreed that the shipowners' appeal on this issue should be dismissed.)

6 Loading

At common law the obligations to load, stow and discharge cargo fall on the shipowner but can be transferred to the charterer by agreement, provided that clear words are used: *Jindal Iron & Steel Co Ltd v Islamic Solidarity Co Jordan Inc* [2003] EWCA Civ 144; [2003] 2 Lloyd's Rep 87. However, it has been said that a term making the shipper responsible for discharge might be implied in the bill of lading in some circumstances: *Tradigrain SA v King Diamond Shipping SA,*

The Spiros C [2000] 2 Lloyd's Rep 315. The cases in this area distinguish between paying for, performing and taking responsibility for an activity. There is no presumption that each of these burdens must fall on the same person, so that if the charterer agrees to pay for loading, there is no presumption that he has agreed to carry it out or to be liable if loading causes damage: *Jindal Iron*, above. Two further factors add complexity to disputes about liability for damage caused in the course of loading. First, where the charterer agrees to load, it is clear that the master of the vessel has a legal right and duty to intervene in that process in some circumstances, most obviously to ensure the stability and safety of the vessel. Second, the conduct of the parties – by interfering in the process or by agreeing to a particular stow or by failing to object – may also affect the incidence of liability. Most of the recent reported decisions in this area turn on the precise terms of the charter in question. The central problems, however, are as old as maritime commerce: the Laws of Oleron in the 13th century protected a master who dropped a tun of wine, but only if the ropes had been shown to and accepted by the merchant. The decision in *The Argonaut* provides a review of the issues and the key decisions.

MSC Mediterranean Shipping Co SA v Alianca Bay Shipping Co, The Argonaut [1985] 2 Lloyd's Rep 216

Facts: *The Argonaut* was trip chartered for a voyage from South Africa to the Mediterranean/Continent/UK. The charter was in the New York Produce Exchange (NYPE) form and provided: '8 . . . Charterers are to load, stow and . . . discharge at their own expense under the supervision and responsibility of the Captain.'

The vessel was ordered by the charterers to Durban where she loaded *inter alia* granite blocks for discharge at Marina di Carrara (MDC) and at Sete. The vessel was damaged at both Sete and MDC when granite blocks were dropped by stevedores.

Held:

Leggatt J: . . . The issue in this appeal is whether, on a proper construction of the charterparty, the owners were responsible for damage to the vessel caused by stevedores employed by the charterers . . . Each of the parties argued before the arbitrator that the other was liable for stevedore damage except where the complainants were guilty of active intervention . . .

In *Blaikie v Stembridge* (1860) 6 CB(NS) 894 it was held that in the absence of custom or agreement to the contrary, it is the duty of the master, on the part of the owner of a ship, to receive and properly stow on board the goods to be carried; and, for any damage to the goods occasioned by negligence by the performance of this duty, the owner is liable to the shipper. In *Sack v Ford*, (1862) 13 CB(NS) 90, the clause in question provided that the cargoes were to be taken on board and discharged by the charterers, the crew of the vessel rendering customary assistance so far as they might be under the orders of the master; and the charterers were to have liberty to employ stevedores and labourers to assist in the loading, stowage and discharge thereof; but such stevedores and labourers, being under the control and direction of the master, the charterers were not in any case to be responsible to the owners for damage or improper stowage. It was held by the Court of Common Pleas that there was nothing in this charterparty to exonerate the owner from responsibility for negligent and improper stowage by the stevedores employed by the charterers under the clause to which I have referred . . . At p 100, Chief Justice Erle said:

> Ordinarily speaking, the shipowner has by law cast upon him the risk of attending the loading, stowing, and unloading of the cargo: and the question is whether by the terms of this charterparty he is exempted from that liability. I think not: on the contrary, it appears to me that the charterer, seeing what were the consequences resulting from the decision in *Blaikie v Stembridge*, has expressly stipulated that the liability of the owner for bad stowage shall continue,

notwithstanding that the charterer was to have liberty to employ stevedores and labourers to assist in the loading, stowage, and discharge of the cargo.

The Chief Justice added at p 101 that the clause which provided that the owners should, in every respect, be and remain responsible as if the ship was loading and discharging her cargo was but a repetition of the same idea. At p 103, Byles J said:

> The master is to have the control of the stevedores – to tell them what they are not to do; and he is to have the direction – to tell them what they are to do. If any difference of opinion should arise as to the proper mode of stowage, between the stevedore and the master, that of the latter is to prevail.

In his judgment all possibility of doubt was removed by the additional clause also relied on by the Chief Justice.

In *The Helene* (1865) 167 ER 426, the charterparty provided that the cargo should be taken alongside by the charterer, and be received and stowed by the master as presented for shipment, the charterer being allowed to appoint a head stevedore at the expense and responsibility of the master for proper stowage. After citing this provision, Dr Lushington said at p 431:

> These words appear to me to answer the objection, and remove the case out of the authority of *Blaikie v Stembridge* where similar words were not contained in the charterparty, and where the court held the true construction of the charterparty to be, that the cargo was to be brought alongside at the risk and expense of the charterer, and that it was to be shipped and stowed by his stevedore, and consequently at his risk – though at the expense of the shipowner, and subject to the control of the master, on behalf of the shipowner, to protect his interests.

. . . In *Union Castle Mail Steamship Co Ltd v Borderdale Shipping Co Ltd* [1919] 1 KB 612, the charterparty provided that the charterers should bear the expense of loading and discharging cargo, but:

> . . . the stowage shall be under the control of the master, and the owners shall be responsible for the proper stowage and correct delivery of the cargo.

Bailhache J held that this clause did not amount to an absolute warranty by the owners, and that it merely meant that they would not be negligent in the stowage of the cargo. Chloride of lime in iron drums, apparently in good condition, was stowed under deck by the charterers' agents, neither they nor the master knowing, or having any reason to suspect, that it would be likely to do harm by being stowed there. The iron drums were in fact defective, and fumes escaping from them damaged other cargo. In those circumstances the judge was not prepared to impute to the master a state of knowledge which was not shared by the charterers' agents. Since no harm would have been done if the drums had been protected in the way suggested, the judge concluded that no negligence was to be imputed to the master, and negligence being necessary to enable the charterers to succeed, the action failed. I see no warrant for importing that necessity and in that respect I decline to follow that case: see *Carver on Carriage by Sea*, 13th edn, s 1097.

In *Ismail v Polish Ocean Lines* [1976] QB 893, stowage instruction had been given by the charterers under the master's supervision and responsibility. At pp 494 and 902E, after referring to the charterers' obligation to load and stow the cargo at their own expense, Lord Denning said:

> Notwithstanding those provisions, the master has an overriding power to supervise the stowage. He must have this as a matter of course . . . The master is responsible for the stowage of the cargo so as to ensure the safety of the ship: and also of the cargo so as to see that it is stowed so as to be able to withstand the ordinary incidents of the voyage. That is the meaning of the last words of cl 49: 'He is to remain responsible for the proper stowage and dunnaging.'

At pp 497 and 907D, Ormrod LJ said of cl 49:

> It would be hard to find a form of words better adapted to promoting disputes between owners and charterers than this. On the face of it it places the master in the impossible position of being under obligations which are, at least potentially, mutually inconsistent. The first part of the clause requires him to comply with the charterer's instructions as to stowage and dunnaging; the second leaves the responsibility for proper stowing and dunnaging on him. So, if he declines to comply with his instructions he may be in breach, and if he does comply with them he may also be in breach if damage occurs due to improper stowage.

It may be relevant to observe that in that case the charterer overrode the master with the result that the court held the charterer to be estopped from complaining about stowage.

Finally, in *Filikos Shipping Corporation of Monrovia v Shipmair BV (The Filikos)* [1981] 2 Lloyd's Rep 555, it was held by Lloyd J that, although certain clauses in the charterparty placed duty and responsibility for discharge upon the charterers, the subsequent clause which provided that, notwithstanding anything to the contrary, the owners were to be responsible towards the charterers as carriers rendered it impossible to hold that as between owners and charterers the owners were not liable for the relevant loss. This decision was unequivocally upheld by the Court of Appeal: see [1983] 1 Lloyd's Rep 9 . . .

The classic exposition of cl 8, albeit without the addition of the words 'and responsibility', is to be found in *Canadian Transport Co Ltd v Court Line Ltd* [1940] AC 934. In that case the House of Lords held that the requirement that cargo was to be stowed under the supervision of the captain did not relieve the charterers of their primary duty to stow safely. But to the extent that the master did supervise the stowage so as to limit the charterers' control of it their liability was correspondingly limited.

Lord Atkin dealt thus with the charterers' argument at pp 166 and 937:

> The first answer which the charterers made was that there was no such liability because the duty of the charterers was expressed to be to stow, etc, 'under the supervision of the captain'. This, it was said, threw the actual responsibility for stowage on the captain; or at any rate threw upon the owners the onus of showing that the damage was not due to an omission by the master to exercise due supervision. This, we were told, was the point of commercial importance upon which the opinion of this House was desired. My Lords, it appears to me plain that there is no foundation at all for this defence; and on this point all the judges so far have agreed. The supervision of the stowage by the captain is in any case a matter of course; he has in any event to protect his ship from being made unseaworthy; and in other respects no doubt he has the right to interfere if he considers that the proposed stowage is likely to impose a liability upon his owners. If it could be proved by the charterers that the bad stowage was caused only by the captain's orders, and that their own proposed stowage would have caused no damage no doubt that might enable them to escape liability. But the reservation of the right of the captain to supervise, a right which in my opinion would have existed even if not expressly reserved, has no effect whatever in relieving the charterers of their primary duty to stow safely . . .

At pp 168 and 943, Lord Wright said:

> It is, apart from special provisions or circumstances, part of the ship's duty to stow the goods properly, not only in the interests of seaworthiness of the vessel, but in order to avoid damage to the goods, and also to avoid loss of space or dead freight owing to bad stowage. In modern times the work of stowage is generally deputed to stevedores, but that does not generally relieve the shipowners of their duty, even though the stevedores are under the charterparty to be appointed by the charterers, unless there are special provisions which

either expressly or inferentially have that effect. But under clause 8 of this charterparty the charterers are to load, stow and trim the cargo at their expense. I think these words necessarily import that the charterers take into their hands the business of loading and stowing the cargo. It must follow that they not only relieve the ship of the duty of loading and stowing, but as between themselves and the shipowners relieve them of liability for bad stowage, except as qualified by the words 'under the supervision of the captain', which I shall discuss later. The charterers are granted by the shipowners the right of performing a duty which properly attaches to the shipowners. Presumably this is for the convenience of the charterers. If the latter do not perform properly the duty of stowing the cargo, the shipowners will be subject to a liability to the bill of lading holders. Justice requires that the charterers should indemnify the shipowners against that liability on the same principle that a similar right of indemnity arises when one person does an act and thereby incurs liability at the request of another, who is then held liable to indemnify. That such a liability on the part of the charterers is contemplated is shown by the last words of clause 8 which supposes that the charterers may incur liability for 'damage to cargo'. So far I think is clear. What then is the effect of the words 'under the supervision of the master'? These words expressly give the master a right, which I think he must in any case have, to supervise the operations of the charterers in loading and stowing. The master is responsible for the seaworthiness of the ship and also for ensuring that the cargo will not be so loaded as to be subject to damage, by absence of dunnage and separation, by being placed near to other goods or to parts of the ship which are liable to cause damage, or in other ways . . . But I think this right is expressly stipulated not only for the sake of accuracy, but specifically as a limitation of the charterers' rights to control the stowage. It follows that to the extent that the master exercises supervision and limits the charterers' control of the stowage, the charterers' liability will be limited in a corresponding degree.

. . . Lord Wright added at pp 169 and 945:

The master's power of supervision is obviously not limited to matters affecting seaworthiness.

Lord Maugham agreed with Lord Atkin, and Lord Romer agreed with Lord Atkin and Lord Wright. Finally, at pp 172 and 951 Lord Porter said:

In my opinion by their contract the charterers have undertaken to load, stow and trim the cargo, and that expression necessarily means that they will stow with due care. *Prima facie* such an obligation imposes upon them the liability for damage due to improper stowage. It is true that the stowage is contracted to be effected under the supervision of the captain, but this phrase does not, as I think, make the captain primarily liable for the work of the charterers' stevedores. It may indeed be that in certain cases as, eg, where the stability of the ship is concerned the master would be responsible for unseaworthiness of the ship and the stevedore would not. But in such cases I think that any liability which could be established would be due to the fact that the master would be expected to know what method of stowage would affect his ship's stability and what would not, whereas the stevedores would not possess any such knowledge. It might be also that if it were proved that the master had exercised his rights of supervision and intervened in the stowage, again the responsibility would be his and not the charterers. The primary duty of stowage, however, is imposed upon the charterers and if they desire to escape from this obligation they must, I think, obtain a finding which imposes the liability upon the captain and not upon them.

This case was considered by Neill LJ in *AB Marintrans v Comet Shipping Co Ltd* [1985] 1 Lloyd's Rep 568 . . . In the course of his judgment, Lord Justice Neill said, referring to *Canadian Transport Co Ltd v Court Line Ltd* (above):

> It is apparent from these speeches, however . . . that the primary responsibility of the charterers may be affected if the captain in fact intervenes by, for example, insisting on his own system of stowage. But in the present case the contract between the parties included the additional words in typescript 'and responsibility'.

The clause had indeed been altered as it was in the present case. After considering the rival submissions in the case before him Neill LJ said at p 575 of the report:

> I have found this question a difficult one to resolve. On the one hand, I see the force of Mr Milligan's submission that the addition of the words 'and responsibility' are apt, when taken in conjunction with cl 32, to transfer responsibility back to the owners and in effect to restore the old rule of maritime law. On the other hand, to limit the responsibility of the charterers to that of providing competent stevedores and paying for them gives little weight to the words in cl 8 . . . Charterers are to load, stow, trim and discharge the cargo . . . Such a narrow construction may also ignore what happens in practice where stowage is treated as a joint undertaking with both the charterers and the ship playing their part.

In the end I have come to the conclusion that the correct approach is to construe the words 'and responsibility' as effecting a *prima facie* transfer of liability for bad stowage to the owners, but that if it can be shown in any particular case that the charterers by, for example giving some instruction in the course of the stowage, have caused the relevant loss or damage the owners will be able to escape liability to that extent. In my judgment, this approach is consistent with that of the House of Lords in the *Court Line* case where it was clearly contemplated that the party primarily responsible might be relieved from liability for loss caused by the other party's intervention. There may therefore be cases where it will be necessary to consider the dominant cause of particular damage.

If this analysis is correct, the added words 'and responsibility' will place the primary duty on the master and owners but with the possibility that their liability will be affected by some intervention by the charterers.

Later in his judgment at p 577 of the report, Neill LJ said:

> . . . having regard to the terms of this charterparty, neither the stevedores nor the surveyor can be treated as the agents of the charterers so as to make their acts or conduct the acts or conduct of the charterers.

I respectfully endorse and follow those conclusions.

[Counsel] argues that the correct approach is to consider causation. The test, he says, is whether the charterers, in carrying out the mechanics of loading or other operations, have caused loss or damage or whether the owners, in the exercise of their duty of control, have caused the loss or damage. He relies also on *Union Castle Mail Steamship Co Ltd v Borderdale Shipping Co Ltd* [1919] 1 KB 612. But, for the reasons which I have given earlier, that case will not, in my judgment, avail him.

I agree that the charterers' obligation to load, stow and trim the cargo, and discharge, requires them to do so with due care. The primary responsibility for stowage is, however, imposed on the master. Although in the *Court Line* case 'it was clearly contemplated that the party primarily responsible might be relieved from liability caused by the other party's intervention', the concept of 'intervention' may not be entirely apt where what is being exercised on behalf of the charterers is not a right to supervise, such as may take the form of intervention, but a duty to stow properly. At any rate in a case such as the present, I see no need to ascertain what is 'the dominant cause of particular damage'. Either a party is responsible for a particular operation (or damage caused by it) or he is not. The exercise of a right of supervision may impinge upon, override or detract from a duty to stow properly; but it is difficult to see why the fact that responsibility is conferred on the owners should have a corresponding effect of limiting the charterers' control of stowage operations. The fact that there are duties cast upon both parties by cl 8 may militate against a construction which makes the owners liable for charterers' breach of their own duty. But the effect of cl 8 was to confer the primary duty on the owners and in the absence of actual intervention by the charterers, as distinct from stevedores employed by them, the owners' liability will not be avoided. A limitation of the scope of the liability accepted by the owners through the master may be implicit in the word 'responsibility' itself. It may be said that if the word is to be reasonably construed, its application must be limited to matters within the power of the master, and that in the sense in which the word is here used, a master cannot properly be said to be 'responsible' for damage which he cannot avoid by the reasonable exercise of his powers of supervision and control. It seems to me that the scope of such powers, which is objectively ascertainable, goes beyond what was regarded by the arbitrators as having been within the master's 'province'...

... I would wish to reserve the question whether in other circumstances a master, and so owners, should be held liable for damage directly caused by charterers, which it was not within the owners' power to prevent, except by the adoption of unusual precautions. It may be that in such a case, as in *Ismail v Polish Ocean Lines* [1976] QB 893, owners' liability may be avoided by operation of the doctrine of estoppel.

The charterers' appeal from the interim award will accordingly be allowed, and that of the owners dismissed.

Notes

1   *The Argonaut* was followed by Steyn J in *The Alexandros P* [1986] 1 Lloyd's Rep 421:

> ... the words 'and responsibility ...' in clause 8 and the transfer of risk comprehended by it, relate to the entire operation of loading, stowing, trimming and discharging the cargo. Specifically, it covers not only the mechanical process of handling the ship's gear and cargo but also matters of stevedores' negligence in strategic planning of loading and discharge of the cargo.

2   The decision in *The Argonaut* includes a quotation from *Court Line*, where Lord Wright said that if the charterer fails to 'perform properly the duty of stowing the cargo, the shipowners will be subject to a liability to the bill of lading holders'. But in *Jindal Iron & Steel Co Ltd v Islamic Solidarity Co Jordan Inc*, where the shipper agreed to load, it was held that the shipowner was not responsible to the receiver.

3   In *The Santamana* (1923) 14 Ll L Rep 159, the court was concerned with claims in respect of a cargo of onions that had been shipped from Alexandria to the UK. The onions were damaged by being in stacks 15 or 16 tiers high with insufficient dunnage. Hill J was referred to a number of earlier authorities on the effect of the knowledge of the shippers about the method of stowage that was being used. At p 163 he said:

> I have considered these cases very carefully. They seem to me to carry the law at least far enough to show that a shipper who takes an active interest in the stowage, and complains of some defects but makes no complaint of others which are patent to him, cannot be heard to complain of that to which he has made no objection. I think that the onions were stowed 15 or 16 tiers high without a temporary deck by the leave and licence of [the shipper] and that he cannot be heard to complain of that. I therefore hold that, for the damage caused by reason of that defect, namely, stowing 15 or 16 tiers high without use of a temporary deck, the [owners] are not answerable to [the shippers]. For the damage caused by the other defects they are answerable.

4 Stowage and estoppel by conduct. In *Ismail v Polish Ocean Lines, The Ciechocinek* [1976] QB 893, CA, the claim related to a cargo of new potatoes shipped from Alexandria to the UK:

> **Lord Denning MR** (p 495): If a shipper or his representative is present when the goods are loaded – and superintends the stowage – or if he insists on their being stowed in a particular manner, he cannot afterwards complain if they are afterwards damaged by being stowed in a bad manner . . . The present case is a classic one of its kind. Here Mr Ismail instructed the master to carry 1,400 tons of potatoes. He told him that no dunnage was necessary, and that the bags were of a new kind, such that the potatoes would not suffer on the voyage. On those representations, I do not see that the master could possibly have refused to load the cargo. If he had refused, he would expose the owners to a claim for damages which they would be quite unable to refute – because they had no evidence that the representations were untrue. Again, Mr Ismail allayed the master's misgivings by promising to get a surveyor's certificate and a guarantee: and on the faith of that promise the master loaded the 1,400 tons. In this situation it would be quite contrary to all fairness and to all justice that the shipper or owner should be able to hold the master liable for improper stowage . . .

5 *The Imvros* was chartered on the NYPE form (as amended) to carry a cargo of sawn timber in bundles from Brazil on terms that the charterers would load, stow and lash at their expense under the supervision and to the satisfaction of the master. Part of the cargo was lost overboard in the course of the voyage because it had been lashed at intervals of 3 m and not at intervals of 1.5 m as required by the International Maritime Organisation (IMO) Code. The vessel was damaged. The charterers argued that the ship was unseaworthy on sailing and that the owners were the authors of their own misfortune. It was held that: (1) on the facts, the limited duty of seaworthiness imposed on the carrier by the charter had not been broken; (2) the charter transferred responsibility to the charterers for lashing in such a way as to ensure seaworthiness; and (3) the master's right to intervene 'does not normally carry with it a liability for failure to do so let alone relieve the actor from his failure': *Transocean Liners Reederei GmbH v Euxine Shipping Co Ltd, The Imvros* [1999] 1 Lloyd's Rep 848. Arguably either the first or the second element in the decision is sufficient to distinguish *The Kapitan Sakharov* [2002] 2 Lloyd's Rep 255, CA and *The Fiona* [1994] 2 Lloyd's Rep 506, CA.

7 Dangerous cargo

Liability of shippers for loss or damage caused by their goods has been the subject of a number of reported decisions, both ancient and modern. In addition to the possibility of liability in tort for negligence or for breach of a statutory duty, possible bases of liability have been held to include breach of the contract of carriage by failing to ship goods which conform to the contractual description (*Islamic Investment Co SA v Transorient Shipping Ltd, The Nour* [1999] 1 Lloyd's Rep 1, CA), breach of an implied warranty or of a collateral contract to ship safe goods or to disclose the identity or nature of goods shipped or to pack goods properly. Liability under an express, implied or statutory agreement to indemnify is also possible. The precise scope of a shipper's duty at common law was disputed for many years: the balance of authority favoured the view that the shipper could be liable even if blamelessly ignorant of the fact that the goods were dangerous. The minority view was that there was no satisfactory ground on which to allocate responsibility to an innocent shipper and that damage should rest where it was suffered. The position was reviewed by the House of Lords in the *Giannis NK*.

Effort Shipping Co Ltd v Linden Management SA, The Giannis NK [1998] AC 605

Facts: A part cargo of ground nut pellets was loaded on the vessel at Dakar under a bill of lading that incorporated the Hague Rules. Unknown to the shippers, the shipment was infested with Khapra beetle which in its larval form was proved to be capable of consuming a grain cargo. Bulk wheat pellets had been loaded at previous loading ports. The presence of the beetles was discovered and discharge from the vessel was prohibited in the Dominican Republic and Puerto Rico. After unsuccessful attempts to fumigate, the shipowners were required to return the cargo to its port of origin or dump it at sea. The shipowners brought proceedings against the shippers seeking damages for delay. The House of Lords held that the owners were entitled to be indemnified by the shippers under Art IV, r 6 of the Hague Rules. The House went on to consider an alternative claim that the owners were entitled to rely on an undertaking implied at common law that a shipper will not ship goods of such a dangerous character that they are liable to cause physical damage to the vessel or its cargo, or to cause detention or delay, without giving notice to the owner of the character of the goods.

Held:

Lord Lloyd of Berwick: ... What is the nature and scope of any implied obligation at common law as to the shipment of dangerous goods? [This] ... question does not need to be decided. But as it has been the subject of differing views over many years, and as we have heard full argument on the point, it seems desirable for us to express an opinion. Even though that opinion will not form part of the *ratio decidendi*, it may at least help to resolve a long-standing controversy ...

The point at issue arises because of a difference of opinion in *Brass v Maitland* (1856) E & B 470. The facts in that case were that the plaintiffs were owners of a general ship. The defendants shipped a consignment of chloride of lime, better known as bleaching powder, on board the plaintiffs' vessel. Chloride of lime is a corrosive substance liable to damage other cargo if it escapes. The plaintiff shipowners were unaware of the dangerous nature of the cargo. They claimed damages from the defendants on two counts. The third plea by way of defence was that the defendants had bought the goods from a third party already packed, and that they had no knowledge, or means of knowledge, that the packing was insufficient, and that they were not guilty of negligence. It was held by the majority that the third plea was bad in law. Lord Campbell CJ said, at p 481:

> Where the owners of a general ship undertake that they will receive goods and safely carry them and deliver them at the destined port, I am of the opinion that the shippers undertake that they will not deliver, to be carried in the voyage, packages of goods of a dangerous nature, which those employed on behalf of the shipowner may not on inspection be reasonably expected to know to be of a dangerous nature, without expressly giving notice that they are of a dangerous nature.

On the question whether absence of knowledge or means of knowledge on the part of the shippers is a good defence, Lord Campbell CJ said, at p 486:

> The defendants, and not the plaintiffs, must suffer, if from the ignorance of the defendants a notice was not given to the plaintiffs, which the plaintiffs were entitled to receive, and from the want of this notice a loss has arisen which must fall either on the plaintiffs or on the defendants. I therefore hold the third plea to be bad.

Crompton J took a different view. He would have held that knowledge on the part of the shipper is an essential ingredient of liability. He said, at p 492:

> I entertain great doubt whether either the duty or the warranty extends beyond the cases where the shipper has knowledge, or means of knowledge, of the dangerous nature of the

goods when shipped, or where he has been guilty of some negligence, as shipper, as by shipping without communicating danger which he had the means of knowing and ought to have communicated.

A little later he said, at p 493:

where no negligence is alleged, or where the plea negatives any alleged negligence, I doubt extremely whether any right of action can exist.

Mr Johnson [counsel] relies heavily on the dissenting judgment of Crompton J and the commentary in *Abbott's Merchant Ships and Seamen*, 13th ed (1892), a work of great authority, where it is said that the powerful reasons urged by Crompton J rendered the decision, to say the least, doubtful. In the 14th ed (1901) it is said, at p 647, that Crompton J's views are more in accordance with later authorities.

But when one looks at the later authorities, and in particular at *Bamfield v Goole and Sheffield Transport Co Ltd* [1910] 2 KB 94 and *Great Northern Railway Co v LEP Transport and Depository Ltd* [1922] 2 KB 742 it is the majority view which has found favour. It was suggested by Mr Johnson that the *Bamfield* and the *Great Northern Railway* cases can be explained on the ground that the plaintiffs in those cases were common carriers. That may or may not be a relevant distinction. What matters is that in both cases the court regarded itself as being bound by the majority decision in *Brass v Maitland*, 6 E & B 470, which was not a case of a common carrier.

Mr Johnson advanced a number of more wide ranging arguments, that to hold the shippers strictly liable for shipping dangerous goods would be impracticable and unreasonable, and create an anomalous imbalance between the rights and liabilities of shippers and carriers. But equally strong arguments of a general nature can be advanced on the other side.

The dispute between the shippers and the carriers on this point is a dispute which has been rumbling on for well over a century. It is time for your Lordships to make a decision one way or the other. In the end that decision depends mainly on whether the majority decision in *Brass v Maitland*, which has stood for 140 years, should now be overruled. I am of the opinion that it should not. I agree with the majority in that case and would hold that the liability of a shipper for shipping dangerous goods at common law, when it arises, does not depend on his knowledge or means of knowledge that the goods are dangerous.

An incidental advantage of that conclusion is that the liability of the shipper will be the same whether it arises by virtue of an implied term at common law, or under article IV, r 6 of the Hague Rules.

For the reasons mentioned earlier I would dismiss the appeal.

8 Arrived ship, laytime and demurrage laytime

The obligation of the charterer to load or discharge the cargo within a fixed time is usually set out in the charter.

As we have previously noted (with regard to cancellation), a common clause is the 'laycan' clause. Alternatively the charterer is under a common law obligation to load or discharge the cargo within a reasonable time. The time allotted in the charterparty of the reasonable time is called 'laytime'.

In practice many disputes arise from laytime, particularly about the question of when laytime is to commence. This is the issue of 'arrived ship'. In general there are three requirements that have to be satisfied for laytime to commence under the law of England and Wales. These are as follows:

1. The vessel has to have arrived at the agreed destination. This may be a port, dock, mooring, berth etc., or an area coupled with a provision that the vessel proceeds to a part of the area nominated by the charterer.

2. The vessel is ready to load or discharge her cargo when she has reached her destination and (or when) a notice of readiness is tendered. This means that the vessel must be available to the charterer, which in turn requires that:

    a) the cargo spaces on the ship are ready for loading or discharge, (note that this will only be relevant at the loading stage);
    b) the ship is properly equipped for loading/discharge;
    c) all relevant documentation is in order.

3. A notice of readiness is tendered to the charterer or its agents. This is only required at the first loading port and is not required at second or subsequent ports (in the case of collection from multiple ports for the same charterer) or for any discharge ports.

When these three requirements are satisfied then the vessel is considered to be arrived and, under English law, laytime commences. Please note that it is common for the parties to vary these requirements, for example by way of 'time lost in waiting' clauses. Additionally there may be agreed variations concerning the issuing of a Notice of Readiness (NOR).

Therefore, merely arriving in the port is not enough to satisfy the obligation to provide an 'arrived ship' she only achieves this status when all three of the above requirements are satisfied.

It is a common feature of voyage charterparties that the ship must tender a valid NOR in order for the laytime period to commence. We should note that the issue of arrival of a commercial ship at a port these days also involves compliance with security requirements, particularly in the EU (Advance Cargo Shipment Data) and the US (eNOAD information- electronic Notice of Arrival and Departure). The International Ship and Port Facility Security Code (the ISPS code), which came into force in 2004, is managed as part of SOLAS (the Safety of Life at Sea Convention). These regulations require that notice of arrival (usually in electronic form) be given to the harbour master/pilot station when a request is made by the vessel to enter the port and so arguably signal that the vessel has 'arrived'. However, in purely commercial terms, i.e. in terms of the private law contractual agreement between the parties, the issue of whether or not the ship has arrived depends upon the nature/wording of the charterparty. This can be either a berth or a port charter. A berth charter is less likely and more demanding because it requires the vessel to be tied up at a named berth within the port.

In the case of a berth charter the vessel cannot be arrived until she gets into berth – in other words, when she is securely moored alongside a berth and in a position to load or unload cargo. It is not necessary for a berth to be named in a charter for it to be a berth charter; it is sufficient that there be an express right to nominate a berth. It is important to read that the charter is carefully drafted in order to avoid ambiguity. An interesting case, which illustrates this, is *The Finnix* (1975) 2 Lloyd's Rep 415 where Donaldson J (as he then was; he went on to become an outstanding judge in the House of Lords) said (*obiter*) that 'one safe berth, London' was a berth charter but that 'London, one safe berth' was a port charter.

Some people find distinctions of this kind to be illogical. They take the view that a berth charter should only be where the berth is named in the charter itself (for example, because the cargo interest owns the dock and so can guarantee the named berth) since, after all, a vessel invariably has to go to a berth in order to load or discharge cargo.

A port charter is the more likely of the two but still presents problems; there is the need to be able to establish at what point can a vessel be said to be 'arrived'? It is a question that arises on a daily basis, for example where there is congestion in the port. In other words the port is so busy that there is no room in the port and so the ship has to wait. Is this 'arrived'? It is very important to know if this is the case because, as we know, it is very expensive to operate any commercial vessel. These expenses include finance costs to buy the vessel, insurance of the vessel, registration fees, crew wages and bunker fuel costs. These will have been proportioned on a 24-hour basis (and for the purpose of quoting a freight rate to the cargo interest port fees and an element of profit will also have been added). Until the vessel is 'arrived' the costs of delay lie with the carrier; once the vessel is 'arrived' these costs fall on the cargo interest.

8.1 Arrival

The time of arrival depends on the destination on which the parties have agreed. In practice, the destination selected is generally either a port, or a specified area within a port such as a dock, or a particular loading place, such as a named berth, quay, wharf, or a mooring. If the stipulated destination is either a dock or a berth, the vessel is an arrived ship when she is in the specified area or at the agreed place. The rule applicable to a port charter has changed over the years. In *Leonis Steamship v Rank* [1908] 1 KB 499, the Court of Appeal held that where a port was referred to in a charterparty – a commercial document – 'the term is to be construed in a commercial sense in relation to the objects of the particular transaction'. On this basis, 'port' meant 'the commercial area of the port'. In *The Aello* [1961] AC 135, the *Leonis* test was held to require that the vessel should be in that part of the port where she was to be loaded when a berth became available, with the result that it was found that the *Aello* had not arrived in the port of Buenos Aires while waiting at a usual waiting area within the port that was 22 miles from the loading area. Influenced by changes 'in the kinds of ships used in maritime commerce, in means of communication and in port facilities and the management of ports' (*per* Lord Diplock) the House of Lords abandoned the *Aello* approach in *The Johanna Oldendorff*, although some phrases and ideas used in the earlier cases continued to be used in the judgments in that case.

EL Oldendorff & Co GmbH v Tradax Export SA, The Johanna Oldendorff [1974] AC 479

Facts: The *Johanna Oldendorff* was chartered to carry a bulk grain cargo from the United States to Liverpool/Birkenhead. No berth was available when the vessel arrived on 2 January 1968, and she was ordered by the port authority to anchor at the bar light vessel. Her owners gave notice of readiness. The vessel lay at anchor at the bar from 3 to 20 January ready, so far as she was concerned, to discharge.

Held:

> **Lord Reid:** . . . The question at issue is who is liable to pay for the delay . . . The argument before your Lordships turned on the time when the vessel became an arrived ship. The main contention for the owners is that she became an arrived ship when she anchored at the bar anchorage because that is within the port of Liverpool, it is the usual place where vessels lie awaiting a berth, and it was the place to which she had been ordered to go by the port authority. The reply of the charterers is that that anchorage is at least 17 miles from the dock area, or commercial area of the port, that arrival at that anchorage is not arrival at the port of Liverpool /Birkenhead and that the ship did not arrive until she proceeded to her unloading berth in the Birkenhead docks . . .
>
> [T]he essential factor is that before a ship can be treated as an arrived ship she must be within the port and at the immediate and effective disposition of the charterer and that her geographical position is of secondary importance. But for practical purposes it is so much easier to establish that, if the ship is at a usual waiting place within the port, it can generally be presumed that she is there fully at the charterer's disposal.
>
> I would therefore state what I would hope to be the true legal position in this way. Before a ship can be said to have arrived at a port she must, if she cannot proceed immediately to a berth, have reached a position within the port where she is at the immediate and effective disposition of the charterer. If she

is at a place where waiting ships usually lie, she will be in such a position unless in some extraordinary circumstances proof of which would lie in the charterer . . .

If the ship is waiting at some other place in the port then it will be for the owner to prove that she is as fully at the disposition of the charterer as she would have been if in the vicinity of the berth for loading or discharge . . .

Lord Diplock: . . . A dock encloses a comparatively small area entered through a gate. There is no difficulty in saying whether a vessel has arrived in it. As soon as a berth is vacant in the dock a vessel already moored inside the dock can get there within an interval so short that for the practical business purpose of loading or discharging cargo it can be ignored. For such purposes she is as much at the disposal of the charterer when at her mooring as she would be if she were already at the actual berth at which the charterer will later make or accept delivery of the cargo, but is unable for the time being to do so.

The area of a port, however, may be much larger. It may sometimes be less easily determinable, because of absence of definition of its legal limits or variations between these and the limits within which the port authority in actual practice exercises control of the movement of shipping; but I do not believe that in practice it is difficult to discover whether a place where ships usually wait their turn for a berth is within the limits of a named port; or is outside those limits as is the case with Glasgow and with Hull . . .

. . . If a port is congested so that on arrival within its limits the chartered vessel cannot proceed immediately to a berth to load or to discharge, it is of no business importance to the charterer where she waits within those limits, so long as it is a place (1) where she counts for turn if the port is one where vacant berths are allotted to waiting vessels in order of arrival; (2) where the charterer can communicate with her as soon as he knows when a berth will become available for the cargo to be loaded or discharged; and (3) from which the vessel can proceed to the available berth when she receives the charterer's communication, so as to arrive there as soon as the berth has become vacant or so shortly thereafter as not to be significant for practical purposes.

. . . Since it is to the interest of all concerned, of port authorities as well as charterers and shippers, that time should not be wasted by leaving berths vacant when they are available for loading or discharging cargo, the usual places for ships to wait their turn for a vacant berth are those which do possess the three characteristics that I have mentioned, if there are any such places within the limits of the port. In days of sailing ships close proximity to berths likely to become vacant may have been necessary in order that a place should possess those characteristics, but distance from the actual berth becomes of less importance as steam and diesel power replaces sail and instantaneous radio communication is available between ship and shore. In modern conditions it is possible for port authorities and charterers to know at least some hours in advance, when a berth presently occupied by a loading or discharging vessel will become vacant and available for use by the chartered vessel. Notice of similar length can be given by the charterer to the waiting vessel so as to enable her to reach the berth as soon as it becomes vacant, if she can make the journey from her waiting place to the berth within that time. And if she can she is as effectively at the disposal of the charterer for loading or discharging while at that waiting place as she would have been if waiting in the immediate vicinity of the berth.

My Lords, this no doubt is why the bar anchorage, which is within the legal limits of the Port of Liverpool and included in the area in which the port authority is entitled to control the movement of shipping, has become the usual place to which vessels are directed by the port authority to wait their turn for a berth. And the same must generally be true of usual waiting places within the limits of other ports where congestion is liable to occur. I would therefore accept as a convenient practical test as to whether a vessel has completed her loading voyage or her carrying voyage under a port charter so as to cast upon the charterer the responsibility for subsequent delay in finding a vacant berth at which her cargo can be loaded or discharged, the test as it is formulated by my noble and learned friend, Lord Reid, at the conclusion of his speech . . .

In *The Johanna Oldendorff* the usual waiting area was within the limits of the port of Liverpool. The next case, which was argued in the House of Lords not long after *The Johanna Oldendorff* had been decided, dealt with a charter to a port where the usual waiting area was outside the port limits. It was almost as though the House of Lords were being asked to confirm that they had meant what was said in the earlier decision about the location of the waiting anchorage. But since *The Johanna Oldendorff* had abandoned the rule in *The Aello* very quickly, perhaps it was reasonable to ask if the House wanted to make a further change.

Federal Commerce and Navigation Co Ltd v Tradax Export SA, The Maratha Envoy [1978] AC 1

Facts: The *Maratha Envoy* was chartered to carry grain to Brake in the river Weser. The usual waiting area for Weser ports was the Weser lightship anchorage, about 25 miles from the mouth of the river and outside the limits of Brake. While waiting for a berth, the vessel sailed up river and, off Brake, served a notice of readiness. She then returned and anchored at the lightship.

Held:

Lord Diplock: . . . My Lords, in *EL Oldendorff & Co GmbH v Tradax Export SA (The Johanna Oldendorff)* [1974] AC 479, the purpose of this House was to give legal certainty to the way in which the risk of delay from congestion at the discharging port was allocated between charterer and shipowner under a port charter which contained no special clause expressly dealing with this matter. The standard form of charterparty used in *The Johanna Oldendorff* was also that used in the instant case – the Baltimore berth grain charterparty – although in each case the destination of the carrying voyage was a port, not a berth. The allocation of this risk under this kind of charterparty depends upon when the vessel becomes an 'arrived ship' so as to enable laytime to start running and demurrage to become payable once laytime has expired . . . After a hearing extending over six days in the course of which the position of ports where the usual waiting place lies outside the limits of the port of discharge was fully considered and cases dealing with such ports were cited, this House substituted for the Parker test [*The Aello*, above] a test which I ventured to describe as the 'Reid test', which in its most summary form is stated by Lord Reid thus, at p 535:

> Before a ship can be said to have arrived at a port she must, if she cannot proceed immediately to a berth, have reached a position within the port where she is at the immediate and effective disposition of the charterer.

. . . The Reid test applies to a port charter in which there is no express provision dealing with how the misfortune risk of delay through congestion at the loading or discharging port is to be allocated between charterer and shipowner. In such a case it allocates the risk to the charterer when the waiting place lies within the limits of the port; but to the shipowner when it lies outside those limits. In a berth charter, on the other hand, it had long been settled law that, in the absence of express provision providing for some other allocation of the risk, the risk is allocated to the shipowner wherever the waiting place lies. In the case of both port and berth charters, however, it is the common practice, by the use of standard clauses, which too have been the subject of judicial exegesis, to provide expressly for the way in which the risk of delay by congestion at the loading or discharging port is to be allocated . . .

There are also standard clauses dealing specifically with the commencement of laytime at individual ports at which the usual anchorage for vessels waiting turn lies outside the limits of the port. A typical clause of this kind relating to the ports of Avonmouth, Glasgow and Hull is cited in the judgment of Roskill LJ in *The Johanna Oldendorff* [1974] AC 479, 505. A similar clause is used in the case of the four ports on the River Weser, for all of which the usual waiting place for vessels of considerable draught is an anchorage at the Weser Lightship which lies outside the limits of any of the ports. The Weser Lightship clause runs as follows:

> If vessel is ordered to anchor at Weser Lightship by port authorities, since a vacant berth is not available, she may tender notice of readiness upon arriving at anchorage near Weser Lightship, as if she would have arrived at her final loading/discharging port. Steaming time for shifting from Weser Lightship to final discharging port, however, not to count.

The use of the time lost clause or of standard clauses relating to particular ports whose waiting place is outside the limits of the port may well seem to be particularly appropriate to cases where the charterparty reserves to the charterer an option to choose a loading or discharging place out of a range of ports at some of which the risk of congestion may be greater than at others or at some of which the usual waiting place lies inside and at others outside the limits of the port; for, in the absence of any such express provision, the existence of the option means that the charterer by the way he requires the contract to be carried out may influence the incidence or extent of the risk to be borne by the shipowner.

Nevertheless, even where the extent of the risk is potentially variable according to the way in which the charterer exercises his options, a shipowner may be willing to assume that risk in the course of bargaining rather than to transfer it to the charterer and accept a lower freight rate or demurrage rate or both. He may be content to back his own knowledge and experience of conditions at the ports included in the option range and to rely also on the fact that it will generally be in the charterer's own interest to exercise his options in such a way as to cause as little delay as possible.

The instant case is about a claim to demurrage upon a vessel the *Maratha Envoy* laden with a cargo of grain for which the discharging port nominated by the charterer under a port charter was the port of Brake. This is one of the four ports on the River Weser. The other three are Bremerhaven at the mouth of the river, Nordenham downstream from Brake, and Bremen upstream, for all of which the usual waiting place for vessels of the *Maratha Envoy*'s draught is the Weser Lightship.

. . . The history of the carrying voyage is set out in detail in the judgments of the courts below. It is sufficient for your Lordships' purpose to mention that the *Maratha Envoy* reached the anchorage at the Weser Lightship on 7 December 1970. She took her turn for discharge at any of the Weser ports on her arrival at the anchorage but no valid nomination of Brake as the discharging port was made by the charterers until 10 December. When this nomination was received, it never crossed the minds of the shipowners or their agents that the *Maratha Envoy* was already an arrived ship while at the Weser Lightship anchorage. They knew she had to get to a place within the limits of the port of Brake itself before she would be entitled to give notice of readiness to discharge. Accordingly on 12 December when the tide was right, she carried out a manoeuvre which has been variously described as 'showing her chimney', 'a charade' and 'a voyage of convenience'. She weighed anchor at the lightship, proceeded up the river until she was opposite the port of Brake, turned round in midstream and went back immediately to the lightship anchorage where she remained until 30 December 1970, when her turn came round and she moved to her discharging berth in Brake. During the ten minutes or so that it took for her to turn round in the river, on 12 December notice of readiness was served upon the charterers' agents.

. . . Donaldson J held that the voyages of convenience did not serve to make the *Maratha Envoy* an arrived ship at the port of Brake.

From this judgment the shipowners appealed to the Court of Appeal [which allowed the appeal on the ground that arrival at the Weser Lightship anchorage constituted the *Maratha Envoy* an arrived ship for discharge at the port of Brake].

. . . My Lords, it is conceded by counsel for the shipowners that the Weser Lightship anchorage is outside the legal, fiscal and administrative limits of the port of Brake. It lies 25 miles from the mouth of the river in an area in which none of the port authorities of Weser ports does any administrative acts or exercises any control over vessels waiting there. It was held by a German court in 1962 that a ship waiting at the Weser Lightship anchorage is not an arrived ship. A similar decision was reached by Donaldson J in *Zim Israel Navigation Co Ltd v Tradax Export SA (The Timna)* [1970] 2 Lloyd's Rep 409, and approved by Megaw LJ when the case came before the Court of Appeal [1971] 2 Lloyd's Rep 91. Counsel also concedes that charterers, shippers and shipowners who use the Weser ports would not regard the waiting area at the lightship as forming part of any of them. All the evidence is to the contrary, the conduct of the parties and their agents, the correspondence and the oral evidence that was accepted by the judge. So is the common use in charterparties of the special Weser Lightship clause, when it is intended that time spent in waiting there for a berth should count as laytime. This way of reconciling loyal adherence to the Reid test with an inclination to find in favour of the shipowners in the instant case is not, in my view, available.

... Your Lordships would be doing a disservice to the shipping community if, so shortly after the Reid test had been laid down by this House in *The Johanna Oldendorff*, you did not reaffirm it and insist upon its application to the instant case.

I turn to the second ground relied on by the Court of Appeal as justifying departing from the Reid test ... The form of charterparty used incorporated as one of the printed clauses dealing with time for discharge:

> Time to count from the first working period on the next day following receipt ... of written notice of readiness to discharge, *whether in berth or not*.

The words italicised are surplusage in a port charter. Their presence, however, is readily explicable. The parties took a printed form appropriate to a berth charter as respects both loading and carrying voyages, and used it for an adventure in which the destination of the carrying, though not the loading voyage, was a range of named ports, not berths. The effect of this well known phrase in berth charters has been settled for more than half a century. Under it time starts to run when the vessel is waiting within the named port of destination for a berth there to become vacant. In effect it makes the Reid test applicable to a berth charter. It has no effect in a port charter; the Reid test is applicable anyway ...

... Finally, there is the voyage of convenience down to Brake and back. This was rejected by Donaldson J and, in the Court of Appeal, by Stephenson and Shaw LJJ. Lord Denning MR characterised it as commercial nonsense but said [1977] QB 324, 341 that he 'would swallow the commercial nonsense if it was the only way in which justice could be done'.

My Lords, I cannot swallow it, nor, for reasons I have stated earlier, do I see that justice would be done if I could bring myself to do so.

Notes

1 *Port charter or berth charter?* A ship was chartered to 'proceed to one or two safe ports East Canada or Newfoundland, place or places as ordered by Charterers and/or Shippers ...'. It was held that these words conferred an express power to nominate the berth or berths at which the ship should load so that the vessel did not become an arrived ship until she berthed: *Stag Line v Board of Trade* [1950] 2 KB 194, CA. In the case of a berth charter, a notice of readiness given before berthing will be invalid, in the absence of a special agreement to the contrary: see *Glencore Grain Ltd v Goldbeam Shipping Inc, The Mass Glory* [2002] EWHC 27 (Comm); [2002] 2 Lloyd's Rep 244, below.

2 *Demurrage in respect of waiting time.* Special agreements intended to deal with the effect of congestion have a long history. The *Werrastein* was chartered for a voyage from Australia to Hull to deliver grain at any customary dock, wharf or pier as ordered by the charterers 'provided that if such discharging place is not immediately available, demurrage in respect of all time waiting thereafter shall be paid ...'. The only discharging place available for grain at Hull at the relevant time was the King George Dock, which was congested. The *Werrastein*

was instructed by port authorities to wait at a customary waiting anchorage off Spurn Head, 22 miles from the King George Dock and outside the geographical, legal and fiscal limits of the port. The charterers had in the circumstances no option as to the dock, but did eventually nominate a particular berth. The shipowner's claim was made against holders and endorsees of bills of lading which incorporated all terms, conditions, clauses and exceptions in the charter. Sellers J said that the claim would have failed if the shipowner had had to show that the *Werrastein* was an arrived ship; but his Lordship held that they did not. The right to 'demurrage' in the clause quoted arose when the vessel was kept waiting because a discharge place was not immediately available; that right was quite independent and distinct from a right to demurrage after lay days had run: *Roland-Linie Schiffart GmbH v Spillers* [1957] 1 QB 109.

3   *Time lost in waiting for a berth to count as laytime.* The *Darrah* was chartered to carry cement from Novorossisk to Tripoli. The charterparty was a port charterparty on the printed GENCON form, with amendments. The fixed laytime was based on an agreed rate of discharge per weather working day of 24 consecutive hours, Fridays and holidays excepted. Time from noon on Thursday or noon on the day before a legal holiday until 8 am on the next working day was not to count. The charter also provided that time lost in waiting for a berth was to count as laytime. The vessel reached the usual waiting place in the port of Tripoli and became an arrived ship. She waited six calendar days for a berth. The shipowners claimed for those six days despite the fact that they included a Friday and a holiday and the periods from noon on the day before each. The House of Lords held: (1) that time lost clauses are superfluous in a port charter so far as concerns time spent in waiting in turn within the limits of the port. 'This counts as laytime anyway; it is laytime': *per* Lord Diplock, p 166. Thus, in a port charter, it is only where the usual waiting area is outside the limits of the port that the clause has any effect; (2) in a berth charter, the effect of the clause is that a waiting vessel which cannot berth because of congestion is treated as though she were in fact in berth. The result is that a waiting vessel cannot count all waiting days against laytime, but only those that would count if she were actually in berth; (3) notice of readiness is not required to start time running under a 'time lost' clause: *Aldebaran Maritima v Aussenhandel* [1977] AC 157.

4   *Time lost to count if cargo inaccessible?* The *Massalia (No 2)* [1962] 2 QB 416 concerned a dispute relating to demurrage under a charterparty of the vessel for a voyage from Antwerp and Bordeaux to Colombo with a part cargo of flour in bags. The owners had liberty to complete cargo en route, which they exercised at Port Said where a small amount of additional cargo (less than 10% by weight of the flour cargo) was loaded and carried under bills of lading. On arrival at Colombo, the flour was mostly overstowed by the Port Said cargo. The *Massalia* waited six days for a berth. The charter provided that time lost in waiting for a berth was to count as discharging time. Diplock J held that the owners were entitled to rely on this clause and rejected the charterers argument that no time has been 'lost' in waiting for a berth because the vessel was not ready to discharge the flour as soon as she got to berth. But compare the next case.

5   *Time lost and overlapping charters.* In *The Agios Stylianos* [1975] 1 Lloyd's Rep 426, the shipowners entered into two separate charterparties (both in the GENCON form) for the carriage of part cargoes from Constanza. One charter was for carriage of 8,800 metric tons of cement, the other for 450 tons of vehicles. Both charters contained time lost clauses and agreements to pay demurrage at the rate of $1,500 a day. The vessel waited 14 days at the discharge port (Lagos) for a berth. Both cargoes were discharged at the same berth. The owners were awarded demurrage at the agreed rate against the vehicle charterers for the 14-day waiting period. They sought to recover a similar amount from the cement charterers. It was common ground between the parties that laytime did not begin to run under the cement charter until the vehicles had been discharged. Donaldson J held that 'time lost waiting for a

berth' meant 'time lost waiting for a cement berth'. The time at Lagos was lost in waiting for a vehicle discharging berth. 'Once the vehicles had been discharged the cement charterers had the right and duty to nominate a berth, but this did not arise at any earlier point in time.' *The Massalia* was to be distinguished because the present point had not been argued in that case.

6   *Berth reachable on arrival.* 'Arrival' in the absence of any other agreement between the parties means the physical arrival of the vessel at the point where the indication or nomination of a particular loading place would become relevant if the vessel were to be able to proceed without being held up: *The Angelos Lusis* [1964] 2 Lloyd's Rep 28. 'Reachable' means able to be reached: *The President Brand* [1967] 2 Lloyd's Rep 338. 'Reachable on arrival' means immediately reachable on arrival: *Nereide v Bulk Oil, The Laura Prima* [1982] 1 Lloyd's Rep 1, noted more fully below.

7   The *Laura Prima* was chartered on the Exxonvoy 1969 form to load at one safe berth Marsa El Hariga (Libya). Clause 6 of the charterparty provided that on arrival at the port of loading, notice of readiness to load could be given 'berth or no berth' and laytime (agreed at 72 hours) would commence either six hours later or when the vessel arrived at her berth if that occurred earlier. But this clause concluded by stating that 'where delay is caused to vessel getting into berth after giving notice of readiness for any reason over which charterer has no control, such delay shall not count as used laytime'.

Clause 7 of the form provided that time consumed by the vessel on moving from loading port anchorage to loading berth would not count as laytime. Clause 9 provided that the loading place to be designated or procured by the charterers would be reachable on arrival.

The *Laura Prima* arrived at her loading port and gave the required six hours' notice of readiness. She could not reach a loading berth at once since all were occupied by other vessels. She waited nine days for a berth. The shipowners claimed demurrage. The charterers claimed to be protected by cl 6, alleging the reason for the delay (congestion) was something over which they had no control. The House of Lords held that 'reachable on arrival' meant immediately reachable on arrival. Clause 6 only protected the charterers once they had designated a loading place that actually was so reachable. It was only thereafter if some intervening event occurred causing delay over which the charterers had no control that the last sentence of cl 6 would apply: *Nereide v Bulk Oil*.

8   *Berth or no berth.* In *SA Marocaine de l'Industrie du Raffinage v Notos Maritime* [1987] 1 Lloyd's Rep 503 the *Notos* was chartered on the STB form for a voyage from Ras Tanura (Saudi Arabia) to Mohammedia (Morocco). Clause 6 of the charterparty was in a form similar to that in *The Laura Prima*. But the charters in this case had not undertaken that a berth would be reachable on arrival. After giving notice of readiness at Mohammedia, the *Notos* was delayed because swell prevented vessels from using the sea line. The shipowners argued that the charterers were obliged to ensure that a berth was available for the vessel on arrival and relied on their right to give notice of readiness 'berth or no berth' under cl 6 of the charter. The House of Lords held those words did no more than provide that a notice of readiness could be given on arrival whether or not a berth was then available. *The Laura Prima* was distinguished on the grounds that that case was concerned with a charter that was materially different in terms. Swell was held to be a cause of delay over which the charterer had no control within the meaning of cl 6.

9   *Whether in berth or not.* The *Kyzikos* was fixed under a berth charterparty to carry a cargo of steel from Italy to the US Gulf. She was ordered to discharge at Houston. A berth was

available on arrival at the port, but she could not proceed to it immediately because the pilot station was closed by fog. The charterparty provided that laytime was to commence whether the vessel was in berth or not. The House of Lord held that WIBON meant 'whether in berth (a berth being available) or not in berth (a berth not being available)'. This agreement did not cause laytime to start in cases where a berth was available on arrival at the port but was unreachable by reason of bad weather: *Seacrystal Shipping Ltd v Bulk Transport Group Shipping Co Ltd, The Kyzikos* [1989] 1 Lloyd's Rep 1.

10 *Duty to provide a cargo.* The House of Lords held in *The Aello* that if the provision of a cargo is necessary to enable a ship to become an arrived ship, the charterer has an absolute obligation to provide the cargo, or at any rate a reasonable part of it, in time to enable the ship to perform its obligation. Where the charterer fails to provide a cargo and prevents the arrival of the vessel, it was held in *Glencore Grain Ltd v Goldbeam Shipping Inc, The Mass Glory* that the shipowner is entitled to recover damages for detention in respect of the delay before she becomes an arrived ship and that those damages are to be calculated without reference to the laytime provisions and exceptions that apply from arrival; only when the vessel reaches her destination, serves notice of readiness and becomes an arrived ship, does delay fall to be regulated by the laytime agreement.

11 *Charterers' duty to facilitate arrival.* In *Sunbeam Shipping v President of India* [1973] 1 Lloyd's Rep 483, the *Atlantic Sunbeam* was chartered for a voyage from the US Gulf to one or two safe berths or ports on the east coast of India. She was ordered to discharge at Madras and Calcutta. She could not become an arrived ship at Calcutta until the consignees (who were for this purpose the same as the charterers) obtained a document called a jetty challan from the port commissioners. The owners alleged that a delay in obtaining the jetty challan delayed the ship and this was the responsibility of the charterers. Arbitrators made an award in the form of a special case in favour of the owners. Kerr J held that a term was to be implied in the charter that 'the charterers were bound to act with reasonable despatch and in accordance with the ordinary practice of the port of Calcutta in doing those acts which had to be done by them as consignees to enable the ship to become an arrived ship' (p 488). It has been suggested that this decision cannot be reconciled with *The Aello*, above, but the difference between a promise to provide a cargo and a promise to act generally to facilitate arrival is a convincing basis for distinguishing the cases.

12 *Order not to berth and load.* The *Ulyanovsk* was chartered to carry a cargo of gas oil from Skikda. The charterers had contracted to pay their suppliers by reference to a formula that depended on a market price around the bill of lading date. Anticipating a fall in price, they ordered the vessel not to berth and load on arrival. In disregard of these instructions, on arrival notice of readiness to load was given by the ship to the refinery and shippers and the vessel proceeded to berth and load. It was held that charterers could make use of the total agreed laytime of 72 running hours as they wished and they were entitled to delay the commencement of loading: *Novorossisk Shipping Co v Neopetro Co Ltd, The Ulyanovsk* [1990] 1 Lloyd's Rep 425.

8.2 Readiness

Very often problems occur with regard to the cleanliness of the cargo spaces prior to loading e.g. the new cargo is flour for human consumption, the immediately previous cargo was herring meal and the hold (cargo space) has not been properly cleaned out and so there is a danger that the previous cargo will "taint" the new cargo.

Absolute readiness is not necessary according to the decision in *The Tres Flores.*

Compania de Naviera Nedelka SA v Tradax Internacional SA,
The Tres Flores **[1974] QB 264**

Facts: The *Tres Flores* was chartered to carry maize in bulk from Bulgaria to Cyprus. The vessel gave notice of readiness at the loading port but on later inspection fumigation for pests was found necessary.

Held:

Lord Denning MR: . . . The dispute is whether laytime commenced at the time for which the master gave his notice of readiness, that is, 14.00 hours on Monday, 23 November, or only at the time when the vessel had been fumigated and was suitable to receive the cargo, that is, at 14.00 hours on Tuesday, 1 December 1970.

It seems to me that this dispute is really covered by the specific sentence in the charterparty which I have already read but which I will repeat now:

> Before tendering notice master has to take necessary measures for holds to be clean, dry, without smell and in every way suitable to receive grain to shippers/charterers' satisfaction.

That lays down a condition precedent to the validity of a notice of readiness to load. That condition precedent was not fulfilled until the fumigation had been completed on 30 November and therefore the notice of readiness could not validly be given until that time.

That is sufficient for the decision of this case; but, as the contrary has been discussed before us, it may be desirable for the members of the court to give their views upon it.

One thing is clear. In order for a notice of readiness to be good, the vessel must be ready at the time that the notice is given, and not at a time in the future. Readiness is a preliminary existing fact which must exist before you can give a notice of readiness: see *per* Atkin LJ in *Aktiebolaget Nordiska Lloyd v J Brownlie & Co (Hull) Ltd* (1925) 30 Com Cas 307, 315.

The next question, when can a ship be said to be ready? Conversely, if some things are yet to be done, what are the things which make her unready to receive cargo?

The leading case is *Armement Adolf Deppe v John Robinson & Co Ltd* [1917] 2 KB 204, where the hatch covers had not been removed at the time when the notice of readiness was given. It would be necessary for them to be removed before discharging could take place. The notice of readiness was held to be good. Then there is *Sociedad Financiera de Bienes Raices SA v Agrimpex Hungarian Trading Co for Agricultural Products, The Aello* [1961] AC 135, where a police permit was necessary before a ship could be loaded. It was held that the absence of a police permit did not prevent the *Aello* from being 'ready to load' while at the anchorage: see *per* Lord Radcliffe at pp 174–75. And finally *Shipping Developments Corporation v V/O Sojuzneftexport (The Delian Spirit)* [1972] 1 QB 103, where the vessel had not obtained free pratique and would need it before she could load. It was held that she was entitled to give notice of readiness.

In considering the cases, it seems to me that the submission which Mr MacCrindle [counsel] put forward was correct. In order to be a good notice of readiness, the master must be in a position to say 'I am ready at the moment you want me, whenever that may be, and any necessary preliminaries on my part to the loading will not be such as to delay you'. Applying this test it is apparent that notice of readiness can be given even though there are some further preliminaries to be done, or routine matters to be carried on, or formalities observed. If those things are not such as to give any reason to suppose that they will cause any delay, and it is apparent that the ship will be ready when the appropriate time arrives, then notice of readiness can be given.

In the present case there were pests in the hold such as to make the ship unready to receive cargo. Fumigation was not a mere preliminary, nor a routine matter, nor a formality at all. It was an essential step which had to be taken before any cargo could be received at all. Until the vessel had been fumigated, notice of readiness could not be given. It has always been held that, for a notice of readiness to be given, the vessel must be completely ready in all her holds to receive the cargo at any moment when she is required to receive it ...

So, both under the specific clause and at common law, I am of opinion that the presence of pests in the hold invalidated the notice of readiness. I think the decision of Mocatta J was right and I would dismiss this appeal.

(Cairns and Roskill LJJ agreed that the charter made fumigation a condition precedent to the giving of notice of readiness.)

Notes

1   *Readiness in respect of overstowed cargo.* In *The Massalia (No 2)* Diplock J held that a require-
    ment under a charterparty to give notice of readiness in respect of 'cargo', means readiness to
    discharge the cargo that is the subject of the charter, not readiness to discharge other cargo
    overstowed on it. Notice of readiness in respect of an inaccessible part cargo could not be
    given until that cargo was actually accessible.
2   *Readiness in respect of the whole of the cargo.* The *Virginia M* was chartered to carry a cargo
    of bagged calcium ammonium nitrate from Constanza to Lagos. She arrived and gave
    notice of readiness with insufficient fresh water on board to enable her to discharge the
    whole cargo by her own steam power. It was held that: (1) readiness means readiness in a
    business and mercantile sense and does not involve the completion of what are mere for-
    malities; and (2) the readiness required is readiness to discharge the whole of the cargo that
    is the subject matter of the charterparty. Readiness to discharge some of the cargo only is
    not sufficient. The case was remitted to arbitrators to decide, among other things, whether
    taking more water on board at a discharge berth was a mere formality that would not
    impede or hold up discharge and not prevent the vessel from being ready to discharge the
    whole cargo: *Unifert International SAL v Panous Shipping Co Inc, The Virginia M* [1989]
    1 Lloyd's Rep 603.

8.3 Notice of readiness

The parties to a charter can agree on any form of notice they wish, even oral notice (*Franco-British Steamship v Watson & Youell* (1921) 9 Ll L Rep 282, p 283) or they can dispense with notice alto-gether. In the absence of special agreement or a legally binding custom, the shipowner must give notice of readiness to load (*Stanton v Austin* (1892) LR 7 CP 651) but is not obliged to give notice of readiness to discharge: *Houlder v GSN* (1862) 3 F & F 170. The reason for the distinction between loading and discharge has been said to be that the charterer can be expected to take an interest in the movements of the vessel once his cargo has been loaded which he would not take prior to loading: *per* Donaldson J, *Christensen v Hindustan Steel* [1975] 1 Lloyd's Rep 398. How-ever, notice of readiness to discharge must be given if the shipowner, as is usual, has contracted to do so, as for example when the bill of lading contains a space for the insertion of the name of the 'party to be notified' and the space has been completed: *Clemens Horst v Norfolk* (1906) 11 Com Cas 141; or where the shipowner intends to rely on a 'near' clause and discharge at a place other than the primary contractual destination: *The Varing* [1931] P 79, p 87.

In order to give a valid notice of readiness, the ship must first be an arrived ship and must in fact be ready to load: *Nelson v Dahl* (1879) 12 Ch D 581. Where a charterparty expressly relates the commencement of laytime to the giving of a notice of readiness, the notice will be premature if the ship is not at the time at the agreed place (*The Agamemnon* [1998] 1 Lloyd's Rep 675) or in a fit condition to load (*Cobelfret NV v Cyclades Shipping Co Ltd, The Lindaros* [1994] 1 Lloyd's

Rep 28) or physically able to discharge (*The Mexico 1* [1990] 1 Lloyd's Rep 507, CA) or in the state required by the charter (*Surrey Shipping v Compagnie Continentale, The Shackleford* [1978] 1 WLR 1080, CA). A premature notice of readiness is a nullity and does not mature into an effective notice when the vessel reaches the right place or becomes ready: *The Mexico 1*. Nor in such a case does laytime start when the charterer knows or ought to have known of the readiness. One reason for this approach was said to be the need to avoid uncertainty about the moment at which laytime starts. However, the practical advice given by the courts to shipowners anxious to avoid disputes about premature notices – serve a further notice on any change in a vessel's circumstances – also produces uncertainty; and a second or later notice runs the risk of being seen as an admission that an earlier notice was invalid.

A notice that is despatched out of hours, just before the earliest moment permitted by the charter, in the knowledge that it would be dealt with at the start of the next working day, has been treated as a proper tender: *The Petr Schmidt* [1998] 2 Lloyd's Rep 1.

The series of decisions dealing with notices of readiness that were invalid for prematurity did not decide what should happen if no further notice was served, but the vessel thereafter started to load or discharge. When did laytime start? Did it start at all? A number of possible answers were discussed in the cases. The Court of Appeal reviewed the problem in *The Happy Day*.

Glencore Grain Ltd v Flacker Shipping Ltd, The Happy Day [2002] EWCA Civ 1068; [2002] 2 Lloyd's Rep 487

Facts: The ship was chartered on the Synacomex form to carry grain from Odessa to Cochin. She missed the tide and could not enter Cochin on arrival on 25 September 1998. Nevertheless the master purported to give notice of readiness immediately. The notice was invalid because the charter was a berth charter and there was no congestion: see *The Kyzikos*, above. The vessel berthed the following day and discharge commenced. No further NOR (notice of readiness) was ever given. Discharge was not completed until 25 December. Langley J on appeal from arbitrators held that as no valid NOR had been given, no demurrage ever became payable. The shipowners appealed to the Court of Appeal and argued that laytime had started at the commencement of discharge or thereafter at the earliest moment that a valid notice could have expired either because the notice had been accepted, or on grounds that the charterers were estopped from denying the validity of the notice or that there had been a waiver or a variation of the contract.

Held:

> **Potter LJ: 18** . . . In the absence of contract or custom, there is no common law requirement that the shipowner must give NOR to unload to the charterers. However, where (as is usual) NOR is required, the proper contents of the notice depend upon the terms of the charter. In the absence of any specific additional requirements it should state (i) that the vessel has arrived at the place (eg a particular port, area or berth) where, under the terms of the charter, she may tender notice and (ii) that the vessel is ready to perform the cargo operation required. A notice which states that the vessel is ready, but which is given at a time when it is not actually ready, is not a valid notice. These matters are not in issue. Nor is it in issue that the purpose of NOR is that of defining the time at, or following which, laytime starts to run for the purpose of calculating the period allowed to the charterers under the charter for loading or discharging; that will in turn regulate the liability of the charterers to pay demurrage if the period for loading is exceeded and charterers' right to payment by owners of despatch in respect of working time saved. That being so, if, having given premature NOR, the vessel arrives at berth and the work of unloading proceeds with the knowledge and consent of the charterers but exceeds the period of

laytime provided for in the charter, the question arises whether the law is such that it permits the charterers to treat laytime as never having commenced, to deny liability for demurrage and, indeed, to claim despatch for the entire period of laytime. It is the submission of the owners on this appeal that that is a surprising proposition productive of injustice and cannot be derived from the authorities relied upon before the judge. The charterers, on the other hand, assert (as the judge held) that such is indeed the effect of the authorities and is in any event the correct position. [His Lordship considered the authorities and continued.]

38 . . . the law at the time of the decision of Langley J was to the following effect. In a case where NOR has been given which is invalid for prematurity, the doctrine of 'inchoate' notice is not available to the owners to start laytime running as soon as the vessel becomes ready to unload (even though the charterers are aware that it is in fact ready). Time will not start to run until valid NOR is given, in the absence of an agreement to dispense with such notice, or unless there is a waiver or an estoppel binding upon the charterers in respect of the necessity for further (valid) notice. The question whether or not such agreement, waiver or estoppel can be established (which is a mixed question of law and fact) must depend upon the circumstances of the case. In particular, in a case where unloading has commenced with the knowledge and consent of the charterers or their agents and without any reservation of the charterers' position, the question arises whether that fact alone gives rise to an (implied) agreement, waiver or estoppel (as suggested by the decision of Horridge J in the *Franco-British Steamship* case (1921) 9 Ll L Rep 282 and of Donaldson J in *The Helle Skou* [1976] 2 Lloyd's Rep 205 but doubted and left for later decision by Mustill LJ in *The Mexico 1* [1990] 1 Lloyd's Rep 507). By his decision, Langley J answered that question in the negative . . .

Variation by agreement

61 Although variation, waiver and estoppel by representation are traditionally treated as virtually interchangeable pleas in support of the assertion that, on the basis of particular facts, a party has lost or may not now enforce his rights under a written contract, they are by no means synonymous. In particular (a) a variation alters the obligations to be performed under the original contract, whereas waiver and estoppel are conduct on the part of one party which does not alter the terms of the contract but merely affects the remedies in respect of a breach of those terms by the other party . . . (b) because the same formalities apply to a variation as to the formation of an original contract, a plea of variation must sustain analysis in terms of offer, acceptance and certainty of terms.

62 Mr Eder [counsel] submits that the appropriate analysis in contractual terms is that of an offer by the owners to allow the charterers to discharge the vessel on the basis that the previously tendered NOR was valid and that laytime would run throughout discharge, which was accepted by charterers without suggesting that the NOR was invalid or that laytime was not running; alternatively, an offer by charterers to discharge the vessel on the basis that the previously tendered NOR was valid and/or that laytime would run during discharge, accepted by owners in allowing discharge to proceed. In this connection he relies upon the principle that the law applies an objective test as to the communications between the parties, whether by words or conduct, and submits that each must be taken to have appreciated that the other was acting on the basis attributed to them.

63 The difficulty with such a formulation however is that the court is being asked to spell positive offer and acceptance out of conduct alone in a situation where the parties' obligations were governed by a formal written contract pursuant to which the owners were at all times purporting to act. There was thus no apparent *bilateral* intention to vary or re-negotiate the express terms of the charter, as opposed to an apparent willingness on the part of the charterer to treat as valid a notice appropriate in form and purportedly served in compliance with the terms of the charter (see 'Waiver' below).

Waiver

64 Broadly speaking, there are two types of waiver strictly so-called: unilateral waiver and waiver by election. Unilateral waiver arises where X alone has the benefit of a particular clause in a contract and decides unilaterally not to exercise the right or to forego the benefit conferred by that particular clause . . .

In such a case, X may expressly or by his conduct suggest that Y need not perform an obligation under the contract, no question of an election by X between two remedies or courses of action being involved. Waiver by election on the other hand is concerned with the reaction of X when faced with conduct by Y, or a particular factual situation which has arisen, which entitles X to exercise or refrain from exercising a particular right to the prejudice of Y. Both types of waiver may be distinguished from estoppel. The former looks principally to the position and conduct of the person who is said to have waived his rights. The latter looks chiefly at the position of the person relying on the estoppel. In waiver by election, unlike estoppel, it is not necessary to demonstrate that Y has acted in reliance upon X's representation . . .

65 So far as waiver by election is concerned, the basic proposition is that where two possible remedies or courses of action are to his knowledge open to X and he has communicated his intention to follow one course or remedy in such a manner as to lead Y to believe that his choice has been made, he will not later be permitted to resile from that position . . .

66 Thus, it is clear that whether or not the party entitled to notice has waived a defect upon which he subsequently seeks to rely, will depend upon the effect of the communications or conduct of the parties, the intention of the party alleged to have waived his rights being judged by objective standards. This being so, it seems to me clear that, in an appropriate commercial context, silence in response to the receipt of an invalid notice in the sense of a failure to intimate rejection of it, may, at least in combination with some other step taken or assented to under the contract, amount to a waiver of the invalidity or, put another way, may amount to acceptance of the notice as complying with the contract pursuant to which it is given.

67 Waiver is closely associated with the law of estoppel in that, in the case of estoppel (and at this point I leave aside estoppel by convention), it is necessary for there to have been an unequivocal representation of fact by words or conduct and, in waiver, there must similarly have been an unequivocal communication of X's intention, whether by words or conduct . . .

68 In relation to waiver, it is important to note certain features of the doctrine around which the submissions of the parties have revolved:

(1) In order to demonstrate awareness of the right waived, it must generally be shown that X had knowledge of the underlying facts relevant to his choice or indication of intention . . .

(2) The court will examine any act or conduct alleged to be unequivocal in its context, in order to ascertain whether or not it is sufficiently clear and unequivocal to give rise to a waiver . . .

(3) The courts will also examine with care any agency relationship between X and any person alleged to have made the unequivocal communication on his behalf. If that person lacked the actual or ostensible authority to waive the right or rights concerned there will be no waiver . . .

69 On the basis of the findings of fact made by the arbitrators in this case, it was, in my view, properly open to them to conclude that, as at the time discharge commenced, the charterers had waived any reliance on the invalidity of the NOR served upon the receivers or their agents in accordance with the requirements of the charterparty as a means of deferring operation of the laytime regime provided for in Clause 30. The context was as follows. The owners had served NOR upon the receivers' agents in purported compliance with the charter at a time shortly before she arrived at berth. Having arrived at berth the vessel was in fact ready to commence the cargo operation required and neither the owners nor the Master received any intimation of rejection or reservation so far as the validity of the NOR was concerned. The charterers were well aware of the matters which the NOR was concerned to convey, namely the arrival of the vessel and its readiness to discharge . . . On an objective construction of those matters, although the charterers were not under a contractual duty to indicate rejection of the NOR, by their failure to do so, coupled with their assent to commencement of discharging operations, they intimated, and a reasonable shipowner would have concluded, that the charterers thereby waived reliance upon any invalidity in the NOR and any requirement for a further notice . . .

73 . . . If, it is to be said that, by participating in the commencement of discharge on Saturday 26 September 1998, the charterers/receivers accepted the validity of the NOR, does that indicate an intention that laytime commences immediately, or does it require that NOR be treated as notionally given at the time discharge commenced, leaving intact *mutatis mutandis* the specific provisions in Clause 30 as to the interval before laytime starts to run and as to the days to be included in it? It seems to me that the latter is plainly the case. Not only was it the conclusion of the arbitrators. It entirely accords with commercial good sense. The unequivocal indication arising from commencement of loading was that the notice previously tendered was at that point accepted as valid, but it was no more than that. On that basis, the detailed provisions as to laytime contained in Clause 30 were apt to apply as from the time of the validation of the notice by acceptance, and neither the conduct of the charterers/receivers nor the circumstances of the case suggested waiver in that respect . . .

76 . . . if the charterparty provides that NOR is to be served not upon the charterers but upon the receivers/agents through whom the charterers propose to perform their obligation to discharge then, so far as the owners are concerned, the receivers are not only the charterer's agent to receive the NOR but also the persons to whom he is entitled to look to make decisions as to the readiness of the vessel and its equipment for such discharge to begin . . .

Estoppel by convention

79 Since I am of that opinion, it is not strictly necessary to consider Mr Eder's alternative submission, namely that at, or as from, the time of commencement of discharge, the parties were operating upon a common assumption that the NOR was valid and/or that it was unnecessary for the owners to serve a further NOR in order to start laytime running, so that an estoppel by convention arose whereby the charterers were precluded from later asserting that the NOR served was invalid.

80 Estoppel by convention may be held to arise where both parties to a transaction:

> . . . act on an assumed state of facts or law, the assumption being either shared by both or made by one and acquiesced in by the other: see *Republic of India v India SS Co Limited (No 2)* [1988] AC 878 at 913. The effect of an estoppel by convention is to preclude a party from denying the assumed facts or law if it would be unjust to allow them to go back on the assumption . . .

82 For the doctrine to operate, there must be some mutually manifest conduct by the parties, which is based on a common assumption which the parties have agreed on, and for that purpose 'Agreement need not be expressed, but may be inferred from conduct or even silence', *per* Staughton LJ, giving the judgment of the Court of Appeal in *Republic of India v India Steamship Co Limited ('The Indian Grace') (No 2)* [1997] 2 WLR 538 at 549.

83 . . . it seems to me that, contrary to the position on waiver, the findings of the arbitrators are inadequate to sustain their decision on the basis of (an inferred) estoppel by convention . . .

Conclusion

85 In the context of this case I would answer the question of law in relation to which leave was granted as follows. Laytime can commence under a voyage charterparty requiring service of a notice of readiness when no valid notice of readiness has been served in circumstances where: (a) a notice of readiness valid in form is served upon the charterers or receivers as required under the charterparty prior to the arrival of the vessel; (b) the vessel thereafter arrives and is, or is accepted to be, ready to discharge to the knowledge of the charterers; (c) discharge thereafter commences to the order of the charterers or receivers without either having given any intimation of rejection or reservation in respect of the notice of readiness previously served or any indication that further notice of readiness is required before laytime commences. In such circumstances, the charterers may be deemed to have waived reliance upon the invalidity of the original notice as from the time of commencement of discharge and laytime will commence in accordance with the regime provided for in the charterparty as if a valid notice of readiness had been served at that time. By answering the question in that way, I should not be thought to doubt that, in appropriate circumstances, the same result may follow by application of the doctrines of variation and estoppel . . .

Notes

1   By a charterparty on the standard form of Richards Bay coal charter, the *Lindaros* was fixed to load a cargo of coal for carriage from Richards Bay, South Africa to Antwerp. The charter provided that laytime would commence 18 hours after notice of readiness and that 'any time lost subsequently by vessels not fulfilling requirements for . . . readiness to load in all respects, including Marine Surveyor's Certificate . . . shall not count as notice time, or as time allowed for loading'. The vessel gave notice of readiness. After berthing the marine surveyor failed her for loading because of water and rust that he found in her hatches. She was subsequently passed on the following morning. It was argued that while in general a valid notice cannot be given unless and until the vessel is in truth ready to load, it was always open to the parties to alter the position by agreement to the contrary. It was held that the clause contemplated a notice being given at a time when the vessel was not in fact ready to load and that the effect of the clause was to contract out of the normal rule requiring that a vessel must be ready at the time of giving notice: *Cobelfret NV v Cyclades Shipping Co Ltd, The Lindaros*. See also to the same effect *The Jay Ganesh* [1994] 2 Lloyd's Rep 358 (WorldFood charterparty form).

2   *Acceptance of notice of readiness/estoppel*. In *Surrey Shipping v Compagnie Continentale, The Shackleford*, the vessel was chartered on the Baltimore form C grain charter for a voyage to Constanza. By a special clause it was agreed that the vessel would obtain customs entry before notice of readiness was given. The master purported to give (to the charterer's agents) notice of readiness before the vessel had been entered with customs at Constanza. The charterer's agents, who had authority to receive a valid notice of readiness, were found also to have authority to accept a premature notice of readiness which, on the facts, they were held to have done. The charterers were estopped from denying that the premature notice of readiness was valid and effective. The shipowners had relied on the acceptance of the notice of readiness to their detriment by not attempting to procure customs entry as soon as they could otherwise have done.

3   The *Helle Skou* was chartered on the GENCON form to carry a cargo of skimmed milk powder. Her previous cargo had been fish meal. By cl 22 of the berth charter she was 'to be presented with holds clean and dry and free from smell'. Notice of readiness was given although she was not in fact free from smell. The charterers were found to have accepted the invalid notice of readiness when they began to load:

> Whether it is labelled as waiver or estoppel or something else, I do not consider that the charterers can resile from this position, save upon grounds of fraud (Donaldson J).

The charterers were not allowed to reject the notice later the same day when the smell became more apparent and it was decided that the milk powder that had been loaded had to be discharged and the vessel cleaned: *Sofial v Ove Skou Rederi* [1976] 2 Lloyd's Rep 205.

9 Fixed laytime

It is conventional law that a charterer who agrees to load or discharge within a fixed period is not excused if cargo operations are delayed by circumstances outside his control, unless perhaps the contract is frustrated. But the charterer may be excused by exceptions in the charter, or if prevented from loading or discharging by the shipowner or those for whom he is responsible ('fault of the shipowner'), and possibly if the shipowner makes use of the ship for his own purposes. The first judgment in this section contains a general statement of the law. The next case – *The Fontevivo* – deals with fault of the shipowner. The final decision is the controversial recent case of the *Stolt Spur*, in which it was held that both laytime and demurrage will be interrupted if the shipowner makes use of the ship, even if there is no interference with loading or discharge.

9.1 General principles

William Alexander & Sons v A/S Hansa [1920] AC 88

Facts: The *Hansa* was chartered to carry to Ayr a cargo of wood that the charterer agreed to discharge in a fixed time. A shortage of labour at Ayr meant that the discharge was delayed.

Held:

Viscount Finlay: . . . On this appeal a great many cases were cited laying down the rule that if the charterer has agreed to load or unload within a fixed period of time (as is the case here, for *certum est quod certum reddi potest*), he is answerable for the non-performance of that engagement, whatever the nature of the impediments, unless they are covered by exceptions in the charterparty or arise through the fault of the shipowner or those for whom he is responsible. I am here adopting in substance the language used by Scrutton LJ in his work upon *Charterparties and Bills of Lading*, art 131 . . . Although no authority upon the point was cited which would in itself be binding upon your Lordships' House, there has been such a stream of authority to the same effect that I think it would be eminently undesirable to depart in a matter of business of this kind from the rule which has been so long applied, even if your Lordships felt any doubt as to the propriety of these decisions in the first instance. I myself have no doubt as to their correctness, and I understand that this is the opinion of all your Lordships. It seems to me that the appeal on this point must fail . . .

Notes

1 *'Exceptions in the charterparty'*. This is a reference to specific exceptions that are expressed to apply to the laytime provisions. A general exceptions clause in a charterparty will not normally be read as applying to provisions for laytime and demurrage unless the language is clear: *The Johs Stove* [1984] 1 Lloyd's Rep 38.

2 *'Whatever the nature of the impediments'*. Charterers have been held liable on an obligation to load or unload within a fixed time notwithstanding that they could not do so because of congestion, as in *Randall v Lynch* (1810) 2 Camp 352; ice, *Barret v Dutton* (1815) 4 Camp 333; bad weather preventing access to the ship, *Thiis v Byers* (1876) 1 QBD 244; strikes of stevedores, *Budgett v Binnington* [1891] 1 QB 35; and even absence of the vessel from the port, the ship having been ordered away by an act of the sovereign authority, *Cantiere Navale*

Triestina v Soviet Naptha [1925] 2 KB 172, CA, where it was said that it was just as if the ship had been driven to sea by stress of weather:

> . . . there can be no reason why the absence of the ship from the harbour, once the lay days have begun to run, without any fault on the part of the owner, should prevent the lay days from continuing to run and the ship going on demurrage (*per* Atkin LJ, p 207).

However, it seems that the charterer may be excused, on the principle of *Ralli v Compania Naviera* [1920] 2 KB 287, if the loading or unloading becomes illegal by the law of the port of loading or unloading. But it is insufficient if the law applied in the port merely limits the time for loading, as opposed to preventing it completely: *Compania Crystal de Vapores v Herman & Mohatta, The Maria G* [1958] 2 QB 196.

9.2 'Fault of the shipowner'

The charterer will not be in breach of an obligation to load or discharge within a fixed period if prevented from doing so by the shipowner or by those for whom the shipowner is responsible.

Gem Shipping of Monrovia v Babanaft, The Fontevivo [1975] Lloyd's Rep 399

Facts: The *Fontevivo*, a tanker, was chartered to carry gasoline from Turkey to Lattakia in Syria. She arrived at Lattakia and began discharging her cargo. However, when part only had been discharged, she sailed away claiming that the port had become unsafe owing to war risks. Three days later she returned and completed the discharge.

Held:

Donaldson J: . . . The issue raised by this award, in the form of a special case, is whether the time she was away from her berth counts as part of the laytime. Mr Cedric Barclay, sitting as the arbitrator, held that it did not.

In the absence of express exceptions, the charterer's obligation to load and discharge the vessel within the lay days is unconditional, once the vessel has reached the appropriate place. Nevertheless, it is subject to the qualification which applies to all contracts that a party is not liable for the commission of a breach if the breach arose because the other party prevented him from performing the contract and did so without lawful excuse. (See *Budgett & Co v Binnington & Co* [1891] 1 QB 35 *per* Lord Esher MR at p 38, Lindley LJ at p 40, and Lopes LJ at p 41.)

Mr Pardoe, who has appeared for the shipowners, submits that if the safety of the ship and cargo requires the removal of the vessel from the discharging berth, the removal is lawfully excused and laytime continues to run. (See *Houlder v Weir* [1905] 2 KB 267, and *Compania Crystal de Vapores of Panama v Herman and Mohatta (India) Ltd* [1958] 2 QB 196.) In the former case laytime was held to run although discharge was temporarily interrupted in order to ballast the vessel. In the latter case it continued to run whilst the vessel was temporarily away from the berth in order to avoid the danger of bore tides.

. . . The reasoning underlying both *Houlder's* case and the *Crystal* case is that the mere fact that the shipowner by some act of his prevents the continuous loading or discharging of the vessel is not enough to interrupt the running of the lay days; it is necessary to show also that there was some fault on the part of the shipowner . . .

The issue in this case is, therefore, whether discharge of the vessel was prevented by some action on the part of the shipowner and, if so, whether that action constituted fault on his part. The initial burden of proof lies on the charterers, but this they discharge by proving the removal of the vessel from the berth in the course of discharging. Thereafter the burden lies upon the shipowner of justifying this action or showing that it was involuntary.

[His Lordship then reviewed the facts and continued:] The long and the short of it is that the crew of this Somali vessel had a severe attack of cold feet in a hot climate and the master decided that the cure was to leave Lattakia. There is no finding that this was necessary for the safety of ship or cargo or that, had he left the ship at the discharging berth, she would not have been at the disposal of the charterers for the purpose of discharging.

Whatever may be the responsibility of a shipowner for the activity or inactivity of his crew in this context – a point which was left open by Lord Esher in *Budgett v Binnington* [1891] 1 QB 35, at p 39 – there is no doubt as to his responsibility for the actions of the master who decided to leave the discharging berth. On the facts found that cannot be justified and accordingly I hold that time does not run against laytime during the period of the vessel's absence from Lattakia.

Notes

1   Neither a justified nor an involuntary act of the shipowner is a 'fault', so that laytime will continue to run where loading or discharge is delayed because the carrying ship is damaged by collision without any negligence on the part of the owner, or is removed from berth to take on necessary ballast (*Houlder v Weir*, above) or to avoid damage by weather or tides (*Compania Crystal de Vapores of Panama v Herman and Mohatta (India) Ltd*, above) or to comply with a governmental order (*Cantiere Navale Triestina v Soviet Naptha*, above). But laytime or demurrage will continue to run if the vessel is removed from berth unnecessarily or only for the convenience of the owner (*Re Ropner* [1927] 1 KB 879) or is negligently run aground, even where the charter excludes liability for negligent navigation (*Blue Anchor Line v Toepfer, The Union Amsterdam* [1982] 2 Lloyd's Rep 432). As this last case shows, it is not necessary to constitute 'fault of the shipowner' that the owner's act should be a breach of contract.

2   In *Overseas Transportation v Mineralimportexport, The Sinoe* [1971] 1 Lloyd's Rep 514, affirmed on appeal [1972] 1 Lloyd's Rep 201, CA, the time allowed for discharging was exceeded because of the incompetence of the stevedores. The owners claimed demurrage. The charterparty provided that the stevedores were to be employed by charterers but 'considered as owners' servants'. Sir John Donaldson held that in employing or causing or allowing these stevedores to be employed, the charterers were in breach of their duty to the owners and could not rely upon the neglect of the stevedores as barring the owners' claim to demurrage. The charterers were, alternatively, liable to the owners in a like amount as damages for breach of their obligation to employ competent stevedores.

9.3 Use of a waiting ship by the owner

The statement of general principle in *Alexander v Hansa*, above, which is repeated in later cases, does not mention the possibility that laytime or demurrage might cease to run if a shipowner makes some use of the vessel while waiting for the charterer to load or unload. It seems likely that this omission was deliberate. In *Alexander v Hansa* the House of Lords accepted the law as laid down by the Court of Appeal in *Budgett v Binnington*. And in that case it was held that it was not an implied term of a voyage charter that the ship would be able and willing to load at every moment after laytime started. On that basis, it was thought that where laytime had begun but no berth or cargo was available, the shipowner could make use of the delay to refuel, clean, maintain or repair the ship without affecting the charterer's obligations, provided that no delay to loading or discharge was caused. However, in the next case, *The Stolt Spur*, the ship was a parcels tanker chartered to carry a part cargo. She was discharged, cleaned and loaded with other cargo while waiting for a berth. The court reviewed the older cases and identified a wider principle – wider than 'fault of the shipowner' – which can result in the interruption of laytime and demurrage.

Stolt Tankers Inc v Landmark Chemicals SA, The Stolt Spur [2002] 1 Lloyd's Rep 786

Facts: The *Stolt Spur*, a parcels tanker designed to carry several distinct liquid cargoes at the same time, was chartered to carry a part cargo from Rotterdam to Bombay. The vessel arrived, gave an effective notice of readiness and laytime commenced. No berth was available for 17 days because of congestion. While the laytime was running, the ship left the waiting anchorage for six days to discharge cargo carried under a concurrent charter and to clean the discharged tanks. While on demurrage she again shifted to load cargo under another part charter.

Held:

> **Andrew Smith J:** ... The charterers ... contend that the law is correctly stated in *Scrutton on Charter Parties* (20th ed) in the following passage (italics added):
>
>> Demurrage becomes payable when the lay-days allowed for loading or unloading have expired ... *However, in order to be entitled to claim demurrage, the shipowner is under an obligation to have the vessel ready and available to load or discharge.* Thus, if the shipowner for his own purposes removes the vessel from the charterer's disposition, eg for bunkering, or if when on demurrage at the first port of loading she is moved to a second loading port named in the charter, no demurrage is payable for the period when the vessel is so removed from the charterer's disposition or is on passage (at p 302, art 155).
>
> The sentence in italics was introduced into the 20th ed of the work which was published in 1996, and is not found in the 19th ed, published in 1984. The authority cited in support of it is the decision of Mr Justice Evans in *Ellis Shipping Corporation v Voest Alpine Intertrading (The Lefthero)* [1991] 2 Lloyd's Rep 599 at p 608.
>
> ... Although these views are expressed in relation to whether demurrage is payable, the same principles must apply to the question whether laytime runs.
>
> *The Lefthero* concerned the charter-party of a vessel for a voyage to Bandar Khomeini in 1983, at the time of Iran/Iraq war. Because of the war the pilot refused to take the vessel north of Bushire, and in the end the parties agreed terms under which the cargo was to be discharged there. Discharge at Bushire took longer than it would have taken at Bandar Khomeini, and the first point that arose for decision upon the owners' claim for demurrage was whether the charterers were protected by a provision exempting responsibility for the result of 'restraint of princes'. Mr Justice Evans held that they were. However, the charterers advanced a second defence to the demurrage claim, that the additional period of delay resulted from the owners' own breach of contract in failing to proceed to Bandar Khomeini, and this 'default' prevented them from claiming demurrage, even though the breach was excused by the 'restraint of princes' provision. Mr Justice Evans held that the owners were not guilty of 'default' or 'fault'. However, he continued as follows:
>
>> It seems to me that charterers, if they are to succeed on this issue, must rely upon the 'wider principle' referred to by Mr Justice Parker, in *The Union Amsterdam* ...

The authorities show . . . that the charterer undertakes an absolute obligation to pay demurrage, subject to exceptions and to 'fault', but this depends in its turn, in my judgment, upon the shipowners' obligation to have the vessel ready and able to give discharge in accordance with contract. This cannot be stated as an absolute obligation . . . but it is nevertheless a qualified obligation, non-performance of which will prevent the shipowner from recovering demurrage. Thus, no claim lies when the ship is proceeding from one loading, or discharging, port to another; not because the time on passage is an exception, but because the ship is proceeding on the voyage, not being detained by the charterers, during that period: *Breynton v Theodorou & Co* (1924) 19 Ll L Rep 409. The wider principle underlying the authorities is like the larger theme which goes through the Enigma Variations, but which is never played.

[After a full review of the cases his Lordship continued] I consider that if a vessel is unavailable for cargo operations, it is natural to regard that in itself as preventing the loading or discharge of the vessel. It is a cause of any delay in cargo operations. This, it seems to me, is why the 'wider principle' in no way conflicts with such authorities as *William Alexander* . . .

Mr Houghton [for the owners] submits that this conclusion would introduce uncertainty into the routine and largely mechanical calculation of laytime and demurrage, and raise questions as to whether it would be necessary for the vessel throughout her wait to maintain an absolute state of readiness to shift to her berth. I am not persuaded by these arguments: the requirement is one of what Mr Justice Hobhouse in *The Virginia M* [1989] 1 Lloyd's Rep 603 at p 606 described as 'readiness in a business and mercantile sense [which] does not involve completion of what are mere formalities'.

Demurrage is payable, as Mr Justice Donaldson pointed out in *Navico AG v Vrontados Naftiki Etaira PE* [1968] 1 Lloyd's Rep 379 at p 383 because the shipowner, having agreed freight to cover the voyage and an agreed time for loading and discharging processes, 'faces serious losses if the processes take longer than he had bargained for and the earning of freight on the ship's next engagement is postponed', and the charterer agrees to compensate him for those losses by way of demurrage. If a vessel is not available for the charterers' cargo operations but being used by the owners for their own purposes, there is no reason that they should pay compensation. She is not being detained by the charterers.

The commercial arbitrators in this case came to the clear view that it would be wrong for the owners to be able to claim that laytime ran during the first period and demurrage accrued during the second period when they were employing the vessel for their own purposes. I agree with that view, and uphold their award.

Note

The 'wider principle' that defeated the claim for demurrage in this case is expressed in the judgment in at least three different ways. First, in the words used by Scrutton, the claim did not succeed because the shipowner failed 'to have the vessel ready and available to load'. *The Lefthero* used a very similar phrase but added a second idea, that the claim in that case failed because the ship was 'not being detained by the charterer'. The third possibility, using the words in the penultimate paragraph above of the judgment in The *Stolt Spur*, is that the claim failed because the vessel was 'was not available for the charterers' cargo operations but being used by the owners for their own purposes'.

All three formulations are open to objection. The first is inconsistent with the decisions of the Court of Appeal in *Budgett v Binnington* and *Cantiere Navale Triestina v Soviet Naptha*, which rejected the notion that continued readiness is a precondition of a claim to demurrage. It is also inconsistent with *The Tres Flores*, above, which recognised that a ship is ready enough if she is ready when wanted.

The second version of the wider principle – *the ship was not detained by the charterer* – raises problems of causation. On the facts if a berth had been available for the *Stolt Spur*, the vessel would not have attempted to discharge, clean or load other cargo; the owners' acts caused no extra delay; no time would have been saved for the charterers if the ship had remained in the waiting anchorage. The effective cause of the 17-day delay was congestion, something for which the charterers had agreed to be responsible, so that the ship could properly be said to have been detained by them.

The third version of the wider principle – *the ship was not available for the charterers' cargo operations but being used by the owners for their own purposes* – treats the ship as unavailable to the charterer because the owners managed to make some economic use of her while waiting. The use made by the owners ought to be treated as irrelevant. They did not contract to keep her in a continuous state of readiness or to keep her inactive if she was detained by the charterer: it is plain that a parcels tanker may be put to profitable use if kept waiting under a part charter. But the reported evidence does not show the nature or extent of the additional benefit, if any, that accrued to the owners by discharging, cleaning and then loading other cargo. It cannot be assumed that the shipowners did receive a windfall, or that if they did, this windfall was unanticipated or was not taken into account in negotiating the relevant charters or that in justice it ought to be shared with these particular charterers. If there is the potential for windfall profit in the case of part charters of parcels tankers, the identification of a fair solution is something that ought to be left for negotiation by the parties themselves. The need for a 'wider principle' is not therefore clear. And wide new principles with alternative formulations are unsettling. In this case, laytime ceased for a period because the owners were cleaning tanks. Must all laytime and demurrage calculations now include extracts from engine and deck logs, so that any beneficial use made of a ship is excluded from the calculations? Will a series of decisions be necessary to settle questions such as the credit to be given to a charterer if an engineer undertakes a routine replacement of a part? Where is the line to be drawn? Must credit be given if the crew of a waiting ship spends their time chipping rust or washing the decks?

10 Calculating fixed laytime

If a charterparty does not contain an express term fixing the time to be taken in loading and discharging cargo, it is implied that those operations will be carried out within a reasonable time. Voyage charters that do not fix laytime are very unusual today, but the older cases are summarised in the next section. Today it is almost invariable practice for laytime to be fixed. This can be done directly, for example cargo to be loaded within five days. It can also be fixed a little less directly by an agreement that a specified weight or measurement of cargo will be loaded or discharged in a particular period of time, for example 100 tons per working day 'and as the burden of the ship was known and *id certum est quod certum reddi potest*, this was equivalent to naming a certain number of days': *Postlethwaite v Freeland* (1880) 5 App Cas 599, p 618, *per* Lord Blackburn.

Where loading or discharge cannot be carried on continuously, as for example in the case of dry cargo that cannot be unloaded in wet weather or in the case of ports that do not work on particular days, it is common for the agreed laytime to be based on an estimate of the actual time that will be needed, with exclusions for periods such as holidays or wet days. The *prima facie* meanings and effect of a number of words or phrases in common use in calculating laytime were considered by Lord Devlin in *Reardon Smith Line v Ministry of Agriculture* [1963] AC 691:

> Day: a calendar day of 24 hours ('in the beginning a day was a day – a Monday, a Tuesday or a Wednesday, as the case may be').
> *Conventional day*: a day of 24 hours which starts from the time when a notice of readiness expires. Replaces calendar day when a charter provides, eg, that time for loading shall commence 12 hours after written notice has been given between 9.00 am and 6.00 pm.

Working day: a description of a type of day of 24 hours, not a reference to the part of a day in which work is carried out. A day for work as distinguished from a day for religious observance or for play or rest.

Weather working day: *prima facie* a species of working day. ('It is well established that whether a day is a weather working day or not depends on the character of the day and not on whether work was actually interfered with.') When bad weather occurs, a reasonable apportionment should be made 'according to the incidence of the weather upon the length of day that the parties either were working or might be expected to have been working at the time'.

Notes

1 *Holidays excepted*. A charterparty provided that the vessel should proceed to and load at one safe port US Gulf, loading at the average rate of 1,000 tons per weather working day of 24 consecutive hours, Saturday afternoon, Sundays and holidays excepted. The vessel was ordered to Lake Charles, Louisiana. The question stated by the arbitrator for the court was whether at that port Saturday mornings did or did not count as laytime. Donaldson J held that: (1) on the evidence, that Saturday was a working day in the port as it was a day on which work was ordinarily done; (2) that a working day could nevertheless be a holiday; and (3) that whether a day was a holiday depended on local law and custom. An act of the Louisiana legislature declared all Saturdays to be holidays in an area that included Lake Charles and that was conclusive: *Controller of Chartering of the Govt of India v Central Gulf Steamship, The Mosfield* [1968] 2 Lloyd's Rep 173.

2 *Holidays worked*. In *James Nelson v Nelson Line* [1908] AC 108, the House of Lords held that where holidays were excepted from laytime but nevertheless loading continued during the holidays, an agreement to treat a holiday as a working day and count it among the lay days could not be inferred. Such an agreement had to be proved.

3 *Time lost through rain*. The contract provided 'should any time be lost whilst steamer is in a loading berth owing to work being impossible through rain ... the amount of actual time so lost during which it is impossible to work owing to rain ... to be added to the loading time'. It was held by Greer and Romer LJJ (Scrutton LJ dissenting) that to take advantage of this provision, the charterers must show: (1) that rain in fact made work impossible; and (2) that, for that reason, time was in fact lost: *Burnett Steamship v Danube and Black Sea Shipping Agencies* [1933] 2 KB 438, CA.

4 *Weather permitting*. It has been held that there is no material difference between a clause that fixes laytime by reference to 'working days weather permitting' and clauses that do so by reference to 'weather permitting working days' (*The Camelia and The Magnolia* [1978] 2 Lloyd's Rep 182) or to 'running days weather permitting' or 'running hours weather permitting' (*Gebr Broere v Saras* [1982] 2 Lloyd's Rep 436). In *Dow Chemical v BP Tanker, The Vorras* [1983] 1 Lloyd's Rep 579, the Court of Appeal held that '72 hours weather permitting' meant '72 hours during which the weather conditions are such that loading or discharging is possible'. In that case, a port charter, the *Vorras* had arrived at the loading port but was awaiting a berth: Sir John Donaldson MR said that in his judgment (p 584):

> the weather prohibited any vessel of this general type from loading and it is nothing to the point that owing to the presence of another vessel in the berth, the prohibition was not the operative cause which prevented the vessel from loading.

5 *Cargo be loaded at the average rate of [100] tons per working hatch*. The alternative expressions working hatch/available working hatch have been held to mean an upper deck hatch that can be worked either because under it is a hold into which cargo can be loaded or a hold

out of which cargo can be discharged, in either event being a hatch that the party responsible for loading or discharging is not for any reason disabled from working: *Cargill v Rionda de Pass, The Giannis Xilas* [1982] 2 Lloyd's Rep 511, *per* Bingham J, following the decision of the Court of Appeal in *The Sandgate* [1930] P 30. On this basis, it has been said that a hatch might be unworkable because the loading or discharging of that hatch has been completed or because of physical damage or perhaps because the master insists that the centre holds are loaded first to preserve the vessel's trim. The reference to an average rate of loading means that there is no obligation to load any particular amount on a particular day.

But in considering workability it is necessary to disregard any unevenness in loading (or discharge) that arises from the shippers' choice as opposed to reasons that disable them from working the hatches evenly: *Cargill v Marpro, The Aegis Progress* [1983] 2 Lloyd's Rep 570, p 574. If the rule were otherwise, and the laytime calculation was based simply on the way in which the holds are in fact loaded or discharged, then charterers might be able unfairly to influence the total of the lay days. For example, suppose a charterer agrees to load a ship at an average rate of 300 tons per working hatch per day, the vessel has three hatches, and a capacity in tons in No 1 hold of 1,200 tons, No 2 hold, 900 tons and No 3 hold, 600 tons. If the charterer loads at the agreed rate but concentrates on one hold at a time, and each were to be treated as 'unworkable' when filled, the loading could take six days. But if all holds were loaded simultaneously at the average rate, loading might be completed in four days, which is the time taken to load the largest hold. To prevent the length of laytime depending on the whim of the charterer, the laytime calculation under this clause therefore ignores the way in which the charterer in fact chooses to load the vessel: *Compania de Navigacion Zita SA v Louis Dreyfus & Cie, The Corfu Island* [1953] 1 WLR 1399, explaining *The Sandgate*. The result of this is that in most cases the length of laytime can be found by taking the quantity of cargo passing through the hatch or hold receiving or discharging the largest quantity and then dividing that figure by the average rate figure fixed by the charterparty.

This approach ('the *Sandgate* formula') has to be modified in exceptional cases, such as *The Aegis Progress*, where more than one hatch had to be taken into account in calculating the laytime. In *The Aegis Progress* the vessel loaded at two ports and different holds were workable in the two ports. Permitted laytime was held to consist of the time required to load the critical hold in Port 1 added to the time required to load the hold that was critical in Port 2.

Although this type of clause was described in *The Sandgate* by Scrutton LJ as 'ambiguous and mysterious', more recently Hobhouse J in *The Aegis Progress* (at p 573) has explained that: 'The convenience of such an approach where one is concerned with an fob shipment such as the present is obvious. The vessel is provided by the buyers. The sellers will normally not know at the time of contracting what the vessel is to be, nor what its capacity will be, nor its number of holds. They do not know whether it will be part laden. They do not know whether it will be loading other cargo. They do not know what draft, trim or stability restrictions it may be subject to. They will not normally have any right to give orders or directions to the vessel. These points are illustrated in the present case. The vessel had seven hatches; she was already partly laden; the master did impose restrictions on the way in which the vessel could be loaded. The workable hatch approach provides a sensible basis for dealing with this situation . . .'

6 *Cargo to be discharged at the average rate of 1,000 metric tons basis five or more available workable hatches pro rata if less number of hatches per weather working day.* The House of Lords

(Lord Templeman dissenting) held that this clause selected an overall rate for the ship that was qualified only to the extent that the overall rate was to be reduced *pro rata* if one or more hatches were unavailable at the start of loading or became unavailable temporarily in the course of discharge. But on this form of words the reference to available workable hatches did not override the overall rate for the ship and substitute a rate per available hatch. The mere fact that discharge of any particular hatch was completed would not itself affect the computation of laytime. Lord Templeman dissented, holding that 'available workable hatch' had an established meaning which could not be ignored: *President of India v Jebsens (UK) Ltd, The General Capinpin* [1991] 1 Lloyd's Rep 1.

7   *Cargo to be loaded at the average rate of 120 metric tons per hatch per weather working day.* The vessel had five hatches. It was held that this clause was no more than a roundabout way of saying that the vessel should be loaded at an average rate of 600 tons per day. *The Sandgate* [1930] P 30 and *Zita v Louis Dreyfus, The Corfu Island* (above) were distinguished by the absence of a reference to 'working' or 'available working' hatches: *Lodza Compania de Navigacione SA v Govt of Ceylon, The Theraios* [1971] 1 Lloyd's Rep 209, CA.

8   *Charterers to have right to average the days allowed for loading and discharging.* In the absence of an agreement of this sort, time for loading and discharging have to be considered and calculated separately: *Marshall v Bolckow Vaughan* (1881) 6 QBD 231. Under this clause if the charterer chooses to exercise the right the two calculations are still kept 'entirely separate until the very end when a balance is struck. If time is saved on discharge it is set against the excess time of loading, or vice versa, and in that way, a net result is arrived at': *Alma v Salgaoncar* [1954] 2 QB 94, *per* Devlin J. The implications of using this method depend on the meaning of 'time saved' and on rates of demurrage and despatch. Where, as is often the case, the despatch rate is half the demurrage rate, it will be in the charterer's interests to be able to average.

9   *Loading and discharge time to be reversible.* The words 'to be reversible' give a charterer the right to choose either to draw up separate time sheets for loading and discharge ports and calculate demurrage/despatch accordingly or, if preferred, to draw up one time sheet dealing with both ports and so, in effect, pool or aggregate the laytime at each end of the voyage: *Fury Shipping v State Trading Corp of India, The Atlantic Sun* [1972] 1 Lloyd's Rep 509.

10 *Completion of loading.* The *Argobec* was chartered on the Baltimore berth grain form and ordered to load a cargo of grain at Sorel for carriage to the UK. The charter provided that the vessel was 'to be loaded according to berth terms, with customary despatch and if detained longer than five days ... charterer to pay demurrage ...'. Regulations of statutory force in the port required grain carried in the *Argobec's* 'tween deck to be in bags. A certificate of the port authorities that the regulations had been complied with was also required before the vessel could sail. At Sorel, the cargo of bulk wheat was put on board by elevators. After the lay days expired, loose grain continued to be poured into the *Argobec's* 'tween deck where it was bagged by stevedores employed on behalf of the ship. Charterers argued that the vessel was 'loaded' once the elevators had stopped and a full cargo of bulk grain had been put on board. The shipowners claimed that the vessel was not loaded until the grain had also been bagged and stowed. The Court of Appeal, upholding the owner's argument, held that the cargo was not loaded until the cargo was so placed in the ship that the ship could proceed on her voyage in safety. It made no different that this work had to be done at the end of the loading operation or that the shipowner had to pay the costs involved: *Argonaut Navigation v Ministry of Food* [1949] 1 KB 14, CA.

On what seems to be the same principle, Webster J held as an alternative ground of decision in *Total Transport v Amoco Transport, The Altus* [1985] 1 Lloyd's Rep 423 that time spent by a tanker in avoiding pollution by flushing pipelines through which the vessel has been loaded, was part of loading. A reasonable time to disconnect terminal hoses is probably also part of loading, although in tanker charters there is often an express agreement on this point.

11 *Concurrent charterparties.* In *Sarma Navigation v Sidermar* [1982] 1 Lloyd's Rep 13, CA, the *Sea Pioneer* was the subject of two charters in the GENCON form between the same parties, for the carriage of part cargoes of, respectively, steel bars and steel coils. In the event, the port of delivery for both cargoes was the same. At that port (Puerto Cabello, Venezuela) she was delayed for approximately three weeks. Both charters provided that time waiting for a berth should count as discharging time. The freight rates differed under the charters, but both provided for discharge at the rate of 1,000 metric tons per weather working day and both provided for demurrage at the rate of $3,000 per running day. The steel coils were discharged first, followed by the bars: there was an overlap of a few hours during which time both cargoes were being discharged concurrently. The owners claimed demurrage under both charters. The Court of Appeal held that the two charters were complementary and were to be read together. But while the charterers were entitled to the laytime allowed by both charters, which was to be added together (that is, the rate of discharge per day was *not* doubled), the owners were only entitled to $3,000 per day for detention.

A result that differs from that in *The Sea Pioneer* was reached in *The Oriental Envoy* [1982] 2 Lloyd's Rep 266. In that case, two charters (the 'June' and 'July' charters) were agreed between the same parties: both charters dealt with cargoes of rice in bags. Both cargoes were eventually discharged at the same port. However, the July agreement was made six weeks after the June charter and the freight rates, demurrage rates and cargo quantities differed as between the two agreements. Neither charter related to a specific vessel, but both gave the owners a right to nominate. The owners, as they were entitled to do, nominated the named vessel to lift the first and part of the second chartered cargo. It was held that the two charterparties had to be read separately. It was also held that the owners became entitled to demurrage under the June charter when laytime expired under that charter (27 December) and under both charters when laytime had also expired under the July charter (7 March).

11 Laytime not fixed

The approach to be applied where laytime is not fixed is summarised by Lord Atkinson in the following extract from *Van Liewen v Hollis.*

Van Liewen v Hollis, The Lizzie [1920] AC 239

Facts: This was an action brought in the Hull County Court to recover 11 days' demurrage allegedly incurred while the ship waited for a berth in the congested Victoria Dock. The claim was based on a custom of the Port of Hull governing discharge of timber cargoes. The House of Lords held that the custom did no more than impose an obligation on charterers to discharge within a time that was reasonable in all circumstances outside their control.

Held:

Lord Atkinson: . . . If by the terms of the charterparty the charterers have agreed to discharge the chartered ship within a fixed period of time, there is an absolute and unconditional engagement for the non-performance of which they are answerable, whatever be the nature of the impediments which prevented them from performing it, and thereby causing the ship to be detained in their service beyond the time stipulated. If no time be fixed expressly or impliedly by the charterparty the law implies an agreement by the charterers to discharge the cargo within a reasonable time, having regard to all the circumstances of the case as they actually existed, including the custom or practice of the port, the facilities available thereat, and any impediments arising therefrom which the charterers could not have overcome by reasonable diligence: *Postlethwaite v Freeland* (1880) 5 App Cas 599; *Hick v Raymond & Reid* [1893] AC 22; and *Hulthen v Stewart & Co* [1903] AC 389.

Notes

1   *Laytime fixed by implication.* A charterparty in the Chamber of Commerce White Sea Wood form ('Merblanc') provided for discharge 'with customary steamship despatch as fast as the steamer can … deliver'. It was argued that the shipowner would know and the charterer could ascertain the time required for delivery of the cargo when the ship was working as fast as she could. Since that time could be measured by days and hours, it was contended that, in effect, the time for discharge had been fixed. The House of Lords rejected this argument. The clause was insufficient to fix laytime. Lord Macnaghten said that: 'in order to impose such a liability the language used must in plain and unambiguous terms define and specify the period of time within which delivery of the cargo is to be accomplished' (*Hulthen v Stewart* [1903] AC 389).

   Similarly, obligations to load or discharge 'with all dispatch according to the custom of the port' (*Postlethwaite v Freeland*, above), or 'with all dispatch as customary' (*Castlegate Steamship v Dempsey* [1892] 1 QB 854, CA and *Lyle Shipping v Cardiff Corp* [1900] 2 QB 638) have also been held to be insufficiently definite and free from ambiguity for the charterparty in question to be treated as having a fixed laytime. In all these cases, therefore, the obligation was to load or unload within a reasonable time.

   References to 'custom' in this context are taken to refer primarily to the customary or established working practices of the port; they are interpreted as references to the manner of loading or discharge rather than to the time that those activities take: *Dunlop v Balfour, Williamson* [1892] 1 QB 507, CA; *Castlegate Steamship v Dempsey*, above.

2   *Reasonable time.* Since 'all the circumstances' are relevant, it is clear that a reasonable time will depend on the terms of the particular contract of affreightment (*Carlton v Castle Mail* [1898] AC 486, p 491, *per* Lord Herschell), which must include both the nature of the cargo and the vessel. Both the normal features of the port and any unusual circumstances can also be taken into account. Thus, both delay caused by tides (*Carlton v Castle Mail*) and by strikes (*Hick v Raymond & Reid* [1893] AC 22) can extend the period that would otherwise be allowed. Delays arising out of the settled and established working practices of the port are also relevant. This is so whether or not the contract expressly incorporates a phrase of the 'according to the custom of the port' type mentioned above: *Postlethwaite v Freeland*, p 613, *per* Lord Blackburn, but compare Lord Herschell in *Hick v Raymond*, at p 30. However, circumstances to be taken into account do not include those caused by a default for which the charterer is held responsible, or which the charterer could be expected to have avoided.

3   A cargo of wheat was shipped under bills of lading on the *Derwentdale* at Taganrog for carriage to London. Time for discharge was not fixed by the bills of lading. The respondents, who were consignees and holders of the bills of lading, employed the dock company to discharge the vessel. After discharge had been commenced, a strike of dock workers began. Completion of discharge was delayed by nearly four weeks. It was admitted that during the

strike it was not possible for the respondents either to find any other person to provide the labour or to obtain the necessary labour themselves. It was held that the respondents' obligation was to discharge within a reasonable time under the circumstances as they actually existed, since those circumstances had not been caused or contributed to by them. The respondents were not therefore liable to damages for detention of the vessel: *Hick v Raymond*.

4   The *Cumberland Lassie* was chartered to deliver at East London at a safe wharf or as near thereto as she could safely get, a cargo of steel rails and fastenings. The cargo was 'to be discharged with all dispatch according to the customs of the port'. The vessel had to be lightened before it could cross the harbour bar at East London. Because of the lack of lighters and the number of ships awaiting discharge the vessel had to wait for 24 working days before lightening could begin. No more lighters could have been obtained from any other source in the time available. Discharge was completed as rapidly as possible in all the circumstances. It was held that the shipowner was not entitled to demurrage for the delay: 'Difficult questions may sometimes arise as to the circumstances which ought to be taken into consideration in determining what time is reasonable. If (as in the present case) an obligation, indefinite as to time, is qualified or partially defined by express or implied reference to the custom or practice of a particular port, every impediment arising from or out of that custom or practice, which the charterer could not have overcome by the use of any reasonable diligence, ought (I think) to be taken into consideration.' (*Postlethwaite v Freeland* (1880) 5 App Cas 599, *per* Lord Selborne LC)

5   The *Ardandearg* was chartered to load a cargo of coal at Newcastle, New South Wales for carriage to Java. Time for loading was not fixed. The cargo was to be loaded in the usual and customary manner. The vessel was delayed for 31 days because the charterers had failed to procure a cargo. Held: the charterers' primary duty to provide a cargo was distinct from their subsequent duty to load that cargo in a reasonable time. The primary duty was, on the facts, absolute and unqualified. An assertion that the charterers did nothing unreasonable was therefore no answer to the shipowners' claims for damages for detention of the vessel where breach of the primary duty caused the delay: *Ardan Steamship v Andrew Weir* [1905] AC 501.

6   The *Julia* was chartered to carry oak logs from Danzig to Millwall Dock. The more usual method of discharge at that dock was to lift the logs direct into railway trucks. It was found that it was also practicable to discharge into lighters. Discharge took an extra four days because too few trucks and no lighters were provided by the defendants, who were receivers of the cargo. The defendants were held liable in an action for damages for detention because they failed to show that they had used reasonable exertions to get either railway trucks or lighters: 'As the result I come to the conclusion that it has not been shown that the defendants used reasonable care to provide for the discharge, and I am of opinion that they did not exhaust all available means. It is therefore unnecessary to discuss all the cases ... Where there are alternative methods of discharge it is clear that the defendant must use all available methods and exhaust all efforts to effect the discharge. There will, therefore, be judgment for the plaintiffs for four days demurrage.' (*Rodenacker v May* (1901) 6 Com Cas 37, *per* Mathew J)

12 Demurrage

Failure by a charterer to load or discharge within the agreed laytime is a breach of contract. The shipowner is then entitled to damages for the period during which he is deprived of the use of his ship: *The Dias* [1978] 1 Lloyd's Rep 325. It is common practice in voyage charters to specify a demurrage rate, that is an amount payable as agreed damages for each day or part of a day that a vessel is detained by the charterer. An agreement to demurrage is not, therefore, the payment of the contractual price for the exercise of a right to detain: *The Lips* [1987] 2 Lloyd's Rep 311. It is no different in nature from any agreement providing for payment of liquidated damages: *Chandris v Isbrandtsen-Moller* [1951] 1 KB 240.

But damages for detention are not always governed by demurrage clauses. A shipowner will be entitled to unliquidated damages for detention for failure to load or discharge within the agreed time, if either: (a) laytime has expired and there is no agreement to pay demurrage; or (b) a demurrage period is fixed and has expired; for example, if the charterparty provides for 72 hours for loading and 72 hours on demurrage and a further delay then occurs. If the demurrage period is not fixed, the demurrage rate applies not just for a reasonable time but for as long as the ship is in fact detained under the contract: *Western Steamship v Amaral Sutherland* [1913] 3 KB 366.

The cases dealt with in this section deal with three questions: to which breaches of contract do demurrage clauses apply? Is demurrage payable continuously after commencement? How long can a charterer insist that a ship wait on demurrage?

12.1 Effect of an agreement to pay demurrage

An agreement to pay demurrage is normally treated as preventing the shipowner recovering from the charterer more than the agreed sum for the wrongful detention of his vessel. This is so however the delay is caused, whether by simply failing to load or discharge within the laytime, even if the delay could be described as deliberate: *Suisse Atlantique v NV Rotterdamsche Kolen Centrale*, below; or by failing to provide a cargo: *Inverkip Steamship v Bunge* [1917] 2 KB 193, CA; or by providing a cargo of the wrong sort: *Chandris v Isbrandtsen-Moller*, noted below. But while a demurrage clause limits damages recoverable for delay, it does not prevent the recovery of damages of some other character (such as deadfreight) if a breach of contract other than failure to load or discharge within the laytime has also occurred: *A/S Reidar v Arcos* [1927] 1 KB 352, noted below.

Suisse Atlantique v NV Rotterdamsche Kolen Centrale [1967] AC 361

Facts: The appellants chartered the *General Guisan* to the respondents to carry coal from the US to Europe; the charter was for a total of two years' consecutive voyages. Loading and discharge times were fixed with demurrage at $1,000 a day. As a result of failures by the charterers to load and discharge within the lay days, the ship did not complete as many voyages as she could have done. The owners claimed damages calculated on the basis of the freights they would have earned if the vessel had not been wrongfully detained. They argued that demurrage provisions ceased to apply where the breach for which a charterer was responsible was such as to entitle the owner to treat the charterparty as repudiated. It was held that: (1) there is no rule of law that deprives demurrage provisions of effect when the breach for which the charterer is responsible is such as to entitle the shipowners to treat the charterparty as repudiated; and (2) it is a question of construction of the contract as a whole whether demurrage provisions apply in the circumstances of a particular breach of contract. The demurrage provisions in this case applied to the whole of the periods of detention.

Held:

Lord Wilberforce: . . . [W]hat is the legal nature of the demurrage clause; is it a clause by which damages for breach of the contract are agreed in advance, a liquidated damages clause as such provisions are commonly called, or is it, as the appellants submit, a clause limiting damages?

... The form of the clause is, of course, not decisive, nor is there any rule of law which requires that demurrage clauses should be construed as clauses of liquidated damages; but it is the fact that the clause is expressed as one agreeing a figure, and not as imposing a limit; and, as a matter of commercial opinion and practice, demurrage clauses are normally regarded as liquidated damage clauses ...

The clause being, then, one which fixes, by mutual agreement, the amount of damages to be paid to the owners of the vessel if 'longer detained' than is permitted by the contract, is there any reason why it should not apply in the present case in either of the assumed alternatives, ie, either that the aggregated delays add up to a 'frustrating' breach of contract, or that the delays were 'deliberate' in the special sense?

... In either case, why should not the agreed clause operate? Or what reason is there for limiting its application to such delays as fall short of such as 'frustrate the commercial purpose' or such as are not 'deliberate'? I can see no such reason for limiting a plain contractual provision ...

Notes

1   In *AS Reidar v Arcos* [1927] 1 KB 352, CA, the *Sagatind* was chartered to load a full and complete cargo of timber (850 standards) at Archangel. She was to be loaded at an agreed rate per day and demurrage at £25 per day was payable if she was detained beyond the time required to load at the agreed rate. There was no provision for a fixed number of days on demurrage. If she had been loaded at the agreed rate she could have carried a full summer cargo of 850 standards to the discharge port (Manchester) to which she was eventually ordered. Because loading was delayed beyond the agreed time, the master could not lawfully carry more than a winter deck load to a UK port, which was in fact loaded. The Court of Appeal held that the shipowners were entitled to recover damages for loss of freight in addition to demurrage at the agreed rate. Although there is little hostility to the outcome of the case, the basis of the decision has long been a matter of dispute: the three judgments given in the Court of Appeal are impossible to reconcile. In *Suisse Atlantique* in the House of Lords it was said that *Reidar v Arcos* was to be treated as a decision that the charterers were in breach of two distinct obligations: (a) failure to load a full and complete cargo; and (b) detaining the vessel beyond the lay days. The provisions as to demurrage quantified only the damages arising from the detention of the vessel.

For another analysis of *Reidar v Arcos*, see *The Altus* [1985] 1 Lloyd's Rep 423, p 435 and *The Adelfa* [1988] 2 Lloyd's Rep 466, p 472, which were not followed in *The Bonde* [1991] 1 Lloyd's Rep 136.

2   In *Chandris v Isbrandtsen-Moller* [1951] 1 KB 240, a voyage charter provided that the cargo was to consist of lawful general merchandise, excluding dangerous cargo. Demurrage was fixed at £100 per day. A general cargo was loaded, which included 1,546 tons of turpentine. The vessel arrived at the discharge port (Liverpool) and began discharging in dock on 27 May 1941. Because of the dangerous nature of the turpentine, she was ordered by the authorities to move out of the dock and unload in the Mersey into lighters. The discharge took 16 days longer than it otherwise would. In arbitration, the shipowner claimed demurrage, damages for detention for the 16 days, and interest. The arbitrator stated a special case for the court. Devlin J held that turpentine was a dangerous cargo and that the charterers were in breach of contract but that the damages recoverable for the delay were limited by the demurrage clause.

12.2 Once on demurrage, always on demurrage

This maxim is misleading. It is not a rule of law but an approach to the interpretation of laytime and demurrage clauses and means only that if the parties to a charter intend that demurrage should not continue to be payable in some circumstances, they must say so clearly. (For exclusion from demurrage of periods of delay caused by the fault of the shipowner or on the principle recognised in *The Stolt Spur*: see above.)

Dias Compania Naviera v Louis Dreyfus, The Dias [1978] 1 Lloyd's Rep 325, HL

Facts: The *Dias* was chartered to carry wheat from the US to China. Demurrage became payable while the vessel was waiting for a berth. While waiting, the cargo was fumigated for a total of 16 days. The fumigation itself caused no additional delay. Clause 15 of the charter provided:

At discharging, Charterers/Receivers have the option at any time to treat at their expense ship's holds/compartments/hatchway and/or cargo and time so used to not count. The Master to cooperate with the Charterers/Receivers or their representative with a view to the treatment being carried out expeditiously.

Held:

Lord Diplock: . . . The only question in this appeal is whether demurrage is payable for the period of 16 days six hours during which fumigation was being carried out . . .

My Lords, the principles that apply to laytime and demurrage under voyage charterparties are clear. What 'laytime' and 'demurrage' mean was stated succinctly by Lord Guest (with the substitution of 'lay days' for 'laytime') in *Union of India v Compania Naviera Aeolus SA* [1964] AC 868 at p 899:

Lay days are the days which parties have stipulated for the loading or discharge of the cargo, and if they are exceeded the charterers are in breach; demurrage is the agreed damages to be paid for delay if the ship is delayed in loading or discharging beyond the agreed period.

. . . As Mocatta J, a judge of great experience in these matters, said in his judgment in the instant case:

In my experience, so far as it goes, phrases like 'to count' or 'not to count' are generally used in charters in reference to laytime.

If laytime ends before the charterer has completed the discharging operation he breaks his contract. The breach is a continuing one; it goes on until discharge is completed and the ship is once more available to the shipowner to use for other voyages. But unless the delay in what is often, though incorrectly, called redelivery of the ship to the shipowner, is so prolonged as to amount to a frustration of the adventure, the breach by the charterer sounds in damages only. The charterer remains entitled to continue to complete the discharge of the cargo, while remaining liable in damages for the loss sustained by the shipowner during the period for which he is being wrongfully deprived of the opportunity of making profitable use of his ship. It is the almost invariable practice nowadays for these damages to be fixed by the charterparty at a liquidated sum per day and *pro rata* for part of a day (demurrage) which accrues throughout the period of time for which the breach continues.

Since demurrage is liquidated damages, fixed by agreement between the parties, it is possible by apt words in the charterparty to provide that, notwithstanding the continuance of the breach, demurrage shall not be payable in respect of the period when some event specified in the charterparty is happening; but the effect of such an agreement is to make an exception to the ordinary consequences that would flow in law from the charterer's continued breach of his contract, *viz*, his liability in damages. As was said by Scrutton LJ in a passage in his work on charterparties that was cited by Lord Reid in the *Union of India* case (above) at p 879:

When once a vessel is on demurrage no exceptions will operate to prevent demurrage continuing to be payable unless the exceptions clause is clearly worded so as to have that effect.

This is but an example of the general principle stated by Lord Guest in the same case in continuation of the passage that I have already cited:

> . . . an ambiguous clause is no protection. 'If a party wishes to exclude the ordinary consequences that would flow in law from the contract that he is making he must do so in clear terms' (*Szymonowski & Co v Beck & Co* [1923] 1 KB 457 at p 466 *per* Scrutton LJ).

With these principles in mind I turn to the clause (cl 15) principally relied upon by the charterers as excluding the accrual of demurrage during the period while fumigation, which did not commence until after the expiration of laytime, was being carried out. Appearing as it does in a set of six clauses dealing with the discharging operation, laytime allowed for it, and demurrage, my immediate reaction, like that of Mocatta J, is that the answer to the question: 'for what purpose is time used in fumigation 'not to count'?' would be: 'for the purpose of calculating laytime'. These words do not seem to me to be an apt way of saying that the time so used is not to be taken into account in assessing the damages payable by the charterer for breach of contract for failing to complete the discharging operation within the stipulated time . . .

For my part, I think that when construed in the light of established principles, cl 15 is unequivocal. It means that time used in fumigation is not to be taken into account only in the calculation of laytime. The provision that time is 'not to count' has no further application once laytime has expired. But even if I were persuaded that the clause was in some way ambiguous, this would not be enough to save the charterers from their liability to pay demurrage during the period while fumigation was being carried out after laytime had expired. For these reasons, and in agreement with Mocatta J and Browne LJ I would allow this appeal.

Notes

1   The reason for the 'clear exceptions only' rule was considered by the House of Lords in *Union of India v Compania Naviera Aeolus* [1964] AC 868, where a clause provided that no claim for damages or demurrage should be made for delay caused by a strike. It was held that the clause did not apply for a strike that began only after laytime had ended. Lord Reid explained that: 'If a strike occurs before the end of the laytime neither party can be blamed in any way. But if it occurs after demurrage has begun to accrue the owner might well say: true, your breach of contract in detaining my ship after the end of the laytime did not cause the strike, but if you had fulfilled your contract the strike would have caused no loss because my ship would have been on the high seas before it began: so it is more reasonable that you should bear the loss than that I should. So it seems to me right that if the respondents are to escape from paying demurrage during this strike they must be able to point to an exceptions clause which clearly covers this case. And in my judgment they cannot do that.'

2   Once laytime has been exceeded, there has been a breach and a clause operating at this time may be of a type that excludes or limits the liability in demurrage or it may be one that suspends the continuing obligation to discharge and therefore, *pro tanto*, suspends the breach that would otherwise have given rise to the obligation to pay demurrage. These types of clauses, whether excusing breaches, relieving *prima facie* obligations, or simply excluding or reducing the liability in liquidated damages are all provisions of the character of exclusion or exceptions clauses and therefore must be clearly expressed if they are to have that effect. Unclear or ambiguous clauses will be ineffective for that purpose. This is an application of the ordinary rules of contractual construction governing such clauses. They must be clearly worded (*The Forum Craftsman* [1991] 1 Lloyd's Rep 81, *per* Hobhouse J).

3   The *Kalliopi A* was chartered for the carriage of a cargo of shredded scrap from Rotterdam to Bombay. She was affected by congestion both during laytime and thereafter. The charterers

claimed to be excused from any liability to pay demurrage by a clause in the charter which provided that '... unavoidable hindrances which may prevent ... discharging ... always mutually excepted'. It was held that the clause was not clear enough to exempt the charterers from liability in respect of periods when the vessel was on demurrage and they were in breach of contract: *The Kalliopi A* [1988] 2 Lloyd's Rep 101, CA, applied in *The Lefthero* [1992] 2 Lloyd's Rep 109, CA and *The Solon* [2000] 1 Lloyd's Rep 292.

4   A typed addition to a charter in the Pacific Coast Grain form provided by cl 62 that 'charterers shall not be liable for any delay in ... discharging ... which delay ... is caused in whole or in part by strikes ... and any other causes beyond the control of the charterers'. Other provisions of the charter dealt with causes beyond the charterers' control that interrupted laytime. The vessel came on demurrage at the discharge port and was then delayed for 26 days by a strike of port workers. It was held that cl 62 did relieve the charterers from liability for demurrage: *President of India v N G Livanos Maritime Co, The John Michalos* [1987] 2 Lloyd's Rep 188.

12.3 How long must a ship remain on demurrage?

If a charterer fails to load, how long must the shipowner wait before he is entitled to sail away, assuming that the charter does not deal with the point? The leading case is *Universal Cargo Carriers v Citati* [1957] 2 QB 401.

Universal Cargo Carriers v Citati [1957] 2 QB 401

Facts: A charterparty in the GENCON form provided that the *Catherine D Goulandris* was to proceed to Basra and load 6,000 tons of scrap iron for Buenos Aires. The lay/can spread was 5 July to 25 July 1951. The vessel arrived at Basrah on 12 July 1951. The charter allowed six weather working days for loading. Despite repeated enquiries, no shipper or berth was nominated and the cargo did not materialise. The owners purported to cancel the charter on 19 July when the lay days had run for only two-thirds of the time allowed. The question stated by the arbitrator for the opinion of the court was whether the owners were entitled to terminate the charterparty on 18 July.

Held:

Devlin J:

(1)   The charterer was on 18 July in breach of the charter in failing to nominate a berth and in failing to provide a cargo in sufficient time to enable the vessel to be loaded within the lay days (the arbitrator had found that on 18 July the cargo could not have been loaded within the laytime which remained).

(2)   For the same reason, the charterer was on 18 July also in anticipatory breach of the express obligation to complete loading by 21 July, or (alternatively) possibly on the same date was in breach of an implied term that he would not by his own act or omission put it out of his power to load by 21 July. 'But whether the breach is said to be an actual breach of an implied term or an anticipatory breach of an express term is not to my mind at all important; and it must be one or the other' (p 429).

(3)   The breaches in question were breaches of warranty not of condition.

(4)   'It follows that the owners were not entitled *ipso facto* to rescind on July 18. But a party to a contract may not purchase indefinite delay by paying damages and a charterer may not keep a ship indefinitely on demurrage. When the delay becomes so prolonged that the breach assumes a character so grave as to go to the root of the contract, the aggrieved party is entitled to rescind. What is the yardstick by which this length of delay is to be measured? Those considered in the arbitration can now be reduced to two: first, the conception of a reasonable time, and secondly, such delay as would

frustrate the charterparty. The arbitrator, it is clear, preferred the first. But in my opinion the second has been settled as the correct one by a long line of authorities.'

(His Lordship reviewed the earlier cases and continued.)

' . . . Having settled the proper yardstick, the next question that arises for determination could, I think, have been put very conveniently in the form adopted in *Stanton v Richardson* (1872) LR 7 CP 421, namely, was the charterer on July 18, 1951, willing and able to load a cargo within such time as would not have frustrated the object of the venture; and the answer to that question would have determined the case. But in the arbitration the main argument was on anticipatory breach, and the emphasis on one mode of it, namely, renunciation. The chief findings of the arbitrator relate entirely to renunciation. I must therefore consider the nature of anticipatory breach and the findings thereon which the arbitrator has made.

The law on the right to rescind is succinctly stated by Lord Porter in *Heyman v Darwins Ltd* [1942] AC 356 as follows:

The three sets of circumstances giving rise to a discharge of contract are tabulated by Anson, *Law of Contract*, 20th edition, p 319 as: (1) renunciation by a party of his liabilities under it; (2) impossibility created by his own act; and (3) total or partial failure of performance. In the case of the first two, the renunciation may occur or impossibility be created either before or at the time for performance. In the case of the third, it can occur only at the time or during the course of performance.

The third of these is the ordinary case of actual breach, and the first two state the two modes of anticipatory breach. In order that the arguments which I have heard from either side can be rightly considered, it is necessary that I should develop rather more fully what is meant by each of these two modes.

(5) A renunciation can be made either by words or by conduct, provided it is clearly made. It is often put that the party renunciating must 'evince an intention' not to go on with the contract. The intention can be evinced either by words or by conduct. The test of whether an intention is sufficiently evinced by conduct is whether the party renunciating has acted in such a way as to lead a reasonable person to the conclusion that he does not intend to fulfil his part of the contract.

. . . Since a man must be both ready and willing to perform, a profession by words or conduct of inability is by itself enough to constitute renunciation. But unwillingness and inability are often difficult to disentangle, and it is rarely necessary to make the attempt. Inability often lies at the root of unwillingness to perform. Willingness in this context does not mean cheerfulness; it means simply an intent to perform. To say: 'I would like to but I cannot' negatives intent just as much as 'I will not' . . . If a man says 'I cannot perform', he renounces his contract by that statement, and the cause of the inability is immaterial.

(6) In considering whether the charterer had renounced by evincing an intention not to perform the charterparty and so committed an anticipatory breach, only events known to the shipowner at the time could be considered.

(7) The arbitration award in the owner's favour on the issue of renunciation could not stand because it was based on an erroneous concept of the length of delay necessary to amount to a repudiation.

(8) Impossibility could arise even if the disability was not deliberately created. However, a party electing to treat 'impossibility' as a repudiatory breach must prove that the inability was still effective at the time fixed for performance.

In my judgment, therefore, if the owners can establish that in the words of Lord Sumner (*British & Beningtons v N W Cachar Tea* [1923] AC 48, 72) the charterer had on July 18 'become wholly and finally disabled' from finding a cargo and loading it before delay frustrated the venture, they are entitled to succeed. Lord Sumner's words expressly refer to the time of breach as the date at which the inability must exist. But that does not mean in my opinion that the facts to be looked at in determining inability are only those which existed on July 18; the determination is to be made in the light of all the events, whether occurring before or after the critical date, put in evidence at trial.

(9) The test of impossibility did not depend on how the matter would have appeared to a reasonable shipowner or to a reasonable and well informed person on 18 July.

An anticipatory breach must be proved in fact and not in supposition. If, for example, one party to a contract were to go to another and say that well informed opinion on the market was that he would be unable to fulfil his obligations when the time came, he might get the answer from his adversary that the latter did not care to have his affairs discussed on the market and did not choose to give any information about them except the assurance that he could and would fulfil his obligations. If that assurance was rejected and the contract rescinded before the time for performance came and the assurance in fact turned out to be well founded, it would be intolerable if the rescinder was entitled to claim that he was protected because he had acted on the basis of well informed opinion.

(10) His Lordship concluded by dealing with procedural and factual submissions and ordered that the award be remitted to the arbitrator to answer the question whether the charterer was on 18 July 1951 willing and able to perform the charterparty within such time as would not have frustrated the commercial object of the adventure. Subsequent proceedings on these issues are reported at [1957] 1 WLR 979 and [1958] 2 QB 254.

13 Despatch

The object of demurrage is to encourage the charterer to load or discharge within agreed laytime and, if he does not, to compensate the shipowner for the delay. However, the prospect of paying demurrage is no encouragement to a charterer to load or discharge in less than the agreed laytime. Unless the parties have agreed that despatch money will be paid by the shipowner if charterers use less than the agreed time (despatch is only payable by agreement) charterers may find it suits them best to spread loading or discharge – as they are entitled to do – over the whole of the period allowed, even if they could have completed their activities more quickly. Thus, if demurrage is a stick for the charterer, despatch is a carrot.

Agreements for the payment of despatch can give rise to difficult questions of interpretation in charters that provide for lay days subject to exceptions such as Sunday and holidays. How is time to be calculated for the purpose of paying despatch money where the charterparty only refers imprecisely in such cases to 'any time saved in loading and/or discharging' or to 'each clear day saved loading' or 'each running day saved'? As Bailhache J said in *Mawson Shipping v Beyer* [1914] 1 KB 304, p 307:

Is despatch money payable in respect only of lay days saved or in respect of all time saved to the ship? In other words is despatch for this purpose on the same footing as demurrage?

In *Mawson*, Sundays were excluded from lay days; the despatch clause referred to 'all time saved in loading'. In cases before *Mawson*, Bailhache J thought that question he formulated had been decided both ways. *Laing v Hollway* (1878) 3 QBD 437, CA and *In re Royal Mail Steam Packet and River Plate Steamship Co* [1910] 1 KB 600 held that time saved meant all the time saved to the ship; *The Glendevon* [1893] P 269, DC and *Nelson & Sons v Nelson Line* [1907] 2 KB 705,

CA decided it meant only laytime saved, so that in neither of those two cases was despatch payable in respect of a Sunday that was saved to the ship.

As a judge at first instance, Bailhache J in *Mawson* loyally attempted to reconcile and to follow the earlier decisions. Nevertheless, his personal views were also clear: 'I should, I fear, have decided all the four reported cases in favour of the charterers.' This has commercial logic. In origin exceptions such as Sundays and holidays were carved out of the agreed loading periods because these were days the charterers could not use (or could not use as cheaply) to load or discharge. But a ship that has completed loading or discharge and left port has always been able to make good use of these excepted periods. Consequently, 'one would naturally expect that this despatch money would be proportionate to the advantage derived by the shipowners from the extra speed in loading . . .': *Nelson & Sons*, p 719, *per* Fletcher Moulton LJ (dissenting).

There is an additional point. Despatch is often dealt with, both in charterparties and in the preceding negotiations, in close relationship with demurrage. And the general rule of construction is that laytime exceptions do not apply while the vessel is on demurrage, in the absence of a clear agreement to the contrary. Since the laytime exceptions do not normally apply when the shipowner is receiving demurrage to compensate for time that is lost, might it not be expected that the exceptions would not normally apply when the shipowner is paying despatch for the advantage of time which he gains?

The conclusion that Bailhache J reached in *Mawson* in his careful reserved judgment was that, on the authorities:

(1) *Prima facie* under this type of despatch clause, shipowners must pay for all time saved to the ship, calculated in the way in which, in the converse case, demurrage would be calculated; that is, taking no account of lay day exceptions: *Laing v Hollway* and *In Re Royal Mail Steam Packet*, above.

(2) The *prima facie* presumption is displaced where either (a) lay days and time saved by despatch are dealt with in the same clause and demurrage in another clause (*The Glendevon*); or (b) lay days, time saved by despatch and demurrage are dealt with in the same clause, on construction of which the court is satisfied that 'days saved' are used in the same sense as 'lay days' and not in the same sense as days lost by demurrage (*Nelson & Sons v Nelson Line*).

In the *Mawson* charterparty, lay time, demurrage and despatch were dealt with in three separate clauses; the case fell within the first of Bailhache J's classes and the charterers succeeded.

The second stage of the *Mawson* approach is probably too mechanical to be generally accepted today. But some support for the basic *Mawson* presumption can be found in *Bulk Transport v Sissy Steamship, The Archipelagos* [1979] 2 Lloyd's Rep 289, Com Ct. That case involved a motion to set aside or remit an arbitration award arising out of a dispute as to the calculation of despatch money. Parker J held that the arbitrators ought to have begun with the *prima facie* presumption laid down in *Mawson* and then gone on to consider whether the wording of the clauses rebutted the presumption. The despatch agreement in this case was in the demurrage clause; but the agreement provided for despatch 'on *all laytime* saved'. Looking at the rest of the charterparty, Parker J held that by 'laytime', the parties were referring to 'laytime used for or required to be used for, in the sense of availability for, loading'. Only time that could be counted as laytime could therefore be saved under that despatch agreement.

In *The Themistocles* (1949) 82 Ll LR 232 Morris J took a quite different approach. There too despatch was dealt with in the same clause as demurrage and laytime was dealt with in another clause. The agreement provided for despatch 'on all time saved at port of loading'. Morris J said:

> Inasmuch as my task is to construe the particular words of the contract now before me, it does not seem to me that cases which decide the meaning of other words in other contexts can be of

governing authority. Indeed, I doubt how far any question of principle is involved in what I have to decide or was involved in the various reported cases … Unless terms of art are used, or unless the court is bound by some decision relating to a contract in virtually identical form, then, while deriving such assistance as the decisions afford, the task of the court, as it seems to me, is merely one of the construction of particular words as used in their context in a particular contract.

On the point in question, Morris J concluded that despatch was payable not just on loading time saved, but on total saving on the time that the vessel might have stayed in port.

14 Freight

Freight is the consideration paid to the shipowner for performing his part of the contract of carriage. Typically this means that an agreed rate is payable according to the weight or volume of cargo (such as £10 per long ton) carried to and delivered at its destination. In general, it is open to the parties to make whatever agreement they want about how freight shall be calculated, earned and paid. But unless a special agreement is made, for example for payment in advance (which is a typical clause in the bulk trade) or for a lump sum, payment of freight and delivery of the cargo at the port of discharge are concurrent conditions: *Black v Rose* (1864) 2 Moore PC(NS) 277; *Paynter v James* (1867) LR 2 CP 348.

15 Delivery freight

A shipowner is entitled to freight if either he is willing and able to deliver in accordance with the contract of carriage or if he is only prevented from delivering by some act or omission of the cargo owner. However, no freight is payable if the shipowner cannot deliver the goods because they have been lost or destroyed. It does not matter how or why the goods are lost or destroyed, or (probably) even if they destroy themselves through inherent vice (see *Matheos v Dreyfus* [1925] AC 655, p 667, *per* Lord Sumner). No freight is payable even where the loss occurs without fault on the part of the shipowner and even if the cause of the loss is an excepted peril: excepted perils may prevent the shipowner from being sued for losing or damaging the cargo, but they do not normally confer a right to freight. Destruction of the merchantable character or commercial identity of a cargo has the same effect on the right to freight as a total destruction of the goods. Where only part of a cargo is delivered, freight is payable on that part; delivery of a complete cargo is not a condition precedent to the recovery of freight: *Ritchie v Atkinson* (1808) 10 East 294. Freight is payable in full on cargo that is delivered damaged. No deductions can be made from or set off against freight that is payable on goods delivered, for the value of other goods that are lost or damaged; but a separate action (or a counterclaim) may be brought to recover damage for which the shipowner is responsible. The leading case is *Dakin v Oxley*.

Dakin v Oxley (1864) 15 CBNS 646, Court of Common Pleas

Facts: The shipowner sued the charterer for the freight on a cargo of coal carried from Newport to Nassau. The charterer alleged that the coal was damaged during the voyage and that on arrival at the port of discharge it was worth less than the freight. He claimed that in these circumstances, as a matter of general maritime law, he had the right to abandon the cargo to the shipowner and to be free of any further liability.

Held:

Willes J (at 660): ... the question for us to consider is, whether a charterer whose cargo has been damaged by the fault of the master and the crew so as upon arrival at the port of discharge to be worth less than the freight, is entitled to excuse himself from payment of freight by abandoning the cargo to the shipowner. We think not: and we should not have taken time to consider, but for the general importance of the subject, and of its having been suggested that our law was silent upon this question, and that the plea was warranted by the usage and law of other maritime countries, which, it was said, we ought to adopt ...

It ought to be borne in mind, when dealing with such cases, that the true test of the right to freight is the question whether the service in respect of which the freight was contracted to be paid has been substantially performed; and, according to the law of England, as a rule, freight is earned by the carriage and arrival of the goods ready to be delivered to the merchant, though they be in a damaged state when they arrive. If the shipowner fails to carry the goods for the merchant to the destined port, the freight is not earned. If he carry part, but not the whole, no freight is payable in respect of the part not carried, and freight is payable in respect of the part carried unless the charterparty make the carriage of the whole a condition precedent to the earning of any freight – a case which has not within our experience arisen in practice ...

Little difficulty exists in applying the above test where the cargo upon arrival is deficient in quantity. Where the cargo, without loss or destruction of any part, has become accidentally swelled (*Gibson v Sturge* 10 Exch 622), or, perhaps, diminished, as, by drying (*Jacobsen's Sea Laws*, Book 3, ch 2, p 220), freight (usage of trade apart) is payable upon the quantity shipped, because that is what the contract refers to ...

In the case of an actual loss or destruction by sea-damage of so much of the cargo that no substantial part of it remains; as, if sugar in mats, shipped as sugar and paying so much per ton, is washed away, so that only a few ounces remain, and the mats are worthless, the question would arise whether practically speaking any part of the cargo contracted to be carried has arrived ...

Where the quantity remains unchanged, but by sea-damage the goods have been deteriorated in quality, the question of identity arises in a different form, as, for instance, where a valuable picture has arrived as a piece of spoilt canvas, cloth in rags, or crockery in broken shreds, iron all or almost all rust, rice fermented or hides rotten.

In both classes of cases, whether of loss of quantity or change in quality, the proper course seems to be the same, *viz*, to ascertain from the terms of the contract, construed by mercantile usage, if any, what was the thing for the carriage of which freight was to be paid, and by the aid of a jury to determine whether that thing, or any and how much of it, has substantially arrived.

If it has arrived, though damaged, the freight is payable by the ordinary terms of the charterparty; and the question of fortuitous damage must be settled with the underwriters, and that of culpable damage in a distinct proceeding for such damage against the ship captain or owners. There would be apparent justice in allowing damage of the latter sort to be set off or deducted in an action for freight; and this is allowed in some (at least) of the United States, *Parsons on Mercantile Law*, 172, n. But our law does not allow deduction in that form; and, as at present administered, for the sake perhaps of speedy settlement of freight and other liquidated demands, it affords the injured party a remedy by cross-action only: *Davidson v Gwyne* 12 East 381; *Stinson v Hall* 1 Hurlst & N 831; *Sheels (or Shields) v Davies* 4 Campb 119, 6 Taunt 65; the judgment of Parke B in *Mondel v Steel* 8 M & W 858; *The Don Francisco* 32 LJ Adm 14, *per* Dr Lushington. It would be unjust, and almost absurd that, without regard to the comparative value of the freight and cargo when uninjured, the risk of a mercantile adventure should be thrown upon the shipowner by the accident of the value of the cargo being a little more than the freight; so that a trifling damage, much less than the freight, would reduce the value to less than the freight; whilst, if the cargo had been much more valuable and the damage greater, or the cargo worth a little less than the freight and the damage the same, so as to bear a greater proportion to the whole value, the freight would have been payable, and the merchant have been put to his cross-action. Yet this is the conclusion we are called upon by the defendant to affirm in his favour, involving no less than that that damage, however trifling, if culpable, may work a forfeiture of the entire freight, contrary to the just rule of our law, by which each party bears the damage resulting from his own breach of contract, and no more.

The extreme case above supposed is not imaginary; for, it has actually occurred on many occasions, and notably upon the cessation of war between France and England in 1748, which caused so great a fall in prices that the agreed freight in many instances exceeded the value of the goods. The merchants in France sought a remission of freight or the privilege of abandonment, but in vain. (2 Boulay-Paty, *Cours de Droit Commercial*, 485, 486.)

It is evident enough from this review of the law that there is neither authority nor sound reason for upholding the proposed defence. The plea is naught, and there must be judgment for the plaintiff.

Note

The general principle adopted in *Dakin v Oxley* is that the shipowner acquires a right to freight only if the service in respect of which the freight was contracted to be paid has been substantially performed. In the case of delivery freight it is therefore necessary to ask if the goods for the carriage of which freight was to be paid have arrived. Damage so serious that it causes a change in the identity of the cargo may prevent arrival, so that no freight is earned, as the decision in *Asfar v Blundell* memorably illustrates.

Asfar v Blundell [1896] 1 QB 123, CA

Facts: Dates were shipped on the vessel *Govino* under bills of lading that made freight payable to the plaintiffs on right delivery in London. The ship collided with another vessel in the Thames and sank. She was raised but the dates were found to be unfit for human consumption. The trial court found the dates were unmerchantable (note that this case is also relevant for consideration of the 'perishing' of goods in a sale contract) as dates although a proportion were still recognisable and the cargo was still valuable and was sold for £2,400 for export for distillation. On a claim against underwriters who had insured the carrier against loss of freight, it was held that no freight was payable.

Held:

Lord Esher MR: I am of opinion that this appeal should be dismissed. The first point taken on behalf of the defendants, the underwriters, is that there has been no total loss of the dates, and therefore no total loss of the freight on them. The ingenuity of the argument might commend itself to a body of chemists, but not to businessmen. We are dealing with dates as subject matter of commerce; and it is contended that, although these dates were under water for two days, and when brought up were simply a mass of pulpy matter impregnated with sewage and in a state of fermentation, there had been no change in their nature, and they still were dates. There is a perfectly well known test which has for many years been applied to such cases as the present – that test is whether, as a matter of business, the nature of the thing has been altered. The nature of a thing is not necessarily altered because the thing itself has been damaged; wheat or rice may be damaged, but may still remain the things dealt with as wheat or rice in business. But if the nature of the thing is altered, and it becomes for business purposes something else, so that it is not dealt with by business people as the thing which it originally was, the question for determination is whether the thing insured, the original article of commerce, has become a total loss. If it is so changed in its nature by the perils of the sea as to become an unmerchantable thing, which no buyer would buy and no honest seller would sell, then there is a total loss. That test was applied in the present case by the learned judge in the court below, who decided as a fact that the dates had been so deteriorated that they had become something which was not merchantable as dates. If that was so, there was a total loss of the dates. What was the effect of this upon the insurance? If they were totally lost as dates, no freight in respect of them became due from the consignee to the person to whom the bill of lading freight was payable – that is, to the charterers – and there was a total loss of the bill of lading freight on these dates ...

Notes

1   In *Duthie v Hilton* (1868) 4 CP 138 (an action for freight), the plaintiffs contracted to carry 300 casks of cement on the *John Duthie* from London to Sydney. Freight was to be paid 'within three days after arrival of ship and before delivery of any portion of the goods'. Before delivery and within three days of arrival, the ship was scuttled in Sydney to extinguish an accidental fire. The cement hardened and the casks were destroyed. The parties agreed on these facts that the cement no longer existed as cement. The plaintiffs admitted that this was a case of total loss but alleged that the freight had become payable on arrival of the vessel and before the loss occurred. It was held that the plaintiffs had to be ready to deliver the goods on demand throughout the agreed period. Since they were not, freight was not payable. If no time had been fixed, the shipowner must be ready to deliver for a reasonable time to earn freight.

2   The holders of a respondentia bond on a cargo (for whom the cargo owners were found to be responsible) obtained an order of the Court of Admiralty for the removal and sale of the cargo. It was held that freight was payable as performance of the contract had been (in effect) prevented by the cargo owners: *Cargo ex Galam* (1863) 33 LJ Adm 97, Privy Council on appeal from the Court of Admiralty.

3   The *Caspian Sea* was chartered for a voyage from Punta Cardon to Genoa with freight payable on delivery. She was loaded with 'Bachaquero Crude', a Venezuelan crude oil normally free of paraffin. The charterers took physical delivery at the port of discharge, but denied that freight was payable because they alleged that the cargo had been contaminated by paraffinic products from residues of a previous cargo. Arbitrators stated a case for the opinion of the court. The award was remitted to the arbitrators, the court finding that the owners would be entitled to freight if what they had delivered could, in commercial terms, bear a description that sensibly and accurately included the words 'Bachaquero Crude'. The arbitrators had to decide whether 'Bachaquero Crude' meant a 'paraffin-free crude'; if it did, the owners were not entitled to freight. Or did it mean 'a crude from the Bachaquero region that in its natural state contains no paraffin'; in this case, the owners would be entitled to freight unless the cargo was so contaminated that it was not possible to describe it even as 'contaminated Bachaquero Crude': *Montedison v Icroma, The Caspian Sea* [1980] 1 Lloyd's Rep 91, *per* Donaldson J.

4   Is the proper starting point in a case such as *The Caspian Sea* to ask, what description did the shipper apply to the goods? Or should we ask instead, what precisely was it that the parties agreed would be the service on performance of which freight would be paid? Does this mean we must consider not only the words the shipper used to describe the cargo, but also what both parties knew or must be taken to have known about, such as any special susceptibilities of that cargo?

5   The idiosyncratic English rule is that, in the absence of an agreement to the contrary, a claim for loss or damage to cargo cannot be asserted by way of deduction from or equitable set off against freight. There is no general agreement on the reason for this rule, although suggested explanations include: (1) alleged judicial tenderness for shipowners that is suggested to have

been appropriate when communications were poor and facilities for transfer of money limited; and (2) a special desire to encourage prompt payment and avoid spurious delaying complaints in case of contracts for carriage by sea. The rule is inconsistent with the law of some other maritime jurisdictions and with the English rule applied to contracts for the sale of goods and for work. Nevertheless, in *Aries Tanker v Total Transport, The Aries* [1977] 1 All ER 398, the House of Lords refused to abandon the rule because the parties had contracted on the basis of and against the background of the established position and to avoid retrospectively disturbing many other contracts similarly entered into. In *Colonial Bank v European Grain & Shipping Ltd, The Dominique* [1989] 1 Lloyd's Rep 431 (noted below), the House of Lords held that a repudiatory breach of a voyage charter, like the non-repudiatory breach considered in *The Aries* (above), was equally incapable of giving rise to a defence by way of equitable set off to a claim for accrued freight under a voyage charterparty. *The Aries* rule is significantly modified in application to time charter hire.

6   It is not unusual in a charterparty for it to be expressly agreed that freight shall be paid in full without deductions for cargo claims, for instance by making freight payable 'in cash without discount', as was done in the *Aries* charter, above. In practice, when a dispute arises, it is common for shipowners to seek payment of freight in full, but for the cargo owner's position to be safeguarded by a guarantee of payment of any damages for which the shipowners are ultimately held responsible to be given by the shipowner's P and I club.

16 Lump sum freight

A lump sum freight is one that is not tied directly to the quantity of cargo actually carried. It is a definite sum agreed to be paid for the hire of a ship for a specified voyage (*Williams v Canton Insurance* [1901] AC 462, p 473, *per* Lord Lindley): for example, £1,000 for a voyage from Y to Z. This may be the easiest way to define the freight obligation when the charterer does not know the exact quantity of cargo that will be loaded or when it is difficult to measure the quantity actually loaded. An alternative, often used in contracts of affreightment that are not tied to a particular vessel, is to fix a rate based on the size of the vessel: for example, £10 per deadweight ton. Freight that is computed on intaken quantity and to be paid on that quantity despite a shortage on out-turn, shares at least some of the characteristics of lump sum freight: *Shell v Seabridge, The Metula* [1978] 2 Lloyd's Rep 5, CA.

The two basic rules about payment of lump sum freight are, first, that if the ship is put at the disposal of the freighter, the whole of the freight is payable even though no cargo or less than a full cargo is loaded: *Robinson v Knights* (1873) 8 CP 465, p 468. Second, the whole sum is payable if any part of the cargo shipped is delivered, at least if the remainder is lost due to excepted perils. But it is not easy to identify a consistent legal theory that explains these rules. The explanation adopted in *The Norway* (1865) 3 Moore PC(NS) 245 and later followed in *Robinson v Knights* (above) was that a charterparty at a lump sum freight was a contract to pay for the use and hire of a ship for a given voyage, rather than a contract to pay for the carriage and delivery of a particular cargo. On this analysis, the shipowner is clearly entitled to full freight even if he only manages to deliver part of the cargo loaded. He earns freight, it could be said, by making the agreed voyage, not by delivering cargo. But this rationalisation implies that freight can be earned even if no cargo ever arrives, so long as the chartered vessel reached the port of discharge; on the other hand, it also suggests that no freight would be earned if the ship herself does not arrive, even if the whole cargo is in fact delivered in perfect condition. It was largely for these reasons that in *Thomas v Harrowing* a different explanation of the nature of a contract at a lump sum freight was adopted.

Thomas v Harrowing Steamship Co [1913] 2 KB 171, CA; affirmed [1915] AC 58, HL

Facts: The *Ethelwalda* was chartered to load a cargo of pit props in Finland for carriage to a dock at Port Talbot for a specified lump sum freight. The freight was payable under art 9 on unloading and right delivery of cargo. The charterparty contained the usual exception of perils of the seas. The *Ethelwalda* arrived with her cargo, which consisted in part of a deckload, outside the port of discharge, when owing to heavy weather she was driven against the breakwater and became a total loss. About two-thirds of the cargo was washed ashore and was collected on the beach by the directions of the master of the *Ethelwalda*, acting on behalf of the plaintiffs, and placed on the dock premises and there delivered to the defendants, the residue of the cargo being lost by perils of the seas. The plaintiffs brought the present action to recover the lump sum freight.

Held:

Kennedy LJ: . . . [T]wo questions of law, each of which is of considerable general importance, have been raised by the appellants . . . They contend, in the first place, that, as the stipulated freight was a lump freight, it could be earned by the plaintiffs only if the cargo was carried to its destination in the *Ethelwalda*, and therefore, inasmuch as she was wrecked outside the breakwater, and the cargo, as it came ashore, was conveyed to the dock in the way in which I have described, no freight could become due, even if the whole cargo had been thus delivered to the defendants. Secondly, they contend that, if they are wrong in this, yet, inasmuch as part of the cargo loaded on board of the *Ethelwalda* was lost and not delivered, that circumstance bars the maintenance of the plaintiffs' claim.

I proceed to consider each of these contentions.

. . . The only sort of authority which the defendants' counsel put forward for their contention consisted of inferences which they invited us to draw from expressions to be found in the judgments in two reported cases, in each of which the freight reserved by the charterparty under consideration was a lump sum. In the judgment of the Privy Council in *The Norway* (cited above) it was said that the lump sum called freight was not properly so called, but was more properly a sum in the nature of a rent to be paid for the use and hire of the ship. In *Robinson v Knights* (above) Keating J described the freight payable under the charterparty in that case as an entire sum to be paid for the hire of the ship for one entire service, and Brett J, as he then was, in regard to it used the expression 'a stipulated gross sum to be paid for the use of the whole ship for the whole voyage'. It appears to me that none of these statements really afford support to the contention of the present appellants. They must, of course, be read in each case in reference to the particular charterparty which was under the consideration of the court and in reference to the particular question which had to be decided in respect of that charterparty. Neither in *The Norway*, nor in the case in the Common Pleas, was there any question as to the arrival of the chartered vessel at the port of destination. In each case the vessel had in fact arrived, and therefore the courts had not to consider any question of the shipowner's right, in Lord Ellenborough's words, to earn the whole freight by forwarding the goods by some other means to the place of destination. What they had to decide was the distinct and different question whether under the particular terms of the charterparty before them the shipowner was entitled to claim payment, without deduction, of the whole freight where only part of the cargo was delivered out of the arrived ship – a question involved in the second contention of the defendants which I shall consider presently. Further, it is to be noted that in each of these cases the terms of the charterparty, as I understand the report, were in a material respect different from those of the charterparty with which we are concerned in the present case. In both of them the lump freight was, as to some portion, expressly made payable at a time to be ascertained by reference to the ship's arrival at her destination. In *The Norway*, as is pointed out in the judgment on p 409 of Browning and Lushington's report, one-third in cash was made payable 'on arrival at the port of delivery'. In *Robinson v Knights* the provision was that freight should be paid in cash half on arrival and the remainder on unloading and right delivery of cargo. I must not be understood to say that even such stipulations in a charterparty ought, if that question should ever arise for decision, to be held to affect the shipowner's right, in case of his ship's disablement in the course of the chartered voyage, to forward the cargo and earn the lump sum freight. But the presence of those stipulations in the particular charterparty in each case under consideration cannot properly be left out of sight when we have to consider the expressions in the judgments to which I have referred, and it differentiates the charterparties which contained such stipulations from the charterparty in the present case, which, except that the freight is to be a lump sum and not calculated per standard or per fathom of the timber shipped, in no way differs from the ordinary charterparty for the services of a ship to carry a particular cargo to a particular port, and which expressly provides for the payment of the lump freight, not in reference to the arrival of the ship, but, according to article 9, 'on unloading and right delivery of cargo'. I agree with Pickford J [the trial judge] when he says:

> I do not say that there may not be lump sum charters in which the freight, being payable for the use of the particular ship, is not to be paid unless the ship completes her voyage. There may be such charters, but I do not think that this is the effect of the present one.

I may add in this connection that it may be worth noting that by the terms of this charterparty in this case the charterers' agents were to load a full and complete cargo.

I now come to that which I have called the second contention of the defendants, which is that only a part of the cargo was delivered, and, therefore, the contract not having been completely performed by the plaintiffs, they are, according to the principle exemplified by the leading case of *Cutter v Powell* (1795) 6 TR 320, not entitled to claim the lump sum which constituted the agreed remuneration for the performance of the contract of affreightment. Upon this point also I am of opinion that the judgment of Pickford J in favour of the plaintiffs was right. What, under the contract contained in the charterparty, was the condition precedent to the plaintiffs' right to the payment of the lump freight? It was, as I construe the document, the right delivery of the cargo. What is, under this charterparty, meant by 'the cargo'? To ascertain this, we must look at the charterparty, and, so looking, we find that what the shipowner has to deliver is not in all circumstances the quantity of cargo shipped, but all which was shipped and of which delivery was not prevented by any of the excepted perils. This is the law as enunciated in the judgments both of Lord Coleridge CJ and Bramwell B in the case of *Merchant Shipping Co v Armitage* (1873) LR 9 QB 99, in which the charterparty under the consideration of the Exchequer Chamber was in its terms, as to payment of a lump sum freight, excepted perils, and right delivery of cargo, like the charterparty in the present case, and in which, as in the present case, part of the cargo had been lost by excepted perils, and therefore the cargo owner had got only a partial delivery ...

... In a comparatively recent case in the House of Lords the law has been laid down in the same way by Lord Lindley. The case was *Williams & Co v Canton Insurance* [above]. A lump sum freight, said his Lordship:

> is a definite sum agreed to be paid for the hire of a ship for a specified voyage; and although only payable on the right and true delivery of the cargo, those words are not taken literally, but are understood to mean right and true delivery, having regard to and excluding excepted perils. In other words, the cargo in this clause of the charterparty does not mean the cargo shipped, but the cargo which the shipowner undertakes to deliver. The non-delivery of some of that [namely, the cargo shipped] affords no defence to a claim for a lump sum freight, although such non-delivery, if wrongful, will give rise to a cross-action. This was settled by the Court of Exchequer Chamber in *Merchant Shipping Co v Armitage*, which followed a decision to the same effect by the Privy Council in *The Norway*.

These authoritative pronouncements of the law . . . constitute, in my judgment, a sufficient answer to the defendants' second contention. It is common ground that the goods not delivered in the present case were not delivered because they had been lost by excepted perils. The defendants' counsel asked in the course of the argument what, as to the right to freight, ought to be the legal consequence of the chartered ship arriving without any of the cargo on board, so that nothing was delivered, and they further asked whether, if the loss had been caused not by excepted perils, but by the wrongful act or negligence of the shipowner, the lump freight would nevertheless be payable. It is, I think, sufficient to say that it is quite unnecessary for the purpose of our judgment in the present case to decide either of these points which are not involved. But it is clear from his judgment in *Merchant Shipping Co v Armitage* that Bramwell B, for the reason that the delivery of cargo is a condition precedent to payment, would have answered the first of the appellants' questions in favour of the owner of cargo, as he there states; and that in regard to the second question he would have concurred in the opinion expressed by Lord Lindley in the concluding sentence of the passage in his judgment in *Williams & Co v Canton Insurance*, which I have already quoted, that, even if the non-delivery of part of the cargo is due to wrongful conduct or negligence on the part of the shipowner, the proper remedy of the cargo owner is by cross-action. It is, however, in my judgment, as I have already intimated, useless, for the purpose of deciding the present case, to consider how these questions ought to be decided, the relevancy of which is excluded by the facts of the case under consideration.

Notes

1   In *Skibs A/S Trolla v United Enterprises, The Tarva* [1983] 2 Lloyd's Rep 385 in the Singapore High Court, Chua J held that where the balance of lump sum freight was payable under a voyage charter on 'right and true delivery' the balance became payable when the cargo that had arrived at the ports of discharge had been completely delivered. The shipowners did not have to prove right and true delivery of the whole cargo originally shipped to earn the freight and the charterers had no right to retain the balance against possible cargo claims by consignees.

2   In *Steamship Heathfield Co v Rodenacher* (1896) 2 Com Cas 55, CA, the *Heathfield* was chartered 'guaranteed by owners to carry 2,600 tons dead weight'. It was also provided she would load 'a full and complete cargo of sugar' to be delivered at a stated freight rate 'all per ton dead weight capacity as above'. The ship was given a lien, *inter alia*, for dead freight. The charterer loaded 2,673 tons of sugar, but refused to load the vessel to her actual capacity of 2,950 tons. At first instance (1 Com Cas 446) Mathew J rejected the argument that this was a lump sum freight and held that: (1) the owners' guarantee meant only that the vessel could carry 2,600 tons at least, not that she could not carry more; (2) that a 'full and complete cargo' meant what it said and was not restricted to 2,600 tons; and (3) that the freight rate was to be computed on the basis of a 'full and complete cargo' (2,950 tons), not on the basis of the guaranteed dead weight (2,600 tons). This judgment was upheld on appeal. T E Scrutton was counsel for the successful plaintiffs.

3   In *Rotherfield v Tweedy* (1897) 2 Com Cas 84 the *Rotherfield* was described in the contract (a 'Danube berth note') as 'of the capacity of 4,250 tons'; the owners also guaranteed that the vessel could carry 4,250 tons dead weight. It was agreed that a full cargo would be loaded. Freight was made payable per ton 'on the guaranteed d-w capacity of 4,250 tons'. The vessel loaded a full cargo of only 3,947 tons; her stated deadweight capacity included bunkers. The plaintiffs sought freight on 4,250 tons. The court rejected Scrutton's argument as counsel for the unsuccessful plaintiffs that the contract was for a lump sum freight and held freight was payable only on the quantity of cargo actually shipped. Successive editions of *Scrutton on*

Charterparties, from the 4th edn, 1899, have stated with justification that both the *Heathfield* and *Rotherfield* decisions seem to strike out of the charters part of their provisions. In *Rotherfield*, the court seems to have been particularly influenced by the fact that, if the parties had intended a lump sum, they could have said so in a simpler way.

4   *Shell v Seabridge*. The *Metula*, a supertanker, was chartered on the Exxonvoy 1969 form to carry a full cargo of petroleum. Freight was to be computed on intake quantity and paid without discount on delivery of cargo at destination. Over 190,000 long tons were loaded at Ras Tanura for carriage to Chile. The vessel stranded in the Magellan Strait and about a third of the cargo was lost; the rest was transhipped and carried to destination. It was held that the owners were entitled to freight on the full amount loaded. The court does not seem to have been impressed by the idea that 'intake quantity' clauses are not intended to deal with accidental losses in known circumstances, but only to avoid disputes where there is, as often occurs, a discrepancy between intake and outturn measurements of bulk cargo because of differences in weighing methods or in the physical circumstances (such as ambient temperature in which the measurements were made); or the normal gains or losses that occur with certain commodities in transit because of, for example, evaporation, sedimentation in ship's tanks or absorption of moisture.

17 *Pro rata* freight and the right to forward

Where freight is to be earned by delivering the agreed goods at the port of discharge, the carrier does not acquire a right to a proportion of the agreed sum by moving the cargo over part of the agreed route unless the parties agree to this, either expressly or by implication. The two cases in this section outline the very limited circumstances in which an agreement to pay a proportionate sum as freight may be implied from the conduct of the parties.

Hunter v Prinsep (1808) 10 East 378

Facts: The *Young Nicholas* was chartered to carry a cargo of timber from Honduras Bay to London. Freight was payable at agreed rates on or after a right and true delivery of the cargo. The ship and cargo were captured by a French privateer, recaptured by an English sloop but then wrecked at St Kitt's, where the Vice-Admiralty Court (on the master's application) ordered a sale of the cargo. The shipowner claimed to be entitled to freight *pro rata itineris*.

Held:

Lord Ellenborough: The principles which appear to govern the present action are these: the ship owners undertake that they will carry the goods to the place of destination, unless prevented by the dangers of the seas, or other unavoidable casualties: and the freighter undertakes that if the goods be delivered at the place of their destination he will pay the stipulated freight: but it was only in that event, viz, of their delivery at the place of destination, that he, the freighter, engages to pay anything. If the ship be disabled from completing her voyage, the shipowner may still entitle himself to the whole freight, by forwarding the goods by some other means to the place of destination; but he has no right to any freight if they be not so forwarded; unless the forwarding them be dispensed with, or unless there be some new bargain upon this subject. If the shipowner will not forward them, the freighter is entitled to them without paying anything. One party, therefore, if he forward them, or be prevented or discharged from so doing, is entitled to his whole freight; and the other, if there be a refusal to forward them, is entitled to have them without paying any freight at all. The general property in the goods is in the freighter; the shipowner has no right to withhold the possession from him, unless he has either earned his freight, or is going on to earn it. If no freight be earned, and he decline proceeding to earn any, the freighter has a right to possession. The captain's conduct in obtaining an order for selling the goods, and selling them accordingly, which was unnecessary, and which disabled him from forwarding the goods, was in effect declining to proceed to earn any freight, and therefore entitled the plaintiff to the entire produce of his goods, without any allowance for freight ...

St Enoch Shipping v Phosphate Mining [1916] 2 KB 624

Held:

Rowlatt J (at p 627): There can be no freight *pro rata* unless there is a new contract express or implied to substitute the carriage which has been effected for the carriage originally contracted for. In *Hopper v Burness* (1876) 1 CPD 137, 140, Brett J said:

> What, then, is the principle governing the question whether such freight is payable? It is only payable when there is a mutual agreement between the charterer or shipper and the captain or shipowner, whereby the latter being able and willing to carry on the cargo to the port of destination, but the former desiring to have the goods delivered to him at some intermediate port, it is agreed that they shall be so delivered, and the law then implies a contract to pay freight *pro rata itineris*.

That is a rule clearly stated of what is not only shipping law, but general law, where there is an agreement between two parties that a thing shall be done but no agreement as to the price to be paid for doing it. Park B in *Vlierboom v Chapman* (1844) 3 M & W 230, 238, laid down the law to the same effect:

> To justify a claim for *pro rata* freight, there must be a voluntary acceptance of the goods at an intermediate port, in such a mode as to raise a fair inference, that the further carriage of goods was intentionally dispensed with.

> The consignee must accept the goods in such a way as to imply that he and the shipowner agree that the goods have been carried far enough and that the shorter transit shall be substituted for that named in the original contract ... In the present case the defendants, who were consignees, merely took their own goods when they were landed. No agreement to modify the contract of carriage can be inferred from that act.

Note

Lord Ellenborough refers in *Hunter* to the possibility of the shipowner earning freight under a 'new bargain'. Such an agreement may be express or implied. But as Lord Ellenborough's judgment also illustrates, the respective rights of the parties under their original agreement are such that there is little room for the implication of a new contract. It follows from the above decisions that *pro rata* freight will not be payable merely because the owner of the cargo receives it at a place other than the contractual port of discharge. The master is not 'able' to carry or forward cargo if, for example, the cargo has been lost, destroyed or justifiably sold by the master without the cargo owner's consent (*Vlierboom v Chapman*; *Hopper v Burness*, above).

'Unwillingness' can be demonstrated simply by a wrongful refusal at an intermediate port to carry the cargo to its destination (*Metcalfe v Britannia Ironworks* (1877) 2 QBD 423); it might also be shown if, for example, the crew justifiably abandon the ship and its cargo in a storm, when the cargo owner can treat the contract of carriage as having ended: *The Cito* (1881) 7 PD 5.

The Law Commission provisionally concluded in 1975 (*Pecuniary Restitution on Breach of Contract*, Working Paper No 65) that the rules as to payment of *pro rata* freight were so firmly established in the business practice of shipowners and insurers that any interference with them (for instance by introducing a general obligation to make a payment in return for any benefit received) would be undesirable. This suggestion was generally approved (Law Commission, *Privity of Contract: Contracts for the Benefit of Third Parties*, Report No 121, 1983, London: HMSO). Compare the approach advocated in (1941) 57 LQR 385 (Glanville Williams) and by Goff and Jones, *Restitution*, 6th edn, 2002, London: Sweet & Maxwell, para 20–006.

18 Advance freight

Instead of agreeing that freight is to be earned by making delivery at an agreed place it is typical for bills of lading to provide that freight shall be earned and paid at a much earlier stage, usually on or around the date of commencement of the voyage, although there are variations in the precise event on which freight becomes due. For example, 'freight due and payable (or alternatively: freight to be considered earned) on shipment/on receipt of goods by carrier/on signing bills of lading/on sailing and non-returnable, ship and/or cargo lost or not lost'. Some clauses make a distinction between the date on which freight is 'earned' (on which the freight risk passes from the shipowner) and a later date on which the freight is actually payable. The decision of the House of Lords in *Allison v Bristol Marine Insurance* settled the effect of an agreement to pay advance freight.

Allison v Bristol Marine Insurance (1876) 1 App Cas 209, HL

Facts: The *Merchant Prince* was chartered to carry coal from Greenock to Bombay. The freight rate was 42 shillings a ton, such freight to be paid 'one half in cash on signing bills of lading . . . less five per cent for insurance . . . and the remainder on right delivery of the cargo'. Half of the freight was paid in London. The shipowner insured the freight that he expected to receive on the delivery of the full cargo. The cargo owner insured his cargo for a sum inclusive of the value of the freight he had prepaid. The ship was wrecked on a reef about eight miles from Bombay. Half the cargo was saved and landed but no further freight was paid. The shipowner claimed on his insurance policies alleging that he had suffered a total loss of half of the freight not paid in advance.

The judges were summoned to assist the House of Lords.

Held:

Brett J (after an extensive review of earlier cases) (at 226): I have drawn attention to all the cases, in order to shew how uniform the view has been as to what construction is to be put upon shipping documents in the form of the present charter-party, and as to the uniform, though perhaps anomalous rule, that the money to be paid in advance of freight must be paid, though the goods are before payment lost by perils of the sea, and cannot be recovered back after, if paid before the goods are lost by perils of the sea.

Although I have said that this course of business may in theory be anomalous, I think its origin and existence are capable of a reasonable explanation. It arose in the case of the long Indian voyages. The length of voyage would keep the shipowner for too long a time out of money; and freight is much more difficult to pledge, as a security to third persons, than goods represented by a bill of lading. Therefore the shipper agreed to make the advance on what he would ultimately have to pay, and, for a consideration, took the risk in order to obviate a repayment, which disarranges business transactions.

[Of the other judges who attended, Baron Pollock agreed with Brett J; Lord Chief Baron Kelly and Grove J also thought the plaintiff shipowner was entitled to succeed. Blackburn and Mellor JJ thought he was not. The House of Lords unanimously found in favour of the shipowner.]

Notes

1   Freight clauses often include an express statement that freight paid in advance is not repayable if the ship and/or cargo are later lost. This is strictly unnecessary under English law (many other legal systems require repayment); but it has a commercial advantage. It is easier to resolve a dispute with a shipper by referring him to a clause in a form that he has used than to attempt to demonstrate a general legal principle.

2   Where advance freight is paid and the goods are subsequently lost in circumstances in which the shipowner is liable in an action for damages for nondelivery (that is, the loss is not covered by an exclusion clause) then the advance freight paid forms part of the value of the goods at their intended destination and is recoverable as part of their value: *Great Indian Peninsula Rly v Turnbull* (1885) 53 LT 325.

3   'Final sailing': the *General Chasse* was chartered for a voyage from Cardiff to San Francisco, with a portion of freight payable on final sailing from the port of loading. The ship cleared customs, passed the dock gates, but, whilst under tow, she grounded in the ship canal that connected the dock with the open sea. The vessel subsequently became a wreck. It was held that 'sailing' meant the time the vessel is fully fit for sea and breaks ground; but 'final sailing' meant departure from the port and being at sea. The advance freight was not payable: *Roelandts v Harrison* (1854) 9 Ex 447.

4   'On signing bills of lading': one-third of freight was payable on signing bills of lading. The cargo was loaded but the vessel sank before reaching the dock gates and before the bills of lading had been signed. It was held that the charterers had an implied duty to present the bills of lading for signature within a reasonable time and that this obligation did not cease when the ship was lost. The charterers were found to have broken this implied contract and the measure of damages was the amount of the advance freight: *Oriental Steamship v Tylor* [1893] 2 QB 518, CA.

5   'If required': in *Oriental Steamship* (above), the earlier case of *Smith v Pyman* [1891] 1 QB 742 was distinguished. In that case advance freight was payable 'if required' and it was held too late to require it after the ship was lost, because the charterer could then no longer insure it.

6   The *Lorna I* was nominated under a freight contract to lift ore from an Albanian port. The contract provided 'freight non-returnable cargo and/or vessel lost or not lost to be paid . . . as follows: 75 per cent . . . within five . . . days after master signed Bills of lading and the balance after right and true delivery'. Bills of lading were signed but the vessel was lost with all hands, within five days, in a gale in the Black Sea. It was held that freight was not payable because the charterers had been under no obligation to pay any freight until the end of the five-day period and before that time the cargo and the vessel had been lost. Robert Goff J at first instance pointed out that the result would have been different if the parties had chosen to provide that freight was earned on shipment, but was not payable for five days thereafter: *Compania Naviera General v Kerametal* [1983] 1 Lloyd's Rep 373, CA.

7 Plaintiff owners let the *Karin Vatis* for a voyage from Liverpool to India with a cargo of scrap. The charter provided:

> Freight deemed earned as cargo loaded . . . 95 per cent of freight to be paid within three banking days after completion of loading and surrender of signed bills of lading . . . vessel and/or cargo lost or not lost . . . Balance of freight to be settled within 20 days after completion of discharge . . .

The initial payment was made, the vessel sailed and sank shortly after passing Suez. The charterers denied that the remaining 5% of freight was due on the grounds that no cargo had been discharged. The Court of Appeal held that the entire freight was earned as soon as cargo was loaded. Completion of discharge was not a condition precedent to the recovery of the outstanding amount, which was payable within a reasonable time: *The Karin Vatis* [1988] 2 Lloyd's Rep 330, CA.

8 In *Colonial Bank v European Grain & Shipping Ltd, The Dominique*, shipowners assigned to the plaintiff bank all the earnings of the *Dominique* including all freight. The vessel was chartered to load agricultural produce in bulk at Kakinada, India, for carriage to European ports. The charterparty provided that:

> Freight shall be prepaid within five days of signing and surrender of final bills of lading, full freight deemed to be earned on signing bills of lading, discountless and non-returnable, vessel and/or cargo lost or not lost and to be paid to [a named bank in Piraeus].

Cargo was loaded and bills of lading signed. At Colombo the vessel was arrested by suppliers and detained. The charterers justifiably elected to treat the owners' conduct as repudiating the charter. The bills of lading were subsequently surrendered to shippers. The plaintiff bank sued to recover the advance freight from the charterers. The charterers argued that, if the right to freight was held to have accrued before the charterparty was brought to an end, they were nevertheless entitled to set off the damage suffered by them as a result of the owners' repudiation. The House of Lords held that:

(i) the proper interpretation of the charterparty was that the owners' right to freight accrued on completion of signing of all the bills of lading, with payment being postponed until five days after the signed bills of lading had been delivered to shippers. In the result, the right to freight accrued before the termination of the charter;

(ii) the right to freight was unconditionally acquired before termination of the charter and survived that termination and was not divested or discharged by termination;

(iii) a repudiatory breach of a voyage charter, like the non-repudiatory breach considered in *The Aries* (above), was not capable of giving rise to a defence by way of equitable set off to a claim for accrued freight.

9 In *Krall v Burnett* (1877) 25 W R 305, QB Div Ct, the plaintiff shipped goods in London for carriage to Rouen in the defendant's ship. The ship was lost. The bill of lading stated 'freight payable in London'. It was held that the words meant only that freight was payable in London and not elsewhere, and had no reference to time of payment. The clause was not ambiguous and no evidence of an alleged custom that it meant freight was payable in advance could be given.

19 Back freight

Back freight is compensation payable to the carrier for extraordinary acts done in cases of 'accident and emergency' for the benefit of the owners of the cargo.

Cargo Ex Argos (1873) LR 5 PC 134

Facts: The defendant shipped petroleum on the plaintiff's vessel for carriage from London to Le Havre. The bill of lading provided that the petroleum was to be taken out by the defendant within 24 hours of arrival. The vessel arrived at Le Havre, but was ordered to leave the following day by the authorities because of the presence of munitions in the port. The master attempted to land the goods at other local ports but failed. He returned to Le Havre and obtained permission to discharge the petroleum temporarily into a lighter in the outer harbour where it remained under his control. Four days later, the *Argos* had discharged the rest of her cargo at the quay and was ready to sail. No request for delivery having been made, the master reshipped the petroleum and brought it back to London. It was held that the shipowner had earned the outward freight. But the case is best known for the decision on the shipowner's claim for freight on the return voyage and for expenses.

Held:

Sir Montague E Smith: . . . The next question to be considered is, whether the plaintiff is entitled to compensation in the shape of homeward freight for bringing the petroleum back to England. It seems to be a reasonable inference from the facts, that after the four days during which the petroleum had been lying in the harbour had expired, the authorities would not have allowed it to remain there. It was still in the master's possession, and the question is, whether he should have destroyed or saved it. If he was justified in trying to save it, their Lordships think he did the best for the interest of the defendant in bringing it back to England. Whether he was so justified is the question to be considered.

As pointed out by the judge of the Admiralty Court, the same kind of question arose in *Christy v Rowe* (1808) 1 Taunt 300. In that case Sir James Mansfield says:

> Where a ship is chartered upon one voyage outwards only, with no reference to her return, and no contemplation of a disappointment happening, no decision, which I have been able to find, determines what shall be done in case the voyage is defeated: the books throw no light on the subject. The natural justice of the matter seems obvious: that a master should do that which a wise and prudent man would think most conducive to the benefit of all concerned. But it appears to be wholly voluntary; I do not know that he is bound to do it; and yet, if it were a cargo of cloth or other valuable merchandise, it would be a great hardship that he might be at liberty to cast it overboard. It is singular that such a question should at this day remain undecided.

The precise point does not seem to have been subsequently decided; but several cases have since arisen in which the nature and scope of the duty of the master, as agent of the merchant, have been examined and defined. (Amongst others *Tronson v Dent* (1853) 8 Moo PC 419; *Notara v Henderson* (1872) LR 7 QB 225; *Australasian Navigation Company v Morse* (1872) LR 4 PC 222.) It results from them that not merely is a power given, but a duty is cast on the master in many cases of accident and emergency to act for the safety of the cargo, in such manner as may be best under the circumstances in which it may be placed; and that, as a correlative right, he is entitled to charge its owner with the expenses properly incurred in so doing.

Most of the decisions have related to cases where the accident happened before the completion of the voyage; but their Lordships think it ought not to be laid down that all obligation on the part of the master to act for the merchant ceases after a reasonable time for the latter to take delivery of the cargo has expired. It is well established that, if the ship has waited a reasonable time to deliver goods from her side, the master may land and warehouse them at the charge of the merchant; and it cannot be doubted that it would be his duty to do so rather than to throw them overboard. In a case like the present, where the goods could neither be landed nor remain where they were, it seems to be a legitimate extension of the implied agency of the master to hold that, in the absence of all advices, he had authority to carry or send them on to such other place as in his judgment, prudently exercised, appeared to be most convenient for their owner; and if so, it will follow from established principles that the expenses properly incurred may be charged to him.

Their Lordships have no doubt that bringing the goods back to England was in fact the best and cheapest way of making them available to the defendant, and that they were brought back at less charge in the *Argos* than if they had been sent in another ship.

If the goods had been of a nature which ought to have led the master to know that on their arrival they would not have been worth the expenses incurred in bringing them back, a different question would arise. But, in the present case, their value, of which the defendant has taken the benefit by asking for and obtaining the goods, far exceeded the cost.

The authority of the master being founded on necessity would not have arisen, if he could have obtained instructions from the defendant or his assignees. But under the circumstances this was not possible. Indeed this point was not relied on at the bar.

Their Lordships, for the above reasons, are of opinion that the plaintiff has made out a case for compensation for bringing back the goods to England. But they think the plaintiff is not entitled to recover the amount claimed for demurrage and expenses in attempting to enter the ports of Honfleur and Trouville. These efforts may have been made by him in the interest of the cargo as well as the ship; but they were made before the ship was ready to deliver at all in the port of Havre, and the expenses of this deviation and of the return to Havre, after permission had been obtained to discharge there, must be treated as expenses of the voyage, and not as incurred for the benefit of the defendant.

The charges for the hire of the vessel and of storing the petroleum in her at Havre, after permission had been obtained for its discharge there, stand on different ground. If the ship had then waited in the outer harbour with the petroleum on board, the defendant would have been liable to pay demurrage at £10.10s a day. It was obviously, therefore, to his advantage under the circumstances for the master to hire the vessel, and thus relieve him from the heavy demurrage payable for the detention of the ship. The whole expense of this operation appears to be about £15 only.

In the result their Lordships think the plaintiff is entitled to recover the outward freight, and the charge made for the carriage back to England . . . and also the £15 for the above expenses at Havre . . .

20 Shipper's liability for freight

In the case of liner shipping, the shipper named in the bill of lading is normally the person who has entered into the contract for carriage with the carrier and is normally the person who is liable to pay the freight. But this is not always the case, as Hobhouse LJ explains below.

Cho Yang Shipping Co Ltd v Coral (UK) Ltd [1997] 2 Lloyd's Rep 641, CA

Facts: Coral contracted with B who agreed to carry containers from Germany to Gulf ports at an agreed rate to be paid to B. B contracted on similar terms with A, who contracted with Cho Yang who carried the containers. Coral paid B who paid A, but A failed to pay Cho Yang, who had issued bills of lading marked 'Freight Prepaid' that named Coral as the shipper. It was held that there was no agreement by Coral to pay freight to the shipowners.

Held:

> **Hobhouse LJ:** ... In the absence of some other consideration, the shipper is contractually liable to the carrier for the freight: *Scrutton*, 20th ed, art 172. This is because the carriage is for reward and the personal liability to pay the reward is a contractual liability (whether the carriage was as a common carrier or pursuant to a 'special' contract). The personal liability is that of the person with whom the performing carrier has contracted to carry the goods. This person is normally the shipper: *Domett v Beckford* (1883) 5 B & Ad 521. But the shipper may be shipping as the agent of the consignee in which case the contract will be with the consignee: eg *Fragano v Long* (1825) 4 B & C 219, *Dickenson v Lano* (1860) 2 F & F 188. A contract to pay the freight will not always be implied from the fact of shipment and the issue of a bill of lading: *Smidt v Tiden* (1874) LR 9 QB 446. It is possible for there to be more complex contractual schemes; the performing carrier may be in contractual relations with others as well, as, for example, where there is a voyage or time charter; this can affect the position.
>
> In English law the bill of lading is not the contract between the original parties but is simply evidence of it: eg *The Ardennes* (1950) 84 Ll L Rep 340; [1951] 1 KB 55. Indeed, though contractual in form, it may in the hands of a person already in contractual relations with the carrier (eg a charterer) be no more than a receipt: *Rodoconachi v Milburn* (1886) 18 QBD 67. Therefore, as between shipper and carrier, it may be necessary to inquire what the actual contract between them was; merely to look at the bill of lading may not in all cases suffice. It remains necessary to look at and take into account the other evidence bearing upon the relationship between the shipper and the carrier and the terms of the contract between them: *Scrutton*, art 33. The terms upon which the goods have been shipped may not be in all respects the same as those actually set out in the bill of lading. It does not necessarily follow in any given case that the named shipper is to be under a personal liability for the payment of the freight.
>
> As will be readily appreciated, the inclusion of the words 'freight prepaid' in the bill of lading does not of itself show that the shipper is not to be under any liability for the freight if it has not in fact been paid: eg *The Nanfri* [1979] 1 Lloyd's Rep 201; [1979] AC 757. Such words are not, in English law, words of contract (eg *Compania Naviera Vasconzada v Churchill* [1906] 1 KB 237) and their insertion in the bill of lading does not without more serve to negative a pre-existing, undischarged, contractual liability to pay the freight. Indeed, a request to the carrier that he issue a freight prepaid bill of lading before the freight has in fact been paid would normally imply a personal undertaking by the person making the request that it would be paid ... Thus, in the present case, the mere inclusion of those words in the bill of lading does not preclude a liability of Coral for the freight but it is part of the evidence to be taken into account when considering whether or not Coral were under a contractual liability to the plaintiffs for the freight ...

(On the facts, it was held that the correct inference was that there was no agreement
by Coral to pay freight to the plaintiffs.)

Notes

1   Delivery of cargo to consignees with no attempt to collect freight will not itself relieve a charterer or shipper from liability to pay: *Domett v Beckford* (1833) 5 B & Ad 521.

2   *Liens*. At common law, the shipowner is entitled to a possessory lien on cargo for freight payable on delivery. The shipowner is similarly entitled to a lien for general average contributions and for extraordinary expenses that have been justifiably incurred for the protection of cargo: *Hingston v Wendt* (1876) 1 QB 367. These common law liens are all possessory in nature so that the shipowner's right is to retain possession of the goods until the freight due is offered to him. Since the common law lien for freight is only possessory, it can be waived or lost by delivering the goods to the person entitled, without insisting on payment. There is no common law or implied lien in respect of freight that is contractually payable in advance of or after delivery:

The decision is, that where the agreed time for payment of freight is not contemporaneous with the time of delivery of the cargo, there is no implied right of lien [*per* Brett J, *Allison v Bristol Marine* (above) referring to *Kirchner v Venus* (1859) 12 Moo P C 361].

Nor is there any lien at common law for dead freight or for demurrage or damages for detention. But liens for advance freight, demurrage, dead freight and other items ('all other charges') can be and frequently are created by agreement.

21 Cesser clauses

It is not unusual for a charterparty to provide that, in some circumstances, the charterer shall escape all liability for freight, for example:

> Charterer's liability to cease on steamer being loaded provided the cargo is worth the freight, the owners having an absolute lien on the cargo for all freight, dead freight, demurrage and average.

This example is taken from Thornton, RN's evocative *British Shipping*, 1945, Cambridge: CUP. Thornton rightly describes the cesser clause as a commercial instrument of real ingenuity and flexibility. He points out that it enables the charterer with a cargo to avoid borrowing and paying interest to finance advance freight charges, and possibly also gives him additional time to sell the cargo; although naturally the cargo must be sold on the basis that the buyer pays the freight. The shipowner for his part is protected by his lien on the cargo. But this is the factor that limits the use of the device: the shipowner is only protected to the extent that the lien is a valid and effective means of securing payment from the receiver in the jurisdiction in which the port of discharge is located. *The Aegis Britannic*, although not a case dealing directly with freight, reviews the traditional approach to the construction of cesser clauses.

Action SA v Britannic Shipping, The Aegis Britannic
[1987] 1 Lloyd's Rep 119, CA

Facts: The vessel was chartered to carry rice from a US Gulf port to Basra in Iraq. During discharge by the stevedores, the cargo was damaged and the owners were held liable to the cargo receivers by an Iraqi court in Basra in respect of that damage. The owners claimed damages and/or an indemnity from the charterers in respect of that liability. The charter contained three relevant clauses. Clause 5 imposed liability on the charterers:

> 5 Cargo to be brought to, loaded, and stowed, respectively discharged at the expense and risk of Shippers/Charterers respectively Receivers/ Charterers.

Clause 20 created a lien:

> 20 Owners shall have a lien on the cargo for freight, dead freight and demurrage. Charterers shall remain responsible for dead freight and demurrage incurred at loading port. Charterers shall also remain responsible for freight and demurrage incurred at discharge port.

Clause 35 was the cesser clause:

> 35 Charterers' liability under this charterparty to cease upon cargo being shipped except as regards payment of freight, dead freight and demurrage incurred at both ends.

Held:

Dillon LJ: . . . Here the lien clause and the cesser clause fit in together, as the judge pointed out, with no difficulty. The owners are to have a lien under the lien clause for freight, dead freight and demurrage. Notwithstanding that lien, the charterers are to remain responsible for freight, dead freight and demurrage. The cesser clause expressly excludes from its scope payment of freight, dead freight and demurrage incurred at both ends. So the lien clause creates no problem as I see it, but the difficulty lies in reconciling the cesser clause with the other provisions of the charterparty, particularly cl 5 which I have read, because if the cesser clause is to be read literally, the liability of the charterers under cl 5, at any rate in respect of discharge, is at once removed by cl 35 of the same document. The same happens with a number of the other additional clauses in the charterparty . . .

The courts have long since considered cesser clauses. The leading authority is the decision of this court in *Clink v Radford & Co* [1891] 1 QB 625. There it so happened that the difficulty of construction was concerned with how the lien clause and the cesser clause were to be read together. Lord Esher, it seems to me, put things on a more general basis. He said the following at p 627:

> It seems to me, without going through the cases that have been referred to, that certain rules have been laid down in them which will enable us to decide this particular case. In my opinion, the main rule to be derived from the cases as to the interpretation of the cesser clause in a charterparty, is that the court will construe it as inapplicable to the particular breach complained of, if by construing it otherwise the shipowner would be left unprotected in respect of that particular breach, unless the cesser clause is expressed in terms that prohibit such a conclusion. In other words, it cannot be assumed that the shipowner without any mercantile reason would give up by the cesser clause rights which he had stipulated for in another part of the contract. If that be true, then the question in this particular case, as in every other case, will depend upon this, whether if we apply the cesser clause to the particular breach complained of, and so hold the charterer to be free, the shipowner has any remedy for his loss. If he has, we should construe the cesser clause in its fullest possible meaning, and say that the charterer is released; but if we find that, by so construing it, the shipowner would be left without any remedy whatever for the breach, then we should say that it could not have been the meaning of the parties that the cesser clause should apply to such a breach.

That language seems to me to be directly applicable to treating the liability of the charterers under cl 5 as immediately discharged by the cesser clause, cl 35. Bowen LJ puts the matter similarly. He says, at p 629, the following:

> There is no doubt that the parties may, if they choose, so frame the clause as to emancipate the charterer from any specified liability without providing for any terms of compensation – to the shipowner; but such a contract would not be one we should expect to see in a commercial transaction. The cesser clauses as they generally come before the courts are clauses which couple or link the provisions for the cesser of the charterer's liability with a corresponding creation of a lien.

I interject that here the lien and the cesser clauses are separate from each other. I now continue the citation:

> . . . There is a principle of reason which is obvious to commercial minds, and which should be borne in mind in considering a cesser clause so framed, namely, that reasonable persons would regard the lien given as an equivalent for the release of responsibility which the cesser clause in its earlier part creates, and one would expect to find the lien commensurate with the release of liability. That is a sound principle of commercial reasoning which has been sanctioned by the courts in the cases cited to us, and which has been recognised in the chain of important and valuable judgments of the present Master of the Rolls. That being the principle of construction

to apply, one would not expect to find a shipowner placing his ship and himself at the mercy of a charterer without some equivalent, or contracting on a given event to release the charterer from all liability unless there were some other mode of protecting himself against the act of the charterer.

Again, the wording is general and is not limited to finding that the other remedy is given by the lien clause. This, as I see it, is all part of the normal process of construction in which all the various relevant clauses of the contract have to be read together, without taking the wording of one standing on its own and looking no further. The appellant's construction of the cesser clause in effect involves striking out the word 'charterers' wherever it appears in the passage from cl 5 which I have read, at any rate in relation to discharge.

It is submitted, very probably rightly by Mr Priday for the charterers, that the references in that passage in cl 5 to shippers and receivers, envisages that by adoption of clauses of the charterparty into the bills of lading, the owners will have protection against any claims of the receivers of the cargo for damage in discharge. In the present case, the clauses of the charterparty were, we are told, adopted into the bills of lading, but the court in Iraq refused to give effect to those clauses and the arbitrator in his award has said that that is generally the case in Iraq. Hence the liability as held by the Iraqi court of the owners to the receivers of the cargo. But where the question has arisen in a context of reconciling a cesser clause and a lien clause, the court has held that the reconciliation is to be effected by holding that the cesser clause only applies in so far as the lien is effective. This was held first in *Hansen v Harrold Brothers* [1894] 1 QB 612. In that case the charterparty permitted the charterers to recharter the ship. The effect of that was that the owners had a lien on the freight under the recharter, but for various reasons that came out as less than the freight payable under the charterparty and therefore it was not an adequate remedy.

Lord Esher, at p 618, cited from the judgments of the Court in *Clink v Radford & Co*. He said the following:

> . . . It seems to me that this reasoning has not been and cannot be answered. Therefore the proposition is true that, where the provision for cesser liability is accompanied by the stipulation as to lien, then the cesser of liability is not to apply in so far as the lien, which by the charterparty the charterers are enabled to create, is not equivalent to the liability of the charterers. Where, in such a case, the provisions of the charterparty enable the charterers to make such terms with the shippers that the lien which is created is not commensurate with the liability of the charterers under the charterparty, then the cesser clause will only apply so far as the lien which can be exercised by the shipowner is commensurate with such liability.

Similarly, in the case of *The Sinoe* [1971] 1 Lloyd's Rep 514 – a decision of Donaldson J which was upheld by this court in [1972] 1 Lloyd's Rep 201 – it was held that the cesser clause did not avail charterers where the owners had a lien on cargo which they could not enforce owing to local conditions. I find that reasoning directly applicable in the present case. If the owners had no alternative remedy against the receivers of the cargo or, for that matter anyone else, the cesser clause cannot be construed as immediately cutting out and extinguishing the charterers' primary liability under cl 5 . . .

(Lloyd and Nicholls LJJ delivered concurring judgments.)

 Further reading

Baughen, S, *Summerskill on Laytime*, 5th edn, 2013, London: Sweet & Maxwell.
Bulow, L, 'Dangerous cargoes' (1989) LMCLQ 342.
Davies, D, *Commencement of Laytime*, 4th edn, 2006, London: Informa.

Girvin, S, 'Shipper's liability for dangerous cargoes' (1996) LMCLQ 487.

Rose, F, 'Cargo risks: Dangerous goods' (1996) 55 CLJ 14.

Schofield, J, *Laytime and Demurrage*, 6th edn, 2011, London: Informa.

Solvang, T, 'Laytime, demurrage and multiple charterparties' (2001) LMCLQ 285.

Tiberg, H, *Demurrage*, 5th edn, 2013, London: Sweet & Maxwell.

Todd, P, 'Start of laytime' (2002) JBL 217.

Chapter 4

Time Charters

Strictly speaking the letting of vessels on time charters is not carriage of goods. Under a time charter the owner agrees to allow the charterer to have the use of a vessel for a fixed period of time. The owner does not agree to carry cargo; rather it allows the charterer to make its own decisions about the use of the vessel. The charterer takes the vessel complete with a crew and so does not have to worry too much about personnel issues but does take the risk of routeing and delay.

From a legal analysis point of view the relationship between owner and charterer is an interesting and at times complex one. It is common practice to use modified standard form contracts in order to draft the time charter and although these naturally vary in the actual words used they cover much the same issues and use very similar terminology.

Among other things, a time charter will contain promises by the owner about the vessel and its maintenance; the contract will also deal with the length of the charter (delivery, period and redelivery), the uses to which the ship may be put and the places to which it can be sent (safe ports, ice and war clauses and trading limits) and with the payment by the charterer of hire and the variable operating expenses such as fuel, port and canal dues which flow from the charterer's decisions.

1 Terminology

When considering the terminology it is worth noting that the words *delivery, redelivery, withdrawal* and *let* and *hire* may suggest that a time charter is an agreement under which possession of the vessel passes from the owner to the charterer. This is not the case, as MacKinnon LJ explains.

Sea & Land Securities Ltd v William Dickinson & Co Ltd [1942] 2 KB 65, CA

Held:

> **MacKinnon LJ:** The rights and obligations of the parties to a time charterparty must depend on its written terms, for there is no special law applicable to this form of contract as such. A time charterparty is, in fact, a misleading document, because the real nature of what is undertaken by the shipowner is disguised by the use of language dating from a century or more ago, which was appropriate to a contract of a different character then in use. At that time a time charterparty (now known as a demise charterparty) was an agreement under which possession of the ship was handed by the shipowner to the charterer for the latter to put his servants and crew in her and sail her for his own benefit . . . The modern form of time charterparty is, in essence, one by which the shipowner agrees with the time charterer that during a certain named period he will render services by his servants and crew to carry the goods which are put on board his ship by the time charterer. But certain phrases which survive in the printed form now used are only pertinent to the older form of demise charterparty. Such phrases, in the charterparty now before the court, are: 'the owners agree to let', and 'the charterers agree to hire' the steamer. There was no 'letting' or 'hiring' of this steamer. Then it is in terms provided that at the end of the period the vessel shall be 'redelivered' by the time charterers to the shipowners. 'Redelivery' is only a pertinent expression if there has been any delivery or handing over of the ship by the shipowner to the charterer. There never had been any such delivery here. The ship at all times was in the possession of the shipowners and they simply undertook to do services with their crew in carrying the goods of the charterers. As I ventured to suggest quite early in the argument, between the old and the modern form of contract there is all the difference between the contract which a man makes when he hires a boat in which to row himself about and the contract he makes with a boatman that he shall take him for a row . . .

2 The interrelationship of clauses and the charterer's right to give legitimate orders

The time charter will contain clauses that set out the terms upon which the vessel can be used. Prominent amongst these are the choice of law and jurisdiction clause, the employment and indemnity clause and the geographical limits clause. The law and jurisdiction clause will point to the law that applies to the contract and frequently this will be English law and so explains why we think that this book is of interest to those in the worldwide shipping community.

The other clauses are to be read together and the existence of one clause has a bearing on the operation of another. This can result in situations where implied duties are subordinated to contractual terms.

The employment and indemnity clause sets out the rights that the charterer (as non-owner) has over the vessel and the obligations that the owner has undertaken to fulfill. The charterer has the right to give orders with regard to the employment of the vessel but this right is not unlimited. All lawful orders must be complied with but unlawful orders can be refused. The clause will usually provide for an indemnity (see later in this chapter) for any damage sustained as a consequence of following a direct order. The scope of the charterer's right to give orders and the interrelation with the master's duty to ensure the safety of the vessel and the geographical limits clause were reviewed by Lord Hobhouse in *Whistler International Ltd v Kawasaki Kisen Kaisha Ltd, The Hill Harmony* [2001] 1 AC 638.

Whistler International Ltd v Kawasaki Kisen Kaisha Ltd, The Hill Harmony [2001] 1 AC 638

Facts: The bulk carrier *Hill Harmony* was chartered for seven/nine months' worldwide trading within Institute Warranty Limits, as ordered by charterers, with an obligation to proceed with the utmost despatch. The ship was ordered to make two laden voyages from Vancouver to Japan, in the months of January and April, by the shortest route (the Great Circle route), which was the route recommended as the most favourable by an independent weather routing agency Ocean Routes. In the period March to May 1994 Ocean Routes provided advice to 360 vessels moving from the Pacific north-west to northerly China, Korea or Japan. There was no evidence of any particular difficulties encountered by the vessels that had taken the northern route. By that route the voyages would have taken about 16 and 13 days. But the *Hill Harmony* followed a longer and more southerly line (the rhumb line route), the master hoping that on this track the weather conditions would be better. As a result, on one voyage she took six days longer to get to her destination and consumed some 130 tons more fuel and on the other she took three days longer and consumed some 69 tons more. The loss to the charterers was about US$89,800. The owners denied liability for the charterers' loss, arguing that the choice of route did not relate to the employment of the vessel but to its navigation and all matters of navigation were within the sole province of the master to decide and, if he was in any way at fault, their liability was excluded under the contract as an error of navigation.

Held:

Lord Hobhouse: . . . The question raised by this dispute is not a new one. It reflects the conflict of interest between owners and charterers under a time charter. Under a voyage charter the owner or disponent owner is using the vessel to trade for his own account. He decides and controls how he will exploit the earning capacity of the vessel, what trades he will compete in, what cargoes he will carry. He bears the full commercial risk and expense and enjoys the full benefit of the earnings of the vessel. A time charter is different. The owner still has to bear the expense of maintaining the ship and the crew. He still carries the risk of marine accidents and has to insure his interest in the vessel appropriately. But, in return for the payment of hire, he transfers the right to exploit the earning capacity of the vessel to the time charterer. The time charterer also agrees to provide and pay for the fuel consumed and to bear the disbursements which arise from the trading of the vessel. The owner of a time chartered vessel does not normally have any interest in saving time . . .

What might be described as the scheduling of the vessel is of critical importance to the charterer so that obligations to others can be fulfilled, employment opportunities not missed and flexibility maintained. The 'utmost dispatch' clause is, as Lord Sumner said in *Suzuki and Co Ltd v J Benyon and Co Ltd* (1926) 42 TLR 269, 274, a merchants' clause with the object of giving effect to the mercantile policy of saving time. As a matter of this mercantile policy and, indeed, as a matter of the use of English a voyage will not have been prosecuted with the utmost dispatch if the owners or the master unnecessarily chooses a longer route which will cause the vessel's arrival at her destination to be delayed. If the charterer has sub-voyage-chartered the vessel to another or has caused bills of lading to be issued, the charterer will be under a legal obligation to ensure that the voyage be prosecuted without undue delay and without unjustifiable deviation. The charterer is entitled to look to the owner of the carrying vessel to perform this obligation and that is one of the reasons why the 'utmost dispatch' clause is included in the usual forms of time charter.

Suppose that the charterer does no more than order the vessel to load at Vancouver and proceed to a port on the east coast of Japan, that order would give rise to an obligation under the clause to proceed from one port to the other with the utmost dispatch and is inconsistent with a liberty to delay the vessel by going by a longer than necessary route. To proceed by an unnecessarily long route delays the vessel just as surely as if the vessel had sailed at something less than full speed. There may of course be countervailing factors such as adverse currents or headwinds which may make an apparently longer route in fact the more expeditious route but, on the arbitrators' findings, none of those factors justified taking the longer route in the present case.

Another difficulty for the owners' argument is the fact that the owners have already agreed in the charterparty what are to be the limits within which the charterers can order the vessel to sail, for present purposes the Institute Warranty Limits, and have undertaken that, barring unforeseen matters, the vessel will be fit to sail in those waters. It is not open to the owners to say that the vessel is not fit to sail from Vancouver to Japan by the shortest route within IWL . . . In fact, upon the findings of the arbitrators, the vessel was fit to sail by the shorter northern route and the master did not have any good reason for preferring the longer southern route. It was not a good reason that he preferred to sail through calm waters or that he wanted to avoid heavy weather. Vessels are designed and built to be able to sail safely in heavy weather. The classification society rules require, as does clause 1 of the NYPE Form, the maintenance of these safety standards. It is no excuse for the owners to say that the shortest route would (even if it be the case) take the vessel through the heavy weather which she is designed to be able to encounter.

The courts below discussed the question of deviation under bill of lading contracts or voyage charterparties. This was not directly material to a time charter where the contract is not a contract of carriage but a contract for the provision of the services of a crewed vessel. However there is a relationship between prosecuting a voyage with the utmost dispatch and doing so without unjustifiable deviation . . .

Under the time charter the obligation is not simply to proceed by a usual route but to proceed with the utmost dispatch. Further, where the vessel should take on bunkers is, subject to emergencies, undoubtedly a matter for the charterers. The provision of bunkers is the charterers' responsibility and the charterers can give orders as to the bunkering ports to be visited; no question of what is usual arises . . . The argument of the owners, from which they did not resile, was that in this situation the choice between the usual routes was entirely a matter for the master and the charterers could not give orders as to which was to be chosen, say, via the Cape of Good Hope or via the Suez Canal, even though the charterers would have to pay the canal and port dues and pay for the fuel consumed. (See also Mr Davenport QC (1998)

LMCLQ 502.) The significance of such choices are commercial and relate to the exploitation of the earning capacity of the vessel. They are within the ambit of the employment of the vessel and are matters about which time charterers can give orders. A time charterer can give an order because he wants the vessel to be well positioned for a commercial opportunity or other commercial reason. A time charterer can order the chartered vessel to proceed at an economical speed; the time charterer may be waiting for a cargo to become available or the laydays at a loading port may not begin until after a certain date.

But even if the courts below should have got involved, which they have not, in a discussion of what was the usual route across the Pacific from Vancouver to the east coast of Japan, the arbitrators' reasons were clear. The northerly route was the shortest route. There was no evidence that any other route was a usual route. There was evidence that the northerly route was the usual route to follow as it had been by 360 vessels over a three month period. It was also incorrect to treat the case as if it left open the possibility that there had been a rational justification for refusing to proceed by the northerly route. The arbitrators found that the master did not have any rational justification for what he did. My Lords, it follows from what I have already said that, on the findings of the arbitrators, the charterers were, by ordering the vessel to proceed by the shortest and most direct route, requiring nothing more than was in any event the contractual obligation of the owners. Therefore the question whether the order was an order as regards the employment of the vessel is academic. But it was in truth such an order. The choice of ocean route was, in the absence of some overriding factor, a matter of the employment of the vessel, her scheduling, her trading so as to exploit her earning capacity. The courts below, by contrast, accepted the owners' argument that it was necessarily a matter of the navigation of the vessel.

In support of this argument, the charterers primarily relied upon *Larrinaga Steamship Co Ltd v The King* [1945] AC 246 . . .

The meaning of any language is affected by its context. This is true of the words 'employment' in a time charter and of the exception for negligence in the 'navigation' of the ship in a charterparty or contract of carriage. They reflect different aspects of the operation of the vessel. 'Employment' embraces the economic aspect – the exploitation of the earning potential of the vessel. 'Navigation' embraces matters of seamanship. Mr Donald Davies [(1999) LMCLQ 461] suggests that the words 'strategy' and 'tactics' give a useful indication. What is clear is that to use the word 'navigation' in this context as if it includes everything which involves the vessel proceeding through the water is both mistaken and unhelpful. As Lord Sumner pointed out [*Suzuki v Beynon*, above], where seamanship is in question, choices as to the speed or steering of the vessel are matters of navigation, as will be the exercise of laying off a course on a chart. But it is erroneous to reason, as did Clarke J, from the fact that the master must choose how much of a safety margin he should leave between his course and a hazard or how and at what speed to proceed up a hazardous channel to the conclusion that all questions of what route to follow are questions of navigation.

The master remains responsible for the safety of the vessel, her crew and cargo. If an order is given compliance with which exposes the vessel to a risk which the owners have not agreed to bear, the master is entitled to refuse to obey it: indeed, as the safe port cases show, in extreme situations the master is under an obligation not to obey the order. The charterers' submissions in the present case and the arbitrators' reasons and decision did not contravert this.

In the present case, the exception did not provide a defence. First, the breach of contract was the breach of both aspects of the owners' obligations under clause 8 of the time charter – to prosecute the voyage with the utmost dispatch and to comply with the orders and directions of the charterers as regards the employment of the vessel. As a matter of construction, the exception does not apply to the choice not to perform these obligations . . . Secondly, any error which the master made in this connection was not an error in the navigation or management of the vessel; it did not concern any matter of seamanship. Thirdly, the owners failed to discharge the burden of proof which lay upon them to bring themselves within the exception. This was clearest with regard to the second of the two relevant voyages where the arbitrators could only guess at, 'suspect', why it was that the master acted as he did . . .

Note

In *The Hill Harmony* the charterers' order seems to have been treated as legitimate because it had commercial implications (or affected profitability) and did not fall within the master's exclusive sphere of competence and responsibility. On this basis, for example, a decision to sail from a given port is one for the charterer if there are no safety or other good reasons to remain (*The Renee Hyaffil* (1916) 32 TLR 83, p 660; *The SS Lord* [1920] 1 KB 846). But wind, current, tide, visibility, traffic, conditions on board and weather forecasts may make the decision about when to sail a navigational matter for the master, as *The Ramon de Larrinaga* [1945] AC 246 shows. See further Davenport, B, 'The Hill Harmony' (1998) LMCLQ 502; Davies, D, 'The Hill Harmony' (1999) LMCLQ 461.

2.1 Time for compliance

In the last case, *The Hill Harmony*, the House of Lords held that the shipowner was in breach of contract in failing to comply with a legitimate order with reasonable despatch. But the shipowner's promise is not an absolute and unconditional undertaking to respond immediately to instructions. The existence of a right and perhaps sometimes a duty to delay was confirmed in *The Houda*: compliance with commercial instructions may have to wait for favourable circumstances.

Kuwait Petroleum Corp v I & D Oil Carriers Ltd, The Houda [1994] 2 Lloyd's Rep 541, CA

Facts: shipowners let their vessel *Houda* on the Shelltime 4 form. On 2 August 1990 when Iraq invaded Kuwait, *Houda* was loading a cargo of crude oil at Mina Al Ahmadi. She sailed with a part cargo, leaving behind blank bills of lading that had been signed by the master. After the invasion the management of the charterers was moved to London and it was from the London offices that the charterers gave sailing and survey orders to the vessel. The vessel remained at anchor off Fujairah until 27 September. The charterers alleged that the shipowners had refused to comply with orders that were lawfully given.

Held:

Neill LJ: . . . It was argued on behalf of the charterers . . . that subject to three exceptions, the owners and the master were obliged to obey the charterers' orders immediately, or at any rate as soon as practicable. Counsel for the charterers identified these exceptions as follows: (1) where obedience to an order might involve a significant risk of endangering the vessel or its cargo or crew; (2) where it was necessary to seek clarification of an ambiguous order; and (3) where the owners had knowledge of circumstances which were not known to the charterers but which might, if known, affect their orders, and the owners needed confirmation that the orders were to stand. It was submitted that there was no room for the implication of a general term whereby the owners were allowed a reasonable time in which to seek confirmation of the authority of those giving the orders or of the lawfulness of the orders. Furthermore, it was submitted that on the facts of this case the owners' conduct amounted not to delayed compliance but to a refusal to comply with the charterers' orders.

It is clear therefore that it is common ground between the parties that a master is entitled to delay in executing an order if to comply would threaten to expose the ship and cargo to a potential peril or if the circumstances otherwise fall within one of these three exceptions. We were referred to four authorities in support of that proposition. I propose to consider these authorities to see whether one can detect any wider principle on which a right to pause before complying with an order can be founded.

In *Pole v Cetcovitch* (1860) 9 CBNS 430 the master of an Austrian vessel declined to comply immediately with an order to sail from Falmouth to Copenhagen. He relied on the fact that war had broken out between

France and Austria and therefore the voyage might expose his vessel to capture by a French cruiser. The Court of Common Pleas upheld a direction to the jury that if they considered that in the circumstances the master was justified in pausing before complying with the order they should find that he was not in breach.

The next case to which we were referred was the decision of the Privy Council in *The Teutonia* (1872) LR 4 PC 171. In giving judgment Mellish LJ said at p 179:

> It seems obvious that, if a Master receives credible information that, if he continues in the direct course of his voyage, his ship will be exposed to some imminent peril, as, for instance, that there are pirates in his course, or icebergs or other dangers of navigation, he must be justified in pausing and deviating from the direct course, and taking any step which a prudent man would take for the purpose of avoiding the danger.

The reference to 'credible information' is of importance because the information which the master had received was premature in the sense that war between France and Prussia was not formally declared until three days later. Counsel for the charterers treated this case as one where the master had some additional information and where there was a risk of danger to the ship or cargo.

A year later the Privy Council gave judgment in a similar case: *The San Roman* (1873) LR 5 PC 301. In the course of a voyage to Europe *San Roman* put in to Valparaiso for repairs. The repairs were completed on or about 23 September 1870 but the vessel delayed sailing until 23 December because war had broken out between France and Prussia and it was believed that if the vessel sailed there was a risk of capture by the French Navy. In the course of the judgment Sir Montague Smith said at p 306:

> . . . the question their Lordships have to determine is entirely a question of fact, namely, whether the German master had during that time such an apprehension of capture founded on circumstances calculated to affect his mind – he being a man of ordinary courage, judgment, and experience – as would justify delay; and their Lordships agree with the judge in the court below that there was a sufficient risk of capture to justify this delay.

> This is not a case where the master has refused to perform the contract at all. No doubt, if the voyage had been abandoned, then it would have been necessary to show that he had been actually prevented from performing it; but this is merely a question of whether there was a reasonable cause for delay.

It was held that the fact that the cargo was an English cargo made no difference. Sir Montague Smith continued at p 307:

> If their Lordships were to look upon this case as a case in which the cargo was German as well as the ship, or a case in which both ship and cargo belonged to the same person, and then were to ask the question: Would a man of reasonable prudence, under such circumstances, have set sail or waited? It appears to their Lordships most clearly that a man of reasonable prudence would have waited.

The fourth case in this quartet was the decision of Donaldson J in *Midwest Shipping Co v DI Henry (Jute) Ltd* [1971] 1 Lloyd's Rep 375. In that case the master under a time charter received orders from the charterers to put back to port. The master did not comply at once because, on the charterers' instructions, he had lied to the port authorities about his destination and he was also concerned as to whether there would be sufficient water to cross the bar at the port. The judge held that the master's actions were justified, but at one point in his judgment he expressed the duty of the master in a way which might suggest that the right to pause may arise in a number of different circumstances including those where there is no threat to expose the ship and cargo to potential peril. Thus at p 379 Donaldson J put the matter in this way:

> . . . It is important to remember that the master of a merchant ship occupies a civilian post. He is not the captain of a naval vessel who might well be expected to comply instantly with

an order and seek verification or reconsideration afterwards. Furthermore, he is not receiving the instruction from somebody who is his professional superior, as would be the case in the services. He is the representative of his owners and also to some extent of the charterers. He occupies a post of very great responsibility, and he occupies that post by virtue of long training and experience. If he was the type of man who would immediately act upon any order from charterers without further consideration, he would probably be unfitted for that post. It seems to me that against that background it must be the duty of the master to act reasonably upon receipt of orders. Some orders are of their nature such that they would, if the master were to act reasonably, require immediate compliance. Others would require a great deal of thought and consideration before a reasonable master would comply with them.

... In the course of the argument in this court counsel for the charterers introduced what might be regarded as a fourth category of exception. Thus he accepted that the owners and a master might pause and seek further information if they knew or had reasonable cause to suspect that the instructions had not been given by the charterers. It was not enough, however, it was said, to justify delay if the owners and the master had merely a vague apprehension.

I am unable to accept that the right, or indeed the duty, to pause can safely be confined to specific categories of cases. I consider that it is necessary to take a broad and comprehensive view of the duties and responsibilities of the owners and the master and to ask, as was suggested in *The San Roman*, above: How would a man of reasonable prudence have acted in the circumstances? Thus, for example, the delivery of a cargo pursuant to an order given by the agent of an invading army may pose just as much a threat to cargo and those who have legitimate rights to it as an iceberg or a foreign frigate. It will depend on the circumstances.

... It is not of course for this court to decide whether on the facts the owners had reasonable grounds to pause, but I am satisfied that in a war situation there may well be circumstances where the right, and indeed the duty, to pause in order to seek further information about the source of and the validity of any orders which may be received is capable of arising even if there may be no immediate physical threat to the cargo or the ship.

... it seems to me that it is at least possible that where a country has been invaded prudent owners may be entitled to guard against the risk that their orders may have come from the 'wrong' side ...

Leggatt LJ: ... It is obvious that lawful orders have to be obeyed, unless to do so would imperil the safety of ship, crew or cargo. It is not obvious that they have to be obeyed unthinkingly. 'Theirs not to reason why' is a creed that neither characterises nor befits masters of chartered vessels. In my judgment when a master receives an order relating to the cargo his duty, which is probably owed to the owners of the cargo as well as the owners of the vessel, is to act reasonably. Orders ordinarily require immediate compliance. But the circumstances in which an order is received or the nature of it may make it unreasonable for the master to comply without further consideration or enquiry. When an order is reasonably regarded as ambiguous, it must be clarified. When the lawfulness of an order is reasonably called in question, it must be established. When the authenticity of an order is reasonably doubted, it must be verified. The delay introduced by any of these processes will usually be brief ...

Millett LJ: ... In my judgment the authorities establish two propositions of general application: (1) the master's obligation on receipt of an order is not one of instant obedience but of reasonable conduct; and (2) not every delay constitutes a refusal to obey an order; only an unreasonable delay does so ...

3 Shipowner's right to an indemnity

To protect the shipowner who agrees to carry out the time charterer's orders, it is common to provide expressly that the charterer will indemnify the shipowner against the consequences of complying with such orders. A right to an indemnity may be implied in some circumstances if not expressed: *The Island Archon* [1994] 2 Lloyd's Rep 227, noted below. In the leading case in this area, *The Ramon de Larrinaga*, it was found that the order that led to the loss was not given under the charter.

Larrinaga Steamship Co Ltd v The King [1945] AC 246

Facts: In 1939, at the start of the Second World War, the *Ramon de Larrinaga* was requisitioned by the Crown on the terms of the government form time charter T 99A (incorporating T 773), which provided in cl 9 that:

> The master . . . although appointed by the owners . . . shall be under the orders and direction of the charterer as regards employment, agency, or other arrangements: and the charterer hereby agrees to indemnify the owners for all consequences or liabilities that may arise from the master or officers . . . complying with such orders . . .

She was ordered to St Nazaire and notified that after discharge there she would return to South Wales for survey, as she was being released from government service. At St Nazaire written orders were given to her by the Naval Sea Transport Officer that she was to proceed that night to Quiberon Bay and join a convoy to be escorted to the Bristol Channel. The order was repeated orally the same day despite the ship's protest against sailing at night in dangerous navigation conditions and at a time when the weather was worsening. The ship sailed as ordered. Approximately five hours after sailing, during a gale, she anchored on the advice of the pilot. The anchor cable broke and the ship drifted onto a sand bank and was damaged. The appellants claimed that the cost of repair should be borne by the Crown on the grounds, amongst others, that the repair costs were the result of complying with the charterers' orders.

Held:

Lord Porter: My Lords, this appeal calls for a . . . consideration of a well known clause in time charterparties by the terms of which the master is placed under the orders and direction of the charterers, as regards employment, agency or other arrangements, and the charterers give the owners an indemnity against the consequences of complying with those orders . . .

The argument . . . was that the order to leave St Nazaire and to proceed to Cardiff was an order as regards employment, and that though generally a marine loss following on such an order would not be its consequence, yet where, as here, the order was to proceed in the face of the danger of a storm and against the protests of the master, the damage which the ship suffered was a consequence of the order. Had he not been compelled to leave port the master would not have sailed, and it was, it is said, the natural and a contemplated result of obeying that order that the ship might suffer marine damage; the respondent was therefore under a duty to indemnify the appellants for their loss.

. . . My Lords, I cannot but think that the word employment in cl 9 does include at any rate certain employments of the ship . . . In its natural sense it includes orders to proceed from one port to another or to undertake a voyage or series of voyages, and therefore the original notification of 7 October and the written order of 13 October in so far as it reiterated and confirmed that order, were authorised and covered by the clause. But this order did not in a legal sense, and I doubt if such an order ever could, cause such a loss. Even the order of 13 October specified no exact moment of departure, except that the ship was to sail after the discharge was complete. This wording left it to the master's discretion to sail at a reasonable time thereafter, and in determining what is a reasonable time all such matters as the state of the weather and the exhaustion of the crew would properly be taken into consideration. In these circumstances it cannot be said that either of these orders caused the damage which the ship suffered. A loss is not, under English law, caused by orders to make or by making a voyage because it occurs in the course of it. Such a loss is merely the fortuitous result of the ship being at a particular place at a particular time, and in no legal sense caused by the charterers' choice of port to which the ship is directed or their instructions to her master to proceed to it. But it was said that the ship sailed not by reason of the written order to proceed, but by the subsequent oral order, and that such an order did cause the loss, since it was the probable and contemplated result of sailing in unfavourable weather that the ship might suffer damage which, had the master been free to choose his own time, would probably have been avoided.

Three answers to this argument have been made by the respondent.

(1) That though an order specifying the voyage to be performed is an order as to employment, yet an order as to the time of sailing is not. That order, it is contended, is one as to navigation, or, at any rate, not as to employment. My Lords, this distinction seems to me to be justified: an order to sail from port A to port B is in common parlance an order as to employment, but an order that a ship shall sail at a particular time is not an order as to employment because its object is not to direct how the ship shall be employed, but how she shall act in the course of that employment. If the word were held to include every order which affected not the employment itself but any incident arising in the course of it almost every other liability undertaken by the charterer would be otiose, since the owners would be indemnified against almost all losses which the ship would incur in prosecuting her voyages. In particular war and marine risk insurance would be unnecessary . . .

(2) The second answer of the respondents was that even if it were conceded that orders to sail in a storm were orders in respect of which an indemnity is due, they must still be orders of the charterers as charterers and such as under this charterparty they are entitled to give. The mere instruction to sail may be such an order, but such an instruction leaves it to the discretion of the master who is responsible for the safety of his ship to choose the time and opportunity for starting on his voyage. I know of no right on the part of a charterer to insist that the safety of the ship should be endangered by sailing at a time when seamanship requires her to stay in port. The naval authorities however have this power . . . The written order to sail, which did not specify any time for compliance except the finish of discharge, left it to the master to choose his time and opportunity but did not cause the loss: the oral order which followed it was not a charterer's but a naval order and therefore not one for which the charterers are responsible.

(3) Finally it was urged that neither the order nor sailing in obedience to it caused the loss. In *Portsmouth Steamship Co Ltd v Liverpool and Glasgow Salvage Association* (1929) 34 Ll L Rep 459, 462, Lord Roche (then Roche J) points out that the clause, where it applies, covers only losses arising directly from charterer's instructions, because, as he says:

> if some act of negligence intervenes or some marine casualty intervenes then the chain of causation is broken and the indemnity does not operate.

I do not think your Lordships are called on to determine the soundness of this argument in the present case. It might be urged that a loss following upon an order to sail into danger which is complied with and results in damage due to the contemplated risk is a consequence of that order, but to decide it in this case is unnecessary and I prefer to express no opinion upon it either in favour or against. For the reasons given above, however, I would dismiss the appeal . . .

Notes

1   *Implied indemnity.* An implied right to an indemnity has been recognised in some circumstances: *The Nogar Marin* [1988] 1 Lloyd's Rep 412, p 422; *The Berge Sund* [1993] 2 Lloyd's

Rep 453, p 462; *Deutsche Ost-Afrika Linie v Legent* [1998] 2 Lloyd's Rep 71. In *The Island Archon*, the vessel was chartered for 36 months on the New York Produce Exchange (NYPE) form. She was ordered to Basrah where unjustified cargo claims were asserted by the receivers of the cargo under bills of lading. The owners had to provide security before the vessel was allowed to depart. There was no express agreement for an indemnity applicable in the circumstances. An implied agreement to indemnify was claimed against the consequences of the charterer's order to proceed to Basrah. The charterers argued that no promise to indemnify could be implied since the order to carry to Basrah was one that they had a contractual right to give. The Court of Appeal held that a right to an indemnity would be implied in the charter.

> . . . the implication is justified . . . first by 'business efficacy' in the sense that if the charterer requires to have the vessel at his disposal, and to be free to choose voyages and cargoes and bill of lading terms also, then the owner must be expected to grant such freedom only if he is entitled to be indemnified against loss and liability resulting from it, subject always to the express terms of the charterparty contract; and secondly by the legal principle underlying the 'lawful request' cases such as *Sheffield Corp v Barclay*; in other words, an implication of law [*Triad Shipping Co v Stellar Chartering & Brokerage Inc, The Island Archon, per* Evans LJ].

The rule applied in *Sheffield Corp v Barclay* [1905] AC 392 was that: 'when an act is done by one person at the request of another which act is not in itself manifestly tortious to the knowledge of the person doing it, and such act turns out to be injurious to the rights of a third party, the person doing it is entitled to an indemnity from him who requested that it should be done.'

2   *Indemnity and fault.* The right to an indemnity does not depend on the charterer being at fault. But there is no right to an indemnity for matters that are the fault of the shipowner: *The Aquacharm* [1982] 1 Lloyd's Rep 7.

3   *Risks accepted by the shipowner.* The owner is not entitled to be indemnified against all losses and expenses that arise whilst engaged in carrying out the charterers' orders. In *Weir v Union Steamship* [1900] AC 525 it was held that the cost of ballasting was not recoverable, even though the ballast was needed to make the voyage that the charterers selected. There are also many statements in decided cases and texts indicating that, in the absence of special and unusual contract terms, the charterer is not obliged to indemnify the shipowner against losses incurred as a result of maritime perils encountered in the course of a voyage on which the charterer has properly sent the ship. But these statements do not explain the reason for this rule of thumb in identical terms, probably because, as Lord Porter's judgment makes clear, there is not one but a number of overlapping reasons why charterers are not normally liable for navigational or weather risks. However, the decision in *The Hill Harmony*, above, makes one of the reasons given in *Ramon de Larrinaga* more difficult to sustain in some circumstances: if a charterer is entitled to and does dictate the route and speed, it becomes more difficult to say with conviction, when a casualty occurs in the course of the voyage, that 'Such a loss is merely the fortuitous result of the ship being at a particular place at a particular time' and that it is not in any sense caused by the charterers' instructions. It remains, of course, perfectly possible to say that *as a matter of law,* the loss is not to be treated as the responsibility of the charterer, that it is too remote (*The Aquacharm* [1980] 2 Lloyd's Rep 237) or to say that the right to indemnity does not extend to the risk that the shipowner has agreed to run, 'hence the exclusion of navigation risks': *The Island Archon, per* Evans LJ.

4   Indemnity for orders that are obviously impermissible? See *The Sagona* and *The Goodpal*, noted after *The White Rose*, below.

3.1 Need for an unbroken chain of causation

The right to indemnity only arises if an unbroken chain of causation can be shown. *The White Rose* contains a valuable review of earlier decisions as well as a clear articulation of the governing principle.

A/B Helsingfors Steamship Co Ltd v Rederiaktiebolaget Rex, The White Rose [1969] 1 WLR 1098

Facts: The vessel was trip chartered on the Baltime form and ordered to load grain at Duluth, Minnesota. Clause 9 of the charter provided that:'... The master shall be under the orders of the charterers as regards employment, agency or other arrangements. The charterers to indemnify the owners against all consequences or liabilities arising from the master ... complying with such orders ...' The charterers, who were obliged to pay for loading, trimming and stowing of cargo, employed independent contractors to carry out those tasks. During loading, one of the agent's employees fell through an unfenced 'tween deck hatch and was injured. The shipowners settled a claim by the injured man for $3,000 and claimed to recover that sum from the charterers.

Held:

> **Donaldson J:** ... Counsel for the shipowners ... submits that the authorities establish that if the shipowner, having complied with an instruction from the charterer, thereby incurs a liability to a third party ... from which he would be protected had the charterer alone been concerned, he is entitled to an indemnity. He says that the basis of the bargain between the parties was summarised by Devlin J in *Royal Greek Government v Minister of Transport* (1950) 83 Ll L Rep 228, when he said at p 234:
>
>> If [the shipowner] is to surrender his freedom of choice and put his master under the orders of the charterer, there is nothing unreasonable in his stipulating for a complete indemnity in return.
>
> As applied to a claim by a stevedore for personal injuries, the shipowner, submits counsel, makes good his claim to an indemnity by the following stages: (i) the shipowner established an order to go to a particular port to load a particular cargo; (ii) the terms of the charterparty expressly place the duty of arranging and paying for loading on the charterer, who, in fulfilment of that obligation, engages independent stevedores whom the shipowner is impliedly obliged to accept; (iii) under the terms of the relevant law, that is the local law, a potential liability on the part of the shipowner towards the stevedore is thereby established; (iv) the charterer fails to clothe the shipowners with the protection against the stevedore's claims which, under cl 13, he would have against similar claims by the charterers. That clause, after dealing with delay in delivery of the vessel, delay during the currency of the charter and loss or damage to goods on board, provides that 'The owners not to be responsible in any other case nor for damage or delay whatsoever and howsoever caused even if caused by the neglect or default of their servants'; (v) as the shipowner has, as a result of complying with the charterers' orders, been placed in a less attractive position than he would have been if the charterers had personally loaded the vessel, he is entitled to an indemnity.
>
> Counsel for the shipowners further submits that this is consistent with the cases in which shipowners have been indemnified against their liability to holders of bills of lading, whose terms were less favourable to the shipowners than were the terms of the time charterparty. (See, for example, *Milburn & Co v Jamaica Fruit Importing & Trading Co of London* [1900] 2 QB 540, where the loss arose from an inability to claim general average contribution from cargo; *Kruger & Co Ltd v Moel Tryvan Ship Co Ltd* [1907] AC 272, where the shipowners became liable for loss of cargo; *Elder Dempster & Co v Dunn & Co* (1909) 15 Com

Cas 49, where the cargo was wrongly marked and by the terms of the bills of lading and/or the provisions of the law of the place of discharge the shipowners could not require the receivers to take delivery of the mismarked goods and were liable as if they had lost them; *The Brabant* [1967] 1 QB 588 and *Bosma v Larsen* [1966] 1 Lloyd's Rep 22, further damage to cargo cases.)

He also submits that it is consistent with the decisions in *Lensen Shipping Co Ltd v Anglo-Soviet Shipping Co Ltd* (1935) 40 Com Cas 320, in which a vessel sustained damage as a result of being ordered to load at an unsafe berth; in *Strathlorne Steamship Co Ltd v Andrew Weir & Co* (1934) 40 Com Cas 168, in which the shipowners incurred a liability to the bill of lading holders as a result of their having delivered the cargo on the instructions of the time charterers to persons who could not produce the bills of lading and were not in fact entitled to receive the goods, and in *Portsmouth Steamship Co Ltd v Liverpool & Glasgow Salvage Association* (1929) 34 Ll L Rep 459, in which the shipowners recovered an indemnity in respect of damage to the vessel caused by the cargo which they loaded on the time charterers' instructions.

Counsel for the charterers accepts much of the submission of counsel for the shipowners, but he says that one vital element has been omitted, namely, that the right to indemnity only arises if and insofar as the loss suffered by the shipowners can be proved to have been caused by the shipowners' compliance with the charterers' instructions. He says that in the bill of lading cases causation is relevant, but it is rarely, if ever, a live issue, because commonly the shipowner is for practical purposes under no liability whatsoever in respect of cargo under the terms of the charterparty and if he is liable under the bills of lading which he has signed under instructions from the charterers, his liability must be caused by his compliance with those instructions. When, however, one looks at the unsafe port cases or cases of damage to the ship resulting from the nature or condition of the cargo (*Portsmouth Steamship Co Ltd v Liverpool & Glasgow Salvage Association*, above, and *Royal Greek Government v Minister of Transport*, above) the element of causation is all important as it is in the present case.

In my judgment the submission of counsel for the charterers is correct, and it is necessary in every case to establish an unbroken chain of causation, although I would not accept as a generalisation that:

> if some act of negligence intervenes or some marine casualty intervenes, then the chain of causation is broken and the indemnity does not operate (*per* Roche J, in *Portsmouth Steamship Co Ltd v Liverpool & Glasgow Salvage Association*, 34 Ll L Rep 459, 462).

A loss may well arise in the course of compliance with the charterers' orders, but this fact does not, without more, establish that it was caused by and is in law a consequence of such compliance and, in the absence of proof of such causation there is no right to indemnity.

The shipowners in the present case have undoubtedly established that their 'potential liability' to Mr de Chambeau [the injured employee] and their actual loss of £2,935.5s.5d. were incidents of and occurred in the course of complying with the charterers' orders to load grain at Duluth; but were they caused by such compliance? The judge of fact, the learned umpire, has found that the accident itself was caused partly by the absence of fencing, but it is clear from his conclusion that the charterers themselves were at no time guilty of any improper or negligent act and that they were not responsible for the lack of fencing. He has found that the shipowners were in breach of Finnish law, but I do not think that that is material. What connected the accident with, and gave rise to, a potential liability and an actual loss was the provisions of Minnesota law. Unless it can be said that this law was so unusual as to constitute Duluth a legally unsafe port to which the vessel should not have been ordered – and no such contention was advanced – or that the charterers engaged stevedores who were incompetent by local standards, which is negatived by the findings of fact, I do not consider that it can be said that there is the necessary causal connection between the order to load and the loss. This view is strengthened by, although not dependent on, the finding that at the time of the accident Mr de Chambeau had 'Left his position at No 2 'tween deck hatch, and for his own private purposes unconnected with his employment made his way aft into No 3 'tween deck'. It is also strengthened, and it may be that I am really precluded from reaching any other conclusion, although I have assumed that this is not the case, by the learned umpire's conclusion that 'the accident was not caused by the [shipowners'] complying with orders of the [charterers]', it not being suggested that in reaching this conclusion he misdirected himself in fact or in law. Accordingly in my judgment the claim under cl 9 fails . . .

Notes

1   *Order to deliver cargo without production of bill of lading.* The *Sagona* was time chartered for a period of 38 months during which she was ordered to carry a cargo of gasoil from Sicily to a port on the river Weser. On arrival the vessel was instructed by the charterers to deliver the cargo to receivers without requiring the production of the bill of lading. The cargo was delivered. The vessel was arrested and detained at the suit of the unpaid shippers. The shippers were later reimbursed by one of the string purchasers of the gasoil, but the shipowner sought to recover from the charterers their loss of earnings while the vessel was under arrest and the expenses of defending the proceedings. It was held that: (a) the charterers' order was not one which the shipowners were obliged to obey; (b) nevertheless, the order was not manifestly illegal or such as ought to have caused the master to refuse to act or likely to excite suspicion in the special circumstances of the oil trade; (c) the master had followed the normal practice and his conduct did not sever the causal connection between the order and the loss: *A/S Hansen-Tangens Rederi III v Total Transport Corp, The Sagona* [1984] 1 Lloyd's Rep 194.

2   *Compliance with obviously impermissible orders.* Partly on the basis of the decision in *The Sagona,* in *The Goodpal* [2000] 1 Lloyd's Rep 638 Colman J said that if owners obey an order where it is or ought to be obvious that the instruction is impermissible, the owners will not be entitled to an indemnity 'if obedience to the order as distinct from the giving of it, is the proximate cause of the loss'. But not every acceptance of an obviously impermissible order with full knowledge of the facts will necessarily break the causal link between the instruction and the loss: see Lord Goff's judgment in *The Kanchenjunga* [1990] Lloyd's Rep 391, HL in the next section of this chapter.

4 Safe ports

It is common for time charters (and voyage charters in some circumstances) to provide that the vessel shall only be employed between safe ports. An order to go to an unsafe port is not one that the charterer is entitled to give. If such an order is given, the owner is entitled to decline to carry it out. At one time it might have been possible to argue that this was the only consequence of such an order. But this approach was decisively rejected in *The Stork* [1955] 2 QB 68 by the Court of Appeal: it was held that nominating an unsafe port was a breach of contract and that when damage followed, the ordinary principles of causation and remoteness of damage would apply. Physical damage to the ship (ranging from total loss, loss of a piece of equipment such as an anchor down to the cost of replacing a damaged aerial or repainting scratches) and expenses such as the cost of tugs and lighters have been held to be recoverable.

In the absence of an express clause, it is not clear whether every charterer has an equivalent implied duty in contract. Opinion is divided. Some charters resolve the issue by expressly excluding the possibility: 'The charterers do not warrant the safety of any place to which they order the vessel' (Shelltime 4). It seems clear, however, that in at least some circumstances a charterer may owe a shipowner a duty of care in tort not to direct a ship to a place known to the charterer to be unsafe.

In *The Eastern City* [1958] 2 Lloyd's Rep 127, Sellers LJ gave us, what has become a classic definition of safe port:

> A port will not be safe unless, in the relevant period of time, the particular ship can reach it, use it and return from it without, in the absence of some abnormal occurrence, being exposed to danger which cannot be avoided by good navigation and seamanship . . .

On the basis of the ideas contained in this passage, ports and loading places have been held to be unsafe because of ice, shoals, sandbanks, wrecks, obstructions, lack of holding ground, war, wind, unsafe mooring systems and liability to confiscation, among other things. On the same basis, for a time, one strand of legal opinion regarded charterers as making an absolute continuing promise of safety from all events save 'abnormal occurrences'. This approach was rightly criticised. It turned charterers into insurers against damage and detention in ports and rivers. Further movement of the law in this direction was halted by the decision of the House of Lords in *The Evia*.

Kodros Shipping Corp of Monrovia v Empresa Cubana de Fletes, The Evia (No 2) [1983] 1 AC 736

Facts: The vessel was time chartered on terms that she was to be employed between safe ports and was ordered to carry cement from Cuba to Basrah. She became trapped in the Shatt-al-Arab waterway on the outbreak of hostilities between Iran and Iraq in September 1980. An arbitrator held that the charter was frustrated in October 1980 and that the charterers were not in breach of the safe port obligation so as to debar themselves from relying on frustration.

Held:

Lord Roskill: . . . 'The vessel to be employed . . . between . . . safe ports'.
. . . [T]he first question is whether, apart from authority, these words are to be construed in the manner suggested. In order to consider the scope of the contractual promise which these eight words impose upon a charterer, it must be determined how a charterer would exercise his undoubted right to require the shipowner to perform his contractual obligations to render services with his ship, his master, officers and crew, the consideration for the performance of their obligation being the charterer's regular payment of time charter hire. The answer must be that a charterer will exercise that undoubted contractual right by giving the shipowner orders to go to a particular port or place of loading or discharge. It is clearly at that point of time when that order is given that that contractual promise to the charterer regarding the safety of that intended port or place must be fulfilled. But that contractual promise cannot mean that that port or place must be safe when that order is given, for were that so, a charterer could not legitimately give orders to go to an ice-bound port which he and the owner both knew in all human probability would be ice-free by the time that vessel reached it. Nor, were that the nature of the promise, could a charterer order the ship to a port or place the approaches to which were at the time of the order blocked as a result of a collision or by some submerged wreck or other obstacles even though such obstacles would in all human probability be out of the way before the ship required to enter. The charterer's contractual promise must, I think, relate to the characteristics of the port or place in question and in my view means that when the order is given that port or place is prospectively safe for the ship to get to, stay at, so far as necessary, and in due course, leave. But if those characteristics are such as to make that port or place prospectively safe in this way, I cannot think that if, in spite of them, some unexpected and abnormal event thereafter suddenly occurs which creates conditions of unsafety where conditions of safety had previously existed and as a result the ship is delayed, damaged or destroyed, that contractual promise extends to making the

charterer liable for any resulting loss or damage, physical or financial. So to hold would make the charterer the insurer of such unexpected and abnormal risks which in my view should properly fall upon the ship's insurers under the policies of insurance the effecting of which is the owner's responsibility under clause 3 unless, of course, the owner chooses to be his own insurer in these respects . . .

My Lords, on the view of the law which I take, since Basrah was prospectively safe at the time of nomination, and since the unsafety arose after the *Evia*'s arrival and was due to an unexpected and abnormal event, there was at the former time no breach of clause 2 by the respondents, and that is the first ground upon which I would dismiss this appeal.

But, my Lords, since the Court of Appeal gave leave to appeal in order that this branch of the law should be fully explored, I think your Lordships may wish further to consider whether . . . there is a residual obligation upon a charterer, whether for time or voyage, given that he has fully complied with his obligation at the time of nomination. My Lords, unless there is something unusual in the relevant express language used in a particular charterparty, the charterer's obligation at the time of nomination which I have been discussing must, I think, apply equally to a voyage charterer as to a time charterer. But in considering whether there is any residual or remaining obligation after nomination it is necessary to have in mind one fundamental distinction between a time charterer and a voyage charterer. In the former case, the time charterer is in complete control of the employment of the ship. It is in his power by appropriate orders timeously given to change the ship's employment so as to prevent her proceeding to or remaining at a port initially safe which has since it was nominated become unsafe. But a voyage charterer may not have the same power. If there is a single loading or discharging port named in the voyage charterparty then, unless the charterparty specifically otherwise provides, a voyage charterer may not be able to order that ship elsewhere. If there is a range of loading or discharging ports named, once the voyage charterer has selected the contractual port or ports of loading or discharge, the voyage charterparty usually operates as if that port or those ports had originally been written into the charterparty, and the charterer then has no further right of nomination or renomination. What, then, is the contractual obligation of such charterers whether for time or voyage if the nominated port becomes unsafe after it was nominated?

My Lords, in the case of a time charterer, I cannot bring myself to think that he has no further obligation to the owner even though for the reasons I have given earlier he is not the insurer of the risks arising from the unsafety of the nominated port. Suppose some event has occurred after nomination which has made or will or may make the nominated port unsafe. Is a time charterer obliged to do anything further? What is a voyage charterer to do in similar circumstances? My Lords, this problem seems never to have been judicially considered in any detail . . .

In my opinion, while the primary obligation of a time charterer under clause 2 of this charterparty is that which I have already stated, namely, to order the ship to go only to a port which, at the time when the order is given, is prospectively safe for her, there may be circumstances in which, by reason of a port, which was prospectively safe when the order to go to it was given, subsequently becoming unsafe, clause 2, on its true construction, imposes a further and secondary obligation on the charterer.

In this connection two possible situations require to be considered. The first situation is where, after the time charterer has performed his primary obligation by ordering the ship to go to a port which, at the time of such order, was prospectively safe for her, and while she is still proceeding towards such port in compliance with such order, new circumstances arise which render the port unsafe. The second situation is where, after the time charterer has performed his primary obligation by ordering the ship to go to a port which was, at the time of such order, prospectively safe for her, and she has proceeded to and entered such port in compliance with such order, new circumstances arise which render the port unsafe.

In the first situation it is my opinion that clause 2, on its true construction (unless the cause of the new unsafety be purely temporary in character), imposes on the time charterer a further and secondary obligation to cancel his original order and, assuming that he wishes to continue to trade the ship, to order her to go to another port which, at the time when such fresh order is given, is prospectively safe for her. This is because clause 2 should be construed as requiring the time charterer to do all that he can effectively do to protect the ship from the new danger in the port which has arisen since his original order for her to go to it was given.

In the second situation the question whether clause 2, on its true construction, imposes a further and secondary obligation on the time charterer will depend on whether, having regard to the nature and consequences of the new danger in the port which has arisen, it is possible for the ship to avoid such danger by leaving the port. If, on the one hand, it is not possible for the ship so to leave, then no further and secondary obligation is imposed on the time charterer. This is because clause 2 should not be construed as requiring the time charterer to give orders with which it is not possible for the ship to comply, and which would for that reason be ineffective. If, on the other hand, it is possible for the ship to avoid the new danger in the port which has arisen by leaving, then a further and secondary obligation is imposed on the time charterer to order the ship to leave the port forthwith, whether she has completed loading or discharging or not, and, assuming that he wishes to continue to trade the ship, to order her to go to another port which, at the time when such fresh order is given, is prospectively safe for her. This is again because clause 2 should be construed as requiring the time charterer to do all that he can effectively do to protect the ship from the new danger in the port which has arisen since his original order for her to go to it was given.

My Lords, what I have said with regard to these further and secondary obligations under clause 2 of this charterparty will apply to any other similarly worded 'safe port' clauses.

My Lords, for the reasons I have given I find it much more difficult to say what are the comparable obligations under a voyage charterparty at any rate where there is no express right to renominate . . . I think, therefore, in a case where only a time charterparty is involved, that it would be unwise for your Lordships to give further consideration to the problems which might arise in the case of a voyage charterparty, and for my part, I would leave those problems for later consideration if and when they arise.

My Lords, on the basis that time charterers were potentially under the further and secondary obligations which I have held that clause 2 may impose on them, it cannot avail the appellants against the respondents since the events giving rise to the unsafety did not occur until after the *Evia* had entered Basrah, and an order to leave the port and proceed to another port could not have been effective . . .

Notes

1   Lord Roskill went on to conclude that: (a) in any event, cl 21 (war clause) of the charterparty freed the charterers from any liability to which they might otherwise be subject; (b) the war clause did not exclude the application of the doctrine of frustration; and (c) the arbitrator's conclusion as to the date on which the charterparty had become frustrated should be upheld.

2   The *Saga Cob* was time chartered for six months' employment in the Red Sea, Gulf of Aden and East Africa. The charterparty provided that the charterers would 'exercise due diligence to ensure that the vessel is only employed between and at safe ports'. She was ordered to Massawa, Ethiopia, with a cargo of aviation fuel. While at anchor she was attacked by Eritrean guerillas; the master was wounded and the ship suffered substantial damage. The Court of Appeal held that 'prospective safety' did not mean 'absolute safety' and that a port should not be regarded as unsafe unless a 'political' risk is sufficient for a reasonable shipowner or master to decline to send or sail his vessel there: *K/S Penta Shipping A/S v Ethiopian Shipping Lines Corp, The Saga Cob* [1992] 2 Lloyd's Rep 545, CA. For analysis of the decision, see Davenport, B, 'The Saga Cob' (1993) LMCLQ 150.

The decision in *The Evia* dealt with the position where neither owner nor charterer is aware of the danger. In the next case the owners undertook the voyage knowing of the circumstances at the port to which they had been ordered.

Motor Oil Hellas (Corinth) Refineries SA v Shipping Corp of India, The Kanchenjunga [1990] 1 Lloyd's Rep 391, HL

Facts: In 1978, the *Kanchenjunga* was chartered under a consecutive voyage charter on the Exxonvoy form, with loading at '1/2 safe ports Arabian Gulf'. On 21 November 1980 the charterers ordered the vessel to proceed to the Iranian port of Kharg Island to load a cargo of crude oil. Arbitrators held that, on that date, Kharg Island was not a prospectively safe port by reason of the Iran/Iraq war. Nevertheless, the vessel undertook the voyage. She arrived and the master gave notice of readiness on 23 November. Before she could berth and load, an Iraqi air attack on 1 December on oil installations on Kharg Island caused the master to sail for a place of safety. Thereafter, the owners called for alternative loading instructions, while the charterers pressed for a return to Kharg; neither side altered its position and both eventually alleged that the other had repudiated the agreement.

Held:

Lord Goff: . . . Here the crucial question is whether, before the vessel sailed away, the owners had, by their words or conduct, precluded themselves from rejecting the charterers' nomination as not complying with the contract. Hence the reliance by the charterers on the principles of waiver and estoppel, unsuccessful before the arbitrators, but successful, so far as waiver is concerned, before the judge and the Court of Appeal. The question whether the courts below were correct in their conclusion depends, in my opinion, upon an analysis of these principles, and their proper application to the facts of the present case.

It is a commonplace that the expression 'waiver' is one which may, in law, bear different meanings. In particular, it may refer to a forbearance from exercising a right or to an abandonment of a right. Here we are concerned with waiver in the sense of abandonment of a right which arises by virtue of a party making an election. Election itself is a concept which may be relevant in more than one context. In the present case, we are concerned with an election which may arise in the context of a binding contract, when a state of affairs comes into existence in which one party becomes entitled, either under the terms of the contract or by the general law, to exercise a right, and he has to decide whether or not to do so. His decision, being a matter of choice for him, is called in law an election . . . In all cases, he has in the end to make his election, not as a matter of obligation, but in the sense that, if he does not do so, the time may come when the law takes the decision out of his hands, either by holding him to have elected not to exercise the right which has become available to him, or sometimes by holding him to have elected to exercise it . . . Once an election is made, however, it is final and binding (see *Scarf v Jardine* (1882) 7 App Cas 345, *per* Lord Blackburn, at p 360). Moreover it does not require consideration to support it, and so it is to be distinguished from an express or implied agreement, such as a variation of the relevant contract, which traditionally requires consideration to render it binding in English law.

Generally, however, it is a prerequisite of election that the party making the election must be aware of the facts which have given rise to the existence of his new right . . . I add in parenthesis that, for present purposes, it is not necessary for me to consider certain cases in which it has been held that, as a prerequisite of election, the party must be aware not only of the facts giving rise to his rights but also of the rights themselves, because it is not in dispute here that the owners were aware both of the relevant facts and of their relevant rights . . .

The present case is concerned . . . with an uncontractual tender of performance. Even so, the same principles apply. The other party is entitled to reject the tender of performance as uncontractual; and, subject to the terms of the contract, he can then, if he wishes, call for a fresh tender of performance in its place. But if, with knowledge of the facts giving rise to his right to reject, he nevertheless unequivocally elects not to do so, his election will be final and binding upon him and he will have waived his right to reject the tender as uncontractual.

... Election is to be contrasted with equitable estoppel, a principle associated with the leading case of *Hughes v Metropolitan Railway Co* (1877) 2 App Cas 439. Equitable estoppel occurs where a person, having legal rights against another, unequivocally represents (by words or conduct) that he does not intend to enforce those legal rights; if in such circumstances the other party acts, or desists from acting, in reliance upon that representation, with the effect that it would be inequitable for the representor thereafter to enforce his legal rights inconsistently with his representation, he will to that extent be precluded from doing so.

There is an important similarity between the two principles, election and equitable estoppel, in that each requires an unequivocal representation ...

These are the principles which fall to be considered in the present case. Here, as I have already indicated, the situation in which the owners found themselves was one in which they could either reject the charterers' nomination of Kharg Island as uncontractual, or could nevertheless elect to accept the order and load at Kharg Island, thereby waiving or abandoning their right to reject the nomination but retaining their right to claim damages from the charterers for breach of contract. Since the owners were in this situation, it is logical first to consider the question of election before considering (if necessary) equitable estoppel.

The arbitrators addressed themselves to the possibility of election, but unfortunately their rejection of it was founded upon a mistaken appreciation of the law. The judge and the Court of Appeal, however, both held that the owners had elected to waive their right to reject the nomination. In my opinion they were right to reach this conclusion.

Because the arbitrators did not approach the issue of election correctly, they failed to consider the correct questions. In particular, they did not ask themselves whether there had been the necessary unequivocal representation by the owners. It is true that they did ask themselves whether there had been the necessary 'clear and unequivocal promise' when considering the alternative principle of equitable estoppel; they held that there was not, on the basis that the mere acceptance of orders without protest does not amount to such a promise. As a general proposition, this is no doubt correct; and it would equally be true if made with reference to the question whether there had been an unequivocal representation by the owners that they were waiving their right to reject the nomination as uncontractual. Moreover, if the relevant evidence had related only to the communications passing between the parties before the vessel arrived at Kharg Island, the question would have arisen whether, on these communications (set of course in their factual context), there had been such an unequivocal representation. But the matter does not stop there, because on arrival at Kharg Island the master proceeded to serve notice of readiness. Thereafter, as the judge pointed out, the owners were asserting that the vessel was available to load; they were also calling upon the charterers to arrange priority berthing, and referring to the fact that laytime was running. In these circumstances, the owners were asserting a right inconsistent with their right to reject the charterers' orders. The right which they were asserting was that laytime had started to run against the charterers at Kharg Island, with the effect that the charterers had become bound to load the cargo there within the laytime fixed by the charter and, if they failed to do so, to pay demurrage to the owners at the contractual rate. In these circumstances, on the principle stated by Lord Diplock in the *Kammins Ballrooms* case [1971] AC 850, at pp 882–83, the owners must be taken in law to have thereby elected not to reject the charterers' nomination, and so to have waived their right to do so or to call for another nomination ...

No doubt the master was entitled to refuse to endanger his ship and crew in the circumstances in which he found himself; but that did not excuse the owners from their breach of contract, after they had elected not to reject the charterers' nomination of Kharg Island in the knowledge of the facts rendering it prospectively unsafe. Furthermore this is not a case in which a new situation had developed at Kharg Island, or some other danger already existed there. If the known danger had become significantly different; or if a new and different danger had developed; or if some other danger, hitherto unknown, already existed at the port – in such circumstances as these, other questions might have arisen. But your Lordships are not troubled with any such questions in the present case. The arbitrators found as a fact that the safety or unsafety of Kharg Island was not changed in any way by the attack on December 1. This was a finding which they were fully entitled to make, and which cannot be challenged.

For these reasons, I would dismiss the owners' cross-appeal on this issue. It follows that it is unnecessary for the purposes of the cross-appeal to consider the alternative question of equitable estoppel.

I turn then to the charterers' appeal which related to the effect of cl 20(vi) of the charter. Clause 20 (vi) reads, so far as relevant, as follows:

> WAR RISKS (a) If any port of loading or of discharge named in this charterparty or to which the vessel may properly be ordered pursuant to the terms of the bills of lading be blockaded, or (b) if owing to any war, hostilities, warlike operations . . . entry to any such port of loading or of discharge or the loading or discharge of cargo at any such port be considered by the master or owners in his or their discretion dangerous or prohibited . . . the charterers shall have the right to order the cargo or such part of it as may be affected to be loaded or discharged at any other safe port of loading or of discharge within the range of loading or discharging ports respectively established under the provisions of the charterparty (provided such other port is not blockaded or that entry thereto or loading or discharge of cargo thereat is not in the master's or owner's discretion dangerous or prohibited) . . .

Both the judge and the Court of Appeal held that this clause was effective to protect the owners from liability in damages, though it did not render the charterers liable in damages in the events which had happened. With this conclusion I agree . . .

The obligation to nominate a safe port has been raised as an issue in a number of arbitration cases recently. In the following case the arbitration was appealed and caused much excitement in the industry. The decision by Teare J that the Japanese port of Kashima was unsafe had important implications both for the drafting of time charters and for the commercial viability of a major, modern port.

Gard Marine & Energy Ltd v China National Chartering Co Ltd, The Ocean Victory and others [2013] EWHC 2199 (Comm)

The facts are set out in the judge's opening remarks:

Teare J: On 24 October 2006 OCEAN VICTORY, a Capesize bulkcarrier, part-laden with a cargo of iron ore, sought to leave the port of Kashima, Japan during a severe gale. As she proceeded along the Kashima Fairway she was confronted by northerly or north-north-westerly winds of about Beaufort scale force 9 and by heavy seas generated both by the winds and by the dominant swell from the north-east. When north-west of the seaward end of the South Breakwater, without steerage way and with her portside exposed to the gale she was set down onto the end of the breakwater. She was then driven southwards by the weather, went aground and was abandoned by her crew who were airlifted ashore. Notwithstanding the assistance of Nippon Salvage on LOF 2000 terms she broke apart just after Christmas 2006. A wreck removal contract was entered into with Fukada Salvage and by August 2008 the wreck had been removed.

This was a remarkable maritime casualty. Although OCEAN VICTORY had the full use of her engines she lost steerage way when leaving a modern, purpose-built port and navigating a fairway which had been used by many ships without incident. The casualty has given rise to a claim in the sum of approximately US$137.6m. made up of the loss of the vessel, some US$88.5m., loss of hire of the vessel until 27 December 2006, some US$2.7m., SCOPIC costs pursuant to LOF 2000 in the sum of US$12m., and wreck removal costs of some US$34.5m. The Claimants, the hull underwriters who are suing as assignees of the owners and demise charterers, say that the casualty was caused by the unsafety of the port of Kashima to which the time charterers had ordered the vessel. The time charterers say that the port of Kashima was not unsafe but that even if it were unsafe the cause of the casualty was not that unsafety but a misapprehension by the master of the vessel that the vessel had been ordered to leave the port and/or by the negligent navigation of the master when leaving the port. The time charterers also say that certain of the losses claimed are irrecoverable for other reasons. The following guide to the contents of this judgment may assist the reader:

The storm was raging so why did the ship's master leave the port? This was because the vessel faced another danger if it remained in port this was because of the presence of so called 'long waves'. These are waves which come in periods of 30 seconds to 5 minutes and although only having a small height of between 0.2 to 0.3 metres they can travel thousands of miles and carry a huge amount of energy with them. Long Waves due to their long wavelength can be diffracted and reflected around breakwaters, much more easily than ordinary swell or sea waves and so can easily enter a harbour with a little loss of energy. The effect of this is that ships can be buffeted by the waves causing damage to the hull and the breaking of mooring lines with the consequent risk of drifting and grounding And indeed the vessel was already affected by Long Waves and was already surging and slamming at the Raw Materials Quay of the Port of Kashima, with few mooring lines had already broken. The vessel had called for a tug assistance in order to minimize her movements, and to relieve some of the strain to the moorings. It was dangerous for the vessel to remain in the port in such conditions, with the forecast showing weather to deteriorate even further. The logical alternative was to vacate the berth and sail out in the open sea, until Long Wave conditions have improved.

Later in his judgment at paragraph 94 he looks at the precedents as to safe port and refers to Lord Sellers' definition in *The Eastern City* as 'classic'.

Counsel for the Charterers submitted that 'a port is not unsafe because its systems fail to guard against every conceivable hazard. The emphasis is upon reasonable safety and the taking of reasonable precautions.' Counsel therefore submitted that "in the light of the fact that no vessel had ever been trapped by a combination of wind and swell at the RMQ and adverse conditions in the channel (whether on 24 October 2006 or before) it is difficult to see upon what basis the port is to be criticised for not having put in place a system to address such a (non) risk.

The submission by counsel for the Charterers that the port had only to be 'reasonably safe' rather than 'safe' raises a question as to the true construction of the safe port warranty. Counsel's submission was based upon what was said to be the 'classic definition' of a safe port by Lord Denning in the *Evia* No.2 [1982] 1 Lloyd's Reports 334 at p.338 where he said in terms that the port must be "reasonably safe" for the vessel. The relevant passage provides as follows:

What then are the characteristics of a 'safe port'? What attributes must it possess and retain if the charterer is to fulfil his warranty? To my mind it must be reasonably safe for the vessel to enter, to remain, and to depart without suffering damage so long as she is well and carefully handled. Reasonably safe, that is, in its geographical configuration on the coast or waterway and in the equipment and aids available for her movement and stay. In short, it must be safe in its set-up as a port. To elaborate a little, every port in its natural state has hazards for the ships going there. It may be shallows, shoals, mudbanks, or rocks. It may be storms or ice or appalling weather. In order to be a 'safe port', there must be reasonable precautions taken to overcome these hazards, or to give sufficient warning of them to enable them to be avoided. There must be buoys to mark the channel, lights to point the way, pilots available to steer, a system to forecast the weather, good places to drop anchor, sufficient room to manoeuvre, sound berths, and so forth. In so far as any of these precautions are necessary – and the set-up of the port is deficient in them – then it is not a 'safe port'. Once the set-up of the port is found to be deficient – such that it is dangerous for the vessel when handled with reasonable care – then the charterer is in breach of his warranty and he is liable for any damage suffered by the vessel in consequence of it. To illustrate this proposition, I will give some of the deficiencies in set-up which have been held to render a port unsafe: Its tendency to be ice-bound during that very winter: see *G. W. Grace & Co. v General Steam Navigation Co. Ltd.,* (1950) 83 Ll.L.Rep. 297; [1950] 2 K.B. 383. Its tendency to sudden storms, endangering a vessel of this size in this bay: see *The Stork,* [1955] 1 Lloyd's Rep. 349; [1955] 2 Q.B. 68. The absence of navigational aids such as a hauling-off buoy or waling-piece: see *The Houston City,* [1956] 1 Lloyd's Rep. 1; [1956] A.C. 266. The lack of reliable holding ground in the anchorage area: see *The Eastern City,* [1958] 2 Lloyd's Rep. 127 . . . The absence of an adequate weather forecasting system: see *The Dagmar,* [1968] 2 Lloyd's Rep. 563. The absence of adequate room to manoeuvre in bad weather: see *The Khian Sea,* [1979] 1 Lloyd's Rep. 545. The tendency of the channel to become silted up so as to produce narrowing or shoaling: see *The Pendrecht,* [1980] 2 Lloyd's Rep. 56 and *Transoceanic Petroleum Carriers v Cook Industries Inc. (The Mary Lou),* [1981] 2 Lloyd's Rep. 272.

On the other hand, if the set-up of the port is good but nevertheless the vessel suffers damage owing to some isolated, abnormal or extraneous occurrence – unconnected with the set-up – then the charterer is not in breach of his warranty. Such as when a competent berthing-master makes for once a mistake, or when the vessel is run into by another vessel, or a fire spreads across to her, or when a hurricane strikes unawares. The charterer is not liable for damage so caused.

This passage was cited in the *Carnival* [1994] 2 Lloyd's Reports 14 at p.26 by Hirst LJ who noted that it had not been questioned when the *Evia* (No.2) was considered by the House of Lords.

However, I was surprised that counsel referred to Lord Denning's explanation of a safe port as the 'classic definition' of a safe port. In so far as there is a classic definition of a safe port that definition has long been regarded as being that of Sellers LJ in the *Eastern City* [1958] 2 Lloyd's Reports 127 at p.131 where he said that

a port will not be safe unless, in the relevant period of time, the particular ship can reach it, use it and return from it without, in the absence of some abnormal occurrence, being exposed to danger which cannot be avoided by good navigation and seamanship.

That statement of principle was made in what was the third of 'a trilogy of decisions' (per Roskill LJ in the *Hermine* [1979] 1 Lloyd's Reports 212 at p.214) in the middle of the last century which analysed and explained the meaning and effect of the safe port warranty. The first of the trilogy was *Compania Naviera Maropan v Bowaters Lloyd Pulp and Paper Mills* [1955] 1 Lloyds Reports 349 (the *Stork*) per Singleton LJ at pp. 363–366, Hodson LJ at pp. 369–370 and Morris LJ at pp. 373–375 and the second was *Reardon Smith Line v Australian Wheat Board* [1954] 2 Lloyds Reports 148 (the *Houston City*) per Dixon CJ at pp. 151–159 whose dissenting judgment was upheld by the Privy Council at [1956] AC 266.

The definition of a safe port by Sellers LJ in the *Eastern City* was expressly approved by Roskill LJ in the *Hermine* [1979] 1 Lloyd's Reports 212 at p.214 and described by him as 'the classic statement . . . of the present state of the law'. In the *Evia* (No.2) in the House of Lords Lord Diplock referred to the definition of a safe port by Sellers LJ in the *Eastern City* as a 'classic passage' which correctly and concisely stated the nature of the contractual promise made by a charterer in a safe port warranty; see [1983] AC 736 at p.749. In *Wilford on Time Charters* 6th.ed. at paragraph 10.3 the definition of Sellers LJ in the *Eastern City* is described as the 'classic definition' of a safe port. It is therefore unsurprising that counsel for the Charterers had accepted in their opening submissions that this was 'the classic dictum'.

> Notwithstanding the absence of any express criticism of Lord Denning's explanation of the safe port warranty by the House of Lords in the *Evia* (No.2) I consider that the authoritative and long recognised statement of the nature of a safe port is that of Sellers LJ in the *Eastern City* which was itself so closely modelled on the definition of a safe port by Morris LJ in the *Stork*. That statement or definition makes no reference to 'reasonable safety' and it would, in my respectful opinion, introduce an unwelcome and inappropriate measure of uncertainty in the meaning of the safe port warranty if safety were to be understood as 'reasonable safety' rather than safety. Safety is not absolute but the measure of safety is not what is 'reasonable' but whether any dangers in a port can be avoided by good navigation and seamanship. It is most improbable that Lord Denning intended to depart from Sellers LJ's statement. First, in a passage not quoted by counsel for the charterers in their closing submissions, Lord Denning noted that where the setup of a port is found to be deficient, that is because 'it is dangerous for the vessel when handled with reasonable care'. That reflects Sellers LJ's definition of a safe port. Second, although Lord Denning referred to both the *Eastern City* and to the *Hermine*, in which Roskill LJ so handsomely endorsed Sellers LJ's statement of principle, Lord Denning did not suggest that that statement of principle should be in any way modified. Finally, it is to be noted that the learned editors of *Wilford on Time Charters* make no reference to a notion of 'reasonable safety'.

On appeal the judges were unanimous in finding for the Appellants.

Gard Marine & Energy Ltd v China National Chartering Co Ltd (Rev 1) [2015] EWCA Civ 16

The judgment was read on behalf of all by Longmore LJ. As you will see from the extract below, much was made of the expression, 'abnormal occurrence'.

At para 50:

> We consider with all due respect that the logic of the judge's approach to the issue of abnormal occurrence is flawed. Our reasons may be stated as follows.
>
> The nature of a charterer's safe port warranty is well established. As Lord Diplock said in *The Evia (No. 2)* [1983] 1 AC 736 at 149:-
>
>> For my part, I would regard the nature of the contractual promise by the charterer that a chartered vessel shall be employed between safe ports ('the safe port clause') as having been well settled for a quarter of a century at the very least. It was correctly and concisely stated by Sellers LJ in *Leeds Shipping Co. Ltd. v Société Francaise Bunge (The Eastern City)* [1958] 2 Lloyd's Rep. 127 in a classic passage which, in its reference to 'abnormal occurrence,' reflects a previous statement in the judgment of Morris LJ in *Compania Naviera Maropan S.A. v Bowaters Lloyd Pulp and Paper Mills Ltd. (The Stork)* [1955] 2 Q.B. 68. Sellers LJ said, at p. 131:-
>> 'a port will not be safe unless, in the relevant period of time, the particular ship can reach it, use it and return from it without, in the absence of some abnormal occurrence, being

exposed to danger which cannot be avoided by good navigation and seamanship . . . It is with the prospective safety of the port at the time when the vessel will be there for the loading or unloading operation that the contractual promise is concerned and the contractual promise itself is given at the time when the charterer gives the order to the master or other agent of the shipowner to proceed to the loading or unloading port.' Lord Roskill (in a speech to which Lord Brandon had contributed and with which the other members of the committee agreed) amplified the nature of the promise, and of the 'abnormal occurrence' exception, in his speech at 757: 'In order to consider the scope of the contractual promise which these eight words impose upon a charterer, it must be determined how a charterer would exercise his undoubted right to require the shipowner to perform his contractual obligations to render services with his ship, his master, officers and crew, the consideration for the performance of their obligation being the charterer's regular payment of time charter hire. The answer must be that a charterer will exercise that undoubted contractual right by giving the shipowner orders to go to a particular port or place of loading or discharge. It is clearly at that point of time when that order is given that that contractual promise to the charterer regarding the safety of that intended port or place must be fulfilled. But that contractual promise cannot mean that that port or place must be safe when that order is given, for were that so, a charterer could not legitimately give orders to go to an ice-bound port which he and the owner both knew in all human probability would be ice-free by the time that vessel reached it. Nor, were that the nature of the promise, could a charterer order the ship to a port or place the approaches to which were at the time of the order blocked as a result of a collision or by some submerged wreck or other obstacles even though such obstacles would in all human probability be out of the way before the ship required to enter. **The charterer's contractual promise must, I think, relate to the characteristics of the port or place in question and in my view means that when the order is given that port or place is prospectively safe for the ship to get to, stay at, so far as necessary, and in due course, leave. But if those characteristics are such as to make that port or place prospectively safe in this way, I cannot think that if, in spite of them, some unexpected and abnormal event thereafter suddenly occurs which creates conditions of unsafety where conditions of safety had previously existed and as a result the ship is delayed, damaged or destroyed, that contractual promise extends to making the charterer liable for any resulting loss or damage, physical or financial. So to hold would make the charterer the insurer of such unexpected and abnormal risks which in my view should properly fall upon the ship's insurers under the policies of insurance the effecting of which is the owner's responsibility** under clause 3 unless, of course, the owner chooses to be his own insurer in these respects.' [Our emphasis in bold text.] The import of these passages is clear. A charterer does not assume responsibility for unexpected and abnormal events which occur suddenly and which create conditions of unsafety after he has given the order to proceed to the relevant port. These are the responsibility of the ship's hull insurers (if owners have insured) or of owners themselves. Moreover the concept of 'safety' is necessarily not an absolute one. As the Court of Appeal said in *The Saga Cob* [1979] 1 Lloyd's Rep. 548 at 551, column 2, in the context of political risk:

> In the latter case [the safe port warranty] one is considering whether the port should be regarded as unsafe by owners, charterers, or masters of vessels. It is accepted that this does not mean that it is unsafe, unless shown to be absolutely safe. It will not in circumstances such as the present be regarded as unsafe unless the 'political' risk is sufficient for a reasonable shipowner or master to decline to send or sail his vessel there.

A similarly realistic approach has in our view to be adopted to the determination of the essentially factual question whether the event giving rise to the particular casualty is to be characterised as an 'abnormal occurrence' or as resulting from some 'normal' characteristic of the particular port at the particular time of year. We emphasise the word 'normal' in the term 'normal characteristic'. It was used by Lord Diplock when he observed in *The Evia (No. 2)* at 749 that:-

> ...it is not surprising that disputes should arise as to whether damage sustained by a particular vessel in a particular port on a particular occasion was caused by an 'abnormal occurrence' rather than resulting from some normal characteristic of the particular port at the particular time of year. The term was also used in *The Saga Cob* at 550, column 2, to 551, column 1, in an illuminating passage which emphasises that the fact that an event (in that case a guerrilla attack) was theoretically foreseeable did not make it an 'normal characteristic' of the port:- 'Be that as it may, there is no evidence whatever that the system introduced after the *Omo Wonz* had any defects until the attack on *Saga Cob* itself when at anchor four or five miles outside the port. This cannot in our judgment be regarded as other than an abnormal and unexpected event unless it is to be said that as from the *Omo Wonz* incident, any vessel proceeding to or from Assab or Massawa was proceeding to an unsafe port. This in our judgment is untenable. The situation in this case was drastically different from that in *The Lucille* when the Shatt-al-Arab had become the centre of hostilities. All that can be said in this case is that since a guerrilla attack may take place anywhere at any time and by any means, that the guerrillas had two boats and that they had made one seaborne attack 65 miles away, it was foreseeable that there could be a seaborne attack either en route from Assab to Massawa or in the anchorage at Massawa. If this were enough it would seem to follow that, if there were a seaborne guerrilla or terrorist attack in two small boats in the coastal waters of a country in which there had been sporadic guerrilla or terrorist activity on land and which had many ports, it would become a normal characteristic of every port in that country that such an attack in the port or whilst proceeding to it or departing from it was sufficiently likely to render the port unsafe. This we cannot accept. *Omo Wonz* was itself clearly an isolated abnormal incident and, until the order to proceed to Massawa almost three months later, nothing further had occurred to suggest that the risk of further attack on the Assab/Massawa voyage or in the anchorage at Massawa had not been contained. In such circumstances, to say that such an attack or even the risk of such an attack was a normal characteristic of the port, is in our view impossible. As to the letter of the master immediately after the *Omo Wonz* incident we do not consider that it can be regarded as of any importance. The master was no doubt at the time alarmed but thereafter he visited Massawa on several occasions despite the provisions of the charter-party entitling him to refuse. The charterers expressly disclaim any arguments that by entering into the charter-party the owners accepted the risks but it appears to us that the master's actions indicate clearly that whatever he may have thought immediately after the *Omo Wonz* incident he, like every one else, considered that Massawa was a safe port. We further consider that what occurred subsequently is relevant on the question whether Massawa was a safe port. We accordingly hold that on the Aug. 26. 1988 Massawa was a safe port.'

Likewise, Mustill J in the *Mary Lou* [1981] 2 Lloyd's Reports 272, at 278, column 2, in his description of what constitutes an abnormal occurrence, implicitly recognised the need to approach the identification of an abnormal occurrence realistically and having regard to whether the event had occurred sufficiently frequently so as to become a characteristic of the port:-

> The abnormal nature of the occurrence which causes the loss is also relevant in a different way, in that it bears upon the question where there is a breach of warranty if the ship does comply with the order and suffers damage in the port. The mere happening of the casualty does not necessarily imply a breach. The warranty does not involve a guarantee that a properly navigated ship will be in all circumstances free from danger in the port. Certain accidents are

due to misfortunes which are not the direct consequence of the order to the port, for instance, if a storm of unprecedented violence catches the ship in the nominated port and drives her ashore. The choice of port is an indirect cause of the loss for the ship would have escaped loss if she had not been ordered to some other port. But it is not the direct cause, for the choice of port does not involve a choice by the charterer of the risk of this unexpected event. In this context, also it is not easy to find a turn of phrase which accurately expresses the notion. It may be said that the loss is not recoverable unless events of this type and magnitude are sufficiently regular or at least foreseeable to say that their occurrence is an attribute or characteristic of a port, or it may be said that abnormal or casual events do not found a claim.

In our view the judge went wrong in his analysis in a number of respects. First of all he failed to formulate the critical – and *unitary* – question which he had to answer: namely, whether the simultaneous coincidence of the two critical features, viz. (a) such severe swell from long waves that it was dangerous for a vessel to remain at her berth at the Raw Materials Quay (because of the risk of damage or mooring break out) and (b) conditions in the Kashima Fairway being so severe because of gale force winds from the northerly/northeasterly quadrant), as to make navigation of the Fairway dangerous or impossible for Capesize vessels, was an abnormal occurrence or a normal characteristic of the port of Kashima? Or put even more simply, was it an abnormal occurrence or a normal characteristic of the port that a vessel might be in danger at her berth at the Raw Materials Quay but unable at the same time safely to leave because of navigation dangers in the Kashima Fairway arising from the combination of long waves and gale force northerly winds which, in fact, occurred.

On the contrary, instead of asking the unitary question directed at establishing the correct characterisation of the critical combination (abnormal occurrence or normal characteristic of the port), the judge merely addressed the respective constituent elements of the combination (swell from long waves making it dangerous for a vessel to remain at the Raw Materials Quay and gale force winds from the northerly/northeasterly quadrant making navigation of the Fairway dangerous or impossible for Capesize vessels) separately. He looked at each component and decided that, viewed on its own, neither could be said to be rare and both were attributes or characteristics of the port. That was the wrong approach; what mattered was not the nature of the individual component dangers that gave rise to the events on 24th October, but the nature of the event (i.e. the critical combination) which gave rise to the vessel (on the judge's findings) effectively being trapped in port.

He then compounded his previous error by concluding that, even if the critical combination was rare, nonetheless it was a characteristic of the port, apparently for two reasons:-

i) first, because, although:-'It may well be a rare event for these two events to occur at the same time but nobody at the port could, I consider, be surprised if they did. There is no meteorological reason why they should not occur at the same time'; and ii) secondly, because:-'Even if the concurrent occurrence of those events is a rare event in the history of the port such an event flows from characteristics or features of the port'. Both reasons in our view are fallacious.

The first reason ('nobody at the port could, I consider, be surprised if they did.') appears to based on the idea that, provided an event is theoretically foreseeable as possibly occurring at the relevant port, because of the port's location, then that is enough to qualify the event as a 'characteristic of the port'. The judge appears to have derived this test from dicta from the judgment of Mustill J in *The Mary Lou* at 278, column 2, which the judge selectively quotes in paragraph 129 of the judgment, where he refers to long waves and northerly gale winds as being 'at least foreseeable'. But satisfaction of the test of mere 'foreseeability' is *per se* clearly not sufficient to turn what the judge himself described as 'a rare event in the history of the port' into a normal characteristic or attribute of the port. The error of the judge, in our view, was to pick up on the words 'at least foreseeable' in his citation from Mustill J's judgment, and to use minimum foreseeability, without more, as some sort of litmus test for establishing whether an event was a characteristic of a port, without having any regard to significant factors such as the actual evidence relating to the past history of the port, the frequency (if any) of the event, the degree of forseeability of the critical combination and the very severe nature of the storm on the casualty date. In doing so, the judge departed from the orthodox and practical approach by Mustill J, as set out in the full passage of his judgment quoted above, and indeed that of Lords Diplock and Roskill in *The Evia (No.2),* to the question of whether an event was abnormal, which necessarily includes an examination of the past history of the port and whether, in that evidential context, the event was unexpected, but also took the phrase 'at least foreseeable' as used by Mustill J out of context. In our view it is clear, when the passage is read in context, that Mustill J certainly was not suggesting that mere, theoretical, forseeability on its own was sufficient. Whether or not, as Mr Kendrick suggested, Mustill J intended the adverb 'sufficiently' to modify the word 'foreseeable', Mustill J was not setting up some sort of alternate test which excluded considerations of questions such as the frequency of past occurrences of the particular event, or the degree of likelihood that the event was to occur in the future.

Moreover, as the Court of Appeal emphasised in *The Saga Cob* in the passage cited above, one has to look at the reality of the particular situation in the context of all the evidence, to ascertain whether the particular event was sufficiently likely to occur to have become an attribute of the port, otherwise the consequences of a mere foreseeability test lead to wholly unreal and impractical results. That point may be illustrated by examples given by charterers in their written argument: does the mere fact that it is 'foreseeable' from the location of San Francisco that earthquakes may occur in its vicinity, or from the location of Syracuse, beneath Mount Etna, that there may be volcanic explosions in its vicinity, predicate that any damage caused to vessels in those ports from such events, were they to occur in the future, would flow from the 'normal characteristics or attributes' of those ports, and therefore necessarily involve a breach of any safe port warranty? The answer is obviously not; whether, in such circumstances, there would be a breach of the safe port warranty, or the event would be a characterised as an abnormal occurrence, would necessarily depend on an evidential evaluation of the particular event giving rise to the damage and the relevant history of the port.

Perhaps most significantly under this head, the judge provides no evidential basis for his apparent factual conclusion that 'nobody at the port could, I consider, be surprised' if the crucial combination occurred, or for the conclusion reached earlier in paragraph 110 of the judgment that 'there must have been . . . a clear risk of gale force winds from the northerly quadrant in the Kashima Fairway at the same time as long waves were affecting the Raw Materials Quay.'

In the light of the evidence to the effect that no vessel in the port's history had been dangerously trapped at the Raw Materials Quay, with a risk of damage or mooring break out, at the same time as the Kashima Channel was not navigable because of gale force winds, it is difficult to see how he reached this conclusion. This may be because he did not adequately focus evidentially on the particular situation which he had to consider, namely one where a vessel was effectively trapped, because the swell from long waves affecting vessels berthed at the Raw Materials Quay was so severe that it was dangerous for a vessel to remain there (as opposed to merely a situation where long waves caused swell and a vessel decided to leave the Raw Materials Quay) and the Kashima Channel not being navigable because of gale force winds. It may also be because he did not give adequate weight to the evidence of Mr. Lynagh (which he gives no cogent reason for rejecting) that the storm which occurred on 24th October was exceptional in terms of its rapid development, its duration and its severity (see para 48 (ix) above).

The second reason given by the judge ('Even if the concurrent occurrence of those events is a rare event in the history of the port such an event flows from characteristics or features of the port') is, in our view, equally flawed. As we have already stated in paragraphs 55 and 56 above, what the judge had to decide was whether 'the concurrent occurrence of those events' (i.e. the critical combination) was itself a normal characteristic of the port or an abnormal occurrence. That was the relevant event which the judge had to characterise. It simply did not follow, logically or otherwise, from the fact that that event arose from (or, as the judge said, 'flow[ed] from') the combination of two individual dangers, which he had held were normal characteristics or attributes of the port, that the 'concurrent occurrence of those events' was also a normal characteristic or attribute of the port.

In deciding whether the critical combination was itself a normal characteristic of the port or an abnormal occurrence, what the judge should have done was to evaluate the evidence relating to the past frequency of such an event occurring and the likelihood of it occurring again. He should have also, in our view, have taken into account what appears to have been the unchallenged evidence of Mr Lynagh referred to above relating to the exceptional nature of the storm that affected Kashima on 24th October 2006 in terms of its rapid development, its duration and its severity. Had he done so, then, on the basis of his own finding that 'the concurrent occurrence of those events was rare', and on the basis of the evidence which we have summarised above, there would, in our view, have been only one conclusion which he could have reached – namely that the event which occurred on 24th October 2006 was indeed an abnormal occurrence.

For the above reasons we conclude that the conditions which affected Kashima on 24th October 2006 were an abnormal occurrence, that there was no breach by the charterers of the safe port obligation, and accordingly that the appeal should be allowed on this ground.

The result has been welcomed by charterers and insurers but owners will be disappointed, since the safe port warranty is perhaps not as fully protective as they may have thought. At the time of writing an appeal to the Supreme Court remains a possibility.

5 Hire and withdrawal

The relationship between the law and commerce is very important to commercial law generally and in carriage of goods by sea particularly with regard to contract terms.

The Baltic Dry Index is provided daily by the Baltic Exchange in London and is a measure of the cost of transporting commodities such as grain and metals by sea. It is a composite of three indices that look at different sizes of dry bulk carriers: Capesize, Panamax and Supramax. The index is expressed in US dollars.

In 2008 it reached a peak of 11,793. By February 2015 the BDI had fallen to 577.

It is commonplace to say that the shipping market is cyclical in nature and that freight rates for carriage under voyage charters or the rates available for time charters will vary under changing market conditions. However, it is as well to note that the oscillation between the heights of the market in 2008 and the subsequent depths following the financial turmoil of that same year has been enormous. Time charters agreed at the height of the market began to look very unappealing to charterers following the financial crash and no doubt presented financial difficulties; these manifested themselves as a reluctance to pay hire promptly or at all. Shipowners therefore experienced difficulties. In a falling market where charterers are not paying hire what should owners do?

Hire is the consideration to be paid to the shipowner for the use and service of the ship and crew. It is usual for charter to deal expressly with the time, place, amount, currency and manner of payment, as well as the moment from which hire accrues and the moment to which it runs. A shipowner may and commonly will reserve the right to withdraw the vessel and terminate the charter if the charterer fails to pay hire in the way agreed. This right must normally be reserved expressly: in the absence of a withdrawal clause, in earlier editions of this book we suggested that a late payment of hire would not usually be regarded at common law as a repudiatory breach entitling the owner to treat the contract as at an end and we relied on *The Georgios C* [1971] 1 Lloyd's Rep 7.

We think it fair to say that much interest has been created in the ship-owning community by the Commercial Court's more recent decision in *Kuwait Rocks Co v AMN Bulkcarriers Inc, The Astra* [2013] EWHC 865 (Comm), a case where, although not central to the decision, the court held that the obligation of timeous payment of hire under a NYPE charterparty is a condition. More recently again the same court has had the opportunity to consider the issue, although once more the case did not turn on this point.

This is the case of *Spar Shipping AS v Grand China Logistics Holding (Group) Co Ltd* [2015] EWHC 718 (Comm). In both cases the question of whether late payment was a breach of a condition or merely of a warranty was argued in some detail.

Kuwait Rocks Co v AMN Bulkcarriers Inc, The Astra [2013] EWHC 865 (Comm)

Facts: By a charterparty dated 6 October 2008 on an amended NYPE 1946 form AMN Bulkcarriers Inc chartered the Astra to Kuwait Rocks Co for a five-year period.

The charter contained the usual cl 5, which provided:

Payment of said hire to be in London net of bank charges in cash in United States Currency 30 days in advance and for the last 30 days or part of same the approximate amount of hire, hire is to be paid for the balance day by day as it becomes due, if so required by owners, otherwise failing the punctual and regular payment of the hire, or bank guarantee, or any breach of this Charter Party, the owners shall be at liberty to withdraw the vessel from the service of the Charterers, without prejudice to any claim they (the owners) may otherwise have on the Charterers. . . .

In addition the charter contained in cl 31 an anti-technicality clause:

. . . Referring to hire payment(s), where there is any failure to make 'punctual and regular payment' due to oversight or negligence or error or omission of Charterers' employees, bankers or agents, owners shall notify Charterers in writing whereupon Charterers will have two banking days to rectify the failure, where so rectified the payment shall stand as punctual and regular payment.

The charterers delayed in paying hire and owners served an anti-technically notice for failure to pay hire in a timely manner. The charterers failed to rectify the situation and owners withdrew the vessel and terminated the charter. In order to mitigate its losses the owners entered into a substitute charter for the remainder of the charter period; however, at a much lower hire rate.

The charter rate was very favourable to the owners and at US$26,800 per day was above the market rate. The charterers attempted to negotiate the rate downwards and warned that they might have to declare bankruptcy if no reduction was forthcoming. They ultimately defaulted.

Following service of an anti-technicality notice as required by cl 31, there was withdrawal and termination by owners in August 2010. Approximately one month later, the owners mitigated their loss by concluding a substitute fixture for the balance of the charter period. However, the rate under the substitute fixture was only US$17,500 per day. Since there was more than three years of the original charter period remaining, owners were left to face a very substantial loss.

In his judgment Flaux J says at para 34:

I have already recorded at [14] above the tribunal's conclusion at [59] of the Reasons that, whatever their instinct as commercial arbitrators, they considered that the generally accepted position under English law is that clause 5 is not a condition. It is clear from the previous two paragraphs of the Reasons that the tribunal were strongly influenced in reaching that conclusion by the view expressed at [16.132] of the current (sixth) edition of *Wilford on Time Charters* (and indeed in previous editions) that despite various dicta to the effect that clause 5 of the NYPE form and other similar hire payment provisions are conditions, to which the editors refer (and which I analyse in more detail below): 'it is thought that the better view is that the obligation to pay hire is by nature an intermediate term, so damages for the loss of the charter are recoverable only where the failure to pay hire by the due date can be shown to be repudiatory. It may be that the judicial remarks recorded above should not be understood as meaning that Clause 5 is a condition, but only that its draftsman, by adding an option to withdraw to the obligation to pay hire, has given to that obligation one characteristic of a condition, namely that any breach gives a right of termination. But uncertainty will remain until the House of Lords has shed more light on this important question'.

That last sentence is evidently a reference back to the citation at [16.129] of the judgment of Brandon J in *The Brimnes* [1973] 1 WLR 386, affirmed by the Court of Appeal [1975] 1 QB 929. It was that decision (which I consider below) which the tribunal in the present case clearly regarded as setting out the position under English law that clause 5 is not a condition. In his written and oral argument on this issue, Mr Bright QC was critical of both the editors of *Wilford* and the tribunal for over-reliance on *The Brimnes* because that was a case where there was no anti-technicality clause and *Wilford* simply fails to recognise that anti-technicality clauses are now commonplace, it being Mr Bright's submission that the effect of such a clause is to make time for payment of hire by the end of the relevant grace period (in the case of clause 31 two banking days after notice) of the essence, so that the clause is a condition.

[Later at paragraph 111 he continues]: In my judgment, an obvious ground of distinction between *The Brimnes* and the present case is the presence in this case of clause 31, the anti-technicality clause, but the question then arises whether that clause makes time of the essence where it would not otherwise be so. In support of their case that it does not, the charterers rely upon the fact that the clause is designed to protect the charterers. However, it seems to me that the fact that, in one sense the anti-technicality clause is intended to protect the charterers from the risk of termination on technical grounds, does not preclude the clause from having the effect of making time of the essence, even if clause 5 alone did not make time of the essence. What a clause like clause 31 does make clear is that there is a defined period of grace, here two banking days, after which, provided the notice has been given, the owners are entitled to withdraw the vessel. I can see no sensible distinction as a matter of principle between clause 31 and the first paragraph of clause 5.05 in *Stocznia v Latco*: they both establish the limit of any period of grace, after which if the other party remains in default, the innocent party is entitled to bring the contract to an end. It seems to me that the reasoning of Rix LJ that this creates a condition of the contract is equally applicable to the present case.

That reasoning, that although the anti-technicality clause is granting the charterers an indulgence in terms of time for payment, it makes the obligation to pay hire a condition of the contract is supported by [31] of the decision of Eder J in *Parbulk II A/S v Heritage Maritime Ltd SA ('The Mahakam')* [2011] EWHC 2917 (Comm); [2012] 1 Lloyd's Rep 87, albeit that the contract in that case provided expressly for time to be of the essence in relation to punctual payment of hire. Furthermore, I do not consider that there is anything in the decision of Christopher Clarke J in *The Qatar Star* which is to contrary effect or otherwise assists the charterers. All the learned judge was saying was that the anti-technicality clause should be interpreted beneficially to the charterers. He was not saying that if, notwithstanding that beneficial interpretation, the charterers were in breach of the obligation to make prompt payment of hire, they were to be relieved in some way of the consequences of that breach. That approach would be to revive the approach to clauses such as clause 5 of the NYPE form and clause 6 of the Baltime form adopted by Lord Denning MR which was disapproved in trenchant terms by the House of Lords.

It follows in my judgment that the presence of the anti-technicality clause in this charter does provide a valid ground for distinguishing Brandon J's judgment in *The Brimnes* and that, even if Brandon J is right that clause 5 standing alone does not make time of the essence, the effect of clause 31, making it clear that there is a limit to the period of grace of two banking days after the notice, does make time of the essence.

However, even if clause 31 were not in the present charter, I would, albeit with some hesitation, decline to follow Brandon J on this issue for a number of reasons. First, his conclusion that the clause is not an essential term cannot really be reconciled with the dicta of the House of Lords to which I have referred. Second, as is clear from the passages in his judgment which I have cited at [67] above, his reasoning was based in large measure upon the decision in *The Georgios C* which was subsequently overruled by *The Laconia*. Third, and following on from the second reason, his conclusion involved acceptance of the argument of Mr Robert Goff QC, that the word 'punctual' added little or nothing to the word 'payment' standing alone, an argument the validity of which depended on the correctness of *The Georgios C*. It is quite clear from the speeches in *The Laconia* that the House of Lords regarded punctual payment of hire as of considerable commercial importance, discrediting the argument that 'punctual' added nothing to 'payment'.

The third reason why in my judgment the obligation to make punctual payment of hire is a condition is related to the second and is the point emphasised time and again in the speeches in the House of Lords to which I have referred, namely the importance to businessmen of certainty in commercial transactions. As I see it, an aspect of that need for certainty is that, if it were the case that the right to withdraw the vessel for non-payment of hire left the owners with no remedy in damages on a falling market, save in cases where the charterers' conduct could be said to be repudiatory, that would leave the owners in a position of uncertainty as to whether to withdraw the vessel or to soldier on with a recalcitrant charterer until such time as the owners were in a position to say that the charterers were in repudiatory breach, essentially what happened on the facts in the present case.

Contrary to Miss Davies' submission that somehow business commonsense supports the charterers' construction of the provision, it seems to me that 'wait and see' approach to breach of charterparty is inimical to certainty. That is undesirable for the reasons given by the House of Lords in *Bunge v Tradax* in the passages I have set out at [83] to [87] above. Equally, if the obligation to make punctual payment of hire is a condition, the charterers have a corresponding certainty, that if they fail to make prompt payment of hire and the owners withdraw the vessel, at a time when the market rate is falling, they will be liable for damages for loss of bargain.

The fourth reason why I consider that the obligation to make punctual payment of hire (whether clause 5 on its own or clause 5 in conjunction with clause 31) is that, not only is that conclusion supported by the dicta in the House of Lords to which I have referred, but also by the *obiter* statements of Rix LJ in *Stocznia v Latco* referred to at [93] above and the reasoning of Moore-Bick LJ in *Stocznia v Gearbulk*. In view of that judicial support, albeit *obiter*, it seems to me that this court need not show any reluctance to hold that the obligation is a condition. The reluctance demonstrated by Lord Mustill in *The Gregos* was really limited to the particular provisions he was considering and did not extend to the obligation to make punctual payment of hire. Furthermore, as Lords Wilberforce and Roskill made clear in *Bunge v Tradax* (in the passages quoted at [84] and [86] above), in the case of so-called time clauses in mercantile contracts, of which this obligation is one, the courts should not show any reluctance to find that such provisions are conditions and, indeed, should usually do so.

For all those reasons, in my judgment the obligation to make punctual payment of hire (whether clause 5 on its own or when combined with clause 31) is a condition of the contract. Once it is recognised that the obligation is a condition, then as Moore-Bick LJ recognises in *Stocznia v Gearbulk* (and as is implicit in [52] of Lord Mance's judgment in *The Kos*) the owners have a right to claim damages upon termination for loss of the bargain. The suggestion in *Wilford* that the various dicta should somehow be understood as meaning not that the obligation is a condition, but that it has one characteristic of a condition, namely that any breach gives rise to a right of termination, seems to me not only contrary to the dicta themselves, which clearly contemplate the obligation being an essential term or condition or time being of the essence, all synonymous as I have said with a condition in the classic sense, but also somewhat heretical. The obligation either is a condition or it is not. If it is not, then it is an innominate term, if it is a condition then all the 'usual consequences' as Moore-Bick LJ puts it, follow, including the right to claim damages for loss of bargain.

Spar Shipping AS v Grand China Logistics Holding (Group) Co Ltd [2015] EWHC 718 (Comm)

The court also examined the leading cases in detail but came to a different conclusion.

In *Spar Shipping*, three long-term NYPE 1993 charters had been agreed on 5 March 2010. Hire was paid punctually on all three until 11 April 2011; thereafter the charterers began to default and the owners withdrew the vessels, reserving a right to claim loss of bargain damages on the basis that the charterers were in breach of condition or in repudiatory breach of an innominate term.

In *Spar Shipping*, Popplewell J refers to *Financings Ltd v Baldock* [1963] 2 QB 104. This is not a shipping case but rather a case concerning hire purchase. In this case the Court of Appeal discussed whether or not a breach of timely payment by the hirer gave rise to a right of termination and sustained a claim for damages for loss of a bargain. It was held that in the absence of a serious breach by the hirer there was no right to loss of bargain damages. In contrast, in *The Astra*, Flaux J had indicated that even trivial breaches of the NYPE charter suggested that the obligation of timeous payment was a condition. In *Spar Shipping* Popplewell J says at para 104:

Financings v Baldock does not immediately provide the answer to the question whether non payment of hire in a time charter is a condition. There are important differences between a time charter and a hire purchase agreement. Moreover the contract in that case provided for termination upon events which were not confined to breaches; and there was a clause providing for interest on late payment which Diplock LJ treated as significant in indicating that time of payment was not intended to be of the essence. These are significant distinctions. The case does, however, illustrate that the mere fact that a contractual right of termination is conferred for any breach of a term, however trivial, does not answer the question whether the term is a condition.

[He then went on to say at para 154:] The starting point is the seminal judgment of Diplock LJ in *Hongkong Fir Shipping Co Ltd v Kawasaki Kishen Kaisha Ltd* [1962] 2 QB 26. His analysis begins by equating events which are sufficiently serious to bring a contract to an end for breach with those which are sufficiently serious for frustration, and treats the various metaphors used to define such seriousness as encapsulated in a test of whether the event deprives the party of substantially the whole benefit of the contract (p. 66). After a survey of the historical development of the law on conditions and warranties he states at pp. 69–70:

No doubt there are many simple contractual undertakings, sometimes express but more often because of their very simplicity ('It goes without saying') to be implied, of which it can be predicated that every breach of such an undertaking must give rise to an event which will deprive the party not in default of substantially the whole benefit which it was intended that he should obtain from the contract. And such a stipulation, unless the parties have agreed that breach of it shall not entitle the non-defaulting party to treat the contract as repudiated, is a 'condition.' So too there may be other simple contractual undertakings of which it can be predicated that no breach can give rise to an event which will deprive the party not in default of substantially the whole benefit which it was intended that he should obtain from the contract; and such a stipulation, unless the parties have agreed that breach of it shall entitle the non-defaulting party to treat the contract as repudiated, is a 'warranty.' There are, however, many contractual undertakings of a more complex character which cannot be categorised as being 'conditions' or 'warranties', if the late nineteenth-century meaning adopted in the Sale of Goods Act, 1893, and used by Bowen LJ in *Bentsen v Taylor, Sons & Co.* be given to those terms. Of such undertakings all that can be predicated is that some breaches will and others will not give rise to an event which will deprive the party not in default of substantially the whole benefit which it was intended that be should obtain from the contract; and the legal consequences of a breach of such an undertaking, unless provided for expressly in the contract, depend upon the nature of the event to which the breach gives rise and do not follow automatically from a prior classification of the undertaking as a 'condition' or a 'warranty'.

This passage identifies that a term is to be categorised as a condition only if any predicated breach would deprive the innocent party of substantially the whole benefit of the contract, in the absence of agreement between the parties that a breach shall entitle the innocent party to treat the contract as repudiated. This qualification is not to be elevated into a principle that a contractual right of termination on any breach of the term is indicative that it is a condition. To have such effect it must be an agreement that the breach shall 'entitle the defaulting party to treat the contract as repudiated', in the words of Diplock LJ. A contractual right to terminate may or may not be such an agreement, depending upon its proper construction; it may be no more than an option to cancel, as Diplock LJ himself made clear in *Financings v Baldock* a year later. I would therefore reject the submission of counsel for the owners in *The Astra*, recorded at paragraph [39], that the logical corollary of Diplock LJ's analysis of what constitutes a condition is that if the contract provides for a right to terminate, that is a very strong indication that the term in question is a condition. This seems to me to turn the passage on its head. The essential test proposed is whether the term is one any predicated breach of which deprives the innocent party of substantially the whole benefit of the contract. This may be modified by the agreement of the parties that a breach will entitle the innocent party to treat the contract *as repudiated*. A contractual termination clause may be one which provides that the agreement is to be treated as repudiated at common law, or may be one which treats the contract as cancelled in futuro as a matter of contractual option. Which of two consequences is intended is a question which falls to be considered as a matter of interpretation of the termination provision and the other terms of the contract. The mere existence of a termination provision tells one nothing about the status of the term without discovering the intention of the parties as to the consequences of the contractual right of termination by this process of interpretation.

So we have two judgments containing close analysis of the precedents with regard to conditions; both given in furtherance of commercial activity but coming to opposing conclusions. It seems inevitable that the Court of Appeal will be asked to examine this issue in the future.

Notes

1   In *Afovos Shipping Co SA v Pagnan* [1983] 1 WLR 195, the House of Lords held where a payment was due on or before a particular day, the charterer has the whole of that day to make the payment and is not in default until midnight. It was also held that where the owner agrees to give notice of default before withdrawing (usually referred to as an anti-technicality clause) a valid notice cannot be given until the charterer is in default. It is of course possible to vary either of these rules by agreement. It is also possible that the right to withdraw in respect of a particular breach may be lost if that breach is waived.

2   A right to withdraw and notice of withdrawal must be given promptly, or the right will be lost. In *The Northern Pioneer* [2002] EWCA Civ 1878; [2003] 1 Lloyd's Rep 212, the Court of Appeal suggested that this rule was better explained as the result of an implied term, although noting that application of principles of election, waiver and estoppel may produce the same result.

5.1 Waiver

Owners may be held to have waived and be unable to rely on a particular default if, for example, they accept a late payment when tendered or if they do not give notice that they reject it within a reasonable time.

Mardorf Peach & Co Ltd v Attica Sea Carriers Corp of Liberia, The Laconia [1977] AC 850

Facts: The *Laconia* was chartered on the NYPE form. The charter provided that the hire was to be paid in cash in US currency semi-monthly in advance into a designated account at a specified branch of the owners' bank and that 'failing the punctual and regular payment of the hire' the owners should be at liberty to withdraw the vessel. The final payment of hire became due on a Sunday. It was conceded by the charterers that, as London banks were closed on Sunday and Saturday, the due date for payment of this instalment was the previous Friday. It was not paid but was tendered or paid to the owners' bank at about 3 pm on the following Monday. At 6.55 pm on that day the owners withdrew the vessel.

Held:

Lord Wilberforce: . . . My Lords, I cannot find any difficulty or ambiguity in this clause. It must mean that once a punctual payment of any instalment has not been made, a right of withdrawal accrues to the owners. Conversely, it is incapable of meaning that a charterer who has failed to make a punctual payment can (unless the owners have waived the default) avoid the consequences of his failure by later tendering an unpunctual payment. He would still have failed to make a punctual payment, and it is on this failure and by reason of it that the owners get the right to withdraw . . .

This leaves the second question, which is whether the right of withdrawal was waived by the owners. The submission of the charterers was that on Monday, 13 April 1970, before the owners purported to withdraw the ship, they accepted the charterers' late payment of the instalment and so affirmed the contract. The arbitrators found that there had not been any waiver, so that the charterers must undertake the task of showing that, upon the facts found, the only possible conclusion must have been there had.

In order to understand the argument, it is necessary to go into the facts in some detail. At about 3 pm, at which time London banks closed for the day, a messenger from the Midland Bank, acting for the charterers, delivered to the owners' bank, the First National City Bank, 34, Moorgate, London (FNCB), a 'payment order' for the amount of the seventh instalment. A payment order is a document issued by one bank to another under a scheme (LCSS) by which banks maintain dollar suspense accounts in which they credit or debit each other with sums in dollars and make periodical settlements. As between banks, a payment order is the equivalent of cash, but a customer cannot draw upon it. The amount must first be credited to his account, but he can, of course, make special arrangements for earlier drawing. At about 3.10 or 3.15 pm the payment order was received and stamped in the sorting office of FNCB. It was then taken to the transfer department. There an official called an editor wrote on the face of the order the formula CR ADV & TT Lausanne, an instruction (to be carried out elsewhere in the bank) meaning 'credit advice and telegraphic transfer Lausanne'. Not perhaps quite simultaneously, but at about the same time, another official telephoned to the owners' agents and said that the bank had received a payment order for the amount of the hire: this was in accordance with instructions received by the bank earlier in the day from the owners' agents. This official was immediately told to refuse the money and to return it. Thereupon the editor deleted the annotation he had made on the payment order and wrote on it: 'Beneficiary has refused payment. Advise remitter by phone.' There was no direct evidence that this was done but such may be presumed. The next day FNCB sent to the Midland Bank a payment order for the same amount as that which the Midland Bank had sent the previous day.

My Lords, much ingenuity and effort was used in order to show that this series of actions, or some part of it, constituted acceptance and waiver by the owners of the right to withdraw. But in my opinion it did not approach success. Although the word 'waiver', like 'estoppel', covers a variety of situations different in their legal nature, and tends to be indiscriminately used by the courts as a means of relieving parties from bargains or the consequences of bargains which are thought to be harsh or deserving of relief, in the present context what is relied on is clear enough. The charterers had failed to make a punctual payment but it was open to the owners to accept a late payment as if it were punctual, with the consequence that they could not thereafter rely on the default as entitling them to withdraw. All that is needed to establish waiver, in this sense, of the committed breach of contract, is evidence, clear and unequivocal, that such acceptance has taken place, or, after the late payment has been tendered, such a delay in refusing it as might reasonably cause the charterers to believe that it has been accepted.

My Lords, if this is, as I believe, what would have to be proved in order to establish a waiver in the situation under review, it must be obvious that the facts in the present case do not amount to it. Looked at untechnically, the facts were that the money was sent to the bank, taken into the banking process or machinery, put in course of transmission to the owners, but rejected by the latter as soon as they were informed of its arrival and as soon as they were called upon, or able, to define their position. Put more technically, the bank, though agents of the owners, had a limited authority. It is not necessary to decide whether, in general, and in the absence of specific instructions, bankers in such situations as these have authority to accept late payments . . . here it is clear that the bankers had no such authority and still less any authority to make business decisions as to the continuance or otherwise of the charterparty but that *per contra* they had express instructions to refer the matter to the owners' agents. On this basis they receive the order (they clearly had no right to reject it out of hand), and, while provisionally starting to process it into the owners' possession, at the same time seek the owners' directions in accordance with the owners' previous instructions. On those directions, they arrest the process and return the money. The acts of the editors – the annotation on the payment order – were internal acts (Brandon J, of a similar situation in *The Brimnes* [1973] 1 WLR 386, 411 called them 'ministerial', ie acts done without any intention or capacity to affect legal relations with third parties), not irrevocable, but provisional and reversible acts, consistent with an alternative decision of the customer which might be to accept or reject. The customer chose to reject, he did so as rapidly as the circumstances permitted, and he could have given no ground to the charterer for supposing that the payment had been accepted. The charterer did not act upon any such supposition.

The pattern of action is to me so clear that I do not find it necessary to decide the rather technical question whether, as regards the owners, there was payment 'in cash' as required by the charterparty, or not. Whatever it was it was not punctual payment, and not accepted in waiver of the unpunctuality. I think then that there is no basis on which the arbitrators' finding against waiver can be attacked.

The result of my conclusions on these two points leaves the matter as follows:

1   Under the withdrawal clause, as under similar clauses, including the Baltime clause properly interpreted, a right of withdrawal arises as soon as default is made in punctual payment of an instalment of hire. Whether or not this rule is subject to qualification in a case of punctual but insufficient payment as some authorities appear to hold, is not an issue which now arises and I express no opinion upon it.

2   The owners must within a reasonable time after the default give notice of withdrawal to the charterers. What is a reasonable time – essentially a matter for arbitrators to find – depends on the circumstances. In some, indeed many cases, it will be a short time – *viz*, the shortest time reasonably necessary to enable the shipowner to hear of the default and issue instructions. If, of course, the charterparty contains an express provision regarding notice to the charterers, that provision must be applied.

3   The owners may be held to have waived the default, *inter alia*, if when a late payment is tendered, they choose to accept it as if it were timeous, or if they do not within a reasonable time give notice that they have rejected it . . .

5.2 Relief from forfeiture

The consequence of withdrawal of a vessel may of course be serious for the charterer. Loss of the ship may seem particularly hard where the failure to pay was accidental and the charter market has risen substantially. In some areas of law – the law of mortgages and landlord and tenant – English courts claim power to grant relief on reasonable terms to parties who are in breach and who are threatened with loss of their interest in a property. The courts were urged in *The Scaptrade* to claim analogous powers.

Scandinavian Trading Tanker Co AB v Flota Petrolera Ecuatoriana, The Scaptrade [1983] 2 AC 694

Facts: The tanker *Scaptrade* was time chartered for three years. The charterers, through a slip in their own office, failed to make a payment at a time when the charter still had a year to run. The owners gave notice to the charterers withdrawing the vessel. Tender of the overdue hire was made on the following day but was refused. After negotiations had taken place, the vessel was rechartered by the owners to the charterers on a 'without prejudice' agreement with the rate of hire (that is, charter rate or market rate) to abide the result of litigation.

Held:

Lord Diplock: . . . In this appeal . . . your Lordships have heard argument upon one question only: 'Has the High Court any jurisdiction to grant relief against the exercise by a shipowner of his contractual right, under the withdrawal clause in a time charter, to withdraw the vessel from the service of the charterer upon the latter's failure to make payment of an instalment of the hire in the manner and at a time that is not later than that for which the withdrawal clause provides?'

. . . A time charter, unless it is a charter by demise, with which your Lordships are not here concerned, transfers to the charterer no interest in or right to possession of the vessel; it is a contract for services to be rendered to the charterer by the shipowner through the use of the vessel by the shipowner's own servants, the master and the crew, acting in accordance with such directions as to the cargoes to be loaded and the voyages to be undertaken as by the terms of the charterparty the charterer is entitled to give to them. Being a contract for services it is thus the very prototype of a contract of which before the fusion of law and equity a court would never grant specific performance: *Clarke v Price* (1819) 2 Wils 157; *Lumley v Wagner* (1852) 1 De GM & G 604. In the event of failure to render the promised services, the party to whom they were to be rendered would be left to pursue such remedies in damages for breach of contract as he might have at law. But as an unbroken line of uniform authority in this House, from *Tankexpress* [1949] AC 76 to *The Chikuma* [1981] 1 WLR 314, has held, if the withdrawal clause so provides, the shipowner is entitled to withdraw the services of the vessel from the charterer if the latter fails to pay an instalment of hire in precise compliance with the provisions of the charter. So the shipowner commits no breach of contract if he does so; and the charterer has no remedy in damages against him.

To grant an injunction restraining the shipowner from exercising his right of withdrawal of the vessel from the service of the charterer, though negative in form, is pregnant with an affirmative order to the shipowner to perform the contract; juristically it is indistinguishable from a decree for specific performance of a contract to render services; and in respect of that category of contracts, even in the event of breach, this is a remedy that English courts have always disclaimed any jurisdiction to grant. This is, in my view, sufficient reason in itself to compel rejection of the suggestion that the equitable principle of relief from forfeiture is juristically capable of extension so as to grant to the court a discretion to prevent a shipowner from exercising his strict contractual rights under a withdrawal clause in a time charter which is not a charter by demise.

...All the analogies that ingenuity has suggested may be discovered between a withdrawal clause in a time charter and other classes of contractual provisions in which courts have relieved parties from the rigour of contractual terms into which they have entered can in my view be shown upon juristic analysis to be false. *Prima facie* parties to a commercial contract bargaining on equal terms can make 'time to be of the essence' of the performance of any primary obligation under the contract that they please, whether the obligation be to pay a sum of money or to do something else. When time is made of the essence of a primary obligation, failure to perform it punctually is a breach of a condition of the contract which entitles the party not in breach to elect to treat the breach as putting an end to all primary obligations under the contract that have not already been performed. In *Tankexpress A/S v Compagnie Financière Belge des Petroles SA* [1949] AC 76 this House held that time was of the essence of the very clause with which your Lordships are now concerned where it appeared in what was the then current predecessor of the Shelltime 3 charter. As is well known, there are available on the market a number of so-(mis)called 'anti-technicality clauses', such as that considered in *The Afovos*, which require the shipowner to give a specified period of notice to the charterer in order to make time of the essence of payment of advance hire; but at the expiry of such notice, provided it is validly given, time does become of the essence of the payment.

My Lords, quite apart from the juristic difficulties in the way of recognising a jurisdiction in the court to grant relief against the operation of a withdrawal clause in a time charter there are practical reasons of legal policy for declining to create any such new jurisdiction out of sympathy for charterers. The freight market is notoriously volatile. If it rises rapidly during the period of a time charter, the charterer is the beneficiary of the windfall which he can realise if he wants to by subchartering at the then market rates. What withdrawal of the vessel does is to transfer the benefit of the windfall from charterer to shipowner.

The practical objections to any extension to withdrawal clauses in time charters of an equitable jurisdiction to grant relief against their exercise are so convincingly expressed by Robert Goff LJ in the judgment of the Court of Appeal [1983] QB 529, 540–41 in the instant case that I can do no better than to incorporate them in my own speech for ease of reference:

> Parties to such contracts should be capable of looking after themselves: at the very least, they are capable of taking advice, and the services of brokers are available, and are frequently used, when negotiating terms. The possibility that shipowners may snatch at the opportunity to withdraw ships from the service of time charterers for non-payment of hire must be very well known in the world of shipping: it must also be very well known that anti-technicality clauses are available which are effective to prevent any such occurrence. If a prospective time charterer wishes to have any such clause included in the charter, he can bargain for it. If he finds it necessary or desirable to agree to a charter which contains no such clause, he can warn the relevant section of his office, and his bank, of the importance of securing timeous payment. But the matter does not stop there. It is of the utmost importance in commercial transactions that, if any particular event occurs which may affect the parties' respective rights under a commercial contract, they should know where they stand. The court should so far as possible desist from placing obstacles in the way of either party ascertaining his legal position, if necessary with the aid of advice from a qualified lawyer, because it may be commercially desirable for action to be taken without delay, action which may be irrevocable and which may have far-reaching consequences. It is for this reason, of course, that the English courts have time and again asserted the need for certainty in commercial transactions – for the simple reason that the parties to such transactions are entitled to know where they stand, and to act accordingly. In particular, when a shipowner becomes entitled, under the terms of his contract, to withdraw a ship from the service of a time charterer, he may well wish to act swiftly and irrevocably. True, his problem may, in any particular case, prove to be capable of solution by entering into a without prejudice agreement with the original time charterer, under which the rate of hire payable in future will

be made to depend upon a decision, by arbitrators or by a court, whether he was in law entitled to determine the charter. But this is not always possible.

He may wish to refix his ship elsewhere as soon as possible, to take advantage of a favourable market. It is no answer to this difficulty that the ship may have cargo aboard at the time, so that her services cannot immediately be made available to another charterer . . . For one thing, the ship may not have cargo on board, and for another she can be refixed immediately under a charter to commence at the end of her laden voyage. Nor is it an answer that the parties can immediately apply to arbitrators, or to a court, for a decision, and that both maritime arbitrators and the Commercial Court in this country are prepared to act very quickly at very short notice. For, quite apart from the fact that some delay is inherent in any legal process, if the question to be decided is whether the tribunal is to grant equitable relief, investigation of the relevant circumstances, and the collection of evidence for that purpose, cannot ordinarily be carried out in a very short period of time.

For all these reasons I would dismiss this appeal. I do so with the reminder that the reasoning in my speech has been directed exclusively to time charters that are not by demise. Identical considerations would not be applicable to bareboat charters and it would in my view be unwise for your Lordships to express any views about them.

5.3 Withdrawal for any other breach

A charter may, as in the case of the NYPE form, provide for withdrawal on nonpayment of hire 'or on any breach of this charter'. The proper interpretation of these words was considered in *The Antaios*.

Antaios Compania Naviera SA v Salen Rederierna AB, The Antaios [1985] AC 191

Facts: Shipowners purported to withdraw the vessel on the grounds of breach of an innominate term in the charterparty relating to the charterers' right to issue bills of lading on behalf of the master, arguing that this breach fell within the words 'any breach of this charterparty' in the NYPE withdrawal clause.

Held:

Lord Diplock: . . . The arbitrators decided this issue against the shipowners. The 78 pages in which they expressed their reasons for doing so contained an interesting, learned and detailed dissertation on the law, so lengthy as to be, in my view, inappropriate for inclusion in the reasons given by arbitrators for an award. Their reasons can be adequately summarised as being . . . that 'any other breach of this charter party' in the withdrawal clause means a repudiatory breach – that is to say: a fundamental breach of an innominate term or breach of a term expressly stated to be a condition, such as would entitle the shipowners to elect to treat the contract as wrongfully repudiated by the charterers, a category into which in the arbitrators' opinion the breaches complained of did not fall . . .

To the semantic analysis, buttressed by generous citation of judicial authority, which led the arbitrators to the conclusions as to the interpretation of the wording of the withdrawal clause that I have summarised, the arbitrators added an uncomplicated reason based simply upon business common sense:

We always return to the point that the owners' construction is wholly unreasonable, totally uncommercial and in total contradiction to the whole purpose of the NYPE time charter form.

The owners relied on what they said was 'the literal meaning of the words in the clause'. We would say that if necessary, in a situation such as this, a purposive construction should be given to the clause so as not to defeat the commercial purpose of the contract.

... your Lordships would not be trespassing on the field of a discretion that a judge upon whom it was conferred had in fact exercised if you were to take this opportunity of stating ... that the arbitrators in the passage in their award that I have cited earlier were not obviously wrong but were obviously right in their decision on the 'repudiatory breach' question ...

5.4 Deductions from hire

Deductions are often permitted by express agreement, for example for advances made by charterers for payments on behalf of the ship. It has also been held in a series of cases, of which *The Nanfri*, below, is the best known, that a charterer may deduct and set off against hire a claim for damages in limited circumstances, that is where in breach of contract the owners have deprived the charterer of the use of the whole or part of the ship. This principle and the way deductions should be quantified are considered in *The Nanfri*.

Federal Commerce & Navigation Co Ltd v Molena Alpha Inc,
The Nanfri [1978] QB 927, CA

Facts: Charterers deducted sums from hire and explained their reasons. The owners argued that charterers were not entitled to make any deduction from hire by way of off-hire or set off (even if the same was in fact due to the charterers) unless prior to such deduction either the owners had accepted the validity thereof or it was supported by vouchers signed by the master or a proper tribunal had pronounced on its validity.

Held:

Lord Denning MR: ... This contention was founded on the proposition that hire payable under a time charterparty is in the same position as freight payable under a voyage charterparty: and that under a settled rule of law freight is payable in full without deduction. Even if cargo is short-delivered, or delivered damaged, there can be no deduction on that account. Any cross-claim must be left to be decided later by the courts or by arbitration. That is well established now for 'freight' in such cases as *Henriksens Rederi A/S v T H Z Rolimpex (The Brede)* [1974] QB 233 and *Aries Tanker Corporation v Total Transport Ltd, The Aries* [1977] 1 WLR 185.

At one time it was common to describe the sums payable under a time charterparty as 'freight'. Such description is to be found used by judges and textbook writers of great distinction. But in modern times a change has come about. The payments due under a time charter are usually now described as 'hire' and those under a voyage charter as 'freight'. This change of language corresponds, I believe, to a recognition that the two things are different. 'Freight' is payable for carrying a quantity of cargo from one place to another. 'Hire' is payable for the right to use a vessel for a specified period of time, irrespective of whether the charterer chooses to use it for carrying cargo or lays it up, out of use. Every time charter contains clauses which are quite inappropriate to a voyage charter, such as the off-hire clause and the withdrawal clause. So different are the two concepts that I do not think the law as to 'freight' can be applied indiscriminately to 'hire'. In particular the special rule of English law whereby 'freight' must be paid in full (without deductions for short delivery or cargo damage) cannot be applied automatically to time charter 'hire'. Nor is there any authority which says that it must. It would be a mistake to suppose that the House of Lords had time charter hire and so forth in mind when they decided *The Aries* [1977] 1 WLR 185 or the *Nova (Jersey) Knit Ltd v Kammgarn Spinnerei GmbH* [1977] 1 WLR 713, or that anything said in those cases can bind this court. Many of us, I know, in the past have assumed that the rule as to 'freight' does apply: and some judges have said so. But now, after full argument, I am satisfied that the 'freight' rule does not apply automatically to 'time charter' hire: and we have to consider the position on principle.

Equitable set off in general

. . . one thing is quite clear: it is not every cross-claim which can be deducted. It is only cross-claims that arise out of the same transaction or are closely connected with it. And it is only cross-claims which go directly to impeach the plaintiff's demands, that is, so closely connected with his demands that it would be manifestly unjust to allow him to enforce payment without taking into account the cross-claim . . .

Equitable set off in this case

So I turn to the problem here. A shipowner has contracted to give a charterer the right to use the vessel for a period of time – six years in fact. In return the charterer has agreed to pay a stated sum of hire monthly in advance. Then let us suppose that, after the charterer has paid his month's hire in advance, the shipowner wrongly declines to allow the charterer to have the use of the vessel for some days during the ensuing month. He may put the vessel perhaps to some more profitable use. He, by his conduct, deprives the charterer of part of the consideration for which the hire was paid. I should have thought it plain that the charterer should in fairness be able to recoup himself by making a deduction from the next month's hire – so as to compensate him for the loss of use for those days – equivalent to the hire of those lost days. Likewise if the shipowner has been guilty of some other wrongful conduct which has deprived the charterer of the use of the ship during some days – or prejudiced the charterer in the use of the ship – then the charterer should in fairness be able to recoup himself by making a deduction from the next month's hire. If the charterer quantifies his loss by a reasonable assessment made in good faith – and deducts the sum quantified – then he is not in default. The shipowner cannot withdraw his vessel on account of non-payment of hire nor hold him guilty at that point of any breach of contract. If it subsequently turns out that he has deducted too much, the shipowner can of course recover the balance. But that is all. This point of view is supported by a score of judges versed in commercial matters over the last 30 to 40 years . . .

. . . I would hold that, when the shipowner is guilty of a breach of contract which deprives the time charterer of part of the consideration for which the hire has been paid in advance, the charterer can deduct an equivalent amount out of the hire falling due for the next month.

I would as at present advised limit the right to deduct to cases when the shipowner has wrongly deprived the charterer of the use of the vessel or has prejudiced him in the use of it. I would not extend it to other breaches or default of the shipowner, such as damage to cargo arising from the negligence of the crew . . .

The special clauses

Thus far I have considered only cases where the shipowner has himself been guilty of a breach of contract in depriving the charterer of the use of the vessel. Now I come to cases where the shipowner has not been guilty of any breach of contract, or is protected by exceptions clauses. In such cases the charterer is often given a right of deduction by express clauses such as the off-hire clause or a clause allowing deductions for disbursements. There is no doubt that the charterer can make the deduction, but the question is when? Have they to be agreed or established before he can make the deduction? There is no authority that I know of to that effect. It seems to me that he is entitled to quantify his loss by a reasonable assessment made in good faith – and deduct the sum so quantified from the hire. Then the actual figures can be ascertained later: either by agreement between the parties: or, failing agreement, by arbitration. That was what the parties did in the present case for the first three years of the charters. The right to deduct would be useless to the charterer if he had to wait until a figure was agreed or established – for then it might be postponed indefinitely . . .

Note

Shipowners let the *Aditya Vaibhav* to charterers on the Shelltime 3 form. The charterers alleged that a failure by the owners to clean the holds properly in breach of the charterparty had resulted in a delay to the vessel of 14 days when the vessel was not available for the service required and had caused them consequential loss and expense, which they claimed to deduct from hire due to the owners. Saville J held that the maximum amount that could be deducted by the charterers, applying *The Nanfri*, was the amount of hire payable for the period during which the vessel was off-hire: *Century Textiles and Industry Ltd v Tomoe Shipping Co (Singapore) Pte Ltd, The Aditya Vaibhav* [1991] 1 Lloyd's Rep 573.

6 Off-hire

The loss-of-time risk under a time charter is allocated to the charterer. In other words, under this type of contract, the charterer loses if the vessel is delayed or is unproductive and the shipowner is not at fault. Another way to put the same point is to say that in general time charters impose an obligation to pay hire continuously. However, it is common to agree that payment is not due for time lost to the charterer in consequence of circumstances 'Which can be attributed to the owner or the vessel and, sometimes, in wider circumstances.' Since off-hire clauses operate as exceptions which cut down the owner's right to hire, it is for the charterer to show that those circumstances have arisen. For the same reason, if the meaning of a clause is uncertain, it has been said that the words must be read in favour of the owner: *Royal Greek Govt v Minister of Transport, The Ilissos* (1948) 82 Ll L Rep 196, p 199, *per* Bucknill LJ. However, off-hire clauses are not identical and the standard forms are in any event frequently amended by the parties. For these reasons it has been said that the only general rule that can be laid down is that one must consider the wording of the off-hire clause in every case: *The Berge Sund* [1993] 2 Lloyd's Rep 453, p 459, *per* Staughton LJ. The issues that commonly arise are:

(1) did an off-hire event, as defined in the contract, actually occur?;
(2) was there in consequence a loss of time to the charterer?; and
(3) on what event did the hire become payable again? All three issues arose in *The Westfalia*.

Hogarth v Miller, The Westfalia [1891] AC 48

Facts: While the vessel was on a voyage from West Africa to Harburg and Antwerp, under charter, her high pressure engine broke down and it was necessary to put back about 100 miles to Las Palmas, which she reached with the aid of a low pressure engine assisted by her sails. As repairs could not be effected in that port, the appellants and respondents agreed that a tug should be employed to tow the ship to Harburg, and that the expense, £1,100, should be treated as general average on cargo, ship, and freight. As their proportion of this expense the respondents eventually paid £867. The ship left Las Palmas on 18 October 1887, towed by the tug and assisted by her own low pressure engine. She arrived at Harburg on 31 October and discharged the cargo with her own power. Repairs to her main engine were completed on 10 November. The charterparty provided that:

> In the event of loss of time from deficiency of men or stores, breakdown of machinery, want of repairs, or damage, whereby the working of the vessel is stopped for more than 48 consecutive working hours, the payment of hire shall cease until she be again in an efficient state to resume her service.

The shipowner admitted that the vessel was off-hire while at Las Palmas, but claimed payment of hire for the whole period of the voyage from Las Palmas to Harburg; the charterer denied liability to pay anything for the period before completion of repairs.

Held:

Lord Halsbury LC: . . . My Lords, the whole of this case, as it appears to me, turns upon the true construction of the contract which regulates the relations between the parties . . .

What the parties to this contract contemplated was this: the hirer of the vessel wants to use the vessel for the purpose of his adventure, and he is contemplating the possibility that by some of the causes indicated in the clause itself . . . the efficient working of the vessel may be stopped, and so loss of time may be incurred; and he protects himself by saying, that during such period as the working of the vessel is stopped for more than 48 consecutive hours, payment shall cease; and now come the words upon which such reliance is placed: 'until she be again in an efficient state to resume her service.' If the contention which has been put forward at your Lordships' Bar were well founded one might have expected that the parties in contemplating what upon that view was said to be the intention of the parties if they had intended that the test should be the efficient state of the vessel as it originally was might very readily have used the words, 'until such time as the deficiency of men or stores has been removed, or the breakdown of the machinery has been set to rights, or the want of repairs has been supplied, or the damage has been remedied', and so forth; or the terms might have been inserted that the resumption of the payment shall be dependent upon the vessel being restored to full efficiency in all respects, as to seaworthiness and otherwise, as she was at the time when she was originally handed over. But the parties have not used such language. On the contrary, the test by which the payment for the hire is to be resumed is the efficient state of the vessel to resume her service; so that each of those words, as it appears to me, has relation to that which both of the parties must be taken to have well understood, namely, the purpose for which the vessel was hired, the nature of the service to be performed by the vessel, and the efficiency of the vessel to perform such service as should be required of her in the course of the voyage.

As to the first part of the claim which has been insisted upon here, I confess that I entertain no doubt whatever that the vessel was not efficient in any sense for the prosecution of her voyage from Las Palmas to Harburg . . . As a matter of fact, this vessel did not and could not pursue her voyage as a vessel from Las Palmas to Harburg. That another vessel took her in tow, that another vessel accomplished the voyage and brought this vessel, not as an efficient steamer, but as a floating barge, whereby the goods were brought to Harburg, seems to me to be nothing to the purpose. I use that phrase because, although I am aware that it is suggested that the low pressure engine was used for the purpose of easing the work of the tug, that appears to me to be entirely irrelevant when one is ascertaining whether this vessel of its own independent power was efficient for the purpose of prosecuting the voyage. All that is suggested is that the tug was assisted by the use of the low pressure engine. I find, as a matter of evidence, as each court I think has found, that the vessel was not seaworthy for the purpose of accomplishing her voyage without the assistance of a tug; she did not accomplish her voyage without the assistance of a tug; and in truth, as it appears to me, upon these facts it is clear that the voyage which was accomplished, and the service which it was contemplated this hired vessel was to perform, was performed by another vessel, and that the auxiliary assistance which she gave to that other vessel was not making the vessel herself an efficient vessel for the working of which the hirer was to pay.

. . . That is conclusive upon the first part of the case, and therefore no payment for the hire was due during the period that she was passing from Las Palmas to Harburg.

With reference to the second question which has been argued it appears to me that one has again to refer to each of these clauses of the contract to see what the parties were bargaining for. I should read the contract as meaning . . . that she should be efficient to do what she was required to do when she was called upon to do it; and accordingly, at each period, if what was required of her was to lie at anchor, if it was to lie alongside the wharf, upon each of those occasions, if she was efficient to do it at that time she would then become, in the language of the contract, to my mind 'efficient', reading with it the other words, 'for the working of the vessel'. How does a vessel work when she is lying alongside a wharf to discharge her cargo? She has machinery there for the purpose. It is not only that she has the goods in the hold, but she has machinery there for the purpose of discharging the cargo. It is not denied that during the period that she was lying at Harburg there was that machinery at work enabling the hirer to do quickly all that this particular portion of her employment required to be done. It appears to me, therefore, that at that period there was a right in the shipowner to demand payment of the hire, because at that time his vessel was efficiently working; the working of the vessel was proceeding as efficiently as it could with reference to the particular employment demanded of her at the time.

Under these circumstances, it appears to me that the pursuer here was entitled to payment for the hire of the vessel during the period of discharge . . .

My Lords, I wish to say one word as to the other view which has been presented, that the shipowner was not entitled to anything in respect of the period during which she was discharging. It has been put in various forms by the learned counsel. What reason or good sense would there be in construing a mercantile contract so that all right for payment should cease when the other party to the contract was getting everything he could out of the use of the vessel if the vessel was in an efficient state? I can see none. And what was put this morning seems to me conclusive: if some other part of the steam-gearing not used for the purpose of navigation had gone out of working in mid-ocean, and there had been no longer any use for that particular thing, the reason why such a breakdown of the machinery in mid-ocean would not have created a cesser of payment under the contract would, I suppose, have been this – it would have been argued, and argued justly, 'It is very true that there has been a breakdown of machinery; but that breakdown of machinery is not the only event contemplated; it does not of itself entitle you to a cesser of payment. There must be to entitle you to a cesser of payment a loss of time arising from a breakdown of machinery. Not even then does the cesser of payment arise; but there must be a loss of time by the breakdown of the machinery whereby the working of the vessel is stopped for the contracted time'. That appears to me to reflect great light upon the other question – What was the breakdown of the machinery which was contemplated by both the parties? It appears to me that the resumption of the right of payment is correlative with that; and inasmuch as when the vessel got to Harburg the vessel became 'efficient' for the purpose for which alone she was wanted at that time, it appears to me that the right of payment arose . . .

Notes

1   In the period between Las Palmas and Harburg the cargo was being moved and time was not being lost. The important point here is that the charterer was contributing to the towage expenses, so that he was not receiving from the owner the service required during that period under the charter.

2   The other members of the court approached the case in different ways. Lord Watson held that: (a) the vessel was not in an efficient state to resume her service when she started from

Las Palmas under tow and that she remained off-hire until she reached port; (b) that a *quantum meruit* might be payable in some cases while a vessel is off-hire where the charterer was benefiting from the use of the vessel, although not in the present case because of the arrangement made to pay for the tow; (c) hire was payable again when the vessel berthed at Harburg because the vessel was then in an efficient state for the service then required. Lord Herschell agreed with the Lord Chancellor and Lord Watson. Lord Morris thought that the vessel was off-hire at Las Palmas and the hire only became payable again when she had been repaired. Lord Bramwell thought that the vessel was efficient at Las Palmas; the charterers had had the benefit of their cargo being taken to Harburg and ought to pay for it.

3   In some circumstances an off-hire event will be the natural result of following charterers' orders, as when it is necessary for a ship to spend time bunkering, ballasting, lightening or cleaning the vessel. In these circumstances the ship will not go off-hire unless the contract clearly so provides: *The Berge Sund* [1993] 2 Lloyd's Rep 453, p 460.

6.1 Loss of time

One aspect of the agreement in *The Westfalia* – that the occurrence of an off-hire event is not in itself enough to put the ship off-hire, there must also be a loss of time – features in many modern charters. The impact of this form of agreement is illustrated by *The Ira*.

Forestships International Ltd v Armonia Shipping and Finance Corp,
The Ira [1995] 1 Lloyd's Rep 103

Facts: The *Ira* was time chartered on the NYPE form. The parties agreed that after discharging cargo at Ravenna, the vessel would drydock in Greece. The vessel proceeded to Piraeus where it was drydocked. When the vessel was ready to resume chartered service, the charterers fixed the vessel to load a cargo at Novorossiysk in the Black Sea. The charterers contended that the vessel was off-hire from dropping the outward pilot at Ravenna; the owners argued that almost none of the duration of the voyage from Ravenna to Piraeus was lost since Piraeus is, with a very slight deviation, on the route from Ravenna to the Black Sea. The off-hire clause provided that 'In the event of loss of time from drydocking preventing the full working of the vessel the payment of hire shall cease for the time thereby lost.' The drydocking did not cause the charterers to lose the whole of the time occupied by the voyage from Ravenna to Piraeus and the vessel was not therefore off-hire for the whole of that period.

Held:

> **Tuckey J:** . . . A net time clause, such as this clause is, requires the charterer to prove the happening and the duration of the off-hire event, and that time has been lost to him thereby. So it is a two-stage operation and it does not follow merely by proof of the off-hire event and its duration that he is able to establish a loss of time to him. That must depend on the circumstances of the particular case.

6.2 Partial inefficiency

Can a ship be off-hire where she is partly working? The answer, bearing in mind Staughton LJ's warning in *The Berge Sund*, must depend on the terms of the off-hire clause as the next two cases seem to demonstrate.

Tynedale Steam Shipping Co Ltd v Anglo-Soviet Shipping Co Ltd, *The Hordern* [1936] 1 All ER 389

Facts: The *Hordern* was chartered on the Baltime 1920 form. In the course of a voyage from Archangel to Liverpool with a deckload of timber, she was struck by a heavy squall; part of the deck cargo fell overboard carrying away the foremast to which the forward winches were attached. Discharge took six days longer than it would normally have taken. The shipowners claimed hire for the period during which the vessel was delayed. Baltime 1920 provided:

> Clause 10 – In the event of loss of time caused by dry-docking or by other necessary measures to maintain the efficiency of steamer, or by deficiency of men or owners' stores, breakdown of machinery, damage to hull or other accident preventing the working of the steamer and lasting more than 24 consecutive hours, hire to cease from commencement of such loss of time until steamer is again in efficient state to resume service. Should steamer be driven into port, or to anchorage by stress of weather, or in the event of steamer trading to shallow harbours, rivers or ports with bars, or in case of accident to cargo, causing detention to steamer, time so lost and expenses incurred shall be for charterers' account even if caused through fault or want of due diligence by owners' servants.

The shipowners argued that the ship was partly efficient and that the clause only put the ship off-hire in the event of complete or total prevention from working the ship, not if there was a mere interference with working.

Held:

Lord Roche: ... There is one fatal objection to that argument, and that is that it has come about 45 years too late. In the year 1890 a clause which I am unable in any way to distinguish from the present clause came up for decision in ... *Hogarth v Miller, Brother & Co* [above]. I say that the language of that clause cannot in my view be distinguished from the language of the clause in this case. The only difference was that the word 'stopped' occurred in that case instead of the word 'preventing' in this case.

... Here, the mast being damaged did not prevent or hinder the ship steaming, but it did hinder or prevent her discharging in the sense that prevention was construed in the House of Lords in *Hogarth v Miller* as preventing discharge or the working of the ship happening in accordance with the contract. That is the full point, it seems to me, between the parties in this case, as it was between the majority of the House in the case of *Hogarth v Miller* and the dissenting Lord Bramwell.

Let me go a little further into the judgments in order to make good my point. I recognise that the facts in *Hogarth v Miller* were in a sense different to those in this case. It was held there that the ship could not have got to a port without a tug. Mr Le Quesne says in this case that they could have discharged slowly and did discharge slowly, but that they did discharge. I am afraid that the answer to that part of the case is that it is a finding of fact. There is a finding of fact here that discharge of the forward part of the ship was impossible by the ship herself by means of her winches and derricks ...

... It seems to me that it follows from [the reasoning in *Hogarth v Miller*] that the vessel was not fit or able to work for the services required and stipulated for by the initial words of the charterparty, and in those circumstances two results follow. Under clause 2 it was the duty of the owners then to put her back into an efficient state in hull and machinery for that purpose. Under clause 10 events had happened which put into operation the cesser of hire clause ...

Now it is really sufficient to dispose of this case to indicate the reasons why I think on this part of the case the learned judge was right and why the appeal fails. There are two matters to be added. We must only answer the questions put by the arbitrators, and it is important in answering them not to be ambiguous. The first question is: 'Whether upon the true construction of the charter and upon the facts as herein found the shipowners are entitled to hire for the vessel in respect of the time occupied in discharge.'

... The answer that I give is this: that upon the true construction of the charter and upon the facts as here found – that is to say, found in the case – the ship-owners' right to be paid hire ceased in respect of the time occupied in discharge; that is to say, they should get no further than that during the continuance of that period.

That answer is really sufficient to dispose of the argument which was developed by Mr Le Quesne in reply: namely, that there should be a sort of assessment of the amount of time lost by reason of the inefficiency, and that for that net loss of time so ascertained hire should be deemed to cease. With respect to that argument, it is sufficient to say that I regard every word which I have read from the judgments of Lord Halsbury and the other noble Lords who formed the majority [in *Hogarth v Miller*] as negativing that argument, which in my view is opposed to the proper construction of the clause, that construction being a stipulation that, if certain events happen, then *ipso facto* hire is to cease and is not to begin again until that state of affairs has ceased to exist. The ascertainment of the net loss is something foreign to the clause as drawn ...

Scott LJ: I agree with the whole of the judgment delivered by Lord Roche and with a little hesitation only add one or two observations ...

Mr Le Quesne submitted to us that in [*Hogarth v Miller*] ... the House accepted as a principle that hire had ceased by reason of prevention within the meaning of the charter before the vessel reached the port of refuge at Las Palmas and before the voyage home with a tug assisting began. He said, therefore, that the House was not considering what caused the charter hire to cease, but what entitled the shipowner to say that the right to charter hire had re-attached. That argument had at first its attractions, but on further reflection, apart from the *obiter dicta* – to which we have to pay the very greatest possible attention in this court – which fell from their Lordships in the House of Lords, I do feel this very strongly: that from a commercial point of view the distinction between what causes the charter hire to go off and what causes it to come on again is, to the commercial man, a distinction which is rather apt to worry him; and I am very loath to construe an ordinary commercial clause in a way that is not simple to the commercial mind if the clause can properly be interpreted in a simple way. And this clause, I think, can be interpreted simply, for this reason: the clause provides that in the event of loss of time caused by damage to hull or other accident preventing the working of the steamer, then hire for a minimum length of time is to cease until the steamer is again in an efficient state to resume the service. As Lord Roche has said, the word 'again' indicates the former state of the ship and the latter state of the ship. The state before she went off-hire and the state to which she must have returned before she goes on hire again are intended to be the same ...

Canadian Pacific (Bermuda) Ltd v Canadian Transport Co Ltd, The HR Macmillan [1974] 1 Lloyd's Rep 311, CA

Facts: By a time charterparty in the New York Produce Exchange form, the owners of the *HR Macmillan*, which was fitted with three Munck gantry cranes, chartered her to the charterers for eight years from the date of delivery. In April 1968 the trolley of the No 1 crane fell overboard and the crane was not operational for nearly three and a half months. The charter contained a special clause to cover a breakdown of the Munck cranes. But in the course of his judgment, Lord Denning also referred to the off-hire clause which provided:

That in the event of the loss of time from deficiency and/or default of men or deficiency of stores, fire, breakdown or damages to hull, machinery or equipment, grounding, detention by average accidents to ship or cargo, drydocking for the purpose of examination or painting bottom, or by any other cause preventing the full working of the vessel, the payment of hire shall cease for the time thereby lost ...

Held:

> **Lord Denning MR:** . . . Taking that clause by itself, it would mean that, if one crane broke down, there would have to be an inquiry as to the time lost thereby. That would be a most difficult inquiry to undertake. For instance, if one broke down and the other two cranes were able to do, and did do, all the work that was required, there would be no 'time lost thereby'; and there would be no cessation of hire. But if there was work for three cranes, and there was some loss of time owing to the one crane breaking down, there would have to be an assessment of the amount of time lost. In that event, as the judge pointed out, the question would have to be asked: 'How much earlier would the vessel have been away from her port of loading or discharge if three Munck cranes, instead of two, had been available throughout?' The judge called that a 'net loss of time' clause . . .

6.3 Inefficiency and external causes

In the cases considered above, the off-hire event occurred on board the ship. None of the vessels were in perfect working order. Can a ship be off-hire if she is efficient in herself; can a cause that is wholly external to the ship be an off-hire event? A line of cases, which started with *Court Line Ltd v Dant and Russell Inc, The Errington Court* (1939) 44 Com Cas 345, have considered these two connected questions. The effect of the line of decisions was reviewed in *The Laconian Confidence*. And see Weale, J, 'Can an efficient vessel be placed off-hire?' (2002) Jo Mar L & Com 133.

Andre & Cie SA v Orient Shipping (Rotterdam) BV,
The Laconian Confidence [1997] 1 Lloyd's Rep 139

Facts: The *Laconian Confidence* was chartered on the NYPE form for one time charter trip from Yangon to Bangladesh. Authorities at Chittagong refused to allow the vessel to proceed to her next business following discharge of her cargo of 10,000 metric tons of rice in bags because of the presence remaining on board of 15 tonnes of residue sweepings. As a result the vessel was delayed for nearly 18 days until she was allowed to dump these residues and thereafter to sail. Charterers argued that the vessel was off-hire during this period.

Held:

> **Rix J:** This is, for the present, the latest in a line of cases arising out of the New York Produce Exchange's off-hire clause and the problem created by the interference of authorities. As a result of such interference, the vessel, although entirely sound and efficient in herself, is prevented from working, that is to say from performing the next task required of her. Is the vessel off-hire, on the ground that she has been prevented from working by some 'other cause', ie by some cause other than the named causes in the clause? Or does she remain on hire, because the vessel remains entirely efficient in herself, and/or because the *ejusdem generis* principle curtails 'any other cause' to causes similar to the named causes?
>
> My reader will recall that the NYPE's off-hire clause (clause 15) provides as follows:
>
> > That in the event of the loss of time from deficiency of [*and/or default*] men or stores, fire, breakdown or damages to hull, machinery or equipment, grounding, detention by average accidents to ship or cargo, dry-docking for the purpose of examination or painting bottom, or by any other cause preventing the full working of the vessel, the payment of hire shall cease for the time thereby lost . . .

The words in italics 'and/or default' were added to the standard clause in the instant case, as they often are. (They were in error slightly misplaced: the obvious intent is that the clause should read 'deficiency and/or default of men'; but nothing turns on that.) The word 'whatsoever' is sometimes added to the phrase 'or by any other cause', but not in the instant case. It is established that the phrase 'preventing the full working of the vessel' qualifies not only the phrase 'any other cause' but also all the named causes: *The Mareva AS* [1977] 1 Lloyd's Rep 368 at 382. It has therefore been said that the first question to be answered in any dispute under the clause is whether the full working of the vessel has been prevented; for if it has not, there is no need to go on to ask whether the vessel has suffered from the operation of any named cause or whether the phrase 'any other cause [whatsoever]' is or is not limited in any way: *The Aquacharm* [1982] 1 Lloyd's Rep 7 at 9; *The Roachbank* [1987] 2 Lloyd's Rep 498 at 507.

The Mareva AS is also cited for the proposition that the qualifying condition 'preventing the full working of the vessel' is not met if 'the vessel in herself remains fully efficient in all respects'.

Ten years later, by time of *The Roachbank*, this had become:

> a judicial gloss . . . so that the question which has to be asked, according to the authorities, is whether the vessel is fully efficient and capable in herself of performing the service immediately required by the charterers . . .

Nevertheless, this judicial gloss has caused problems in cases where the cause of delay is the interference of authorities operating on a vessel which is herself fully efficient. Four cases in particular illustrate this problem. In *The Apollo* [1978] 1 Lloyd's Rep 200 the vessel was denied free pratique and thus prevented from berthing and discharging while the suspicion of typhus in two of her crew members was investigated and, as it turned out, eliminated. In *The Aquacharm* [1980] 2 Lloyd's Rep 237, Lloyd J [1982] 1 Lloyd's Rep 7, CA, the vessel was delayed by the authorities at the entrance to the Panama Canal until she had lightened part of her cargo. In *The Mastro Giorgis* [1983] 2 Lloyd's Rep 66 the vessel was arrested by receivers as a result of alleged cargo damage on the voyage. In *The Roachbank* the vessel was delayed in being permitted to enter port because of the presence on board her of 293 Vietnamese refugees. In the first and third of those cases the vessel was held to be off-hire, in the second and fourth on hire. The word 'whatsoever' lies on both sides of that divide for, although it was absent in *The Aquacharm*, it was present in the other cases . . .

The authorities
. . . I would . . . observe at the outset of my discussion of those authorities that there appear to be two inter-related concepts which run here and there through them. One is that the typical off-hire clause does not cover an 'extraneous' cause, by which is, I think, meant a cause extraneous to the vessel itself. This concept I suppose relates to the meaning or possible width of meanings of 'cause' in the expression 'any other cause' or 'any other cause whatsoever'. The other concept is that a vessel cannot be off-hire unless there is some defect or incapacity of or in the vessel itself which affects her working. This concept relates of course to the phrase 'preventing the full working of the vessel'.

Both concepts may be said to go back to what in a sense is for these purposes the leading case of *Court Line Limited v Dant and Russell Incorporated* (1939) 44 Com Cas 345. That concerned a vessel, the *Errington Court*, which got caught by a boom placed in the Yangtze River by Chinese forces. For a leading case the relevant part of the judgment is brief. At pp 352–53 Branson J merely opined that the words 'any other cause preventing the full working of the vessel':

> are not apt to cover a case where the ship is in every way sound and well found, but is prevented from continuing her voyage by such a cause as this.

. . . The concept of an extraneous cause was not . . . in issue in *The Mareva AS*, nor was that expression used in the *Court Line* case. But in *The Apollo* counsel for shipowners based a submission upon *Court Line* and *The Mareva AS* to the effect that:

the off-hire clause applied to matters internal to the ship and her crew and not to external interferences or delays (at p 205).

However, Mocatta J rejected that submission. He said (*ibid*):

I find it very difficult to lay down criteria of this kind. For example if a surveyor from a classifica-tion society required tests to be made to the machinery, would the delay consequent upon this bring the off-hire clause into play?

So far the concept of extraneous or external cause had not perhaps got very far: but in *The Aquacharm* [1980] 2 Lloyd's Rep 237 at 240 Lloyd J relied expressly on *Court Line* to eliminate 'some external cause, such as the boom' as a possible off-hire cause at any rate when the vessel remained 'fully efficient in her-self'. Those decisions were in turn relied on by the Court of Appeal in *Harmony Shipping Co SA v Saudi-Europe Line Ltd, The Good Helmsman* [1981] 1 Lloyd's Rep 377 at 422.

Then in *The Mastro Giorgis* Lloyd J held that a distinction should be made, in deciding whether a cause prevents the full working of a vessel:

between causes which are totally extraneous, such as the boom in *Court Line Ltd v Dant & Rus-sell Inc*, and causes which are attributable to the condition of the ship itself, such as engine breakdown (at p 69).

Lloyd J then went on to decide that a vessel's susceptibility to arrest by reason of an allegation of cargo damage was sufficient to prevent the arrest itself being totally extraneous . . .

. . . It follows that in *The Mastro Giorgis* Lloyd J was not giving to the words 'preventing the full work-ing of the vessel' a meaning that required the vessel to be inefficient in herself. Her full working was only prevented inasmuch as she was under arrest . . .

. . . *The Mastro Giorgis* is therefore a decision to the effect that a vessel's inability to perform the service immediately required of her by reason of the interference of authorities fulfils the requirements of the words 'preventing the full working of the vessel', at any rate if the authorities' interference is not totally extraneous. A vessel may of course be susceptible to the interference of authorities for a whole variety of reasons: the arrest jurisdiction is one such reason, but in truth any vessel visiting a port becomes immediately subject to the law of the country in which the port is situated and to the requirements and directives of the local authorities.

The off-hire clause in *The Mastro Giorgis* contained the word 'whatsoever'. That meant, said Lloyd J at p 92, that any cause may suffice to put the vessel off-hire, whether physical or legal. Lloyd J's reasoning thereafter appears to be concerned with the qualification of 'preventing the full working of the vessel'. The effect of his reasoning, however, appears to be that under a 'whatsoever' clause outside interference which prevents the vessel performing her service, provided that it is not 'totally extraneous', will put the vessel off-hire.

I would comment that, if Lloyd J was wrong in his conclusion that an efficient vessel may be pre-vented from working by the action of the authorities, then it would be odd if the addition of the word 'whatsoever' could make any difference. If a vessel efficient in herself cannot be within the words 'prevent-ing the full working of the vessel', then it does not seem to me that the nature of the cause which operates on such a vessel can alter the fact that the vessel is efficient in herself. In such a case, widening the ambit of 'cause' by adding the word 'whatsoever' ought not in logic to affect the position.

In *The Roachbank*, however, Lloyd J's conclusion in *The Mastro Giorgis* was not applied. In that case the vessel was prevented for a while from entering port by the authorities because of the presence on board of Vietnamese refugees who had been rescued in pitiful condition at sea during the vessel's voyage. The off-hire clause contained the word 'whatsoever' . . . Webster J felt required by previous authorities to place upon the words 'preventing the full working of the vessel' a judicial gloss:

> so that the question which has to be asked, according to the authorities, is whether the vessel is fully efficient and capable in herself of performing the service immediately required by the charterers (at p 507).

In the circumstances it was inevitable that he should uphold the award, for he was bound by the arbitrators' finding on that question. Equally, it would be irrelevant for him that the vessel could not work in the different sense that she was prevented from entering port and discharging by the action of the port authorities. In the circumstances, having been asked by counsel (see at p 502) to differ from the conclusions of Lloyd J in *The Mastro Giorgis,* he expressed his diffident disagreement with that decision in these terms (at p 507):

> . . . for two reasons; first, because it seems to me to give undue emphasis to the cause of the prevention of the full working, as distinct from the fact that full working is prevented; and, secondly because, for the reasons that I have already expressed, in the case of an amended clause in my view it is probably unnecessary to consider the nature of the cause at all, something which Lloyd J himself acknowledged in the way in which he stated his second reason: 'any cause may suffice'. Moreover, for my own part, I do not think it either necessary or helpful to attempt to categorise causes with a view to distinguishing between totally extraneous and other causes.

I feel bound to say, however, with equal diffidence, that in my judgment the real point of difference between Lloyd J and Webster J (and perhaps both of them, reading this, would disagree with me) was that Lloyd J was willing to say that a vessel wholly efficient in herself might nevertheless, under certain circumstances, come within the words 'preventing the full working of the vessel', whereas Webster J was of the view, based upon his reading of the authorities, that such a reading was not possible where the vessel was fully efficient and capable in herself . . .

So, as it seems to me, the critical question may well be whether Webster J was right to say that a judicial gloss had been put upon the phrase so as to require, for a vessel to be off-hire, that she should not be efficient in herself to perform the next service required. The authorities considered by Webster J were *Court Line*, *The Mareva AS*, *The Apollo*, and *The Aquacharm*.

I have already considered *Court Line* and *The Mareva AS*. In my opinion there is nothing in those cases to require the judicial gloss which Webster J found to exist. *Court Line* differed perhaps from all other cases in that the boom there was a totally extraneous matter – I know of no other way in which to point up that idiosyncrasy. Although it was man-made, it was akin to a geographical impediment. A vessel is not off-hire just because she cannot proceed upon her voyage because of some physical impediment, like a sand bar, or insufficiency of water, blocking her path. While remarking that the vessel was 'in every way sound and well found' Branson J ultimately founded his reasoning, it seems to me, on the fact that 'such a cause as this' was not within the clause. As for *The Mareva AS,* I have already made the point that that case was not concerned at all with the interference of authorities. The language of a vessel's inherent efficiency is there found, but in circumstances where there was no interference with the vessel's service, and the distinction that had to be made was between the efficiency of the vessel herself and the increased time involved in the discharge of a damaged cargo. In such circumstances it comes as no surprise that Kerr J used the language which he did, nor that he found that the cargo damage had not prevented the full working of the vessel. The vessel, after all, was working fully.

Similarly I do not think that *The Apollo* supports the judicial gloss determined by Webster J, nor did he found any reliance on it. On the contrary, Mocatta J said (at 205):

> In my judgment the action taken by the port health authorities did prevent the full working of the vessel and did bring the off-hire clause into play.

It seems to me that in saying this Mocatta J was recognising that a vessel could be prevented from working by an outside bar on her working. That is not consistent with glossing the critical phrase as requiring some failure of the vessel's efficiency in herself. Of course I bear in mind that in that case there was suspected typhus of the crew.

The last case considered by Webster J was *The Aquacharm*. It was Lloyd J himself who, at first instance, introduced the judicial test of whether:

> the vessel is fully efficient in herself, that is to say, whether she is fully capable of performing the service immediately required of her (at p 240).

I would comment in passing first that the test of 'fully efficient in herself' is not necessarily the same as the test of 'fully capable of performing the service immediately required of her' as Lloyd J was himself to recognise in *The Mastro Giorgis*; and secondly, that on the facts of that case, once the vessel had to be lightened to transit the Panama Canal, there could have been no difference between the service required by the charterers and that required by the canal authorities, *viz*, the lightening of the vessel.

In the Court of Appeal in *The Aquacharm*, Lord Denning MR did not adopt the gloss of 'fully efficient in herself'. He merely said (at 9):

> I do not think the lightening of the vessel does 'prevent the full working of the vessel'. Often enough cargo has to be unloaded into a lighter – for one reason or another – to get her off a sandbank – or into a basin. The vessel is still working fully, but she is delayed by the need to unload part of the cargo.

Griffiths LJ did, however, adopt the judicial gloss. For instance he said (at p 11):

> *Aquacharm* remained at all times in herself fully efficient in all respects. She could not pass through the canal because the canal authorities decided she was carrying too much cargo, but that decision [in] no way reflected upon the *Aquacharm*'s efficiency as a ship. By contrast, in *The Apollo* . . . A ship suspected of carrying typhus is prevented from working fully until it is cleared, for no responsible person would use it in such a condition. The incapacity of the ship to work in such a case is directly attributable to the suspected condition of the ship itself . . .

Shaw LJ said that he agreed entirely with the judgments of Lord Denning and of Lloyd J and would dismiss the appeal for the reasons stated in the judgment of Lord Denning (at p 12).

The judgment of Griffiths LJ and his explanation of *The Apollo* have been influential; but the reasoning of the majority in the Court of Appeal is that contained in the judgment of Lord Denning, and that in my view does not support, and *a fortiori* does not require, the judicial gloss found by Webster J. Of course, *The Aquacharm* was fully efficient in herself, that was one of the facts of the case. Equally, it was a fact of the case that the vessel was fully working when she was waiting to lighten and actually lightening. That, however, may be contrasted with the situation in *The Apollo*, where the vessel was not working at all during the period when free pratique was refused; and could also be contrasted perhaps with a hypothetical situation where the Panama Canal authorities perversely refused entrance to the canal on grounds of draught, even though the vessel plainly was not overladen, a problem with which the Court of Appeal did not have to contend . . .

In these circumstances I would for my part respectfully differ from Webster J's conclusion that he was bound by authority to impose the judicial gloss he adopted upon the phrase 'preventing the full working of the vessel'. I would prefer myself to accept that it could be legitimate to find that the full working of a vessel had been prevented by the action of authorities in preventing her working . . .

Two further decisions cited to me but not mentioned by Webster J are *The Manhatton Prince* [1985] 1 Lloyd's Rep 140 and *The Bridgestone Maru No 3* [1985] 2 Lloyd's Rep 62. It may be that they were not cited to Webster J, or if cited not mentioned in his judgment, because they are both decisions on the Shelltime 3 clause with its slightly different language 'preventing the *efficient* working of the vessel' (emphasis added). The efficiency of the vessel is mentioned twice in the clause, thus:

> In the event of loss of time . . . due to deficiency of . . . or any other cause preventing the efficient working of the vessel . . . hire shall cease to be payable from the commencement of such loss of time until the vessel is again ready and in an efficient state to resume her service . . .

In *The Manhatton Prince* the vessel was arrested by the ITF on the ground that her owners were in breach of their agreement with the ITF to employ crew in accordance with ITF rates for worldwide trading. Leggatt J considered the authorities down to *The Mastro Giorgis* and held that the vessel remained on hire. He said (at p 146):

> It is plain that what the charterers have to show is that the efficient working of the vessel was indeed prevented by the ITF. One starts then by asking: what is the natural meaning of the words in that context? One may take account of the *ejusdem generis* principle in the sense that the causes of loss of time which are specified may indeed throw light upon the proper meaning to be ascribed to the phrase 'efficient working of the vessel'.

It seems to me that the true interpretation of the phrase in its context demands that it should apply, and apply only, to the physical condition of the vessel, with the result that, as Mr Phillips contends, the phrase 'efficient working' must enjoy the connotation of efficient physical working. In my judgment the vessel worked, even though she was prevented from working in the way the charterers would have wished by the action of the ITF. She was indeed fully operational and as such was not within the scope of the off-hire clause.

In *The Bridgestone Maru No 3* it will be recalled that the vessel was unable to remain and discharge at Livorno because her booster pump was not a fixed installation as required by local RINA regulations. She was nevertheless in every way an efficient vessel. Hirst J considered the same authorities and held that the vessel was off-hire on the ground that the delay was attributable to the suspected condition of the ship . . .

I find nothing in these two cases, or in their examination of the NYPE authorities, to alter the view I have formed of those authorities. On the contrary, it seems to me that the Shelltime 3's emphasis upon the efficiency of the vessel is a real difference from the language of the NYPE, fully justifying Leggatt J's conclusion that the former's off-hire clause applies only to the physical condition of the vessel or at any rate to her efficiency as a vessel (including, I would readily accept, her suspected efficiency). It seems to me that Leggatt J pointed up the difference in the language of the two forms when he said:

> the vessel worked, even though she was prevented from working in the way the charterers would have wished . . .

In my judgment therefore, the qualifying phrase 'preventing the full working of the vessel' does not require the vessel to be inefficient in herself. A vessel's working may be prevented by legal as well as physical means, and by outside as well as internal causes. An otherwise totally efficient ship may be prevented from working. That is the natural meaning of those words, and I do not think that there is any authority binding on me that prevents me from saying so. The question remains, of course, whether a ship has been prevented from working by a cause within the clause. Moreover, it will generally be relevant to find whether the ship is efficient in herself: either, as in *The Mareva AS,* because, even on the assumption of the operation of a named cause, it may be relevant to point out that the vessel's working had not been prevented; or, as in *Court Line*, because, in considering whether an alleged cause of off-hire is a cause within the clause, it may be very pertinent to point out that the vessel was otherwise efficient in herself.

Those comments bring me back to consider the phrase 'any other cause' in the light of the authorities. In my judgment it is well established that those words, in the absence of 'whatsoever', should be construed either *ejusdem generis* or at any rate in some limited way reflecting the general context of the charter and clause: see *The Apollo* at p 205, *The Aquacharm* at p 239 (Lloyd J), *The Mastro Giorgis* at p 68, *The Manhatton Prince* at p 146, *The Roachbank* at p 507. A consideration of the named causes indicates that they all relate to the physical condition or efficiency of either vessel (including its crew) or, in one instance, cargo. There is, moreover, the general context, emphasised for instance by Kerr J in *The Mareva AS* (at p 382), that it is for the owners to provide an efficient ship and crew. In such circumstances it is to my mind natural to conclude that the unamended words 'any other cause' do not cover an entirely extraneous cause, like the boom in *Court Line*, or the interference of authorities unjustified by the condition (or reasonably suspected condition) of ship or cargo. *Prima facie* it does not seem to me that it can be intended by a standard off-hire clause that an owner takes the risk of delay due to the interference of authorities, at any rate where that interference is something beyond the natural or reasonably foreseeable consequence of some named cause. Where, however, the clause is amended to include the word 'whatsoever', I do not see why the interference of authorities which prevents the vessel performing its intended service should not be regarded as falling within the clause, and I would be inclined to say that remains so whether or not that interference can be related to some underlying cause internal to the ship, or is merely capricious. That last thought may be controversial, but it seems to me that if an owner wishes to limit the scope of causes of off-hire under a clause which is deliberately amended to include the word 'whatsoever', then he should be cautious to do so.

The decision

It follows in my judgment that, although I would for my part accept Mr Kendrick's submission that the full working of a vessel may be prevented for legal as well as physical reasons, this appeal must nevertheless fail. In the absence of the word 'whatsoever', the unexpected and unforeseeable interference by the authorities at Chittagong at the conclusion of what was found to be a normal discharge was a totally extraneous cause, (save in a 'but for' sense) unconnected with, because too remote from, the merely background circumstance of the cargo residues of 15.75 tonnes. There was no accident to cargo, and there was nothing about the vessel herself, her condition or efficiency, nor even anything about the cargo, which led naturally or in the normal course of events to any delay. If the authorities had not prevented the vessel from working, she would have been perfectly capable of discharging the residues or of sailing and dumping them without any abnormal delay. In such circumstances I reject Mr Kendrick's submission that the action of the authorities was in any sense *ejusdem generis* any of the named causes within the clause. There is no finding that they suspected an average accident to cargo, or, to pick up the award's reference to a certificate for non-radioactivity, that there was any suspected problem in regard to radioactive contamination. I would be extremely doubtful in any event that a capricious suspicion could bring their action within the clause. As it is we do not know why on this occasion the authorities delayed the vessel for so long, other than the arbitrators' finding that their procedures were remarkably bureaucratic.

Having decided the issue before me, I should perhaps go no further. But out of deference to the submissions made to me, I would venture the following thoughts, but emphasising their *obiter* nature.

I would suggest that if the clause had been amended to contain the word 'whatsoever', then the position would probably have been otherwise. The vessel would have been prevented from working, albeit in unexpected circumstances. The cause would not have been *ejusdem generis*, but with the addition of the word 'whatsoever' would not have to be. It would not seem to me to matter that the authorities' actions may have been capricious.

The authorities suggest, moreover, that where the authorities act properly or reasonably pursuant to the (suspected) inefficiency or incapacity of the vessel, any time lost may well be off-hire even in the absence of the word 'whatsoever'. Thus in *The Apollo* (albeit the presence of 'whatsoever' may have facilitated the decision) Mocatta J stressed that there was good cause for the careful testing and disinfection that was carried out before free pratique was granted (at p 205); and Griffiths LJ pointed out (in *The Aquacharm* at p 11) that no responsible person would use a ship suspected of carrying typhus. Moreover in *The Bridgestone Maru No 3* Hirst J held that the vessel was off-hire even in the absence of the word 'whatsoever' on the basis that the regulations had been properly applied and that the failure of the pump to comply with the regulations was a potential (*sc* and reasonable) challenge to the efficiency of the ship herself.

Finally, suppose time lost due to the detention of a vessel by the authorities arising out of the discovery of contraband on board her, an example debated before me. In such a case the position may well depend on who was responsible for the presence of the contraband. If the owners (or their crew) were responsible, the vessel might well be off-hire, particularly under an amended clause, but even perhaps in the absence of amendment. If, however, the charterers were responsible, it would seem to be absurd to hold the vessel off-hire: how would that square under an amended clause with my construction, seeing that the detention by the authorities under my construction would be 'any other cause whatsoever preventing the full working of the vessel'? It seems to me that there would be an implicit exclusion of causes for which the charterers were responsible.

Considerations such as these indicate that there will always be difficult decisions to make in borderline cases or unusual combinations of circumstances. In many if not most cases the ultimate decision will depend on findings of fact or mixed fact and law made by the arbitrators, which could not be easily, if at all, faulted. So in the present case, even upon the construction of the words 'preventing the full working of the vessel' which I have preferred, and even after taking into account the charterers' shift of position, it seems to me that ultimately my decision is concluded for me by the arbitrators' findings.

7. Redelivery

Time charters typically require redelivery at the end of the period of the charter in good order at a port or place within an agreed range. The charter period may include an express or implied margin, as Lord Denning's judgment in *The Dione* explains.

Alma Shipping Corp of Monrovia v Mantovani,
The Dione [1975] 1 Lloyd's Rep 115, CA

Facts: The agreement was 'for a period of six months' time charter 20 days more or less'. The Court of Appeal considered whether an additional margin could be implied.

Held:

Lord Denning MR:

(a) *Implied margin or allowance*

When a charterparty is for a stated period – such as 'three months' or 'six months' – without any express margin or allowance, then the court will imply a reasonable margin or allowance. The reason is because it is not possible for anyone to calculate exactly the day on which the last voyage will end. It is legitimate for the charterer to send her on a last voyage which may exceed the stated period by a few days. If the vessel does exceed the stated period – and the market rate has gone up – nevertheless the charterer is only bound to pay the charter rate until she is actually redelivered, see *Gray and Co v Christie*

(1889) 5 TLR 577: *Watson Steamship Co v Merryweather & Co* (1913) 18 Com Cas 294 at p 300 (without the handwritten words).

(b) *No margin or allowance express or implied*

But it is open to the parties to provide in the charterparty – by express words or by implication – that there is to be no margin or allowance. In such a case the charterer must ensure that the vessel is redelivered within the stated period. If he does not do so – and the market rate has gone up – he will be bound to pay the extra. That is to say, he will be bound to pay the charter rate up to the end of the stated period, and the market rate thereafter, see *Watson v Merryweather* (1913) 18 Com Cas 294 (with the handwritten words).

(c) *Express margin or allowance*

It is also, in my opinion, open to the parties themselves to fix expressly what the margin or allowance shall be. In that case the charterer must ensure that the vessel is redelivered within the permitted margin or allowance. If he does not do so – and the market rate has gone up – he will be bound to pay the extra. That is to say, he will be bound to pay the charter rate up to the end of the expressly permitted margin or allowance, and the market rate for any overlap thereafter . . .

In view of those three propositions, when I speak of the 'charter period', I mean the stated period plus or minus any permitted margin or allowance, express or implied. There follows these two propositions:

(d) If the charterer sends the vessel on a legitimate last voyage – that is, a voyage which it is reasonably expected will be completed by the end of the charter period, the shipowner must obey the directions. If the vessel is afterwards delayed by matters for which neither party is responsible, the charter is presumed to continue in operation until the end of that voyage, even though it extends beyond the charter period. The hire is payable at the charter rate until redelivery, even though the market rate may have gone up or down, see *Timber Shipping Co SA v London & Overseas Freighters Ltd* [1972] AC 1.

(e) If the charterer sends the vessel on an illegitimate last voyage – that is, a voyage which it cannot be expected to complete within the charter period, then the shipowner is entitled to refuse that direction and call for another direction for a legitimate last voyage. If the charterer refuses to give it, the shipowner can accept his conduct as a breach going to the root of the contract, fix a fresh charter for the vessel, and sue for damages. If the shipowner accepts the direction and goes on the illegitimate last voyage, he is entitled to be paid – for the excess period – at the current market rate, and not at the charter rate, see *Meyer v Sanderson* (1916) 32 TLR 428. The hire will be payable at the charter rate up to the end of the charter period, and at the current market rate for the excess period thereafter.

. . . If this clause had said simply 'six months time charter' without any express margin or allowance, I should have thought that there would be implied a reasonable margin or allowance. But this clause expressly defines the margin as '20 days more or less'. That leaves no room for any implied margin or allowance. The express margin is greater than any period which would normally be implied . . .

Note

Paragraphs (a) to (c) in Lord Denning's judgment, dealing with the charter period and margins, are conventional and widely accepted. But paragraph (d) has been criticised and said not to be settled law: *Hyundai Merchant Marine Co Ltd v Gesuri Chartering Co Ltd, The Peonia* [1991] 1 Lloyd's Rep 100, CA. In that case it was said, *obiter*, that 'if charterers send a vessel on a legitimate last voyage and the vessel is thereafter delayed for any reason (other than the fault of the owners) so that it is redelivered after the final terminal date, the charterers will (in the absence of agreement to the contrary) be in breach of contract and accordingly, if the market rate has gone up, will be obliged to pay by way of damages the market rate for any excess period after the final terminal date up to redelivery' (*per* Slade LJ). The phrase *final terminal date* here means the date at the end of the charter period and any agreed or implied margin or tolerance. It was acknowledged in *The Peonia* that charter hire remains payable until actual delivery, so that the practical difference between the two cases is that only hire is payable if the market has dropped, but damages are payable in addition if owners have suffered because the market has risen. The technical difference between the two positions is that *The Peonia* treats a charterer who fails to redeliver by the final terminal date as in breach of contract while *The Dione* does not, provided the final voyage instructions were legitimate. *The Peonia* was cited with approval in the House of Lords in *Torvald Klaveness A/S v Arni Maritime Corp, The Gregos*, below, by Lord Mustill.

7.1 The legitimate final voyage

The judgment in *The Dione* used the phrase *legitimate final voyage* to refer to a voyage that can reasonably be expected to be completed within the charter period. The reference to the effect of a subsequent delay in Lord Denning's judgment suggested that the legitimacy of the instruction was to be considered at the moment the order was given. But when this point was fully argued in the House of Lords in *The Gregos*, a different solution was adopted. An apparently valid order was said to be 'no more than a contingency' so that if circumstances change and compliance with the order would call for a service that the owner had not undertaken to perform, the obligation to comply would fall away.

Torvald Klaveness A/S v Arni Maritime Corp, The Gregos [1994] 1 WLR 1465, HL

Facts: The *Gregos* was chartered 'for about 50 to maximum 70 days' (thus excluding any further margin). The charterers ordered the vessel to carry a cargo of iron ore from Palau, on the Orinoco river, to Fos, prior to redelivery. If judged when the order was given, compliance with the order could reasonably have been judged to allow redelivery by the last permissible date. But obstructions in the Orinoco caused delays, which meant that if the orders were followed, the vessel could not be redelivered in time. The owners then declined to perform the laden voyage and called for fresh instructions. No such orders were given but the voyage was in fact performed on terms that gave the owners an increased rate of hire if subsequent proceedings found that they had been entitled to decline the final instruction. Two issues were argued before the House of Lords: (1) Should the validity of the order for the final voyage be judged as at the time when it was given or as at the time when it fell to be complied with? (2) If the validity of the order was to be judged in the light of matters as they stood when the owners declined to comply, so that the voyage was not one for which a legitimate order could be given, what was the effect of the charterers having given the order and their refusal to replace it by another?

Held:

> **Lord Mustill:** . . . I begin with the first issue, concerning the date for judging the validity of the charterers' order. Here, it seems to me that the inquiry has been led astray by concentrating too much on the order and too little on the shipowner's promise to furnish the services of the vessel, which is what the contract is about. Initially, the practical implications of the promise are undefined, since they depend on how in the future the charterer decides to employ the vessel; but they are not unlimited, being constrained from the start as to duration, nature and extent by express terms in the charter (concerning for example the types of cargo to be carried and the geographical limits of trade) and also by important implied terms. Later, when the time for performance has arrived, this broad promise is converted to a series of specific

obligations by the charterer's orders for employment, but the constraints expressly or impliedly accepted by the charterer in the original contract continue to apply. Whatever the charterer may order, a service which falls outside the range encompassed by the owner's original promise is not one which he can be compelled to perform; and this is so as regards not only the duration of the chartered service, but also all the other limitations imposed by the charterparty on the charterer's freedom of choice. There is thus to be a measuring of the service called for against the service promised. As a matter of common sense, it seems to me that the time for such measurement is, primarily at least, the time when performance falls due.

My Lords, I have qualified this statement with the words 'primarily at least' because in practice the interests of both parties demand that the charterer is entitled to give orders in advance of the time for performance; and this must entail at least a provisional judgment on the validity of the order. If it can be seen at this early stage that compliance will involve a service which lies outside the shipowner's undertaking the latter can say so at once, and reject the order. But if the order is apparently valid its validity is no more than contingent, since the time for matching the service against the promise to serve does not arrive until the nature of the service is definitively known; and this will not usually be until the service is due to begin, or in some instances until it is already in progress. Thus, if and for so long as the service required conforms with those which the shipowner promised in advance to render the specific order creates a specific obligation to perform them when the time arrives. But only for so long as that state of affairs persists. If circumstances change, so that compliance with the order will call for a service which in the original contract the shipowner never undertook, the obligation to comply must fall away. As I see it, the charterers' order in advance amounts to a continuing requirement, the validity of which may change with the passage of time . . .

I turn to the issue of repudiation. Although the appeal is concerned with an invalid order for a final voyage this is only a special case of an order issued for the performance of a service which lies outside the scope of the shipowner's promise. Since orders for employment and compliance with them lie at the heart of a time charter the question is of general importance, and the solution arrived at should hold good for all types of order . . .

The original order having become ineffectual the charterers were obliged by cl 11 to replace it with one which they were entitled to give. Whether at the time of the cancellation they had committed an actual breach of this obligation is debatable, but at all events the breach was not final, since (if I correctly understand the arbitrator's reasons) there would have been time if all else failed for the charterers to ballast the vessel back to the redelivery area before the final date, or conceivably to issue an order for a revised laden voyage. But it is plain from the facts stated by the arbitrator that the charterers had no intention of doing this, and that the critical time would pass without any valid orders being given. This is the significance of the changed circumstances which rendered the original order invalid. Not that the order constituted a repudiation in itself, but that the charterers' persistence in it after it had become invalid showed that they did not intend to perform their obligations under the charter. That is to say, they 'evinced an intention no longer to be bound' by the charter. This was an anticipatory breach, which entitled the owners to treat the contract as ended . . .

7.2 Redelivery in disrepair

Most time charters call for redelivery in repair. But good repair is not normally a condition precedent to redelivery. *The Puerto Buitrago* related to a demise charter, but the judgment cites cases dealing with time charters and the principle applied was said to be common to both forms of contract.

Attica Sea Carriers Corp v Ferrostaal Poseidon Bulk Reederei GmbH, The Puerto Buitrago [1976] 1 Lloyd's Rep 250, CA

Facts: The *Puerto Buitrago* was to be redelivered in good repair. Repairs would have cost twice the value of the vessel. The owners claimed that the charterers had to pay charter hire until repairs were complete.

Held:

Lord Denning MR: The first question is as to the true construction of the charterparty. I will not set it out in full, but in substance the question is whether or not, on the wording of the charterparty, the charterers are entitled to redeliver the vessel now: or must wait until after the ship has been surveyed and all repairs done (ordinary wear and tear excepted) and passed in class without recommendations . . .

. . . it is plain that the charterer is under an obligation to put the vessel in good repair before redelivery. But the question is whether that stipulation is a condition precedent to his right to redeliver the vessel (so that he is not entitled to redeliver the vessel until he has performed it): or whether it is merely a stipulation which, if broken, gives a remedy in damages but does not prevent him from redelivering the vessel to the owner. This is the sort of question which has come before the courts for the last 200 or 300 years. I summarised the history in *Cehave NV v Bremer mbH* [1975] 3 WLR 447 at pp 453–54.

The parties can, by clear words, provide that complete performance of a particular stipulation can be a condition precedent: but, in the absence of clear words, the court looks to see which of the rival interpretations gives the more reasonable result. Lord Reid said so in *Wickman v Schuler* [1974] AC 235 at p 251E. He said:

> The fact that a particular construction leads to a very unreasonable result must be a relevant consideration. The more unreasonable the result, the more unlikely it is that the parties can have intended it, and if they do intend it, the more necessary it is that they shall make that intention abundantly clear.

There are only two cases in the books where the courts have had to apply this principle to the obligation to repair a ship. They were both cases of ordinary time charters (not by demise). The first is the *Wye Shipping* case [1922] 1 KB 617. McCardie J looked to see what was reasonable. He said:

> In my opinion they [the charterers] are not liable for hire after they have tendered redelivery at the proper time. If the rule were otherwise, it seems to me that absurd situations would arise.

and he gave an illustration of such an absurdity. That case was followed in *Black Sea v Goeland* (1942) 74 Ll L Rep 192 by Atkinson J, who regarded it as authority that 'the contract terminated on redelivery whether the repairs had been effected or not'.

Those were both cases of ordinary time charters in which the word 'redelivery' is used in a different sense from that in a demise charterparty . . . But the distinction makes no difference to our present question. The illustration given by McCardie J of an absurdity can be applied equally to a charterparty by demise. Another illustration was given in the present case. Suppose some spare parts were needed for the turbo-generator (so as to maintain classification without recommendations or qualifications), and it would take some months to get them. It would be most unreasonable to require the charterer to keep the vessel – and pay the hire – for the months that would elapse. It was suggested that the doctrine of frustration would apply, but I do not think it would. The correct answer is that the obligation to repair in cl 15 (in class without recommendations) was not a condition precedent to the right to redeliver, but only a stipulation giving a remedy in damages . . .

7.3 Redelivery at the wrong place

The owner has a contractual right to have the ship kept in employment at the charter rate of hire until the ship reaches the agreed place of redelivery. Breach of the obligation gives a right to damages calculated on the basis of the hire that would have been earned by the shortest voyage to the agreed place.

Santa Martha Baay Scheepvaart and Handelsmaatschappij NV v Scanbulk A/S, The Rijn [1981] 2 Lloyd's Rep 267

Facts: Charterers redelivered the ship at Galveston rather than at a Japanese port as required by the charter. The owners claimed damages.

Held:

Mustill J: ... For the charterers it is pointed out that where a charterer has tendered the vessel for redelivery at a port within the redelivery range, the tender is valid even 'if the vessel is not, as she ought to be, in the same good order and condition as on delivery': *Wye Shipping Co Ltd v Compagnie du Chemin de Fer Paris-Orleans* (1922) 10 Ll L Rep 55, and *The Puerto Buitrago* [1976] 1 Lloyd's Rep 250. They say that there should be a similar result where the complaint is reversed. If the charter terminates when the ship is redelivered at the right port in the wrong condition, then it should equally come to an end when she is redelivered at the wrong port in the right condition.

This argument sounds attractive, but I do not accept it. There is no true analogy between the two situations. Both legal and commercial considerations demand that the charter shall come to an end, even if the condition of the vessel on redelivery is unsatisfactory. So far as concerns the law, the contractual service is defined in terms of the place or time, or both, at which the vessel is redelivered. The stipulation concerning the vessel's condition on redelivery is not part of this definition. Once the stated time has expired, or the stated port or range has been reached, the period of hiring is accomplished, even if the charterer is in breach at the time. Equally, from a commercial point of view, it would be absurd if the charter were to run on indefinitely, with the charterer obliged to retain the ship in service, even though there was no longer any voyage upon which she could permissibly be sent.

The position is quite different where the ship is tendered at a port which is not within the redelivery range. Here there is no question of the charterer breaking a collateral obligation attaching at the moment of redelivery, nor is it the owner's sole complaint that the ship has been returned to him in the wrong place. He has a contractual right to have the ship kept in employment at the charter rate of hire until the service is completed. This does not happen until the ship reaches the redelivery range, and the voyage to that range forms part of the chartered service. In a case such as the present, therefore, the tender is not only in the wrong place but also at the wrong time; and full compensation for the breach requires the charterer to restore to the owner the hire which he would have earned if the voyage had in fact been performed.

I therefore consider that the arbitrators were right in basing their award of damages on the cost of a notional final voyage to Japan ...

This is not the end of the question of damages, for there remains a dispute as to the basis on which to calculate loss of hire on the notional redelivery voyage. For how long should that voyage be presumed to have lasted?

Apart from any express agreement as to the nature of the voyage, there is little room for doubt. It is quite clear that where a promisor has the choice of how his promise shall be performed, it is presumed for the purpose of calculating damages that he would have chosen the way which would have brought least benefit to the promisee. This principle, that an option is presumed to have been exercised in the way which reduces damages to a minimum, is too well established to require citation in support. Applying this approach to the present case yields the conclusion that the loss should be assessed in terms of the voyage which would have yielded the least hire. This was a voyage to the nearest safe port within the redelivery range, namely, Yokohama; and it would have been a voyage in ballast, because this would have saved time which would otherwise have been occupied.

 ## Further reading

Gay, R, 'Unsafe berth obligations, repairs to a berth and exceptions to laytime' (2011) LMCLQ 24.

Chapter 5

Bills of Lading

Given the distance involved and the lack of mutual trust between the relevant parties in the shipping arrangements and relationships, the use of a document issued by a trusted third party makes international trade much more efficient. An example might be this – for good commercial reasons, the seller of goods when putting the goods on board a ship would seek a receipt from the ship that the goods had been properly received for carriage. When the vessel arrives at the port of discharge, the carrier will require the buyer or consignee to produce some proof of entitlement to the goods. Otherwise he could be liable for conversion to the person with a legitimate right to possession if the goods are handed over to some rogue. Hence, if the seller could transmit the document he received from the carrier at the port of shipment to the buyer, the buyer would be able to rely on it to show the carrier that he was the legitimate consignee. As for the carrier, the document had originally been issued by them making it easy for them to properly identify it and ascertain its veracity. A document that has been used over the centuries for that purpose is the bill of lading.

1 A bit of the historical context

Lord Justice Aikens, Richard Lord QC, Michael Bools, *Bills of Lading*, 1st edn, 2006, London: Informa, paras 1.7–1.27 (footnotes removed):

1.7 The bill of lading originated purely as a receipt for the goods shipped, a copy of which could be sent to advise the correspondent of the goods sent and the purpose to which they were to be put. There was no need for a document which proved the consignee's entitlement to the goods since the carrier knew from the register or his own copy of the receipt to whom delivery was to be made. The need for a document which indicated entitlement to the goods would only arise when the goods were despatched before the shipper had finally determined to whom they were to be sent. This might have been because the shipper had not decided whether the goods should be consigned to an agent for sale or should be sold afloat. It is the possibility of the goods being traded whilst at sea that must have given rise to the need for a document that could be transferred, by the shipper at least, and which would evidence entitlement to receive the cargo at the port of destination.

1.8 Bennett's [Bennett, *The History and Present Position of the Bill of Lading* (1914)] conclusion that the bill at this stage did evidence entitlement is questionable, given that there is no evidence that the bills of the fourteenth century were transferable and consequently that there is no evidence that bills of this period were traded. It will be recalled that the bill of lading from 1390 provided for delivery to a named consignee and then provided that the carrier would deliver to the agent of the consignee. There is no indication that the document was intended to be traded. Such a conclusion would only follow either from there being an indorsement on the bill showing that it had been transferred to a new holder after it was made out or from bills being made out to order or to bearer.

1.9 Transferability only arises in the second quarter of the sixteenth century when bills of lading made their appearance in the files of libels of the High Court of Admiralty. The majority of the bills contain provisions importing some degree of transferability. They are of two kinds: (1) those that provide for delivery to the shipper (or his agent) or their assigns; and (2) those that provide for delivery to a third person (presumably a buyer of the goods) or his assigns.

1.10 This change in the form of the bill of lading was probably caused by a change in trading practice. Although cargoes do not seem to have been traded many times during transit, as they are today, they were often despatched before the shipper knew for whom they were finally destined. The change in form, therefore, reflects a change in the function of the bill. It was at this point that the bill needed to evidence entitlement to the goods as, unlike the bills of the fourteenth century, neither the bill itself, nor the ship's register, indicated to the carrier the person to whom the goods should be delivered.

1.11 The presence, in the majority of the bills from this period, of words importing transferability and of the clause, 'one accomplished, the others to stand void' or equivalent, suggests that these bills were seen as giving the holder some right against the carrier: such a clause was only necessary to protect the carrier from multiple suits if the bill was, by this time, seen as giving its holder some rights against the carrier. This represents a logical and important step in the document's development. That said, it is much easier to state that the right existed than to explain from where it came. It is likely that merchants, by course of experience, regarded the bill in this way, rather than regarding it as embodying an agreement which bound the carrier. This follows not only from the fact that merchants are unlikely to analyse the foundations of the right, but also from the fact that, contrary to Bennett's assertion above, most bills of this period were not regarded as embodying an agreement for carriage.

The contract of carriage

1.12 If the earliest bills of lading did not perform a contractual function at all, there is no reason why, given that their function was to act as a separate record of the goods shipped, they should usurp the role of the charterparty. Whilst the number of cargoes per ship remained small, the bill of lading need not perform a contractual function. The bill did, though, adopt this function and it seems to have done so during the course of the sixteenth century. In the fourteenth-century bills discussed above there are no provisions that imply a contractual function. The sixteenth-century bills are of two distinct types, as might be expected in a transitional period. There are still bills that contain no independent terms. The undertakings in these bills all make reference to an existing charterparty. Thus, freight is payable as per charterparty between the shipper and carrier. Two interpretations of these bills are possible: first, that they were intended merely to incorporate the terms of the charterparty into a bill of lading contract, or, secondly, they might equally suggest that the carriage was to be governed by the charterparty alone. The latter is inherently more likely given the origins of the bill, and occasionally the bills of lading refer to the fact that the shipper was a party to the charterparty. There is some evidence, then, that there were bills from this period which were not intended to operate as an agreement for carriage, and this is supported by evidence of mercantile usage in the seventeenth century, which did not regard these bills as separate contracts.

1.13 It would, however, be an over-simplification to assert that no bills from this period performed a contractual function. There were bills which made no reference to another agreement and contained terms which governed the shipment, implying that they alone contained the agreement between the parties. This implication is strengthened by the evidence of the bill in *The White Angel* [(1549) Select Pleas, vol. II, p. 59]. It provides that freight is to be paid '. . . according as it is mentioned by an other chartre partie made in the name of an other merchaunte' and later 'Paying hym the freight and avaries as ys abovesayed although the chartre partie be made in the name of an other merchaunte'. Further, the bill is also around three times as long as any of the other bills of this period because, unlike the others, it contains a full agreement:

> 'And it is aggreed that in case the sayed mechaundize should be loste or spoyled through the defaulte of the sayed maister of the shipp or the company of the same, the sayed maister shalbe bounde to make it good.'

1.14 There then follow clauses giving the master a lien over the goods and stating that the parties submit to the law of the place of shipment or elsewhere and that they renounce any customs that conflict with the agreement. All in all, the document is a very different beast from the others of this period: it was almost certainly intended to act as a contractual document, incorporating by reference the terms of a charterparty made with a different shipper.

1.15 With the increasing number of cargoes per vessel, entering into a charterparty with all the shippers became impracticable, and, in these cases, as today, the carriage contract was embodied in the bill of lading. However, the seventeenth-century works on mercantile law suggest that the number of cases where no charterparty was concluded was still small.

1.16 The first, and best, of these works was the seminal treatise of Gerard Malynes in 1622. Chapter 21 of that work deals with the freighting of ships, charterparties and bills oflading. Malynes begins by stating that no ship should be freighted without a charterparty. It is clear that he anticipates that all shippers will be party to the charterparty. He says:

> 'The ordinarie Charter-parties of fraightments of Ships, made and indented betweene the Master of a Ship and a Merchant, or many Merchants in fraighting a ship together by the tunnage, where every Merchant taketh upon him to lade so may Tunnes in certainty: are made as follows, Mutatis, Mutandis, which is done before Notaries or Scrivenors.'

1.17 He proceeds to give a precedent for a charterparty which states, inter alia, that the merchant shall:

> '. . . deliver all the said goods, well-conditioned, and in such sort as they were delivered unto him, to such a Merchant of Factor, as the Merchant the fraightor shall nominate and appoint, according to the Bills of lading made or to be made thereof.'

1.18 He further writes that:

> 'No ship should be fraighted without a Charterpartie, meaning a Charter or Covenant betweene two parties, the Master and the Merchant: and Bills of lading do declare what goods are laden, and bindeth the Master to deliver them well conditioned to the place of discharge, according to the contents of the Charterpartie, binding himselfe, his ship, tackle, and furniture of it, for the performance thereof.'

1.19 It is difficult to interpret the phrase 'and Bills of lading do declare what goods are laden, and bindeth the Master and the Merchant to deliver them well conditioned to the place of discharge'. It might be that, even given the charterparty, the bill was intended to bind the carrier contractually when in the hands of a transferee (the charterparty being only the contract between the carrier and shipper). Such a view is made unlikely by the fact that Malynes never refers to the bill being transferred and never states expressly that the holder of the bill has an action upon it against the carrier. It is almost inconceivable that, if the bill did give the holder an action against the carrier based upon contract, Malynes would not mention it at all. It is possible, therefore, that the phrase means that the carrier's obligations are fixed by the charterparty and the bill of lading only 'binds' him by virtue of its being evidence against him of the quantity and quality of goods loaded. Substantial support for this proposition lies in the other seventeenth- and eighteenth-century works. It is clear from the wording of these that Malynes's work was enormously influential upon them, but they clarify his statement about the role of the bill. Four of these works [Molloy, *De Jure Maritimo et Navali: or a Treatise of Affaires Maritime and of Commerce* (1676); Jacob, *Lex Mercatoria: or, The Merchant's Companion* (1729); Anon, *A General Treatise of Naval Trade and Commerce* (1738) and Beawes, *Lex Mercatoria, Rediviva The Law Merchant* (1752)] all explain the interaction of the bill of lading and charterparty in substantially similar terms to those used by Jacob [Jacob, *Lex Mercatoria: or, The Merchant's Companion* (1729), p. 82.] in 1729 who said:

> 'Charterparties of Affreightment settle the Agreement, and the Bills of Lading the Contents of the Cargo, and bind the Master to deliver the Goods in good Condition at the Place of Discharge according to the Agreement; and the master obliges himself, Ship, Tackle, and Furniture, for performance.'

1.20 The bill of lading, therefore, was not usually conceived of as fulfilling a contractual function because each shipper would be a party to the charterparty made with the carrier.

1.21 These works contain no reference to the bill of lading ever being issued without a charterparty to which the shipper was a party. Read alone, they suggest that every cargo wasshipped under a charter-party, and that the practice discussed above, of not entering a charter-party and including the contractual terms in the bill of lading had died out. Their silence implies that such a course was uncommon, but there is evidence in the comments of Postelthwayt [Postelthwayt, *The Universal Dictionary of Trade and Commerce; Translated from the French of the Celebrated Monsieur Savory* (2nd edn, 1757)] that it was neverthe-less followed occasionally. He wrote:

> 'Bill of Lading, is a memorandum, of acknowledgement, signed by the master of the ship; and given to a merchant, or any other person, containing an account of the goods which the master has received on board from that merchannt or other person, with a promise to deliver them at the intended place, for a certain salary.'

And later:

> 'It must be observed that a bill of lading is used only when the merchandizes sent on board a ship are but part of the cargo; for, when a merchant loads a whole vessel for his own personal account the deed passed between him and the master or owner of the ship, is called CHARTER-PARTY.'

1.22 The bill of lading is here conceived of as a contract, when there is no charterparty, as it is today.

1.23 It is possible to conclude, therefore, that the majority of bills of lading were issued to shippers who were also parties to the charterparty. The practice of issuing bills of lading alone was, however, beginning to develop.

1.24 If the majority of bills were not regarded as embodying a contract of carriage in the hands of the shipper, and there is no evidence to suggest that they were regarded as contracts in the hands of a trans-feree, it seems that the entitlement to delivery must have arisen from the custom of merchants.

1.25 It was a natural progression that, when bills came to be drawn up before the shipper had determined for whom the cargo was destined, the carrier in practice delivered to the first presenter of a bill and that by continued usage the holder came to be thought of as entitled to delivery such that carriers were regarded as under an obligation to compensate holders for their failure to deliver. The document can, therefore, tentatively be said to have entitled the holder to possession as a result of the custom of merchants. It is impossible to say whether or not this custom was ever legally recognised, but it was later impliedly rejected by the English common law.

An indicium of title

1.26 It is tempting to conclude that the reason that the bill was regarded as giving the holder a right to delivery was because it was regarded as giving him title to the goods. Though this may have been the case, there is no evidence to permit such a conclusion. None of the works dealing with bills of lading, discussed above, refer to it having this capacity, and it would surely be too important to be overlooked by them all. Further, although little can be hung upon it, when billsof lading came to be considered by the common law courts, they did not, for 80 years at least, consider the bill of lading as possessing a propri-etary function.

Conclusions

1.27 It can be concluded that the bill of lading of the fourteenth century was purely a receipt. During the sixteenth and seventeenth centuries, when it ceased to be possible to enter a charterparty with every shipper, some bills were issued that contained the contract of carriage, although these do not seem to have been prevalent. Further, during this period, bills came to represent the holder's entitlement to delivery of the goods by virtue of the custom of merchants.

In modern shipping there are different types of bills of lading; it is important to note that there are different legal incidences for different bills.

Types of B/Ls

(a) Liner B/L: A liner bill of lading derives its name from break bulk general dry cargo vessels trading on a regular 'liner' service and the term covers any non-charterparty bill of lading. A fully set out liner bill can stand alone, although it is often preceded into existence by a booking note or space charter.

(b) Charterparty B/L: A charterparty bill is a bill of lading that is designed for use with a voyage charterparty and derives the majority of its terms from the governing charterparty.

(c) Negotiable and Non-Negotiable B/Ls:

If a B/L uses the words 'to order' or 'bearer' or 'holder' or is left blank in terms of who is the consignee, then the B/L is negotiable and can be transferred by delivery or endorsement. A Non-Negotiable B/L is a B/L which is only transferable from the shipper to the consignee. If the consignee box in the B/L is filled in with a name and the words 'to order' or similar are not included, then the B/L is non-negotiable. If a B/L is not negotiable it cannot be transferred to any other person. Also known as a Straight B/L.

(d) Bearer B/Ls: a bill need not contain the name of the person or entity intended to take delivery of the cargo. In some cases, the identity of such entity will be unknown at the time of shipment or it will be confidential. In these circumstances, the 'Consignee' box is left blank and possession of the bill is crucial: whoever has physical possession of a bearer bill may demand delivery of the cargo.

(e) Charterer's B/L: If a charterer signs the B/L in his own capacity, and not as agent for the shipowner, then the charterer will be the carrier under the B/L responsible for the safe delivery of the cargo. This would be rare in the tanker business. The normal course if for the signature to be by, or on behalf of, the owner or demise charterer or his servant (employee), which makes the bill an 'owner's' bill.

(Source: ESSDOCS website: http://www.essdocs.com/resources/paper-bills-lading (2014))

2 Bill of lading as contract and evidence of contract

Lord Selborne in *Glyn Mills & Co v East and West India Dock Co* [1882] 7 App Cas 591 described the bill of lading in these terms: 'The primary office and purpose of a bill of lading, although by mercantile law and usage it is a symbol of the right of property in the goods, is to express the terms of the contract between the shipper and the shipowner.'

So we find that the bill of lading is not only a document of title but also the embodiment of the contract of carriage. It has often thus been said that the bill of lading is 'not in itself the contract between the shipowner and the shipper of goods, though it has been said to be excellent evidence of its terms.' (*per* Goddard CJ, *The Ardennes* [1951] 1 KB 55, 59–60).

Ardennes (Cargo Owners) v Ardennes (Owners) [1951] 1 KB 55

Facts: The plaintiffs shipped 3,000 cases of mandarin oranges on *The Ardennes* at Cartagena after the defendants had orally agreed to carry this cargo direct to London. When the cargo had been loaded, a bill of lading was issued that contained liberty to call at intermediate ports, to proceed by any route directly or indirectly and to overcarry. Instead of sailing direct to London, the vessel went first to Antwerp. By the time she arrived in London there had been an increase in the import tax payable on mandarins and the market price of the fruit had fallen. The plaintiffs were awarded damages in respect of the increase in import duty and their loss of profit due to the foreseeable fall in the market price.

Held:

> **Lord Goddard:** The defences raised were in substance that there was no oral agreement, and reliance is placed on one of the conditions in the bill of lading. I have no hesitation in finding that there was a promise made to the shippers' representative that the ship should go direct to London, and that they shipped in reliance on that promise. I therefore have now to consider the defence which arises out of the terms of the bill of lading ...
>
> It is, I think, well settled that a bill of lading is not in itself the contract between the shipowner and the shipper of goods, though it has been said to be excellent evidence of its terms: *Sewell v Burdick* (1884) 10 App Cas 74, 105 per Lord Bramwell and *Crooks v Allan* (1879) 5 QBD 38. The contract has come into existence before the bill of lading is signed; the latter is signed by one party only, and handed by him to the shipper usually after the goods have been put on board. No doubt if the shipper finds that the bill contains terms with which he is not content, or does not contain some term for which he has stipulated, he might, if there were time, demand his goods back; but he is not, in my opinion, for that reason, prevented from giving evidence that there was in fact a contract entered into before the bill of lading was signed different from that which is found in the bill of lading or containing some additional term. He is no party to the preparation of the bill of lading; nor does he sign it. It is unnecessary to cite authority further than the two cases already mentioned for the proposition that the bill of lading is not itself the contract; therefore in my opinion evidence as to the true contract is admissible ...

Note

The Lord Chief Justice's statement that the 'shipper is no party to the preparation of the bill of lading' is not correct for all carriers and all circumstances: see Chapter 1.

However *The Ardennes* is not the perfect example of the use and issue of the bill of lading in modern shipping practice. Although classical contract law as demonstrated in *The Ardennes* would suggest that the bill of lading is always issued after the conclusion of the contract of carriage, it should be noted that that is not reflective of modern shipping practice. Modern shipping practice involves many commercial entities and, as such, there may be a number of contractual relationships arising prior to the issue of the bill of lading and these should not all be considered to be contracts of carriage. They may be contracts simply for the arrangement of carriage (the person in question acting as agent) or contracts for carriage (which are different from contracts *of* carriage in that here the party in question undertakes as a principal to arrange for the carriage of the goods); or mere booking notes to reserving space on board a ship. These contracts may provide, at times, for the bill of lading to supersede them. In *Electrosteel Castings v Scan-Trans Shipping & Chartering Sdn Bhd* [2003] 1 Lloyd's Rep 190 for example the Conline form of booking note used stipulated that the contract 'shall be superseded (except as to deadfreight and demurrage) by the terms of the bill of lading, the terms of which (in full or extract) are found on the reverse side hereof ...'. In such cases, it is not appropriate to analyse the contractual rights and obligations on some simple proposition that the bill of lading is always merely evidence of an existing contract.

Electrosteel Castings v Scan-Trans Shipping & Chartering Sdn Bhd
[2003] 1 Lloyd's Rep 190

Facts: The carriage in question was for the transportation of ductile iron pipes and rubber gaskets from Calcutta to Algiers. Negotiations for the carriage of the cargo were conducted between Scan-Trans (from its Malaysian office) and Electrosteel through Marcons Shipmanagement Pvt. Ltd. of Mumbai (Marcons).

A booking note was drawn up by Marcons and signed by Electrosteel and by Scan-Trans as agents only on 30 October 2000. Electrosteel argued that the booking note contained the contract between the parties. Scan-Trans submitted that, at most, it evidenced the contract (already made in or evidenced by the recap telex). The booking note contained a super-cession clause, which provided that the bill of lading would supersede the terms in the booking note. A bill of lading was subsequently issued by the carrier. Electrosteel's contention was that Scan-Trans were not a party to the contract in question because Scan-Trans was only referred to in the booking note as agent. However, the bill of lading contained a reference that Scan-Trans was a carrier, hence a party to the contract.

Held:

24. Issue (1): What documents contain or evidence the contract? It is plain that no binding contract came into existence at the time of the recap telex; as already observed, at that stage, two subjects remained outstanding. I do, however, think that the arbitrator was right to infer that those subjects came to be lifted before the signature of the booking note; insofar as there is evidence from Mr. Taylor (Electrosteel's solicitor) to the contrary, I am unable to accept that evidence. For my part, I reach that conclusion on the simple ground that it would have been curious to execute the formal booking note while subjects remained outstanding, ex hypothesi leaving the parties free of contractual obligation. At all events, had the subjects remained outstanding when the booking note came to be executed, I would at least have expected some reference to be made to this feature in the booking note; but the booking note says nothing about any subjects. If no more happened than that the 'carrier's' subjects were lifted or waived by entry into the booking note, then in my judgment that lifting came instantaneously before entry into the booking note. It follows that a concluded contract on terms of the recap telex came into existence before the conclusion of the booking note. In the present context, such a conclusion is unsurprising: see, Voyage Charters (2nd ed., 2001), at pars. 1.14–1.15. For completeness, my conclusion here does not place any reliance on the precise timing of the exchanges between the parties and Marcons (no easy matter given the different time zones involved), nor do I rest it on Electrosteel's own request for 'all carrier's subs to be lifted by 14.00 hours IST on 30/10/2000'....

25. I turn to the booking note. I do not think it follows from the determination that there was a prior concluded contract, that the booking note enjoys no status greater than constituting evidence of that contract. The booking note was signed and stamped; it was complete and self-contained and, as Mr. Collett put it in his skeleton argument 'there is no suggestion on its face that it was intended that the terms of the contract were contained in any other document'. In these circumstances, I am satisfied that the booking note was intended to embody the contract between the parties thereto – not merely to evidence a prior contract. I do not think that it is mere habit which leads to countless pleadings in analogous charter-party cases referring to the contract as being contained in – not simply evidenced by – the charter-party itself, even when, in many such cases, there will have been a prior concluded agreement evidenced by a fixture recap; so too with the booking note here. I respectfully disagree with the arbitrator on this point.

26. In summary therefore, I answer issue (I) as follows: There were two contracts: (1) The booking note contained a contract between the parties thereto; (2) The recap telex evidenced a prior contract between the parties thereto, concluded once the subjects had been lifted before entry into the booking note contract.

. . .

> **31.**... (1) Primarily, looking at the arrangements between the parties in their wider context, I am satisfied that what was intended was (a) a contract for carriage, contained in the booking note to be followed by (b) separate and subsequent contracts of carriage, contained in or evidenced by the bills of lading. I can infer an intention that the terms of the two contracts should be consistent, so far as possible; I am unable to discern any intention to unite the two contracts into a single contract with the registered owners of the vessel. But that, in a nutshell, would be the effect of incorporating cl. 17 [of the bill of lading] into the booking note. Viewed in this light, cl. 17 was only intended to apply when bills of lading came to be issued.

Notes

1   In *Electrosteel* Gross J, after evaluating the factual and contractual matrix, found that not all the conditions in the bill of lading had formed part of the initial contract. Although there was a super-cession clause, whether and the extent the bill of lading would supersede the terms of the original contract depends on other factors including a proper construction of the contract. In *Electrosteel*, the judge decided that the super-cession was only partial.

2   On the function of the bill of lading as a contract in the hands of an indorsee, see section 'Transfer of Contractual Rights' below.

3 Bill of lading without contractual force

A bill of lading issued to a charterer is normally a receipt, not a new contract, at least while it remains in the charterer's hands. The contract of carriage remains to be contained in the original charterparty and not the bill of lading. (On the bill of lading as a receipt, see below at p 287.)

Rodoconachi v Milburn (1886) 18 QBD 67, CA

Facts: The plaintiffs chartered the defendants' ship to carry a cargo of cotton seed from Alexandria to the United Kingdom. The cargo was shipped under the charterparty at Alexandria by and on account of the charterers. A bill of lading was issued that contained an exception that was not in the charterparty and that purported to relieve the shipowners from liability for damage arising 'from any act, neglect, or default of the pilot, master, or mariners'. The cargo was lost by the negligence of the master.

Held:

> **Lindley LJ:** . . . The authorities shew that *prima facie*, and in the absence of express provision to the contrary, the bill of lading as between the charterers and the shipowners is to be looked upon as a mere receipt for the goods. There is nothing here to shew any intention to the contrary; so far from there having been in fact any *animus contrahendi* when the bill of lading was signed, the jury have found upon the evidence that there was none, and that the bill of lading was taken as a mere receipt . . .

Notes

1   Older authorities suggest that the bill of lading is a mere receipt in the hands of a charterer who is also the shipper, but not when he is an indorsee (*Calcutta SS v Weir* [1910] 1 KB 759, *Hogarth SS Co v Blyth* [1917] 2 KB 534, 551). However, in *The Dunelmia* [1970] 1 QB 289

Lord Denning rejected that orthodox view. There, the charterparty contained an arbitration clause that was not incorporated into the bills of lading. The bills were issued to shippers and indorsed to the charterers. Lord Denning held that the charter and not the bill of lading prevailed as to the terms of the contract:

'. . . in a case such as this the relations between shipowner and charterer are governed by the charterparty. Even though the charterer is not the shipper and takes as indorsee of a bill of lading, nevertheless their relations are governed by the charter, at any rate when the master is only authorised to sign bills of lading without prejudice to the charter.'

2   It might be noted that the rule could be extended to cases where the underlying contract of carriage is contained not in a charterparty but in a booking note or contract of affreightment.

3   Where a bill of lading is issued to a charterer and then indorsed to a third party, it then attains contractual status or force upon indorsement because 'a new contract appears to spring up between the ship and the consignee on the terms of the bill of lading' (*Tate & Lyle Ltd v Hain Steamship Co* (1936) 55 Ll L Rep 159, 174).

4 The terms of the contract: Incorporation of charterparties in bills of lading

Where bills of lading are issued to a shipper by a shipowner in respect of goods loaded on a chartered ship, both the charterer and the owner may wish to ensure that the shipowner's rights and duties as against the holder of the bill of lading are the same as those contained in the charter. The shipowner may want to avoid exposure to risks or claims that he has not agreed in the charter to undertake; and the charterer will want to avoid consequential claims to indemnify the owner: see Chapter 4. These aims can sometimes be achieved. If the obligations that will arise under the bills of lading are inescapable, one solution may be to make the charter mirror the bills. Where the parties have unfettered freedom of contract, another approach is to see that relevant clauses of the charter are reprinted as terms of the bills of lading. This requires time and effort so that it may be tempting to try to achieve the same result by a single clause in the bill of lading that purports to incorporate some or all of the terms of the charter by reference. Some forms do this in a well-planned way, with the charter attached to and forming an appendix to the bill of lading. Other forms refer specifically to the charter clauses that are to be incorporated so that there is no doubt what was intended. But in many of the cases mentioned in this section the incorporation clause used very general words. The extract from *The Varenna* reveals the general approach taken by English courts to interpretation of incorporation clauses, as well as the history of the interpretation of some forms of words.

Skips A/S Nordheim v Syrian Petroleum Co, The Varenna [1984] QB 599

Facts: Crude oil was shipped at Tartous for carriage to Wilhelmshaven under a bill of lading signed by the master of the Varenna. The shipowners brought proceedings against the consignee on the bills of lading to recover demurrage alleged to be due under the charter, the charterers having defaulted. The consignees sought to stay the proceedings at a preliminary stage on the grounds that the charter contained an agreement that any disputes would be settled by arbitration and that this agreement had been incorporated into the bill of lading. The bill of lading provided that the cargo was: 'to be delivered (subject to the undermentioned conditions and exception) . . . unto order P or to their assigns upon payment of freight as per charterparty, all conditions and exceptions of which charterparty including the negligence clause, are deemed to be incorporated in bill of lading.'

Held:

Hobhouse J: . . . [Counsel for the consignees] advanced and developed an argument . . . that the word 'condition' must, in the context, be read as 'term'.

The shipowners submitted that the word 'condition' has, in the context of an incorporation clause in a bill of lading, a well-recognised limited meaning and does not suffice to incorporate an arbitration clause and, secondly, that in any event the provisions of this charterparty are not clear enough . . .

The question of the incorporation of charterparty provisions, and specifically arbitration clauses, into bills of lading has been the subject of many cases. The problems discussed in these cases arise primarily from the simple fact that charterparties by their nature normally contain many more provisions and stipulations than are relevant to the simple contract of bailment between a bill of lading holder and a shipowner. The courts have therefore recognised that *prima facie* only provisions directly germane to the subject matter of the bill of lading, that is the shipment, carriage and delivery of goods, should be incorporated: *The Annefield* [1971] P 168. A charterparty arbitration clause is not normally germane to the bill of lading contract and therefore a clear intention to incorporate it has to be found. Although earlier cases may have disclosed an element of judicial prejudice against arbitration clauses (*TW Thomas & Co v Portsea Steamship* [1912] AC 1) that element is wholly absent from the more recent authorities and is not the basis on which they have proceeded. Some decisions have also reflected the principle that exclusions of liability, if they are to be relied upon by the carrier, must be clearly expressed.

Another point which is apparent from the authorities, and indeed from any consideration of principle, is that the primary task of the court is to construe the bill of lading. The bill of lading contract is the contract between the parties before the court and it is in that document that their intention must be found: *The Rena K* [1979] QB 377 and *Gray v Carr* (1871) LR 6 QB 522, 537, *per* Brett J. The breadth of the intention disclosed by the bill of lading is critical. There are many gradations of such intention . . . The oldest and narrowest form of wording was 'he or they paying freight as per charterparty': see *Abbott on Merchant Ships and Seamen*, 5th ed (1827), p 286. Then there was a wider form 'paying freight and all other conditions as per charterparty': see, for example, *Russell v Niemann* (1864) 17 CBNS 163. Express reference to 'exceptions' or to 'negligence clause' were introduced: see, for example, *The Northumbria* [1906] P 292. Also in this century much wider expressions came into use such as: 'The terms, conditions and exceptions contained in the charterparty': see, for example, *Crossfield v Kyle Shipping* [1916] 2 KB 885, or 'all the terms, conditions, clauses and exceptions contained in the said charterparty': see, for example, *The Merak* [1965] P 223. For many years it has been commonplace to find bills of lading using any of these various alternatives. Sometimes wider forms are used, sometimes narrower ones . . .

In this type of situation . . . where a particular type of clause has received a certain judicial interpretation and become established as such in commercial law, a later tribunal will not substitute its own view of that clause's meaning for that previously stated.

This proposition is essential to the proper recognition of contractual intention in commercial transactions. In the present context of bill of lading clauses this principle has been expressly stated and acted on in more than one case . . .

It is also a well-recognised principle that courts do not distinguish between similar forms of wording unless there are significant differences between them. Mere verbal changes in the way a well-known clause is expressed do not form the basis for attributing a different meaning to the clause . . .

The use of the word 'conditions' in bill of lading charterparty incorporation clauses has a long history, going back to at least the middle of the last century. It has throughout been consistently interpreted as meaning the conditions which have to be performed on the arrival of the ship by the consignee who is asserting his right to take delivery of the goods. Typically such a condition is the discharge of any lien on the goods or the performance of any unloading obligations . . .

The 19th century decisions on the words, 'deliver unto order or assigns they paying freight for the goods and all other conditions as per charterparty' were undoubtedly based on an *ejusdem generis* construction derived from the reference to freight: see *Serraino & Sons v Campbell* [1891] 1 QB 283 and the cases cited therein. In the present century the emphasis has simply been upon the use of the word 'conditions' as opposed to the wider words 'terms' or 'clauses' . . .

The position is that over some 150 years the question whether the word 'condition' should be construed as a synonym for 'term' or 'clause' has been before the courts on many occasions and on every occasion the wider construction has been rejected. There can be no doubt that the narrower construction represents the established meaning in the present context of bills of lading and charterparties.

It is in recognition of this meaning of the word 'conditions' that the alternative wider words 'terms' and 'clauses' have been and are used by parties when they wish to effect a wider incorporation . . .

The correct construction of the present bill of lading therefore is that when it refers to conditions it refers only to conditions properly so called to be performed by the consignee on the arrival of the vessel. On no view is an arbitration clause such a condition. An arbitration clause is a collateral provision: *Heyman v Darwins Ltd* [1942] AC 356. It is a clause or a term. It is not a condition . . .

The consignees' application accordingly is dismissed.

On appeal

Donaldson MR: . . . The issue, in a nutshell, is whether the wording of the bill of lading is apt to introduce the provisions of the charterparty arbitration clause and apply it to the bill of lading contract . . .

The starting point for the resolution of this dispute must be the contract contained in or evidenced by the bill of lading, for this is the only contract to which the shipowners and the consignees are both parties. What the shipowners agreed with the charterers, whether in the charterparty or otherwise, is wholly irrelevant, save in so far as the whole or part of any such agreement has become part of the bill of lading contract. Such an incorporation cannot be achieved by agreement between the shipowners and the charterers. It can only be achieved by the agreement of the parties to the bill of lading contract and thus the operative words of incorporation must be found in the bill of lading itself.

Operative words of incorporation may be precise or general, narrow or wide. Where they are general, and in particular where they are general and wide, they may have the effect of incorporating more than can make any sense in the context of an agreement governing the rights and liabilities of the shipowner and of the bill of lading holder. In such circumstances, what one might describe as 'surplus', 'insensible' or 'inconsistent' provisions fall to be 'disincorporated', 'rejected' or ignored as 'surplusage'. But the starting point must always be the provisions of the bill of lading contract producing the initial incorporation. And what must be sought is incorporation, not notice of the existence or terms of another which is not incorporated . . .

[In] *TW Thomas & Co v Portsea Steamship* [1912] AC 1, [it was held that] . . . 'terms and conditions' only incorporated 'matters which have to be dealt with both by the shippers and the consignees in relation to the carriage, discharge and delivery of the cargo' . . . I can find no trace of *TW Thomas & Co v Portsea Steamship* ever having been doubted or modified and that decision is in my judgment fatal to the appeal . . .

As in my judgment the arbitration clause was never incorporated, it is unnecessary to consider whether, if it was, it has to be rejected as being insensible in view of its references to 'this charter', 'under this charter' and the appointment of arbitrators by 'owners and charterers'. Clearly the clause would have required 'manipulation' to use the colourful phrase of Lord Denning MR in *The Annefield* [1971] P 168, 184. Whether such manipulation could be justifed . . . is an interesting point but not one which, in my judgment, arises for decision on this appeal.

I would dismiss the appeal. [Oliver and Watkins LJJ delivered judgments agreeing that the appeal should be dismissed.]

The Varenna refers to the important case of *TW Thomas & Co v Portsea Steamship* [1912] AC 1; it is useful to consider the reasons behind the insistence that general words of incorporation are insufficient, especially with reference to arbitration or jurisdiction clauses.

TW Thomas & Co v Portsea Steamship [1912] AC 1

Facts: The bill of lading provided that the goods shipped thereunder should be delivered to the shipper or to his assigns, 'he or they paying freight for the said goods, with other conditions as per charter party,' and in the margin was written, in ink, 'Deck load at shipper's risk, and all other terms and conditions and exceptions of charter to be as per charter party, including negligence clause.' The charter party provided that 'Any dispute or claim arising out of any of the conditions of this charter shall be adjusted at port where it occurs, and same shall be settled by arbitration.'

Held:

Lord Gorell: To my mind the question is one of construction, and when one turns to the marginal clause in question I have very serious doubt whether it carries the question one bit further than the clause which is found in the body of the bill of lading, except, of course, so far as it brings in the exceptions in the charter party, and those exceptions are to include the negligence clause; because it adds, in words, nothing more than that all other terms and conditions are to be those of the charter party, to the words in the body 'with other conditions as per charter party.'

Now the case of *Hamilton & Co. v Mackie & Sons* has already decided that the words 'all other terms and conditions as per charter party' have not the effect of bringing the arbitration clause into the bill of lading. We have not had a full report of that case so as to enable us to judge whether there was a cesser clause in that case or not; but I cannot help thinking myself, having regard to the date of the decision and the fact that there was a full cargo, as I understand the report, that it is extremely probable that there was in that case a cesser clause, which had become quite common at the date when that decision was given; and the conclusion to which I come is that that case was rightly decided and that it governs the present case. But, whether it does so or not, it seems to me that the marginal clause does not contain words in it which incorporate the arbitration clause in the present case. I think the true view to take of such a clause is that the 'terms and conditions' do not really include more than refers to those matters which have to be dealt with by both the shipowner and the consignee in relation to the carriage, discharge, and delivery of the cargo. To what extent they include what refers to those matters I do not pause to consider, but I do not see that they expressly in any way deal with the arbitration clause; and, of course, it is sufficient for present purposes to say that they do not; but my view is that what they deal with is no more than what I have already stated.

That being so, if one considers this case a little more broadly, the shipper is not likely, I think, to have been desirous of consenting to an arbitration clause which places upon him possibly the obligation of deciding by arbitration at any port where a dispute occurs a question on which there is any dispute. Certainly no consignee would ever naturally be likely to assent to such a proposition, because he might find himself landed in the difficulty of having to go to arbitration at a port of shipment with which he had no further connection than the mercantile one of correspondence.

It therefore seems to me, when one looks at the matter broadly, that the true construction to place upon this clause is what I have already suggested; and that the point may be made still plainer by trying to see what would be the effect produced if this clause of arbitration were actually written into the bill of lading. If it were written in, it would at once be seen that it is not a clause which in its terms is consistent with the bill of lading – it is consistent with disputes arising under a charter party; and that again leads to the conclusion that it was never intended to be inserted as part of a bill of lading which was to pass from hand to hand as bills of lading, being negotiable instruments, usually do.

But there is a wide consideration which I think it is important to bear in mind in dealing with this class of case. The effect of deciding to stay this action would be that the bill of lading holder or shipowner (in this case it would be the shipowner, but it might just as well occur where a bill of lading holder is concerned who does not wish for an arbitration,) – that either party is ousted from the jurisdiction of the Courts and compelled to decide all questions by means of arbitration. Now I think, broadly speaking, that very clear language should be introduced into any contract which is to have that effect, and I am by no means prepared to say that this contract, when studied with care, was ever intended to exclude, or does carry out any intention of excluding, the jurisdiction of the Courts in cases between the shipowner and the bill of lading holder. It seems to me that the clause of arbitration ought properly to be confined, as drawn, to disputes arising between the shipowner and the charterer; and therefore I concur in the motion which my noble and learned friend on the woolsack has made, that this appeal should be dismissed.

Lord Robson: There are two references in the bill of lading which purport to incorporate all or some of the terms of the charter. With regard to the clause in the body of the document which expresses the obligation of the shipowner to deliver the goods to the consignee, 'he or they paying freight, with other conditions as per charter,' very little need be said. These words have been the subject of a series of decisions which establish that such a reference does not incorporate every clause or term of the charter, but only those terms which are ejusdem generis with that for the payment of freight.

There is written, however, in the margin of this bill of lading a clause which deals with the incorporation of the provisions of the charter in somewhat wider terms. It says 'Deck load at shipper's risk, and all other terms and conditions and exceptions of the charter are to be as per charter party, including negligence clause.' In these words we have no specific reference to the payment of freight so as to import a limitation on their generality, but I do not think they differ in effect from the clause in the body of the bill of lading so far as the question in the present case is concerned. Both clauses are subject to the rule that the terms of the charter party when incorporated or written into the bill of lading shall not be insensible or inapplicable to the document in which they are inserted, and it is not absolutely clear that, when thus tested, this arbitration clause is applicable to a dispute between persons other than the parties to the charter. It expressly relates only to disputes 'arising out of the conditions of this charter party' and would stand in the bill of lading with that limitation. In one sense it is perhaps difficult to imagine any dispute relating to the chartered voyage which might not be said to arise out of the conditions of the charter, but we are here dealing with obligations founded primarily on the bill of lading, which is a different contract and is made between different parties, though it relates in part to the same subject-matter as the charter. The limitation of the clause to the conditions of 'this charter party' is therefore, to say the least, embarrassing and ambiguous when it comes to be written into the bill of lading. It requires, indeed, some modification to make it read even intelligibly in its new connection.

It is to be remembered that the bill of lading is a negotiable instrument, and if the obligations of those who are parties to such a contract are to be enlarged beyond the matters which ordinarily concern them, or if it is sought to deprive either party of his ordinary legal remedies, the contract cannot be too explicit and precise. It is difficult to hold that words which require modification to read as part of the bill of lading and then purport to deal only with disputes arising under a document made between different persons are quite sufficiently explicit for the appellants' purpose.

On the whole, therefore, I think their contention fails.

Lord Gorell's observation that it is a matter of construction is an important one. It should not be assumed that incorporation depends on some general technical rule of law providing for what types of cases where incorporation is permissible and which are not. That paradigm emphasised by Lord Gorell in the early 20th century is re-emphasised more recently a hundred or so years later.

Caresse Navigation Ltd v Office National de L'Electricite and others, The Channel Ranger [2013] EWHC 3081 (Comm)

Facts: The voyage charterparty contained an English law and jurisdiction clause. The bill of lading was issued to the charterer but indorsed and transferred subsequently to M. The bill of lading was on the Congenbill 1994 form. A box on the front contained the printed words 'Freight payable as per CHARTER-PARTY dated . . .', while on the reverse clause 1 of the conditions of carriage provided: 'All terms and conditions, liberties and exceptions of the Charter Party, dated as overleaf, including the Law and Arbitration Clause, are herewith incorporated.'

The box on the front of the form included the following typed clause: 'Freight payable as per Charter Party. All terms, conditions, liberties and exemptions including the law and arbitration clause, are herewith incorporated.'

The shipowners, following a dispute, tried to rely on the English law and jurisdiction clause in the charterparty against M.

Held:

> **Males J: 40.** . . . Mr Byam-Cook for the owners submitted that the specific incorporating words of the bill of lading (which included typed words on the face of the bill to which it was important to give meaning and effect: see *Homburg Houtimport BV v Agrosin Private Ltd (The Starsin)* [2003] 1 Lloyd's Rep 571; [2004] 1 AC 715) demonstrated an intention to incorporate the charterparty dispute resolution clause, and could only refer to clause 5 of the charterparty providing for English law and court jurisdiction. He submitted that where, as here, the bill of lading contained specific words of incorporation, there was no need to give those words a strict construction, and that if it was clear that the parties had made a mistake (by referring to 'arbitration' when they clearly meant 'jurisdiction'), the bill of lading contract could be read in accordance with what a reasonable person would have understood them to have meant (see *Chartbrook Ltd v Persimmon Homes Ltd* [2009] 1 AC 1101).
>
> **41.** Mr Whitehead for the receiver and insurers, however, submitted that the rules about incorporation give effect to the need for clarity and certainty, that arbitration is (and is well understood to be) different from litigation in court for a variety of important reasons (privacy, flexible procedures, parties' choice of tribunal which may include members with special expertise, ease of enforcement of awards, etc), that there is no reason to suppose that the parties made a mistake in referring to arbitration, and that effect would be given to the words of incorporation by construing them to mean that the charterparty arbitration clause 'if any' would be incorporated.
>
> **42.** I accept that there is a need for clarity and certainty in this area, and that arbitration and litigation are (or at least can be) very different. Indeed parties sometimes choose to arbitrate precisely because they do not want their disputes to go to court. I accept also Mr Whitehead's submission that the typed words in the central box on the face of the bill ('Freight payable as per Charter Party. All terms, conditions, liberties and exemptions including the law and arbitration clause, are herewith incorporated') appear to add nothing to the meaning of printed clause 1 on the reverse, when read together with the lower box dealing with payment of freight in which the date of the charterparty has been inserted. Even if that typed repetition adds a degree of emphasis, and notwithstanding the greater weight attaching to typed clauses than to standard printed conditions, I would be reluctant to conclude that these words make a critical difference in the present case.
>
> **43.** Nevertheless, on balance I accept Mr Byam-Cook's submissions. It seems to me that the question here is essentially one of construction rather than incorporation. Thus, although it can be posed by asking whether the jurisdiction clause in the charterparty is incorporated into the bill of lading, the real question

is what the parties should reasonably be understood to have meant by the words 'law and arbitration clause' which plainly contemplate the incorporation of at least one kind of ancillary clause. That is a question to be answered objectively, having regard to the background circumstances, which include the fact that the charterparty does not contain an arbitration clause, but does contain a law and jurisdiction clause. Special rules, to the effect that ancillary clauses will not be incorporated unless specific words are used, are of comparatively little weight in deciding whether specific words which are accepted to be effective to incorporate at least one kind of ancillary clause (an arbitration clause) can properly be read as extending also to another kind of ancillary clause.

44. It is clear, as Mr Byam-Cook submitted, that the only clause in the charterparty to which the parties could have intended their words to refer is the law and jurisdiction clause. There is no other candidate. That being so, it seems to me to be a more natural construction of the bill of lading to read it as referring to that clause, rather than to read it as referring to an arbitration clause in the charterparty 'if any'. I can see no basis for adding the words 'if any' into the bill of lading when the original parties to that contract either knew or must be taken to have known that the charterparty contained no such clause. That would render the specific incorporating words empty of content.

45. Accordingly, I accept Mr Byam-Cook's submission that the principle stated by Lord Hoffmann in *Chartbrook v Persimmon Homes* at para 25 applies here:

> 'What is clear from these cases is that there is not, so to speak, a limit to the amount of red ink or verbal rearrangement or correction which the court is allowed. All that is required is that it should be clear that something has gone wrong with the language, and that it should be clear what a reasonable person would have understood the parties to have meant. In my opinion, both of these requirements are satisfied.'

46. Does this conclusion run counter to the need for clarity and certainty, particularly bearing in mind that the bill may come into the hands of other parties (such as the receiver in this case) who are not aware of the terms of the charterparty? In my judgment it does not.

47. It is true that without reference to the charterparty a consignee taking up and paying for the bill of lading cannot know in what forum any claim for breach of the bill of lading contract must be brought. But that would be true even if the charterparty provided for arbitration (in which case Mr Whitehead accepted that the consignee would be bound to arbitrate). The consignee could assume that the arbitration clause was one which was usual in the trade (if it was not, the consignee would not be bound by it), but it could not know without seeing the charterparty whether any arbitration was to be held in London or in some other city, whether the tribunal was to be a sole arbitrator or three arbitrators, and so on. In all these respects the consignee would be bound by whatever the original parties to the bill of lading had agreed by their incorporation of the charterparty arbitration clause. Indeed, the consignee would not necessarily know what governing law applied to the bill of lading contract.

48. None of this offends against the need for clarity and certainty. On the contrary, the consignee would know from the specific words of incorporation that the incorporation of charterparty terms was not confined to terms which were 'germane to the shipment, carriage and delivery of the goods' (to use the phrase found in the authorities going back to *T W Thomas & Co Ltd v Portsea Steamship Co Ltd* [1912] AC 1) but extended to at least some ancillary clauses concerned with choice of law and dispute resolution. That being so, I conclude that the consignee is equally bound by a clause in the charterparty which can be identified as the clause which the parties to the bill of lading contract clearly had in mind when referring to the charterparty 'law and arbitration clause', at any rate provided that (as here) the clause in question is one which was usual in the trade.

49. I am reinforced in this conclusion by the decision of Gloster J in *Y M Mars Tankers Ltd v Shield Petroleum (Nigeria) Ltd* [2012] EWHC 2652 (Comm). That was a case involving a Congenbill form including the standard wording incorporating 'the Law and Arbitration Clause' of the charterparty, but the charterparty in question included a clause, headed 'Law and Litigation', which provided for disputes involving an amount in excess of US$50,000 to be subject to the jurisdiction of the English court, while disputes involving lesser amounts were to go to arbitration in accordance with the LMAA Small Claims Procedure. The cargo receiver argued that the bill did not on its true construction provide for the jurisdiction of the English court over a claim for an amount in excess of US$50,000. Gloster J rejected this argument. She said at para 30 that:

> 'In my judgment, the "Law and Arbitration Clause" referred to in the Bill of Lading clearly should be, and would be, construed as a reference to the "Law and Litigation Clause" in the Head Charterparty. It would be un-commercial to suggest that, simply because the "Law and Litigation Clause" in the Head Charterparty provides that arbitration should be limited to disputes below a certain level, that somehow meant that only the arbitration provision should be carved out for the purpose of the Bill of Lading. The High Court provisions are all part of the same clause and scheme. It is absurd to suggest that once claims exceed a certain threshold, no jurisdictional provisions are incorporated.'

50. While this case is not on all fours, because the 'Law and Litigation' clause did at least contain some provision for arbitration, it demonstrates that the question for decision is a question of construction of the bill of lading and that at least in some circumstances a reference to 'arbitration' in the bill of lading may properly be read as providing for court jurisdiction – indeed, it goes further by saying that in some circumstances any other conclusion would be 'uncommercial' and 'absurd'.

51. I should mention one further argument. Mr Whitehead submitted that because the charterparty in this case takes the form of a fixture recap into which the terms of a previous charterparty between Glencore and Eitzen (a third party) were incorporated, this is what was described by Christopher Clarke J in *Habas Sinai ve Tibbi Gazlar Isthisal Endustri AS v Somatel* SAL [2010] 1 Lloyd's Rep 661 as a 'two contract' case. He submitted that the jurisdiction clause in the Glencore/Eitzen charterparty was not even incorporated into the charterparty dated 6 January 2011 between U-Sea and Glencore, and therefore could not have been incorporated into the bill of lading by a reference to that charterparty, however specific. That, said Mr Whitehead, was because the recap did not contain specific words of incorporation, but only the general words 'otherwise as per pro forma C/P Glencore/Eitzen . . . logically amended'.

52. Referring to the situation where parties make a contract incorporating terms agreed between one of them and a third party, Christopher Clarke J observed at para 49 that:

> 'There is a particular need to be clear that the parties intended to incorporate the arbitration clause when the incorporation relied on is the incorporation of the terms of a contract made between different parties, even if one of them is a party to the contract in suit. In such a case it may not be evident that the parties intended not only to incorporate the substance of provisions of the other contract, but also provisions as to the resolution of disputes between different parties, particularly if a degree of verbal manipulation is needed for the incorporated arbitration clause to work. These considerations do not, however, apply to a single contract case.'

53. I would respectfully agree that there is a need for clarity and that, depending on the circumstances, it may not be evident in such a case that the parties intend to incorporate a dispute resolution clause. Conversely, it may be evident that they do. The conclusion of a charterparty by means of a fixture recap together with the incorporation of terms from some earlier charter by means of wording such as 'otherwise as per proforma . . . logically amended' is very common. In my judgment the parties to a charter concluded in this way do intend to incorporate the dispute resolution clause of the earlier charter thus identified. If, as generally happens, their contract is subsequently set out in a formal signed charterparty drawn up by the brokers, it will include that dispute resolution clause, but even if that does not happen (as is also common and as appears to be the present case) they still intend that clause to apply to disputes between them. The alternative would mean that their charter contains no dispute resolution clause at all, either for arbitration or for a specified court jurisdiction, which (if not unprecedented) would at least be extremely unusual. I have no doubt that the dispute resolution clause in the Glencore/Eitzen charterparty did form part of the charterparty between U-Sea and Glencore, which charterparty was in turn incorporated into the bill of lading. I suspect that, if a dispute were to arise between U-Sea and Glencore, those parties would be amazed to be told that the jurisdiction clause did not apply.

54. Accordingly I conclude that the bill of lading contained a term requiring any dispute to be submitted to the exclusive jurisdiction of the English court.

Males J's judgment was subsequently affirmed by the Court of Appeal.

Caresse Navigation Ltd v Office National de L'Electricite and others, The Channel Ranger [2014] EWCA Civ 1366

Held:

Beatson LJ: [15] English law has long recognised the particular need for certainty that follows from the negotiable nature of a bill of lading, which may come into the hands of a person in another jurisdiction who has no ready means of ascertaining the terms of the charterparty. It has developed special rules for the incorporation of the terms of the charterparty into the bill of lading. These include the now well-established principle that general words of incorporation in the bill of lading only incorporate provisions from the charterparty which are directly 'germane' or 'relevant' to the shipment, carriage, discharge and delivery of the cargo and not charterparty terms such as arbitration and jurisdiction clauses which are ancillary. That principle and the authorities in this frequently litigated area are discussed by Sir Guenter Treitel in *Carver on Bills of Lading* (3rd ed) para 3–021–3–023.

[16] The Appellants' case in this court was substantially the same as that put to the judge. Mr Whitehead relied on the ordinary and natural meaning of the words of the reference in the bill of lading to the 'law and arbitration clause', which he submitted was plainly a reference to an agreement to arbitrate and not to one submitting disputes to the exclusive jurisdiction of a particular national court. He also relied on five other matters. The first was the principle that general words of incorporation in the bill of lading do not suffice to incorporate ancillary terms of the charterparty. He argued that in this context the interests of commercial certainty are paramount, particularly where what is at issue is the meaning of a standard term in a widely used form of bill of lading. The others were precedent, inconsistency of the jurisdiction clause in the charterparty and the express terms of the bill of lading, the presumption against surplusage in commercial contracts, and the decision of this court in *The Merak* [1965] P 223, [1965] 1 All ER 230, [1965] 2 WLR 250, which he submitted decided that the court is not able to correct a mistake in the bill of lading.

[17] At various points in his submissions, Mr Whitehead contended that, because of the need for certainty and clarity, particularly in relation to the provisions of a standard form, the charterparty is not part of the admissible background to construing words in a bill of lading and that it should never be necessary to look beyond the words of the bill of lading to ascertain what clauses of the charterparty are incorporated. He, however, accepted that even this may not, in fact, achieve the certainty which he maintained was paramount because knowing from the words of the bill of lading that it was subject to an arbitration clause in the charterparty, although sufficient for the clause to be incorporated, would not identify the seat of the arbitration or the nature of the tribunal. He was unable to give a reason of principle justifying that departure from the certainty for which he contended, and relied simply on the fact that it was established by authorities binding on this court.

[18] As to the distinction in the authorities between the insufficiency of the words 'all the terms' in the bill of lading's incorporation clause to incorporate an arbitration clause (eg *The Federal Bulker* [1989] 1 Lloyd's Rep 103) and the fact that the words 'all the . . . clauses' which (subject to a test of consistency) has been held to be sufficient to do so, (eg *The Merak* [1965] P 223 (discussed at 32ff below) and *The Annefield* [1971] P 168, [1971] 1 All ER 394, [1971] 2 WLR 320.) Mr Whitehead's inability to give a reason of principle for this reflects the approach of Bingham LJ, in *The Federal Bulker* ([1989] 1 Lloyd's Rep 103 at 107–108) and Hobhouse J and Oliver LJ, in *The Varenna* ([1984] QB 599 at 608 and 621–622, [1983] 3 All ER 645, [1984] 2 WLR 156) They appeared to justify the distinction simply on the ground that earlier decisions had so interpreted the use of the words 'all the . . . clauses' in an incorporation clause in a bill of lading.

[19] In *The Varenna*, Oliver LJ, describing himself as a tyro in the area, observed that it was 'discouraging . . . to find what appears to be a simple construction point overlaid by a great weight of authority which it is claimed, compulsively restricts the inquiry to predestinate grooves'. (Ibid, at 618.) It is, however, not surprising in a commercial context, that where a settled construction has been given to a particular form of words, courts will recognise that other commercial parties are entitled to rely and act on it. (See Sir Guenter Treitel in *Carver on Bills of Lading* (3rd ed) para 3–014 and 3–034) If, however, a settled construction involves courts having to make fine distinctions between the particular form of words given the construction and very similar forms of words that cannot be explained by reference to differences in the ordinary meaning of the two forms of words or the objectively ascertained intention of the parties, the certainty achieved may come at a cost. That cost arises because any deviation from the form that has been sanctified by the construction may lead to a different result which can be explained only in formal terms and not on the basis of any substantial linguistic difference or principle. While the consequent complexity may not, in itself, be objectionable, ultimately such differences may not be healthy for the coherence of the law and perceptions as to its fairness.

[20] Mr Whitehead's starting point was to seek to rely on the ordinary and natural meaning of the words 'arbitration clause' in the bill of lading. The literal meaning of the words themselves is obvious. However, the modern approach (See the cases cited at 32 below.) is to construe a contract in its context, and the relevant question here is whether, as the judge found, in all the circumstances of this case the words had another meaning. I acknowledge, as the judge did, the particular need for certainty in this context: see the summary of the judge's views at 12(1) above. But, as Mr Whitehead acknowledged (see 17 above), even the approach for which he contends will not provide full certainty.

[21] The next question is the legitimacy of looking beyond the words of the bill of lading and considering the language of the charterparty. This may arise in two situations. The first is when considering the initial question of incorporation of charterparty terms into the bill. The second is whether language in the bill which prima facie suffices to incorporate a charterparty clause will not be effective because the language of the charterparty clause is inconsistent with it or because the words of the charterparty cannot be 'verbally manipulated' to reflect their operation in the different context of a bill of lading contract. This case is concerned only with the first, the initial question of incorporation of charterparty terms into the bill, and I make no observations on the second situation.

[22] I turn to the legitimacy of looking beyond the terms of the bill of lading when considering the initial question of incorporating charterparty terms into it. Gross J (as he then was) stated in *The Siboti* (at 26) that the more recent decisions in *The Varenna* and *The Federal Bulker* provide court of Appeal authority for the proposition that the inquiry not only begins but ends with the bill of lading, but that the authorities do not all speak with one voice. He, however, made it clear (at 29 and 33) that he considered the more

recent authorities to be correct. He did not have to resolve any differences between their approach and the approach in the earlier decisions in *The Annefield* [1971] P 168 and *The Merak* [1965] P 223. Nor, for the reasons I give at 26–29 below, does this court.

[23] The next limb of Mr Whitehead's submissions is precedent. He maintained that the words ' . . . and arbitration clause' in the Congenbill form have a settled meaning in the case law, which establishes that they incorporate the charterparty arbitration clause. He relied on *The Delos* [2001] 1 Lloyd's Rep 703 at 12 per Langley J, and on the earlier decisions, *The Rena K* [1979] QB 377 at 390–391, [1979] 1 All ER 397, [1978] 3 WLR 431 and *The Nerano* [1994] 2 Lloyd's Rep 50 at 55, [1996] 1 Lloyd's Rep 1 at 4, considered in that case. I do not consider that Mr Whitehead is assisted by those cases.

[24] *The Delos* is distinguishable because the charterparty in that case contained separate clauses dealing with governing law and arbitration (cl 13) and venue and arbitration (cl 18). Langley J held that the reference in the Congen bills to 'the law and arbitration clause' of the charterparty was sufficient only to incorporate cl 13. It was obvious that the reference to 'the law and arbitration clause' incorporated the arbitration clause in the charterparty. Clause 13 was in fact a law and arbitration clause. The position in the charterparty in that case is different to that in this case. Although the reference in the bill of lading in that case was to a single clause in the charterparty, there were two separate clauses in the charterparty. The charterparty dealt with venue and arbitration in cl 18 but with law and arbitration in cl 13. It is not surprising a reference to 'law and arbitration' was held only to incorporate cl 13 into the bill. The reference in the bill of lading in this case is also to a single clause of the charterparty. However, because cl 5 of the AmWelsh form of charterparty which was incorporated into the charterparty in this case is a single clause dealing with law and jurisdiction, there is only one charterparty clause with the potential to be incorporated.

[25] *The Rena K* was principally concerned with the question of manipulation of words in a charterparty to give effect to it in a bill of lading contract, and not the question before this court. *The Nerano* was principally concerned with whether there was inconsistency with a provision on the face of the bill of lading in that case that 'English law and jurisdiction applies' and cl 1 of the conditions of carriage on the back of the document, which provided inter alia 'all terms and conditions liberties exceptions and arbitration clause of the charterparty, dated as overleaf, are herewith incorporated.'

[26] I turn to Mr Whitehead's reliance on the principle that general words of incorporation in a bill of lading, even if they are comparatively wide, are insufficient to incorporate provisions of the charterparty such as arbitration and jurisdiction clauses which are ancillary in the sense of not being directly relevant to the shipment, carriage, and delivery of the goods. It is important to remember that this principle about the effect of general words is an exception to the general approach of English law which in principle accepts incorporation of standard terms by the use of general words. (See eg *The Athena* [2006] EWHC 2530 (Comm) at 65, [2007] 1 All ER (Comm) 183, [2007] Bus LR D5 per Langley J) Although in some cases the distinction between 'general' words and 'specific' words may not be as clear as it appears at first sight to be, (See Sir Guenter Treitel in *Carver on Bills of Lading* (3rd ed) para 3–016.) that is not a problem in this case. Caresse do not seek to rely on some generic phrase referring to a group of charterparty terms as referring to the ancillary clause. The bill of lading specifically refers to and seeks to incorporate one kind of ancillary clause, an arbitration clause.

[27] The issue in this case is thus not the effect of general words falling within the exception. It is as to the effect of a specific reference in the bill to one kind of charterparty ancillary provision and the construction of the words 'law and arbitration clause' in the bill of lading, in particular the word 'arbitration'. Does the fact that the clause in the bill of lading is effective to incorporate one kind of ancillary clause mean that, in the context of the case, it can properly be read as meaning another kind of ancillary clause, a jurisdiction clause? For that reason and those given by the judge (see 43, summarised at 12(4) and (5) above), Mr Whitehead's reliance on the principle about the insufficiency of general words is misplaced.

[28] Once it is recognised that the question is one of construction, it is established that the rules that apply to the construction of contracts generally are applicable to the construction of the bill of lading. The words of the bill must be looked at as a whole in their context. (See eg *The Nerano* [1996] 1 Lloyd's Rep 1, at 3.) In *The Siboti* Gross J stated (at 36) '[i]n every case, the court is seeking to ascertain the intention of the parties and, when construing the language, it is necessary to have regard to the individual context and commercial background.'

[29] It is true that, in *The Siboti* Gross J held that the 'governing law/dispute resolution' clause in the charterparty which provided that 'all bills of lading under this Charter Party shall incorporate this exclusive jurisdiction clause' was not incorporated into the bill of lading. The cargo interests' submissions about the effect of that case, however, significantly underplay an important distinction between it and the present case. In that case the incorporation clause in the bill of lading did not supply the date of the charterparty, the names of the parties to it or contain an explicit reference to any dispute resolution clause in the charterparty. So all that it contained were 'general words' of the sort that do not suffice. Gross J stated (at 48) that the only bridge between the bill of lading and the charterparty relied on by the Claimant in that case was the governing law/dispute resolution clause in the charterparty. But, what had to be construed to determine the initial question whether an ancillary term in the charterparty was incorporated into the bill, were the terms of the bill of lading, not those of the charterparty. The case was thus a classic example of the application of the proposition that general words of incorporation in a bill of lading are, even if they are comparatively wide, insufficient to incorporate ancillary provisions of the charterparty. In the present case, there are two bridges in the bill of lading. The first, ineffective in itself, is the date of the charterparty. The second bridge consists of the words 'law and arbitration clause' in the bill of lading's incorporation clause.

[30] Mr Whitehead also submitted that the clauses in the charterparty in this case are inconsistent with the provisions in the bill of lading. Accordingly, they cannot and will not be incorporated. This part of his argument overlapped with that based on the ordinary natural meaning of the words in the bill of lading. A reference to an arbitration clause, he maintained, is not a reference to a jurisdiction clause. Accordingly, incorporating a jurisdiction clause from the charterparty is inconsistent with the express provision in the bill of lading. I reject the submission that the reference to an arbitration clause is inconsistent with the incorporation of the jurisdiction clause in the circumstances of this case. As the judge stated (at 43, summarised at 12(5) above), in this context the question is not one of incorporation but of construing the meaning of the word used in the bill of lading. It is only after a meaning is attributed to it that one can consider whether there is a problem of inconsistency. Moreover, the argument that the clauses are inconsistent has an element of circularity because it proceeds on the basis of an assumption about the meaning of the words of incorporation rather than determining that meaning by the usual means and then considering whether there is inconsistency.

[31] I also reject the submission based on *The Eurus* [1998] 1 Lloyd's Rep 351 at 357, [1998] CLC 90 that because it is well-established that, in the interpretation of commercial contracts, the presumption against surplusage is of little value it followed that there is no need to strive to search for an alternative meaning to the term 'arbitration clause' in the incorporation provisions in the bill of lading. Mr Whitehead's approach would denude the words of any meaning. The argument that the words meant 'arbitration clause if any' is in my judgment wholly uncommercial because the original parties to the bill of lading (Glencore and Caresse) knew or must be taken to have known of the terms of the charterparty and thus that it did not contain an arbitration clause. This is particularly so since they chose to repeat the wording of cl (1) of the printed conditions of the Congenbill form in the typed clause on the front of the bill of lading.

[32] Finally, I turn to *The Merak* [1965] P 223 and its effect. An important component of Mr Whitehead's submissions was the proposition that in *The Merak* this court held that it is not possible to read the

words of a bill of lading in a way which seeks to correct what was said to be an obvious mistake in it. It followed, he argued, that there is no justification in principle or on the authorities, as a matter of construction, for reading a reference to the arbitration clause in the incorporation clause of the bill of lading in this case as a reference to a jurisdiction clause in the charterparty which he contended was wholly inept and irrelevant to the bill of lading. Before setting out the material terms of the bill of lading and charterparty in that case, and considering the judgments, I observe that it is a case that predates the modern contextual approach to construction and implication in cases such as *Chartbrook Ltd v Persimmon Homes Ltd* [2009] UKHL 38, reported at [2009] 1 AC 1101, [2009] 4 All ER 677, and its precursors notably *Mannai Investment Co Ltd v Eagle Star Life Assurance Co Ltd* [1997] AC 749 at 774, [1997] 3 All ER 352, [1997] 2 WLR 945 (per Lord Hoffmann), and see also 767E–768D, 770F–771B, and 772H (per Lord Steyn), *and Investors Compensation Scheme Ltd v West Bromwich BS* [1998] 1 All ER 98, [1998] 1 BCLC 493, [1998] 1 WLR 896, at 912–913 (per Lord Hoffmann).

[33] The charterparty in *The Merak*, dated 21 April 1961, was on the Nubaltwood form. It provided that the bills of lading should be prepared in the form endorsed upon the charter ' . . . and all terms, conditions, clauses (including cl 32 [the arbitration clause]) . . . as per this charter'. The bill of lading stated that the voyage was 'as per charter dated 21 April 1961' and contained a clause incorporating 'all the terms, conditions, clauses . . . including cl 30 contained in the said charterparty'. The arbitration clause in the former version of the Nubaltwood form of charter was cl 30, but cl 30 of the form used in *The Merak* was concerned with the shipowner's right to substitute another vessel and had no relevance to the bill of lading contract.

[34] The Plaintiffs issued proceedings under the bill of lading against the shipowner in respect of damage to the cargo, contending that the arbitration clause was not incorporated into the bill of lading. The court rejected this contention, unanimously holding that the words 'including cl 30' in the bill of lading's incorporation clause were mere surplusage and could be struck out and that the remaining words of the clause were adequate and effective to incorporate the arbitration clause in the charterparty.

[35] In reaching that conclusion, although Davies and Russell LJJ (at 254G and 259D) stated that a bill of lading, as a negotiable instrument, must be construed according to its terms without reference to any extrinsic facts or documents, they in fact relied on the fact that the charterparty expressly provided in cl 32 that that clause applied to disputes arising out of the bills of lading. Davies LJ (at 254) stated that since the bill referred to the charter it was impossible to construe the bill without reference to the charter, and Russell LJ (at 259) relied on the fact that the charterparty arbitration clause expressly referred to disputes arising out of 'any bill of lading issued hereunder'. Sellers LJ stated (at 250) '[T]he incorporating clause is clear and wide, and to be understood requires a reference to the charterparty. In order to discover what the terms of the bill of lading are, that is to construe or interpret it, the holder has to refer to the charterparty and select therefrom the clauses which apply.' It is possible that the language used means that insufficient attention was paid to the differences between the two situations to which I refer at 21 about the question of considering the language of the charterparty. This part of the decision may, in the light of the subsequent decisions in *The Varenna* and *The Federal Bulker*, only be justifiable because of the use of the word 'clauses' in the bill of lading's reference to the charterparty: see *The Siboti* at 46(ii) and (iii) and see my observations at 20–21 above. This is because the court's reliance on the provisions of the charterparty in construing the incorporation clause in the bill of lading may not reflect the more modern approach: see *The Siboti* at 26–29.

[36] What Mr Whitehead relied on was the basis on which a majority of the court, Sellers LJ dissenting, rejected another argument advanced for holding that the arbitration clause was incorporated. Davies and Russell LJJ stated that there was no justification, as a matter of construction, for reading the incorporation clause in the bill of lading as if the reference to cl 30 was a reference to the arbitration clause, cl 32, because this would be contrary to all the canons of construction. Mr Whitehead submitted that *The Merak*

is therefore binding authority for the proposition that there is no power to correct a mistaken reference in a bill of lading in the way the judge did when acceding to Caresse's submissions. He relied in particular on the words of Russell LJ at 259 that 'it is true that clause 30 is wholly irrelevant to the bill of lading and must have been inserted in error. But there is no room for the application of *the maxim falsa demonstratio non nocet cum decorpore constat* for there is no corpus evident, as there would have been had the bill said 'including cl 30 (arbitration)''. He also relied on the statements of Davies and Russell LJJ at 254G and 259D to which I refer at 35 above.

[37] In my view, Mr Whitehead is not assisted by *The Merak*. In concluding that the court is not entitled to remedy an obvious mistake Davies and Russell LJJ took what to modern eyes is a very old-fashioned and outdated approach to interpretation. The case was described as 'an unusual case' by Bingham LJ in *The Federal Bulker* ([1989] 1 Lloyd's Rep 103 at 108) In *The Merak* Davies LJ (at 254), but not the other two members of the court, considered that it was important that the Plaintiffs, who it happened were both the charterer and the shipper, were themselves parties to the charter. Sir Guenter Treitel's explanation of the case is inconsistent with Mr Whitehead's submission based on it. Sir Guenter stated (*Carver on Bills of Lading* (3rd ed) para 3–034) that the unusual feature in the case was that the parties 'had plainly intended to incorporate the charterparty arbitration clause and would have succeeded in doing so but for their 'slip of drafting'', and that, 'in these special circumstances, the Court of Appeal took account of the fact that there had been such a slip and gave effect to the evident intention of the original parties to the bill, even though the court was not able to correct the error by rectifying the bill.'

[38] As my Lord, Sir Robin Jacob, observed during the hearing, had *The Merak* been decided today, in the light of Chartbrook and other decisions of the House of Lords and the Supreme Court on the construction of contracts, it is very likely that the approach of Sellers LJ in his dissenting judgment would have prevailed. Sellers LJ recognised the negotiable nature of the bill of lading and the fact that it may be acquired by a party with no knowledge of the charterparty. Despite this, he stated (at 250) that:

> '. . . [T]he bill of lading clause can properly be read by substituting "32" for "30" . . . on two grounds. Anyone reading the charterparty, as the bill of lading holder would have to do, would know that the arbitration clause was intended, and I cannot see why the court should shut its eyes to the obvious on some technical ground of construction. A practical, not an abstract, construction is called for.'

[39] I also accept Mr Byam-Cook's submissions that *The Merak* is not authority for Mr Whitehead's proposition that the words of incorporation in the bill of lading must be construed and interpreted in isolation from, and without regard to, the charterparty. The majority judgments do not purport to lay down a proposition to this effect but represent a decision on the specific facts of that case. This is seen from the statements about the charterparty to which I refer at 35 above. It is seen particularly clearly from the judgment of Russell LJ who, in the passage set out at 36 above, gave an example of circumstances in which it would have been possible to correct a mistake. He considered that it would have been possible to do this had the bill of lading included the words 'including cl 30 (arbitration)'. It also appears that the majority may have accepted the submission of Mr Willmer on behalf of the charterers (see 241) that, notwithstanding the mistake, in that case the words in the bill of lading could not be read differently.

[40] Finally, I observe that the decision of this court was anticipated by Aikens LJ when refusing the cargo interests' application for permission to appeal against the judge's dismissal of their challenge to the court's jurisdiction. He stated ' . . . the reasoning of the judge leading to the conclusion that the jurisdiction clause was incorporated is compelling . . .'. I respectfully agree. It is for these reasons that I concluded at the end of the hearing that the appeal was to be dismissed.

[Lord Dyson MR and Sir Robin Jacob agreed with the judgment.]

Notes

1 In *The Federal Bulker* [1989] 1 Lloyd's Rep 103, p 105, CA, Bingham LJ explained why incorporation clauses in bills of lading receive special treatment:

> Generally speaking, the English law of contract has taken a benevolent view of the use of general words to incorporate by reference standard terms to be found elsewhere. But in the present field a different, and stricter, rule has developed, especially where the incorporation of arbitration clauses is concerned. The reason no doubt is that a bill of lading is a negotiable commercial instrument and may come into the hands of a foreign party with no knowledge and no ready means of knowledge of the terms of the charterparty. The cases show that a strict test of incorporation having, for better or worse, been laid down, the courts have in general defended this rule with some tenacity in the interests of commercial certainty. If commercial parties do not like the English rule, they can meet the difficulty by spelling out the arbitration provision in the bill of lading and not relying on general words to achieve incorporation.

2 The judgments in *The Varenna* show that a staged approach to the interpretation should be adopted. The operative words of incorporation must normally be found in the bill of lading itself, since incorporation can only be achieved by agreement of the parties to that contract (see also *Kallang Shipping SA Panama v AXA Assurances Senegal (The Kallang No 2)* [2008] EWHC 2761 (Comm)). Normally, the language of the charterparty only becomes relevant at a second stage of the inquiry. If the language of a bill of lading is wide enough to effect a *prima facie* incorporation of a clause in a charterparty, the next question is whether that clause makes any sense at all in the context of the bill of lading contract. In *Hamilton & Co v Mackie & Sons* (1889) 5 TLR 677, Lord Esher MR said: '. . . the conditions of the charterparty must be read verbatim into the bill of lading as though they were printed there *in extenso*. Then, if it was found that any of the conditions of the charterparty on being so read were inconsistent with the bill of lading they were insensible, and must be disregarded.'

3 *Verbal manipulation.* If a general incorporation clause in a bill of lading catches terms in a charterparty, must those terms be read literally and rejected if they are inappropriate in the bill of lading contract, or is it possible to embark on a wider search for the parties' intentions? In *The Varenna* and *The Nerano* [1996] 1 Lloyd's Rep 1, CA, it seems to have been accepted that the wish to incorporate a particular clause might be so clearly expressed as to require, 'by necessary implication, some modification of the language incorporated so as to adapt it to the new contract into which it is inserted': *The Varenna, per* Oliver LJ, above.

4 A bill of lading was issued to shippers by shipowners in respect of goods shipped on board a vessel that was under charter. The bill of lading provided that 'all terms and conditions, liberties, exceptions and arbitration clause of the charter party, dated as overleaf, are herewith incorporated'. The arbitration clause in question referred to disputes 'between the Owners and the Charterers'. The Court of Appeal held that by identifying and specifying the charterparty arbitration clause, the parties to the bill of lading contract had agreed to arbitrate and that to give effect to that intention, the words in the clause had to be construed as applying to those parties; the words in the clause would therefore be manipulated or adapted so that they covered disputes arising under the bill of lading contract: *The Nerano*.

5 The result of this line of development so far as arbitration clauses are concerned is the decision in *The Delos* [2001] 1 Lloyd's Rep 703, where it was held that to incorporate an arbitration clause required an express reference to it in the bill of lading, or, if general words could be construed to include it, that they did so only when the arbitration clause in the charterparty itself expressly provided that bills were to be subject to its provisions, so that no 'manipulation' was required for that result to be achieved.

6   But 'verbal manipulation' in search of the parties' intentions is problematic. In *Miramar Maritime Corp v Holborn Oil Trading Ltd* [1984] 1 AC 676, the bill of lading provided for the incorporation of 'all the terms whatsoever of the said charter except the rate and payment of freight'. It was argued, on the basis of *dicta* in *The Annefield*, that this resulted in the incorporation in the bill of lading of the demurrage clause in the charterparty and that, because the clause was directly germane to the shipment, carriage and delivery of goods, a degree of verbal manipulation of the clause was permissible and 'charterer' in the demurrage clause could and should be read as 'consignee' or 'bill of lading holder'. If correct, this argument would have meant that every consignee of every parcel of goods carried on a chartered voyage using the standard forms in question might become liable for an unknown and wholly unpredictable sum for demurrage without any ability on his part to prevent it. The House of Lords rejected the claim. Lord Diplock said: 'My Lords, I venture to assert that no businessman who had not taken leave of his senses would intentionally enter into a contract which exposed him to a potential liability of this kind; and this, in itself, I find to be an overwhelming reason for not indulging in verbal manipulation of the actual contractual words used in the charterparty so as to give to them this effect when they are treated as incorporated in the bill of lading ... [W]here in a bill of lading there is included a clause which purports to incorporate the terms of a specified charterparty, there is not any rule of construction that clauses in that charterparty which are directly germane to the shipment, carriage or delivery of goods and impose obligations upon the 'charterer' under that designation, are presumed to be incorporated in the bill of lading with the substitution of (where there is a cesser clause), or inclusion in (where there is no cesser clause), the designation "charterer", the designation "consignee of the cargo" or "bill of lading holder".'

7   *Freight.* 'Freight payable as per charterparty' was held in *India Steamship Co v Louis Dreyfus Sugar Ltd, The Indian Reliance* [1997] 1 Lloyd's Rep 52 to incorporate the whole of the relevant charter's terms as to the payment of freight, not only the rate of freight payable but also 'the manner of payment, when and where and to whom freight shall be payable'. However, the carrier may be entitled to redirect payment to himself: *Tradigrain SA v King Diamond Shipping SA, The Spiros C* [2000] 2 Lloyd's Rep 319, CA.

8   Failure to insert, in a space provided in a bill of lading, the date of the relevant charter will not automatically negative incorporation: *The San Nicholas* [1976] 1 Lloyd's Rep 8; *The SLS Everest* [1981] 2 Lloyd's Rep 389.

9   An incorporation clause in a bill of lading will not normally have the effect of incorporating oral terms which have not been reduced into writing: *The Heidberg* [1994] 2 Lloyd's Rep 287; but such a clause may affect incorporation where the charter contract is contained in or evidenced by a recap telex and a standard form to which the telex refers: *The Epsilon Rosa* [2003] EWCA Civ 938; [2003] 2 Lloyd's Rep 509.

10 An incorporated clause (such as an arbitration or jurisdiction clause) could be superseded by a validly agreed new agreement. In *Viscous Global Investment Ltd v Palladium Navigation Corp, The Quest* [2014] EWHC 2654 (Comm), although the relevant bills of lading had incorporated the arbitration clause from the charterparty, the parties by subsequently agreeing to a P&I Club Letter of Undertaking (which contained a different arbitration clause) were found by the court to have intended for the new LOU to replace the arbitration undertakings properly incorporated by the bills of lading in question.

5 The terms of the contract: Incorporation of international carriage conventions

A distinction has to be made between charterparty and non-charterparty bills of lading. The latter are usually subject to the mandatory application of the relevant international carriage convention (for example, the Hague Rules, Hague-Visby Rules, Hamburg Rules). On the mandatory application of these international conventions, please see Chapter 7 on Hague-Visby Rules below.

As regards charterparty bills (usually voyage charters), it is clear that the contract of carriage is not subject to mandatory application of international carriage conventions. However, it is sometimes considered useful by the shipowner and charterer that their contract should be subject to the relevant international transport convention. Sometimes that is to ensure that there is a sense of consistency between the charterparty and any bill of lading contracts made under the charterparty with other cargo interests.

A commonly used clause for contractual incorporation of the Hague or Hague-Visby Rules is the so-called 'clause paramount'. It is so called because the intention of the parties is that the Rules as incorporated by it were to be 'paramount' and would take precedence over any inconsistent clauses to the contrary.

Lord Denning famously defined it in these terms:

> The parties have expressly stated that 'Paramount clause' is deemed to be incorporated into this charterparty. We should strive to give effect to this incorporation, rather than render it meaningless. We should make all reasonable implications to this end, just as the House of Lords did in W. N. Hillas & Co. Ltd. v Arcos Ltd. (1932) 38 Com. Cas. 23, 37 and 38. What does 'Paramount clause' or 'clause paramount' mean to shipping men? Primarily it applies to bills of lading. In that context its meaning is, I think, clear beyond question. It means a clause by which the Hague Rules are incorporated into the contract evidenced by the bill of lading and which overrides any express exemption or condition that is inconsistent with it. As I said in *Adamastos* Shipping Co. Ltd. v Anglo-Saxon Petroleum Co. Ltd. [1957] 2 Q.B. 233, 266: 'When a paramount clause is incorporated into a contract, the purpose is to give the Hague Rules contractual force: so that, although the bill of lading may contain very wide exceptions, the rules are paramount and make the shipowners liable for want of due diligence to make the ship seaworthy and so forth'. (*The Agios Lazaros* [1976] QB 933, 943.)

Lord Denning's definition is however not universally adopted. However, whatever definition or description we might take, the issue is increasingly being resolved as a matter of construction of the clause paramount against the charterparty's commercial and factual matrix.

Seabridge Shipping AB v AC Orsleff's Eftf's A/S [1999] 2 Lloyd's Rep 685

Facts: By a charterparty on the Gencon form, the owners, a Danish company, chartered to the charterers, a Swedish company, a vessel to be nominated for five voyages with cargoes of equipment to the Avondale shipyard at New Orleans. The charter provided:

> 'P and I bunkering clause, Both to blame collision Clause, New Jason Clause and Paramount Clause are deemed to be incorporated into this Charter Party.'

The charter was expressly governed by English law. The owners nominated the vessel *Fjellvang*. She loaded a cargo at Gdynia, Poland under bills of lading issued by both owners and charterers and completed discharge at the Avondale shipyard.

The cargo interests under a bill of lading issued by the charterers brought a claim against the charterers in respect of the cargo carried. That bill of lading incorporated the Hague Rules as enacted in the country of shipment. Poland had however brought the Hague-Visby Rules into force by the time of that shipment (which means that as the shipment was from Poland, ordinarily, the Hague-Visby Rules would thus apply to that bill of lading).

The question was whether the paramount clause had incorporated the Hague Rules or the Hague-Visby Rules into the charterparty.

Held:

Thomas J (holding that the Hague Rules had been incorporated, not the Hague-Visby Rules): . . . the approach to the question must remain governed by the approach of the Court of Appeal in *The Agios Lazaros*. Lord Denning's approach was to ask the question (at p. 50 of the report), 'What does 'paramount clause' or 'clause paramount' mean to shipping men?'

It seems to me that when the 'paramount clause' is incorporated, without any words of qualification, it means that all the Hague Rules are incorporated. If the parties intend only to incorporate part of the rules (for example, art. IV), or only so far as compulsorily applicable, they say so. In the absence of any such qualification, it seems to me that a 'clause paramount' is a clause which incorporates all the Hague Rules. I mean, of course, the accepted Hague Rules and not the Hague-Visby Rules which are of later date.

[The approach of **Goff LJ** was different. At p 53 of the report he said this]: It is clear that the term 'paramount clause' is a term of art and means a clause incorporating the Hague Rules either simpliciter or if and as made compulsorily applicable by whatever may be the relevant local law . . . This being so, in my judgment the direction to include a paramount clause is not one requiring the incorporation in particular form designated by name, but one describing by description what is comprehended by the term of art 'paramount clause' . . .

That being so, there remain only two possible areas of uncertainty to be explored. First, does this mean the Hague Rules simpliciter, or if, and as made compulsory by the relevant law, and, secondly, does it mean the Hague Rules as originally agreed, or in the form commonly called the Hague-Visby Rules as amended by the protocol signed in Brussels of Feb. 23, 1968.

The first of these presents no difficulty because in my judgment one must apply the proper law of the charter-party which is English and on the facts of this case that law by the Carriage of Goods by Sea Act, 1924 imports the Hague Rules in toto. Mr. Hallgarten argued that possibly one should apply the law of the country of shipment, namely Greece, and that might create a difficulty because that country had not adopted the Hague Rules at all. In my judgment, however, there is no warrant to that construction. The Court always struggled to give a meaning to what the parties have said, if it can. The conclusion that it is open to uncertainty is really a counsel of despair . . .

[After referring to authority, Goff LJ continued]: Here the provision is capable of having effect and an important effect, and one is being asked so to construe it to prevent it doing so.

On the same principle, it seems clear to me that the second point also does not give rise to any uncertainty either. It is simply a matter of choosing between the two possibilities as this Court did in *The San Nicholas* where the question arose between a head and sub-charter-party. For my part, I have no difficulty in saying that the reference in cl. 31 is the Hague Rules in their original form.

At the date of the charter-party, the Visby rules had not been adopted in any country, nor indeed I think have they even now, but that does not matter. The form taken from a bill of lading entitled Hague-Visby Paramount Clause had not been published and the Visby variant was not in any kind of general use.

[**Shaw LJ** approached the matter in a way much more similar to that of Lord Denning. He said at p. 57 of the report]: A more productive approach in the circumstances of this case is to ask what the shipowners would have supposed the charterers had in mind when the words 'paramount clause' were inserted and then to ask the same question with the parties reversed. In the absence of any express words of variation or abbreviation or extension, each party must have assumed that the other party had the Hague Rules in mind in their original form without modification or qualification. This approach does provide a clue as to what the respective party had in contemplation, namely that by the phrase 'paramount clause' they meant simply the Hague Rules.

It seems to me clear from the judgments of Lord Denning and Lord Justice Shaw that the correct approach is to ask what would shipowners, or shipping men in general, and these shipowners in particular, have had in mind when referring to a paramount clause.

Unfortunately, there is nothing in the award which assists on this point. The arbitrator simply took the view that the Hague Rules applied because the cargo had been discharged in the United States. Miss Melwani bravely tried to adduce evidence in relation to what shipping men thought, but as this is an appeal from an arbitration award, this was plainly an impermissible course. As the P&I clubs in this case decided to proceed by way of preliminary issue before an arbitrator, and not, as is more usual in this type of case, by an application to the Court, it was not open to the charterers to provide proper evidence necessary to support their argument.

Although Mr. Goldstone, who appeared for the owners, did not contend the decision in *The Agios Lazaros* was necessarily binding as to the meaning of the words 'clause paramount' for all time, he submitted that on the materials before the Court in this appeal, there was nothing which showed there had been a change in the position from that which was before the Court of Appeal in 1976.

In my view he was correct in this contention. Although in other circumstances where proper materials were available, Miss Melwani's attractive argument might have been successful, there was nothing before the Court in this case which justified this Court in taking the view that shipping men in general, or these owners and charterers in particular, had intended a different view to that current at the time of *The Agios Lazaros*. There is, I consider, force in the point that parties to a particular charterparty would regard the term 'clause paramount' as a term of art as characterized by Lord Justice Goff – that its meaning would therefore not vary depending on factors such as where the port of loading was or who the charterer or owners were. It would cause great uncertainty, in my view, if the term 'clause paramount' referred to the Hague Rules in one charter-party, but meant the Hague-Visby Rules in another charter-party. I cannot readily envisage particular owners or charterers intending the meaning of the term to vary as between different charter-parties depending on the parties or the port of loading.

The shipping trade commonly uses terms – 'clause paramount', 'general clause paramount', 'Canadian clause paramount', 'U.S. clause paramount'. For over 20 years the meaning of 'clause paramount' has been certain. Persons in the shipping trade have been free to use the phrase 'general clause paramount' if they wished to incorporate the Hague-Visby Rules into trades where those rules are compulsorily applicable. Thus, on the evidence before me I see no warrant for departing from the views of shipping men which the Court ascertained and gave effect to in *The Agios Lazaros*.

In reaching this view I have taken into account what is set out in two of the works on charter-parties. In *Voyage Charters* (1993 edition) written by Mr. Julian Cooke and others, the authors state that the point remains to be decided. However, in *Time Charters* by Wilford, Coughlin & Kimball (4th ed., 1995) the following view is expressed,

> However, if a 'Paramount clause' is incorporated into a Baltime charter governed by English law, it is likely, following the coming into force in 1977 of the Carriage of Goods by Sea Act 1971, that the Hague-Visby Rules would be regarded as incorporated.

I do not, however, regard the mere bringing into force of the Hague-Visby Rules in the United Kingdom brings about the consequence that a clause paramount in a charter-party governed by English law incorporates the Hague-Visby Rules. The approach of the majority in the Court of Appeal in *The Agios Lazaros* was to ask what shipping men intended, and the bringing into force of the legislation enacting the Hague-Visby Rules can only be a factor in determining what shipping men intended. The legislation does not apply to charter-parties and, in my view, reading the whole of Lord Justice Goff's judgment, the fact that the law of England and Wales now subjects bills of lading on voyages within its scope to the Hague-Visby Rules does not, of itself, bring about the incorporation of the rules by the use of the term 'clause paramount'. More is needed and the majority decision in the Court of Appeal makes that plainly clear.

I therefore, though for different reasons, uphold the decision of the arbitrator on this first issue.'

See too *Yemgas Fzco and others v Superior Pescadores SA Panama* [2014] EWHC 971 (Comm) where many of the prevailing authorities on incorporation clause in a charterparty are considered.

6 Which rules are incorporated by virtue of the clause paramount?

Yemgas Fzco and others v Superior Pescadores SA Panama
[2014] EWHC 971 (Comm)

Facts: Machinery and equipment for the construction of a gas facility in Yemen was carried by the *Superior Pescadores* from Antwerp to Balhaf in Yemen. The contract was represented by several bills of lading, each of which also contained a Paramount Clause in the following familiar terms:

> 'The Hague Rules contained in the International Convention for the Unification of certain rules relating to Bills of Lading, dated Brussels 25 August 1924 as enacted in the country of shipment shall apply to this contract. When no such enactment is in force in the country of shipment, the corresponding legislation of the country of destination shall apply, but in respect of shipments to which no such enactments are compulsorily applicable, the terms of the said Convention shall apply.'

When the vessel was crossing the Bay of Biscay, the cargo in one of the holds shifted, causing damage to part of the cargo. The claim was agreed to be resolved applying English law. The question was whether the Paramount Clause had incorporated the Hague Rules or the Hague-Visby Rules.

Held:

Males J: **[12]** The premise for the Claimants' argument that they are entitled to rely on the Hague Rules limit where this is higher is that it is the Hague Rules and not the Hague-Visby Rules which are incorporated into the bill of lading by virtue of the clause paramount set out at 4 above. The Claimants recognise that in a case such as the present, where the carriage is from a port in a contracting state, the Hague-Visby Rules apply compulsorily by reason of s 1(2) of the 1971 Act and art X of the Hague-Visby Rules themselves, but they rely on the permission given by those Rules to agree contractually on a higher package limitation figure than that for which the Rules provide. They say that the parties have so agreed (to the extent that it produces a higher limit) by incorporating the limit provided for by the Hague Rules.

[13] The first question is therefore whether the parties have indeed incorporated the Hague Rules and not the Hague-Visby Rules by virtue of the clause paramount. That depends on what is meant, in this bill of lading, by the phrase 'the Hague Rules contained in the International Convention for the Unification of certain rules relating to Bills of Lading, dated Brussels 25 August 1924 as enacted in the country of shipment . . .' It is common ground that if this does not refer (or is not capable of referring) to the Hague-Visby Rules which have been enacted in Belgium, the Hague and not the Hague-Visby Rules are incorporated by virtue of the second sentence of the clause.

The Parties' Submissions

[14] Mr Robert Thomas QC for the Claimant cargo interests submitted, in summary, that this question is determined in his favour by the judgment of Tomlinson J in *The Happy Ranger* [2001] 2 Lloyd's Rep 530 and is also supported by other authority; and in any event that the clause is clear in incorporating the original Hague Rules and not the Hague Rules 'as amended', as the words 'the Hague Rules contained in the International Convention for the Unification of certain rules relating to Bills of Lading, dated Brussels 25 August 1924' are only capable of referring to the original Hague Rules.

[15] Mr David Goldstone QC for the Defendant shipowners sought to distinguish *The Happy Ranger* and submitted, again in outline, that the Hague-Visby Rules are capable of falling within the expression 'the

Hague Rules . . . as enacted in the country of shipment' and should be construed as doing so if there is no contrary indication in the clause (such as a distinction drawn elsewhere in the clause between the Hague and Hague-Visby Rules).

The Authorities

[16] In considering the authorities it is necessary to distinguish between cases (usually charterparty cases) which have addressed the question of what is meant by general expressions such as 'clause paramount' without spelling out what the terms of such a clause paramount are intended to be and other cases (usually bill of lading cases) which have addressed the terms of particular clauses. It is also necessary to bear in mind that in a charterparty case there is freedom of contract, so that the parties are entitled to agree whatever they wish. That will not necessarily be so in a bill of lading case, where (under English law) the application of the Hague-Visby Rules is compulsory in the cases falling within s 1 of the 1971 Act and art X of the Rules, although not in other cases. Taking them chronologically, the authorities relied on by counsel are as follows.

[17] *The Agios Lazaros* [1976] QB 933, [1976] 2 All ER 842, [1976] 2 Lloyd's Rep 47 was a charterparty case which provided for the incorporation of a 'clause paramount' into the charter but without identifying further the terms of that clause. Lord Denning MR held that the right approach was to ask 'what would 'paramount clause' or 'clause paramount' mean to shipping men?' and that this referred to the original Hague Rules:

> 'It seems to me that when the "paramount clause" is incorporated, without any words of qualification, it means that all the Hague Rules are incorporated. If the parties intend only to incorporate part of the rules (for example, art IV), or only so far as compulsorily applicable, they say so. In the absence of any such qualification, it seems to me that a "clause paramount" is a clause which incorporates all the Hague Rules. I mean, of course, the accepted Hague Rules and not the Hague-Visby Rules which are of later date.'

[18] Although Goff LJ's conclusion was the same, his reasoning depended to some extent on the fact that the Hague-Visby Rules were not in any kind of general use at that time. Shaw LJ's approach, however, was the same as Lord Denning's:

> 'A more productive approach in the circumstances of this case is to ask what the shipowners would have supposed the charterers had in mind when the words "paramount clause" were inserted and then to ask the same question with the parties reversed. In the absence of any express words of variation or abbreviation or extension, each party must have assumed that the other party had the Hague Rules in mind in their original form without modification or qualification. This approach does provide a clue as to what the respective party had in contemplation, namely that by the phrase "paramount clause" they meant simply the Hague Rules.'

[19] While this is an authoritative decision as to the meaning of the phrase 'clause paramount' without more in a charterparty, which remains binding in the absence of evidence that this meaning has changed in the intervening years, it is of only limited assistance in construing the terms of any specific clause. It does, however, demonstrate that what shipping men (in those days it was men and to a large extent it still is) meant by a 'clause paramount' is the Hague Rules.

[20] *The Marinor* [1996] 1 Lloyd's Rep 301 was also a charterparty case, which included a Canadian clause paramount incorporating 'the provisions of the Carriage of Goods by Water Act . . . as amended, enacted by the Parliament of Canada'. At the relevant time Canada had repealed its original Carriage of Goods by Water Act enacting the Hague Rules and had passed new legislation enacting the Hague-Visby Rules. Counsel for the charterers (as it happens, Mr Stephen Tomlinson QC) submitted that since the original Canadian

Act was repealed and not 'amended' in 1993, the clause did not incorporate the Hague-Visby Rules. Colman J was not impressed by this distinction and held that the Hague-Visby Rules were incorporated:

> 'The words "as amended" in Rider A are, in my view, intended to provide for legislative changes which may subsequently be made in respect of the subject-matter of the existing Act identified in the clause paramount. Whether those changes were effected by a subsequent Act which introduced amendments into the Act specified or by a subsequent Act which repealed the specified Act and replaced it with an Act containing amended provisions in respect of the same subject-matter would be wholly irrelevant to the owners and charterers of Marinor. The obvious purpose of incorporating the rider is to make sure that throughout the period of the time charter the current Canadian Carriage of Goods by Sea legislation is contractually incorporated.
>
> I therefore hold that the 1993 Canadian Act came to be incorporated and with it the Hague-Visby Rules.'

[21] The next case was *The Bukhta Russkaya* [1997] 2 Lloyd's Rep 744, a charterparty case where the clause in question referred to 'the general paramount clause' without further detail. Again the question was whether this incorporated the Hague or Hague-Visby Rules into the charterparty. As in *The Agios Lazaros*, this was treated simply as a question of construction of the phrase 'the general paramount clause'. What would shipping men mean by that phrase? That question was answered, on the evidence in that case, by reference to a BIMCO general paramount clause which provided as follows:

> '(a) The Hague Rules contained in the International Convention for the Unification of certain rules relating to Bills of Lading dated Brussels 25 August 1924, as enacted in the country of shipment, shall apply to this Bill of Lading. When no such enactment is in force in the country of shipment, the corresponding legislation of the country of destination shall apply, but in respect of shipments to which no such enactments are compulsorily applicable the terms of the said convention shall apply.
>
> (b) Trades where Hague-Visby Rules apply: in trades where the International Brussels Convention 1924 as amended by the protocol signed at Brussels on 23 February 1968 – the Hague-Visby Rules – apply compulsorily, the provisions of respective legislation shall apply to this Bill of Lading.
>
> (c) The carrier shall in no case be responsible for loss of or damage to cargo howsoever arising prior to the loading into and after discharge from the Vessel or while the cargo is in the charge of another Carrier, nor in respect of deck cargo or live animals.'

[22] Having set out that typical example of a general paramount clause, Thomas J continued:

> 'There appear to be some very minor variations in the wording of several of the clauses that have been put before me. However each of the clauses described as "the general paramount clause" has the following essential terms: (1) if the Hague Rules are enacted in the country of shipment, then they apply as enacted; (2) if the Hague Rules are not enacted in the country of shipment, the corresponding legislation of the country of destination applies or, if there is no such legislation, the terms of the Convention containing the Hague Rules apply; (3) if the Hague-Visby Rules are compulsorily applicable to the trade in question, then the legislation enacting those rules applies.
>
> . . .
>
> Thus, on the evidence before me I am satisfied that shipping men would have understood "the general paramount clause" to have referred to a clause with the essential features which I have spelt out. Applying the terms of that clause to the circumstances of this case, it is clear on

what is common ground as to the applicable legislation at the ports of shipment and destination, that the Hague Rules apply.'

[23] This is a decision as to what is meant by the phrase 'general paramount clause' and identifies the essential features of such a clause. It does not directly address the question of what is meant by 'the Hague Rules . . . as enacted in the country of shipment', a question which did not arise as neither the country of shipment (Mauritania) nor the country of destination (Japan) had enacted either the Hague or Hague-Visby Rules. However, Thomas J's statement as to the essential features of a 'general paramount clause' was made in the context of standard clauses which expressly draw a distinction between the Hague Rules and trades where the Hague-Visby Rules apply. That would suggest a general understanding that the first part of the clause would not be effective to incorporate the Hague-Visby Rules, for which separate provision was necessary.

[24] *Seabridge Shipping AB v AC Orsleff's Eftf's A/S* [1999] 2 Lloyd's Rep 685, [2000] 1 All ER (Comm) 415 was another charterparty case where the same question arose. The charter incorporated a 'Paramount Clause' but without identifying its terms. Thomas J held that there was no reason to depart from the approach of the majority of the Court of Appeal in *The Agios Lazaros*. In particular, the facts that the Hague-Visby Rules had since been brought into force in the United Kingdom (on 23 June 1977 – the 1971 Act was not yet in force when *The Agios Lazaros* and *The Bukhta Russkaya* were decided) and that this was a case where the country of shipment (Poland) had enacted the Hague-Visby Rules did not justify a different approach, not least because the legislation did not apply to charterparties.

[25] The decision in this case therefore affirms the continuing application of the approach in *The Agios Lazaros* case despite the changes brought about by the intervening years.

[26] The principal case relied on by Mr Thomas is *The Happy Ranger* [2002] 1 All ER (Comm) 176, [2001] 2 Lloyd's Rep 530 at first instance. The contract of carriage contained a general paramount clause which provided as follows:

> 'General paramount clause
>   The Hague Rules contained in the International Convention for the Unification of certain rules relating to Bills of Lading, dated Brussels 25 August 1924, as enacted in the country of shipment shall apply to this contract. When no such enactment is in force in the country of shipment, Articles I to VIII of the Hague Rules shall apply. In such case the liability of the Carrier shall be limited to £100 – sterling per package.
>   Trades where Hague-Visby Rules apply
>   In trades where the International Brussels Convention 1924 as amended by the Protocol signed at Brussels on 23 February 1968 – the Hague-Visby Rules – apply compulsorily, the provisions of the respective legislation shall be considered incorporated in this Bill of Lading. . . .'

[27] This was similar to the BIMCO clause considered by Thomas J in *The Bukhta Russkaya*, save for the exclusion of art IX of the Hague Rules when not enacted in the country of shipment. The contract was for carriage from Italy, which had enacted the Hague-Visby Rules. Accordingly it might have been expected that the effect of the 1971 Act would be that the Hague-Visby Rules would apply compulsorily. However, Tomlinson J held that this was not so because the contract of carriage was not a bill of lading or similar document of title within the meaning of the 1971 Act. Accordingly the Rules would only apply if incorporated by contract. The Claimant cargo interests contended (see 19 of the judgment) that 'the version of the Hague Rules enacted in Italy is the Hague-Visby Rules so that those rules are applicable pursuant to the first sentence of cl 3', while the Defendant shipowners' argued (see 21) that the Hague-Visby Rules were not the Hague Rules as enacted in Italy. That was said to be so 'not only because of the various important differences between the two codes but also because, as they contend, the wording of cl 3 itself draws a clear distinction between enactment of the Hague Rules and enactment of [the] Hague-Visby Rules.'

[28] Tomlinson J held that the Hague and not the Hague-Visby Rules were applicable, saying at 31:

> 'I also reject the argument that the Hague-Visby Rules are to be regarded as the Hague Rules "as enacted" in Italy so as to be incorporated by reason of the first limb of clause 3 of the specimen bill of lading. Quite apart from the important differences between the two codes, in the first two sub-clauses of clause 3 a clear distinction is drawn between the Hague and the Hague-Visby Rules and their enactment. Italy has repealed its enactment of the Hague Rules and has enacted the Hague-Visby Rules. That is not the situation to which the first sub-clause of clause 3 refers.'

[29] The point that repeal of the Hague Rules and enactment of the Hague-Visby Rules was not within the first paragraph of the clause appears to contain at least an echo of the argument which did not find favour with Colman J in *The Marinor*.

[30] When the case reached the Court of Appeal ([2002] EWCA Civ 694, [2002] 2 Lloyd's Rep 357), the arguments appear to have been different. The cargo Claimants no longer suggested that the first sentence of the clause ('The Hague Rules . . . as enacted in the country of shipment') referred to the Hague-Visby Rules. Instead they contended that the Hague-Visby Rules applied by virtue of the second part of the clause in that case, referring to trades where the Hague-Visby Rules applied. That argument was rejected as a matter of construction: the majority (Tuckey and Aldous LJJ, Rix LJ dissenting) held that the second part of the clause only operated when the Hague-Visby Rules applied compulsorily, which would only be the case when there was a bill of lading or similar document of title. However, reversing Tomlinson J, all three members of the court held that there was such a bill in this case and therefore the Hague-Visby Rules did apply compulsorily. It did not matter, therefore, whether the clause purported to apply the Hague or Hague-Visby Rules. It is nevertheless of interest that Tuckey LJ said at 11 'The Hague Rules are not enacted in Italy so the first sentence of the first paragraph of cl 3 of the bill is not applicable.'

[31] Although strictly this point did not arise for decision in view of the fact that the shipowners' reliance on this part of the clause as a route to the application of the Hague-Visby Rules was no longer pursued, this constitutes a clear statement of the position for which Mr Thomas contends in the present case.

[32] *The MSC Amsterdam* [2007] EWCA Civ 794, [2008] 1 All ER (Comm) 385, [2007] 2 Lloyd's Rep 622 was another bill of lading case, but the terms of the relevant clause were materially different from the clause in the present case.

Decision

[33] In circumstances where the Hague-Visby Rules are widely applied all over the world and have been enacted by legislation in many countries, I would be inclined to hold that the expression 'the Hague Rules contained in the International Convention for the Unification of certain rules relating to Bills of Lading, dated Brussels 25 August 1924 as enacted in the country of shipment . . . ' is capable of referring to the Hague-Visby Rules, and (as submitted by Mr Goldstone) that they do so refer in the absence of any contrary indication in the clause. Such a contrary indication would include a distinction drawn elsewhere in the clause between the Hague and Hague-Visby Rules, as in the BIMCO clause and the clause considered in *The Happy Ranger*. However, there is no such distinction in the clause in the present case.

[34] The Hague-Visby Rules are in fact an amended version of the Hague Rules. The 1968 Protocol by which they were agreed was described as a 'Protocol to Amend the International Convention for the Unification of Certain Rules of Law Relating to Bills of Lading ('Visby Rules') (Brussels, 23 February 1968)' and went on to identify the amendments rather than to enact an entirely new code. I would see no real difficulty, if the point were free of authority, in holding that the version of the Hague Rules which is enacted in the country of shipment in the present case is the Hague-Visby Rules, with the consequence that those

Rules apply not just as a result of the compulsory application of the 1971 Act but also as a matter of contract. It appears that in the United States the Second Circuit Court of Appeals has taken a similar view: *The Seijin* 124 F3d 132 (1997).

[35] It would seem odd that in a case where English law applies and the parties must be taken to have known that the Hague-Visby Rules would therefore apply compulsorily to a shipment from Belgium, a clause which provides for the application of the Hague Rules as enacted in the country of shipment would be construed as an agreement for the Hague and not the Hague-Visby Rules to apply. Because the Hague-Visby Rules do apply compulsorily anyway, the parties must have realised that a contractual choice of the Hague Rules would be largely ineffective. It would therefore seem implausible to attribute to them such a contractual choice. I would, moreover, be inclined to agree with Colman J in *The Marinor* that it should make no difference to the application of the clause whether the legislative technique adopted in the country of shipment was to amend the existing Hague Rules legislation in the same way as the 1968 Protocol does or to repeal that legislation and enact the Hague-Visby Rules.

[36] However, the point is not free from authority. While in theory the cases reviewed above can all be distinguished as being concerned with different clauses (in particular, clauses which unlike the present case do draw an express distinction between the Hague and Hague-Visby Rules) or with the meaning of a phrase such as 'clause paramount' in a charterparty where no specific clause is identified, I do not think that this would be a valid ground of distinction. The decision of Tomlinson J in *The Happy Ranger* is a decision that the language of the present clause is not apt to refer to the Hague-Visby Rules, while Tuckey LJ's statement in the Court of Appeal is to the same effect. Even if not strictly binding, these are highly persuasive statements and I should follow them, supported to some degree as they are by the charterparty cases to which I have referred.

[37] I conclude, therefore, that the clause paramount at cl 2 of the bill of lading constitutes a contractual agreement that the Hague Rules shall apply, albeit one which the parties must have realised would be largely ineffective in the present case.

Note

It might of course be doubted whether in the fast-moving world of commercial shipping, an approach that is so dependent on an inquiry into the factual matrix is useful. Would it be economically efficient to rely on the production of extraneous evidence (such as the practice and understanding of 'shipping men') to explain and construe the clause paramount?

7 The terms of the contract: Relevant rules of construction

A subject which has become of much significance and relevance in recent times is how the terms contained in the bill of lading should be construed or interpreted. The general starting point is the oft-cited proposition that the bill of lading, like any other commercial contract, should be construed in a commercial sense to give effect to the presumed intention of the parties.

Homburg Houtimport BV v Agrosin Private Ltd, The Starsin [2003] UKHL 12; [2003] 1 Lloyd's Rep 571

Lord Bingham: 9. When construing a commercial document in the ordinary way the task of the court is to ascertain and give effect to the intentions of the contracting parties. Here, the task is to ascertain who, on one side, the contracting party was. But a similar approach is appropriate. Mr Milligan urged that the House should not seize on a single canon of construction and give it effect to the exclusion of all others. I am sure that warning is salutary. But there are a number of rules, some of very long standing, which give valuable guidance.

10. First is the rule to which Lord Halsbury alluded in *Glynn v Margetson & Co* [1893] AC 351 at 359, 'that a business sense will be given to business documents'. The business sense is that which businessmen, in the course of their ordinary dealings, would give the document. It is likely to be a reasonably straightforward sense since, as Lord Mansfield famously observed (*Hamilton v Mendes* (1761) 2 Burr 1198 at 1214, 97 ER 787 at 795),

> 'The daily negotiations and property of merchants ought not to depend upon subtleties and niceties; but upon rules, easily learned and easily retained, because they are the dictates of common sense, drawn from the truth of the case.'

In the present case, the suggestion that CPS contracted jointly on its own behalf and on behalf of the shipowner loses credibility when one notes that this possibility, although not objectionable in legal principle, first occurred to a member of the Court of Appeal during argument: [2001] 1 Lloyd's Rep 437 at 452, para 75.

11. Secondly, it is common sense that greater weight should attach to terms which the particular contracting parties have chosen to include in the contract than to pre-printed terms probably devised to cover very many situations to which the particular contracting parties have never addressed their minds. It is unnecessary to quote the classical statement of this rule by Lord Ellenborough in *Robertson v French* (1803) 4 East 130 at 136; 102 ER 779 at 782, cited with approval by Lord Halsbury in *Glynn v Margetson* [1893] AC 351 at 358 and by Scrutton LJ in *In re an Arbitration between L Sutro & Co and Heilbut, Symons & Co* [1917] 2 KB 348 at 361-2.

12. Thirdly, it has long been recognised by very distinguished commercial judges that to seek perfect consistency and economy of draftsmanship in a complex form of contract which has evolved over many years is to pursue a chimera: see, for example, *Simond v Boydell* (1779) 1 Dougl 268; 99 ER 175; *James Nelson & Sons Ltd v Nelson Line (Liverpool) Ltd* [1908] AC 16 at 20–21; *Hillas & Co Ltd v Arcos Ltd* (1932) 43 Ll. L. Rep 359 at 367; *Chandris v Isbrandtsen-Moller Co Inc* [1951] 1 KB 240 at 245. The court must of course construe the whole instrument before it in its factual context, and cannot ignore the terms of the contract. But it must seek to give effect to the contract as intended, so as not to frustrate the reasonable expectations of businessmen. If an obviously inappropriate form is used, its language must be adapted to apply to the particular case: The Okehampton [1913] P 173 at 180, per Hamilton LJ.

13. Fourthly,

> 'In all mercantile transactions the great object should be certainty: and therefore, it is of more consequence that a rule should be certain, than whether the rule is established one way or the other. Because speculators in trade then know what ground to go upon': *Vallejo v Wheeler* (1774) 1 Cowp 143 at 153; 98 ER 1012 at 1017.

This observation is, I suggest, particularly pertinent where the issue is one which, like that now under consideration, has been the subject of repeated litigation over the years in cases which have included *The Berkshire* [1974] 1 Lloyd's Rep 185; *The Venezuela* [1980] 1 Lloyd's Rep 393; *The Rewia* [1991] 2 Lloyd's Rep 325; *MB Pyramid Sound MV v Briese Schiffahrts GmbH (The Ines)* [1995] 2 Lloyd's Rep 144; *Sunrise Maritime Inc v Uvisco Ltd (The Hector)* [1998] 2 Lloyd's Rep 287; and *Fetim BV v Oceanspeed Shipping Ltd (The Flecha)* [1999] 1 Lloyd's Rep 612. In his accomplished extempore judgment in the last of these cases, on a form of bill and on facts indistinguishable from the present, Moore-Bick J concluded that the contract of carriage was made with the owners of the vessel and not with CPS, a decision which Colman J declined to follow in the present case.

In the construction of a bill of lading, like any other commercial contract, the Supreme Court has stressed the importance of using the relevant factual matrix to help ascertain the commercial sense of the contract. The following case provides a useful summary of the relevant principles of construction of contracts including a round-up of some of the most important authorities on the matter.

Rainy Sky SA and others v Kookmin Bank [2011] UKSC 50

Lord Clarke (with whom Lord Phillips, Lord Mance, Lord Kerr and Lord Wilson agree): **14.** For the most part, the correct approach to construction of the Bonds, as in the case of any contract, was not in dispute. The principles have been discussed in many cases, notably of course, as Lord Neuberger MR said in *Pink Floyd Music Ltd v EMI Records Ltd* [2010] EWCA Civ 1429; [2011] 1 WLR 770 at para 17, by Lord Hoffmann in *Mannai Investment Co Ltd v Eagle Star Life Assurance Co Ltd* [1997] AC 749, passim, in *Investors Compensation Scheme Ltd v West Bromwich Building Society* [1998] 1 WLR 896, 912F-913G and in *Chartbrook Ltd v Persimmon Homes Ltd* [2009] 1 AC 1101, paras 21–26. I agree with Lord Neuberger (also at para 17) that those cases show that the ultimate aim of interpreting a provision in a contract, especially a commercial contract, is to determine what the parties meant by the language used, which involves ascertaining what a reasonable person would have understood the parties to have meant. As Lord Hoffmann made clear in the first of the principles he summarised in the Investors Compensation Scheme case at page 912H, the relevant reasonable person is one who has all the background knowledge which would reasonably have been available to the parties in the situation in which they were at the time of the contract.

15. The issue between the parties in this appeal is the role to be played by considerations of business common sense in determining what the parties meant. Sir Simon Tuckey said at para 19 of his judgment that there was no dispute about the principles of construction and the Bank so submitted in its skeleton argument. However, I do not think that is quite correct.

16. At para 18 Sir Simon identified the question of construction substantially as set out in para 9 above and said at para 19:

> 'There is no dispute about the principles of construction to be applied in order to answer this question. The court must first look at the words which the parties have used in the bond itself. The shipbuilding contract is of course the context and cause for the bond but is nevertheless a separate contract between different parties. If the language of the bond leads clearly to a conclusion that one or other of the constructions contended for is the correct one, the Court must give effect to it, however surprising or unreasonable the result might be. But if there are two possible constructions, the Court is entitled to reject the one which is unreasonable and, in a commercial context, the one which flouts business common sense. This follows from the House of Lords decisions in *Wickman Machine Tools Sales Limited v Schuler AG* [1974] AC 235, where at 251 Lord Reid said: "The fact that a particular construction leads to a very unreasonable result must be a relevant consideration. The more unreasonable the result, the more unlikely it is that the parties can have intended it, and if they do intend it the more necessary it is that they shall make that intention abundantly clear" and *The Antaios* [1984] AC 191, where at 201 Lord Diplock said: "If detailed and syntactical analysis of words in a commercial contract is going to lead to a conclusion that flouts business common sense it must yield to business common sense."'

17. As I read his judgment, Patten LJ did not put the question in quite the same way. This can be seen from paras 35 to 44 of his judgment. At para 35 he referred to Sir Simon Tuckey's approach at para 19 (as quoted above). He also referred to para 18(iii) of the Judge's judgment, where the Judge described the Bank's construction of the Bond as having the surprising and uncommercial result of the guarantee not being available to meet the Builder's repayment obligations in the event of insolvency. Patten LJ noted that the Judge appeared to have taken that into account as a factor in favour of the Buyers' construction of paragraph [3] of the Bonds. Patten LJ added that the Judge's approach was the same as that of Sir Simon Tuckey.

18. Patten LJ then referred to the cases mentioned above and expressed his conclusion in principle thus at para 42:

> 'In this case (as in most others) the Court is not privy to the negotiations between the parties or to the commercial and other pressures which may have dictated the balance of interests which the contract strikes. Unless the most natural meaning of the words produces a result which is so extreme as to suggest that it was unintended, the Court has no alternative but to give effect it its terms. To do otherwise would be to risk imposing obligations on one or other party which they were never willing to assume and in circumstances which amount to no more than guesswork on the part of the Court.'

19. Finally, at paras 43 and 44, Patten LJ quoted from the speeches of Lord Wilberforce in *Prenn v Simmonds* [1971] 1 WLR 1381, 1384–5 and of Lord Hoffmann in *Chartbrook* at para 20, where they discussed the reason for the rule excluding evidence of pre-contractual negotiations. In particular they stressed the irrelevance of the parties' subjective intentions and noted that the mere fact that a term in the contract appears to be particularly unfavourable to one party or the other is irrelevant. As Lord Hoffmann put it, the term may have been agreed in exchange for some concession made elsewhere in the transaction or it may simply have been a bad bargain.

20. I entirely accept those caveats. However, it seems to me to be clear that the principle stated by Patten LJ in para 42 is different from that stated by the Judge in his para 18(iii) and by Sir Simon Tuckey in para 19. It is not in my judgment necessary to conclude that, unless the most natural meaning of the words produces a result so extreme as to suggest that it was unintended, the court must give effect to that meaning.

21. The language used by the parties will often have more than one potential meaning. I would accept the submission made on behalf of the appellants that the exercise of construction is essentially one unitary exercise in which the court must consider the language used and ascertain what a reasonable person, that is a person who has all the background knowledge which would reasonably have been available to the parties in the situation in which they were at the time of the contract, would have understood the parties to have meant. In doing so, the court must have regard to all the relevant surrounding circumstances. If there are two possible constructions, the court is entitled to prefer the construction which is consistent with business common sense and to reject the other.

22. This conclusion appears to me to be supported by Lord Reid's approach in Wickman quoted by Sir Simon Tuckey and set out above. I am of course aware that, in considering statements of general principle in a particular case, the court must have regard to the fact that the precise formulation of the proposition may be affected by the facts of the case. Nevertheless, there is a consistent body of opinion, largely collated by the Buyers in an appendix to their case, which supports the approach of the Judge and Sir Simon Tuckey.

23. Where the parties have used unambiguous language, the court must apply it. This can be seen from the decision of the Court of Appeal in *Co-operative Wholesale Society Ltd v National Westminster Bank plc* [1995] 1 EGLR 97. The court was considering the true construction of rent review clauses in a number of different cases. The underlying result which the landlords sought in each case was the same. The court regarded it as a most improbable commercial result. Where the result, though improbable, flowed from the unambiguous language of the clause, the landlords succeeded, whereas where it did not, they failed. The court held that ordinary principles of construction applied to rent review clauses and applied the principles in *The Antaios (Antaios Compania Naviera SA v Salen Rederierna AB)* [1985] AC 191. After quoting the passage from the speech of Lord Diplock cited above, Hoffmann LJ said, at p 98:

'This robust declaration does not, however, mean that one can rewrite the language which the parties have used in order to make the contract conform to business common sense. But language is a very flexible instrument and, if it is capable of more than one construction, one chooses that which seems most likely to give effect to the commercial purpose of the agreement.'

24. The court also comprised Leggatt and Simon Brown LJJ. Simon Brown LJ at p 101 said that, having regard to the improbable result for which the landlords contended, only the most unambiguous of such clauses could properly be found to bear the landlords construction and that in the case of only one of the leases did the clause 'unambiguously . . . achieve the improbable result for which the landlords contend'. The case is of interest because Simon Brown LJ considered that, of the other three cases, one unambiguously failed to achieve the result sought by the landlords, whereas, of the other two, he said this at p 102:

'For my part, I would accept that the more obvious reading of both favours the landlord's construction. I am persuaded, however, that they are capable of being, and therefore, for the reasons already given, should be, construed differently.'

That case is therefore an example of the adoption and application of the principle endorsed by the Judge and by Sir Simon Tuckey. See also *International Fina Services AG v Katrina Shipping Ltd, The Fina Samco* [1995] 2 Lloyd's Rep. 344, where Neill LJ said at page 350 it was necessary when construing a commercial document to strive to attribute to it a meaning which accords with business common sense.

25. In 1997, writing extra-judicially ('Contract Law: Fulfilling the reasonable expectations of honest men') in 113 LQR 433, 441 Lord Steyn expressed the principle thus:

'Often there is no obvious or ordinary meaning of the language under consideration. There are competing interpretations to be considered. In choosing between alternatives a court should primarily be guided by the contextual scene in which the stipulation in question appears. And speaking generally commercially minded judges would regard the commercial purpose of the contract as more important than niceties of language. And, in the event of doubt, the working assumption will be that a fair construction best matches the reasonable expectations of the parties.'

I agree. He said much the same judicially in *Society of Lloyd's v Robinson* [1999] 1 All ER (Comm) 545, 551:

'Loyalty to the text of a commercial contract, instrument, or document read in its contextual setting is the paramount principle of interpretation. But in the process of interpreting the meaning of the language of a commercial document the court ought generally to favour a commercially sensible construction. The reason for this approach is that a commercial construction is likely to give effect to the intention of the parties. Words ought therefore to be interpreted in the way in which a reasonable commercial person would construe them. And the reasonable commercial person can safely be assumed to be unimpressed with technical interpretations and undue emphasis on niceties of language'.

26. Similar assistance is at hand nearer at home. In *Gan Insurance Co Ltd v Tai Ping Insurance Co Ltd* [2001] CLC 1103, 1118–1119; [2011] EWCA Civ 1047; [2001] 2 All ER (Comm) 299, Mance LJ said:

'**13.** Construction, as Sir Thomas Bingham MR said in *Arbuthnott v Fagan* [1995] CLC 1396 at p 1400 is thus "a composite exercise, neither uncompromisingly literal nor unswervingly purposive". To para (5), one may add as a coda words of Lord Bridge in *Mitsui Construction Co Ltd v A-G of Hong Kong* (1986) 33 BLR 14, cited in my judgment in *Sinochem International Oil (London) Ltd v Mobil Sales and Supply Corp* [2000] CLC 878 at p 885. Speaking of a poorly drafted and ambiguous contract, Lord Bridge said that poor drafting itself provides: "no reason to depart from the fundamental rule of construction of contractual documents that the intention of the parties must be ascertained from the language that they have used interpreted in the light of the relevant factual situation in which the contract was made. But the poorer the quality of the drafting, the less willing the court should be to be driven by semantic niceties to attribute to the parties an improbable and unbusinesslike intention, if the language used, whatever it may lack in precision, is reasonably capable of an interpretation which attributes to the parties an intention to make provision for contingencies inherent in the work contracted for on a sensible and businesslike basis." . . . 16 . . . in my judgment the subclause has no very natural meaning and is, at the least, open to two possible meanings or interpretations – one the judge's, the other that it addresses two separate subject-matters. In these circumstances, it is especially important to undertake the exercise on which the judge declined to embark, that is to consider the implications of each interpretation. In my opinion, a court when construing any document should always have an eye to the consequences of a particular construction, even if they often only serve as a check on an obvious meaning or a restraint upon adoption of a conceivable but unbusinesslike meaning. In intermediate situations, as Professor Guest wisely observes in *Chitty on Contracts* (28th edn) vol 1, para. 12–049, a "balance has to be struck" through the exercise of sound judicial discretion.'

27. More generally, in *Homburg Houtimport BV v Agrosin Private Ltd: The Starsin* [2004] 1 AC 715, para 10 Lord Bingham referred to

'the rule to which Lord Halsbury LC alluded in *Glynn v Margetson & Co* [1893] AC 351, 359, 'that a business sense will be given to business documents. The business sense is that which businessmen, in the course of their ordinary dealings, would give the document.'

28. Three other cases merit brief reference. The same approach was adopted by Arden LJ in *In the Matter of Golden Key Ltd (In Receivership)* [2009] EWCA Civ 636, paras 29 and 42 and by this Court in *In Re Sigma Finance Corporation (in administrative receivership)* [2009] UKSC 2; [2010] 1 All ER 571, where Lord Mance said at para 12 that the resolution of an issue of interpretation in a case like the present was an iterative process, involving checking each of the rival meanings against other provisions of the document and investigating its commercial consequences.

29. Finally, it is worth setting out two extracts from the judgment of Longmore LJ in *Barclays Bank plc v HHY Luxembourg SARL* [2010] EWCA Civ 1248; [2011] 1 BCLC 336, paras 25 and 26:

'**25.** The matter does not of course rest there because when alternative constructions are available one has to consider which is the more commercially sensible. On this aspect of the matter Mr Zacaroli has all the cards. . . .

26. The judge said that it did not flout common sense to say that the clause provided for a very limited level of release, but that, with respect, is not quite the way to look at the matter. If a clause is capable of two meanings, as on any view this clause is, it is quite possible that neither meaning will flout common sense. In such circumstances, it is much more appropriate to adopt the more, rather than the less, commercial construction.'

30. In my opinion Longmore LJ has there neatly summarised the correct approach to the problem. That approach is now supported by a significant body of authority. As stated in a little more detail in para 21 above, it is in essence that, where a term of a contract is open to more than one interpretation, it is generally appropriate to adopt the interpretation which is most consistent with business common sense. For these reasons I prefer the approach of the Judge and Sir Simon Tuckey to that of Patten LJ, which is to my mind significantly different on this point.

8 Whose contract? Identifying the carrier

Bills of lading do not always clearly identify the party who contracts to carry and deliver the goods. The problem of identifying the contracting carrier can be acute where bills of lading are issued to shippers for goods that are loaded on a chartered ship. In English law a contracting carrier need not necessarily be the performing carrier or, to put the point another way, a contract to carry and deliver is not invariably a contract to carry and deliver personally. The result is that a bill of lading for goods on a chartered ship may show a contract with either the shipowner or the charterer or possibly with both.

Shipowners and charterers may have their own views on what arrangement makes the most sense. They might agree that the charterer will find the shippers but that the shipowner will issue the bills of lading: this arrangement is common in time chartering. On the other hand, a charterer may wish to contract with shippers in its own name: a liner service, for example, that happens to make use of chartered tonnage from time to time, may want to use the line's standard terms and conditions and to issue bills of lading in its own name to all its customers. But whatever a shipowner and charterer may agree between themselves, matters may look quite different from the perspective of a shipper.

If the parties have not made their intentions clear, the general approach in English courts is to ask first if the charter is by demise. Where the charter is by demise, possession of the vessel will pass to the charterer and the master will normally be an employee/agent of the charterer, but not the shipowner. Goods loaded on the ship will normally be in the possession of the demise charterer and a bill of lading signed by the master will normally show a contract with the demise charterer. In the case of any other form of charter, possession of the vessel and the goods carried will be in the owner, the master will normally be the employee/agent of the owner and a bill of lading signed by the master will normally show a contract with the shipowner.

Sandeman v Scurr (1866) LR 2 QB 86

Facts: The defendants were owners of the ship *the Village Belle*. The ship was chartered to a Mr Hodgson to load from the charterer's agents at Oporto a full cargo of wine for carriage to a safe port in the United Kingdom. The cargo was to be loaded and discharged at the merchant's risk and expense. The captain was to 'sign bills of lading at any rate of freight, without prejudice to the charter'. The claim was for damage caused by bad stowage to goods shipped by the plaintiffs.

Held:

Cockburn CJ: . . . The ship accordingly proceeded to Oporto, consigned to the agents of the charterer. She was by them put up as a general ship, but without it being at all made known that the vessel was under charter. The plaintiffs delivered their goods on board without any knowledge that the ship was not entirely at the disposition of the owner. Bills of lading for the goods in question were signed by the master in the usual form. The cargo was stowed by stevedores employed and paid by the charterer's agents, but the amount so paid by the latter was repaid to them by the master.

The goods having been damaged by reason of improper stowage, the plaintiffs have brought their action against the defendants, as owners of the vessel; and the question is whether the defendants, under the circumstances stated, are liable. We are of opinion that they are liable, and that the action against them lies.

On the argument, it was contended on behalf of the defendants, that, as the use of the ship had been made over to Hodgson, the charterer, and the ship had been put up as a general ship by his agents, and the bill of lading had been given by the captain in furtherance of a contract for freight of which the charterer was to have the benefit, the captain must be considered as having given the bill of lading as the agent of the charterer, and the contract as having been made with the latter, and not with the defendants, the owners of the vessel; and that, consequently, the charterer was alone responsible for the negligent stowing of the goods in question.

It is unnecessary to decide whether the charterer would or would not have been liable, if an action had under the circumstances been brought against him. Our judgment proceeds on a ground, wholly irrespective of the question of the charterer's liability, and not inconsistent with it, namely, that the plaintiffs, having delivered their goods to be carried in ignorance of the vessel being chartered, and having dealt with the master as clothed with the ordinary authority of a master to receive goods and give bills of lading on behalf of his owners, are entitled to look to the owners as responsible for the safe carriage of the goods.

The result of the authorities, from *Parish v Crawford* (1746) 2 Strange 1251 downwards, and more especially the case of *Newberry v Colvin* (1832) 1 Cl & F 283, in which the judgment of the Court of Exchequer Chamber, reversing the judgment of the Court of Queen's Bench, was affirmed on appeal by the House of Lords, is to establish the position, that in construing a charterparty with reference to the liability of the owners of the chartered ship, it is necessary to look to the charterparty, to see whether it operates as a demise of the ship itself, to which the services of the master and crew may or may not be superadded, or whether all that the charterer acquires by the terms of the instrument is the right to have his goods conveyed by the particular vessel, and, as subsidiary thereto, to have the use of the vessel and the services of the master and crew.

In the first case, the charterer becomes for the time the owner of the vessel, the master and crew become to all intents and purposes his servants, and through them the possession of the ship is in him. In the second, notwithstanding the temporary right of the charterer to have his goods loaded and conveyed in the vessel, the ownership remains in the original owners, and through the master and the crew, who continue to be their servants, the possession of the ship also. If the master, by the agreement of his owners and the charterer, acquires authority to sign bills of lading on behalf of the latter, he nevertheless remains in all other respects the servant of the owners; in other words, he retains that relation to his owners out of which by the law merchant arises the authority to sign bills of lading by which the owner will be bound.

It appears to us clear that the charterparty in the present instance falls under the second of the two classes referred to. There is here no demise of the ship itself, either express or implied. It amounts to no more than a grant to the charterer of the right to have his cargo brought home in the ship, while the ship itself continues, through the master and crew, in the possession of the owners, the master and crew remaining their servants.

It is on this ground that our judgment is founded. We think that so long as the relation of owner and master continues, the latter, as regards parties who ship goods in ignorance of any arrangement whereby the authority ordinarily incidental to that relation is affected, must be taken to have authority to bind his owner by giving bills of lading. We proceed on the well known principle that, where a party allows another to appear before the world as his agent in any given capacity, he must be liable to any party who contracts with such apparent agent in a matter within the scope of such agency. The master of a vessel has by law authority to sign bills of lading on behalf of his owners. A person shipping goods on board a vessel, unaware that the vessel has been chartered to another, is warranted in assuming that the master is acting by virtue of his ordinary authority, and therefore acting for his owners in signing bills of lading. It may be that, as between the owner, the master, and the charterer, the authority of the master is to sign bills of lading on behalf of the charterer only, and not of the owner. But, in our judgment, this altered state of the master's authority will not affect the liability of the owner, whose servant the master still remains, clothed with a character to which the authority to bind his owner by signing bills of lading attaches by virtue of his office. We think that until the fact that the master's authority has been put an end to is brought to the knowledge of a shipper of goods, the latter has a right to look to the owner as the principal with whom his contract has been made ...

Notes

1   In this extract the Chief Justice referred to an agreement that the master would sign bills of lading on behalf of the charterer. It is more common today to find agreements authorising the charterer, or the charterer's agent, to sign bills as agent for the master or the shipowner. In *The Rewia* [1991] 2 Lloyd's Rep 325, the Court of Appeal held that a bill of lading signed for a master could not be a charterer's bill unless the contract was made with the charterer alone and the person signing had authority to sign and did sign on behalf of the charterer and not the owners.

2   The usual assumption in the case of a chartered ship is that the contracting carrier is either the owner or a charterer. Cockburn CJ hints in this extract that in some circumstances both might be liable, an idea that was said in *The Starsin*, below, to be 'unobjectionable in legal principle', but which has not been developed in decided cases.

3   Demise clauses. The original aim of these clauses (see an example below, in the extract from *The Starsin*) was to ensure that time charterers, who could not claim the protection of the legislation limiting the liability of shipowners, would not be held liable as carriers: (1990) 106 LQR 403, *per* Lord Roskill. The right to limit liability was, as the law then stood, only available to a shipowner or demise charterer. The right to limit liability was extended to time charterers in 1958. Nevertheless demise clauses continued to be included in bills of lading and were treated as effective in English courts: *The Berkshire* [1974] 1 Lloyd's Rep 185; *The Vikfrost* [1980] 1 Lloyd's Rep 560; *The Jalamohan* [1988] 1 Lloyd's Rep 443. The decision of the House of Lords in *The Starsin* now leaves little future for these clauses in liner shipping, unless perhaps they are printed prominently on the front of a bill of lading and do not contradict other statements that appear there. However, see also the recent case of *Golden Endurance Shipping SA v RMA Watanya SA* [2014] EWHC 3917 (Comm) where the judge said: 'But it is clear from the very passages from their Lordships' speeches cited that *The Starsin* was in no way a decision that the content of the first page of a bill of lading should be preferred to the content of the reverse page. In this case the Conditions of Carriage are set out clearly and legibly on the reverse of the Bill. There is no need for anyone to cross-refer to the content of the relevant edition of those standard terms in order to cross-check them. It is only if somebody either already knows the contents of that edition by heart or takes the trouble so to check, that the inconsistency will appear, and the very words of Lord Steyn emphasise the speed of international trade and the natural choice of the reader to trust what is written in the bill rather than to wade through small print, particularly small print which is not even contained in the bill itself. I am entirely satisfied that, construing the Bill of Lading in a business sense, the conditions which are incorporated are those which are set out in the Bill, rather than those which are said to be incorporated by a reference on the top left hand corner of the first page.'

4   Further reading: Pejovic, C, 'The identity of carrier problem under time charters' (2000) J Mar L & Com 379 (a comparative treatment).

Makros Hout BV v Agrosin Private Ltd, The Starsin
[2003] UKHL 12; [2003] 1 Lloyd's Rep 571

Facts: The defendants' vessel *The Starsin* was time chartered to Continental Pacific Shipping, who operated a liner service from the Far East to Europe. Timber and plywood arrived seriously damaged by fresh water. The plaintiffs were purchasers and receivers of the cargo and sued the shipowners on the bill of lading contracts (for tort claims, see Chapter 2). The bills of lading were issued on printed forms bearing the name and logo of Continental Pacific Shipping. The printed form was designed to be signed by the master and to create a contract with the shipowner, but the bills were in fact signed by agents 'As Agent for Continental Pacific Shipping (The Carrier)'. On the back of the bills, 'in barely legible tiny print', the terms included a clause dealing with the identity of the carrier (cl 33) and a demise clause (cl 35). Continental Pacific Shipping had authority to issue bills on behalf of the shipowners. The shipowners argued that the carriage contracts had been entered into by the charterers, who had become insolvent. The cargo owners claimed that the bills were contracts with the shipowners. The shipowners pointed out that where written words or clauses are added to a printed form, *prima facie* the added words have greater effect than printed ones. The cargo owners responded that parties were free to stipulate in printed conditions that written provisions added to a printed form were not to prevail over printed terms.

The terms printed on the bills of lading provided:

> **1** DEFINITIONS . . . (c) 'Carrier' means the party on whose behalf this Bill of Lading has been signed . . .

> **33** IDENTITY OF CARRIER The contract evidence by this Bill of Lading is between the merchant and owner of the vessel . . . and . . . the . . . shipowner only shall be liable for any damage . . . arising out of the contract of carriage . . .

> **35** If the ocean vessel is not owned or chartered by demise to the company or line by whom this Bill of Lading is issued (as may be the case notwithstanding anything that appears to the contrary) this Bill of Lading shall take effect only as a contract of carriage with the owner . . . as principal made through the agency of the said company or line who act solely as agent and shall be under no personal liability whatsoever . . .

Held:

Lord Bingham: [6] The first and most crucial issue between the parties on these appeals is whether the contracts to carry these various parcels of cargo were made by or on behalf of the shipowner, as the cargo owners contend, or by or on behalf of CPS, the charterers of the vessel, as the shipowner contends. Put another way, the question is whether these were shipowner's bills or charterer's bills . . .

[14] . . . [A] very cursory glance at the face of the bill is enough to show that the master has not signed the bill. It has instead been signed by agents for CPS which is described as 'The Carrier'. I question whether anyone engaged in maritime trade could doubt the meaning of 'carrier', a term of old and familiar meaning, but any such doubt would be quickly resolved by resort to the first condition overleaf in which the term is defined to mean the party on whose behalf the bill of lading has been signed, that is, the party contracting to carry the goods . . .

[15] I can well understand that a shipper or transferee of a bill of lading would recognise the need to consult the detailed conditions on the reverse of the bill in any one of numerous contingencies which might arise and for which those conditions make provision. He would appreciate that the rights and obligations of the parties under the contract are regulated by those detailed conditions. But I have great difficulty in accepting that a shipper or transferee of a bill of lading would expect to have to resort to the detailed conditions on the reverse of the bill (and to persevere in trying to read the conditions until reaching conditions 33 and 35) in order to discover who he was contracting with. And I have even greater difficulty in accepting that he would expect to do so when the bill of lading contains, on its face, an apparently clear and unambiguous statement of who the carrier is . . . I am further fortified in taking this view of market practice by noting its adoption (since 1994) in the ICC Uniform Customs and Practice for Documentary Credits . . . Article 23(v) makes plain that banks will not examine terms and conditions on the back of the bill of lading. The ICC's Position Paper No 4 reiterates that the name of the carrier must appear as such on the front of the bill and that banks will not examine the contents of the terms and conditions of carriage . . .

[17] I would note, lastly on this point, that the decision of the Court of Appeal majority has not earned the approval of some academic commentators expert in this field . . .

[18] I agree with these opinions and would hold, in agreement with Colman J and Rix LJ, and for essentially the reasons which they gave, that the bill contained or evidenced a contract of carriage made with CPS as carrier.

Lord Hoffmann: [80] . . . The construction given to the bill of lading must be objective and uniform and, in the case of the identity of the carrier, determined by an unequivocal statement on the face of the document . . .

[85] . . . I think that if the carrier is plainly identified by the language on the front of the document, one never gets to the demise clause on the back.

Lord Hobhouse: [128] In my judgment the salient fact is that the signatures contradict the form. The signature is not neutral or equivocal, nor, for that matter is the form. Where the (original) parties . . . have expressly agreed that Container Pacific Shipping [sic] shall be the contracting party, they have implicitly agreed that inconsistent clauses will be overriden. The special words, typed or stamped, placed in the signature box demonstrate a special agreement. Effect must be given to that agreement. The contracts contained in these bills of lading are contracts with Continental Pacific Shipping . . .

[129] There are two observations to make about this conclusion. The first is that 'shipped on board' bills of lading . . . will normally have been preceded by some anterior contract . . . However, there is no evidence or finding on this aspect so it cannot assist either side on the appeal. The second observation is that the claimants are subsequent holders of the bills of lading by endorsement. Their contractual rights must be ascertained by reference to the bill of lading document itself.

Note

The works cited in para 17 of Lord Bingham's judgment were Debattista, C, 'Is the end in sight for chartering demise clauses' (2001) Lloyd's List 5; Gaskell, N et al, *Contracts for the Carriage of Goods by Land, Sea and Air*, Yates, D (Editor in Chief), London: Lloyds of London; Girvin, S and Bennett, H, 'English Maritime Law 2000' (2001) LMCLQ 76. The decision is considered in Girvin, S, 'Himalaya clauses and tort in the House of Lords' (2003) LMCLQ 311.

9 A contractual right under the bill of lading to demand delivery of goods

A person who is a party to the contract of carriage contained in, or evidenced by, the bill of lading is contractually entitled to delivery of the goods on board on presentation of the bill of lading. Under s 2 of the Carriage of Goods by Sea Act 1992 (infra), it therefore follows that if the carrier does not deliver the goods to a lawful consignee or indorsee of the bill of lading, he would be in breach of the contract contained in or evidenced by the bill of lading.

Consequently, where a lawful holder of the bill is a transferee of rights of suit against the carrier pursuant to COGSA 1992, s 2(1), and the bill provides, as it usually will, that the carrier will deliver to the presenter of the bill, the carrier is in breach of the contract contained in, or evidenced by, the bill of lading if he refuses to deliver the goods and has no contractual justification for doing so.

Motis Exports Ltd v Dampskibsselskabet AF 1912 Aktieselskab; Aktieselskabet Dampskibsselskabet Svendborg [1999] 1 Lloyd's Rep 837 (affirmed by the Court of Appeal in [2000] 1 Lloyd's Rep 211)

Facts: Goods were carried from Hong Kong to certain ports in West Africa. The goods were delivered to rogues who had used forged bills of lading to take delivery of the goods. The contract of carriage was represented by liner bills of lading issued by Maersk.

The issue was whether the carriers were liable for the loss of the goods after discharge from their vessel, where the cause of the loss was the use of forged bills of lading to obtain delivery orders in respect of and thus delivery of the goods at the discharge ports.

Rix J held that the carriers had caused a misdelivery. A forged bill of lading was in the eyes of the law a nullity; it was simply a piece of paper with writing on it, which had no effect whatever. That being so the delivery of the goods was not in exchange for the original bill but for a worthless piece of paper. The Court of Appeal agreed. For our purposes, it is Rix J's judgment which is of interest.

Held:

Rix J:

Contract

One must start with the nature of a bill of lading contract, irrespective of any special clauses like cl. 5.3.b. It is of the essence of such a contract that a shipowner is both entitled and bound to deliver the goods against production of an original bill of lading, provided he has no notice of any other claim or better title to the goods: see Glyn Mills Currie & Co. *v* East and West India Dock Co., (1882) 7 App. Cas. 591, *The Stettin*, (1889) 14 P.D. 142, *Carlberg v Wemyss*, 1915 S.C. 616 at p. 624, *Sze Hai Tong Bank Ltd. v Rambler Cycle Co. Ltd.*, [1959] 2 Lloyd's Rep. 114; [1959] A.C. 576, *Barclays Bank Ltd. v Commissioners of Customs and Excise*, [1963] 1 Lloyd's Rep. 81, and most recently *The Houda*, [1994] 2 Lloyd's Rep 541, see especially at pp. 550, 552–553 and 556. As Lord Denning said in *Sze Hai Tong Bank v Rambler Cycle* at p. 120, col. 1; p. 586:

It is perfectly clear law that a shipowner who delivers without production of the bill of lading does so at his peril. The contract is to deliver, on production of the bill of lading, to the person entitled under the bill of lading. In this case it was 'unto order or his or their assigns,' that is to say, to the order of the Rambler Cycle Company, if they had not assigned the bill of lading, or to their assigns, if they had. The shipping company did not deliver the goods to any such person. They are therefore liable for breach of contract unless there is some term in the bill of lading protecting them. And they delivered the goods, without production of the bill of lading, to a person who was not entitled to receive them. They are therefore liable in conversion unless likewise so protected.

In *The Houda* Lord Justice Neill put it in this way (at p. 550):

'The case for the owners is based on the general principle that once a bill of lading has been issued only a holder of the bill can demand delivery of the goods at the port of discharge. It is because of the existence of this principle that a bill of lading can be used as a document of title so that the transfer of the document transfers also the right to demand the cargo from the ship at discharge.'

Lord Justice Leggatt said this (at p. 553):

'Under a bill of lading contract a shipowner is obliged to deliver goods upon production of the original bill of lading. Delivery without production of the bill of lading constitutes a breach of contract even when made to the person entitled to possession . . .

It is an incident of the bill of lading contract that delivery is to be effected only against the bill of lading.'

Lord Justice Millett explained the matter as follows (at p. 556):

'A bill of lading is not only a potential contract for the carriage of goods, it is also a negotiable receipt for the cargo. Once the master has signed a bill of lading and parted with it, he has subjected the shipowners to a contractual obligation, enforceable at the suit of any person to whom the bill of lading has been negotiated, to deliver the cargo to that person . . .

Conversely the master takes an obvious risk if he delivers the goods without production of the bill of lading. He does not obtain a good discharge unless the person to whom he delivers is the person entitled to them, and he has no means of satisfying himself that he is the person entitled except he produce the bill of lading. In a case like the present, where bills of lading have been signed in triplicate, the others to be void when one is accomplished, he has no means of defending himself against a later claimant who produces a copy of the bill of lading unless he has obtained a copy himself from the person to whom he delivered the goods.'

To this line of authority Mr. Dunning objects that it does not take account of the situation where the goods have been delivered against a bill of lading, but, unfortunately, a forged one. That the rule requiring a bill of lading is not a universal rule without exception is, he submits, illustrated by the following dicta. In *The Sormovskiy 3068* Mr. Russell's submission on behalf of cargo recognized 'exceptional circumstances' (at p. 270), and Mr. Justice Clarke himself accepted the possibility of such exceptions (at p. 272), although they were unspecified. Mr. Berry's submission on behalf of the ship (at p. 270) cited *Barclays Bank Ltd. v Commissioners of Customs and Excise*, [1963] 1 Lloyd's Rep. 81 at p. 89 for an exception where the bill of lading's absence 'has been satisfactorily accounted for'. That submission likewise was accepted by Mr. Justice Clarke at p. 272, in these terms:

'. . . I would add the following fourth proposition. Subject to the particular terms of the contract concerned (which may and often does include a provision whereby the master is to deliver the cargo in return for a letter of indemnity), a master or shipowner is not entitled to deliver goods otherwise than against an original bill of lading unless it is proved to his reasonable satisfaction both that the person seeking the goods is entitled to possession of them and that there is some reasonable explanation of what has become of the bills of lading.'

So also, Mr. Justice Clarke developed his view as to the general rule and the exception to it in this passage (at p. 274):

'It makes commercial sense to have a simple rule that in the absence of an express term of the contract the master must only deliver the cargo to the holder of the bill of lading who presents it to him. In that way both the shipowners and the persons in truth entitled to possession of the cargo are protected by the terms of the contract.

Where the master or shipowner delivers the cargo in breach of contract otherwise than in return for an original bill of lading the person entitled to possession will of course only be entitled to recover substantial damages if he proves that he has suffered loss and damage as a result. So for example if the cargo is delivered to the person entitled to possession he will not ordinarily be able to show that he has suffered a loss.

In trades where it is difficult or impossible for the bills of lading to arrive at the discharge port in time the problem is met by including a contractual term requiring the master to deliver the cargo against a letter of indemnity or bank guarantee. That is commonplace and indeed there was a provision to that effect here. The simple rule to which I have referred does require some exceptions because the bill of lading might have been lost or stolen. In order to cater for that problem it is no doubt necessary to imply a term that the master must deliver cargo without production of an original bill of lading in circumstances where it is proved to his reasonable satisfaction both that the person seeking delivery of the goods is entitled to possession and what has become of the bills of lading. The precise nature of the exceptions will no doubt require further consideration in the future.'

The Sormovskiy 3068 does not appear to have been cited to the Court of Appeal in *The Houda*: be that as it may, it would seem that the Court of Appeal did not consider this exception to exist. Thus the case where delivery is made to the true owner in the absence of a bill of lading was explained by Lord Justice Leggatt in the following terms (at p. 553):

'Delivery without production of the bill of lading constitutes a breach of contract even when made to the person entitled to possession . . .

It is necessarily implicit in the power to order the issue of bills of lading which make the goods deliverable 'to order' that the obligation is accepted to deliver to the holder upon production of the bill of lading. It is an incident of the bill of lading contract that delivery is to be effected only against the bill of lading. It is nothing to the point that if there were no bill of lading contract the time charterer could give a lawful order to deliver with which the master would be obliged to comply. In my judgment delivery to a time charterer entitled to possession without production of the bill of lading is a breach of the bill of lading contract.

In practice, if the bill of lading is not available, delivery is effected against an indemnity. Where the bill of lading is lost, the remedy, in default of agreement, is to obtain an order of the Court that on tendering a sufficient indemnity the loss of the bill of lading is not to be set up as a defence. Clause 50 provides expressly that, if the master complies with the charterer's orders to deliver goods without presentation of bills of lading, the owners are indemnified by the charterers. In default of production of the bill of lading an indemnity is afforded to the shipowner not on account of the lawfulness of the order to deliver but so as to protect him if he does what he is not contractually obliged to do.'

It seems to me that the judgment of Lord Justice Neill similarly approves what he calls the 'simple working rule' that delivery without production of a bill of lading is at the shipowner's peril (at p. 552). He cites (at p. 550) the passage from *Barclays Bank v Commissioners of Excise* as being consistent with the following clear statement of principle from Lord Johnson's judgment in *Carlberg v Wemyss*, 1915 S.C. 616 at p. 624 –

'A shipowner is not bound to deliver goods except in exchange for the bill of lading. He is not bound to take on trust that he knows the consignee and that no intermediate rights had been created . . . Neither the owner, his agent, nor the master can, I think, be called upon to accept a banker's or any other guarantee of an indemnity, though such a thing is not unknown, and in the event of total loss of the bill of lading might have to be resorted to, if necessary at the sight of the court.'

There is, it seems to me, no support there, at any rate not without the intervention of the Court, for the concept that a shipowner can be obliged to deliver not against a bill of lading but against a reasonable explanation of its loss. Lord Justice Millett is to similar effect (at p. 558):

> 'But the real difficulty of the Judge's conclusion is that it leads to this: the charterers can lawfully require the shipowners to deliver the cargo without presentation of the bills of lading if, but only if, the person to whom the cargo is to be delivered is in fact entitled to receive it. If that is indeed the law, it places the master in an intolerable dilemma. He has no means of satisfying himself that it is a lawful order with which he must comply, for unless the bills of lading are produced he cannot know for certain that the person to whom he has been ordered to deliver the cargo is entitled to it. One solution, no doubt, is that, since the master's duty is not one of instant obedience but only of reasonable conduct, he can delay complying with the order for as long as is reasonably necessary to satisfy himself that the order is lawful, possibly by obtaining the directions of the Court in the exercise of its equitable jurisdiction to grant relief in the case of lost bills.
>
> But in my judgment the charterers are not entitled to put the master in this dilemma . . .'

In my judgment a true owner cannot in the absence of some special arrangement oblige a shipowner to deliver his goods to him without presenting his bill of lading: either he must have agreed in his contract with the shipowner that an indemnity will suffice, or he must persuade the shipowner to deliver against an indemnity, or he must seek the assistance of the Court. In practice, a suitable indemnity will be likely to satisfy the shipowner, all the more so where the goods owner has a reasonable explanation for the absence of his bill of lading. The upshot is that in my judgment the exception which Mr. Dunning seeks to derive from *The Sormovskiy 3068* does not exist.

The question remains whether a forged bill of lading is as good as a genuine bill of lading for the purposes of the 'simple working rule'. The question only has to be asked, to make it seem unlikely that the answer will be in the positive.

I suppose the question can be asked in two forms. First, is a shipowner entitled to deliver against a forged bill of lading? Second, can a shipowner be obliged to deliver against a forged bill of lading? Mr. Dunning is interested in the former question, but the answer must make sense in both cases. Clearly, if the forgery is known or suspected, or if the shipowner is on notice of the possibility of forgery, the answer to both questions must be 'No', nor would Mr. Dunning seek to submit otherwise.

Let me suppose, however, that the forgery could not reasonably be detected. Can a shipowner be obliged to deliver against such a bill? It seems impossible to think that he can. He may of course be deceived, but if he obstinately refuses, despite his ignorance of the deception, to deliver against the forged bill, can he be liable for that refusal to the holder of the forged bill? It cannot be. He may have acted in ignorance, but he did right. An analogy can be made with a paying bank faced with a forged cheque. If the bank refuses to pay, knowing of the forgery, it obviously acts rightly. If the bank refuses to pay, ignorant of the forgery, it cannot by means of its ignorance be turned into a wrongdoer. It is justified in its refusal by the fact of forgery.

Now suppose that the question is whether the shipowner is entitled to deliver, that is to say has a defence in delivering, against a forged bill, in ignorance of the forgery? If that is so, it can only be by reason of an implied term. It is hard to think, however, that it is necessary to imply such a term. It would favour the shipowner at the expense of the true owner of the goods. It would subvert the rule that a bill of lading is the key to the warehouse. Certainly no true owner would think that such an implication would be reasonable. It is wrong to imply a term unless it is both reasonable and necessary. The fact is that the law does not in general protect those who act on forgeries, but rather those whose true title is attacked by forgery. Thus, a paying bank which debits its customer, even in the absence of any negligence by the bank, on a forged cheque must repay its customer; it has acted beyond its mandate: see the Bills of Exchange

Act, s. 24 and *National Westminster Bank v Barclays Bank*, [1975] 1 Q.B. 664 at p. 666, *Barclays Bank Ltd. v W.J. Simms Son & Cooke (Southern) Ltd.*, [1980] Q.B. 677 at p. 699. Thus a forgery is regarded in general as a nullity: see *Ruben v Great Fingall Consolidated Ltd.*, [1906] A.C. 439.

In the last case a share certificate was fraudulently issued by the secretary of a company: it was accepted in good faith by a third party as security for the advance of moneys; nevertheless it did not bind the company and was regarded as a nullity. Lord Macnaghten said (at p. 444):

> 'Every statement in the document is a lie. The only real thing about it is the signature of the secretary of the company, who was the sole author and perpetrator of the fraud. No one would suggest that this fraudulent certificate could of itself give rise to any right or bind or effect the company in any way. It is not the company's deed.'

That shows that the company was not obliged to recognize the certificate as its own. Similarly, where a company was induced by a forged transfer to deregister a true owner of shares and to issue a certificate in favour of a fraudster, it cannot claim to be free of liability to the true owner, even though it can claim an indemnity against the presenter of the forged instrument: see *Sheffield Corporation v Barclays*, [1905] A.C. 392. So, it seems to me, a shipowner is not free to release goods on the basis of a forged bill of lading, but may be able to claim an indemnity.

I do not think that the question turns on a matter of policy, but in any event I would agree with the submission of Mr. Meeson that policy favours the same answer. If a shipowner was entitled to deliver goods against a forged bill of lading, then the integrity of the bill as the key to a floating warehouse would be lost. Moreover, as between shipowner and true goods' owner, it is the shipowner who controls the form, signature and issue of his bills, even if as a matter of practice he may delegate much of that to his time charterers or their agents. If one of two innocent people must suffer for the fraud of a third, it is better that the loss falls on the shipowner, whose responsibility it is both to look to the integrity of his bills and to care for the cargo in his possession and to deliver it aright, rather than on the true goods' owner, who holds a valid bill and expects to receive his goods in return for it.

In my judgment, therefore, it is no defence to a shipowner or to the defendants in this case, innocently to be deceived by production of a forged bill of lading into release of cargo. When the proper bill of lading is produced, he has no defence. He cannot say: I have already delivered the goods without production of the original bill of lading. Nor does it avail him to say: although I have already delivered the goods without production of the original bill of lading, I did so without negligence in return for a worthless forgery.

Notes

1   Rix J's judgment refers to *The Sormovskiy 3068* where Clarke J characterised the duty of the carrier to deliver the goods, even in the absence of a bill of lading. The judge said: 'In trades where it is difficult or impossible for bills of lading to arrive at the discharge port in time the problem is met by including a contractual term requiring the master to deliver the cargo against a letter or indemnity or bank guarantee. That is common place and indeed there was a provision to that effect here. The simple rule [that in the absence of an express term of the contract the master must only deliver to the holder of the bill of lading] does require some exceptions because the bill of lading might have been lost or stolen. In order to cater for that problem it is no doubt necessary to imply a term that the master must deliver cargo without production of an original bill where it is proved to his reasonable satisfaction both that the person seeking delivery of the goods is entitled to possession and what has become of the bills of lading. The precise nature of the exceptions will no doubt require further consideration in the future.' ([1994] 2 Lloyd's Rep 266, 274.)

2   It seem clear that Clarke J's emphasis was on there being in existence an implied term that could affect the strict express duty of the carrier to deliver against tender of the bill of lading. The nature of the implied term, from Clarke's judgment, was very much one implied by fact as derived from the business efficacy test and not one implied by law. Such an approach, if correct, means that the attendant facts and circumstances of the specific case become highly relevant.

3   The correctness of that approach, however, was doubted by Rix J in *Motis Export*. Rix J considered that such an implied term was inconsistent with *dicta* of the Court of Appeal in *Kuwait Petroleum Corp v I&D Oil Carriers Ltd, The Houda* [1994] 2 Lloyd's Rep 541, CA. He thought, as we see in the excerpt from his judgment above, that a true owner cannot without some special arrangement compel the carrier to deliver the goods to him without production of the bill of lading. Either there should be an indemnity or there should be a court order permitting the carrier to deliver the goods contrary to the contractual duty to insist on the original bill of lading.

4   It is clear thus a letter of indemnity is a useful protective measure for the carrier.

Sze Hai Tong Bank Ltd v Rambler Cycle Co Ltd [1959] AC 576, PC

Facts: Rambler shipped bicycle parts on Glengarry under a bill of lading that provided for delivery to order or assigns. The purchasers of the goods were named as the notify party. After discharge of the goods at Singapore, the carrier's agents (relying on an indemnity agreement with the purchasers and their bank) delivered the goods to the purchasers without insisting on production of the bill of lading. The purchasers could not produce the bill of lading because they had not paid the purchase price and taken up the documents.

Held:

Lord Denning: . . . It is perfectly clear law that a shipowner who delivers without production of the bill of lading does so at his peril. The contract is to deliver, on production of the bill of lading, to the person entitled under the bill of lading. In this case it was 'unto order or his or their assigns', that is to say, to the order of the Rambler Cycle Company, if they had not assigned the bill of lading, or to their assigns, if they had. The shipping company did not deliver the goods to any such person. They are therefore liable for breach of contract unless there is some term in the bill of lading protecting them. And they delivered the goods, without production of the bill of lading, to a person who was not entitled to receive them. They are therefore liable in conversion unless likewise so protected.

In order to escape the consequences of the misdelivery, the appellants say that the shipping company is protected by clause 2 of the bill of lading, which says that:

During the period before the goods are loaded on or after they are discharged from the ship on which they are carried by sea, the following terms and conditions shall apply to the exclusion of any other provisions in this bill of lading that may be inconsistent therewith, viz, '(a) so long as the goods remain in the actual custody of the carrier or his servants' (here follows a specified exception);'(b) whilst the goods are being transported to or from the ship' (here follows another specified exemption); '(c) in all other cases the responsibility of the carrier, whether as carrier or as custodian or bailee of the goods, shall be deemed to commence only when the goods are loaded on the ship and to cease absolutely after they are discharged therefrom'.

The exemption, on the face of it, could hardly be more comprehensive, and it is contended that it is wide enough to absolve the shipping company from responsibility for the act of which the Rambler Cycle Company complains, that is to say, the delivery of the goods to a person who, to their knowledge, was not entitled to receive them. If the exemption clause upon its true construction absolved the shipping company from an act such as that, it seems that by parity of reasoning they would have been absolved if they had given the goods away to some passer-by or had burnt them or thrown them into the sea. If it had been suggested to the parties that the condition exempted the shipping company in such a case, they would both have said: 'Of course not.' There is, therefore, an implied limitation on the clause, which cuts down the extreme width of it: and, as a matter of construction, their Lordships decline to attribute to it the unreasonable effect contended for.

But their Lordships go further. If such an extreme width were given to the exemption clause, it would run counter to the main object and intent of the contract. For the contract, as it seems to their Lordships, has, as one of its main objects, the proper delivery of the goods by the shipping company, 'unto order or his or their assigns', against production of the bill of lading. It would defeat this object entirely if the shipping company was at liberty, at its own will and pleasure, to deliver the goods to somebody else, to someone not entitled at all, without being liable for the consequences. The clause must therefore be limited and modified to the extent necessary to enable effect to be given to the main object and intent of the contract: see *Glynn v Margetson & Co* [1893] AC 351, 357; *GH Renton & Co Ltd v Palmyra Trading Corporation of Panama* [1956] 1 QB 462, 501.

To what extent is it necessary to limit or modify the clause? It must at least be modified so as not to permit the shipping company deliberately to disregard its obligations as to delivery. For that is what has happened here. The shipping company's agents in Singapore acknowledged: 'We are doing something we know we should not do.' Yet they did it. And they did it as agents in such circumstances that their acts were the acts of the shipping company itself. They were so placed that their state of mind can properly be regarded as the state of mind of the shipping company itself. And they deliberately disregarded one of the prime obligations of the contract. No court can allow so fundamental a breach to pass unnoticed under the cloak of a general exemption clause: see *The Cap Palos* [1921] P 458, 471.

The appellants placed much reliance, however, on a case which came before their Lordships' Board in 1909, *Chartered Bank of India, Australia and China v British India Steam Navigation Co Ltd* [1909] AC 369. There was there a clause which said that in all cases and under all circumstances the liability of the company shall absolutely cease when the goods are free of the ship's tackle. The goods were discharged at Penang and placed in a shed on the jetty. Whilst there a servant of the landing agents fraudulently misappropriated them in collusion with the consignees. Their Lordships' Board held that the shipping company were protected by the clause from any liability.

Their Lordships are of opinion that that case is readily distinguishable from the present, as the courts below distinguished it, on the simple ground that the action of the fraudulent servant there could in no wise be imputed to the shipping company. His act was not its act. His state of mind was not its state of mind. It is true that, in the absence of an exemption clause, the shipping company might have been held liable for his fraud, see *United Africa Co Ltd v Saka Owoade* [1955] AC 130. But that would have been solely a vicarious liability. Whereas in the present case the action of the shipping agents at Singapore can properly be treated as the action of the shipping company itself . . . their Lordships will humbly advise Her Majesty that this appeal should be dismissed.

Notes

1   It should, however, be remembered that the letter of indemnity is effective only where it had been properly and validly issued (for example, if the person issuing the letter of indemnity lacks the authority to do so, subject to the agency law principle of ostensible authority (*Pacific Carriers v BNP Paribas* [2004] HCA 35 (Australian High Court)). The letter of indemnity as a contract, also, may not have sufficient clarity in its terms to provide for the sort of protection that the carrier seeks – the commercial interpretation of the instrument is essential (*Farenco Shipping Co Ltd v Daebo Shipping Co Ltd, The Bremen Max* [2009] 1 Lloyd's Rep 81).

2   Exclusion or limitation of liability clauses have also been deployed by carriers to protect themselves against misdelivery of the goods.

Chartered Bank of India, Australia and China v British India Steam Navigation Co Ltd [1909] AC 369, PC

Facts: The bank held, as security for a loan, bills of lading relating to goods carried to Penang on the steamship *Teesta*, one of a line of steamers belonging to British India Steam Navigation. On arrival in Penang, the cargo was delivered overside into lighters and taken to the wharf by landing agents. The goods were taken away by fraud without production of the bills of lading by a representative of the receivers acting in collusion with a representative of the landing agents.

Held:

Lord Macnaghten: ... Both here and in the courts below the respondent company disclaimed all liability, relying on conditions subject to which the bills of lading were expressed to be issued. They are printed at the foot of the bill of lading, and attention is called to them in the body of the bill. The only conditions material in the present case are those intended to be applicable on the arrival of the carrying vessel at the port of destination. They are contained in the following clause:

> The company is to have the option of delivering these goods or any part thereof into receiving ship or landing them at the risk and expense of the shipper or consignee as per scale of charges to be seen at the agent's office, and is also to be at liberty until delivery to store the goods or any part thereof in receiving ship, godown, or upon any wharf, the usual charges therefor being payable by the shipper or consignee. The company shall have a lien on all or any part of the goods against expenses incurred on the whole or any part of the shipment. In all cases and under all circumstances the liability of the company shall absolutely cease when the goods are free of the ship's tackle, and thereupon the goods shall be at the risk for all purposes and in every respect of the shipper or consignee.

On behalf of the respondents the contention was that the obligations they undertook were fulfilled by delivering the goods to the landing agents, and that at any rate their liability ceased when the goods were once 'free of the ship's tackle'.

On the other hand it was said on behalf of the bank that the landing agents were neither the assigns nor the agents of the shippers or consignees, and that the goods had never been delivered in accordance with the bills of lading. As regards the provision for cesser of liability, the suggestion was that it applied only to the interval between the removal of the goods from the ship and their being landed on the quay.

... Now it may be conceded that the goods in question were not delivered according to the exigency of the bills of lading by being placed in the hands of the landing agents, and it may be admitted that bills of lading cannot be said to be spent or exhausted until the goods covered by them are placed under the absolute dominion and control of the consignees. But their Lordships cannot think that there is any ambiguity in the clause providing for cesser of liability. It seems to be perfectly clear. There is no reason why it should not be held operative and effectual in the present case. They agree with the learned Chief Justice that it affords complete protection to the respondent company.

Their Lordships therefore will humbly advise His Majesty that the appeal should be dismissed

Note

There is some debate as to whether there is another defence open to the carrier who has delivered goods without requiring production of the bill of lading. In *The Sormovskiy 3068*,

Clarke J stated: 'where it is proved to [the master's] reasonable satisfaction that the person seeking possession of the goods is entitled to possession of them and that there is some reasonable explanation of what has become of the bills of lading'. However, from Rix J's *dicta* in *Motis Export* and, more recently, Teare J's comments in *The Erin Schulte* [2013] EWHC 808 (Comm), it must be said that the correctness of Clarke J's exception to the strict rule of delivery against bills of lading is to be doubted. It seems more probable that there is only the 'simple rule that, in the absence of an express term of the contract, the master must only deliver the cargo to the holder of the bill of lading who presents it to him'. (Todd, P, 'Bank as Holder under Carriage Of Goods By Sea Act 1992 – *The Erin Schute*' [2013] LMCLQ 276)

10 A carrier is entitled to deliver against production of one original bill

Bills of lading are traditionally issued in sets with a minimum of three originals. This practice originated in the days of sail, when the merchant would retain one copy and would send two others by different vessels in the hope that at least one would arrive. The practice of issuing sets of multiple originals has continued, although there is a clear danger of fraud when a set of originals is separated. Cargo interests, rather than carriers, bear this risk.

Glyn Mills Currie & Co v East and West India Dock Co
(1882) 7 App Cas 591

Facts: Twenty hogsheads of sugar were shipped in Jamaica on the *Mary Jones* and consigned to Cottam & Co in London. The master signed a set of three bills of lading marked 'First', 'Second', and 'Third', respectively, which made the goods deliverable to Cottam & Co, or their assigns, freight payable in London, 'the one of the bills being accomplished, the others to stand void'. During the voyage Cottam & Co endorsed the bill of lading marked 'First' to a bank in consideration of a loan. Upon the arrival of the ship at London the goods were landed and placed in the custody of a dock company in their warehouses. The dock company *bona fide* and without notice or knowledge of the bank's claim delivered the goods to other persons who produced delivery orders signed by Cottam & Co.

Held:

Lord Blackburn: . . . If there were only one part of the bill of lading, the obligation of the master under such a contract would be clear, he would fulfil the contract if he delivered to Cottam & Co on their producing the bill of lading unindorsed; he would also fulfil his contract if he delivered the goods to anyone producing the bill of lading with a genuine indorsement by Cottam & Co. He would not fulfil his contract if he delivered them to anyone else, though if the person to whom he delivered was really entitled to the possession of the goods, no one might be entitled to recover damages from him for that breach of contract. But at the request of the shipper, and in conformity with ancient mercantile usage, the master has affirmed to three bills of lading all of the same tenor and date, the one of which bills being accomplished the others to stand void.

. . . But where the person who produces a bill of lading is one who – either as being the person named in the bill of lading which is not indorsed, or as actually holding an indorsed bill – would be entitled to demand delivery under the contract, unless one of the other parts had been previously indorsed for value to some one else, and the master has no notice or knowledge of anything except that there are other parts of the bill of lading, and that therefore it is possible that one of them may have been previously indorsed, I think the master cannot be bound, at his peril, to ask for the other parts.

... unless this was the practice, the business of a shipowner could not be carried on, unless bills of lading were made in only one part ...

... where the master has notice that there has been an assignment of another part of the bill of lading, the master must interplead or deliver to the one who he thinks has the better right, at his peril if he is wrong. And I think it probably would be the same if he had knowledge that there had been such an assignment, though no one had given notice of it or as yet claimed under it. At all events, he would not be safe, in such a case, in delivering without further inquiry. But I think that when the master has not notice or knowledge of anything but that there are other parts of the bill of lading, one of which it is possible may have been assigned, he is justified or excused in delivering according to his contract to the person appearing to be the assign of the bill of lading which is produced to him ...

(Lord Selborne LC, Lord O'Hagan, Lord Watson and Lord Fitzgerald agreed with Lord Blackburn. Earl Cairns also delivered a judgment in favour of dismissing the appeal.)

Notes

1   The Civil Procedure Rules 1998 provide in Parts 85 and 86 for 'Claims on Controlled and Executed Goods' and 'Stakeholder Applications' respectively. These actions allow the carrier who is faced with competing claims on the goods to seek directions from the court as to the appropriate action to take. These were formerly known as interpleaders.
2   See further in Wilson, J, 'The presentation rules revisited' (1995) LMCLQ 289.

11 The bill of lading as a receipt of cargo

As we have seen, the bill of lading originated as a receipt for the goods shipped. It should contain a statement made by the carrier attesting that he had received certain specified goods into his control.

It is quite clear that busy commercial people would rely largely on the information on the face of the bill of lading to ascertain for themselves that the goods have been shipped according to the agreed terms of carriage. They are unlikely to scrutinise the detailed conditions on the back of the bill of lading. It is therefore important for commercial shipping law to recognise this behaviour of the shipping community.

The law would therefore place a legal bearing on the statements made on the face of the bill of lading. However, the effect of a particular statement would depend on the nature of the statement, its content and the position of the party who may rely on it.

As a receipt of cargo, the bill of lading may be held in law to be evidence of the quantity of goods shipped, the condition and quality of goods, and the date of the bill of lading. At common law, in the shipper's hands, the bill will constitute only *prima facie* evidence of the quantity and quality of goods shipped. That means that the carrier bears the burden of rebutting that presumption. The position is similar where the Hague-Visby Rules apply (see Art III, r 4). In the hands of a transferee of the bill of lading, the statements in the bill of lading may give rise to an estoppel by representation at common law. Hence, where a transferee sues the carrier for short delivery or defective delivery it could rely on the carrier statements in the bill of lading as proof of what was shipped and the condition of the goods shipped. The carrier would be estopped from denying the truth of his representations and statements. Where the Hague-Visby Rules apply, Art III, r 4 states that the bill of lading shall be *prima facie* evidence of the receipt by the carrier of the goods as therein described and proof to the contrary shall not be admissible when the bill of lading has been transferred to a third party acting in good faith.

11.1 Evidence of quantity

At common law a statement in a bill of lading as to quantity ('received, 10 bales of silk') was *prima facie* evidence of the truth of the facts stated: *Smith v Bedouin Steam Navigation* [1896] AC 70. But *prima facie* evidence is capable of being explained and displaced. Under the rule in *Grant v Norway* (1850) 10 CB 665 a shipowner who was able to prove that, in a bill signed by the master, a statement of quantity was incorrect because the goods had never been loaded, could escape liability even to an endorsee of that bill of lading who had purchased the goods in reliance on the statement. The justification for this rule was said to be that it is no part of the duty of a master to sign a bill of lading for goods that both the master and the shipper know or ought to know have not been received, and that everyone dealing with a bill of lading understands this limitation on the master's powers and accepts the risk that a bill of lading may contain an inaccurate and unreliable statement of the quantity. The first part of this justification was correct; the second was not and the rule in *Grant v Norway* was consequently unpopular. Nevertheless, it survived unchanged for most of the last century, even though it made no sense in the context in which it operated and was inconsistent with the general approach taken by English law to the liability of principals for the fraud of their agents. The rule has now been altered by s 4 of the Carriage of Goods by Sea Act 1992 which makes a statement that goods have been received or loaded conclusive evidence in favour of a person who has become the lawful holder of the bill, provided that the bill is signed by the master or some other person with authority to sign from the carrier.

At common law it was also possible to prevent a statement of quantity amounting to *prima facie* evidence by use of a phrase such as 'weight or quantity unknown'. This rule too has been modified by statute: when the Hague-Visby Rules (see Chapter 7, section 7 generally) apply to a contract, then, with exceptions, the carrier must on request issue a bill of lading showing the number of packages or pieces or the quantity or weight as furnished in writing by the shipper.

Attorney-General of Ceylon v Scindia Steam Navigation Co, India [1962] AC 60, PC

Facts: Bills of lading acknowledged receipt of 100,652 bags of rice 'weight, contents and value when shipped unknown' for carriage from Burma to Ceylon. Only 100,417 bags were delivered. The appellants claimed damages.

Held:

Lord Morris of Borth-y-Gest: . . . The first question which arises is whether the plaintiff established that 100,652 bags were shipped at Rangoon for delivery to the Director of Food Supplies at Colombo. The onus of proving that fact undoubtedly rested upon the plaintiff. It was forcibly pointed out by the respondent that the plaintiff had chosen to rely for proof solely upon producing the bills of lading, and that the plaintiff had not traced the bills of lading to their source or supported them by producing and proving mate's receipts and tally men's books. The respondent further submitted that the bills of lading did not yield *prima facie* evidence of the number of bags that had been shipped.

. . . three bills of lading were actually issued. They contained respectively the admissions or acknowledgments that 2,187 bags and 47,992 bags and 50,473 bags 'being marked and numbered as per margin' were shipped. Their Lordships consider that, though these statements in the bills of lading as to the numbers of bags shipped do not constitute conclusive evidence as against the shipowner, they form strong *prima facie* evidence that the stated numbers of bags were shipped unless it be that there is some provision in the bills of lading which precludes this result. Was there, then, any such provision in the present case? There was a condition in the terms: 'weight, contents and value when shipped unknown'. That meant that in signing a bill of lading acknowledging the receipt of a number of bags there was a disclaimer of knowledge in regard to the weight or contents or value of such bags. There was, however, no disclaimer as to the numbers of bags. Their Lordships cannot agree with the view expressed in the judgment of the Supreme Court that the conditions in the bills of lading disentitled the plaintiff from relying upon the admissions that bags to the numbers stated in the bills of lading were taken on board.

The present case differs from *New Chinese Antimony Co Ltd v Ocean Steamship Co Ltd* [1917] 2 KB 664. In that case a bill of lading for antimony oxide ore stated that 937 tons had been shipped on board: in the margin was a typewritten clause: 'A quantity said to be 937 tons', and in the body of the bill of lading (printed in ordinary type) was a clause: 'weight, measurement contents and value (except for the purpose of estimating freight) unknown'. It was held that the bill of lading was not even *prima facie* evidence of the quantity of ore shipped, and that in an action against the shipowners for short delivery the onus was upon the plaintiff of proving that 937 tons had in fact been shipped . . .

In *Hogarth Shipping Co Ltd v Blyth, Greene, Jourdain & Co Ltd* [1917] 2 KB 534 a captain signed a bill of lading for a specified number of bags of sugar: one of the exceptions and conditions of the bill of lading read 'weight, measure, quality, contents and value unknown'. It was held by Lush J that the bill of lading was conclusive only as to the number of bags in the sense of skins or receptacles and not as to their contents.

Even though the plaintiff called no evidence from Rangoon and took the possibly unusual course of depending in the main upon the production of the bills of lading, their Lordships conclude that the bills of lading did form strong *prima facie* evidence that the *SS Jalaveera* had received the stated numbers of bags for shipment to Colombo and delivery to the Director of Food Supplies. (See *Henry Smith & Co v Bedouin Steam Navigation Co Ltd* [1896] AC 70, HL.) The shipowners would, however, be entitled to displace the *prima facie* evidence of the bills of lading by showing that the goods or some of them were never actually put on board: to do that would require very satisfactory evidence on their part. In his speech in the case last cited Lord Halsbury said (page 76):

> To my mind, the cardinal fact is that the person properly appointed for the purpose of checking the receipt of the goods has given a receipt in which he has acknowledged, on behalf of the person by whom he was employed, that those goods were received. If that fact is once established, it becomes the duty of those who attempt to get rid of the effect of that fact to give some evidence from which your Lordships should infer that the goods never were on board at all.

Unless the shipowners showed that only some lesser number of bags than that acknowledged in the bills of lading was shipped then the shipowners would be under obligation to deliver the full number of bags. (See *Harrowing v Katz & Co* (1894) 10 TLR 400, CA; *Hain Steamship Co Ltd v Herdman & McDougal* (1922) 11 Ll L Rep 58 and *Royal Commission on Wheat Supplies v Ocean Steam Ship Co*.)

Though by relying upon the bills of lading the plaintiff presented *prima facie* evidence that 100,652 bags (marked and numbered as in the margins of the bills) were shipped, the bills of lading were not even *prima facie* evidence of the weight or contents or value of such bags. This was the result of the incorporation in the bills of lading of the provision above referred to. (See *New Chinese Antimony Co Ltd v Ocean Steamship Co Ltd*, above.) It was for the plaintiff to prove the contents of the bags and the weight of the bags, and it was for him to prove his loss by proving what it was that the bags contained and by proving what was the value of what the bags contained. The respondent company submitted that such proof was lacking. The respondent company further submitted (a) that there was evidence which displaced the *prima facie* evidence of the shipment of 100,652 bags and which led to the conclusion that there never were 235 missing bags, and (b) that if, alternatively, 100,652 bags were in fact shipped, the evidence showed that all the contents of such bags were discharged at Colombo – with the result that the liability of the respondent company would be limited to the value of 235 empty bags.

In support of the respondent company's submission under (a) above it was urged that it was improbable that 235 bags had been put on board at Rangoon and had then been in some manner removed. It was further urged that inasmuch as the ship sailed directly from Rangoon to Colombo and carried no other cargo than was shipped by the State Agricultural Marketing Board Union of Burma, and that it was not suggested that any rice was retained in the ship's hold after discharge at Colombo, the probabilities were that the number of bags shipped was not 100,652 but 100,417. Their Lordships cannot accept the view that these circumstances are of sufficient weight to displace the *prima facie* evidence of the shipment of 100,652 bags. Nor do their Lordships consider that any useful purpose would be served by speculating as to possible explanations as to what might have happened. It was for the shipowners to explain away their acknowledgment of the number of bags that they had received.

On the basis that 100,652 bags were shipped the evidence clearly established a short delivery of 235 bags. The result of the double tally at the time of discharge was that it was satisfactorily proved that only 100,417 bags were discharged. It was not contended by Mr Michael Kerr, appearing for the respondent company, that the 235 original bags were in fact discharged and were missed in the two tallies at Colombo.

It remains to be considered whether the plaintiff proved the loss that he alleged: linked with the points raised in that issue are those which are involved in the submission of the respondent company referred to under (b) above.

It was for the plaintiff to prove what was in the missing bags. Their Lordships consider that there was abundant evidence that the missing bags contained rice . . . On the assumption that the bags contained rice the next question is whether there was evidence as to their weight. The provision of the bill of lading which has been quoted above expressly precludes any dependence upon the particulars as to weight which were declared by the shipper . . .

In this connection reference may again be made to the decision of Lush J in *Hogarth Shipping Co Ltd v Blyth, Greene, Jourdain & Co Ltd,* above. In his judgment Lush J pointed out that if a certain number of bags had been lost, and if one had to ascertain what was in the bags that were lost, then as a matter of evidence one would almost necessarily infer that the lost bags were bags containing similar goods to those which were not lost . . .

In the present case their Lordships consider that it was shown that there was a short delivery of 235 bags and that such bags had been shipped with rice in them, and that each had weighed approximately 160 lbs . . .

Noble Resources Ltd v Cavalier Shipping Corp, The Atlas [1996] 1 Lloyd's Rep 642

Facts: A cargo of steel billets was loaded in Russia with bills of lading specifying the number of bundles and the weight of the cargo. A second set of bills (switch bills) were prepared with the quantity and weight expressed as being 'unknown'. The charterers (cargo interest) argued that the weight and quantity of billets were less than disclosed in the first set of bills. The issue was whether the bill of lading was *prima facie* evidence of these facts and whether the tally documents were admissible evidence of weight.

Held:

Longmore J: It was accepted law before 1924 that a document acknowledging receipt of a certain quantity of goods constituted prima facie evidence of such receipt, which the carrier would have to displace if he wished to contradict it, *Smith & Co v The Bedouin Steam Navigation Co Ltd* [1896] AC 70; it was also established that a bill of lading which acknowledged a quantity of goods 'said to be' of a certain weight with the additional words 'weight unknown' did not constitute evidence of any particular quantity of goods shipped. *New Chinese Antimony Co Ltd v Ocean Steamship Co Ltd* [1917] 2 KB 664. Mr Jacobs, for cargo-owners, submitted, however:

(1)   that, although he did not rely on the three Russian bills as evidencing a contract of carriage, he could rely on them as receipts and that, since they (and the switch bills) contained no equivalent of 'said to be' but only 'weight unknown', he could rely on the bills as prima facie evidence of the quantity shipped;

(2)   that the effect of the Hague Rules was to make any bill of lading prima facie evidence of quantity shipped, because (i) it was contrary to art. III, r. 3 or r. 8 for shipowners to include or rely on clauses such as 'said to be' or 'weight unknown' and (ii) art. III, r. 4 provided for the statements in the bill to be prima facie evidence.

The first argument is plainly wrong; it is impossible to imagine that the New Chinese Antimony case would have been decided differently if the bill in that case had said merely 'weight unknown'; one has to construe the bill of lading to determine whether it is an unqualified assertion or representation of the shipment of a particular quantity of goods. If the bill of lading provides that the weight is unknown it cannot be an assertion or representation of the weight in fact shipped. Mr Jacobs said the typed figures should prevail over the printed 'weight unknown' but, if the Russian bills are construed as a whole, they must be held to mean that the shipowners are not committing themselves, one way or the other, as to the weight of cargo shipped.

Mr Jacobs' second argument is somewhat more forceful and appears to have been accepted by at least some Federal courts in the United States, see *Spanish American Skin Co v M/S 'Ferngulf'* [1957] AMC 611 and *Westway Coffee Corp v MV 'Netuno'* [1982] AMC 1640. Mr Baker submitted it was not in accordance either with the wording of the Hague Rules themselves or with English law.

Mr Baker is right on both counts. The words of art. III, r. 4, 'Such a bill of lading shall be prima facie evidence of the receipt by the carrier of the goods', refer back to the words of art. III, r. 3:

'the carrier . . . shall . . . issue to the shipper a bill of lading showing . . . (b) Either the number of packages . . . or the quantity, or weight, as the case may be, as furnished in writing by the shipper.'

Do the Russian bills show the number of packages or weight (as furnished in writing by the shipper)? In one sense it can be said they do, because the bills have figures which were in fact provided by the shipper in writing. But if the bills provide 'Weight . . . number . . . quantity unknown' it cannot be said that the bills 'show' that number or weight. They 'show' nothing at all because the shipowner is not prepared to say what the number or weight is. He can, of course, be required to show it under art. III, r. 3 but, unless and until he does so, the provisions of art. III, r. 4 as to prima facie evidence cannot come into effect.

This seems to me to be right as a matter of language but there is authority to the same effect. In *Canada and Dominion Sugar Co Ltd v Canadian National (West Indies) Steamships Ltd* [1947] AC 46 there was a statement in the bill of lading qualifying the words 'apparent good order and condition'. The Privy Council held that there was 'no reason under the rules or otherwise for refusing effect to the bill of lading according to its construction' see p. 57 per Lord Wright. *Attorney-General of Ceylon v Scindia Steam Navigation Co Ltd* [1962] AC 60 is closer on the facts. The bills of lading stated that a number of bags had been shipped 'weight, contents and value when shipped unknown.' The Privy Council held that this clause was not a disclaimer as to the number of bags so that the bills of lading, governed by the Hague Rules, did constitute prima facie evidence of the number of bags shipped. In delivering the advice of the Judicial Committee, however, Lord Morris said (at p. 75):

'the bills of lading were not even prima facie evidence of the weight or contents or value of such bags . . . It was for the plaintiff to prove the contents of the bags and the weight of the bags, and it was for him to prove his loss by proving what it was that the bags contained and by proving what was the value of what the bags contained.'

The plaintiff in fact won by discharging that onus of proof in relation to weight and value, although he was only entitled to rely on the bills as prima facie evidence of the number of bags. Mr Jacobs can say that his point was conceded by Mr Gratiaen QC (see p. 71), but in my opinion Mr Gratiaen's concession was correctly made, cf. Hobhouse J's construction of the words 'number of bags/packages as signed for in the bills of lading' in *The Herroe and Askoe* [1986] 2 Ll Rep 281.

Even the American cases do not appear to speak with one voice, see *Tokio Marine and Fire Insurance Co Ltd v Retla Steamship Co* [1970] 2 Ll Rep 91.

I therefore conclude that neither the Russian bills nor the switch bills constitute prima facie evidence of the number of bundles or quantity shipped and I must look at the underlying facts of shipment without the assistance of any evidentiary presumption. No oral evidence was called; various statements and documents were put in under the Civil Evidence Act 1968. Except in one respect, which I have already mentioned and with which I shall deal in its place, both parties agreed that I could treat such documents as evidence of the truth of their contents subject, of course, to all due reservation about the weight of any such evidence.

11.2 Evidence of quality

It may be reasonable in many cases to expect a carrier to be able to make accurate statements of quantity. But statements about the quality of goods fall into a different category.

Cox, Paterson & Co v Bruce & Co (1886) 18 QBD 147, CA

Facts: A bill of lading signed by the master in respect of a shipment of bales of jute stated that a specified proportion of the bales were marked with particular marks. The marks were an indication of their superior quality. On discharge it was found that the number of bales of superior quality had been overstated. The Court of Appeal first rejected an argument by the endorsee of the bill of lading based on breach of a special term of the contract. The court went on to reject a more general argument based on estoppel.

Held:

Lord Esher MR: . . . it is said that, because the plaintiffs are indorsees for value of the bill of lading without notice, they have another right, that they are entitled to rely on a representation made in the bill of lading that the bales bore such and such marks, and that there is consequently an estoppel against the defendants. That raises a question as to the true meaning of the doctrine in *Grant v Norway* (1851) 10 CB 665. It is clearly impossible, consistently with that decision, to assert that the mere fact of a statement being made in the bill of lading estops the shipowner and gives a right of action against him if untrue, because it was there held that a bill of lading signed in respect of goods not on board the vessel did not bind the shipowner. The ground of that decision, according to my view, was not merely that the captain has no authority to sign a bill of lading in respect of goods not on board, but that the nature and limitations of the captain's authority are well known among mercantile persons, and that he is only authorised to perform all things usual in the line of business in which he is employed. Therefore the doctrine of that case is not confined to the case where the goods are not put on board the ship. That the captain has authority to bind his owners with regard to the weight, condition, and value of the goods under certain circumstances may be true; but it appears to me absurd to contend that persons are entitled to assume that he has authority, though his owners really gave him no such authority, to estimate and determine and state on the bill of lading so as to bind his owners the particular mercantile quality of the goods before they are put on board, as, for instance, that they are goods containing such and such a percentage of good or bad material, or of such and such a season's growth. To ascertain such matters is obviously quite outside the scope of the functions and capacities of a ship's captain and of the contract of carriage with which he has to do. It was said that he ought to see that the quality marks were not incorrectly inserted in the bill of lading. But, apart from the special terms of the contract with regard to the quality marks, with which I have already dealt, I do not think it was his duty to put in these quality marks at all; all he had to do was to insert the leading marks . . .

11.3 Evidence of condition

At common law a statement in a bill of lading of the apparent order and condition in which goods are received by a carrier ('received, 10 bales of silk in apparent good order and condition') is *prima facie* evidence in favour of the shipper. When the bill of lading reaches the hands of a bona fide third party who has given value – a consignee or endorsee of an order bill – the carrier is not ordinarily permitted to deny the truth of this kind of statement. The two cases in this section explain how this conclusion can be justified at common law. But this is far from saying that the carrier who issues a clean bill of lading guarantees that the goods were received in good order. 'Apparent' means no more than apparent on an external inspection: *The Peter der Grosse* (1875) 1 PD 414. The Hague-Visby Rules, when they apply (Chapter 7), oblige a carrier to make a statement as to apparent order and condition, which is treated as *prima facie* evidence in the hands of the shipper: proof to the contrary is not admissible when the bill has been transferred to a third party acting in good faith.

Silver v Ocean Steamship Co Ltd [1930] 1 KB 416, CA

Facts: Frozen eggs were shipped at Shanghai for delivery in London. They were packed in rectangular metal cases which were not protected by padding. The cases were said to have been damaged before loading.

Held:

Scrutton LJ: On May 25 a bill of lading is signed stating that a number of tins are shipped 'in apparent good order and condition'. After issuing such a bill can the ship prove that at that time: (1) the tins were perforated or punctured, or (2) that they were insufficiently packed, or must it be taken that on shipment the tins, so far as reasonable inspection would discover, were not perforated or punctured and were by all reasonable inspection sufficiently packed?

. . . Two questions seem to arise at this stage. First, under the law prior to the Carriage of Goods by Sea Act 1924 [which applied by agreement] a shipowner who received goods which he signed for 'in apparent good order and condition' to be delivered in the like good order and condition, and who delivered them not in apparent good order and condition, had the burden of proving exceptions which protected him for the damage found. The present bill of lading runs 'Shipped in apparent good order and condition for delivery subject to Conditions', etc. Has any difference been made in the old law by this wording? In my opinion no difference has been made. I agree with the view expressed by Wright J in *Gosse Millard v Canadian Government Merchant Marine* [1927] 2 KB 432, on similar words, that there is still an obligation to deliver in the like apparent good order and condition unless the shipowner proves facts bringing him within an exception covering him. Lord Sumner in *Bradley & Sons v Federal Steam Navigation Co* (1927) 27 Ll L Rep 395, 396, appears to express the same view.

The second point of law is this. It has been decided by Channell J in *Compania Naviera Vasconzada v Churchill & Sim* [1906] 1 KB 237 and affirmed by the Court of Appeal in *Brandt v Liverpool, Brazil and River Plate Steam Navigation Co* [1924] 1 KB 575 that the statement as to 'apparent good order and condition' estops (as against the person taking the bill of lading for value or presenting it to get delivery of the goods) the shipowner from proving that the goods were not in apparent good order and condition when shipped and therefore from alleging that there were at shipment external defects in them which were apparent to reasonable inspection. Art III, r 4, of the Carriage of Goods by Sea Act 1924, which says the bill shall be *prima facie* evidence (not *prima facie* evidence only, liable to be contradicted), can hardly have been meant to render the above decisions inapplicable. For the information relates to the shipowner's knowledge; he is to say what is 'apparent', that is, visible by reasonable inspection to himself and his servants, and on the faith of that statement other people are to act, and if it is wrong, act to their prejudice.

I am of opinion that r 4 of Art III, has not the effect of allowing the shipowner to prove that goods which he has stated to be in apparent good order and condition on shipment were not really in apparent good order and condition as against people who accepted the bill of lading on the faith of the statement contained in it. Apparent good order and condition was defined by Sir R Phillimore in *The Peter der Grosse* (1875) 1 PD 414, 420 as meaning that 'apparently, and so far as met the eye, and externally, they were placed in good order on board this ship'. If so, on the *Churchill & Sim* decision (above) the shipowner is not allowed to reduce his liability by proving or suggesting contrary to his statement in the bill that the goods in respect of matters externally reasonably visible were not in good condition when shipped.

Now what was reasonably apparent to the shipowner's servants loading at Shanghai at night but under clusters of electric lights? The ultimate damage was classed by the surveyors as (1) serious damage where the tins were gashed or punctured, damage easily discernible in handling each tin; (2) minor damage, pinhole perforations, which on tins covered with rime were not easily discernible but which were found when the tins were closely examined. I have considered the evidence and I find that the first class of damage was apparent to reasonable examination; the second, having regard to business conditions, was not apparent. The result of this is that the shipowner is estopped against certain persons from proving or suggesting that there were gashes or serious damage when the goods were shipped. He may raise the question whether there was not minor or pinprick damage at that time, but having regard to the small quantity of goods rejected for visible damage I should not estimate the amount of such minor damage at shipment as very high.

Canada and Dominion Sugar Co Ltd v Canadian National (West Indies) Steamship Co Ltd
[1947] AC 46, PC

Facts: The appellants were holders of a bill of lading covering sugar shipped at Demerera on the respondents' steamship *Colborne* for delivery at Montreal. The bill of lading stated that the sugar was 'Received in apparent good order and condition'. But it was also endorsed 'Signed under guarantee to produce ship's clean receipt'. The sugar was found to be damaged on arrival.

Held:

Lord Wright: . . . If the statement at the head of the bill, 'Received in apparent good order and condi-tion', had stood by itself, the bill would have been a 'clean' bill of lading, an expression which means, at least in a context like this, that there was no clause or notation modifying or qualifying the statement as to the condition of the goods. But the bill did in fact on its face contain the qualifying words 'Signed under guarantee to produce ship's clean receipt': that was a stamped clause clear and obvious on the face of the document, and reasonably conveying to any business man that if the ship's receipt was not clean the statement in the bill of lading as to apparent order and condition could not be taken to be unqualified. If the ship's receipt was not clean, the bill of lading would not be a clean bill of lading, with the result that the estoppel which could have been set up by the indorsee as against the shipowner if the bill of lading had been a clean bill of lading, and the necessary conditions of estoppel had been satisfied, could not be relied on. That type of estoppel is of the greatest importance in this common class of commercial transactions; it has been upheld in a long series of authoritative decisions . . . But if the statement is qualified, as in the opinion of their Lordships and the judges of the Supreme Court it was, the estoppel fails . . .

Breffka & Hehnke GMBH & Co KG and others v Navire Shipping Co Ltd and others
[2012] All ER (D) 81

Facts: Steel pipes were shipped on the *MV Saga Explorer* from South Korea to the US. The bill of lading contained the following clauses:

SHIPPED in apparent good order and condition, weight, measures, marks, numbers, quality, con-tents, and value unknown, for carriage to the Port of Discharge . . . to be delivered in the like good order and condition at the aforesaid Port unto Consignees or their Assigns . . . In accepting this Bill of Lading, the Merchant expressly accepts and agrees to all its stipulations on both pages, whether written, printed, stamped or otherwise incorporated as fully as if they were all signed by the Merchant. One original Bill of Lading must be surrendered in exchange for the Goods or delivery order.

RETLA CLAUSE: If the Goods as described by the Merchant are iron, steel, metal or timber prod-ucts, the phrase 'apparent good order and condition' set out in the preceding paragraph does not mean the Goods were received in the case of iron, steel or metal products, free of visible rust or moisture or in the case of timber products free from warpage, breakage, chipping, moisture, split or broken ends, stains, decay or discoloration. Nor does the carrier warrant the accuracy of any piece count provided by the Merchant or the adequacy of any banding or securing. If the Merchant so requests, a substitute Bill of Lading will be issued omitting this definition and setting forth any nota-tions which may appear on the mate's or tally clerk's receipt.

The steel pipes arrived in a rusted condition. It was alleged that the representations about good order and condition had been made fraudulently.

Held:

Simon J: 31. Under s.3(3)(c) of US COGSA, after shipment of the cargo on board the vessel the Master (or his agent) is bound on demand to issue to the shipper a bill of lading showing 'the apparent order and condition of the goods'. [This provision is similar to Art III, r. 3 of the Hague-Visby Rules which applies in England and Wales.]

32. Before he can do that the Master (or his agent) must form an honest and reasonable, non-expert view of the cargo as he sees it and, in particular, as to its apparent order and condition. The Master may ask for expert advice from a surveyor but ultimately it will be a matter of his own judgement on the appearance of the cargo being loaded. See for example *The David Agmashenebeli* [2002] EWHC 104 (Comm), [2003] 1 Lloyd's Rep 92, at 104–6 and *Sea Success Maritime v African Maritime Carriers* [2005] EWHC 1542 (Comm), [2005] 2 Lloyd's Rep 692 at 699.

33. The Bills of Lading in the present case contained a statement on their face that the cargo was shipped 'in apparent good order and condition'. If there had been no RETLA clause, this would amount to a representation of fact which could be relied on as reflecting the reasonable judgement of a reasonably competent and observant master; see *The David Agmashenebeli* (above) at 106 and Carver, *Bills of Lading*, 3rd Ed. §2–006.

34. In the case of *Tokio Marine & Fire Insurance Company Ltd v Retla Steamship Company* [1970] 2 Lloyd's Rep 91 (US 9th Circuit CA), the Court was concerned with construing provisions as to the apparent good order and condition of the cargo and a Rust clause in the following terms:

> The term 'apparent good order and condition' when used in this Bill of Lading with reference to iron, steel or metal products does not mean that the goods when received, were free of visible rust or moisture. If the shipper so requests, a substitute Bill of Lading will be issued omitting the above definition and setting forth any notations which may appear on the mates' or tally clerks' receipts.

35. These are the words used under the heading 'Retla Clause' in the Mate's Receipts in the present case, although the wording of the RETLA clause in the present case is slightly different.

36. In the *Tokio Marine* case there was rust and wetness which was described in the Mate's receipts as 'heavy rusty', 'white rusty', 'rusty', 'heavy flaky rust' and 'wet before loading.' The US 9th Circuit, having referred to the Privy Council case of *Canada and Dominion Sugar Company Ltd v Canadian National Steamships Ltd* [1947] AC 46, held (p.95–96) held that,

> . . . the bills of lading here, 'read fairly as a whole', show that the term 'good order and condition' was qualified by the clause defining the term with respect to iron, steel or metal products.

37. This part of the reasoning is uncontroversial. The conclusion of the Court is more debateable. Having referred to the fact that the Rust clause appeared boldly and capitalised on the bill of lading and to the shippers' express right to request substitute bills setting out any notations in the Mate's receipts; the Court found that there was no affirmative representation by the owners that the pipe was free of rust or moisture when it was received by the carrier. In summary, all surface rust of whatever degree was excluded from the representation of apparent good order and condition.

38. Mr Swaroop (for the Owners) submitted that English law should follow the *Tokio Marine* case in holding that the RETLA clause was not limited to rust which was in some sense, 'minor' or 'superficial.' He drew attention to the inherent ambiguity and uncertainty of such terms; and referred to *Scrutton on Charterparties* where he submitted the case was cited with approval.

39. In the 21st edition, the editors noted (at Artcle 63):

> The practice is now developing of including in the bill of lading a definition of 'good order and condition' which makes it clear that the representation does not imply that the cargo is free from the type of defect which commonly affects the cargo in question, e.g. rust (metal goods) or moisture (timber). There appears to be no reason why these clauses should not be valid: and they do not appear to offend the Hague-Visby Rules.

In the 22nd edition, the editors reframed their view of the law in Article 77 at 8–031,

... wording may clarify (and restrict) the representation being made. Thus, a bill of lading may attest to the apparent good order and condition while including a definition of 'good order and condition' which makes it clear that the representation does not import that the cargo is free from certain defects, often a type of defect that commonly affects the cargo in question, e.g. rust (metal goods) or moisture (timber).

In each of the two editions there is a foot-note reference to the *Tokio Marine* case.

40. For B&H Mr Thomas QC submitted that the RETLA clause did not render the words 'apparent good order and condition' meaningless. The provisions should be read together and each provision given proper effect. To the extent that the RETLA clause was designed to except from liability it should be read restrictively, see for example Aikens and Bools, *Bills of Lading*, 2006 at §4.30 and *Attorney-General of Ceylon v Scindia Steam Navigation Co. Ltd* [1962] AC 60 at 74.

41. He argued that the RETLA clause only excludes (surface) rust which is likely to be found in any normal cargo and which would not detract from its overall quality and affect its merchantability.

42. There would seem to be a number of problems with this formulation, for example: what is the degree of 'surface rust' which falls outside the representation, what is a 'normal' cargo of steel and why is merchantability relevant to the representation by the Master of the carrying vessel?

43. I have come to the following conclusions as to the proper construction of the two provisions in the Bills of Lading.

44. (1) The RETLA clause can and should be construed as a legitimate clarification of what was to be understood by the representation as to the appearance of the steel cargo upon shipment. It should not be construed as a contradiction of the representation as to the cargo's good order and condition, but as a qualification that there was an appearance of rust and moisture of a type which may be expected to appear on any cargo of steel: superficial oxidation caused by atmospheric conditions. The exclusion of 'visible rust or moisture' from the representation as to the good order and condition is thus directed to superficial appearance of a cargo which is difficult, if not impossible, to avoid. It is likely to form the basis of a determination as to whether there has been a further deterioration due to inherent quality of the goods on shipment under s.4(2)(m) of US COGSA, or Article 4(2)(m) of the Hague-Visby Rules.

45. (2) It follows that I reject the Owner's argument, based on the facts of the decision in the *Tokio Marine* case, that the RETLA clause applies to all rust of whatever severity.

46. First, because such a construction would rob the representation as to the good order and condition of the steel cargo on shipment of all effect.

47. Secondly, because of what appears to be a misapprehension as to the nature of the trade. One of the grounds for the decision in the *Tokio Marine* case was that the Rust clause provided that it was always open to the shipper to call for a substitute bill of lading showing the true condition of the cargo as set out in the Mate's Receipt, (see p.961 of the report). However, the objection to this part of the reasoning is that it is highly unlikely that a shipper of cargo would ask for a claused bill of lading reflecting the terms of a Mate's Receipt: rather the contrary, as the present case reveals. The matter has been put in clear and emphatic terms by Professor Michael F Sturley in an article in the 'Journal of Maritime Law and Commerce' (April 2000) pages 245–248.

Some courts, led by the Ninth Circuit in *Tokio Marine* & Fire Insurance Co. V Retla Steamship Co., have nevertheless permitted carriers to include standard clauses in their bills of lading that essentially disclaim all responsibility for the required statement. Although COGS A § 3(8) explicitly prohibits any clause lessening a carrier's liability 'otherwise than as provided in this Act', 'rust clauses' have been justified on the ground that that the shipper had the option of demanding a different bill of lading that did not contain the offending clause. In practice, such a demand would be unlikely, for the typical effect of a rust clause is to permit a seller to ship rusty steel to its customer while still obtaining the 'clean' bill of lading that enable it to be paid under a letter of credit.

. . .

Permitting the carrier to escape liability for the statement of apparent order and condition undermines the Hague Rules' goal of protecting the bill of lading as a commercial document on which third parties can rely. Indeed, one of the principal abuses that the Hague Rules were intended to correct was the carriers' use of 'reservation clauses' to exonerate themselves from responsibility for the description of the goods. Thus the rules required the bill of lading (if one were issued) to include the specified information without reservation unless the exception (found in the proviso to COGSA § 3(3)) applied. A carrier's use of a reservation clause when the exception did not apply would be 'null and void' under COGSA § 3(8).

. . .

The phrase 'on demand of the shipper,' upon which the Retla court relied so heavily, does not alter the carrier's obligation to include the information required by COGSA § 3(3) wherever it does issue a bill of lading.

48. This critical analysis of the *Tokio Marine* case is supported by Professor John F Wilson in *'Carriage of Goods by Sea'* 4th edition at p.131 and by the author of the 4th edition of *'Marine Cargo Claims'*, Professor William Tetley QC, in a highly unfavourable analysis at p.698–9.

49. (3) If the *Tokio Marine* case had been consistently followed since 1970 the advantages of giving similar effect to mercantile clauses in different jurisdictions might have been a reason for following it now. However, although the researches of counsel have not been exhaustive, Professor Sturley's article suggests that the decision has not been consistently followed; and this impression is reinforced by a bulletin issued by the UK P&I Club (221–11/01). After referring to the reason why US Courts have upheld the Retla Clause, the bulletin continues.

However, there remains a risk to Members using such clauses as, whilst some courts in the United States may have upheld the clause, other U.S. courts and courts in other jurisdictions have not. The only safe means of avoiding claims arising from pre-shipment damage is to ensure that the bill of lading is claused to reflect the apparent order and condition of the goods at the time of loading. Failure to properly describe the condition of the cargo leaves the carrier open to allegations of being a party to a misrepresentation, particularly from third-party purchasers of the cargo who have only contracted to do so based on a bill of lading and who have not been shown any pre-shipment survey by the sellers.

The final sentence is both accurate and pertinent.

11.4 Incorrect dating of the bill of lading

The date is a material part of a bill of lading. In the case of a shipped bill of lading, the insertion of a particular date is a representation that the goods have actually been loaded on or before the specified time: *Stumore, Weston & Co v Breen* (1886) 12 App Cas 698. It was held in the next case that the principle on which *Grant v Norway*, above, was based – that a shipowner is not responsible for unauthorised misstatements by the master – does not apply to the way that a bill of lading is dated.

The Saudi Crown [1986] 1 Lloyd's Rep 261

Facts: The plaintiffs agreed to purchase ricebran extract that was to be shipped under bills of lading dated on or before 15 July 1982. Bills were issued, signed by agents for the carrier, dated 15 July, but loading of the cargo was not completed until 26 July. The plaintiffs claimed damages for misrepresentation as to the date when the cargo was loaded and said that if the bills of lading had been correctly dated they would have rejected them. It was submitted that their agents had no authority to ante-date the bills so that the carrier was not liable for their agents' acts.

Held:

Sheen J: [If the agents] were authorized to sign bills of lading on behalf of the shipowners, as is admitted, they must have had authority to insert the name of the place at which and the date on which each bill of lading was issued. It is clearly within the authority of an agent to put the date of issue on a bill of lading. If that agent puts the wrong date on the bill of lading he may do so by mistake or deliberately. It can be assumed that the agent has no actual authority to insert the wrong date on a bill of lading but the question is: can that affect any liability of the principal which may arise from the fact that his agent was acting within the scope of his apparent authority when inserting the wrong date?

. . . The general principle is well known. An innocent principal is civilly responsible for the fraud of his authorizied agent, acting within his authority, to the same extent as if it was his own fraud. See Lord Macnaghten in *Lloyd v Grace Smith and Co* [1912] AC 716 at p 736 . . .

Putting the correct date on a bill of lading is a routine clerical task which does not require any skill. An erroneous date may be inserted negligently or fraudulently. There is nothing on the document to put its recipient on enquiry. The date may or may not be of any materiality. But when it is material, as in this case, it seems to me that great injustice may be done to the innocent third party if he is left to pursue whatever remedy he may have against a person of unknown financial means in some distant land . . .

If the bills of lading had been correctly dated the plaintiffs would have rejected them. In their claim for damages for misrepresentation the plaintiffs are not relying upon the rights of suit which they have by reason of being endorsees of the bills of lading. The complaint made by the plaintiffs is that they were induced to become endorsees by reason of a misrepresentation as to the date when the cargo was loaded. That misrepresentation was made by the agents of the shipowners in the course of their normal duties. It was a fraud committed by the defendants' representatives in the course of their employment . . .

The parties have . . . agreed that if I find in favour of the plaintiffs in respect of their right to claim for loss of opportunity to reject the bills of lading by reason of fraudulent misrepresentation as to the date on which the cargo was shipped the amount of the damages to which the plaintiffs are entitled is £20,967.66. Accordingly I hold that the plaintiffs are entitled to judgment.

Notes

1   The decision in *The Saudi Crown*, and a statement, *obiter*, to the same effect at first instance in *The Starsin* [2000] 1 Lloyd's Rep 85, were followed in *Alimport v Soubert Shipping Co Ltd*

[2000] 2 Lloyd's Rep 447 where an owner's bill of lading was signed on behalf of the master by the time charterer's agent. Cf *The Hector* [1998] 2 Lloyd's Rep 287, p 298.

2 In *Standard Chartered Bank v Pakistan National Shipping Corp (No 2)* [2003] UKHL 43; [2003] 1 Lloyd's Rep 227, *Lalazar* was chartered to carry bitumen in drums from Badar Abbas to Ho Chi Min City by O Ltd, a cif seller and the beneficiary under a letter of credit that required shipment to be effected not later than 25 October. Loading was delayed. By agreement with M, managing director of O Ltd, on 8 November, before the goods had been shipped, PNSC issued bills of lading dated 25 October. In a letter signed by M, O Ltd presented the falsely dated bills of lading to SCB to obtain payment under the letter of credit. SCB paid, but were unable to obtain reimbursement from the issuing bank because of discrepancies in the documents that SCB had not noticed. SCB sued PNSC, O Ltd and M for deceit, alleging that they had all joined in issuing a false bill of lading intending it to be used to obtain payment from SCB. All were held liable. On appeal to the House of Lords, M argued that he was not personally liable because his acts had been those of O Ltd. He was held to be personally liable: 'No one can escape liability for fraud by saying "I wish to make it clear that I am committing this fraud on behalf of someone else"' (*per* Lord Hoffmann). For an analysis of this case, see Parker, B, 'Bills of lading and banker's commercial credits' (2003) LMCLQ 1.

3 Liability of agent to principal. In *Stumore, Weston & Co v Breen*, bills of lading dated 12 and 14 September were signed by the master on 19 September. The House of Lords held that the master was liable in negligence and breach of duty to his owners, who had compensated consignees who had relied on the incorrect date.

12 The bill of lading as a document of title

As we have alluded to earlier, the common law rules dealing with the transfer of bills of lading are derived from the custom of merchants. Custom (and it follows the common law) has established that the bill of lading is a 'symbol of possession'.

> **Pollock & Wright, *Possession in the Common Law* (1888), p. 68:**
> ...The key [and the bill of lading] is not a symbol in the sense of representing the goods, but the delivery of the key [and of a bill of lading] gives the transferee a power over the goods which he had not before, and at the same time is an emphatic declaration (which being by manual act, instead of words, may be called symbolic) that the transferor intends no longer to meddle with the goods.

The leading case on the nature of the bill of lading as a document of title involved competing claims to a single cargo from Holland. A City of London jury of merchants was asked to give a special verdict on specific questions that were put to them. The judgment of the Court of King's Bench on the verdict crystallised, as part of the common law, the mercantile custom identified by the jury.

Lickbarrow v Mason (1794) 5 Term Rep 683

Facts: In 1786, Turing & Son of Middelburg shipped a cargo of corn (beans, according to one report) on the *Endeavour* for delivery at Liverpool. A set of four original bills of lading were signed by the master. The bills were drawn 'unto order or assigns'. Turing kept one bill, sent another with the ship and endorsed the remaining two in blank and forwarded them to the buyer, James Freeman of Rotterdam. Freeman passed the bills to Lickbarrow. Hearing that Freeman, who had not paid cash for the goods, was bankrupt, Turing endorsed the last bill to Mason. On arrival of the *Endeavour* Mason took delivery and sold the goods. It was argued that Turing had lost any right to stop the goods in transit when Freeman passed the bills to Lickbarrow, to whom it was said that title had passed.

Held:

The jury on a special verdict found that (p 685): by the custom of merchants, bills of lading, expressing goods or merchandises to have been shipped by any person or persons to be delivered to order to assigns, have been, and are, at any time after such goods have been shipped, and before the voyage performed, for which they have been or are shipped, negotiable and transferable by the shipper or shippers of such goods to any other person or persons by such shipper or shippers endorsing such bills of lading with his, her, or their name or names, and delivering or transmitting the same so indorsed, or causing the same to be so delivered or transmitted to such other person or persons; and that by such indorsement and delivery, or transmission, the property in such goods hath been, and is transferred and passed to such other person or persons. And that, by the custom of merchants, indorsements of bills of lading in blank, that is to say, by the shipper or shippers with their names only, have been, and are, and may be, filled up by the person or persons to whom they are so delivered or transmitted as aforesaid, with words ordering the delivery of the goods or contents of such bills of lading to be made to such person or persons; and, according to the practice of merchants the same, when filled up, have the same operation and effect, as if the same had been made or done by such shipper or shippers when he, she, or they indorsed the same bills of lading with their names as aforesaid.

13 Intention of the parties

The verdict in *Lickbarrow v Mason* did not say that endorsement and delivery of an order bill of lading always moves the ownership of goods at sea to the endorsee, or if this only happens where the parties so intend. Later cases make the position clear.

Sanders Bros v Maclean & Co (1883) 11 QBD 327

Bowen LJ: The law as to the indorsement of bills of lading is as clear as in my opinion the practice of all European merchants is thoroughly understood. A cargo at sea while in the hands of the carrier is necessarily incapable of physical delivery. During this period of transit and voyage, the bill of lading by the law merchant is universally recognised as its symbol, and the indorsement and delivery of the bill of lading operates as a symbolical delivery of the cargo. Property in the goods passes by such indorsement and delivery of the bill of lading, whenever it is the intention of the parties that the property should pass, just as under similar circumstances the property would pass by an actual delivery of the goods. And for the purpose of passing such property in the goods and completing the title of the indorsee to full possession thereof, the bill of lading, until complete delivery of the cargo has been made on shore to some one rightfully claiming under it, remains in force as a symbol, and carries with it . . . the full ownership of the goods . . .

   The above effect and power belong to any one of the set of original bills of lading which is first dealt with by the shipper . . .

14 Nature of the interest passed

The nature of the interest passed depends on the intention of the parties; property in goods on a ship at sea may pass independently of a bill of lading.

Sewell v Burdick, The Zoe (1884) 10 App Cas 74

Facts: Goods were shipped under bills of lading making them deliverable to the shipper or assigns. Freight was payable at destination. After the goods had arrived and been warehoused the shipper endorsed the bills of lading in blank and deposited them with the defendant bankers as security for a loan. The defendants did not take possession or claim delivery of the goods. The shipowner brought an action against the lender to recover the freight due under the bill of lading. They argued that the endorsement and delivery of a bill of lading necessarily passed the general property in the goods to the defendants, even if this was not what the parties had intended.

The House of Lords held that the endorsement and delivery of a bill of lading did not necessarily move an absolute or general interest in the property in the goods to the endorsee, but only such an interest in the property as the parties intended to transfer. The result was that the passing of an openly endorsed bill of lading to a lender would only impose bill of lading contractual liabilities on the lender under the Bills of Lading Act 1855 (now repealed and replaced by the Carriage of Goods by Sea Act 1992: see below) if and when the latter acquired a general property in the goods by exercising his rights under the pledge.

Held:

> **Lord Selborne LC:** . . . In principle the custom of merchants as found in *Lickbarrow v Mason* (above) seems to be as much applicable and available to pass a special property at law by the indorsement (when that is the intent of the transaction) as to pass the general property when the transaction is, eg one of sale. In principle also there seems to be nothing in the nature of a contract to give security by the delivery of a bill of lading indorsed in blank, which requires more in order to give it full effect, than a pledge accompanied by a power to obtain delivery of the goods when they arrive, and (if necessary) to realise them for the purpose of the security. Whether the indorsee when he takes delivery to himself may not be entitled to assume, and may not be held to assume towards the shipowner, the position of full proprietor, is a different question. But, so long at all events as the goods are *in transitu*, there seems to be no reason why the shipper's title should be displaced any further than the nature and intent of the transaction requires.
>
> **Lord Blackburn:** . . . I think that all the judges below were of opinion that if the right reserved was the general right to the property at law, what was transferred being only a pledge (conveying no doubt a right of property and an immediate right to the possession, so that the transferee would be entitled to bring an action at law against anyone who wrongfully interfered with his right), though 'a' property, and 'a' property against the indorser, passed 'upon and by reason of the indorsement', yet the property did not pass. And I agree with them. I do not at all proceed on the ground that this being an indorsement in blank followed by a delivery of the bill of lading so indorsed, had any different effect from what would have been the effect if it had been an indorsement to the appellants by name.
>
> **Lord Bramwell:** . . . I take this opportunity of saying that . . . the property does not pass by the indorsement, but by the contract in pursuance of which the indorsement is made. If a cargo afloat is sold, the property would pass to the vendee, even though the bill of lading was not indorsed. I do not say that the vendor might not retain a lien, nor that the non-indorsement and non-handing over of the bill of lading would not have certain other consequences. My concern is to shew that the property passes by the contract. So if the contract was one of security – what would be a pledge if the property was handed over – a contract of hypothecation, the property would be bound by the contract, at least as to all who had notice of it, though the bill of lading was not handed over.

Notes

1 Endorsement and delivery of an order bill of lading will not pass a title to the endorsee if the transferee has none to give. Although the verdict in *Lickbarrow* contains the word 'negotiable', a bill of lading is not a negotiable document in the sense in which a bill of exchange is negotiable. It cannot give to the transferee a better title than the transferor has got, but it can by endorsement and delivery give as good a title. 'Negotiable', when used in relation to a bill of lading, means simply transferable. The transferee of the bill can only acquire such interest as the transferor is capable of transferring: *Kum v Wah Tat Bank Ltd* [1971] 1 Lloyd's Rep 439, PC; *The Future Express* [1993] 2 Lloyd's Rep 542, CA, p 547.

2 *Right to possession.* Endorsement and delivery of a bill of lading is capable of passing a right to possession: *The Berge Sisar* [2001] UKHL 17, para 18; [2002] 2 AC 205, although whether it actually has this effect depends on the intention of the parties, objectively ascertained: *P&O Nedlloyd v Utaniko* [2003] EWCA Civ 83, para 41; [2003] 1 Lloyd's Rep 239.

15 Straight bills of lading and sea waybills

The verdict in *Lickbarrow* deals with a bill of lading made out 'unto order or assigns'. What is the position if these magic words are omitted?

CP Henderson & Co v The Comptoir D'Escompte de Paris (1873) LR 5 PC 253

Held:

Sir Robert P Collier: It appears that a bill of lading was made out, which is in the usual form, with this difference, that the words 'or order or assigns' are omitted. It has been argued that, notwithstanding the omission of these words, this bill of lading was a negotiable instrument, and there is some authority at *nisi prius* for that proposition; but, undoubtedly, the general view of the mercantile world has been for some time that, in order to make bills of lading negotiable, some such words as 'or order or assigns' ought to be in them. For the purposes of this case, in the view their Lordships take, it may be assumed that this bill of lading was not a negotiable instrument.

Note

Order, bearer and straight consigned bills. A bill of lading making goods deliverable to a named person 'or order' or 'or order or assigns' is an order bill and is transferable by endorsement and delivery. A bill making goods deliverable to bearer or to '[name left blank] or order' is a bearer bill and can pass from hand to hand by delivery. An order bill endorsed in blank is also treated as a bearer bill. A bill making goods deliverable to a named person only is a straight consigned bill.

A debate that has captured the imagination of many commentators is the status of straight bills of lading. There was a view the straight bills are not proper bills of lading or similar document of title for the purposes of international carriage conventions such as the Hague-Visby Rules or indeed the common law (Art I(b) and COGSA 1971, s 1(4)). A minority academic view, however, took the line that the straight bill of lading is nevertheless a document of title albeit only in relation to the consignor and named consignee and does not possess an element of negotiability (see Chuah, J, *Law of International Trade*, 1998; London: Sweet & Maxwell, pp 17, 155–159). There are varying degrees of evidence of ownership – limited negotiability, however, does not necessarily mean the absence of title.

There was also the thorny question as to whether the carrier was entitled or required to deliver to the named consignee without insisting on the production of the bill, given that the straight bill is not a document of title. Indeed, the Law Commission had taken the view that ('Rights of Suit in respect of Carriage of Goods by Sea' (HC 250, March 1991)):

(1) a straight bill of lading was not a document of title at common law;
(2) it did not have to be produced before the consignee could obtain delivery and thus was often retained by the shipper; and
(3) the Bills of Lading Act 1885 had no application to straight bills of lading, which had not been 'invented' at the date it was passed.

However, The House of Lords' decision in *The Rafaela S* [2005] UKHL 11, upholding that of the Court of Appeal, in which Rix LJ gave the leading judgment, has now substantially rejected that conventional viewpoint. In particular the view that a straight bill of lading need not be produced to obtain delivery was held to be wrong. The House of Lords also stressed that a straight bill is a bill of lading (or, at the very least, a similar document of title) for the purposes of the Hague and Hague-Visby Rules. The goods could and should thus be delivered against the production of the bill.

The Rafaela S [2005] UKHL 11

Held:

Lord Bingham: . . . **5.** It is always the task of the court to determine the true nature and effect of a legal document, and in performing that task the court is not bound by the label which the parties have chosen to apply to it. Where, however, the court is considering a bona fide mercantile document, issued in the ordinary course of trade, it will ordinarily be slow to reject the description which the document bears, particularly where the document has been issued by the party seeking to reject the description. This document called itself a bill of lading. It was not a bill transferable by endorsement, and so was not 'negotiable' in the somewhat inaccurate sense in which that term is used in this context: *Kum and Another v Wah Tat Bank Limited* [1971] 1 Lloyd's Rep 439, 446. But if this document was a mere receipt or sea waybill there was no purpose in following the traditional practice of issuing more than one original, and the time honoured language used in the attestation clause (see para 4 (6) above) was entirely meaningless. The contract conditions clearly envisage that the consignee and bill of lading holder may become a party to the contract of carriage, and the conveyance of contractual rights by transfer of the bill of lading has been a, if not the, distinctive feature of a bill of lading, at any rate since the Bills of Lading Act 1855. The conditions of this contract make no sense if the consignee, although holding the bill of lading, remains a stranger to the contract of carriage. They are unlike the standard terms of non-negotiable sea waybills of which examples are given in Gaskell, *Bills of Lading: Law and Contracts* (LLP, 2000), pp 727–733.

6. The carrier responds to this argument by pointing out that the form may be used in the case of either an order bill or a straight bill, and that if it is used for the latter purpose some of the stated conditions (such as the attestation clause quoted in para 4 (6) above) are inapposite. The first of these points is plainly correct: if 'order of' or words to that effect are added in box (2) the bill becomes an order bill, and if they are not it is a straight bill. It is also true that it is necessary in some cases (as in *Homburg Houtimport BV v Agrosin Private Limited* [2003] UKHL 12, [2004] 1 AC 715) to reject some printed conditions of a contract as inconsistent with other provisions. Here the requirement that one of the bills must be surrendered 'duly endorsed' in exchange for the goods could not in all cases be given effect, since even in the case of an order bill the named consignee might require delivery as holder of the bill, and in that case there could be no endorsement. It would, however, be extraordinary to treat the detailed terms of this contract as inapplicable to a named consignee holding a straight bill. In particular, I can see no reason not to give effect to the requirement that an original bill be surrendered in exchange for the goods. This provision is of course even more efficacious in the case of an order bill, since until such a bill is presented the carrier will not know the identity of the party entitled to delivery, and it has long been the 'undoubted practice' to deliver 'without inquiry' to the holder of such a bill of lading: *Glyn Mills Currie & Co v The East and West India Dock Company* (1880) 6 QBD 475, 492; (1882) 7 App Cas 591, 603. But the requirement does not lack a commercial rationale in the case of a straight bill: the shipper will not wish to part with an original bill to the consignee or buyer until that party has paid, and requiring production of the bill to obtain delivery is the most effective way of ensuring that a consignee or buyer who has not paid cannot obtain delivery. In this case, therefore, as in the case of an order bill, the bill is 'a key which in the hands of a rightful owner is intended to unlock the door of the warehouse, floating or fixed, in which the goods may chance to be' (*Sanders v Maclean*, above, p 341, per Bowen LJ).

. . .

10. In *C P Henderson & Co v The Comptoir d'Escompte de Paris* (1873) LR 5 PC 253 the Privy Council considered a straight bill. The decision was that a bill not drawn to order or assigns was not a negotiable instrument. But it is noteworthy that Sir Richard Baggallay QC in his argument, while submitting that the bill differed from an ordinary bill, did not contend that it was not a bill of lading at all, and Sir Robert Collier in giving the judgment of the Board consistently described it as such. The document considered in *The Marlborough Hill*, above, was, if a bill of lading, an order bill, and the question was whether the document was a bill at all. Lord Phillimore, giving the judgment of the Privy Council, observed at p 452 that 'If this document is a bill of lading, it is a negotiable instrument', perhaps suggesting that negotiability was in his opinion a necessary feature of a bill of lading. But he went on to point out (pp 452–453) that the parties had agreed to call the document a bill of lading, that the parties had acquired rights and incurred obligations proper to a bill of lading, that the detailed provisions properly belonged to a bill of lading, that it repeatedly described itself as a bill of lading, that it was expressly subject to the Harter Act and that it contained the time-honoured attestation clause. All these features led him to conclude that it was a bill of lading. I agree with Rix LJ in para 43 of his judgment that Lord Phillimore was not holding negotiability to be essential to the existence of a bill of lading or even its defining aspect but was, instead, emphasising that the document before the Board would work as merchants would expect a bill of lading to work.

11. *Thrige v United Shipping Company Limited* (1923) 16 Lloyd's Rep 198 and (1924) 18 Lloyd's Rep 6 is of interest because its progress through the English courts coincided with the last stages of the Hague Rules negotiations and because, in the Court of Appeal, it came before a bench which included Scrutton LJ. Save that the case concerned a straight bill, the facts are not significant. Scrutton LJ, with his immense authority and experience, expressed doubt whether a carrier was in breach if he delivered goods without production of the bill where the bill was made out to a named consignee and property in the goods passed on shipment. But he did not express any doubt that a bill drawn in that form was properly to be regarded as a bill, and he left open the question whether such a bill was a negotiable instrument.

12. By section 1 of the Harter Act 1893, the restriction on stipulations relieving from liability for negligence was applied to any bill of lading or shipping document. The Pomerene Bills of Lading Act 1916 applied to carriage by land as well as by sea. It distinguished between straight bills (section 2) and order bills (section 3). The former were to have placed plainly, upon their face, by the carrier issuing them, the words 'nonnegotiable' or 'not negotiable' (section 6), but carriers were to be justified in delivering to the consignee named in a straight bill without production of the bill (sections 8–9).

13. From evidence given to Butt J in *The Stettin* (1889) 14 PD 142 it is plain that German law had by that date distinguished between an order bill (orderkonnossement) and a straight bill (namenskonnossement).

The judge concluded that, at least in the case of an order bill, delivery could only be obtained by producing the bill, and there was evidence that that rule applied in either case. This is, as I understand, the current law in Germany: Tiberg, 'Legal Qualities of Transport Documents' (1998) 23 Mar. Law. 1, 32. Goren and Forrester, *The German Commercial Code* (Colorado, 1979), articles 445(1)4, 447(1), 448, 450.

14. The French Commercial Code provided in article 281, as early as 1808, that a bill of lading might be to order, or to bearer, or to a person named therein ('à personne dénommée').

15. In Scandinavia the same distinction has been recognised between running (or order) bills and straight (or recta) bills: see Tiberg, above, p 8. It appears (ibid, p 10) that 'because the recta bill should also serve as security for the seller's possible payment claims, it is not possible to dispense with the need for the consignee's or other title holder's presentation of the document'. A bill of lading is presumed to be an order document unless it is stated, by a recta clause, that the bill is not to order (ibid, p 13). As in Germany, the requirement of presentation applies equally to both types of bills (ibid, p 32). Professor Tiberg concludes (ibid, pp 43–44) that there are three distinctive types of documents: the order (or running) bill, the straight (or recta) bill and the sea waybill.

16. This brief survey shows that straight bills (however described) were a familiar mercantile phenomenon in the early 1920s and, as already observed, they were not ignored in the Hague Rules negotiations. Thus one would incline to infer that the Rules were intended to apply to straight as well as order bills unless either (a) there was any persuasive reason why they should be excluded or (b) the text of the Rules, broadly interpreted, suggests an intention to exclude them.

17. I cannot for my part see any reason why it should have been intended to exclude straight bills from the scope of the Rules. It may be accepted that the need for regulation was greater in the case of those becoming party to the contract by virtue of endorsement, partly because, order bills being standard in the commodity trades, they were more numerous. But where, as perhaps in the present case, the goods consigned were for the use of the named consignee, that party would not ordinarily be involved in negotiating the terms of the contract of carriage and would, like an endorsee, be liable to suffer loss if he became a party to the contract and found his rights attenuated by restrictive conditions imposed by the carrier.

18. From articles I (b) and V of the Hague and Hague-Visby Rules, which do not differ in any way material for present purposes, it is plain that the Rules do not apply to charterparties at all and that they apply to bills of lading issued under charterparties only 'from the moment at which such bill of lading or similar document of title regulates the relations between a carrier and a holder of the same'. This is explained by the intention of the Rules to afford protection not to the immediate parties to the contract of carriage but to third parties. Subject to that exclusion, the scope of the Hague Rules and, relevantly to this case, the Hague-Visby Rules, is generously expressed. Thus section 1(6) of the 1971 Act provides:

'(6) Without prejudice to Article X(c) of the Rules, the Rules shall have the force of law in relation to –

(a) any bill of lading if the contract contained in or evidenced by it expressly provides that the Rules shall govern the contract, and

(b) any receipt which is a non-negotiable document marked as such if the contract contained in or evidenced by it is a contract for the carriage of goods by sea which expressly provides that the Rules are to govern the contract as if the receipt were a bill of lading . . ..'

This provision is supplemented by article VI, reproducing the text of article VI of the Hague Rules (although in 1924 the United Kingdom, by section 4 of the 1924 Act, qualified its acceptance of the article in relation to the goods referred to and in relation to the territorial application of the proviso):

'Notwithstanding the provisions of the preceding Articles, a carrier, master or agent of the carrier and a shipper shall in regard to any particular goods be at liberty to enter into any agreement in any terms as to the responsibility and liability of the carrier for such goods, and as to the rights and immunities of the carrier in respect of such goods, or his obligation as to seaworthiness, so far as this stipulation is not contrary to public policy, or the care or diligence of his servants or agents in regard to the loading, handling, stowage, carriage, custody, care and discharge of the goods carried by sea, provided that in this case no bill of lading has been or shall be issued and that the terms agreed shall be embodied in a receipt which shall be a non-negotiable document and shall be marked as such.

Any agreement so entered into shall have full legal effect.

Provided that this Article shall not apply to ordinary commercial shipments made in the ordinary course of trade, but only to other shipments where the character or condition of the property to be carried or the circumstances, terms and conditions under which the carriage is to be performed are such as reasonably to justify a special agreement.'

Thus a carrier and shipper can in effect contract out of the Rules but only if (a) no bill of lading has been or is to be issued, (b) the agreed terms are embodied in a receipt, (c) the receipt is a non-negotiable document marked as such, (d) the shipments in question are not ordinary commercial shipments made in the ordinary course of trade, and (e) the character or condition of the property to be carried or the circumstances, terms and conditions under which the carriage is to be performed are such as reasonably to justify a special agreement. It is evident that the contracting-out conditions laid down in article VI are very restrictive and hard to satisfy. Reading section 1(6) and article VI together, I infer that the Hague and Hague-Visby Rules were intended, subject to the charterparty exclusion already mentioned, to govern the great majority of ordinary commercial shipments. It seems plain that the concern of those negotiating the Hague Rules was not to restrict the scope of the Rules but to prevent their circumvention, as Rix LJ explained in paras 66 and 68 of his judgment.

19. In paras 56–75 of his judgment Rix LJ reviewed the travaux préparatoires of the Hague Rules, assessing in a judicious and even-handed way the extracts on which the parties had respectively relied. He concluded (para 75):

'At the end of the day, I do not think that there is anything in the travaux préparatoires which I have seen which unequivocally states that such a case [ie. an ordinary, commercial, contract providing for delivery to a third party, with title remaining in the shipper until transfer of documents] is outside the scope of the Rules, and there is much in that material which points in the opposite direction.'

I would not disagree. It must be remembered that in a protracted negotiation such as culminated in adoption of the Hague Rules there are many participants, with differing and often competing objects, interests and concerns. It is potentially misleading to attach weight to points made in the course of discussion, even if they appear at the time to be accepted. In the present case, I do not think that either party can point to such a clear, pertinent and consensual resolution of the issue before the House as would provide a sure ground of decision.

20. I would accordingly give an expansive interpretation to the expression 'bill of lading or any similar document of title', which seems to me apt to cover the document issued in this case. I have no difficulty in regarding it as a document of title, given that on its express terms it must be presented to obtain delivery of the goods. But like Rix LJ (para 145) I would, if it were necessary to do so, hold that production of the bill is a necessary pre-condition of requiring delivery even where there is no express provision to that effect.

21. The most recent decisions on this subject, as I understand them, support these conclusions. In *The Duke of Yare* (ARR-RechtB Rotterdam, 10 April 1997) the Dutch court considered a straight bill of lading, and observed in para 4.1 of its judgment, as translated:

'First of all, the question needs to be answered as to whether the documents . . . can be considered as bills of lading or as "similar documents". As stated before under 3.1, the documents contain the wording "Bill of Lading" in the top right hand corner and are in the name of the addressee. According to Dutch Law – in which the Hague-Visby Rules are incorporated [references omitted] – the straight bill of lading, also called "rektacognossement", exists alongside the bearer or order bill of lading. The fact that a straight bill of lading cannot be treated in the same way as a bearer or order bill of lading does not detract from the fact that the present straight bill of lading meets the legal requirements to be considered as such.

As opposed to a non-negotiable seaway bill – said document not normally considered "a similar document" in English and Dutch literature – the holder of a straight bill of lading has the exclusive right to delivery of the goods, therefore delivery of the bill of lading is a requirement for obtaining the load.'

The Court of Appeal of Singapore also considered a straight bill, although not in the context of the Hague or Hague-Visby Rules, in *Voss v APL Co Pte Limited* [2002] 2 Lloyd's Rep 707. The issue was whether a straight bill had to be produced by the consignee to obtain delivery, and it was held that it had. The main characteristics of a bill of lading (para 48) were its negotiability and its recognition as a document of title, requiring presentation to obtain delivery of the cargo. While a straight bill lacked the first of these characteristics, there was no reason to infer that the parties intended to do away with the other also. This conclusion was, in the court's opinion, supported by considerations of commercial efficacy and convenience. The decision of the 2nd Division of the Court of Appeal of Rennes on appeal from the Commercial Court of Le Havre in *The MSC Magallanes* also concerned straight bills of lading. The court observed (as translated):

'These documents bear the comment "on board" proving that the merchandise had been loaded; by making this comment the common carrier acknowledged that the merchandise was loaded on board the vessel and guaranteed the delivery of the cargo to the bearer of the original bills of lading. It is of little relevance [therefore] that, following the example of the sea waybill, this bill of lading is nominative and non-negotiable.'

The court continued:

'It follows that these documents constitute bills of lading, it is the responsibility of MSC [as carrier] to hand over the merchandise to the consignee Delta Shipping, as stipulated in the bills of lading . . .

In effect, having given the original bills of lading and documents of title of the merchandise to Delta Shipping, MSC could only follow the instructions given by the legitimate bearer of the bills of lading, these documents giving rights . . .

Calberson [the shipper's agent] cannot therefore reproach MSC for having committed a fault in executing the contract of carriage, in accordance with particulars of the bill of lading. Far from contravening its obligations the carrier has ensured the respect owed to the documents of title to the merchandise, . . .

. . . Calberson could not be unaware of the fact that MSC could only deliver the merchandise to the bearer of the original bills of lading.'

22. It is plain, as Rix LJ accepted in para 94 of his judgment, that a straight bill of lading is not a bill of lading for the purposes of the Carriage of Goods by Sea Act 1992. It is also correct, as appears from para 2.50 of their report 'Rights of Suit in respect of Carriage of Goods by Sea' (HC 250, March 1991), quoted by Rix LJ in para 88 of his judgment, that the Law Commission and the Scottish Law Commission did not consider a straight bill of lading to be a document of title at common law. The conclusion of such bodies, following wide consultation, must command respect. But a 1991 report and a 1992 statute cannot govern the meaning of Rules given statutory force in 1924 and 1971, and the question before the House is not whether a straight bill of lading is a document of title at common law but whether it is 'a bill of lading or any similar document of title' for purposes of the Hague and Hague-Visby Rules. It is noteworthy that, by section 5(5) of the 1992 Act, the provisions of the Act are to have effect without prejudice to the application, in relation to any case, of the rules (the Hague-Visby Rules) having the force of law by virtue of the 1971 Act.

23. In paragraphs 117–133 of his judgment, Rix LJ reviewed in some detail the leading academic and practitioner texts applicable to the present issue, some of them heavily and understandably relied on by the carrier. He concluded in para 133:

> '[Counsel for the carrier] submitted that the textbooks were almost uniformly in favour of the carrier's case. However, in my judgment the position is more complex and mixed, and it can also be said that, on the basis that the bill of lading expressly requires its surrender to obtain delivery, there is something like uniformity in the opposite direction.'

> This seems to me a fair assessment.

24. Like Professor Sir Guenter Treitel QC, FBA (*'The Legal Status of Straight Bills of Lading'* (2003) 119 LQR 608, 620) I am a little puzzled by the third sentence of para 145 of Rix LJ's judgment. Subject to that minor qualification, I agree with his conclusions set out in paras 134–146, for the reasons which he gives, and also with the reasons and conclusions of Jacob J. I am also in agreement with the opinions of my noble and learned friends Lord Steyn and Lord Rodger of Earlsferrry, which I have had the benefit of reading in draft.

> Lord Nicholls: . . . 43. The question is whether a straight bill of lading triggers the application of the Rules, that is the provision that the Rules are only engaged in respect of contracts of carriage 'covered by a bill of lading or any similar document of title'. Before the adoption of the Hague Rules the practice of issuing straight bills of lading was known, and such documents were described and treated as bills of lading. For the United Kingdom this proposition is made good by the decision of the Privy Council in *C P Henderson & Co v Comptoir d'Escompte de Paris* (1873) LR 5 PC 253, 259–260. In the United States the straight bill of lading was sufficiently recognised to be regulated by the Pomerene Bills of Lading Act 1916; see the judgment of Rix LJ, paras 47 and 48, at 721F-722A. In continental legal systems the straight bill of lading was well known and treated as a bill of lading: Tiberg, Legal Qualities of Transport Documents (1998) 23 Mar. Law 1 and Treitel, *The Legal Status of Straight Bills of Lading*, (2003) 119 LQR 608. It is true, of course, that the vast preponderance of transactions took place on the basis of order bills of lading. But it is a matter of contextual significance that straight bills of lading were in use before the Hague Rules were adopted. The travaux préparatoires of the Hague Rules are plainly inconclusive and cannot be used to determine the intentions of the framers on the precise question before the House. But it is a fair inference that the framers of the Hague Rules could not have been unaware of the relatively widespread mercantile use of straight bills of lading at that time. If it had been intended to exclude these bills of lading, special provision to that effect would surely have been made. Instead the gateway to the application of the Hague Rules was expressed in the wide and general terms of the existence of a bill of lading or any similar document of title.

44. The very words in question – 'bills of lading or any similar document of title' – are words of expansion as opposed to restriction. They postulate a wide rather than narrow meaning. The attempt by the carriers to treat those words as importing a restrictive meaning of a conforming document under article I(b) involves a distortion of the plain language. It also reveals a preoccupation with notions of domestic law regarding documents of title which ought not to govern the interpretation of an international maritime convention. Instead the Rules must be construed by reference to 'broad principles of general acceptance' appropriate to the international mercantile subject matter: see *Stag Line v Foscolo Mango & Co* [1932] AC 328, at 350. This view is reinforced if one considers the French text of the 1924 Hague Rules, which was at the time the authoritative version of the Rules: *Pyrene v Scindia* [1954] 2 QB 402, at 421, per Devlin J. The French text refers in article I(b) to a 'contrat constaté par un connaissement ou par tout document similaire formant titre pour le transport des merchandises par mer . . .'. It contains no reference to the English concept of a 'document of title' at all. Instead it focuses on the right to possession of the goods vesting in the holder of the document. This makes it singularly inappropriate to invoke the meaning of 'document of title' at common law. But even the English text is more consistent with an interpretation of article I(b) which treats straight bills of lading as included rather than excluded.

45. The attestation clause expressly provides that 'One of the bills of lading must be surrendered duly endorsed in exchange for the goods or delivery order.' The carrier argued that the words 'duly endorsed' signify that this provision is inapplicable to a straight bill of lading. I would reject this argument. The words 'duly endorsed' merely indicate that the bill of lading must be endorsed if appropriate or as may be necessary to perform the right of the presenting party to claim delivery. In any event, the issue of a set of three bills of lading, with the provision 'one of which being accomplished, the others to stand void' necessarily implies that delivery will only be made against presentation of the bill of lading. In my view the decision of the Court of Appeal of Singapore in *Voss v APL Co Pte Ltd* [2002] 2 Lloyds LR 707 at 722 that presentation of a straight bill of lading is a requirement for the delivery of the cargo is right. A connected point is that the logic of the carrier's position is that some standard terms on the reverse side of the bill of lading must be deemed to be inapplicable. That too is not how traders, bankers and insurers would understand a straight bill of lading.

46. The carrier tried to equate the function of a straight bill of lading with that of a sea waybill. In Schmitthoff's *Export Trade: The Law and Practice of International Trade*, 10th ed, 2000, edited by Leo D'Arcy and others, a sea waybill is described as follows (paras 15–033, at p 281):

> 'A sea waybill is a non-negotiable transport document and its great advantage is that its presentation by the consignee is not required in order for him, on production of satisfactory identification, to take delivery of the goods, thus avoiding delay both for him and the carrier where the goods arrive before the waybill. It is not a document of title but contains, or is evidence of, the contract of carriage as between the shipper and carrier in that it incorporates the standard terms of the carrier on its face. However, unlike a bill of lading, these terms are not detailed on the reverse of the waybill which is blank. A waybill is usually issued in the 'received for shipment' form but may, like a bill of lading, be notated once the goods have been loaded.'

The suggested comparison is plainly unrealistic. In the hands of the named consignee the straight bill of lading is his document of title. On the other hand, a sea waybill is never a document of title. No trader, insurer or banker would assimilate the two. The differences between the documents include the fact that a straight bill of lading contains the standard terms of the carrier on the reverse side of the document but a sea waybill is blank and straight bills of lading are invariably issued in sets of three and waybills not. Except for the fact that a straight bill of lading is only transferable to a named consignee and not generally, a straight bill of lading shares all the principal characteristics of a bill of lading as already described.

47. Moreover, no policy reason has been advanced by the carrier why the draftsmen of the Hague Rules would have wanted to distinguish between a named consignee who receives an order bill of lading and a named consignee who receives a straight bill of lading. There is simply no sensible commercial reason why the draftsmen would have wished to deny the CIF buyer named in a straight bill of lading the minimum standard of protection afforded to the CIF buyer named in an order bill of lading. The importance of this consideration is heightened by the fact that straight bills of lading fulfil a useful role in international trade provided that they are governed by the Hague-Visby Rules, since they are sometimes preferred to order bills of lading on the basis that there is a lesser risk of falsification of documentation.

48. On a broader footing it is apparent that the interpretation advanced by the carrier depends on fine and technical distinctions and arguments. Traders, bankers and insurers would be inclined to take a more commercial view of straight bills of lading. This view is supported by Schmitthoff's *Export Trade: The Law and Practice of International Trade*, 10th ed, 2000, at 276.

49. The academic response to the decision of the Court of Appeal is also important. Professor Sir Guenter Treitel QC, *The Legal Status of Straight Bills of Lading*, (2003) 119 LQR 608, at 611) observed about the Court of Appeal decision that 'there seems to be no good policy reason for distinguishing between straight and order bills, so that one can express one's respectful agreement with the actual decision that the Hague-Visby Rules apply to both kinds of bill alike'. Professor Charles Debattista, Straight Bills Come In From the Cold – Or Do They?, Lloyd's List 23 April 2003, at 6, also welcomed the decision.

50. It is common ground that the Carriage of Goods by Sea Act 1992 treats straight bills of lading as sea waybills. That assumption comes from the view of the Law Commission to that effect: The Law Commission Report No 196, Rights of Suit in Respect of Carriage of Goods by Sea, paras 2.50 and 4.10–4.12. The 1992 Act was enacted three years after the contract of carriage in this case came into existence. Moreover, and more fundamentally, section 5(5) of the 1992 Act specifically provides that it will not affect the Hague-Visby Rules. The terms of the 1992 Act cannot alter the proper construction of article I(b) of the Rules.

That decision is to be welcomed. There is no good commercial reason why a straight bill should not be treated as a proper document of title. The artificiality in suggesting that the rights of ownership are limited (by means of the bill being only transferable once) is difficult to defend.

Although the decision has provided better clarity on the matter, there are a few interesting doctrinal questions which have not been fully resolved.

Treitel, G, 'The legal status of straight bills of lading' (2003) LQR 608

. . . Towards the end of his judgment in *The Rafaela S*, Rix LJ discusses a point that it was 'unnecessary to decide' in that case, viz.'whether a straight bill of lading is in principle a document of title, even in the absence of an express provision requiring its production to obtain delivery.' He gives an affirmative answer to this question ('in my judgment it is') and adds 'that was also the view of the Law Commission' (in its Report No.196 (1991), which led to the passing of the Carriage of Goods by Sea Act 1992). The reference here to the Law Commission's Report is at first sight puzzling, since para.2.50 of that Report contains the statement that 'A 'straight' consigned bill of lading, such as one made out 'to X' without any such words as 'to order', is not a document of title at common law'. . . . Rix LJ cannot have overlooked this sentence, for he quotes it in an earlier passage of his judgment in *The Rafaela S*. So the question arises: exactly what was the point that it was 'unnecessary to decide' in that case and what was the 'view of the Law Commission' that was cited in support of the conclusion. It is tempting to say that the whole passage is to be read in the context of the preceding discussion of the scope of the Hague Rules, i.e. that a straight bill is 'in principle' a 'document of title' within these Rules even if it contains no express provision requiring its production to obtain delivery of the goods because such a requirement was inherent in the nature of such a document. But this interpretation of the passage will not do since the policy reasons given in the part of the judgment here under discusssion have nothing to do with the Hague Rules: they are that it is desirable for the protection both of the carrier and of the shipper to treat straight bills as 'documents of title' for other purposes. These policy considerations have been discussed above; they are relevant 'in principle' to the question whether such a bill is a 'document of title' in the common law sense, and not merely for the purpose of legislation using that expression. The answer to that question depends partly on how one defines the concept of a 'document of title' and partly on further policy considerations.

With regard to the first of these points, a number of statements in *The Rafaela S* seem to make the issue whether a straight bill is a 'document of title' depend on whether such a document has to be produced to the carrier to obtain delivery of the goods. According to one such statement, the question 'has been seen possibly to depend on whether the consignee is obliged to present the document'; another refers to 'a document of title in the sense that presentation is necessary to obtain possession of the goods'; and in a third it is said that 'Everyone seems to agree that if a straight bill expressly provides, as it commonly does, that its surrender is required for delivery to take place, then it is a "document of title"'. But even if one accepts that a document of title has to be produced to claim delivery, and that a straight bill has to be produced for this purpose, it does not follow that a straight bill is a document of title. Such a conclusion would, with respect, raise the question whether, even if the need for production were a necessary condition for a document's being a document of title, it was also a sufficient condition. As was pointed out above, the common law concept of a document goes back to *Lickbarrow v Mason*, where an order bill of lading was recognised as such a document by virtue of proof of a custom of merchants to that effect; and when, nearly 200 years later, it was alleged in *Kum v Wah Tat Bank Ltd* that certain mates' receipts were documents of title in the common law sense, it was again by virtue of proof of a custom to that effect that the argument was accepted in principle (though it was held not to apply to the particular receipt issued in that case as it was marked 'not negotiable'). In neither of these cases was there any suggestion that, in the absence of proof of such a custom, a document can become a document of title merely because (whether by virtue of one of its express provisions or for some other reason) it has to be produced by the person claiming delivery of the goods to which it refers. The fact that the document does not have to be produced may, indeed, be a ground for denying it the status of a document of title, but the fact that it does have to be produced does not suffice to give it that status. As has been suggested in an earlier part of this comment, the requirement of production of the document to secure delivery of the goods is the consequence of its recognition as a document of title, not the cause of that recognition. In the terms of Bowen LJ's famous metaphor, an order bill has to be produced because it is the key to the warehouse: you cannot get in if you have not got the key or if you keep it in your pocket. But the converse is not true: a document does not become a key merely because it has to be produced to gain admittance; it may have to be produced to induce someone else to unlock the door. Therefore it is respectfully suggested that the mere fact that a straight bill may (by its terms or its nature) have to be produced does not, in the absence of proof of custom, turn it into a document of title in the common law sense, that is, (again in Bowen LJ's words) into a document, the transfer of which operated as 'symbolical delivery' of the goods and which if so intended, can result in the passing of the property in them.

The common law is, it is submitted, right in having (at least up to now) refused to grant this quality to documents without proof of mercantile custom satisfying the usual requirements of being notorious, certain and reasonable. The judgment in *The Rafaela S* stresses that recognition of straight bills as documents of title can help to protect carriers and shippers; but if they can have that effect it must follow that it can equally prejudice third parties who, in good faith, deal with goods themselves in circumstances in which they cannot rely on any of the exceptions to nemo dat quod non habet. Recognition of a document as a document of title requires a careful balancing of such conflicting interests and should not be afforded to a document merely because it provides that it has to be produced in order to obtain delivery. It is surely no accident that *Lickbarrow v Mason* was also (at an earlier stage of proceedings from that referred to above) the source of Ashurst J's famous dictum that 'wherever one of two innocent persons must suffer by the acts of a third, he who has enabled such third person to occasion the loss must sustain it.' In situations of the kind here under discussion, the answer to the question, who must sustain the loss, may well depend on whether the document is recognised as having the quality of transferability possessed by an order bill; and it is at least arguable that the courts should be slow to extend the categories of documents which possess that quality.

It remains to consider one further argument relevant to this issue. This is that the law already recognises that a 'straight' bill can be transferred; in this respect, it differs from an order bill only in that, while an order bill can be transferred repeatedly, for a theoretically infinite number of times by endorsement and delivery, a 'straight' bill can be transferred only once, i.e. to the named consignee. This was the argument of counsel in *The Rafaela S*, and the judgment supports view that 'although a [straight bill] cannot be transferred more than once, for it is not negotiable, it can be transferred by delivery (just like a classic bill) to the named consignee.' No doubt a straight bill can be, and often may be, delivered to the named consignee, but one has then to ask what legal consequences (if any) flow from such a delivery. Three possible consequences call for consideration. They concern the transfer of contractual rights, the receipt function of the document and (most significantly in the present context) the effect of such delivery on possessory and proprietary rights in the goods.

So far as transfer of contractual rights against the carrier is concerned, the transfer in English law is accomplished without delivery of the bill: as noted above, for this purpose, a 'straight' bill is treated by the Carriage of Goods by Sea Act 1992 in the same way as a sea waybill, so that the consignee named in the document acquires such rights simply by virtue of being so named, without the need to have become the holder of it (see s.2(1)(b)). The document may, indeed, by its terms make the acquisition of contractual rights dependent on the consignee's having acquired possession of it, but the mere fact that it contained words requiring its production in exchange for delivery of the goods would not have this effect; such words would not apply to the situation in which the goods had been lost and the named consignee was claiming, not delivery, but damages for breach of the contract of carriage leading to the loss. The only other possible consequence of the transfer of the document might be to deprive the shipper of his right to redirect the goods; but s.2(5) of the Act preserves this right and makes no exception on the ground that the document has been delivered to the consignee.

The receipt function of the document is only marginally relevant to the present discussion. The delivery to the named consignee of a straight bill clearly does not enable a consignee to rely on the conclusive evidence provision of s.4 of the 1992 Act, since for the purpose of this Act a straight bill is not a 'bill of lading.' Whether such delivery entitles the consignee of a straight bill to rely on the 'conclusive evidence' provision of Art.III 4 of the Hague-Visby Rules, as limited by s.1(6) of the Carriage of Goods by Sea Act 1971, is more doubtful. The reasoning of *The Rafaela S* may suggest an affirmative answer to this question; but the point need not be pursued here, as the issue has no direct bearing on the status of a straight bill as a document of title.

The question whether delivery of a straight bill to the named consignee can transfer constructive possession of the goods depends on whether such a bill is a document of title in the common law sense. One cannot argue that merely because the document can be 'transferred' (i.e. delivered), though only once, it can therefore achieve this object and so is in principle a document of title in the common law sense, for this line of argument assumes the very point in issue: i.e. that delivery of the document amounts to a constructive delivery of the goods. Of course, if the relationship between the shipper and the consignee were that of buyer and seller, or that of pledgor and pledgee, then constructive possession of the goods and proprietary interests in them might pass to the consignee for the reason given by Lord Devlin in *Kum v Wah Tat Bank Ltd*: i.e. on the ground that delivery of the goods to the carrier was delivery to him as bailee for the named consignee. But such delivery would result from dealings with the actual goods rather than from transfer of the document; and it can so result, as it did in that case, even though the document is not a document of title in the common law sense.

By way of footnote to the foregoing discussion, it may be noted that, in the United States, the concept of the 'transfer' of a 'straight' or (now) 'nonnegotiable' bill is quite different. The starting point is that an order or (now) 'negotiable' bill is negotiable in a sense in which an English bill is not: that is, in the sense that the transferee can acquire title even where the transferor had none, e.g. because he had acquired the bill by theft. The 'transferee' of a straight or (now) nonnegotiable bill on the other hand, does not by virtue of the transfer get any 'additional right'. So it was necessary to distinguish between the 'negotiation' of a negotiable bill and the 'transfer' of a nonnegotiable bill. The latter process is achieved 'by delivery and agreement to transfer title to the bill or to the goods represented by it.' The concept of the 'transfer' of a straight bill may be derived from this source. If so, it seems to be inapposite to a discussion of English law, in which there is no direct counterpart to the American distinction here discussed since, in English law, even an 'order' bill is not fully 'negotiable' in the American sense.

On the application of the Hague and Hague-Visby Rules to straight bills see Chapter 7.

A seawaybill is usually used for short sea voyages and is not negotiable. It is not a document of title. The carrier should therefore insist on proof of identity and entitlement before releasing the goods to the bearer. See the Report of the United Nations Conference on Trade and Development (UNCTAD), 'The Use of Transport Documents in International Trade', UNCTAD/SDTE/ TLB/2003/3, dated 26 November 2003 concerning a survey conducted by UNCTAD with large container operators and several national shipping lines, as well as shippers and their associations, freight forwarders and banks. The survey showed that 88% of respondents had used, issued or required negotiable bills of lading and 70% of these used such bills of lading mainly or exclusively. The main reason given was the security provided by negotiable bills of lading under letter of credit transactions. The security of delivery and payment were also cited as reasons for the continuing preference for bills of lading. As a contrast, only 51% stated that they had used, issued or required sea waybills. Out of these, 23% used waybills for the majority of transactions and a mere 18% reported that they used waybills for only 10% or less of all transactions.

It was stated in a Singapore case, *Voss v APL Co Pte Ltd* [2002] 2 Lloyd's Rep 707, 722, that: 'The sea waybill is retained by the shipper and all the consignee need show to take delivery is poof of his identity. It is a receipt, not a document of title. It, unlike a bill of lading, cannot be used as a security to obtain financing.' It seems thus to follow that a sea waybill is more likely to be used when no letters of credit financing is required.

See also the CMI Uniform Rules for Sea Waybills 1990 at sub-r 7(i): 'The carrier shall deliver the goods to the consignee upon production of proper identification.' It should however be noted that no special form of identification is needed. In practice, sometimes presentation of the pro forma invoice (this is not the commercial invoice but a price quotation originally sent to the consignee by the seller usually to enable the consignee to secure an import licence or trade financing) would be requested.

What about received bills of lading? Are they documents of title under the transport conventions and/or common law?

The Marlborough Hill [1920] 5 Ll L Rep 362, PC

Lord Phillimore: . . . The first point taken on behalf of the appellant is that this purports to be a claim by the assignee of a Bill of Lading, and that the shipping instrument on which reliance is placed is not a Bill of Lading; and this point requires some careful consideration. The document is not in the old form of a Bill of Lading. The old form starts with a statement or acknowledgment that the goods have been shipped. It runs 'shipped on board,' &c. But this document runs 'received in apparent good order and condition from . . . for shipment.' The old form is precise that the goods have been shipped on board the particular vessel, though the conditions of the Bill of Lading may proceed afterwards to permit of transhipment.

This document runs to the effect that the goods have been received for shipment by the sailing vessel called the Marlborough Hill, or by some other vessel owned or operated by the Commonwealth &

Dominion Line, Ltd., Cunard Line, Australasian Service; and the first term which is expressed to be mutually agreed is to the effect that the shipowner may substitute or tranship the whole or any portion of the goods by any other prior or subsequent vessel at the original port of shipment, or at any other place. The contract, therefore, is not one by which the shipment in the particular vessel proceeded against is admitted, nor one whereby the shipowner or his agent or the Master contracts to carry and deliver by that ship. It is one whereby the agents for the Master put their signature to the contract, admit the receipt for shipment and contract to carry and deliver, primarily by the named ship Marlborough Hill, but with power to substitute any other vessel owned and operated by the specified line, or possibly under the first condition by any other ship whatsoever. but the contract does contain the further obligation that, subject to the excepted conditions and perils, either the named ship or the substituted ship shall duly and safely carry and deliver.

It is a matter of commercial notoriety, and their Lordships have been furnished with several instances of it, that shipping instruments which are called Bills of Lading, and known in the commercial world as such, are sometimes framed in the alternative form 'received for shipment' instead of 'shipped on board,' and further with the alternative contract to carry or procure some other vessel (possibly with some limitations as to the choice of the other vessel) to carry, instead of the original ship. It is contended, however, that such shipping instruments, whatever they may be called in commerce or by men of business, are nevertheless not Bills of Lading within the Bills of Lading Act of 1855, and it is said therefore not Bills of Lading within the meaning of the Admiralty Court Act of 1861.

Their Lordships are not disposed to take so narrow a view of a commercial document. To take the first objection first. There can be no difference in principle between the owner, Master or agent acknowledging that he has received the goods on his wharf, or allotted portion of quay, or his storehouse awaiting shipment, and his acknowledging that the goods have been actually put over the ship's rail. The two forms of a Bill of Lading may well stand, as their Lordships understand that they stand, together. The older is still in the more appropriate language, for whole cargoes delivered and taken on board in bulk; whereas 'received for shipment' is the proper phrase for the practical business like way of treating parcels of cargo to be placed in a general ship which will be lying alongside the wharf taking in cargo for several days, and whose proper stowage will require that certain bulkier or heavier parcels shall be placed on board first, while others, though they have arrived earlier, wait for the convenient place and time of stowage.

Then as regards the obligation to carry either by the named ship or by some other vessel; it is a contract which both parties may well find it convenient to enter into and accept. The liberty to tranship is ancient and well established, and does not derogate from the nature of a Bill of Lading; and if the contract begin when the goods are received on the wharf, substitution does not differ in principle from transhipment.

If this document is a Bill of Lading, it is a negotiable instrument. Money can be advanced upon it, and business can be done in the way in which maritime commerce has been carried on for at least half a century, throughout the civilised world. Both parties have agreed to call this a Bill of Lading; both, by its terms, have entered into obligations and acquired rights such as are proper to a Bill of Lading. All the other incidents in its very detailed language are such as are proper to such a document. The goods are marked and numbered as stated in the margin, and are to be delivered to the order of the shipper or his assignees, on payment of freight and charges. There are the usual, now in modern times very detailed, provisions and excepted perils. There are provisions for the payment of general average; that the shipper is to be liable to the shipowner for damage owing to his having shipped dangerous goods; and that he shall pay all expenses for reconditioning and gathering of loose cargo. The shipowner is to have a lien on the goods, not only for freight, but for fines, damages, costs and expenses which may be incurred by any defect in insufficient marking or description of contents. It is called a Bill of Lading many times in the course of the fifteen provisions, and particularly in the last, where it is provided that the shipment, being from New York, shall be subject to all the provisions of certain statutes of the United States, and specially to the well-known Harter Act. The list closes as follows:-

'In accepting this Bill of Lading, the shipper, owner and consignee of the goods, and holder of the Bill of Lading, agrees to be bound by all its stipulations, exceptions and conditions, whether written, stamped or printed, as tully as if they were all signed by the shipper, owner, consignee or holder, any local customs or privileges to the contrary notwithstanding. If required by the shipowner, one signed Bill of Lading, duly endorsed, must be surrendered on delivery of the goods.'

And then the document ends in the time-honoured form-

'In Witness whereof the Master or agent of sail vessel has signed three Bills of Lading, all of this tenor and date, of which if one is accomplished, the others shall be void.'

No doubt it appears from the margin that it is the form in use by the Commonwealth & Dominion Line, Ltd., Cunard Line, Australasian Service, trading from New York to Australia and New Zealand, with Funch, Edye & Co., Incorporated, as the American agents; and it may be said that it is not signed by the Master, but by that firm as agents for the Master. It is, however, well known that in general ships the Master does not usually sign. The Bills of Lading are signed in the agents' office by the agents. It should perhaps be added that it is evidently contemplated by the document that the shipper will assign his rights and that the assignee or holder of the Bill of Lading will present the document at the port of delivery, and that his receipt, and not that of the shipper, will be the discharge to the shipowner.

Their Lordships conclude that it is a Bill of Lading within the meaning of the Admiralty Court Act, 1861.

The Marlborough Hill is not universally accepted as setting forth the correct pronouncement of law.

Diamond Alkali Export Corp v FL Bourgeois [1921] 3 KB 443

Facts: The bill of lading in question stated, 'Received in apparent good order and condition from D. A. Horan to be transported by the S.S. Anglia now lying in the port of Philadelphia and bound for Gothenburg, Sweden, with liberty to call at any port or ports in or out of the customary route or failing shipment by said steamer in and upon a following steamer, 280 bags Dense Soda.'

Held:

McCardie J: . . . The document seems to me to be (in substance) a mere receipt for goods which at some future time and by some uncertain vessel are to be shipped. It is not even in the form of the New York Produce Exchange bill of lading set out in Carver, 6th ed., Appendix A, p. 971. The buyer is left in doubt as to actual shipment and actual ship.

The sellers, however, submit that I am bound by the opinion of the Privy Council in *Marlborough Hill (Ship) v Cowan & Sons*. The buyers, on the other hand, contend that that opinion is erroneous and that I ought not to follow it. I need scarcely state the deep diffidence and embarrassment which I feel in discussing that weighty opinion. As Lord Phillimore himself, however, pointed out in *Dulieu v White & Sons* [[1901] 2 K. B. 669], a Privy Council advice is not binding on the King's Bench Division even as to the res decisa. I wish to point out first that the actual decision in the *Marlborough Hill Case* was merely that the bill of lading there in question (which closely resembles the one now before me) fell within s. 6 of the Admiralty Court Act, 1861. It may be that the phrase 'bill of lading' in that section permits of a board interpretation. I point out next that there is no express statement in the *Marlborough Hill Case* that the document there in question actually fell within the Bills of Lading Act, 1855. In the third place it seems to me to be clear that the Board did not consider the nature and effect of an ordinary c.i.f. contract or the decisions thereon in relation to the question before them. The case of *Bowes v Shand* [(1876–77) 2 App. Cas. 455] moreover was not even cited to the Board. Lord Phillimore, in reading the advice of the Privy Council, said : 'There can be no difference in principle between the owner, master, or agent acknowledging that he has received the goods on his wharf, or allotted portion of quay, or his storehouse awaiting shipment, and his acknowledging that the goods have been actually put over the ship's rail.' With the deepest respect I venture to think that there is a profound difference between the two, both from a legal and business point of view. Those differences seem to me clear. I need not state them. If the view of the Privy Council is carried to its logical conclusion, a mere receipt for goods at a dock warehouse for future shipment might well be called a bill of lading. Again the Board say: 'Then as regards the obligation to carry either by the named ship or by some other vessel; it is a contract which both parties may well find it convenient to enter into and accept. The liberty to tranship is ancient and well established, and does not derogate from the nature of a bill of lading, and if the contract begin when the good are received on the wharf, substitution does not differ in principle from transshipment.' I do not pause to analyse these words. I only say that in my own humble view substitution and the right of transshipment are distinct things, and rest on different principles. The passage last cited can, I think, have no application at all to a c.i.f. contract, which provides for a specific date of shipment. It will suffice if I say two things. First, that in my view the *Marlborough Hill Case* does not apply to a c.i.f. contract such as that now before me. Secondly, that grounds for challenging and dicta of the Privy Council will be found in Art. 22, and the notes and cases there cited, in *Scrutton on Charterparties*, 10th ed., as to what are called 'through bills of lading,' in the lucid article in the Law Quarterly Review of October, 1889, vol. v., p. 424, by Mr. Bateson, K.C.; and of July, 1890, vol. vi., p. 289, by the late Mr. Carver, and in Carver on Carriage, 6th ed., notes to Sect. 107. I do not doubt that the document before me is a 'shipping document' within the U.S.A. Harter Act, 1893. I feel bound to hold, however, that it is not a bill of lading within the c.i.f. contract of sale made between the present parties.

It should perhaps be noted that *The Marlborough Hill* was a case largely about whether the relevant New South Wales court had jurisdiction and jurisdiction depended on whether the dispute concerned a bill of lading. That said there does not appear to be a good commercial reason for McCardie J in *Diamond Alkali* to suggest that a received bill of lading is any different from a shipped bill for the purposes of title. See also *Ishag v Allied Bank International* [1981] 1 Lloyd's Rep 92.

Other documents such as mates receipts and delivery orders are not recognised as documents of title. See *Nippon Yusen Kaisha v Ramjiban Serowgee* [1938] AC 429, 444 and *Hathesing v Laing* (1873) LR 17 Eq 92 where it was held that a mates receipt was not a document of title at common law. Delivery orders are widely used. However, they are not issued by the holder of the goods. As such, they could never be documents of title.

For a document to be considered a document of title under the common law, it needs to satisfy the following requirements:

- It must be capable of giving the necessary degree of control over the good.
- When it is transferred, it must be able to give rise to a presumption of the transferor's intention to give up possession and of the transferee's intention to take possession of the goods.

In *Kum v Wah Tat Bank Ltd* [1971] 1 Lloyd's Rep 439, where there is evidence in trade custom that a particular mates receipt gives rise to these presumptions, then that mates receipt could be treated as a document of title. In that case however it was found that in shipping trades in Malaya, Borneo and Singapore in the 1950s there was a custom treating a mates receipt used in certain trades as a document of title, the mates receipt in question had been marked 'non-negotiable'. Such markings were inconsistent with that local custom and, as such, the mates receipt in question could not be regarded as a document of title.

As for a delivery order, it would be difficult to show the requisite intention on the part of the bailee to give the holder a sufficient degree of control over the goods to give him symbolic possession. Therefore, even if we are able to strain a finding of the existence of a relevant custom, it is virtually impossible to contend that a delivery order is a document of title.

16 Exhaustion of transferability

How long does a bill of lading remain 'negotiable and transferable'? Can a bill of lading be used to transfer title only when goods are loaded on board a ship at sea and so are incapable of physical delivery? Or does efficient and secure commerce demand a different rule? Can a bill of lading continue to be used to transfer title and the right to possession when the cargo has been landed, or perhaps even when part of the cargo has been handed over to the receiver? The latest possible moment must surely be when delivery is given against production of a bill of lading, given the traditional statement that accompanies the signature of a bill: 'In witness whereof the Master of the said vessel has signed . . . original Bills of Lading all of this tenor and date one of which being accomplished the others to stand void.'

Meyerstein v Barber (1870) LR 4 HL 317, HL

Facts: A cargo of cotton was shipped from India to England. There were three bills of lading making one set. They were in the usual form, except as to the last sentence, which concluded thus: 'In witness whereof I, the said master of the said ship, have affirmed to three bills of lading, all of this time and date, one of which being accomplished, the others to stand void.' Abraham, the consignee, held the set of three bills. In exchange for a cheque he gave two of the bills to Meyerstein. Meyerstein did not ask for the third bill assuming that it was being retained by the carrier. Abraham who had retained that third bill fraudulently, then sold the third bill to Barber.

Held:

> **Lord Harheley LC:** . . . The question has really turned upon one point, and I may almost say upon one point alone, namely, whether or not the bills of lading had fully performed their office, and were discharged and spent at the time that the Plaintiff took his security. Whether, in other words, the landing of those goods at the sufferance wharf in the name of the consignee, but subject to the stop which was put upon them by the shipowner, and the stop put upon them by the mortgagees, was, or was not, a delivery which had exhausted the whole effect of the bill of lading. That, I think, is the single point to which the case becomes reduced.
>
> It appears to me, my Lords, that there are one or two points of law which must be taken to be clearly established, although very able efforts, employed with considerable ingenuity and resource, have been directed to the shaking of those well-established points of law. I refer particularly to the very able argument we have heard from Mr. Grantham in this case with reference to the first step, if I may so call it, in the proceeding, namely, the fact of the first assignment for value of a bill of lading when the goods are not

landed, but are still at sea. Now, if anything could be supposed to be settled in mercantile law, I apprehend it would be this, that when goods are at sea the parting with the bill of lading, be it one bill out of a set of three, or be it one bill alone, is parting with the ownership of the goods.

Mr. Grantham has raised this argument upon the frame of the bill of lading itself, which I apprehend is in the common form where three bills are given. The form of the bill of lading to which he specially referred, and upon which he founded the argument I now advert to, is this, that the shipper undertakes to deliver these goods, the cotton, to the Souzas or order, or to their assigns, he or they paying the freight for the goods at the rate there mentioned; and then, at the end of the document we have these words, "In witness whereof I, the master of the ship, have affirmed to three bills of lading, all of this tenor and date, one of which being accomplished the others to stand void." The argument has been this, that the bill of lading has not accomplished its office until not only the goods are landed, but the freight is paid, and the whole matter which is the subject of the contract of the shipowner has been achieved; and that, accordingly, if that be law, it follows that if one bill of lading be assigned while the ship is at sea, and a second bill of lading be assigned to a second person, fraudulently, of course, and a third bill of lading be assigned to a third person, also fraudulently, of course, it becomes simply a matter of expedition and race between the several parties who have taken those different assignments of the bills of lading; because until the goods have actually been landed and fully delivered, each bill of lading, according to the argument, is to be considered as of equal force until one of the bills has been, according to the argument, accomplished.

Now, I apprehend that it would shake the course of proceeding between merchants, as sanctioned by decided cases (which the learned counsel admitted to have been decided, and never yet to have been altered or reversed), if we were to hold that the assignment of the bill of lading, the goods being at the time at sea, does not pass the whole and complete ownership of the goods, so that any person taking a subsequent bill of lading, be it the second or be it the third, must be content to submit to the loss which would result from that state of facts. I apprehend that no decision can be found to the effect that any person taking an assignment of a bill of lading, knowing that others existed, is to be held to have been guilty of fraud simply from the fact of his so acting. No authority, at all events, has been cited for that proposition. And no authority has been cited at the Bar to shew that the transaction is not entire and complete when once the bill of lading has been assigned, as respects, at all events, goods in transitu, whether the assignment be by mortgage or by sale. If it were by sale other considerations would intervene which would give still greater efficacy to the assignment of the goods without delivery or possession. But when the vessel is at sea and the cargo has not yet arrived, the parting with the bill of lading is parting with that which is the symbol of property, and which, for the purpose of conveying a right and interest in the property, is the property itself. It appears to me that to shake any conclusion of that kind would be entirely to annihilate the course of mercantile procedure which has existed for a long period of time – far longer, probably, than I can at this moment accurately state.

That being so, the Judges have reasonably assumed that proposition as a point of undeniable law. Then, if the property so passes when the goods are at sea, the whole question resolves itself into this: What is the effect of the assignment of the bill of lading under the circumstances of this case, when the goods were not at sea at the time when the interest was passed, but were at a sufferance wharf in the name and by the order of the consignee, Abraham, who represented the original consignees, the Souzas, subject to the stop-order in respect of freight, and subject to the stop-order given to the chartered bank.

. . .

Then, the first proposition of law being clear – that an indorsement of the bill of lading carries with it the property in the goods when the goods are at sea, the next proposition of law that we have to consider is this, laid down by all the Judges who have delivered their opinions in this case, and, as it appears to me, correctly laid down by them. It is stated by Mr. Justice Willes in his very elaborate judgment, in which he says: 'I think the bill of lading remains in force at least so long as complete delivery of possession of the goods has not been made to some person having a right to claim them under it.' Mr. Justice Keating says, in the same way, that he considers that 'there can be no complete delivery of goods under a bill of lading until they have come to the hands of some person who has a right to the possession under it.' And afterwards, in the Exchequer Chamber, Mr. Baron Martin, putting the case on somewhat different grounds, says: 'For many years past there have been two symbols of property in goods imported; the one the bill of lading, the other the wharfinger's certificate or warrant. Until the latter is issued by the wharfinger the former remains the only symbol of property in the goods. When, therefore, Abraham delivered the bill of lading to the Plaintiff on the 4th of March, 1865, as a security for the advance then made to him, such delivery amounted to a valid pledge of the goods, and the Plaintiff thereby acquired a right to hold them as against Abraham and all persons claiming title thereto under him.' The principle seems to be the same, according to the view which Mr. Baron Martin takes, which is this: There has been adopted, for the convenience of mankind, a mode of dealing with property the possession of which cannot be immediately delivered, namely, that of dealing with symbols of the property. In the case of goods which are at sea being transmitted from one country to another, you cannot deliver actual possession of them, therefore the bill of lading is considered to be a symbol of the goods, and its delivery to be a delivery of them. When they have arrived at the dock, until they are delivered to some person who has the right to hold them the bill of lading still remains the only symbol that can be dealt with by way of assignment, or mortgage, or otherwise. As soon as delivery is made, or a warrant for delivery has been issued, or an order for delivery accepted (which in law would be equivalent to delivery), then those symbols replace the symbol which before existed. Until that time bills of lading are effective representations of the ownership of the goods, and their force does not become extinguished until possession, or what is equivalent in law to possession, has been taken on the part of the person having a right to demand it.

It appears to me that that is the legal sense of the transaction. The shipowner contracts that he will deliver the goods on the payment of freight. He discharges his contract when he delivers the goods. But, unless he chooses to waive his rights, he is not bound so to deliver the goods, or to hand them over to the person who is the original consignee to whom he has contracted to make the delivery, until all the conditions on which he contracted to deliver them are fulfilled. One of those conditions is, that the freight should be paid; and until the freight has been paid he is not bound to make the delivery.

…

It is said that a frightful amount of fraud may be perpetrated if persons are allowed to deal in this way with bills of lading drawn in sets, if you allow efficacy be given to the first assignment of one of those bills, to the detriment of persons who may take, for value, subsequent assignments of the others. All that we can say is, that such has been the law hitherto, and that the consequences of the supposed evil, whatever they may be, have not been considered to be such as to counterbalance the great advantages and facilities afforded by the transfer of bills of lading. There is no authority or reason for holding that the person who first obtains the assignment of a bill of lading, and has given value for it, shall not acquire the legal ownership of the goods it represents. It seems to be required by the exigencies of mankind. It may be a satisfaction to be told by Mr. Justice Willes (though it is a matter upon which I put no reliance), that other nations concur with us in holding that (whatever inconveniences there may be attending it), the person who gets the first assignment for value is the person to be preferred.

The reasoning of the learned Judges in this case establishes clearly these two propositions: First, that the holder of the first assignment for value obtains a priority over those who obtain possession of the other bills. And, secondly (following the reasoning of Mr. Justice Willes), 'The wharfinger under these circumstances was, at the lowest, the common agent for the shipowner and for the consignee or holder of the bill of lading – agent for the consignee or holder, upon his producing the bill of lading shewing that he was entitled to the goods, and upon his paying the freight, to transfer the goods into his name, and to deliver them to him, or give him a warrant for them – and agent for the shipowner to retain possession of the goods and to permit no one to exercise any control over them until the claim for freight had been satisfied. During this period, therefore, the bill of lading would not only, according to the usage, and for the satisfaction of the wharfinger that he was delivering to the right person, be a symbol of possession, and practically the key of the warehouse, but it would, so far at least as the shipowner was concerned, retain its full and complete operation as a bill of lading, there having been no complete delivery of possession of the goods.' The other learned Judges take the same view; and I apprehend that the correct view in substance is this – that this being the possession of the wharfinger, the bill of lading remains in force so long as complete delivery and possession has not been given to some person having the right to claim such delivery and possession.

As to the argument founded on the possibility of fraud, I agree very much with one of the learned Judges, Mr. Justice Willes, who says, that as to any argument upon that subject, 'all arguments founded upon the notion that the Court is to pronounce a judgment in this case which will protect those who deal with fraudulent people, are altogether beside the facts of this case, and foreign from transactions of this nature.' I am afraid that the protection of parties against fraud is a matter of difficulty with which the Legislature must cope, as far as it can possibly do so, from time to time, when frauds of a serious character are practised; but the Courts of Law, which have to administer the law as it exists, cannot alter their course of proceeding because those who ought to do that which is right and just to their neighbours find means of defrauding them in spite of all the protection which the law may have thrown around the innocent holders of property. Judicature has no power to interfere with the course of proceeding in such cases. It must be left to the Legislature alone. But, on the other hand, we should consider that our mercantile laws, which are founded on long usage, have been found to work well for the general convenience of those engaged in those large adventures which are familiar to the enterprise of this country, and that although occasional inconvenience may have been caused by the fraudulent behaviour of some parties, yet these laws have, upon the whole, been felt to operate beneficially.

The principles which, as I have stated, form the foundation of the judgment in the present case are, that the parting with the symbol of property the possession of which cannot be delivered is the parting with the property itself; and that persons who have not a complete ownership and possession of the property cannot be said to have such a title to that property as to divest the operation of the symbol to give a title to it, until something occurs which brings the symbol and the property itself into contact – and that for the purpose of so bringing the property and the symbol into contact, there must be a complete concurrence of title in the person who holds the symbol and the person who has the right to demand the property; and until that happens the symbol, as in the present case, has not exhausted its office.

I am, therefore, of opinion that the learned Judges have come to the right conclusion, and I have to move your Lordships to affirm the two decisions which are complained of in this appeal.

The law suggests that when a bill of lading becomes spent, it loses its character as document of title. In *Central Trading & Exports Ltd v Fioralba Shipping Company* [2014] EWHC 2397 (Comm) we can see why this issue can be important. In that case, the claimant's claim was for loss and damage to a cargo of bagged rice carried from Thailand to Nigeria. Five bills of lading were issued by the carrier. The voyage was completed, and discharge was commenced, as long ago as 17 September 2009. The bills were subject to English law and each contained a London arbitration clause. The claimant claimed that it became the holder of the bills and that rights of suit were transferred to it pursuant to the provisions of the Carriage of Goods by Sea Act 1992. It accepted that it became the holder at a time when the bills were spent, discharge having taken place without production of the bills pursuant to letters of indemnity, but contended that it did so 'by virtue of a transaction effected in pursuance of any contractual or other arrangements made before the time when such a right to possession ceased to attach to production of the bill'. If that is so, it has title to sue in accordance with the Act. The defendant challenged this contention, pointing to evidence that suggests that any such arrangements may only have been put in place at a later stage. A hearing date in October 2014 has been set to deal with these issues but for our purposes it suffices to point out the significance of the proposition.

It has been suggested that a bill would not be spent until the goods have been delivered to the *rightful* holder (namely the completion of the fundamental obligations of the contract of carriage). See *The Future Express* [1992] 2 Lloyd's Rep 79, affd [1993] 2 Lloyd's Rep 542 where HHJ Diamond held thus that a bill of lading does not become exhausted if the goods are delivered against the presentation of other documentation (such as a letter of indemnity). It is respectfully submitted that it is difficult to see how the bill could continue to be the symbolic representation of the goods when the goods have been lawfully delivered to a person fully entitled to taking possession of the goods.

In *Glyn Mills Currie & Co. v East & West India Dock Co* (1882) 7 App Cas 591, it was said, '... the bill of lading remains in force at least so long as complete delivery of possession of the goods has not been made to some person having a right to claim under it.'

Barclays Bank Ltd v Commissioners of Customs & Excise [1963] 1 Lloyd's Rep 81

Facts: A bill of lading was issued at Rotterdam by Bristol Steam Navigation Company Ltd in respect of a consignment of washing machines shipped on the motor vessel *Echo* for delivery at Cardiff to order of shippers or assigns. The goods were landed and warehoused to the order of the shipowners. Two months later B, the holder of the bill of lading, pledged it to the plaintiffs as security. The plaintiffs subsequently presented the bill of lading to the carriers and received a delivery order addressed to the warehouse, but before delivery could be obtained, the goods were seized on behalf of the defendants who were judgment creditors of B. The question for the court was whether, on the date of the pledge, the bills of lading were still documents of title to the goods, by endorsement and delivery of which the rights and property in the goods would be transferred.

Held:

Diplock LJ (sitting as an additional judge of the Queen's Bench Division): . . . The contention of the Customs and Excise is that as soon as (1) a contract of carriage by sea is complete, or at any rate the contract of carriage evidenced by the bill of lading is complete, and (2) the bill of lading is in the hands of the person entitled to the property in, and possession of, the goods, and is in a form which would entitle him upon mere presentation to obtain delivery of the goods from the shipowner – that is indorsed to him or indorsed in blank – it ceases to be a document of title by delivery and indorsement of which the rights and property in the goods can be transferred. This is indeed a startling proposition of law which, if correct, would go far to destroy the value of a bill of lading as an instrument of overseas credit. It would mean that no bank could safely advance money on the security of a bill of lading without first making inquiries at the port of delivery, which may be at the other side of the world, as to whether the goods had been landed with the shipowner's lien, if any, discharged or released. It would also mean that no purchaser of goods could rely upon delivery and indorsement to him of the bill of lading as conferring upon him any title to the goods without making similar inquiries, for it would follow that once the goods had been landed and any lien of the shipowner released or discharged, the owner of the goods could divest himself of the property in them without reference to the bill of lading. It would also follow that the shipowner, once the goods had been landed in the absence of any lien, could not safely deliver the goods to the holder of the bill of lading upon presentation because the property in and right to possession of the goods, might have been transferred by the owner to some other person. To hold that this was the law would be to turn back the clock to 1794 before the acceptance by the court of the special verdict of the jury as to custom of merchants in the case of *Lickbarrow v Mason* (1794) 5 Term 683, and which laid the foundation for the financing of overseas trade and the growth of commodity markets in the 19th century.

The contract for the carriage of goods by sea, which is evidenced by a bill of lading, is a combined contract of bailment and transportation under which the shipowner undertakes to accept possession of the goods from the shipper, to carry them to their contractual destination and there to surrender possession of them to the person who, under the terms of the contract, is entitled to obtain possession of them from the shipowners. Such a contract is not discharged by performance until the shipowner has actually surrendered possession (that is, has divested himself of all powers to control any physical dealing in the goods) to the person entitled under the terms of the contract to obtain possession of them.

So long as the contract is not discharged, the bill of lading, in my view, remains a document of title by indorsement and delivery of which the rights of property in the goods can be transferred. It is clear law that where a bill of lading or order is issued in respect of the contract of carriage by sea, the shipowner is not bound to surrender possession of the goods to any person whether named as consignee or not, except on production of the bill of lading (see *The Stettin* (1889) 14 PD 142). Until the bill of lading is produced to him, unless at any rate, its absence has been satisfactorily accounted for, he is entitled to retain possession of the goods and if he does part with possession he does so at his own risk if the person to whom he surrenders possession is not in fact entitled to the goods.

... It is not necessary in this case to consider what is a much more difficult question of law ... as to what the position would be if the shipowners had given a complete delivery to B of the goods without production of the bill of lading, at the date when they were entitled under its terms to deliver, and B had subsequently purported to pledge the goods by deposit of the bill of lading. That question does not arise because in this case not only had complete delivery of possession not been given to B, but no delivery of possession at all at the relevant time on 2 June had been given. In my opinion the pledge made on 2 June by deposit of the bill of lading was a valid pledge and as a consequence I think that I can give judgment for the plaintiffs in this case.

Notes

1 In *Enichem Anic SpA v Ampelos Shipping Co Ltd, The Delfini* [1990] 1 Lloyd's Rep 252, at first instance, it was said that where short delivery was alleged, the bill of lading ceased to be a document of title when the majority of the cargo was delivered. On appeal, Mustill J said that it was clear from *Meyerstein v Barber* (1870) LR 4 HL 317, especially at pp 330 and 335, that when the goods have been actually delivered at destination to the person entitled to them, or placed in a position where the person is entitled to immediate possession, the bill of lading is exhausted 'and will not operate at all to transfer the goods to any person who has either advanced money or has purchased the bill of lading'. It was also said to be clear that until the buyer has actually received delivery, the fact that the goods have been discharged at destination subject (say) to a lien for freight, does not entail that the bill is exhausted.

2 *Carriage of Goods by Sea Act 1992*. The Act, below, provides for the statutory transmission of rights of action under the bill of lading contract from the shipper to a person who becomes the holder of a transferable bill of lading: s 2(1). But, with exceptions, no rights of suit pass once the bill of lading has ceased to carry the right as against the carrier to possession of the goods: s 2(2).

17 Statutory transfer of rights of action

The cases included in the first part of this chapter show that the ownership of cargo on board a ship on bill of lading terms may be transferred by endorsement and delivery of an order bill of lading.

However, at common law the transfer of the property in the goods did not pass to the endorsee the contractual rights and duties contained in the bill of lading. The result was that if the cargo was lost or damaged by the carrier, an endorsee who had purchased the goods while they were at sea could not normally make a claim for damages against the contracting carrier on the basis of the contract contained in or evidenced by the bill of lading; nor could the carrier make a claim under the bill of lading for freight or other charges against anyone other than the party on whose behalf the goods were shipped. Several devices were employed to minimise the inconvenience of this position.

One possibility where the consignee was the owner of the goods was to find as a fact that that the bill of lading contract had been entered into by the consignor as agent for the consignee, so that the consignee named in the bill of lading might sue or be sued on its terms. This solution was, however, of little use where the goods were only purchased after the carriage contract had been concluded. An alternative approach – the rule in *Dunlop v Lambert* (1839) Cl & Fin 600 – permitted the shipper to sue and recover substantial damages on behalf of the consignee or endorsee to whom the goods had been sold. A third possibility was to treat presentation of the bill of lading and the giving and taking of delivery of the cargo at discharge as facts from which a contract between the carrier and the receiver – a *Brandt* contract – could be implied.

These three devices could help in individual cases, but they did not provide a comprehensive and reliable solution. In 1855 Parliament offered assistance. The Bills of Lading Act 1855 provided a statutory transfer of rights of action in cases where the general property in the goods on a ship passed on or by reason of the consignment or endorsement of the bill of lading. However, this scheme came to be regarded in the 20th century as too narrow and restrictive. It did not operate when property passed independently of the consignment or endorsement of the goods or in cases – such as a sale of goods forming part of an undivided bulk – where the property could not pass at all while the goods were at sea. Also, the Act only applied to bills of lading, not to other contractual forms such as sea waybills and ship's delivery orders or of course to electronic commerce. The English and Scottish Law Commissions, in a joint report *Rights of Suit in Respect of Carriage of Goods by Sea* (Law Com 196, London: HMSO; Scot Law Com 130) proposed changes. The 1855 Act was repealed and replaced by the Carriage of Goods by Sea Act 1992. The 1992 Act follows the statutory assignment model of the 1855 Act, but abandons the idea that the transmission of rights of action against the carrier should be linked to the passing of property in the goods carried. The passing of contractual rights is also separated from the passing of liabilities.

18 Carriage of Goods by Sea Act 1992

1 Shipping documents etc to which Act applies

(1)   This Act applies to the following documents, that is to say:
   (a)   any bill of lading;
   (b)   any sea waybill; and
   (c)   any ship's delivery order.
(2)   References in this Act to a bill of lading:
   (a)   do not include references to a document which is incapable of transfer either by indorsement or, as a bearer bill, by delivery without indorsement; but
   (b)   subject to that, do include references to a received for shipment bill of lading.
(3)   References in this Act to a sea waybill are references to any document which is not a bill of lading but:
   (a)   is such a receipt for goods as contains or evidences a contract for the carriage of goods by sea; and

(b) identifies the person to whom delivery of the goods is to be made by the carrier in accordance with that contract.

(4) References in this Act to a ship's delivery order are references to any document which is neither a bill of lading nor a sea waybill but contains an undertaking which:

(a) is given under or for the purposes of a contract for the carriage by sea of the goods to which the document relates, or of goods which include those goods; and

(b) is an undertaking by the carrier to a person identified in the document to deliver the goods to which the document relates to that person.

(5) The Secretary of State may by regulations make provision for the application of this Act to cases where a telecommunication system or any other information technology is used for effecting transactions corresponding to:

(a) the issue of a document to which this Act applies;

(b) the indorsement, delivery or other transfer of such a document; or

(c) the doing of anything else in relation to such a document.

(6) Regulations under subsection (5) above may:

(a) make such modifications of the following provisions of this Act as the Secretary of State considers appropriate in connection with the application of this Act to any case mentioned in that subsection; and

(b) contain supplemental, incidental, consequential and transitional provision;

and the power to make regulations under that subsection shall be exercisable by statutory instrument subject to annulment in pursuance of a resolution of either House of Parliament.

2 Rights under shipping documents

(1) Subject to the following provisions of this section, a person who becomes:

(a) the lawful holder of a bill of lading;

(b) the person who (without being an original party to the contract of carriage) is the person to whom delivery of the goods to which a sea waybill relates is to be made by the carrier in accordance with that contract; or

(c) the person to whom delivery of the goods to which a ship's delivery order relates is to be made in accordance with the undertaking contained in the order,

shall (by virtue of becoming the holder of the bill or, as the case may be, the person to whom delivery is to be made) have transferred to and vested in him all rights of suit under the contract of carriage as if he had been a party to that contract.

(2) Where, when a person becomes the lawful holder of a bill of lading, possession of the bill no longer gives a right (as against the carrier) to possession of the goods to which the bill relates, that person shall not have any rights transferred to him by virtue of subsection (1) above unless he becomes the holder of the bill:

(a) by virtue of a transaction effected in pursuance of any contractual or other arrangements made before the time when such a right to possession ceased to attach to possession of the bill; or

(b) as a result of the rejection to that person by another person of goods or documents delivered to the other person in pursuance of any such arrangements.

(3) The rights vested in any person by virtue of the operation of subsection (1) above in relation to a ship's delivery order:

(a) shall be so vested subject to the terms of the order; and

(b) where the goods to which the order relates form a part only of the goods to which the contract of carriage relates, shall be confined to rights in respect of the goods to which the order relates.

(4) Where, in the case of any document to which this Act applies:

   (a) a person with any interest or right in or in relation to goods to which the document relates sustains loss or damage in consequence of a breach of the contract of carriage; but

   (b) subsection (1) above operates in relation to that document so that rights of suit in respect of that breach are vested in another person,

the other person shall be entitled to exercise those rights for the benefit of the person who sustained the loss or damage to the same extent as they could have been exercised if they had been vested in the person for whose benefit they are exercised.

(5) Where rights are transferred by virtue of the operation of subsection (1) above in relation to any document, the transfer for which that subsection provides shall extinguish any entitlement to those rights which derives:

   (a) where that document is a bill of lading, from a person's having been an original party to the contract of carriage; or

   (b) in the case of any document to which this Act applies, from the previous operation of that subsection in relation to that document;

but the operation of that subsection shall be without prejudice to any rights which derive from a person's having been an original party to the contract contained in, or evidenced by, a sea waybill and, in relation to a ship's delivery order, shall be without prejudice to any rights deriving otherwise than from the previous operation of that subsection in relation to that order.

3 Liabilities under shipping documents

(1) Where subsection (1) of section 2 of this Act operates in relation to any document to which this Act applies and the person in whom rights are vested by virtue of that subsection:

   (a) takes or demands delivery from the carrier of any of the goods to which the document relates;

   (b) makes a claim under the contract of carriage against the carrier in respect of any of those goods; or

   (c) is a person who, at a time before those rights were vested in him, took or demanded delivery from the carrier of any of those goods,

that person shall (by virtue of taking or demanding delivery or making the claim or, in a case falling within paragraph (c) above, of having the rights vested in him) become subject to the same liabilities under that contract as if he had been a party to that contract.

(2) Where the goods to which a ship's delivery order relates form a part only of the goods to which the contract of carriage relates, the liabilities to which any person is subject by virtue of the operation of this section in relation to that order shall exclude liabilities in respect of any goods to which the order does not relate.

(3) This section, so far as it imposes liabilities under any contract on any person, shall be without prejudice to the liabilities under the contract of any person as an original party to the contract.

. . .

5 Interpretation etc

(1) In this Act:

   'bill of lading', 'sea waybill' and 'ship's delivery order' shall be construed in accordance with section 1 above;

   'the contract of carriage':

(a)   in relation to a bill of lading or sea waybill, means the contract contained in or evidenced by that bill or waybill; and

(b)   in relation to a ship's delivery order, means the contract under or for the purposes of which the undertaking contained in the order is given;

'holder', in relation to a bill of lading, shall be construed in accordance with subsection (2) below;

'information technology' includes any computer or other technology by means of which information or other matter may be recorded or communicated without being reduced to documentary form; and

'telecommunication system' has the same meaning as in the Telecommunications Act 1984.

(2)   References in this Act to the holder of a bill of lading are references to any of the following persons, that is to say:

(a)   a person with possession of the bill who, by virtue of being the person identified in the bill, is the consignee of the goods to which the bill relates;

(b)   a person with possession of the bill as a result of the completion, by delivery of the bill, of any indorsement of the bill or, in the case of a bearer bill, of any other transfer of the bill;

(c)   a person with possession of the bill as a result of any transaction by virtue of which he would have become a holder falling within paragraph (a) or (b) above had not the transaction been effected at a time when possession of the bill no longer gave a right (as against the carrier) to possession of the goods to which the bill relates;

and a person shall be regarded for the purposes of this Act as having become the lawful holder of a bill of lading wherever he has become the holder of the bill in good faith.

(3)   References in this Act to a person's being identified in a document include references to his being identified by a description which allows for the identity of the person in question to be varied, in accordance with the terms of the document, after its issue; and the reference in section 1(3)(b) of this Act to a document's identifying a person shall be construed accordingly.

(4)   Without prejudice to sections 2(2) and 4 above, nothing in this Act shall preclude its operation in relation to a case where the goods to which a document relates:

(a)   cease to exist after the issue of the document; or

(b)   cannot be identified (whether because they are mixed with other goods or for any other reason);

and references in this Act to the goods to which a document relates shall be construed accordingly.

(5)   The preceding provisions of this Act shall have effect without prejudice to the application, in relation to any case, of the rules (the Hague-Visby Rules) which for the time being have the force of law by virtue of section 1 of the Carriage of Goods by Sea Act 1971.

Notes

1   Section 1 of COGSA 1992 applies the Act to 'documents' including any 'bill of lading' and in s 5(1) a '"bill of lading" shall be construed in accordance with s 1 above'. However, s 1(2)(a) expressly excludes 'straight' bills of lading from the statutory definition. It explicitly excludes all documents which would otherwise have fallen within the term bill of lading but that are 'incapable of transfer either by indorsement or, as a bearerbill, by

delivery without indorsement'. Consequently, although the Act does attempt to define the bill of lading, the description is limited. Reference to the common law's definition thus remains vital.

2   Section 1(3) suggests that a straight bill of lading would be treated as a sea waybill for the purposes of the 1992 Act. NB. However, for the purposes of the Hague-Visby Rules (and Carriage of Goods by Sea Act 1971) it would be treated as a bill of lading: *The Rafaela S* [2005] UKHL 11.

3   The Act also anticipates the increasing use and reliance on electronic shipping documents by carriers, consignors and consignees. Section 1(5) and (6) of COGSA 1992 make provision for the making of regulations to cases where 'a telecommunication system or any other information technology' is used for effecting transactions involving bills of lading. Although no such regulations have been made by the government as yet, the presence of these provisions suggest that an electronic bill of lading is likely to be treated as a bill of lading for the purposes of the Act.

19 Transfer of contractual rights

The 1992 Act transfers to and vests 'all rights of suit under the contract of carriage' in the holder of a shipping document. In the *East West Corp* case [2003] EWCA Civ 83; [2003] 2 All ER 700, below, 'rights of suit' was said at trial to mean all the rights arising under the contract. But what is meant by 'the contract of carriage'? Section 5 of the Act provides that in the case of a bill of lading these words are to be treated as meaning 'the contract contained in or evidenced by that bill'. What then is the position where a bill of lading was not originally a contract at all, but merely a receipt issued to a charterer? And what if the bill, when issued, was no more than 'some evidence' of a contract. Does s 5 mean that other evidence of the terms of the contract is also admissible against a holder?

Leduc & Co v Ward (1888) 20 QBD 475, CA

Facts: The claimants were endorsees of a bill of lading that contained the usual exception of sea perils and stated that the goods were shipped in apparent good order and condition on the steamship *Austria*, now lying in the port of Fiume, and bound for Dunkirk, with liberty to call at any ports in any order, and to deviate for the purpose of saving life or property; 3,123 bags of rape seed, being marked and numbered as per margin, and to be delivered in the like good order and condition at the aforesaid port of Dunkirk unto order or assigns.

The ship, instead of proceeding direct for Dunkirk, sailed for Glasgow, and was lost, with her cargo, off the mouth of the Clyde, by perils of the sea. In an action brought by the plaintiffs against the shipowners for non-delivery of the goods, evidence was given to show that the shippers of the goods, at the time when the bill of lading was given, knew that the vessel was intended to proceed via Glasgow.

Held:

Lord Esher MR: In this case the plaintiffs, the owners of goods shipped on board the defendants' ship, sue for non-delivery of the goods at Dunkirk in accordance with the terms of the bill of lading. The defence is that delivery of the goods was prevented by perils of the sea. To that the plaintiffs reply that the goods were not lost by reason of any perils excepted by the bill of lading, because they were lost at a time when the defendants were committing a breach of their contract by deviating from the voyage provided for by the bill of lading. The plaintiffs were clearly indorsees of the bill of lading to whom the property passed by reason of the indorsement; and, therefore, by the Bills of Lading Act [1855], the rights upon the contract contained in the bill of lading passed to them. The question, therefore, arises what the effect of that contract was. It has been suggested that the bill of lading is merely in the nature of a receipt for the goods, and that it contains no contract for anything but the delivery of the goods at the place named therein. It is true that, where there is a charterparty, as between the shipowner and the charterer the bill of lading may be merely in the nature of a receipt for the goods, because all the other terms of the contract of carriage between them are contained in the charterparty; and the bill of lading is merely given as between them to enable the charterer to deal with the goods while in the course of transit; but, where the bill of lading is indorsed over, as between the shipowner and the indorsee the bill of lading must be considered to contain the contract, because the former has given it for the purpose of enabling the charterer to pass it on as the contract of carriage in respect of the goods . . .

The terms of the Bills of Lading Act shew that the legislature looked upon a bill of lading as containing the terms of the contract of carriage . . .

Note

An unequivocal explanation of the position is contained in the judgment in *The Heidberg* [1994] 2 Lloyd's Rep 287 where Judge Diamond QC said:

> Bills of lading are transferrable documents which come into the hands of consignees and indorsees who may be the purchasers of goods or banks. The transferee of the bill of lading does not, however, take precisely the same contract as that made between the shipper and the shipowner (of which the bill of lading is merely the evidence). What is transferred to the consignee or indorsee consists, and consists only, of the terms which appear on the face and reverse of the bill of lading. Thus collateral oral terms are not transferred; see *Leduc v Ward* (1888) QBD 475; *The Ardennes* [1951] 1 KB 55. This rule facilitates the use of bills of lading in international commerce since it enables a prospective transferee of a bill of lading to see, merely by inspecting the bill, whether it conforms to his contract (whether it be a sale contract or a letter of credit) and what rights and obligations will be transferred to him if he takes up the bill. The transferee, or prospective transferee, need not enquire whether any collateral oral agreements have been made between the shipper and the shipowner as, for example, a waiver by the shipper of any obligation undertaken by the shipowner in the bill . . .

It should also be noted that the underlying policy for introducing the 1992 Act was also to provide for the case where cargo is discharged against a letter of indemnity and where under those circumstances, there would be no right of recourse under the Bills of Lading Act 1855, s 1.

Pace Shipping Co Ltd v Churchgate Nigeria Ltd, The Pace [2010] 1 Lloyd's Rep 183

Facts: CN were the holders of seven bills of lading for a cargo of bagged rice loaded in Thailand on board the *MV Pace* bound for Nigeria. They brought a claim against P, the owners, for cargo damage and a small short delivery. CN became holders of the bills of lading in due course after the bills were endorsed to it by its bankers, G, and then handed over to an employee of CN. The cargo was discharged, in the absence of the bills of lading, to the charterers of the *MV Pace* under a letter of indemnity.

A question was whether CN had title to sue pursuant to the Carriage of Goods by Sea Act 1992, s 2(2)(a). The arbitrators, by a majority, found that C did have rights of suit under s 2(2)(a) because CN became the holders of the bills of lading by virtue of a transaction, namely the endorsement and delivery of the bills pursuant to contracts of sale entered into by it as principal for the purchase of the cargo. They also ruled that the immediate and proximate cause of the transfer of the bills of lading was the contracts of sale that predated the discharge of the cargo. While CN's payment under the contracts of sale could not have been made strictly in accordance with their terms, the tribunal was satisfied, albeit just, that payment for the cargo was made pursuant to the contracts of sale.

P submitted that the endorsement and delivery of the bills of lading could only have been effected 'in pursuance of' the sale contracts if CN had been entitled to receive the bills of lading under the contracts of sale. They argued that the tribunal either rejected that proposition or failed adequately to address it. P applied to have the arbitrators' award set aside.

Held: (claim dismissed)

42. Having reviewed the submissions put to the tribunal before it made the second award I have concluded that the first question of law on which the applicant seeks leave to appeal was not one which the tribunal was asked to determine. The applicant's case was that, following the decision of Aikens J in *The Ythan*, the words 'in pursuance of' in section 2(2)(a) required that the contractual or other arrangements must be 'the reason or cause' of the endorsement and delivery of the bills. It is true that in support of its case the applicant submitted that the respondent cannot have had an entitlement under the contracts of sale to the endorsement and delivery of the bills but this was one of several points, albeit described as the key point, which led to the conclusion that the respondent had failed to discharge the burden of proving that the contracts of sale were the reason or the cause of the endorsement and delivery of the bills. The tribunal was asked to consider all the circumstances of the case when deciding a question of fact.

43. For this reason, namely, that the first question of law on which leave to appeal is sought was not one which the tribunal was asked to determine, I must refuse leave to appeal on that first question of law.

44. In case I am wrong in concluding that the first question of law was not one which the tribunal was asked to decide I shall nevertheless consider that question upon the assumption that it is a question of general public importance and that the decision of the tribunal is open to serious doubt. In the unusual circumstances of this case I have heard full argument upon it before deciding whether leave to appeal upon that question should be granted.

45. In *The David Agmashenebeli* [2003] 1 Lloyd's Rep 92 Colman J said that the key question in applying section 2(2)(a) was whether the transfer of the bills of lading was 'called for' by the contractual or other arrangements made before the bills were spent. This seems to me to be consistent with the applicant's submission that the section requires the transferee to be 'entitled' to the transfer of the bills pursuant to the terms of the contractual or other arrangements. In that case a contract of sale made before the bills had become spent had been replaced by a later agreement made after the bills had become spent. It was held that the buyers had acquired the bills under the later contract.

46. In *Primetrade AG v Ythan Ltd* (*The Ythan*) [2006] 1 Lloyd's Rep 457 at para 84 Aikens J, as I have already noted, agreed with a statement in *Carver on Bills of Lading* (see now the 2nd Edition at para 5–059 by Treitel and Reynolds) that the words 'contractual or other arrangements' refer to the 'reason or cause for the transfer'. In that case the vessel suffered an explosion the day after the cargo was loaded. The bills of lading were eventually delivered to the insurance brokers acting for the buyers and there was an issue as to whether that 'transaction' was in pursuance of the marine open cover that was in place before the vessel and cargo were lost or in pursuance of a compromise agreement between the buyers and the underwriters made long after the vessel and cargo were lost. Aikens J held that the reason for the delivery of the bills was because it was 'contemplated' that underwriters would pay under the compromise agreement. He accepted that it could be said that the delivery of the bills of 'arose out of the open cover' but in his view 'the immediate reason and proximate cause of the transfer of the bills' was the compromise agreement.

47. This decision is also consistent with the applicant's submission because the buyers may be said to have been entitled to receive the bills under the compromise agreement. However, the terms in which Aikens J himself expressed the test were that the contractual or other arrangements had to be the 'reason or the cause' of the endorsement and delivery of the bills.

48. In considering the meaning of the phrase 'in pursuance of' it is appropriate to bear in mind the purpose of section 2(2)(a) of the Act. It provided that the rights of suit would only be transferred to those who became holders of the bills after the bills had been spent where they became holders 'in pursuance of' contractual or other arrangements made before the bills had been spent. That was to prevent 'trafficking in bills of lading simply as pieces of paper which give causes of action against sea carriers' (see The Law Commission Report on Rights of Suit in Respect of Carriage of Goods by Sea at para 2.43). Bearing that purpose in mind I consider that the words 'in pursuance of' can most appropriately be understood to mean that the contractual or other arrangements must be the reason or cause for the transfer of delivery of the bills. In this regard I respectfully agree with Aikens J's understanding of section 2(2)(a) based as it was on the observations in Carver. Of course, that test will usually be satisfied where the holder receives the bills because he has a contractual entitlement to receive them (or to 'call for' them) under the contractual or other arrangements in existence before the bills were spent. Those will be the typical circumstances in which the test is satisfied. But I do not consider that section 2(2)(a) should be restricted to cases where there is such a contractual entitlement. First, section 2(2)(a) does not use such words. Second, the objective or aim of section 2(2)(a) to avoid trafficking in bills of lading will be achieved if the reason or cause of the transfer is the contractual or other arrangements in existence before the bills were spent. Such an interpretation may have a wider scope than one based upon contractual entitlement in that it may be satisfied in the absence of a contractual entitlement but it is nevertheless consistent with the aim or object of section 2(2)(a). It will avoid trafficking in bills of lading.

49. The majority of the tribunal concluded that 'CN [the respondent] were parties to the sale contracts, that payment was made and that as a result CN became the lawful holders of the bills'. That is consistent with a finding that the reason or cause of the delivery of the bills was the sale contracts. No finding had been made that the respondent had paid for the goods and the majority accepted that payment cannot have been made strictly in accordance with the terms of the contract of sale. But the majority found as a fact that the respondent entered into the contracts of sale as principals and remained principals and that the payment (albeit by NBIC) had been made under the sale contracts. In those circumstances the majority inferred that the transfer of the bills to the respondent was a result of the payment made under the contracts of sale. That is an inference they were entitled to draw, though in the absence of evidence as to precisely what had happened between payment by NBIC and endorsement and delivery of the bills by the Guaranty Trust Bank, others might not have not done and Mr Harris did not do so. The facts that the respondent entered into the contracts of sale as principals and remained as principals and that the payment by NBIC was under the sale contracts are, at the least, consistent with this not being a case of trafficking in bills of lading.

50. The essence of the applicant's complaint is that once the price had been paid by NBIC and the bills had been delivered to NBIC by the sellers the contracts of sale had been 'exhausted' and there was no longer any entitlement on the part of the respondent to delivery of the bills from the sellers. However, the respondent was and remained the principal to the contracts of sale and 'the payment for the goods, by whatever means, was under the sale contracts'. Whether or not the obligation of the sellers to deliver the bills in exchange for the price had been 'exhausted' the respondent in due course had the bills of lading endorsed and delivered to it, which was what the contracts of sale had contemplated by their terms and what would be expected in the ordinary course of international trade. I do not consider that the conclusion of the majority reveals an approach to section 2(2)(a) which is inconsistent with its meaning and purpose. The majority held that the contracts of sale entered into by the respondent as principal before the bills became spent were the reason or cause of the endorsement and delivery of the bills to the respondent.

51. Thus, had I decided that the first question of law had been a question which the tribunal had been asked to determine and given leave to appeal I would have dismissed that appeal.

52. The second alleged error of law is that the majority either misdirected itself as to the difference between a proximate cause and a causa sine qua non in concluding that the underlying contracts of sale were the proximate and immediate cause of the endorsements and delivery of the bills or reached a conclusion which a properly directed tribunal could not properly have reached.

53. It was not said, and could not be said, that the question of proximate cause was not one which the tribunal had been asked to determine. Having concluded that the respondent became the holders of the bills as a result of the payment of the price under the contracts of sale the majority stated that: 'it follows from our findings in our immediately preceding paragraph that we are also satisfied that the immediate and proximate cause of the transfer of the bills was the sale contracts and the payments made thereunder to CN's respective sellers'.

54. Just as the conclusion of the majority that the respondent became the holder of the bills as a result of the payment of the price under the contracts of sale was an inference they were entitled to draw so the majority were entitled to conclude that the immediate and proximate cause of the transfer of the bills was the sale contracts and the payments made thereunder. Others might not have been prepared to draw that inference in the absence of clear evidence as to the circumstances in which Guaranty Trust Bank endorsed the bills to the respondent but I do not consider that it is possible to say that the majority must have misdirected itself or reached a decision which a properly directed tribunal could not have reached. This was not a case where a competing cause was suggested (as was the case in both *The Ythan* and *The David Agmashenebeli*) and the tribunal expressly stated that there was nothing to suggest that CN became the holders other than lawfully. (It was only after the second award had been published that the applicant suggested that 'trafficking' in bills of lading might have been the reason for the transfer of the bills.) The decision of the majority on this question of causation was neither obviously wrong nor open to serious doubt (as those expressions are used in section 69(3)(c) of the Arbitration Act 1996) notwithstanding that in assessing the evidence and in particular the significance of those matters that had not been proved others might have reached, and Mr Harris did reach, a different conclusion.

Note

From this judgment, it seems to follow that the words 'in pursuance of' in s 2(2)(a) should be taken to mean that the contractual or other arrangements had to be the reason for or cause of the transfer of delivery of the bills. That test should therefore be met if the holder received the bills because he had a contractual entitlement to receive them under the contractual or other arrangements in existence before the bills were spent. It, however, does not follow that s 2(2)(a) should be confined *only* to cases where there was such a contractual entitlement. The words of the subsection clearly do not employ such wording. Other arrangements may also be sufficient. The case does not discuss what such arrangements are likely to be.

20 Transmission of liabilities under the 1992 Act

The 1992 Act provides that liabilities under shipping documents pass to the holder of the document only when the holder takes or demands delivery or makes a claim under the contract. This part of the Act was new, although it was intended to reflect the broad effect of previous law. The new provisions were considered by the House of Lords for the first time in *The Berge Sisar*. For analysis of the case, see 'Further Reading', below.

Borealis AB v Stargas Ltd, The Berge Sisar [2001] UKHL 17; [2002] 2 AC 205

Facts: Stargas sold liquid propane to Borealis and chartered the *Berge Sisar* to carry the propane from Saudi Arabia to Sweden. Bills of lading were signed by the master. On arrival routine sampling showed that the propane was contaminated and Borealis, to whom title to the propane had passed, refused to receive the cargo and sold it on to Dow who had facilities to deal with it in a contaminated condition. The cargo was delivered to Dow, without production of the bills of lading, on the instructions of the charterers and against a letter of indemnity from them. Nearly two months later the bills of lading were endorsed to Borealis and then endorsed on to Dow. Bergesen, the shipowners, alleged that the cargo became contaminated before it was loaded and claimed damages for costs of cleaning the ship from the charterers and also from Borealis, under the terms of the 1992 Act.

Lord Hobhouse: 17 The question raised . . . is whether Bergesen has a good arguable case in contract against Borealis. The question breaks down into two subsidiary questions. First, did Borealis ever become liable to Bergesen under section 3 of the 1992 Act? It is the case of Bergesen that Borealis became liable when they received the endorsed bills of lading from Stargas on 19 or 20 January 1994 . . . If the answer to this question is in the affirmative, the second subsidiary question is whether Borealis ceased to be so liable when they endorsed the bills of lading over to Dow Europe on 20 January. Bergesen submit that, once liable, Borealis remained liable under section 3(1) of the Act notwithstanding that they had endorsed the bills of lading over to another. Borealis submitted that they did cease to be liable . . .

The drafting of the 1992 Act

30 This Act . . . makes separate provision for the rights and the liabilities of a bill of lading holder. Section 2(1) makes being the lawful holder of the bill of lading the sole criterion for the right to enforce the contract which it evidences and this transfer of the right extinguishes the right of preceding holders to do so: section 2(5). There are two qualifications: in simplified terms, the holder can sue and recover damages on behalf of another with an interest in the goods (section 2(4)), and the transfer of a bill of lading after it has ceased to give a right to the possession of the goods does not confer any right of suit against the carrier unless the transfer was pursuant to an earlier contract or to the revesting of that right after a rejection by a buyer: sections 2(2) and 5(2). In the present case the provisions of section 2 do not give rise to any problem. Until, anyway, the discharge of the propane from the vessel at Terneuzen to Dow Europe in the second half of November 1993, the bills of lading remained effective to give a right to the possession to the cargo as against Bergesen. Both the contract between Stargas and Borealis and that between Borealis and Dow Europe were made before that time. Therefore, Borealis and Dow Europe were in January 1994 successively holders of the bills of lading who came within the provisions of section 2(1) and (2) and the extended definition of 'holder' in section 5(2).

31 . . . Section 3(1) imposes additional requirements before a holder of a bill of lading comes under any contractual liability to the carrier. The solution adopted by the draftsman was to use the principle that he who wishes to enforce the contract against the carrier must also accept the corresponding liabilities to the carrier under that contract. This . . . is a principle of mutuality . . .

32 In giving effect to this intention, section 3 of the Act postulates first that the holder in question must be a person in whom the contractual rights of suit have been vested by section 2(1). The language of section 2(1) adopts and is identical to the corresponding words in section 1 of the 1855 Act: 'shall have transferred to and vested in him all rights of suit.' Section 3(1)(a) and (b) relate to a person who, being a person who has those rights, chooses to exercise them either (a) by taking or demanding delivery of the goods or (b) by making a claim under the contract of carriage contained in or evidenced by the bill of lading. Both involve an enforcement by the endorsee of the contractual rights against the carrier transferred to him by section 2(1). Under (a) it is by enjoying or demanding the performance of the carrier's contractual delivery obligation. Under (b) it is by claiming a remedy for some breach by the carrier of the contract of carriage. Each of (a) and (b) involves a choice by the endorsee to take a positive step in relation to the contract of carriage and the rights against the carrier transferred to him by section 2(1). It has the character of an election to avail himself of those contractual rights against the carrier. There are however difficulties which neither the drafting nor the report faces up to. Whilst taking delivery is a clear enough concept – it involves a voluntary transfer of possession from one person to another – making a 'demand' or 'claim' does not have such a specific character and, what is more, may be tentative or capable of being resiled from, a point commented upon by Millett LJ in the Court of Appeal [1999] QB 863, 884c–d. Delivery brings an end to the actual bailment of the goods and is (save in special circumstances) the final act of contractual performance on the part of the carrier. Claims or demands may on the other hand be made at any stage (although usually only made after the end of the voyage) and there may at the time still be performance obligations of the carrier yet to be performed.

33 To 'make a claim' may be anything from expressing a view in the course of a meeting or letter as to the liability of the carrier to issuing a writ or arresting the vessel. A 'demand' might be an invitation or request, or perhaps, even implied from making arrangements; or it might be a more formal express communication, such as would have sufficed to support an action in detinue. From the context in the Act and the purpose underlying section 3(1), it is clear that section 3 must be understood in a way which reflects the potentially important consequences of the choice or election which the bill of lading holder is making. The liabilities, particularly when alleged dangerous goods are involved, may be disproportionate to the value of the goods; the liabilities may not be covered by insurance; the endorsee may not be fully aware of what the liabilities are. I would therefore read the phrase 'demands delivery' as referring to a formal demand made to the carrier or his agent asserting the contractual right as the endorsee of the bill of lading to have the carrier deliver the goods to him. And I would read the phrase 'makes a claim under the contract of carriage' as referring to a formal claim against the carrier asserting a legal liability of the carrier under the contract of carriage to the holder of the bill of lading.

34 But this is not the end of this problem. The use of the word 'demand' is problematic . . . If the carrier accedes to the demand and gives delivery as demanded, the demand is subsumed in the taking of delivery. If the carrier rejects the demand, a new scenario arises: is the endorsee going to make a claim against the carrier for refusing to comply with the demand? If the endorsee chooses to let the matter drop and not to make a claim, what significance of the demand remains? What principle of mutuality requires that the endorsee shall nevertheless be made subject to the liabilities of a contracting party? What if the endorsee chooses to endorse over the bill of lading to another to whom the carrier is willing to and does deliver the goods? The task of the judge, arbitrator or legal adviser attempting to construe section 3(1) is not an easy one and it is necessary to try and extract from it some self-consistent structure.

35 So far I have been concentrating on paragraphs (a) and (b). Paragraph (c) presents further problems. It raises the relatively common situation where the vessel and its cargo arrive at the destination before the bills of lading have completed their journey down the chain of banks and buyers. The intended receiver has not yet acquired any rights under section 2(1). He is not entitled to demand delivery of the goods from the carrier. He may or may not be the owner of the goods but he quite probably will not at that time have the right to the possession of the goods; an earlier holder of the bill of lading may be a pledgee of the goods. This situation is dealt with commercially by delivering the goods against a letter of indemnity provided by the receiver (or his bank) which will include an undertaking by the receiver to surrender the bill of lading to the carrier as soon as it is acquired and will include any other stipulations and terms which the situation calls for. It may well at that time, either expressly or by implication, give rise to a *Brandt v Liverpool* type of contract (*Brandt v Liverpool, Brazil and River Plate Steam Navigation Co Ltd* [1924] 1 KB 575) on the terms of the bill of lading. But again the question arises: what is the character and the role of the demand referred to in paragraph (c)? *Ex hypothesi*, the intended receiver had no right to make the demand and the carrier had no obligation to accede to it unless there was some other contract between the receiver and the carrier, eg a charterparty, which gave rise to that right and obligation in which case sections 2 and 3 have no application to that transaction. Paragraph (c) clearly involves an anticipation that the section 2(1) rights will be transferred to the receiver. The parenthesis which follows emphasises this: 'by virtue . . . of having the rights vested in him.' This shows that it is a necessary condition of the receiver's becoming liable under section 3(1) that the rights are vested in him by the operation of section 2(1). The inclusion of the word 'demanded' remains problematical. A rightly rejected demand for delivery by one who is not entitled to delivery is an act devoid of legal significance. What is significant is if the carrier decides (voluntarily) to accede to the demand and deliver the goods to the receiver notwithstanding the non-arrival of the bill of lading. Paragraph (c) does not include the making of a claim. The draftsman has accepted the irrelevance of a claim made by one who has no contractual standing to make it. Unless facts occur which give a relevance to the inclusion of the word 'demanded' in paragraph (c), in my view the scheme of sections 2 and 3 requires that any such demand be treated as irrelevant for the purposes of section 3(1) and that the Act be construed accordingly. A 'demand' made without any basis for making it or insisting upon compliance is not in reality a demand at all. It is not a request made 'as of right', which is the primary dictionary meaning of 'demand'. It is not accompanied by any threat of legal sanction. It is a request which can voluntarily be acceded to or refused as the person to whom it is made may choose. Accordingly it will be unlikely in the extreme that paragraph (c) will ever apply save where there has been an actual delivery of the cargo.

36 Taking delivery in paragraphs (a) and (c) means, as I have said, the voluntary transfer of possession from one person to another. This is more than just co-operating in the discharge of the cargo from the vessel. Discharge and delivery are distinct aspects of the international carriage of goods . . . Although the normal time for delivering cargo to the receiver may be at the time of its discharge from the vessel, that is not necessarily so. There may be a through contract of carriage. The goods may need to be unpacked from a container. The vessel may need to discharge its cargo without delay into a terminal. The discharge of the vessel is a necessary operation in the interests of the ship as well as of the cargo and requires the co-operation of others besides the shipowner. Providing that co-operation should not be confused with demanding delivery. The unloading of one cargo is for the shipowner the necessary preliminary to the loading of the next. Damaged or contaminated cargoes may need especial discharge because they may cause damage or pollution. Any unnecessary delays will cost the shipowner money and a loss to the charterer through incurring demurrage or forfeiting dispatch. Where the vessel is operating under a charterparty it is more likely than not that the obligation to discharge will be that of the charterer. The charterer will be responsible for providing or arranging a berth at which the vessel can discharge. Where the cargo is a bulk cargo which has been sold by the charterer to the intended receiver, the contract of sale may require the buyer to perform the seller's charterparty obligations in relation to the discharge of the vessel. The delivery to which section 3 is referring is that which involves a full transfer of the possession of the relevant goods by the carrier to the holder of the bill of lading. The surrender of the relevant endorsed bill of lading to the carrier or his agent before or at the time of delivery will ordinarily be an incident of such delivery. Where that is not done, the carrier will ordinarily require a letter of indemnity. The letter of indemnity will probably be the best evidence of what arrangement has been and will probably contain appropriate express terms . . .

The facts: The 'demand'

38 It will be apparent that in my judgment what occurred fell far short of amounting to the making of any demand for delivery on the part of Borealis. The vessel was under charter to Stargas. It was Stargas (or their agents) who gave orders to Bergesen. It was Stargas who offered and then gave the letter of indemnity to Bergesen against their agreement to deliver to Borealis without production of the bills of lading. The only thing done by Borealis appears to have been to direct the master to their import jetty and then, having allowed her to berth there, to take the routine samples from the cargo tanks before clearing the vessel for discharge into their terminal. These are exactly the type of co-operative acts, assisting the shipowners and charterers, to which I have referred earlier and which cannot on any view be treated as a demand by Borealis to deliver. Further, the trade in which these parties were involved necessitates the routine sampling of the cargo before it can be decided whether the vessel can be allowed to discharge its cargo into the terminal. It is elementary that in the ordinary course the nature and quality of the cargo must be established first. As the facts of the present case illustrate, it is always possible that the cargo may unexpectedly turn out to be contaminated or have some other characteristic which makes it unfit or unsafe for discharge into the terminal. What occurred did not get even as far as the stage of expressing their willingness to receive this cargo into their terminal. It fell a long way short of amounting to any demand or request that it should be. Once Borealis knew what the true characteristics of the cargo were, they refused to accept it from the ship.

39 It follows that, as a matter of fact, Bergesen have failed on the agreed primary facts to make out even an arguable case that Borealis demanded the delivery of this cargo. If the facts had disclosed something more positive on the part of Borealis, it is difficult to visualise that it could have had an appropriately unequivocal character or could have amounted to a demand for the purposes of paragraph (c) of section 3(1). The considerations discussed in paragraphs 35 and 36 above would apply both as a matter of the proper use of language and as a matter of the interpretation of section 3(1) in its schematic context including the guidance given by a consideration of the joint report of the Law Commission and the Scottish Law Commission on rights of suit in respect of carriage of goods by sea (Law Com No 196; Scot Law Com No 130).

The secondary question: Endorsement on and section 3(1)

40 The answer which I have given to the question whether there was a demand is decisive of the appeals. If there was no demand by Borealis, there cannot be any liability of Borealis under section 3(1) whatever answer is given to the secondary question which was decisive in the Court of Appeal. The secondary question is easily formulated: when an endorsee of a bill of lading who has both had transferred to and vested in him all the rights of suit under the contract of carriage pursuant to section 2(1) and become subject to the liabilities under that contract pursuant to section 3(1), does he cease to be so liable when he endorses over the bill of lading to another so as to transfer his rights of suit to that other?

41 The remarkable thing is that the report does not refer to this question at all and the Act contains no express provision covering it even though there are express provisions dealing with similar matters such as section 2(5) (extinction of rights) and section 3(3) (preservation of liabilities). It clearly was not foreseen as being a live issue . . .

43 I agree with the sentiment of Professor Reynolds (1999) LMCLQ 161 that it is likely that the particular facts will be of importance in any subsequent case concerning the interrelation of sections 2 and 3 of the Act. It is possible that the conduct of one or other party may give rise to estoppels as where one party has been led to exercise forbearance in reliance upon some conduct of the other. In most cases there will be other documents or agreements to take into account besides the bill of lading such as charterparties, letters of indemnity, non-separation agreements, or ad hoc agreements. With these caveats, I will shortly state my conclusion on the secondary question itself as a matter of the construction of the 1992 Act unqualified by any special factors.

44 I consider that there are two principles which are stated in the report and reflected in the drafting of the Act which show an intention on the part of the draftsman to preserve the decision in *Smurthwaite v Wilkins* 11 CBNS 842. The first is the intention to preserve the well tried and familiar of the 1855 Act . . .

45 The second principle is that of mutuality (or, if preferred, reciprocity or fairness). I have already quoted passages from the report demonstrating that this was the guiding principle in arriving at the recommendations which have led to section 3(1). Section 3(1) is drafted following this principle because it makes it fundamental that, for a person to be caught by section 3(1), he must be the person in whom the rights of suit under the contract of carriage are vested pursuant to section 2(1). The liability is dependent upon the possession of the rights. It follows that, as there is no provision to the contrary, the Act should be construed as providing that, if the person should cease to have the rights vested in him, he should no longer be subject to the liabilities. The mutuality which is the rationale for imposing the liability has gone. There is no longer the link between benefits and burdens. I have already commented upon the fact that the report refers to *Smurthwaite v Wilkins* and adopts it without criticism. It was in that case that Erle CJ said, at p 848:

> the contention is that the consignee or assignee shall always remain liable, like the consignor, although he has parted with all interest and property in the goods by assigning the bill of lading to a third party before the arrival of the goods. The consequences which this would lead to are so monstrous, so manifestly unjust, that I should pause before I consented to adopt this construction of the Act of Parliament.
>
> I recognise, and emphasise yet again, that it is likely that individual cases will be more complicated than that here visualised by Erle CJ and other factors are likely to come into play which, maybe decisively, will affect the respective rights and liabilities of the relevant parties. But as a matter of the construction of the Act *per se*, what he says remains apt and reflects the same principle as that adopted by the report and is supported, not contradicted, by the Act.

21 Right to sue after extinction of shipper's contractual rights

Where rights under a bill of lading are transferred by s 2 of the 1992 Act, the transfer extinguishes the shipper's entitlement to those rights. In the next case, *East West Corp*, it was held that the shipper's rights in contract are extinguished even where the shipper remains the owner of the goods, the consignee is merely the shipper's agent and has no interest in the goods at all. But in these circumstances, if the shipper's rights in contract have been extinguished, can an action be brought in tort for negligence or conversion or alternatively by the shipper as bailor?

**P & O Nedlloyd BV v Utaniko Ltd Dampskibsselskabet AF 1912 A/S
(Maersk Line v East West Corp) [2003] EWCA Civ 83; [2003] 2 All ER 700**

Facts: The claimants agreed to sell goods to a buyer in Chile, cash against delivery. The goods – watches, clocks and miscellaneous other items – were packed in containers and shipped in Hong Kong on liner services operated by the defendants, Maersk and P & O Nedlloyd. On discharge, the containers were warehoused and subsequently released to the buyer by the carriers' agents without presentation of the bills of lading. The bills of lading named the claimants as shippers and the buyer as the notify party. The goods were consigned to the order of named Chilean banks. The bills of lading were endorsed by the claimants and sent to the banks to obtain payment from the buyer in return for the bills of lading. The goods remained the property of the claimants at all times and the banks had no property interest in them. The buyer did not pay for the goods. The banks returned the bills of lading to the claimants without indorsing them. At trial, Thomas J held the 1992 Act had transferred to the banks not only the shippers' rights of suit in contract but also their right to possession of the goods, so that they had no right of action as bailors; nevertheless as owners of the goods they could sue in tort for negligence. Both the shippers and the carriers appealed.

Held:

Mance LJ:

Title to sue – the claim in bailment and/or as reversionary owners

42 . . . In the present case, leaving aside the effect of the 1992 Act, the Chilean banks were named as consignees, and the bills were transferred to them, not as pledgees, but simply for convenience, so that they could freely use them to collect the price for the respondents. They were to hold them (and if it ever became material, the goods which they represented or symbolised) for the respondents. I do not accept the appellants' proposition that the Chilean banks must themselves have had the sole or any right to immediate possession in order to be able to pass on such a right by endorsing and delivering the bills to the intended receivers against payment of the price. An authorised agent can transfer a right belonging to his principal, and so *a fortiori* can an agent who appears from the language and his physical possession of the bill to be the person entitled thereto. Although the Chilean banks had physical possession of the bills, I would therefore doubt that they thereby acquired at common law a sufficient possessory title in respect of the goods to sue in tort for loss of or damage to the goods . . .

43 . . . Prior to the 1992 Act, the right to possession of goods and the contractual rights under a bill of lading could be held in different hands . . . The appellants submit that the effect of the 1992 Act is to ensure that the two are held in the same hands. The contractual right to delivery vests in a holder of the bill under s 2(1). The right to immediate possession which suffices to found a claim in bailment must, they submit, vest in the (sole) person having the contractual right to delivery. They point out that Lord Hobhouse in *The Berge Sisar* said at para 31 that it was the contractual rights, not the proprietary rights (be they general or special) that were, under the Act, to be relevant. That is no doubt so, wherever there is an overlap. But it does not answer the question whether or when contractual and proprietary or possessory rights do overlap.

44 The first observation to be made on the appellants' submission is that the 1992 Act does not expressly modify any rights other than contractual rights. The definition of a holder is in terms of possession of the bill, not in terms of any possessory right in respect of the goods that such possession may bring with it . . . The mischief at which the 1992 Act was aimed was that rights under the bill of lading contract could remain vested in persons other than those having the property or risk in the goods. This might occur either because the general property did not pass at all, or because it did not pass upon or by reason of the endorsement of the bill, so that the 1855 Act was of no assistance. The remedy adopted by the 1992 Act was to transfer contractual rights to any holder of the bill, as defined in s 5(2). The result is, however, to create a new class of cases in which the bill of lading contract may be vested in a person other than the person at risk. The pendulum has thus swung.

45 The question is whether the statutory transfer carries with it anything more than purely contractual rights. Again, it seems to me that this may be a false question. Even if the Act were treated as giving the transferee of contractual rights a sufficient possessory interest to hold the shipowners responsible, in circumstances where none was intended or could, therefore, prior to the Act have passed, it does not follow that the transferor loses all right to immediate possession or, therefore, all right of suit in bailment. If it were necessary, however, I would conclude that the sole effect of the 1992 Act is on contractual rights, and, where there is no intention to pass any possessory right, possessory rights sounding in bailment remain unaffected. But in my view it is unnecessary even to reach any such conclusion. Whatever the position in that regard, I do not consider that the 1992 Act can be treated as working an automatic transfer of any rights in bailment, so that they enure *exclusively* to the person entitled under its provisions to exercise the contractual rights. Were that the case, it would simply increase the difficulties that the Law Commission recognised might arise from creating a new class of cases in which the bill of lading contract is vested in someone other than the person at risk.

46 Not only is there nothing express in the 1992 Act to that effect, but the Law Commission clearly did not contemplate it. Their report at paragraphs 2.39 said this:

> Even in those ex ship or arrival contracts where the seller retains risk and property during transit, and yet transfers the bill of lading to someone who has no interest in suing having suffered no loss, there would be nothing in our recommendations to prevent the seller suing in tort by reason of being the owner of the goods, which he can do under the present law.

In paragraphs 2.45 and 5.24 the report explained the Law Commission's decision not to recommend any exclusion of the right of an owner to sue in tort... So it is clear that the Law Commission contemplated that claims by owners against carriers as bailees would remain possible and in some circumstances counterbalance the automatic transfer of contractual rights instituted by the Act. The Law Commission cannot have thought that the 1992 Act would itself frustrate such claims, by working an automatic transfer of any immediate right of possession necessary to found such a claim. On the contrary, the Law Commission regarded claims in bailment by goods owners as some mitigation of the transfer of all contractual rights to persons who could in some cases have no conceivable interest in pursuing them. Such persons could indeed in some circumstances have a very considerable disincentive to the pursuit of any claim – for example where a claim against shipowners for cargo lost by sinking might elicit a counterclaim that the ship sank because the cargo was dangerous and caught fire, so that the claimant should indemnify the shipowners for the loss of their ship.

47 I see nothing impossible or surprising in the idea that one party should, as a result of the statutory transfer, possess the contractual right to delivery against the contracting carrier, while another person, the real owner and party at risk, should possess a right of suit in bailment against anyone, including the carrier, for loss or damage caused by their negligence as bailees in possession of the goods. It does not mean that the shipping lines were exposed to conflicting claims, since they were entitled and bound to deliver against an original bill of lading (*Barber v Meyerstein*, above, and *Glyn Mills v The East and West India Dock Co* (1882) LR 7 AC 591). Like the judge, I would also question whether it would be any justification for delivery to someone, who was not entitled to the goods and did not present such a bill, that those making such delivery thought reasonably that the recipient was the person entitled, and had received an apparently reasonable explanation for the absence of the bill (cf *The Sormorksy 3068* [1994] 2 Lloyd's Rep 266, *Motis Exports Ltd v Dampskibsselskabet AF 1912* [1999] 1 Lloyd's Rep 837; [2000] 1 Lloyd's Rep 213). Quite apart from this, there are certain cases in which two different persons, such as an owner entitled to immediate possession and an immediate bailor or person in possession, are both entitled to pursue claims for the same loss or damage, with no major practical problems arising for reasons identified in Palmer, N, *Bailment*, 2nd ed, 1991, London: Sweet & Maxwell, at pp 335 and 354 *et seq*.

48 The appellants' case could, on the other hand, lead to some surprising consequences. If an owner loses any immediate right of possession of the goods, together with any right of suit in bailment, as soon as the bill of lading and contractual rights pass to a holder under the 1992 Act, even though the holder is no more than an agent, the owner must, on the appellants' case, be unable to sue *anyone* in bailment. If the disability derives from a deemed transfer of the immediate right to possession as soon as there is any transfer of contractual rights, there is no obvious basis to limit it. So, on the appellants' case, the effect of the 1992 Act must have been to preclude actions in bailment not merely against the contracting carrier, but also against any sub-contractor or bailee who loses or damages the goods.

49 I can summarise my conclusions as follows:

i.   The appellants were under the bills of lading the original bailors of the containerloads of goods to the respondents . . .

ii.   That bailment continued despite the delivery of the bills of lading to the Chilean banks named in them as consignees, and despite the transfer of contractual rights under the bills to such banks under the 1992 Act . . .

iii.   Whether or not the Chilean banks themselves acquired sufficient possessory title to pursue claims in bailment is not the critical issue: paragraphs 27, 37–38 and 45. Having said that:

    a.   In my view, they did not: paragraphs 42 and 45.

    b.   But, assuming that they did, they were never more than agents at will in relation to the respondents, who retained a sufficient immediate right to possession throughout to enable them to pursue claims in bailment: paragraphs 38 and 44–48.

    c.   Even if that were wrong, the respondents could claim for any loss of or damage to their reversionary proprietary interest, and any such claim would (contrary to the appellants' apparent concession) constitute a claim in or to be determined by the same principles as govern a claim in bailment: paragraphs 31–32.

50 In these circumstances, it is unnecessary to examine the authorities and arguments deployed for and against the proposition that, if the appellants had no other potential responsibility towards the respondents, they must at least be regarded as owing the respondents an ordinary duty of care. *The Aliakmon* rejected such a proposition in a case where the buyer at risk was attempting to hold the carriers responsible in negligence, without having any proprietary or possessory basis for so doing. The House of Lords was unable to understand how any purely tortious duty of care could be treated as modified so to equate with the intricate blend of responsibilities and liabilities constituted by the Hague Rules, which governed the shipowners' bill of lading liability (p 818). Similar considerations would have presented a formidable impediment to the recognition of any purely tortious duty, if I had not concluded that the appellants owed duties towards the respondents in or paralleling those owed in bailment, notwithstanding the delivery to the Chilean banks of the bills of lading. On that basis, well-recognised duties exist in law and the doctrine of bailment on terms is potentially available as a controlling mechanism. So it is unnecessary for me to consider further whether the impediment would have been insuperable. It simply does not arise . . .

86 In summary:

i.   The respondents are unable to claim in contract, whether as original parties or as principals of the Chilean banks, or on any other basis . . .

ii.   The respondents retained the right to immediate possession of the goods at all material times, and were on that basis entitled to hold the appellants responsible in bailment for any loss or damage resulting from breach by the appellants of duty as bailees: paragraphs 49(i), (ii) and (iii)(b).

iii.   Even if that was not so, the respondents would have been entitled by virtue of their reversionary proprietary interest as owners to hold the appellants responsible in or on a basis analogous to bailment for any loss or damage caused to such respondents' interest: paragraph 49(iii)(c).

iv.   The appellants were in breach of duty in bailment, or alternatively on a basis analogous to bailment, by virtue of their failure either to deliver up the goods to a person entitled to them against presentation of an original bill of lading or, when they parted with possession of the goods to third parties, to arrange for such third parties to be under any similar obligation regarding delivery up; and such breach was causative of the loss by the respondents of their goods: paragraph 68.

v.   The doctrine of bailment on terms applies to afford the appellants with the benefit, in relation to the respondents, of any relevant exemptions or protective conditions in the terms of the appellants' bills of lading: paragraph 69.

vi.   Upon the true construction of such bills of lading, there are no relevant exemptions or protective conditions . . .

Notes

1   Endorsement of the returned bills of lading by the banks might seem a simple way to avoid the need to find any other cause of action against the carriers. But holders of commercial documents are often reluctant to make voluntary endorsements, fearing that it may expose them to claims.

2   *Claim in bailment.* This decision is another example of a general trend that treats bailment not just as a description of the relationship between persons and things but as a cause of action *sui generis*, arising out of possession of goods and independent of both contract and tort: thus 'the claims were put before the judge under the heads of bailment, conversion and negligence' (para 51). Bailment's apparent emancipation from its earlier dependence on forms of action in contract and tort has not been fully explored by appeal courts in England, where the position rests more on assumption than authority.

3   The Court of Appeal did not deal with the shipper's tort claim in negligence but was clearly concerned that such an action might unfairly circumvent the bill of lading terms. Would this be so? The 1992 Act extinguishes the shipper's rights in contract when another becomes holder of the bill of lading: it does not extinguish the carrier's rights.

4   The approach taken in the Court of Appeal treats the rights arising as between bailor and bailee as the same as but separable from those arising under the bill of lading contracts. A bailment can of course come into existence without any need for a contract. But the bailments in question here – and the duties of the carriers as bailees for reward – only arose under a contract. 'Bailment and contract often go hand in hand': see Chapter 6 on 'Carriage Contracts and Third Parties'. This decision treats them as parting company where the 1992 Act transfers and extinguishes the shipper's rights in contract.

An action in conversion, where the contractual right had been extinguished, may be available.

Baughen, 'Bailment or conversion? Misdelivery claims against non-contractual carriers'
[2010] LMCLQ 411
(footnotes omitted, other than citations)
  . . . This paper will consider the three non-contractual ways in such a claim may be brought – in conversion, in bailment, and in negligence – all of which were subject to judicial scrutiny in the East West case. The Court of Appeal there found for the shipper on the basis that the carrier was in breach of its obligations, as bailee. This paper will argue that a right to sue in conversion exists in such circumstances and, from the claimant's perspective, is a preferable way of bringing a non-contractual misdelivery claim.
  . . .

II. Conversion

The three elements of the tort of conversion were defined by Lord Nicholls of Birkenhead in *Kuwait Airways Corp v Iraqi Airways Corp (Nos 4 and 5)* [2002] UKHL 19; [2002] 2 AC 883, [39] as follows:

> 'First, the defendant's conduct was inconsistent with the rights of the owner (or other person entitled to possession). Second, the conduct was deliberate, not accidental. Third, the conduct was so extensive an encroachment on the rights of the owner as to exclude him from use and possession of the goods. The contrast is with lesser acts of interference. If these cause damage they may give rise to claims for trespass or in negligence, but they do not constitute conversion.'

Delivery of cargo to a party that is not entitled to possession thereof, satisfies all three of these elements. The first element is satisfied by the act of delivering to a party that is not entitled to possession of the goods, which is clearly 'conduct inconsistent with the rights of the owner (or other person entitled to possession)'. This element may also be established by an inability to deliver the goods. In *The MSC Amsterdam* [2007] EWHC 944 (Comm); [2007] 2 All ER (Comm) 149; affd [2007] EWCA 794; [2007] 2 Lloyd's Rep 622, Aikens J held that there were two instances of conversion. The first was when the carrier put in motion the delivery process at the Chinese discharge port following the presentation to its agents of a forged bill of lading. The second was when the Chinese customs authorities refused to release the goods following the presentation of the true bill of lading on account of the release that had already been made against the forged bill. It may also be established where one party orders another party in possession of the cargo to deliver the cargo to a party that is not entitled to the cargo. However, a transfer of possession from one bailee to another will not satisfy this element as it will not be an act inconsistent with the rights of the owner. An example would be where a carrier transfers the goods into the custody of a terminal operator at the discharge port. It is likely, though, that in this situation the bailee converts the cargo if it releases it without requiring that the terminal operator deliver only on presentation of a bill of lading. The second element requires the delivery to be effected as a result of a voluntary act of the defendant but there is no defence if the defendant believes that it is delivering to a party with no right to possession, no matter how reasonable that belief. In [*Motis Exports Ltd v Dampskibsselskabet AF 1912 A/S (No 1)* [1999] 1 Lloyd's Rep 837 (QB); affd [2000] 1 Lloyd's Rep 211 (CA).], a carrier was still liable even when it delivered against what appeared to be an original bill of lading, but which was, in fact, a forgery. Rix J held this to be 'an intentional act inconsistent with the true owner's rights, albeit done in ignorance of them and without intending to challenge them ...'. The third element will be satisfied by a delivery to a party other than the party with the immediate right to possession of the goods, notwithstanding that such party's rights over the goods are not extinguished by the misdelivery.

The one defence available to a party that delivers to a party without the right to possession is where delivery is made against surrender of an original bill of lading, provided the party effecting delivery has no actual or constructive knowledge of the bill of lading holder's want of title.

1 Successors in title and the right to sue in conversion

Title to sue in conversion is based on possession, which can be actual possession or the immediate right to possession. With misdelivery claims, the claim will be asserted by the party with the immediate right to possession of the goods at the time of their misdelivery. This right will generally be vested in the party in possession of the bill of lading at that time. However, physical possession of the bill does not always mean that the holder has the immediate right to possession of the goods referred to in the bill. For instance, in *The Aliakmon* [1986] AC 785 the buyers had possession of the bill but held it as agents for the seller and were, therefore, unable to sue the shipowners in negligence for the loss of the cargo. In *The Future Express* [1993] 2 Lloyd's Rep 542 a bank which was named as consignee in the bill of lading came into possession of the bill some considerable time after the goods had been delivered pursuant to an indemnity. The Court of Appeal held that the seller had intended to pass both property and possession of the goods to its buyer when it had agreed that the goods should be discharged against provision of an indemnity to the shipowner. At the time it passed on the bill of lading to the bank, several months later, it had therefore disabled itself from passing on the immediate right to possession of the goods.

Where the claimant has the immediate right to possession at the date of the misdelivery, it can claim in conversion notwithstanding that it is a successor in title to the original bailor. The immediate right to possession is transferable by transfer of the bill of lading without the need for an attornment, unlike the position where the claim is one for breach of the bailment. Once the goods have been delivered to the party who has the immediate right to their possession, the bill of lading will be exhausted as a document of title. Where delivery is made to a party that does not have the immediate right to possession of the goods in question, it is generally accepted that the bill of lading will not be exhausted as a document of title. It is therefore possible for the immediate right to possession in the goods to be transferred after the time of their delivery to the wrong party. The carrier will be unable to set up its own prior wrongful act by way of defence.

Such a transferee must, however, make a fresh demand for delivery of the carrier to establish its right to sue in conversion. In *Motis Exports Ltd v Dampskibsselskabet AF 1912 Aktieselskab, Aktieselskabet Damp-skibsselskabet Svendborg* Moore-Bick J declined to give summary judgment for a bank suing in conversion in respect of a misdelivery occurring before it had obtained the immediate right to possession of the goods covered by the bill of lading. This was because it was uncertain whether the claimant had obtained the immediate right to possession in the goods, or had become their owner, at the date of the misdelivery. The evidence was also uncertain as to whether the claimant had made a fresh demand for delivery.

. . .

3 Conversion and the terms of the bill of lading

In the event that a claim in conversion can be sustained, the issue then arises whether the shipowner may set up the terms of the bill of lading by way of defence, as is the case where the suit is in bailment. This was the position as regards one of the claimants, PEAG, in *The Captain Gregos (No 2)* [1990] 2 Lloyd's Rep 395. The shipowners argued that they were entitled to rely on the bailment contained in the bill of lading, so as to take advantage of the one-year Hague Rule time bar. The Court of Appeal held that PEAG were not the original bailors of the cargo, although they had obtained ownership when it was loaded onto the vessel, and the shipowners had not attorned in their favour. The shipowners also argued that plaintiffs which had to rely on a bailment to establish their cause of action could not disown the terms on which the bailment had been made, relying on observations of Donaldson J in *Johnson Matthey & Co Ltd v Constantine Termi-nals Ltd* [1976] 2 Lloyd's Rep 215 to the effect that:

> 'If Constantine Terminals had themselves damaged the silver, quite different considerations would have been involved. The plaintiffs could then have set out to prove negligent conduct without any reference to the bailment. Whether, in those circumstances, Constantine Terminals could have relied upon the contract of sub-bailment to which the plaintiffs were strangers or upon the contract of head-bailment to which they themselves were strangers, seems to me a problem of some nicety to be tackled only when it arises'.

Bingham LJ rejected this argument, as follows:

> 'If, as with the plaintiffs in Constantine Terminals, there had been a bailment and PEAG could only succeed by establishing a bailment, then we would accept that they could not conveni-ently ignore the terms of the bailment, whatever those might be found to be. But the essence of Mr Milligan's case here was that the shipowners deliberately appropriated the cargo to their own use by consuming it, transshipping it and making off with it. These were torts, he argued, for which any owner of goods could sue entirely irrespective of bailment or the duty on a bailee to take care. In this we think he was substantially correct . . . We do not think it arises here, since there was in our view no bailment by PEAG, and no relevant sub-bailment, and PEAG's case is not essentially founded on an alleged failure to take care.'

However, the shipowner's argument would have been stronger if PEAG's title to sue had been based on their immediate right to possession of the goods through the bill of lading. Although a claim in conversion would still have been based on a denial of title, rather than of any failure to take reasonable care, the claimant's possessory title would derive from the undertaking of the carrier to the original bailor to deliver the cargo only on production of the original bill of lading. Where the misdelivery was effected by the carrier's agents at the port of discharge, the claimant would have to invoke the bailment to make the carrier liable for the defaults of its independent contractors. It would therefore be subject to the terms of the bailment.

It is also possible that a claim in conversion may be subject to the provisions of the bill of lading by way of an estoppel by convention. However, in *The Captain Gregos (No 2)*, Bingham LJ pointed out that such an estoppel "requires communications to pass across the line between the parties". On the facts of that case, there was no such estoppel, as "nothing whatever passed between PEAG and the shipowners until after the cargo had been delivered to BP".

. . .

VI Conclusion

Misdelivery of cargo by a shipowner usually gives rise to a claim in contract under the bill of lading, together with a parallel claim in the tort of conversion. The shipowner will remain liable both contractually and in tort where the actual misdelivery is effected by its agents at the port of discharge, on the basis that it has assumed a non-delegable duty to deliver the cargo only against surrender of an original bill of lading. However, the position appears to be different where there is no contractual link between the claimant and the shipowner and the claim can only be advanced in tort. The approach of the Court of Appeal in the East West case means that, where delivery is effected by port agents rather than through discharge direct to the receiver, the claimant will be unable to sue in conversion and will, instead, have to base its claim on a breach of bailment. This has several disadvantages over an action in conversion, most notably the requirement of an attornment by the shipowner if successors in title of the original bailor are to have title to sue under the bailment. This seems an initially surprising conclusion until one realises that the obligations undertaken by the carrier under the bailment are fundamental to the issue of whether the carrier can be held liable for the conversion committed by the port agents. The carrier's obligations in bailment are non-delegable and this would form the basis for a finding of personal liability in conversion when the conversion has been effected by an independent contractor. In such circumstances the carrier would be able to rely on the terms of the bailment as a defence to an action in conversion, as the non-delegable duty arising under the bailment would be essential to holding the carrier liable for a conversion effected by its independent contractor. It would also be possible to find a liability in conversion based on failure to give adequate instructions regarding delivery to one's independent contractor. Liability for this form of conversion would look very similar to the liability in bailment that was found in East West, although there would be no requirement of attornment, as is the case with an action in bailment.

However, misdelivery effected by port agents raises the issue of what obligations the non-contractual carrier has assumed, as bailee, as regards delivery of cargo. Where the bailment was initially contractual, as in the East West case, it is clear that the shipowner has undertaken to deliver the cargo only on presentation of an original bill of lading. Accordingly, the shipowner in that case should have been held liable in conversion. The position, though, is different when the shipowner has never had a contract with the claimant. The shipowner is clearly a bailee, or a sub-bailee, but the nature of the undertaking under the bailment as regards delivery of the cargo, carried under another party's contract, has received no judicial attention by the English courts. Where a time charterer's bill of lading has been issued, the undertaking by the shipowner as bailee could be analysed in two ways. One view, that taken in the US courts in *The Finn Amer*, would be that the shipowner's undertaking parallels that of the time charterer as contractual carrier under the bill of lading. Another view would be that the shipowner's responsibility is limited to its care of the cargo whilst in its custody, and that no responsibility has been assumed for care of the cargo once it leaves its custody and is transferred into the custody of the charterer's agents at the port of discharge. It is submitted that this is the better view. Similar issues arise when considering the potential liability for misdelivery of the second carrier where the cargo has been transshipped. However, there is the additional issue of whether the second carrier has a defence in delivering according to the instructions of its bailor, the first carrier. This will depend on whether the second carrier has knowledge that third parties are interested in the goods. If this is the case, the second carrier will have no defence in delivering as instructed by its bailor.

22 Bills of lading and technology

Modern shipping operations rely on fast technology to increase operational and supply chain efficiency. It is therefore of little surprise to the industry when electronic solutions are being offered for the replacement of the paper bill of lading (and other shipping and commercial papers).

Electronic Commerce and International Transport Services – A Report by UNCTAD Secretariat TD/B/COM.3/EM.12/2 (31 July 2001)
© 2011 United Nations. Reprinted with the permission of the United Nations, C. Attempts to facilitate development of electronic transport documents (www.unctad.org/en/PublicationsLibrary/td bcom3em12d2_en.pdf) (footnotes omitted)

I Contractual approaches
a SeaDocs Registry
51. The first attempt to facilitate the bill of lading process took place in 1986 through the launching of the SeaDocs Registry by Chase Manhattan Bank and the International Association of Independent Tanker Owners (Intertanko). It was to act as a depository and central registry of the original paper bills of lading instead of their free circulation. Any endorsement of the bill of lading reflecting its negotiation would be carried out, by electronic means, through the Registry, acting as agent for the parties. The project was abandoned after less than a year. The reasons suggested failure included questions of costs, insurance, liability and confidentiality of information.

b CMI Rules for Electronic Bills of Lading 1990
52. The CMI Rules aim at providing a contractual mechanism for replacing the traditional paper bill of lading with an electronic alternative by imitating the functions of the bill of lading in an electronic environment. The CMI Rules do not have the force of law and only apply whenever the parties so agree (Rule 1). The main feature of the CMI Rules is the creation of an electronic bill of lading by the carrier, who acts as a depository or central registry for negotiations. Any endorsement/negotiation of the bill of lading takes place through the use of a secret code or what is called a 'private key'. The 'private key' is unique to the holder and is non-transferable (Rule 8). Its possession is considered to place the holder in the same position as being in possession of a paper bill of lading. Thus, the holder of the private key is the only party that can claim delivery of the goods, nominate the consignee or substitute a nominated consignee for any other party, or transfer the right of control and transfer to another party.

53. From a strictly legal standpoint serious doubts have been expressed about whether the private key is the equivalent of the paper bill of lading. The Rules further provide that electronic transfer 'shall have the same effects as the transfer of such rights under a paper bill of lading' (Rule 7 (d)). The 'difficulty with this provision is that mandatory rules of law cannot be discarded by mere agreement of the parties'.

54. The problems which may arise from the requirement, under certain national laws, that the contract of carriage be evidenced in writing are addressed by stipulating that an electronic recording or a computer print-out would satisfy that requirement. In agreeing to adopt the CMI Rules the parties are taken to have agreed not to raise the defence that the contract is not in writing (Rule 11). The legal effect and validity of such provisions, however, will depend on the applicable law.

55. The CMI Rules have not received a wide support from the industry. They have been criticized for placing excessive liability on the carrier (arising from his involvement in the process of negotiation of the bill of lading), for failure to address the allocation of liability for system breakdown and for the lack of a specific security system.

c Bolero

56. The Bolero system provides a mechanism for exchange of trade documentation, including transfer of rights from the holder of a bill of lading to a new holder replicating the functions of the traditional paper bill of lading in an electronic environment. It began operation in September 1999 and its services are available only to members on subscription. All Bolero members trade with each other under a legal framework embodied in the Rule Book, which is binding on them. It constitutes a multilateral contract between all the users of the Bolero system and is governed by English law.

57. The transfer of rights and title to the Bolero Bill of Lading (BBL) is achieved by a separate Title Registry run by Bolero. The BBL, which is created by the carrier through electronic messages, will state whether it is to be transferable (electronic equivalent of 'to order' bill of lading) or not, and will inform the Registry who is to be the 'Holder' of the BBL, i.e. the person who is to control it initially. The transfer of control takes place by the Holder giving the Registry an electronic instruction by use of its digital signature and the Registry acting upon such instruction by cancelling the control rights of the first Holder (the seller) and transferring it to the next Holder (the buyer). As this process does not involve any function traditionally recognized by the custom of merchants or by any of the legal regimes regulating the transfer of the paper bill of lading, the Rule Book achieves the same end by agreement and by use of the English law concepts of novation and attornment.

58. The system also enable users to 'switch to paper' (Rule 3.7), for example in cases where the goods are sold to a party who is not a member of Bolero. In such a case, the BBL is placed in 'end status' by the Title Registry and the carrier releases the paper bill of lading, including a statement to the effect that it originated as a BBL.

59. The risks associated with the use of electronic transport documents are at present difficult to assess. Under the Bolero system, the maximum liability of Bolero is limited to US$ 100,000 per incident. The members of the International Group of Protection and Indemnity (P&I) Clubs, while supportive of the aims of Bolero, have introduced into their Rules a Paperless Trading Endorsement which excludes from the normal P&I Cover liabilities arising as a result of electronic trading unless and to the extent that it can be shown that liability would have been incurred in any event had a paper document been used. To assist those members who wish to use Bolero, the International Group has arranged for a separate cover against such risks up to a limit of US$ 50 million for any one accident or occurrence.

60. Bolero clearly offers advantages over paper trading in terms of speed and security. The risks and uncertainties may not be so significant as long as transactions are taking place between those who are members of Bolero and bound by its Rules. The situation may be different when interaction with third parties is required or when the cargo is sold to a party outside Bolero and the 'switch to paper' procedure is followed.

d @GlobalTrade Secure Payment and Trade Management System

61. The @GlobalTrade Secure Payment and Trade Management System was created by CCEWeb Corp., Canada. A pilot of the system is being run from April to August 2001 and will be followed by a commercial launch in the autumn of 2001. The system aims at performing functions equivalent or similar to the functions of some key trade and transport documents, including letters of credit and bills of lading, by the use of electronic messages.

62. Under the @GlobalTrade system, an electronic sea waybill is created by the carrier and accepted by the seller as shipper. The waybill is a receipt and a contract of carriage, but not a document of title. It can nevertheless facilitate the concurrent exchange of control over goods and payment between seller and buyer. This effect is created by nominating the buyer as consignee in the waybill and including a statement in it that the shipper irrevocably renounces any right to nominate another party as consignee when a bank has accepted the waybill against an electronic letter of credit arrangement and confirmed the acceptance to the carrier. After receiving the confirmation, the carrier will be under an obligation not to carry out any instruction from the shipper (seller) and only to deliver the goods to the nominated consignee (buyer).

Notes

1   Since the publication of the Report, there has now been a new player in the industry – ESS Databridge (http://www.essdocs.com/).

2   An electronic bill of lading properly so called should have the following characteristics:

(a) A legitimate governing framework enabling its use – this can be achieved either by a contract involving all relevant parties or a statutory/legislative framework (such as the Rotterdam Rules). The legal framework should to an appreciable extent enable or provide for the electronic bill of lading to replicate the rights and obligations of the parties under a paper B/L. The legal framework would also ensure that the risks and obligations are properly allocated between the relevant parties (for example, the title registry facilitating the electronic endorsements on the database should be properly insured).

(b) Information technology framework: the technology must ensure that there is integrity, authenticity, security and privacy in the system.

(c) Functional perspective: the electronic bill of lading system or scheme should be able to perform the following functions:
   •   allow the electronic bill to 'move' from one party to another mirroring the manner a paper bill is transferred. This functionality must be able to transfer the right to demand possession for the goods, to provide a security interest in the goods and to recognise any modifications to the terms.
   •   be convertible into paper if the need arises

International organisations, both private and public, are concerned first that technology should not be stifled but, secondly, that technology is properly regulated.

CMI rules for electronic bills of lading

(http://www.comitemaritime.org/Rules-for-Electronic-Bills-of-Lading/0,2728,12832,00.html#)

1 Scope of Application

These Rules shall apply whenever the parties so agree.

2 Definitions

(a)   'Contract of Carriage' means any agreement to carry goods wholly or partly by sea.

(b)   'EDI' means Electronic Data Interchange, i.e. the interchange of trade data effected by teletransmission.

(c)   'UN/EDIFACT' means the United Nations Rules for Electronic Data Interchange for Administration, Commerce and Transport.

(d)   'Transmission' means one or more messages electronically sent together as one unit of dispatch which includes heading and terminating data.

(e)   'Confirmation' means a Transmission which advises that the content of a Transmission appears to be complete and correct, without prejudice to any subsequent consideration or action that the content may warrant.

(f)   'Private Key' means any technically appropriate form, such as a combination of numbers and/or letters, which the parties may agree for securing the authenticity and integrity of a Transmission.

(g)   'Holder' means the party who is entitled to the rights described in Article 7(a) by virtue of its possession of a valid Private Key.

(h)   'Electronic Monitoring System' means the device by which a computer system can be examined for the transactions that it recorded, such as a Trade Data Log or an Audit Trail.

(i)   'Electronic Storage' means any temporary, intermediate or permanent storage of electronic data including the primary and the back-up storage of such data.

3 Rules of procedure a When not in conflict with these Rules, the Uniform Rules of Conduct for Interchange of Trade Data by Teletransmission, 1987 (UNCID) shall govern the conduct between the parties.

(a)   The EDI under these Rules should conform with the relevant UN/EDIFACT standards. However, the parties may use any other method of trade data interchange acceptable to all of the users.

(b)   Unless otherwise agreed, the document format for the Contract of Carriage shall conform to the UN Layout Key or compatible national standard for bills of lading.

(c)   Unless otherwise agreed, a recipient of a Transmission is not authorised to act on a Transmission unless he has sent a Confirmation.

(d)   In the event of a dispute arising between the parties as to the data actually transmitted, an Electronic Monitoring System may be used to verify the data received. Data concerning other transactions not related to the data in dispute are to be considered as trade secrets and thus not available for examination. If such data are unavoidably revealed as part of the examination of the Electronic Monitoring System, they must be treated as confidential and not released to any outside party or used for any other purpose.

(e)   Any transfer of rights to the goods shall be considered to be private information, and shall not be released to any outside party not connected to the transport or clearance of the goods.

4 Form and content of the receipt message

(a)   The carrier, upon receiving the goods from the shipper, shall give notice of the receipt of the goods to the shipper by a message at the electronic address specified by the shipper.

(b)   This receipt message shall include:

   i.   the name of the shipper;

   ii.   the description of the goods, with any representations and reservations, in the same tenor as would be required if a paper bill of lading were issued;

   iii.   the date and place of the receipt of the goods;

   iv.   a reference to the carrier's terms and conditions of carriage; and

   v.   the Private Key to be used in subsequent Transmissions.

The shipper must confirm this receipt message to the carrier, upon which Confirmation the shipper shall be the Holder.

(c) Upon demand of the Holder, the receipt message shall be updated with the date and place of shipment as soon as the goods have been loaded on board.

(d) The information contained in (ii), (iii) and (iv) of paragraph (b) above including the date and place of shipment if updated in accordance with paragraph (c) of this Rule, shall have the same force and effect as if the receipt message were contained in a paper bill of lading.

5 Terms and conditions of the Contract of Carriage

a. It is agreed and understood that whenever the carrier makes a reference to its terms and conditions of carriage, these terms and conditions shall form part of the Contract of Carriage.

b. Such terms and conditions must be readily available to the parties to the Contract of Carriage.

c. In the event of any conflict or inconsistency between such terms and conditions and these Rules, these Rules shall prevail.

6 Applicable law

The Contract of Carriage shall be subject to any international convention or national law which would have been compulsorily applicable if a paper bill of lading had been issued.

7 Right of Control and Transfer

(a) The Holder is the only party who may, as against the carrier:

   (1) claim delivery of the goods;

   (2) nominate the consignee or substitute a nominated consignee for any other party, including itself;

   (3) transfer the Right of Control and Transfer to another party;

   (4) instruct the carrier on any other subject concerning the goods, in accordance with the terms and conditions of the Contract of Carriage, as if he were the holder of a paper bill of lading.

(b) A transfer of the Right of Control and Transfer shall be effected: (i) by notification of the current Holder to the carrier of its intention to transfer its Right of Control and Transfer to a proposed new Holder, and (ii) confirmation by the carrier of such notification message, whereupon (iii) the carrier shall transmit the information as referred to in article 4 (except for the Private Key) to the proposed new Holder, whereafter (iv) the proposed new Holder shall advise the carrier of its acceptance of the Right of Control and Transfer, whereupon (v) the carrier shall cancel the current Private Key and issue a new Private Key to the new Holder.

(c) If the proposed new Holder advises the carrier that it does not accept the Right of Control and Transfer or fails to advise the carrier of such acceptance within a reasonable time, the proposed transfer of the Right of Control and Transfer shall not take place. The carrier shall notify the current Holder accordingly and the current Private Key shall retain its validity.

(d) The transfer of the Right of Control and Transfer in the manner described above shall have the same effects as the transfer of such rights under a paper bill of lading.

8 The private key

a. The Private Key is unique to each successive Holder. It is not transferable by the Holder. The carrier and the Holder shall each maintain the security of the Private Key.

b. The carrier shall only be obliged to send a Confirmation of an electronic message to the last Holder to whom it issued a Private Key, when such Holder secures the Transmission containing such electronic message by the use of the Private Key.

c. The Private Key must be separate and distinct from any means used to identify the Contract of Carriage, and any security password or identification used to access the computer network.

9 Delivery

a. The carrier shall notify the Holder of the place and date of intended delivery of the goods. Upon such notification the Holder has a duty to nominate a consignee and to give adequate delivery instructions to the carrier with verification by the Private Key. In the absence of such nomination, the Holder will be deemed to be the consignee.

b.   The carrier shall deliver the goods to the consignee upon production of proper identification in accordance with the delivery instructions specified in paragraph (a) above; such delivery shall automatically cancel the Private Key.

c.   The carrier shall be under no liability for misdelivery if it can prove that it exercised reasonable care to ascertain that the party who claimed to be the consignee was in fact that party.

10 Option to receive a paper document

a.   The Holder has the option at any time prior to delivery of the goods to demand from the carrier a paper bill of lading. Such document shall be made available at a location to be determined by the Holder, provided that no carrier shall be obliged to make such document available at a place where it has no facilities and in such instance the carrier shall only be obliged to make the document available at the facility nearest to the location determined by the Holder. The carrier shall not be responsible for delays in delivering the goods resulting from the Holder exercising the above option.

b.   The carrier has the option at any time prior to delivery of the goods to issue to the Holder a paper bill of lading unless the exercise of such option could result in undue delay or disrupts the delivery of the goods.

c.   A bill of lading issued under Rules 10(a) or (b) shall include: the information set out in the receipt message referred to in Rule 4 (except for the Private Key); and (ii) a statement to the effect that the bill of lading has been issued upon termination of the procedures for EDI under the CMI Rules for Electronic Bills of Lading. The aforementioned bill of lading shall be issued at the option of the Holder either to the order of the Holder whose name for this purpose shall then be inserted in the bill of lading or 'to bearer'.

d.   The issuance of a paper bill of lading under Rule 10(a) or (b) shall cancel the Private Key and terminate the procedures for EDI under these Rules. Termination of these procedures by the Holder or the carrier will not relieve any of the parties to the Contract of Carriage of their rights, obligations or liabilities while performing under the present Rules nor of their rights, obligations or liabilities under the Contract of Carriage.

e.   The Holder may demand at any time the issuance of a print-out of the receipt message referred to in Rule 4 (except for the Private Key) marked as 'non-negotiable copy'. The issuance of such a print-out shall not cancel the Private Key nor terminate the procedures for EDI.

11 Electronic data is equivalent to writing

The carrier and the shipper and all subsequent parties utilizing these procedures agree that any national or local law, custom or practice requiring the Contract of Carriage to be evidenced in writing and signed, is satisfied by the transmitted and confirmed electronic data residing on computer data storage media displayable in human language on a video screen or as printed out by a computer. In agreeing to adopt these Rules, the parties shall be taken to have agreed not to raise the defence that this contract is not in writing.

As regards public international organisations, the UNCITRAL has made significant inroads into the facilitation of dematerialisation or digitisation of shipping relationships.

UNCITRAL Model law on electronic commerce

Chapter I   Carriage of goods

Article 16   Actions related to contracts of carriage of goods

Without derogating from the provisions of part one of this Law, this chapter applies to any action in connection with, or in pursuance of, a contract of carriage of goods, including but not limited to:

(a)   (i) furnishing the marks, number, quantity or weight of goods; (ii) stating or declaring the nature or value of goods; (iii) issuing a receipt for goods; (iv) confirming that goods have been loaded;

(b)   (i) notifying a person of terms and conditions of the contract; (ii) giving instructions to a carrier;

(c)   (i) claiming delivery of goods; (ii) authorizing release of goods; (iii) giving notice of loss of, or damage to, goods;

(d)   giving any other notice or statement in connection with the performance of the contract;

(e)   undertaking to deliver goods to a named person or a person authorized to claim delivery;

(f)   granting, acquiring, renouncing, surrendering, transferring or negotiating rights in goods;

(g)   acquiring or transferring rights and obligations under the contract.

Article 17   Transport documents

(1) Subject to paragraph (3), where the law requires that any action referred to in article 16 be carried out in writing or by using a paper document, that requirement is met if the action is c e granted to, or an obligation is to be acquired by, one person and no other person, and if the law requires that, in order to effect this, the right or obligation must be conveyed to that person by the transfer, or use of, a paper document, that requirement is met if the right or obligation is conveyed by using one or more data messages, provided that a reliable method is used to render such data message or messages unique. (4) For the purposes of paragraph (3), the standard of reliability required shall be assessed in the light of the purpose for which the right or obligation was conveyed and in the light of all the circumstances, including any relevant agreement.

(5) Where one or more data messages are used to effect any action in subparagraphs (f) and (g) of article 16, no paper document used to effect any such action is valid unless the use of data messages has been terminated and replaced by the use of paper documents. A paper document issued in these circumstances shall contain a statement of such termination. The replacement of data messages by paper documents shall not affect the rights or obligations of the parties involved.

(6) If a rule of law is compulsorily applicable to a contract of carriage of goods which is in, or is evidenced by, a paper document, that rule shall not be inapplicable to such a contract of carriage of goods which is evidenced by one or more data messages by reason of the fact that the contract is evidenced by such data message or messages instead of by a paper document.

. . .

 Further reading

Beatson, J and Cooper, J, 'Rights of suit in respect of carriage of goods by sea' (1991) LMCLQ 196.

Berman, H and Kaufman, C, 'The law of international commercial transactions (Lex Mercatoria)' (1978) 19 Harv Int'l LJ 221.

Caplehorn, R, 'Bolero.Net – The global electronic commerce solution for international trade' (1999) 10 JIBFL 421.

Chandler, G, 'Maritime electronic commerce for the twenty first century' (1997) 32 ETL 647.

Clarke, M, 'Transport documents: Their transferabilityas documents of title; electronic documents' (2002) LMCLQ 356.

Lee, D and Sooksripaisarnkit, P, 'The straight bill of lading: Past, present, and future' (2012) 18(1) JIML 39.

Murray, D, 'History and development of the bill of lading' (1983) 37 U Miami L Rev 689.

Reynolds, F, 'The Carriage of Goods by Sea Act 1992' (1993) LMCLQ 436.

Treitel, G, 'Bills of lading: Liabilities of transferee' (2001) LMCLQ 344.

Treitel, G, 'The legal status of straight bills of lading' (2003) 119 LQR 608.

Chapter 6

Carriage Contracts and Third Parties

At common law, in general, a third party cannot claim the benefit of, and is not bound by, a term of a contract made between others. The last chapter dealt with the special statutory scheme created by the Carriage of Goods by Sea Act 1992 for the holders of bills of lading and sea waybills, equivalent electronic transactions and ship's delivery orders. The cases in this chapter deal with the common law devices by which rights and liabilities may be transmitted to third parties, but the chapter opens with the general legislation – the Contracts (Rights of Third Parties) Act 1999 – that enables third parties to enforce contractual terms. The 1999 Act tries to avoid interfering with the operation of the earlier statute by providing that it shall confer no rights on third parties in the case of any of the shipping contracts covered by the 1992 scheme, apart from the right, where the general requirements of the 1999 Act are satisfied, to rely on an exclusion or limitation of liability clause.

1 Contracts (Rights of Third Parties) Act 1999

An Act to make provision for the enforcement of contractual terms by third parties (11 November 1999).

1 Right of third party to enforce contractual term
(1) Subject to the provisions of this Act, a person who is not a party to a contract (a 'third party') may in his own right enforce a term of the contract if–

   (a)   the contract expressly provides that he may, or
   (b)   subject to subsection (2), the term purports to confer a benefit on him.

(2) Subsection (1)(b) does not apply if on a proper construction of the contract it appears that the parties did not intend the term to be enforceable by the third party.

(3) The third party must be expressly identified in the contract by name, as a member of a class or as answering a particular description but need not be in existence when the contract is entered into.

(4) This section does not confer a right on a third party to enforce a term of a contract otherwise than subject to and in accordance with any other relevant terms of the contract.

(5) For the purpose of exercising his right to enforce a term of the contract, there shall be available to the third party any remedy that would have been available to him in an action for breach of contract if he had been a party to the contract (and the rules relating to damages, injunctions, specific performance and other relief shall apply accordingly).

(6) Where a term of a contract excludes or limits liability in relation to any matter references in this Act to the third party enforcing the term shall be construed as references to his availing himself of the exclusion or limitation.

(7) In this Act, in relation to a term of a contract which is enforceable by a third party–

   'the promisor' means the party to the contract against whom the term is enforceable by the third party, and
   'the promisee' means the party to the contract by whom the term is enforceable against the promisor.

2 Variation and rescission of contract
(1) Subject to the provisions of this section, where a third party has a right under section 1 to enforce a term of the contract, the parties to the contract may not, by agreement, rescind the contract, or vary it in such a way as to extinguish or alter his entitlement under that right, without his consent if–

   (a)   the third party has communicated his assent to the term to the promisor,
   (b)   the promisor is aware that the third party has relied on the term, or

(c)   the promisor can reasonably be expected to have foreseen that the third party would rely on the term and the third party has in fact relied on it.

(2) The assent referred to in subsection (1)(a)–

(a)   may be by words or conduct, and
(b)   if sent to the promisor by post or other means, shall not be regarded as communicated to the promisor until received by him.

(1) Subsection (1) is subject to any express term of the contract under which–

(a)   the parties to the contract may by agreement rescind or vary the contract without the consent of the third party, or
(b)   the consent of the third party is required in circumstances specified in the contract instead of those set out in subsection (1)(a) to (c).

(2) Where the consent of a third party is required under subsection (1) or (3), the court or arbitral tribunal may, on the application of the parties to the contract, dispense with his consent if satisfied–

(a)   that his consent cannot be obtained because his whereabouts cannot reasonably be ascertained, or
(b)   that he is mentally incapable of giving his consent.

(3) The court or arbitral tribunal may, on the application of the parties to a contract, dispense with any consent that may be required under subsection (1)(c) if satisfied that it cannot reasonably be ascertained whether or not the third party has in fact relied on the term.

(4) If the court or arbitral tribunal dispenses with a third party's consent, it may impose such conditions as it thinks fit, including a condition requiring the payment of compensation to the third party.

(5) The jurisdiction conferred on the court by subsections (4) to (6) is exercisable by both the High Court and a county court.

3 Defences etc available to promisor

(1) Subsections (2) to (5) apply where, in reliance on section 1, proceedings for the enforcement of a term of a contract are brought by a third party.

(2) The promisor shall have available to him by way of defence or set-off any matter that–

(a)   arises from or in connection with the contract and is relevant to the term, and
(b)   would have been available to him by way of defence or set-off if the proceedings had been brought by the promisee.

(3) The promisor shall also have available to him by way of defence or set-off any matter if–

(a)   an express term of the contract provides for it to be available to him in proceedings brought by the third party, and
(b)   it would have been available to him by way of defence or set-off if the proceedings had been brought by the promisee.

(4) The promisor shall also have available to him–

(a)   by way of defence or set-off any matter, and
(b)   by way of counterclaim any matter not arising from the contract, that would have been available to him by way of defence or set-off or, as the case may be, by way of counterclaim against the third party if the third party had been a party to the contract.

(5) Subsections (2) and (4) are subject to any express term of the contract as to the matters that are not to be available to the promisor by way of defence, set-off or counterclaim.

(6) Where in any proceedings brought against him a third party seeks in reliance on section 1 to enforce a term of a contract (including, in particular, a term purporting to exclude or limit liability), he may not do so if he could not have done so (whether by reason of any particular circumstances relating to him or otherwise) had he been a party to the contract.

...

6 Exceptions

(1) Section 1 confers no rights on a third party in the case of a contract on a bill of exchange, promissory note or other negotiable instrument.

...

(5) Section 1 confers no rights on a third party in the case of–

(a)   a contract for the carriage of goods by sea, or
(b)   a contract for the carriage of goods by rail or road, or for the carriage of cargo by air, which is subject to the rules of the appropriate international transport convention, except that a third party may in reliance on that section avail himself of an exclusion or limitation of liability in such a contract.

(6) In subsection (5) 'contract for the carriage of goods by sea' means a contract of carriage–

(a)   contained in or evidenced by a bill of lading, sea waybill or a corresponding electronic transaction, or
(b)   under or for the purposes of which there is given an undertaking which is contained in a ship's delivery order or a corresponding electronic transaction.

(7) For the purposes of subsection (6)–

(a)   'bill of lading', 'sea waybill' and 'ship's delivery order' have the same meaning as in the Carriage of Goods by Sea Act 1992, and
(b)   a corresponding electronic transaction is a transaction within section 1(5) of that Act which corresponds to the issue, indorsement, delivery or transfer of a bill of lading, sea waybill or ship's delivery order.

(8) In subsection (5) 'the appropriate international transport convention' means –

(a)   in relation to a contract for the carriage of goods by rail, the Convention which has the force of law in the United Kingdom under section 1 of the International Transport Conventions Act 1983,
(b)   in relation to a contract for the carriage of goods by road, the Convention which has the force of law in the United Kingdom under section 1 of the Carriage of Goods by Road Act 1965, and
(c)   in relation to a contract for the carriage of cargo by air–
   (i)   the Convention which has the force of law in the United Kingdom under section 1 of the Carriage by Air Act 1961, or
   (ii)   the Convention which has the force of law under section 1 of the Carriage by Air (Supplementary Provisions) Act 1962, or
   (iii) either of the amended Conventions set out in Part B of Schedule 2 or 3 to the Carriage by Air Acts (Application of Provisions) Order 1967.

For example as to how the 1999 Act might apply to third parties associated with a contract of carriage, see:

Navig8 Pte Ltd v Al-Riyadh Co for Vegetable Oil Industry, The Lucky Lady [2013] 2 Lloyd's Rep 104

Facts: The dispute concerned a shipment of palm oil and palm olein from Malaysia to Jordan, which was apparently delivered in poor condition and was rejected by R. R had bought the cargo from the shipper (P), a Malaysian company, which sub-chartered the vessel from N. The sub-charter was governed by English law and provided for arbitration in London. The bills of lading incorporated the terms of the sub-charter and further provided that, if a person other than the shipowner or demise charterer was judged to be a carrier or bailee of the shipment, that person would be entitled to all limitations of or exonerations from liability and/or defences provided by law or by the terms of the contract of carriage. R issued proceedings for damages in Jordan against P as seller and N as carrier under the bills.

Andrew Smith J: 16 Thus, Navig8 [the carriers] contend that the Jordanian proceedings would defeat, and are designed to defeat, their rights under English law, the governing law of the bills of lading contracts. Mr Collett emphasised that English law governs the contracts because of the parties' choice in that they incorporated the terms of the sub-charter, which contained an express choice of English law: see Dicey, Morris & Collins, *The Conflict of Laws* (15th edn, 2012) para 32–061.Navig8 also contend that under English law, although they are not party to the bills of lading contracts, they are protected by the exclusion provision because of the Contracts (Rights of Third Parties) Act, 1999 (the '1999 Act'), which allows a third party to enforce a contractual term that purports to confer a benefit on him (provided that the third party is sufficiently identified in the contract and subject to and in accordance with the relevant terms of the contract); and by section 1(6), 'Where a term of a contract excludes or limits liability in relation to any matter references in this Act to the third party enforcing the term shall be construed as references to his availing himself of the exclusion or limitation'. By section 6 of the 1999 Act, although third parties generally have no such statutory rights in relation to a contract for the carriage of goods by sea (including contracts evidenced by bills of lading), they may avail themselves of an exclusion or limitation of liability in such a contract.

. . .

21 . . . His argument is, I think, that the parties to the bills chose English as the governing law, and under English law Navig8 have a right under the 1999 Act to the protection of the exclusion provision. Since the Jordanian proceedings threaten that right, Navig8 are entitled to have them restrained and, in that their right arises from the bills of lading contracts, such a claim for an anti-suit injunction is 'in respect of' a contract governed by English law and covered by the Practice Direction. He also formulated a claim for damages for breach of such a right. He submitted that the position is analogous to that in *West Tankers Inc v Ras Riunione Adriatica di Sicurta (The Front Comor)* [2005] EWHC 454 (Comm); [2005] 1 CLC 347, in which the claimants had an arbitration agreement with the defendants' insured and an anti-suit injunction against the defendant insurers to restrain them from pursuing a claim against the claimants was made in order to protect the claimants' right to have the dispute arbitrated. To put it another way, since Al-Riyadh assert a claim against Navig8 on the basis that they are party to the bills of lading contracts, the matter must be considered on the basis that Al-Riyadh and Navig8 chose English law to govern their relationship: the implication of that choice is that neither party would act so as to defeat the rights of the other or to circumvent their duties under English law.

22 I reject this argument: I do not think that this is a good arguable claim. The 1999 Act does not confer a right comparable to that in the Front Comor case, and in any case I cannot accept that by bringing or pursuing the Jordanian proceedings Al-Riyadh are contravening any (contractual or other) duty owed to Navig8. Navig8's argument assumes that they cannot invoke the exclusion provision in the Jordanian proceedings. Even if so, it is not because the Jordanian courts would not recognise the exclusion provision or rights under the 1999 Act, but, it appears, because Jordanian private international law would hold that the relationship is governed by Jordanian law. (It was common ground before me that the 1999 Act only applies to contracts of which the governing law is English: see Dicey, Morris and Collins, *The Conflict of Laws* (cit sup) para 12–11.) In effect, therefore, Navig8's argument asserts a right, deriving apparently from the choice of English law, not to be sued in any jurisdiction that does not give effect to a choice of English law that is recognised by English private international law, at least unless the foreign jurisdiction recognises rights similar to those recognised by English law. There is no proper basis for so wide a proposition. In any case, as Mr Pearce explained, Al-Riyadh's claim in Jordan does not seek to circumvent any protection that Navig8 would have under the 1999 Act under English law. Their contention is that on the proper interpretation of the bills of lading contracts the expression 'Owners' refers to Navig8 and so as a matter of contractual interpretation they are not protected by the exclusion provision. I conclude that Navig8 should not be permitted to serve out of the jurisdiction a claim for an injunction or for damages.

Notes

1   It should be noted that there were other issues in *The Lucky Lady* on private international law and declaratory relief. The excerpt above should therefore be read in the light of the narrow issue of the role of the 1999 Act.

2   Although the Contracts (Rights of Third Parties) Act 1999 has limited application to contracts for the carriage of goods (s 6(5)), there are specific instances where shipping parties may find themselves having to resort to the Act. One such instance is where there is a settlement agreement made between the insurers and claimant following the finding of liability in the carriage/shipping relationship, that agreement is a simple contract and as such the 1999 Act would apply entitling a named or referred to third party in the settlement agreement to rely on the benefit in the settlement agreement (*Starlight Shipping Co v Allianz Marine and Aviation Versicherungs AG* [2014] EWHC 3068 (Comm)). See also *San Evans Maritime Inc v Aigaion Insurance Co SA* [2014] EWHC 163 (Comm); [2014] 2 Lloyd's Rep 265 where it was stressed that the benefit for the third party should be properly identified.

2 *Himalaya* clauses

Over the last 50 years, a great deal of effort and imagination has been devoted to the search for ways in which – consistent with the doctrines of privity of contract and consideration – the benefit of terms of contracts for the carriage of goods by sea can be extended to the carrier's employees and agents. Crew, sub-carriers, commercial associates and stevedores all reasonably expect to be able to rely on at least some of the terms secured by carriers; carriers and many shippers share the same expectation, at least at the moment a bill of lading contract is made. Two common law devices have had some success: the *Himalaya* clause, considered in this section, and the doctrine of bailment on terms, which is dealt with next. But these devices do not provide a reliable and comprehensive solution, one that is good for all cases; hence the need for legislation. In addition to the Carriage of Goods by Sea Act 1992 and the Contracts (Rights of Third Parties) Act 1999, the Hague-Visby Rules make a limited statutory alteration to the common law position.

The Law Reform Commission in its paper recommending the enactment of the 1999 Act provides a good summary of the law, especially in regards shipping contracts.

Privity of Contract: Contracts for the Benefit of Third Parties
[1996] EWLC 242(2) (31 July 1996)

(g) Techniques Used to Enable Third Parties to Take the Benefit of Exclusion Clauses

2.19 A problematic issue, that has been raised in numerous cases, has been the extent to which third parties to contracts may take the benefit of clauses in those contracts excluding or limiting liability for loss or damage. The tangled case law in this area provides an excellent illustration of the tension between, on the one hand, the formal adherence by the judiciary to the privity doctrine, which would prevent third parties taking the benefit of exclusion clauses, and the judiciary's desire to find ways round the doctrine so as to effect the contracting parties' intentions.

2.20 In the first leading case of the twentieth century, (73) *Elder, Dempster & Co Ltd v Paterson, Zochonis & Co Ltd*, (74) the question was whether, as a defence to a shipper's action in tort for negligently stowing cargo, shipowners could rely on an exclusion clause in the bills of lading, despite the fact that the contract of carriage was between the shipper and the charterer. The House of Lords held that they could do so, although the reasoning on which the result was based has proved very difficult to understand. (75)

2.21 Perhaps the most significant point (76) is that some of their Lordships seemed to accept a principle of vicarious immunity, according to which a servant or agent who performs a contract is entitled to any immunity from liability which his employer or principal would have had. Hence, although the shipowners may not have been privy to the contract of carriage (between shipper and charterer) they took possession of the goods on behalf of, and as agents for, the charterers and so could claim the same protection as their principals. (77)

2.22 Although the principle of vicarious immunity was subsequently generally accepted by the lower courts, (78) it did not survive the decision of the House of Lords (Lord Denning dissenting) in *Midland Silicones Ltd v Scruttons Ltd*. (79) The defendant stevedores, engaged by the carrier, negligently damaged a drum containing chemicals. When the cargo-owners sued in tort, the stevedores unsuccessfully attempted to rely on a limitation clause contained in the bill of lading between the carriers and the cargo-owners. The majority of the House of Lords confirmed English law's adherence to the privity of contract doctrine and was not prepared to hold that the principle of vicarious immunity was the ratio of *Elder, Dempster*. (80)

2.23 However, the possibility of third party stevedores taking advantage of exemption clauses was not entirely ruled out. Lord Reid said that there could exist a contract between the shipper and the stevedore made through the agency of the carrier, provided certain conditions were met: (81) (i) the bill of lading makes it clear that the stevedore is intended to be protected by the provisions therein; (82) (ii) the bill of lading makes it clear that the carrier, in addition to contracting on its own behalf, is also contracting as agent for the stevedore; (iii) the carrier has authority from the stevedore so to act, or perhaps later ratification by the stevedore would suffice; (iv) there is consideration moving from the stevedore.

2.24 Lord Reid's speech encouraged the use of "Himalaya" clauses, (83) which purport to extend the defences of the carrier to servants, agents and independent contractors engaged in the loading and unloading process. In *New Zealand Shipping Co Ltd v A M Satterthwaite & Co Ltd (The Eurymedon)*, (84) the Privy Council considered the extent to which such an exclusion clause contained in a bill of lading could be relied on by the third party stevedore, an independent contractor employed by the carrier, who was sued by the consignees of goods for negligently damaging the goods while unloading them.

2.25 The majority of the Privy Council gave effect to the clause by regarding the shipper as having made an offer of a unilateral contract to the stevedores to unload the goods on terms incorporating the exclusion clause. This offer was accepted by the stevedores by commencing work. In the words of Lord Wilberforce, the bill of lading:

... brought into existence a bargain initially unilateral but capable of becoming mutual, between the shipper and the [stevedores], made through the carrier as agent. This became a full contract when the [stevedores] performed services by discharging the goods. The performance of these services for the benefit of the shipper was the consideration for the agreement by the shipper that the [stevedores] should have the benefit of the exemptions and limitations contained in the bill of lading. (85)

2.26 The exclusion clause in question was expressed to be entered into by the carrier as agent for its servants, agents and independent contractors, and therefore "the exemption is designed to cover the whole carriage from loading to discharge, by whomsoever it is performed: the performance attracts the exemption or immunity in favour of whoever the performer turns out to be". (86) Further,

In the opinion of their Lordships, to give the appellant the benefit of the exemptions and limitations contained in the bill of lading is to give effect to the clear intentions of a commercial document, and can be given within existing principles. They see no reason to strain the law or the facts in order to defeat these intentions. It should not be overlooked that the effect of denying validity to the clause would be to encourage actions against servants, agents and independent contractors in order to get round exemptions .... (87)

2.27 Nevertheless, the reasoning of Lord Wilberforce in *The Eurymedon* has been criticised as artificial, (88) primarily because it effectively rewrites the Himalaya clause, which was an agreement between the shipper and the carrier and from which it is difficult to detect an offer of a unilateral contract made by the shipper to the stevedore. (89)

2.28 *The Eurymedon* was not received with enthusiasm in other jurisdictions, (90) and in *Port Jackson Stevedoring Pty Ltd v Salmond and Spraggon (Australia) Pty Ltd (The New York Star)*, (91) the High Court of Australia sought to restrict its application. (92) Unloaded goods were stolen from the stevedores' possession, and the consignees sued the stevedores in negligence. The stevedores unsuccessfully attempted to rely on a Himalaya clause in the bill of lading. Stephen and Murphy JJ thought that, as a matter of policy, a decision in favour of the consignees would encourage carriers to insist on reasonable diligence on the part of their employees and contractors. Furthermore, a policy of extending protection to stevedores would merely benefit shipowning nations to the detriment of those countries, such as Australia, which relied on these fleets for their import and export trade. The Privy Council unanimously reversed the High Court of Australia. It warned against confining *The Eurymedon* to its facts, and stated that in the normal course of events involving the employment of stevedores by carriers, accepted principles enabled and required stevedores to enjoy the benefit of contractual provisions in the bill of lading. (93)

2.29 In other contexts the courts have been less attracted by this unilateral contract device though similar results have been achieved by other means. In *Southern Water Authority v Carey*, (94) engineering subcontractors, who were being sued in the tort of negligence, sought to rely on an exclusion clause in the main contract between the employer and the head-contractors which excluded liability on the part of all subcontractors, agents and independent contractors. Judge David Smout QC, sitting as an Official Referee, doubted that unilateral contract reasoning could be applied beyond the specialised practice of carriers and stevedores and described it as "uncomfortably artificial". (95) In particular, *The Eurymedon* was held inapplicable because it could not be said that the head-contractors were agents for the subcontractors. Nevertheless, effect was given to the exclusion clause in an alternative way by finding that it negatived the duty of care which would otherwise have existed. (96) A similar result was achieved in *Norwich City Council v Harvey*, (97) where a building was damaged by fire as a result of the negligence of the sub-contractor. The main contract provided that the building owner was to bear the risk of damage by fire, and the subcontractor contracted on the same terms and conditions as in the main contract. The owner sued the sub-contractor in tort. The Court of Appeal held that, although there was no direct contractual relationship between the owner and the subcontractor, nevertheless they had both contracted with the main contractor on the basis that the owner had assumed the risk of damage by fire. Hence, the subcontractor owed the owner no duty of care in respect of the damage which occurred. May LJ said:

> I do not think that the mere fact that there is no strict privity between the employer and the subcontractor should prevent the latter from relying upon the clear basis upon which all the parties contracted in relation to damage to the employer's building caused by fire, even when due to the negligence of the contractors or subcontractors. (98)

The reasoning in both cases represents a controversial application of the normal principles for ascertaining whether a duty of care in tort exists. This was particularly so in respect of *Norwich CC v Harvey*, where the finding of a duty of care should have been non-problematic because the harm in question was property damage and not pure economic loss.

2.30 Thus there have been several ways in which third parties have taken the benefit of exemption clauses limiting liability for negligence. These include the now rejected doctrine of vicarious immunity, the unilateral contract device and the idea of a contract limiting the scope of a duty of care in tort. By each of these rather artificial techniques, the courts have striven to achieve commercially workable results, despite the privity doctrine.

2.31 The Supreme Court of Canada has recently gone even further than the English courts in enabling third parties to take the benefit of exclusion clauses by in effect accepting the doctrine of vicarious immunity even where the employee has not been expressly referred to in the exclusion clause. In *London Drugs Ltd v Kuehne & Nagel International Ltd*, (99) the plaintiff bailors entered into a contract of bailment with a warehouseman. The contract contained a limitation clause as follows:

> The warehouseman's liability on any one package is limited to $40 unless the holder has declared in writing a valuation in excess of $40 and paid the additional charge specified to cover warehouse liability.

The bailed goods (an electrical transformer) were damaged through the negligent handling of the warehouseman's employees. In the plaintiffs' claim against the employees in the tort of negligence, the question at issue was whether the employees could rely on the limitation clause in the contract. It should be emphasised that there was no express mention of the employees in that limitation clause.

2.32 A majority of the Supreme Court (100) held that employees could take the benefit of a contractual limitation clause where (i) the limitation of liability clause, expressly or impliedly, extends its benefit to the employees seeking to rely on it; and (ii) the employees seeking the benefit of the limitation of liability clause have been acting in the course of their employment and have been performing the very services provided for in the contract between their employer and the plaintiff customer when the loss occurred. On the facts of the case, the majority held that:

> [W]hen all the circumstances of this case are taken into account, including the nature of the relationship between employees and their employer, the identity of interest with respect to contractual obligations, the fact that the appellant knew that employees would be involved in performing the contractual obligations, and the absence of a clear indication in the contract to the contrary, the term 'warehouseman' in s 11(b) of the contract must be interpreted as meaning 'warehousemen'. As such, the respondents are not complete strangers to the limitation of liability clause. Rather, they are unexpressed or implicit third party beneficiaries with respect to this clause. (101)

2.33 Finally, in the very recent case of *The Mahkutai* (102) the question before the Privy Council was whether shipowners, who were not parties to the bill of lading contract, (which was between the charterers, who were carriers, and the cargo-owners, the bill of lading being a charterers' bill) could enforce against the cargo-owners an exclusive jurisdiction clause contained in that contract. The Privy Council held that they could not because the Himalaya clause in the bill of lading, which extended the benefit of all "exceptions, limitations, provision, conditions and liberties herein benefiting the carrier" to "servants, agents and sub-contractors of the carrier " did not include the exclusive jurisdiction clause because an exclusive jurisdiction clause is a mutual agreement and does not benefit only one party. Rather the rights conferred entail correlative obligations. Hence there was no question of the third party taking the benefit of the exclusive jurisdiction clause whether by application of the Eurymedon principle or under what Lord Goff referred to as the principle of "bailment on terms" deriving from Lord Sumner's speech in the Elder Dempster case. (103)

2.34 Of particular importance to this Report, however, was the Privy Council's recognition that, while the Eurymedon principle, or something like it, was commercially necessary, the principle rested on technicalities that would continue to throw up difficulties unless and until it was recognised that, in this area, there should be a fully-fledged exception to the third party rule. Lord Goff said the following:

> [T]here can be no doubt of the commercial need of some such principle as this, and not only in cases concerned with stevedores; and the bold step taken by the Privy Council in *The Eurymedon*, and later developed in *The New York Star*, has been widely welcomed. But it is legitimate to wonder whether that development is yet complete. Here their Lordships have in mind not only Lord Wilberforce's discouragement of fine distinctions, but also the fact that the law is now approaching the position where, provided that the bill of lading contract clearly provides that (for example) independent contractors such as stevedores are to have the benefit of exceptions and limitations contained in that contract, they will be able to enjoy the protection of those terms as against the cargo owners. This is because (1) the problem of consideration in these cases is regarded as having been solved on the basis that a bilateral agreement between the stevedores and the cargo owners, entered into through the agency of the shipowners may, though itself unsupported by consideration, be rendered enforceable by consideration subsequently furnished by the stevedores in the form of performance of their duties as stevedores for the shipowners; (2) the problem of authority from the stevedores to the shipowners to contract on their behalf can, in the majority of cases, be solved by recourse to the principle of ratification; and (3) consignees of the cargo may be held to be bound on the principle in *Brandt v Liverpool Brazil and River Plate Steam Navigation Co Ltd*. Though these solutions are now perceived to be generally effective for their purpose, their technical nature is all too apparent; and the time may well come when, in an appropriate case, it will fall to be considered whether the courts should take what may legitimately be perceived to be the final, and perhaps inevitable, step in this development, and recognise in these cases a fully-fledged exception to the doctrine of privity of contract, thus escaping from all the technicalities with which courts are now faced in English law. It is not far from their Lordships' minds that, if the English courts were minded to take that step, they would be following in the footsteps of the Supreme Court of Canada (see *London Drugs Ltd v Kuehne & Nagel International Ltd*) [1992] 3 SCR 299 and, in a different context, the High Court of Australia (see *Trident General Insurance Co Ltd v McNiece Bros Pty Ltd*). [1988] HCA 44. Their Lordships have given consideration to the question whether they should face up to this question in the present appeal. However, they have come to the conclusion that it would not be appropriate for them to do so, first, because they have not heard argument specifically directed towards this fundamental question, and second because, as will become clear in due course, they are satisfied that the appeal must in any event be dismissed.

2.35 While our proposed reform would reach the same result as in *The Mahkutai* (because, as we shall explain in Part XIV below, exclusive jurisdiction clauses fall outside our proposals), it would bring about at a stroke what Lord Goff regarded as a desirable development in that it would sweep away the technicalities applying to the enforcement by expressly designated third parties of exclusion clauses.

[footnotes]

(73) For 19th century cases, which normally involved carriage by rail, see eg, *Hall v North Eastern Railway Company* (1875) 10 QB 437, a case where the reasoning has been described as artificial but face-saving for privity. See Treitel, *The Law of Contract* (9th ed, 1995) p 568. See also *Bristol and Exeter Ry v Collins* (1859) 7 HLC 194; 11 ER 78; *Martin v Great Indian Peninsular Ry* (1867) LR 3 Ex 9; *Foulkes v Metropolitan District Ry Co* (1880) 5 CPD 157.

(74) [1924] AC 522.

(75) Lord Reid in *Midland Silicones Ltd v Scruttons Ltd* stated that the task of extracting a ratio from the case was "unrewarding" [1962] AC 446, 479. See also *Johnson Matthey & Co Ltd v Constantine Terminals Ltd* [1976] 2 Lloyd's Rep 215, 219 (per Donaldson J, "something of a judicial nightmare") and *The Forum Craftsman* [1985] 1 Lloyd's Rep 291, 295 (per Ackner LJ, "heavily comatosed, if not long-interred"). See also Treitel, *The Law of Contract* (9th ed, 1995) pp 568–569; N Palmer, Bailment (2nd ed, 1991) pp 1638–1640. *Carver's Carriage by Sea* (13th ed, 1982) p 529, refers to the case as a "mystery". *Scrutton on Charterparties* (19th ed, 1984) p 251 n 36, contends that no general principle is to be extracted from the case.

(76) For the alternative line of reasoning see Lord Sumner, [1924] AC 522, 564, with whom Lord Dunedin and Lord Carson agreed. Lord Sumner talked of there being a "bailment on terms" which appears to mean that by entrusting the goods to the shipowners, the shipper may be taken to have impliedly agreed that the shipowner received the goods on the terms of the bill of lading which included the exemption from liability for bad storage. Lord Goff has recently given some support to this line of thinking in *obiter* dicta in *The Pioneer Container* [1994] 2 AC 324, 339–340 and, most importantly, in *The Mahkutai* [1996] 3 WLR 1 (see para 2.33 below).

(77) This was the basis of Scrutton LJ's judgment in the Court of Appeal: [1923] 1 KB 421, 441, and was supported by Viscount Cave, at p 534, with whom Lord Carson agreed. See also Viscount Finlay, at p 548.

(78) See, for instance, Scrutton LJ in *Mersey Shipping & Transport Co Ltd v Rea Ltd* (1925) 21 Lloyd's Rep 375; *Pyrene Co Ltd v Scindia Steam Navigation Co Lt*d [1954] 2 QB 402. For a discussion of the *Pyrene* case, see Consultation Paper No 121, para 5.37. But cf *Cosgrove v Horsfall* (1945) 62 TLR 140 (where *Elder, Dempster* was not cited) and *Adler v Dickson* [1955] 1 QB 158.

(79) [1962] AC 446. It should be noted that Art IV bis rule 2 of the Hague-Visby Rules, enacted in the UK by the Carriage of Goods by Sea Act 1971, provides that servants or agents of the carrier (but not independent contractors, eg stevedores, employed by it) are to have the benefit of the exceptions and limitations of liability given to the carrier under the Hague-Visby Rules themselves. Similar provisions are contained in the Geneva Convention on the Contract for the International Carriage of Goods By Road (CMR) (implemented in England by the Carriage of Goods by Road Act 1965); in the Warsaw Convention (implemented in England by the Carriage by Air Act 1961); and in the Berne Convention Concerning International Carriage by Rail 1980 (COTIF) (implemented in England by the International Transport Convention Act 1983): see para 12.14, note 21, below.

(80) Lord Denning, in his dissenting speech, [1962] AC 446, 487–488, argued that, if the buyer is able to sue a sub-contractor (eg a stevedore) in tort for what was in truth a breach of the main contract, and the stevedore is not allowed the benefit of the terms of that contract, there exists an easy way for the buyer to avoid the terms of the main contract. He held that the stevedores could take advantage of the exclusion clause, since the earlier decision of the House in *Elder, Dempster & Co Ltd v Paterson, Zochonis & Co Ltd* [1924] AC 522 had determined this point in favour of stevedores.

(81) [1962] AC 446, 474.

(82) The exclusion clause was expressed to exclude the liability of the " carrier ", and the stevedores suggested that the word " carrier " could be read as including stevedores. This proposition was rejected by a majority of their Lordships: see [1962] AC 446, 471 (per Viscount Simonds), 474 (per Lord Reid), 495 (per Lord Morris).

(83) So called after the vessel in *Adler v Dickson* [1955] 1 QB 158.

(84) [1975] AC 154. Although sometimes overlooked, the negligence claim in the case was being brought by the buyers (consignees) not the shipper. The buyers were held to be bound by the shipper's contract with the stevedore by reason of a so-called *Brandt v Liverpool* [1924] 1 KB 575 contract which arose when the buyers presented the bill of lading and took delivery. See Treitel, *The Law of Contract*, (9th ed 1995) p 570–571.

(85) [1975] AC 154, 167–8.

(86) [1975] AC 154, 167.

(87) [1975] AC 154, 169. Lord Wilberforce emphasised the difficulty of analysing many of the common transactions of daily life within the classical "slots" of offer, acceptance and consideration; [1975] AC 154, 167. In dissenting speeches, Viscount Dilhorne and Lord Simon of Glaisdale emphasised that artificial reasoning should not be employed in contractual interpretation with the effect of rewriting contractual provisions. Viscount Dilhorne stated that " . . . clause 1 of the bill of lading was obviously not drafted by a layman but by a highly qualified lawyer. It is a commercial document but the fact that it is of that description does not mean that to give it efficacy, one is at liberty to disregard its language and read into it that which it does not say and could have said or to construe the English words it contains as having a meaning which is not expressed and which is not implied." [1975] AC 154, 170. At p 172, he referred with approval to the judgment of Fullagar J in *Wilson v Darling Island Stevedoring and Lighterage Co Ltd* (1956) 95 CLR 43, 70, where Fullagar J decried the seeming anxiety of some courts and judges to save grossly negligent people from the normal consequences of their negligence, despite the established tendency of the law to construe exclusion clauses strictly.

(88) See generally F Reynolds, 'Himalaya Clause Resurgent' (1974) 90 LQR 301; B Coote, 'Vicarious Immunity by an Alternative Route – II' (1974) 37 MLR 453; N Palmer, 'The Stevedore's Dilemma: Exemption Clauses and Third Parties – I' [1974] JBL 101; A Duggan, 'Offloading the Eurymedon' (1974) 9 Melbourne ULR 753; F Rose, 'Return to Elder Dempster?' (1975) 4 Anglo-Am LR 7; G Battersby, 'Exemption Clauses and Third Parties: Recent Decisions' (1978) 28 U of Toronto LJ 75; S Waddams, Comment (1977) 55 Can Bar Rev 327; P Davies and N Palmer, 'The Eurymedon Five Years On' [1979] JBL 337. For discussion of whether the better analysis is a unilateral or a bilateral contract, see N Palmer, *Bailment* (2nd ed, 1991) pp 1610–1611. In *The Mahkutai* [1996] 3 WLR 1, Lord Goff referred to, and appeared to support, Barwick CJ's description, in *The New York Star* [1979] 1 Lloyd's Rep 298, of the contract as bilateral.

(89) Since the carrier desires the result that holders of the bill of lading should not sue his servants or independent contractors, he can achieve this by procuring that they promise not to sue, by contracting to indemnify the servants or agents against claims, and by making it clear to the consignor and holder of the bill that he has done so. The carrier would then be able to obtain the staying of any action against the third party in breach of this agreement. See F Reynolds (1974) 90 LQR 301, 304.

(90) It was distinguished by the Supreme Court of British Columbia in *The Suleyman Stalskiy* [1976] 2 Lloyd's Rep 609, and by the Kenyan High Court in *Lummus Co Ltd v East African Harbours Corpn* [1978] 1 Lloyd's Rep 317, 322–323, because it was not shown that the carrier had authority to contract on behalf of the stevedore. See also *Herrick v Leonard and Dingley Ltd* [1975] 2 NZLR 566.

(91) [1981] 1 WLR 138 (PC). See N Palmer, *Bailment* (2nd ed, 1991) pp 1600–1601, for the view that the case might have been decided on the basis of bailment.

(92) Even though they were considering a situation in which all four of Lord Reid's conditions could be said to have been satisfied.

(93) At p 143. Treitel, *The Law of Contract* (9th ed, 1995) pp 571–572, submits that the principle of *The Eurymedon* should not be confined to cases where carriers and stevedores are associated companies or where there is some previous connection between them. He accepts that the protection of Himalaya clauses does not cover acts wholly collateral to contractual performance, see *Raymond Burke Motors Ltd v The Mersey Docks and Harbour Co* [1986] 1 Lloyd's Rep 155 (goods damaged while they were stored and not during any loading or unloading).

(94) [1985] 2 All ER 1077.

(95) At p 1084.

(96) The judge applied the speech of Lord Wilberforce in *Anns v Merton London Borough Council* [1978] AC 728, 751–752 to determine whether a duty of care in tort arose between the client and the sub-contractors. He found that sufficient proximity existed to render it reasonably foreseeable by the subcontractors that a failure by them to exercise care would lead to loss or damage to the client. He then asked whether there were any considerations which suggested that the scope of that duty should be reduced, and said that the contractual exemption clause, which defined the area of risk which the client was entitled to regard the contractors as undertaking responsibility for, meant that no duty of care arose. Although this precise approach to the establishment of duties of care in negligence is now out of favour, the courts will presumably employ similar reasoning to determine whether it is "just and reasonable" to impose a duty of care: see *Caparo Industries plc v Dickman* [1990] 2 AC 605; *Murphy v Brentwood DC* [1991] 1 AC 398.

(97) [1989] 1 WLR 828. See also *Pacific Associates Inc v Baxter* [1990] 1 QB 993 in which the Court of Appeal held that if, contrary to its view, there would otherwise have been a duty of care owed by the defendant engineer (C) to the plaintiff main contractor (A) for pure economic loss, it would have been negatived by the exclusion clause in the contract between A and the employer (B) excluding C's liability to A: see on this case *Chitty on Contracts* (27th ed) para 14–044.

(98) At p 837. This reasoning does not, however, explain the non-liability (at pp 833–834) of the sub-contractor's employee who was also sued. This may be the ghost of Elder, Dempster rising from its watery grave, the reasoning being reminiscent of the now rejected doctrine of vicarious immunity; N Palmer, *Bailment* (2nd 1991) pp 1609–1610; C Hopkins ?Privity of Contract: The Thin End of the Wedge?' [1990] CLJ 21, 23.

(99) (1992) 97 DLR (4th) 261. Noted by J Adams and R Brownsword, 'Privity of Contract – That Pestilential Nuisance' (1993) 56 MLR 722; S Waddams, 'Privity of Contract in the Supreme Court of Canada' (1993) 109 LQR 349; J Fleming 'Employee's Tort in a Contractual Matrix: New Approaches in Canada' (1993) OLJS 430; C MacMillan, 'Privity and the Third Party Beneficiary: The Monstrous Proposition' [1994] LMCLQ 22; R Wintemute, 'Don't look to me: The Negligent Employee's Liability to the Employer's Customer' (1994–95) 5 KCLJ 117. See also para 2.67, note 178, below.

(100) Iacobucci J with whom L'Heureux-Dube, Sopinka and Cory JJ concurred; McLachlin J concurred on different grounds; La Forest J dissented in part.

(101) (1992) 97 DLR (4th) 261, 369.

(102) [1996] 3 WLR 1.

(103) See para 2.21, note 76, above.

The Mahkutai [1996] AC 650, PC

Facts: Time charterers of *Mahkutai* issued a bill of lading in respect of a cargo of plywood, which was to be carried from Jakarta to Shantou, People's Republic of China. At Shantou the cargo was found to have been damaged by sea water. Cargo owners brought proceedings in Hong Kong against the shipowners. The shipowners sought to stay proceedings on the grounds that the charterer's bill provided for the exclusive jurisdiction of the courts of Indonesia and that they were entitled to the benefit of this agreement by virtue of a *Himalaya* clause or the doctrine of bailment on terms. For the judgment on this last point, see the next section of this chapter.

Held:

Lord Goff of Chieveley: . . . In the present case, shipowners carrying cargo shipped under charterers' bills of lading are seeking to claim the benefit of a *Himalaya* clause in the time charterers' bills of lading, or in the alternative to invoke the principle of bailment on terms. However, they are seeking by these means to invoke not an exception or limitation in the ordinary sense of those words, but the benefit of an exclusive jurisdiction clause. This would involve a significantly wider application of the relevant principles; and, to judge whether this extension is justified, their Lordships consider it desirable first to trace the development of the principles through the cases . . .

The Midlands Silicones case

This was a test case in which it was sought to establish a basis upon which stevedores could claim the protection of exceptions and limitations contained in the bill of lading contract . . . [The stevedores argued, among other things, that they had contracted with the receivers through the agency of the shipowners and could claim the benefit of the Hague Rules limitation of liability that was incorporated in the bill of lading.]

. . . Lord Reid in the *Midlands Silicones* case, while rejecting the agency argument on the facts of the case before him, nevertheless indicated how it might prove successful in a future case. He said ([1962] AC 446 at 474):

I can see a possibility of success of the agency argument if (first) the bill of lading makes it clear that the stevedore is intended to be protected by the provisions in it which limit liability (secondly) the bill of lading makes it clear that the carrier, in addition to contracting for these provisions on his own behalf, is also contracting as agent for the stevedore that these provisions should apply to the stevedore (thirdly) the carrier has authority from the stevedore to do that, or perhaps later ratification by the stevedore would suffice, and (fourthly) that any difficulties about consideration moving from the stevedore were overcome.

It was essentially on this passage that the *Himalaya* clause (called after the name of the ship involved in *Adler v Dickson* [1955] 1 QB 158) was later to be founded . . .

The Eurymedon and The New York Star

Their Lordships have already quoted the terms of cl 4 (the *Himalaya* clause) of the bill of lading in the present case. For the purposes of this aspect of the case, the essential passage reads as follows:

Without prejudice to the foregoing, every such servant, agent and sub-contractor shall have the benefit of all exceptions, limitations, provision, conditions and liberties herein benefiting the Carrier as if such provisions were expressly made for their benefit, and, in entering into this contract, the Carrier, to the extent of these provisions, does so not only on [his] own behalf, but also as agent and trustee for such servants, agents and sub-contractors.

The effectiveness of a *Himalaya* clause to provide protection against claims in tort by consignees was recognised by the Privy Council in *The Eurymedon* [1975] AC 154 and *The New York Star* [1981] 1 WLR 138 . . . In both cases, the bill of lading contract incorporated a one-year time bar, and a *Himalaya* clause which extended the benefit of defences and immunities to independent contractors employed by the carrier. The stevedores relied upon the *Himalaya* clause to claim the benefit of the time bar as against the consignees . . .

Critique of the Eurymedon principle
In *The New York Star* [1981] 1 WLR 138 at 144 Lord Wilberforce discouraged 'a search for fine distinctions which would diminish the general applicability, in the light of established commercial practice, of the principle'. He was there, of course, speaking of the application of the principle in the case of stevedores. It has however to be recognised that, so long as the principle continues to be understood to rest upon an enforceable contract as between the cargo owners and the stevedores entered into through the agency of the shipowner, it is inevitable that technical points of contract and agency law will continue to be invoked by cargo owners seeking to enforce tortious remedies against stevedores and others uninhibited by the exceptions and limitations in the relevant bill of lading contract . . .

Nevertheless, there can be no doubt of the commercial need of some such principle as this, and not only in cases concerned with stevedores; and the bold step taken by the Privy Council in *The Eurymedon*, and later developed in *The New York Star*, has been widely welcomed. But it is legitimate to wonder whether that development is yet complete. Here their Lordships have in mind not only Lord Wilberforce's discouragement of fine distinctions, but also the fact that the law is now approaching the position where, provided that the bill of lading contract clearly provides that (for example) independent contractors such as stevedores are to have the benefit of exceptions and limitations contained in that contract, they will be able to enjoy the protection of those terms as against the cargo owners. This is because (1) the problem of consideration in these cases is regarded as having been solved on the basis that a bilateral agreement between the stevedores and the cargo owners, entered into through the agency of the shipowners, may, though itself unsupported by consideration, be rendered enforceable by consideration subsequently furnished by the stevedores in the form of performance of their duties as stevedores for the shipowners; (2) the problem of authority from the stevedores to the shipowners to contract on their behalf can, in the majority of cases, be solved by recourse to the principle of ratification; and (3) consignees of the cargo may be held to be bound on the principle in *Brandt & Co v Liverpool Brazil and River Plate Steam Navigation Co Ltd* [1924] 1 KB 575. Though these solutions are now perceived to be generally effective for their purpose, their technical nature is all too apparent; and the time may well come when, in an appropriate case, it will fall to be considered whether the courts should take what may legitimately be perceived to be the final, and perhaps inevitable, step in this development and recognise in these cases a fully-fledged exception to the doctrine of privity of contract, thus escaping from all the technicalities with which courts are now faced in English law. It is not far from their Lordships' minds that, if the English courts were minded to take that step, they would be following in the footsteps of the Supreme Court of Canada . . .

Application of the Eurymedon principle
Their Lordships now turn to the application of the principle in *The Eurymedon* to the facts of the present case. Two questions arose in the course of argument which are specific to this case. The first is whether the shipowners qualify as 'sub-contractors' within the meaning of the *Himalaya* clause (cl 4 of the bill of lading). The second is whether, if so, they are entitled to take advantage of the exclusive jurisdiction clause (cl 19). Their Lordships have come to the conclusion that the latter question must be answered in the negative. It is therefore unnecessary for them to answer the first question; and they will proceed to address the question of the exclusive jurisdiction clause on the assumption that the shipowners can be regarded as sub-contractors for this purpose.

The exclusive jurisdiction clause

The *Himalaya* clause provides that, among others, sub-contractors shall have the benefit of 'all exceptions, limitations, provision, conditions and liberties herein benefiting the Carrier as if such provisions were expressly made for their benefit'. The question therefore arises whether the exclusive jurisdiction clause (cl 19) falls within the scope of this clause.

In *The Eurymedon* [1975] AC 154 at 169 and *The New York Star* [1981] 1 WLR 138 at 143 Lord Wilberforce stated the principle to be applicable, in the case of stevedores, to respectively 'exemptions and limitations' and 'defences and immunities' contained in the bill of lading. This is scarcely surprising. Most bill of lading contracts incorporate the Hague-Visby Rules, in which the responsibilities and liabilities of the carrier are segregated from his rights and immunities, the latter being set out primarily in art IV, rr1 and 2, exempting the carrier and the ship from liability or responsibility for loss of or damage to the goods in certain specified circumstances; though the limitation on liability per package or unit is to be found in art IV, r 5, and the time bar in art III, r 6. Terms such as these are characteristically terms for the benefit of the carrier, of which sub-contractors can have the benefit under the *Himalaya* clause as if such terms were expressly made for their benefit.

It however by no means follows that the same can be said of an exclusive jurisdiction clause ... Such a clause can be distinguished from terms such as exceptions and limitations in that it does not benefit only one party, but embodies a mutual agreement under which both parties agree with each other as to the relevant jurisdiction for the resolution of disputes. It is therefore a clause which creates mutual rights and obligations. Can such a clause be an exception, limitation, provision, condition or liberty benefiting the carrier within the meaning of the clause?

First of all, it cannot in their Lordships' opinion be an exception, limitation, condition or liberty. But can it be a provision? That expression has, of course, to be considered in the context of the *Himalaya* clause; and so the question is whether an exclusive jurisdiction clause is a provision benefiting the carrier, of which servants, agents and sub-contractors of the carrier are intended to have the benefit, as if the provision was expressly made for their benefit. Moreover, the word 'provision' is to be found at the centre of a series of words, viz 'exceptions, limitations . . . conditions and liberties', all of which share the same characteristic, that they are not as such rights which entail correlative obligations on the cargo owners.

In considering this question, their Lordships are satisfied that some limit must be placed upon the meaning of the word 'provision' in this context. In their Lordships' opinion, the word 'provision' must have been inserted with the purpose of ensuring that any other provision in the bill of lading which, although it did not strictly fall within the description 'exceptions, limitations . . . conditions and liberties', nevertheless benefited the carrier in the same way in the sense that it was inserted in the bill for the carrier's protection, should enure for the benefit of the servants, agents and sub-contractors of the carrier. It cannot therefore extend to include a mutual agreement, such as an exclusive jurisdiction clause, which is not of that character.

Their Lordships draw support for this view from the function of the *Himalaya* clause. That function is, as revealed by the authorities, to prevent cargo owners from avoiding the effect of contractual defences available to the carrier (typically the exceptions and limitations in the Hague-Visby Rules) by suing in tort persons who perform the contractual services on the carrier's behalf. To make available to such a person the benefit of an exclusive jurisdiction clause in the bill of lading contract does not contribute to the solution of that problem. Furthermore, to construe the general words of the *Himalaya* clause as effective to make available to servants, agents or sub-contractors a clause which expressly refers to disputes arising under the contract evidenced by the bill of lading, to which they are not party, is not easy to reconcile with those authorities such as *TW Thomas & Co Ltd v Portsea Steamship Co Ltd* [1912] AC 1 which hold that general words of incorporation are ineffective to incorporate into a bill of lading an arbitration clause which refers only to disputes arising under the charter.

Furthermore, it is of some significance to observe how adventitious would have been the benefit of the exclusive jurisdiction clause to the shipowners in the present case. Such a clause generally represents a preference by the carrier for the jurisdiction where he carries on business. But the same cannot necessarily be said of his servants, agents or sub-contractors. It could conceivably be true of servants, such as crew members, who may be resident in the same jurisdiction; though if sued elsewhere they may in any event be able to invoke the principle of *forum non conveniens*. But the same cannot be said to be true of agents, still less of sub-contractors. Take, for example, stevedores at the discharging port, who provide the classic example of independent contractors intended to be protected by a *Himalaya* clause. There is no reason to suppose that an exclusive jurisdiction clause selected to suit a particular carrier would be likely to be of any benefit to such stevedores; it could only conceivably be so in the coincidental circumstance that the discharging port happened to be in the country where the carrier carried on business. Exactly the same can be said of a shipowner who performs all or part of the carrier's obligations under the bill of lading contract, pursuant to a time or voyage charter. In such a case, the shipowner may very likely have no connection with the carrier's chosen jurisdiction. Coincidentally he may do so, as in the present case where the shipowners happened, like Sentosa, to be an Indonesian corporation. This of course explains why the shipowners in the present case wish to take advantage of the exclusive jurisdiction clause in Sentosa's form of bill of lading; but it would not be right to attach any significance to that coincidence.

In the opinion of their Lordships, all these considerations point strongly against the exclusive jurisdiction clause falling within the scope of the *Himalaya* clause. However, in support of his submission that the exclusive jurisdiction clause fell within the scope of the *Himalaya* clause in the present case, Mr Gross QC for the shipowners invoked the decision of the Privy Council in *The Pioneer Container* [1994] 2 AC 324. That case was however concerned with a different situation, where a carrier of goods sub-contracted part of the carriage to a shipowner under a 'feeder' bill of lading, and that shipowner sought to enforce an exclusive jurisdiction clause contained in that bill of lading against the owners of the goods. The Judicial Committee held that the shipowner was entitled to do so because the goods' owner had authorised the carrier so to sub-contract 'on any terms', with the effect that the shipowner as sub-bailee was entitled to rely on the clause against the goods' owner as head bailor. The present case is however concerned not with a question of enforceability of a term in a sub-bailment by the sub-bailee against the head bailor, but with the question whether a sub-contractor is entitled to take the benefit of a term in the head contract. The former depends on the scope of the authority of the intermediate bailor to act on behalf of the head bailor in agreeing on his behalf to the relevant term in the sub-bailment; whereas the latter depends on the scope of the agreement between the head contractor and the sub-contractor, entered into by the intermediate contractor as agent for the sub-contractor, under which the benefit of a term in the head contract may be made available by the head contractor to the sub-contractor. It does not follow that a decision in the former type of case provides any useful guidance in a case of the latter type; and their Lordships do not therefore find *The Pioneer Container* of assistance in the present case.

In the event, for the reasons they have already given, their Lordships have come to the conclusion that the *Himalaya* clause does not have the effect of enabling the shipowners to take advantage of the exclusive jurisdiction clause in the bill of lading in the present case . . .

In this case Lord Goff of Chieveley said that it was inevitable that cargo owners would continue to invoke technical points of contract and agency law in order to circumvent *Himalaya*-based defences to tort claims. In the next case, *The Starsin*, the cargo owners invoked the Hague Rules, which led the Court to refine the analysis of nature of the agreement created by a *Himalaya* clause.

Makros Hout BV v Agrosin Private Ltd, The Starsin [2003] UKHL 12; [2003] 1 Lloyd's Rep 571

Facts: Cargo owners sued shipowners in tort for negligence in stowing and caring for cargo that was carried under charterers' bills of lading. The shipowners claimed that they were protected by a *Himalaya* clause in the bills of lading, which provided (paragraph numbers were added by the court for ease of reference):

5 (1) It is hereby expressly agreed that no servant or agent of the carrier ... including every independent contractor from time to time employed by the carrier shall in any circumstance whatsoever be under any liability whatsoever to the shipper, for any loss or damage ...

(2) without prejudice to the generality of the provisions of this Bill of Lading, every exemption limitation, condition and liberty herein contained and every right exemption from liability, defence and immunity ... applicable to the carrier or to which the carrier is entitled hereunder shall also be available to and shall extend to protect every such servant or agent of the carrier acting as aforesaid and for the purpose of all the foregoing provisions of this clause, the carrier is or shall be deemed to be acting on behalf of ... his servants or agents ... including every independent contractor ...

(3) and all such persons shall to this extent be deemed to be parties to the contract contained in or evidenced by this Bill of Lading.

(4) The shipper shall indemnify the carrier against any claim by third parties against whom the carrier cannot rely on these conditions ...

The cargo owners argued that part 1 of this clause was inconsistent with Art III, r 8 of the Hague Rules and was void. Five reasoned judgments were delivered. It was held that:

- The shipowners were 'independent contractors' for the purpose of cl 5.
- Reversing the Court of Appeal, that part 1 of the clause was not merely an agreement with the contracting carrier that the cargo owners would not sue servants, agents and independent contractors, but was a *Himalaya* agreement with the third parties, notwithstanding the apparent overlap between part 1 and 2 of the clause: 'Probably the draftsman thought it might be prudent to wear belt as well as braces.'
- By a majority, the resulting contract to which the shipowner became a party was one to which the Hague Rules applied, with the result that part 1 of the clause was rendered ineffective by Art III, r 8. The result was that the defences to which the shipowner was entitled were only those which were compatible with the Hague Rules.

In the following judgment, a contract created by a *Himalaya* clause is referred to as a *Barwick* contract, after Sir Garfield Barwick CJ whose analysis of *Himalaya* clauses was adopted in *The New York Star*.

Held:

Lord Hobhouse (after reviewing the decided cases, continued):

152 What emerges from these cases?

Where no bailment is involved, the only contract which should be looked at (save for the purpose of authority) is the bill of lading contract. It is in the bill of lading that the mutual contract between the relevant persons must be found.

The 'Barwick' contract, although mutual, does not involve an exchange of promises but, rather, an exchange of the performance of a service for protection in relation to that performance.

The requirement of consideration is real not fictional but can be achieved by entering upon performance and thereby converting an arrangement into a mutual contract in respect of that service.

Through the agency of the contracting carrier, the third party becomes a party to a contract contained in the bill of lading.

A complete exemption from all legal liability may be inconsistent with the enforceability of the clause.

The question of authority has not arisen in any of the cases but remains part of the necessary structure of the enforceability of the clause.

The point for examination in the present case is what is the effect of applying the principles in *The Eurymedon* and *The New York Star* to the facts of the present case and whether the shipowners' argument should succeed.

Discussion: the shipowners as a carrier:

153 The first point is that the shipowners are the actual owners of the ship named on the front of the bill of lading, the *Starsin*, and the employers of her crew. They took possession of the goods and carried them. The consideration which they are giving to the shipper in order to make clause 5 enforceable between them – to 'enact' the arrangement in the clause, to use Barwick CJ's language – is the actual carriage of the goods. That is the service – the 'act or acts' – which they are performing for the cargo owners. They assumed the possession of the goods as carriers by way of sub-bailment and entered into a bailee-bailor relationship with the shipper (see Lord Pearson, *sup*). The bill of lading previously contained an inchoate contract of carriage – or 'arrangement' – capable of becoming an enforceable contract when the shipowners enter upon the carriage of the shipper's goods. The shipowners have thus entered into a contract *of* carriage with the shipper. Both Lord Wilberforce and Barwick CJ treated the resultant contract as a mutual one but the mutuality arises from the performance of the service by the one party, here the carrying of the goods by the shipowners, and the agreement by the other that, should he do so, he shall be entitled to the stated protective provisions. Barwick CJ excluded an analysis involving an exchange of promises. Thus the person (the shipowners) performing the service (the carriage of the goods) does not promise in advance that he will do so nor that he will continue to do so. The 'Barwick' contract is not a contract with executory obligations; it is not a contract *for* the carriage of the goods. But it is a mutual contract *of* carriage which lasts as long as the shipowners remain the bailees of the goods as the actual performing carriers. The element of consideration and mutuality which the shipowners render to the shipper under the contract is their entering into this bailor/carrier relationship with the cargo owners and performing the carriage. In the event, they carried the cargo from Malaysia to Europe. Further, the contract is one which is 'covered' by a bill of lading. Thus both the relevant person, here the shipowners, and the contract come within the definitions of 'contract of carriage' and 'carrier' in Article I (b) and (a) of the Hague Rules. Likewise, a contract of carriage which lasts only so long as the carrier concerned remains in possession of the goods as a carrier conforms to the Hague Rules definition of 'carriage of goods' as covering 'the period from the time when the goods are loaded on to the time they are discharged from the ship': Article I(e). (See also Article VII and the standard 'Period of Responsibility' clause in the bills of lading.) The scheme of the Hague Rules is that they deal with the terms of the carriage not the destination to which they should be carried . . .

155 It is argued that the 'Himalaya' clause contract is 'collateral' to the bill of lading contract and therefore is not to be affected by such considerations as the Hague Rules. Why the use of the epithet 'collateral' should have this effect is not clear. It does not address or affect the essential question: what is the 'Barwick' contract? In so far as a 'Himalaya' clause may include additional stipulations as between the person issuing the bill of lading and the shipper such as jurisdiction clauses or covenants not to sue, it may well be correct to use the word 'collateral'. But even then the substance may have to be looked at not just the form: *The Hollandia* [1983] 1 AC 565. But, as regards the persons referred to in the clause, clause 5 says that it is, for the purposes of all the provisions of the clause, made on behalf of such persons and to that extent all such persons shall 'be deemed to be parties to the contract contained in or evidenced by this bill of lading'. As between those persons and the shipper the resultant contract is not 'collateral'; it is *the* contract. The purpose of the additional use of these express words is to procure that transferees of the bill of lading shall be bound as well as the shipper: see the final sentence of the quotes from Lord Reid (*sup*) and Lord Wilberforce (*sup*). Clause 5 deliberately makes the contract between such persons and the shipper part of the bill of lading contract so as to obtain the benefit of it against other persons besides the shipper. Were it not for the inclusion of these words in the clause the shipowners would not have been able to rely upon it as against any of the claimants in this litigation.

156 Then it is said that the contract is a 'contract of exemption'; it merely exempts the other person. This may be a valid observation where the completion of the 'Barwick' contract does not involve the assumption of any special relationship towards the cargo owner. But, when the completion of the 'Barwick' contract involves becoming the sub-bailee of the goods and the actual performing carrier, the 'Barwick' is a contract of carriage, albeit purportedly on terms of complete exemption. True the contract does not include promises or executory obligations and will come to an end as soon as the relationship ceases, but that does not prevent the contract from being a contract and, while it subsists, a contract of carriage. To deny that it is a contract of carriage is to ignore the fact that the service being provided (and which makes the contract enforceable between them) and its subject matter is the carriage of the goods by the shipowners for the goods' owner . . .

159 . . . [Clause 5] starts with a blanket and comprehensive exclusion of any liability whatsoever. It is upon this part of the clause that the shipowners rely as containing the exemption. It is drafted widely enough to cover a very wide range of persons (including 'any person who performs work on behalf of the vessel (*sic*) on which the goods are carried'). This part may present no problem for any entity, such as a stevedoring company, which is not a carrier and has no contract of carriage with the shipper. But for the shipowners it is by reason of clause 2 [a clause paramount incorporating the Hague Rules] as ineffective as the preceding paragraph. It is not until one gets to the next part of the paragraph which contains the words given effect to in *The Eurymedon* and *The New York Star*, that the conflict with clause 2 of the bill of lading is resolved . . . These words add the exemptions etc 'applicable to the carrier or to which the carrier is entitled hereunder'. This specifically avoids any conflict with clause 2. The exemptions applicable to the carrier under this bill of lading are those compatible with the Hague Rules as are those to which he is entitled. This part of the clause reflects the function of a *Himalaya* Clause. This is fatal to the shipowners' case. They want more but this is inconsistent with their reliance upon clause 5 as actual carriers and clause 2 . . .

162 Therefore, applying *The Eurymedon* and *The New York Star*, the shipowners' attempt to get round clause 2 of the bill of lading and the Hague Rules fails and accordingly their defence fails. It is reassuring that this conclusion also conforms to the judicial statements as to the purpose (or function) of the *Himalaya* clause and to the outcome which would be arrived at in jurisdictions which are not circumscribed by contractual criteria or by common law concerns with privity and consideration. Nor would a different conclusion have been arrived at under the Hague-Visby or Hamburg Rules. Nor would it be different if the Contracts (Rights of Third Parties) Act 1999 had applied; it would still have been necessary to see what exemptions this bill of lading on its proper construction, including clause 2, conferred upon the shipowners . . .

Notes

1 The House of Lords struggled here to fix the performing carrier with liability. Why do so? The shippers were content to make a contract with the charterers and to confer a wide express exemption on everyone else.

2 Under part 3 of the *Himalaya* clause in this case, the shipowner became a party to the bill of lading contract with the result that the Hague Rules applied and invalidated part 1 of the clause. The same result will not necessarily follow where the clause does not include this feature.

3 '*A complete exemption from all legal liability may be inconsistent with the enforceability of the clause.*' Why so? An agreement conferring complete exemption is not the same thing as an agreement without legal content. An agreement for a release is not invalid at common law; nor is an agreement to waive liability in tort.

4 The usefulness of a *Himalaya* clause also depends on how it is drafted – the courts would not unduly stretch the words of the clause just to extend protection to the third parties (*Whitesea Shipping & Trading Corp v El Paso Rio Clara Ltda, The Marielle Bolten* [2010] 1 Lloyd's Rep 648).

5   On the validity of the *Himalaya* clause and Art III, r 8 of the Hague-Visby Rules, see Chapter 7, section 9 below.

3 Bailment on terms

Recognition of the effectiveness of *Himalaya* clauses means that it is possible for the terms of a bill of lading to be invoked in some circumstances by someone who is not a holder of the bill or a party to the primary contract. A second common law device that may produce the same result is the doctrine of bailment on terms. This doctrine rests, according to the leading case, on the voluntary taking of possession of goods with an obligation to the owner to look after them on terms to which the owner of the goods has consented. The doctrine does not depend on the existence of a contract between the owner of cargo and the person in possession who loses or damages them, so that in appropriate circumstances it can be invoked by a sub-carrier or a stevedore who takes possession of goods on terms but is not in contract with their owner.

KH Enterprise (Cargo Owners) v Pioneer Container (Owners), The Pioneer Container [1994] 2 AC 324, PC

Facts: The claimants were the owners of goods loaded on the containership *KH Enterprise*, which sank with all her cargo off the coast of Taiwan following a collision in fog. Some of the containers were loaded under direct contract between the shipowners and the shippers. Others were on board under sub-contracts with Hanjin and Scandutch shipping lines, to each of whom the shipowners issued a single feeder bill of lading. There was no contract between the shipowners and the plaintiff owners of the 229 parcels of goods packed in the Hanjin and Scandutch containers. Under their contracts with the plaintiffs, both Hanjin and Scandutch had the right to subcontract all or part of their duties on any terms. The shipowners asked the court to stay the claims on the grounds that there was a bailment to them of the goods on the terms of their bills of lading, which provided by cl 26 that:

> This bill of lading contract shall be governed by Chinese law. Any claim or other dispute arising thereunder shall be determined at Taipei in Taiwan unless the carrier otherwise agrees in writing.

The Court of Appeal of Hong Kong held that all the claimants were bound by the exclusive jurisdiction clause and stayed the proceedings. The claimants appealed to the Privy Council. The Privy Council held that:

(1)   by voluntarily receiving the goods into their custody from the shipping lines with notice that they were owned by other persons, the shipowners assumed the duty to the owners of the goods of a bailee for reward and were obliged to take reasonable care of the goods;

(2)   the shipowners could invoke the terms on which the goods were sub-bailed to them, including the exclusive jurisdiction clause, because by agreeing to allow sub-contracting on any terms, the owners of the goods had consented to the sub-bailment and its terms.

Held:

Lord Goff of Chieveley: . . . Their Lordships turn immediately to the central problem in the case, which is whether the shipowners can rely, as against the Scandutch and Hanjin plaintiffs, on the exclusive jurisdiction clause (clause 26) in the feeder bills of lading to which these plaintiffs were not parties. They think it right to observe, at the outset, that in commercial terms it would be most inconvenient if these two groups of plaintiffs were not so bound. Here is a ship, upon which goods are loaded in a large number of containers; indeed, one container may contain goods belonging to a number of cargo owners. One incident may affect goods owned by several cargo owners, or even (as here) all the cargo owners with goods on board. Common sense and practical convenience combine to demand that all of these claims should be dealt with in one jurisdiction, in accordance with one system of law. If this cannot be achieved, there may be chaos . . . It is scarcely surprising therefore that shipowners seek to achieve uniformity of treatment in respect of all such claims, by clauses designed to impose an exclusive jurisdiction and an agreed governing law, as in the present clause 26 in the shipowners' standard form of bill of lading. Within reason, such an attempt must be regarded with a considerable degree of sympathy and understanding.

However, so far as English law and the law of Hong Kong are concerned, a technical problem faces shipowners who carry goods, for example under the feeder bills of lading in the present case, where there is no contractual relationship between the shipowners and certain cargo owners. This is because English law still maintains, though subject to increasing criticism, a strict principle of privity of contract, under which as a matter of general principle only a person who is a party to a contract may sue upon it. The force of this principle is supported and enhanced by the doctrine of consideration, under which as a general rule only a promise supported by consideration will be enforceable at common law. How long these principles will continue to be maintained in all their strictness is now open to question . . . The present case is concerned with the question whether the law of bailment can here be invoked by the shipowners to circumvent this difficulty.

Bailment and sub-bailment

Their Lordships are here concerned with a case where there has been a sub-bailment – a bailment by the owner of goods to a bailee, followed by a sub-bailment by the bailee to a sub-bailee – and the question has arisen whether, in an action by the owner against the sub-bailee for loss of the goods, the sub-bailee can rely as against the owner upon one of the terms upon which the goods have been sub-bailed to him by the bailee . . . The question is whether the shipowners can in these circumstances rely upon the exclusive jurisdiction clause in the feeder bills of lading as against both groups of plaintiffs, notwithstanding that the plaintiffs in neither group were parties to the contract with the shipowners contained in or evidenced by such a bill of lading, having regard to the fact that the plaintiffs are seeking to hold the shipowners liable for failing to care for the goods so entrusted to them or failing to deliver them to the plaintiffs – in other words, for committing a breach of duty which is characteristic of a bailee.

The question whether a sub-bailee can in circumstances such as these rely upon such a term, and if so upon what principle he is entitled to do so, is one which has been considered in cases in the past, but so far neither by the House of Lords nor by the Privy Council. It has been much discussed by academic writers. Their Lordships are grateful to counsel for the citation to them of academic writings, especially Palmer, N, *Bailment*, 2nd ed, 1991: London: Sweet & Maxwell and Bell, A, *Modern Law of Personal Property in England and Ireland*, 1989, London: Butterworths, to which they have repeatedly referred while considering the problems which have arisen for decision in the present case.

In approaching the central problem in the present case, their Lordships wish to observe that they are here concerned with two related questions. The first question relates to the identification of the relationship between the owner and the sub-bailee. Once that question is answered, it is possible to address the second question, which is whether, given that relationship, it is open to the sub-bailee to invoke as against the owner the terms upon which he received the goods from the bailee.

The relationship between the owner and the sub-bailee

Fortunately, authoritative guidance on the answer to the first question is to be found in the decision of the Privy Council in *Gilchrist Watt and Sanderson Pty Ltd v York Products Pty Ltd* [1970] 1 WLR 1262, an appeal from the Court of Appeal of New South Wales. There two cases of clocks were shipped from Hamburg to Sydney. On arrival of the ship at Sydney the goods were unloaded, sorted and stacked on the wharf by the defendants, who were ship's agents and stevedores. The plaintiffs were the holders of the relevant bills of lading. When their agents sought delivery of the two cases from the defendants, one was missing and was never found. The plaintiffs sought to hold the defendants responsible as bailees of the goods. The Privy Council proceeded on the basis that there was a bailment to the shipowners, and a sub-bailment by the shipowners to the defendants; and that the defendants as sub-bailees received possession of the goods for the purpose of looking after them and delivering them to the holders of the bills of lading, who were the plaintiffs. Accordingly, the defendants 'took upon themselves an obligation to the plaintiffs to exercise due care for the safety of the goods, although there was no contractual relation or attornment between the defendants and the plaintiffs': see p 1267 *per* Lord Pearson, delivering the judgment of the Judicial Committee . . .

The terms of the collateral bailment between the owner and the sub-bailee

On the authority of the *Gilchrist Watt* case [1970] 1 WLR 1262, their Lordships have no difficulty in concluding that, in the present case, the shipowners became on receipt of the relevant goods the bailees of the goods of both the Hanjin plaintiffs and the Scandutch plaintiffs. Furthermore, they are of the opinion that the shipowners became the bailees of the goods for reward. In Pollock and Wright, *Possession in the Common Law*, 1888, Oxford: Stevens, it is stated that both the owner of the goods and the bailee have concurrently the rights of a bailor against the sub-bailee according to the nature of the sub-bailment. Their Lordships, like Lord Denning MR in *Morris v CW Martin & Sons Ltd* [1966] 1 QB 716, 729, consider that, if the sub-bailment is for reward, the obligation owed by the sub-bailee to the owner must likewise be that of a bailee for reward, notwithstanding that the reward is payable not by the owner but by the bailee. It would, they consider, be inconsistent in these circumstances to impose on the sub-bailee two different standards of care in respect of goods so entrusted to him.

But the question then arises whether, as against the owners (here the two groups of plaintiffs), the sub-bailees (here the shipowners) can invoke any of the terms on which the goods were sub-bailed to them, and in particular the exclusive jurisdiction clause (clause 26).

In *Morris v CW Martin & Sons Ltd* Lord Denning MR expressed his opinion on this point in clear terms, though on the facts of the case his opinion was *obiter*. He said, at p 729: 'The answer to the problem lies, I think, in this: the owner is bound by the conditions if he has expressly or impliedly consented to the bailee making a sub-bailment containing those conditions, but not otherwise.'

. . . In order to decide whether . . . to accept the principle so stated by Lord Denning MR, it is necessary to consider the relevance of the concept of 'consent' in this context. It must be assumed that, on the facts of the case, no direct contractual relationship has been created between the owner and the sub-bailee, the only contract created by the sub-bailment being that between the bailee and the sub-bailee. Even so, if the effect of the sub-bailment is that the sub-bailee voluntarily receives into his custody the goods of the owner and so assumes towards the owner the responsibility of a bailee, then to the extent that the terms of the sub-bailment are consented to by the owner, it can properly be said that the owner has authorised the bailee so to regulate the duties of the sub-bailee in respect of the goods entrusted to him, not only towards the bailee but also towards the owner . . .

Such a conclusion, finding its origin in the law of bailment rather than the law of contract, does not depend for its efficacy either on the doctrine of privity of contract or on the doctrine of consideration. That this may be so appears from the decision of the House of Lords in *Elder Dempster & Co Ltd v Paterson, Zochonis & Co Ltd* [1924] AC 522. In that case, shippers of cargo on a chartered ship brought an action against the shipowners for damage caused to the cargo by bad stowage, for which the shipowners were responsible. It is crucial to observe that the cargo was shipped under charterers' bills of lading, so that the contract of carriage contained in or evidenced by the bills of lading was between the shippers and the charterers. The shipowners nevertheless sought to rely, as against the shippers, upon an exception in the bill of lading which protected the charterers from liability for damage due to bad stowage. It was held that the shipowners were entitled to do so, the preferred reason upon which the House so held (*see* *Midland Silicones Ltd v Scruttons Ltd* [1962] AC 446, 470, *per* Viscount Simonds, following the opinion of Fullagar J in *Wilson v Darling Island Stevedoring and Lighterage Co Ltd* [1956] 1 Lloyd's Rep 346, 364; 95 CLR 43, 78) being found in the speech of Lord Sumner [1924] AC 522, 564:

> in the circumstances of this case the obligations to be inferred from the reception of the cargo for carriage to the United Kingdom amount to a bailment upon terms, which include the exceptions and limitations of liability stipulated in the known and contemplated form of bill of lading.

Of course, there was in that case a bailment by the shippers direct to the shipowners, so that it was not necessary to have recourse to the concept of sub-bailment. Even so, notwithstanding the absence of any contract between the shippers and the shipowners, the shipowners' obligations as bailees were effectively subject to the terms upon which the shipowners implicitly received the goods into their possession. Their Lordships do not imagine that a different conclusion would have been reached in the *Elder, Dempster* case if the shippers had delivered the goods, not directly to the ship, but into the possession of agents of the charterers who had, in their turn, loaded the goods on board; because in such circumstances, by parity of reasoning, the shippers may be held to have impliedly consented that the sub-bailment to the shipowners should be on terms which included the exemption from liability for bad stowage.

. . . On this approach, a person who voluntarily takes another person's goods into his custody holds them as bailee of that person (the owner); and he can only invoke, for example, terms of a sub-bailment under which he received the goods from an intermediate bailee as qualifying or otherwise affecting his responsibility to the owner if the owner consented to them. It is the latter approach which, as their Lordships have explained, has been adopted by English law and, with English law, the law of Hong Kong.

Their Lordships wish to add that this conclusion, which flows from the decisions in *Morris v CW Martin & Sons Ltd* [1966] 1 QB 716 and the *Gilchrist Watt* case [1970] 1 WLR 1262, produces a result which in their opinion is both principled and just. They incline to the opinion that a sub-bailee can only be said for these purposes to have voluntarily taken into his possession the goods of another if he has sufficient notice that a person other than the bailee is interested in the goods so that it can properly be said that (in addition to his duties to the bailee) he has, by taking the goods into his custody, assumed towards that other person the responsibility for the goods which is characteristic of a bailee. This they believe to be the underlying principle. Moreover, their Lordships do not consider this principle to impose obligations on the sub-bailee which are onerous or unfair, once it is recognised that he can invoke against the owner terms of the sub-bailment which the owner has actually (expressly or impliedly) or even ostensibly authorised. In the last resort the sub-bailee may, if necessary and appropriate, be able to invoke against the bailee the principle of warranty of authority . . .

The Mahkutai [1996] AC 650, PC

Facts: See p 366, above.

Held:

Lord Goff of Chieveley:

Application of the principle of bailment on terms in the present case

In the light of the principle stated by Lord Sumner in the *Elder Dempster* case [1924] AC 522 at 564, as interpreted by Fullagar J in the *Darling Island* case 95 CLR 43 at 78, the next question for consideration is whether the shipowners can establish that they received the goods into their possession on the terms of the bill of lading, including the exclusive jurisdiction clause (cl 19), ie whether the shipowners' obligations as bailees were effectively subjected to the clause as a term upon which the shipowners implicitly received the goods into their possession (see *The Pioneer Container* [1994] 2 AC 324 at 340 *per* Lord Goff of Chieveley). This was the ground upon which Bokhary JA ([1994] 1 HKLR 212 at 229–230) expressed the opinion, in his dissenting judgment, that the shipowners were entitled to succeed.

Their Lordships feel able to deal with this point very briefly, because they consider that in the present case there is an insuperable objection to the argument of the shipowners. This is that the bill of lading under which the goods were shipped on board contained a *Himalaya* clause under which the shipowners as sub-contractors were expressed to be entitled to the benefit of certain terms in the bill of lading but, as their Lordships have held, those terms did not include the exclusive jurisdiction clause. In these circumstances their Lordships find it impossible to hold that, by receiving the goods into their possession pursuant to the bill of lading, the shipowners' obligations as bailees were effectively subjected to the exclusive jurisdiction clause as a term upon which they implicitly received the goods into their possession. Any such implication must, in their opinion, be rejected as inconsistent with the express terms of the bill of lading.

Notes

1 Possession is an elusive idea. It is not always easy to decide who, if anyone, is in possession of particular goods at a given moment or to identify the special terms, if any, on which they hold those goods. In *Lotus Cars Ltd v Southampton Cargo Handling plc* [2000] 2 Lloyd's Rep 532, CA, a Lotus car intended for export on *Rigoletto* was stolen from an insecure compound at Southampton docks operated by ABP. It was common ground that Lotus were entitled to a received for shipment bill of lading on the shipowner's standard form, which included a *Himalaya* clause. The car was delivered to SCH, stevedores acting for the owners of *Rigoletto*, on the stevedores' standard conditions of business and parked in the compound. Despite the agreement that *Rigoletto* had received the car it was held that: (1) SCH had taken possession of the vehicle for storage, as opposed to simply handling during loading or discharge, and were in possession on their standard business terms; (2) the *Himalaya* clause was inconsistent with SCH's own terms, on which SCH had chosen to rely, and so was inapplicable; (3) (Chadwick LJ dissenting) possession of the car was transferred from SCH to ABP when it was parked in the compound and ABP thus owed Lotus a duty of care as bailees or sub-bailees or alternatively were liable in negligence. Comment: the question whether a person has taken possession of goods is a mixed question of fact and law. Control of a compound or an area used for storage does not necessarily demonstrate possession of everything in it. Here the Court of Appeal attached importance to a list of factors that tend to indicate possession, including a clause in ABP's terms that acknowledged that ABP might take possession of stored goods.

2 *Bailment and contract often go hand in hand.* This handy epigram comes from *Sandeman Coprimar SA v Transitos y Transportes Integrales SL* [2003] 3 All ER 108, CA, a road transport case, where it was said that principles of the law of bailment have always overlapped with those of the law of contract so that where a bailee has the consent, and thus the authority, of the bailor to enter into a sub-bailment on particular terms and does so, and where those terms purport to govern the relationship not merely between the sub-bailee and the bailee, but between the sub-bailee and the bailor, all the elements of a collateral contract binding the sub-bailee and the bailor will be present, for there will be privity, via the agency of the bailee, and no difficulty in identifying consideration, at least if the terms are capable of resulting in benefit to each of the parties.

3 See further Bell, A, 'Sub-bailment on terms' (1995) LMCLQ 177; Wilson, J, 'A flexible contract of carriage' (1996) LMCLQ 187; Baughen, S, 'Bailment's continuing role in cargo claims' (1999) LMCLQ 393. See also Chapter 5 section 16.

4 *Brandt* contracts

If the Carriage of Goods by Sea Act 1992 does not operate to transfer to the holder of a bill of lading the rights under the contract, it may nevertheless be possible in some circumstances to imply a contract between carrier and the receiver to give and receive delivery on the terms of the bill of lading. In some cases decided before 1992 courts seem to have been prepared to find contracts of this type – *Brandt* contracts – without a strong factual basis, almost treating these agreements as arising by operation of law. The Court of Appeal rejected this approach in the next case.

The Aramis [1989] 1 Lloyd's Rep 213, CA

Facts: The *Aramis* was trip chartered for a voyage from South America to Europe. The ship loaded a cargo of linseed expellers at Necochea in Argentina. Two parcels were to be delivered from this bulk at Rotterdam. One parcel was the subject of bill of lading 5 (204 tons), the other of bill of lading 6 (255 tons). On discharge at Rotterdam, it became clear that there was a considerable shortage of cargo, possibly because of over delivery at an earlier port of call. No delivery at all was made under bill of lading 5. Only 11.55 tons was delivered on presentation of bill of lading 6. Despite the fact that separate bills of lading had been issued, the goods in question were said to have formed part of a single undivided bulk cargo. On this basis, no property in the goods had passed to the plaintiff purchasers, who were not therefore entitled to sue the shipowners on the bill of lading contract under s 1 of the Bills of Lading Act 1855. The plaintiffs alleged that, applying *Brandt v Liverpool, Brazil and River Plate Steam Navigation Co Ltd* [1924] 1 KB 575, CA, an implied contract had arisen, even though the shipowners had no lien over the cargo and were bound to deliver to any holder of these bills of lading claiming delivery. Freight had been pre-paid; no payments were due to the carrier on discharge. The Court of Appeal held that mere presentation of a bill of lading coupled with delivery is not sufficient material on which to find an implied contract.

Held:

Bingham LJ: . . . Like most important legal decisions, that in *Brandt's* case did not lack ancestors and has not lacked progeny. We were referred to a number of cases before *Brandt* and since . . .

These cases may be said to decide no more than that whether a contract is to be implied is a question of fact and that a contract will only be implied where it is necessary to do so. But the cases certainly show that there is evidence from which a contract may be inferred where a shipowner who has a lien on cargo for unpaid freight or demurrage or other charges makes or agrees to make delivery of the cargo to the holder of a bill of lading who presents it and seeks or obtains delivery and pays outstanding dues or agrees to pay them or is to be taken to agree to pay them. The parties may also . . . show an intention to adopt and perform the bill of lading contract in other ways. There does not, however, appear to have been a case in which a contract has been implied from the mere facts (a) that an endorsee, entitled as holder of the bill of lading to demand delivery, does so, and (b) that the shipowner, bound by contract with his shipper (and perhaps his charterer) to deliver goods to any party presenting the bill of lading, duly makes such delivery. Whether on such facts (without more) a contract may be implied must be considered in the light of ordinary contractual principles.

Most contracts are, of course, made expressly, whether orally or in writing. But here, on the evidence, nothing was said, nothing was written. So regard must be paid to the conduct of the parties alone. The questions to be answered are, I think, twofold: (1) whether the conduct of the bill of lading holder in presenting the bill of lading to the ship's agent would be reasonably understood by the agents (or the shipowner) as an offer to enter into a contract on the bill of lading terms; (2) whether the conduct of the ship's agent in accepting the bill or the conduct of the master in agreeing to give delivery or in giving delivery would be reasonably understood by the bill of lading holder as an acceptance of his offer.

I do not think it is enough for the party seeking the implication of a contract to obtain 'it might' as an answer to these questions, for it would, in my view, be contrary to principle to countenance the implication of a contract from conduct if the conduct relied upon is no more consistent with an intention to contract than with an intention not to contract. It must, surely, be necessary to identify conduct referable to the contract contended for or, at the very least, conduct inconsistent with there being no contract made between the parties to the effect contended for. Put another way, I think it must be fatal to the implication of a contract if the parties would or might have acted exactly as they did in the absence of a contract.

If this approach is correct, I think it is impossible to imply a contract on the bare facts of this case. Nothing that the shipowners or the bill of lading holders did need have been different had their intention been not to make a contract on the bill of lading terms. Their business relationship was entirely efficacious without the implication of any contract between them. Although the bill of lading holders had no title to any part of the undivided bulk cargo they had a perfectly good right to demand delivery and the shipowners had no right to refuse or to impose conditions . . .

I fully recognise the good sense and the commercial convenience underlying the learned judge's decision. Unless the parties understood s 1 of the 1855 Act (which is not necessarily so) they probably thought that their rights and duties were governed by the bill of lading anyway. It would be perfectly reasonable in a general sense to treat the parties' rights and duties as so governed. Once an intention to contract is found no problem on consideration arises, since there would be ample consideration in the bundle of rights and duties which the parties would respectively obtain and accept. Had the boot been on the other foot it seems very likely that the shipowners would have sought to assert the bill of lading contract. But I do not think these matters entitle one to cast principle aside and simply opt for a commercially convenient solution . . .

Note

The decision in *The Aramis* has been criticised: Treitel, G, 'Bills of lading and implied contracts' (1989) LMCLQ 612 and Davenport, B, 'Problems in the Bill of Lading Act' (1989) 105 LQR 174. But it was cited without disapproval in the House of Lords in *The Berge Sisar* [2001] UKHL 17; [2002] 2 AC 205 and in the Court of Appeal in *The Captain Gregos (No 2)* [1990] 2 Lloyd's Rep 395, CA and *The Gudermes* [1993] 1 Lloyd's Rep 311, CA, where it said that it was not enough to show that the parties had done something more than, or something different from, what they were already bound to do under obligations owed to others. What they do must be consistent only with there being a new contract implied, and inconsistent with there being no such contract. And in any event, terms could not be implied which one party had refused to accept.

5 The rule in *Dunlop v Lambert*

If for some reason a buyer of cargo carried by sea is not able to make a claim for damages against the carrier, can the shipper or charterer sue on the receiver's behalf? The general rule in English law is that a party to a contract who suffers no loss or damage as a result of a breach can recover no more than nominal damages. The rule in *Dunlop v Lambert* (1839) 6 CP & Fin 600 creates an exception to the general rule. But *The Albazero*, below, restricted the rule to a very narrow range, which has been narrowed even further by the enactment of the Carriage of Goods by Sea Act 1992.

Owners of cargo lately laden on board ship or vessel Albacruz v Ship or vessel Albazero (Owners), The Albazero [1977] AC 774

Facts: The *Albacruz* was time chartered under a five-year time charter. Crude oil was loaded at La Salina, Venezuela, for carriage to Antwerp. A bill of lading, which named the charterter as consignee, was endorsed to another company in the charterer's group. In the course of the voyage the *Albacruz* and her cargo became a total loss owing to breaches by the shipowners of the charterparty. The charterer brought an action against the shipowners for breach of the time charter. The cargo owners were not parties to the action; they had lost their right to claim under the bill of lading owing to the expiry of the one-year limitation period fixed by the Hague Rules. The charterer claimed that the measure of the damages that they were entitled to recover was the arrived value of the goods lost, notwithstanding that at the time the goods were lost the charterer had no longer any property in the goods and had suffered no loss themselves by reason of their non-delivery at their destination.

Held:

Lord Diplock: . . . *Dunlop v Lambert* (1839) 6 Cl & Fin 600 was a Scots case . . . The argument before this House took place some 15 months before judgment was delivered. The only speech was that of Lord Cottenham LC and its reasoning is baffling. The pursuer had shipped a puncheon of whisky for carriage by sea in the defender's ship from Leith to Newcastle under a bill of lading issued by the defender in which the pursuer was named as shipper and Robson, the buyer of the whisky from the pursuer, was named as consignee. The goods were lost by what appears to have been a general average sacrifice and the pursuer had in fact made good the loss to his buyer.

Nine-tenths of Lord Cottenham LC's speech appears to be directed to the question whether the pursuer as consignor and seller had contracted with the shipowner on his own behalf or as agent for his buyer who was named as consignee, and to relate this to the terms of the contract of sale between the consignor and consignee as respects the passing of property in the goods and the passing of risk. So far this was what by 1839 had become the classic approach to the question whether the consignor or consignee was entitled to sue on the contract of carriage. The same approach is also reflected in the order of the House directing that . . . it ought to have been left to the jury to determine, first, whether the goods had been delivered to the carrier on the risk of the consignor or of the consignee and, secondly, whether there was a special contract between the consignor and the consignee which might have enabled the pursuers to recover in the action.

There is, however, a penultimate paragraph in the speech immediately preceding the direction as to the order to be made. This appears to bear little relation to any of the reasoning that goes before or to the direction that comes after unless 'consignee' in the second part of the direction is a mistake for 'carrier'. It reads as follows:

> These authorities, therefore, establish in my mind the propositions which are necessary to be adopted, in order to overrule this direction of the Lord President. I am of opinion, that although, generally speaking, where there is a delivery to a carrier to deliver to a consignee, he is the proper person to bring the action against the carrier should the goods be lost; yet that if the consignor made a special contract with the carrier, and the carrier agreed to take the goods from him, and to deliver them to any particular person at any particular place, the special contract supersedes the necessity of showing the ownership in the goods; and that, by the authority of the cases of *Davis v James* (1770) 5 Burr 2680 and *Joseph v Knox* (1813) 3 Camp 320, the consignor, the person making the contract with the carrier, may maintain the action, though the goods may be the goods of the consignee.

My Lords, there might have been room for argument for some years after *Dunlop v Lambert* as to what principle of law it did lay down and whether it was really a decision of this House that privity of contract sufficed not only to entitle the consignee to bring suit against the carrier (which would be trite law today) but also to enable him to recover substantial damages whether or not he had himself sustained them. It has however been uniformly treated ever since by textbook writers of the highest authority, Abbott, Maude and Pollock, Blackburn and (implicitly) by Scrutton in each of its successive editions, as authority for the broad proposition that the consignor may recover substantial damages against the shipowner if there is privity of contract between him and the carrier for the carriage of goods; although, if the goods are not his property or at his risk, he will be accountable to the true owner for the proceeds of his judgment.

... It has been urged on your Lordships on behalf of the shipowners that if *Dunlop v Lambert* really is authority for the rule that it has for so long been understood to have laid down, it constitutes an anomalous exception to the general rule of English law that a party to a contract apart from nominal damages, can only recover for its breach such actual loss as he has himself sustained; and that ... your Lordships should now declare that it is no longer the law.

My Lords ... the Bills of Lading Act 1855 and the subsequent development of the doctrine laid down in *Brandt v Liverpool, Brazil and River Plate Steam Navigation Co Ltd* have reduced the scope and utility of the rule in *Dunlop v Lambert* where goods are carried under a bill of lading. But the rule extends to all forms of carriage, including carriage by sea itself where no bill of lading has been issued, and there may still be occasional cases in which the rule would provide a remedy where no other would be available to a person sustaining loss which under a rational legal system ought to be compensated by the person who has caused it. For my part, I am not persuaded that your Lordships ought to go out of your way to jettison the rule.

On the other hand, I do not think your Lordships should extend it beyond what is justified by its rationale so far as this can be discerned ...

The only way in which I find it possible to rationalise the rule in *Dunlop v Lambert* so that it may fit into the pattern of the English law is to treat it as an application of the principle, accepted also in relation to policies of insurance on goods, that in a commercial contract concerning goods where it is in the contemplation of the parties that the proprietary interests in the goods may be transferred from one owner to another after the contract has been entered into and before the breach which causes loss or damage to the goods, an original party to the contract, if such be the intention of them both, is to be treated in law as having entered into the contract for the benefit of all persons who have or may acquire an interest in the goods before they are lost or damaged, and is entitled to recover by way of damages for breach of contract the actual loss sustained by those for whose benefit the contract is entered into.

With the passing of the Bills of Lading Act 1855 the rationale of *Dunlop v Lambert* could no longer apply in cases where the only contract of carriage into which the shipowner had entered was that contained in a bill of lading, and the property in the goods passed to the consignee or endorsee named in the bill of lading by reason of the consignment or indorsement. On that happening the right of suit against the shipowner in respect of obligations arising under the contract of carriage passes to him from the consignor ...

The rationale of the rule is in my view also incapable of justifying its extension to contracts for carriage of goods which contemplate that the carrier will also enter into separate contracts of carriage with whoever may become the owner of goods carried pursuant to the original contract.

A charterparty which provides for the issue of bills of lading covering the carriage of particular goods shipped on the chartered vessel is such a contract ... The complications, anomalies and injustices that might arise from the co-existence in different parties of rights of suit to recover, under separate contracts of carriage which impose different obligations on the parties to them, a loss which a party to one of those contracts alone has sustained, supply compelling reasons why the rule in *Dunlop v Lambert* should not be extended to cases where there are two contracts with the carrier covering the same carriage and under one of them there is privity of contract between the person who actually sustains the loss and the carrier by whose breach of that contract it was caused ...

Notes

1   Lord Diplock here points out that for some years after *Dunlop v Lambert* was decided, the proper interpretation of that case was open to dispute. In the House of Lords, in *Alfred McAlpine Construction Ltd v Panatown Ltd* [2001] AC 530, Lord Clyde and Lord Jauncey demonstrate that the rule in *Dunlop v Lambert*, as it eventually emerged, was based on a misunderstanding of the original decision. Nevertheless, the rule, as interpreted in *The Albazero*, was treated in *Panatown* as too well established to be challenged.

2   The function of the rule is to prevent a carrier avoiding liability when the consignee has no cause of action. It is, therefore, fatal to the application of *The Albazero* that the person who has the property and risk in the cargo also has a direct remedy against the carrier.

3   In *Panatown*, the rule in *Dunlop v Lambert* was said to be a rule of law (which can be excluded by agreement) but not a result that can be created by contract.

4   See further Coote, B, '*Dunlop v Lambert:* the search for a rationale' (1998) 13 JCL 91.

5   A majority in *Panatown* recognised that in the case of some contracts, an innocent party who suffers no personal financial loss – as where A employs B to repair property belonging to C, a relative – may nevertheless recover the loss of the value of performance of the contract, provided that C has no direct cause of action.

 Further reading

Battersby, G, 'Exemption clauses and third parties: Recent decisions' (1978) 28 U Toronto LJ 75.

Baughen, S, 'Bailment's continuing role in cargo claims' (1999) LMCLQ 393.

Bell, A, 'Sub-bailment on terms' (1995) LMCLQ 177.

Browne, J, 'The rise and demise of the *Brandt v Liverpool* contract' (2005) 11(3) JIML 221.

Coote, B, 'Vicarious immunity by an alternative route – II' (1974) 37 MLR 453.

Davies, P and Palmer, N, '*The Eurymedon* five years on' (1979) JBL 337.

Duggan, A, 'Offloading the Eurymedon' (1974) 9 Melbourne ULR 753.

Glenn, B, 'Responsibilities of owner and charterer to third parties – Consequences under time and voyage charters' (1974–1975) 49 Tul L Rev 995.

Hopkins, C, 'Privity of contract: The thin end of the wedge?' (1990) CLJ 21.

Law Commission, 'Reforming privity of contract' Report No 242 (1996).

Palmer, N, 'The Stevedore's dilemma: Exemption clauses and third parties – I' (1974) JBL 101.

Rawlings, P, 'Third party rights in contract' (2006) 1(Feb) LMCLQ 7.

Reynolds, F, 'Himalaya clause resurgent' (1974) 90 LQR 301.

Rose, F, 'Return to elder dempster?' (1975) 4 Anglo-Am LR 7.

Tetley, W, 'The Himalaya clause – revisited' (2003) 9(1) JIML 40.

Waddams, S, 'Comment' (1977) 55 Can Bar Rev 327.

Wilson, J, 'A flexible contract of carriage' (1996) LMCLQ 187.

Chapter 7

Contractual Liabilities between Carrier and Cargo Interest – The Hague-Visby and Hamburg Regimes

Before 1800 it was unusual for English bills of lading to include extensive exclusion clauses. Practice changed dramatically in the first half of the 19th century and in due course provoked a reaction on the part of cargo interests. Carriers claimed that freedom of contract was the right approach and robustly exercised that freedom. Shippers responded that the only freedom of contract they enjoyed was the freedom either to ship on terms dictated by the sea carrier or the freedom not to ship at all. Consignees, endorsees and their bankers usually had even less opportunity than shippers to influence the terms of bills of lading by negotiation. In England, these considerations led to the promotion of model bills of lading and to unsuccessful demands for legislation. In other jurisdictions, cargo interests were powerful enough to obtain legislation to adjust the balance in their favour. This was done in the US in the Harter Act in 1893 and later in Australia (Sea Carriage of Goods Act 1904), Canada (Water Carriage of Goods Act 1910) and in New Zealand (Shipping and Seamen Act 1903).

A number of attempts were made to secure a uniform international approach.

After considerable discussion among the representatives of leading shipowners, underwriters, shippers and bankers of the big maritime nations, a set of rules was finally drafted by the Maritime Law Committee of the International Law Association at a meeting held at The Hague in 1921. '[They] came to be known as the Hague Rules, but . . . were not immediately adopted . . . The Rules were amended at the London Conference of CMI in 1922. A draft convention drawn up at that conference was amended at Brussels in 1923, and in due course an international Convention was ultimately signed there by the most important trading nations on 25 August 1924. Each State was expected to give the Hague Rules statutory force with regard to all outward bills of lading . . .' (UNCTAD (United Nations Conference on Trade and Development), 'Bills of Lading', 1971, para 62).

In Great Britain, the draft Convention of 1923 was given statutory effect by the Carriage of Goods by Sea Act 1924. Subsequently, the draft of 1923 was signed at Brussels on 25 August 1924, although only after further amendments, which were not incorporated in the 1924 Act.

It was said (Wright J, *Gosse Millerd v Canadian Govt Merchant Marine Ltd* [1927] 2 KB 432, KBD, p 434) that the Hague Rules:

> radically changed the legal status of sea carriers under bills of lading. According to the previous law, shipowners were generally common carriers, or were liable to the obligations of common carriers, but they were entitled to the utmost freedom to restrict and limit their liabilities, which they did by elaborate and mostly illegible exceptions and conditions. Under the Act and the Rules, which cannot be varied in favour of the carrier by any bill of lading, their liabilities are precisely determined, and so also are their rights and immunities . . . .

In 1963 the CMI adopted (at Visby on the Swedish island of Gotland) the text of a draft document intended to make limited amendments to the 1924 Convention. This draft was considered at the 12th session of the Brussels Diplomatic Conference on Maritime Law in 1967 and 1968. The result was the Protocol signed on 23 February 1968. In the United Kingdom, the Carriage of Goods by Sea Act 1971 was passed to give effect to that Protocol. The Act was brought into force on 23 June 1977. It repealed the 1924 Act and re-enacted the Hague Rules in their amended Hague-Visby form.

The Hague Rules (and their successor the Hague-Visby Rules) form an internationally recognised code adjusting the rights and duties existing between shipowners and those shipping goods under bills of lading. 'As Sir John Donaldson MR said in *Leigh & Sillivan Ltd v Aliakmon Shipping Co Ltd* [1985] QB 350, 368, "the rules create an intricate blend of responsibilities and liabilities, rights and immunities, limitations on the amount of damages recoverable, time bars, evidential provisions, indemnities and liberties, all in relation to the carriage of goods under bills of lading'" (Saville LJ, *The Nicholas H* [1994] 1 WLR 1071, p 1080).

Although the 1968 Protocol made important changes, it did not radically alter the compromise between the interests of carriers and cargo owners that had been reached in 1924. The case for a more fundamental revision of the Hague Rules was argued in *Bills of Lading*, a report by the secretariat of UNCTAD, published by the United Nations in 1971. The movement for reform, which began with the UNCTAD report, led to the UN Conference on the Carriage of Goods by Sea at Hamburg in 1978 and the adoption of a new convention, the Hamburg Rules. Those Rules, however, attracted little support in the UK.

Work then commenced again in the 1990s by the Comité Maritime International (CMI) for the creation of a new convention to take on board the then pressing issues such as containerisation, electronic shipping docuemntation, multi-modal transportation, door-to-door cover, etc. Their work was subsequently followed up by the UNCITRAL and on 3 July 2008, the UNCITRAL Commission officially adopted a new transport convention called 'The Convention on Contracts for the International Carriage of Goods wholly or partly by Sea'– now commonly known as the Rotterdam Rules. This new convention will come into force one year after the date of deposit of the 20th instrument of ratification, acceptance, approval or accession. The UK has not expressed much support for the new convention and at present does not represent the law of the UK in relation to carriage of goods by sea. It is therefore proposed that the provisions of the Rotterdam Rules are best addressed in a separate chapter.

1 The Hague (Visby) regime in English law

The Hague-Visby Rules are given effect to in English law by means of the Carriage of Goods by Sea Act 1971. Where the Carriage of Goods by Sea Act 1971 applies, the Hague-Visby Rules will apply to the relevant contract of carriage as a matter of law. In charterparty cases, it is open to the parties to agree to incorporate the Rules into their contract of carriage. That is achieved usually by means of a paramount clause contained in the charterparty bill of lading (see Chapter 5 section 5).

The effect of such an incorporation is neatly summarised by Hamblen J in *Onego Shipping and Chartering BV v JSC Arcadia Shipping, M/V 'Socol 3'* [2010] EWHC 777 (Comm):

... where the Hague/Hague-Visby Rules are incorporated into a charterparty:

(1) The charterparty 'must ... be read as if the provisions of the Act were written out therein and thereby gained such contractual force as a proper construction of the document admits'. Only provisions in the Rules that are 'insensible' or 'inapplicable' in the context of a time charter will be disregarded – see *Adamastos Shipping Co Ltd v Anglo-Saxon Petroleum Ltd* [1959] AC 133, 152, 155 (per Viscount Simonds); 'The provisions of the Act are, therefore, to be incorporated as terms of the contract [ie the Charterparty] as far as applicable' – *Adamastos* (Lord Somervell at 184).

(2) As the House of Lords made clear in *Adamastos*, an important purpose of incorporating the Rules into a charterparty is 'to import into the contractual relation between owners and charterers the same standard of obligation, liability, right and immunity as under the rules subsists between carrier and shipper' – (Viscount Simonds at 154).

A key difference thus is that where the Rules had only been incorporated as a matter of contract, they could be derogated from by means of appropriately worded exclusion or limitation of liability clauses. In *Trafigura Beheer BV v Navigazione Montanari Spa* [2014] EWHC 129 (Comm) as Andrew Smith J said, owners seldom agree to absolute undertakings in charterparty bills of lading.

Carriage of Goods by Sea Act 1971
An Act to amend the law with respect to the carriage of goods by sea (8 April 1971; in force 23 June 1977; printed as amended).

1 Application of Hague Rules as amended
(1) In this Act, 'the Rules' means the International Convention for the unification of certain rules of law relating to bills of lading signed at Brussels on 25 August 1924, as amended by the Protocol signed at Brussels on 23 February 1968, and by the Protocol signed at Brussels on 21 December 1979.

(2) The provisions of the Rules, as set out in the Schedule to this Act, shall have the force of law.

(3) Without prejudice to subsection (2) above, the said provisions shall have effect (and have the force of law) in relation to and in connection with the carriage of goods by sea in ships where the port of shipment is a port in the United Kingdom, whether or not the carriage is between ports in two different States within the meaning of Article X of the Rules.

(4) Subject to subsection (6) below, nothing in this section shall be taken as applying anything in the Rules to any contract for the carriage of goods by sea, unless the contract expressly or by implication provides for the issue of a bill of lading or any similar document of title.

...

(6) Without prejudice to Article X(c) of the Rules, the Rules shall have the force of law in relation to:

(a)   any bill of lading if the contract contained in or evidenced by it expressly provides that the Rules shall govern the contract, and

(b)   any receipt which is a non-negotiable document marked as such if the contract contained in or evidenced by it is a contract for the carriage of goods by sea which expressly provides that the Rules are to govern the contract as if the receipt were a bill of lading, but subject, where paragraph (b) applies, to any necessary modifications and in particular with the omission in Article III of the Rules of the second sentence of paragraph 4 and of paragraph 7.

(7) If and so far as the contract contained in or evidenced by a bill of lading or receipt within paragraph (a) or (b) of subsection (6) above applies to deck cargo or live animals, the Rules as given the force of law by that subsection shall have effect as if Article I(c) did not exclude deck cargo and live animals.

In this subsection 'deck cargo' means cargo which by the contract of carriage is stated as being carried on deck and is so carried.

1A Conversion of special drawing rights into sterling
[Section added by the Merchant Shipping Act 1995, s 314(2), Sched 13, para 45(3). In force 1 January 1996.]

(1) For the purposes of Article IV of the Rules the value on a particular day of one special drawing right shall be treated as equal to such a sum in sterling as the International Monetary Fund have fixed as being the equivalent of one special drawing right:

(a)   for that day; or

(b)   if no sum has been so fixed for that day, for the last day before that day for which a sum has been so fixed.

(2) A certificate given by or on behalf of the Treasury stating:

(a)   that a particular sum in sterling has been fixed as aforesaid for a particular day; or

(b)   that no sum has been so fixed for a particular day and that a particular sum in sterling has been so fixed for a day which is the last day for which a sum has been so fixed before the particular day, shall be conclusive evidence of those matters for the purposes of subsection (1) above; and a document purporting to be such a certificate shall in any proceedings be received in evidence and, unless the contrary is proved, be deemed to be such a certificate.

(3) . . . [Fees for certificates.]

2 Contracting states, etc
(1) If Her Majesty by Order in Council certifies to the following effect, that is to say, that for the purposes of the Rules:

(a)   a State specified in the Order is a Contracting State, or is a Contracting State in respect of any place or territory so specified; or
(b)   any place or territory specified in the Order forms part of a State so specified (whether a contracting State or not),

the Order shall, except so far as it has been superseded by a subsequent Order, be conclusive evidence of the matters so certified.

(2) An Order in Council under this section may be varied or revoked by a subsequent Order in Council.

3 Absolute warranty of seaworthiness not to be implied in contracts to which Rules apply
There shall not be implied in any contract for the carriage of goods by sea to which the Rules apply by virtue of this Act any absolute undertaking by the carrier of the goods to provide a seaworthy ship.

4 Application of Act to British possessions, etc
. . .

5 Extension of application of Rules to carriage from ports in British possessions, etc
. . .

6 Supplemental
(1) This Act may be cited as the Carriage of Goods by Sea Act 1971.

(2) It is hereby declared that this Act extends to Northern Ireland.

(3) The following enactments shall be repealed, that is:

(a)   the Carriage of Goods by Sea Act 1924,
(b)   section 12(4)(a) of the Nuclear Installations Act 1965,

and without prejudice to section 17(2) of the Interpretation Act 1978, the reference to the said Act of 1924 in section 1(1)(i)(ii) of the Hovercraft Act 1968 shall include a reference to this Act.

(4) It is hereby declared that for the purposes of Article VIII of the Rules section 186 of the Merchant Shipping Act 1995 (which entirely exempts shipowners and others in certain circumstances for loss of, or damage to, goods) is a provision relating to limitation of liability [*Subsection added by s 314(2), Sched 13, para 45(4) of the Merchant Shipping Act 1995. In force 1 January 1996.*]

(5) . . . [*Commencement.*]

Schedule
The Hague Rules
as amended by the Brussels Protocol 1968

Article I
In these Rules the following words are employed, with the meanings set out below:

(a) 'Carrier' includes the owner or the charterer who enters into a contract of carriage with a shipper.
(b) 'Contract of carriage' applies only to contracts of carriage covered by a bill of lading or any similar document of title, in so far as such document relates to the carriage of goods by sea, including any bill of lading or any similar document as aforesaid issued under or pursuant to a charter party from the moment at which such bill of lading or similar document of title regulates the relations between a carrier and a holder of the same.
(c) 'Goods' includes goods, wares, merchandise, and articles of every kind whatsoever except live animals and cargo which by the contract of carriage is stated as being carried on deck and is so carried.
(d) 'Ship' means any vessel used for the carriage of goods by sea.
(e) 'Carriage of goods' covers the period from the time when the goods are loaded on to the time they are discharged from the ship.

Article II
Subject to the provisions of Article VI, under every contract of carriage of goods by sea the carrier, in relation to the loading, handling, stowage, carriage, custody, care and discharge of such goods, shall be subject to the responsibilities and liabilities, and entitled to the rights and immunities hereinafter set forth.

Article III
1 The carrier shall be bound before and at the beginning of the voyage to exercise due diligence to:

(a) Make the ship seaworthy.
(b) Properly man, equip and supply the ship.
(c) Make the holds, refrigerating and cool chambers, and all other parts of the ship in which goods are carried, fit and safe for their reception, carriage and preservation.

2 Subject to the provisions of Article IV, the carrier shall properly and carefully load, handle, stow, carry, keep, care for, and discharge the goods carried.

3 After receiving the goods into his charge the carrier or the master or agent of the carrier shall, on demand of the shipper, issue to the shipper a bill of lading showing among other things:

(a) The leading marks necessary for identification of the goods as the same are furnished in writing by the shipper before the loading of such goods starts, provided such marks are stamped or otherwise shown clearly upon the goods if uncovered, or on the cases or coverings in which such goods are contained, in such a manner as should ordinarily remain legible until the end of the voyage.
(b) Either the number of packages or pieces, or the quantity, or weight, as the case may be, as furnished in writing by the shipper.
(c) The apparent order and condition of the goods.

Provided that no carrier, master or agent of the carrier shall be bound to state or show in the bill of lading any marks, number, quantity, or weight which he has reasonable ground for suspecting not accurately to represent the goods actually received, or which he has had no reasonable means of checking.

4 Such a bill of lading shall be *prima facie* evidence of the receipt by the carrier of the goods as therein described in accordance with paragraph 3(a), (b) and (c). However, proof to the contrary shall not be admissible when the bill of lading has been transferred to a third party acting in good faith.

5 The shipper shall be deemed to have guaranteed to the carrier the accuracy at the time of shipment of the marks, number, quantity and weight, as furnished by him, and the shipper shall indemnify the carrier against all loss, damages and expenses arising or resulting from inaccuracies in such particulars. The right of the carrier to such indemnity shall in no way limit his responsibility and liability under the contract of carriage to any person other than the shipper.

6 Unless notice of loss or damage and the general nature of such loss or damage be given in writing to the carrier or his agent at the port of discharge before or at the time of the removal of the goods into the custody of the person entitled to delivery thereof under the contract of carriage, or, if the loss or damage be not apparent, within three days, such removal shall be *prima facie* evidence of the delivery by the carrier of the goods as described in the bill of lading.

The notice in writing need not be given if the state of the goods has, at the time of their receipt, been the subject of joint survey or inspection.

Subject to paragraph 6 *bis* the carrier and the ship shall in any event be discharged from all liability whatsoever in respect of the goods, unless suit is brought within one year of their delivery or of the date when they should have been delivered. This period may, however, be extended if the parties so agree after the cause of action has arisen.

In the case of any actual or apprehended loss or damage the carrier and the receiver shall give all reasonable facilities to each other for inspecting and tallying the goods.

7 *bis* An action for indemnity against a third person may be brought even after the expiration of the year provided for in the preceding paragraph if brought within the time allowed by the law of the Court seized of the case. However, the time allowed shall be not less than three months, commencing from the day when the person bringing such action for indemnity has settled the claim or has been served with process in the action against himself.

8 After the goods are loaded the bill of lading to be issued by the carrier, master, or agent of the carrier, to the shipper shall, if the shipper so demands, be a 'shipped' bill of lading, provided that if the shipper shall have previously taken up any document of title to such goods, he shall surrender the same as against the issue of the 'shipped' bill of lading, but at the option of the carrier such document of title may be noted at the port of shipment by the carrier, master, or agent with the name or names of the ship or ships upon which the goods have been shipped and the date or dates of shipment, and when so noted, if it shows the particulars mentioned in paragraph 3 of Article III, shall for the purpose of this article be deemed to constitute a 'shipped' bill of lading.

9 Any clause, covenant, or agreement in a contract of carriage relieving the carrier or the ship from liability for loss or damage to, or in connection with, goods arising from negligence, fault, or failure in the duties and obligations provided in this article or lessening such liability otherwise than as provided in these Rules, shall be null and void and of no effect. A benefit of insurance in favour of the carrier or similar clause shall be deemed to be a clause relieving the carrier from liability.

Article IV
1 Neither the carrier nor the ship shall be liable for loss or damage arising or resulting from unseaworthiness unless caused by want of due diligence on the part of the carrier to make the ship seaworthy, and to secure that the ship is properly manned, equipped and supplied, and to make the holds, refrigerating and cool chambers and all other parts of the ship in which goods are carried fit and safe for their reception, carriage and preservation in accordance with the provisions of paragraph 1 of Article III. Whenever loss or damage has resulted from unseaworthiness the burden of proving the exercise of due diligence shall be on the carrier or other person claiming exemption under this article.

2 Neither the carrier nor the ship shall be responsible for loss or damage arising or resulting from:

(a) Act, neglect, or default of the master, mariner, pilot, or the servants of the carrier in the navigation or in the management of the ship.
(b) Fire, unless caused by the actual fault or privity of the carrier.
(c) Perils, dangers and accidents of the sea or other navigable waters.
(d) Act of God.
(e) Act of war.
(f) Act of public enemies.
(g) Arrest or restraint of princes, rulers or people, or seizure under legal process.
(h) Quarantine restrictions.
(i) Act or omission of the shipper or owner of the goods, his agent or representative.
(j) Strikes or lockouts or stoppage or restraint of labour from whatever cause, whether partial or general.
(k) Riots and civil commotions.
(l) Saving or attempting to save life or property at sea.
(m) Wastage in bulk or weight or any other loss or damage arising from inherent defect, quality or vice of the goods.
(n) Insufficiency of packing.
(o) Insufficiency or inadequacy of marks.
(p) Latent defects not discoverable by due diligence.
(q) Any other cause arising without the actual fault or privity of the carrier, or without the fault or neglect of the agents or servants of the carrier, but the burden of proof shall be on the person claiming the benefit of this exception to show that neither the actual fault or privity of the carrier nor the fault or neglect of the agents or servants of the carrier contributed to the loss or damage.

3 The shipper shall not be responsible for loss or damage sustained by the carrier or the ship arising or resulting from any cause without the act, fault or neglect of the shipper, his agents or his servants.

4 Any deviation in saving or attempting to save life or property at sea or any reasonable deviation shall not be deemed to be an infringement or breach of these Rules or of the contract of carriage, and the carrier shall not be liable for any loss or damage resulting therefrom.

(a) Unless the nature and value of such goods have been declared by the shipper before shipment and inserted in the bill of lading, neither the carrier nor the ship shall in any event be or become liable for any loss or damage to or in connection with the goods in an amount exceeding [666.67 units of account] per package or unit or [2 units of account per kilogramme] of gross weight of the goods lost or damaged, whichever is the higher.
(b) The total amount recoverable shall be calculated by reference to the value of such goods at the place and time at which the goods are discharged from the ship in accordance with the contract or should have been so discharged.
(c) The value of the goods shall be fixed according to the commodity exchange price, or, if there be no such price, according to the current market price, or, if there be no commodity exchange price or current market price, by reference to the normal value of goods of the same kind and quality.
(d) Where a container, pallet or similar article of transport is used to consolidate goods, the number of packages or units enumerated in the bill of lading as packed in such article of transport shall be deemed the number of packages or units for the purpose of this paragraph as far as these packages or units are concerned. Except as aforesaid such article of transport shall be considered the package or unit.
(e) [The unit of account mentioned in this Article is the special drawing right as defined by the International Monetary Fund. The amounts mentioned in subparagraph (a) of this paragraph shall be converted into national currency on the basis of the value of that currency on a date to be determined

by the law of the court seized of the case.] [*Words in square brackets substituted by s 2(3), (4) of the Merchant Shipping Act 1981, and by s 314(2), Sched 13, para 45(5) of the Merchant Shipping Act 1995; para 45(6) states that Art IV, para 5(d) 'shall continue to have effect as if the date there mentioned were the date of the judgment in question'.*]

(f)   Neither the carrier nor the ship shall be entitled to the benefit of the limitation of liability provided for in this paragraph if it is proved that the damage resulted from an act or omission of the carrier done with intent to cause damage, or recklessly and with knowledge that damage would probably result.

(g)   The declaration mentioned in subparagraph (a) of this paragraph, if embodied in the bill of lading, shall be *prima facie* evidence, but shall not be binding or conclusive on the carrier.

(h)   By agreement between the carrier, master or agent of the carrier and the shipper other maximum amounts than those mentioned in subparagraph (a) of this paragraph may be fixed, provided that no maximum amount so fixed shall be less than the appropriate maximum mentioned in that subparagraph.

(i)   Neither the carrier nor the ship shall be responsible in any event for loss or damage to, or in connection with, goods if the nature or value thereof has been knowingly misstated by the shipper in the bill of lading.

5 Goods of an inflammable, explosive or dangerous nature to the shipment whereof the carrier, master or agent of the carrier has not consented with knowledge of their nature and character, may at any time before discharge be landed at any place, or destroyed or rendered innocuous by the carrier without compensation and the shipper of such goods shall be liable for all damages and expenses directly or indirectly arising out of or resulting from such shipment. If any such goods shipped with such knowledge and consent shall become a danger to the ship or cargo, they may in like manner be landed at any place, or destroyed or rendered innocuous by the carrier without liability on the part of the carrier except to general average, if any.

Article IV bis

1 The defences and limits of liability provided for in these Rules shall apply in any action against the carrier in respect of loss or damage to goods covered by a contract of carriage whether the action be founded in contract or in tort.

2 If such an action is brought against a servant or agent of the carrier (such servant or agent not being an independent contractor), such servant or agent shall be entitled to avail himself of the defences and limits of liability which the carrier is entitled to invoke under these Rules.

3 The aggregate of the amounts recoverable from the carrier, and such servants and agents, shall in no case exceed the limit provided for in these Rules.

4 Nevertheless, a servant or agent of the carrier shall not be entitled to avail himself of the provisions of this article, if it is proved that the damage resulted from an act or omission of the servant or agent done with intent to cause damage or recklessly and with knowledge that damage would probably result.

Article V

A carrier shall be at liberty to surrender in whole or in part all or any of his rights and immunities or to increase any of his responsibilities and obligations under these Rules, provided such surrender or increase shall be embodied in the bill of lading issued to the shipper. The provisions of these Rules shall not be applicable to charter parties, but if bills of lading are issued in the case of a ship under a charter party they shall comply with the terms of these Rules. Nothing in these Rules shall be held to prevent the insertion in a bill of lading of any lawful provision regarding general average.

Article VI

Notwithstanding the provisions of the preceding articles, a carrier, master or agent of the carrier and a shipper shall in regard to any particular goods be at liberty to enter into any agreement in any terms as to the responsibility and liability of the carrier for such goods, and as to the rights and immunities of the carrier in respect of such goods, or his obligation as to seaworthiness, so far as this stipulation is not contrary to public policy, or the care or diligence of his servants or agents in regard to the loading, handling, stowage, carriage, custody, care and discharge of the goods carried by sea, provided that in this case no bill of lading has been or shall be issued and that the terms agreed shall be embodied in a receipt which shall be a non-negotiable document and shall be marked as such.

Any agreement so entered into shall have full legal effect.

Provided that this article shall not apply to ordinary commercial shipments made in the ordinary course of trade, but only to other shipments where the character or condition of the property to be carried or the circumstances, terms and conditions under which the carriage is to be performed are such as reasonably to justify a special agreement.

Article VII

Nothing herein contained shall prevent a carrier or a shipper from entering into any agreement, stipulation, condition, reservation or exemption as to the responsibility and liability of the carrier or the ship for the loss or damage to, or in connection with, the custody and care and handling of goods prior to the loading on, and subsequent to the discharge from, the ship on which the goods are carried by sea.

Article VIII

The provisions of these Rules shall not affect the rights and obligations of the carrier under any statute for the time being in force relating to the limitation of the liability of owners of sea-going vessels.

Article IX

These Rules shall not affect the provisions of any international Convention or national law governing liability for nuclear damage.

Article X

The provisions of these Rules shall apply to every bill of lading relating to the carriage of goods between ports in two different States if:

(a)   the bill of lading is issued in a contracting State, or

(b)   the carriage is from a port in a contracting State, or

(c)   the contract contained in or evidenced by the bill of lading provides that these Rules or legislation of any State giving effect to them are to govern the contract,

whatever may be the nationality of the ship, the carrier, the shipper, the consignee, or any other interested person.

(The last two paragraphs of this Article are not reproduced. They require contracting States to apply the Rules to bills of lading mentioned in the Article and authorise them to apply the Rules to other bills of lading.)

(Articles 11 to 16 of the International Convention for the unification of certain rules of law relating to bills of lading signed at Brussels on 25 August 1924 are not reproduced. They deal with the coming into force of the Convention, procedure for ratification, accession and denunciation, and the right to call for a fresh conference to consider amendments to the Rules contained in the Convention.)

2 Interpretation of the convention

The Hague-Visby Rules are expressed to have two official languages – English and French. However, for the purposes of English law and the Carriage of Goods by Sea 1971, it should follow that only the English text would be relevant. That said, as an international convention where a degree of international uniformity is desirable, an English court would be guided by international judicial practice including any relevant languages the convention is expressed or applied. That is consistent with English legal principles on the interpretation and construction of statutes.

Stag Line v Foscolo Mango [1932] AC 328

Held:

> **Lord Wright** (referring to the Hague Rules as contained in the now repealed Carriage of Goods by Sea Act 1924): It is important to remember that the Act of 1924 was the outcome of an International Conference and that the rules in the Schedule have an international currency. As these rules must come under the consideration of foreign Courts it is desirable in the interests of uniformity that their interpretation should not be rigidly controlled by domestic precedents of antecedent date, but rather that the language of the rules should be construed on broad principles of general acceptation.
>
> The law also allows the judge to consider the travaux preparatoire (see *Jindal Iron and Steel Co. Ltd. v Islamic Solidarity Shipping Co. Jordan Inc., The Jordan II* [2005] 1 W.L.R. 1363, [2005] Lloyd's Rep. 57, para 20). That said, it might be noteworthy that some English judges have often been less inclined to do so despite the change in law on statutory interpretation (see see Michael Mustill Q.C., *Arkiv for Sjorett*, vol. ii, issue 4/5 (1972) pp. 688–689). In *The Rafaela S* [2003] 2 Lloyd's Rep. 113, 126, affd [2005] 2 A.C. 423 although Rix LJ allowed himself to be guided by the travaux preparatoire, His Lordship commented that on using the travaux preparatoire as a stautory interpretation aid, 'only a bull's eye counts'.

3 Article I

The Hague-Visby Rules only apply to certain types of contract. Article II is the principal operative provision; it applies the rights and duties set out in the Rules to the carrier under 'every contract of carriage of goods by sea'. But Art I defines these words narrowly, so that only contracts 'covered by a bill of lading or any similar document of title' attract the operation of the convention. Article X provides further limitations: the carriage must be between ports in two different states and either the bill of lading must be issued in a contracting state, or the carriage must be from a port in a contracting state, or the contract contained in or evidenced by the bill of lading must provide that the Rules or the legislation of any state giving effect to them are to govern the contract.

The Carriage of Goods by Sea Act 1971 gives the Rules the force of law in the UK: s 1(2). The Rules are extended to UK coastal shipping by s 1(3).

3.1 Carrier

Article I, para (a) defines 'carrier' as including the owner or the charterer who enters into a contract of carriage with a shipper. This definition directs attention to the contracting rather than the performing carrier, as Robert Goff J indicates in the following extract.

Freedom General Shipping SA v Tokal Shipping Co Ltd, The Khian Zephyr [1982] 1 Lloyd's Rep 73

Held:

> **Robert Goff J:** . . . the function of art I(a), in providing that the word 'carrier' includes the owner or charterer who enters into a contract of carriage with a shipper, is to legislate for the fact that you may get a case . . . where the bills of lading are charterers' bills; and where there are charterers' bills, of course, the charterer is in a contractual relationship with the cargo owner and is responsible under the bills of lading to the cargo owners . . .
>
> There is a suggestion that as the Hague-Visby Rules refer to "the owner or the charterer who enters into a contract of carriage with a shipper", an implied joint venture between the owner and charterer could bind both the owner and charterer to the liability regime of the Hague-Visby Rules. For example, if the charterer issues the bill of lading but that is endorsed and facilitated by the owner, both the owner and charterer could be liable to the shipper under the Hague-Visby Rules. That concept does not represent English law – it is clear that in English law, the court would always look to the contracting carrier as the subject of the Hague-Visby Rules carrier liability regime (*The Starsin* [2004] 1 AC 715) . A clear rejection of the concept is best seen in the Canadian case below.

Jian Sheng Co v Great Tempo SA [1998] 3 FCR 418

Facts: The claim for loss of cargo was served on both the charterer and owners. The bill of lading was issued by the charterer 'as agents' of the owners.

Held:

> **Décary JA:**
>
> **The identity of the carrier**
> In shipowners' bills of lading, there is a presumption that the shipowner is the carrier. In charterers' bills of lading, on the other hand, the presumption is that the demise charterer is the carrier. Any other can be the carrier only where the above presumptions have been rebutted, and such rebuttal occurs only when there is evidence that such other has actually assumed the role of carrier under the contract of carriage with the shipper (see *Paterson SS Ltd. v Aluminum Co. of Can.*, 1951 CanLII 48 (SCC), [1951] S.C.R. 852, at page 854, Rand J.; *Aris Steamship Co. Inc. v Associated Metals & Minerals Corporation*, 1980 CanLII 211 (SCC), [1980] 2 S.C.R. 322, at page 328 ff, Ritchie J.; *Cormorant Bulk-Carriers Inc. v Canficorp (Overseas Projects) Ltd.* (1984), 54 N.R. 66 (F.C.A), at page 76, Stone J.A.; *Carling O'Keefe Breweries of Canada Ltd. v CN Marine Inc.*, [1990] 1 F.C. 483 (C.A.), at page 501, Stone J.A.; *Union Carbide Corp. et al. v Fednav Ltd. et al.* (1997), 131 F.T.R. 241 (F.C.T.D.), at page 254 ff, Nadon J. and *The Rewia* at page 333).
>
> Counsel for the appellant has suggested that there could be more than one carrier in the present case, one being the shipowner, the other being an alleged demise charterer or an alleged time charterer who would have assumed the role of carrier. He relies for this proposition on the decision of Reed J. in *Canastrand Industries Ltd. v Lara S* (The), 1993 CanLII 2934 (FC), [1993] 2 F.C. 553 (T.D.), which was confirmed orally by this Court ((1994), 176 N.R. 31 (F.C.A.)). Reed J. had relied on comments by Professor Tetley in *Marine Cargo Claims*, 3rd ed. (Montréal: Yvon Blais, 1988) at page 242, to the effect that:
>
> > Carriage of goods is effectively a joint venture of owners and charterers (except in the case of a bareboat charter) and, consequently, they should be held jointly and severally responsible as carriers.

Professor Tetley's concept of an implicit joint venture of owners and charterers was qualified by this Court as an "American-influenced principle" (*Lantic Sugar Ltd. v Blue Tower Trading Corp. et al.* (1993), 163 N.R. 191 (F.C.A.), at page 194, MacGuigan J.A.) and referred to as a "suggestion" by Stone J.A. in Carling O'Keefe, in a footnote, at page 501.

The implicit joint venture concept is in my respectful view incompatible with the gist of the decisions of the Supreme Court in Paterson SS and in Aris Steamship and of the decisions of this Court in Cormorant and in Carling O'Keefe. The concept has been found "unsound" by Nadon J. in Union Carbide, at page 264 and I entirely agree with his reasons for reaching that conclusion. The law, in my view, is clearly stated by Nadon J., at pages 264–265:

> The position taken by the learned authors appears to be that in circumstances where the charterer will be liable on the contract of carriage, the shipowner will not. I agree with this point of view. A charterer will issue and sign a bill of lading either on his own behalf or on behalf on the master. Where he signs on behalf of the master, and is so authorized, the shipowner will be bound by the issuance of the bills of lading but not the charterer. Where the charterer issues and signs bills of lading on his own behalf, he shall be bound by those bills. Consequently, in most cases, the word "or" in article 1(a) of the Hague Rules will mean exactly that. The carrier shall either be the owner or the charterer, but not both. I need not discuss a situation where a charterer issues and signs a bill of lading on behalf of the master and on his own behalf. That is certainly not the situation in the present case.

There may be cases where a shipowner and a charterer actually decide to carry on a joint venture or form a partnership, but it would then be the joint venture or the partnership that assumes the role of carrier.

I appreciate that the Lara S was confirmed by this Court, but the oral reasons of the Court did not address the issue of implicit joint venture and a careful perusal of the voluminous factums filed by counsel has persuaded me that the issue had not been raised as such in the appeal. The Lara S cannot, therefore, be seen as an endorsement of Professor Tetley's comments.

3.2 Contract of carriage

These words are said by Art I, para (b) to apply only to contracts of carriage covered by a bill of lading or any similar document of title. The word 'covered' is interpreted broadly. A contract can be 'covered' by a bill of lading even though no bill is ever actually issued.

Pyrene Co Ltd v Scindia Navigation Co Ltd [1954] 2 QB 402

Facts: The plaintiffs sold machinery, including a fire tender, to the Government of India. While the tender was being lifted on to the vessel by the ship's tackle, and before it was across the rail it was, through the fault of the ship, dropped and damaged. The plaintiffs sued in tort to recover £966, which was the cost of repairing the tender. The defendants admitted liability but claimed to limit the amount recoverable under Art 4 r 5 of the Hague Rules to £200. A bill of lading had been prepared to cover the whole shipment and was later issued, but with the fire tender deleted from it. It was not disputed that the contract of carriage was actually created before loading began.

Held:

> **Devlin J:** The . . . contention on behalf of the plaintiffs is that the rules are incorporated in the contract of carriage only if a bill of lading is issued. The basis for this is in the definition of Article I(b) of 'contract of carriage'; I have already quoted it, and it 'applies only to contracts of carriage covered by a bill of lading'. The use of the word 'covered' recognises the fact that the contract of carriage is always concluded before the bill of lading, which evidences its terms, is actually issued. When parties enter into a contract of carriage in the expectation that a bill of lading will be issued to cover it, they enter into it upon those terms which they know or expect the bill of lading to contain. Those terms must be in force from the inception of the contract; if it were otherwise the bill of lading would not evidence the contract but would be a variation of it. Moreover, it would be absurd to suppose that the parties intend the terms of the contract to be changed when the bill of lading is issued: for the issue of the bill of lading does not necessarily mark any stage in the development of the contract; often it is not issued till after the ship has sailed, and if there is pressure of office work on the ship's agent it may be delayed several days. In my judgment, whenever a contract of carriage is concluded, and it is contemplated that a bill of lading will, in due course, be issued in respect of it, that contract is from its creation 'covered' by a bill of lading, and is therefore from its inception a contract of carriage within the meaning of the rules and to which the rules apply . . .

Notes

1   Devlin J concluded that the Hague Rules applied to the contract and that the defendants were entitled to limit their liability to £200.
2   The word 'covered' in Art I, para (a) is clarified so far as UK law is concerned by s 1(4) of the 1971 Act, which provides that the contract must expressly or by implication provide for the issue of a bill of lading or similar document of title.
3   The judgment in this case noted that the bill of lading to be issued was to contain the terms on which the parties had agreed. In the next case, it did not.

3.3 Contract not in bill of lading

A contract can still be covered by a bill of lading even though the bill does not contain the terms of the contract.

Parsons Corp v CV Scheepvaartonderneming, The Happy Ranger [2002] EWCA Civ 694; [2002] 2 Lloyd's Rep 357

Facts: The defendant owners of the heavy-lift vessel the *Happy Ranger* contracted to carry three reactors from Porto Marghera in Italy to Al Jubail in Saudi Arabia. One of the reactors was damaged by the carrier while being loaded. The contract between the parties consisted of three documents: a printed front page, which was signed, a rider consisting of six pages and an attached specimen form of bill of lading. The rider clauses contained provisions (for example, for laytime) that would ordinarily be found in a voyage charter but not in a liner bill of lading. The shipowners argued that the contract was not subject to the Hague-Visby Rules because the bill of lading did not contain the terms of the contract or alternatively because the contract was a voyage charter.

Held:

> **Tuckey LJ** (para 24): It does not seem to me that the Rules are concerned with whether the bill of lading contains terms which have been previously agreed or not. It is the fact that it is issued or that its issue is contemplated which matters. As it was put in one of the cases, 'the bill of lading is the bedrock on which the mandatory code is founded'. If a bill of lading is or is to be issued the contract is 'covered' by it or 'provides for its issue' within the definitions of art I(b) and s 1(4) of the 1971 Act . . . As to Mr Teare's [counsel] alternative submission I do not think it is possible to characterize the contract in this case as a voyage charter-party. It was obviously a carefully drawn document and although it does contain terms which are to be found in voyage charter-parties, it emphatically calls itself a contract of carriage and that is what I think it is. The fact that the goods to be carried were a part cargo supports this conclusion, although I accept that this factor is not conclusive . . .

3.4 Straight bill of lading

Despite longstanding doubts, it has recently been held that a straight bill of lading is a bill of lading for the purposes of the Rules.

JI MacWilliam Co Inc v Mediterranean Shipping Co SA, The Rafaela S
[2003] EWCA Civ 556; [2003] 2 Lloyd's Rep 113

Facts: Printing machinery was shipped to MacWilliam at Boston, US from Felixstowe in England and was damaged on the way. No bill of lading was in fact issued but the parties accepted that the carriage was to be treated as governed by a straight bill of lading in the same form as that used for an earlier voyage. That bill of lading in three identical original parts was based on a printed form with a box layout and could be completed either as an order bill or as a straight bill. The attestation clause provided that: 'One of the Bills of Lading must be surrendered duly endorsed in exchange for the goods or delivery order.'

Held:

> **Rix LJ: 134** The first question is whether a straight bill of lading, but otherwise in the form of any classic bill of lading, is a bill of lading within the meaning of the Rules . . . It is common ground that the point is open. It is open today. It was open and uncertain immediately before the agreement of the Hague Rules.
>
> **135** In my judgment, a straight bill of lading, for all that it is non-negotiable, should be viewed as a bill of lading within the meaning of the Rules. I say that for the following reasons.
>
> **136** First, the Hague Rules are predominately concerned with the content of a contract of carriage in circumstances where such a contract as found in a bill of lading may come to affect a third party into whose hands such a bill is transferred. It seems to me to be plain as a matter of commonsense but also on a review of the material cited in this judgment, that in this connection a named consignee under a straight bill of lading, unless he is the same person as the shipper, is as much a third party as a named consignee under a classic bill. Therefore I would view such a named consignee under a straight bill as *prima facie* within the concern of the Rules.
>
> **137** Secondly, while it is I suppose true that a straight bill of lading can be used in circumstances where there is no intention of transferring it to the consignee, the authorities considered demonstrate that in practice it is used, just like a classic bill, as a document against which payment is required and the transfer of which thus marks the intended transfer of property. Therefore, as Professor Tetley says

[*Marine Cargo Claims*, 3rd edn, 1998, Montreal: BLAIS], its nature is that, although it cannot be transferred more than once, for it is not negotiable, it can be transferred by delivery (just like a classic bill) to the named consignee. In these circumstances, the shipper and his bankers and insurers need the same protection as the shipper under a classic bill; and the consignee himself and his insurers in turn need to have rights against the carrier under the contract of carriage. I can see no reason why straight bills of lading have not always been within the 1855 Act. Those needs are in any event recognised under the 1992 Act.

138 Thirdly, whatever may be the position as a matter of principle and in the absence of express agreement, the practice appears to be that a straight bill of lading, unlike a mere sea waybill, is written on the form of an otherwise classic bill and requires production of the bill on delivery, and therefore transfer to a consignee to enable him to obtain delivery. (In this respect the position of a straight bill under the Pomerene Act appears to be different, but even so the US Harter Act, one of the forerunners of the Hague Rules, would seem to cover straight as well as negotiable bills.)

139 Fourthly, suppose the question is asked, in the context of the Hague Rules, in these, terms: What of the straight bill? Is this a 'bill of lading' or, being non-negotiable, something else, more akin to a non-negotiable receipt? Then, as it seems to me, the straight bill of lading is in principle, function, and form much closer to a classic negotiable bill, than to a non-negotiable receipt, which, to judge from article VI of the Rules, was viewed as something far more exotic.

140 Fifthly, the *travaux preparatoires* of the Hague Rules, despite lacking unequivocal cogency, to my mind are not only consistent with the view I would prefer, but go far to support it.

141 Sixthly, I am unimpressed by the argument derived from the terms of the 1971 and 1992 Acts. They may reflect a developing English view about how to categorise bills of lading and nonnegotiable receipts and sea waybills, but, as the learned authors of *Benjamin* and *Carver* point out, they are ultimately dealing with different purposes. In any event, I do not see how they can control the meaning of the Hague Rules, which are not only much earlier, but also of international and not merely domestic scope.

142 The next question is as to the effect of the attestation clause in the bill of lading in the present case. Is it applicable only to the use of the bill in its negotiable form, or does it survive to control its use as a straight bill? In my judgment, for the reasons stated in para 106 above and in *Gaskell* [*Bills of Lading: Law & Contracts*, 2nd edn, 2002, London: Lloyd's of London] the attestation clause is to be construed as applicable in either event. If it had been intended that it should not apply when the bill was used in a non-negotiable form, then it could very easily have said so. Against the background of the common forms of sea waybills, it is truly remarkable that it does not say so.

143 The third question is, then, whether such a straight bill of lading, which has to be produced to obtain delivery, is a document of title? In my judgment it is. I consider that the authorities and textbooks discussed above support that view. Whatever the history of the phrase in English common or statutory law may be, I see no reason why a document which has to be produced to obtain possession of the goods should not be regarded, in an international convention, as a document of title. It is so regarded by the courts of France, Holland and Singapore.

144 Is it a 'similar' document of title? If I am right to consider that negotiability is not a necessary requirement of a 'bill of lading' within the meaning of the Rules, then plainly it is. But I also think that the good sense of regarding a straight bill whose production is required for delivery of the goods as a document of title in turn supports the answer to the prior question of whether a straight bill is a 'bill of lading'.

145 The final question is whether a straight bill of lading is in principle a document of title, even in the absence of an express provision requiring its production to obtain delivery? It would seem that *Peer Voss v*

APL Co Pte Ltd [2002] 2 Lloyd's Rep 707, Singapore Court of Appeal, concluded that it was (at any rate if it is issued in traditional form in three originals). That was also the view of the Law Commission. It is unnecessary to decide the point, but in my judgment it is. It seems to me to be undesirable to have a different rule for different kinds of bills of lading – which I think was the view of Butt J in *The Stettin* as well. It is true, as *Benjamin* states, that in the case of a negotiable bill the carrier needs to have the bill produced in order to be able to police the question of who is entitled to delivery. Yet an analogous problem arises with a straight bill. A shipper needs the carrier to assist him in policing his security in the retention of the bill. He is entitled to redirect the consignment on notice to the carrier, and, although notice is required, a rule of production of the bill is the only safe way, for the carrier as well as the shipper, to police such new instructions. In any event, if proof of identity is necessary, as in practice it is, what is wrong with the bill itself as a leading form of proof? That is of course an inconvenient rule where the carriage is very short, as in cross-Channel shipments, and that is why sea waybills are used in such trades. But it is clear that straight bills are used in intercontinental carriage and therefore the inconvenience argument fades.

146 I am not unhappy to come to these conclusions. It seems to me that the use of these hybrid forms of bill of lading is an unfortunate development and has spawned litigation in recent years in an area which for the previous century or so has not caused any real difficulty. Carriers should not use bill of lading forms if what they want to invite shippers to do is to enter into sea waybill type contracts. It may be true that ultimately it is up to shippers to ensure that the boxes in these hybrid forms are filled up in the way that best suits themselves; but in practice I suspect that serendipity often prevails. In any event, these forms invite error and litigation, which is best avoided by a simple rule.

3.5 No right to a bill of lading

The primary statutory application of the 1971 Act is excluded if the shipper is not entitled under the contract of carriage to demand a bill of lading at or after shipment.

Browner International Ltd v Monarch Shipping Co Ltd, The European Enterprise [1989] 2 Lloyd's Rep 185

Facts: The defendants operated a roll-on roll-off ferry between Dover and Calais and, in common with all other English operators in that trade, would not issue a bill of lading for goods taken on board, but offered only non-negotiable receipts. While entering port during heavy weather, goods overturned and were damaged. The defendants claimed to be entitled to limit their liability under the conditions of carriage to a sum, which was less than the amount stated in Art IV, r 5.

Held:

Steyn J: It follows that shipowners, if they are in a strong enough bargaining position, can escape the application of the rules by issuing a notice to shippers that no bills of lading will be issued by them in a particular trade. Subject to the limited restriction introduced by the Unfair Contract Terms Act 1977 in favour of carriage for consumers . . . the position is that freedom of contract prevails . . .

Note

Article X and s 1(6)(b) make specific provision for the application of the Rules by agreement.

3.6 A bill of lading, etc, is necessary but not sufficient to engage the Rules

Compania Portorafti Commerciale SA v Ultramar Panama Inc,
The Captain Gregos [1990] 1 Lloyd's Rep 310, CA

Facts: The *Captain Gregos* was chartered for the carriage of a cargo of crude oil from Egypt to Rotterdam. The bills of lading incorporated the Hague-Visby Rules. More than one year after discharge of the cargo, the cargo owners alleged that the ship had made short delivery and that part of the cargo had been deliberately misappropriated. The shipowners commenced proceedings for a declaration that this claim was time-barred under Art III, r 6. The cargo owners argued that they were not parties to the bills of lading and that they were not therefore bound by the Rules.

Held:

Bingham LJ: The shipowners' argument was in essence very brief. They could rely on the time bar in Article III, rule 6 because the rules have the force of law and apply to any bill covered by Article X, as these bills admittedly were. Article IV *bis* rule 1 expressly provides that the rules shall apply in any action against the carrier in respect of loss or damage to goods covered by a contract of carriage whether the action be founded in contract or in tort. It would frustrate the purpose of an international convention if its application were to depend on questions of privity to which (as we know) different legal systems may yield different answers. The issue of a bill of lading to which the rules apply is a necessary but also a sufficient condition of the right of shipowner or cargo owner to rely on the rules, even though neither is a party to the bill. Reliance was placed in particular on views expressed by Mr Diamond QC in his article on 'The Hague-Visby Rules' (1978) 2 *LMCLQ* 225 at 248–49 and on *Gillespie Bros v Roy Bowles Ltd* [1973] QB 400 at p 412 where Lord Denning MR cited Article IV *bis* rule 1 to show how a non-party could become bound.

The cargo owners' response was even briefer. The effect of the Act is to give statutory force to a mandatory contractual regime. The language of the Act and the rules shows that they were intended to regulate the rights and duties of the parties to the bill of lading contract, not nonparties. That was what Mr Mustill QC thought in 1972 ('Carriage of Goods by Sea Act 1971', *Arkiv for Sjorett* at p 710). The issue of a bill of lading was a necessary, but not in itself a sufficient, condition of the application of the rules.

We are again (no doubt unavoidably) obliged to resolve this issue without the help which the decisions or opinions of foreign judges or jurists might have given us. I have not for my part found it an easy question. I am particularly concerned at the risk that idiosyncratic legal rules on privity might yield different results in different countries. But on balance I prefer the cargo owners' argument for three main reasons:

(1) As section 1(4) of the Act and Articles I(b) and X of the rules in particular make clear, the bill of lading is the bedrock on which this mandatory code is founded. A bill of lading is a contractual document with certain commercially well known consequences when endorsed and transferred. It is not clear to me why the code should treat the existence of a bill of lading as a matter of such central and overriding importance if the code is to apply with equal force as between those who are not parties to the contract which the bill contains or evidences.

(2) Much of the language in the Act and the rules suggests that the code is intended to govern the relations between the parties to the bill of lading contract. Section 1(4) speaks of applying the rules to a contract. Article I(a) defines the carrier as including the party who enters into a contract of carriage with a shipper. Article I(b) speaks of regulating relations between a carrier and a holder of a bill or similar document of title. Most significantly of all, Article II defines the application of the rules 'under every contract of carriage'. Articles V and VI are concerned with agreements between contracting parties. Article X applies the rules to the bill of lading, not the carriage. If it had been intended to

regulate relations between non-parties to the bill of lading contract, it is hard to think the language would not have been both different and simpler.

(3) Whatever the law in other jurisdictions, the general principle that only a party to a contract may sue on it is well established here. If the draftsmen of the 1924 or 1971 Acts had intended the respective rules to infringe that principle or appreciated that that was their effect, I think they would have sought to make that clear in the Acts. It would be strange if so fundamental a principle were to be so inconspicuously abrogated.

In reaching this conclusion I recognise the unattractiveness to carriers of exposure to claims by non-parties to bills not subject to limits in time or amount. But the notion that bill of lading terms may be held to regulate relations between those who were not parties to the bills was, as I understand, specifically disavowed by Lord Donaldson MR and the House of Lords in *The Aliakmon* [1985] QB 350 at p 368; [1986] AC 785 at p 818.

3.7 Deck cargo

The definition of 'goods' in Art I, para (c) is expressed to include goods, wares, merchandise, and articles of every kind whatsoever except live animals and cargo that, by the contract of carriage, is stated as being carried on deck and is so carried.

Deck cargo only falls outside the Rules if the contract allows the carrier to carry on deck, the cargo is in fact carried on deck and the bill of lading contains on its face a statement that the cargo is so carried.

Svenska Traktor Aktiebolaget v Maritime Agencies (Southampton) Ltd **[1953] 2 QB 295**

Held:

Pilcher J: The policy of the Carriage of Goods by Sea Act 1924, was to regulate the relationship between the shipowner and the owner of goods along well known lines. In excluding from the definition of 'goods', the carriage of which was subject to the Act, cargo carried on deck and stated to be so carried, the intention of the Act was, in my view, to leave the shipowner free to carry deck cargo on his own conditions, and unaffected by the obligations imposed on him by the Act in any case in which he would, apart from the Act, have been entitled to carry such cargo on deck, provided that the cargo in question was in fact carried on deck and that the bill of lading covering it contained on its face a statement that the particular cargo was being so carried. Such a statement on the face of the bill of lading would serve as a notification and a warning to consignees and indorsees of the bill of lading to whom the property in the goods passed under the terms of s 1 of the Bill of Lading Act 1855, that the goods which they were to take were being shipped as deck cargo. They would thus have full knowledge of the facts when accepting the documents and would know that the carriage of the goods on deck was not subject to the Act. If, on the other hand, there was no specific agreement between the parties as to the carriage on deck, and no statement on the face of the bill of lading that goods carried on deck had in fact been so carried, the consignees or indorsees of the bill of lading would be entitled to assume that the goods were goods the carriage of which could only be performed by the shipowner subject to the obligations imposed on him by the Act. A mere general liberty to carry goods on deck is not in my view a statement in the contract of carriage that the goods are in fact being carried on deck. To hold otherwise would in my view do violence to the ordinary meaning of the words of Article I(c)

. . .

Note

See also 'Article IV Rule 4', below. The 1855 Act was repealed and replaced by the Carriage of Goods by Sea Act 1992.

Sideridraulic Systems SpA v BBC Chartering & Logistics GmbH & Co KG
[2011] EWHC 3106 (Comm)

Facts: The case concerns the carriage of ten sand filter tanks for a water treatment plant from Porto Marghera, Italy to Mobile, Alabama on board the m/v *BBC Greenland*. The carriage was provided for by a bill of lading. The tanks were carried on deck and the bill of lading contained the following statement:

Master's remarks

–all cargo loaded from open storage area

All cargo carried on deck at shipper's/charterer's/receiver's risk as to perils inherent in such carriage, any warranty of seaworthiness of the vessel expressly waived by the shipper/charterer/receiver.

And in all other respects subject to provisions of the United States Carriage of Goods by Sea Act 1936."

It was also stated in a box on the front of the bill: 'Special terms as per Booking note dated: 16/09/2009'. It is not clear from the evidence whether this refers to the 'fixture recap', but there is no other document that could be so described in evidence. The fixture recap (namely the booking form for the carriage) included a provision giving the carrier liberty to carry the tanks as deck cargo: 'shipment under/on deck in owners option, deck cargo at merchant risk and b/l to be marked accordingly'.

The question for the court was whether the cargo was 'deck cargo' for the purposes of the Hague-Visby Rules.

Held:

Andrew Smith J:

. . .

Mr Buckingham argued as follows:

i)   The tanks were 'deck cargo' because they were carried on deck and stated by the contract of carriage in the bill of lading to be carried on deck.

ii) Therefore the tanks were not 'goods' within the meaning of the Rules, the contract was not for the carriage of 'goods' and the Rules do not apply to it.

iii) Therefore the carriage was subject to COGSA 1936 because the bill of lading expressly so provided.

iv) In any event, even if the tanks were not 'deck cargo' and the Rules apply to their carriage, the carriage would still be subject to COGSA 1936 because the parties' agreement that it should apply would be displaced only if it were shown (or agreed) that COGSA 1936 would relieve the defendants of liability or lessen their liability and therefore article III rule 8 of the Rules had effect, and it has not been so shown (nor agreed).

. . .

Mr Kulkarni's argument was as follows:

i)   By clause 4 of the bill of lading the dispute is to be referred to arbitration in London 'except as provided elsewhere'.

ii) English law governs the contract under clause 4 of the bill, and the Rules would apply to carriage of goods under it because of article X, the carriage being from Italy, a convention country, and because the parties expressly so provided by clause 3(a).

iii) The contract was for the carriage of goods within the meaning of the Rules, because, although they were carried on deck, they were not 'by the contract of carriage . . . stated as being carried on deck'.

iv) The bill of lading did not 'provide elsewhere' for anything other than London arbitration. The statement on the front of the bill of lading that the carriage was 'in all other respects subject to' COGSA 1936 does not do so because it is displaced by article III rule 8 of the Rules, and therefore the provision in special clause B for exclusive jurisdiction of a 'court of proper jurisdiction in the United States' does not apply.

v) Even if the tanks were 'deck cargo', under sections 1(6) and 1(7) of COGSA 1971, the Rules apply to their carriage where, as here, the parties by their contract incorporate them into their contract of carriage.

. . .

Were the tanks 'deck cargo'?

18. Although they were carried on deck, the tanks were not deck cargo unless the bill of lading stated that they would be so carried. Mr. Buckingham accepts that it would not suffice that the parties had agreed and the bill of lading stated that the carriers were at liberty to carry them on deck. The question is whether the bill of lading so stated. There was no such statement in the 'fixture recap': that only provided for a carrier's liberty that they might be deck cargo.

19. Mr. Buckingham submitted that the master's remark on the front of the bill is such a statement. In effect, he advocated a meaning that would insert into the remark the word 'is' in the pivotal sentence so that it would read, 'All cargo [is] carried on deck at shipper's/charterer's/receiver's risk as to perils inherent in such carriage. . .'; and he argued that the remark is not to be understood as merely permitting the carriers to carry the tanks on deck because such a provision in the bill would have been pointless, the parties having already agreed in the fixture recap that the carriers were free to do this and that the bill was to be 'marked accordingly'.

20. Mr Kulkarni disputed that the master's remark means that the tanks were to be carried on deck. He did not, however, contend that it repeated the provision of the fixture recap that the carriers should be at liberty to carry them on deck, but submitted that it provided for an exclusion of liability that, if cargo was carried on deck, applied to that cargo. In effect, his interpretation would insert the word 'is' after the expression 'carried on deck': 'All cargo carried on deck [is] at shipper's/charterer's/receiver's risk as to perils inherent in such carriage. . .'. Mr Kulkarni went on to argue that, if the meaning of the statement is uncertain or ambiguous, it is to be interpreted in the claimants' favour because of the principle that documents are to be construed contra proferentem. He cited a 'Summary of English and US Law' produced by the defendants' insurers, Gard, that 'The crucial question appears to be whether a third party transferee of the bill of lading would be able to ascertain from the terms of the bill of lading whether the goods were stowed on or under deck', and argued that a reasonable person (or 'a third party transferee') on seeing the master's remark would not realise that all the cargo was being carried on deck.

21. I accept that it is for the defendants to establish that the master's remark states that the tanks were carried on deck, and if its meaning is uncertain, the uncertainty is to be resolved against them. They are (in the language of Staughton LJ in *Youell v Bland Welch & Co Ltd*, [1992] Lloyd's LR 127 at p. 134) the proferens coram iudice in that they need to rely upon the document to establish that the tanks were deck cargo. This principle applies not only where a party asserts a contractual exception but equally to the defendants' argument that the carriage was not covered by the compulsory statutory regime of the Rules because of the exception for deck cargo: in *Nimmo v Alexander Cowan & Sons Ltd*, [1968] AC 107, Lord Wilberforce referred to '. . . the orthodox principle (common to both the criminal and the civil law) that exceptions etc., are to be set up by those who rely upon them'. Further, the defendants produced the bill (and the statement was made as a master's remark), and for that reason too, the defendants being proferens in contrahendo or analogous thereto, ambiguity is to be resolved against them. That said, the court does not readily resort to the either rule of construing contra proferentem: see *K/S Victoria Street v House of Fraser*, [2011] EWCA (Civ) 904 at para 68, '. . . such rules are rarely if ever of any assistance when it comes to construing commercial contracts . . .. The words used, commercial sense, and the documentary and factual context, are, and should be, normally enough to determine the meaning of a contractual provision'.

22. The ordinary and natural meaning of the master's remark is largely a matter of impression, but to my mind the defendants' interpretation is the more natural. The claimants' meaning would more naturally be conveyed by the statement that 'Any cargo carried on deck at shipper's/charterer's/receiver's risk. . .'. Moreover, the defendants' interpretation is supported by considerations other than the language of the remark itself:

i)   First, the statement is made by way of a master's remark. This would not be an obvious or usual place to state a contractual provision. The remark is more readily taken to be, or at least to include, a statement of fact about how the cargo was to be carried or otherwise handled.

ii) Moreover, the bill contained another master's remark that 'All cargo loaded from open storage area'. There (a) 'All cargo' means all of the tanks (and not 'any cargo') and (b) a verb ('was' or 'has been') is to be interpolated after the word 'cargo' in order to give the remark grammatical structure. In both respects, on the defendants' interpretation both the master's remarks are similar.

23. These reasons are sufficient to justify the defendants' interpretation, but they have another argument based upon previous dealings between the parties. Mr Buckingham invoked the master's remarks on the bills for the shipment on the 'BBC Gibraltar', the first shipment under the fixture recap, and for the shipment on the 'BBC Zarate'. These can, in my judgment, only be understood as stating which filter or filters were carried on deck. Accordingly it is argued that against this background the master's remark on the bill of 24 November 2009 is to be understood similarly, and I accept that argument. Generally, bills of lading are subject to the same principles of construction as other contracts, and 'The general approach is therefore an objective one by which the courts will ascertain the intention of the parties by considering what meaning the document would convey to a reasonable person having all the background knowledge which would reasonably have been available to the parties in the situation in which they were at the time of the contract': *Scrutton on Charterparties* and Bills of Lading (2011) 22nd Ed para 1–045. In particular, assistance may be found in a course of conduct before the parties entered into the contract on the bill of lading if its words are fairly capable of having more than one meaning: Scrutton (loc cit) at para 10–59, citing *Houlder Bros v Public Works Commissioner*, [1908] AC 276 at p. 285 per Lord Atkinson. I do not need to consider the application of this approach in circumstances where the original parties expected that the bill would be transferred to third parties unfamiliar with relevant previous dealings between them: this case is concerned with a straight consigned bill and the named consignee was the second claimant and was similarly named in the earlier bills.

24. Mr Buckingham also sought support for his argument in forms of wording recommended by the Steamship Mutual and suggested in Hazelwood and Semark's 'P&I Clubs, Law and Practice (2010) 4th Ed. at p. 426. It is not clear when the use of these wordings is recommended or suggested, and I do not consider that they assist his argument.

25. I therefore conclude that the ten tanks carried on the 'BBC Greenland' were deck cargo.

What does it mean by 'cargo which by the contract of carriage is stated as being carried on deck and is so carried' in art I(c)? In most cases, that would be the bill of lading itself. However, where there is a charterparty bill of lading and the Hague-Visby Rules are incorporated into the contract of carriage by means of a paramount clause (or similar device), the matter may pose some challenges. That is because the Hague-Visby Rules use the terms 'bills of lading' and 'contract of carriage' quite distinctively and specifically. The latter usually referring to the charterparty. However when a charterparty is expressed to have incorporated the Hague-Visby Rules as its terms, it may be necessary to read the terms 'bill of lading' and 'contract of carriage' as actually referring to the charterparty.

Onego Shipping and Chartering BV v JSC Arcadia Shipping, M/V 'Socol 3' [2010] EWHC 777 (Comm)

Facts: The charterparty had incorporated the Hague/Hague-Visby Rules and envisaged that deck cargo will or may be carried. It did not however state and/or identify what and/or how much deck cargo would be so carried ('an on-deck statement'). The question, following loss caused to the cargo shipped on deck, was whether the Rules applied to the carriage of deck cargo or whether their application was excluded by virtue of art I(c) of the Hague/Hague-Visby Rules.

Held:

> **Hamblen J:**
>
> [21] The Charterers contended that the 'contract of carriage' referred to in art I(c) is the Charterparty and that since the Charterparty does not contain the necessary on-deck statement, the exclusion of deck cargo does not apply. The Owners contended that the 'contract of carriage' refers to the bill(s) of lading issued for the deck cargo, not the Charterparty.
>
> [22] As was common ground between the parties, where the Hague/Hague-Visby Rules are incorporated into a charterparty:
>
> (1) The charterparty 'must ... be read as if the provisions of the Act were written out therein and thereby gained such contractual force as a proper construction of the document admits'. Only provisions in the Rules that are 'insensible' or 'inapplicable' in the context of a time charter will be disregarded – see *Adamastos Shipping Co Ltd v Anglo-Saxon Petroleum Ltd* [1959] AC 133, 152, 155 (per Viscount Simonds); 'The provisions of the Act are, therefore, to be incorporated as terms of the contract [ie the Charterparty] as far as applicable' – *Adamastos* (Lord Somervell at 184).
>
> (2) As the House of Lords made clear in *Adamastos*, an important purpose of incorporating the Rules into a charterparty is 'to import into the contractual relation between owners and charterers the same standard of obligation, liability, right and immunity as under the rules subsists between carrier and shipper' – (Viscount Simonds at 154).
>
> [23] The Charterers submitted that *Adamastos* supported a further 'principle', namely that to give effect to the Rules as incorporated words will be manipulated so that (1) references to 'this bill of lading' will be read as references to 'this charterparty' and (2) references to 'the contract of carriage' will be read as references to the charterparty.
>
> [24] In support of that argument they relied in particular on the following passages from the *Adamastos* case:
>
>> By the paramount clause, the provisions just quoted are deemed to be incorporated in the charterparty. It is only by virtue of section 2 that the rights and immunities on which the

owners rely can come into operation, since it is section 2 which confers these rights and immunities; and it is impossible to incorporate section 4 in the charterparty without also incorporating the section which provides that the 'carrier' shall be entitled to the rights and immunities set forth in section 4.

Applying section 2 to the present charterparty, which is, of course, a contract for the carriage of goods by sea, the section only brings these rights and immunities into operation . . . (Lord Morton at 163–4) . . .

As the parties have chosen to incorporate in a charterparty provisions which are designed to apply, and only to apply, to bills of lading, one must, I think, infer that they intended these provisions to be incorporated mutatis mutandis; and in order to see what this involves I would begin by trying to read references to bills of lading in the Act as if they were references to charterparties. That necessarily involves the rejection as insensible of the provisions of section 5 of the Act that its provisions shall not be applicable to charterparties, and I find little difficulty in taking that step.

Then there are a number of provisions in the Act which, from their very nature, can only apply to bills of lading, and which become meaningless if one tries to make them apply to a charterparty . . . (Lord Reid at 170)

. . .

Turning to the document incorporated by the paramount clause, namely, the United States Act, one finds, as was to be expected, that it applies only to contracts of carriage of goods by sea covered by a bill of lading or similar document of title, and the outlook of the various sections of the Act is necessarily on such contracts. To give any effect to the contractually incorporated document it must be construed, so far as possible, with reference to a charterparty and not a bill of lading. This is necessarily involved in the step that has already been taken of regarding as inapplicable the words, 'The provisions of the Act shall not be applicable to charterparties.' The next step, in my opinion, is to read 'contract of carriage' as meaning a contract between a carrier and a charterer and not one between a carrier and a shipper. A charterparty is one form of contract for the carriage of goods by sea.' (Lord Keith at 178)

[25] The Charterers further submitted that:

(1) It is art II of the Hague/Hague-Visby Rules which imposes the responsibilities of Art III, and the immunities of art IV to 'contracts of carriage of goods by sea' with 'contracts of carriage' having been defined by art 1(b).

(2) Article II needs to be satisfied since 'It is only by virtue of [art] 2 that the rights and immunities on which the owners rely can come into operation since it is [art] 2 which confers these rights and immunities.' *Adamastos* per Lord Morton at 164.

(3) It is because one reads the references to contract of carriage as being a reference to the charterparty that the Rules apply at all. Just as the 'contract of carriage' in art II is the charterparty and not the bill of lading so too the 'contract of carriage' in art 1(c) is also the charterparty and not the bill of lading.

[26] I accept that in order to make sense of the Rules as incorporated it will generally be necessary to read 'bill of lading' or 'contract of carriage' as referring to the governing charterparty. However, there is no 'principle' or 'rule' that this must always be so. Verbal manipulation is a process which should be carried out intelligently rather than mechanically and only in so far as it is necessary to avoid insensible results.

[27] I also accept that Lord Keith puts the matter generally when he says that the 'next step is to read 'contract of carriage' as meaning a contract between a carrier and a charterer and not one between a carrier and a shipper' and that, given the wording used at the beginning of the paragraph, he may well have been here referring to the definition set out in art 1(b). However, the House of Lords were not considering the specific issue of construction which arises in the present case. Further, given the general principle that provisions which are 'insensible' or 'inapplicable' to a charterparty are to be disregarded, art 1(b) might well be regarded as being such a provision, and indeed *Cooke on Voyage Charters* (6th edition) cites it as a 'clear example' of this (para 85.10).

[28] In my judgment whether 'contract of carriage' in the Rules refers to the bill(s) of lading or the charterparty depends on the context in which it is being used. Unlike in relation to the opening paragraph of art II, there is no necessary reason for construing 'contract of carriage' in art I(c) as referring to the charterparty as opposed to the bill of lading. Indeed it is a provision which can only sensibly apply to the bill of lading since it is only the bill of lading which is ever likely to contain an on-deck statement.

[29] Time charters are, by definition, entered into before any cargo is loaded on to the vessel. Time charters can last for a few weeks or months or for years. Unless the contract in question happens to be a trip time charter (as the present one happened to be) the charter will be concluded before it is even known what voyages are to be undertaken or (save in the case of specialist tankers/carriers) what cargoes are to be carried. Although a time charter might give liberty to carry cargo on deck, in most cases it will be not be known whether any cargo is ever going to be loaded on deck at all at the time the charter is concluded. Further, it will in any event be virtually impossible for the parties to know at the time the time charter is concluded how much cargo is actually going to be loaded on deck. The practical effect of the Charterers' construction would therefore be that the carriage of deck cargo under the NYPE charterparty will almost invariably be subject to the Hague/Hague-Visby Rules and to render the art I(c) liberty to contract out of the Rules illusory.

[30] Moreover, it makes good sense for the liability for deck cargo under the time charter to be co-extensive with that under the bill of lading. As was made clear in *Adamastos*, the parties incorporate the Rules because 'they wish to import into the contractual relation between owners and charterers the same standard of obligation, liability, right and immunity as under the rules subsists between carrier and shipper' – [1959] AC at 154, per Viscount Simonds.

[31] As stated by Clarke LJ in *The Fjord Wind* [2000] 2 Lloyd's Rep 191, 197, para 15:

> 'The general approach in *Adamastos* would to my mind be included in the background knowledge (referred to by Lord Hoffmann) which the parties would have had in mind if they had thought about it. In short I accept the submissions made by Mr Hamblen QC that it is extremely unlikely that the parties would have agreed a different regime for cargo damage under a bill of lading and the charter-party. They would be expected to apply a Hague or Hague-Visby Rules' regime and not to have agreed an absolute warranty of seaworthiness. In particular they would not be likely to have agreed a different regime for different voyages which were both subject to the same contract in respect of which the charterers were to pay freight.'

[32] These considerations equally apply in the present case. The consequence of the Charterers' construction is a dislocation between the contractual regime applicable to the carriage of deck cargo under the bill of lading and that under the Charterparty. Under the bill of lading an on-deck statement means that the Rules are inapplicable and that a different regime of responsibility applies, whilst under the Charterparty the Rules will invariably govern the carriage.

[33] Further, it is the Charterers' case that the effect of Art III, r 8 is to render null and void any provision in the charter 'relieving the carrier or the ship from liability for loss or damage to or in connection with the goods arising from the negligence, fault or failure in the duties and obligations provided in this Article'. This means that, in contrast to the position under the bill of lading, owners would not be free to carry deck cargo on their own conditions or as may be differently stipulated for in the Charterparty.

[34] Nor do I accept the Charterers' argument that there is anything uncommercial about the terms governing carriage of deck cargo being determined by the bill(s) of lading rather than the Charterparty.

It is generally appropriate that the terms governing carriage of a particular deck cargo should be related to the cargo in question, and in any event under a time charter the terms of the bill(s) of lading will generally be a matter within the control of the Charterers since the Master is obliged to sign bills 'as presented'.

[35] For all these reasons I conclude that when written out in the Charterparty, art I(c) requires the bill(s) of lading rather than the Charterparty to contain the on-deck statement and that this is the relevant 'contract of carriage'.

It is conventional for some freight forwarders when placing a shipment for the cargo interest to issue some sort of confirmation as to how the goods are to be carried. This is often known in the industry as a warranty. What is the nature of the freight forwarder's legal liability if the warranty proves to be inaccurate?

Geofizika DD v MMB International Ltd [2010] EWCA Civ 459

Facts: The freight forwarders had arranged for the carriage of three ambulances from the UK to Tripoli, Libya. The consignor had expressly requested for RO-RO terms (thereby implying that the ambulances would be carried under deck). The freight forwarders subsequently also issued a certificate stating that the ambulances were insured on the terms of the Institute Cargo Clauses (A) with the following additional condition 'Warranted shipped under deck.' However, the bill of lading contained a clause permitting the carrier to carry the goods on deck. The ambulances were thus carried on deck and two were washed overboard when the ship was travelling over the Bay of Biscay. The question, amongst others, was whether the freight forwarder was liable for the warranty in the certificate.

Held:

Thomas LJ: I approach this question on the basis that it is clear that the freight forwarders' duty is to procure a contract of carriage in accordance with the instructions of the client and that the freight forwarders are not in any way responsible for the supervision of the carriers' performance of the contract of carriage or for the carriers' failure to perform it. Nonetheless, in the circumstances of this case, in my view, the judge was right. The freight forwarders were negligent in giving the warranty. It seems to me clear that it was incumbent on the freight forwarders, who were in no different a position to insurance brokers, to check that the facts they were warranting were true were in fact true. Although I have not reached the same view as the judge in relation to meaning of the booking confirmation, I nonetheless conclude that the judge was, in my view right, to find that in circumstances where they had not dealt with the carriers before, they simply could not rely upon the fact that they had arranged a contract with the carriers that, if performed in accordance with its terms, would have resulted in the matters warranted being true being true. The consequences of a breach of warranty are so severe, the warranty should not have been given without due care being taken to check that the cargo was under deck. This conclusion does not involve any guarantee by the freight forwarder that the carrier will perform his contract or any supervision by the freight forwarders of the carrier's obligation. It is a conclusion simply that on the facts of this case, the judge was entitled to conclude that the freight forwarders should not have given a warranty in relation to a fact without taking reasonable steps to check that that fact was accurate.

4 Article II

Subject to the provisions of Art VI, under every contract of carriage of goods by sea the carrier, in relation to the loading, handling, stowage, carriage, custody, care and discharge of such goods, shall be subject to the responsibilities and liabilities, and entitled to the rights and immunities hereinafter set forth.

A problem of interpretation is considered in the cases reproduced in this section. Article II uses the words 'carriage of goods', which are defined in Art I, para (e) as covering the period from the time when the goods are loaded on to the time when they are discharged from the ship. The two articles do not sit happily together: the activities listed in Art II may straddle the moments in time fixed by Art I. The three extracts in this section deal with the relationship between these provisions.

Pyrene Co Ltd v Scindia Navigation Co Ltd [1954] 2 QB 402

Facts: See above. It was argued that, as the fire tender had not passed across the ship's rail when it was dropped, it had never been loaded on the ship so that the accident occurred before the time specified in Art I, para (e).

Held:

Devlin J: . . . In my judgment this argument is fallacious, the cause of the fallacy perhaps lying in the supposition inherent in it that the rights and liabilities under the rules attach to a period of time. I think that they attach to a contract or part of a contract. I say 'part of a contract' because a single contract may cover both inland and sea transport; and in that case the only part of it that falls within the rules is that which, to use the words in the definition of 'contract of carriage' in Article I(b), 'relates to the carriage of goods by sea'. Even if 'carriage of goods by sea' were given by definition the most restricted meaning possible, for example, the period of the voyage, the loading of the goods (by which I mean the whole operation of loading in both its stages and whichever side of the ship's rail) would still relate to the carriage on the voyage and so be within the 'contract of carriage'.

Article II is the crucial article which for this purpose has to be construed. It is this article that gives the carrier all his rights and immunities, including the right to limit his liability. He is entitled to do that 'in relation to the loading' and 'under every contract of carriage'. . . .

. . . In my judgment, no special significance need be given to the phrase 'loaded on'. It is not intended to specify a precise moment of time. Of course, if the operation of the rules began and ended with a period of time a precise specification would be necessary. But they do not. It is legitimate in England to look at section 1 of the Act, which applies the rules not to a period of time but 'in relation to and in connection with the carriage of goods by sea'. The rules themselves show the same thing. The obligations in Article III, r 1, for example, to use due diligence to make the ship seaworthy and man and equip her properly are independent of time. The operation of the rules is determined by the limits of the contract of carriage by sea and not by any limits of time. The function of Article I(e) is, I think, only to assist in the definition of contract of carriage. As I have already pointed out, there is excluded from that definition any part of a larger contract which relates, for example, to inland transport. It is natural to divide such a contract into periods, a period of inland transport, followed perhaps by a period of sea transport and then again by a period of inland transport. Discharging from rail at the port of loading may fall into the first period; loading on to the ship into the second. The reference to 'when the goods are loaded on' in Article I(e) is not, I think, intended to do more than identify the first operation in the series which constitutes the carriage of goods by sea; as 'when they are discharged' denotes the last. The use of the rather loose word 'cover', I think, supports this view.

... It is no doubt possible to read Article I(e) literally as defining the period as being from the completion of loading till the completion of discharging. But the literal interpretation would be absurd. Why exclude loading from the period and include discharging? How give effect to the frequent references to loading in other rules? How reconcile it with Article VII which allows freedom of contract 'prior to the loading on and subsequent to the discharge from'? Manifestly both operations must be included. That brings me back to the view that Article I(e) is naming the first and last of a series of operations which include in between loading and discharging, 'handling, stowage, carriage, custody and care'. This is, in fact, the list of operations to which Article II is by its own terms applied. In short, nothing is to be gained by looking to the terms of Article I(e) for an interpretation of Article II ...

Compania Portorafti Commerciale SA v Ultramar Panama Inc, The Captain Gregos [1990] 1 Lloyd's Rep 310, CA

Facts: See above. Cargo owners argued that the time bar under Art III, r 4 could only be invoked in suits relating to events occurring between loading and discharge and not in relation to later events such as misdelivery of cargo.

Held:

Bingham LJ: ... The contract of carriage here was of an entirely normal kind. The cargo owners counterclaim as parties to the bill of lading (which I shall at this stage assume them to have been) against the shipowners as carriers. It is a paradigm situation.

The definition in Article I(e) does, I accept, assign a temporal term to the 'carriage of goods' under the rules, supporting an argument that the rules do not apply to events occurring before loading or after discharge. (See also Article VII.) I read Article II as defining the scope of the operations to which the responsibilities, rights and immunities in the rules apply. Apart from the obligation of seaworthiness imposed by Article III rule 1 (not in issue here), the carrier's central obligation is (per Article III rule 2) properly and carefully to load, handle, stow, carry, keep, care for and discharge the goods carried.

It seems to me that the acts of which the cargo owners complain are the most obvious imaginable breaches of Article III rule 2. A bailee does not properly and carefully carry, keep and care for goods if he consumes them in his ship's boilers or delivers them to an unauthorised recipient during the voyage. A bailee does not properly and carefully discharge goods if, whether negligently or intentionally, he fails to discharge them and so converts them to his own use. If the cargo owners were to establish the fact they allege, and had brought suit within the year, I cannot see how a claim based on breach of the rules could fail ...

Mayhew Foods Ltd v Overseas Containers Ltd [1984] 1 Lloyd's Rep 317

Facts: OCL agreed to carry a refrigerated container of chicken and turkey from Mayhew's premises to Jeddah, Saudi Arabia. The contract contemplated that the container would be carried on *Benalder* from Southampton direct to Jeddah. But the contract gave the carrier a wide power to choose the route and method of transport and, after collection, the container was in fact taken to Shoreham, loaded on *Voline* and carried to Le Havre where it was discharged. The container was then stored for six days before being loaded on *Benalder* and carried to Jeddah, where permission to discharge was refused because the meat had decayed. The temperature control on the container, instead of being set at −18°C, as it should have been, had been set at +2°C to +4°C. OCL accepted that they had failed to carry, keep and care for the same properly and carefully.

Held:

> **Bingham J:** OCL's second submission took as its starting point the fact already noted that the Act and the rules only apply:
>
> > ... in relation to and in connection with the carriage of goods by sea in ships ...
>
> It was accordingly argued that even if the statutory provisions governed carriage from Shoreham to Le Havre, they did not apply while the goods were lying ashore at Le Havre any more than they applied before the goods were loaded at Shoreham or after they were discharged at Jeddah. In short, it was said that the interval of storage at Le Havre was not carriage by sea and so not covered by the rules ... The answer to this problem is again to be found in the principle that the rights and liabilities under the rules attach to a contract. They do not apply to carriage or storage before the port of shipment or after the port of discharge, because that would be inland and not sea carriage. But between those ports the contract was, despite the wide language of cl 21, for carriage by sea. If, during that carriage, OCL chose to avail themselves of their contractual right to discharge, store and tranship, those were, in my judgment, operations 'in relation to and in connection with the carriage of goods by sea in ships', to use the language of the Act, or were 'within the contractual carriage', to use the language of cl 21(2) of the bill of lading conditions. It would, I think, be surprising if OCL could, by carrying the goods to Le Havre and there storing the goods before transhipment, rid themselves of liabilities to which they would have been subject had they, as contemplated, shipped the goods at Southampton and carried them direct to Jeddah, the more so since Mayhew had no knowledge of any voyage to Le Havre. My conclusion is that the rules, having applied on shipment at Shoreham, remained continuously in force until discharge at Jeddah ...

5 Article III, rule 1: Seaworthiness

The 1971 Act and the Rules alter the position at common law. Section 3 of the Act provides that an absolute warranty of seaworthiness is not to be implied in contracts to which the Rules apply. In its place, Art III, provides a duty to exercise due diligence 'before and at the beginning of the voyage'. Unlike the common law duty, which can be excluded by agreement, the obligation under the Rules to exercise due diligence has been held to be 'inescapable', an idea that has been explored in recent cases. By Art IV, r 1 the carrier is made liable only for loss or damage caused by want of care; the burden of proving due diligence is placed on the carrier.

The meaning of 'before and at the beginning of the voyage' was settled by the decision in *Maxine Footwear*, a case that also established that if the obligation in Art III, r 1 is not fulfilled and the non-fulfilment causes damage to cargo, the immunities in Art IV, r 2 cannot be relied on.

5.1 An overriding obligation

Maxine Footwear Co Ltd v Canadian Govt Merchant Marine Ltd [1959] AC 589, PC

Facts: The appellants were shippers and consignees of cargo loaded on the *Maurienne* at Halifax NS for carriage to Kingston, Jamaica. The contract was subject to the Hague Rules as enacted by the Canadian Water Carriage of Goods Act 1936. Shortly before the vessel was due to sail an attempt was made to thaw a frozen drainpipe with an acetylene torch. A fire was started in the cork insulation around the pipe. The fire eventually forced the master to scuttle the ship.

Held:

Lord Somervell of Harrow: . . . Before proceeding to consider the arguments it is convenient to state certain conclusions which appear plain to their Lordships. From the time when the ship caught on fire she was unseaworthy. This unseaworthiness caused the damage to and loss of the appellants' goods. The negligence of the respondents' servants which caused the fire was a failure to exercise due diligence.

Logically, the first submission on behalf of the respondents was that in cases of fire Article III never comes into operation even though the fire makes the ship unseaworthy. All fires and all damage from fire on this argument fall to be dealt with under Article IV, r 2(b). If this were right there was at any rate a very strong case for saying that there was no fault or privity of the carrier within that rule, and the respondents would succeed.

In their Lordships' opinion the point fails. Article III, r 1, is an overriding obligation. If it is not fulfilled and the non-fulfilment causes the damage the immunities of Article IV cannot be relied on. This is the natural construction apart from the opening words of Article III, r 2. The fact that that rule is made subject to the provisions of Article IV and r 1 is not so conditioned makes the point clear beyond argument.

The further submissions by the respondents were based, as they had to be, on the construction of Article III, r 1. It was submitted that under that article the obligation is only to exercise due diligence to make the ship seaworthy at two moments of time, the beginning of the loading and the beginning of the voyage.

It is difficult to believe that this construction of the word 'before' could have been argued but for the fact that this doctrine of stages had been laid down in relation to the absolute warranty of seaworthiness in English law.

It is worth, therefore, bearing in mind words used by Lord Macmillan with reference to the English Carriage of Goods by Sea Act 1924, which embodied the Hague Rules, as does the present Act:

It is important to remember that the Act of 1924 was the outcome of an International Conference, and that the rules in the Schedule have an international currency. As these rules must come under the consideration of foreign courts it is desirable in the interests of uniformity that their interpretation should not be rigidly controlled by domestic precedents of antecedent date, but rather that the language of the rules should be construed on broad principles of general acceptation (*Stag Line Ltd v Foscolo, Mango & Co* [1932] AC 328, 350).

In their Lordships' opinion 'before and at the beginning of the voyage' means the period from at least the beginning of the loading until the vessel starts on her voyage. The word 'before' cannot in their opinion be read as meaning 'at the commencement of the loading'. If this had been intended it would have been said. The question when precisely the period begins does not arise in this case, hence the insertion above of the words 'at least'.

On that view the obligation to exercise due diligence to make the ship seaworthy continued over the whole of the period from the beginning of loading until the ship sank. There was a failure to exercise due diligence during that period. As a result the ship became unseaworthy and this unseaworthiness caused the damage to and loss of the appellants' goods. The appellants are therefore entitled to succeed . . .

It becomes therefore unnecessary to consider whether the Supreme Court were justified in holding that the appellants' goods were not stowed until after the commencement of the fire.

It is also unnecessary to consider the earlier cases as to 'stages' under the common law. The doctrine of stages had its anomalies and some important matters were never elucidated by authority. When the warranty was absolute it seems at any rate intelligible to restrict it to certain points of time. It would be surprising if a duty to exercise due diligence ceased as soon as loading began, only to reappear later shortly before the beginning of the voyage.

For these reasons their Lordships will humbly advise Her Majesty that this appeal should be allowed.

Notes

1   *Lack of due diligence is negligence*: *The Amstelslot* [1963] 2 Lloyd's Rep 223, p 225, *per* Lord Devlin. The exercise of due diligence is equivalent to the exercise of reasonable skill and care: *The Eurasian Dream* [2002] EWHC 118 (Comm); [2002] 1 Lloyd's Rep 719.

2   *Unseaworthiness and the carrier's right to limit liability*: The carrier's duty to ensure seaworthiness is overriding in that a breach of the duty, if it causes loss or damage, prevents the carrier relying on the defences in Art IV, r 2 and on the right to indemnity contained in Art IV, r 6. However, a carrier is entitled to limit financial liability under Art IV, r 5 notwithstanding a failure to exercise due diligence to make the ship seaworthy. The words in r 5: "'in any event" mean what they say. They are unlimited in scope': *The Happy Ranger, per* Tuckey LJ.

5.2 An inescapable obligation

The obligation under the Rules to exercise due diligence has been held to be 'inescapable' in the sense that the carrier is liable for lack of due diligence on the part of anyone involved in keeping or making the vessel seaworthy. The authorities for this interpretation were reviewed in *The Muncaster Castle*.

Riverstone Meat Co Pty Ltd v Lancashire Shipping Co Ltd,
The Muncaster Castle [1961] AC 807

Facts: Cases of canned ox tongue were shipped on board the *Muncaster Castle* for carriage from Sydney to London under a bill of lading that was subject to the Hague Rules as enacted by the Australian Sea Carriage of Goods Act 1924. When the goods were discharged, most of the cases were found damaged by sea water that had entered the hold through storm valves. Shortly before starting the voyage, the storm valve inspection covers had been removed during a survey of the vessel. The covers had not been properly refitted by the independent firm of ship repairers who had been instructed in connection with the survey. The cargo owners alleged that the carriers had not exercised due diligence to make the ship seaworthy.

Held:

Viscount Simonds: My Lords, the question, then, is whether the respondents discharged this burden, and it is conceded that they did unless they are to be held responsible for the negligence of the fitter employed by Alexander Stephen & Sons Ltd. This is the single issue in the case . . . Its solution depends on the meaning of the words occurring in article III, rule 1, and repeated in article IV, rule 1, 'due diligence to make the ship seaworthy'. To ascertain their meaning it is, in my opinion, necessary to pay particular regard to their history, origin and context . . . The Hague Rules, as is well known, were the result of the Conferences on Maritime Law held at Brussels in 1922 and 1923. Their aim was broadly to standardise within certain limits the rights of every holder of a bill of lading against the shipowner, prescribing an irreducible minimum for the responsibilities and liabilities to be undertaken by the latter. To guide them the framers of the rules had amongst other precedents the American Harter Act of 1893, the Australian Sea Carriage of Goods Act 1904, the Canadian Water Carriage of Goods Act 1910, and, though they had no British Act as a model, they had decisions of the English courts in which the language of the Harter Act had fallen to be construed by virtue of its provisions being embodied in bills of lading. In all these Acts the relevant words, 'exercise due diligence to make the ship seaworthy', are to be found. It was in these circumstances that these words were adopted in the Hague Rules.

My Lords, the question how far their meaning should be governed by previous decisions in the courts of America or this country has been more than once discussed in this House. Notwithstanding some apparent qualification of the proposition which is to be found in the speeches of Lords Atkin and Macmillan in *Stag Line Ltd v Foscolo Mango & Co Ltd* [1932] AC 328, I think I am at liberty to adopt emphatically what was said by Lords Sumner and Hailsham in *Gosse Millard Ltd v Canadian Government Merchant Marine Ltd* [1929] AC 223. The former of them said:

By forbearing to define 'management of the ship'... the legislature has, in my opinion, shown a clear intention to continue and enforce the old clause as it was previously understood and regularly construed by the courts.

The latter said:

I am unable to find any reason for supposing that the words as used by the legislature in the Act of 1924 leave any different meaning to that which has been judicially assigned to them when used in contracts for the carriage of goods by sea before that date; and I think that the decisions which have already been given are sufficient to determine the meaning to be put upon them in the statute now under discussion.

Mutatis mutandis these statements I apply to the words we have to construe...

First I would refer to *G E Dobell & Co v Steamship Rossmore Co Ltd* [1895] 2 QB 408, a case often referred to in the courts of this country and of the United States and never, so far as I am aware, dissented from. In that case the ship was unseaworthy owing to the negligence of the ship's carpenter. Into the bill of lading the words of the Harter Act were introduced, 'which', said Lord Esher MR 'I decline to construe as an Act, but which we must construe simply as words occurring in this bill of lading'. Then he proceeds:

In section 3 of the Act so incorporated the exception which is to relieve the ship owner is made to depend on the condition that the owner of the ship... shall exercise due diligence to make the vessel in all respects seaworthy. If he does not do that the exceptions in his favour do not take effect. It is contended that the meaning of the clause is that if the owner personally did all that he could do to make the ship seaworthy when she left America, then, although she was not seaworthy, by the fault of some agent or servant, the owner is not liable.

And the learned Master of the Rolls, after rejecting this contention, went on:

It is obvious to my mind... that the words of section 3 which limit the owner's liability if he shall exercise due diligence to make the ship in all respects seaworthy, must mean that it is to be done by the owner by himself or the agents whom he employs to see to the seaworthiness of the ship before she starts out of that port.

So also Kay LJ:

It seems to me to be plain on the face of this contract that what was intended was that the owner should, if not with his own eyes, at any rate by the eyes of proper competent agents, ensure that the ship was in a seaworthy condition before she left port, and that it is not enough to say that he appointed a proper and competent agent.

I have cited from these judgments at some length because they determine decisively the meaning attached by the courts of this country to the relevant words. It is true that the negligence was that of a servant of the shipowner, but the reasoning and the language of the judgments embrace any agent employed by him. These are wise words.

I turn now to a case decided two years later in the District Court, SD New York, *The Colima* (1897) 82 Fed Rep 665 and I quote at some length from the judgment of Judge Brown. In that case the vessel was unseaworthy owing to negligent loading by the stevedores which was done under the supervision and direction of the master and first officer of the ship. The learned judge said:

> This section [that is, section 3 of the Harter Act] has been in several cases adjudged to require due diligence, not merely in the personal acts of the owner, but also on the part of the agents he may employ, or to whom he may have committed the work of fitting the vessel for sea. The Act requires in other words, due diligence in the work itself . . .

On any other construction, owners would escape all responsibility for the seaworthiness of their ships by merely employing agents of good repute, whether any diligence and care to make their vessels seaworthy were in fact exercised or not. On reason and sound policy no such intent in the statute can be supposed. The context and the pre-existing law indicate that the intent of the Act is to relieve the shipowner from his previous warranty of absolute seaworthiness in fact, and to substitute for that warranty a warranty only of diligence, to make the ship seaworthy. This difference is of great importance, as it avoids responsibility for latent and undiscoverable defects. But the warranty of diligence remains: and this requires the application of the usual rule, that the acts and negligences of the agent are deemed those of the principal.

. . . My Lords, I have without reluctance ventured on this long quotation because I can find no words more apt to express my own view as to the meaning of words taken from the Harter Act and embodied in the Hague Rules. To one thing in particular I call attention . . . Here I may quote words of MacKinnon LJ in *Smith, Hogg & Co Ltd v Black Sea and Baltic General Insurance Co Ltd* [1939] 2 All ER 855:

> The limitation and qualification of the implied warranty of seaworthiness by cutting down the duty of the shipowner to the obligation to use 'due diligence . . . to make the ship seaworthy' is a limitation or qualification more apparent than real, because the exercise of due diligence involves not merely that the shipowner personally shall exercise due diligence, but that all his servants and agents shall exercise due diligence. That is pointed out in a note in *Scrutton on Charterparties* (14th edn, 1939, London: Sweet & Maxwell, p 110) which says that this variation will not be 'of much practical value in face of the dilemma that must constantly arise on the facts. In most cases if the vessel is unseaworthy due diligence cannot have been used by the owner, his servants, or agents; if due diligence has been used the vessel in fact will be seaworthy. The circumstances in which the dilemma does not arise (eg a defect causing unseaworthiness, but of so latent a nature that due diligence could not have discovered it) are not likely to occur often'.

In the same case on appeal to this House, Lord Wright said [1940] AC 997, 1001:

> The unseaworthiness, constituted as it was by loading an excessive deck cargo, was obviously only consistent with want of due diligence on the part of the shipowner to make her seaworthy. Hence the qualified exception of unseaworthiness does not protect the shipowner. In effect such an exception can only excuse against latent defects. The overloading was the result of overt acts.

. . . I come, then, to *W Angliss & Co (Australia) Proprietary Ltd v P & O Steam Navigation Co* [1927] 2 KB 456 which is said to be the first case in which the Hague Rules were discussed in an English court . . . It is important to note what was the point of decision. It was whether, when the carrier has contracted for the building of a ship, he is liable for lack of due diligence on the part of the shipbuilders or their workmen if he has engaged builders of repute and has adopted all reasonable precautions, such as requiring the builders to satisfy one of the recognised classification societies and engaged skilled naval architects who advise him and skilled inspectors who supervise the work with due diligence. The learned judge, Wright J, as he then was, held that in such circumstances the carrier was not liable. I see no reason to question the correctness of this decision, and need say no more about it, for it does not in the present appeal fall to be reviewed. Of greater significance is that, except in a single passage where the learned judge was dealing with the employment of an inspector to supervise the work, no mention is made of the employment of agents to repair a ship. That passage is as follows: 'Again, the need of repairing a ship may cast on the carrier a special duty to see, as far as reasonably possible, by special advisers for whom he is personally responsible, that the repairs adequately make good the defects.'

It is not possible to extract from this somewhat speculative *dictum* that the learned judge thought that the carrier would not in any case, with or without inspection, be liable for negligence on the part of those to whom (in the words of Brown J in *The Colima*) 'he committed the work of fitting the vessel for sea'. It was not a matter for his decision and he did not, in my opinion, purport to decide it. But it is upon this authority that the whole fabric of the respondents' case appears to rest. It is a reasonable construction of the words, which once again I quote, 'to exercise due diligence to make the ship seaworthy' to say that in the case of a ship built for the carrier, or newly come into his hands by purchase, the carrier fulfils his obligation if he takes the precautions which the learned judge suggests. Until the ship is his he can have no further responsibility. I am aware of no case either in the United States under the Harter Act or this country when its words fell to be construed in which the contrary has been suggested. But it is far otherwise where the shipowner puts his ship in the hands of third parties for repair. To such a case the words that I have cited from *The Rossmore* and *The Colima* are precisely applicable. An attempt was made to draw a distinction between negligence shown by the shipowner's servants, his agents and independent contractors. But this could but fail. For no sensible reason could be found for such a distinction . . .

The plea that the shipowner is not liable for the negligence of an independent contractor failing as a general proposition, as it was bound to fail, it was then urged that it was a question of fact in each case, and that upon the facts of the present case the respondents were not liable for the negligence of the fitter employed by the ship repairers. It was for this reason that I stated the facts fully at the beginning of this opinion. Having done so, I must say at once that I find it impossible to distinguish between one independent contractor and another, or between one kind of repair and another. I have no love for the argumentative question 'Where is the line to be drawn?' but it would be an impossible task for the court to examine the facts of each case and determine whether the negligence of the independent contractor should be imputed to the shipowner. I do not know what criterion or criteria should be used, nor were any suggested. Take the case of repair. Is there to be one result if the necessary repair is slight, another if it is extensive? Is it relevant that the shipowner might have done the work by his own servants but preferred to have it done by a reputable shipyard? These and many other questions that will occur to your Lordships show that no other solution is possible than to say that the shipowner's obligation of due diligence demands due diligence in the work of repair by whomsoever it may be done.

. . . I will end by categorically repelling the second and third formal reasons in the respondents' case. They did not on the facts of the case by entrusting the vessel to reputable ship repairers perform their duty to exercise due diligence. They were vicariously liable for negligence of a servant of an independent contractor, namely, the fitter of Alexander Stephen & Sons Ltd . . .

Lord Keith of Avonholm: My Lords, I agree. I would only add a few words . . .

The obligation is a statutory obligation imposed in defined contracts between the carrier and the shipper. There is nothing novel in a statutory obligation being held to be incapable of delegation so as to free the person bound of liability for breach of the obligation, and the reasons for this become, I think, more compelling where the obligation is made part of a contract between parties. We are not faced with a question in the realm of tort, or negligence. The obligation is a statutory contractual obligation. The novelty, if there is one, is that the statutory obligation is expressed in terms of an obligation to exercise due diligence, etc. There is nothing, in my opinion, extravagant in saying that this is an inescapable personal obligation. The carrier cannot claim to have shed his obligation to exercise due diligence to make his ship seaworthy by selecting a firm of competent ship repairers to make his ship seaworthy. Their failure to use due diligence to do so is his failure.

The question, as I see it, is not one of vicarious responsibility at all. It is a question of statutory obligation. Perform it as you please. The performance is the carrier's performance . . .

(Lord Merriman, Lord Radcliffe and Lord Hodson also delivered reasoned judgments
in favour of allowing the appeal.)

Note

An inescapable and unlimited personal obligation? The approach adopted in *The Muncaster Castle* makes the carrier liable under the Rules for lack of due diligence by anyone involved in keeping or making the vessel seaworthy. In *The Kamsar Voyager* [2002] 2 Lloyd's Rep 57 this was held to include the suppliers of equipment or spare parts. In this case an engine failed at sea. A spare piston was fitted. One dimension of the spare made it incompatible with the engine and, when the engine was run, a major breakdown occurred. The shipowners could not be criticised for ordering and carrying a spare made by the reputable builders of the engine, for failing to notice the small difference in dimensions of the spare, or for fitting it when the failure occurred. But the shipowners could not prove that the engine builders had exercised due diligence in supplying the spare piston and the ship was held to be unseaworthy at the start of the voyage. So understood, the obligation is extensive as well as inescapable. But is it unlimited? In the next case, it was argued that the carrier was responsible not only for those involved in keeping or making a ship seaworthy, but also for the acts or defaults of all those who ship cargo.

5.3 Due diligence

Parsons Corp and others v C V Scheepvaartonderneming Happy Ranger, The Happy Ranger [2006] EWHC 122 (Comm)

Facts: Whilst the *Happy Ranger* was loading the cargo, her lifting cranes broke causing the cargo to be seriously damaged. It was proved that the 'safe working load' (swl) of cranes had not been properly tested. If the cranes had been tested, they would have snapped during the test and thus, the casualty would not have arisen. The claim was for breach of Art III, r 1 and Art III, r 2.

Held:

Gloster J: . . .it was common ground that, under Article III Rule 1 of the Hague-Visby Rules, a shipowner will not, in principle, be liable for any defects in the construction of the vessel because this would involve 'an almost unlimited retrogression' in relation to a shipowner's non-delegable duties. As Wright J. stated in *W. Angliss v Peninsular and Oriental Steam Navigation Co.* [1927] 1 KB 456 at 460–461:

. . . The Carriage of Goods by Sea Acts have introduced a new and obligatory code of responsibilities and immunities as affecting carriers under bills of lading in place of the former rule that carriers by sea, while generally under the liability of common carriers, were free by contract to vary and limit their liabilities. In particular, the Acts have expressly abolished the previous absolute obligation to provide a seaworthy ship and have substituted an obligation to use due diligence to that effect. The carrier may not be the owner of the ship, but merely the charterer;

he may not have contracted for the building of the ship, but merely have purchased her, possibly years after she has been built. In the two latter cases the builders and their men cannot possibly be deemed to have been the agents or servants of the carrier and it is illogical that there should be such difference in the carrier's obligations merely because he has bought the ship by the method of contracting with the builders to build it for him. In addition, if the carrier were held liable for the bad workmanship of the builders' men, he might equally be held liable for bad workmanship by the men employed by the various sub-contractors who supply material for the builders, such as steel-workers in furnaces and rolling mills, or who supply special articles such as castings, pumps or proprietary machines, which would involve an almost unlimited retrogression.

20. The same principle was applied more recently in *The 'Kapitan Sakharov'* [2000] 2 Ll.R. 255 at 271–3 (per Auld LJ); see, also, *Scrutton on Charterparties* (20th Ed.) – page 429. *The 'Kapitan Sakharov'* illustrates that the relevant failure to exercise due diligence must relate to the performance of a function undertaken (by the sub-contractor) as a carrier or on behalf of the carrier rather than in an alternative capacity, namely shipper as in *The 'Kapitan Sakharov'*. The Court of Appeal also confirmed (by reference to W. Angliss & Co. (Australia) *v* P & O Navigation Company (supra)) that a carrier: (a) should not be exposed to an infinite liability in time; and (b) is not, without more, liable for latent defects in a vessel before it acquired it. Both these propositions are relevant to the instant case.

21. Further, in 'The Muncaster Castle' [1961] AC 807 the House of Lords unanimously considered that a shipowner's/carrier's duty under Article III, Rule 1 would not start and he would not be responsible for work carried out until the transfer of ownership, or possession of the vessel, or until the vessel came into his 'orbit', service or 'control': see per Viscount Simonds at 8402a-b, per Lord Merriman at 860b-c, per Lord Radcliffe at 867f-868b, and per Lord Keith at 870c-d and f-g. Further, having referred in detail to Angliss, Lord Radcliffe stated (at 847E-G):

> It is plain to me that this conclusion turns on the consideration that the causative carelessness took place at a time before the carrier's obligation under article III (1) had attached and in circumstances, therefore, when the builders and their men could not be described as agents for the carrier 'before and at the beginning of the voyage to . . . make the ship seaworthy'. This is a tenable position for those who engage themselves upon the work of bringing the ship into existence. The carrier's responsibility for the work itself does not begin until the ship comes into his orbit, and it begins then as a responsibility to make sure by careful and skilled inspection that what he is taking into his service is in fit condition for the purpose and, if there is anything lacking that is fairly discoverable, to put it right. This is recognised in the judgment. But if the bad work that has been done is 'concealed' and so cannot be detected by any reasonable care, then the lack of diligence to which unseaworthiness is due is not to be attributed to the carrier.

22. The Claimants claim damages for breach of the contract of carriage and in particular for breach of Article III, Rules 1 and/or 2. Their primary case is under Article III, Rule 1. The Claimants contend that the Defendant was itself at fault in allowing the lift to go ahead in the circumstances, and also in law responsible for the fault of others including the crane manufacturers and Lloyd's, the classification society which oversaw the testing regime for the cranes and granted a special exemption certificate for this particular loading. They contend that the Defendant is also liable for the failings of others prior to the date of delivery on 16 February 1998. As an alternative case, the Claimant say the actual lifting was carried out in such a way as to put extra loading on the hook, causing the breakage.

23. The Defendant denies liability. It contends that, for the purpose of Article III Rule 1 of the Hague-Visby Rules, the Vessel came into the Defendant's 'orbit' on 16 February 1998. Accordingly it contends that, prior to 16 February, it cannot be liable for the negligence of any one or more of the builders, De Merwede and De Schelde, the foundry, SGR, the crane manufacturers, or Huisman, Lloyd's or DHI. In principle the Defendant accepts that it could be liable in tort for its own negligence prior to 16 February. However, it submitted that: (a) the scope of its duty of care owed to the Claimants prior to 16 February is limited; and (b) the Defendant in any event was neither negligent nor did it act in breach of its duty of care prior to 16 February 1998. It further submits that, on and at all material times after 16 February 1998, the Defendant, its servants or agents, exercised due diligence to make the Vessel seaworthy within the meaning of Article III Rule 1 of the Hague-Visby Rules. In particular the Defendant submitted that:

i) On handover of the Vessel the Defendants received all necessary certification. A separate hook certificate would not have been provided to the Defendants because: (1) the hook should have been proof tested and certified by the foundry and all the Defendants were concerned to receive was the 'complete' crane certificate; and (2) the hook would not constitute 'loose gear' so as to attract a separate certificate on handover;

ii) Mr Piet Mast, the Lloyd's surveyor in charge of the Flushing office reasonably granted the swl extension temporarily increasing the swl of each crane to 424 t.;

iii) Mr. T.P.R Moolenaar, of Mammoet, the cargo inspector and port captain at the lift, acted reasonably in permitting the load to take place, especially in the light of the Mast extension; and

...

24. Thus the issues which the Court has to decide may be summarised as follows:

i) Did the Vessel come into the Defendant's 'orbit' prior to 16 February 1998 for the purpose of its having responsibility under Article III, Rule 1 for any failure to exercise due diligence in relation to the manufacture or testing of the crane or the hook, prior to that date? If so, when?

ii) If the Defendant was responsible at any time prior to 16 February 1998, has it discharged the burden of proof of showing that it (or its sub-contractors or others) exercised due diligence to make the Vessel seaworthy?

iii) If not, was such failure to exercise due diligence to make the Vessel seaworthy causative of the accident's occurrence?

iv) Has the Defendant discharged the burden of proof of showing that it (or its sub-contractors or others) exercised due diligence to make the Vessel seaworthy, after 16 February 1998?

v) If not, was such failure to exercise due diligence in relation to seaworthiness causative of the accident's occurrence?

....

37. I accept the submission of Mr Nigel Jacobs, counsel on behalf of the Defendant, that, in the circumstances set out above, prior to 16 February 1998, the Vessel did not come under the Defendant's control or service, or in that sense, 'within its orbit'. In *The 'Muncaster Castle'* (supra), the term 'orbit' is used co-extensively with ownership or service or control, and I do not consider that it should be construed in any looser sense. The Shipbuilding Contract itself shows how, contractually, the Defendant did not assume responsibility for the Vessel until 16 February. Mr Dailey (the Claimants' heavy lift expert) accepted in evidence that responsibility shifted to the Defendants on 16 February. Moreover, the fact that the Master and/or Chief Officer were on board the Vessel prior to delivery for familiarisation purposes did not in my judgment mean that the Vessel passed into the Defendant's orbit prior to 16 February. The evidence, not surprisingly, showed that, in contracts in relation to shipbuilding and ship sale, it is standard practice for a buyer to place officers on board the Vessel for familiarisation prior to the completion of purchase. If a vessel were to be in a ship purchaser's 'orbit' by reason of familiarisation alone, there would be few ship sale cases in which the vessel had not passed into the prospective owners' orbit prior to delivery, which I would find a surprising conclusion. Further, the fact that the Defendant prepared lifting plans for the performance of its contract with the Claimants, before the Vessel had been delivered to the Defendants cannot bear on this issue. The Defendant obviously could not wait until 16 February (when the lift was to be carried out at the beginning of March), especially when the contract of carriage was concluded the previous October and the operation needed considerable pre-planning. This was accepted by Mr Dailey, who agreed in cross-examination that the planning of the lifting operation might take some time. Moreover, although the Defendant had Captain Alblas as its representative at the yard and present during the various tests, the reality is that, at that stage, the Defendant was entitled to entrust the testing regime to Huisman and Lloyd's, as was accepted by Mr Dailey in evidence.

. . .

39. Thus, whilst I conclude, contrary to the submissions of Mr Richard Lord QC, who appeared on behalf of the Claimants, that the Defendant was not responsible, without more, for any negligence of others prior to the delivery of the Vessel (because I do not consider that the Vessel's was under the Defendant's control or within its 'orbit' before that date), that is not, in my judgment, the critical issue, or the end of the story. What matters, in my view, is what actions were, or were not, taken by Mammoet and the Defendant after the latter took delivery of the Vessel, in the light of the knowledge that they clearly had: (a) as a result of the certificates which had been handed over; (b) as a result of the tests which they knew had been carried out and those which they knew had not been carried out; (c) as to the design of the ramshorn hooks and the lifting equipment; and (d) as to the properties of the process vessel that had to be loaded. It is to this issue which I now turn.

Issues (ii) and (iii)

40. In the circumstances these issues do not arise for determination.

Issue (iv): Has the Defendant discharged the burden of proof of showing that it (or its sub-contractors or others) exercised due diligence to make the Vessel seaworthy, after 16 February 1998?

. . .

41. I heard extensive evidence from witnesses on both sides, both factual and expert, and received lengthy detailed submissions, both written and oral, from counsel, both during and after the hearing. I have carefully considered all of these, but it is not feasible to attempt to summarise all the evidence and arguments. In my judgment, the Defendant has failed to discharge the burden of showing that it did indeed exercise due diligence to make the Vessel seaworthy, after it took delivery on 16 February 1998.

. . . .

Northern Shipping Co v Deutsche Seereederei GmbH, The Kapitan Sakharov [2000] 2 Lloyd's Rep 255, CA

Facts: C shipped tank containers of the flammable liquid isopentane on NSC's vessel *Kapitan Sakharov*. The containers were improperly stowed under-deck in a hold without mechanical ventilation, which was held to be an obvious danger and a contravention of the International Convention for Health and Safety of Life at Sea (SOLAS), the International Maritime Dangerous Goods Code (IMDG) and MOPOG (Russian version of IMDG) and to render the ship unseaworthy. D unwittingly shipped other dangerous cargo, which exploded and caused a fire. The fire ignited the isopentane, resulting in the sinking of the vessel. Two seamen died. The vessel would not have been lost if the isopentane had been stowed on deck. It was held that the vessel was unseaworthy in respect of both shipments. The unseaworthiness in respect of D's container was not caused by lack of due diligence by the shipowner: a carrier's duty of due diligence did not extend to verification of the contents of a sealed container packed by the shipper, in the absence of notice of the need to do so. But the unseaworthiness in respect of C's cargo was on the facts caused by lack of due diligence and was a cause of the sinking. Claims were made against the carrier by other shippers, the dependants of the deceased seamen and by Iranian authorities for pollution damage. D was held liable for the shipowner's loss from the initial explosion but was not obliged to indemnify the carrier against claims arising from the isopentane fire and sinking.

Held:

Auld LJ: . . .

Due diligence

NSC was required under art III, r 1, of the Hague Rules to exercise due diligence to make the vessel seaworthy. The Judge correctly took as the test whether it had shown that it, its servants, agents or independent contractors, had exercised all reasonable skill and care to ensure that the vessel was seaworthy at the commencement of its voyage, namely, reasonably fit to encounter the ordinary incidents of the voyage. He also correctly stated the test to be objective, namely to be measured by the standards of a reasonable shipowner, taking into account international standards and the particular circumstances of the problem in hand.

The Judge held that NSC was in breach of art III, r 1, of the Hague Rules in failing to exercise due diligence to make the ship seaworthy in respect of the stowage of the isopentane below deck . . .

Compliance or otherwise with codes like MOPOG is not necessarily determinative of the issue of due diligence. Depending on the facts of the case, a reasonable misconstruction or misunderstanding of such an instrument may not amount to want of due diligence. Here, though the Judge found that there had been a genuine misunderstanding of the document, it was coupled with what, on the evidence before him, he was entitled to find was plainly unreasonable conduct in stowing isopentane below deck. It was an obvious risk . . .

NSC's entitlement to an indemnity from D – art IV, r 6

. . . Art III, r 1, of the Hague Rules requires a carrier before and at the beginning of a voyage to exercise due diligence to make the ship seaworthy. Article IV, r 6, of the rules renders the shipper of inflammable, explosive or otherwise dangerous goods, who gives no notice of their nature and dangerous character, liable to the carrier 'for all damages and expenses directly or indirectly arising out of or resulting from . . . [their] shipment'. The shipper is so liable irrespective of its knowledge of the dangerous nature of the goods; see *Effort Shipping Co Ltd v Linden Management SA (The Giannis NK)* [1998] 1 Lloyd's Rep 337; [1998] AC 605. But what if another effective cause of the loss is the carrier's want of due diligence in providing an unseaworthy ship?

The Judge held that, as NSC's want of due diligence in failing to render the vessel seaworthy was an effective, albeit not the only, cause of its loss of the ship and most of the cargo, it could not recover damages for, or an indemnity in respect of, that loss against D under art IV, r 6, or at common law . . .

In my view, the Judge was correct for the reasons he gave. The essential question was whether NSC's lack of due diligence in the stowage of the isopentane – breach of contract – causing unseaworthiness in the vessel was an effective cause of the fire in hold 3 and her loss. The Judge held that it was and that, therefore, NSC was not entitled to rely on art IV, r 6, to seek an indemnity against D in respect of loss caused by that breach. It is immaterial that there was another cause or as to which of them was the dominant cause or their respective timings. The principle is the same as that applicable to a breach of art III, r 1, resulting in damage to or loss of cargo where the shipowner pleads an excepted peril under art IV, r 2, where it is for the shipowner to establish that the whole or a specific part of the damage or loss was caused by the excepted peril. See eg *The Torenia* [1983] 2 Lloyd's Rep 210, per Mr Justice Hobhouse at 219. As the House of Lords held in the pre-Hague Rules' case of *Smith Hogg & Co Ltd v Black Sea & Baltic General Insurance Co Ltd* (1940) 67 Ll L Rep 253; [1940] AC 997, the obligation to furnish a seaworthy ship is the 'fundamental obligation' or, now, as Lord Somervell in *Maxine Footwear Co Ltd v Canadian Merchant Marine Ltd* [1959] 2 Lloyd's Rep 105 at p 113; [1959] AC 589 at pp 602–603, and Lord Justice Hirst in *The Fiona*, at p 519, put it, art III, r 1, is the 'overriding' obligation.

As to Mr Macdonald's [counsel] submission that the general rule does not apply where the cooperating causes are concurrent, as causes they are almost never truly concurrent though they may be in their consequences. The unseaworthiness, where it is a co-operating cause of loss, will in all or most cases precede other co-operating causes, since it must exist at the commencement of the voyage . . .

NSC's 'non-delegable' duty of due diligence in respect of D's undeclared and dangerous cargo

. . . Mr Milligan [counsel] submitted that the Judge should have found that NSC had not exercised due diligence in relation to D's undeclared dangerous cargo since it had a non-delegable duty to exercise such due diligence in all the stages of progress of the cargo to shipment. He argued that it was not enough for NSC to show that it could not itself have reasonably known what was in the offending container; it had to establish that due diligence was exercised by all concerned in the manufacture, packing, transport and storage of the cargo before shipment. He said that NSC was thus liable to C, even if not on notice of the undeclared and dangerous cargo, for the acts of D or of some other third party previously concerned with the cargo or D's container, and that it had a corresponding right of indemnity against D as contemplated by art IV, r 2, of the Hague Rules.

The sole authority upon which Mr Milligan relied for that ambitious proposition was *Riverstone Meat Co Pty Ltd v Lancashire Shipping Co Ltd* [1961] 1 Lloyd's Rep 57; [1961] AC 807 . . . :

The Judge, on my reading of his judgment, clearly found it beyond argument that the vessel was unseaworthy because of the dangerous and undeclared cargo on deck. On the evidence before him and on the authorities to which I have referred, I consider that he was right to do so.

As to the separate question of due diligence . . . Lord Keith, in *Riverstone Meat*, at p 87; p 871, described the duty as 'an inescapable personal obligation'. However, it is plain from context of the case – disrepair of a ship – and of his reasoning in the passage from his speech I have set out, that he did not extend it to a responsibility for the conduct of manufacturers or exporters, or of shippers in their stuffing of containers and description of their contents; see also *Maxine Footwear Co Ltd v Canadian Government Merchant Marine Ltd*, per Lord Somervell at p 113; p 602. In my view, there is no warrant in the facts of those cases or the *rationes* of them for extending a carrier's duty of due diligence as to the structure and stowage of its ship to a physical verification of the declared contents of containers or other packaging in which cargo is shipped, unless put on notice to do so. As Mr Macdonald [counsel] observed, in the case of shipper-packed containers – the norm nowadays – the containers are, in any event, closed with a customs seal and not capable of internal examination by the carrier or his agents . . .

Mr Milligan [argued] . . . that where the issue is one of due diligence in providing a seaworthy ship, as distinct from one of the careful handling of cargo, the carrier has an absolute duty rendering it responsible for the misconduct of shippers and others over whom it has no control and whether or not it is on notice of such misconduct.

The difficulty in that submission, as he acknowledged, involves an open ended extension of *Riverstone Meat*, itself an unseaworthiness case, the *ratio* of which was that a carrier cannot absolve itself from its personal duty of due diligence by delegating its responsibility as a carrier to an independent contractor. The shipper's and the carrier's respective orbits of responsibility are normally quite distinct and neither is agent of the other outside its own orbit; cf, per Lord Radcliffe in *Riverstone Meat*, at p 82; p 863. Those responsible for the manufacture, stuffing and shipping of containers are plainly not carrying out any part of the carrier's function for which he should be held responsible. I can find nothing in the Hague Rules or at common law to make a carrier responsible for the unseaworthiness of its vessel resulting from a shipper's misconduct of which it, the carrier, has not been put on notice. Nor can I see any reason in principle or logic why a carrier should be exposed to such an infinite liability in time, place and people. It is not liable for latent defects in a vessel before it acquired it; see *Riverstone Meat, per* Lord Radcliffe at p 85; p 867 and cf *W Angliss & Co (Australia) Pty v Peninsular & Oriental Steam Navigation Co* (1927) 28 Ll L Rep 202; [1927] 2 KB 456. So why, as a matter of unseaworthiness, should it be liable for latent defects in cargo shipped on it?

On the facts found by the Judge – a shipper-packed and sealed container containing undeclared dangerous cargo – he was clearly justified in finding that NSC could not, with the exercise of reasonable skill and care have detected the presence of that cargo. Accordingly, I am of the view that he was justified in holding that NSC had exercised due diligence in this respect . . .

Note

The decision in *The Kapitan Sakharov* followed an earlier case, *The Fiona*, where an explosion occurred while the vessel was preparing to discharge a cargo of fuel oil. The explosion was caused by the ignition of gasses derived partly (and unknown to the carrier) from the cargo and partly from the remains of a previous cargo that the owners had failed to wash from the ship's ducts and lines. Both the parties were therefore at fault. The shipowners claimed an indemnity, under Art IV, r 6, from the shippers of the cargo. The claim failed. It was held that a carrier was not entitled to invoke the indemnity under Art IV, r 6 if he was in breach of his obligation under Art III, r 1 to exercise due diligence to make the vessel seaworthy and that was a total or partial cause of the loss: *Mediterranean Freight Services Ltd v BP Oil International Ltd, The Fiona* [1994] 2 Lloyd's Rep 506, CA.

5.4 Seaworthiness: 'The voyage'

At common law, the carrier's duty to provide a seaworthy ship is not continuous but arises only at particular points of time. It was argued in the next case that the duty under the Rules was no different.

Island Tug and Barge v Makedonia, The Makedonia [1962] P 190

Facts: The plaintiffs shipped timber on board the vessel for carriage from various British Columbian ports to ports in the UK. The bills of lading incorporated the Canadian Water Carriage of Goods Act 1936. The *Makedonia* broke down in mid-ocean and had to take salvage assistance. The plaintiffs brought proceedings to recover the shares of the salvage award which they had had to pay.

Held:

Hewson J: Before proceeding to the consideration of whether the breakdown was caused by actionable fault on the part of the defendants, I propose to decide first what 'voyage' under Article III(1) of the Hague Rules means. There has been much argument about it. Mr Brandon [counsel] submitted that the Hague Rules substituted for the absolute warranty of seaworthiness at each bunkering stage at common law a qualified obligation upon the owners to exercise due diligence to make her seaworthy at each bunkering port. If she was unseaworthy on leaving any bunkering port through defective bunkers being shipped there or through loading good fuel oil into tanks already containing sea water, thereby contaminating the fuel and making it unburnable, the owners are responsible for the lack of diligence on the part of the engineers at the beginning of that stage and they cannot, therefore, rely on the exceptions in Article IV (2) of those Rules.

There is no decision on what is meant or implied by 'voyage' in Article III(1) of the Hague Rules ... In *Northumbrian Shipping Co Ltd v E Timm & Son Ltd* [1939] AC 397 Lord Wright said:

> ... the warranty of seaworthiness is subdivided in respect of bunkers. Instead of a single obligation to make the vessel seaworthy in this respect, which must be satisfied once for all at the commencement of the voyage, there is substituted a recurring obligation at each bunkering port at which the owners or those who act for the owners decide she shall bunker, thereby fixing the particular stage of the voyage.

In the *Northumbrian Shipping Co* case, s 6 of the Canadian Water Carriage of Goods Act 1910, applied. This section provided that if the shipowner exercised due diligence to make the ship in all respects seaworthy and properly manned, he should not be responsible for any loss resulting from faults or errors in the navigation of the ship. The House of Lords held that that qualified obligation, referred to by Mr Brandon, applied to the owners at each bunkering stage, that is, the owners were bound to exercise due diligence regarding bunkers at each stage.

Has the different wording of the Hague Rules or the rules of the Canadian Act of 1936 altered the position? Mr Brandon argued that the importation of the words 'before and at the beginning of the voyage' has added nothing, and that the words are simply declaratory of the law as it was at the time or up to the time the Rules were formulated. In my view, the position in this country before the Carriage of Goods by Sea Act 1924, was clear without any further words. Mr Brandon argued that 'seaworthy at the beginning of the voyage' had already been defined by a long line of cases, and therefore the qualified obligations to use due diligence of seaworthiness at each stage should be read into the words.

... I see no obligation to read into the word 'voyage' a doctrine of stages, but a necessity to define the word itself. The word does not appear in the Canadian Act of 1910. 'Voyage' in this context means what it has always meant; the contractual voyage from the port of loading to the port of discharge as declared in the appropriate bill of lading. The rule says 'voyage' without any qualification such as 'any declared stage thereof'. In my view, the obligation on the shipowner was to exercise due diligence before and at the beginning of sailing from the loading port, to have the vessel adequately bunkered for the first stage to San Pedro, and to arrange for adequate bunkers of a proper kind at San Pedro and other selected intermediate ports on the voyage so that the contractual voyage might be performed. Provided he did that, in my view, he fulfilled his obligation in that respect.

I find that the shipowner exercised due diligence to ensure sufficient and proper bunkers at each stage of the voyage ...

Note

Unseaworthiness: burden of proof. In *Ministry of Food v Reardon-Smith Line* [1951] 2 Lloyd's Rep 265, McNair J said that the burden of proving that loss was caused by unseaworthiness lies on the claimant and that it is not until that burden has been discharged that any question of any burden of proof on the carrier under Art IV, r 1 can arise. This decision was followed and applied in *The Hellenic Dolphin* [1978] 2 Lloyd's Rep 336, which was followed in *The Theodegmon* [1990] 1 Lloyd's Rep 52. If the claimant proves that the vessel was unseaworthy and that the unseaworthiness caused the loss or damage, the burden passes to the defendants to prove that they and those for whom they are responsible exercised due diligence in the relevant respects: *The Toledo* [1995] 1 Lloyd's Rep 40, p 50. In *The Eurasian Dream* [2002] EWHC 118 (Comm), para 123; [2002] 1 Lloyd's Rep 719, Cresswell J made it plain that as regards Art III r 1, the claimant has to show that unseaworthiness was the cause of the damage, not necessarily the sole or even the dominant cause. The extent of the obligation is to exercise due diligence to make the ship seaworthy before and at the beginning of the voyage. Once unseaworthiness is established the burden then passes to the defendant to show that all due diligence has been exercised to make the vessel seaworthy.

6 Article III, rule 2

Subject to the provisions of Art IV, the carrier shall properly and carefully load, handle, stow, carry, keep, care for, and discharge the goods carried.

The extracts reprinted in this section deal with the meaning of the phase 'shall properly and carefully', which gives rise to two questions. Does 'shall' oblige the carrier to undertake – or at least accept liability for – all the activities listed in the rule? Does 'properly' add anything to 'carefully'?

Pyrene Co Ltd v Scindia Navigation Co Ltd [1954] 2 QB 402

Held:

> **Devlin J:** The phrase 'shall properly and carefully load' may mean that the carrier shall load and that he shall do it properly and carefully: or that he shall do whatever loading he does properly and carefully. The former interpretation perhaps fits the language more closely, but the latter may be more consistent with the object of the rules. Their object as it is put, I think correctly, in *Carver's Carriage of Goods by Sea*, 9th ed, 1952, page 186, is to define not the scope of the contract service but the terms on which that service is to be performed. The extent to which the carrier has to undertake the loading of the vessel may depend not only upon different systems of law but upon the custom and practice of the port and the nature of the cargo. It is difficult to believe that the rules were intended to impose a universal rigidity in this respect, or to deny freedom of contract to the carrier. The carrier is practically bound to play some part in the loading and discharging, so that both operations are naturally included in those covered by the contract of carriage. But I see no reason why the rules should not leave the parties free to determine by their own contract the part which each has to play. On this view the whole contract of carriage is subject to the rules, but the extent to which loading and discharging are brought within the carrier's obligations is left to the parties themselves to decide.

Note

This statement was approved by the Court of Appeal in *The Coral* [1993] 1 Lloyd's Rep 1 and by a majority of the House of Lords in *Renton v Palmyra* [1957] AC 149, where it was held that 'shall carry' means no more than 'shall undertake the carrying obligation defined in the contract'; and see note to Art III, r 8, below. *Pyrene* and *Renton v Palmyra* were followed by the Court of Appeal in *Jindal Iron and Steel Co Ltd v Islamic Solidarity Co Jordan Inc* [2003] EWCA Civ 144 where the shipper agreed with the shipowner that the shipper would load a cargo of steel coils and be responsible for any damage in loading and that the receiver would discharge the cargo and be responsible. The cargo was damaged either during loading or discharge. The Court of Appeal held that Art III, r 2 did not compel the shipowner to take responsibility for loading or discharge: 'it simply compels the shipowner to load and unload properly if he undertakes those functions' (*per* Waller LJ, para 47).

Albacora SRL v Wescott & Laurance Line [1966] 2 Lloyd's Rep 53, HL

Facts: The owners of *Maltasian* carried a consignment of wet salted fish from Glasgow to Genoa. Both parties were aware that the vessel's holds were not refrigerated but neither knew that the cargo could not be carried safely at the relevant time of year. The fish deteriorated. The cargo owners argued that the shipowners were in breach of Art III, r 2.

Held:

Lord Reid: . . . The argument is that in this Article 'properly' means in the appropriate manner looking to the actual nature of the consignment, and that it is irrelevant that the shipowner and ship's officers neither knew nor could have discovered that special treatment was necessary. The obligation under the Article is to carry goods properly and if that is not done there is a breach of contract. So it is argued that in the present case it is proved that the only proper way to carry this consignment on this voyage was in a refrigerated hold, and there the obligation of the respondents was to do that, even if the appellants' agents who were parties to the contract were aware that there was no refrigeration in this ship.

This construction of the word 'properly' leads to such an unreasonable result that I would not adopt it if the word can properly be construed in any other sense. The appellants argue that, because the article uses the word 'properly' as well as 'carefully', the word 'properly' must mean something more than carefully. Tautology is not unknown even in international conventions, but I think that 'properly' in this context has a meaning slightly different from 'carefully'. I agree with Viscount Kilmuir LC, that here 'properly' means in accordance with a sound system (*GH Renton & Co Ltd v Palmyra Trading Corporation of Panama* [1957] AC 149, at p 166) and that may mean rather more than carrying the goods carefully. But the question remains by what criteria it is to be judged whether the system was sound.

In my opinion, the obligation is to adopt a system which is sound in light of all the knowledge which the carrier has or ought to have about the nature of the goods. And if that is right, then the respondents did adopt a sound system. They had no reason to suppose that the goods required any different treatment from that which the goods in fact received. That is sufficient to dispose of the appellants' case on breach of contract . . .

Lord Pearce: . . . . The word 'properly' presumably adds something to the word 'carefully'. In *GH Renton & Co Ltd v Palmyra Trading Corporation of Panama* [1957] AC 149, this House construed it as meaning 'upon a sound system'. A sound system does not mean a system suited to all the weaknesses and idiosyncrasies of a particular cargo, but a sound system under all the circumstances in relation to the general practice of carriage of goods by sea. It is tantamount, I think, to efficiency . . .

Lord Pearson: . . . Article III, r 2, is expressly made subject to the provisions of Article IV. The scheme is, therefore, that there is a *prima facie* obligation under Article III, r 2, which may be displaced or modified by some provision of Article IV. Article IV contains many and various provisions, which may have different effects on the *prima facie* obligation arising under Article III, r 2. The convenient first step is to ascertain what is the *prima facie* obligation under Article III, r 2.

It is not an obligation to achieve the desired result, ie the arrival of the goods in an undamaged condition at their destination. It is an obligation to carry out certain operations properly and carefully. The fact that goods, acknowledged in the bill of lading to have been received on board in apparent good order and condition, arrived at the destination in a damaged condition does not in itself constitute a breach of the obligation, though it may well be in many cases sufficient to raise an inference of a breach of the obligation. The cargo owner is not expected to know what happened on the voyage, and, if he shows that the goods arrived in a damaged condition and there is no evidence from the shipowner showing that the goods were duly cared for on the voyage, the court may well infer that the goods were not properly cared for on the voyage.

In *Gosse Millerd v Canadian Government Merchant Marine Ltd* [1927] 2 KB 432, at p 434, Wright J said:

> The words 'properly discharge' in Article III, r 2, mean, I think, 'deliver from the ship's tackle in the same apparent order and condition as on shipment', unless the carrier can excuse himself under Article IV . . .

In my view, that is not the right construction of Article III, r 2. Rightly construed, that rule only provides that the operations referred to, including the operation of discharging the goods, shall be carried out properly and carefully. That this is the right construction appears from the judgment of Mr Justice Devlin in *Pyrene Company Ltd v Scindia Navigation Company Ltd* [1954] 2 QB 402 and from the speeches in the House of Lords in *GH Renton & Co Ltd v Palmyra Trading Corporation of Panama* [1957] AC 149.

. . . The word 'properly' adds something to 'carefully', if 'carefully' has a narrow meaning of merely taking care. The element of skill or sound system is required in addition to taking care. In my opinion, there was no breach of the *prima facie* obligation under Article III, r 2 . . .

(Lord Guest and Lord Upjohn agreed with Lord Reid.)

Notes

1   It might be suggested that the duty properly and carefully to handle and carry the cargo implies a duty to ensure the expeditious delivery of the cargo; hence the carrier could be liable for delays under Art III, r 2. That would be the case even if there is no damage or loss caused; i.e. the carrier could be found liable under the Hague-Visby Rules regime for pure economic loss. (*The Limnos* [2008] EWHC 1036 (Comm)).

2   As to the issue of the burden of proof, it is well-established, since the earliest days of the Rules, that where the cargo owner establishes that the goods were shipped in good order and condition and have been delivered in a damaged condition, that is *prima facie* evidence of a breach of the shipowner's obligations under Art III, r 2 and the onus is then on the shipowner to show that the damage was due to one of the excepted causes in Art IV. If, or to the extent that, the cause of the damage is unexplained, the shipowner will be liable: see *Gosse Millard v Canadian Government Merchant Marine* [1927] 2 KB 432, at 434 and 437, *per* Wright J and [1929] AC 223, at 234, *per* Viscount Sumner. (See also *Ceroilfood Shandong Cereals and Oils and another v Toledo Shipping Corporation* [2006] EWHC 2054 (Comm) and *Exportadora Valle de Colina SA and others v A P Moller Maersk A/S (t/a Maersk Line)* [2010] EWHC 3224 (Comm).)

7   Article III, rule 3: Carrier's duty to issue a bill of lading

The cargo interest relies on a clean bill of lading in order to be paid by the buyer of the goods. The importance of a clean bill of lading is recognised by the Hague-Visby Rules, hence Art III, r 3.

Breffka & Hehnke GmbH & Co KG and others v Navire Shipping Co Ltd and others [2012] All ER (D) 81

Simon J: . . . after shipment of the cargo on board the vessel the Master (or his agent) is bound on demand to issue to the shipper a bill of lading showing 'the apparent order and condition of the goods'.

32. Before he can do that the Master (or his agent) must form an honest and reasonable, non-expert view of the cargo as he sees it and, in particular, as to its apparent order and condition. The Master may ask for expert advice from a surveyor but ultimately it will be a matter of his own judgement on the appearance of the cargo being loaded. See for example *The David Agmashenebeli* [2002] EWHC 104 (Comm), [2003] 1 Lloyd's Rep 92, at 104–6 and *Sea Success Maritime v African Maritime Carriers* [2005] EWHC 1542 (Comm), [2005] 2 Lloyd's Rep 692 at 699.

33. The Bills of Lading in the present case contained a statement on their face that the cargo was shipped 'in apparent good order and condition'. . . . this would [normally] amount to a representation of fact which could be relied on as reflecting the reasonable judgement of a reasonably competent and observant master; see *The David Agmashenebeli* . . . at 106 and Carver, *Bills of Lading*, 3rd Ed. §2–006.

34. In the case of *Tokio Marine & Fire Insurance Company Ltd v Retla Steamship Company* [1970] 2 Lloyd's Rep 91 (US 9th Circuit CA), the Court was concerned with construing provisions as to the apparent good order and condition of the cargo and a Rust clause in the following terms:

> The term 'apparent good order and condition' when used in this Bill of Lading with reference to iron, steel or metal products does not mean that the goods when received, were free of visible rust or moisture. If the shipper so requests, a substitute Bill of Lading will be issued omitting the above definition and setting forth any notations which may appear on the mates' or tally clerks' receipts.

35. These are the words used under the heading 'Retla Clause' in the Mate's Receipts in the present case, although the wording of the RETLA clause in the present case is slightly different.

36. In the *Tokio Marine* case there was rust and wetness which was described in the Mate's receipts as 'heavy rusty', 'white rusty', 'rusty', 'heavy flaky rust' and 'wet before loading.' The US 9th Circuit, having referred to the Privy Council case of *Canada and Dominion Sugar Company Ltd v Canadian National Steamships Ltd* [1947] AC 46, held (p.95-96) held that,

> . . . the bills of lading here, 'read fairly as a whole', show that the term 'good order and condition' was qualified by the clause defining the term with respect to iron, steel or metal products.

37. This part of the reasoning is uncontroversial. The conclusion of the Court is more debateable. Having referred to the fact that the Rust clause appeared boldly and capitalised on the bill of lading and to the shippers' express right to request substitute bills setting out any notations in the Mate's receipts; the Court found that there was no affirmative representation by the owners that the pipe was free of rust or moisture when it was received by the carrier. In summary, all surface rust of whatever degree was excluded from the representation of apparent good order and condition.

38. Mr Swaroop (for the Owners) submitted that English law should follow the *Tokio Marine* case in holding that the RETLA clause was not limited to rust which was in some sense, 'minor' or 'superficial.' He drew attention to the inherent ambiguity and uncertainty of such terms; and referred to *Scrutton on Charterparties* where he submitted the case was cited with approval.

39. In the 21st edition, the editors noted (at Artcle.63 [sic]):

> The practice is now developing of including in the bill of lading a definition of 'good order and condition' which makes it clear that the representation does not imply that the cargo is free from the type of defect which commonly affects the cargo in question, e.g. rust (metal goods) or moisture (timber). There appears to be no reason why these clauses should not be valid: and they do not appear to offend the Hague-Visby Rules.

In the 22nd edition, the editors reframed their view of the law in Article 77 at 8-031,

... wording may clarify (and restrict) the representation being made. Thus, a bill of lading may attest to the apparent good order and condition while including a definition of 'good order and condition' which makes it clear that the representation does not import that the cargo is free from certain defects, often a type of defect that commonly affects the cargo in question, e.g. rust (metal goods) or moisture (timber).

In each of the two editions there is a foot-note reference to the *Tokio Marine* case.

40. For B&H Mr Thomas QC submitted that the RETLA clause did not render the words 'apparent good order and condition' meaningless. The provisions should be read together and each provision given proper effect. To the extent that the RETLA clause was designed to except from liability it should be read restrictively, see for example Aikens and Bools, *Bills of Lading*, 2006 at §4.30 and *Attorney-General of Ceylon v Scindia Steam Navigation Co.Ltd* [1962] AC 60 at 74.

41. He argued that the RETLA clause only excludes (surface) rust which is likely to be found in any normal cargo and which would not detract from its overall quality and affect its merchantability.

42. There would seem to be a number of problems with this formulation, for example: what is the degree of 'surface rust' which falls outside the representation, what is a 'normal' cargo of steel and why is merchantability relevant to the representation by the Master of the carrying vessel?

43. I have come to the following conclusions as to the proper construction of the two provisions in the Bills of Lading.

44. (1) The RETLA clause can and should be construed as a legitimate clarification of what was to be understood by the representation as to the appearance of the steel cargo upon shipment. It should not be construed as a contradiction of the representation as to the cargo's good order and condition, but as a qualification that there was an appearance of rust and moisture of a type which may be expected to appear on any cargo of steel: superficial oxidation caused by atmospheric conditions. The exclusion of 'visible rust or moisture' from the representation as to the good order and condition is thus directed to superficial appearance of a cargo which is difficult, if not impossible, to avoid. It is likely to form the basis of a determination as to whether there has been a further deterioration due to inherent quality of the goods on shipment under s.4(2)(m) of US COGSA, or Article 4(2)(m) of the Hague-Visby Rules.

45. (2) It follows that I reject the Owner's argument, based on the facts of the decision in the *Tokio Marine* case, that the RETLA clause applies to all rust of whatever severity.

46. First, because such a construction would rob the representation as to the good order and condition of the steel cargo on shipment of all effect.

47. Secondly, because of what appears to be a misapprehension as to the nature of the trade. One of the grounds for the decision in the *Tokio Marine* case was that the Rust clause provided that it was always open to the shipper to call for a substitute bill of lading showing the true condition of the cargo as set out in the Mate's Receipt, (see p.961 of the report). However, the objection to this part of the reasoning is that it is highly unlikely that a shipper of cargo would ask for a claused bill of lading reflecting the terms of a Mate's Receipt: rather the contrary, as the present case reveals. The matter has been put in clear and emphatic terms by Professor Michael F Sturley in an article in the 'Journal of Maritime Law and Commerce' (April 2000) pages 245-248.

> Some courts, led by the Ninth Circuit in *Tokio Marine & Fire Insurance Co. v Retla Steamship Co.*, have nevertheless permitted carriers to include standard clauses in their bills of lading that essentially disclaim all responsibility for the required statement. Although COGSA § 3(8) explicitly prohibits any clause lessening a carrier's liability 'otherwise than as provided in this

Act', 'rust clauses' have been justified on the ground that that the shipper had the option of demanding a different bill of lading that did not contain the offending clause. In practice, such a demand would be unlikely, for the typical effect of a rust clause is to permit a seller to ship rusty steel to its customer while still obtaining the 'clean' bill of lading that enable it to be paid under a letter of credit.

...

Permitting the carrier to escape liability for the statement of apparent order and condition undermines the Hague Rules' goal of protecting the bill of lading as a commercial document on which third parties can rely. Indeed, one of the principal abuses that the Hague Rules were intended to correct was the carriers' use of 'reservation clauses' to exonerate themselves from responsibility for the description of the goods. Thus the rules required the bill of lading (if one were issued) to include the specified information without reservation unless the exception (found in the proviso to COGSA § 3(3)) applied. A carrier's use of a reservation clause when the exception did not apply would be 'null and void' under COGSA § 3(8).

...

The phrase 'on demand of the shipper,' upon which the Retla court relied so heavily, does not alter the carrier's obligation to include the information required by COGSA § 3(3) wherever it does issue a bill of lading.

48. This critical analysis of the *Tokio Marine* case is supported by Professor John F Wilson in 'Carriage of Goods by Sea' 4th edition at p.131 and by the author of the 4th edition of 'Marine Cargo Claims', Professor William Tetley QC, in a highly unfavourable analysis at p.698-9.

49. (3) If the *Tokio Marine* case had been consistently followed since 1970 the advantages of giving similar effect to mercantile clauses in different jurisdictions might have been a reason for following it now. However, although the researches of counsel have not been exhaustive, Professor Sturley's article suggests that the decision has not been consistently followed; and this impression is reinforced by a bulletin issued by the UK P&I Club (221-11/01). After referring to the reason why US Courts have upheld the Retla Clause, the bulletin continues.

However, there remains a risk to Members using such clauses as, whilst some courts in the United States may have upheld the clause, other U.S. courts and courts in other jurisdictions have not. The only safe means of avoiding claims arising from pre-shipment damage is to ensure that the bill of lading is claused to reflect the apparent order and condition of the goods at the time of loading. Failure to properly describe the condition of the cargo leaves the carrier open to allegations of being a party to a misrepresentation, particularly from third-party purchasers of the cargo who have only contracted to do so based on a bill of lading and who have not been shown any pre-shipment survey by the sellers.

The final sentence is both accurate and pertinent.

There is little authority in English law dealing with the liability of a carrier who unnecessarily clauses a bill of lading. In *The David Agmashenebeli*, the court concluded that the carrier's duty is limited to making and expressing an honest and reasonable assessment of the goods.

The David Agmashenebeli [2002] EWHC 104 (Comm); [2003] 1 Lloyd's Rep 92

Facts: A bulk cargo of urea was carried from Kotka, Finland, to Behai, South China. Despite protests, the shipowners insisted that the bills of lading must be claused: 'cargo discoloured also foreign materials eg Plastic, Rust, Rubber, Stone, Black particles found in cargo'. The contract for the sale of the urea provided for payment against clean bills of lading. The buyer's bank declined to accept the claused bills when they were presented. Terms of settlement were agreed between buyer and seller and the cargo was released to the buyer at a reduced price, the market price having fallen. The shippers brought proceedings against the shipowners alleging that the bills had been improperly claused and that they had suffered damage as a result. The total overall discoloration in the cargo was found to be about 1% and the quantity of contaminants miniscule.

Held:

> **Colman J:** . . . Clean bills of lading are essential documents for the purpose of triggering the right to receive payment under documentary credits issued in respect of contracts for the international sale of goods. If claused bills of lading are presented under such documentary credits they will ordinarily be rejected by the buyers' banks and sellers will be unable to obtain payment in the absence of special agreements with the buyers to permit the banks to make payment. Indeed, the inability of sellers to present clean bills of lading may operate as a repudiatory breach of the sale contract . . .

The clausing issue: Discussion

It is necessary to keep in mind two areas of distinction which underlie the analysis of this issue.

Firstly, a bill of lading has two distinct functions: (i) as evidence of the contract of carriage and (ii) as a receipt and document of title to the goods laden on board.

Secondly, whether the carrier's duty in respect of the statement in the bill of lading as to the apparent order and condition is of a contractual nature is a distinct issue from the question what scope that duty has and in particular whether it is duty of care or analogous to a duty of care or whether it is merely a duty honestly to state the apparent order and condition of the goods.

The starting point in this analysis is to identify the function of the statement of the order and condition of the goods in a bill of lading. For this purpose it is necessary to go back to the issue of the bill. It is the shipper or the shipper's agent who in the ordinary way tenders the bill to the carrier or the carrier's agent, usually the master, for signature. In so doing, the shipper invites the carrier to acknowledge the truth of the statement in the tendered bill as to the order and condition of the goods which the shipper has delivered into the possession of the carrier pursuant to the contract of affreightment. In determining whether the carrier by the master's or other agent's signature accepts contractual responsibility for the accuracy of the statement as to the condition of the goods it is relevant to take account of the fact that it is the shipper or his agent who is delivering the goods and that accordingly any such statement would be as to facts of which he must already have actual or imputed knowledge. Further, because the shipper already has that knowledge he cannot be said to rely on the accuracy of the statement. His requirement goes no further than the need to obtain from the carrier a receipt for the goods in appropriate form. The tender for signature of a bill which states the order and condition of the goods is thus an invitation to the carrier to express his acknowledgment of the truth of the statements in the bill. As such it is an invitation to make a representation of fact as distinct from a binding promise as to the accuracy of the represented facts. The purpose of making that representation is to record the carrier's evidence as to his receipt of the goods and as to their apparent condition when he did receive them for carriage. Given that bills of lading are negotiable instruments, the specific function of recording that evidence is to inform subsequent holders of the facts represented, for those facts are likely to be relevant to their exercise of contractual rights against sellers of the goods or, indeed, the carriers themselves.

Against this background, it is not difficult to see why it has been said in many of the authorities on the Harter Act, the Hague Rules and the Hague-Visby Rules that those codes stop short of imposing on the carrier any contractual obligation as to the accuracy of that which is stated in the bill as to the order and condition of the goods.

Moreover, the wording of Article III Rules 3, 4 and 5 of the Hague Rules and their successor, the Hague-Visby Rules, is clearly consistent with this analysis. It imposes a contractual duty to issue a bill of lading containing the information specified but by Rule 4 provides only that such statements are to be *prima facie* evidence of the facts stated . . .

That the effect of Article III Rule 3 is to impose *some* contractual duty on the carrier is beyond argument. The master or carrier's agent must at least issue to the shipper on demand a bill of lading showing the specified information. Refusal to issue any bill of lading accurate or not in respect of the goods received on board would thus be a breach of the contract of carriage in respect of which the shipowner would be liable to the shipper. But that duty is more specifically defined in as much as Rule 3(a), (b) and (c) specify those matters which the bill of lading is required to show, including 'the apparent order and condition of the goods'.

A refusal to issue a bill which made any statement as to the apparent order and condition of the goods would thus be a failure to comply with the contractual obligation imposed by the rule.

If there is a contractual obligation to the shipper that the bill of lading should state the apparent order and condition of the goods, how is that duty to be performed? In my judgment, the general effect of the authorities is that the duty requires that the master should make up his mind whether in all the circumstances the cargo, in so far as he can see it in the course and circumstances of loading, appears to satisfy the description of its apparent order and condition in the bills of lading tendered for signature. If in doubt, a master may well consider it appropriate to ask his owners to provide him with expert advice, but that is a matter for his judgment. In the normal case, however, he will be entitled to form his own opinion from his own observations and the failure to ask for expert advice is unlikely to be a matter of criticism. For this purpose the law does not cast upon the master the role of an expert surveyor. He need not possess any greater knowledge or experience of the cargo in question than any other reasonably careful master. What he is required to do is to exercise his own judgment on the appearance of the cargo being loaded. If he honestly takes the view that it is not or not all in apparent good order and condition and that is a view that could properly be held by a reasonably observant master, then, even if not all or even most such masters would necessarily agree with him, he is entitled to qualify to that effect the statement in the bill of lading. This imposes on the master a duty of a relatively low order but capable of objective evaluation . . . In so far as the observations of the Court of Appeal in *The Arctic Trader* [1996] 2 Lloyd's Rep 449, which were strictly *obiter*, suggest any higher duty on the master, I am not persuaded that they accurately express the effect of Article III Rule 3.

Likewise, the extent to which and the terms in which the master considers it appropriate to qualify the bills of lading statement as to the order and condition of the cargo is again a matter for his judgment. Reasonably careful masters might use different words to describe the reason why and the extent to which the cargo was not in their view in apparent good order and condition. In many cases they may only have a limited command of English and little knowledge of the nature of the cargo. The approach which, in my judgment, properly reflects the master's duty is that the words used should have a range of meaning which reflects reasonably closely the actual apparent order and condition of the cargo and the extent of any defective condition which he, as a reasonable observant master, considers it to have.

Against this background, the shipowners' duty is to issue a bill of lading which records the apparent order and condition of the goods according to the reasonable assessment of the master. That is not, as I have indicated, any contractual guarantee of absolute accuracy as to the order and condition of the cargo or its apparent order and condition. There is no basis, in my judgment, for the implication of any such term either on the proper construction of Article III Rule 3 or at common law. The shipper is taken to know the actual apparent order and condition of his own cargo. What the Hague-Visby Rules require is no more than that the bill of lading in its capacity of a receipt expresses that which is apparent to the master or other agent of the carrier, according to his own reasonable assessment . . .

Notes

1   On the facts, Colman J concluded that the actual pre-loading condition of the cargo did not justify the language used in the bills of lading, but equally did not justify the issue of clean bills. An appropriate clause would also have led to the rejection of the bills by the buyer's bank, so that the shipper could not show that the master's acts had caused them any loss.

2   On the law, Colman J rejected alternative submissions that a higher duty of care should be implied as a term of the contract or arose by virtue of the bailment relationship. A claim that the carrier was liable in tort for failure to take reasonable care not to misrepresent the apparent order and condition of the goods was also rejected on the grounds that tort liability would inhibit masters, might cause delay and should not be superadded to the international code contained in the Hague and Hague-Visby Rules: 'At least where the Hague Rules or Hague-Visby Rules govern the bills of lading, the third "test" in *Caparo v Dickman* [1990] 2 AC 605 – that it is fair, just and reasonable to impose a duty of care in all the circumstances – is not satisfied.'

3   In *The Arctic Trader*, referred to in the extract above, it was held in the High Court that no term could be implied into a time charter that the shipowner would take reasonable care to clause mate's receipts if the cargo was not in apparent good order and condition. The Court of Appeal concluded that the existence of such a duty was not relevant on the facts because the shipowner could not have been in breach of it. But in the course of the judgment it was said that 'one should not, in our judgment, lose sight of the fact that the duty is to make an accurate statement in the circumstances of the case'.

4   See further, Parker, B, 'Liability for incorrectly clausing bills of lading' (2003) LMCLQ 201.

8 Article III, rule 6: Time limit on suits

Subject to para 6 *bis* the carrier and the ship shall in any event be discharged from all liability whatsoever in respect of the goods, unless suit is brought within one year of their delivery or of the date when they should have been delivered. This period may, however, be extended if the parties so agree after the cause of action has arisen.

Transworld Oil (USA) Inc v Minos Compania Naviera SA, The Leni [1992] 2 Lloyd's Rep 486

Held:

> **Judge Diamond QC:** There were a number of objectives which Article III, r 6 sought to achieve; first, to speed up the settlement of claims and to provide carriers with some protection against stale and therefore unverifiable claims; second, to achieve international uniformity in relation to prescription periods; third, to prevent carriers from relying on 'notice-of-claim' provisions as an absolute bar to proceedings or from inserting clauses in their bills of lading requiring proceedings to be issued within short periods of less than one year.

Compania Portorafti Commerciale SA v Ultramar Panama Inc,
The Captain Gregos [1990] 1 Lloyd's Rep 310, CA

Facts: See Chapter 7, section 3.6, above. Cargo owners alleged that part of a cargo of crude oil had been deliberately misappropriated by the carrier and argued that the time bar could not be invoked in response to such a claim.

Held:

Bingham LJ: . . . Article III, r 6 provides that the carrier and the ship shall:' . . . *in any event* be discharged from *all liability whatsoever in respect of the goods* (my emphasis) unless suit is brought within the year.' I do not see how any draftsman could use more emphatic language . . . I would hold that 'all liability whatsoever in respect of the goods' means exactly what it says. The inference that the one-year time bar was intended to apply to all claims arising out of the carriage (or miscarriage) of goods by sea under bills subject to the Hague-Visby Rules is in my judgment strengthened by the consideration that Article III, r 6 is, like any time bar, intended to achieve finality and, in this case, enable the shipowner to clear his books (*The Aries* [1977] 1 Lloyd's Rep 334 at p 336) . . .

There is an obvious attraction in the argument that a party should not be able to rely on a one-year time bar to defeat a claim based on his own dishonesty. It is, however, to be remembered that claims such as these are made not infrequently (although how often they are established I do not know). I would moreover be slow to suppose that the experienced shipping interests represented at the conferences which led to these rules were not alert to the possibility of almost any form of skulduggery. But I think the rules themselves provide the solution. If damage to the goods is caused by wilful or reckless misconduct the shipowner loses the benefit of the financial limitation (Article IV, r 5(e)). If a servant or agent of the carrier damages the goods by wilful or reckless misconduct he cannot rely on the provisions of Article IV (Article IV *bis*, r 4), although still perhaps able to rely on the time bar (see the commentary in *Scrutton* at p 459). There is, however, no provision which deprives the shipowner of his right to rely on the time bar, even where he has been guilty of wilful or reckless misconduct. I cannot regard the omission as other than deliberate. This approach gains some small support from the Court of Appeal decision in *The Antares* [1978] 1 Lloyd's Rep 424.

I would be more reluctant to accept the shipowners' argument if I thought it would lead to injustice. A limitation provision can lead to injustice if a party's cause of action may be barred before he knows he has it. But that should not, as it seems to me, happen here. A cargo owner should know whether he has received short delivery at or about the time of delivery. With a cargo of crude oil such as this he will quickly be able to consider, and if necessary investigate, whether the shortage is reasonably explicable by evaporation, wastage, clingage, unpumpable residue etc. He can investigate what quantity was loaded. If he finds an unjustifiable shortage during carriage he is in a position to sue, and it is not crucial how or why the shortage occurred. He should be ready to sue well within the year, as the rules intend. The only reason why the cargo owners seek to found on the shipowners' alleged misconduct rather than on the breaches of the rules is, as I infer, that for whatever reason they let the year pass without bringing suit. That is in my view precisely the result the rules were intended to preclude.

For these reasons I differ from the judge and conclude that he was wrong to make the declaration he did on the ground he did. In reaching my conclusion I am not greatly influenced by the *travaux preparatoires*, which seem to me to have been concentrating on a different problem namely delivery to a party who does not present the bills, but I hold the view, if it be relevant, that the *travaux* certainly do disclose the legislative intention which the judge found. I am pleased to find that my conclusions broadly reflect those of Mr Brian Davenport QC in the *Law Quarterly Review* (vol 105, p 521, October, 1989) . . .

Notes

1   *Time bar: terminus a quo.* Where goods are not loaded, time begins to run from the moment the goods ought to have been delivered, assuming the loading obligation had been fulfilled: *The Ot Sonja* [1993] 2 Lloyd's Rep 435, CA.

2   *Time bar: 'suit'.* The commencement of an arbitration is a 'suit' within the meaning of Art III, r 6: *The Merak* [1965] P 223, CA.

3   *Time bar: 'brought'.* This means brought by a competent plaintiff (*Compania Columbiana de Seguros v Pacific Steam Navigation Co* [1965] 1 QB 101) in a competent court (*The Nordglimpt* [1988] QB 183) and brought to enforce a relevant claim (*The Leni* [1992] 2 Lloyd's Rep 48).

4   *Time bar: effect.* In *The Aries* [1977] 1 Lloyd's Rep 334, the House of Lords held that the effect of Art III, r 6 of the Hague Rules is to extinguish the claim (that is to say the substantive claim), not merely to bar the remedy while leaving the claim against the carrier in existence (see also *Röhlig (UK) Ltd v Rock Unique Ltd* [2011] EWCA Civ 18 where a contractual clause using similar language was held to be an attempt to extinguish substantive liability and not merely a procedural time bar provision). Nevertheless, the time bar does not prevent a carrier's negligence being relied on as a defence to a claim by the carrier to be indemnified under Art IV, r 6: *The Fiona* (above). And see *Goulandris v Goldman* [1958] 1 QB 74.

9 Article III, rule 8

Any clause, covenant, or agreement in a contract of carriage relieving the carrier or the ship from liability for loss or damage to, or in connection with, goods arising from negligence, fault, or failure in the duties and obligations provided in this article or lessening such liability otherwise than as provided in these Rules, shall be null and void and of no effect. A benefit of insurance in favour of the carrier or similar clause shall be deemed to be a clause relieving the carrier from liability.

It is not always immediately clear whether a contractual clause has the effect of relieving the carrier from liability provided for by the Hague-Visby Rules.

The Hollandia [1983] 1 AC 565

Facts: The respondents shipped machinery on the appellants' vessel *Haico Holwerda* at Leith for carriage to Bonaire in the Netherlands Antilles. A through bill of lading, providing for transhipment at Amsterdam, was issued. The cargo was damaged during the course of discharge at Bonaire as a result of the negligence of the servants of the carrying vessel which for the ocean leg of the voyage was a ship under the Norwegian flag, the *Morviken*, of which the carriers were charterers. The shippers commenced an action *in rem* in the High Court against the *Hollandia*, a sister ship of the *Haico Holwerda*. The carriers sought to stay proceedings on the grounds that the bill of lading included a choice of forum clause that provided for the exclusive jurisdiction of the Court of Amsterdam. The bill of lading also provided that the proper law of the contract should be the law of the Netherlands and stated 'The maximum liability per package is DFL 1,250' (para 1, condition 2). It was common ground that if the dispute was tried by a Dutch court, that court would apply Dutch law and the Hague Rules limit of liability, which would limit recovery to £250, but that if an English court tried it, the Hague-Visby limit would be £11,000.

Held:

Lord Diplock: My Lords, the provisions in section 1 of the Act . . . appear to me to be free from any ambiguity perceptible to even the most ingenious of legal minds. The Hague-Visby Rules, or rather all those of them that are included in the Schedule, are to have the force of law in the United Kingdom: they are to be treated as if they were part of directly enacted statute law. But since they form part of an international convention which must come under the consideration of foreign as well as English courts, it is, as Lord Macmillan said of the Hague Rules themselves in *Stag Line Ltd v Foscolo, Mango and Co Ltd* [1932] AC 328, 350:

> desirable in the interests of uniformity that their interpretation should not be rigidly controlled by domestic precedents of antecedent date, but rather that the language of the rules should be construed on broad principles of general acceptance.

They should be given a purposive rather than a narrow literalistic construction, particularly wherever the adoption of a literalistic construction would enable the stated purpose of the international convention, *viz*, the unification of domestic laws of the contracting states relating to bills of lading, to be evaded by the use of colourable devices that, not being expressly referred to in the Rules, are not specifically prohibited.

The bill of lading issued to the shippers by the carriers upon the shipment of the goods at the Scottish port of Leith was one to which the Hague-Visby Rules were expressly made applicable by Article X; it fell within both paragraph (a) and paragraph (b); it was issued in a contracting state, the United Kingdom, and it covered a contract for carriage from a port in a contracting state. For good measure, it also fell directly within s 1(3) of the Act of 1971 itself.

The first paragraph of condition 2 of the bill of lading, prescribing as it does for a per package maximum limit of liability on the part of the carriers for loss or damage arising from negligence or breach of contract instead of the higher per kilogram maximum applicable under the Hague-Visby Rules, is *ex facie* a clause in a contract of carriage which purports to lessen the liability of the carriers for such loss or damage otherwise than is provided in the Hague-Visby Rules. As such it is therefore rendered null and void and of no effect under Article III, paragraph 8. So much indeed was conceded by counsel for the carriers, subject to a possible argument to the contrary which was briefly mentioned but not elaborated upon. I shall have to revert to this argument later, but can do so with equal brevity ...

[The carriers argued for a stay on the grounds that a choice of forum clause] is to be classified as a clause which only prescribes the procedure by which disputes arising under the contract of carriage are to be resolved. It does not *ex facie* deal with liability at all and so does not fall within the description 'Any clause, covenant, or agreement in a contract of carriage ... lessening ... liability', so as to bring it within Article III, paragraph 8; even though the consequence of giving effect to the clause will be to lessen, otherwise than is provided in the Hague-Visby Rules, the liability of the carrier for loss or damage to or in connection with the goods arising from negligence, fault or failure in the duties and obligations provided in the Rules.

My Lords, like all three members of the Court of Appeal, I have no hesitation in rejecting this narrow construction of Article III, paragraph 8, which looks solely to the form of the clause in the contract of carriage and wholly ignores its substance. The only sensible meaning to be given to the description of provisions in contracts of carriage which are rendered 'null and void and of no effect' by this rule is one which would embrace every provision in a contract of carriage which, if it were applied, would have the effect of lessening the carrier's liability otherwise than as provided in the Rules. To ascribe to it the narrow meaning for which counsel contended would leave it open to any shipowner to evade the provisions of Article III, paragraph 8 by the simple device of inserting in his bills of lading issued in, or for carriage from a port in, any contracting state a clause in standard form providing as the exclusive forum for resolution of disputes what might aptly be described as a court of convenience, *viz*, one situated in a country which did not apply the Hague-Visby Rules or, for that matter, a country whose law recognised an unfettered right in a shipowner by the terms of the bill of lading to relieve himself from all liability for loss or damage to the goods caused by his own negligence, fault or breach of contract.

My Lords, unlike the first paragraph of condition 2 a choice of forum clause, such as that appearing in the third paragraph, does not *ex facie* offend against Article III, paragraph 8. It is a provision of the contract of carriage that is subject to a condition subsequent; it comes into operation only upon the occurrence of a future event that may or may not occur, *viz*, the coming into existence of a dispute between the parties as to their respective legal rights and duties under the contract which they are unable to settle by agreement. There may be some disputes that would bring the choice of forum clause into operation but which would not be concerned at all with negligence fault or failure by the carrier or the ship in the duties and obligations provided by article III; a claim for unpaid freight is an obvious example. So a choice of forum clause which selects as the exclusive forum for the resolution of disputes a court which will not apply the Hague-Visby Rules, even after such clause has come into operation, does not necessarily always have the effect of lessening the liability of the carrier in a way that attracts the application of Article III, paragraph 8.

My Lords, it is, in my view, most consistent with the achievement of the purpose of the Act of 1971 that the time at which to ascertain whether a choice of forum clause will have an effect that is proscribed by Article III, paragraph 8 should be when the condition subsequent is fulfilled and the carrier seeks to bring the clause into operation and to rely upon it. If the dispute is about duties and obligations of the carrier or ship that are referred to in that rule and it is established as a fact (either by evidence or as in the instant case by the common agreement of the parties) that the foreign court chosen as the exclusive forum would apply a domestic substantive law which would result in limiting the carrier's liability to a sum lower than that to which he would be entitled if Article IV, paragraph 5 of the Hague-Visby Rules applied, then an English court is in my view commanded by the Act of 1971 to treat the choice of forum clause as of no effect.

The rule itself speaks of a proscribed provision in a contract of carriage as a 'clause, covenant, or agreement in a contract of carriage' and describes the effect of the rule on the offending provision as being to render it 'null and void and of no effect'. These pleonastic expressions occurring in an international convention (of which the similarly pleonastic version in the French language is of equal authenticity) are not to be construed as technical terms of legal art. It may well be that if they were to be so construed the most apt to be applied to a choice of forum clause when brought into operation by the occurrence of a particular dispute would be the expression 'of no effect', but it is no misuse of ordinary language to describe the clause in its application to the particular dispute as being *pro tanto* 'null' or 'void' or both ...

As foreshadowed at an earlier point in this speech I must return in a brief postscript to an argument based on certain passages in an article by a distinguished commentator, Dr FA Mann, 'Statutes and the Conflict of Laws' which appeared in (1972–73) 46 BYIL 117, and which, it is suggested, supports the view that even a choice of substantive law, which excludes the application of the Hague-Visby Rules, is not prohibited by the Act of 1971 notwithstanding that the bill of lading is issued in and is for carriage from a port in, the United Kingdom. The passages to which our attention was directed by counsel for the carriers I find myself (apparently in respectable academic company) unable to accept. They draw no distinction between the Act of 1924 and the Act of 1971 despite the contrast between the legislative techniques adopted in the two Acts, and the express inclusion in the Hague-Visby Rules of Article X (absent from the Hague Rules), expressly applying the Hague-Visby Rules to every bill of lading falling within the description contained in the article, which article is given the force of law in the United Kingdom by section 1(2) of the Act of 1971. The Act of 1971 deliberately abandoned what may conveniently be termed the 'clause paramount' technique employed in section 3 of the Act of 1924, the Newfoundland counterpart of which provided the occasion for wide-ranging *dicta* in the opinion of the Privy Council delivered by Lord Wright in *Vita Food Products Inc v Unus Shipping Co Ltd* [1939] AC 277.

Although the actual decision in that case would have been the same if the relevant Newfoundland statute had been in the terms of the Act of 1971, those *dicta* have no application to the construction of the latter Act and this has rendered it no longer necessary to embark upon what I have always found to be an unrewarding task of trying to ascertain precisely what those *dicta* meant. I would dismiss this appeal.

Note

Liberty clauses. The holders of bills of lading argued that a clause that permitted discharge at a substitute port, including the port of loading, in the event of a strike, was a clause that purported to relieve the carrier from loss arising from failure in the duty 'properly to carry ... and discharge the goods carried' (Art III, r 2) and so was rendered null and void by Art III, r 8. The House of Lords rejected this claim on the grounds that:

(a) Art III, r 2 did not require goods to be transported from one place to another if the contract said they need not be moved in a certain event;

(b) the obligation to 'discharge properly' meant 'in accordance with a sound system' and not at a particular place (*per* Viscount Kilmuir LC);

(c) the clause did not purport to extend the power to deviate permitted by the Rules, but rather defined the contractual voyage to be performed in certain circumstances: *GH Renton & Co Ltd v Palmyra Trading Corporation of Panama*. (For the facts and the decision of the House of Lords in this case on the construction of the liberty clause, see Chapter 2, section 36, above.)

As to whether Art III, r 8 could be relied on when a *Himalaya* clause is in issue, there is useful guidance from the following case.

Whitesea Shipping and Trading Corporation and another v El Paso Rio Clara Ltd and others, The Marielle Bolten [2009] EWHC 2552 (Comm)

Facts: The contract of carriage contained a Himalaya clause (Clause 3b) which read: '[1] The merchant undertakes that no claims or allegations shall be made against any servant, agent, stevedore or subcontractor of the carrier which imposes or attempts to impose upon any of them or any vessel owned or chartered by any of them any liability whatsoever in connection with the goods, [2] and if such claim or allegation should nevertheless be made, to indemnify the carrier against all consequences thereof. [3] Without prejudice to the foregoing, every servant, agent, stevedore and subcontractor shall have the benefit of all provisions herein benefiting the carrier as if such provisions were expressly for their benefit, and all limitations of and exonerations from liability provided to the carrier by law and by the terms hereof shall be available to them, and in entering into this contract the carrier, to the extent of those provisions, does so not only on its own behalf, but also as agent and trustee for such servants, agents, stevedores and subcontractors.'

The question was whether the clause was in breach of Art III, r 8.

(Note: For simplicity, the claimants were the owners; the defendants were the cargo interests and their insurers.)

Held:

Flaux J: [21] The Claimants' case against the insurer Defendants for present purposes is straightforward. They contend that each of the third parties being sued by the insurer Defendants in Brazil is either their servant or agent or a sub-contractor within the wide definition of 'sub-contractor' in cl 1f. By virtue of the first part of cl 3b, all the insurer Defendants are bound in equity (as subrogated insurers) by a covenant to the Claimants that they will not sue those third parties and the proceedings in Brazil are vexatious. The Claimants are entitled to enforce that covenant by injunction, since they can show a sufficient practical interest in the enforcement of the covenant: see the decision of Ackner J as he then was in *The Elbe Maru* [1978] 1 Lloyd's Rep 206 at 209–210.

The insurer defendants' objection: The application of Art III, r 8
[22] Mr Jacobs contends that the Claimants cannot rely upon the first part of cl 3b, because it is equivalent to conferring on the third parties a blanket immunity from liability, which is contrary to Art III, r 8 of the Hague Rules. That provides as follows:

'Any clause, covenant or agreement in a contract of carriage relieving the carrier or the ship from liability for loss or damage to or in connection with the goods, arising from negligence, fault, or failure in the duties and obligations provided in this section, or lessening such liability otherwise than as provided in this chapter, shall be null and void and of no effect.'

[23] The reasoning by which Mr Jacobs urges that conclusion runs thus:

(1)   The first part of cl 3b is a covenant not to sue given not only to the Claimants as carriers but to any third party who falls within the third part of the clause, the so-called Himalaya contract. One of the provisions of which the third party has the benefit by virtue of the third part of the clause is the first part of the clause.

(2)   Once the third party is performing 'carriage' obligations (as it is alleged the third parties who are being sued in Brazil were), then, even though the third party is not actually a party to the bill of lading contract, the Himalaya contract is itself a contract of carriage which is subject to the Hague Rules.

(3)   The effect of entitling either the carrier under the bill of lading contract or the third party to enforce the covenant not to sue in the first part of cl 3b would be to confer blanket immunity upon the third party, which is contrary to Art III, r 8 of the Hague Rules to which the Himalaya contract is subject. Accordingly, the first part of cl 3b is null and void and of no effect.

[24] This argument relies heavily on the decision of the House of Lords in *The Starsin* [2003] UKHL 12, [2004] 1 AC 715, [2003] 1 All ER (Comm) 625, which it will thus be necessary to look at in a little detail. That was a somewhat unusual case in the sense that it was the shipowners who had performed the actual carriage of the goods who were seeking to contend that they were under no liability. The vessel was on time charter to a charterer, CPS, which subsequently became insolvent. The cargo having suffered damage on the voyage, the cargo interests sued the owner and demise charterer of the vessel.

[25] The judge at first instance, Colman J concluded that the bills of lading were charterers' bills so that the relevant contract of carriage was with CPS. Rix LJ in the Court of Appeal agreed, but the other members of the Court of Appeal (Sir Andrew Morritt V-C and Chadwick LJ) concluded that they were owners' bills so that the owners were parties to the contract of carriage. The House of Lords considered that the bills were charterers' bills and the contract of carriage was with CPS.

[26] The owners were contending that the clause in the bill of lading which corresponded with cl 3 in the bills of lading in the present case conferred a complete immunity from liability on them as independent contractors. The clause in that case was not in the same terms as cl 3b in the present case. It provided:

(1)   'It is hereby expressly agreed that no servant or agent of the carrier (including any person who performs work on behalf of the vessel on which the goods are carried or of any of the other vessels of the carrier, their cargo, their passengers or their baggage, including towage of and assistance and repairs to the vessels and including every independent contractor from time to time employed by the carrier) shall in any circumstances whatsoever be under any liability whatsoever to the shipper, for any loss, damage or delay of whatsoever kind arising or resulting directly or indirectly from any act neglect or default on his part while acting in the course of or in connection with his employment and,

(2)   without prejudice to the generality of the provisions in this Bill of Lading, every exemption limitation, condition and liberty herein contained and every right exemption from liability, defence and immunity of whatsoever nature applicable to the carrier or to which the carrier is entitled hereunder shall also be available to and shall extend to protect every such servant or agent of the carrier [*] is or shall be deemed to be acting on behalf of and for the benefit of all persons who are or might be his servants or agents (including any person who performs work on behalf of the vessel on which the goods are carried or of any of the other vessels of the carrier, their cargo, their passengers or their baggage, including towage of and assistance and repairs to the vessels and including every independent contractor from time to time employed by the carrier)

(3) and all such persons shall to this extent be deemed to be parties to the contract contained in or evidenced by this Bill of Lading.

(4) The shipper shall indemnify the carrier against any claim by third parties against whom the carrier cannot rely on these conditions, in as far as the carrier's liability would be excepted if said parties over bound by these conditions.'

[27] The numbering within the clause was that adopted by their Lordships for ease of reference, as I have adopted in relation to the present clause. It will be immediately apparent that there are two principal distinctions between that clause and the present clause, that the first part of that clause does not in terms set out an undertaking or covenant not to sue and that the present clause does not contain a 'deeming provision' such as is contained in the third part of the clause in that case.

[28] The Court of Appeal in *The Starsin* [2001] EWCA Civ 56, [2001] 1 All ER (Comm) 455, [2001] 1 Lloyd's Rep 437 had upheld Colman J's conclusion at first instance that, despite the absence of express words to that effect, the first part of the clause was a covenant not to sue, which inured only to the benefit of the carrier under the bill of lading, not also to the benefit of third parties who fell within the Himalaya part of the clause. The fullest exposition of this conclusion is in the judgment of Rix LJ at paras 115 to 117 of his judgment:

'**115** Mr Jacobs on behalf of the Claimants, on the other hand, submits that part 1 of the clause applies only to the carrier, who alone is entitled to enforce by means of this provision a total prohibition on any collateral attack on him by means of any suit by the shipper against third parties; that it is only part 2 with its more limited exemption that applies to such third parties and that the introductory words are intended to signify the insulation of part 2 from part 1; that the words of part 3 look back ("to this extent") to the words of part 2 and not to the clause as a whole; and that, in accordance with the purpose of the clause as a whole, which is to extend to third parties the protection enjoyed by the carrier under the bill of lading, no less and no more, the Hague Rules paramount provision contained in article III, rule 8, incorporated with the rest of the Hague Rules, ensures that third parties, like the carrier itself, cannot enjoy a blanket exclusion of liability.

116 Colman J preferred the submissions of the Claimants to those of the owner (see at 99/100) and I agree. The essence of the matter is that part 1 of the clause does not give to the carrier a personal blanket exemption of liability, which is then extended to third parties within the clause, but is only concerned with granting to the carrier an exceptional right, not granted to any other party, to enforce, if necessary by injunction, a complete prohibition on any suit by holders of the bill against third parties within the clause: see *Nippon Yusen Kaisha v International Import & Export Co Ltd (The Elbe Maru)* [1978] 1 Lloyd's Rep 206. I do not think I can put the various considerations better than Colman J has put them himself, but I would seek to refer to them briefly as follows:

(1) There is no sign in the leading cases on the Himalaya clause, *The Eurymedon*, *The New York Star*, and *The Makhutai*, each of them in the Privy Council, of any reliance on part 1 of the clause or of finding there a complete exemption of liability for the benefit of third parties. Mr Berry submits that that is not surprising in that at any rate the first two of those cases relied on the bills' Hague Rules one year time bar – and that a time bar is as good as a blanket exemption, so that there was no need to raise an additional point under part 1 of the clause. That may be so, but it does not explain why the additional point was not taken, if there to be taken, nor why in *The New York Star* at 142E/F and again at 143E/F Lord Wilberforce explained the function of the Himalaya clause, which was present there in very similar (albeit not identical terms) to clause 5 here, as being, for instance, to extend "the benefit of defences and immunities conferred by

the bill of lading upon the carrier to independent contractors employed by the carrier"; nor why in *The Makhutai*, where again the clause was similar but not identical, and where the issue was whether an exclusive jurisdiction clause was available for the benefit of the shipowner, the shipowner did not simply apply to strike out the claim as a whole. There it was this time Lord Goff of Chieveley who described the function of the Himalaya clause (at 666G) as – "to prevent cargo owners from avoiding the contractual defences available to the carrier (typically the exceptions and limitations in the Hague-Visby Rules) by suing in tort persons who perform the contractual services on the carrier's behalf."

(2) In *The Elbe Maru*, the clause read "The Merchant undertakes that no claim or allegation shall be made against any servant, agent or sub-contractor of the Carrier which imposes or attempts to impose . . . any liability whatsoever . . . and, if any such claim or allegation should neverthe-less be made, to indemnify the Carrier against all consequences thereof." That may be a clause which states the obligation not to sue third parties more clearly than the wording of clause 5: but I am not concerned with the effectiveness of part 1 as a promise not to sue, and it will be seen that in essence parts 1 and 4 of clause 5 amount or are intended to amount to the same promise given to the carrier by the shipper not to impose any liability whatsoever on the carrier's servants or agents. Thus part 4 is a promise by the shipper to the carrier to indem-nify the carrier against any claim by parties against whom the carrier cannot rely on "these conditions . . .". It will be seen moreover that part 1 of the clause taken by itself is not extended to benefit third parties, unlike part 2, and that this emphasises that the function of part 1 is to benefit the carrier itself rather than its servants or agents.

(3) If part 1 had the effect contended for by Mr Berry, then part 2 would be redundant and unnecessary. The argument against surplusage may not be the strongest of weapons, but it is certainly an unsatisfactory and dangerous way of drafting for a blanket exception to go on in part 2 to provide third parties the merely inferior protection of the benefit of the carrier's own protection, if they had already been granted a complete exemption, beyond the carrier's own protection, under part 1 of the clause. Moreover the link words between part 1 and part 2 ("without prejudice" etc) do not say "without prejudice to the foregoing", which is how Mr Berry would wish to read them, but look forward rather than back.

(4) While it is true that the word "right" appears among the other nouns in part 2, nothing in its surrounding context suggests that it looks backwards to the right of the carrier under part 1 to have its servants and agents exonerated of all liability whatsoever. Surrounded as it is by words of exemption, defence, immunity and so on, the word "right" must rather refer to rights which go to protect the carrier itself, such as a right for instance to commence a limitation action. Mr Berry concedes that "right" cannot be given its natural meaning to include all rights given to a carrier under its bill of lading contract, because it is accepted that the function of the Himalaya clause is not to transfer to third parties the carrier's rights, eg to freight or other payments, but only its defences.

(5) The words in part 3 "to this extent" do not apply to the whole of the preceding clause, but naturally look back to the words in part 2 "shall extend to protect every such person".

(6) Article III, rule 8 of the Hague Rules is incompatible with the idea that third parties to whom the benefit of the carrier's defences are extended, should have a blanket exemption from liability.

117 For these reasons, I consider, in agreement with Colman J, that clause 5 only protects the owner to the same extent as the carrier is itself protected by the bill of lading provisions under its contract of carriage. Since the carrier would have no exemption for negligent stowage, it follows that its independent contractor, typically a stevedore but here the shipowner itself, can have no exemption either.'

[29] Mr Ashcroft for the Claimants relied upon this part of the judgment of Rix LJ in support of his argument that the covenant not to sue in the first part of the present case only inured to the benefit of the Claimants as carriers under the bills of lading, and not to the benefit also of the various third parties being sued in Brazil, as Mr Jacobs contended.

[30] The House of Lords decided that the provision in that case could not be regarded as a covenant not to sue. In doing so, however, they did not suggest that Rix LJ's reasoning was wrong, to the effect that, if it was a covenant not to sue, it inured only to the benefit of the carrier under the bill of lading and not third parties. In my judgment, his reasoning as to why, if the first part of the clause is a covenant not to sue (as it undoubtedly is in the present case), it inures only to the benefit of the contractual carrier and not third parties, remains compelling. Accordingly, the first stage of Mr Jacobs' argument is incorrect.

[31] However, Mr Jacobs submits that such a conclusion is not fatal to his argument. Even if the first part of the clause only inures to the benefit of the Claimants as carriers under the bills of lading, he still contends that any attempt to enforce the covenant, by way of injunction or otherwise, amounts to the conferring of a blanket immunity on the third parties who performed 'carriage' obligations, and thus falls foul of Art III, r 8 of the Hague Rules. He relies upon the conclusion of the majority of the House of Lords, that the provision in that case did purport to confer blanket immunity on the owners and that, as such, the provision was contrary to Art III, r 8.

[32] In the present context, the argument that cl 3b is contrary to Art III, r 8 is dependent upon the conclusion that the Himalaya contract, to which the relevant third parties (such as the charterers and sub-charterers, VOC and Bossclip) became parties when they allegedly performed the relevant 'carriage' obligations, was a 'contract of carriage' within the meaning of the Hague Rules. Mr Jacobs contended that this conclusion flows from the decision of the majority of the House of Lords in *The Starsin*. In these circumstances, it is important to ascertain the ratio of the decision of the majority of their Lordships in that case.

[33] The fullest analysis of the construction and effect of the clause in that case is contained in the judgment of Lord Hobhouse of Woodborough. He set out the history of how the common law in England and the Commonwealth had developed the Himalaya clause to provide protection for servants, agents and independent contractors of the contractual carrier, from being sued outside the regime of the Hague Rules, culminating in the decisions of the Privy Council in *New Zealand Shipping v Satterthwaite (The Eurymedon)* [1975] AC 154, [1974] 1 All ER 1015, [1974] 2 WLR 865 and *Port Jackson Stevedoring Pty Ltd v Salmond & Spraggon (Australia) Pty Ltd (The New York Star)* [1980] 3 All ER 257, [1981] 1 WLR 138, [1980] 2 Lloyd's Rep 317.

[34] Mr Jacobs relied on Lord Hobhouse's judgment at paras 153–6 in support of the proposition that, whenever the third party under the Himalaya contract performs carriage functions, the Himalaya contract is a 'contract of carriage' within the meaning of the Hague Rules. Certainly para 153 is stated in general terms, which might be thought to support that proposition, but on closer analysis, it seems to me to be clear that the reason why Lord Hobhouse concluded that cl 5 (the Himalaya clause in that case) constituted a contract of carriage was because of the presence of the 'deeming' provision in the third part of the clause.

[35] This emerges from the last two sentences of para 154 and from para 155, where his Lordship said this:

'The shipowners have escaped from being the original contracting carriers by relying upon the doctrine of privity of contract and the way in which the bills of lading were signed. They have brought themselves back in as a contracting carrier by relying upon clause 5 in the bills of lading and the privity of contract which it expressly creates.'

155 It is argued that the 'Himalaya' clause contract is 'collateral' to the bill of lading contract and therefore is not to be affected by such considerations as the Hague Rules. Why the use of the epithet 'collateral' should have this effect is not clear. It does not address or affect the essential question: what is the 'Barwick' contract? In so far as a 'Himalaya' clause may include additional stipulations as between the person issuing the bill of lading and the shipper such as jurisdiction clauses or covenants not to sue, it may well be correct to use the word 'collateral'. But even then the substance may have to be looked at not just the form: *The Hollandia* [1983] 1 AC 565. *But, as regards the persons referred to in the clause, clause 5 says that it is, for the purposes of all the provisions of the clause, made on behalf of such persons and to that extent all such persons shall 'be deemed to be parties to the contract contained in or evidenced by this bill of lading'. As between those persons and the shipper the resultant contract is not 'collateral'; it is the contract.* The purpose of the additional use of these express words is to procure that transferees of the bill of lading shall be bound as well as the shipper: see the final sentence of the quotes from Lord Reid (sup) and Lord Wilberforce (sup). Clause 5 deliberately makes the contract between such persons and the shipper part of the bill of lading contract so as to obtain the benefit of it against other persons besides the shipper. *Were it not for the inclusion of these words in the clause the shipowners would not have been able to rely upon it as against any of the Claimants in this litigation.* (My emphasis)

[36] The passages I have underlined demonstrate that it was only because those deeming words made the relevant third party (there the actual shipowner who had carried the goods) a party to the bill of lading contract, that it could be said to be party to a contract of carriage. On the basis of that conclusion, Lord Hobhouse went on to conclude that since that contract of carriage was subject to the Hague Rules, reliance on the first part of the clause by the shipowner was an attempt by it to obtain a blanket immunity from liability, which was contrary to Art III, r 8.

[37] The judgments of Lord Hoffmann and Lord Millett reached the same result by a similar process of reasoning. Lord Hoffmann said at paras 113 and 114:

'**113** That brings me to the fourth argument, which is that the complete exemption conferred by part (1) is cut down by Article III.8 of the Hague Rules, which provides that any clause in a contract of carriage relieving 'the carrier or the ship' from liability for negligence shall be null and void. I confess that on this point my opinions have fluctuated but in the end I have been persuaded that the reasoning of Lord Hobhouse of Woodborough is correct and that Article III.8 does have this effect.

114 Putting the argument in my own words, it seems to me to run as follows. I do not think that the collateral contract between shipper and independent contractor is a 'contract of carriage' so as to attract the application of the Hague Rules. But part (3) says that the independent contractor 'shall to this extent be deemed to be parties to the contract contained in or evidenced by this Bill of Lading'. That means, as I said earlier, that he is a party only for the purpose of taking the benefit of the exemption clause against the shipper and any transferee of the bill of lading. But, for that purpose only, the provisions of the bill of lading, insofar as they are relevant, apply to him. The only provision which has been suggested as relevant in the present case is Article III.8, which applies by virtue of the paramountcy provision in part (2). That does apply to exemption clauses and restricts their effect.'

[38] Lord Millett at paras 205 and 207 of his judgment analysed the Himalaya contract as follows:

'**205** Such a contract cannot properly be characterised as a contract of carriage. It is rather a contract of exemption which is ancillary or collateral to other contractual arrangements (the time charter and the bill of lading) which were necessary to achieve the carriage of the goods on the chosen vessel . . .

207 Accordingly, I am satisfied that the Himalaya Clause is not itself a contract of carriage of goods by sea, and that merely by taking the benefit of such a Clause the owner or demise charterer of the ship does not become a party to a contract of carriage and so a carrier within the meaning of Article I(a) of the Hague Rules.'

[39] He went on to say that the matter did not rest there, because the 'deeming' provision in the third part of the clause deemed the third party to be a party to the contract of carriage contained in or evidenced by the bill of lading. He concluded, not without some considerable doubt, that the shipowner could not rely on the first part of the clause, because it fell foul of Art III, r 8.

[40] Lord Bingham put the matter on a more general basis in his judgment, concluding at para 34 that on the facts of that case (in contradistinction to the stevedore cases in which the Himalaya clause is usually invoked), because the shipowners were actually carrying the goods, the Himalaya contract was a contract of carriage to which the Hague Rules applied:

'The present case however is factually different, because the act performed to bring any contract into existence between the shipowner and the cargo owners is the carrying of the goods. The question is whether that factual difference gives rise to a legal difference, whether (in short) the resulting contract is properly to be regarded for Hague Rules purposes as a contract of carriage and the shipowner as entering into it with a shipper. I have not found these to be easy questions, but I conclude that to answer them negatively would be to elevate form over substance and to invest what is essentially a legal device with a wholly disproportionate legal significance. If the act performance of which brings a contract into existence between the shipowner and the cargo owners is the carrying of the cargo owners' goods it would seem to me anomalous to give the shipowner the benefit of clause 5 but take no account of article III rule 8 of the Hague Rules which were incorporated into the contract by clause 2 (where they were described as the 'BASIS OF CONTRACT'). Thus the shipowner is not protected by an exemption provision invalidated by article III rule 8.'

[41] Lord Steyn dissented on the issue whether the Himalaya contract could be regarded as a contract of carriage within the meaning of the Hague Rules, concluding that it could not, even with the deeming provision in the third part of the clause (see paras 59 to 63 of his judgment).

[42] I accept Mr Ashcroft's submission that the ratio of the decision of the House of Lords on the Art III, r 8 issue was that the Himalaya contract was to be regarded as a 'contract of carriage' within the meaning of the Hague Rules, not because the relevant third party had performed 'carriage functions' as Mr Jacobs put it, but because of the 'deeming' provision in the third part of the clause. Of the majority, only Lord Bingham put the matter on the wider basis which would support Mr Jacobs' argument, but, as I have demonstrated, on this point he was in a minority of one. Accordingly, in my judgment, *The Starsin* is not an authority for the wide proposition for which Mr Jacobs contends, that merely because the third party performs what might be regarded as 'carriage functions', it is to be regarded as a party to a contract of carriage governed by the Hague Rules.

[43] Mr Jacobs nonetheless relied upon a number of other arguments in support of his proposition. He contended that even if only the Claimants as carriers under the bills of lading could rely upon the covenant not to sue in the first part of cl 3b, this would have an effect, albeit indirect, of circumventing the Hague Rules, which would still be contrary to Art III, r 8 (see *The Hollandia* [1983] 1 AC 565, [1982] 3 All ER 1141, [1982] 3 WLR 1111). I have already stated my conclusion that the decision of the House of Lords in *The Starsin* does not support this broad proposition. In so far as the matter has been considered in earlier decisions or in the textbooks, there is little to assist one way or the other.

[44] I was referred for the sake of completeness to three decisions of the courts of New South Wales which antedate the decision of the House of Lords in *The Starsin*, the decisions of Yeldham J in *Broken Hill Pty Ltd v Hapag Lloyd* [1980] 2 NSWLR 572 and *Sidney Cooke Ltd v Hapag Lloyd* [1980] 2 NSWLR 587 and the decision of Emmett J in *Chapman Marine Pty Ltd v Wilhelmsen Lines A/S* [1999] FCA 178. Although those cases are concerned with enforcement by contractual carriers of covenants not to sue in Himalaya clauses and similar provisions, and the conclusion was reached (at least in the latter two cases) that such enforcement to prevent the pursuit of claims against third party sub-contractors was not contrary to Art III, r 8, in none of them was the third party performing the carriage of the goods itself. Accordingly, they are of limited assistance in the present context: see Lord Hobhouse's discussion of the latter two cases at paras 169 and 170 of his judgment in *The Starsin*.

[45] Viewed in isolation, the passage at para 116(6) of the judgment of Rix LJ in the Court of Appeal in *The Starsin* which I quoted above, that 'art III, r 8 of the Hague Rules is incompatible with the idea that third parties to whom the benefit of the carrier's defences are extended, should have a blanket exemption from liability' might be thought to support Mr Jacobs' proposition. However, as Mr Jacobs himself submitted, the particular point did not arise and was not argued in the Court of Appeal, no doubt because the majority concluded that the bills of lading were owners' bills.

[46] In any event, if anything can be gleaned from Rix LJ's judgment on this point, it seems to me that it is to be inferred from the whole of para 116 that he did not consider that the enforcement by the contractual carrier of a covenant not to sue sub-contractors, which covenant was only in favour of the contractual carrier, would be contrary to Art III, r 8. However, I accept that, since the point was not expressly addressed, it would be dangerous to seek to draw too much from that judgment.

[47] As for the leading textbooks, the new edition of *Scrutton on Charterparties* does not address this area of law at all. Professors Treitel and Reynolds in *Carver on Bills of Lading*, 2nd edition, are evidently of the view that the contractual carrier can enforce a covenant not to sue, at least when the third party has been sued. However, they regard such a provision as not operating on substantive rights, but procedurally, so that it is not affected by Art III, r 8: see para 9–198. However, I am not sure that analysis can be correct. Commenting on it, the editors of *Cooke on Voyage Charters* 3rd edition at para 85.226 say:'This may well be so in some cases but each case should be considered as to the substantive effect of a particular clause in a particular contract and the decision in *The Starsin* might suggest there is no universal answer.' This somewhat tentative statement does not seem to me really to be of any great assistance.

[48] Mr Jacobs relied upon a passage in Tetley: Marine Cargo Claims 4th edition at p 1893, considering what Professor Tetley describes as the 'circular indemnity clause' (ie the covenant not to sue) where, having cited the Australian cases where the clause had been upheld, to which I have referred, he considers that a claim under the clause would be contrary to Art III, r 8 of the Hague Rules, if the claim related to the period when the Hague Rules applied. However, he cites no authority for the proposition he puts forward and does not elucidate further whether he means that even the contractual carrier could not invoke the clause in such a situation. Ultimately I did not find the passage of much assistance.

[49] In my judgment it is important to test Mr Jacobs' proposition by reference to the functions which the relevant third parties were actually performing. The time charterers VOC and/or the sub-time charterers, Bossclip, were responsible through their agents for the preparation and issue of bills of lading on behalf of the Master, pursuant to cl 30 of the respective charterparties. The managers of the vessel were just that, agents of the Claimants, but not responsible as principals for the actual carriage of the goods. Gard likewise as P&I insurers insured the owners against, inter alia, liability to cargo interests. All these third parties may thus be said to have performed services incidental to the goods or to the carriage of the goods (a matter to which I return below). However, by no stretch of the imagination can any of them be said to have undertaken the actual carriage of the goods. The actual carriage was undertaken by the Claimants alone, pursuant to bills of lading which were owners' bills.

[50] That conclusion cannot be affected by the fact that, for their own tactical purposes in the Brazilian proceedings, the insurer Defendants have alleged that all these third parties, in common with the Claimants, provided services as maritime carriers of the goods. The court is entitled to look at the substance, not the form, the real facts as they appear from the evidence before this court, as opposed to the way in which the insurer Defendants have chosen to categorise their claim in Brazil.

[51] Mr Jacobs urged on the court that his construction of the covenant not to sue in cl 3b as null and void and of no effect under Art III, r 8 gave the Hague Rules a purposive and not a literalistic construction and would give effect to the purpose for which the Rules were enacted, to prevent cargo interests from avoiding the effect of contractual defences. In my judgment, to accede to his proposition would have completely the opposite effect. It is clear that Mr Jacobs' clients are pursuing claims against the third parties in Brazil not on the basis that, as parties to a contract of carriage constituted by cl 3b they are entitled to rely on the defences under Art IV, r 2 of the Hague Rules, but on the basis that, in common with the Claimants as the actual contractual carriers, they are liable under some theory of strict liability under Brazilian law. There is no question of his clients being prepared to limit their claim in Brazil to a contractual one, subject to the Hague Rules and the defences under them. As already noted above, the Rules have no application in Brazil. The insurer Defendants are avowedly seeking to take advantage of that by pursuing claims in Brazil.

[52] Once it is seen that none of the third parties undertook the sea carriage or was in fact the carrier within the meaning of the Hague Rules (unlike the owners in *The Starsin*), the conclusion that the enforcement of the covenant not to sue is not contrary to Art III, r 8 is clearly correct.

10 Article IV, rule 2

10.1 Article IV, r 2(a): Fault in the navigation or management of the ship

These words contain two surprises. The idea that the Rules should excuse carriers from the consequences of the negligence of their employees at sea looks odd; odder still when it is remembered that the Rules also create a virtually inescapable duty to be careful in making the ship ready for sea. The words contain a second surprise for anyone unfamiliar with the general approach adopted in English courts to the interpretation of exclusion clauses in bills of lading.

Gosse Millard Ltd v Canadian Govt Merchant Marine Ltd [1929] AC 223

Facts: The appellants shipped boxes of tinplates on the respondents' ship *Canadian Highlander* at Swansea for carriage to Vancouver. On arrival it was found that the cargo had been damaged by fresh water. The trial judge found that rain entered the hold at a port of call when the hatch cover was removed during discharge of other cargo and during a period in dry dock when there was carelessness in moving and replacing tarpaulins that were supposed to cover the hatch when repair and maintenance work was being done to the vessel.

Held:

Lord Hailsham LC: My Lords, this is an action brought by the appellants against the respondents, claiming damages for injury done to their tinplates on a voyage from Swansea to Vancouver in a ship belonging to the respondents and known as the *Canadian Highlander*.

At the trial there was a great conflict as to the cause of the damage to the tinplates; but on the hearing before the Court of Appeal and at your Lordships' bar, both sides accepted the findings of fact of the learned trial judge . . .

The appellants relied on rule 2 of Article III of the rules . . . but the respondents relied upon rule 2 (a) of Article IV; this rule provides that:

> Neither the carrier nor the ship shall be responsible for loss or damage arising or resulting from – (a) Act, neglect, or default of the master, mariner, pilot, or the servants of the carrier in the navigation or in the management of the ship.

. . . The argument at the bar turned mainly upon the meaning to be placed upon the expression 'management of the ship' in that rule. The words in question first appear in an English statute in the Act now being considered; but nevertheless they have a long judicial history in this country. The same words are to be found in the well known Harter Act of the United States, and as a consequence they have often been incorporated in bills of lading which have been the subject of judicial consideration in the courts in this country. I am unable to find any reason for supposing that the words as used by the Legislature in the Act of 1924 have any different meaning to that which has been judicially assigned to them when used in contracts for the carriage of goods by sea before that date; and I think that the decisions which have already been given are sufficient to determine the meaning to be put upon them in the statute now under discussion.

In the year 1893, in the case of *The Ferro* [1893] P 38, certain oranges had been damaged by the negligent stowage of the stevedore. It was held by the Divisional Court that the negligent stowage of the cargo was not neglect or default in the management of the ship. Gorell Barnes J says:

> I think it is desirable also to express the view which I hold about the question turning on the construction of the words 'management of the ship', I am not satisfied that they go much, if at all, beyond the word 'navigation'.

Sir Francis Jeune says:

> It would be an improper use of language to include all stowage in such a term [ie 'mismanagement of the ship']. It is not difficult to understand why the word 'management' was introduced, because, inasmuch as navigation is defined as something affecting the safe sailing of the ship . . . it is easy to see that there might be things which it would be impossible to guard against connected with the ship itself, and the management of the ship, which would not fall under navigation. Removal of the hatches for the sake of ventilation, for example, might be management of the ship, but would have nothing to do with the navigation.

In the case of *The Glenochil* [1896] P 10, the same two learned judges, sitting as a Divisional Court, held that the words did protect the shipowner for damage done by pumping water into the ballast tank in order to stiffen the ship without ascertaining that a pipe had become broken, and thereby let the water into the cargo. Gorell Barnes J says:

> There will be found a strong and marked contrast in the provisions which deal with the care of the cargo and those which deal with the management of the ship herself; and I think that where the act done in the management of the ship is one which is necessarily done in the proper handling of the vessel, though in the particular case the handling is not properly

done, but is done for the safety of the ship herself, and is not primarily done at all in connection with the cargo, that must be a matter which falls within the words 'management of the said vessel'.

Sir Francis Jeune says:

It seems to me clear that the word 'management' goes somewhat beyond – perhaps not much beyond – navigation, but far enough to take in this very class of acts which do not affect the sailing or movement of the vessel, but do affect the vessel herself.

And referring to his own judgment in *The Ferro*, he says:

It may be that the illustration I gave in that case, as to the removal of the hatches for the sake of ventilation, was not a very happy one; but the distinction I intended to draw then, and intend to draw now, is one between want of care of cargo and want of care of the vessel indirectly affecting the cargo.

The principles enunciated in this case have repeatedly been cited since with approval in this country and in America . . .

In the case of *Hourani v Harrison* (1927) 32 Com Cas 305 the Court of Appeal had to consider the meaning to be attached to the words of Article IV, rule 2, in a case in which loss was caused by the pilfering of the stevedore's men whilst the ship was being discharged. The court held that this did not fall within the expression 'management of the ship'; but both Bankes LJ and Atkin LJ (as he then was) discussed the meaning to be placed on the expression. Bankes LJ reviews the authorities both in this country and in the United States; he points out that the principle laid down in *The Glenochil* has been accepted in the Supreme Court of the United States as being correct, and he adopts and applies that principle to the case which he is then considering. The learned judge expresses the distinction as being between:

damage resulting from some act relating to the ship herself and only incidentally damaging the cargo, and an act dealing, as is sometimes said in some of the authorities, solely with the goods and not directly or indirectly with the ship herself.

Atkin LJ says:

that there is a clear distinction drawn between goods and ship; and when they talk of the word 'ship', they mean the management of the ship, and they do not mean the general carrying on of the business of transporting goods by sea.

My Lords, in my judgment, the principle laid down in *The Glenochil* and accepted by the Supreme Court of the United States in cases arising under the American Harter Act, and affirmed and applied by the Court of Appeal in the *Hourani* case under the present English statute, is the correct one to apply. Necessarily, there may be cases on the borderline, depending upon their own particular facts; but if the principle is clearly borne in mind of distinguishing between want of care of cargo and want of care of vessel indirectly affecting the cargo, as Sir Francis Jeune puts it, there ought not to be very great difficulty in arriving at a proper conclusion . . .

My Lords, it appears to me plain that if the test which I have extracted from the earlier cases is the correct one, it follows that the appellants are entitled to recover in the present case. It is clear that the tinplates were not safely and properly cared for or carried; and it is for the respondents then to prove that they are protected from liability by the provisions of Article IV, and that the damage was occasioned through the neglect or default of their servants in the management of the ship. In my judgment they have not even shown that the persons who were negligent were their servants; but even if it can be assumed that the negligence in dealing with the tarpaulins was by members of the crew, such negligence was not negligence in the management of the ship, and therefore is not negligence with regard to which Article IV, rule 2(a), affords any protection . . .

Viscount Sumner: . . . Now the tarpaulins were used to protect the cargo. They were put over the hatch, as they always are, to keep water out of cargo holds. They should have been so arranged, when the hatch boards were taken off, as to prevent water from getting to the cargo. It was not a question of letting light into the 'tween decks. They were lit by electricity. There is no evidence that an amount of water entered that would have done any harm to an empty hold or to the ship as a ship. Water, sufficient when soaked into the wood of the boxes to rust the tinplates in the course of a voyage through the tropics, might well have been harmless if it merely ran into the bilges. There is neither fact nor finding to the contrary. I think it quite plain that the particular use of the tarpaulin, which was neglected, was a precaution solely in the interest of the cargo. While the ship's work was going on these special precautions were required as cargo operations. They were no part of the operations of shifting the liner of the tail shaft or scraping the 'tween decks . . .

Compania Sud American Vapores v Hamburg and another [2006] EWHC 483 (Comm)

Facts: There was an explosion on board the vessel causing damage to the cargo. There was a question as to whether, if the bunkers had been heated to a temperature above what was required to keep the fuel oil reasonably thin and that was the cause of the explosion, the carrier was entitled to rely on the defence in Art IV(2)(a).

Held:

Morison J:

B Bunker tank heating
[54] The facts as found by the Arbitrators are these. The relevant tank is identified as No 3 FFOTS ['the tank']. Steam heating to the tank, to thin the oil in it, was applied for the first time during the morning of 22 December 1998. '[F]uel temperatures of 53°C and 63.3°C were recorded at the transfer pump in the engine room at some time prior to the explosion and fire' [paras 98 and 100 of the Award]. The practice adopted by the Chief Engineer to heat bunker fuel in the storage tanks to a temperature of between 50° and 60° was probably commonplace at sea [para 107]. Although it may have been strictly unnecessary to heat the fuel to more than a temperature of perhaps 38°C, the:

'unarguable technical point that it would be operationally possible to achieve the same result at a lower temperature did not seem to us to be sufficient to brand [the chief engineer's] practice as unreasonable or negligent in the circumstances.' [paras 114 and 116].

[55] The Arbitrators reached their conclusions in this way:

'It was common ground between the parties that the relevant test, approved by the House of Lords in *Gosse Millard v Canadian Government Merchant Marine* [1929] AC 223 (HL), was that of Greer LJ, dissenting, in the Court of Appeal:

"If the cause of the damage is solely, or even primarily, a neglect to take reasonable care of the cargo, the ship is liable, but if the cause of the damage is a neglect to take reasonable care of the ship or some part of it, as distinct from the cargo, the ship is relieved from liability; but if the negligence is not negligence towards the ship, but only negligent failure to use the apparatus of the ship for the protection of the cargo, the ship is not so relieved." [1928] 1 KB 717 at p 749.

Again, both parties were agreed that the effect of the judgment is accurately paraphrased in *Cooke on Voyage Charters* (2nd edn) at para 85.261:

"The principal inquiry, therefore, is whether the act or default which caused loss or damage was done (or left undone) as part of the care of the cargo or as part of the running of the ship, not specifically related to the cargo. Some functions of machinery on board are clearly related only to cargo."

The Charterers said that, however the test is put, the overheating of bunkers causing the heating of cargo adjacent thereto, contrary to ordinary deck and engine room practice, is a neglect to take reasonable care of the cargo and was a default in the care of the cargo. It was not some failure to "run the ship as a ship" or to take care for the ship which incidentally led to cargo damage. They said that proper bunker heat management is a matter directly concerned with the proper preservation of the cargo where heat sensitive. It has nothing to do with the care of the ship (in the sense that the cases discuss it). They said that even if it is to do with both care of cargo and ship, it is like improper management of hatch covers (ie capable of both damaging cargo and sinking the ship).

We did not find the analogy of hatch covers helpful, because, as pointed out in *Cooke* at paragraph 85.262, negligence in the management of hatch covers will not often be within the exception, because one major purpose of having holds covered is to keep the elements out and away from the cargo. The bunker tanks fell into a completely separate category. They had nothing at all to do with the cargo.

We found more apt the situations in the authorities cited by the Owners: The "GLENOCHIL" [1896] P 10 (pumping water into the ballast tanks to secure stability) and The "RODNEY" [1900] P 112 (breaking a pipe whilst trying to free it in order to get water out of the forecastle and thereby wetting cargo).

The Charterers' case effectively meant that the exception would almost never apply, because the question only arises where there has been damage to the cargo. As Greer LJ said in a slightly earlier passage in *Gosse* Millard:

"The effect of it is that, in the words of Gorell Barnes J in *The Rodney*, 'Faults and errors in the management of the vessel include improper handling of the ship as a ship which affects the safety of the cargo,' and that construction merely follows, I think, and was intended by the learned judge to follow, his decision in *The Glenochil*. Both these cases of *The Glenochil* and *The Rodney* are supported in terms by Stirling LJ in *Rowson v Atlantic Transport Co*, to which my Lord has referred, and I think that those statements of the meaning of the word 'management' must be taken, so far as this court is concerned, as being authoritative."

In short, we agreed with the Owners that heating of bunker oil for transfer to the engine room is patently something done as part of the running of the ship not specifically related to the cargo.'

[56] The criticism which Mr Rainey QC makes of this part of the Award is as follows:

[57] The arbitrators erred in four respects:

(1) They never asked themselves the correct question, namely was the failure by the ship to control the heating of the bunker tank so as to protect the heat sensitive cargo adjacent to it from want of harm, a want of care of cargo or a want of care of the vessel indirectly affecting the cargo and was the cause of the damage primarily a neglect to take reasonable care of the cargo rather than of the ship? On the facts, the cargo was a heat sensitive cargo, which the Owners were under a duty to care for under Art III, r 2; the bunkers could have been heated to a low temperature which would not affect the

cargo; whereas the oil in the tank was heated to a much higher temperature than was operationally necessary.

(2) Instead the arbitrators asked themselves the wrong question which was directed to the question namely 'for what purpose was the tank being heated'? This 'purpose' test was precisely the error into which Scrutton and Sargant LJJs fell in *Gosse Millerd*.

(3) The Arbitrators wrongly drew an analogy with cases relating to ballast tanks and then relied upon that as a ground for automatically categorising all bunker tank operations as: 'management of the ship . . . They did not seek to derive or apply any statement of principle from those cases but merely referred to the factual situation being 'more apt' and therefore as governing the outcome.' [paragraph 96 of the skeleton argument].

(4) The Arbitrators wrongly rejected the Charterers' argument because of their view that if right it would mean that the exception would almost never apply.

The Owners' Arguments

(1) The Charterers' arguments fail to recognise that there are effectively two questions:
    (a) what is the relevant 'act neglect or default' and
    (b) is that 'act neglect or default' one that is properly described as being 'in the management of the ship'?

(2) The court must ask itself what was the primary purpose of heating the bunkers, which is identified as the act relied upon. In *Gosse* at page 744 Greer LJ said:

'In my judgment, the reasonable interpretation to put on the Articles is that there is a paramount duty imposed to safely carry and take care of the cargo, and that the performance of this duty is only excused if the damage to the cargo is the indirect result of an act, or neglect, which can be described as either (1) negligence in caring for the safety of the ship; (2) failure to take care to prevent damage to the ship, or some part of the ship; or (3) failure in the management of some operation connected with the movement or stability of the ship, or otherwise for ships' purposes. . . . '

(3) The position is properly summarised in *Cooke on Voyage Charters* which was cited by the Arbitrators. The correct question is, therefore, was the heating of the bunkers 'some operation connected with the movement of the hip or otherwise for ship's purposes' or was it done as part of the care of the cargo? The Arbitrators answered this question at para 125 of their Reasons:

'heating of bunker oil for transfer to the engine room is patently something done as part of the running of the ship not specifically related to the cargo.'

The Decision

[58] I regard the question as to the application of art IV.2(a) as quintessentially one of fact for experienced Arbitrators. The legal principles are clear and the parties accepted the statement of them in *Cooke*. There is no doubt that the Arbitrators were aware of the correct legal principles and I find it odd that it should now be submitted that in some way or another they have failed to apply the very test which they carefully set out in their Award, and which was common ground.

[59] At the end of the day, I have come to the conclusion that Mr Rainey QC's arguments are quite unsustainable. Indeed, I think I can say that I would not have given permission for this point to be argued on the s 69 procedure.

[60] Taking the *Cooke* test as right, an element of purpose is brought into the picture when the question arises as to whether the act [the heating of the bunker tanks] 'was done as part of the care of the cargo or as part of the running of the ship, not specifically related to the cargo.' 'Is an act done as part of this or that'

begs the question 'why was the act done' or 'for what purpose was the act done'? In my view there can only be one answer to the question whether the [excessive] heating of the bunker oil was done as part of the care of the cargo or was done as part of the running of the ship not specifically related to the cargo. That is, the answer which the Arbitrators gave. The heating of the bunker tank was to facilitate the transfer of oil from it to the engines. It was a single act which did not relate in any way to the care of the cargo; albeit it may have indirectly adversely affected the cargo.

[61] What Mr Rainey QC is arguing, I think, is that the Owners ought to have realised that by heating the bunkers adjacent to this dangerous cargo they were creating a risk of damage to cargo; therefore what they were doing was directly affecting the cargo and therefore the act was done as part of the care of the cargo. But this is perverting the structure of the Article, as interpreted by the courts. The fact that the act damages the cargo is, so to speak, a given, otherwise the issue does not arise at all. By asserting that an act directly causes damage to the cargo does not alter the nature of the act itself. If the act was done as part of the running of the ship, then the damage to the cargo is indirectly caused by that act, whereas one would say that an act which was done as part of the care of the cargo and which caused cargo damage, directly caused that damage.

[62] In my judgment, this ground of appeal is hopeless and should be dismissed.

Petroleum Oil and Gas Corporation of South Africa (Pty) Ltd v FR8 Singapore Pte Ltd [2008] EWHC 2480 (Comm)

Facts: This case concerned the carriage of diesel and gas to South Africa. The cargo was found to be defective on arrival. It was alleged that the cause of the damage was the crew's failure to close the relevant IG (inert gas) valves and/or to take other steps to ensure the segregation of the vapour phases of the cargoes from the common IG line. The contract contained the following clause:

12 Inert Gas System ('IGS')

12.1 Owners undertake that the Vessel is equipped with a fully functional IGS which is in full working order, and is or is capable of being fully operational on the date hereof and that they shall so maintain the IGS for the duration of the Charter, and that the Master, officers and crew are properly qualified (as evidenced by appropriate certification) and experienced in, the operation of the IGS. Owners further undertake that the Vessel shall arrive at the loading port with her cargo tanks fully inerted and that such tanks shall remain so inerted throughout the voyage and the subsequent discharging of the cargo. Any time lost owing to deficient or improper operation of the IGS shall not count as laytime or, if the vessel is on demurrage, as demurrage.

12.2 The Vessel's IGS shall fully comply with Regulation 62, Chapter 11–2 of the SOLAS Convention 1974 as modified by its protocol of 1978 and any subsequent amendments and Owners undertake that the IGS shall be operated by the Master, officers and crew in accordance with the operational procedures as set out in the IMO publication entitled 'Inert Gas Systems' (IMO 860E) as amended from time to time . . .

The owners argued that the crew's failure (if proved) constituted an act, neglect or default of the master and/or servants of the carrier in the management of the vessel within Art IV, r 2(a) of the Hague/Hague-Visby Rules.

Held:

David Steel J:

Issue 3

[22] I turn now to the . . . issue . . . whether any failure to close the isolation valves of the IGS or any failure to maintain the valves in good condition are to be characterised as a failure in the management of the vessel.

[23] Of course, the purpose of an IGS taken as a whole might be regarded as the protection of the vessel. Indeed such a system comes into its own when the vessel concerned is in ballast. But protection against tank explosion by introducing inert gas is one thing whilst the avoidance of contamination of different parcels through the inert gas main is quite another.

[24] In *The Iron Gippsland* [1994] 1 Lloyd's Rep 335, 34 NSWLR 29 it was held by Carruthers J in the Supreme Court of New South Wales in a contamination claim of like kind to the present that the defence under Art IV, r. 2(a) of the Hague-Visby Rules was not available:

> It is true that inert gas systems were installed on tankers fundamentally for the protection of the vessel. However, the purpose of the inert gas system is primarily to manage the cargo, not only for the protection of the cargo but for the ultimate protection of the vessel from adverse consequences associated with that cargo. Thus, essentially the inert gas system is concerned with the management of the cargo and, in my view, damage occasioned to cargo by misman-agement of the inert gas system cannot be categorized as neglect or fault in the management of the ship.
>
> Consistently with the principles enunciated in *The Tenos*, I must hold that the subject damage was not occasioned by an act of neglect or default in the management of the ship but rather in the management of the cargo.

[25] Whether or not it is appropriate to start from the proposition that 'the purpose of the inert gas system was primarily to manage the cargo', I have no doubt that failure to operate (or maintain) properly those parts of the IGS available for the purpose of avoiding contamination of cargo 'cannot be categorised as neglect or default in the management of the ship'.

[26] The separation valves have two purposes: one purpose being the avoidance of contamination: the other to facilitate gas freeing: see IMO Publication on IGS supra. Dual purpose fittings can give rise to borderline cases. In *Gosse Millerd v Canadian Government Merchant Marine* [1928] 1 KB 717, 97 LJKB 193, 29 Ll L Rep 190 the principle was set out as follows:

> If the cause of the damage is solely, or even primarily, a neglect to take reasonable care of the cargo, the ship is liable, but if the cause of the damage is a neglect to take reasonable care of the ship, or some part of it, as distinct from the cargo, the ship is relieved from liability; but for if the negligence is not negligence towards the ship, but only negligent failure to use the appa-ratus of the ship for the protection of the cargo, the ship is not so relieved.

[27] Against that background it is my judgment that the cause of the damage in the present case was indeed primarily a failure to care for the cargo. The Claimants placed some reliance on the decision in *The Hector* [1955] 2 Lloyd's Rep 218 where seawater entered cargo holds when tarpaulins came adrift from the hatches due to the failure of the crew to lash them or fit locking bars. The carrier was held to be protected under art IV. Rule 2 on the basis that the whole of the appliances which go to make a properly seaworthy hatch are to be regarded as part of the mechanism for securing the safety of the ship.

[28] This decision has been subjected to justifiable academic criticism. But in any event it is no direct assistance. Here there was a failure to use or maintain the equipment the primary purpose of which at the relevant time was the avoidance of damage to cargo. The vessel was not engaged in gas freeing at any material time so that the distinction that is sought to be drawn by the Defendants that the want of care only indirectly affected the cargo does not arise.

[29] For all those reasons I accept the Charterers' submission on issue 3.

10.2 Article IV, r 2(q): Any other cause

Leesh River Tea v British India Steam Navigation [1967] 2 QB 250, CA

Facts: The plaintiffs shipped tea on *Chyebassa* for carriage from Calcutta to London, Hull and Amsterdam via Port Sudan. While the vessel was at Port Sudan it discharged other cargo and loaded cotton seed. The work was carried out by stevedores who were the agents of the shipowners. In the course of discharge or loading, one or more of the stevedores stole a brass cover plate from one of the ship's storm valves. As a result, when the vessel left port, water entered the hold and damaged the tea.

Held:

Sellers LJ: . . . The shipowners established that the theft was without their actual fault or privity and they have to establish also that it was without the fault or neglect of their agents or servants. *RF Brown & Co Ltd v T & J Harrison* (1927) 43 TLR 633 held that 'and' has to be substituted for 'or' . . . If a complete stranger had entered the hold unobserved and removed the plate, sub-clause (q) would, I think, apply if the shipowner could prove that it was a stranger who removed the cover and reasonable care had been taken to prevent strangers getting aboard the ship and due diligence generally had been exercised. In the present case the act of the thief ought, I think, to be regarded as the act of a stranger.

Notes

1   *Excepted perils: burden of proof.* The burden of proof of an excepted peril under Art IV, r 2, falls on the carrier 'by virtue of the common law principle that he who seeks to rely upon an exception in his contract must bring himself within it': *The Antigoni* [1991] 1 Lloyd's Rep 209, CA, p 212, *per* Staughton LJ.
2   *Excepted peril and concurrent cause: burden of proof.* 'Where the facts disclose that the loss was caused by the concurrent causative effects of an excepted and a non-excepted peril, the carrier remains liable. He only escapes liability to the extent he can prove that the loss or damage was caused by the excepted peril alone': *The Torenia* [1983] 2 Lloyd's Rep 211, *per* Hobhouse J.

11 Article IV, rule 4

Any deviation in saving or attempting to save life or property at sea or any reasonable deviation shall not be deemed to be an infringement or breach of these Rules or of the contract of carriage, and the carrier shall not be liable for any loss or damage resulting therefrom.

The meaning of 'reasonable' in this rule was considered by the House of Lords in *Stag Line*. Lord Atkin's approach enjoys wide support today.

Stag Line Ltd v Foscolo, Mango & Co [1932] AC 328

Held:

Lord Buckmaster: My Lords, the appellants are the owners of the steamship *Ixia* . . . The vessel was chartered to carry a cargo of coal . . . and to proceed from Swansea, where the coal was to be loaded with all possible despatch, to Constantinople . . . The usual and customary route for the voyage was from Swansea, south of Lundy, from thence in a straight line to a point about five miles off Pendeen, on the north coast of Cornwall, and then with a slight alteration to the east to Finisterre and so on.

The ship had been fitted with a heating apparatus designed to make use of the heat which might otherwise be wasted as steam and so to diminish the bill for fuel. This apparatus had not been working satisfactorily, and the owners therefore arranged to send representatives of the engineers to make a test when the vessel started on her next voyage. Two engineers accordingly joined the boat, the intention being that they should leave the ship with the pilot somewhere off Lundy.

The firemen on board the ship were not in possession of their full energies when the boat started at 1.45 in the morning on [30] June 1929, owing to excessive drinking before they joined the ship. The result was that a proper head of steam necessary for making the test was not got up in time to enable the test to be made before the pilot was discharged. Accordingly they proceeded on the voyage until the ship was off St Ives, when the ship was turned about five miles out of its course to enter the St Ives Harbour in order that the engineers might be landed. After landing them, the ship did not go straight back to the recognised route that she ought to have pursued, but hugged too closely the dangerous coast of Cornwall, and ran on a rock called the Vyneck Rock, with the result that the vessel and cargo were totally lost though, fortunately, there was no loss of life. The accident took place at about 3.20 pm, there was a moderate wind from ENE, the weather was cloudy, but visibility was moderately good up to six miles.

The respondents sought to recover damages for loss of their cargo upon the ground that there had been an unlawful deviation from the contracted course. The appellants . . . said (that) by the Carriage of Goods by Sea Act 1924, the rules in the Schedule must be regarded as incorporated in the contract and, by those rules, they were entitled to make the deviation which led to the disaster . . .

The appellants' argument upon the statute is, firstly, that the accident was a peril of the sea; and, secondly, that the deviation in question was a reasonable deviation and consequently was not an infringement of the contract of carriage . . . the first point can, I think, be disregarded. It involves the view that perils and accidents of the sea are not qualified by the provisions as to deviation, and that such perils exempted the shipowner from responsibility for damage if they arise from or in the course of deviation, whether such deviation be reasonable or not. In my opinion clause 4 must be given its full effect without rendering it to a large extent unnecessary by such an interpretation, for it would follow from the arguments that a peril encountered by deviation, wholly unreasonable and wholly unauthorised, would be one for which the shipowner would be exempted from loss. In other words, the reasonable deviation would then only apply to questions of demurrage whatever the deviation might be.

The real difficulty in this case, and it is one by which I have been much oppressed, is whether in the circumstances the deviation was reasonable. It hardly needed the great authority of Lord Herschell in *Hick v Raymond* [1893] AC 22 to decide that in construing such a word it must be construed in relation to all the circumstances, for it is obvious that what may be reasonable under certain conditions may be wholly unreasonable when the conditions are changed. Every condition and every circumstance must be regarded, and it must be reasonable, too, in relation to both parties to the contract and not merely to one . . . I do not think elaborate definitions, whether contained in dictionaries or judgments, are of much use in determining the value of a word in common use which means no more in this context than a deviation which where every circumstance has been duly weighed commends itself to the common sense and sound understanding of sensible men . . .

Lord Atkin: ... The position in law seems to be that the plaintiffs are *prima facie* entitled to say that the goods were not carried safely: the defendants are then *prima facie* entitled to rely on the exception of loss by perils of the sea: and the plaintiffs are *prima facie* entitled in reply to rely upon a deviation. For unless authorised by the charterparty or the Act the departure to St Ives from the direct course to Constantinople was admittedly a deviation. I pause here to say that I find no substance in the contention faintly made by the defendants that an unauthorised deviation would not displace the statutory exceptions contained in the Carriage of Goods by Sea Act. I am satisfied that the general principles of English law are still applicable to the carriage of goods by sea except as modified by the Act: and I can find nothing in the Act which makes its statutory exceptions apply to a voyage which is not the voyage the subject of 'the contract of carriage of goods by sea' to which the Act applies. It remains therefore for the shipowners to show that the suggested deviation was authorised by the contract including the terms incorporated by the Act ...

(Article IV, r 4 provides that) 'Any deviation in saving or attempting to save life or property at sea, or any reasonable deviation shall not be deemed to be an infringement or breach of these Rules or of the contract of carriage, and the carrier shall not be liable for any loss or damage resulting therefrom'. In approaching the construction of these rules it appears to me important to bear in mind that one has to give the words as used their plain meaning, and not to colour one's interpretation by considering whether a meaning otherwise plain should be avoided if it alters the previous law. If the Act merely purported to codify the law, this caution would be well founded. I will repeat the well known words of Lord Herschell in the *Bank of England v Vagliano Brothers* [1891] AC 107. Dealing with the Bills of Exchange Act as a code he says:

> I think the proper course is in the first instance to examine the language of the statute and to ask what is its natural meaning, uninfluenced by any considerations derived from the previous state of the law, and not to start with inquiring how the law previously stood, and then, assuming that it was probably intended to leave it unaltered, to see if the words of the enactment will bear an interpretation in conformity with this view ... The purpose of such a statute surely was that on any point specifically dealt with by it, the law should be ascertained by interpreting the language used instead of, as before, by roaming over a vast number of authorities in order to discover what the law was.

He then proceeds to say that of course it would be legitimate to refer to the previous law where the provision of the code was of doubtful import, or where words had previously acquired a technical meaning or been used in a sense other than their ordinary one. But if this is the canon of construction in regard to a codifying Act, still more does it apply to an Act like the present which is not intended to codify the English law, but is the result (as expressed in the Act) of an international conference intended to unify certain rules relating to bills of lading. It will be remembered that the Act only applies to contracts of carriage of goods outwards from ports of the United Kingdom: and the rules will often have to be interpreted in the courts of the foreign consignees. For the purpose of uniformity it is, therefore, important that the courts should apply themselves to the consideration only of the words used without any predilection for the former law, always preserving the right to say that words used in the English language which have already in the particular context received judicial interpretation may be presumed to be used in the sense already judicially imputed to them.

Having regard to the method of construction suggested above, I cannot think that it is correct to conclude, as Scrutton LJ does, that r 4 was not intended to extend the permissible limits of deviation as stated in *The Teutonia* (1872) LR 4 PC 171, 179. This would have the effect of confining reasonable deviation to deviation to avoid some imminent peril. Nor do I see any justification for confining reasonable deviation to a deviation in the joint interest of cargo owner and ship, as MacKinnon J appears to hold, or even to such a deviation as would be contemplated reasonably by both cargo owner and shipowner, as has been suggested by Wright J in *Foreman and Ellams Ltd v Federal Steam Navigation Co* [1928] 2 KB 424, 431, approved by Slesser LJ in the present case. A deviation may, and often will, be caused by fortuitous circumstances never contemplated by the original parties to the contract; and may be reasonable, though it is made solely in the interests of the ship or solely in the interests of the cargo, or indeed in the direct interest of neither: as for instance where the presence of a passenger or of a member of the ship or crew was urgently required after the voyage had begun on a matter of national importance; or where some person on board was a fugitive from justice, and there were urgent reasons for his immediate appearance. The true test seems to be what departure from the contract voyage might a prudent person controlling the voyage at the time make and maintain, having in mind all the relevant circumstances existing at the time, including the terms of the contract and the interests of all parties concerned, but without obligation to consider the interests of any one as conclusive ... The decision has to be that of the master or occasionally of the shipowner; and I conceive that a cargo owner might well be deemed not to be unreasonable if he attached much more weight to his own interests than a prudent master having regard to all the circumstances might think it wise to do.

Applying then this test, was this deviation reasonable? I do not discuss the facts except to say that I see no ground for suggesting that the deviation was due to some default of the shipowner in respect of the firemen. In the absence of evidence directed to that issue it does not seem right to impute blame to the owners in that respect ... I think that Greer LJ is plainly right in applying the test of reasonableness to the deviation as a whole. It could not, however, be laid down that as soon as the place was reached to which deviation was justified, there was an obligation to join the original course as directly as possible. A justified deviation to a port of refuge might involve thereafter a shorter and more direct route to the port of destination compared with a route which took the shortest cut to the original course. On the other hand, though the port of refuge was justifiably reached, the subsequent voyage might be so conducted as to amount to an unreasonable deviation. Taking all the facts into account I am pressed with the evidence which the learned judge accepted, that after St Ives the coasting course directed by the master was not the correct course which would ordinarily be set in those circumstances. It is obvious that the small extra risk to ship and cargo caused by deviation to St Ives, was vastly increased by the subsequent course. It seems to me not a mere error of navigation but a failure to pursue the true course from St Ives to Constantinople which in itself made the deviation cease to be reasonable. For these reasons I agree that this appeal should be dismissed.

Note

Deck cargo and deviation. In *Kenya Railways v Antares, The Antares* [1986] 2 Lloyd's Rep 626; [1987] 1 Lloyd's Rep 424, machinery was shipped at Antwerp for carriage to Mombasa under two bills of lading that were subject to the Hague or Hague-Visby Rules and that also contained arbitration clauses. On discharge at Mombasa it was found that part of the machinery had been loaded on deck and had been seriously damaged in the course of the voyage. The bills of lading were on the form of the Mediterranean Shipping Company (MSC) but each contained a demise clause. MSC had chartered the vessel from the defendant owners. The plaintiffs made a claim against MSC by letter and informed MSC that they had appointed an arbitrator under the arbitration clause in the bills of lading. One year and two days after the final discharge of the cargo, MSC's solicitors informed the plaintiffs' solicitors that MSC were not the owners of the vessel. The plaintiffs then attempted to claim against the owners, who asserted that the claim was time-barred. The plaintiffs sought a declaration that the owners were in fundamental breach of contract by stowing the goods on deck and that this precluded the owners from relying on the one-year time bar in Art III, r 6 of the Hague-Visby Rules.

Steyn J held that the question was one of construction of Art III, r 6 and that the word 'whatsoever' in the rules made it clear that the time limit applied to cases of wrongful stowage of cargo on deck. His Lordship also said that it would be wrong to approach this question of construction by supposing that the Hague-Visby Rules were intended to codify or reflect pre-existing English law. He concluded that the rule made no distinction between fundamental and non-fundamental breach of contract or between breaches that do and breaches that do not amount to deviations: [1986] 2 Lloyd's Rep 626, p 633.

The Court of Appeal agreed that the time limit in Art III, r 6 applied to claims arising from unauthorised carriage on deck, although the question whether the time limit also applied to 'a deviation strictly so called' was not determined. In delivering the leading judgment, Lloyd LJ (Glidewell and O'Connor LJJ concurring) noted that it was 'sometimes said that the so-called "deviation cases" may have survived the abolition (in *Suisse Atlantique* [1967] 1 AC 361) of the doctrine of fundamental breach' and that the plaintiffs argued that improper loading on deck should be treated in the same way as a geographical deviation. After referring to *Photo Production v Securicor* [1980] AC 827 his Lordship said that: 'Whatever may be the position with regard to deviation cases strictly so called (I would myself favour the view that they should now be assimilated into the ordinary law of contract), I can see no reason for regarding the unauthorised loading of deck cargo as a special case.'

The effect of unauthorised stowage on deck was considered again by the Court of Appeal in *Daewoo Heavy Industries Ltd v Klipiver Shipping, The Kapitan Petko Voivoda* [2003] EWCA Civ 451; [2003] 2 Lloyd's Rep 1, where charterers contracted to carry 34 new excavators from Korea to Turkey on bill of lading terms that provided for under-deck carriage and incorporated the Hague Rules. All the excavators were initially stowed under deck, but, in breach of contract at an intermediate port, 26 were restowed on deck without consent. Eight of the excavators were subsequently lost overboard in heavy weather; the others were damaged by rust or water. The Court of Appeal held that the words 'in any event' in Art IV, r 5 of the Hague Rules meant 'in every case', so that the charterers were entitled to limit liability.

12 Article IV, rule 5

We have already seen that there are strict time limits on the bringing of a claim for breach of the duties contained in the Hague-Visby Rules. There is yet another type of limitation – these are the so-called financial limits on the carrier's liability. Article IV, r 5(a) provides that 'Unless the nature and value of such goods have been declared by the shipper before shipment and inserted in the bill of lading, neither the carrier nor the ship shall in any event be or become liable for any loss or damage to or in connection with the goods in an amount exceeding [666.67 units of account] per package or unit or [2 units of account per kilogramme] of gross weight of the goods lost or damaged, whichever is the higher.'

M.Huybrechts, Chapter 7: 'Package limitation as an essential feature of the modern maritime transport treaties: a critical analysis'

in Thomas, DR, *Carriage of Goods under the Rotterdam Rules*, 2000, London: Informa (footnotes omitted)

7.13 The historic origin of the limitation per package or shipping unit finds its roots in the common practice of early bills of lading in the nineteenth century. Contractual freedom was a predominant feature at that time and resulted in many clauses by which the carrier excluded his liability in almost all possible situations. A bill of lading had become a document of irresponsibility.

7.14 The United States Harter Act 1893 tried to put a stop to the excesses and the abuses of this freedom of contract, which always benefited the carrier. The Harter Act 1893 prohibited most of the exoneration clauses but did not prohibit the limitation of liability of the carrier to a certain agreed amount which was to equal or which was to approach the real value of the goods so carried.

7.15 This solution offered by the US Harter Act 1893 also inspired the drafters of the 1924 Hague Rules. A US court has adequately described the purpose of the limitation provisions of the 1924 Hague Rules.

7.16 However over the years the emphasis moved quickly towards genuine limitation and the concept is now seen as a pure limitation device rather than a vehicle for just compensation for the cargo-owners.

. . .

7.17 As a consequence we may say that in the present system of the Hague-Visby Rules (the Hague-Visby Rules are still the industry standard in international shipping), we have moved far away from the initial purpose of the package limitation concept, i.e. just compensation for cargo damage.

7.18 The limitation per package or unit carried is now really seen as a genuine limitation in favour of the carrier and this limitation concept has lost its initial connection with the equitable and just compensation approach in favour of shippers and or cargo-owners. The compromise that was initially reached in the Hague Rules was seen as a 'minimum minimorum', beyond which the carrier could not go.

7.19 Article 3 rule 8 of the Hague Rules explicitly states:

'Any clause, covenant, or agreement, in a contract of carriage, relieving the carrier or the ship from liability for loss or damage to, or in connection with, goods arising from negligence, fault or failure in the duties and obligations provided in this article or lessening such liability, otherwise than as provided in this convention, shall be null and void and of no effect. A benefit of insurance in favour of the carrier or similar clause shall be deemed to be a clause relieving the carrier from liability.'

What other language does one need to make absolutely clear that the Hague-Visby Rules provide an absolute limit?

7.20 Beyond the compromise that was reached and the many exclusions (they are called 'immunities') which the carrier has been given under the Hague Rules, he cannot go. Nonetheless, the case history of the application of the Hague-Visby Rules has been a history of repeated attempts by carriers to cross that borderline despite the radical message which is so clearly spelled out in article 3 rule 8 HVR.

The formation of the Hague Rules, the principle of limitation is not challenged and the 'no joke' approach

7.21 On the occasion of the discussion leading to the Hague Rules, the issue of limitation was not really questioned anymore. The discussions concentrated more on the question of the amount of the limit as such. It was strongly argued that the limit should not be 'a joke' or as it was said in the French language 'une farce', lest the Rules would become useless and irrelevant.

7.22 Ultimately, the Hague Rules have retained the £100 Sterling, but this posed a very serious problem as it was difficult to evaluate or fix the value of £100 Sterling. This resulted in the gold standard issue. Many countries have converted the £100 Sterling into their national currencies, but in doing so even more discrepancies were created.

7.23 The United States converted the limit to USD500 per unit and Belgium converted that to Bfrs.17.500 per unit, but on account of the currency erosion, these amounts got to such a point that they were unrealistically low and indeed became a 'farce' or a 'joke'.

The 1968 Visby Rules: What changes have been introduced?

7.24 In 1968, the Visby Rules were adopted, one of the last major conventions prepared by the CMI. The Visby Rules were added to the Hague Rules and are now known as Hague-Visby Rules.

7.25 In these Rules, the pound Sterling was replaced by a French currency known as the Franc Poincare, and the limitation amount was set at 10.000 Franc Poincaré per package or unit.

7.26 But again inflation and currency erosion compelled the international legislator to take action. This happened when the special drawing right, the SDR, was introduced replacing the Franc Poincaré; the special drawing right reflects the value of a basket containing the main international currencies and in doing so, the effects of a sharp inflation or currency devaluation of one particular national currency are overcome.

7.27 The Visby amendment in 1968 also introduced another improvement. Not only was a limitation amount per package or per unit maintained, but also a limitation on the basis of weight per kilogram was introduced and this limitation amount was set at 2 SDR per kilogram whereas the limitation per package was set at 676.6 special SDR.

7.28 Indeed it had become increasingly clear that the 1924 solution based on limitation of liability per package or per unit was no longer satisfactory. It had in any case always been imperfect, because in certain cases it led to unacceptable results, while in others it provided no definite solutions. From the report filed by Professor Van Ryn we quote two of his conclusions:

1) Liability limited per package or per unit becomes very derisory in the case of machinery or heavy engineering products such as locomotives and electrical transformers for example.
2) In the case of bulk cargoes it has been necessary to have recourse to some form of fiction and consider every ton or every item as separate units or packages, according to whether the freight is calculated per ton or per item.

7.29 The imperfect 1924 solution was becoming more and more cumbersome in view of the present transport trends, both from the technical and legal point of view. Ultimately a Norwegian proposal won the day; this proposal combined the package or a unit limitation and alternatively the weight limitation. This resulted in the text of the present article 4 rule 5 c. The cargo-owner can henceforth choose whichever limit will give him the highest amount; when a unit weighs more than 333 kilogram, he has good reasons to switch to the limitation amount as expressed on the basis of kilos or the weight of the unit in order to get the largest amount in terms of compensation.

7.30 The Visby Rules also dealt with a new phenomenon: palletisation and container transport. Article II, litera c of the Visby Rules clearly made a provision for the carriage of goods in a container and/or a pallet or similar article of transport. The new article 5 c states:

> 'where a container, pallet or similar article of transport is used to consolidate goods, the number of packages or units enumerated in the bill of lading as packed in such article of transport, shall be deemed the number of packages or units for the purpose of this paragraph as far as these packages or units are concerned. Except as aforesaid such article of transport shall be considered the package or unit.'

7.31 For the purposes of our further analysis it is useful to quote the French version of the Visby amendment, which is equally authentic, as the words 'as packed'/'étant inclus' will play a vital role in understanding this paragraph:

> 'Lorsqu'un cadre, une palette ou tout engin similaire est utilisé pour grouper des marchandises, tout colis ou unité énuméré au connaissement comme étant inclus dans cette engin

sera considéré comme un colis ou unité au sens de ce paragraphe. En dehors du cas prévu ci-dessus, cet engin sera considéré comme colis ou unité.'

7.32 During the debates leading to the 1968 Visby amendment, the CMI working group tried to formulate a new definition of the words 'package and unit'. The Belgian Professor Van Ryn was chairing the committee which was involved with this aspect of the drafting work. Regretfully all the efforts failed as no consensus could be reached. This was his conclusion:

'Le Président (J. Van Ryn):

'[2] . . .

Nous pouvons alors revenir en arrière et examiner les deux questions que nous avions laissées en suspens.

La première est celle de savoir s'il est possible de trouver [3–10] une formule qui rempla-cerait dans l'art. 4 (5) les mots "colis et unité". Nous avions chargé un groupe de travail d'examiner cette question. J'ai été informé ce matin qu'après de longs échanges de vues, le groupe de travail est arrivé à la conclusion qu'il etait préférable de demander à la commission d'approuver purement et simplement les conclusions sur ce point de la commission inter-nationale, cette conclusion étant qu'il y a lieu de maintenir le statu quo en ce qui concerne l'expression "colis et unité". Telle est donc la conclusion de la recherche, des échanges de vues du groupe de travail.

Dans ces conditions, je mets directement aux voix à moins que quelqu'un ne demande la parole.

La parole est a M. M. Hill de la délégation britannique.'

7.33 The words 'package or a unit' could not be replaced nor redefined. It was then Mr Martin Hill who summed up what must be understood by 'package and unit':

'Mr. Martin Hill (United Kingdom). Mr. Chairman, as Chairman of the little Working Group: "The general trend, and I put it rather carefully in that way, the general trend I think of our discussion this morning was that a package is a package and you only move away from the package to the unit, when you are definitely not dealing with a package, then the line of thought and it was only a line of thought and we are not attempting to express any opinion was that a unit is a single article – one unit, one single article – and the only problem you then come up against is that arising in the case of bulk cargo; our line of thought this morning was that it would be interpreted in the case of bulk cargo to mean the freight unit. However, as I said the decided recommendation of the Sub-Committee this morning is that the recommendation of the International Sub-Commission be adopted by this meeting. Thank you." (General applause).'

7.34 Article II, litera e dealt also with the loss of the benefit of limitation of liability.

'Neither the carrier, nor the ship shall be entitled to the benefit of limitation of liability provided for in this paragraph, if it is proved that the damage resulted from an act or omission of the carrier, done with intent to cause damage or recklessly with knowledge that damage would probably result.'

The parameters of Art IV, r 5 have also caused courts and tribunals much inconvenience as is seen in the following case.

*Serena Navigation Ltd and another v Dera Commercial Establishment and
another, The Limnos* **[2008] EWHC 1036 (Comm)**

Facts: The cargo of corn had suffered some wet damage. The physical damage was relatively small but the entire cargo was required by the Jordanian authorities to be fumigated and chemically treated. This operation resulted in a large number of broken kernels (around 250 tonnes). The value of the corn was thus seriously devalued (loss claimed to be around USD 360,000). The cargo then acquired a reputation of a distressed cargo, which depressed its arrived value even more (resulting in a loss of approximately USD 570,000).

The cargo interest argued that this claim for consequential economic loss fell within Art IV, rule 5(a) as 'loss or damage to or *in connection with* the goods' and therefore the limitation of liability should be by reference to the gross weight of the whole cargo (namely, 43,999.86 tonnes). The carrier argued on the other hand that 'gross weight of the goods *lost or damaged'* refers to goods physically lost or damaged – at most only around 250 tonnes.

Held:

Burton J: [7] The relevant Article of the Hague-Visby Rules, which has been the subject of the dispute before me, is Art IV, r 5(a), which I cite below (as amended by the substitution of Special Drawing Rights for 'Units of account' as originally provided):

> '5(a) Unless the nature and value of such goods have been declared by the shipper before shipment and inserted in the bill of lading, neither the carrier nor the ship shall in any event be or become liable for any loss or damage to or in connection with the goods in an amount exceeding 666.77 [Special Drawing Rights] per package or unit or 2 [Special Drawing Rights] per kilogram of gross weight of the goods lost or damaged, whichever is the higher.'

[8] The Carrier's case is that the limit of liability under art IV.5(a) where, as here, gross weight is the applicable test, and loss of the goods is not in issue, is by reference to the gross weight of the goods physically damaged – in this case the conceded tonnage. Hence, if that be right, the limit will be, at 2SDRs per kilo, 14,000 SDRs (7 tons) or 24,000 SDRs (12 tons) or up to 52,400 SDRs (the 12+ < 250 tons). The Cargo Owner asserts that the limit is applicable by reference to the whole cargo of 43,999.86 tons, which would more than cover the entirety of the sum claimed.

Common ground
[9] There were some areas of common ground as to the legal background to the issue before me. The first related to the approach to construction of the Rule. Both sides drew my attention to the seminal passages in the authorities: the words of Lord Macmillan in *Stag Line Ltd v Foscolo, Mango & Co Ltd* [1932] AC 328 at 350, 101 LJKB 165, 18 Asp MLC 266, of Longmore LJ in *CMA CGM SA v Classica Shipping Co Ltd* [2004] EWCA Civ 114, [2004] 1 All ER (Comm) 865, [2004] 1 Lloyd's Rep 460 at 463–4 (making express reference to arts 31 and 32 of the 1969 Vienna Convention on the Law of Treaties, to which the United Kingdom is a party), and of Lord Steyn, both in *Jindal Iron & Steel Co Ltd and others v Islamic Solidarity Shipping Co (Jordan) Inc (The Jordan II)* [2004] UKHL 49, [2005] 1 All ER (Comm) 1, [2005] 1 Lloyds Rep 57 at 64 and, in relation to travaux préparatoires, in *The Giannis NK* [1998] AC 605 at 623, [1998] 1 All ER 495, [1998] 2 WLR 206. From these passages the proposition can be drawn that what the court is seeking to do is to deduce the ordinary meaning of the words used (especially per Longmore LJ at 464), by reference to broad and generally acceptable principles of construction rather than a rigid domestic approach, and without English law

preconceptions (Lord Macmillan at 350 and Longmore LJ at 463): and consistently with the evident object and purpose of the Convention or international rule in question, as to which regard may be had to travaux préparatoires (per Longmore LJ at 464), which, however, will only be determinative of the question of construction if they amount to a 'bull's-eye' (per Lord Steyn in *The Giannis NK* in 623F).

[10] I have endeavoured, with the assistance of the parties, to apply that approach in this judgment. As for any other assistance to questions of construction, Mr Akka did not, before me, although Mr Rainey QC in his skeleton asserted that he thought that he might (and was ready to deal with it), rely on any contra proferentem approach. However, he rested a good deal of his argument, as will be seen, on the well established canon of construction articulated in relation to commercial contracts by Lord Diplock in *The Antaios* [1985] AC 191 at 200–201, [1984] 3 All ER 229, [1984] 3 WLR 592, namely that 'if detailed semantic and syntactical analysis of words in a commercial contract is going to lead to a conclusion that flouts business common sense, it must be made to yield to business common sense'. Notwithstanding that this canon was prescribed for the purpose of construing commercial contracts, Mr Rainey QC did not suggest that it was not also an available tool with regard to the construction of an international rule applicable in, and incorporated into, commercial transactions.

[11] The second matter of common ground was that, if it ever had been, it was, and was rightly, not in dispute before me that, whatever be the proper construction of the controversial words in art IV.5(a) 'goods lost or damaged', the limit to be applied was by reference only to that part of the cargo which could be so described, as opposed to the whole cargo (although, of course, in this case Mr Akka submitted that, on the assumed facts, the whole cargo fell within that definition). Thus, although Mr Rainey dedicated some part of his skeleton argument to this proposition – by reference for example to the words of the editors of *Carver on Bills of Lading* (2nd edition, 2005) at 9–267 'Is the limit calculated by reference to the weight of the damaged goods or by reference to the weight of the whole consignment? . . . It seems clear that reference should be made to the weight of what is damaged' – this was not in issue between the parties and the passage in Carver was not addressed to the question now before me.

[12] The third matter of common ground is that economic loss and damage is recoverable by a cargo owner within the Hague-Visby Rules. Thus, a claim in respect of loss or damage, to include economic loss, may form the basis of a notice, and is subject to the time bar, in art III.6, and liability for loss or damage to or in connection with goods (including economic loss) cannot by reason of art III.8 be excluded (but could be excluded where it arose or resulted from unseaworthiness, by reference to art IV.1). As to this, the decisions of the courts, in relation either to those or similar clauses, are clear: see *GH Renton & Co Ltd v Palmyra Trading Corporation of Panama* [1957] AC 149, [1956] 3 All ER 957, [1957] 2 WLR 45 (re art III.8) especially at 169 per Lord Morton of *Henryton, Goulandis Brothers Ltd v R Goldman & Sons Ltd* [1958] 1 QB 74, [1957] 3 All ER 100, [1957] 2 Lloyds Rep 207 (in relation to art III.6) per Pearson J, *Anglo-Saxon Petroleum Co Ltd v Adamastos Shipping Co Ltd* [1957] 2 QB 233, [1957] 1 All ER 673, [1957] 1 Lloyds Rep 79 per Devlin J (especially at 88, referring to art III.8), and to similar effect in the House of Lords in 1958 1 Lloyds Rep 73, especially per Viscount Simmonds at 83, and *The OT Sonja* [1993] 2 Lloyd's Rep 435 per Hirst LJ at 443–4.

[13] Mr Akka submits that, because it is thus not in dispute that loss and damage in the first part of the disputed art IV.5(a), prior to the imposition of the limit, must therefore also include economic loss, so, as a matter of consistency, and what he calls co-extensiveness (drawing from the OT Sonja at 443–444), or of uniformity (which he draws from a decision of the United States Court of Appeals (2nd Circuit), *Comercio Transito Internationale Ltd v Lykes Bros Steamship Co* [1957] AMC 1188), the words lost or damaged goods must carry a similar meaning. To achieve this, he puts forward, as will be seen, constructions to that effect:

i)   Damaged includes and means economically damaged, and/or

ii)   In order to emphasise that the words goods lost or damaged are to be construed as the same as what is referred to in the first part of the clause, whereby the carrier is liable for any loss or damage to or in connection with the goods, they must be construed as meaning the goods in respect of (or in connection with) which the loss and damage was suffered: or the goods affected or the goods the subject of the claim or dispute which letter would both feature in other/later Conventions or formalities – see paras 16(i) and 16(iii) below.

[14] If, Mr Akka submits, the limit is by reference to goods physically damaged, then what if there are no goods lost or damaged, such as will arise in relation to a claim for delay (which it is common ground can be brought within the Hague-Visby Rules)? Or what if substantial expenses are incurred in successfully eliminating most of the loss or damage, but such that only a very small quantity of damage is left – why should there be such a low and irrelevant limit as would arise if it was by reference only to the small amount of physical damage?

[15] Mr Rainey QC submits that there is nothing odd about the straightforward meaning and approach of the clause, namely that the losses suffered, including economic and consequential losses, are then limited by reference to the weight of the goods physically damaged. As to Mr Akka's two questions, to which I shall return below, Mr Rainey submits, in relation to the first of them, that, where the claim is entirely for economic loss, such as a claim for delay, there is no limit: with regard to the possibility that substantial expenses may be incurred in mitigation of loss, that would be a rare scenario, and not one such as to lead to any need to move away form the ordinary meaning of art IV.5(a).

[16] The last area of common ground relates to other Conventions, at which we had a brief look, not least because (particularly by reference to the judgment of Bingham J, as he then was, in *Datacard Corp and others v Air Express International Corp and others* [1983] 2 All ER 639, [1984] 1 WLR 198, [1983] 2 Lloyd's Rep 81 ('*Datacard*'), to which I shall refer below) it was of some assistance to do so to understand the context:

i)   The Warsaw Convention, as most recently amended in Montreal in 1975, provides by art 22(2)(c) that: 'In the case of loss, damage or delay of part of registered baggage or cargo, or of any object contained therein, the weight to be taken into consideration in determining the amount to which the carrier's liability is limited shall be only the total weight of the package or packages concerned. Nevertheless, when the loss, damage or delay of a part of the registered baggage or cargo, or of an object contained therein, affects the value of other packages covered by the same baggage check or the same airway bill, the total weight of such package or packages shall also be taken into consideration in determining the limit of liability.'

ii) The Hamburg Rules, pursuant to the United Nations Convention on the Carriage of Goods by Sea 1978, provide, as, on the submissions of Mr Rainey QC, the Hague-Visby Rules do not, a limit of liability in respect of the liability of the carrier for delay in delivery, by art 6(1)(b). Article 6(1)(a) reads as follows: 'The liability of the carrier for loss resulting from loss of or damage to goods according to the provisions of Article 5 is limited to an amount equivalent to . . . per kilogram of gross weight of the goods lost or damaged, whichever is the higher.'

iii) The United Nations Commission on International Trade Law ('UNCITRAL') presently has a working group engaged upon proposing a new draft Convention to replace the Hague-Visby Rules. The latest version, as at April 2007, also has a proposed limit of liability for loss caused by delay in the draft art 63. As for the proposed limitation of the carrier's liability in cases other than delay, that is covered by the proposed art 62, which, as presently drafted, reads (in material part) 'The carrier's liability for breaches of its obligations under this Convention is limited to . . . per kilogram of the gross weight of the goods that are the subject of the claim or dispute.'

[17] It is common ground that the contents of other Rules, or of subsequent amendments or proposed amendments to these Rules, are of no materiality, although it is noteworthy, as will be seen, that Bingham J in Datacard did look at the subsequent amendment to the form of the Warsaw Convention with which he was then dealing. The contents of the above Rules are consequently in no way determinative of my conclusion: indeed, of course, as is so often the case in relation to subsequent statutory amendment, one side could assert that the subsequent amendment only indicates that, prior to the amendment, the law was otherwise, while the contrary, namely that the subsequent law is only clarificatory of the earlier, is also usually argued. Nevertheless, it can be seen that some of Mr Akka's submissions set out in para 13(ii) above can be said to draw life from one or more of the above wordings, while the Hamburg Rules, which of course have an entirely different business base to the Hague-Visby Rules, appear to be close to the wording presently in issue.

Object and purpose of the rules

[18] I turn then to consideration of the matters which were in issue. I consider first the question of the evident object and purpose of the Rules, if such can be ascertained, with a view to addressing purposive interpretation, as per para 9 above. I found nothing that was put before me of any material assistance. A learned article on the Hague-Visby Rules in Lloyds Maritime and Commercial Law Quarterly 1978 by Anthony Diamond QC, as he then was, addressed the historical background to the Rules and suggested (at p 226) that, apart from producing standardisation of the most important terms of bills of lading, the Rules had 'redressed the imbalance which had formerly existed as between ship and cargo as regard the risk of loss or damage occurring to goods in the course of a sea transit', such that (at p 239) he determined that:

> 'when the limit was first set in 1924 one of the intentions . . . was to fix a liberal amount so as to preclude ship owners from inserting value clauses in their bills of lading which might otherwise have limited their liability to ridiculously low amounts'.

Tomlinson J, in *Linea Naviera Paramaconi SA v Abnormal Load Engineering Ltd* [2001] 1 All ER (Comm) 946, [2001] 1 Lloyd's Rep 763 at 769 recorded that 'the Hague Rules represent a negotiated bargain between ship owners whose interest lies in maximum immunity and cargo owners whose interest lies in maximum redress'. But Lord Steyn's words in *The Giannis NK* at 621 ring very true:

> 'This much we know about the broad objective of the Hague Rules: it was intended to rein in the unbridled freedom of contract of owners to impose terms which were 'so unreasonable and unjust in their terms as to exempt from almost every conceivable risk and responsibility' (1992) 108 LQR 501, 502; it aimed to achieve this by a pragmatic compromise between the interests of owners and shippers; and the Hague Rules were designed to achieve a part harmonisation of the diverse laws of trading nations, at least in the areas which the convention covered. But these general aims tell us nothing about the meaning of Article IV rule 3 or Article IV rule 6. One is therefore remitted to the language of the relevant part of the Hague Rules as the authoritative guide to the intention of the framers of the Hague Rules.'

[19] This is, in my judgment, also the case here. I see no guidance from a purposive construction in order to assess whether the limit now arrived at should be interpreted more favourably towards cargo owners than to carriers. If a purposive construction is to embrace what Mr Akka called, by reference to the *OT Sonja* at 443 'co-extensiveness' whereby 'good sense required the scope of the limitation provisions to be co-extensive with the scope of the liabilities', I am again unpersuaded that it is necessary that, though economic loss is recoverable, it should not be limited in the way Mr Rainey QC contends. Nevertheless this principle may be of assistance when I turn below to consider the meaning of the words 'lost or damaged goods'.

Travaux préparatoires

[20] There is no 'bull's-eye'. With the assistance of Counsel I have searched through the extracts that have been put before me for some indication. Mr Rainey has submitted that the use of the words 'actually lost or damaged' in a proposed amendment put forward by the Government of the Federal Republic of Germany is of some assistance – but there would still be dispute as to its meaning, such as there would not be if the words were 'physically damaged'; and in any event the word 'actually' did not in fact survive through to the final draft.

[21] The chronology seems to be that the United States suggested an amendment which was said to propose 'the same limitation as that of the CMR, namely 25 germinal francs per kg of goods lost or averaged'. This amendment was almost the one eventually adopted, but the United Kingdom made a slight adjustment. The Federal Republic of Germany then suggested an amendment whereby the limit was in part to be by reference to '25 francs per kilogram of the goods actually lost or damaged', which, in their accompanying comments, was in fact said to deal with the issue raised by Carver discussed in para 11 above, namely 'to avoid that in case of large packages, eg containers, the often considerable weight of the whole package practically will abolish the limitation of liability at all'.

[22] Then the United Kingdom proposed a further amendment, which was to superimpose an additional upper limit, had it gone through, with an overriding cut-off based upon the value of the goods, only a residue of which has survived into what is now art IV.5(b), referred to in para 35(iv) below. The amendment which the United Kingdom suggested, by way of an additional clause, was as follows:

> 'When, under the provisions of this Convention the carrier and/or the ship is liable for any loss or damage to or in connection with goods, the extent of such liability shall not exceed the value of such goods at the place and time at which the goods are discharged or should have been discharged from the ship and no further damages shall be payable.'

[23] On the face of it, this wording could support the contentions of Mr Akka, because of the reference to 'such goods' rather than to 'goods lost or damaged', not to speak of 'goods actually lost or damaged'. However:

i)   The amendment was not adopted.
ii) It was accompanied by an explanatory memorandum by the United Kingdom Government, which makes clear their interpretation of it, as its author. They explained the proposed superimposed new limit as follows: 'It is the value of the actual cargo lost or damaged which is in the majority of cases the true measure of the cargo owners' loss. . . . Accordingly it is suggested that the fairest and most practical solution of the problem is to adopt as the measure of the carrier's upper or maximum limitation of liability the value of the cargo actually lost or damaged at the place and time at which such cargo is discharged.' They thus seem to have regarded the reference in the amendment to 'such goods' as implicitly to goods lost or damaged.

[24] There is accordingly something for everyone in the travaux préparatoires which, as Bingham J said in *Datacard* with regard to the travaux préparatoires to which he was invited to pay regard at 644B-C, 'perusal of these materials in the present case serves only to highlight the wisdom of the courts' cautious approach to such material'. I am taken no further forward by reference to them.

Authorities
[25] Before addressing the words of the Rule itself, I turn to any assistance that could be gained from authority. I have already indicated in para 2 above that there is no previous decision of any court to which I have been referred on this point. The authorities to which I referred in para 12 above are all dedicated to whether economic loss falls within the Hague-Visby Rules, which it does. The only authority which approaches anywhere near the issue in this case is *Datacard*. This was a decision by Bingham J on the construction of the unmended Warsaw Convention (not that set out in para 16(i) above). The relevant clause, art 22(2), provided as follows (in material part) 'In the carriage of . . . cargo, the liability of the carrier is limited to a sum of 250 francs per kilogram'.

[26] Short and sweet. The issue, naturally, was 'per kilogram' of what? The factual context of *Datacard* is not entirely clear from the judgment, even though it incorporates a set of agreed facts. One package was dropped from a forklift truck, causing the contents severe damage, in circumstances for which the carrier was liable. This package formed part of a total consignment of eight packages. The other seven packages were not damaged. However it formed part of the agreed statement of facts (set out at 640j) that:

'. . . each complete system was designed to operate as a single unit and . . . none of the individual items separately quoted could function on its own. Further each system was designed and constructed by the Plaintiffs to an individual customer's specification and was thus unique . . . Without the one damaged item, the whole system was useless to the consignee or any one else. Accordingly the damage to that one item affected the value of the other items.'

[27] What is not clear is the way the claim was put. It is not stated whether the claimants were claiming (subject to the contested limit) the value of all eight packages, or whether they were seeking only the value of the damaged package but arguing that the limit should be set by reference to the affected packages. It seems to have been assumed that there was no liability for economic loss – although art 18(1) of the then Convention, set out at p 641 of the judgment, would seem to suggest the availability of recovery for economic loss. That no recovery for economic loss is assumed appears from Bingham J's summary of the submissions of Counsel at 643a-b:

'. . . he had no liability except for goods lost or damaged. He had no liability for goods which arrived safely. It was very odd, counsel submitted, if the limitation of damages had reference to goods for which there was no liability at law anyway. Why should the limit escalate in proportion to the number of undamaged packages?'

This appears to suggest that there was not a claim for economic damage to the seven packages, but simply a claim for physical damage to the one package, while the limit was sought to be increased by reference to the economic consequential loss.

[28] As can be seen from the material passage from the then art 22(2), cited in para 25 above, there were no words, such as in our case, expressly pinning the kilograms to the gross weight of the goods lost or damaged. This was the carrier's contention, namely (at 642d) 'that the limit was determined by the weight of the package lost or damaged, in this case the weight of the package which was dropped'. Bingham J had no difficulty (at 643f) in accepting that contention:

'The words "250 francs per kilogram" do, I accept, pose the question "per kilogram of what?", but the natural and grammatical answer to derived from the clause itself seems to me to be "per kilogram of the package that was handed over to the carrier". A requirement that the limit should be calculated by reference to goods neither lost nor damaged would, as it seems to me, require express language or clear implication which is not to be found in the paragraph.'

[29] On the face of it, this is powerfully in favour of the Carrier's interpretation in this case, albeit that the decision is on a different convention, but it might be said to be a fortiori, by virtue of Bingham J's having regarded it as obvious that the words 'of the goods lost or damaged' should be understood. However, Mr Akka forcefully points out that, if indeed there were, or were assumed, agreed or conceded to be, no liability for, or recoverability of, economic loss under the Convention of which art 22(2) formed part, then the conclusion that Bingham J set out above would be obvious; and such conclusion gives no guidance whatsoever for this case, in which there is such liability. It is, Mr Akka suggests, for this reason, that the argument was not even considered to be the cargo owner's best point, their 'strongest point', albeit also rejected by Bingham J, being that which I too have cast aside in para 11 above, namely that it was, or should be, a more easily calculable approach to base a claim on the total weight shown on the air waybill (643g).

[30] In relation therefore to the only potentially relevant authority, Datacard, I am also, for those reasons, left unassisted in relation to the construction point now before me. It is however worth pointing out in the context of para 17 above, that the claimant in that case sought to construe the words of art 22.2 in the unamended Warsaw Convention by reference to the words of the subsequently amended Convention. This was a not unattractive proposition, given how clear it was, at least by reference to the agreed facts, that the value of the other seven packages was affected by the damage to the one. Bingham J however was himself unaffected by this argument (642cd, 644h):

> '... the Plaintiffs contended that damages should be assessed on the basis that, for the purposes of art 22(2), the liability of the air carrier for damage to part of the cargo is limited to a sum of 250 francs per kilogram of the actual total weight of such packages of cargo covered by the air waybill as had their value affected by such damage. This basis has been referred to as "the affected weight".
>
> When the Warsaw Convention was amended at the Hague in 1955, art 22 was amended so as to achieve this result. . . .

The affected weight
This was, as I have said, the solution adopted by the Hague amendment to the Warsaw Convention. I find nothing whatever in the wording of the unamended Warsaw Convention, in travaux preparatoires of the Warsaw Convention, in any authority or any academic writing to suggest that art 22(2) in its unamended form was intended to have the meaning which it later bore after being amended at the Hague.

The words of the rule
[31] Mr Rainey's case is straightforward. 'Goods lost or damaged' means goods physically lost or physically damaged. Mr Akka submits that lost or damaged should be construed in accordance with the presumption of consistency (per Hirst LJ in *The OT Sonja* at 442) with other parts of the Rules. Although, he submits, the words lost or damaged do not appear, what does appear is loss or damage, and so the construction of lost or damaged must be consistent with:

i)   The words loss or damage in arts III.6, III.8 and IV.1, all of which include economic loss/damage, and in particular:
ii) The words in the first part of art IV.5(a) 'any loss or damage to or in connection with the goods'.

Hence either the words lost or damaged goods must be interpreted in accordance with (ii) above, so that they mean goods in respect of which the loss and damage was suffered, or damaged goods must include 'economically damaged' goods. This was the case in relation to the balance of the cargo which suffered very substantial depreciation as referred to in para 4(i) and (iii) above. The value of those goods was affected just as was the value of the seven other packages in *Datacard*, but in this case, unlike as was, or was assumed to be, the case under the then Warsaw Convention, economic loss is recoverable.

     . . . .

Conclusions

The words of the rule
[37] I am not persuaded by Mr Akka's submission that lost or damaged goods are necessarily to be construed in the same way as loss or damage. Loss and damage is a familiar expression in the field of tort and contract. It normally, though not necessarily, suggests that loss is economic and damage is physical, though there seems to be no etymological reason why that should be so. The words are very frequently found together to cover all kinds of loss, in the sense of loss incurred. However, in my judgment the expression lost or damaged goods is referring to two categories of goods, goods that are lost in the sense of vanished, gone, disappeared, destroyed, and goods that are damaged, in the

sense of not being lost, but surviving in damaged form. The two expressions, in my judgment, in this context do not carry the same meaning, and so Mr Akka's attempt to construe the latter by reference to the former fails.

[38] Further, Mr Akka's submissions appear on analysis to disclose a degree of confusion as to precisely what is sought to be achieved by way of construction. Rather as in *Datacard*, it is not clear to me in this case what it is that the Cargo Owner is claiming:

i) Is it physical damage in respect of the conceded tonnage (and, if physical damage is permitted to be recoverable itself when it occurs after discharge, then also in relation to the goods damaged in the silo) plus 'economic damage' to the balance of the cargo?

ii) Or is it physical damage to the conceded tonnage etc with consequential economic loss (including the loss by reference to the balance of the cargo)?

[39] If it is the former:

i) It is in my judgment not possible to describe the undamaged goods in this case as 'economically damaged'. Their value may have been affected. There may be depression in respect of their price. The goods may be depreciated. But in my judgment they cannot sensibly be described as damaged.

ii) As Mr Rainey points out, the case is not pleaded on this basis: see para 5 above. Paragraph 28(a) claims the market value of damaged goods (the 12 tons) and (b) claims losses/expenses incurred in reasonable mitigation etc. Of course a pleading point could be resolved hereafter, but it is significant in the context of the argument.

iii) The effect on the value of the balance of the cargo and the monies spent on them were plainly (on the assumptions made) consequential upon the damage to the conceded tonnage. Mr Rainey points to the words of Lord Morton in *Renton* at 169, where he is referring to the words in art III.8 'loss or damage to or in connection with goods'. He says as follows:

'In my view, the phrase covers four events – (a) loss 'to' goods (whatever that may mean) [presumably loss of goods]; (b) damage to goods; (c) loss in connection with goods; (d) damage in connection with goods.'

This in my judgment assists in the conclusion that the goods by reference to which losses have been suffered consequential to the damage to the originally (physically) damaged goods fall into a different category from the goods originally damaged.

iv) I prefer Mr Rainey's submissions, set out in para 35 above, as to the test for when and whether goods are damaged being as at the time of discharge/delivery, and for the reasons he gives. If therefore it is an appropriate question to ask whether goods are 'economically damaged', then this must be tested as at the time of discharge/delivery. Although this might be possible (subject to my conclusion in (i) above), it would not achieve the end which the Cargo Owner would wish. The 'economic damage' would have to be assessed as at that date, by reference to whether the goods had then depreciated, and whether there was then a likelihood that some monies might need to be spent in relation to them. This would of course be a different measure of damage from that which is sought in this case, which is the actual consequential economic loss. It might then mean that there would be contention as to whether a notice within art III.6 giving the general nature of such loss or damage could be or had been given, when what would eventually be claimed would bear little relationship with the economic damage as assessed at the time of discharge.

I reject the suggestion that this, or any, claim for consequential loss is a claim in respect of economically damaged goods.

[40] I turn to consider the alternative basis, which at least has the merit of being in accordance with Mr Akka's pleaded case. This needs the construction not that the goods themselves have been economically damaged, but that goods lost or damaged must be construed as meaning goods in connection with which loss or damage has been suffered. There is a real problem for Mr Akka in this regard. Looking at Lord Morton's four categories, his first category does not apply, there having been no loss of any goods. The conceded tonnage would fall within his category (b), the economic consequential loss would fall within his category (c) and the damage in the silos would presumably fall within his category (d). So far in particular as concerns the latter, the goods that were allegedly damaged in the silo were so damaged at a time when they had ceased to be in the custody of the Carrier.

[41] It is plain in my judgment that all the loss or damage which was incurred after discharge was 'loss or damage in connection with the goods' within the first part of art IV.5(a). The goods in question are the goods which were damaged while in the Carrier's custody in connection with which other loss (partly in respect of other, undamaged, goods) was suffered. In those circumstances the reference in the last part of the clause is to those same 'goods lost or damaged'.

[42] Thus, even if, instead of the words 'goods lost or damaged', there had been used the phrase 'such goods', as in the proposed UK amendment referred to in paras 22 and 23 above, that would have been a reference back to the goods in connection with which loss or damage had been incurred. In my judgment therefore, what is permitted in art IV.5(a) is a claim in respect of (lost or) damaged goods, and a claim for loss or damage in connection with those (lost or) damaged goods, but in the second part of the clause the weight of those (lost or) damaged goods is then taken as the limit. If Mr Akka's alternative construction were used, namely that it is the gross weight of the goods 'in respect of which the loss or damage was suffered', it would still be the lost or damaged goods (the dropped package for example, in the Datacard case), in connection with which consequential loss or damage would have been suffered, which would provide the weight limit.

[43] I agree with Mr Akka that there are anomalies both as to construction and as to effect, by reference to the submissions he has made as summarised in paras 32–33 and 34 above . However, I am satisfied that such anomalies do not begin to drive me to adopt the Antaios canon of construction in this case, so as to conclude that the construction which I have determined to be the correct one, by reference to the analysis of the Article and the Rules, flouts business common sense. A claim for economic loss, without physical loss, by reference to delay is not frequent. The scenario which he posited of substantial sums expended on mitigation would be rare and unusual. Many, if not all, provisions, particularly ones arrived at after very considerable international negotiation and compromise, will have unusual or unwanted effects. I am not driven by Mr Akka's arguments to conclude, and do not consider, that to have an entitlement to claim economic loss, but one which is limited by reference to the weight of the physical damage caused while the goods were in the custody of the carrier, is inappropriate or contrary to commercial good sense.

Notes

1   The judgment does not however deal with the issue as to how package limitation would work when there is no physical damage to the goods (i.e. when the claim is for pure economic loss). It would be interesting to see how the courts would address such an issue – would it proceed on the basis that where the claim is for pure economic loss, normal rules of remoteness should apply and no limits of liability would apply?

2   In the case where there is minimal physical damage and substantial pure economic loss, the package limitation would apply and compensation would be calculated by reference to that small amount of damaged cargo. Burton J did not think that such a result went against commercial sensibility. Moreover, the judge thought that claims for economic loss without physical damage would be rare.

Article IV rule 5(c) makes it plain that 'where a container, pallet or similar article of transport is used to consolidate goods, the number of packages or units enumerated in the bill of lading as packed in such article of transport shall be deemed the number of packages or units for the purpose of this paragraph as far as these packages or units are concerned. Except as aforesaid such article of transport shall be considered the package or unit.' (See also *The River Guarara* [1998] QB 610.)

The maximum liability however would not apply if the damage is the result of an act or omission of the carrier done with intent to cause damage or recklessly and with the knowledge that damage would probably result (Art IV, r 5(e)). In *Browner International Ltd v Monarch Shipping Co Ltd, The European Enterprise* [1989] 2 Lloyd's Rep 185 Steyn J held that Art IV, r 5(e) does not impose on the carrier a non-delegable duty and drawing an analogy from the Warsaw Convention (an international convention on carriage by air), the word 'carrier' should only mean the carrier himself or his alter ego in the case of a company or association.

13 The Hamburg Rules

13.1 Introduction

Chuah, J, *Law of International Trade: Cross-Border Commercial Transactions,* **2013, London: Sweet & Maxwell, pp 392–393**

The chief complaint about the Hague and Hague-Visby Rules is that they primarily favour the carrier in a contract of carriage of goods by sea. Cargo exporting countries without a strong presence of shipowners are concerned with the limitations of the Hague-Visby Rules, particularly in respect of the following:

- the Hague-Visby Rules only have mandatory application where the contract is evidenced by a bill of lading; anything less, such as a sea waybill which is used frequently for shorter voyages, is not accommodated;
- the Hague-Visby Rules only apply to contracts of carriage by sea, they do not extend to any period of storage or consolidation of the cargo at the port of shipment even though the goods have already been received into custody by the carrier;
- the burden of proof under the Hague-Visby Rules weighs too heavily on the shipper;
- the Hague-Visby Rules contain no rules on how jurisdiction is to be allocated; and
- the low financial limits in the Hague-Visby Rules.

The United Kingdom is however not a signatory to the Hamburg Rules, and is unlikely to be in the near future. However, some contracts of carriage which are litigated or arbitrated here are those which have incorporated the Hamburg Rules, contractually or otherwise.

Transport Canada, *Marine Liability Act, Part 5: Liability for the Carriage of Goods by Water* (2009/2010 Report to the Canadian Parliament) ((TP 14947E) (https://www.tc.gc.ca/eng/policy/report-acf-hamburg-menu-1099.htm)

The preparatory work for the Hamburg Rules was done by the United Nations Commission on International Trade Law (UNCITRAL), leading to a diplomatic conference held in 1978 in Hamburg, Germany, which adopted the new Rules under their official title 'The United Nations Convention on the Carriage of Goods by Sea'.

The Hamburg Rules were viewed as an improvement over the Hague/Visby Rules since they extended the scope of a carrier's liability for loss of or damage to cargo to the entire period that the goods are in his charge rather than just for the time that the goods are physically aboard the vessel. The Hamburg Rules also established liability of the carrier when economic loss occurs due to delay in delivery and place the onus on the carrier to prove that all reasonable measures were taken to avoid damage or loss rather than requiring the claimant to prove the carrier's negligence. They also increased the carrier's limit of liability.

Having been adopted by the United Nations with the participation of traditional maritime nations and developing countries, the Hamburg Rules were considered to have a broader political base than the Hague/Visby regime.

...

Extensive consultations with various industry groups failed to reach a consensus on the appropriate regime for Canada. However, agreement on a two-pronged approach to cargo liability eventually emerged. It was agreed that Canada should immediately implement the Hague/Visby Rules with a provision to bring into force the Hamburg Rules when a sufficient number of Canada's trading partners have ratified them. This approach is embodied in section 44 of the MLA, which requires the Minister of Transport to conduct a periodic review of the Act to determine if the Hamburg Rules should replace the Hague/Visby Rules and to report to Parliament on the outcome of that review. This provision reflected Canada's intention to accept the Hamburg Rules, if and when they become a viable liability regime for international trade. Until then, Canada is committed to promoting wider international acceptance of the Hamburg Rules and exploring other practical options to promote uniformity in international law.

In 2005, the government completed its second review of the Hamburg Rules3 and the Report to Parliament submitted by the Minister concluded that:

1. The Hague/Visby Rules should be retained until the next review period, ending January 1, 2010; and
2. Transport Canada should continue to make efforts, in consultation with industry and in cooperation with like-minded countries, with a view to developing practical options for a new international regime of liability for the carriage of goods by sea which would achieve a greater uniformity than the Hague/Visby Rules.

IV International developments

The Hamburg Rules entered into force in November 1993, 15 years after their adoption by the United Nations. To date, 34 States have ratified the Hamburg Rules, but Canada and other major trading nations have not acceded to them, nor implemented them fully in national legislation. The 15-year delay between adoption and entering into force testifies to the reluctance of governments to adopt these rules.

Currently, the Hamburg Rules apply to a very small portion of international maritime trade in comparison to the trade covered by their predecessors, the Hague Rules and the Hague/Visby Rules. As the chart below indicates, over 60 percent of Canada's trade is with countries that subscribe to one of those two, closely aligned, liability regimes ...

Initial expectations were that the Hamburg Rules would prove to be the key to the development of an international regime and contribute to uniformity in the area of cargo liability. Unfortunately, the overall lack of support they received from the international community has resulted in their no longer being considered a viable replacement for the Hague/Visby Rules.

13.2 Scope of application

Carr, I, 'The scope of application of Hamburg Rules and Hague-Visby Rules: a comparison' (1992) *International Company and Commercial Law Review* 214

(footnotes omitted)

Introduction
The Hamburg Rules, the United Nations Convention on Carriage of Goods by Sea 1978, will be in force from 2 November 1992. The Convention needed 20 signatories to become effective ...

Once this Convention comes into force it will exist alongside the other two well-established and highly successful Conventions – the Hague Rules 1924 and the Hague-Visby Rules 1968. Among others, provisions relating to the scope of application, the extent of carrier liability, the contents of transport documents and their effects on the responsibilities and liabilities of the contracting parties are different from those of the Hague Rules and Hague-Visby Rules. This article will concentrate on the scope of application of the Hamburg Rules (hereinafter the Rules). It will accordingly deal with the following areas: (1) the range of voyages affected; (2) the types of contracts of carriage affected; (3) the period of coverage; and (4) the kinds of cargo affected.

In considering the above, comparisons will be drawn where pertinent with the Hague-Visby Rules (hereinafter H/V Rules) to illustrate better the novel approach adopted by the Rules. (Comparison with the Hague Rules is not made, since the H/V Rules are for the most part identical to the Hague Rules.)

The range of voyages affected by the rules

The geographic scope of the Rules is set out in Article 2(1) which states:

The provisions of this convention are applicable to all contracts of carriage by sea between two different states, if:

(a) the port of loading as provided for in the contract of carriage by sea is located in a Contracting State; or

(b) the port of discharge as provided for in the contract of carriage by sea is located in a Contracting State, or

(c) one of the optional ports of discharge provided for in the contract of carriage by sea is the actual port of discharge and such port is located in a Contracting State, or

(d) the bill of lading or other document evidencing the contract of carriage by sea is issued in a Contracting State.

The basic requirements for triggering the Rules are: (1) the contract for carriage must be for carriage by sea; and, (2) an element of internationality must be present in that the contract for carriage must be between two different states. Similar requirements are also specified for bringing the H/V Rules into operation. It is not however a necessary condition of the Rules that the different states involved in the contract of carriage are all Contracting States. The Rules can be applied to the contract if one of the operations involved in the handling of goods takes place in a Contracting State. So, if the port of loading is located in a Contracting State (Article 2(1)(a)) or, if the port of discharge is located in a Contracting State (Article 2(1)(b)), then the Rules are applicable. This means that both inward shipments to and outward shipments from Contracting States are subject to the Rules, and this is a major advance on the H/V Rules which only apply to shipments leaving a Contracting State (Article X(b)). It is not inconceivable that the wide approach taken here could raise interesting questions in the sphere of conflicts of law. For example, which Convention relating to carriage of goods by sea will determine the rights and obligations of the parties where a bill of lading is issued in State A, a Contracting State of the H/V Rules, and the port of discharge is situated in State B, a Contracting State of the Rules? Although questions like these are worthy of further consideration, they are beyond the scope of this article.

Article 2(1)(c) extends the applicability of the Rules where an optional port situated in a Contracting State and named in the contract of carriage becomes the actual port of discharge. Article 2(1)(d) like Article X(a) of the H/V Rules provides for the applicability of the Rules where a bill of lading or document evidencing the contract of carriage is issued in a Contracting State. The important difference from the equivalent provision in the H/V Rules is that the Rules also allow for any document evidencing a contracting of carriage. This means that documents other than documents of title issued in a Contracting State will also be governed by the Rules.

It must be mentioned that a contract of carriage may trigger the operation of the Rules despite the lack of contact with a Contracting State in circumstances mentioned in the above paragraphs. This can be achieved through express incorporation; that is, by providing that the provisions of the Rules or the legislation of any state giving effect to them are to govern the contract (Article 2(1)(e)). A similar provision is to be found in Article X(c) of the H/V Rules.

The types of contracts of carriage affected

The applicability of the H/V Rules is determined by the kind of document that covers the contract of carriage. It is only where a bill of lading or similar document of title is issued that the H/V Rules become relevant in determining the responsibilities and liabilities of the parties to the carriage (Article 1(b)). The meaning of 'covered' is not provided and there is ambiguity whether the H/V Rules can be applied when there is a time lapse between the contract of carriage and the issue of a bill of lading. However, it seems that where the parties envisage at the time of the conclusion of the contract that the contract will be covered by a bill of lading the H/V Rules take effect even though no such document is in fact issued.

The H/V Rules also refer to documents of title similar to a bill of lading. A document of title similar to a bill of lading is unknown in British shipping practice. What constitutes similar documents of title will presumably depend on the particular facts. The custom of the trade, for instance, may play a role in determining whether the document is similar to a bill of lading. The H/V Rules are not designed to apply to non-negotiable documents like way-bills though it is possible to make them applicable by express stipulation.

The issue of a document having qualities similar to those possessed by a bill of lading is not essential for the Rules to come into operation, since Article 2(1) states that the provisions of the Convention are applicable to all contracts of carriage. Therefore the Rules will govern way-bills, short-sea notes and other contracts of carriage used in the trade, and this is a significant advance on the H/V Rules.

The Rules, like the H/V Rules (Article 1(b)), exclude charterparties except where bills of lading are issued pursuant to a charterparty from the scope of the Convention in Article 2(3). However this exception is applicable only in some circumstances and these are: (1) where the bill of lading issued under a charterparty to the charterer is subsequently endorsed by him to a third party; and (2) where a bill of lading is issued to the shipper who is not the charterer. In other words, the issue of whether the Rules are to be applied to a bill of lading issued under a charterparty is to be determined in terms of the holder's identity.

The Rules under Article 2(4) also govern 'volume' or 'tonnage' contracts which are contracts of carriage in which the carrier agrees to future carriage of goods in a series of shipments during an agreed period. However, where such an agreement is in the form of a charterparty, then it will be subject to Article 2(3) of the Rules.

The period of coverage

The H/V Rules in Article 1(e) define carriage of goods by sea by reference to the period from the 'time when the goods are loaded to the time when they are discharged from the ship'. This formula causes problems because no general principle can be enunciated to determine at what point loading begins and discharge finishes, since varied methods are used in cargo handling. This means that each operation has to be examined on its own particular facts, and there is nothing to stop the parties from determining the part which each has to play in cargo handling in the contract of carriage. It seems that where tackle is used the H/V Rules come into operation from the moment when the ship's tackle is hooked at the port of loading until the moment that cargo is landed and the ship's tackle released at the port of discharge.

Apart from the problem of deciding the precise moment at which loading and discharge takes place, there are problems where the goods are unloaded on to a lighter or where there is transhipment of the goods. The reason for this is that Article 1(e) of the H/V Rules makes the actual presence of the goods on the vessel carrying them a condition for its application.

In the event of lightering operations the extent to which these are included in the ambit of the definition of carriage of goods by sea is not decided and presumably will depend on the particular contract of carriage and whether the carrier has contracted to perform the lightering operation as part of the discharging state. However, where discharge on to a lighter is not complete the H/V Rules are still operative.

In the event of transhipment once again no general principle can be formulated regarding the applicability of the H/V Rules to the period during which the goods are awaiting transhipment. The applicability will be determined by the courts by looking at the particular terms of the contract of carriage. It seems that where a liberty to tranship clause is invoked and the shipper is unaware that there would be transhipments the H/V Rules would cover the whole journey despite intermediate transhipments. However, where separate bills of lading for different legs of the journey are issued this would raise a strong presumption that transhipments were envisaged thereby bringing the period when the goods are awaiting transhipment outside the ambit of the H/V Rules.

The Rules have adopted a different approach set out in Article 4(1) as follows:

> The responsibility of the carrier for the goods under this Convention covers the period during which the carrier is in charge of the goods at the port of loading, during the carriage and at the port of discharge.

This means that the precise moment of the applicability of the Rules is calculated not from the time the goods are placed on board the ship but is determined from the time the carrier can exercise the right of control and supervision of the goods. The carrier is regarded as in charge of the goods when he takes over the goods from the shipper, or a person acting on his behalf or an authority or third party to whom the goods must be handed for shipment (Article 4(2)(a)). The carrier is regarded as having delivered the goods when he hands them over to the consignee, or by placing them at the disposal of the consignee in accordance with the contract, by handing over the goods to an authority or third party to whom the goods must be handed over (Article 4(2)(b)).

The question of when the goods are taken over or delivered by the carrier will presumably be decided from the terms of the contract. The formula adopted by the Rules should cause no problems in relation to lighterage operations, since the question will be decided in terms of who was in charge of the goods. If an independent contractor is employed, then this would suggest that the carrier took over the goods when they were loaded on to the ship. Where the lightering operations are conducted for the carrier, this suggests that he is in charge of the goods thereby bringing the Rules into effect during this process.

As far as transhipment is concerned it seems that the Rules will apply to the period when the goods are awaiting transhipment, since Article 4 suggests that the carrier is responsible for the entire period – that is, from the time the goods are taken over to the time they are delivered to the relevant party at the port of discharge. In these circumstances, it would not be unusual for a through bill of lading to be issued.

Where a through bill of lading is issued it appears from Article 10 that the carrier is responsible throughout the carriage of goods by sea unless the carrier excludes his liability under Article 11(1). The exclusion is effective provided the actual carrier is named in the contract of carriage and details are given in the contract of carriage of that part of the carriage to be undertaken by the actual carrier. Where these requirements are met, the actual carrier is responsible for the goods while they are in his charge.

The kinds of cargo affected

Under the H/V Rules both deck cargo and live animals fall outside their ambit thereby leaving the parties to the contract of carriage to negotiate its terms. However, in order to make the H/V Rules inoperative in relation to deck cargo two requirements need to be satisfied – first, the deck cargo must be stated as carried on deck and second, it must as matter of fact be so carried. A clause giving the ship liberty to stow the goods on deck and absolving the shipowner of responsibility for any loss, damage, or claim to goods so carried is insufficient to restrict the operation of the H/V Rules, since the clause is not tantamount to a statement that the goods in fact are being carried on deck.

The provisions in relation to deck cargo in the Rules are to be found in Article 9 which states:

1. The carrier is entitled to carry the goods on deck only if such carriage is in accordance with an agreement with the shipper or with the usage of the particular trade or is required by statutory rules or regulations.

2. If the carrier and the shipper have agreed that the goods shall or may be carried on deck, the carrier must insert in the bill of lading or other document evidencing the contract of carriage by sea a statement to that effect.

It appears from this Article that deck cargo will be regarded as normal cargo and will be subject to the Rules. In the absence of a definition of deck cargo the gist of what may qualify as deck cargo is to be gathered from Article 9(1), which sets out the circumstances in which the ship may carry the cargo on deck. Accordingly, cargo may be carried on deck:

(1) if there is usage to do so (Article 9(1)). As to what usage may be will presumably depend on the trade practices. This suggests that containers that are normally carried on deck will qualify as deck cargo.
(2) if there are statutory rules or regulations to that effect (Article 9(1)). This covers situations where statute may require the ship to carry dangerous goods such as explosives on deck.
(3) if there is an agreement (Article 9(1)). Where there is an agreement this must be inserted in the bill of lading or other document evidencing the contract of carriage (Article 9(2)). This is perhaps the most problematic of the three situations circumscribed by Article 9(1). What form must the agreement take? Does the agreement have to be express and appear on the face of the bill of lading or will a liberty clause allowing the carrier to carry on deck qualify as sufficient to constitute an agreement for the purposes of this provision? It will be possible to argue that a liberty clause will be regarded as an agreement, since the Rules do use the phrase 'express agreement' in Article 9(4), which suggests that the drafters were aware of the conceptual distinction between agreement and express agreement.

Where the carrier carries cargo on deck in circumstances stipulated by Article 9(1), the carrier can take advantage of the limitation of liability set out in Article 6 of the Rules. The carrier however will lose this entitlement where:

(1) cargo is carried on deck in the absence of usage or agreement or statutory rule, and it can be shown by the claimant as required by Article 8 that deck carriage was done with the 'intent to cause such loss, damage or delay in delivery resulted from an act or omission of the carrier done with the intent to cause such loss, damage or delay, or recklessly, and with knowledge that such loss, damage or delay would probably result'.
(2) cargo is carried on deck contrary to an express agreement to carry below deck, since this is deemed to be an act or omission within the meaning of Article 8 (Article 9(4)).

As far as the carriage of live animals is concerned the Rules have gone further than the H/V Rules in making their carriage subject to the Rules. The carrier is not liable only where he can show that he has complied with the special instructions given by the shippers but the damage, loss or delay in delivery was caused by the special risks inherent in the kind of cargo carried. Presumably, special risks will be determined in relation to the type of animal carried and the risks generally present in the transportation of animals by sea. Article 5(5) sets this out as follows:

With respect to live animals, the carrier is not liable for loss, damage or delay in delivery resulting from any special risks inherent in that kind of carriage. If the carrier proves that he has complied with any special instructions given to him by the shipper respecting the animals and that, in the circumstances of the case, the loss, damage or delay in delivery was so caused, unless there is proof that all or a part of the loss, damage or delay in delivery resulted from fault or neglect on the part of the carrier, his servants or agents.

Conclusion
The aims of the Convention were to improve upon the Hague and Hague-Visby Rules and to achieve greater international uniformity. Among others, the Rules have made some significant (and sometimes

controversial) advances in the area of the scope of its application. The most noticeable of these are that the Rules are applicable to inward shipments, to live animals, and to contracts of carriage by sea other than bills of lading like way-bills, and short-seaway notes. . . .

13.3 Exclusion of the Rules

The Hamburg Rules nullify not only those contractual provisions which directly derogate from the Rules (when the Rules apply as a matter of law, and not simply by means of a paramount clause) but also those provisions that indirectly derogate from them. It would be interesting to see how the courts deal with the issue.

Article 23
Contractual stipulations
1. Any stipulation in a contract of carriage by sea, in a bill of lading, or in any other document evidencing the contract of carriage by sea is null and void to the extent that it derogates, directly or indirectly, from the provisions of this Convention. The nullity of such a stipulation does not affect the validity of the other provisions of the contract or document of which it forms a part. A clause assigning benefit of insurance of the goods in favour of the carrier, or any similar clause, is null and void.
2. Notwithstanding the provisions of paragraph 1 of this article, a carrier may increase his responsibilities and obligations under this Convention.
3. Where a bill of lading or any other document evidencing the contract of carriage by sea is issued, it must contain a statement that the carriage is subject to the provisions of this Convention which nullify any stipulation derogating therefrom to the detriment of the shipper or the consignee.
4. Where the claimant in respect of the goods has incurred loss as a result of a stipulation which is null and void by virtue of the present article, or as a result of the omission of the statement referred to in paragraph 3 of this article, the carrier must pay compensation to the extent required in order to give the claimant compensation in accordance with the provisions of this Convention for any loss of or damage to the goods as well as for delay in delivery. The carrier must, in addition, pay compensation for costs incurred by the claimant for the purpose of exercising his right, provided that costs incurred in the action where the foregoing provision is invoked are to be determined in accordance with the law of the State where proceedings are instituted.

13.4 Who is a carrier?

Article 10
Liability of the carrier and actual carrier
1. Where the performance of the carriage or part thereof has been entrusted to an actual carrier, whether or not in pursuance of a liberty under the contract of carriage by sea to do so, the carrier nevertheless remains responsible for the entire carriage according to the provisions of this Convention. The carrier is responsible, in relation to the carriage performed by the actual carrier, for the acts and omissions of the actual carrier and of his servants and agents acting within the scope of their employment.
2. All the provisions of this Convention governing the responsibility of the carrier also apply to the responsibility of the actual carrier for the carriage performed by him. The provisions of paragraphs 2 and 3 of article 7 and of paragraph 2 of article 8 apply if an action is brought against a servant or agent of the actual carrier.

3. Any special agreement under which the carrier assumes obligations not imposed by this Convention or waives rights conferred by this Convention affects the actual carrier only if agreed to by him expressly and in writing. Whether or not the actual carrier has so agreed, the carrier nevertheless remains bound by the obligations or waivers resulting from such special agreement.

4. Where and to the extent that both the carrier and the actual carrier are liable, their liability is joint and several.

5. The aggregate of the amounts recoverable from the carrier, the actual carrier and their servants and agents shall not exceed the limits of liability provided for in this Convention.

6. Nothing in this article shall prejudice any right of recourse as between the carrier and the actual carrier.

Article 11
Through carriage

1. Notwithstanding the provisions of paragraph 1 of article 10, where a contract of carriage by sea provides explicitly that a specified part of the carriage covered by the said contract is to be performed by a named person other than the carrier, the contract may also provide that the carrier is not liable for loss, damage or delay in delivery caused by an occurrence which takes place while the goods are in the charge of the actual carrier during such part of the carriage. Nevertheless, any stipulation limiting or excluding such liability is without effect if no judicial proceedings can be instituted against the actual carrier in a court competent under paragraph 1 or 2 of article 21. The burden of proving that any loss, damage or delay in delivery has been caused by such an occurrence rests upon the carrier.

2. The actual carrier is responsible in accordance with the provisions of paragraph 2 of article 10 for loss, damage or delay in delivery caused by an occurrence which takes place while the goods are in his charge.

13.5 Carrier's liability and limits of liability

Article 5
Basis of liability

1. The carrier is liable for loss resulting from loss of or damage to the goods, as well as from delay in delivery, if the occurrence which caused the loss, damage or delay took place while the goods were in his charge as defined in article 4, unless the carrier proves that he, his servants or agents took all measures that could reasonably be required to avoid the occurrence and its consequences.

2. Delay in delivery occurs when the goods have not been delivered at the port of discharge provided for in the contract of carriage by sea within the time expressly agreed upon or, in the absence of such agreement, within the time which it would be reasonable to require of a diligent carrier, having regard to the circumstances of the case.

3. The person entitled to make a claim for the loss of goods may treat the goods as lost if they have not been delivered as required by article 4 within 60 consecutive days following the expiry of the time for delivery according to paragraph 2 of this article.

The carrier is liable

(I) for loss of or damage to the goods or delay in delivery caused by fire, if the claimant proves that the fire arose from fault or neglect on the part of the carrier, his servants or agents;

(II)   for such loss, damage or delay in delivery which is proved by the claimant to have resulted from the fault or neglect of the carrier, his servants or agents, in taking all measures that could reasonably be required to put out the fire and avoid or mitigate its consequences.

In case of fire on board the ship affecting the goods, if the claimant or the carrier so desires, a survey in accordance with shipping practices must be held into the cause and circumstances of the fire, and a copy of the surveyor's report shall be made available on demand to the carrier and the claimant.

4.   With respect to live animals, the carrier is not liable for loss, damage or delay in delivery resulting from any special risks inherent in that kind of carriage. If the carrier proves that he has complied with any special instructions given to him by the shipper respecting the animals and that, in the circumstances of the case, the loss, damage or delay in delivery could be attributed to such risks, it is presumed that the loss, damage or delay in delivery was so caused, unless there is proof that all or a part of the loss, damage or delay in delivery resulted from fault or neglect on the part of the carrier, his servants or agents.

5.   The carrier is not liable, except in general average, where loss, damage or delay in delivery resulted from measures to save life or from reasonable measures to save property at sea.

6.   Where fault or neglect on the part of the carrier, his servants or agents combines with another cause to produce loss, damage or delay in delivery the carrier is liable only to the extent that the loss, damage or delay in delivery is attributable to such fault or neglect, provided that the carrier proves the amount of the loss, damage or delay in delivery not attributable thereto.

There are thus some important differences between the Hague-Visby Rules and the Hamburg Rules as regards carrier liability.

1.   The Hamburg Rules apply from port-to-port instead of from tackle-to-tackle.
2.   They also apply to all contracts of carriage by sea and not merely to bills of lading or similar documents of title.
3.   The Hamburg Rules do not contain a long list of defences for the carrier unlike the Hague-Visby Rules. That of course does not mean that there are no defences available to the carrier under the Hamburg Rules but any defence raised would be constrained or qualified by the requirement of the carrier to take reasonable care of the goods.
4.   Another important difference is that the Hamburg Rules adopt a single standard of care on the owner as regards seaworthiness and proper care of the cargo; whereas in the Hague-Visby Rules, seaworthiness and care of cargo are contained in two separate and distinct articles.
5.   Importantly, the Hamburg Rules do away with the error in navigation and ship management as a defence.
6.   It has also been suggested that the burden of proof rules under the Hamburg Rules are more straightforward – once the cargo interest is able to show that loss or damage occurred during the carriage, the carrier then bears the burden of proof throughout under Art 5(1). (NB. The position is slightly different in the case of fire damage or loss: see Art 5(4)(b)). That said, through the passage of time, case law has rendered the issue of burden of proof as regards the Hague-Visby Rules much more pellucid.
7.   It should be noted that Art 5(1) requires the use of reasonable care throughout the carriage/transit. The Hague-Visby Rules adopts a different language – that expressed as 'due diligence'. It remains to be seen whether the two concepts would be construed by the courts as being the same.
8.   The Hamburg Rules clearly extend liability of the carrier for delay (Art 5(1)(2)) – that is not explicit in the Hague-Visby Rules.

Article 6
Limits of liability

    (a)   The liability of the carrier for loss resulting from loss of or damage to goods according to the provisions of article 5 is limited to an amount equivalent to 835 units of account per package or other shipping unit or 2.5 units of account per kilogramme of gross weight of the goods lost or damaged, whichever is the higher.

    (b)   The liability of the carrier for delay in delivery according to the provisions of article 5 is limited to an amount equivalent to two and a half times the freight payable for the goods delayed, but not exceeding the total freight payable under the contract of carriage of goods by sea.

    (c)   In no case shall the aggregate liability of the carrier, under both subparagraphs (a) and (b) of this paragraph, exceed the limitation which would be established under subparagraph (a) of this paragraph for total loss of the goods with respect to which such liability was incurred.

1.   For the purpose of calculating which amount is the higher in accordance with paragraph 1(a) of this article, the following rules apply:

    (a)   Where a container, pallet or similar article of transport is used to consolidate goods, the package or other shipping units enumerated in the bill of lading, if issued, or otherwise in any other document evidencing the contract of carriage by sea, as packed in such article of transport are deemed packages or shipping units. Except as aforesaid the goods in such article of transport are deemed one shipping unit.

    (b)   In cases where the article of transport itself has been lost or damaged, that article of transport, if not owned or otherwise supplied by the carrier, is considered one separate shipping unit.

2.   Unit of account means the unit of account mentioned in article 26.

3.   By agreement between the carrier and the shipper, limits of liability exceeding those provided for in paragraph 1 may be fixed.

Article 7
Application to non-contractual claims

1.   The defences and limits of liability provided for in this Convention apply in any action against the carrier in respect of loss or damage to the goods covered by the contract of carriage by sea, as well as of delay in delivery whether the action is founded in contract, in tort or otherwise.

2.   If such an action is brought against a servant or agent of the carrier, such servant or agent, if he proves that he acted within the scope of his employment, is entitled to avail himself of the defences and limits of liability which the carrier is entitled to invoke under this Convention.

3.   Except as provided in article 8, the aggregate of the amounts recoverable from the carrier and from any persons referred to in paragraph 2 of this article shall not exceed the limits of liability provided for in this Convention.

Article 8
Loss of right to limit responsibility

1.   The carrier is not entitled to the benefit of the limitation of liability provided for in article 6 if it is proved that the loss, damage or delay in delivery resulted from an act or omission of the carrier done with the intent to cause such loss, damage or delay, or recklessly and with knowledge that such loss, damage or delay would probably result.

2.   Notwithstanding the provisions of paragraph 2 of article 7, a servant or agent of the carrier is not entitled to the benefit of the limitation of liability provided for in article 6 if it is proved that the loss, damage or delay in delivery resulted from an act or omission of such servant or agent, done with the intent to cause such loss, damage or delay, or recklessly and with knowledge that such loss, damage or delay would probably result.

13.6 Shipper liability

In contrast to the Hague-Visby Rules, the Hamburg Rules make specific provision for shipper liability.

Article 12

General rule

The shipper is not liable for loss sustained by the carrier or the actual carrier, or for damage sustained by the ship, unless such loss or damage was caused by the fault or neglect of the shipper, his servants or agents. Nor is any servant or agent of the shipper liable for such loss or damage unless the loss or damage was caused by fault or neglect on his part.

Article 13

Special rules on dangerous goods

1. The shipper must mark or label in a suitable manner dangerous goods as dangerous.
2. Where the shipper hands over dangerous goods to the carrier or an actual carrier, as the case may be, the shipper must inform him of the dangerous character of the goods and, if necessary, of the precautions to be taken. If the shipper fails to do so and such carrier or actual carrier does not otherwise have knowledge of their dangerous character:
   (a) the shipper is liable to the carrier and any actual carrier for the loss resulting from the shipment of such goods, and
   (b) the goods may at any time be unloaded, destroyed or rendered innocuous, as the circumstances may require, without payment of compensation.
3. The provisions of paragraph 2 of this article may not be invoked by any person if during the carriage he has taken the goods in his charge with knowledge of their dangerous character.
4. If, in cases where the provisions of paragraph 2, subparagraph (b), of this article do not apply or may not be invoked, dangerous goods become an actual danger to life or property, they may be unloaded, destroyed or rendered innocuous, as the circumstances may require, without payment of compensation except where there is an obligation to contribute in general average or where the carrier is liable in accordance with the provisions of article 5.

...

Article 17

Guarantees by the shipper

1. The shipper is deemed to have guaranteed to the carrier the accuracy of particulars relating to the general nature of the goods, their marks, number, weight and quantity as furnished by him for insertion in the bill of lading. The shipper must indemnify the carrier against the loss resulting from inaccuracies in such particulars. The shipper remains liable even if the bill of lading has been transferred by him. The right of the carrier to such indemnity in no way limits his liability under the contract of carriage by sea to any person other than the shipper.
2. Any letter of guarantee or agreement by which the shipper undertakes to indemnify the carrier against loss resulting from the issuance of the bill of lading by the carrier, or by a person acting on his behalf, without entering a reservation relating to particulars furnished by the shipper for insertion in the bill of lading, or to the apparent condition of the goods, is void and of no effect as against any third party, including a consignee, to whom the bill of lading has been transferred.
3. Such letter of guarantee or agreement is valid as against the shipper unless the carrier or the person acting on his behalf, by omitting the reservation referred to in paragraph 2 of this article, intends to defraud a third party, including a consignee, who acts in reliance on the description of the goods in the bill of lading. In the latter case, if the reservation omitted relates to particulars furnished by

the shipper for insertion in the bill of lading, the carrier has no right of indemnity from the shipper pursuant to paragraph 1 of this article.

4.   In the case of intended fraud referred to in paragraph 3 of this article the carrier is liable, without the benefit of the limitation of liability provided for in this Convention, for the loss incurred by a third party, including a consignee, because he has acted in reliance on the description of the goods in the bill of lading.

13.7 Carrier's duties in respect of documentation

The provisions in the Hamburg Rules on the carrier's duty to issue the appropriate transport document/s are more detailed than those in the Hague-Visby Rules. In this connection, international traders have tended to prefer the less interventionist Hague-Visby Rules.

Article 14
Issue of bill of lading
1.   When the carrier or the actual carrier takes the goods in his charge, the carrier must, on demand of the shipper, issue to the shipper a bill of lading.
2.   The bill of lading may be signed by a person having authority from the carrier. A bill of lading signed by the master of the ship carrying the goods is deemed to have been signed on behalf of the carrier.
3.   The signature on the bill of lading may be in handwriting, printed in facsimile, perforated, stamped, in symbols, or made by an other mechanical or electronic means, if not inconsistent with the law of the country where the bill of lading is issued.

Article 15
Contents of bill of lading
1.   The bill of lading must include, inter alia, the following particulars:
(a)   the general nature of the goods, the leading marks necessary for identification of the goods, an express statement, if applicable, as to the dangerous character of the goods, the number of packages or pieces, and the weight of the goods or their quantity otherwise expressed, all such particulars as furnished by the shipper;
(b)   the apparent condition of the goods;
(c)   the name and principal place of business of the carrier;
(d)   the name of the shipper;
(e)   the consignee if named by the shipper;
(f)   the port of loading under the contract of carriage by sea and the date on which the goods were taken over by the carrier at the port of loading;
(g)   the port of discharge under the contract of carriage by sea;
(h)   the number of originals of the bill of lading, if more than one;
(i)   the place of issuance of the bill of lading;
(j)   the signature of the carrier or a person acting on his behalf;
(k)   the freight to the extent payable by the consignee or other indication that freight is payable by him;
(l)   the statement referred to in paragraph 3 of article 23;
(m)   the statement, if applicable, that the goods shall or may be carried on deck;
(n)   the date or the period of delivery of the goods at the port of discharge if expressly agreed upon between the parties; and
(o)   any increased limit or limits of liability where agreed in accordance with paragraph 4 of article 6.

2. After the goods have been loaded on board, if the shipper so demands, the carrier must issue to the shipper a 'shipped' bill of lading which, in addition to the particulars required under paragraph 1 of this article, must state that the goods are on board a named ship or ships, and the date or dates of loading. If the carrier has previously issued to the shipper a bill of lading or other document of title with resect to any of such goods, on request of the carrier, the shipper must surrender such document in exchange for a 'shipped' bill of lading. The carrier may amend any previously issued document in order to meet the shipper's demand for a 'shipped' bill of lading if, as amended, such document includes all the information required to be contained in a 'shipped' bill of lading.

3. The absence in the bill of lading of one or more particulars referred to in this article does not affect the legal character of the document as a bill of lading provided that it nevertheless meets the requirements set out in paragraph 7 of article 1.

Article 16
Bills of lading: Reservations and evidentiary effect

1. If the bill of lading contains particulars concerning the general nature, leading marks, number of packages or pieces, weight or quantity of the goods which the carrier or other person issuing the bill of lading on his behalf knows or has reasonable grounds to suspect do not accurately represent the goods actually taken over or, where a 'shipped' bill of lading is issued, loaded, or if he had no reasonable means of checking such particulars, the carrier or such other person must insert in the bill of lading a reservation specifying these inaccuracies, grounds of suspicion or the absence of reasonable means of checking.

2. If the carrier or other person issuing the bill of lading on his behalf fails to note on the bill of lading the apparent condition of the goods, he is deemed to have noted on the bill of lading that the goods were in apparent good condition.

3. Except for particulars in respect of which and to the extent to which a reservation permitted under paragraph 1 of this article has been entered:

   (a) the bill of lading is prima facie evidence of the taking over or, where a 'shipped' bill of lading is issued, loading, by the carrier of the goods as described in the bill of lading; and

   (b) proof to the contrary by the carrier is not admissible if the bill of lading has been transferred to a third party, including a consignee, who in good faith has acted in reliance on the description of the goods therein.

4. A bill of lading which does not, as provided in paragraph 1, subparagraph (k) of article 15, set forth the freight or otherwise indicate that freight is payable by the consignee or does not set forth demurrage incurred at the port of loading payable by the consignee, is prima facie evidence that no freight or such demurrage is payable by him. However, proof to the contrary by the carrier is not admissible when the bill of lading has been transferred to a third party, including a consignee, who in good faith has acted in reliance on the absence in the bill of lading of any such indication.

...

Article 18
Documents other than bills of lading

Where a carrier issues a document other than a bill of lading to evidence the receipt of the goods to be carried, such a document is prima facie evidence of the conclusion of the contract of carriage by sea and the taking over by the carrier of the goods as therein described.

13.8 Time limit

Article 19
Notice of loss, damage or delay

1. Unless notice of loss or damage, specifying the general nature of such loss or damage, is given in writing by the consignee to the carrier not later than the working day after the day when the goods were handed over to the consignee, such handing over is prima facie evidence of the delivery by the carrier of the goods as described in the document of transport or, if no such document has been issued, in good condition.
2. Where the loss or damage is not apparent, the provisions of paragraph 1 of this article apply correspondingly if notice in writing is not given within 15 consecutive days after the day when the goods were handed over to the consignee.
3. If the state of the goods at the time they were handed over to the consignee has been the subject of a joint survey or inspection by the parties, notice in writing need not be given of loss or damage ascertained during such survey or inspection.
4. In the case of any actual or apprehended loss or damage the carrier and the consignee must give all reasonable facilities to each other for inspecting and tallying the goods.
5. No compensation shall be payable for loss resulting from delay in delivery unless a notice has been given in writing to the carrier within 60 consecutive days after the day when the goods were handed over to the consignee.
6. If the goods have been delivered by an actual carrier, any notice given under this article to him shall have the same effect as if it had been given to the carrier, and any notice given to the carrier shall have effect as if given to such actual carrier.
7. Unless notice of loss or damage, specifying the general nature of the loss or damage, is given in writing by the carrier or actual carrier to the shipper not later than 90 consecutive days after the occurrence of such loss or damage or after the delivery of the goods in accordance with paragraph 2 of article 4, whichever is later, the failure to give such notice is prima facie evidence that the carrier or the actual carrier has sustained no loss or damage due to the fault or neglect of the shipper, his servants or agents.
8. For the purpose of this article, notice given to a person acting on the carrier's or the actual carrier's behalf, including the master or the officer in charge of the ship, or to a person acting on the shipper's behalf is deemed to have been given to the carrier, to the actual carrier or to the shipper, respectively.

Article 20
Limitation of actions

1. Any action relating to carriage of goods under this Convention is time-barred if judicial or arbitral proceedings have not been instituted within a period of two years.
2. The limitation period commences on the day on which the carrier has delivered the goods or part thereof or, in cases where no goods have been delivered, on the last day on which the goods should have been delivered.
3. The day on which the limitation period commences is not included in the period.
4. The person against whom a claim is made may at any time during the running of the limitation period extend that period by a declaration in writing to the claimant. This period may be further extended by another declaration or declarations.
5. An action for indemnity by a person held liable may be instituted even after the expiration of the limitation period provided for in the preceding paragraphs if instituted within the time allowed by the law of the State where proceedings are instituted. However, the time allowed shall not be less than 90 days commencing from the day when the person instituting such action for indemnity has settled the claim or has been served with process in the action against himself.

13.9 Initial reception

Waldron, AJ, 'The Hamburg Rules – a boondoggle for lawyers?' (1991) JBL 305

[footnotes omitted]

The Hamburg Rules have certainly generated significant opposition among shipowning interests and little active enthusiasm as is shown by the very sluggish rate at which states have become parties. However, if the Hague Rules had used the same machinery governing their entry into force, it would have taken over 30 years before they became effective.

There has also been some rather churlish criticism of the status of the current parties to the Convention as playing an insignificant part in World trade. In a recent BIMCO Bulletin, members of the organisation are given the unequivocal advice that, 'the current pro Hamburg Rules campaign by shippers and their organisations must be resisted at every opportunity and any moves by government administrations towards ratification of the Hamburg Rules [must] be discouraged.' In advancing this case the following potent observation is made, 'it is clear that the Hamburg Rules would cast aside the results of half a century of expensive litigation and pave the way for another half century of legal debate on a new and different regime uniformity and certainty would be lost and litigation lawyers would be the sole beneficiaries.' This point has much force, but it has at its core a reaction to change and reform of the system based on the Hague Rules, an ageing and imperfect regime whose need for reform is testified to by the widespread acceptance of the Visby Protocol. The adoption of a new system of carrier liability has much to commend it, over piecemeal reforms which countries can either accept or reject.

The claim that the Hamburg Rules overly favour cargo owners is predictable, and suggested by the 'Common Understanding' of the Final Conference, but so far as the effect of the Rules is concerned it does not bear close scrutiny. This is no system of strict carrier liability, it has at its core, the principle of liability based on carrier fault. It is true that in general carrier fault is presumed but this is subject to important exceptions. The imposition of the burden of proof upon carriers, (except in the case of fire, an important exception) is hardly an unbearable burden as they will be in a position to control the carriage and ascertain the cause of any loss. They need only show that they were not negligent. Carrier liability is subject to very modest limitation levels which will only be lost in the most exceptional of circumstances. Deviation is deprived of its singular effect, and deck cargo is treated more tolerantly than was previously the case. From a purely legal viewpoint the forecast of radically increased freight rates when the Hamburg Rules become operative is unjustified, and seems a little alarmist. In any event the costs would inevitably be passed on to the long-suffering consumer.

The single test of carrier liability should be welcomed in principle, as should its application to both inbound and outbound voyages. However the test lacks clarity, and uniformity of definition in the Convention. This is a serious weakness and can only generate litigation. There is some force in the argument that the abolition of the battery of defences in Art. IV(2) of the Hague Rules will deprive those involved in shipping of a useful guide to liability, but most of the defences would be covered by the 'reasonable measures' defence to liability under the Hamburg Rules, and therefore the case law generated by Art. IV(2) would not be entirely redundant. It is a great shame that the lucidity of drafting which characterises provisions relating, for example, to the question of forum, is not applied evenly throughout the Convention, but considering the fact that the Rules were necessarily a compromise measure, this is perhaps inevitable. Despite its weaknesses, an international momentum now seems to be developing which will lead to the Convention's operation in the near future and it is quite possible that its acceptance by a major trading nation would give it the critical mass it needs to overthrow the ancien regime based on the Hague Rules.

Note

It is highly unlikely now that the Hamburg Rules will have the impetus to 'overthrow the ancien regime based on the Hague Rules'; the international community have more or less given up hope that the Hamburg Rules could gain any more traction towards international acceptance. The hope for some is for the Rotterdam Rules to overthrow the Hague regime. We shall consider this ambitious new convention in the next chapter.

 Further reading

Boyd, S, Burrows, A and Foxton, D, *Scrutton on Charterparties and Bills of Lading*, 20th edn, 1996, London: Sweet & Maxwell.

Chuah, J, 'Application of the Hague-Visby Rules: By force of law or contract' (2008) 54(Sum) SL Rev 47.

Clarke, M, 'Misdelivery and time bars' (1989) LMCLQ 394.

Clarke, M, 'The carrier's duty of seaworthiness under the Hague Rules', in Rose, F (ed), *Lex Mercatoria: Essays in Honour of Francis Reynolds*, 2000, London: Lloyd's of London, p 105.

Comité Maritime International, *The Travaux Preparatoires of the Hague Rules and of the Hague-Visby Rules*, 1997, Antwerp: CMI.

Davenport, B, 'Problems in the Bills of Lading Act' (1989) 105 LQR 521.

Debattista, C, 'Sea waybills and the Carriage of Goods by Sea Act 1971' (1989) LMCLQ 403.

Diamond, A, 'The Hague-Visby Rules' (1978) LMCLQ 225.

Diplock L, 'Conventions and morals – Limitation clauses in international maritime conventions' (1969–70) JMLC 525.

Gaskell, N, Asariotis, R and Baatz, Y, *Bills of Lading: Law and Contracts*, 2000, London: Lloyd's of London.

Girvin, S, 'The 37th Comité Maritime International Conference' (2001) LMCLQ 406.

Institute of Maritime Law, University of Southampton Colloquium, 'CMI/UNCITRAL Preliminary Draft Instrument' (2002) 3 LMCLQ 304–441.

Margetson NJ, 'Liability of the carrier under the Hague (Visby) Rules for cargo damage caused by unseaworthiness of its containers' (2008) 14(2) JIML 153.

Reynolds, F, *The Butterworth Lectures 1990–91*, 1991, London: Butterworths.

Sturley, M, *Legislative History of the Carriage of Goods by Sea Act and the Travaux Preparatoires of the Hague Rules*, 1990, Littleton, CO: Rothman.

Sturley, M, 'The history of COGSA and the Hague Rules' (1991) JMLC 1.

Sturley, M, 'Uniformity in the law governing the carriage of goods by sea' (1995) JMLC 553.

Sze, P-F, 'The period of responsibility for contracting and actual carriers under the Hague/Hague-Visby and Hamburg Rules' (2000) 3(Sep) CLL Rev 207.

Tetley, W, *Marine Cargo Claims*, 3rd edn, 1988, Montreal: BLAIS; 4th edn available at www.tetley.law.mcgill.ca.

Tetley, W, 'Interpretation and construction of the Hague, Hague/Visby and Hamburg Rules' (2004) 10(1) JIML 30.

Tomlinson, S, 'Due diligence and delegation', in Rose, F (ed), *Lex Mercatoria: Essays in Honour of Francis Reynolds*, 2000, London: Lloyd's of London, p 157.

Treitel, G and Reynolds, F, *Carver on Bills of Lading*, 2001, London: Sweet & Maxwell.

Waldron, AJ, 'The Hamburg Rules – a boondoggle for lawyers?' (1991) Jul JBL 305.

White, R, 'The human factor in unseaworthiness claims' (1995) 2(May) LMCLQ 221.

Chapter 8

The Rotterdam Rules

We have already commented that the international community had not been satisfied with the Hamburg Rules and have since the 1990s been involved in the design and enactment of a new international transport convention applicable to carriage of goods by sea. That work culminated in the UN Convention on Contracts for the International Carriage of Goods Wholly or Partly by Sea (the so-called Rotterdam Rules) 2009.

1 Rationale

UN General Assembly Resolution 63/122

[footnotes omitted]

The General Assembly,

Recalling its resolution 2205 (XXI) of 17 December 1966, by which it established the United Nations Commission on International Trade Law with a mandate to further the progressive harmonization and unification of the law of international trade and in that respect to bear in mind the interests of all peoples, in particular those of developing countries, in the extensive development of international trade,

Concerned that the current legal regime governing the international carriage of goods by sea lacks uniformity and fails to adequately take into account modern transport practices, including containerization, door-to-door transport contracts and the use of electronic transport documents,

Noting that the development of international trade on the basis of equality and mutual benefit is an important element in promoting friendly relations among States,

Convinced that the adoption of uniform rules to modernize and harmonize the rules that govern the international carriage of goods involving a sea leg would enhance legal certainty, improve efficiency and commercial predictability in the international carriage of goods and reduce legal obstacles to the flow of international trade among all States,

Believing that the adoption of uniform rules to govern international contracts of carriage wholly or partly by sea will promote legal certainty, improve the efficiency of international carriage of goods and facilitate new access opportunities for previously remote parties and markets, thus playing a fundamental role in promoting trade and economic development, both domestically and internationally,

Noting that shippers and carriers do not have the benefit of a binding and balanced universal regime to support the operation of contracts of carriage involving various modes of transport

Recalling that, at its thirty-fourth and thirty-fifth sessions, in 2001 and 2002, the Commission decided to prepare an international legislative instrument governing door-to-door transport operations that involve a sea leg,

Recognizing that all States and interested international organizations were invited to participate in the preparation of the draft Convention on Contracts for the International Carriage of Goods Wholly or Partly by Sea and in the forty-first session of the Commission, either as members or as observers, with a full opportunity to speak and make proposals,

Noting with satisfaction that the text of the draft Convention was circulated for comment to all States Members of the United Nations and intergovernmental organizations invited to attend the meetings of the Commission as observers, and that the comments received were before the Commission at its forty-first session,

Taking note with satisfaction of the decision of the Commission at its forty first session to submit the draft Convention to the General Assembly for its consideration,

Taking note of the draft Convention approved by the Commission,

Expressing its appreciation to the Government of the Netherlands for its offer to host a signing ceremony for the Convention in Rotterdam,

1. Commends the United Nations Commission on International Trade Law for preparing the draft Convention on Contracts for the International Carriage of Goods Wholly or Partly by Sea;
2. Adopts the United Nations Convention on Contracts for the International Carriage of Goods Wholly or Partly by Sea, contained in the annex to the present resolution;
3. Authorizes a ceremony for the opening for signature to be held on 23 September 2009 in Rotterdam, the Netherlands, and recommends that the rules embodied in the Convention be known as the "Rotterdam Rules";
4. Calls upon all Governments to consider becoming party to the Convention.

67th plenary meeting
11 December 2008

2 Contracts to which the Rules apply

It must be recalled that the Rotterdam Rules do not apply to all contracts of carriage or for carriage of goods by sea.

Thomas, DR, 'Chapter 1: The emergence and application of the Rotterdam Rules'

Thomas, DR (ed.), *Carriage of Goods under the Rotterdam Rules*, 2010, London: Informa (footnotes omitted)

1.10 The Rules do not apply to all categories of marine commercial contracts which may in one way or another be directly or indirectly associated with the carriage of goods by sea. In their generality the Rules apply to contracts for the international carriage of goods wholly or partly by sea, and which have a specified connection with Contracting States. The Rules never appear to succeed in making this point succinctly and clearly, consequently it has to be deduced from several of their relevant provisions. The Rules, therefore, regulate international contracts under which the obligation of the carrier is 'to carry goods' according to the terms of the contract, in other words, in the language of the common law bailment contracts. Other categories of commercial maritime transport contracts, which may involve the international carriage of goods but under which the carrier undertakes not to carry goods but to make the vessel available for hire or contracts out the use of the vessel, are not within the regulatory regime of the Rules, notwithstanding that the ulterior purpose of such contracts is the carriage of goods.

1.11 It is now proposed to expound on this introductory statement describing the application of the Rules by analysing the several constituent elements.

Contract of carriage
1.12 A 'contract of carriage' is defined in article 1.1 as meaning:

> 'a contract in which a carrier, against the payment of freight, undertakes to carry goods from one place to another. The contract shall provide for carriage by sea and may provide for carriage by other modes of transport in addition to the sea carriage.'

1.13 The primary definition, in defining the carrier as a party who 'undertakes to carry goods', follows the traditional position. What, in the first place, is alluded to is a contractual bailment in relation to sea carriage, the kind of contracts associated with liner trades [defined in Art 1.3] and which in contemporary shipping practice are described as bill of lading and sea waybill contracts. It is an interesting question whether volume contracts which are defined as contracts that 'provide for carriage' [defined in Art 1.2] fall within this definition.

1.14 The second sentence of the definition makes it clear that other modes of transport may be added to the sea carriage without affecting the category. This extension lays down the foundation to the application of the Rules beyond port-to-port contracts to include place-to-place contracts with a sea leg, in other words multimodal contracts with a sea leg.

1.15 Although the principal kinds of contract regulated are what in commercial language would be described as liner trade contracts, the association is not universal. Bulk cargoes are carried principally in chartered vessels, more often than not under voyage charterparties, but there would be nothing to preclude such carriage being undertaken under a contractual bailment. However rare this possibility might be, should it occur the contract of carriage would be within the Rules.

1.16 Contracts, other than bailment contracts, are not within the definition and therefore not regulated. This exclusion includes simple charterparties, such as time, voyage and hybrid charterparties, which are contracts for the use of a ship; and demise or bareboat charterparties, which are contracts of hire. It is equally clear that contracts of affreightment (COAs) are excluded, these being in their essence framework contracts to provide shipping and/or cargo according to agreed contractual terms.

1.17 It is noteworthy that the issuance of a negotiable or non-negotiable transport document is not an essential component of the definition. In most instances a bill of lading or sea waybill will be issued, which the shipper has a conditional right to demand, in keeping with contemporary practice, but this is not essential for the application of the Rules. Even if a transport document is not issued the Rules may still apply providing they are otherwise applicable. In this regard the Rules follow the policy of the Hamburg Rules and are to be contrasted with the Hague Rules, which require the issuance of a bill of lading or at least the contractual contemplation that a bill of lading will be issued.

1.18 The contract exists between the contractual carrier and contractual shipper. Carrier is defined as 'a person that enters into a contract of carriage with a shipper' [Art 1.5], and 'shipper' as 'a person that enters into a contract of carriage with a carrier' [Art 1.8]. The 'carrier', therefore, does not include the physical carrier, who may, nonetheless, be a 'maritime performing party' under the Convention [Art 1.7] and in that capacity be burdened with legal duties and liabilities corresponding with those of the contractual carrier [Art 19]. Nor does the reference to 'shipper' in this context include 'documentary shipper', who is defined as 'a person, other than the shipper, that accepts to be named as 'shipper' in the transport document or electronic transport record' [Art 1.9]. The documentary shipper is therefore not a contractual shipper but is, nonetheless, a party who is burdened with the same duties and potential liabilities as a contracting shipper [Art 33].

1.19 The consideration for the carriage or promise to carry must be in the form of freight, which is monetary payment, and defined as meaning, 'the remuneration payable to the carrier for the carriage of goods under a contract of carriage' [Art 1.28]. In the event that the consideration takes some other form, such as the provision of goods or services, the contract is not within the Rules.

...

Contracts to which the Rotterdam Rules do not apply: Excluded contracts

Introduction

1.41 The contracts specifically excluded from the province of the Rules are set out in the two sub-articles of article 6. In general terms the excluded contracts are charterparties and analogous contracts. But under the article the excluded contracts are clothed in a wider distinction between liner and non-liner transportation, both of which are terms defined in article 1. This is a curious and, it would seem, unhelpful methodology because it appears to be purposeless. It achieves no positive function in defining the application of the Rules, but, regrettably, it does possess the capacity to confuse and perplex. An aspect of the application of the Rules that ought to be straightforward has consequently been rendered less so.

1.42 It does not necessarily follow that because a contract is not excluded under article 6 it must be a contract to which the Rules apply. It remains the case that such a contract must fall within the definition of contracts to which the Rules apply.

Exclusion of certain contracts in liner transportation
1.43 Article 6.1 provides:

'This Convention does not apply to the following contracts in liner transportation: (a) Charterparties; and (b) Other contracts for the use of a ship or of any space thereon.'

1.44 'Liner transportation' is defined in the following terms in article 1.3:

'means a transportation service that is offered to the public through publication or similar means and includes transportation by ships operating on a regular schedule between specific ports in accordance with publicly available timetables of sailing dates.'

1.45 The clear implication of article 6.1 is that the Rules apply, as previously discussed, to contracts of carriage associated with the liner trade, namely contracts of carriage which in contemporary practice are likely to be evidenced by bills of lading or sea waybills and other bailment contracts. The sub-article makes an equally clear express statement that charterparties and other contracts for the use of a ship which may regulate ships operating in the liner trade are excluded from the Rules.

1.46 Consequently, if a carrying ship in the liner trade is operated under a time charterparty, as is often the case, contracts of carriage entered into by or on behalf of the owners or time charterers are capable of being regulated by the Rules but not the charterparty. The same is true should the vessel be operating under a voyage charterparty, which is less likely in practice.

1.47 The exclusion applies to charterparties (which are contracts for the use of a ship) and to other contracts for the use of a ship or any space thereon. The latter words extend the exclusion to include slot charterparties and, more widely, charter-parties for the use of part of a ship and hybrid charterparties. It is, however, a little odd to refer to 'charterparties and other contracts for the use of a ship' when a charterparty is a contract for the use of a ship. If the extended words possess any usefulness, it is probably to indicate that a contract may be characterised as a charterparty notwithstanding that it has not been described as such by the parties.

1.48 In strictness the reference to charterparties does not include bareboat (demise) charterparties, which in English law are understood to be contracts of hire, but which are nevertheless excluded from the Rules because they do not fall within the definition of contracts to which the Rules do apply. It is, however, not impossible that as a question of interpretation the understanding of demise or bareboat charterparties in English law might not be carried forward into the meaning of the words of the sub-article and with them consequently interpreted to include a reference to bareboat charterparties. But for reasons just explained, such a strained interpretation is not necessary in order to give full effect to the intention underlying the Rules.

Inclusion of certain contracts in non-liner transportation
1.49 Article 6.2 provides:

'The Convention does not apply to contracts of carriage in non-liner transportation except when: (a) There is no charter party or other contract between the parties for the use of a ship or of any space thereon; and (b)A transport document or an electronic transport record is issued.'

1.50 Non-liner trade is defined in the following way in article 1.4: 'means any transportation that is not liner transportation.'

1.51 This sub-article reinforces indications found elsewhere in the Rules and previously discussed that they do not apply to any category of charterparty, which is the typical contract found in non-liner transportation or what many would describe as tramp shipping. But, at the same time, the sub-article recognises that charterparties are not necessarily universally synonymous with non-liner transportation and that even within this sector of shipping contracts of carriage may be entered into which are bailment contracts and, therefore, within the ambit of the Rules.

1.52 For a contract, in these circumstances, to be within the Rules there must not exist a charterparty or analogous contract between the parties, meaning, in the light of article 7, the original contracting parties, and a transport document or electronic record must have been issued. Although, in general, the Rules apply to bailment contracts, whether or not a transport document or electronic record has been issued, article 6.2 establishes an exception to this general approach.

1.53 The following are suggested as examples of how the sub-article might operate.

1.54 In very exceptional circumstances a bulk cargo or heavy lift cargo or any other cargo similar in kind may be carried on bailment and not charterparty terms, with only a transport document issued. When this occurs the Rules apply.

1.55 Probably a more readily identifiable example is when a sub-charterer is also the shipper of bulk cargo and receives a transport document (invariably a bill of lading) from the actual, quasi or desponent owner, other than his own desponent owner. In this situation the sub-charterer has not entered into a charterparty with the party that has issued the transport document, but a transport document has been issued to the sub-charterer in respect of the shipment which establishes a contract of carriage between the issuer of the document and the sub-charterer. By virtue of article 6.2 this contract is governed by the Rules.

1.56 The contractual hierarchy of time and voyage charterparties regulating the operation of a sole vessel engaged in non-liner transportation may be numerous in number and productive of a complex whole, but whenever in this context a contractual relationship emerges between parties based solely on a transport document or electronic record, and who are, therefore, not also parties to a charterparty, the contract of carriage is within the Rules.

1.57 Article 7 further reinforces the point, albeit indirectly and in different language, that the Rules do not apply as between the original parties to a contract of carriage excluded pursuant to article 6.

Articles 6 and 7 have been criticised for introducing a level of complexity which had not caused difficulties under the present transport regimes. For a counter-argument, see the following article.

Berlingieri, F, 'Revisiting the Rotterdam Rules' (2010) LMCLQ 583, 589–592

[footnotes omitted]

After quoting the definitions of 'liner transportation' and 'non-liner transportation' and Arts 6 and 7, Diamond [Diamond [2009] LMCLQ 445] says that the attempts to define charterparties had failed and the meaning of 'charter parties' and of the subsequent phrase in Art 6, 'other contracts for the use of a ship or of any space thereon', will have to be determined by the courts. He then stresses that a point of some importance is likely to be whether a contract can be a charterparty if no ship or ships are named or identified in it and says that his tentative view is that such a contract may well be held not to be a charterparty.

A further example he gives is that of an agreement by a freight contractor to supply ships in the course of a long future period for a series of shipments of goods at specified intervals and says that he would have difficulty in characterising the contract as a charterparty as well as a contract 'for the use of a ship or any space thereon'. He consequently doubts that a contract of affreightment, if used in liner transportation, would be excluded.

I suggest that the overall structure of Art 6 should first be considered, such structure being based on the distinction between liner trade and non-liner trade. Although formulated in a negative manner, the basic rule is that the Rotterdam Rules apply to contracts of carriage in the liner trade and do not apply to contracts of carriage in the non-liner trade.

Contracts that may be qualified as charterparties or contracts 'for the use of a ship or any space thereon' are excluded from the scope of the Rotterdam Rules. Therefore, since such contracts are not ordinarily used in the liner trade, the doubts expressed by Diamond relate to marginal situations. In any event, I believe that, on the basis of the correct interpretation of Art 6.1, the concerns expressed by him are not justified.

The lack of a definition of 'charter party' should not be a cause for concern, since no such definition exists in the Hague-Visby Rules (nor does it exist in the Hamburg Rules) and it does not appear that there has been any difficulty in identifying a document evidencing a contract of affreightment as a charterparty. Diamond is right when he says that the need for a definition was considered. The attempts to draft a satisfactory definition failed, in consideration, inter alia, of the new forms of charterparty that the trade had created as well as, and perhaps in particular because of, the fact that any definition would probably fail to cover new forms that may be used in the future.

As regards the subsequent reference, in Art 6.1(b), to 'other contracts for the use of a ship or of any space thereon', I think that that wording covers any type of contract for the use of a ship, including charterparties. The wording of this provision, drafted by an informal working group during the 14th session of the Working Group, contained originally, as Diamond indicates, a reference to 'volume contracts, contracts of affreightment, and similar contracts providing for the future carriage of goods in a series of shipments, whether used in connection with liner services or not'. No specific comments were made by the Working Group on that specific provision, which subsequently appears in the annex to a Note to the Secretariat dated 17 February 2005. At the 15th session of the Working Group, several issues were considered, including whether OLSAs should be included within the scope of application of the instrument or not; and the Working Group decided that that issue should be answered in the affirmative. After all issues had been discussed, on the instructions of the Working Group an informal drafting group prepared a revised version of the relevant provisions, including Art 3, wherein, amongst the contracts excluded from the scope of application of the instrument, reference was made, in addition to charterparties, to 'contracts for the use of a ship or of any space thereon'.

It does not appear that the change in the wording was made with a view to changing the substance of the previous text, since the only comment made on it was that 'the proposed redraft of Art 3.1 was intended mainly to exclude contracts of carriage in non-liner transportation from the scope of application of the draft instrument'. Although draft Art 3 was incorporated (becoming Art 6 in the subsequent edition of the draft instrument), the subsequent discussion of this provision took place on the basis of the new draft contained in a proposal of Finland; this, however, differed from the previous draft, mainly in that the basic approach was that of the type of trade – liner and non-liner transportation – and therefore Art 9.1 was formulated in a negative manner, and stated that the Convention does not apply to the contracts of carriage in liner transportation subsequently mentioned, such contracts being '(a) charter parties and (b) contracts for the use of a ship or of any space thereon, whether or not they are charter parties'. Subsequently subparagraph (b) was amended by adding 'other' before 'contracts' and by deleting the final words 'whether or not they are charter parties'.

From the travaux préparatoires it appears, therefore, that the words 'contracts of affreightment and similar contracts' were replaced by 'other contracts for the use of a ship or any space thereon' with a view to widening the categories of contracts that, if used in liner transportation, are excluded from the scope of the Rotterdam Rules.

In order to clarify the notion of 'contracts for the use of a ship', reference must be made to the very wording of the provision, from which it appears that charterparties are contracts for the use of a ship and, secondly, to its employment in other Conventions, such as the Arrest Convention 1952, Art 1.1 of which mentions, under (d) amongst the maritime claims, 'agreement relating to the use or hire of any ship whether by charter party or otherwise'.

My opinion, therefore, is that it was appropriate to avoid any definition, in order to allow the application of the provision to any future type of contract 'for the use of a ship of any space thereon', and that courts will have no difficulty in deciding which types of contract used in the liner trade are not subject to the Rotterdam Rules. With reference to the specific questions raised by Diamond, I think the following answers may be given: (a) a contract in which no ship is named would come under the scope of Art 6.1(a) or (b) if it identifies the characteristics of the ship the use of which is agreed or the amount of space on a ship that should be placed at the disposal of the shipper; (b) an agreement to supply ships in the course of a long future period for a series of shipments of goods at specified intervals would come under the definition of volume contract and, therefore, would be subject to the Rotterdam Rules.

Diamond is of the view that the wording of Art 6.2 may also give rise to problems, and mentions the situation where a transport document is issued pursuant to a contract of affreightment and such contract is not a charterparty or a contract for the use of a ship or any space thereon, since in such case the Convention will apply even though the contract is for 'non-liner transportation'. I think that that situation cannot materialise, for a contract of affreightment comes under the terms of Art 6.1(a) or (b).

Finally, problems are also envisaged by Diamond in respect of Art 7. He says that the wording used is less precise than that used in the corresponding provisions of the Hague-Visby and Hamburg Rules. Perhaps it would be more appropriate to say that such wording is different. And the reason is obvious, since in the Hague-Visby and Hamburg Rules the provision applies only to bills of lading, whereas in the Rotterdam Rules it applies to all contracts of carriage, whether a negotiable or non-negotiable transport document is issued or not or even whether any transport document is issued or not. With reference to the situation where, in case a non-negotiable transport document is issued, a claim is brought by an original party to the contract or by a third party, Diamond says that uncertainty will be caused in either case due to the fact that the Convention does not provide any guidance on what party to the contract has the right to sue for loss or damage to goods but leaves such question to national law. This is correct except where the claim is for loss of or damage to the goods or delay in delivery, for in such case the Rotterdam Rules provide a clear indication with their provisions in the chapter on delivery: it is in fact obvious that the person entitled to delivery is normally the person entitled to claim and that such person is normally not a party to the contract. I therefore find it difficult to understand Diamond's concern. Similarly, I have some difficulty in understanding why he considers Arts 6 and 7 over-complex

It might be suggested that Prof Berlingieri's perspective is largely guided by his civilian legal background, whilst Anthony Diamond QC's insights are based on the often litigious nature of the common law tradition. The civilian approach tends to less prescriptive in legislation drafting enjoining judicial and arbitration tribunals to take a more teleological or purposive reading of the wording. On the other hand, the common law system places much emphasis on precision and explicit clarity in legislative drafting.

2.1 Volume contracts

Where volume contracts are concerned, the parties may choose to contract out of the Rotterdam Rules.

Diamond, 'The Next Sea Carriage Convention' (2008) LMCLQ 135, 146–148

[footnotes omitted]

Volume contracts

The US delegation drew attention to the fact that much international trade was carried under competitively negotiated liner service contracts and proposed that, while 'ocean liner service agreements' (OLSAs) should be subject to the Instrument, it should be possible for the contracting parties expressly to agree to derogate from all or part of the Instrument's provisions; and that, where a transport document was issued pursuant to an OLSA, then the derogation would not be binding on a holder, consignor or consignee who was not a party to the OLSA except to the extent that such party consented to be bound by it or by terms different from those set forth in the Instrument. The proposal was opposed by some delegations, who have argued that it is unfair in principle to smaller shippers for the parties to liner service contracts to be permitted to agree their own special terms.

In subsequent discussions the term 'volume contract' has been adopted and extensive negotiations have taken place as to how a 'volume contract' should be defined, on the extent to which original parties should be allowed to negotiate their own terms of carriage and on the circumstances in which their bargain should be binding on third parties. This, however, has not been sufficient to satisfy the opponents of any kind of special treatment for volume contracts.

A 'volume contract' is defined (Art 1.2) as follows:

> a contract of carriage that provides for the carriage of a specified quantity of goods in a series of shipments during an agreed period of time. The specification of the quantity may include a minimum, a maximum or a certain range.

Critics have pointed to the lack of limitation to this definition, whether in terms of duration, the number of shipments or the quantities carried. It is said that, in principle, the great majority of contracts for the carriage of goods could be framed so as to fall within the definition of 'volume contracts'.

The legal regime applicable to volume contracts is to be found in Art 82 ('Special rules for volume contracts') and may be summarized as follows:

1. As between a carrier and a shipper a volume contract may provide for greater or lesser rights, obligations and liabilities than those imposed by the Convention.
2. However, this does not apply to two out of the three aspects of the duty relating to seaworthiness – the duty to 'make and keep the ship seaworthy' and the duty to 'properly crew, equip and supply the ship and keep the ship so crewed and equipped throughout the voyage'; nor does it apply to Art 30 ('Shipper's obligation to provide information' etc); nor to Art 33 ('Special rules on dangerous goods'); nor to liability arising from an act or omission referred to in Art 63 ('Loss of the benefit of limitation').
3. There are safeguards: the contract must contain a 'prominent statement that it derogates from the Convention'; it must be 'individually negotiated' and 'prominently specify the sections of the volume contract containing the derogations'; the shipper must be given an opportunity and notice of the opportunity to conclude a contract on terms that comply with the Convention without any derogation; and the derogation must not be incorporated by reference from another document or be included in a contract of adhesion that is not subject to negotiation; nor must it be contained solely in a public schedule of prices and services or transport document or electronic transport record.

4. If these conditions are met, the terms apply between the carrier and any person other than the shipper but only if further conditions are satisfied. The person other than the shipper must have received information that prominently states that the volume contract derogates from the Convention and must have given its express consent to be bound by the derogation. The consent must not be solely set forth in the carrier's public schedule of prices and services, transport document or electronic transport record.

5. The party claiming the benefit of the derogations bears the burden of proving that the conditions for derogation have been fulfilled.

These are provisions of potentially wide impact. There seems no reason why individual negotiations that satisfy the conditions should not be concluded between carriers and regular shippers but greater difficulty will probably be experienced in enforcing volume contracts against parties other than the shipper, due to the requirement that such party must have given its express consent to be bound by the derogations, and due to the safeguard that such consent cannot be inferred solely from acceptance of the carrier's schedule of prices or transport document.

It is said that in the cross-Atlantic liner trades the majority of goods are currently carried under service agreements. The Convention, if it comes into force, may well reinforce this trend. It can be seen, therefore, why the provisions on volume contracts have been controversial.

2.2 Definitions relating to the parties, goods and vessel

Article 1

24. 'Goods' means the wares, merchandise, and articles of every kind whatsoever that a carrier undertakes to carry under a contract of carriage and includes the packing and any equipment and container not supplied by or on behalf of the carrier.

25. 'Ship' means any vessel used to carry goods by sea.

26. 'Container' means any type of container, transportable tank or flat, swapbody, or any similar unit load used to consolidate goods, and any equipment ancillary to such unit load.

27. 'Vehicle' means a road or railroad cargo vehicle.

28. 'Freight' means the remuneration payable to the carrier for the carriage of goods under a contract of carriage.

3 Scope of application

Article 5
General scope of application
1. Subject to article 6, this Convention applies to contracts of carriage in which the place of receipt and the place of delivery are in different States, and the port of loading of a sea carriage and the port of discharge of the same sea carriage are in different States, if, according to the contract of carriage, any one of the following places is located in a Contracting State:
    (a) The place of receipt;
    (b) The port of loading;
    (c) The place of delivery; or
    (d) The port of discharge.

2. This Convention applies without regard to the nationality of the vessel, the carrier, the performing parties, the shipper, the consignee, or any other interested parties.

Honka, H, *Scope of Application and Freedom of Contract,* **pp 3–6**
(http://www.rotterdamrules2009.com/cms/uploads/Def.%20tekst%20Hannu%20Honka.pdf)

The scope issue starts with the RR article 5.1 where it is stated that the Convention applies to contracts of carriage. Clarification on what this reference means is found in the abovementioned definitions in article 1.1. and 1.2. I shall return to the geographical scope later on, it also being a part of article 5.1.

But, the reference in article 5.1 does not suffice without necessary further specifications found in article 6. Without repeating the exact wording of this article, the main message is that contracts of carriage in liner transportation are within the Convention, while contracts of carriage in non-liner transportation are outside the Convention. The above-mentioned definitions again are necessary for the proper understanding of article 6.

One could presume that this setting would suffice, but as said above, a pure trade approach was not the proper way to go. It would have two major problems. First, it would leave unclear specific transport arrangements within liner transportation where it would not be generally considered necessary to include those arrangements under the RR. Second, it was early on considered necessary not to decrease the scope of application of the RR compared with the Hague and the Hague-Visby Rules. As the latter two cover more than just liner transportation due to the requirement of a bill of lading or a similar document of title having been issued, as long as not based on charterparties, it was necessary to have a clarifying provision in the Rotterdam Rules whereby the same result would be achieved. In this general setting it was also clear that what was outside the Hague and the Hague-Visby Rules would also be outside the RR. The main category in this respect includes charterparties. The result in the RR is more sophisticated and has more nuances than what was at one point of the work considered to be enough. Previous versions had in general terms excluded charterparties, contracts of affreightment and volume contracts, but such references caused more confusion than clarification. Legislatively, liner transportation was clarified in article 6.1, considering that liner transportation was automatically included by the general definition of contract of carriage read together with article 5.1. Thus, the specific situations in liner carriage that would not, however, fall under the Convention were in consensus considered to be charterparties used in liner transportation and other contracts for the use of a ship or of any space thereon used in liner transportation. The type of trade yielded to these specific parts. For example, slot charters and space charters on a liner ship in liner trade would fall outside the RR. Quite naturally and, one could say, fully in accordance with tradition, non-liner trade is as said outside the RR according to the chapeau of article 6.2. To coordinate with the Hague and the Hague-Visby Rules an addition was necessary as specified in the same article. Contracts of carriage in non-liner trade are within the RR provided that there is no charterparty or similar contract between the parties and a transport document or an electronic transport record is issued. This is the rule necessary for the Hague and Hague-Visby coordination. To recall, the Hague and the Hague-Visby Rules are applicable when a bill of lading or a similar document of title is issued. Those rules have no explicit exclusion of non-liner trade. It may well happen that a ship carries goods in non-liner trade where no charterparty is issued. The carriage could, for example, concern some specific goods where the carrier does not trade in line transportation, such as a return voyage where the incoming leg is liner based, but the outgoing leg not. Cargo interests might need carriage on the outgoing leg. Some times this arrangement is called on-demand carriage. The above-mentioned addition of inclusion in the RR article 6.2 gives in principle the same result as by the Hague and the Hague-Visby Rules. The relevant difference between the RR and the Hague system is that the RR do not require the use of a particular transport document or corresponding electronic transport record. In this way the RR are the same as the Hamburg Rules. The one exception in view of the RR is that the above-mentioned on-demand carriage does need a particular transport document or electronic transport record as clarified in article 6.2 after the chapeau. Transport document and electronic transport record are defined in article 1.14. and 1.18 respectively. The definition of transport document includes the requirements of the transport document being the receipt of the goods and evidencing or containing the contract of carriage as further specified in the definition. The corresponding requirements are found in article 1.18. In view of on-demand carriage there must not be a charterparty or similar contract underlying the arrangements. There is no problem in the RR covering third party interests where they exist to the extent that the above-mentioned provisions make the RR applicable. Thus, in an ordinary liner trade situation where the RR apply, for example, the consignee is covered in addition to the contracting shipper. Once outside the application of the RR in non-liner trade, but not being on-demand carriage, the status of third parties needs clarification. This is a policy matter – in other words should third parties be included at all. The Hague, the Hague-Visby and the Hamburg Rules all protect a third party bill of lading holder, not being the shipper, in non-liner trade where a charterparty has been concluded between the shipper and the carrier. The protective needs have long since been considered relevant. For the RR, there was no need to change this approach. A third party was to be covered by the RR. While the present regimes require the third party, not being the shipper, to possess a (shipped-on-board) bill of lading, discussion arose in Working Group III on the need to maintain such a requirement. Views were pretty much divided between keeping the traditional approach and a new approach where the protected party would be named in the RR directly. The latter view prevailed, partly based on the fact that the bill of lading is not a guiding line in the RR in general. The name is not used once in this new setting. Also, by naming the third parties the rules were, at least to my mind, clearly simplified compared with the present regimes. With this background in mind, article 7 states that the RR apply as between the carrier and the consignee, controlling party or holder that is not an original party to the charterparty or other contract of carriage excluded from the application of the RR. However, the RR do not apply as between the original parties to a contract of carriage excluded pursuant to article 6. The basic traditional protective concept has been maintained, but the concrete solution on defining third parties is different compared with the present regimes.

As to the geographical scope of the RR, it is necessary to return to article 5.1. For the RR to apply the contract of carriage must include international carriage. As the RR are maritime plus by nature it has been held appropriate that in multimodal operations involving a sea leg both the overall carriage and the sea carriage must be international. The one and same sea carriage must be international. In other words, two separate national sea carriages in two different states under the same contract of carriage does not suffice. There is of course no hindrance for contracting states to extend the application of the RR to national carriage or to extend the application of the RR otherwise on national legislative basis.

The geographical scope has also to do with the fact that there must be a sensible connecting factor to a Contracting State. The place of receipt, the port of loading, the place of delivery or the port of discharge must be situated in a Contracting State.

In this context it has been felt that there is no possibility to deal with certain other issues that could at least relate to the scope of application issue. Multimodal regulation in view of conflict of conventions is regulated in article 82. This provision becomes understandable when looking at the maritime plus nature of the RR in view of article 1.1 and article 26. As said, these specific matters have to be dealt with elsewhere.

4 Carrier's obligations

4.1 Carriage and delivery of the goods

Article 11
Carriage and delivery of the goods
The carrier shall, subject to this Convention and in accordance with the terms of the contract of carriage, carry the goods to the place of destination and deliver them to the consignee.

4.2 Period of responsibility of the carrier

Article 12
Period of responsibility of the carrier
1.   The period of responsibility of the carrier for the goods under this Convention begins when the carrier or a performing party receives the goods for carriage and ends when the goods are delivered.
     (a)   If the law or regulations of the place of receipt require the goods to be handed over to an authority or other third party from which the carrier may collect them, the period of responsibility of the carrier begins when the carrier collects the goods from the authority or other third party.
     (b)   If the law or regulations of the place of delivery require the carrier to hand over the goods to an authority or other third party from which the consignee may collect them, the period of responsibility of the carrier ends when the carrier hands the goods over to the authority or other third party.
2.   For the purpose of determining the carrier's period of responsibility, the parties may agree on the time and location of receipt and delivery of the goods, but a provision in a contract of carriage is void to the extent that it provides that:
     (a)   The time of receipt of the goods is subsequent to the beginning of their initial loading under the contract of carriage; or
     (b)   The time of delivery of the goods is prior to the completion of their final unloading under the contract of carriage.

4.3 Specific obligations

Article 13
Specific obligations
1.   The carrier shall during the period of its responsibility as defined in article 12, and subject to article 26, properly and carefully receive, load, handle, stow, carry, keep, care for, unload and deliver the goods.
2.   Notwithstanding paragraph 1 of this article, and without prejudice to the other provisions in chapter 4 and to chapters 5 to 7, the carrier and the shipper may agree that the loading, handling, stowing or unloading of the goods is to be performed by the shipper, the documentary shipper or the consignee. Such an agreement shall be referred to in the contract particulars.

The period of responsibility provided for in Art 12 demonstrates what the drafters meant when they described the Rotterdam Rules as a 'maritime plus' convention – that is to say, the convention provides cover for not only the sea leg of the carriage but also the legs before and after the sea voyage. The intention is to provide as best as possible for a multimodal carriage regime given that the 1980 UN Multimodal Transport Convention never received sufficient international support for proper implementation. There is criticism from some quarters that the Rotterdam Rules do not properly provide for multimodalism or door-to-door carriage.

Tetley, W, *Transports de cargaison par mer, les Règles de Rotterdam, leur adoption par les EtatsUnis, le Canada, l'Union Européenne et les pays transporteurs du monde?* (2011)
Published at http://cisdl.org/gonthier/public/pdfs/papers/Conf%C3%A9rence%20Charles%20D%20Gonthier%20-%20William%20Tetley.pdf

B Failure to provide a binding multimodal regime

(i) Door-to-door contract of carriage
The R Rules failed to provide a truly updated, binding multimodal regime which would have been required to modernize the law of the carriage of goods by sea. Perhaps one of the greatest pitfalls of the R. Rules in unifying the international carriage of goods wholly or partly by sea is that they do not always apply 'door-to-door'. Although the R. Rules would normally be expected to adopt the 'door-to-door' principle, Article 12(3) explicitly permits contractual parties to 'agree on the time and location of receipt and delivery of goods'. Since the carrier's period of responsibility under this provision ultimately depends on the terms of the contract, it makes it possible for parties to enter into a traditional 'port-to-port' – or even a 'tackle-to-tackle' – contract of carriage.

There are only two restrictions to the application of the principle of freedom of contract under Article 12(3), namely: (a) the time of receipt of the goods cannot be subsequent to the beginning of the initial loading, and (b) the time of delivery cannot be before to the completion of the final unloading. It must be noted, however, that nothing in the R. Rules prevents the parties to enter into a 'door-to-door' contract of carriage, where the carrier also assumes responsibility for land legs.

In a hypothetical case where the parties enter into a 'door-to-door' contract, it would be possible under Article 12(3)(a)(b) of the R. Rules to agree on a period of responsibility that begins after the loading onto the truck/train/aircraft, which is considered the initial loading under the R. Rules. It should be noted that in the hypothetical case noted above where goods are damaged prior to loading onto a ship or after discharge from a ship the parties would be obliged to refer to other international liability regimes in order to fix responsibility for loss or damage. This is another example of the failure of the R. Rules to provide a truly multimodal instrument for the carriage of goods. Evidently, they must be in sync.

The basic difficulty with the R. Rules is that its original draft was drafted by CMI which is essentially sea related in its interests and the drafting came out of a central core consideration of international sea carriage. To give credit to CMI its initial draft left the additional multimodal aspect in square brackets and gave precedence to a full network liability system including national law. This was presumably because much of what is part of an international movement is essentially domestic and the expectation of the ability to widen the Convention to something beyond coverage of international sea carriage was limited. (It should not be forgotten that the Multimodal Convention 1980 never came into force having found insufficient support and that was a concerted effort from the outset to create a true international multimodal regime.)

Sea carriage does not have the same risks as air carriage which does not have the same risks as road carriage which does not have the same risks as rail carriage. All these different modes of carriage have something intrinsically different about them and to give precedence to one type of carriage was to approach the project form a flawed basis. This is not about possibility or convenience but about why an international movement by sea should be stretched beyond an international sea movement to include port movements and other land or air based movements so long as they are not covered by other transport regimes. The problem with that approach made in an effort not to interfere with other international conventions covering the same mode of transport is to fail to consider on what basis it is just or equitable or even appropriate for an international regime to impinge on an essentially domestic movement. CMR covers international road movements; CIM covers international rail movements and the Montreal convention covers international air movements.

Had the original work done by CMI focused on door to door movements rather than a sea core with other aspects tacked on in square brackets it is suggested that a very different draft would have emerged. Those who were responsible for creating this draft have a particular interest in international sea carriage whereas what has in fact emerged is something of a hybrid which has been termed Maritime Plus meaning that the parts additional to the sea carriage are effectively incidental and only partially covered. This has the unfortunate effect of interfering with a complex but perfectly working body of law that has grown up on a regional if not national basis to deal with multimodal transport.

The network liability system of the Rotterdam Rules does not represent a novelty.

Nevertheless, the extension of the Rotterdam Rules to permit the inclusion of nonmaritime transport ('may include') aggravates the problem. In particular, it may be difficult to ascertain from time to time whether Rotterdam Rules carriers will make use of the option to include non-maritime transport. Further, the exclusion of mandatory national law from the network is particularly harmful for States with mandatory regulation of domestic transport used in connection with maritime transport.

4.4 Specific obligations applicable to the voyage by sea

Article 14
Specific obligations applicable to the voyage by sea
The carrier is bound before, at the beginning of, and during the voyage by sea to exercise due diligence to:

(a) Make and keep the ship seaworthy;
(b) Properly crew, equip and supply the ship and keep the ship so crewed, equipped and supplied throughout the voyage; and
(c) Make and keep the holds and all other parts of the ship in which the goods are carried, and any containers supplied by the carrier in or upon which the goods are carried, fit and safe for their reception, carriage and preservation.

Nicholas, A, Chapter 6: 'The duties of carriers under the conventions:
care and seaworthiness'
in Thomas, DR (ed), *Carriage of Goods under the Rotterdam Rules*, 2010, London: Informa

Introduction
6.1 It is perhaps appropriate that a convention that has its genesis in the liner container trade should address certain points that were not in the minds of those who drafted the Hague Rules. By this I am referring to voyages involving multiple ports of loading and/or discharge as well as clarifying the position of containers in relation to whether or not they are a 'part' of a ship.

Relevant provisions of the Hague/Hague-Visby Rules and the Rotterdam Rules
6.2 It is probably prudent to re-visit the relevant articles of the competing Conventions. Article III of the Hague/Hague-Visby Rules provides as follows:

'1. The carrier shall be bound before and at the beginning of the voyage to exercise due diligence to-
    (a) Make the ship seaworthy.
    (b) Properly man, equip and supply the ship.
    (c) Make the holds, refrigerating and cool chambers and all other parts of the ship in which goods are carried, fit and safe for their reception, carriage and preservation.
2. Subject to the provisions of Article IV, the carrier will properly and carefully load, handle, stow, carry, keep, care for, and discharge the goods carried.'

6.3 Turning to the Rotterdam Rules, as appears to be the case more often than not, there is more flesh put on the bones of the basic provisions. The obligations of the carrier with regard to care for the cargo and seaworthiness are split into two articles as follows:

'**Article 13.**
Specific Obligations
1. The carrier shall during the period of its responsibility . . . properly and carefully receive, load, handle, stow, carry, keep, care for, unload and deliver the goods.
2. Notwithstanding paragraph 1 of this article . . . the carrier and the shipper may agree that the loading, handling, stowing or unloading of the goods is to be performed by the shipper, the documentary shipper or the consignee. Such an agreement shall be referred to in the contract particulars.

Article 14
Specific obligations applicable to the voyage by sea
The carrier is bound before, at the beginning of, and during the voyage by sea to exercise due diligence to:

(a) Make and keep the ship seaworthy
(b) Properly crew, equip and supply the ship and keep the ship so crewed, equipped and supplied throughout the voyage; and
(c) Make and keep the holds and all other parts of the ship in which the goods are carried, and any containers supplied by the carrier in or upon which the goods are carried, fit and safe for their reception, carriage and preservation.'

6.4 It may appear, superficially at least, that there is a great similarity between article III of the Hague/ Hague-Visby Rules and articles 13 and 14 of the Rotterdam Rules. However, as I will go on to elaborate, there are some notable and (potentially) crucial differences between the two.

The locus standi of containers
6.5 It is perhaps an oddity of carriage of goods by sea authorities in English law that the exact position of containers, that is, whether they are to be considered as a part of the ship or not, has never been subject to judicial scrutiny. This might simply be a reflection of the reluctance of parties to engage in prolonged and expensive litigation where defects with single containers are involved. I would ask you to consider for just one moment the limited liability of a carrier when the limitation is calculated by reference, in particular, to the weight of goods stowed in a single dry box or reefer container. Even if there is a particularly expensive piece of machinery carried in a dry box which, for the sake of argument, has corrosion holes in the roof, the limit of liability is unlikely to be much more than US$120,000. Such an amount may pale into insignificance when compared with the costs on both sides of taking a piece of litigation to trial in England. Whilst I have personally been involved in a large number of cases where the exact status of defective containers has been considered, none have ever been fought to a trial.

6.6 The Hague/Hague-Visby Rules did not spell out the status of containers, whereas the Rotterdam Rules have now sought to codify the issue.

6.7 It seems to me that the containerisation of cargo is for the benefit of all parties. It allows for ease of transit and reduced freight rates. As is seen in the context of vessels such as the Kate Maersk, container ships have vastly outgrown their break-bulk predecessors. Indeed, the containerisation of cargo may be seen as having been crucial for the development of the economic world as we know it today. However, from a pro-cargo position, there has always been debate as to why any carrier should be able to escape their cargoworthiness obligations as a result of using containers. It appears that those involved in the drafting of the Rotterdam Rules agree with that view. However, they stop short of holding a carrier responsible for all containers carried and simply restrict the obligation to 'any container supplied by the carrier'. This is particularly important in the reefer trade where liner operators such as Maersk will supply the reefer boxes.

6.8 It is notable that the Rotterdam Rules will, in effect, render void any provisions in bills of lading which attempt to transfer liability for defective containers to cargo interests. Such provisions have been common in the container trade whereby carriers have sought to avoid liability by placing on shippers the burden of inspecting containers. It seems to me that such terms would now fall foul of the provisions of article 79, i.e. such a provision of bill of lading would be a derogation from the rules.

'Jordan II': Codification

6.9 In *Jindal Iron & Steel Co Ltd & Others v Islamic Solidarity Company Jordan Inc (The Jordan II)*[2] the House of Lords considered the question of whether or not a 'FIOST' term in a charterparty incorporated into a bill of lading issued on the Congenbill form fell foul of article III rule 8 of the Hague-Visby Rules in that it was, in effect, a derogation from the carrier's obligations under article III rule 2 (as set out above). The leading judgment in the case was given by Lord Steyn who observed that there was a long-standing precedent that made it clear that such re-allocation of risk by agreement is acceptable and, in circumstances such as these, the carrier is not liable insofar as damage occurs during loading or discharge operations (depending on the terms of the 'FIOST' clause). This is a reflection of the common law position. That precedent had existed since the House of Lords judgment in *Renton v Palmyra*.[3]

6.10 For the purposes of this chapter it is interesting to note that Lord Steyn observed in his leading judgment that the operation of the Hague/Hague-Visby Rules was under constant review. Indeed, he referred to the revision being considered by UNCITRAL, which has resulted in the Rotterdam Rules. Lord Steyn noted that such revision of international conventions was the way 'in which such problems are best addressed' and, therefore, he reached the conclusion that it was 'singularly inappropriate to re-examine the *Renton* decision now'.

6.11 It should be noted that the essence of the *Renton* and *The Jordan II* decisions is now codified at paragraph 2 of article 13 of the Rotterdam Rules. It seems to me that it must be a good thing that any uncertainty on the point is removed and all parties are aware from the inception of a set of rules as to which responsibilities or duties are subject to freedom of contract and which are not. Perhaps one pertinent question is whether or not a carrier would remain liable to cargo interests for a mis-delivery in circumstances where it is stevedores appointed by charterers or cargo interests who effect that mis-delivery. No doubt this is a point which other chapters touch upon.

6.12 The only other potential area of uncertainty in the operation of the terms of article 13 paragraph 2 is the requirement that '[s]uch an agreement shall be referred to in the contract particulars'. This gives rise to interesting questions as to the position when a charterparty with 'FIOST' terms is incorporated into a bill of lading contract without specific reference to the transfer of the obligations with regard to loading, handling, stowing and unloading of goods. It is possible that a cargo interest might, at some point in the future, argue that contractual terms incorporated by reference do not fall within the phrase 'referred to in the contract particulars'. That is, no doubt, a debate for another day.

On-going duties of seaworthiness and cargo-worthiness

6.13 There are some fairly subtle, yet potentially crucial, changes between the wordings of article III rule 1 of the Hague/Hague-Visby Rules and article 14 of the Rotterdam Rules. In brief, these changes amount to imposing on the carrier an on-going duty of due diligence throughout the course of a voyage. Under the Hague/Hague-Visby Rules the obligation of due diligence 'expires' upon sailing from the load port. The addition of the words 'and during the voyage by sea' in article 14 of the Rotterdam Rules is an improvement of the position for cargo interests. This would appear to be relevant in two sets of circumstance, namely (1) where a defect in a vessel manifests itself after sailing from the load port and (2) in respect of 'staged' voyages. I will consider each in turn.

6.14 The on-going duty is one of due diligence as opposed to an absolute duty. This raises the issue as to whether or not a defect which manifests itself after the commencement of a voyage but which is not capable of being repaired during the course of a voyage would lead to any less favourable finding for carriers than would have been the case under the Hague/Hague-Visby Rules. The English court has expressed the relevant test as being:' . . . would a prudent shipowner, if he had known of the defect, have sent the ship to sea in that condition?' Perhaps the test to be applied under the Rotterdam Rules is:' . . . would a prudent shipowner, if he had known of the defect, have continued the voyage without effecting any possible repairs?' Surely if repairs are not possible mid-voyage, it is not possible for a carrier to exercise due diligence in an effort to 'keep the ship seaworthy'? Equally, one may wonder aloud as to whether the advent of the Rotterdam Rules might lead to shipowners equipping themselves to a higher standard to react to this type of situation.

6.15 Turning to staged carriages, the English court looked at the issue in *Leesh River Tea Co v British India Steam Navigation Co.*[4] In that case, stevedores at an intermediate port removed a brass cover plate from one of the vessel's storm valves. This was clearly a defect that arose after the commencement of the voyage and one which could not have been discoverable by the exercise of due diligence prior to the vessel sailing.

6.16 In the age of containerised traffic, perhaps this type of scenario has become even more relevant. We are all familiar with container vessels being on pre-planned schedules involving large numbers of ports of loading and discharge. By way of example the MSC Napoli would have had cargo on board during the casualty voyage which was loaded in South Africa but was destined for Portugal. In the age of containerisation it seems that the existence of a number of intermediary ports in a vessel's schedule is more likely than ever before. This is where the on-going duty of due diligence becomes more important. Under the Hague/Hague-Visby Rules regime it is possible that two containers sat next to each other on the same vessel could be subject to different findings on the question of the liability of the carrier depending on the port of loading. It seems to me that the change brought about by the wording of article 14 of the Rotterdam Rules is likely to lead to a 'fairer' result in such circumstances.

Conclusion

6.17 It might be thought that articles 13 and 14 of the Rotterdam Rules contain in microcosm the agenda set when the Rules were drafted, i.e. the Rules are seen as a response to the proliferation of containerised traffic, the Rules are more 'wordy' than the Hague/Hague-Visby Rules and they look to maintain a balance between the competing interests of cargo-owners and carriers.

Endnotes

. . .

2   [2005] 1 Lloyd's Rep 57.

3   [1957] AC 149.

4   [1966] 1 Lloyd's Rep 450.

4.5 Goods that may become a danger

Article 15
Goods that may become a danger
Notwithstanding articles 11 and 13, the carrier or a performing party may decline to receive or to load, and may take such other measures as are reasonable, including unloading, destroying, or rendering goods harmless, if the goods are, or reasonably appear likely to become during the carrier's period of responsibility, an actual danger to persons, property or the environment.

Article 16
Sacrifice of the goods during the voyage by sea Notwithstanding articles 11, 13, and 14, the carrier or a performing party may sacrifice goods at sea when the sacrifice is reasonably made for the common safety or for the purpose of preserving from peril human life or other property involved in the common adventure.

4.6 Liability of the carrier for loss, damage or delay

Article 17
Basis of liability
1.   The carrier is liable for loss of or damage to the goods, as well as for delay in delivery, if the claimant proves that the loss, damage, or delay, or the event or circumstance that caused or contributed to it took place during the period of the carrier's responsibility as defined in chapter 4.
2.   The carrier is relieved of all or part of its liability pursuant to paragraph 1 of this article if it proves that the cause or one of the causes of the loss, damage, or delay is not attributable to its fault or to the fault of any person referred to in article 18.
3.   The carrier is also relieved of all or part of its liability pursuant to paragraph 1 of this article if, alternatively to proving the absence of fault as provided in paragraph 2 of this article, it proves that one or more of the following events or circumstances caused or contributed to the loss, damage, or delay:
     (a)   Act of God;
     (b)   Perils, dangers, and accidents of the sea or other navigable waters;
     (c)   War, hostilities, armed conflict, piracy, terrorism, riots, and civil commotions;
     (d)   Quarantine restrictions; interference by or impediments created by governments, public authorities, rulers, or people including detention, arrest, or seizure not attributable to the carrier or any person referred to in article 18;
     (e)   Strikes, lockouts, stoppages, or restraints of labour;
     (f)   Fire on the ship;
     (g)   Latent defects not discoverable by due diligence;
     (h)   Act or omission of the shipper, the documentary shipper, the controlling party, or any other person for whose acts the shipper or the documentary shipper is liable pursuant to article 33 or 34;
     (i)   Loading, handling, stowing, or unloading of the goods performed pursuant to an agreement in accordance with article 13, paragraph 2, unless the carrier or a performing party performs such activity on behalf of the shipper, the documentary shipper or the consignee;
     (j)   Wastage in bulk or weight or any other loss or damage arising from inherent defect, quality, or vice of the goods;
     (k)   Insufficiency or defective condition of packing or marking not performed by or on behalf of the carrier;

(l)   Saving or attempting to save life at sea;

(m)   Reasonable measures to save or attempt to save property at sea;

(n)   Reasonable measures to avoid or attempt to avoid damage to the environment; or

(o)   Acts of the carrier in pursuance of the powers conferred by articles 15 and 16.

4.   Notwithstanding paragraph 3 of this article, the carrier is liable for all or part of the loss, damage, or delay:

(a)   If the claimant proves that the fault of the carrier or of a person referred to in article 18 caused or contributed to the event or circumstance on which the carrier relies; or

(b)   If the claimant proves that an event or circumstance not listed in paragraph 3 of this article contributed to the loss, damage, or delay, and the carrier cannot prove that this event or circumstance is not attributable to its fault or to the fault of any person referred to in article 18.

5.   The carrier is also liable, notwithstanding paragraph 3 of this article, for all or part of the loss, damage, or delay if:

(a)   The claimant proves that the loss, damage, or delay was or was probably caused by or contributed to by (i) the unseaworthiness of the ship; (ii) the improper crewing, equipping, and supplying of the ship; or (iii) the fact that the holds or other parts of the ship in which the goods are carried, or any containers supplied by the carrier in or upon which the goods are carried, were not fit and safe for reception, carriage, and preservation of the goods; and

(b)   The carrier is unable to prove either that: (i) none of the events or circumstances referred to in subparagraph 5 (a) of this article caused the loss, damage, or delay; or (ii) it complied with its obligation to exercise due diligence pursuant to article 14.

6.   When the carrier is relieved of part of its liability pursuant to this article, the carrier is liable only for that part of the loss, damage or delay that is attributable to the event or circumstance for which it is liable pursuant to this article.

Diamond, A, 'The Rotterdam Rules' (2009) LMCLQ 445, 472–478

Article 17

The article provides, in essence, for an enquiry into the carrier's liability to be conducted in a number of stages, stating, in relation to each stage, which party has the burden of proof, what needs to be proved and the consequence of so doing. I do not mean by this that the stages are required to follow in sequence with the evidence on one issue being given before the next is addressed, though one cannot exclude that in some cases this may be appropriate.[55] What I think is required by the article is that in its judgment the court determines each issue in turn, in so far as each has been canvassed.

At each stage the result of success in proving the relevant matter is that 'the carrier is liable' (art 17.1, 17.4 and 17.5) or that 'the carrier is relieved of all or part of its liability' (art 17. 2 and 17. 3). The words used might suggest an element of finality, but it is clear from the context that what is intended is that the carrier is liable, or relieved from liability, unless something further is established at the next stage. The article is thus structured on the basis of a series of provisional impositions of or exonerations from liability. Previous cargo Conventions have contained provisions dealing with the burden of proof; eg the Hague Rules, arts IV.1 and IV. 2(q) and the Hamburg Rules, art 5.1 and 5.4. The burden of proof under art 17 is of unparalleled complexity.

Before examining art 17 in detail it is important to observe that, while the article is structured on the basis of a series of impositions or exonerations from liability, the Convention is one under which the carrier's liability is based on 'fault', a word which is not defined but which occurs throughout the article. The relevant context includes the Hague-Visby Rules, art IV. 2(q) (where the words 'privity' and 'neglect' also occur) and the Hamburg Rules, Annex ('principle of presumed fault or neglect'). None of the exceptions contained in art 17.3

purports to exempt the carrier from the consequences of fault or negligence. There are, however, exceptions reversing the ordinary burden of proof in a bailment situation, eg art 17.3(f) ('Fire on the ship'). These may have the indirect effect of relieving the carrier from liability for fault, as all the evidence relating to the matter will usually be in the possession of the carrier and, even with the benefit of disclosure of documents and cross-examination of witnesses, it may be difficult for the claimant to prove fault on the part of the carrier. I do not see how such reverse burden of proof provisions can be justified save as a trade-off for the abolition of the exceptions relating to act neglect or default in the navigation or management of the ship.

It is to be noted that the article applies only to 'loss of or damage to the goods' and to 'delay'. It does not refer to other loss which may be incurred in connection with the carriage or the goods.[56]

Stage 1

It is for the claimant to prove either that the loss, damage or delay took place during the period of the carrier's responsibility or that the event or circumstance that caused or contributed to it took place then. The claimant does not need to prove a breach of one of the 'specific obligations' contained in arts 13 or 14; and in most cases the claimant will, no doubt, rely on a 'clean' bill of lading, as either prima facie or conclusive evidence that the goods were in apparent good order and condition at the time of receipt by the carrier, and evidence that the goods were not delivered or were damaged at the time of delivery. This corresponds to the general position under English law which was not materially altered by the Hague-Visby Rules. The Hamburg Rules, art 5.1 require the claimant to prove that 'the occurrence which caused the loss damage or delay took place while the goods were in (the carrier's) charge'. This test could be more difficult for the claimant to satisfy but the claimant might need to satisfy it if the goods were apparently delivered in good condition. The Convention enables the claimant to bring a case on either basis.

Stage 2

The carrier may seek to be relieved of liability under either of art 17.2 or 17.3. In either case the carrier will have the burden of proving how the loss or damage occurred. If the cause of the loss is unexplained, it is difficult to see how the carrier can prove either that one of the causes of the loss was not attributable to its fault or that one of the excepted perils caused or contributed to it.

Article 17.2 may have been derived from the Hague-Visby Rules, art IV.2(q) but it is a very different provision. The carrier does not have to prove that neither its fault nor the fault or neglect of its servants or agents contributed to the loss; it has to prove only that 'the cause or one of the causes' was not attributable to its fault or to the fault of a person for whom it is responsible. The article does not require that cause to be the dominant cause of the loss; it seems to require only that it be a substantial cause.[57] Success in so proving will result in the carrier's being relieved 'of all or part of its liability'. It is not stated when the carrier will be relieved of 'all' and when of 'part' and I return to this in due course.

The alternative is for the carrier to seek to be relieved of liability under art 17.3 by proving that one or more of the listed events or circumstances (which I will call the 'excepted perils') 'caused or contributed' to the loss, damage or delay. Again the paragraph does not require proof that the excepted peril was the dominant cause of the loss but only that it was a substantial cause. Again, success in proving this will result in the carrier being relieved 'of all or part of its liability'. Again, it is unclear when the carrier will be relieved of 'all' and when of 'part' of its liability.

I refer to a few of the more significant exceptions:

'Act of God'

This exception in English law requires the carrier to prove that the loss was due exclusively to natural causes without human intervention and could not have been prevented by any amount of reasonable precaution. It is rarely invoked and is unlikely to cause problems.

'Perils, dangers and accidents of the sea or other navigable waters'

Much difficulty has been felt in defining the expression 'perils of the sea' in both carriage and insurance contexts.[58] In carriage cases it has been said to include 'any damage to the goods caused by seawater, storms, collision, stranding, or other perils peculiar to the sea or to a ship at sea which could not be foreseen and guarded against by the shipowner or his servants as necessary or probable incidents of the adventure'.[59] Before the introduction of the Hague Rules it was possible for the shipowner to establish a prima facie case of perils of the sea by showing the accidental incursion of seawater into a vessel at a part of the vessel, and in a manner, where seawater was not expected to enter, thus throwing the burden of proof of negligence or unseaworthiness onto cargo;[60] but under the Hague-Visby Rules the balance of authority is to the effect that the carrier must disprove causation by negligence in order to bring itself within the exception of perils of the sea.[61] It is submitted that a similar approach should be adopted under the Convention, notwithstanding art 17.4(a).

'War, hostilities . . . piracy, terrorism'

If the carrier proves that one or more of these perils caused or contributed to the loss, damage or delay, the burden of proof will shift to the claimant to prove that the fault of the carrier caused or contributed to the peril, for example by showing that the carrier should have foreseen and guarded against the loss (eg, by avoiding the area of risk) and or by showing that the loss or damage was increased negligently or unreasonably.

'Fire on the ship'

The traditional exception has been retained in an amended form. It is subject to art 17.4(a) and 17.5(a), and I refer below[61a] to the alternative ways in which it may be interpreted.

'Loading, handling, stowing, or unloading of the goods performed pursuant to an agreement in accordance with article 13, paragraph 2, unless the carrier or a performing party performs such activity on behalf of the shipper, the documentary shipper or the consignee'

This exception is designed to clarify that, where there is an agreement for loading, stowing or discharge to be performed by the shipper or the consignee, and loss of or damage to the goods is caused by the performance of those operations, the carrier is not to be liable for the resulting loss or damage. The qualification 'unless . . . consignee' may cause difficulties in the carriage of bulk cargoes, where the contract may place the responsibility for loading, stowage or discharge on the shipper or consignee, and require the shipper or consignee to pay for it, but where the persons engaged to do the work may have been engaged by the carrier.

'Wastage in bulk or weight or any other loss or damage arising from inherent defect, quality, or vice of the goods'

The exception is identical to the exception under the Hague-Visby Rules, art IV.2(m). It refers to loss or damage due to the pre-shipment characteristics of the goods; and, to establish a loss by inherent vice, the carrier may have to disprove causation through improper carrying conditions. It is, however, possible for the amount of the loss or damage to be increased by the fault of the carrier, or for a loss to be partly due to pre-shipment causes and partly due to neglect in the course of the carriage. In such cases, in order to ascertain whether, despite the carrier's having proved that inherent vice caused or contributed to the loss or damage, the carrier may nevertheless have incurred liability for a part or proportion of the loss, it is will be necessary to proceed to apply art 17.4, 17.5 or 17.6.

Stage 3

If the carrier succeeds under art 17.2 or 17.3, the enquiry moves on to the third stage. The claimant now has three possible courses;

(1) The claimant may prove that the fault of the carrier or of a person for whom it is responsible caused or contributed to the event or circumstance on which the carrier relies, in which case 'the carrier is liable for all or part of the loss, damage or delay' (art 17.4(a)).

(2) The claimant may prove that an event or circumstance not listed in art 17.3 'contributed to the loss, damage or delay', in which case, as in (1), 'the carrier is liable for all or part of the loss, damage or delay' (art 17.4(b)).

(3) The claimant may prove that the loss, damage or delay 'was or was probably caused or contributed to by' the unseaworthiness of the ship, improper crewing or supplying of the ship or the fact that the

holds and other carrying spaces were not fit and safe for the reception, carriage and preservation of the goods, in which case (subject to stage 4) the carrier 'is also liable . . . for all or part of the loss, damage or delay'(art 17.5(a)).

Stage 4

If the claimant succeeds under stage 3, a possible fourth stage may ensue.

If under stage 3(2) the claimant proves that an event or circumstance not listed in art 17.3 'contributed to the loss damage or delay', the carrier may seek to prove that 'this event or circumstance is not attributable to its fault or to the fault' of any person for whom it is responsible (art 17. 4 (b)). If under stage 3(3) the claimant proves that the loss, damage or delay 'was or was probably caused or contributed to by the unseaworthiness of the ship' etc., the carrier may prove that the loss, damage or delay was not caused by unseaworthiness or that it exercised due diligence (art 17.5(b)).

These provisions present a number of problems.

First, it will not be easy to relate the concept of 'the unseaworthiness of the ship' in art 17.5(a) to the list of excepted perils in art 17.3. Certain of the excepted perils, for example 'perils of the sea' and 'fire on the ship' can have the immediate effect of making the ship unseaworthy and thereby causing loss or damage to goods. Consequently, as 'unseaworthiness' in art 17.5 does not refer exclusively to unseaworthiness at the commencement of the voyage, one has to ask: Is it sufficient under art 17.5(a) for the claimant to prove that the loss, damage or delay was caused by or contributed to by the unseaworthiness of the ship occurring at any stage of the voyage, even if that unseaworthiness was itself caused by an excepted peril? If so, whenever the integrity of the ship is breached by a peril of the sea or a fire breaks out on board ship, the claimant will be able to prove that the resulting loss or damage was caused by unseaworthiness and one and the same event will result both in the carrier being provisionally relieved from liability under art 17.3 and also in the carrier being provisionally liable for the loss under art 17.5(a). The alternative solution may be to hold that, under art 17.5(a), the claimant must prove that the unseaworthiness of the ship was caused prior to or independently of the excepted peril. But how can such a concept be expected to work? And can it be reconciled with the wording of the 'chapeau' to art 17.5 'notwithstanding paragraph 3 of this article'?

It is possible, however, that the exception of 'Fire on the ship' will place the claimant in a significantly worse position than under the Hague-Visby Rules since, if the fire arose or was caused before the beginning of the voyage, the burden under those rules is on the carrier to prove due diligence; under the Convention it is possible that, before this stage arises, the claimant may have to prove either that the fire was caused by the fault of the carrier (art 17.4(a)) or that the loss was caused by some unseaworthiness of the ship prior to or independent of the fire (art 17.5(a)).

Another aspect of the same problem is that, when a ship becomes unseaworthy from whatever cause, the carrier is thereupon obliged by art 14 to exercise due diligence to restore the ship to a seaworthy state. In many cases this will take time and the claimant may contend that much of the loss was caused or contributed to by the failure of the carrier to act with sufficient expedition to make the ship seaworthy again, but, under art 17.5(b), the burden is on the carrier to prove the exercise of due diligence. The claimant only has to prove that the loss was contributed to by unseaworthiness, which, in this example, was a continuing state of affairs. Will there be cases where the carrier will have to prove that it exercised due diligence pursuant to art 17.5(b) and art 14 in order that it can prove that the loss or damage was caused or contributed to by an excepted peril?

A second problem relates to the burden of proving unseaworthiness and the meaning of 'was or was probably caused by or contributed to by' unseaworthiness. If art 17.5(a) stood alone, the addition of 'or was probably' after 'was' might not lessen the burden on the claimant, as the burden in civil issues in common law countries is normally to prove a case on a balance of probabilities. But here proof of the relevant matter by the claimant is not to be final; if the necessary proof is offered, the carrier has subsequently the opportunity under paragraph 5(b) to prove that 'none of the events referred to in paragraph 5(a) of this article caused the loss damage or delay'. A possible construction is that the inclusion of 'probably' imports that the burden on the claimant is to establish a prima facie case[62] of a loss by unseaworthiness, leaving it to the carrier to prove that unseaworthiness did not cause the loss. But the concept of a prima facie case does not fit well with a system of impositions of and exonerations from liability. The alternative construction is that there are to be two consecutive contests, one following the other like two sets of a tennis match; in the first the burden is on the claimant to prove a fact; in the second it is on the carrier to negative that fact. This is indeed absurd and one would hope that the court would find the relevant facts after all the evidence has been given, so that it will rarely matter where the onus of proof originally lay.[62a] I conclude that the language of art 17.5 derives from a laudable, but not entirely successful, attempt to conciliate two opposing points of view.

A third problem relates to the problem of loss due to concurrent causes for one of which the carrier is liable and in respect of another, or others, the carrier is relieved from liability. Article 17 refers in three places to the carrier being 'relieved of all or part of its liability' (see paragraphs 2, 3 and 6) and in two places to the carrier being liable for 'all or part of the loss, damage, or delay' (see paragraphs 4 and 5). There are references to concurrent causes; for example 'caused or contributed to' occurs in paragraphs 1, 3, 4 and 5, and 'the cause or one of the causes' is found in paragraph 2. There is, however, no guidance given in art 17 as to how, or on what principles, liability for a loss due to concurrent causes is to be apportioned. Article 17.6, which provides that, 'when the carrier is relieved of part of its liability pursuant to this article, the carrier is liable only for that part of the loss, damage or delay that is attributable to the event or circumstance for which it is liable pursuant to this article' serves only to exacerbate the problem, rather than to resolve it.

Some help may perhaps be derived from looking at the article in its original form. As agreed in the 14th session, it provided as follows:

> 'When the carrier is relieved of part of its liability pursuant to the previous paragraphs of this article, then the carrier is liable only for that part of the loss, damage, or delay that is attributable to the event or occurrence for which it is liable under the previous paragraphs, and liability must be apportioned on the basis established in the previous paragraphs'.[63]

When the UNCITRAL Secretariat distributed the updated text in February 2007 (in preparation for the 19th session), it took the opportunity 'to improve the drafting by simplifying the structure of the draft article', stating that it 'is not intended to change the content of the provision in any way'.[64] At that stage the words italicised above were amended or deleted and the wording took its final form.

At one stage the draft contained a proposal for the amount of the carrier's liability to be determined 'in proportion to the extent to which the loss damage or delay is attributable to its fault';[65] but in the final text these words do not appear. At this stage there was a further proposal to add 'The court may only apportion liability on an equal basis if it is unable to determine the actual apportionment or if it determines that the actual apportionment is on an equal basis'. It was, however, decided that further drafting was required to take into account that 'The intention of the draft paragraph was to grant courts the responsibility to allocate liability where there existed concurrent causes leading to the loss damage or delay, some of which the carrier was responsible for and for some of which it was not responsible'.[66]

To summarise, the original text, as set out above, indicates that there are situations in which liability must be apportioned; but the final text conveys no information as to when, how, or on what principles the apportionment is to be made. It is clear, however, that all such matters are left to the courts, though it is unclear whether the question of apportionment is a matter for national law[67] or for some uniform convention principles which the delegates were unable to formulate. I suggest that, if the Convention is adopted, national courts should fill the gap by seeking solutions that seem reasonable in the light of the text and prevailing local law, including the procedural law and tradition of the jurisdiction in which the court operates.

In English law, under well-accepted principles of the law of bailment, there can in general be no question of any apportionment in a case where there were two cooperating causes of a loss of or damage to goods, for one of which the carrier is liable; but, where some cargo damage is attributable to a cause for which the carrier is not liable, and further damage was caused by the carrier's fault (for example, a loss due to the inherent vice of the cargo may have been increased due to improper carrying conditions), the burden is on the carrier to prove the amount of the loss for which it is not liable: it must show how much of the loss was due to a cause for which it has a defence.[68] Under art 17 these principles may continue to be applicable. It is, however, arguable that, where some cargo damage is due to a cause for which the carrier is not liable and further damage was caused by the carrier's fault, a court will be more ready under art 17 to make an apportionment than under the Hague-Visby and Hamburg Rules.[69]

In general I have to say that the terms of art 17 are, to my mind, unnecessarily complex. They will create uncertainty and be difficult to apply in practice

Endnotes

55. Cf Thomas (2008) 14 JIML 496, 501–503.

56. See under Art 11, ante, 468–469.

57. See the Report of the 14th Session of the Working Group, A/CN.9/572, para 32: 'Concern was raised that this second proposed redraft of paragraphs (1) and (2) would allow the carrier to escape 'all or part of its liability' by proving that there was at least one cause, however incidental, of the loss, damage or delay that was not the fault of the carrier, even where the loss, damage or delay in its entirety would not have occurred without the carrier's fault. In response, there was support for the view that the provisions were to be interpreted as referring to causes that were legally significant and that national courts could be relied upon to interpret the provisions in that fashion and to apportion liability for those legally significant events accordingly.'

58. See S Boyd QC et al (eds), *Scrutton on Charterparties*, 21st edn (2008) (hereafter 'Scrutton'), art 112, pp 206–211; Carver, §§9.213–9.214; Sir R Aikens, M Bools and R Lord, *Bills of Lading* (2009), §§10.213–10.218; N Gaskell, R Asariotis and Y Baatz, *Bills of Lading: Law and Contracts* (2000), §§8.61–8.68; and J Gilman QC et al (eds), Arnould's *Law of Marine Insurance and Average*, 17th edn (2008), §§23.10–23.19.

59. Scrutton, 206.

60. *The Glendarroch* [1894] P 226.

61. See supra, n 58 and the cases there cited.

61a. . . .

62. Cf Asariotis (2008) 14 JIML 537, 547; and see the discussion in the 14th Session of the Working Group at A/CN.9/572, paras 23–25 and 29–30, which, however, does not greatly assist except to show that a compromise was being sought on the question of the burden of proof on the claimant to prove that unseaworthiness caused the loss.

62a. See *McWilliams v Arroll* [1962] 1 WLR 259, 307 per Lord Reid: 'when all the evidence has been brought out, it rarely matters where the onus of proof originally lay, the question is which way the balance of probability has come to rest'.

63. A/CN.9/572, para 75.

64. . . .

65. A/CN.9/WG.III/WP.36, para 7, draft text distributed on 23 March 2004.

66. Report of 14th Session, A/CN.9/572, para 74.

67. The argument that questions of causation and apportionment were intended to be left to national law deserves support from the discussion of the draft article at the 19th session of the Working Group: A/CNA.9/621, para 66.

68. See *Gosse Millerd v Canadian Government Merchant Marine* [1929] AC 223, 241; (1928) 32 Ll L Rep 91, 98; and the Hamburg Rules, art 5.7 .

69. See Asariotis (2008) 14 JIML 537, passim.

Note

It is clear that the Rotterdam Rules have done away with the ship management and error of navigation exception in the Hague-Visby Rules. That is, however, not to say that ship management or navigational error could never be a defence – but for such a defence to work, the carrier must be able to bring himself under the terms of Art 17.

Article 18
Liability of the carrier for other persons
The carrier is liable for the breach of its obligations under this Convention caused by the acts or omissions of:

(a) Any performing party;
(b) The master or crew of the ship;
(c) Employees of the carrier or a performing party; or
(d) Any other person that performs or undertakes to perform any of the carrier's obligations under the contract of carriage, to the extent that the person acts, either directly or indirectly, at the carrier's request or under the carrier's supervision or control.

5 Special provisions on particular stages of carriage

Article 24
Deviation
When pursuant to applicable law a deviation constitutes a breach of the carrier's obligations, such deviation of itself shall not deprive the carrier or a maritime performing party of any defence or limitation of this Convention, except to the extent provided in article 61.

Article 25
Deck cargo on ships
1. Goods may be carried on the deck of a ship only if: (a) Such carriage is required by law; (b) They are carried in or on containers or vehicles that are fit for deck carriage, and the decks are specially fitted to carry such containers or vehicles; or (c) The carriage on deck is in accordance with the contract of carriage, or the customs, usages or practices of the trade in question.
2. The provisions of this Convention relating to the liability of the carrier apply to the loss of, damage to or delay in the delivery of goods carried on deck pursuant to paragraph 1 of this article, but the carrier is not liable for loss of or damage to such goods, or delay in their delivery, caused by the special risks involved in their carriage on deck when the goods are carried in accordance with sub-paragraphs 1 (a) or (c) of this article.
3. If the goods have been carried on deck in cases other than those permitted pursuant to paragraph 1 of this article, the carrier is liable for loss of or damage to the goods or delay in their delivery that is exclusively caused by their carriage on deck, and is not entitled to the defences provided for in article 17.
4. The carrier is not entitled to invoke subparagraph 1(c) of this article against a third party that has acquired a negotiable transport document or a negotiable electronic transport record in good faith, unless the contract particulars state that the goods may be carried on deck.

5. If the carrier and shipper expressly agreed that the goods would be carried under deck, the carrier is not entitled to the benefit of the limitation of liability for any loss of, damage to or delay in the delivery of the goods to the extent that such loss, damage, or delay resulted from their carriage on deck.

Article 26
Carriage preceding or subsequent to sea carriage

When loss of or damage to goods, or an event or circumstance causing a delay in their delivery, occurs during the carrier's period of responsibility but solely before their loading onto the ship or solely after their discharge from the ship, the provisions of this Convention do not prevail over those provisions of another international instrument that, at the time of such loss, damage or event or circumstance causing delay: (a) Pursuant to the provisions of such international instrument would have applied to all or any of the carrier's activities if the shipper had made a separate and direct contract with the carrier in respect of the particular stage of carriage where the loss of, or damage to goods, or an event or circumstance causing delay in their delivery occurred; (b) Specifically provide for the carrier's liability, limitation of liability, or time for suit; and (c) Cannot be departed from by contract either at all or to the detriment of the shipper under that instrument.

Notes

1   It is important to note that as regards deviation, that is a matter largely for the applicable law (national law) but what is plain is that the carrier who deviates could not be deprived of the limits and defences in the Rotterdam Rules. That means where English law is the applicable law, what constitutes deviation and what constitutes reasonable or acceptable deviation would be decided by English law but the effects of the deviation would not entirely be decided by English law.

2   Article 24 contains the proviso 'to the extent provided in article 61'. Article 61 excludes the carrier and the maritime performing party from the benefit of the limitation of liability provided for in Articles 59 and 60 if the claimant proves that the breach was attributable to, or the delay in delivery resulted from, a personal act or omission of the person claiming a right to limit, done with the intent to cause such loss or recklessly and with knowledge that such loss would probably result. It should however be observed that Art 61 only concerns the limitation of liability provisions contained in Arts 59 and 60. That implies that the carrier or maritime performing party could nevertheless rely on the time limit and the excepted perils provisions in the Rotterdam Rules.

3   As regards deck cargo, Baatz et al, *The Rotterdam Rules: A Practical Annotation*, 2009, London: Informa at [25–04] noted: 'Under the mini-regime created by Article 25 of the Rules, the carrier is liable for the loss of, damage to or delay in the delivery of goods carried on deck, irrespective of any mention thereof in the bill. However, such liability is excluded in cases where the carrier can prove that loss, damage or delay is caused by the special risks involved in carrying cargo on deck in all instances in which this is done pursuant to contractual agreement, law or customary rules. This rule creates two sub-regimes for deck cargo: goods carried on deck by virtue of 25.1(a) and (c) for which the carrier is entitled to exclude its liability for losses due to the inherent dangers of carrying cargo at sea, and containerised cargo and vehicles fit for deck carriage, where liability cannot be so excluded. There is a further complication: the liberty to carry on deck ex Article 25.1(c) – and its consequences as to liability – cannot be invoked against a third party that has acquired a negotiable transport document or a negotiable electronic transport record in good faith, unless the contract particulars state that

the goods may be carried on deck. This may come as an unwelcome surprise to a bank which has extended credit relying on the security offered by being the lawful holder of a negotiable transport document.' (footnotes omitted)

6 Limits on liability

Article 59
Limits of liability

1. Subject to articles 60 and 61, paragraph 1, the carrier's liability for breaches of its obligations under this Convention is limited to 875 units of account per package or other shipping unit, or 3 units of account per kilogram of the gross weight of the goods that are the subject of the claim or dispute, whichever amount is the higher, except when the value of the goods has been declared by the shipper and included in the contract particulars, or when a higher amount than the amount of limitation of liability set out in this article has been agreed upon between the carrier and the shipper.

2. When goods are carried in or on a container, pallet or similar article of transport used to consolidate goods, or in or on a vehicle, the packages or shipping units enumerated in the contract particulars as packed in or on such article of transport or vehicle are deemed packages or shipping units. If not so enumerated, the goods in or on such article of transport or vehicle are deemed one shipping unit.

3. The unit of account referred to in this article is the Special Drawing Right as defined by the International Monetary Fund. The amounts referred to in this article are to be converted into the national currency of a State according to the value of such currency at the date of judgement or award or the date agreed upon by the parties. The value of a national currency, in terms of the Special Drawing Right, of a Contracting State that is a member of the International Monetary Fund is to be calculated in accordance with the method of valuation applied by the International Monetary Fund in effect at the date in question for its operations and transactions. The value of a national currency, in terms of the Special Drawing Right, of a Contracting State that is not a member of the International Monetary Fund is to be calculated in a manner to be determined by that State.

Article 60
Limits of liability for loss caused by delay

Subject to article 61, paragraph 2, compensation for loss of or damage to the goods due to delay shall be calculated in accordance with article 22 and liability for economic loss due to delay is limited to an amount equivalent to two and one-half times the freight payable on the goods delayed. The total amount payable pursuant to this article and article 59, paragraph 1, may not exceed the limit that would be established pursuant to article 59, paragraph 1, in respect of the total loss of the goods concerned.

Article 61
Loss of the benefit of limitation of liability

1. Neither the carrier nor any of the persons referred to in article 18 is entitled to the benefit of the limitation of liability as provided in article 59, or as provided in the contract of carriage, if the claimant proves that the loss resulting from the breach of the carrier's obligation under this Convention was attributable to a personal act or omission of the person claiming a right to limit done with the intent to cause such loss or recklessly and with knowledge that such loss would probably result.

2. Neither the carrier nor any of the persons mentioned in article 18 is entitled to the benefit of the limitation of liability as provided in article 60 if the claimant proves that the delay in delivery resulted from a personal act or omission of the person claiming a right to limit done with the intent to cause the loss due to delay or recklessly and with knowledge that such loss would probably result.

Chuah, J, *Law of International Trade: Cross Border Commercial Transactions*, 2013, London: Sweet & Maxwell, pp 410–411

Chapters 12 and 13 of the Rotterdam Rules deal with this very important subject.

As regards financial limits, art.61 states that the carrier's liability shall be limited to 875 units of account per package or other shipping unit or three units of account per kilogram of the gross weight, whichever is the higher. This provision will not apply where the carrier and shipper had agreed to higher limits, or where there is a declaration of value in the contract particulars. It should be noted that art.61 refers not to 'any loss or damage to or in connection with the goods' as is the case with the Hague-Visby Rules, but, 'the carrier's liability for breaches of its obligations under this Convention'. The reference to 'breaches of it obligations under this Convention' is clearly wider. The Australian delegation expressed concern that this might be detrimental to the shipper. The example they gave is this – art.61 would thus cover a case where the carrier negligently failed to provide appropriate documents relating to the goods to customs resulting in the shipper being given a steep fine. The shipper should be able to claim compensation in tort against the carrier but the amount of damages would be limited by art 61. Much however depends on whether such an obligation to hand over documents to customs is an obligation 'under [the] Convention'.

Article 61(2) explains that where goods are carried in or on a container, pallet or similar article of transport used to consolidate the foods, or in or on a road or railroad cargo vehicle, the packages or shipping units enumerated in the contract particulars as packed in or on such articles of transport or vehicle are deemed packages or shipping units.60 If not enumerated, the goods in or on such article of transport or vehicle are deemed one shipping unit (art.61(3)). This provision is substantially similar to art.4(5)(c) Hague-Visby Rules; the minor difference is that 'road or railroad cargo vehicle' is made explicit.

As for compensation for delay, liability for economic loss due to delay is limited to an amount equivalent to two-and-a-half times the freight payable on the goods delayed and in any case, not exceeding the total loss of the goods concerned (art.62). The reference to economic loss is intentional – a claim where the delay causes physical loss or damage would normally be treated as a claim for loss or damage, not delay. However, what does 'economic loss' mean? A lost contract for resale could well fall within 'economic loss' but what about the loss of a highly lucrative contract not known to the carrier or a depreciation of value due to market movements? Are these to be dealt with by national law instead of the convention?

The benefit of the limits would be lost if the loss is attributable to a 'personal act or omission' of the defendant done 'with intent to cause such loss or recklessly and with knowledge that such loss would probably result' (art.63).

As far as the time limit is concerned, art.64 provides that the claimant has two years from the time the goods were delivered or should have been delivered to sue.

7 Time limits

Article 62

Period of time for suit

1. No judicial or arbitral proceedings in respect of claims or disputes arising from a breach of an obligation under this Convention may be instituted after the expiration of a period of two-years.

2. The period referred to in paragraph 1 of this article commences on the day on which the carrier has delivered the goods or, in cases in which no goods have been delivered or only part of the goods have been delivered, on the last day on which the goods should have been delivered. The day on which the period commences is not included in the period.

3. Notwithstanding the expiration of the period set out in paragraph 1 of this article, one party may rely on its claim as a defence or for the purpose of set-off against a claim asserted by the other party.

Article 63

Extension of time for suit

The period provided in article 62 shall not be subject to suspension or interruption, but the person against which a claim is made may at any time during the running of the period extend that period by a declaration to the claimant. This period may be further extended by another declaration or declarations.

Article 64

Action for indemnity

An action for indemnity by a person held liable may be instituted after the expiration of the period provided in article 62 if the indemnity action is instituted within the later of: (a) The time allowed by the applicable law in the jurisdiction where proceedings are instituted; or (b) Ninety days commencing from the day when the person instituting the action for indemnity has either settled the claim or been served with process in the action against itself, whichever is earlier.

Article 65

Actions against the person identified as the carrier

An action against the bareboat charterer or the person identified as the carrier pursuant to article 37, paragraph 2, may be instituted after the expiration of the period provided in article 62 if the action is instituted within the later of: (a) The time allowed by the applicable law in the jurisdiction where proceedings are instituted; or (b) Ninety days commencing from the day when the carrier has been identified, or the registered owner or bareboat charterer has rebutted the presumption that it is the carrier, pursuant to article 37, paragraph 2.

M. Huybrechts, Chapter 7, 'Package limitation as an essential feature of the modern maritime transport treaties: a critical analysis'
in Thomas, DR, *Carriage of Goods under the Rotterdam Rules*, 2010, London: Informa

. . . .

Limitation of actions under the Rotterdam Rules

7.85 Professor Sturley adequately describes limitation of actions or time bars as 'time for suit'. This is dealt with by Chapter 13 of the Rotterdam Rules, articles 62 to 65.

7.86 Luckily enough, article 62.1, has retained the two-year period as it was already established under the Hamburg Rules. Practical experience has shown that one year to institute a cargo suit under the Hague-Visby Rules is, in many instances, much too short. The two-year period will start on the day on which the carrier has delivered the goods or on the last day on which he should have delivered the goods (62.2 Rotterdam Rules). The starting point is the day of delivery or when the goods should have been delivered!

7.87 Notwithstanding the expiration of the time for suit, a party may rely on its claim as a defence or as a set-off in an action brought against that party. And evidently, as used to be the case under the Hague-Visby Rules, the time for suit may be extended by consent of parties. As was also the case under the Hague-Visby Rules, extra time is allocated for possible recourse action (articles 64 and 65 of the Rotterdam Rules). After the expiration of the time for suit, the claimant loses the right, not simply the remedy, which means that the prescription period is pretty final, except in cases of a defence raised against a new main claim.

7.88 There may be danger in the fact that the treaty gives rather open-ended definitions on 'delivery of goods' as defined in Chapters 9 and 10, the articles 43 to 53 of the Rotterdam Rules.

7.89 Furthermore, giving a carrier the possibility of 'defining time and place for delivery' could open the door to abuses; delivery may soon become a fiction as it is already in some continental jurisdictions. Bill of lading clauses often mention that 'Delivery is to take place on board of the vessel' at a time when the consignee or the receiver of goods can hardly be available or have access to the vessel.

7.90 The final word has to be mentioned with reference to the time to file protest or notice. Also here we note a minor small improvement. Article 23.1 of the Rotterdam Rules makes it clear that for apparent damage, notice or 'protest' has to be filed at the time of delivery and for non-apparent damage within 7 working days after the delivery of goods. An improvement to the Hague-Visby Rules to be sure, but we are of the opinion that in the container business 7 days is still too short as a proper notice period. Quite often containers are opened somewhere in a faraway warehouse many days after discharge from the oceangoing vessel.

7.91 With reference to damage caused by delay, notice is to be given within 21 consecutive days after delivery. If no such notice is given, the claimant loses his right altogether to start an action on account of damage caused by delay as is spelled out by article 23.4 of the Rotterdam Rules.

7.92 A rather remarkable feature is the fact that the treaty says that failure to file timely notice does not reverse the burden of proof as set out in article 17 of the Rotterdam Rules; however, in the absence of a timely filed notice, the carrier is presumed to have delivered the goods as described in the contract particulars and it is now up to the consignee-claimant to establish that the carrier is liable for the damage sustained by the goods while in his custody according to articles 23.1 and 23.2 of the Rotterdam Rules.

8 Third parties

Article 19

Liability of maritime performing parties

1. A maritime performing party is subject to the obligations and liabilities imposed on the carrier under this Convention and is entitled to the carrier's defences and limits of liability as provided for in this Convention if:
   (a) The maritime performing party received the goods for carriage in a Contracting State, or delivered them in a Contracting State, or performed its activities with respect to the goods in a port in a Contracting State; and
   (b) The occurrence that caused the loss, damage or delay took place: (i) during the period between the arrival of the goods at the port of loading of the ship and their departure from the port of discharge from the ship and either (ii) while the maritime performing party had custody of the goods or (iii) at any other time to the extent that it was participating in the performance of any of the activities contemplated by the contract of carriage.
2. If the carrier agrees to assume obligations other than those imposed on the carrier under this Convention, or agrees that the limits of its liability are higher than the limits specified under this Convention, a maritime performing party is not bound by this agreement unless it expressly agrees to accept such obligations or such higher limits.
3. A maritime performing party is liable for the breach of its obligations under this Convention caused by the acts or omissions of any person to which it has entrusted the performance of any of the carrier's obligations under the contract of carriage under the conditions set out in paragraph 1 of this article.
4. Nothing in this Convention imposes liability on the master or crew of the ship or on an employee of the carrier or of a maritime performing party.

Article 20

Joint and several liability

1. If the carrier and one or more maritime performing parties are liable for the loss of, damage to, or delay in delivery of the goods, their liability is joint and several but only up to the limits provided for under this Convention.
2. Without prejudice to article 61, the aggregate liability of all such persons shall not exceed the overall limits of liability under this Convention.

J. Chuah, Chapter 15, 'Impact of the Rotterdam Rules on the Himalaya Clause;
The Port Terminal Operator's Case'

in Thomas, DR (ed), *Carriage of Goods under the Rotterdam Rules*, 2010, London: Informa (some footnotes omitted)

15.1 The Australian Federal Court once said that it is commercially unrealistic to expect that, in the international carriage of goods by sea, a carrier will itself perform all of the activities concerned with the carriage. In sea transportation contracts, the carrier cannot be physically and logistically with the cargo continually even though the expectation is that he assumes responsibility for the cargo as soon as it comes into his control. It is inconceivable that a sea carrier could be present to direct the movement and handling of the containers at every leg of the journey. It could not therefore be suggested that a consignor or merchant would enter into a contract of carriage with an expectation that the carrier will perform all the activities relevant to the carriage. Sub-contracting and outsourcing are inevitable. The third party will naturally wish to benefit from the defences and limitation of liability the carrier had negotiated for himself from the cargo interest given that the third party is so closely involved in handling the cargo's interest's goods. The reality is even more acute in today's world of highly computerised multimodal transportation. The sharing of computing systems and the fact that parties in the logistic chain can remotely access each other's computerised cargo handling and distribution systems mean that it is frequently impractical and artificial to delineate who was responsible for what part of the computer-controlled cargo management process. In these circumstances, it would be unfair for a third party not to be able to benefit from the protection of the contract of carriage when the boundaries of responsibility cannot be easily drawn.

15.2 However, it does not need pointing out that the contract of carriage is made between the cargo interest and the carrier, not between the cargo interest and the third party concerned. As such, this raises the question as to whether the third party, as a stranger to the contract, is entitled to rely on any defences or limitations of liability contained in the contract of carriage. Most readers will be familiar with the case of *Adler v Dickson*. It was a personal injury case involving a passenger on the steamship Himalaya. The passenger was prevented from pursuing her action against the carrier because of certain exculpatory clauses in the contract of carriage. She thus commenced action against the master and boatswain for negligence. The court held that the defendants were not allowed to benefit from the same exculpatory clauses because they were not privy to the contract of carriage. The shipping industry very quickly responded to this decision by extending protection from liability clauses expressly to benefit the servants and agents of the carrier. There is no absolute consistency in how these Himalaya clauses are drafted but they mostly provide that 'agents, servants and independent contractors whose services have been used in order to perform the contract shall be entitled to the defences, exception, limitation, condition or liberty benefiting the carrier'. Some also carry an indemnifying provision whereby the carrier or the shipper agrees to indemnify the third party for any claims or liabilities the third party has incurred in the course of performing the services associated with the contract of carriage.

15.3 What is of particular significance is that in the context of maritime law, these 'defences, exception, limitation, condition or liberty benefiting the carrier' are not merely those which are found in the contract of carriage but also those provided for by applicable statute law and international conventions. In 1962, the Himalaya clause was properly recognised and fully given effect to by the House of Lords in *Scruttons Ltd v Midland Silicones Ltd*. Readers will also know that it was in the famous case of *The Eurymedon* where the Privy Council reasoned that the consideration from the stevedores for the protection in the exculpatory clauses was the discharge of the goods from the ship. These strenuous findings of consideration and/or an implied contract were to avoid the strictures of the doctrine of privity. In 1999, the Contracts (Rights of Third Parties) Act made it possible for third party beneficiaries to rely on the benefit of such clauses without the need to prove consideration of an implied contract.

...

The scope of the application of the Rotterdam Rules and port terminal operators
15.20 A port terminal operator is not a term known in general law. However, in the 1991 Convention on the Liability of Operators of Transport Terminals in International Trade we have a useful working definition. Article 1(a) defines a terminal operator as

> 'a person who, in the course of his business, undertakes to take in charge goods involved in international carriage in order to perform or to procure the performance of transport-related services with respect to the goods in an area under his control or in respect of which he has a right of access or use.'

However, article 1(a) goes on to stress that a person is not considered to be an operator whenever he is a carrier under applicable rules of law governing carriage. The convention thus recognises that in law the port terminal operator should be treated differently from the carrier. Where a same entity takes on the functions of either role, it will be treated as a carrier in law[35] and would not be allowed to shield itself behind the law relating to port terminal operators. However, the reality is that the distinction between the roles is not always clear.[36]

15.21 In this regard, the Rotterdam Rules provide that maritime performing parties, the master, crew or any other person that performs services on board the ship and the employees of the carrier or a maritime performing party may avoid or limit their liability for cargo loss, damage or delay in delivery or breach of any other obligation under the Rules by invoking any provision of the convention that may provide a defence for, or limit the liability of, the carrier. A maritime performing party is defined in article 1(7) as:

> 'a performing party to the extent that it performs or undertakes to perform any of the carrier's obligations during the period between the arrival of the goods at the port of loading of a ship and their departure from the port of discharge of a ship. An inland carrier is a maritime performing party only if it performs or undertakes to perform its services exclusively within a port area.'

The object of the definition is to restrict the application of the convention only to those persons who are involved in the provision of maritime services.

15.22 The Rotterdam Rules clearly extend beyond where their predecessors have gone; the reference to 'performs or undertakes to perform' makes it clear that even though the performing party who has not actually commenced its services could rely on the defences if it is upon its omission that the cargo interest is suing it. What sort of services should a maritime performing party be providing, as far as the protective provisions of the Rotterdam Rules are concerned? Article 1(6) states that the 'performing party' is

> 'a person other than the carrier that performs or undertakes to perform any of the carrier's obligations under a contract of carriage with respect to the receipt, loading, handling, stowage, carriage, care, unloading or delivery of the goods, to the extent that such person acts, either directly or indirectly, at the carrier's request or under the carrier's supervision or control.'[37]

The exclusion of the carrier from its definition coincides with the terms of the Convention on the Liability of Operators of Transport Terminals. The carrier's liability is primary whilst that of the maritime performing party is secondary. Article 1(6) goes on to assert that 'performing party' does not include any person that is retained, directly or indirectly, by a shipper, by a documentary shipper, by the controlling party or by the consignee instead of by the carrier.

15.23 Reading article 1(6) together with article 1(7), the concept of a maritime performing party appears quite complex. Port terminal operators will clearly fall within this definition as long as they had performed or undertaken to perform their services within a port area. The word 'port' is not explicitly defined. This lack of a definition would seem to be intentional but problematic. A question is whether cargo consolidation areas would also count as the port area. In the light of the increasing need for cargo consolidation near a port, it seems unrealistic to make an artificial distinction between inland and port without looking at the logistic chain. However, given the fact that the Rotterdam Rules claim to be a maritime rather than a multimodal convention, the rules naturally favour a geographic test as to what constitutes the maritime side of its coverage contrary to how the shipping industry views cargo logistics.[38] Containerisation means multimodal transport; in the context of performing parties, the Rotterdam Rules only offer limited recognition of the multimodal reality although they do purport to provide for a door-to-door coverage. There is some merit in Professor Tetley's view that the Multimodal Convention offers a more streamlined solution.[39] Its basic premise for statutory Himalaya protection is sound – we recall that article 20 provides, 'If an action is brought against any other person of whose services the multimodal transport operator had used, that other person shall also be entitled to those same defences and limits of liability if he could prove that he acted within the performance of the contract.' Only a little modulation is needed to ensure that a third party who has undertaken to provide services but has yet to execute those services should also be covered (as is the case in article 1(6) the Rotterdam Rules).

15.24 Another question, not fully attended to by the Rules, is the question of association or connection between the defences claimed and the services provided. Take this example, D is a port terminal operator. It has agreed, as is standard, to consolidate cargo and provide cargo loading services to the carrier. The goods are delayed, it is claimed, as a result of D's fault. The cargo interest sues D. Under article 4(1) will D be entitled to rely on the defences and limits of liability in the Rotterdam Rules generally or should it be shown that the delay was caused as a result of the loading operations instead of the cargo consolidation operations which took place outside the port area before D can rely on the statutory Himalaya protection? On the one hand, if the port terminal operator is treated as being in the carrier's shoes, the carrier's period of responsibility for which he is entitled to the defences is from the time he[40] receives the cargo to the time he delivers up the goods.[41] On that proposition, the port terminal operator would be able to rely on the Himalaya-type protection without needing to link the delay to actions carried out during port operations. On the other hand, article 1(7) defines a maritime performing party (namely the person seeking to rely on article 24(1)) quite narrowly.

15.25 In such a situation, the third party may be able to take advantage of the more specific statutory Himalaya-type protection in article 19. Article 19 states:

'(1)   A maritime performing party is subject to the obligations and liabilities imposed on the carrier under this Convention and is entitled to the carrier's defences and limits of liability as provided for in this Convention if:

(a)   The maritime performing party received the goods for carriage in a Contracting State, or delivered them in a Contracting State, or performed its activities with respect to the goods in a port in a Contracting State; and

(b)   The occurrence that caused the loss, damage or delay took place: (i) during the period between the arrival of the goods at the port of loading of the ship and their departure from the port of discharge from the ship; (ii) while the maritime performing party had custody of the goods; or (iii) at any other time to the extent that it was participating in the performance of any of the activities contemplated by the contract of carriage.'

In our example, the port terminal operator must show that it has the requisite link with a Contracting State. Although in our example, D would seem to meet this requirement, it should be emphasised that it is not extraordinary for a contract of carriage to be subject to the Rotterdam Rules without the relevant port terminal operator having the requisite connecting factor with a Contracting State. After all under article 5, as long as a port of receipt, or the port of loading, or the port of delivery or the port of discharge is located in a Contracting State the Rotterdam Rules will apply but the maritime performing party could be involved in servicing any part of the port-to-port leg.

15.26 As to the relevance of paragraph (b), sub-paragraph (i), by referring to the period of time between the arrival of the goods at the port of loading and their departure from the port of discharge re-emphasises the concept of a maritime performing party and thus adds very little to article 4(1) (reading together with article 1(7)). More complicated are sub-paragraphs (ii) and (iii). These paragraphs refer to the occurrence of events while the maritime performing party was in possession of the goods or at any other time when the performing party was participating in the performance of the contract of carriage. Whilst it would appear to be the intention of the article to extend automatic Himalaya-type protection beyond that encompassed in paragraph (i), it raises a tricky problem.

15.27 Article 19 specifically refers to the maritime performing party, not a mere performing party. Does it therefore mean that a person who is engaged as a maritime performing party but does an act (whilst in custody of the goods or at any other time contributing to the performance of the contract of carriage) outside the maritime sector would not be able to seek cover under article 19? There is little clarity in the convention or the travaux préparatoires about this potential conflict.

15.28 Moreover, what if the maritime performing party had acted beyond the scope of his contract with the carrier? Article 19(1)(b)(ii) simply refers to the maritime performing party having custody of the goods, not lawful or contractual custody of the goods. It would seem that article 19 as is set out would extend the Himalaya-type protection to a maritime performing party who incurs liability whilst in non-contractual or unauthorised possession of the goods (where, for example, the goods come into his possession outside the scope of his employment). Although in theory it might be possible for national legal norms such as equity[42] or good faith[43] to prevent reliance by the third party who is in unlawful or extra-contractual possession of the goods, it is submitted that for an international harmonising legal measure, article 19 is somewhat deficient in failing to anticipate such difficulties. In the case of a Himalaya clause, at common law it is arguable that the third party would not be entitled to such benefit because of an implied term or for failure to provide consideration for the benefit of the clause. Article 19, however, is not a contractual but statutory device dispensing with the need for consideration or implied contracts.

15.29 The same is true for article 19(1)(b)(ii) which refers to participating in the performance of any of the activities contemplated by the contract of carriage; it does not explicitly exclude the extra-contractual or non-contractual performance of those activities. If a maritime performing party does an act which is outside the scope of his employment but is part of the activities contemplated by the contract of carriage, article 19 seems to avail to him the Himalaya-type protections a maritime performing party acting contractually would. A commercially realistic example might be this. D is a port terminal operator offering various cargo services. D agrees to provide terminal operations (at port) for C. W is the cargo consolidator. D also offers cargo consolidation services but, in this case, had not undertaken to do so for C. Indeed, C had engaged the services of W, an entity not associated with D. During cargo consolidation operations outside the port area, D's employees assisted W's despite there being no contract between W and D. Would D subsequently be entitled to rely on article 19 if it was sued by the cargo interest for delay or damage caused as a result of its employees' actions during cargo consolidation?

15.30 In fairness, a maritime performing party would lose the benefit of the convention's limitation of liability rules if the damage, loss or delay is 'attributable to [his] personal act or omission' (article 61). It is conceivable that 'personal' would cover acts done outside the scope of the third party's contract. However, article 61 requires that the claimant must additionally prove that there was 'the intent to cause such loss or recklessly and with knowledge that such loss would probably result'. It is submitted that the mere acting outside the scope of one's contractual employment is not such an act. Furthermore, article 61 narrowly refers to the provisions on limitation of liability in articles 59[44] and 60.[45]

Himalaya-type protection and the period of responsibility

15.31 The importance of the carrier's period of responsibility and the defences and limits of liability provisions has already been alluded to. In both articles 4 and 19, the maritime performing party's entitlement to rely on the automatic protective provisions depends largely on their performance of operations in the maritime leg of the carriage. Article 12(1) states quite peremptorily that 'the period of responsibility of the carrier for the goods under this Convention begins when the carrier or a performing party receives the goods for carriage and ends when the goods are delivered'. However, article 12(3) allows the carrier and shipper to 'agree on the time and location of receipt and delivery of the goods' subject to two conditions, namely that:

(a) 'The time of receipt of the goods is subsequent to the beginning of their initial loading under the contract of carriage; or

(b) The time of delivery of the goods is prior to the completion of their final unloading under the contract of carriage.'

The intention is to allow the carrier and shipper to continue to make so-called 'tackle-to-tackle' contracts.[46] Hence, it would be possible for the Rotterdam Rules to apply where the shipper delivers the goods to the container yard of the port of loading and the carrier unloads the goods at the container yard of the port of discharge, with the carrier being responsible only for the carriage between the two container yards.[47]

15.32 As far as a tackle-to-tackle arrangement is agreed to, pursuant to article 12(3), it would follow that the maritime performing party is a performing party who performs (or undertakes to perform) the carrier's obligations during that period. Therefore, it is at least arguable that the maritime performing party's period of responsibility would also shorten in line with the carrier's. Although articles 4 and 19 are not explicit as to whether a third party who does anything falling outside the tackle-to-tackle period could benefit from the Himalaya-type protection, the natural conclusion is that they would no longer be treated as a maritime performing party and would not be protected by articles 4 and 19.

15.33 In a tackle-to-tackle type of arrangement, it is probable that the port terminal operator actually is the shipper's independent contractor. Under the Rotter-dam Rules, the shipper owes the carrier a number of significant duties including the duty to deliver cargo packed in an appropriate manner,[48] the duty to cooperate with the carrier[49] and the duty to provide relevant handling instructions[50] etc. The shipper will be liable for breaches caused by the acts or omissions of any person, including employees, agents and subcontractors, to which it has entrusted the performance of any of its obligations.[51] In the circumstances, the Rotterdam Rules leave it to the shipper and his employee agent or independent contractor to make provisions for a Himalaya clause.

What constitute the 'defences' under articles 4 and 19?

15.34 Articles 4 and 19 both provide for the maritime performing party's entitlement to the carrier's defences as provided for in the Rules. An important starting point is the travaux préparatoires where one is exhorted to give the word 'defences' a capacious reading.[52] Thus, it would seem that the provisions in the convention dealing with the time for bringing an action,[53] arbitration,[54] jurisdiction clauses,[55] and excepted perils etc. should potentially be encompassed by the two articles.[56] That said, the provisions dealing with process rather than substance such as jurisdiction and arbitration remain a little problematic in this context.

15.35 First, it should be noted the Rotterdam Rules allow states to opt in[57] to the provisions dealing with jurisdiction[58] and arbitration.[59] As regards jurisdiction, if contracting states do not make a declaration to opt in, the effect will be that whilst the parties will have the right to make exclusive jurisdiction clauses in volume contracts (the so-called service contracts),[60] there is no such liberty given to the holders of any paper or electronic transport document issued under a volume contract. It is therefore not open to parties to a non-volume contract to make an exclusive jurisdiction clause prior to the dispute arising.[61] Jurisdictional matters will be resolved using the provisions of the Rotterdam Rules exclusively. Article 66 provides that the carrier could be sued at a competent court[62] in any of the following places:

(a) place where the carrier has his domicile;
(b) place of receipt of the goods under the contract of carriage;
(c) place of delivery as agreed in the contract of carriage; and
(d) the place where the goods are first loaded onboard a ship or the place where the goods are finally discharged from the ship.

As for the maritime performing party, the range of places where he could be sued is more narrow. Under article 68, the claimant could bring action against him at a competent court[63] located in the place where:

(a) the maritime performing party has his domicile, or
(b) the port where the goods are received by the maritime performing party, the port where the goods are delivered by the maritime performing party or the port where he performs activities with respect to the goods.

It would appear that the general presumption is that there should be some connecting factor linking the place, the contract and the maritime performing party. Notions of the forum conveniens doctrine feature quite prominently in the deliberations leading to the rules.[64] This premise is bolstered by article 69 which states that 'no judicial proceedings under this Convention against the carrier or a maritime performing party may be instituted in a court not designated pursuant to article 66 or 68'. This therefore limits the range of possible fora where the maritime performing party could and should be sued. The assumption is that this is for their benefit and coincides with the notion of forum conveniens.[65] It is, however, not beyond reasonable boundaries that a maritime performing party may insist on being sued at a place listed in article 66 instead of article 68 using the capacious reading recommended for articles 4 and 19. That is to say, could a maritime performing party rely on the provisions of article 66 which purportedly confer the benefit of jurisdiction on the carrier? At one level, it might be suggested the terms of Chapter 14[66] are to draw a clear delineation between the jurisdictional domain of the carrier and that of the maritime performing party. Also, if considerations of the doctrine of forum conveniens were applicable, it could be argued that the maritime performing party should be denied the right to rely on article 66. This would be made on the basis that as they are maritime performing parties, their connection to the dispute is chiefly tied to where they perform activities associated with the carriage. However, there are basically no explicit terms to that effect. Article 69, for example, does not carry the word 'respectively'. The omission is understandable in that it was not anticipated that a maritime performing party would conceivably wish to be sued in a country other than those listed in article 68. It is permissible under article 72, however, for the claimant and maritime performing party to agree, after the dispute has arisen, to a competent court not in the place listed in article 68 to have jurisdiction.

15.36 Both articles 66 and 68 refer to a 'competent court'. Article 1(3) defines this to be a 'court in a Contracting State that, according to the rules on the internal allocation of jurisdiction among the courts of that State, may exercise jurisdiction over the dispute' (emphasis added). That means if a maritime performing party is not domiciled in a Contracting State and does not carry out its activities in a Contracting State, article 68 will have no effect because there is no competent court.[67] The claimant is therefore not given a choice of forum against the maritime performing party under the Rotterdam Rules. He will be bound by ordinary rules of private international law of the country where he wishes to pursue the action to establish jurisdiction but that country may not apply the Rotterdam Rules. The maritime performing party would thus not be able to rely on the protection of the Rotterdam Rules even though the contract of carriage itself might be subject to the Rotterdam Rules. In such a case, a Himalaya clause might still be the best solution where the applicable law recognises a jurisdiction conferring Himalaya clause.[68]

15.37 Another not unrealistic prospect is where the claimant wishes to sue both carrier and the maritime performing party jointly. Article 71(1) provides that such an action may be instituted only in a court designated pursuant to both articles 66 and 68. If the maritime performing party operates at either the port of loading or the port of discharge, either of those places will qualify as the common forum. However, in practical terms, this is not always the case. In that case the action should be brought before a competent court of the place where the maritime performing party performed activities related to the contract of carriage (i.e. the place designated by article 68(b)).[69] The attempt to make specific provisions for maritime performing parties as regards jurisdictional matters is intended to provide certainty for these third parties who actually do the majority of the actual work of cargo transportation.[70] However, it is wondered if a Himalaya clause might be just as or more efficient.

Endnotes

35 [*Homburg Houtimport BV v Agrosin Pte, Ltd (The Starsin)* [2003] 1 Lloyd's Rep 571; [2003] UKHL 12.]

36 The Rotterdam Rules therefore adopt a geographical divide – the carrier's period of responsibility is for door-to-door carriage whilst the maritime performing party is only responsible for services provided at the port area. See para. 15.23 below on the lack of a definition for 'port'.

37 Emphasis added.

38 See especially the empirical work by Mason, Ribera, Farris and Kirk, 'Integrating the warehousing and transportation functions of the supply chain', Transportation Research Part E: Logistics and Transportation Review Vol. 39, Issue 2, March 2003, 141–159.

39 Tetley, A summary of the criticisms of the UNCITRAL Convention (Rotterdam Rules) at http://www.mcgill.ca/files/maritimelaw/Summary_of_Criticism_of_UNCITRAL__No_1.pdf (published in December 2008).

40 Or his performing party; supra n. 36.

41 Art. 12.

42 See Hudson, Equity & Trust (Cavendish Publishing, London, 4th edn, 2005) p. 776.

43 As far as the common law is concerned, though, Bingham LJ made it quite plain in *Interfoto Picture Library v Stiletto Visual Programmes* [1988] 1 All ER 348, at 352–353 that: 'In many civil law systems, and perhaps in most legal systems outside the common law world, the law of obligations recognises and enforces an overriding principle that in making and carrying out contracts parties should act in good faith. This does not simply mean that they should not deceive each other, a principle which any legal system must recognise; its effect is most aptly conveyed by such metaphorical colloquialisms as 'playing fair', 'coming clean' or 'putting one's cards face upwards on the table'. It is in essence a principle of fair and open dealing . . . English law has, characteristically, committed itself to no such overriding principle, but has developed piecemeal solutions in response to demonstrated problems of unfairness . . .'.

44 In general, for loss or damage to goods, the defendant's liability is limited to 875 units of account per package or other shipping unit, or 3 units of account per kilogram of the gross weight of the goods that are the subject of the claim or dispute, whichever amount is the higher, except when the value of the goods has been declared by the shipper and included in the contract particulars, or when a

higher amount than the amount of limitation of liability set out in this article has been agreed upon between the carrier and the shipper.

45 The 'compensation for loss of or damage to the goods due to delay shall be calculated in accordance with article 22 and liability for economic loss due to delay is limited to an amount equivalent to two and one-half times the freight payable on the goods delayed'.

46 See the CMI's Questions and Answers on the Rotterdam Rules (10 October 2009) at http://www. comitemaritime.org/draft/pdf/QandAnsRR.pdf (question 4).

47 Ibid.

48 Art. 27.

49 Art. 28.

50 Art. 29.

51 Art. 34; the article goes on to state that the shipper would not be liable for acts or omissions of the carrier or a performing party acting on behalf of the carrier, to which the shipper has entrusted the performance of its obligations.

52 Report of the 19th session, 2007, paras. 15 and 89.

53 See generally Baatz, Chapter 13 in Baatz et al, *The Rotterdam Rules: A Practical Annotation* (Informa, London) (2009).

54 Ibid., Baatz, Chapter 14.

55 Ibid., Baatz, Chapter 15.

56 See [Nikaki, T. *Shipping law: the statutory Himalaya-type protection under the Rotter-dam Rules: capable of filling the gaps? Journal of Business Law* (London) 4:403–421, 2009]

57 On whether maritime conventions should actually contain rules dealing with jurisdiction and arbitration, see Herber, 'Jurisdiction and Arbitration – Should the new Convention contain rules on these subjects?' [2002] LMCLQ 405.

58 Art. 74 provides that 'the provisions of this chapter [chapter 14 dealing with jurisdiction] shall bind only Contracting States that declare in accordance to art. 91 that they will be bound by them'.

59 Art. 78 uses exactly the same words as art. 74.

60 Volume contracts are to be treated differently and in these exclusive jurisdiction clauses may continue to be incorporated. A 'volume contract' is defined in art. 1(2) as 'a contract of carriage that provides for the carriage of a specified quantity of goods in a series of shipments during an agreed period of time. The specification of the quantity may include a minimum, a maximum or a certain range.'

61 The only type of jurisdiction agreement permitted is one which is made between the parties after the dispute has arisen (art. 72).

62 See para. 15.36 below.

63 See ibid. below.

64 See, for example, 14th Session Report paras. 120, 128 (Fall 2004); 15th Session Report para. 121 (Spring 2005); 16th Session Report paras. 10–13, 17 (Fall 2005). See also Sturley, 'Jurisdiction under the Rotterdam Rules', a paper presented at the Colloquium of the Rotterdam Rules 2009, held at De Doelen on 21 September 2009 and published at http://www.rotterdamrules2009.com/cms/uploads/Def.%20tekst%20Michael%20Sturley%2023%20OKT29.pdf

65 Ibid.

66 The chapter in the Rotterdam Rules dealing with the jurisdictional rules.

67 In a similar vein, the parties' right to choose a court under art. 72 (namely after the dispute has arisen) is restricted to a competent court. The specific reference to a 'competent court' in arts. 66, 68 and 72 is to prevent the claimant from losing his rights under the Rotterdam Rules if the country having jurisdiction is not a Contracting State; see 14th Session Report paras. 114–115 (Fall 2004).

68 Cf. *The Mahkutai*, supra n. 9.

70 See Sturley, supra n. 64 at fn. 155.

9 Transport documentation and electronic records

The Rotterdam Rules give the shipper the right to obtain a transport document or an electronic transport record from the carrier. That is similar in tenor to Art III, r 3 of the Hague-Visby Rules but the reader should note the following points:

(1) Under the Hague-Visby Rules, the shipper is expected to demand the issuance of the document. Under the Rotterdam Rules, it does not appear that the shipper has to make a demand.
(2) The entitlement to the transport document or electronic transport record is subject to agreement to the contrary between the shipper and carrier. That is not consistent with current trade practice and it might be thought that that could give rise to misunderstandings between the parties.
(3) The Rotterdam Rules do not make it clear as to the type of transport document the carrier should issue; it is a matter of agreement or trade custom as to whether the carrier should issue a negotiable or non-negotiable transport document.

Article 1

14. 'Transport document' means a document issued under a contract of carriage by the carrier that:

(a) Evidences the carrier's or a performing party's receipt of goods under a contract of carriage; and
(b) Evidences or contains a contract of carriage.

15. 'Negotiable transport document' means a transport document that indicates, by wording such as 'to order' or 'negotiable' or other appropriate wording recognized as having the same effect by the law applicable to the document, that the goods have been consigned to the order of the shipper, to the order of the consignee, or to bearer, and is not explicitly stated as being 'nonnegotiable' or 'not negotiable'.

16. 'Non-negotiable transport document' means a transport document that is not a negotiable transport document.

17. 'Electronic communication' means information generated, sent, received or stored by electronic, optical, digital or similar means with the result that the information communicated is accessible so as to be usable for subsequent reference.

18. 'Electronic transport record' means information in one or more messages issued by electronic communication under a contract of carriage by a carrier, including information logically associated with the electronic transport record by attachments or otherwise linked to the electronic transport record contemporaneously with or subsequent to its issue by the carrier, so as to become part of the electronic transport record, that:

(a) Evidences the carrier's or a performing party's receipt of goods under a contract of carriage; and
(b) Evidences or contains a contract of carriage.

19. 'Negotiable electronic transport record' means an electronic transport record:

(a) That indicates, by wording such as 'to order', or 'negotiable', or other appropriate wording recognized as having the same effect by the law applicable to the record, that the goods have been consigned to the order of the shipper or to the order of the consignee, and is not explicitly stated as being 'nonnegotiable' or 'not negotiable'; and
(b) The use of which meets the requirements of article 9, paragraph 1.

20. 'Non-negotiable electronic transport record' means an electronic transport record that is not a negotiable electronic transport record.

21. The 'issuance' of a negotiable electronic transport record means the issuance of the record in accordance with procedures that ensure that the record is subject to exclusive control from its creation until it ceases to have any effect or validity.

22. The 'transfer' of a negotiable electronic transport record means the transfer of exclusive control over the record.

. . .

Article 8
Use and effect of electronic transport records

Subject to the requirements set out in this Convention: (a) Anything that is to be in or on a transport document under this Convention may be recorded in an electronic transport record, provided the issuance and subsequent use of an electronic transport record is with the consent of the carrier and the shipper; and (b) The issuance, exclusive control, or transfer of an electronic transport record has the same effect as the issuance, possession, or transfer of a transport document.

. . .

Article 10
Replacement of negotiable transport document or negotiable electronic transport record

1. If a negotiable transport document has been issued and the carrier and the holder agree to replace that document by a negotiable electronic transport record: (a) The holder shall surrender the negotiable transport document, or all of them if more than one has been issued, to the carrier; (b) The carrier shall issue to the holder a negotiable electronic transport record that includes a statement that it replaces the negotiable transport document; and (c) The negotiable transport document ceases thereafter to have any effect or validity. 2. If a negotiable electronic transport record has been issued and the carrier and the holder agree to replace that electronic transport record by a negotiable transport document: (a) The carrier shall issue to the holder, in place of the electronic transport record, a negotiable transport document that includes a statement that it replaces the negotiable electronic transport record; and (b) The electronic transport record ceases thereafter to have any effect or validity.

. . .

Article 35
Issuance of the transport document or the electronic transport record

Unless the shipper and the carrier have agreed not to use a transport document or an electronic transport record, or it is the custom, usage or practice of the trade not to use one, upon delivery of the goods for carriage to the carrier or performing party, the shipper or, if the shipper consents, the documentary shipper, is entitled to obtain from the carrier, at the shipper's option: (a) A non-negotiable transport document or, subject to article 8, subparagraph (a), a non-negotiable electronic transport record; or (b) An appropriate negotiable transport document or, subject to article 8, subparagraph (a), a negotiable electronic transport record, unless the shipper and the carrier have agreed not to use a negotiable transport document or negotiable electronic transport record, or it is the custom, usage or practice of the trade not to use one.

Article 36
Contract particulars

1. The contract particulars in the transport document or electronic transport record referred to in article 35 shall include the following information, as furnished by the shipper: (a) A description of the goods as appropriate for the transport; (b) The leading marks necessary for identification of the goods; (c) The number of packages or pieces, or the quantity of goods; and (d) The weight of the goods, if furnished by the shipper. 2. The contract particulars in the transport document or electronic transport record referred to in article 35 shall also include: (a) A statement of the apparent order and condition of the goods at the time the carrier or a performing party receives them for carriage;

(b) The name and address of the carrier;

(c) The date on which the carrier or a performing party received the goods, or on which the goods were loaded on board the ship, or on which the transport document or electronic transport record was issued; and (d) If the transport document is negotiable, the number of originals of the negotiable transport document, when more than one original is issued. 3. The contract particulars in the transport document or electronic transport record referred to in article 35 shall further include: (a) The name and address of the consignee, if named by the shipper; (b) The name of a ship, if specified in the contract of carriage; (c) The place of receipt and, if known to the carrier, the place of delivery; and (d) The port of loading and the port of discharge, if specified in the contract of carriage. 4. For the purposes of this article, the phrase 'apparent order and condition of the goods' in subparagraph 2 (a) of this article refers to the order and condition of the goods based on: (a) A reasonable external inspection of the goods as packaged at the time the shipper delivers them to the carrier or a performing party; and (b) Any additional inspection that the carrier or a performing party actually performs before issuing the transport document or electronic transport record.

Article 37
Identity of the carrier

1. If a carrier is identified by name in the contract particulars, any other information in the transport document or electronic transport record relating to the identity of the carrier shall have no effect to the extent that it is inconsistent with that identification.
2. If no person is identified in the contract particulars as the carrier as required pursuant to article 36, subparagraph 2 (b), but the contract particulars indicate that the goods have been loaded on board a named ship, the registered owner of that ship is presumed to be the carrier, unless it proves that the ship was under a bareboat charter at the time of the carriage and it identifies this bareboat charterer and indicates its address, in which case this bareboat charterer is presumed to be the carrier. Alternatively, the registered owner may rebut the presumption of being the carrier by identifying the carrier and indicating its address. The bareboat charterer may rebut any presumption of being the carrier in the same manner.
3. Nothing in this article prevents the claimant from proving that any person other than a person identified in the contract particulars or pursuant to paragraph 2 of this article is the carrier.

Note

Article 37 attempts to provide some certainty as to the sort of disputes we saw in *The Starsin* over who the contracting carrier is from the face and tenor of the bill of lading.

Article 38
Signature

1. A transport document shall be signed by the carrier or a person acting on its behalf.
2. An electronic transport record shall include the electronic signature of the carrier or a person acting on its behalf. Such electronic signature shall identify the signatory in relation to the electronic transport record and indicate the carrier's authorization of the electronic transport record.

Article 39
Deficiencies in the contract particulars

1. The absence or inaccuracy of one or more of the contract particulars referred to in article 36, paragraphs 1, 2 or 3, does not of itself affect the legal character or validity of the transport document or of the electronic transport record.

2. If the contract particulars include the date but fail to indicate its significance, the date is deemed to be: (a) The date on which all of the goods indicated in the transport document or electronic transport record were loaded on board the ship, if the contract particulars indicate that the goods have been loaded on board a ship; or (b) The date on which the carrier or a performing party received the goods, if the contract particulars do not indicate that the goods have been loaded on board a ship.

3. If the contract particulars fail to state the apparent order and condition of the goods at the time the carrier or a performing party receives them, the contract particulars are deemed to have stated that the goods were in apparent good order and condition at the time the carrier or a performing party received them.

Article 40
Qualifying the information relating to the goods in the contract particulars

1. The carrier shall qualify the information referred to in article 36, paragraph 1, to indicate that the carrier does not assume responsibility for the accuracy of the information furnished by the shipper if: (a) The carrier has actual knowledge that any material statement in the transport document or electronic transport record is false or misleading; or (b) The carrier has reasonable grounds to believe that a material statement in the transport document or electronic transport record is false or misleading.

2. Without prejudice to paragraph 1 of this article, the carrier may qualify the information referred to in article 36, paragraph 1, in the circumstances and in the manner set out in paragraphs 3 and 4 of this article to indicate that the carrier does not assume responsibility for the accuracy of the information furnished by the shipper.

3. When the goods are not delivered for carriage to the carrier or a performing party in a closed container or vehicle, or when they are delivered in a closed container or vehicle and the carrier or a performing party actually inspects them, the carrier may qualify the information referred to in article 36, paragraph 1, if: (a) The carrier had no physically practicable or commercially reasonable means of checking the information furnished by the shipper, in which case it may indicate which information it was unable to check; or (b) The carrier has reasonable grounds to believe the information furnished by the shipper to be inaccurate, in which case it may include a clause providing what it reasonably considers accurate information.

4. When the goods are delivered for carriage to the carrier or a performing party in a closed container or vehicle, the carrier may qualify the information referred to in: (a) Article 36, subparagraphs 1 (a), (b), or (c), if: (i) The goods inside the container or vehicle have not actually been inspected by the carrier or a performing party; and (ii) Neither the carrier nor a performing party otherwise has actual knowledge of its contents before issuing the transport document or the electronic transport record; and (b) Article 36, subparagraph 1 (d), if: (i) Neither the carrier nor a performing party weighed the container or vehicle, and the shipper and the carrier had not agreed prior to the shipment that the container or vehicle would be weighed and the weight would be included in the contract particulars; or (ii) There was no physically practicable or commercially reasonable means of checking the weight of the container or vehicle.

Article 41
Evidentiary effect of the contract particulars

Except to the extent that the contract particulars have been qualified in the circumstances and in the manner set out in article 40:

(a) A transport document or an electronic transport record is prima facie evidence of the carrier's receipt of the goods as stated in the contract particulars;

(b) Proof to the contrary by the carrier in respect of any contract particulars shall not be admissible, when such contract particulars are included in:

    (I) A negotiable transport document or a negotiable electronic transport record that is transferred to a third party acting in good faith; or

    (II) A non-negotiable transport document that indicates that it must be surrendered in order to obtain delivery of the goods and is transferred to the consignee acting in good faith;

(c) Proof to the contrary by the carrier shall not be admissible against a consignee that in good faith has acted in reliance on any of the following contract particulars included in a non-negotiable transport document or a non-negotiable electronic transport record: (i) The contract particulars referred to in article 36, paragraph 1, when such contract particulars are furnished by the carrier; (ii) The number, type and identifying numbers of the containers, but not the identifying numbers of the container seals; and (iii) The contract particulars referred to in article 36, paragraph 2.

Notes

1   Article 40 is important as it tries to regulate the current mess as to what qualifications may be made and what their consequences are. Articles 40(3) and (4) would liberate the carrier from a number of legal consequences if he qualified the transport document in accordance with the provisions of Art 40:

    (a) a qualified statement would not constitute even *prima facie* evidence vis-à-vis the shipper of what has been shipped (see Art 41(a) – this is very similar to the position under English law);

    (b) a qualified statement would not bind the carrier vis-à-vis the holder or consignee for the purposes of the statutory estoppel provided for by Arts 41(b) and (c).

2   Article 41 is enlarged version of Art III, r 4 of the Hague-Visby Rules. As with English law, if a particular had not been properly qualified (namely in a manner consistent with Art 40), the transport document or an electronic transport record is *prima facie* evidence vis-à-vis all parties concerned of the carrier's receipt of the goods as stated in the contract particulars.

3   In the case of a negotiable transport document or electronic transport record, when the document or record is transferred to a third party acting in good faith, the particulars contained in it will become conclusive evidence against the carrier. This seems to be consistent with s 4 of the Carriage of Goods by Sea Act 1992.

4   In the case of a non-negotiable transport document or electronic transport record that required its own surrender to the carrier in order to obtain delivery of the goods, as regards the consignee who receives the document or record in good faith the particulars will become conclusive evidence against the carrier. This appears to conflict with s 4 of the Carriage of Goods by Sea Act 1992, which provides only for the statutory estoppel in the case of a negotiable document. Section 4 reads: 'a bill of lading which – (a) represents goods to have been shipped on board a vessel or to have been received for shipment on board a vessel; and (b) has been signed by the master of the vessel or by a person who was not the master but had the express, implied or apparent authority of the carrier to sign bills of lading, shall, in favour of a person who has become the lawful holder of the bill, be conclusive evidence against the carrier of the shipment of the goods or, as the case may be, of their receipt for shipment.'

10 Shipper's obligations

The Hague-Visby Rules are not especially explicit about the obligations of the shipper toward the carrier and the shipment of the goods. The Rotterdam Rules on the other hand set out some very precise duties to be imposed on the shipper.

Article 27
Delivery for carriage

1. Unless otherwise agreed in the contract of carriage, the shipper shall deliver the goods ready for carriage. In any event, the shipper shall deliver the goods in such condition that they will withstand the intended carriage, including their loading, handling, stowing, lashing and securing, and unloading, and that they will not cause harm to persons or property.
2. The shipper shall properly and carefully perform any obligation assumed under an agreement made pursuant to article 13, paragraph 2.
3. When a container is packed or a vehicle is loaded by the shipper, the shipper shall properly and carefully stow, lash and secure the contents in or on the container or vehicle, and in such a way that they will not cause harm to persons or property.

Article 28
Cooperation of the shipper and the carrier in providing information and instructions

The carrier and the shipper shall respond to requests from each other to provide information and instructions required for the proper handling and carriage of the goods if the information is in the requested party's possession or the instructions are within the requested party's reasonable ability to provide and they are not otherwise reasonably available to the requesting party.

Article 29
Shipper's obligation to provide information, instructions and documents

1. The shipper shall provide to the carrier in a timely manner such information, instructions and documents relating to the goods that are not otherwise reasonably available to the carrier, and that are reasonably necessary: (a) For the proper handling and carriage of the goods, including precautions to be taken by the carrier or a performing party; and (b) For the carrier to comply with law, regulations or other requirements of public authorities in connection with the intended carriage, provided that the carrier notifies the shipper in a timely manner of the information, instructions and documents it requires.
2. Nothing in this article affects any specific obligation to provide certain information, instructions and documents related to the goods pursuant to law, regulations or other requirements of public authorities in connection with the intended carriage.

Article 30
Basis of shipper's liability to the carrier

1. The shipper is liable for loss or damage sustained by the carrier if the carrier proves that such loss or damage was caused by a breach of the shipper's obligations under this Convention.
2. Except in respect of loss or damage caused by a breach by the shipper of its obligations pursuant to articles 31, paragraph 2, and 32, the shipper is relieved of all or part of its liability if the cause or one of the causes of the loss or damage is not attributable to its fault or to the fault of any person referred to in article 34.
3. When the shipper is relieved of part of its liability pursuant to this article, the shipper is liable only for that part of the loss or damage that is attributable to its fault or to the fault of any person referred to in article 34.

Article 31

Information for compilation of contract particulars

1. The shipper shall provide to the carrier, in a timely manner, accurate information required for the compilation of the contract particulars and the issuance of the transport documents or electronic transport records, including the particulars referred to in article 36, paragraph 1; the name of the party to be identified as the shipper in the contract particulars; the name of the consignee, if any; and the name of the person to whose order the transport document or electronic transport record is to be issued, if any.
2. The shipper is deemed to have guaranteed the accuracy at the time of receipt by the carrier of the information that is provided according to paragraph 1 of this article. The shipper shall indemnify the carrier against loss or damage resulting from the inaccuracy of such information.

Article 32

Special rules on dangerous goods

When goods by their nature or character are, or reasonably appear likely to become, a danger to persons, property or the environment: (a) The shipper shall inform the carrier of the dangerous nature or character of the goods in a timely manner before they are delivered to the carrier or a performing party. If the shipper fails to do so and the carrier or performing party does not otherwise have knowledge of their dangerous nature or character, the shipper is liable to the carrier for loss or damage resulting from such failure to inform; and (b) The shipper shall mark or label dangerous goods in accordance with any law, regulations or other requirements of public authorities that apply during any stage of the intended carriage of the goods. If the shipper fails to do so, it is liable to the carrier for loss or damage resulting from such failure.

Baatz, Y, Debattista, C, Lorenzon, F, Serdy, A, Staniland, H, Tsimplis, M, *Rotterdam Rules: A Practical Annotation,* **2009, London: Informa**

(footnotes modified)

It must be noted at the outset that dangerous goods may be refused for shipment, discharged or destroyed by the carrier without incurring in any liability for breach of Article 11 of the Rotterdam Rules.[62]

[32–02] Dangerous goods. Under the new Convention there is no definition of dangerous cargo and hence – it is submitted – where English law applies, the current definition given by the House of Lords in *The Giannis NK*[63] will stand.[64] However, the duty owed by the shipper is in relation to 'goods [which] by their nature or character are, or reasonably appear likely to become, a danger to persons, property or the environment'. Whether this phrase adds or detracts from the current position as far as the duty of the shipper is concerned is hard to tell. 'Persons' is arguably a broader term than 'crew'[65] and the word 'property' is more comprehensive than 'ship'[66] and 'other cargo'[67] although it seems to focus on physical harm rather than legal harm, thus leaving the common law position on damages for detention and other economic losses[68] arguably unchanged.[69] The word 'nature' in the Hague-Visby Rules[70] has now become 'nature and character'; this may have the effect of expressly tackling the case where cargo which would not be naturally dangerous may so become because of its being off-spec or contaminated.[71] If this is the case, the effects of *The Giannis NK*[72] would appear to remain unaffected. There is, however, a brand new concept created by the Rotterdam Rules in this context: goods that by their nature or character are, or reasonably appear likely to become, a danger to the environment. The effect of such an extension to the concept of dangerous cargo appears to be that – under the new regime – the mere fact of shipping pollutants, even if inert, as in the case of crude oil or very stable chemical fertilizers, would trigger the shipper's obligations and liabilities provided for by this article.[73] Whether the notion of 'environment' is broad enough to include micro-ecosystems or individual species remains to be seen.[74]

[32–03] Reasonably appear likely to become. The declared purpose of this phrase is to make the special regime capable of covering all risks.[75] The aim is to 'allow for the widest possible scope for the prevention of accidents involving dangerous goods, such that it would include those that were dangerous prior to and during the voyage'.[76] The expression, with respect, is particularly unhappy and likely to generate litigation as to what exactly the concept of reasonable appearance of the likelihood to become may amount to in practice. The proviso fails to clarify to whom the goods should reasonably appear likely to become a danger: a further difficulty, as it is not hard to anticipate how the view of a reasonable master may differ from that of an equally reasonable shipper.[77] This definition purposely excludes goods that become dangerous, where they did not reasonably appear likely to become so.[78]

[32–04] The information duty. When goods are or appear likely to become dangerous in the sense and circumstances specified above, the shipper has a duty to inform the carrier of such dangerous nature or character of the consignment in a timely manner before they are delivered to the carrier or a performing party. The duty to notify the carrier of the dangerous nature of the cargo remains substantially unvaried from that imposed by the Hague-Visby Rules in Article IV rule 6, although the timing of such notice is now legislatively provided for. The notice can be given in any form[79] but must be given in good time to allow the carrier to take account of it while preparing the loading manifest, the stowage plan and – at any rate – before the goods are delivered to the carrier or to a performing party. Failure to give notice, as well as tender of a notice which is inaccurate[80] or given late, carries strict liability.[81]

[32–05] Avoiding liability for failure to comply with the information duty. The shipper may avoid its liability for failure to fulfil its information duty if it can prove that the carrier or performing party does otherwise have knowledge of the dangerous nature or character of the consignment. The knowledge required under the Hague-Visby system is that 'which a prudent shipowner, seeking to inform himself of the correct method of carrying [the cargo entrusted to it] could have been reasonably expected to become aware'.[82] However, the knowledge required under the Rotterdam Rules seems to be designed as a defence for the shipper and hence – it is submitted – proof of actual knowledge will be required to relieve the shipper of its statutory duty.[83] The express reference to the performing party in Article 32(a) implies that proof of knowledge of such performing party – although not of the carrier – shall suffice.[84] The liability of the shipper towards the carrier is not limited by the provisions of Chapter 12.[85]

[32–06] The marking duty. The Rotterdam Rules impose on the shipper the duty to mark or label dangerous goods in accordance with any law, regulations or other requirements of public authorities that apply during any stage of the intended carriage of the goods.[86] The duty is most notable as it is both new and rather burdensome. A shipper of a container carried by road, sea and rail must mark such container in accordance with the rules applicable to all three stages of the voyage and as provided for by any national law of the countries through which the container has to travel. As Article 32(b) does not indicate the time by which the marking should be performed, it seems that the shipper may fulfil its obligation up to the time when marking is still physically possible or the time of issue of the transport document, whichever is the earlier.

[32–07] The failure to comply with the marking duty. If the shipper fails to mark or label dangerous goods, it is liable to the carrier for loss or damage resulting from such failure. Again, such liability is strict[87] and unlimited.

[32–08] Avoiding liability for failure to comply with the marking duty. Proving the actual knowledge of the carrier or any of its performing parties is of no avail to the shipper.

[32–09] Damages and causation. If compared with the wording of Article IV rule 6 of the Hague-Visby Rules, the absence of the words 'direct or indirect' may mean that the Rotterdam Rules do not intend to interfere with the ordinary rules of remoteness applicable under national laws. If this is the case, the current position under English law would remain unaltered.[88]

[32–10] To whom are these duties owed? Article 32 is very clear in providing that both duties arising therefrom are owed by the shipper – and, by virtue of Article 33, by the documentary shipper – exclusively to the carrier, ie to the person that enters into a contract of carriage with the shipper.[89]

[Endnotes]

62 ...

63 [1998] AC 605; [1998] 1 Lloyd's Rep 337. See also *Bunge SA v ADM Do Brasil Ltda and Ors (The Darya Radhe)* [2009] EWHC (Comm) 845, at [25].

64 See G Treitel, FMB Reynolds, *Carver on Bills of Lading*, 2nd edn, Sweet & Maxwell 2005.

65 *Bamfield v Goole & Sheffield Transport Co Ltd.*

66 *Losinjska Plovidba v Transco Overseas Ltd (The Orjula)* [1995] 2 Lloyd's Rep 395.

67 *William Brass and James Stanes v Frederick Charles Maitland and John Dick Crum Ewing* (1856) 6 E&B 470; 119 ER 940.

68 *Mitchell Cotts & Co v Steel Brothers & Co Ltd ; Effort Shipping Co Ltd v Linden Management SA (The Giannis NK)* [1998] 1 Lloyd's Rep 337. Some element of danger however is required, T*ransoceanica Società Italiana di Navigazione v HS Shipton & Son* (1922) 10 Ll L Rep 153.

69 *The Giannis NK* [1994] 2 Lloyd's Rep 171 (QBD); per Longmore J, at 180; the point was not reversed on appeal; and *Bunge SA v ADM Do Brasil Ltda and Ors (The Darya Radhe)* [2009] EWHC (Comm) 845, at [31]. See also *Carver on Bills of Lading*, G Treitel, FMB Reynolds, 2nd edn, Sweet & Maxwell 2005, at [9–280]; and S Baughen, "Obligations of the Shipper to the Carrier" (2008) 14 JIML 555, at 556.

70 Art. IV r. 6 of the Hague-Visby Rules.

71 The current position under English law appears to depend on whether the degree of contamination is such as to pose a different kind of danger from the one a prudent shipowner would expect; *The Athanasia Comninos* [1990] 1 Lloyd's Rep 277; *The Fiona* [1993] 1 Lloyd's Rep 257.

72 *Effort Shipping Co Ltd v Linden Management SA (The Giannis NK)* [1998] 1 Lloyd's Rep 337.

73 Including the burden of proving the carrier's knowledge; see below.

74 ...

75 UN doc A/CN.9/621, para. 250.

76 Ibid.

77 ...

78 Ibid. When actual harm to person or property is caused by such goods, the shipper may be anyway liable under Art. 27.1.

79 A contrario, Art. 3.

80 Art. 30.2.

81 See Art. 30.2, and Notes thereto. *William Brass and James Stanes v Frederick Charles Maitland and John Dick Crum Ewing* (1856) 6 E&B 470; 119 ER 940; *Effort Shipping Co Ltd v Linden Management SA (The Giannis NK)* [1998] 1 Lloyd's Rep 337. For the same conclusion in the US see *Senator Linie GmbH & Co v Sunway Lines Inc* 291 F 3d 145; [2002] AMC 1217 (2nd Circ, 2002). See also *Scholastic Inc v M/V Kitano* USDC 362 F Supp 2d 449 [2005] AMC 1049.

82 *The Athanasia Comninos* and Georges Chr Lemos [1990] 1 Lloyd's Rep 277; per Mustill J, at 284. For the position in the US see *M/V DG Harmony* [2008] AMC 1848 CA (2nd Cir 2008). See also *Contship Containerlines Ltd v PPG Industries Inc* 442 F 3d 74, 77 (2nd Cir 2006) [2006] AMC 686.

83 Art. 32(a).

84 In this sense also S Baughen, 'Obligations of the Shipper to the Carrier' (2008) 14 JIML 555, at 561.

85 ...

86 Art. 32(b).

87 *Effort Shipping Co Ltd v Linden Management SA (The Giannis NK)* [1998] 1 Lloyd's Rep 337.

88 The latest account of which may be found in *Transfield Shipping Inc v Mercator Shipping Inc (The Achilleas)* [2008] UKHL 48; [2008] 2 Lloyd's Rep 275.

89 Rotterdam Rules, Art. 1.8.

Article 33

Assumption of shipper's rights and obligations by the documentary shipper

1. A documentary shipper is subject to the obligations and liabilities imposed on the shipper pursuant to this chapter and pursuant to article 55, and is entitled to the shipper's rights and defences provided by this chapter and by chapter 13.

2. Paragraph 1 of this article does not affect the obligations, liabilities, rights or defences of the shipper.

Article 34

Liability of the shipper for other persons

The shipper is liable for the breach of its obligations under this Convention caused by the acts or omissions of any person, including employees, agents and subcontractors, to which it has entrusted the performance of any of its obligations, but the shipper is not liable for acts or omissions of the carrier or a performing party acting on behalf of the carrier, to which the shipper has entrusted the performance of its obligations.

11 Delivery of the cargo

Article 43

When the goods have arrived at their destination, the consignee that demands delivery of the goods under the contract of carriage shall accept delivery of the goods at the time or within the time period and at the location agreed in the contract of carriage or, failing such agreement, at the time and location at which, having regard to the terms of the contract, the customs, usages or practices of the trade and the circumstances of the carriage, delivery could reasonably be expected.

Notes

1   UNCITRAL Report A/63/17 states that this article was a legislative response to 'the specific problem of consignees that were aware that their goods had arrived but wished to avoid delivery of those goods by simply refusing to claim them', a problem with which, according to the Report, 'carriers were regularly faced' (at para 140).

2   It is important to note that this article does not apply to consignees *per se* but consignees who demand delivery of the goods under the contract of carriage. The consignee is defined in Art 1.11 as, 'a person entitled to delivery under a contract of carriage or a transport document or electronic transport record'. That means Art 43 could only impose a duty to accept delivery on a consignee who is entitled to delivery under the conditions adumbrated in Art 45, 46 or 47 (see below). On that basis, the carrier would not be able to sue a consignee under Art 43 unless those conditions are met.

Article 44

On request of the carrier or the performing party that delivers the goods, the consignee shall acknowledge receipt of the goods from the carrier or the performing party in the manner that is customary at the place of delivery. The carrier may refuse delivery if the consignee refuses to acknowledge such receipt.

Article 45
Delivery when no negotiable transport document or negotiable electronic transport record is issued

When neither a negotiable transport document nor a negotiable electronic transport record has been issued:

(a) The carrier shall deliver the goods to the consignee at the time and location referred to in article 43. The carrier may refuse delivery if the person claiming to be the consignee does not properly identify itself as the consignee on the request of the carrier;

(b) If the name and address of the consignee are not referred to in the contract particulars, the controlling party shall prior to or upon the arrival of the goods at the place of destination advise the carrier of such name and address;

(c) Without prejudice to article 48, paragraph 1, if the goods are not deliverable because

    (i) the consignee, after having received a notice of arrival, does not, at the time or within the time period referred to in article 43, claim delivery of the goods from the carrier after their arrival at the place of destination,

    (ii) the carrier refuses delivery because the person claiming to be the consignee does not properly identify itself as the consignee, or

    (iii) the carrier is, after reasonable effort, unable to locate the consignee in order to request delivery instructions, the carrier may so advise the controlling party and request instructions in respect of the delivery of the goods. If, after reasonable effort, the carrier is unable to locate the controlling party, the carrier may so advise the shipper and request instructions in respect of the delivery of the goods. If, after reasonable effort, the carrier is unable to locate the shipper, the carrier may so advise the documentary shipper and request instructions in respect of the delivery of the goods;

(d) The carrier that delivers the goods upon instruction of the controlling party, the shipper or the documentary shipper pursuant to subparagraph (c) of this article is discharged from its obligations to deliver the goods under the contract of carriage.

Article 46
Delivery when a non-negotiable transport document that requires surrender is issued

When a non-negotiable transport document has been issued that indicates that it shall be surrendered in order to obtain delivery of the goods:

(a) The carrier shall deliver the goods at the time and location referred to in article 43 to the consignee upon the consignee properly identifying itself on the request of the carrier and surrender of the non negotiable document. The carrier may refuse delivery if the person claiming to be the consignee fails to properly identify itself on the request of the carrier, and shall refuse delivery if the non-negotiable document is not surrendered. If more than one original of the non-negotiable document has been issued, the surrender of one original will suffice and the other originals cease to have any effect or validity;

(b) Without prejudice to article 48, paragraph 1, if the goods are not deliverable because (i) the consignee, after having received a notice of arrival, does not, at the time or within the time period referred to in article 43, claim delivery of the goods from the carrier after their arrival at the place of destination, (ii) the carrier refuses delivery because the person claiming to be the consignee does not properly identify itself as the consignee or does not surrender the document, or (iii) the carrier is, after reasonable effort, unable to locate the consignee in order to request delivery instructions, the carrier may so advise the shipper and request instructions in respect of the delivery of the goods. If, after reasonable effort, the carrier is unable to locate the shipper, the carrier may so advise the documentary shipper and request instructions in respect of the delivery of the goods;

(c) The carrier that delivers the goods upon instruction of the shipper or the documentary shipper pursuant to subparagraph (b) of this article is discharged from its obligation to deliver the goods under the contract of carriage, irrespective of whether the non-negotiable transport document has been surrendered to it.

Article 47
Delivery when a negotiable transport document or negotiable electronic transport record is issued

1. When a negotiable transport document or a negotiable electronic transport record has been issued:
    The holder of the negotiable transport document or negotiable electronic transport record is entitled to claim delivery of the goods from the carrier after they have arrived at the place of destination, in which event the carrier shall deliver the goods at the time and location referred to in article 43 to the holder:
    (i) Upon surrender of the negotiable transport document and, if the holder is one of the persons referred to in article 1, subparagraph 10 (a) (i), upon the holder properly identifying itself; or
    (ii) Upon demonstration by the holder, in accordance with the procedures referred to in article 9, paragraph 1, that it is the holder of the negotiable electronic transport record;
    The carrier shall refuse delivery if the requirements of subparagraph (a) (i) or (a) (ii) of this paragraph are not met;
    (a) If more than one original of the negotiable transport document has been issued, and the number of originals is stated in that document, the surrender of one original will suffice and the other originals cease to have any effect or validity. When a negotiable electronic transport record has been used, such electronic transport record ceases to have any effect or validity upon delivery to the holder in accordance with the procedures required by article 9, paragraph 1.

2. Without prejudice to article 48, paragraph 1, if the negotiable transport document or the negotiable electronic transport record expressly states that the goods may be delivered without the surrender of the transport document or the electronic transport record, the following rules apply:
    (a) If the goods are not deliverable because (i) the holder, after having received a notice of arrival, does not, at the time or within the time period referred to in article 43, claim delivery of the goods from the carrier after their arrival at the place of destination, (ii) the carrier refuses delivery because the person claiming to be a holder does not properly identify itself as one of the persons referred to in article 1, subparagraph 10 (a) (i), or (iii) the carrier is, after reasonable effort, unable to locate the holder in order to request delivery instructions, the carrier may so advise the shipper and request instructions in respect of the delivery of the goods. If, after reasonable effort, the carrier is unable to locate the shipper, the carrier may so advise the documentary shipper and request instructions in respect of the delivery of the goods;
    (b) The carrier that delivers the goods upon instruction of the shipper or the documentary shipper in accordance with subparagraph 2 (a) of this article is discharged from its obligation to deliver the goods under the contract of carriage to the holder, irrespective of whether the negotiable transport document has been surrendered to it, or the person claiming delivery under a negotiable electronic transport record has demonstrated, in accordance with the procedures referred to in article 9, paragraph 1, that it is the holder;
    (c) The person giving instructions under subparagraph 2 (a) of this article shall indemnify the carrier against loss arising from its being held liable to the holder under subparagraph 2 (e) of this article. The carrier may refuse to follow those instructions if the person fails to provide adequate security as the carrier may reasonably request;
    (d) A person that becomes a holder of the negotiable transport document or the negotiable electronic transport record after the carrier has delivered the goods pursuant to subparagraph 2 (b)

of this article, but pursuant to contractual or other arrangements made before such delivery acquires rights against the carrier under the contract of carriage, other than the right to claim delivery of the goods;

(e) Notwithstanding subparagraphs 2 (b) and 2 (d) of this article, a holder that becomes a holder after such delivery, and that did not have and could not reasonably have had knowledge of such delivery at the time it became a holder, acquires the rights incorporated in the negotiable transport document or negotiable electronic transport record. When the contract particulars state the expected time of arrival of the goods, or indicate how to obtain information as to whether the goods have been delivered, it is presumed that the holder at the time that it became a holder had or could reasonably have had knowledge of the delivery of the goods.

Notes

1   The International Federation of Freight Forwarders Associations (FIATA) Working Group has initially expressed concerns about these provisions in para 5.3 of their position paper (http://www.uncitral.org/pdf/english/texts/transport/rotterdam_rules/FIATApaper.pdf):

> A most cumbersome – and indeed absolutely unacceptable – option has been accorded to carriers to issue negotiable transport documents or electronic equivalents and nevertheless retaining the right to deliver the goods without getting the negotiable transport document in return (Art. 47.2). So, the Rotterdam Rules accept that a document is called 'negotiable' when in fact it is not! It goes without saying that, if the Rotterdam Rules come into force, freight forwarders must never issue such documents themselves. Also, they must ensure that such documents are not tendered to their customers by carriers. Indeed, such documents may well constitute important tools in maritime fraud, when a seller fraudulently sells the goods to a second buyer who could convince the carrier that he is entitled to get the goods, although he is unable to tender an original Bill of Lading, leaving the unfortunate first buyer with a right to get limited (cf. 'any breach' above) compensation from the carrier. Freight forwarders must take care not to be associated with such malpractice with the risk of being held liable through 'guilt by association'.

More recently, FIATA has said: 'FIATA is entirely neutral on the Rotterdam Rules and it is for individual National Associations to make their own decisions accordingly.'

2   It should also be remembered that the carrier may refuse to deliver to a consignee who refuses to acknowledge receipt of the goods on his (the carrier's) request (Art 43). It seems clear that Art 43 could apply to the situations envisaged in Arts 45, 46 and 47. The consignee's obligation, on the carrier's request, to acknowledge receipt is alien to English law.

Baatz, et al, *Rotterdam Rules – A Practical Annotation*, 2009, London: Informa)
(footnotes omitted)
[47–01] Delivery against negotiable document. In essence, this article deals with delivery of the goods where, in the paper world, a negotiable bill of lading is issued, sometimes also known as a transferable or 'order' bill of lading. The Article also applies where an electronic transport record, equally in negotiable form, is issued instead of a paper bill of lading. There are other articles which deal with delivery of goods where non-negotiable documents or equivalent electronic transport records are issued: see Articles 45 and 46.

[47–02] In broad terms, the article provides for the delivery of the goods, in the paper world, to a holder of a negotiable transport document who surrenders the document and identifies itself to the carrier; and, in the electronic world, to a person who identifies itself as a holder of that record. Although the article is targeted mainly at negotiable transport documents the presentation (or, in the words of the Rotterdam Rules, 'surrender') of which has traditionally been required for delivery of the goods, the article also introduces into the Rules a negotiable document which expressly dispenses with the requirement of surrender by the holder. This is a hybrid document, negotiable in the sense that the rights it represents can be transferred from one holder to another so that each holder is a holder in possession of the document, yet sharing with typical non-negotiable documents the feature that they need not be surrendered for delivery of the goods.

[47–03] Article 47 envisages the issue of a transport document or electronic transport record which is negotiable. In terms of the definitions of 'negotiable transport document' and 'negotiable electronic transport record' given at Articles 1.15 and 1.19 respectively, this means that Article 47 applies where the document or electronic transport record issued is one which indicates through appropriate wording that the goods have been consigned to the order of the shipper, to the order of the consignee, or to bearer. For Article 47 to apply, the transport document issued must consequently contain the words 'to order', 'to shipper's order', 'to the order of the named consignee' or 'to bearer'.

The document must not, consequently, contain the phrases 'non-negotiable' or 'not negotiable' – or, it is suggested, 'not transferable' or 'non-transferable'. It will be noticed that the phrase 'bill of lading' has been eschewed in the definition of 'negotiable transport document', although in practice Article 47 will be taken to refer to the document which the shipping markets have long labelled the transferable or negotiable bill of lading.

[47–04] For the article to apply to a negotiable electronic record, that record must, apart from being negotiable in the sense just described, satisfy the requirements of Article 9.1, ie it must be subject to procedures providing for the issuance, transfer and integrity of the record itself, for the manner in which the holder can identify itself as such, the manner in which delivery to the holder can be confirmed and finally the manner in which the record ceases to have effect on delivery.

[47–05] Carrier's duty to deliver the goods. It will be recalled that, where Articles 45 and 46 apply, each of those Articles starts off by simply stating to whom the carrier 'shall deliver the goods'. Article 47 starts in a slightly different way.

Where the article applies, the holder of the document or record 'is entitled to claim delivery of the goods' after their arrival at destination, 'in which event' the carrier shall deliver to the holder on certain conditions. This formulation raises the question: what if the event does not occur, ie what if the holder does not claim delivery of the goods? This question entails two issues, one practical, the other legal: what is the carrier to do with the goods; and is the carrier liable for any loss or damage to the unclaimed goods vis-à-vis the holder? The answer to both questions is provided by article 48: in broad terms, as we shall see, the carrier may store or have the goods sold free of liability so long as it takes reasonable steps to preserve the goods.

[47–06] Where Article 47.1 applies, the 'holder' of a negotiable transport document is entitled to claim delivery of the goods on their arrival at destination if it (a) surrenders the document and, if it is in possession of a negotiable transport document made out to its order as shipper or consignee or to whom it is endorsed in full, (b) properly identifies itself. The carrier 'shall' refuse delivery if these requirements are not met. This position results from a combined reading of Articles 47.1(a)(i) and (b) and Article 1.10(a), the article which defines the word 'holder'.

[47–07] Surrender of the documents. The first condition, surrender of the negotiable bill of lading, would effect no change to current English law. Both as a matter of the common law and under COGSA 1992, the party with rights of suit, including the right to demand delivery of the goods, is the consignee or endorsee 'with possession of' a transferable bill of lading: possession of the document is necessary for presentation, and presentation necessary for delivery of the goods. Moreover, as is currently the position under English law, if the negotiable bill of lading has been issued in a set of more than one original, then the surrender of one original will satisfy the condition of surrender, the other originals in the set ceasing to have any effect or validity.

[47–08] Identification as holder. The change to current English law comes, however, in the second require-ment in Article 47.1(a), ie the requirement that the holder properly identifies itself if it is in possession of a negotiable transport document made out to its order as shipper or consignee or to whom it is endorsed in full. The position in English law is that where such a bill of lading is issued, all the holder needs to do to claim possession of the goods is to present the bill of lading in exchange for delivery of the goods; it is equally clear that all the carrier needs to do to avoid an action for misdelivery is to require the presentation of the bill of lading before delivery of the goods. There is no additional requirement that the holder identi-fies itself or that the carrier requires the holder so to do. The presentation of the negotiable document is all the means of identification that the holder needs to show – and all the means of identification that the carrier is entitled or bound to require. Where a non-negotiable bill of lading does not expressly require presentation, ie where the document is one covered by Article 45 of the Rotterdam Rules, identification is necessary because presentation is not. Where, however, surrender of a negotiable document is required, as it is by Article 47.1(a)(i), then it is difficult to see what identification adds to presentation and surrender of the document.

[47–09] It is true that the Court of Appeal in *Motis Exports v Dampskibsselskabet AF* [[2000] 1 Lloyd's Rep 211] decided that the carrier is liable for misdelivery if a bill of lading appears to be – but later turns out not to be – genuine. To allocate the risk of forgery in bills of lading on the carrier is not, however, the same as imposing upon the carrier a duty or a right to require the holder to identify itself before delivery of the goods. Such a duty in the case of negotiable bills of lading is not only unnecessary but may cause delay and cost in the delivery of goods. It raises above all the question as to what 'proper' identification is: in particular, what is it exactly that the carrier must do to check that the holder is who it says it is? Is it enough that the carrier simply asks the holder for identification or must the carrier check that identifica-tion? These questions are likely to raise difficult questions of application, questions which have not to date arisen in English law in the context of transferable bills of lading.

[47–10] While where a negotiable transport document is issued, the holder must surrender the document and identify itself, where a negotiable electronic transport record has been issued, Article 47.1(a)(ii) requires only identification: there is no 'document' to surrender and the Rules do not therefore require any such sur-render. Given that surrender of a paper document is impossible given the medium used, it is clear that iden-tification of the holder is necessary and this is why it is required – and justifiably so – by the Rotterdam Rules. Once delivery has been effected on such identification, the electronic transport record ceases to have effect.

[47–11] There is, in the context of negotiable transport documents a third, and in the context of negotia-ble electronic transport records a second, condition which needs to be satisfied for delivery of the goods. It will be recalled that the carrier may refuse to deliver to a consignee who refuses to acknowledge receipt of the goods on the request of the carrier. This is the result of Article 43: there is nothing in that Article that limits its application to any one of the three Articles dealing with the right to delivery, ie Articles 45, 46 or 47 and Article 43 must therefore be taken to apply to the situations envisaged in all three articles. It was observed in the Notes to that Article that the consignee's obligation, on the carrier's request, to acknowl-edge receipt is new to English law.

[47–12] Where the operation of Article 47.1 is triggered by a claim for delivery being made by a holder of a negotiable transport document or electronic transport record not expressly stating that goods may be delivered without the surrender of the document or record, which holder meets the conditions set out in that Article, the carrier shall deliver the goods to the holder at the time and location referred to in Article 43.

[47–13] Negotiable document allowing delivery without surrender. Where, on the other hand, the negotiable transport document or electronic transport record expressly states that delivery can be made without surrender of the document or record, a wholly different set of rules is stated at Article 47.2. Under this part of Article 47, where a negotiable transport document or record is issued which expressly dispenses with the need for surrender, the carrier 'may' advise the shipper that the goods are not deliverable because the holder (a) having received a notice of arrival, fails to claim delivery of the goods at the time and at the place referred to in Article 43; (b) fails to identify itself as the holder and the carrier refuses to deliver the goods on this ground; or (c) is not located despite reasonable efforts by the carrier for the purpose of requesting delivery instructions. In any of these three circumstances, the carrier 'may so advise' (which presumably means that the carrier may notify which of the three sets of circumstances has rendered the goods undeliverable) and request delivery instructions of the shipper or, if the shipper cannot be located despite reasonable efforts, the documentary shipper. Article 47.2 raises several difficulties.

[47–14] First, does the holder of a document or record covered by Article 47.2 still need to identify itself as required by Article 47.1? It is suggested that the answer is Yes. Article 47.1 is drawn in terms general enough to apply the requirement of identification to all transport documents and records whether they dispense with the need for surrender or not. Indeed, if, for the reasons set out above at paragraph 47–08, it is hard to justify the need for identification where a transport document is surrendered for delivery, it is extremely easy to justify that need where the document dispenses with surrender: in this case, how else other than through identification can the carrier be sure that it is delivering to the right person? For both these reasons, it is suggested that where Article 47.2 applies, the requirement of proper identification in Article 47.1(a)(i) applies and the carrier must require the holder properly to identify itself.

[47–15] Secondly, where goods are undeliverable for the reasons described at Article 47.2 but a document or record is issued which does not dispense with surrender, can the carrier still follow the steps described at Article 47.2, which applies in terms to documents and records which do dispense with the need of surrender? Moreover, if the carrier does follow those steps, would it equally be discharged if it follows the delivery instructions given by the shipper or documentary shipper, as it would be under Article 47.2(b) had the document dispensed with the need of surrender?

[47–16] Again, it is suggested that the answer to both questions is Yes. Any of the circumstances described at Article 47.2(a) might well arise in the context of a normal document or record not dispensing with the need of surrender. The language in Article 47.2(b) is permissive and there is nothing either in Article 47.1 or in Article 47.2 which appears to bar the steps described in Article 47.2 where a transport document or record does not dispense with the need for surrender.

[47–17] Thirdly, what is it exactly that documents and records envisaged by Article 47.2 purport to dispense with? Money turns on the question because of the general requirement in English law that negotiable bills of lading need to be presented before the goods are delivered. Article 47.2 talks of documents and records which expressly state that the goods may be delivered without the 'surrender' of the document or record. Article 47.2 says nothing about the possession of the document or record; indeed, the article talks throughout of the 'holder', a person defined at Article 1.10 as being someone, at any rate in the paper world, as being 'in possession' of a document. It would seem, therefore, that where Article 47.2 applies, the holder must still possess the bill but need not surrender it for delivery of the goods. On this construction, where Article 47.2 applies, there are still two conditions which would need to be satisfied for delivery: possession of the bill of lading, manifested through presentation but not surrender; and identification of the holder. Thus interpreted, Article 47.2 documents would represent little challenge to English lawyers: they would need to be presented, but not surrendered to the carrier.

[47–18] Fourthly, it is not entirely certain why negotiable electronic transport records dispensing with the need of surrender are covered by the rules set out at Article 47.2 when Article 47.1(a)(ii) already dispenses with that need. If Article 47.1 does not require surrender of an electronic transport record, why would the record itself need to dispense with the requirement of surrender? Moreover, would a record expressly dispensing with that requirement be covered by Article 47.1, which states, like the record, that there is no need for surrender; or by Article 47.2, which appears to cover electronic records which themselves expressly state that surrender is not required?

[47–19] Fifthly, there is no obligation on the carrier to follow the steps set out at Article 47.2(a), ie, to advise non-delivery and to seek alternative delivery instructions. The language in that sub-article is permissive throughout and it would seem therefore that a carrier who fails to act as indicated in Article 47.2(a) incurs no resulting liability. However, if a carrier does advise and seek instructions as set out in Article 47.2(a) and then follows the delivery instructions it receives under that sub-article, its delivery duties are discharged and it is free from liability for misdelivery, irrespective of whether the negotiable document was surrendered or whether the holder of the electronic record identified itself as the holder: see Article 47.2(b), which states as much in terms. It would seem to follow that, by the same token, if it ignores those instructions, when sought, and delivers the goods to the wrong person, then it is liable for misdelivery.

[47–20] It will be recalled that one of the circumstances described in Article 47.2(b) is the carrier's refusal to deliver because of the holder's failure to identify itself: see Article 47.2(a)(ii). In the context of the identification of the holder, it is suggested that the effect of Article 47.2 in the context of the carrier's liability for misdelivery under a document or record expressly dispensing with surrender is as follows. The carrier is safe from such action if (i) it does not seek alternative delivery instructions under Article 47.2(a); and, if it does so seek, (ii) it follows those instructions. On the other hand, if it seeks such instructions and ignores them, and delivers the goods to the wrong person, the carrier exposes itself to liability for misdelivery.

[47–21] Sixthly, it should be noted that the steps described at Article 47.2(a) are without prejudice to Article 48.1 of the Rotterdam Rules, which Article sets out further consequences arising from goods remaining undelivered.

[47–22] The effect of Article 47.2(a) is that the carrier will deliver the goods to someone other than the holder of a negotiable transport document or record dispensing with the need for surrender of the document or record. There are risks here and a balance to be struck between conflicting interests. On the one hand, the carrier has had to seek alternative delivery instructions because of the inaction of the holder; on the other hand, the holder needs to be protected against loss caused by those alternative delivery instructions.

[47–23] The remaining sub-articles of article 47.2 represent a somewhat complex mosaic seeking to reconcile these conflicting interests, a mosaic of discharges and indemnities which would, of course, be new to English law given that the circumstances giving rise to them are not currently envisaged in current statutes.

[47–24] The assumption behind Articles 47.2(c), (d) and (e) is that the goods have been delivered by the carrier on the basis of alternative instructions sought and received under Article 47.2(a). As we have seen, delivery pursuant to such instructions discharges the carrier of its delivery obligations towards the holder: see Article 47.2(b). The problem, however, is: what if the holder of the document turns up after delivery and proves that, although the carrier followed the instructions it received, those instructions nonetheless caused the holder loss? Following the alternative instructions provides the carrier with a complete defence to an action for misdelivery (Article 47.2(b)) unless the holder did not and could not reasonably have known of the delivery when it became a holder of the document or record (Article 47.2(e)). On the other hand, the discharge in Article 47.2(b) applies only to the holder's rights to delivery: it does not extend to other rights which the holder may have under the contract of carriage, so long as the holder came to possess the transport document under contractual or other arrangements made before the goods were delivered pursuant to the alternative instructions received by the carrier (Article 47.2(d)). It is clear that, despite the discharge effected by Article 47.2(b), the carrier may still find itself exposed to liability towards the holder either under Articles 47.2(e) or (d) for losses caused to the holder by the carrier's having followed alternative delivery instructions. It is in order to cover the carrier against such exposure that Article 47.2(c) imposes an obligation on the person giving such instructions to indemnify the carrier against such exposure and allows the carrier to refuse to follow those instructions if the person giving them fails to provide adequate security against such exposure (Article 47.2(c)). It is not clear whether, if the carrier ignores the alternative delivery instructions in these latter circumstances, ie because the person giving the instructions fails to provide adequate security, the carrier remains liable for misdelivery to the holder: strictly construed, the discharge effected by Article 47.2(b) applies only where the carrier follows the alternative delivery instructions. It would seem harsh on the carrier, however, to deprive it of that discharge where it refuses to follow those instructions in the circumstances allowed in Article 47.2(c).

Article 48
Goods remaining undelivered

1. For the purposes of this article, goods shall be deemed to have remained undelivered only if, after their arrival at the place of destination: (a) The consignee does not accept delivery of the goods pursuant to this chapter at the time and location referred to in article 43; (b) The controlling party, the holder, the shipper or the documentary shipper cannot be found or does not give the carrier adequate instructions pursuant to articles 45, 46 and 47; (c) The carrier is entitled or required to refuse delivery pursuant to articles 44, 45, 46 and 47; (d) The carrier is not allowed to deliver the goods to the consignee pursuant to the law or regulations of the place at which delivery is requested; or (e) The goods are otherwise undeliverable by the carrier.

2. Without prejudice to any other rights that the carrier may have against the shipper, controlling party or consignee, if the goods have remained undelivered, the carrier may, at the risk and expense of the person entitled to the goods, take such action in respect of the goods as circumstances may reasonably require, including: (a) To store the goods at any suitable place; (b) To unpack the goods if they are packed in containers or vehicles, or to act otherwise in respect of the goods, including by moving them; and (c) To cause the goods to be sold or destroyed in accordance with the practices or pursuant to the law or regulations of the place where the goods are located at the time.

3. The carrier may exercise the rights under paragraph 2 of this article only after it has given reasonable notice of the intended action under paragraph 2 of this article to the person stated in the contract particulars as the person, if any, to be notified of the arrival of the goods at the place of destination, and to one of the following persons in the order indicated, if known to the carrier: the consignee, the controlling party or the shipper.

4. If the goods are sold pursuant to subparagraph 2 (c) of this article, the carrier shall hold the proceeds of the sale for the benefit of the person entitled to the goods, subject to the deduction of any costs incurred by the carrier and any other amounts that are due to the carrier in connection with the carriage of those goods.

5. The carrier shall not be liable for loss of or damage to goods that occurs during the time that they remain undelivered pursuant to this article unless the claimant proves that such loss or damage resulted from the failure by the carrier to take steps that would have been reasonable in the circumstances to preserve the goods and that the carrier knew or ought to have known that the loss or damage to the goods would result from its failure to take such steps.

Article 49
Retention of goods
Nothing in this Convention affects a right of the carrier or a performing party that may exist pursuant to the contract of carriage or the applicable law to retain the goods to secure the payment of sums due.

Notes

1   Article 48 is a new concept – in the Hague-Visby Rules and Hamburg Rules (and indeed, Carriage of Goods by Sea Act 1971 and Carriage of Goods by Sea Act 1992), there are no express provisions dealing with the consequences when the goods failed to be delivered other than for the matter to be resolved by general principles of contract law.

2   There is a requirement in Article 48 that the carrier's actions should be reasonable. Any tribunal or court attempting to apply this provision must thus look at trade practice and, given the international nature of the Rotterdam Rules, the decisions or norms applied by other countries applying the same provision.

12 Transfer of rights

Article 57
When a negotiable transport document or negotiable electronic transport record is issued

1.   When a negotiable transport document is issued, the holder may transfer the rights incorporated in the document by transferring it to another person: (a) Duly endorsed either to such other person or in blank, if an order document; or (b) Without endorsement, if: (i) a bearer document or a blank endorsed document; or (ii) a document made out to the order of a named person and the transfer is between the first holder and the named person.

2.   When a negotiable electronic transport record is issued, its holder may transfer the rights incorporated in it, whether it be made out to order or to the order of a named person, by transferring the electronic transport record in accordance with the procedures referred to in article 9, paragraph 1.

Article 58
Liability of holder

1.   Without prejudice to article 55, a holder that is not the shipper and that does not exercise any right under the contract of carriage does not assume any liability under the contract of carriage solely by reason of being a holder.

2.   A holder that is not the shipper and that exercises any right under the contract of carriage assumes any liabilities imposed on it under the contract of carriage to the extent that such liabilities are incorporated in or ascertainable from the negotiable transport document or the negotiable electronic transport record.

3.   For the purposes of paragraphs 1 and 2 of this article, a holder that is not the shipper does not exercise any right under the contract of carriage solely because: (a) It agrees with the carrier, pursuant to article 10, to replace a negotiable transport document by a negotiable electronic transport record or to replace a negotiable electronic transport record by a negotiable transport document; or (b) It transfers its rights pursuant to article 57.

Notes

1   It is worth comparing s 2 of the Carriage of Goods by Sea Act 1992 with Art 57. Section 2, by providing that 'all rights of suit under the contract of carriage' would vest in the transferee of the bill of lading, makes clear that the right to delivery is passed to the consignee/holder. Article 57, however, extends the right to the right of control as defined in Art 50; namely, '(a) the right to give or modify instructions in respect of the goods that do not constitute a variation of the contract of carriage; (b) The right to obtain delivery of the goods at a scheduled port of call or, in respect of inland carriage, and place en route; and (c) The right to replace the consignee by any other person including the controlling party.'

2   It is clear that whilst s 2 of COGSA 1992 extends to seawaybills, straight bills of lading and to ship's delivery orders, Art 57 is narrower in that it only applies to negotiable documents.

3   As regards Art 58, there too are some differences with s 3 of COGSA 1992. Article 58 lays down three conditions:

   a.   the holder must exercise 'any right under the contract of carriage';
   b.   the liability in question must be one that the contract of carriage imposes on the holder; and,
   c.   that liability must be 'incorporated in or ascertainable from' the transport document or record.

Section 3 of COGSA 1992 on the other hand requires:

   a.   The holder must (i) take or demand delivery from the carrier of any of the goods to which the document relates; (ii) make a claim under the contract of carriage against the carrier in respect of any of those goods; or is a person who, at a time before those rights were vested in him, took or demanded delivery from the carrier of any of those goods.
   b.   The liabilities in question are 'the same liabilities under that contract as if he had been a party to that contract'.

And there is no requirement that the liability be incorporated in or ascertainable from the bill of lading or transport document.

13 Conclusion

The Rotterdam Rules have naturally attracted much support and criticism. The following excerpts show the intensity of the debate within the shipping industry.

13.1 Shippers

US Shippers – The National Industrial Transportation League's Response

(http://www.uncitral.org/pdf/english/texts/transport/rotterdam_rules/NITL_ResponsePaper.pdf) (footnotes omitted)

   The League disagrees strongly with the positions taken by the ESC in its paper and opposes its recommendations which would perpetuate the application of outdated and inconsistent cargo liability rules around the world. The League supports adoption and ratification of the Rotterdam Rules in the United States and globally because the new Convention takes account of present-day shipping arrangements and commercial practices involving sea carriage, and would replace the decades old patchwork of liability regimes currently applied by trading nations. The League served as an industry advisor to the United States delegation involved in the negotiation of the Rotterdam Rules. In this regard, the League actively participated in all of the negotiating sessions before UNCITRAL between the Spring of 2002 and the Spring of 2008, which ultimately led to the adoption of the draft Convention by the UN General Assembly. The League believes that the Rotterdam Rules carefully balance the affected maritime and other interests and reflect a package of reforms that will result in significant benefits for shippers, carriers, and other stakeholders, when viewed as a whole. The ESC, in contrast, did not engage in the complex and delicate treaty negotiations until the very end of the process and now mistakenly evaluates the new Convention in a piecemeal fashion.

Not having participated in the negotiation of the treaty, the ESC also misunderstands many of the provisions of the new Convention.

...

II Shipper benefits under the Rotterdam Rules

ESC surprisingly asserts in its paper that there is nothing in the new Convention which justifies a departure from the status quo. The League strongly disagrees and notes that there are many new enhancements brought about by the Rotterdam Rules which would serve the interests of shippers involved in global trade. The following list sets forth a number of the improvements arising from the new Convention that would be realized by all shippers including those based in Europe. The Rotterdam Rules:

- Eliminate the nautical fault defense, which currently allows carriers to escape liability based on the negligent navigation or management of the vessel.
- Expand the carrier's due diligence obligation to apply during the entire voyage by sea, not just at the beginning of the voyage.
- Increase the liability protection afforded to shippers to 875 SDRs per package or 3 SDRs per kilogram, limits which are significantly higher than those provided under any existing maritime cargo liability regimes, including the Hague-Visby and Hamburg Rules and U.S. COGSA.
- Eliminate limits of liability if the contracting carrier or a maritime performing party engages in reckless or intentional acts.
- Include liability protection for shippers arising from economic losses incurred as a result of deliveries delayed beyond an agreed upon time in the amount of two and one-half times freight.
- Allow shippers and carriers to contract for customized liability arrangements that reflect the shipper's individual business requirements in volume contracts, but require parties that choose to derogate from the Convention to adhere to procedures that protect companies with smaller volumes of cargo. The rules prohibit derogation from certain key carrier and shipper obligations (e.g. carrier's seaworthiness obligation and shipper's dangerous goods obligations).
- Permit countries to opt-in to apply new rules governing jurisdiction and arbitration which would allow the claimant to select the place of adjudication of cargo claims in certain cases, based on a list of potential locations which bear a significant relationship to the involved contract of carriage. This would limit the application of jurisdiction clauses selected by carriers in their bills of lading.
- Extend the statute of limitations applicable to civil claims from one to two years.
- Apply to door-to-door (i.e. inland point-to-inland point) shipments.
- Recognize the increasing use of electronic commerce for shipping transactions (e.g. bills of lading and transport documents) and sets forth new rules governing their use.

The above-listed benefits to shippers directly contradict the ESC's contention that shippers would be better served by the status quo and that the new Convention would place shippers in a worse position than that of the pre-1924 liability environment.

III The concerns of the ESC demonstrate a lack of understanding of the new Convention
The ESC raises a series of specific concerns in its paper which demonstrate a lack of understanding of the workings of the new Convention.

(1) Conflict with Other Conventions
ESC contends that the door-to-door scope of the Rotterdam Rules would potentially conflict with the European Conventions, CMR and CIM, which apply to road and rail carriage respectively. However, Article 82 of the Rotterdam Rules expressly provides that such international conventions would supersede the new Convention to the extent that they apply to multimodal transportation arrangements involving road or rail carriage. Thus, there is an express carve-out for the CMR and CIM conventions.

ESC further asserts that, even if CMR and CIM trump the new Convention, it may be difficult to apply the European road and rail conventions in situations where it is unclear where the damage occurred. However, this possibility exists today under the patchwork of maritime liability rules that exist under Hague-Visby, Hamburg, and COGSA, among other national regimes. Under the new Convention, it will remain possible for European shippers to argue for application of CMR and CIM in cases where the place of damage is not clear. However, to the extent that the Rotterdam Rules are determined to apply in such cases, the League believes that the public policy in favor of international uniformity strikes an appropriate balance.

In addition, ESC asserts that shippers may be discouraged from engaging in short-sea shipping since such arrangements may be governed by the new Convention as opposed to CMR and CIM. However, this concern is more appropriately directed at the limited scope of CMR and CIM, and it ignores the fact that the economics of short-sea shipping arrangements will be the primary factor in determining whether shippers engage in such practices.

(2) Unequal obligations/liabilities
ESC claims that under the new Convention '[c]arriers would be able to continue to offer purely sea carriage. . . . and to limit their period of responsibility to exclude loading, handling, stowing and unloading if the shipper agrees.'. . . In point of fact, if a carrier were to choose to offer only sea carriage, the shipper would be no worse off then they are today under existing maritime liability regimes which apply only tackle-to-tackle (for the Hague Rules and the Hague-Visby Rules) and at most port-to-port (for the Hamburg Rules). In addition, ESC's concern about limitations of the carrier's responsibility for loading, unloading, etc. simply codify the existing commercial practice that arises more frequently in the bulk trades, in which the shipper or consignee prefers to control the loading, handling, stowing, and unloading of its cargo. Most importantly, the rules require the shipper's agreement before a carrier can be relieved of its loading, handling, stowing and unloading responsibilities, and such agreement must be set forth in the contract particulars. Thus, in many cases, the shipper would be the party that requests the carrier to give up its responsibilities for loading, unloading, etc., but even if that were not the case, a shipper need not accept such a unilateral proposal from the carrier.

(3) Volume contracts
The ESC is most concerned with the new Convention's provisions on volume contracts, which allow shippers and carriers to contract to apply terms different from that of the Convention, except with respect to certain key shipper and carrier obligations. ESC's perspective on volume contracts is one which assumes that carriers will always seek to take advantage of smaller volume shippers by forcing them to accept liability and other terms to the shippers' detriment.

However, this perspective is directly contrary to the substantial experience that U.S. shippers have had when negotiating service contracts with ocean liner carriers. Service contracts are formally recognized under the shipping law of the United States, and have been used widely by both large and small shippers for than a decade. Thus, like U.S. based service contracts, volume contracts would be bilateral, individually negotiated agreements that allow for customized rate, service and liability agreements to be entered into between shippers and carriers. If the parties to a volume contract choose not to negotiate special liability terms, the provisions of the Rotterdam Rules will still apply. See Rotterdam Rules, Article 6(1). Thus, departures from the Convention would be the exception, rather than the norm. Furthermore, ESC overstates the risks to shippers that arise from the volume contracts exception and ignores the specific protections and procedures that must be followed to deviate from the Convention in a volume contract. The volume contracts provision expressly conditions any derogation from the terms of the Convention upon compliance with all of the following requirements:

- The volume contract must contain a prominent statement that it is derogating from the convention.
- The volume contract must be individually negotiated or it must prominently specify the sections of the volume contract that contain the derogation.
- The shipper must be given the opportunity to conclude a contract that does not derogate from the Convention.
- The derogation may not be incorporated by reference from another document (e.g. tariff) nor may it be included in a contract of adhesion (e.g. bill of lading).

Under the above protections, any derogation must be 'prominently stated' and will be readily apparent from a review of the volume contract. Thus, a shipper (or carrier) will have clear notice of any terms in a volume contract that derogate from the Convention and will not be caught by surprise. A carrier may not include a derogating term in a bill of lading or tariff, documents that typically are not subject to negotiation. A shipper that does not agree with a volume contract presented by a carrier can refuse to ship under such contract. Rather, the Convention requires the carrier to offer terms that are consistent with the Convention.

The above protections directly address many of the issues raised by the ESC on volume contracts, and the ESC's other concerns are unlikely to occur. For example, the ESC worries that a carrier would exclude the application of international or national law in a volume contract, creating a legal vacuum. However, such an approach is nonsensical from a legal or business perspective, as the parties to a volume contract would have no interest in negotiating a contract that is not subject to either international or national law. As to its concern over the application of competition rules, the Rotterdam Rules would have no impact on such laws and, based on the removal of the block exemption in Europe, carriers could not collaborate on contract prices and service terms.

Furthermore, even without considering the protections in the Convention itself, most shipping markets are sufficiently competitive and offer ample alternatives, especially when competition both among VOCCs, and between VOCCs and NVOCCs or freight forwarders, is considered. In short, shippers have ample choices of service providers in most trades which further mitigate the concerns of ESC that shippers will be forced to accept unreasonable service and liability terms in volume contracts. Stated simply, if a carrier presents unacceptable terms to any shipper, that shipper always remains free to seek another carrier.

ESC's assertion that a carrier may rewrite bill of lading terms to be less shipper-friendly is a risk that exists today under all of the existing maritime cargo liability regimes; but, as explained above, carriers are prohibited under the new Convention from deviating from the terms of the Convention in their bills of lading. Lastly, ESC's assertion that the current economic recession will lead shippers to accept unfavorable liability terms in exchange for lower rates, ignores the negotiating leverage that shippers presently have based on substantial excess vessel capacity that exists around the world.

For those shippers and carriers that choose to address liability-related terms in a volume contract, it will be incumbent upon such parties to review the terms and conditions included in the contract. Shippers that decide to ship under a volume contract must engage in prudent business practices. The League does not accept the apparent position of ESC that shippers should be protected from their own failure to read and negotiate the terms of a contract before accepting its terms.

In short, the volume contracts provision reflects present day contracting practices and provides for commercial flexibility so that shippers and carriers can develop customized shipping contracts that meet their unique business requirements, while also providing for protections to parties that may have limited negotiating leverage.

(4) Proving fault

The ESC is also concerned with the burdens of proof included in the new Convention. Under the new rules, the claimant must first show that the loss or damage to the goods occurred during the carrier's period of responsibility for the goods but it need not establish the fault of the carrier. See Rotterdam Rules, Art. 17(1). The carrier then may defend against the claim by proving that the cause of the loss or damage was not its fault or it may prove that one of the exceptions to liability set forth in the Convention caused or contributed to the loss or damage. See Rotterdam Rules Art. 17(2) and (3). As noted above, the list of exceptions to carrier liability no longer includes an 'error of navigation.'

However, even if a carrier can establish that one of the listed exceptions applied, it may still be held liable if the claimant proves that (1) the fault of the carrier caused or contributed to the event on which the carrier relies; or (2) an event not listed as an exception contributed to the loss or damage and the carrier cannot prove that such event was not its fault; or (3) the loss or damage was caused or contributed to by (i) unseaworthiness of the ship; (ii) the improper crewing, equipping, and supplying of the ship; or (iii) the holds or containers were not fit and safe for the receipt, carriage and preservation of the goods and the carrier is not able to prove that such events did not cause the loss or damage or that it complied with its due diligence obligation. See Rotterdam Rules, Art. 17(4) and (5). The Convention also allows for the liability of the carrier to be apportioned based on that which is attributable to an event or circumstance for which it is liable.

The ESC is concerned with the ability of shippers to prove the fault of the carrier in situations where the carrier asserts that one of the listed exceptions to liability applies. While the League concurs that proving the fault of another party can sometimes be a difficult burden, this burden exists today under the Hague-Visby rules, COGSA, and other regimes that are based on the original Hague Rules. In contrast to the ESC, the League supports a fault-based liability system and it does not believe that the new rules pose an insurmountable burden to establishing the liability of the carrier. Regarding the new rule that would apportion liability based on events within the control of the carrier when there is more than one cause for the loss or damage, the League believes that this was a reasonable compromise based on the elimination of the error of navigation defense and other benefits received by shippers under the new Convention. See Section II above.

(5) Claiming compensation

In its paper, the ESC criticizes the new liability provisions applicable to loss, damage and delay. However, it fails to mention that the liability limits in the Rotterdam Rules (i.e. 875 SDRs per package or 3 SDRs per kilogram, whichever is higher) are greater than any existing international maritime liability regime. See Rotterdam Rules, Art. 59. The ESC also complains about the application of the package rule in Article 59(2), but this rule is intended to apply the package limitation to the smallest package unit enumerated in the bill of lading (e.g. to the carton or boxes listed, as opposed to the number of pallets or containers), which is a benefit to the shipper. Although the new Convention would provide shippers with the long-desired recovery of economic losses caused by delayed deliveries (which liability does not exist under the Hague Rules, COGSA, or the Hague-Visby Rules), and would provide for compensation at two and one-half times freight – a level higher than that provided for under the Hamburg Rules – the ESC fails to recognize this new protection as a benefit to its members. Rather, the ESC expresses concern over the need for the shipper and carrier to 'agree' to a time for delivery in order to trigger the potential liability of the carrier. Rotterdam Rules, Art. 21 and 60. However, the League believes that it is reasonable for the shipper to provide notice of its required delivery date and for the carrier to agree to perform within the stated period of time. In addition, the explanatory report of the new Convention states that a number of delegations believe that the agreement between the parties as to the time for delivery need not be express and, thus, may be inferred or implied based on the facts and circumstances.

The ESC also asserts that it is not typical for the parties to reach agreements as to delivery times in today's contracts and that this may prove more difficult for smaller volume shippers that use the services of transportation intermediaries. However, the lack of performance requirements in existing contracts is likely due to the fact that delay liability is presently unavailable, except for those few nations that have adopted the Hamburg Rules. If the Rotterdam Rules are widely adopted, then the League believes that agreements on delivery times would become more commonplace. Moreover, shippers that choose to use freight forwarders or other intermediaries can readily communicate their delivery requirements to the forwarder and require the forwarder to contract on such terms with a carrier.

As to the new jurisdiction rules, the ESC recognizes that such rules only apply if a country 'opts-in' but it fails to mention that this approach was adopted in large measure to accommodate the desires of the European Union. Furthermore, ESC notes that jurisdiction provisions in volume contracts would be enforceable but it inaccurately asserts that 'carriers would no doubt continue to dictate jurisdiction in many instances.' In the United States, shippers commonly negotiate service contracts which are a form of volume contract, as defined by the new Convention. However, in our experience, shippers have little difficulty negotiating jurisdiction provisions that require foreign carriers to litigate cargo claims in the United States and that is the case in most service contracts. Thus, it is inappropriate to assume that carriers will control jurisdiction clauses in volume contracts.

(6) Shipper obligations

The ESC also objects to the inclusion of certain shipper obligations in the new Convention that require the shipper to tender cargos in a condition that will withstand the carriage, including their loading, handling, stowing, lashing and securing, and unloading, and that they will not cause harm to persons or property (Art. 28), and require the shipper to furnish information, instructions and documents relating to the goods (Art. 29). However, the League believes that such obligations are reasonable and simply codify current practices already followed by most shippers. Additionally, the Convention appropriately recognizes the joint responsibility of shippers and carriers in ensuring the security of the cargo, since the carrier must 'properly and carefully receive, load, handle, stow, carry, keep, care for, unload and deliver the goods', unless otherwise agreed based on the contract particulars. Rotterdam Rules, Art. 13(1) and (2).

The ESC points out that shippers must comply with a new obligation to furnish timely and accurate information to the carrier which relates to the contract particulars (e.g. name of the shipper, name of consignee, if any, and name of the 'to order' party, if any, description of the goods, and the goods marks, quantity and weight) and are deemed to have guaranteed the accuracy of such information at the time of receipt by the carrier. Rotterdam Rules, Art. 31. However, these new requirements are intended to reflect enhanced responsibilities of shippers in a post-9/11 world, in which international and national antiterrorism measures have become an important consideration around the world.

The ESC comments that the Convention imposes on shippers special rules relating to dangerous goods. These provisions require the shipper to provide notice to the carrier of the dangerous nature of the cargo and to mark or label the goods in accordance with applicable laws. Rotterdam Rules, Art. 32. The shipper is to be held strictly liable for a breach of this obligation. Rotterdam Rules, Art. 30. However, the Convention's treatment of dangerous goods was broadly supported by most delegations for public policy and safety reasons, and the specific requirements are substantially similar to other existing legal requirements for hazardous cargo. Thus, the Convention does not impose any greater burden on shippers with respect to dangerous goods than that which already exists under other applicable national and international laws and regulations.

In essence, the shipper's obligations arising under the Convention reflect existing laws and commercial practices, as well as new responsibilities that are reasonable based on changes that have occurred (e.g. in response to terrorist attacks) since the existing cargo liability regimes were adopted.

IV Conclusion

For the foregoing reasons, the League disagrees with the positions of the ESC in opposition to the Rotterdam Rules, as set forth in its March 2009 paper.

13.2 Freight forwarders

The International Federation of Freight Forwarders Associations (FIATA) Position Paper
(http://www.uncitral.org/pdf/english/texts/transport/rotterdam_rules/FIATApaper.pdf)
FIATA Working Group Sea Transport recommends that Association members should advise their governments not to accept the Rotterdam Rules.

1. In general, the Convention is far too complicated. This leads to additional transaction costs and invites misunderstandings and misinterpretations. At worst, the Convention States may end up with different interpretations, so that the Rotterdam Rules will fail in reaching their main objective to unify the law of carriage of goods by sea.

2. Although freight forwarders, as carriers or logistics service providers, gain from the benefits according to carriers by the Rotterdam Rules – such as the right to limit liability not only for loss of or damage to cargo but for any breach (Art. 59.1) and no liability for delay unless agreed (Art. 21) – the Rotterdam Rules work to the disadvantage of freight forwarders when acting as shippers or when demanding compensation from the performing carriers. It is expected that the expansion of freedom of contract in case of volume contracts (Art. 1.2 and Art. 80) will lead to additional difficulties in getting compensation from the performing carriers.

3. As shippers, freight forwarders will be liable without any right to limit liability for incorrect information to the carriers (Art. 79.2(b)), although the carriers enjoy the right to limit their liability for incorrect information to the shippers ('any breach').

4. Freight forwarders are frequently engaged in various capacities in the seaports. Such activities will expose them to liability as 'maritime performing parties' (Art. 1.7 and Art. 19). At present, stevedores and warehousemen enjoy freedom of contract allowing them to escape liability, at least to the extent that their customers are or could be covered by insurance for loss or damage. In countries where stevedoring and warehousing enterprises are owned or controlled by governments or municipalities, any moves towards ratification of the Rotterdam Rules would for this reason presumably be strongly opposed in order to avoid escalation of liability insurance premiums. Multipurpose cargo terminals engaged as distribution centres in logistics operations would strongly oppose a sort of maritime law injection into their business, which presumably will be governed by more sophisticated liability regimes.

5. The administrative burden of freight forwarders will increase significantly with any entering into force of the Rotterdam Rules.

5.1 FIATA has consistently opposed the so-called maritime plus (wholly or partly by Sea) and opted for a convention port-to-port. Although Article 26 permits the liability in some cases to be resolved by mandatory provisions of international instruments (not national law even if mandatory!) relating to non-maritime transport, this does not solve the problem where, at the time of the conclusion of the contract, the mode of transport to be used is not yet known ('unspecified transport'). Surely, it is unacceptable having to look into the after-events (i.e. the way in which the transport was actually performed) in order to decide which rules apply to the contract. Suffice it to mention the impossibility to apply such a methodology to liability for non-performance! How should one decide which of all the hypothetically applicable conventions listed in Art. 82 apply in order to ensure that the correct transport document is issued? Also, it may well be inappropriate to apply the rather low limits of liability of the Rotterdam Rules to cases where it cannot be established where loss or damage occurred during a carriage which involves different modes of transport (so-called 'concealed damage'). An escape from the Rotterdam Rules may well be permitted for multimodal transports or contracts by logistics service providers, when the maritime transport segment is over-shadowed by other elements. But, again, the uncertainty created by the maritime plus of the Rotterdam Rules is disturbing. In the unlikely event that the Rotterdam Rules gain worldwide acceptance, which policy would FIATA prefer with respect to the FBL and the UNCTAD/ICC Rules for Multimodal Transport Documents? Should FIATA work under the hypothesis that multimodal transports, or logistics transport operations, are of their own kind and remain unaffected by the Rotterdam Rules? Or should FIATA use the perhaps more prudent alternative to wait and see if the UNCTAD/ICC Rules will be amended?

5.2 The introduction of a 'joint and several liability for documentary shippers' (Art. 1.9 and Art. 33) and 'real shippers' will call upon freight forwarders to exercise due diligence in avoiding mentioning exporters as 'shippers' in the transport document when they have been selling on the delivery terms EXW, FCA or FOB. In these cases, sellers/shippers are not under a duty to contract for carriage. Needless to say, such sellers would like to avoid being trapped into a joint and several liability (Art. 33.1) with their buyers (the real shippers), particularly when they have protected themselves by getting paid upon shipment under a documentary credit. This is how they protect themselves against the risk of insolvency of their buyers and they certainly do not expect to incur that risk by a backlash from the carrier when his contracting party – the real shipper – becomes insolvent.

NB – FIATA has since departed from their Working Group's position paper and states that they will remain neutral about the Rules and will leave the matter to national representatives.

13.3 Carriers/owners

The International Chamber of Shipping (ICS) Response

(http://www.uncitral.org/pdf/english/texts/transport/rotterdam_rules/ICS_PositionPaper.pdf)

III Political context
The number of States (representing shipping and shipper interests and all major trading nations), Industry representatives and academics that participated in the UNCITRAL discussions was almost unprecedented. The Convention was approved by a huge majority of those participating, signifying a successful and acceptable compromise which raises the very real prospect of an international solution coming into effect.

Importantly, for many States, this Convention represents the last attempt to obtain international agreement after the previous unsuccessful attempts. The US has made it clear, for example, that having deferred its own national proposals in 1993, if there is not widespread ratification of the Rotterdam Rules, it will proceed with its own regional plan. Such a step by the US will almost certainly result in a failure of the UNCITRAL Convention and the end of the prospect of an internationally accepted regime.

ICS is also aware that the EU Commission has plans to introduce its own EU-wide multi-modal solution which might also apply to matters and trades that would otherwise be governed by the UNCITRAL Convention. If such proposals are introduced and this prevents EU Member States from ratifying, it is inevitable that other key States such as the US will walk away from the Convention.

For this reason alone, it is absolutely imperative that full support is given to the international UNCITRAL Convention and that the EU Commission sees that there is a strong international political will in favour of the Convention. It is only by showing strong political support that the attempts to introduce conflicting and overlapping regional rules will be eliminated – an absolute priority for not only the international shipping industry but all interests and ultimately, for the consumer.

IV Overview of the convention
Very broadly, the aim of the Rotterdam Rules is twofold: first to modernise the regime generally for the traditional 'tackle-to-tackle' and 'port-to-port' carriage of goods and secondly, to introduce innovative solutions to meet the demands of carriage of goods on 'door-to-door' terms by which the carrier undertakes

responsibility for not only the maritime leg but also the intermediate and final land, inland waterway or air leg, from receipt of the goods from the shipper until final delivery to the receiver. Existing regimes such as the Hague-Visby Rules are restricted in their scope of application to the maritime leg. The Rotterdam Rules regulate multimodal carriage terms provided that an international maritime leg is contemplated in the contract of carriage. The Convention is best described as a 'maritime plus' instrument rather than providing a full uniform multimodal liability regime for all modes of transport. By limiting the scope in this way it was possible to apply the provisions for the maritime leg to damage which cannot be local-ised ('concealed damage'). Application of the maritime rules to concealed damage was found to be quite appropriate because a maritime transport always has to be part of the whole transport. Furthermore, application of the maritime rules made it unnecessary to establish a separate liability system for such concealed damage, thereby avoiding yet another set of liability rules.

For localised damage, the Convention adheres to the concept of 'network' liability. Thus liabil-ity and the applicable limits of liability for loss of or damage to the goods occurring before or after the sea-leg will be determined by any unimodal international instrument compulsorily applicable to the relevant mode of transport where the loss or damage occurs, for example, the Convention on the Contract for the International Carriage of Goods by Road (CMR 1956) if the damage takes place on the road leg.

The Convention also has a very broad geographic scope of application in that it applies to inter-national contracts of carriage with an international maritime leg where the place of receipt, loading, delivery or discharge is situated in a contracting state. In other words, like the Hamburg Rules, it will apply to both outward and inward carriage. Thus by virtue of if its own provisions, the Convention will enhance uniformity and is to be contrasted with the Hague-Visby Rules which apply only to an outgo-ing carriage.

V Industry's view of the 'Rotterdam Rules'

Shipowners will see a significant increase in the cost of cargo liability claims due to certain provisions of the Convention, namely:

- Loss of the right to the nautical fault defence;
- Extension of the obligation to exercise due diligence to make the ship seaworthy;
- Higher limits of liability;

Balanced against the increased liability for shipowners, however, the Convention contains many valuable provisions that seek to facilitate and regulate modern trade practices and shipowners welcome the following:

- As stated, the Convention modernises the liability regime for carriage of goods by sea and also, importantly, addresses the lacuna that presently exists for maritime carriage where there is also mul-timodal carriage and a sea leg, and regulates such carriage.
- The Convention will extend not only to outgoing maritime carriage but also to incoming maritime carriage.
- The beneficial aspects of existing non-maritime conventions which are known and well-understood and applicable to EU Member States in particular, are retained. Specifically, the new Convention adheres to the concept of 'network' liability whereby liability and the applicable limits of liability for loss and damage to the goods occurring before or after the sea-leg will be determined by any unimodal Convention compulsorily applicable to the relevant mode of transport where the loss or damage occurs, e.g. CMR and COTIF.
- The Convention provides a much needed solution for the problem of how to deal with 'concealed damage' during multimodal carriage by providing that where it is not known when the damage took place and on which mode of transport, the Convention will govern liability and limits of liability, etc.

- The Convention makes provisions for and regulates e-commerce. In particular, the Convention gives functional equivalence to traditional bills of lading and other transport documents such as way bills and electronic trading systems. In this way, e-commerce will no longer be impeded by shipper rights to demand paper documentation before delivery. The use of encrypted electronic systems will help to reduce fraudulent transactions while instantaneous transmission means that documentation will no longer be delayed in postal systems. This will go a long way toward overcoming the age-old problem often leading to pressure on carriers to release cargo without surrender of documentation.
- The Convention applies to all transport documents in liner trade, not only bills of lading, and provides detailed rules on all documentary aspects thereby ensuring uniformity and certainty in an area which has been dominated by divergent national rules and court decisions.
- The Convention allows parties in the liner trade greater freedom of contract where this is appropriate while at the same time giving mandatory protection where needed. For example, it permits volume contracts in liner traffic to derogate from the Convention by contractual arrangement and according to certain strict conditions to ensure that all parties are adequately protected before embarking on terms outside of the Convention.
- The Convention applies to cargo whether carried on or under deck and thereby avoids the legal difficulties which follow from the Hague and Hague-Visby Rules general exclusion of deck cargoes from the scope of those conventions.
- The Convention provides for a much improved regime for deviation when compared with the Hague-Visby Rules, in that where under a national law there is a deviation, the Convention will not deprive the shipowner of the right to defences and limitations;
- The Convention contains comprehensive and more systematic provisions on carrier and shipper liability and provides a balanced allocation of risk between these parties.
- Where the consignee has not obtained possession of a negotiable transport document, the Convention permits the carrier under certain circumstances, to deliver the goods without presentation of the negotiable transport document while at the same time protecting the interests of all the parties involved.
- The Convention deals with jurisdiction and arbitration, however the provisions are subject to an opt-in by States. It is most unlikely that EU Member States will optin whereas the US is expected to exercise the option to opt-in.

The features mentioned above are distinct improvements over existing regimes and the fact that they are encased in an international convention lead shipowners to believe that this instrument is the most effective mechanism to govern international maritime carriage of goods and that it should be supported by all States in the interests of achieving international uniformity and certainty.

VI Conclusion

There seems little doubt that, if the Rotterdam Rules are not ratified, the status quo of existing regimes will not remain because they do not meet the needs of today's trading environment, the likelihood being, in particular, that the USA would enact its own domestic legislation. That would be regionalism, and would result in lack of uniformity and conflicts between liability regimes leading to legal uncertainty and legal and administrative costs incurred in navigating the various legal jurisdictions. International trade would inevitably suffer as result.

To all those involved in international trade, uniform international solutions are of vital importance and regionalism must be avoided. The Rotterdam Rules represent the only international solution. They provide a considerable number of valuable provisions to the advantage of international trade which clearly outweigh the small number of less attractive provisions. Accordingly, the Rotterdam Rules should be supported, promoted and quickly ratified.

Further reading

Alba, M, 'Electronic commerce provisions in the UNCITRAL convention on contracts for the international carriage of goods wholly or partly by sea' (2009) 44 Tex Int'l LJ 387.

Asariotis, R, 'The Rotterdam Rules: Brief overview of some of their key features' (2009) 3 EJCCL 111–125.

Fujita, T, 'The comprehensive coverage of the new convention: Performing parties and the multimodal implication' (2009) 44 Tex Int'l LJ 349.

Nikaki, T, 'Himalaya Clauses and the Rotterdam Rules' (2011) 17 J Int'l Mar L 20.

Nikaki, T and Soyer, B 'A new international regime for carriage of goods by sea: Contemporary, certain, inclusive and efficient, or just another one for the shelves?' (2012) 30 Berkeley J Int'l Law 303.

Sturley, MF, 'Transport law for the twenty-first century: An introduction to the preparation, philosophy, and the potential impact of the Rotterdam Rules' (2008) 14 J Int'l Mar L 461.

Zekos, GI, 'The contractual role of documents issued under the CMI draft instrument on transport law' (2004) 35(1) JMLC 99.

Index